BLOOMSBURY GUIDES TO ENGLISH LITERATURE

The Novel

A Guide to the Novel from its Origins to the Present Day
Edited by Andrew Michael Roberts

BLOOMSBURY

First published in 1994
by Bloomsbury Publishing Plc
2 Soho Square, London WIV 5DE

The moral right of the author has been asserted.

Copyright © Bloomsbury 1993

A copy of the CIP entry for this book is available from the British Library.

ISBN 0 7475 1951 X

Typeset by Hewer Text Composition Services, Edinburgh
Printed in Britain by Cox & Wyman Ltd, Reading, Berks

BLOOMSBURY GUIDES TO ENGLISH LITERATURE

The Novel

The Bloomsbury Guides to English Literature

General Editor: Marion Wynne-Davies

Guide to English Renaissance Literature
  Marion Wynne-Davies

Guide to Restoration and Augustan Literature
  Eva Simmonds

Guide to Romantic Literature
  Geoff Ward

Guide to Nineteenth-Century Literature
  Jane Thomas

Guide to the Novel
  Andrew Michael Roberts

Guide to Twentieth-Century Literature
  Linda R. Williams

Contents

Acknowledgements

General Editor
Marion Wynne-Davies

Editor
Andrew Michael Roberts

Originator
Christopher Gillie

Contributors
Janet Barron (18th-century prose)
Catherine Byron (Irish literature) Loughborough College of Art and Design
Gail Cunningham (19th century prose) Kingston University
John Drakakis (Critical theory) University of Stirling
David Jarrett (Science Fiction) University of North London
Lesley Johnson (Medieval Literature) University of Leeds
Mark Kermode (Horror Fiction) Journalist
David Nokes (18th-century prose) Kings College, University of London
John O'Brien (French literature) University of Liverpool
Valerie Pedlar (Context of literature) University of Liverpool
Andrew Michael Roberts (20th-century novel) Royal Holloway, University of London
Jonathan Sawday (Renaissance poetry) University of Southampton
Mercer Simpson (Welsh literature)
John Thieme (Commonwealth literatures) University of Hull
Geoff Ward (Additional Romantic entries) University of Liverpool
Linda R. Williams (Additional 20th-century entries) University of Liverpool
Marion Wynne-Davies (Additional Renaissance entries)

Advisor
Elizabeth Maslen, Queen Mary and Westfield College, University of London

Editorial
Editorial Director Kathy Rooney
Project Editor Tracey Smith

General Editor's Preface

The Bloomsbury guides to English literature derive directly from *The Bloomsbury Guide to English Literature* (1989), and are intended for those readers who wish to look at a specific period or genre, rather than at the wide-ranging material offered in the original text. As such, the guides include material from the larger and earlier work, but they have been updated and supplemented in order to answer the requirements of their particular fields. Each individual editor has selected, edited and authored as the need arose. The acknowledgements appropriate for the individual volumes have been made in the respective editors' prefaces. As general editor I should like to thank all those who have been involved in the project, from its initial conception through to the innovative and scholarly volumes presented in this series.

Marion Wynne-Davies

Editor's Note

Cross References

A liberal use of cross references has been made. In both the essays and the reference entries, names, titles and topics are frequently marked with an arrow (▷) to guide the reader to the appropriate entry in the reference section for a more detailed explanation. Cross-reference arrows appear both in the text and at the end of entries.

Dates

Dates after the names of people indicate their life spans, except when they follow the names of monarchs when they show the length of the reign.

Editor's Preface

This book aims to provide a stimulus to the reading and appreciation of a wide range of fiction written in English over the last three hundred years and to offer information which may assist enjoyment and study. The first two essays establish the critical context for an understanding of the novel by considering such issues as: the definition of the novel; where its origins lie and how it came to develop as a separate form; its relationship to other literary forms; its engagement with that tricky concept 'reality'; the ideas put forward by novelists themselves about their art; the models of interpretation advocated by the sometimes bewildering variety of modern literary and cultural theorists. The third, fourth and fifth essays examine the development of the novel over the three centuries during which it has been one of the most popular and admired of literary genres. These essays discuss authors, works and movements and some of the historical and social factors which affected writers and readers alike. The reference section of the book provides further information on such topics as: novelists and novels; other relevant writers and texts; critics, philosophers and other thinkers; literary terms, especially those used in the analysis of narrative; relevant historical, political, psychological and philosophical terms; journals and literary movements; other information relevant to the reading of novels. There is extensive cross-referencing from the essays to the reference entries, and between different reference entries, to make supplementary information readily available and to encourage the pursuit of lines of enquiry.

I am grateful to David Nokes, Janet Barron and Gail Cunningham, who wrote the original essays on eighteenth-century prose and the nineteenth-century novel as these appeared in *The Bloomsbury Guide to English Literature*. In order to adapt these essays to the context and aims of the present volume, I have made some minor changes: in the case of the eighteenth-century article this involved adding a new first paragraph and removing a section on non-fictional prose, while the nineteenth-century article has been given an additional concluding paragraph.

Extra reference entries for this volume were supplied by Linda R. Williams, Marion Wynne-Davies, Geoff Ward and myself. In choosing new entries, I have concentrated on broadening the range of authors covered (with particular attention to women novelists and post-colonial writing) and on explanation of the terms and concepts used in novel criticism. I would like to thank Elizabeth Maslen for her scrupulous reading and her unfailing and invaluable advice, Marion Wynne-Davies for her patience and encouragement and Tracey Smith at Bloomsbury for remaining good humoured and supportive throughout the writing process.

I would also like to thank Sally Kilmister for her support, advice and encouragement: this book is dedicated to her.

Andrew Michael Roberts
London 1993

Essay section

Introduction: The Novel as a Genre

Andrew Michael Roberts

What is a Novel?

The novel is at once one of the most varied, one of the most complex and one of the most popular of literary genres. But what is a novel? While we can use the word with little fear of misunderstanding, a clear-cut definition is not as easy to formulate as might first appear. A broad definition would be: 'an extended fictional narrative in written form'. This would probably accommodate any examples we might care to name, but it would also include such works as ▷ Homer's verse epic ▷ *The Odyssey*, ▷ Chaucer's poetic romance ▷ *Troilus and Criseyde* and ▷ Dante's mystical narrative ▷ *The Divine Comedy*. While it may be true that modern readers, accustomed to the pleasures of the novel, appreciate what might be termed novelistic aspects of these works, such as psychological insight or the skilful handling of plot, what is certain is that neither the authors nor the contemporary readers of these works would have called them novels, since the English term in its modern sense only emerged in the early eighteenth century. Thus a narrower definition would be: 'a genre of written prose fictional narrative which emerged in the early eighteenth century and is characterized by a strong interest in plot, by a degree of psychological and/or social realism, and frequently by the presence of elements of moral, political or social comment'. However, there have always been novels which do not quite seem to fit such a definition: for example the ▷ Gothic novel is not readily assimilated to ▷ 'realism' and its didactic intentions are questionable. Furthermore, twentieth-century experiments in the novel have been characterized by the varying of almost all these features: there are novels almost without plot (such as ▷ Samuel Beckett's *The Unnameable*) or with plots that unravel themselves (such as ▷ Flann O'Brien's *At Swim-Two-Birds*); novels of fantasy (such as works of ▷ magic realism or the novels of ▷ Angela Carter); novels in verse (such as ▷ Vikram Seth's *The Golden Gate*); ▷ 'faction' or non-fictional novels (such as Truman Capote's *In Cold Blood*). Most of these have precedents in earlier centuries (it would be possible to see ▷ Daniel Defoe's ▷ *A Journal of the Plague Year* as a form of faction) making it possible to argue for multiple traditions within the novel.

There is, then, no definitive answer to our initial question. This is not really surprising, since literary forms are not timeless essences, but the product of shared ideas and practices. Such ideas and practices emerge within particular social and historical contexts and evolve through the complex processes of cultural circulation. Literary forms are used, questioned, defined, re-defined, attacked, defended, subverted and rescued by authors, critics, reviewers, academics, readers and others. The *concept* of the novel emerged through a gradual process in which it became distinguished from the romance, the epic, the history and the satire, though these terms continued to be applied, by some authors and critics, to works now seen as constitutive of the emerging novel (for example Defoe referred to his works as histories, though the eighteenth-century sense of that word differed somewhat from the modern one). Once the idea was established, the novel was frequently defined both in *contrast* to the forms out of which it emerged and which it rivalled, and through claims of continuity. The emphasizing of difference is perhaps the more common strategy, because the novel continued to draw on other forms; the establishing of boundaries implies the possibility of their transgression. Thus the fact that many writers have contrasted the romance and the novel tells us, not how different these forms are, but the extent to which they interpenetrate.

One of the earliest writers to distinguish the novel from the romance was ▷ William Congreve (1670–1729), who describes his work *Incognita: or, Love and Duty Reconciled* (1691) as a novel, and in his Preface argues that novels 'are of a more familiar Nature' than romances and 'delighteth us with Accidents and odd Events, but not such as are wholly unusual or unpresidented, such which being not so distant from our Belief bring also the pleasure nearer us'. Around 1740 Lord Chesterfield described the novel as 'a kind of abbreviation of a romance', and the distinction by length is not insignificant, since seventeenth-century romances such as ▷ Madeleine de Scudéry's *Artamène, or the Great Cyrus* (1649–53), ran to ten volumes. ▷ Samuel Richardson, whose own novel ▷ *Clarissa* is over a million words long, but who irritably exclaimed in a letter, 'What a deuce, do you think I am writing a Romance? Don't you see that I am copying Nature', makes more moralistic distinctions. Through his heroines Lady Charlotte and Pamela he attacks both epic and romance on moral grounds; the former as the occasion of 'violence, murder, depredations', the latter as 'unnaturally *inflaming* to the passions' and 'calculated to *fire* the *imagination*, rather than to *inform* the *judgment*'. Defoe was similarly critical of the Homeric epics, tersely summing up the plot of ▷ *The Iliad* as 'the rescue of a Whore'. ▷ Henry Fielding, on the other hand, describes his own ▷ *Joseph Andrews* (1742) as a 'comic epic in prose', while distinguishing it from the long romances of the seventeenth century. In *The Progress of Romance* (1775), ▷ Clara Reeve, through her persona Euphrasia, gives the following account: 'The word *Novel* in all languages signifies something new. It was first used to distinguish these works from Romance, though they have lately been confounded together . . . The Romance is an heroic fable, which treats of fabulous persons and things. – The Novel is a picture of real life and manners, and of the times in which it was written'. Reeve, while commenting on the use of the old romances 'to wrap a pound of sugar', points out the inconsistency of venerating the epic and decrying the romance. In 1824 ▷ Sir Walter Scott sums up something approaching a consensus when he identifies the interest of the romance as based upon 'marvellous and uncommon incidents' as opposed to 'the ordinary train of human events, and the modern state of society' represented in the novel.

This recurrent stress on plausibility, the natural, the ordinary and the contemporary contributed to the idea of the novel as a realist form, but should not be allowed to obscure the continuing importance of the marvellous, and of non-contemporary settings, in its development. Plausibility is relative, so that ▷ Horace Walpole, in his Preface to ▷ *The Castle of Otranto* (1765), could claim to avoid the implausible behaviour depicted in old romances, even though his own novel is full of supernatural events and scarcely less incredible reactions. Indeed, *The Castle of Otranto* helped to inaugurate the tradition of the Gothic novel, which continues to incorporate many romance elements (Clara Reeve praised Walpole's novel as 'an attempt to unite the various merits and graces of the ancient Romance and the modern Novel').

To conclude this section on defining the novel, and to preface the wider question of the novel's relationship to reality, it is worth recalling that definitions may be used not only to draw generic boundaries but to make claims for significance and status, and that the novel is a form to which, over the last three hundred years, considerable social and historical importance has been attributed. The Hungarian Marxist critic Georg Lukács, in *The Theory of the Novel* (1920), describes the novel as 'the epic of a world that has been abandoned by God'. The liberal critic and novelist Lionel Trilling argues that 'for our time the most effective agent of the moral imagination has been the novel'. ▷ D.H. Lawrence claims that 'the novel is the highest example of subtle inter-relatedness that man has discovered' and, more simply, states that 'the novel is the book of life'. Clearly individuals redefine the novel to suit their own interests and beliefs. However, these rather grandiloquent descriptions all claim that the novel has a specially indicative relationship to what is important in the life of its time. Whether or not we accept such claims, we may at least observe that the novel has turned out to be a highly receptive and flexible literary form, so that there seems to be no aspect of experience which it cannot embrace: the documenting of social conflict and political debate, as in the ▷ social problem novels of ▷ Elizabeth Gaskell or the political novels of ▷ Anthony Trollope; scrupulous minute descriptions of sense impressions in Alain Robbe-Grillet's novel *The Voyeur* (an example of the French ▷ *nouveau roman*); details of incomes, rents and domestic arrangements in the novels of ▷ Arnold Bennett; supernatural events in the Gothic novel; future or alternative worlds in ▷ science fiction; the most subtle and elusive aspects of an invidual's inner life in the work of ▷ Virginia Woolf or ▷ Henry James. Yet the novel is often thought to have a specific allegiance to reality (however that may be defined), to be the literary genre which we interpret as closest to life itself. How valid is such a claim?

The Novel and the Real

The idea of art as ▷ mimesis, as an imitation of life, goes back to the writings of ▷ Plato and ▷ Aristotle. As we have seen, eighteenth-century definitions of the emergent novel genre tended to stress that it was truer to ordinary, contemporary life than the epic, romance or lyric. This line of argument leads to one sort of paradigm of what the novel should be – a mirror of ordinary social reality, or (to alter the metaphor) a transparent window on the world. Because both romance and epic (from classical times to the Renaissance) had been particularly concerned with aristocratic characters, 'realism' in the novel came to be associated with the portrayal of characters in more humble circumstances: sometimes living in actual poverty, with associated social problems; sometimes middle-class characters struggling for wealth or position. Such novels were unlikely to take an idealized view of human nature, or to represent characters who consistently behaved honourably. This element is strong in the work of Defoe and Fielding: Moll Flanders steals and commits bigamy; Tom Jones, though he is shown as having a certain innate nobility of character, engages in sexual adventures (Fielding defends his protagonist with the comment that 'though he did not always act rightly, yet he never did otherwise without feeling and suffering for it'). However, it was the portrayal of 'low life' and 'immoral' behaviour in the work of nineteenth-century French writers such as ▷ Honoré de Balzac and ▷ Gustave Flaubert which led to the use of 'realism' (French *réalisme*) as a literary term (it had a long history as a philosophical term, but with a very different meaning), and to the somewhat misleading tendency to think of realism as a matter of content (what was portrayed) rather than of mode (how it was portrayed), and as the opposite of idealism. As Ian Watt points out, in his influential study *The Rise of the Novel*, 'if the novel were realistic merely because it saw life from the seamy side, it would only be an inverted romance; but in fact it surely attempts to portray all the varieties of human experience'. These issues formed part of the debate about the morality of the novel: writers such as ▷ Stendhal and Balzac, who described behaviour regarded as socially unacceptable, without the moralizing with which Defoe surrounds Moll Flander's story, defended their work on the grounds of accuracy to life. Balzac, in his 1842 Preface to his series of novels *The Human Comedy*, complained that 'As I was depicting the whole of Society . . . it was bound to happen that one particular story contained more evil than good . . . and criticism cried immorality'. Stendhal, in his novel *The Red and the Black*, made striking use of the traditional realist metaphor of the mirror:

> *Why, my good sir, a novel is a mirror journeying down the high road. Sometimes it reflects to your view the azure blue of heaven, sometimes the mire in the puddles on the road below. And the man who carries the mirror in his pack will be accused by you of being immoral!*

This line of argument culminated in the claim for scientific objectivity which was central to the ▷ naturalism of ▷ Émile Zola, who argued that 'the writer is simply an analyst who may have become engrossed in human corruption, but who has done so as a surgeon might in an operating theatre' (Preface to the second edition of *Thérèse Raquin*). It is noteworthy, however, that the understanding of human motivation contained in Zola's fiction tends to undermine his theoretical claims: in the same Preface he claims that, as a naturalist novelist, he is in the position of those painters who 'copy the nude without themselves being touched by the slightest sexual feeling', yet his novel contains a character who pretends to be a painter largely in order to leer at and proposition the models.

Twentieth-century literature, literary criticism and literary theory have posed radical challenges to the idea of realism. In part these challenges are a result of philosophical ▷ relativism, just as the nineteenth-century idea of scientific realism had been influenced by the empirical philosophy of the eighteenth century, which had taken sense impressions as its basis. So, in the wake of thinkers such as ▷ Nietzsche, ▷ Freud and ▷ Bergson, who in different ways revealed the subjective and relative nature of what each individual sees as 'real', we find literary redefinitions of realism, including Virginia Woolf's privileging of the texture of consciousness over external facts (quoted below). Moreover, ▷ structuralist and ▷ post-structuralist literary theory has questioned the whole concept of mimesis by arguing that words cannot refer in any direct way to a pre-existing reality. According to structuralism, language is a system of signs whose meaning is defined by their difference from each other, not their correspondence with real objects; the linguist ▷ Ferdinand de Saussure asserted that, 'dans la langue, il n'y a que des différences sans termes positifs' (in language, there are only differences, without positive terms; *Course in General Linguistics*, 1915). Post-structuralism takes this separation of language from reference even further, as in ▷ Derrida's claim that 'Il n'y a pas de hors-texte' (there is nothing outside the text, or, the text has no outside). Language in general, and within languages, a range of discourses (structures of power embedded in particular forms of language-use and institutional practice) are seen by theorists such as ▷ Michel Foucault as constructing our view of reality, not as reflecting an independent, pre-existing reality. This points to the extent to which realism in the novel is, paradoxically, an illusion; a matter of inducing the reader to accept as real on an imaginative level something which he or she, on another level, knows to be a verbal construct.

This can be illustrated with reference to one of the classic nineteenth-century realist novels, Flaubert's *Madame Bovary* (1867). The eponymous heroine of this novel is the daughter of a French farmer. Trapped in an early marriage with a husband whom she soon begins to find boring and unambitious, she dreams of romance, riches and high living, and these fantasies are inspired in part by romantic ballads and historical novels. For example, we find her at one point trying to make her feelings for her husband fit the model of love that she has derived from her reading: 'she tried, according to theories she considered sound, to make herself in love. By moonlight in the garden she used to recite to him all the love poetry she knew . . . It left her as unmoved as before.' Later she attempts to make her dreams real through two love affairs which, combined with reckless spending, lead eventually to disaster. The character has lent her name to an adjective – Bovaryism – which means the indulgence of unreal fantasies based on fiction. What is worth noting here is that the unattainability of her fantasies make her 'ordinary' life, as described by Flaubert, seem 'real' in comparison. 'Bovaryism', in Flaubert's accomplished hands, is a subject for tragedy and psychological insight, but it is also a rhetorical manoeuvre, which encourages us to forget that we are reading an invented story, a construct in a language which is not only metaphorical, not only shaped by Flaubert's opinions and assumptions, but also the embodiment of ideological and conceptual structures which are neither universal nor inevitable. Since the education or disillusionment of a character are common subjects for novels, this manoeuvre is frequently found, whenever a character learns that he or she has been mistaken in interpreting the world, and comes to a better understanding of this fictional 'reality'. Examples include ▷ Don Quixote and Catherine Morland in ▷ Jane Austen's ▷ *Northanger Abbey* (1818) – both characters are led astray by reading fiction. Quixote is driven out of his wits by reading 'books of knight errantry' (romances) while Catherine's imagination is fired by Gothic novels. Discovering that her dreadful suspicions of murder are unfounded, Catherine is forced to conclude (with a dry wit typical of Austen) that 'charming as were all Mrs Radcliffe's works, and charming even as were the works of her imitators, it was not in them perhaps that human nature, at least in the midland counties of England, was to be looked for'.

While references to novels in novels can serve to create the illusion of a transparent window on reality, they can also draw attention to the textuality of the work we are reading. Sometimes, indeed, either effect is possible depending on the reader, which is one reason why the boundaries of realism are never clear-cut. However, certain works constantly refer to themselves and the processes of their own construction in a way which seems designed to maintain the reader's awareness of textuality, fictionality and materiality (the novel as text, as invention and as material object). Such foregrounding of textuality goes back, in English prose narrative, at least as far as ▷ Thomas Nashe's ▷ *The Unfortunate Traveller or the Life of Jack Wilton* (1594) (where we find the ▷ narrator making frequent comments such as, 'Stay, let me looke about, where am I? in my text, or out of it'). It finds its pre-twentieth-century apogee in ▷ Laurence Sterne's ▷ *Tristram Shandy* (1759–67), one of the most playful and self-referential of novels, in which the narrator Tristram frequently discusses with the reader the progress he is making (or failing to make) with writing the novel. For example, in a digression on the subject of digressions, Tristram claims that 'in this long digression which I was accidentally led into, as in all my digressions (one only excepted) there is a master-stroke of digressive skill', but he is soon lamenting the dilemma of the writer: 'if he begins a digression, – from that moment, I observe, his whole work stands stock still; – and if he goes on with his main work, – then there is an end of his digresssion.'

One might think that such effects would break the illusion and destroy the reader's pleasure in the invented world. Some readers do feel this. On the other hand, the reflexive or self-conscious text has a special fascination of its own – and also a special reality. *Tristram Shandy* announces itself as a fictional verbal construct, which is precisely what it is. The realist and the reflexive novel might be compared with two styles of theatrical production: the West End drawing-room comedy – in which the set, behind a proscenium arch, authentically reproduces every decanter, curtain and coffee table – and the blank, black, open stage. In the first case the stage copies reality, but in so doing pretends not to be a stage. In the second case the stage admits to being what it is, and asks the audience to use its imagination.

It is important not to be too schematic in classifying texts. For example, *Don Quixote* includes both realist and reflexive manoeuvres. Like Madame Bovary's fantasies, Quixote's romantic delusions (that the windmills are giants, that he is a knight errant, and so on) are continually played off against a more mundane reality (the windmills are just windmills). Yet in many ways the narrative of the novel undermines the illusion of reality, through its playful self-criticism, as in the prologue, where the narrator describes his own book as 'full of varied fancies that no one else has ever imagined'. The extent to which a particular novel appears 'realistic' depends as much on the sophistication of the reader, or the theoretical assumptions made by the critic, as it does on inherent qualities of the text. It is possible to trace two traditions in novel criticism: one which sees the novel in realist and mimetic terms and another which sees it as discourse and artifice.

The realist/mimetic tradition, dominant in most writing about the novel before the twentieth century, understands the novel as basically a representation of reality. While by no means neglecting matters of form, technique and artifice, such criticism understands these ultimately as means for representing and commenting upon the world. This kind of criticism tends to base its paradigm of the novel on texts which are amenable to realist assumptions, such as the work of Defoe, of Jane Austen or of ▷ George Eliot, though these assumptions are capable of surviving critical, ideological or aesthetic realignments which seemed radical at the time. A major example would be the modernist (▷ modernism) emphasis on subjectivity, which implies that 'reality' is seen differently by different individuals. Both Virgina Woolf and Henry James use famous metaphors to reassess the nature of the novel in the light of such relativism, but both retain the concept of mimesis by interiorizing it. Woolf writes that 'reality is not a series of gig lamps symmetrically arranged; life is a luminous halo, a semi-transparent envelope surrounding us from the beginning of consciousness to the end'. James compares fiction to a house with many windows, the scene outside corresponding to the 'choice of subject' and the window to the 'literary form', but asserts that these 'are nothing without . . . the consciousness of the artist'. In each case the novel is still seen as reflecting reality, though in Woolf's metaphor it is the reality of the internal mental flux that is reflected, and in James's metaphor reality is filtered through the unique artistic sensibility of the writer. Ian Watt's *The Rise of the Novel*, which relates the emergence of the eighteenth-century novel to the increasing social and literary power of the commercial middle class and to the rise of individualism and ▷ empiricism, argued that the 'main tradition' of the novel was the realist line, starting with Defoe and Richardson and continuing via Jane Austen, and that 'formal or presentational realism . . . is typical of the novel genre as a whole'. In supporting this view, Watt tends to marginalize those novels which do not accord with it, such as the Gothic, the romantic novel, or the work of ▷ Tobias Smollett. His comments on Sterne are especially revealing of his critical bias; acknowledging Sterne's 'living authenticity', he denies him the leading place among eighteenth-century novelists on the grounds that *Tristram Shandy* is 'not so much a novel as a parody of a novel'; that is, Sterne is denied Watt's ultimate accolade for failing to conform to Watt's idea of the novel. Such critical manoeuvring indicates the danger of attempts to define a typical novel or a single main tradition.

The ability of a mimetic model to survive radical questioning is evident in a work like Linda Hutcheon's *Narcissistic Narrative: the Metafictional Paradox* (1980). This is a sophisticated theoretical study of the sort of contemporary novel which most overtly calls into question the possibility of language reflecting reality. 'Metafiction', which Hutcheon defines as 'fiction that includes within itself a commentary on its own narrative and/or linguistic identity' is notably practised by such novelists as the American John Barth, the Argentinian ▷ Jorge Luis Borges, the Italian Italo Calvino and, in England ▷ John Fowles, ▷ Julian Barnes and others. Hutcheon argues for a 'dialectical literary progression from one kind of novelistic mimesis to another', in which the 'mimesis of product' characteristic of nineteenth-century realism is distinguished from a 'process mimesis', in which it is the act of reading that is imitated by the novel.

An alternative critical approach to the novel rejects mimesis altogether in favour of an emphasis on the novel as ▷ discourse, as a verbal construct; on ▷ intertextuality; and on the acts of writing and reading as processes embedded in the network of social practices. This approach, which focuses on the way in which meaning is created, is primarily associated with structuralism, its antecedents, such as ▷ Russian Formalism, and its successors, such as ▷ deconstruction. Some of the implications of these theories are explored in the next essay. But even within a more traditional critical framework, there has been an alternative history of the novel, which has stressed the elements of playfulness, of artifice, of self-consciousness, of parody. Such a history would point to the work of Cervantes, ▷ Denis Diderot and Sterne in tracing the early history of the novel. Thus Robert Alter, in his book *Partial Magic: The Novel as a Self-Conscious Genre* (1975), rather than seeing nineteenth-century realism as the culmination of the novel as a genre, sees it as a temporary diminution of the self-consciousness found in eighteenth-century and twentieth-century fiction. Whereas Ian Watt argues that 'it is surely very damaging for a novel to be in any sense an imitation of another literary work' because 'the novelist's primary task is to convey the impression of fidelity to human experience', the Russian theorist ▷ Mikhail Bakhtin argues that the novel is inherently parodic and intertextual. Certainly many novels do produce meaning at least in part through intertextuality (their relations with other novels or texts). *Don Quixote*, often seen as the first modern novel, is, amongst other things, a parody of chivalric romance; Defoe's *Moll Flanders* presents itself as within the popular form of prison memoirs; *Northanger Abbey* mocks the Gothic novel; ▷ *The Rainbow* (1915) draws on the Book of Genesis and ▷ *Ulysses* on *The Odyssey*. Of these at least *Don Quixote*, *Northanger Abbey* and *Ulysses* contain significant elements of parody. Thus it is possible to argue, as does Frank Kermode in *The Sense of an Ending* (1966), that 'the history of the novel is a history of anti-novels' (▷ anti-novel).

Antecedents of the Novel

There are various opinions as to the date of the first novel and the true antecedents of the novel as a form. The view of these questions taken by critics and historians of the novel tends to depend on their conception of what defines a novel. A critic who regards the novel as essentially or predominantly a realist form, which emerged in association with the decline of romance and the rise of the middle class, might well claim that ▷ *Robinson Crusoe* (1719) was the first English novel, with ▷ *The Pilgrim's Progress* (1678, 1684) and *Don Quixote* as important English and European precursors respectively. However, a wider conception of the novel, less tied to psychological realism and embracing the grotesque, the fantastic and the playful, would support the case for the existence of the Elizabethan and Jacobean novel.

The strongest contenders for inclusion in this category are the works of Thomas Nashe, whose affinities with the later tradition of self-conscious and parodic fiction have already been mentioned: *The Unfortunate Traveller or the Life of Jack Wilton* (1594), a playful, grotesque and episodic picaresque romance, *Pierce Penniless, His Supplication to the Devil* (1592), a satire on the sins of contemporary London and *Nashes Lenten Stuff* (1599), a comic celebration of the red herring and the town of Yarmouth, including parodic elements such as a burlesque of the story of Hero and Leander. Other significant works of Elizabethan prose fiction include the popular works of ▷ Thomas Deloney (?1543–?1600); stories such as *Jack of Newbury* (1597) and *Thomas of Reading* (1600) which revolve around the comic and heroic activities of working men, based on real personages. On the boundaries of memoir, fiction, ▷ tract and moral tale, ▷ Robert Greene's *Groatsworth of Wit, Bought with a Million of Repentance* (1592) discourses about the author's own vices and forms part of a tradition of moralizing memoirs, with which *Moll Flanders* has obvious affinities. The interest of the many Elizabethan prose romances is largely in the discussion of ideas, in set-piece rhetorical descriptions and in the elegant and lyrical style rather than in plot or character: they include, apart from the most famous example, *The Arcadia* (1580, 1590) of ▷ Sir Philip Sidney, ▷ Lyly's ▷ *Euphues* (1578, 1580), Robert Greene's *Pandosto, or The Triumph of Time* (1588), ▷ Thomas Lodge's *Rosalynde, Euphues Golden Legacy* (1590) and *A Margarite of America* (1596) and ▷ Lady Mary Wroth's *Urania* (1621). Many such prose romances include sections in verse. Between the Jacobean period and the early eighteenth-century, French romantic fiction was popular in England, but the emergence of the novel was also prepared for by such forms as letters (▷ letter-writing), ▷ travel literature and historical writing. Letters are employed as a specifically literary form by ▷ Aphra Behn in her *Love Letters Between a Nobleman and his Sister* (1683), while the ▷ epistolary novel was later to find a major exponent in Samuel Richardson. Travel writing was a popular Elizabethan form; for example Richard Hakluyt published *Divers voyages touching the discoverie of America* in 1582, followed by other accounts of voyages of exploration. Aphra Behn, a playwright notable as one of the earliest professional woman writers in England, used a fictional version of travel writing in her novel ▷ *Oroonoko, or the History of the Royal Slave* (1688). Based on a visit to Surinam, the novel attacks the hypocrisy and cruelty of the slave trade. A little later the politician ▷ Edward Hyde, Earl of Clarendon wrote what was to become one of the most influential works of history in England, *The True Historical Narrative of the Rebellion and Civil Wars in England* (1702–4).

The humour, multiple voices and resistance to generic categorization of *The Unfortunate Traveller*, or the roots of *Jack of Newbury* in popular tales, would accord in particular with the conception of the novel as a polyphonic, parodic and open-ended form derived from the richness of unofficial culture, a conception developed by Bakhtin. The Russian critic located the roots of the novel not only in literary forms but in a whole range of cultural practices, from classical to medieval times, which he saw as engaging with contemporary life in a spirit of laughter, rather than, like the epic, viewing with reverence a sacrosanct past. In his essays 'Epic and Novel' and 'From the Prehistory of Novelistic Discourse', Bakhtin argues that the novel draws on 'that broadest of realms, the common people's creative culture of laughter'. The influences from classical times on novelistic language that he identifies include: bucolic poems, ▷ fable, memoirs, ▷ pamphlets, Socratic dialogue, parodic satyr plays, farces and satires, especially Menippean satire (such as the *Satyricon* of Petronius, a series of parodic and pornographic stories and verses from the 1st century AD). From the Middle Ages, he lists such 'sacred parody' as *Cyprian Feasts* (a pseudo-biblical narrative composed to be recited at table) and the activities of carnivals and holidays. For Bakhtin, these elements culminate in 'the great Renaissance novel of Rabelais and Cervantes'.

Bakhtin's account of the antecedents of the novel is distinctive and polemical (although influential). However, most would agree that Cervantes's *Don Quixote* and Rabelais's ▷ *Gargantua and Pantagruel* (1534–64) are key works in the evolution of the European novel. The rich duality of *Don Quixote* – its participation in both realism and ▷ metafiction – has already been noted. *Gargantua and Pantagruel*, a comic romance originally published in five volumes, is not concerned with psychological interiority but it clearly anticipates elements of the work of James Joyce in its combination of learning and multiple allusions with energy, zest, parody and the frankness about the functions of the human body which has produced the adjective 'Rabelaisian'.

Suspending for the moment both the debate about the precise nature of the novel and the exclusion of poetry from consideration, we may identify many earlier forms of narrative which in some way prefigure or influence novelistic narrative. The most celebrated and admired narrative form before the novel was the verse epic, of which famous early examples include not only Homer's ▷ *Odyssey* and *Iliad* (written down c 600 BC) and ▷ Virgil's ▷ *Aeneid* (19 BC), but also the Babylonian epic of *Gilgamesh* (c 1400 BC). Even earlier than this, however, are a number of Egyptian prose 'novels' – tales of various sorts, on themes such as love or travel – which survive on papyrus rolls dated from c 2000 BC. Of these *Sinahue* tells a tale of shipwreck, exile and homecoming – an outline story found in various versions in many later novels, from *Robinson Crusoe* and ▷ *Gulliver's Travels* to ▷ *Lord of the Flies* and various works of science fiction. Better known than these Egyptian works are the Greek 'novels' of the 1st and 2nd centuries AD, such as Longus's *Daphnis and Cloe*, and the Latin 'novels' of the 1st century AD, such as Apuleius's *The Golden Ass*. There are parallels between the Greek 'novel' and the eighteenth-century English novel in that both found a readership among an emergent middle class and that both tended to be looked down upon by contemporary scholars.

Collections of tales are an ancient form, but the most significant for the novel are probably ▷ *Arabian Nights Entertainments* (c 900), Boccaccio's ▷ *The Decameron* (1353) and, in England, ▷ *The Canterbury Tales*. Chaucer's best-known work anticipates the novel in its vividness of characterization and story-telling skill, but his romance *Troilus and Criseyde*, although entirely in verse, is more consistently novelistic. Although its concluding book requires that it be seen as a form of extended exemplum or ▷ Boethian debate (▷ Boethius), the preceding four books resemble a novel in their single coherent plot and use of scenes of action and dialogue to suggest subtleties of character, motivation and social interaction. The romance, and the pastoral with which it often overlaps, are two further pre-novelistic genres with a significant influence on later fiction. We have noted the role of romance in what some call the 'Elizabethan novel', and the way in which the emergent novel of the eighteenth century defined itself in opposition to romance, while incorporating romance elements and coming to include the sub-genre of the romantic novel (such as the historical romances of Walter Scott). While the word 'novel' derives from the Italian 'novella', meaning something new, many European languages other than English refer to the novel by words related to the French 'roman', a word also used of medieval and later romances, so that the antithesis between the novel and the romance had less linguistic support outside England.

Many medieval romances used versions of the Arthurian legends (derived in part from history and chronicle, notably Geoffrey of Monmouth's *Historia Regum Britanniae*, c 1136). English Arthurian romances include not only fourteenth-century poems, but also the prose *La Morte D'Arthur* of Malory (finished 1470). On the continent the chivalric romance flourished in Spain during the sixteenth century (for example *Amadis de Gaula*, 1508), but was already dying out by the time of Cervantes's parodic use of the form in *Don Quixote*. In France the pastoral romance produced Honoré d'Urfée's *Astrée* (1607–27) which influenced the multi-volume romances of Madeleine de Scudéry, such as *Artamène, or the Great Cyrus* (1649–53). It is these episodic, sentimental works with their antique settings that eighteenth-century novelists are most likely to have had in mind in their strictures on the romance. Indeed Fielding, in his Preface to *Joseph Andrews* (1742), seeks to associate his novel with the epic, and to distance it from 'the voluminous works, commonly called Romances, namely Clelia, Cleopatra, Astraea, Cassandra, the Grand Cyrus ... which contain ... very little instruction or entertainment'. 'Chapbook' is a modern term for the cheap, popular, illustrated collections of ballads and stories that were widely sold in Britain from the sixteenth century to the eighteenth century and these often included versions of romances.

The ▷ picaresque tale, the story of the adventures of a *picaro* or rogue, usually involving a series of semi-comic episodes held together by a journey, is a form which is closely interwoven with the early development of the novel. Well-established in Spain from the time of *Lazarillo de Tomes* (1554; author unknown), and used by Nashe in *The Unfortunate Traveller*, by ▷ Alain-René Lesage in ▷ *Gil Blas* and by Cervantes in *Don Quixote*, the picaresque is a major element in both *Moll Flanders* and *Tom Jones*. Whole *Don Quixote* is the most popular candidate for the first modern European novel, it is in France that the novel develops earliest, emerging out of the romances in the form of *The Princess of Clèves* (1678) by ▷ Marie-Madeleine de La Fayette. Though the setting of this novel suggests chivalric romance, the story of an unhappy but faithful wife is told with sustained psychological insight.

To conclude this overview of the antecedents of the novel we should perhaps return to Bakhtin, and his emphasis on diversity. The novel has been a form capable of assimilating elements of many other genres, and a total account of its antecedents, were such a thing possible, would have to include not only epic, romance, pastoral, picaresque, pamphlets, chapbooks, travel narratives, letters, histories, chronicles, memoirs, biographies, autobiographies and collections of tales, together with the multitude of forms listed by Bakhtin, but also elements of drama (clearly influential on dialogue in the novel) and of poetry (for example the sonnet sequence, as practised by Shakespeare and Sidney, with its implicit plot). The word 'fiction' derives from the Latin *'fingere'*, to fashion (in clay) while 'history' comes from the Greek *'historia'* (finding out, narrative, history; from *'histor'* = wise man) and 'novel' from the Italian *'novella storia'* (new story). Fashioning, finding out, knowing, narrating, the new: such conceptions and impulses interacted at many levels in the discourses of early modern culture within which the novel gradually took its place.

Theories of the Novel 2

Andrew Michael Roberts

Novelists on the novel

As the first essay suggested, the earliest theorists of the novel were generally the novelists themselves, often concerned to defend an emergent form which was not recognized within the classical generic scheme of epic, dramatic and lyric, and which was sometimes subject to attack on the grounds of the supposed immorality or triviality of events which it portrayed, or even on the grounds of its very fictionality (stigmatized as lying). Indeed, prior to the twentieth century the most influential theorizing about the novel – its nature, forms, purpose and techniques – was done by novelists. When not directly engaged in defending their genre, their ideas were often a matter of developing a theoretical basis for their own creative practice or promoting a group or movement with which they were identified. Sometimes such theorizing takes place within novels themselves. In ▷ *Tom Jones* (1749) ▷ Fielding defends the value, as examples, of characters with faults as well as virtues; as we have seen in the previous essay, ▷ Sterne defends the practice of digression in ▷ *Tristram Shandy*; ▷ Anthony Trollope, in *Barchester Towers* (1857), argues that reader and author must trust each other. Other comments are found in letters, diaries, records of conversations or, more formally, in prefaces and essays. So ▷ Stendhal, in 1840, claims that he writes best without planning and argues for simplicity of style; ▷ Thackeray, in the preface to ▷ *Pendennis* (1850), defends frankness and the 'Natural' against what he saw as the limiting prudery of his day, looking back with regret to the freedom enjoyed in this respect by Fielding; ▷ George Eliot argues in 1879 that the novelist must be a 'teacher or influencer of the public mind'; ▷ Dostoevsky, in a letter of 1869, claims that the apparently fantastic is often true. Some of these comments, and many others, are gathered together in Miriam Allott's valuable anthology of quotations *Novelists on the Novel* (1959). It was probably the French novelists of the nineteenth century, ▷ Balzac, ▷ Flaubert, ▷ Stendhal and ▷ Zola, who developed the most systematic theory of the novel, centring on the debate concerning realism. In his Preface to *The Human Comedy*, Balzac explains his huge project in terms of an inclusive portrayal of the life of his times, dividing the volumes up into Studies of Morals, Philosophical Studies and Analytical Studies, sub-dividing the first of these into scenes of Private, Provincial, Parisian, Political, Military and Country Life, and claiming to present 'two or three thousand outstanding types of character of a period . . . that is the sum of types which each generation produces'. Implicit here is a theory of the novel as sociological and moral survey.

Twentieth-century traditions: Anglo-American and Continental

This tendency for theorization by novelists has by no means diminished in the twentieth century; indeed, it has become very much the norm for novelists to be influential critics. In the early part of the century ▷ Henry James, ▷ Virginia Woolf, ▷ D.H. Lawrence, ▷ F.M. Ford and ▷ E.M. Forster all wrote noted studies of other novelists or of the novel in general, and post-war novelists such as ▷ David Lodge, ▷ Malcolm Bradbury, ▷ Gabriel Josipovici and ▷ John Berger have been prominent theorists of the novel. The tradition of commenting on the novel within novels themselves has received a boost from the habitual reflexivity of post-modernism, as for example in the novels of ▷ Julian Barnes. Usually, though not invariably, the theories of novelists remain closely linked to their practice; for example D.H. Lawrence's *Study of Thomas Hardy*, although an interesting discussion of Hardy's fiction, is probably just as revealing in the way it reflects back on Lawrence's own work. However, the twentieth century has also seen numerous attempts by critics and schools of critics to elaborate systematic theories of the novel and of narrative in general, based on explicitly-stated philosophical premises concerning the way in which meaning is created, the nature of language and the social and ideological significance of literature. Until the 1960s this remained largely a continental project, centred in particular on Russia, Germany and France, while Anglo-American novel criticism developed on the whole within exegetical, historical, technical, biographical or evaluative frameworks; that is to say it interpreted the meanings of novels, explored the history of the novel, analysed the techniques of writing, related texts to the lives of their authors, or assessed their value in terms of the insights they offered to the reader and the (usually liberal and humanist) values which they propounded.

The continental tradition, on the other hand, was more influenced by philosophy (especially German philosophy, and notably that of ▷ Kant, Hegel, ▷ Nietzsche and ▷ Marx) and by linguistics, especially the work of ▷ Ferdinand de Saussure, who is regarded as the founder of ▷ structuralism.

Russian Formalism and Bakhtin

One of the earliest schools of linguistics-based theory was Russian ▷ Formalism, which flourished in Moscow and St Petersburg between 1914 and the mid-1920s. Prominent members were Roman Jakobson (who, after a period in Prague, carried the influence of Formalism to the United States in 1941) and Viktor Skhlovsky. The Formalists emphasized the effect of ▷ defamiliarization produced by the special qualities and conventions of literary language. In relation to narrative, they distinguished the ▷ *fabula* (the chronological series of events which are represented in a novel) from the *syuzhet* (the order, manner and techniques of their presentation in the narrative), a distinction which became crucial to the later development of ▷ narratology. Reversing the mimetic view of fiction, the Formalists argued that the literary devices of the *syuzhet* are not determined by the need to convey the *fabula*; rather the *syuzhet* serves to defamilarize and construct the *fabula*.

The Formalists are most important for their influence on later schools of theory. Like Jakobson, René Wellek was a member of the Prague Linguistic Circle (largely a continuation of Formalism), and he too moved to the USA, where he became prominent among the exponents of ▷ New Criticism, who argued that the literary text should be examined as an autonomous object, not in relation to the intentions of the author or the historical context in which it was written. In a 1937 public exchange of letters with ▷ F.R. Leavis, who epitomized the anti-theoretical stance in English criticism, Wellek argued that criticism should make explicit its own theoretical assumptions. ▷ Bakhtin, whose distinctive view of the antecedents of the novel has already been mentioned, began his career with a critique of Formalism's tendency to divorce language from its social context. Bakhtin's influence on English-speaking critics and readers was considerably delayed, because it was not until the late 1960s that his work began to be translated into English, but he has gradually emerged as one of the most important twentieth-century theorists of the novel. He laid great stress on the uniqueness and autonomy of the novel as a genre, a uniqueness which he saw in terms of its openness to continual change, its 'spirit of process and inconclusiveness', its ability to criticize itself, its use of parody and of different languages, its focus on the present and future (contrasted with the epic's concern with the past), its historicity, its revelation of the constantly unrealized potential of the individual in his or her 'zone of contact with an inconclusive present', above all its heteroglossia (multiplicity of voices) or dialogic qualities. In Bakhtin's terms, the dialogic involves an interplay between multiple voices, each the embodiment of a social context and a way of understanding the world, including the voices of the author, of the narrator(s), of characters, and of other texts and styles imitated or quoted within the text. This interest in the interplay of different voices led Bakhtin to attend in particular to narrative techniques such as ▷ free indirect discourse, a blending of the voice of narrator and character which he regarded as a 'zone of dialogical contact'. His work is open to the objection that he essentializes the novel, making it more a metaphysical principle than a descriptive generic term. For example, when other genres, such as the narrative poem, show features which he claims as part of the uniqueness of the novel, he simply argues that such genres have been subject to a process of 'novelization'. Nevertheless, his concepts of the dialogic and of carnival have become key terms for the subsequent analysis of political and ideological aspects of fiction.

Henry James and F.R. Leavis

Anglo-American novel criticism of the first half of the twentieth century was greatly influenced by the elegant subtleties of Henry James's writings on the novel, including his essays (especially those on nineteenth-century novelists such as Balzac and ▷ Dickens) and his Prefaces to the revised New York Edition of his own novels (1907–9). James emphasized the importance of formal perfection (criticizing the novels of ▷ Tolstoy and ▷ Dostoevsky as 'fluid puddings'), advanced such humanist value criteria as 'the amount of felt life' in a novel and advocated an 'impersonal' mode of narration, in which there are no intrusive comments by an omniscient narrator or ▷ implied author, but events are seen through the eyes of a reflector, observer or ▷ focal character, often a character with an intensely aware, finely-developed consciousness; but with crucial limitations of perspective. This conception of impersonal narration had hardened into something like a dogma by the 1920s, in the form of a preference for 'showing' rather than 'telling' in narrative. This over-simplistic antithesis contributed to a relatively low valuation of novelists such as George Eliot (ironically a writer whom Henry James himself greatly admired), who use an authorial voice to offer judgements and observations to the reader, to 'tell' the reader things, rather than 'showing' the thoughts and words of the characters and leaving the reader to draw their own conclusions. Eliot's reputation was, however, restored (on moral rather than technical grounds) by F.R. Leavis, probably the most influential English critic of the first half of the century. In *The Great Tradition* (1948), Leavis asserted that the 'great English novelists are Jane Austen, George Eliot, Henry James and Joseph Conrad'. Leavis's work is relentlessly evaluative, dividing major from minor authors on the basis of criteria such as whether their novels promote 'human awareness' of 'the possibilities of life'; criteria which are based on the widest claims for the importance of literature to human culture, but which are in themselves so subjective as to be hardly open to debate. Leavis radically revised the existing canon of major writers, but tended to replace it with his own equally exclusive canon; novelists whom he dislikes, such as Sterne, may be dismissed by him in a footnote. Leavis was an advocate of high moral seriousness and drew his central value of 'life' from the work of D.H. Lawrence; his work has provoked both passionate discipleship and (especially since the 1960s) passionate opposition. Much of the latter has focused on the weaknesses inherent in his anti-theoretical position, and Leavis has come to stand for everything which various forms of post-structuralist and political theories seek to reject.

Narrative theory: Wayne Booth and Gérard Genette

E.M. Forster, in ▷ *Aspects of the Novel* (1927), considers some of the elements of narrative and introduces the rather vague but highly memorable categories of ▷ 'flat' and 'round' characters. But it was in the 1960s, with Wayne Booth's *The Rhetoric of Fiction*, that attempts at a systematic study of narrative technique – including such matters as point of view, narrative distance, temporal variation, use of narrators and so on – gathered pace within Anglo-American criticism. Booth, a neo-Aristotelian critic of the Chicago school of criticism, overturned the post-Jamesian orthodoxy of indirect, impersonal narration by analysing the limits of 'objectivity', so as to suggest that 'showing' always includes an element of implicit 'telling'. Booth sees the novel as a communicative act which transmits the author's vision, but his own values of morality and order tend to bias him against ambiguous or paradoxical forms of narrative, which are precisely those forms which develop rapidly in the post-war novel. Booth's work on the categorization and analysis of narrative has been largely superseded by the work of German and French structuralist and post-structuralist critics, notably ▷ Roland Barthes and ▷ Gérard Genette. Genette provides probably the most complete and rigorous set of terms for the analysis of narrative in his books, including *Narrative Discourse* (1972), but understands the limits of precise definition and formal categories. Structuralism applies a linguistics-based model, derived from Saussure, to a wide range of cultural activities and artefacts: anthropology and myth, fashion, exhibitions, advertisements, sporting events, literary and other texts and so on. In its earlier forms it had scientific aspirations and aimed for a precise and objective analysis of such systems of meaning. So, in relation to the novel, the most ambitious form of the pseudo-scientific structuralist/narratological project was to construct a 'grammar of narrative' such that any narrative could be exhaustively and rigorously analysed in terms of a pre-established set of rules, procedures, categories and variables. This aim cannot be achieved with any but the simplest narratives without reducing fiction to a set of rigid patterns, although the attempt to achieve the impossible in this respect can be highly illuminating. However, the more perceptive narratological theorists, such as Genette, realise that the most interesting insights of narratology often arise at the very points at which a particular text places the theoretical model under strain, by eluding, subverting or modifying its categories. So Genette's *Narrative Discourse* combines the elaboration of categories with a close reading of ▷ Proust's multi-volume novel *Remembrance of Things Past* (1913–27), and Genette shows himself highly sensitive to the paradoxes, ambiguities and instabilities of Proust's complex narrative.

Structuralism and deconstruction

Textual paradox and instability are main points of attention for ▷ deconstruction, the form of post-structuralist theory (▷ post-structuralism) associated with the name of ▷ Jacques Derrida, but also with Gilles Deleuze, ▷ Paul de Man and others. Genette's *Narrative Discourse* partakes of elements of both the structuralist and deconstructive projects, and the same could be said of Roland Barthes's most influential work on the novel, *S/Z* (trans. 1974), a work which identifies, in the form of a series of codes, the basis of the classic realist text in the form of a short story by Balzac. As ▷ Jonathan Culler points out in *On Deconstruction: Theory and Criticism after Structuralism* (1983), this metalinguistic project of naming and classification seems to exemplify the scientific and rationalist spirit of structuralism, yet Barthes also renounces structuralism in *S/Z* by exploring what Culler terms the text's 'difference from itself, the way in which it outplays the codes on which it seems to rely'. Barthes is a mercurial figure whose work crosses many boundaries; one of the most famous aspects of *S/Z* is his assertion of the value of the writerly (*scriptible*) text, which allows the reader to be a producer of meaning (the reader can 're-write' the text in the process of reading), as against the more traditional readerly (*lisible*) text, of which the reader is only a consumer. This is a distinction which points towards the area of literary theory known as reader-response criticism. As its name implies, such criticism redirects attention from the text and the author to the reader and to reading processes, working with concepts such as the ▷ 'implied reader', the 'ideal reader' and the 'interpretative community'. Prominent exponents of reader-response criticism include Wolfgang Iser and Stanley Fish.

While deconstructive elements may be found in readings of the novel by Genette and Barthes, deconstruction (like structuralism) is a philosophical and cultural project extending beyond literary criticism. Since the 1960s the nature of literary criticism has been transformed by the influence of a whole range of such projects: deconstruction, ▷ feminism, psychoanalysis, Marxism, ▷ New Historicism, ▷ post-modernism, post-colonial theory, theories of ▷ discourse. These projects are often referred to, simply but confusingly, as 'theory'; sometimes as 'literary theory' when they are applied to literature and sometimes, in their more general applications, as 'critical theory' (which implies not only the criticism of literature but the criticism of philosophy, of psychology, of politics, of sociology and so on). From this point on, then, it is often less appropriate to refer to theories *of* the novel than to the influence or application of theory *to* the novel. Of course, more traditional methods and ideas of literary criticism continue to be applied and to interact with such theory, whether polemically or dialogically.

The work of Jacques Derrida is a far-reaching critique of Western thought and its categories, including rationality, the use of binary oppositions, 'logocentrism' (the privileging of speech and self-presence over writing) and the conception of the self or subject. Perhaps most significant for the interpretation of literary texts is the Nietzschean scepticism with which deconstruction rejects, not only the idea that language can refer outside itself, but also the quest for stable meaning. Instead, Derrida conceptualizes texts in terms of an infinite play of *différance*, a French term which puns on the words for difference and deferral. The structuralist conception of textual meaning as a system of difference is transformed by an idea of radical instability, in which the moment of definite, defined meaning is constantly deferred along a chain of shifting signifiers. The anti-referentiality of deconstruction has itself influenced the contemporary novel, inspiring or providing a theoretical support for various forms of self-referential metafiction. While the interpretation of literary texts in the traditional sense of 'literary' is not the main project of deconstruction (much of its attention being directed to philosophical texts), deconstructive practices have proved productive in various ways for readings of the novel. For example, deconstruction has questioned ideas of identity and similarity and analysed the relationship between difference and repetition. This has allowed critics such as J. Hillis Miller (*Fiction and Repetition: Seven English Novels*, 1982) and Steven Connor (*Samuel Beckett: Repetition, Theory and Text*, 1988) to reveal new and complex effects of meaning in what might at first sight seem an unremarkable feature of fictional narratives: their use of repetition.

Psychoanalytical criticism

Since psychoanalysis is primarily a clinical theory of the human mind, two obvious ways of applying it to the novel are to analyse the psyches of authors or their characters. The founder of psychoanalysis, ▷ Sigmund Freud, did both: analysing the personality of Dostoevsky in 'Dostoevsky and Parricide' (1928) and that of Lady Macbeth (a character from drama, not the novel, but the principle is here the same) in 'Some Character-Types Met with in Psychoanalytical Work' (1916). Certainly Freudian and post-Freudian theories of development and motivation have contributed to the sophistication of accounts of characterization in the novel and biographical studies of novelists. There are, however, serious objections to any attempt directly to 'psychoanalyse' authors or characters. Psychoanalysis is an interactive process, in which the evolving relationship of analyst and analysand (especially the ▷ transference) is crucial, and in which the analysand responds to, rather than passively accepting, the interpretations offered by the analyst; interpretations which are strategic and provisional rather than authoritative and fixed. Furthermore, the analysand has to choose to commit himself or herself to analysis. Since neither characters nor authors have made such a commitment, and since neither is generally in a position to interact with the critics and modify interpretations, naive psychoanalytical readings, which treat characters as real people or claim to reveal the unconscious of the author, implicitly assert a knowledge and authority on the part of the critic which is not only dubious, but alien to the practice of psychoanalysis itself. A more satisfactory concept of psychoanalytical literary theory may be represented by imagining that the text occupies the role of the analysand. Critics and readers do interact with the text in the process of reading; readers interpret the text but are also interpreted by it. The post-structuralist re-readings of Freud proposed by ▷ Jacques Lacan have strengthened the basis for the psychoanalytical interpretation of the text because of Lacan's use of a linguistic model of mind, specifically his claim that 'the unconscious is structured like a language'. In Lacan's own well-known 'Seminar on "The Purloined Letter"' (1956), he analyses a short story by the American writer Edgar Allan Poe in terms of the circulation of meaning and desire, so as to make the story into an allegory of processes of writing, reading and interpretation. The mutual interrogation of text and reader can also be extended to the relationship of literature and psychoanalysis, given the latter's reliance on narratives (such as Freud's case-histories of his patients). Thus Shoshana Felman argues, in a 1977 special edition of *Yale French Studies* devoted to psychoanalysis, that 'in the same way that psychoanalysis points to the unconscious of literature, *literature, in its turn, is the unconscious of psychoanalysis*'.

Feminist criticism

The Lacanian view of subjectivity as inherently fractured and as constructed in the symbolic realm of language has proved valuable for certain feminist analyses, as have some Freudian concepts, such as the 'uncanny', although the work of Freud and Lacan has also been much criticized by feminist thinkers. While deconstruction is a philosophical project and psychoanalysis originally a medical one, feminism is social and political in its aims, although it extends to every area of culture. However, there are several reasons why feminist theories are of particular importance to the novel, and vice versa. One is the historical fact that the novel is a form which has often been associated with women, both as writers and as readers. This has not necessarily been a positive association (sometimes it has taken a derogatory form, seeing novels as concerned with trivial 'feminine' issues), nor has it prevented the frequent exclusion or marginalization of woman writers from the canon of recognized 'masters' of the novel. On the one hand, the traditional canon of 'great novelists' includes a number of women writers: Jane Austen, George Eliot, the ▷ Brontë sisters, Virginia Woolf. On the other, there are very large numbers of women novelists, from ▷ Aphra Behn on, who were, until recently, relatively or totally neglected. One of the achievements of feminist novel criticism has been the rediscovery and revaluation of women's writing, accomplished in combination with various publishing houses and imprints, notably Virago, Women's Press and Pandora Press, which have produced paperback editions of many neglected novels by women. The process of identifying and analysing a tradition of women's writing and considering the nature of feminine literary creativity – a combination of aims sometimes termed 'gynocritics' – has been carried out by critics such as Elaine Showalter (*A Literature of Their Own: British Women Novelists from Brontë to Lessing*, 1977), Sandra M. Gilbert and Susan Gubar (*The Madwoman in the Attic: The Woman Writer and the Nineteenth-Century Imagination*, 1979). Gilbert and Gubar also argue that the very act of writing has been understood in the West in terms of patriarchal metaphors: the author as father, the pen as penis and instrument of power. These critics are engaged in rewriting literary history to redress some of the effects of sexism, and this brings us to another point of connection between feminism and the novel. The understanding that history cannot be written objectively, but necessarily reflects (to varying extents) the prejudices and priorities of the historian, has been important to feminists seeking to write what is sometimes termed 'herstory' – the relatively neglected experiences and achievements of women. The novel has provided a source for the writing of herstory, but also in some sense a model. Fiction, and especially modern fiction, has often called into question the boundaries of fiction and fact and can therefore assist in the reshaping of our understanding of how we interpret the past.

Another aspect of feminist novel criticism has been 'feminist critique', the study of representations of women (often focused on the misogyny such representations reveal) in the novel and in novel criticism. The analysis of gender-based structures in fiction has generated re-reading of numerous well-known novelists such as ▷ Hardy, ▷ Conrad and Lawrence. Taking a wider perspective, Gilbert and Gubar's three-volume study, *No Man's Land: The Place of the Woman Writer in the Twentieth Century* (1988, 1989), combines a critique of the (often violent) misogyny of a number of modern male novelists with an analysis of the social and ideological underpinnings of this misogyny and an examination of the strategies of women writers.

The explicitly philosophical forms of feminist theory often known as 'French feminism' are exemplified by the writers ▷ Hélène Cixous, Luce Irigaray and ▷ Julia Kristeva. These thinkers tend to combine feminism with the methods or theories of psychoanalysis, Marxism, or deconstruction, while also contesting what some see as patriarchal structures or assumptions within those theories, such as the phallocentrism of Lacanian psychoanalytical theory, or the neglect of gender issues in some Marxist writing in favour of an exclusive privileging of class issues.

Marxist criticism

Marxist literary theory has, in one way or another, been concerned to relate literature to social and historical factors, which has tended to give it a special interest in the realist novel. Indeed, Friedrich Engels, one of the founders of Marxism as a political doctrine, argued that Balzac's realism led him to represent in his novels the historical necessity of the decline of the French aristocracy, despite the novelist's explicitly conservative political views. The Hungarian Marxist Georg Lukács judged novels according to the correctness with which they objectively reflected the structure of historical and social reality. His idea of objective reality was based on the Marxist view of history as a dialectical class-struggle. So Lukács, in *Studies in European Realism* (1950), saw Tolstoy, Balzac and Scott as the most 'correct' novelists and, in 'The Ideology of Modernism' (1955) objected to modernist novels on the grounds of their 'anti-realist' subjectivity. Lukács published from the 1920s on, and lived most of his career under the constraints of Stalinism. In western Europe, Marxist political views attracted much attention from writers and critics during the 1930s but receded as the oppressive nature of Stalinism became known. In the 1960s (a time when Lukács's work became extensively available in translation), interest in Marxist thought re-emerged strongly, but in new forms. Both the determinism of 'vulgar Marxism' (in which the social and political 'superstructure' is held to be wholly determined by an economic 'base') and the reflective model of literature were largely abandoned. Instead of the former, the French theorist ▷ Louis Althusser developed a theory of social formation in terms of the 'relative autonomy' of a range of different structures and institutions, existing in a complex relationship of overdetermination with each other and with the economic base. This base was seen as the ultimate determining factor, but as depending for its continuing reproduction on elements of the superstructure, such as the 'ideological state apparatuses', which include not only education and religious, political and social organization, but also art and literature. While this freed fiction from simple determination or reflection, it raised the problem of the precise relationship between literature and ideology, which has remained a key focus of Marxist criticism. Althusser argues that literature, specifically the novels of Balzac and Solzhenitsyn, can 'make us "perceive" [but not know] in some sense from the inside, by an internal distance, the very ideology in which they are held' ('A Letter on Art'). Similarly, Pierre Macherey, another of the most influential Marxist critics of this period, argues that the writer's ideology is an element in a novel, but that the novel does not simply reflect that ideology, but produces and transforms it, so that 'literature challenges ideology by using it'. Althusser drew on Freudian and deconstructive theory in his account of 'symptomatic reading' (a reading of the ideology which a text hides from itself), on Lacanian reading for his theory of the ▷ interpellation of the subject in language through the individual's (mis)recognition of himself or herself in the mirror of ideology. The later development of these ideas is exemplified in Frederic Jameson's *The Political Unconscious: Narrative as a Socially Symbolic Act* (1981), which develops a Marxist, historicized and collective version of the Freudian unconscious. In reading the novels of Conrad, ▷ George Gissing, Balzac and others, Jameson argues that the most complex and historically revealing novels set up a tension between the illusions of ideology and the resistance of history. History is here conceived as an 'absent cause . . . inaccessible to us except in textual form' and approachable only through 'its narrativization in the political unconscious'.

Michel Foucault and New Historicism

Althusserian Marxism is subject to criticism from a deconstructive point of view, on the grounds that it seeks to preserve a 'scientific' metalanguage, capable of describing ideology from outside. Since the 1960s political criticism of a broadly left-wing persuasion has developed in various ways. One of the most influential has been the work of ▷ Michel Foucault, who analyses social institutions and practices in terms of discourse. Discourses are systems of representation within which knowledge is *produced*, and include the languages specific to institutions such as education, the law and medicine. Discourse, for Foucault, is both an effect of power and the realm within which power is circulated and contested. In works such as *Discipline and Punish: The Birth of the Prison* (trans. 1977) and his three-volume *History of Sexuality* (trans. 1978, 1985, 1986), Foucault eschews a totalizing theory of the structure of society and a teleological or causal conception of history in favour of an account of the ▷ genealogy of the discursive practices through which social control takes place. His essay 'What is an Author?' (1969) argues that the very idea of the author is the discursive product of a certain individualizing historical era.

An important development of Foucault's ideas is ▷ New Historicism, a critical approach which focuses on what Louis A. Montrose terms 'the historicity of texts and the textuality of history'. New Historicism, which has affinities with the British school of Cultural Materialism derived from the work of ▷ Raymond Williams, does not study literary texts in relation to a historical 'context' or 'background', rejecting these notions in favour of an understanding of the past in terms of the inseparable circulation of literary and non-literary texts. In the field of explicitly political criticism there has been a shift of emphasis in favour of attention to specific marginalized and oppressed groups, a move which has promoted the growth of post-colonial criticism and theory.

Theories of Post-colonial Writing

Post-colonial theory has in common with feminism the double project of affirmation and critique. In this case the affirmation involves the discovery, rediscovery and revaluing of novelists silenced or marginalized by their subjected or 'subaltern' position in the power-structures of colonialism or neo-colonialism, while the critique attacks racism within fiction and criticism. The racist myths of empire play a significant role in many English novels, from Defoe's ▷ *Robinson Crusoe*, in which the story provides a sort of paradigm for the act of colonization, to Conrad's ▷ *Heart of Darkness*. The latter has become something of a *cause célèbre* since 1975, when Conrad was attacked as a racist by the Nigerian novelist ▷ Chinua Achebe; the ensuing debate has focused a number of the key issues of political interpretation. This is because Conrad's text uses modernist strategies of ambiguity and two-level narrative in a way that makes it difficult to identify the ideological position of the writer. Furthermore, the story combines explicit criticism of certain aspects of colonialism and racism (economic exploitation and cruelty) with the use of certain racist and colonialist clichés (Africa as a place of 'primitive' darkness, Africans as lower down the evolutionary scale). Achebe's criticism, combined with his own novels, many of which study Nigerian society at various stages of its history, illustrate the fact that the double project of post-colonial criticism takes place both within the novel and through theoretical writings. Re-writing of both history and fiction plays an important role in post-colonial fiction: ▷ Ama Ata Aidoo's *Our Sister Killjoy* re-writes *Heart of Darkness* in oppositional form, from the point of view of an African woman, a subject position that implies a double heritage of oppression, by colonialism and by patriarchy.

Post-colonial theory includes models of literary creativity and interpretation springing from the philosophical and cultural traditions of those peoples who have suffered colonization (such as African, Caribbean, Asian, Indian, Maori, Inuit) and also models generated within the Western tradition. The former group includes, for example, Indian criticism that draws on the 2000-year tradition of Sanskrit scholarship or the writings of Achebe on the African novel which understand it specifically in the context of African social history. Given that the history of colonialism has been a history of exploitation and appropriation by the West, in which the suppression or marginalization of non-European cultures and languages was a major tool of oppression, the relationship between these two elements within post-colonial theory is clearly politically sensitive and of key importance if post-colonial theorizing is not to repeat the colonizing mentality. In this respect Rhonda Cobham makes a point analogous to Shoshana Felman's view of the necessary reciprocity of literary and psychoanalytical discourse, suggesting that while 'sometimes African literature by women writers may be read usefully through models derived from Western theories', this process 'may also provide modes of perception through which to examine and qualify Western theory'.

Theories of post-modernism

▷ Post-modernism would, by its name, seem to invite some comparison or connection with post-colonialism. The relationship is, however, a potentially uneasy one, since post-modernism has been seen by Frederic Jameson as a 'cultural dominant' which 'is the internal and superstructural expression of a whole new wave of American military and economic domination throughout the world'. On the other hand, the French theorist ▷ François Lyotard presents a more affirmative view of post-modernism in terms of the dismantling of the legitimating grand narratives of science and other 'metanarratives', and offers a utopian vision of a possible society in which free public access to computer memory banks would allow language games based on 'perfect information'. The terms 'post-modernism' and 'post-modernity' are often used without clear distinction, but it is probably helpful to reserve 'post-modernity' for the broad philosophical and political debates between such figures as Jameson, Lyotard and the German philosopher Jürgen Habermas about the existence and nature of a distinctly new phase in world-wide social and economic and cultural structures. 'Post-modernism' is often used in a narrower, though related, sense, to refer to a style or mood in architecture, literature, art, film, music and other areas of cultural production. As regards the novel, post-modernism has been identified with the ironic, the playful and the parodic; with the creation of multiple and often fantastic worlds; with self-reference and a foregrounding of fictionality which nevertheless embraces history. Some novels, such as ▷ Salman Rushdie's *Midnight's Children* (1981), do indeed combine post-colonial themes with post-modernist techniques, while the style known as magic realism, as it has evolved in English fiction under the influence of Latin American novelists such as Gabriel Garcia Marquez, has affinities with post-modernism. The work of the Argentinian writer Jorge Luis Borges typifies the post-modernist taste for paradox and invented worlds. Within fiction in English, post-modernism is in many ways anticipated by ▷ James Joyce's late novel ▷ *Finnegans Wake* (1939) and by the novels of Samuel Beckett, while since the 1950s there has developed a wide range of Anglo-American and European post-modernist fiction, including such British writers as ▷ Angela Carter and Julian Barnes as well as those authors of ▷ metafiction who have already been mentioned.

Conclusion: from the novel to narrative

In looking briefly at some of the implications of literary theory for the interpretation of the novel, this essay has found it helpful to categorize theories under names such as 'deconstruction', 'psychoanalytical criticism' and so on. However, it will perhaps have become apparent that much of the most exciting contemporary critical work springs from a creative interaction of theories, combining, say, feminism, Marxism and psychoanalysis, or post-colonial and post-modernist theories. The diversity of theoretical approaches and the possibility of dialogic exchange which this produces is crucial to the productivity of theory, so that a total synthesis would be neither possible nor desirable. However, if one sought to identify a single problematic which is of importance in most literary theory since the 1960s, the problematic of the subject (*ie* the self) would be a likely candidate. The psychoanalytical theory of the unconscious, the Marxist conception of the subject as interpellated in ideology, the deconstructive subversion of belief in origins or the self-presence of the speaking subject, the post-colonial critique of the attribution of spurious universality to culturally specific images of the self, and the feminist analysis of the imposition of socially-constructed gender roles: all of these tend to call into question the belief in the autonomy and unity of the free individual in favour of a conception of subjectivity as divided, as constructed, as traversed and intersected by discursive and social formations. This is not to say, of course, that ideas of personal autonomy and authenticity are being abandoned on all sides: many theorists, and notably those working in post-colonial, feminist and psychoanalytical areas, are concerned to generate new possibilities for the understanding of the self. However, certain assumptions about the self as a discrete, unproblematic entity (based in the Western tradition deriving largely from the Christian idea of the soul), are now more difficult to make. Because the idea of the individual has been so influential in the development and interpretation of the novel, new ways of reading fiction may be required. Indeed, it may still seem obvious to many to read a novel as the expression of the vision of one individual (the author), including mimetic representations of fictional individuals (the characters), communicated via the text to another individual (the reader) and interpreted by him or her in terms of universal features of 'human nature'. However, literary theory (together, it should be emphasized, with many works of fiction, from this and from other centuries) has systematically questioned all the assumptions, explicit and implicit, of such an 'obvious' model: individuality, mimesis, self-expression, universality, human nature, referentiality.

Where does this leave the novel? Its popularity as a genre does not, of course, depend on the development of academic theories, although such theories have influenced many novelists, while the processes of rediscovery and revaluing within feminist and post-colonial criticism have played their part in making available to a wide reading public many works of past and contemporary fiction. Transformations in the role of the novel are more likely to be effected by developments in electronic media: television, cinema, video, virtual reality and interactive computer software. Some people would take a pessimistic view of the likely fate of the novel, seeing both the spread of theory in academic circles and the increasing dominance of electronic media in society in general as likely to undermine the social attitudes and practices which promoted novel reading and made the novel seem an important way of understanding or interpreting experience. If we consider, however, not a purist or traditional conception of 'the novel', but a wider category of 'narrative', there is evidence for a far more positive assessment. Forms of narrative are pervasive in film, video and television, and these media generate new forms of narrative which nevertheless continue to interact fruitfully with novelistic narrative. The element of narrative in computer-based technology is harder to assess with confidence at the present stage of rapid change, but however radically different the forms of narrative within such media may be, the elements of narrative itself seem inescapably present: temporal sequences existing in combination with the spatial and the problematic of meaning as representation or construction. Meanwhile, within the equally rapidly changing context of academic theory, narrative seems if anything to be becoming more and more prominent. The understanding of the relative and contingent nature of any opposition between 'fact' and 'fiction' and of the extent of the textual or linguistic mediation of many forms of knowledge has led to the application of the category of narrative, not only to 'fiction' as traditionally understood, but to history, science, literary criticism and other disciplines. Whatever the arguments, there seems little likelihood that we are about to stop telling ourselves, and each other, stories.

3

Market, Morality and Sentiment: the Eighteenth-century Novel

Janet Barron and David Nokes

The literary market-place

The gradual emergence during the eighteenth century of the novel as a distinctive, recognized and popular literary form in Britain was influenced by a number of historical factors, including the growth of an economically powerful middle class, an associated spirit of secular individualism, a rapid increase in literacy and the development of commercial printing and bookselling. Some critics see the novel as an essentially middle-class genre, although it clearly was, and remains, a site of ideological conflict, capable of embodying aristocratic and working-class attitudes, views and assumptions. Ideological pressures are present in fiction, not only because novels are sometimes written specifically in support of ideological positions, but also because texts are written, circulated and read within social and economic structures which condition, though do not always determine, elements of theme and form and the processes of interpretation. So, just as an understanding of the novel's literary antecedents and subsequent evolution requires a consideration of a wide range of genres which preceded or continued alongside it, so an understanding of the process by which the novel emerged involves attending to the social and economic conditions of eighteenth-century writing in general.

'No man but a blockhead ever wrote except for money.' ▷ Samuel Johnson's peremptory dictum, though expressed in characteristically provocative manner, highlights a significant development in the prose writing of the eighteenth century. There were, of course, many other motives, apart from the hope of financial gain, which might lead writers to take up their pens: some were inspired by moral or religious convictions; others by the desire to expound a political argument, or the itch for satirical mischief-making; while others still were inspired by the simple authorial vanity of seeing the offsprings of their imagination bound up in folio or octavo volumes. Yet it was the eighteenth century which saw the emergence of the professional writer; the man, or woman, who wrote not as a genteel pastime, or to flatter the self-esteem of a generous patron, but directly for money. For the first time, the spread of literacy, together with the emergence of commercial bookseller-publishers eager to feed the imaginations of an expanding reading public, made the trade of letters a viable, if not always lucrative, profession.

In the early years of the century most of the leading writers still relied more on institutional sinecures, or on a combination of public and private patronage, than on the literary market-place for their support. ▷ Richard Steele was a Commissioner for stamps; William Congreve was nominally in charge of licensing hackney-carriages, ▷ Daniel Defoe was a government spy; ▷ Jonathan Swift held the livings of two country parishes in Ireland; Joseph Addison was a career civil servant, finally achieving the position of Secretary of State.

Yet the qualifications required for entry to the professions excluded some authors who had to rely solely on the income from their writing. As a Catholic, Alexander Pope was unable to hold public office, though he made a virtue of his social exclusion by celebrating his Twickenham retreat as a symbol of independence. His accomplished marketing of the subscription editions of his translations of ▷ Homer netted him an astonishing £10,000 (something in excess of £500,000 in today's terms). It was a commercial coup that other writers could only envy. By contrast, Swift was paid £200 for ▷ *Gulliver's Travels* (1726), and ▷ Oliver Goldsmith £60 for ▷ *The Vicar of Wakefield* (1761–2).

In recent years critical interpretations of eighteenth-century literature have increasingly questioned the traditional image of the period as an 'age of reason', a peaceful haven of political stability and classical values. Recent studies have revealed the commercial realities that lay behind the classical façade of the eighteenth-century literary pantheon. By exploring the subculture of ▷ Grub Street, and by focusing attention on the many previously neglected women writers of the period, modern scholarship has provided a new perspective on this fascinating era in literary history, reminding us of the valuable contributions made by those excluded from the clubs and coffee-houses of the Augustan establishment.

▷Aphra Behn, debarred from the professions as a woman, attempted to attract state patronage by her political writings. The *Ode on the Coronation* would, she hoped, secure her a pension or a grace and favour house. But no money was forthcoming, and she turned instead to more lucrative markets for her talents in romantic fiction and theatrical comedies.

The career of Samuel Johnson demonstrates the precariousness of the literary life. Forced by poverty to abandon his studies at Oxford University, he thereby relinquished all hopes of a career in the law or the church. After an unsuccessful attempt at school-teaching, he arrived in London, virtually penniless, and began to support himself by his writings. Regular contributions to ▷ *The Gentleman's Magazine* provided part of his income, yet his independent projects were also undertaken for commercial reasons. According to legend, ▷ *Rasselas* (1759) was written rapidly to pay the expenses of his mother's funeral; Johnson encouraged such stories as proof of his independence.

In 1755, at the culmination of his labours on the ▷ *Dictionary of the English Language*, Johnson delivered a celebrated epistolary snub to his self-styled patron, the Earl of Chesterfield: 'Is not a patron, my lord, one who looks with unconcern on a man struggling for life in the water and when he has reached ground encumbers him with help?' His letter is a declaration of literary independence that signals the end of the era of the private patron. Ironically, it was the commercial project of the *Dictionary* which brought Johnson academic recognition, as Oxford awarded him the degree he had been unable to obtain by more conventional means. In 1762, the award of a Crown pension of £300 a year relieved Johnson of some of the drudgery of hack work, though he was careful to insist that this was not a reward for political services, but a recognition of literary achievements.

Just before the start of the century, the lapsing of the Licensing Act in 1695 provided the opportunity for a massive expansion of the printing trade. Entrepreneurial publishers ranging from society figures like Jacob Tonson to Grub Street pirates like Edmund Curll played a vital, though sometimes unrecognized, part in shaping the literary culture of the eighteenth century. The 'Augustan Age' is often, and rightly, portrayed as a period when classical models and formal rules were of paramount literary importance; yet the commercial judgements of men like these were equally influential in promoting and developing the variety of eighteenth-century literature, with it works ranging from translations of the classics to lurid Newgate yarns.

It was a time when, according to Martin Scriblerus (alias Pope), 'paper became so cheap and printers so numerous that a deluge of authors cover'd the land'. What is remarkable about the prose writings of the eighteenth century, when compared with those of earlier centuries, is their sheer diversity. The rise of the novel and the development of periodical journalism are only the two most obvious features of this expansion of the literary market. Fabulous adventures, travellers' tales, secret histories, spiritual lives, satires, sermons, pastorals and panegyrics and works of every conceivable style and tone, calculated to appeal to all tastes and pockets, rolled from the presses. The pages of Pope's mock-heroic satire *The Dunciad* (1728–43) are filled with the names of forgotten Grub Street authors, such as Ned Ward, ▷ Eliza Haywood and Charles Gildon, many of whom eked out a precarious living in the kind of literary sweat-shops hilariously described by ▷ Henry Fielding in his play *The Author's Farce* (1730).

Establishment authors, like Pope and Swift, frequently deplored the promiscuous vitality of this new literary world, foreseeing the death of civilized values in publishers' lists as the works of classical authors were outnumbered by the ephemeral products of those whom they dubbed the 'moderns' or 'dunces'. The novelists themselves often appeared embarrassed at their own imaginative freedom, prefacing their works with statements which sought to legitimize the seductive appeal of fiction by appealing to some external authority. In referring to his early novels as 'comic epics in prose', Fielding endeavoured to claim a niche for them in the traditional classical pantheon. Defoe preferred to describe his tales as 'true histories', faking his fictions to read like facts, and filling in the broad sweeps of his adventure stories with minute circumstantial details. To ▷ Samuel Richardson, the only justification for fiction was its clear commitment to moral reform, and he presented his novels as exemplary parables in which vice is routed and virtue rewarded. Yet even the sternest critics of literary self-indulgence found the lure of fictional licence irresistible. Swift's ▷ *A Tale of a Tub* (1704) is, among other things, a satire on the ephemerality of modern culture. 'I have remarked,' says the *Tale's* narrator, 'that nothing is so very tender as a modern piece of wit'. But, while affecting to deplore this cultural perishability, Swift revels in the world of literary ephemera, turning topical tit-bits into enduring metaphors for human vanity.

Thus to speak of 'the rise of the novel' in the early eighteenth century, as if assuming that by then the novel had attained a clear, recognizable identity, is somewhat misleading. There was no single literary genre which sprang, fully-formed, to life with the publication of ▷ *Robinson Crusoe* in 1719. Instead, a variety of contrasting fictional forms competed for attention, ranging from the vivid Grub Street pseudo-biographies published in the down-market *Applebee's Journal* (1715–36) to witty anecdotal sketches of the ▷ de Coverley family presented in ▷ *The Spectator* (1712); or from salacious secret histories, such as ▷ Delarivière Manley's *The New Atalantis* (1709) to satiric fantasies, such as Swift's *Gulliver's Travels* (1726). As late as 1711 *The Tatler* was still using the word 'novelist' to mean a newspaperman. In much the same way Johnson's *Dictionary* (1755) continued to define 'journal' as 'any paper published daily', whereas most of the periodicals so described were not in fact daily publications. In both cases it is clear that the regulatory constraints of etymology had little inhibiting influence on the dynamic growth of the genres themselves. For, despite the Augustan predilection for neo-classical rules and critical categories, the novel, like journalism, grew up happily innocent of prescriptive theories. Indeed, the emergence of the novel form in the early eighteenth century, which often appears an inevitable consequence of changing social conditions, can equally well be presented as the result of a series of felicitous accidents. Defoe was almost 60, and nearing the end of an indefatigably varied career during which he had tried his hand at innumerable forms of business enterprise (all failures) as well as journalism and espionage when he published *Robinson Crusoe*. Fielding was a celebrated young playwright until Sir Robert Walpole's introduction of stage censorship with the new Licensing Act of 1737 forced him to find an alternative outlet for his literary talents. Richardson was a successful printer, whose decision to turn author was partly inspired by a prudent desire to utilize the spare capacity of his press. This process of 'serendipity', a word coined by ▷ Horace Walpole, continued throughout the century, and it was Walpole's own fortuitous success with his fantasy ▷ *The Castle of Otranto* (1764) which inspired the later vogue for Gothic fiction.

The career and reputation of ▷ Daniel Defoe offers some useful insights into one type of literary enterprise. The son of a dissenting tallow-chandler, he was a lifelong bankrupt, a tireless entrepreneur and a prolific journalist whose collected works could fill several hundred volumes. For nine years, from 1704 to 1713 he wrote single-handedly his thrice-weekly journal *The Review*; for much of the same period he was also one of the government's leading spies, sending back secret reports from Edinburgh on the political manoeuvring surrounding the negotiations for the Act of Union between England and Scotland in 1707. Simultaneously, he was also striving to extricate himself from massive debts, and contriving to stay out of the hands of his many creditors. In both his business ventures and his journalism one finds the same spirit of brinkmanship, the same flirting with disaster. The energy and excitement of his writings co-exist with a kind of literary carelessness and an apparent impatience with more studied effects which led on occasions to disaster. His ironic pamphlet *The Shortest Way with*

Dissenters (1702), which counterfeited the violent language of a High Church zealot, backfired badly when its irony was mistaken for incitement, and Defoe was sentenced to punishment at the pillory. More recently, critics have reassessed the apparent carelessness of Defoe's writing, finding in it the poker-face of a more accomplished literary gamesmanship. The 'failure' of *The Shortest Way* succeeded in exposing the covert menace of High Church policies in a way that more conventional irony could not have achieved. Similar subtleties may be detected in the 'mistakes' and contradictions which abound in Defoe's novels. Generations of readers have noted the glaring contradictions between what characters say in one part of a novel, and how they behave elsewhere. Well on in her narrative, Moll Flanders is seized by a sudden maternal instinct and delivers a sober lecture on the depravity of mothers who neglect or abandon their offspring. Yet by this stage she herself has happily abandoned innumerable children of her own without a word or a qualm. Her flair for criminality is accompanied by a constant moral patter as she alternately presents herself as a victim of circumstances and an agent of social education. The unconvincingness of her final 'repentance', which conveniently allows her to retire in comfort on her ill-gotten gains, has often appeared to undermine the novel's moral seriousness. Contradictions like these – and there are many other celebrated examples in all the novels – have often been taken as evidence of a slap-dash journeyman approach to the business of authorship. Yet the pattern of these contradictions, in which characters preach like Puritan moralists yet act like ruthless opportunists, goes to the heart of Defoe's fiction. For all their concentration on mundane details, his novels are fantasies of survival, heroic adventures of social mobility in which individuals single-handedly confront and conquer a host of adverse circumstances. Despite the apparent crudity of their episodic narratives, Defoe's novels are animated by a quality more usually identified with a more self-consciously sophisticated form of fiction, in the characters of his unreliable narrators.

Likewise the unravelling of ▷ Jonathan Swift's ironies has been the key to the twentieth-century reappraisal of his status as a writer. Earlier critics, like ▷ Thackeray, viewed his writings as misanthropic and malign: 'A monster gibbering shrieks, and gnashing imprecations against mankind – tearing down all shreds of modesty, past all sense of manliness and shame; filthy in word, filthy in thought, furious, raging, obscene.'

Judgements like these derive from the tendency to identify Swift with the narrators of his satires, seeing in Gulliver's hysterical reaction to the Yahoos a representation of Swift's supposed alienation from humanity. But Swift is the master of literary disguises, and his chosen narrators are utopians or fanatics, projectors or madmen whose plausible rhetoric of half-truths leads inexorably to such savage conclusions as the eating of babies or the abandonment of human society in favour of life in a stable. As a satirist, Swift's prime target is the irrational utopianism which founds its hopes of progress on a refusal to acknowledge the perversities and flaws of human nature itself. From *A Tale of a Tub* (1704) with its ironic epigraph 'Written for the Universal Improvement of Mankind', to the Academy of Lagado in *Gulliver's Travels* (1726) whose scientists are engaged in projects to produce sunbeams out of cucumbers, Swift ridicules the visionary enthusiasm which finds inspiration in the belchings of a fanatical preacher, and sublime wisdom in the neighing of a horse.

Born and educated in Ireland, Swift took holy orders and became a clergyman in the Church of Ireland. Yet he spent most of Queen Anne's reign in London, pursuing an alternative career as a political journalist. His *Examiner* articles and his pamphlet *The Conduct of the Allies* (1711) provided a magisterial defence of the Tory (▷ Whig and Tory) government's policy for ending the war with France, and even today offer excellent models of the art of political journalism. Forced to return to his native land on the death of Queen Anne, Swift felt like a virtual exile, and it was several years before he could bring himself to relaunch his journalistic career with a series of powerful pamphlets deploring the miserable economic plight of Ireland. His most celebrated pamphlet, ▷ *A Modest Proposal* (1729), ironically recommends that the people of Ireland should rear their children as food for the tables of their English landlords. The scheme has a savage logic; it is methodically costed, and the arguments are financially flawless. With its plausible phrases and deadpan tone, this satire is a brilliant indictment of a society in which economic exploitation has abnegated the natural ties of humanity and love.

While it is undoubtedly true that Swift's satires dwell on the darker side of human nature, his love of jokes, riddles and *jeux d'esprit* should not be forgotten. From his *Bickerstaff Papers* (1708–9) to his *Directions to Servants* (published posthumously in 1745), a spirit of mischievous and subversive anarchy runs through all his writings. In his most famous poem *Verses on the Death of Dr Swift* (1731), he provided his own obituary, declaring, among other things, that 'fair liberty was all his cry'. The liberty that Swift cherished was less political than intellectual and his satires offer a consistent challenge to our own reasoning power to find a way through the maze of utopian delusions and political lies.

'The Female Wits'

At one point in her career, Delarivière Manley worked as Swift's assistant on *The Examiner*, taking over from him as editor in 1711. Manley was already notorious for salacious society scandals: *The Secret History of Queen Zarah* (1705), using the device of a fictional history to avoid prosecution, was an instant success, with its separately published key revealing the code names. In 1709 a further *roman à clef*, *The New Atlantis*, continued this combination of transparent allegory and sexual innuendo. The ▷ Whig ministry, worried by her revelations, issued a warrant for the arrest of printer, publisher and author, and Manley was required to name her informers. Exploiting the ambiguities of fictions-as-facts, Manley declared her only source was divine inspiration. Manley's reputation as an erotic scandalmonger contributed to the stereotype of the immoral female author. Pope's image of the Grub Street hacks and booksellers as literary whores and pimps takes on further implications in the light of Manley's own life; supplementing her income by a series of affairs, she eventually became the mistress of Alderman Barber, her publisher.

Women writers anxious to avoid such notoriety often published their works anonymously, or prefaced them with humble pleas that they were written in distress. And, though scandalous works sold well, novels which conformed to social mores were more widely acceptable as serious literary efforts. The decline of the patronage system made a clear distinction between the aristocratic lady writing as a graceful accomplishment, and the woman who went against the nature of her sex and engaged in disreputable trade.

Even writers with no literary ambitions tailored their products to the changing literary tastes. Eliza Haywood's early works were titillating confections, and *Love in Excess* (1719) was, with *Robinson Crusoe* and *Gulliver's Travels*, one of the three best-selling works before ▷ Samuel Richardson's ▷ *Pamela* (1740–1). But by the 1740s and 50s Haywood takes on a new tone of conventional conformity, and the 'women's novel' became increasingly associated with the values of hearth and home. It was a compromise which allowed the critic both to praise women for their delicate understanding, and to confine them to 'feminine' gentility which could be disparaged as frivolous.

Similar arguments were often advanced in condescending appraisal of some of the more chatty periodicals. Swift was in no doubt as to the main audience for Addison's *Spectator* when he remarked, 'let them fair-sex it to the world's end', and Eliza Haywood exploited this market with the launch of *The Female Spectator* (1744–6). If anything, Addison seems rather to have relished than repudiated his paper's reputation as providing a genteel education of ladies. When he boasted of taking philosophy out of the schools and Colleges, and into 'clubs and assemblies, tea tables and coffee-houses', he made explicit the intention to mingle morality and manners, philosophy and fashion, in an urbane and witty miscellany. And despite a tinge of polite condescension in the tone of its more lightweight contributions, *The Spectator* was remarkably successful in maintaining a style of well-mannered wit. There was, however, a serious side to this endeavour to promote the refined tone and rational debate of coffee-house society to a wider reading public. In the previous century, the Puritan moralist and the fashionable

Cavalier had stood on opposite sides in the Civil War. Addison and Steele endeavoured to heal this breach, by putting a smile on the face of morality, and restraining the more licentious habits of town rakes and courtly roués. In the genial atmosphere of a fictitious Spectator club, the Whig merchant Sir Andrew Freeport and the Tory squire Sir Roger de Coverley could discuss their differences over a glass of port rather than settling them on the battlefield. One form of anti-social behaviour that Addison particularly deplored was the writing of satires, which he described as 'poisoned darts' that gave 'secret stabs to a man's reputation'. In *The Spectator* he promised he would never 'draw a faulty character which does not fit at least a thousand people, or publish a single paper that is not written in the spirit of benevolence, with love to mankind'.

However, it was the growing popularity of the novel rather than Addison's benevolent pieties which gradually killed off the vogue for satire in the middle years of the century. In broad terms, one might say that satire deals essentially with types, whereas the novel presents us with individuals. Eighteenth-century satire is concerned less with the redemption of individual sinners than with the regulation of general standards of conduct. But the novel, particularly under the influence of Richardson, was more interested in questions of moral identity and the expression of individual consciousness. The distinction between the two genres is not always as clear-cut as this might imply. When in ▷ *Joseph Andrews* (1742) Henry Fielding declares 'once for all, I describe not men but manners; not an individual, but a species', he writes as both satirist and novelist. In the preface to that book, he draws a distinction between comic fiction and satire, and like ▷ *Shamela* (1741), the first ten chapters comprise a burlesque satire on Samuel Richardson's *Pamela*. It is only after this point in the novel that Fielding attempts to transform Joseph's chastity from an absurd parody of Pamela's much vaunted virtue into a mark of fidelity for his beloved Fanny. Similarly, ▷ *Jonathan Wild* (1743), with its consistent ironic attacks on 'greatness', might be regarded more as an extended lampoon than as a novel. It is not until ▷ *Tom Jones* (1749) that Fielding finally achieved his own distinctive form of comic fiction, though that novel too contains many incidental satiric and parodic moments.

In Johnson's view there was as great a difference between the literary talents of Richardson and Fielding 'as between a man who knew how a watch was made, and a man who could tell the hour by looking on the dial plate'. Although the terms of the relative judgment has sometimes altered, the temptation to draw comparisons between the literary achievements of these two men has persisted ever since. As authors, they embody two rival traditions of the English novel, appearing as contending 'fathers' of the novel, each disputing the legitimacy of the other's offspring. From Fielding we derive the tradition of comic fiction, a style of writing that revels in its own vivacity and wit, offering its readers a rich and varied diet of social comedy, urbane irony and literary sophistication. From Richardson, we derive the novel of moral introspection and psychological insight; his epistolary style offers a kind of fictional confessional dramatizing the dilemmas of individual moral choice.

The morality of *Tom Jones* is based on a simple antithetical contrast; natural instinct versus social hypocrisy, goodness of heart versus cunning of head. Part of the satisfaction of the book comes from the combination of the formal symmetry of its structure (Coleridge referred to it as one of the three best plots ever written) with the apparent freedom and randomness of its ▷ picaresque episodes. In the same way, Tom's artless and impulsive vitality is made acceptable by the artful manipulations of the narrator's tone.

Pamela (1740–1), Richardson's inspired first-person narrative of a young servant girl's triumph over repeated attempts at seduction by her employer, was an immediate commercial success. 'If all the books in England were to be burnt, this book, next the Bible, ought to be preserved', enthused one reader. Nowadays its reputation is less secure. Modern readers are apt to side with Fielding in regarding its notorious subtitle, 'Virtue Rewarded', as evidence that Pamela is a model of policy rather than purity.

Richardson's next novel, ▷ *Clarissa* (1747–8) is an undisputed literary masterpiece. Again using the epistolary form, Richardson interweaves four narrative voices to construct a novel of great psychological complexity. In its treatment of the contradictions between 'virtue' as reputation and virginity as an extension of moral integrity, Richardson highlights the social hypocrisies where the marriage market puts a high price on maidenhood. Anne Howe, Clarissa's friend, urges the conventional solution of marrying the seducer, but Clarissa follows the path of self-imposed martyrdom. The novel escapes any simplistic morality, reverberating beyond a reductive summary.

The distinction which Johnson drew between the novels of Fielding and those of Richardson, was reapplied by Richardson himself to the novels of ▷ Sarah Fielding, Henry Fielding's sister. Johnson and Richardson both encouraged Sarah Fielding to publish her work. Her best-known novel, *The Adventures of David Simple* (1744), provides a notable contrast to the male novelists' treatment of female characters. Where Pamela and Clarissa struggle with threatening seducers, Sarah Fielding's heroines wryly recognize sexual harassment as a part of the social structure.

It was the development of the ▷ circulating libraries in the later decades of the century which provided the largest market for the mass of novelistic fiction. Many critics were alarmed by the proliferation of light romantic fiction which resulted from these cheaper sources of entertainment. 'This branch of the literary trade', one reviewer remarked, 'appears, now, to be almost entirely engrossed by women'. The naive country girl who has her head turned by these frothy fantasies became a stock figure of fictional stereotypes. From the dramatist Richard Brinsley Sheridan's Lydia Languish to ▷ Jane Austen's Catherine Morland, the harmful effects on the uneducated *ingénue* were a favourite topic for literary parody. In ▷ Charlotte Lennox's *The Female Quixote* (1752), the heroine, Arabella, turns from the sterner labours of her father's study to while away her hours with her mother's library, a collection of lengthy French romances which she mistakes for historical accounts. By creating an ironic distance between the heroine and the narrator, Lennox uses this familiar theme to make a social comment on women's education. ▷ Fanny Burney's major novels also focus on the entry of the *ingénue* into a potentially corrupting society. ▷ *Evelina* (1778) uses the epistolary narrative of a woman asking her male mentor for advice. *Cecilia* (1782), her most successful novel, shows an intelligent but naive girl tricked out of her inheritance by an exploitative friend's husband. In drawing attention to the dangers faced by the good-natured but ill-advised heroine, Burney contributes to the social debate on the status of women, using the novel as an entertaining medium of discussion.

Sentiment and sensation

In the second half of the century two new styles of writing became suddenly fashionable and all but dominated the fiction market. The first of these was the sentimental novel. 'What, in your opinion, is the meaning of the word *sentimental*, so much in vogue among the polite?' Lady Bradshaigh asked Richardson. 'I am frequently astonished to hear such a one is a sentimental man; we were a sentimental party; I have been taking a sentimental walk.' Some twenty years later the Methodist John Wesley (1703–91) continued to protest against the word as a meaningless foreign neologism. 'Sentimental? What is that? It is not English; he might as well say Continental. It is not sense. It conveys no determinate idea.' Probably the most celebrated of sentimental novels was Henry Mackenzie's *The Man of Feeling* (1771) in which the tears of the hero, Harley, flow freely throughout the narrative. As a benevolent innocent with the most delicate sensibility, Harley is constantly cheated, deceived and hurt by the more worldly figures he encounters; yet his sufferings carry with them a *tendresse* of pleasure; his humiliations discover the exquisite sensations of injured integrity. Towards the end of the novel his apparently unrequited love for Miss Watson results in his physical decline until, on his deathbed, she reveals her love for him and he dies of sheer happiness. A similar pattern of innocent suffering can be found in Oliver Goldsmith's novel *The Vicar of Wakefield* (published

1766) which presents a parallel confrontation between naive benevolence and unscrupulous power. Goldsmith's vicar, Primrose, is a man who takes his 'consummate benevolence' to 'a romantic extreme'. With an authentically sentimental relish for the moral authority of suffering, Goldsmith dwells on the vicar's 'pleasing distress' at the repeated trials and tragedies heaped upon him by Thornhill, the malicious libertine squire.

Mackenzie's novel was an immediate best-seller. Robert Burns wore out two copies of the work, calling it 'a book I. prize next to the Bible'. Johnson was less impressed, commenting scornfully on 'the fashionable whine of sensibility'. In 1773 ▷ Mrs Barbauld offered a psychological justification for this type of fiction in her *Inquiry into the kind of distress which exerts agreeable sensations*, emphasizing the evocation of a sympathetic tenderness on the part of the reader. 'Tenderness,' she wrote, 'is, much more properly than sorrow, the spring of tears'.

For modern readers the best-known fictional example of the cult of sensibility is in fact a partial parody of the genre. ▷ Laurence Sterne's ▷ *A Sentimental Journey through France and Italy* (1768) exploits many features of the sentimental style, yet does so with a tone of ironic self-consciousness that constantly trembles on the brink of satire. Like Mackenzie's Man of Feeling whose face is bathed in tears while listening to another's tale of woe, Sterne's Yorick, hearing of the death of a monk to whom he had behaved uncharitably, 'bursts into a flood of tears'. But whereas Harley's tears are the sign of his refined sensibility, Yorick's tears are produced with a sudden and comic exaggeration. Yorick is a virtuoso of the nervous system, conjuring up both tears and blushes with a facility which testifies less to his goodness of heart than to his incorrigible instinct for self-dramatization. Sterne's masterpiece, ▷ *Tristram Shandy* (1760–7) is another teasing work whose success transformed Sterne from an obscure Yorkshire clergyman into a leading literary celebrity, but whose eccentricities have divided critical opinion ever since. Johnson declared 'nothing odd will do long; *Tristram Shandy* did not last', but a formalist critic in our own century has asserted that '*Tristram Shandy* is the most typical novel of world literature'.

'In a word, my work is digressive, and it is progressive too, – and at the same time', announces Tristram in the book's first volume. It is significant that he puts the word 'digressive' first. With its black and marbled pages, its flash-backs and interpolations, its asterisks, blanks and dashes, *Tristram Shandy* is a novel which denies any conventional notions of narrative development. The first four volumes take place while Tristram, the hero/narrator, is still in the womb, and the book ends before it begins. Yet this work, which seems to break all the rules, and which consistently demonstrates the inability of rules, plans, theories and systems to cope with the accidents and vagaries of human life, is nevertheless held together by a curious pseudo-logic of its own. This is the absurd determinism of the association of ideas, as expressed in ▷ Locke's ▷ *Essay concerning Human Understanding* (1690), which Tristram describes as 'a history-book of what passes in a man's own mind'. Each of Sterne's characters, Walter, Toby and Trim, is locked in his own private world of associations; their conversations present the collisions of words rather than the communication of thoughts; their actions are all bounded by accident.

Beside the inventiveness of Sterne, the more conventional comic skills of ▷ Tobias Smollett may seem stolid and predictable. Trained as a surgeon, Smollett published his first, and some would say his best, novel, ▷ *Roderick Random*, in 1748, when he was still only twenty-six. Like all Smollett's novels, this work is a robust picaresque, episodic in form, slapstick in humour and brisk in pace. Some of its best moments are autobiographical, drawing on Smollett's own experience as a ship's surgeon. His next novel, ▷ *Peregrine Pickle* (1751), also has a nautical flavour, with its collection of old sea-dog characters such as Commodore Hawser Trunnion and the peg-legged Lieutenant Hatchway. His final novel, ▷ *Humphry Clinker* (1771), is epistolary in form though the tone owes more to Fielding than to Richardson. In it a group of assorted characters including the irascible old valetudinarian Matthew Bramble and a Methodist coachman Humphry Clinker (who turns out to be Bramble's son) make a grand tour of Britain from Bristol, Bath and London, to Edinburgh and the Highlands, presenting us with a broad panorama of eighteenth-century society. The idiomatic clashes of the different letter-writing styles provide a constant humorous tone, and the book is rich in comic misadventures, though the plot itself is highly derivative. As one recent critic has written, 'it is as though Tom Jones has given way to Baedeker'.

The other fictional form which enjoyed considerable popularity in the later decades of the century was the Gothic novel. In terms of the market place, the date at which the Richardsonian novel of moral instruction began to give way to the Gothic novel of crepuscular phantoms can be pin-pointed with some accuracy. In 1777 Clara Reeve published a novel called The Champion of Virtue, a title which clearly suggests a continuation of Richardsonian preoccupations. The following year, however, she reissued the same novel in a revised form and with a new title, The Old English Baron, A Gothic Story, evidently attempting to exploit the new trend in public tastes. However, the origins of the Gothic novel are usually traced back to Horace Walpole's The Castle of Otranto (1761), a self-indulgent fantasy of fake medievalism which deliberately revels in its extravagant use of supernatural and 'marvellous' elements. One recent critic (Pat Rogers) has written: 'The Castle of Otranto is preposterous; its setting is Hollywood-medieval, a Ruritanian version of chivalric times. Its plot is frankly incredible, jumpily constructed and flatly recounted.' Yet much of the novel's overt implausibility is a calculated device to move away from the classical symmetries and rational morality of Augustan literature. Walpole was a fashionable dilettante whose spirit of whimsicality led him to create his 'little Gothic castle' at Strawberry Hill, and also inspired this little Gothic tale. Like the young ill-fated poet Thomas Chatterton (1752–70), who passed off his 'Rowley' poems as genuine medieval manuscripts, and the fraudulent James Macpherson (1736–96) who claimed to be 'translating' his pastiche Celtic epic ▷ Ossian, Walpole at first maintained a pretence that The Castle of Otranto was an authentic medieval story. For all of these writers, medievalism was a kind of fancy-dress, enabling them to evade the sober responsibilities of neo-classical literary forms and indulge their imaginations in a world of supernatural fantasy. For the Gothic novel entailed a reversal or rejection of many classical values. Instead of Pope's cherished landscape of 'Nature methodiz'd' with its well-proportioned country houses and Palladian villas, the Gothic landscape consists of dark forests and ruined castles, with gloomy dungeons and secret labyrinthine passageways. In place of the daylight world of rational debate and urbane ironies, Gothic fiction presents a nightmare world of torture and fantasies, irrational fears, ancient curses and nameless threats.

Gothic fiction can be divided into two broad categories, the novel of terror and the novel of horror. Practitioners of the novel of terror, from Clara Reeve to ▷ Ann Radcliffe, were interested in using the Gothic form as a means of exploring the psychology of fear. In her most famous novel, ▷ The Mysteries of Udolpho (1794), Radcliffe described the effect of terror on the mind. 'A terror of this nature, as it occupies and expands the mind, and elevates it to a high expectation, is purely sublime, and leads us, by a kind of fascination, to seek even the object from which we appear to shrink.' Echoing here some of the sentiments in ▷ Burke's treatise On the Sublime and the Beautiful (1759), Radcliffe also demonstrates an affinity with Wordsworth who, in his autobiographical poem The Prelude (1799–1805), describes how he 'grew up / Fostered alike by beauty and by fear'. In fact all of the apparently supernatural phenomena in Radcliffe's novels turn out to have perfectly rational, if somewhat contrived, explanations; the ghostly, diabolic presences that haunt her heroines are invariably products of illusionist trickery working on terrified imaginations. Unlike some other Gothic writers, Radcliffe has a perfect control of her plots, and part of the appeal of her novels lies in the ingenuity with which she supplies psychologically convincing explanations for the most apparently mysterious events. Nor is this merely a thriller-writer's gimmick. Radcliffe is interested in the gradations of intimidation and characteristically explores two related levels of fear. The abbeys, castles, dungeons and convents where her heroines find themselves are always reputedly cursed or haunted. Consequently when nocturnal apparitions occur, her heroines are thrown into the kind of superstitious dread satirized by Jane Austen in Northanger Abbey (published 1818).

But typically, in the morning these imaginary terrors are replaced by a yet more insidious fear, as the heroines gradually realize that they are at the mercy not of ghosts and goblins, but of malevolent human beings. It is some indication of the popularity of Gothic fiction that Radcliffe earned £500 for *The Mysteries of Udolpho*, whereas Jane Austen was paid only £10 for her parody of the genre in *Northanger Abbey*.

A good example of the novel of horror is ▷ Matthew 'Monk' Lewis's *The Monk* (1796), which Byron described as representing 'the philtered ideas of a jaded voluptuary'. In this extravagant sadistic fantasy Lewis exploits all the charnel-house images that have since become the clichés of Hammer horror films. His heroine, Agnes, having been separated from her lover, is condemned to perpetual incarceration among rotting corpses in the vaults beneath her convent. With undisguised relish Lewish pictures bloated toads and slimy lizards crawling across her flesh, and describes how, on waking, Agnes would often find 'my fingers ringed with the long worms which bred in the corrupted flesh of my infant'. The monk Ambrosio, the villain of the novel, crowns a career of vice by raping and killing Antonia, a fifteen-year-old girl, among these rotting bodies in the vault, having already murdered her mother Elvira. In order to escape the soldiers of the Inquisition, Ambrosio sells his soul to the Devil, who transports him to a mountain peak. There, before being hurled to his death, he is told that Elvira was in fact his mother, and Antonia his sister. Yet this conclusion is less a form of moral retribution, than a final gloating irony in this lurid sensationalist tale.

Loosely based on Arabian sources, ▷ William Beckford's *Vathek* (French edition 1782, English edition 1787) is another orgiastic tale of hedonism, sorcery and murder, that culminates in damnation. Although Beckford's work, like Lewis's, is filled with a self-indulgent horror, this aspect of Gothic fiction also has its serious side. Throughout the Gothic literature of the late eighteenth and early nineteenth centuries, writers as diverse as Beckford, ▷ James Hogg (*The Private Memoirs and Confessions of a Justified Sinner*, 1824) and ▷ Mary Shelley ▷ *Frankenstein*, 1817) explored Faustian themes and Satanic images that represented the dark side of ▷ Enlightenment thought.

Society, History and the Reader: the Nineteenth-century Novel

4

Gail Cunningham

Background: Authors, readers and publishers

It is a commonplace of modern criticism that the nineteenth century – or perhaps more specifically the Victorian age – was dominated by the novel. 'Fiction' is the word which sits naturally, in literary terms, with ▷ 'Victorian', in the same way that poetry does with 'Romantic' or drama with 'Restoration'. It is not only that the century produced a consistent stream of indisputably major practitioners of the form (a conservative listing of whom would need to include ▷ Jane Austen, ▷ Charles Dickens, ▷ William Thackeray, ▷ Charlotte and Emily Brontë, ▷ George Eliot, ▷ Thomas Hardy and ▷ Henry James, a total difficult to match for a single genre in any other century); more significant, perhaps, is the strength in depth, the immense range and variety of interest to be found amongst novelists of less settled reputation. Fiction in the nineteenth century could and did address every topic, enter every dispute, reflect every ideal of an age perceived by those who lived through it to be one of unprecedentedly rapid change. 'Novels are in the hands of us all; from the Prime Minister down to the last appointed scullery-maid,' wrote ▷ Anthony Trollope in 1870. And of the novels they could have chosen from (an estimated 40,000 titles published in the course of the nineteenth century), an extraordinarily large number have remained in the common currency of popular rather than scholarly reading habits.

The reasons for this enduring popularity are naturally difficult to pin down; and one immediate answer – that such writers as the Brontës and Dickens are still widely read because they are said to have written good novels – must be considered. But this explanation begs the more interesting question of what exactly is a 'good' novel. Shakespeare and Wordsworth, for example, both major influences on most nineteenth-century writers, are not read by the general public to the same extent or for the same reasons as Victorian novelists of considerably lesser claims. There is of course a sense in which the novel is more approachable than drama or poetry. It addresses itself directly to 'life', without the intervening artistic medium of verse or dramatic form, in a way which other literary genres do not. It tells stories, reworks the mundane material of everyday life into something significant, and (most nineteenth-century readers would add) it teaches moral lessons. More interestingly, perhaps, it could be argued that the nineteenth-century novel is the first art form to deal explicitly and realistically with issues which speak directly to some of the central concerns of twentieth-century consciousness.

The novels of this period sprang from a society undergoing a more massive upheaval under the influence of industrialization than in any previous era. Not only was the population shifting irrevocably from an agricultural to an urban base, with all the profound changes in social, working and family patterns that this entailed; there were also the dramatic visible changes resulting from technological invention which altered people's perceptions and their world. The railway boom of the 1840s did not merely affect the landscape; its more profound repercussions lay in revolutionizing expectations of speed, mobility and permanence. When in ▷ *Dombey and Son* (1847–48) Dickens describes 'the first great shock of the earthquake' which the building of the railway brings, he is expressing a now familiar paradox inherent in such change: 'from the very core of all this dire disorder, [the railway] trailed smoothly away, upon its mighty course of civilization and improvement'. The chaotic but humane little community of Staggs's Gardens has been 'cut up root and branch' to make way for the 'crowds of people and mountains of goods' to be shifted by the railway: the individual and the idiosyncratic have been sacrificed to the corporate and the homogeneous. ▷ Thomas Carlyle's famous definition of this period as 'the Mechanical Age' focused the anxieties of many contemporaries about the relationship of the individual to society. 'Men are grown mechanical in head and in heart, as well as in hand,' wrote Carlyle, and the development and preservation of individuality within a society dominated by various kinds of mechanistic systems (moral, social, political, economic, even historical) formed a major theme of fiction throughout the century.

However, whereas Carlyle's mechanized individual is tacitly assumed to be a man, the novel of this period belongs in certain crucial respects to women. Not only were women the major consumers of fiction, forming as they did the majority of the readership throughout the century; they were also, to a degree never seen previously, producers as well. Women novelists take equal status with men both as generally acknowledged 'great writers' (fifty per cent of our earlier listing of major novelists were women) and also as part of the huge array of novel writers who produced everything from minor master-pieces to worthless pot-boilers. In the first two decades of the century Jane Austen was writing novels of sophisticated realism, while ▷ Mary Shelley's ▷ *Frankenstein* (1817) was to become the definitive ▷ Gothic romance. Throughout the period, writers like ▷ Charlotte Mary Yonge, ▷ Elizabeth Gaskell, ▷ Harriet Martineau, ▷ Ouida and ▷ Margaret Oliphant were producing novels ranging from serious social comment to wild sensationalism. And in the 1890s the single most popular novelist (though very far from the best) was another woman, ▷ Marie Corelli, whose *The Sorrows of Satan* (1895) sold more copies than any previous English novel. The subject matter of fiction, moreover, fell characteristically into a woman's sphere: even in novels whose thematic interests lie primarily elsewhere, the standard plot and setting were almost invariably domestic and family-orientated, with courtship and marriage providing a major part of the narrative thrust. As George Eliot pointed out, the novel form, more than any other, offered opportunities to women in a society which elsewhere constrained their every activity: 'No restrictions can shut women out from the materials of fiction, and there is no species of art which is so free from rigid requirements.' The nineteenth-century novel was the first art form in which women could take equal status with men.

For George Eliot, though, as for many others, the unusually dominant role of women as both producers and consumers of fiction was not an unequivocally good thing. Her comments are taken from an essay entitled 'Silly Novels by Lady Novelists', in which she draws attention to the self-gratifying and unreal stereotypes which the lady novelists offer to an uncritical female readership. In other respects, too, this female orientation had an unfortunate influence on the sphere of the English novel. The popular picture of the Victorian *pater familias* reading out suitable material to his devoted family was not far from the truth and was felt by many practising novelists to be a major restriction on their art. Dickens's Miss Podsnap in ▷ *Our Mutual Friend* (1864–65), the archetypal 'young person', placed a crippling constraint on the material thought proper for inclusion in the novel: 'The question about everything was, could it bring a blush into the cheek of the young person? And the inconvenience of the young person was, that, according to Mr Podsnap, she seemed liable to burst into blushes when there was no need at all.' As Thackeray lamented in his preface to ▷ *Pendennis* (1848–50): 'Since the author of "Tom Jones" was buried, no writer of fiction among us has been permitted to depict to his utmost power a MAN'; where ▷ Henry Fielding was at liberty to portray a lovable male libertine, Thackeray and his contemporaries looked constantly over their shoulders for the blushes of the young person and the pursed lips of that mythical guardian of morality, ▷ Mrs Grundy. This provided a field of tacit warfare throughout the century: where Trollope recorded complacently that 'no girl has risen from the reading of my pages less modest than she was before', other novelists, such as the popular feminist writer of the 1890s Mona Caird, chafed furiously against such artificial restraints: 'Mrs Grundy in black silk, with a sceptre in her hand, on the throne of the Ages, surrounded by an angel-choir of Young Persons! Is this to be the end of our democracy?'

Thus for a large part of the nineteenth century the English novel was significantly limited by the necessity to conform to a moral code which aimed to protect a predominantly female readership from exposure to sexual corruption. Extreme circumspection was required in the depiction of any sort of sexual contact, whether in or outside marriage, often with ludicrous results. Jane Eyre's unusually frank accounts of her feelings for Mr Rochester (which included the confession that she had sat on his knee prior to marrying him) brought accusations of coarseness from several critics. The scene in Hardy's ▷ *Tess of the D'Urbervilles* (1891) in which Angel Clare carries the milkmaids across a flooded lane had to be altered to expunge the image of a man lifting a personable young lady in his arms: in the serialized version, Clare had to be equipped with a wheelbarrow. And in broader terms, too, the novel upheld middle-class morality in matters of sexual conduct. Women were to be pure, and morally superior to men; marriage was for life; sex was unmentionable. Where a novel depicted deviation from these values, the appropriate moral lesson had to be firmly underlined, so that the 'fallen woman' who features in so much fiction of the period was invariably seen to be punished. ▷ Mrs Henry Wood's melodramatic and best-selling tale of adultery, *East Lynne* (1861), rammed home these lessons with almost sadistic relish, warning potential adulteresses that their fate 'will be found far worse than death' and proving the point with a story of startlingly ingenious retributive suffering. More commonly, the fallen woman was brought to a dramatic death (like Lady Dedlock in ▷ *Bleak House*) or banished (like ▷ *David Copperfield*'s Little Em'ly). Even in a work which pleaded for the moral rights of the fallen woman, such as Elizabeth Gaskell's *Ruth* (1853), the sinner had to be removed from society by the end of the novel.

This circumspection had a more profound and potentially damaging effect on the portrayal of women in the nineteenth-century novel than it did on the representation of men. Thackeray was to some extent right to envy Fielding his Tom Jones, but he might have done better to regret his own inability to portray a Moll Flanders. Ironically, it was Thackeray himself who in ▷ *Vanity Fair* (1847–48) encapsulated the Victorian double visions of women which was seen by many nineteenth-century commentators to characterize contemporary attitudes. In Amelia Sedley he satirizes the good woman of conventional ideals, destructively doting and cloyingly sentimental, passive, long-suffering and ultimately parasitical; in Becky Sharp he portrays a woman of wit and initiative, who uses her sexuality and intelligence to exploit a society richly deserving her machinations, but who must finally be condemned as a neglectful mother, adulteress and, possibly, a murderer. Charlotte Brontë's ▷ *Shirley* (1849) explicitly attacks this male polarizing of supposed female attributes: 'Men are often under an illusion about women: they do not read them in a true light: they misapprehend them, both for good and evil: their good woman is a queer thing, half doll, half angel; their bad woman always a fiend.' The bad woman, as we have seen, was habitually disposed of by death; but it was the good woman, half doll, half angel, who forms the common twentieth-century conception of the typical Victorian heroine. Dickens's Agnes Wickfield, who in David Copperfield's image of her is 'forever pointing upward', is a typical role model for the sort of female perfection which is morally impeccable, spiritually uplifting and a well-earned reward for the world-weary hero. It was an ideal whose falsity was under constant attack throughout the period and which was largely discredited by the end of the century: in ▷ Havelock Ellis's phrase, the stereotyped woman was 'a cross between an angel and an idiot'.

How, then, did what now appears such a patently distorted view of women retain such a hold in fictional conventions? We must not dismiss out of hand the notion that Victorian portrayals of women are more reflective of their repression in reality than we would care to believe. ▷ George Gissing argued that women actually were intellectually and developmentally feebler than men, when in typically gloomy mood he stated that 'more than half the misery of life is due to the ignorance and childishness of women. The average woman pretty closely resembles . . . the average male *idiot.*' In a society which, for the greater part of the century, denied women access to higher education and the professions, encased them physically in whalebone and voluminous skirts, and imbued them with the notion that their highest function was to serve and inspire men, it is little wonder that the conformist woman of the time should appear to modern eyes an unacceptably compliant creature – or, as Edmund Carpenter (1844–1929) more waspishly expressed it, 'a bundle of weak and flabby sentiments, combined with a wholly undeveloped brain'. However, there is ample evidence from both the numerous examples of independent and religious women of nineteenth-century history, and from the many original and individualized heroines of fiction, that the conventional ideal was not the whole reality. More pervasively influential on characterization, as well as on the form and content of novels, were the actual conditions under which most of them were published.

At the beginning of the nineteenth century, the majority of novels were published in three, or sometimes four, volumes and the 'three decker' retained its popularity until almost the end of the Victorian period. The standard cost of each volume of the novel was half a guinea, a stiff enough price for most middle-class readers and beyond the means of the working class. However, for a subscription of one guinea a year, readers could borrow a volume at a time from one of the ▷ circulating libraries, by far the most influential of which was ▷ Charles Mudie's, opened in 1842. Mudie exercised an influence over the Victorian novel which amounted to a form of ▷ censorship, for he prided himself upon selecting his stock according to its suitability for family consumption. Just as Mudie's moral approval of an author, which could translate into mass buying of copies from the publisher and advance orders for future works, could launch a career in fiction, so his refusal to stock a novel of dubious morality could spell financial disaster. Few novelists could afford the risk of offending the circulating libraries and thus a form of guilty self-censorship constrained the creative freedom of most writers.

Alternatives to publication in three-volume form were initiated by the revival of the monthly serialization of Dickens's ▷ *Pickwick Papers* in 1836. Novels published in this manner were issued as slim volumes appearing at the beginning of each month, continuing as a rule for nineteen numbers. Clearly this form of publication deeply influenced the form of works in a way largely obscured by their subsequent appearance in a single volume. Writers who wished their readers to continue buying their work over a long period had to end each issue with some form of cliff-hanging incentive to purchase the next volume, and needed also to ensure the memorability of characters whose last appearance could have occurred several months earlier. This may in part account for what is now sometimes taken to be a melodramatic form of plotting and exaggeration in characterization on the part of such habitual practioners of the monthly serial as Dickens or Thackeray. On the other hand, publication in parts did allow a writer to adjust his or her work in response to readers' preferences: a popular character could boost sales (as Sam Weller did for *Pickwick*) and a narrative red herring could be expeditiously abandoned. As single volume serialization gradually gave way to part publication in family and literary magazines, the questions of sales and censorship moved from the author's to the editor's domain. Hardy was one of the prime sufferers from editorial restraint in his initial serial publication of novels, and frequently had to wait for one-volume publication before he was able to present his work in the form intended. Both Dickens and Thackeray had experience of the business from both ends, the first as editorial instigator of the family weeklies ▷ *Household Words* and ▷ *All the Year Round*, the second as editor of the prestigious ▷ *Cornhill*. Amongst major Victorian novelists, only the Brontës never published in any sort of serial form.

Development through the century

Given the wealth and variety of nineteenth-century fiction, as well as the inevitable historical shifts in critical judgments, it is hardly surprising to find widely diverging assessments of how the novel developed over the period. ▷ George Saintsbury's *A History of Nineteenth-century Literature*, first published in 1896, gives almost as much space to ▷ Maria Edgeworth as to Jane Austen and George Eliot, and treats ▷ Walter Scott more fully than Dickens: Hardy receives no mention at all. ▷ F. R. Leavis's immensely influential *The Great Tradition* (1948) opens with the characteristically combative statement that 'The great English novelists are Jane Austen, George Eliot, Henry James and Joseph Conrad'; Charlotte Brontë is noted as having 'permanent interest of a minor kind', Dickens as being a 'great entertainer' who lacks 'sustained seriousness'. While few modern critics would wish to eliminate from the canon these four writers, contemporary interest in the nineteenth-century novel ranges far beyond his vaguely defined but insistently urged criterion of 'significant creative achievement'. Individual writers and sub-genres of the novels which would have been relegated to areas of minor interest by many mid-twentieth-century critics now attract serious study, and the reputations of many well-known novelists have notably shifted. Of those most highly regarded in the nineteenth century itself, Scott and ▷ George Meredith have suffered the most serious depression in critical interest; neither is now much read by the general public or widely taught on literature degrees. Dickens, on the other hand, has been reclaimed from the realm of mere entertainer and praised as an incisive social critic of profound symbolic significance. And Hardy, ignored by Saintsbury and patronizingly dismissed by Leavis, now commands as wide a critical industry on both sides of the Atlantic as any nineteenth-century novelist.

There is no simple way of subdividing the mass of fictional material published during the period, nor, despite Leavis's claim for a great tradition, is there any single line of development which can easily be traced. Conventionally, the pre-Victorian period, where the major figures are Scott and Jane Austen, is seen as having a separate identity, which then gives way to the explosion of talent in the first decades of Victoria's reign, with the emergence of Dickens, Thackeray and the Brontës. The mid-Victorian novel can be seen as dominated by the later Dickens and George Eliot, and the late-nineteenth century by Hardy. These periods will be dealt with separately in conjunction with the major authors within them. However, to identify the major practitioners of the form during the period is very far from finding a consistent train of development. While there is a sense in which James's novels can be seen as a more self-consciously artistic development of Jane Austen's fictional mode, there is no obvious way in which Hardy may be said to emerge from the same tradition. Charlotte Brontë, notoriously, found little to admire in Jane Austen, and Hardy recorded that he was unable to finish reading ▷ *Wuthering Heights* (1847). Arguably, the nineteenth century saw the emergence in the novel of a privileging of 'realism', both in the presentation of psychological depth of characterization and in the depiction of humankind's inevitable inter-relation with the newly perceived complexities of social and historical contexts. There is also a clear change, in the Victorian period at least, in the material thought permissible for inclusion in the novel. The tyranny of the circulating libraries and the family magazines was gradually eroded to allow greater frankness in the fictional portrayal of sexuality. By the 1890s outspokenness on questions of sexual behaviour – particularly in women – had become to some extent fashionable, and a host of popular novels which examined such questions in an overtly polemical manner enjoyed a brief vogue. Even so, the violently antagonistic reception of Hardy's ▷ *Jude the Obscure* (1895), which saw the novel reviled in the press and burnt by a bishop, showed how severely limited this increased tolerance could be.

More importantly, an attempt to treat nineteenth-century fiction as a smoothly developing series of 'great writers' severely distorts the picture of the novel as it would have been viewed by both readers and authors during the period itself. It ignores too much of what was seriously offered and received by contemporary writers and readers, and which is now the subject of increasing critical interest, both as reflections of the nineteenth-century consciousness and as significant and legitimate variations on the novel form. Late twentieth-century taste is perhaps more open to the claims of romance and fantasy, more sympathetically interested in the overt wrestling with ideas, than was the case when Leavis made high moral seriousness and mastery of form his main criteria of excellence. Minor novelists, and the sub-genres in which they frequently wrote, are an essential and illuminating part of the nineteenth-century fictional scene.

Sub-genres of the novel

During the early decades of the nineteenth century most popular fiction grew out of the traditions of romance and Romanticism. The two terms are of course closely linked, but should not be equated. A romance, in David Masson's phrase of 1859, was 'a fictitious narrative ... the interest of which turns upon marvellous and uncommon incidents', and the debate between romance and realism formed a continuous part of nineteenth-century thinking about the theory of fiction. The influence of the Romantic movement was most apparent in the late eighteenth-century Gothic novel (▷ Gothic revival), a form not lacking in marvellous and uncommon incidents, but which also played on the Romantic interest in the supernatural and in the dark and untapped areas of the human psyche. Jane Austen, writing novels of pragmatic realism during the height of the Romantic period, mercilessly satirized the implausibility of the Gothic through the credulous Catherine of ▷ *Northanger Abbey* (1818), and neatly pinned down the possible self-indulgence of the Romantic sensibility in ▷ *Persuasion*'s Captain Brandon. ▷ Thomas Love Peacock's spoof Gothic novel, ▷ *Nightmare Abbey* (1818), also lampooned the form as well as parodying the Romantic excesses of some of that movement's major poets. But the Gothic was still kept vividly alive in Mary Shelley's *Frankenstein* (1817), published in the same year as Peacock's parody, and reappears, subtly transformed, in the works of Charlotte and Emily Brontë. It could also be argued that the historical novel, first popularized by Scott, and continued less successfully in the works of, for example, ▷ Harrison Ainsworth, owed much to the Romantic and Gothic preoccupation with the past.

In many ways, though, it was romance rather than Romanticism which informed the main sub-genres of the first three decades of the nineteenth century. Writers of popular fiction were concerned to entertain their readers with dramatic incidents and to draw them imaginatively into worlds remote from their own. The historical novel could obviously offer limitless scope here, in terms both of high drama and (often ponderously academic) period detail. Where Ainsworth's novels catered to the contemporary taste for luridly reconstructed English history, one of the other popular practitioners of the form, Edward Bulwer (▷ Lytton), mainly remembered now for *The Last Days of Pompeii* (1834), took the wider sweep of Western historical movements as his subject. His historical romances tend to focus on the closing of eras, and may thus be seen as signifying contemporary unease in the face of change and instability. But his writings are too clogged with the fruits of meticulous historical research, and too stilted in the rendering of dialogue, to have lasted well. However, forms of the historical novel continued to be practised throughout the century by major as well as minor writers. George Eliot ventured into historical fiction, not wholly successfully, in ▷ *Romola*, and it is a fact often overlooked by modern readers that large numbers of major Victorian novels are 'historical' in the sense of being set some thirty to forty years before their date of publication.

The historical novel could be both an escape from and a comment on the profound changes which were perceived to be occurring in the contemporary social order. Of less obvious relevance were the other popular sub-genres of the early nineteenth century, the ▷ Newgate novel and the ▷ silver-fork school. The Newgate novel played on morbid tastes for violence and death in ways which relate it to some extent to the Gothic, and in romanticizing its criminals it removed such socially disruptive elements safely into the realm of fantasy. The silver-fork school, on the other hand, displayed the sort of high society life to which increasingly prosperous members of the middle class might hope to aspire and which they could certainly be expected to envy. Novels of this class paraded details of the food, fashions and furniture of the rich and well-bred before a readership which could now begin to dream of emulating such manners. Writers of silver-fork fiction included ▷ Benjamin Disraeli in his early novel *Vivian Grey* (1826), and the now largely forgotten Theodore Hook (1788–1841) and ▷ Catherine Gore. Both Dickens and Thackeray capture and to some degree satirize the mood of envious interest amongst the socially mobile on which these novels played, Thackeray in his portrayal of the *nouveaux riches* Osborne and Sedley families in *Vanity Fair*, Dickens, for example, in his parody 'The Lady Flabella' in ▷ *Nicholas Nickleby* or with the Veneerings in *Our Mutual Friend*. Interestingly both the Newgate and silver-fork forms have modern counterparts in recent popular fiction in what have been neatly designated the 'bodice-ripping' school of historical fiction (in which sex replaces death as the focus) and the 'sex-and-shopping' novel which caters for the emulative dreams of the upwardly mobile.

Of more immediate social relevance, however, as well as in general possessing more lasting literary merit, were the novels which addressed the 'condition of England' question. These works, also known as 'social problem' novels, arose out of the social and political upheavals which followed the Reform Act of 1832 (▷ Reform Bills). The 1830s and 1840s marked the beginnings of a conscious effort both by Parliament and by social commentators to address the problems caused by the rapid industrialization of the preceding decades. The first Factory Act and the ▷ Poor Law Amendment Act of 1834 reflected the stirrings of governmental conscience and, from the other side, the rise of ▷ Chartism marked the beginnings of concerted working-class demands for reform. The economic depression of the 1840s produced deprivation amongst the industrial workers of the north on a scale which could not be ignored, and Chartist riots and marches on Westminster made poverty and disaffection visibly threatening to the comparatively untouched middle-class southerner. It was Carlyle who first drew attention to the social effects of the ▷ industrial revolution in his essay 'Signs of the Times' (1829) and who, in coining the phrase 'condition of England question' in *Chartism* (1839), provided a focus for what to many novelists of the early Victorian period seemed to be the central matter for fiction. Writers like Elizabeth Gaskell, Disraeli, ▷ Charles Kingsley and the Dickens of ▷ *Hard Times* (1854), addressed themselves directly to the question and produced novels which dealt realistically and sympathetically with the problems of the industrialized working class.

Probably the major strength of the social problem novel lay in its educational rather than its polemical function. Written by and for the middle classes, these novels laid out with passionate clarity the plight of a section of the community of which most readers, for geographical and social reasons, were simply ignorant. The new cities of the north of England, where industrial workers were herded into hastily erected housing built round smoke-belching factories, were uncharted territory for large parts of the novel-reading public, and the divisive effects of such developments were repeatedly stressed by novelists. In giving his 'condition of England' novel ▷ *Sybil* (1845) the sub-title 'The Two Nations', Disraeli encapsulated his perception of a country tragically and dangerously split between rich and poor, and Elizabeth Gaskell's ▷ *North and South* (1854–5) explores the differences in values and living conditions between the two halves of the country. The vividly realistic descriptions of working-class life provided by many social problem novels were as educative to contemporary readers as to later social historians, and the pressing issues of Chartism, ▷ trade unions, strikes and master–worker relations receive sensitive if rarely revolutionary treatment in such novels as Gaskell's ▷ *Mary Barton* (1848), Kingsley's *Alton Locke* (1850) and Disraeli's *Sybil*. Dickens's *Hard Times*, the only one of his novels to be set exclusively in the north of England, contrasts the mechanistic, and as he sees them, inhuman principles of ▷ utilitarian philosophy with the personal and warm-hearted values of imaginative sympathy, and his handling of the question of solidarity amongst the factory hands is symptomatic of the ambivalence apparently inherent in the genre. His working-class protagonist, Stephen Blackpool, is a saintly victim, his union leader a blustering agitator and the men good-hearted innocents temporarily swayed into an unworthy form of protest against a system portrayed as patently wrong. Blackpool's repeated lament in the face of bafflingly obvious injustice, "Tis all a muddle', sums up the helplessness of worker and novelist alike in the face of the enormity of the problem.

Indeed, the one major criticism of the genre, levelled by contemporaries as well as by modern critics, was that it proffered inadequate and often sentimental solutions to questions of great social and political complexity. As Thackeray put it, 'At the conclusion of these tales ... there somehow arrives a misty reconciliation between the poor and the rich; a prophecy is uttered of better times for the one, and better manners in the other ... and the characters make their bow, grinning, in a group, as they do at the end of a drama when the curtain falls.' This is largely true of the novels mentioned: the symbolic handshake between master and man at the end of *North and South*, Mary Barton's escape to Canada with her newly-wed husband, or Stephen Blackpool's martyrdom in the cause of truth and understanding, all substitute reconciliation at a personal level for long-term political solutions. However, there is no reason to expect novelists to be in possession of answers which escaped legislators, whereas in articulating and making imaginatively immediate the social problems of the time, writers of the 'condition of England' novels not only provided a valuable information service but also produced works of significant realism and insight.

The social condition of a newly industrialized Britian was a preoccupation of novelists mainly during the 1840s and 1850s. During the same period the spiritual condition of the country also became of pressing concern and novels dealing with religious questions formed another recognizable sub-genre which retained its currency to the end of the century. In some sense all nineteenth-century novels are 'religious' in so far as they are the product of a society in which Christian observance was the norm amongst the middle classes, and thus the moral and spiritual values of Christianity are necessarily either implicit in or deliberately explored by all writers of fiction. However, the crisis of faith which arose in the middle decades of the nineteenth century predictably gave rise to works which set out to discuss the problems explicitly, in much the same way in which the 'condition of England' novel articulated social and political questions. The three main influences on religious thought during this time were the ▷ Oxford Movement of the 1830s and 1840s, which sought to restore High Church ideals within the Church of England, and culminated in ▷ John Newman's defection to Roman Catholicism in 1845; the new German biblical criticism, first made accessible to English readers with the publication of George Eliot's translation of Strauss's *Leben Jesu* in 1846; and of course the impact of ▷ Charles Darwin's *On the Origin of Species* (1859). Spiritual crises and ecclesiastical quarrellings form the subject of such novels as J. A. Froude's *The Nemesis of Faith* (1849), Disraeli's *Lothair* (1870) and ▷ Mrs Humphry Ward's *Robert Elsmere* (1883), as well as being the basis of Trollope's ▷ Barsetshire novels and Margaret Oliphant's imitations of them, 'The Chronicles of Carlingford'.

Nineteenth-century consumers of fiction were thus very much more receptive to the exposition of ideas in fiction than are most modern readers, who tend to resent being preached at under the guise of fiction. Problem novels, or 'novels with a purpose', tackled issues of all kinds throughout the period. Again, the main beneficiaries of this discursive tendency were probably women, whose problems, lumped under the catch-all phrase 'the woman question', were repeatedly examined. The fallen woman was, as mentioned above, a particularly popular subject, featuring as a dreadful warning in works such as *East Lynne* or as a repentant Magdalen figure in *Ruth*. Charlotte Mary Yonge's *The Clever Woman of the Family* (1865) cautions young women against the temptations of the intellect as memorably as Mrs Henry Wood does against the lure of the flesh. And by the last decade of the century there had arisen a distinct class of novel, the ▷ 'New Woman fiction', which dealt with the current feminist questions of sex, marriage and work.

There is, then, continuous interaction in terms of themes, issues and genres, between different writers, and between recognizable sub-groups of the novel and what is now regarded as mainstream fiction. The novelists of the period should be viewed within the artistic as well as the social and political context in which they worked.

The pre-Victorian period: Jane Austen

To select Jane Austen (1775–1817) as the single major writer of this period is at once to make a critical judgement which would not always have been accepted. To later nineteenth-century readers and many earlier twentieth-century ones, Walter Scott would have appeared probably the more influential figure. In initiating the historical romance he popularized a form which retained its appeal throughout the century and he was read with admiration by most subsequent nineteenth-century novelists. Charlotte Brontë, unsurprisingly, much preferred his Romantic sweep to Jane Austen's tightly controlled realism, and Henry James praised his 'responding imagination before the human scene'. Interestingly, though, it was Scott himself who was one of the first to identify and appreciate Jane Austen's particular contribution to the development of the English novel at the time. In his review of ▷ *Emma* (1816) he discusses at length the limitations and diminishing returns of the predominating romance form, praising her novels for 'presenting to the reader, instead of the striking representation of an imaginary world, a correct and striking representation of that which is daily taking place around him'.

Jane Austen was herself, as is widely known, acutely conscious of the self-imposed restrictions of her range. When she wrote of the 'little bit (two inches wide) of ivory on which I work with so fine a brush as produces little effect after much labour', she was being characteristically both self-deprecating about her limitations and astute about her strengths. As a realist in an age dominated by romance, her fine brush reworked the material of fiction into tones which set standards for the investigation of the individual within a closely observed social framework for later realists to emulate if they could. For a long time her reputation was somewhat distorted by the indulgent cooings of 'Janeites' who praised her 'gentle' irony and indulgent humour, thus creating an impression of a softly female orientation within the safe sphere of domestic concerns, untroubling to the larger issues of life. Nothing could be further from the truth. Her irony, far from being gentle, is habitually savage in its condemnation of the foolish, hypocritical and self-deceiving; her humour is razor-sharp in its exposure of human weakness in a morally flawed society. Her heroines are set painful lessons in personal knowledge and moral self-discipline which entirely deny the possibilities of sentimental or coincidental resolution to which later Victorian novelists often have recourse. If, in keeping with the comic mode, they succeed finally in securing their desirable ends, it is not through a conventional coincidence of circumstance but because moral maturity secures an appropriate partnering. Nor is Jane Austen's world as prim and restricted as is sometimes unguardedly assumed. While never condoning sexual misdemeanour, her treatment of the subject owes more to hard-headed eighteenth-century worldliness than to Victorian repression. Where the Victorian female innocent is habitually seduced, abandoned and condemned to a lonely fate, Lydia Bennet (▷ *Pride and Prejudice*) bounces exuberantly into Wickham's bed with no thoughts in her head beyond immediate gratification, and after her hastily patched up marriage is received by at least some members of her family.

Jane Austen's values, then, are more eighteenth-century than Victorian, more classical than Romantic. She portrays a society in which foolishness, hypocrisy and avarice abound, but where an agreed standard of moral principle may be assumed and where rationality may be invoked to counterbalance the disruptive lure of unbridled emotionalism. Her characters may suffer but they must also understand, and their understanding derives from a proper exercise of rational thought rather than from emotional or subconscious enlightenment. Through Marianne in ▷ *Sense and Sensibility* (1811) she attacks the idea that feeling can be a reliable guide to conduct and in *Persuasion* (1818) she satirizes, though with more sympathetic indulgence, Romantic emotion. But perhaps no single factor marks Jane Austen off more distinctly from the Victorian novelists that followed her than her treatment of children. Amongst her heroines, only Fanny Price in ▷ *Mansfield Park* (1814) is portrayed in childhood, and children in general figure merely as convenient plot devices or as social distractions. By contrast, the Victorian novelist frequently makes the child, often an orphan, and the process of growth to maturity a central thematic focus. After Jane Austen, the influence of Romantic thought on ideas about childhood, innocence, imagination and feeling is everywhere apparent.

The mid-nineteenth century: Dickens, Thackeray, the Brontës

It is notable, then, that while biographers of Jane Austen find difficulty in giving dramatic interest to a life of largely uneventful calm, those of the great mid-century novelists have a wealth of misery, neglect and misunderstanding to relate in their subjects' early years. This has the obvious effect of producing answering autobiographical portrayals of children in the novels, but also tends to create a sense of the fictional protagonist as alienated from or at odds with society. In the early Victorian novel the depiction of society generally expands unrecognizably from Jane Austen's little bit of ivory to a consciously panoramic perspective in which the individual is likely to be embattled and forlorn. The figure of the innocent child, often lonely and neglected, becomes a powerful symbol of society's guilt; the education and growth from childhood show the process of adjustment within a largely hostile social structure. While the Romantic movement discovered and articulated the moral potency of the child, it was the Victorian novel which produced the first sustained portrayals of children in literature.

Of the major novelists of the period, William Makepeace Thackeray (1811–63) is probably least directly concerned with children, though his best novel, *Vanity Fair* (1847–48), does make use of significant incidents from the childhood of his protagonists in order to account for their subsequent development. Though often astute and original in his perception of his characters' psychology, his main strengths as a writer lay in his sharp eye for the particular kinds of human weakness thrown up by a newly complex society and his ability, in *Vanity Fair* at least, to bind all levels of the social structure into a comprehensive vision of moral and spiritual inadequacy. When Charlotte Brontë described him as 'the first social regenerator of the day', she was responding to qualities which were abundantly present in his early work but which faded notably in his later career. *Vanity Fair*, 'A Novel without a Hero', depicts English society in the years surrounding Waterloo as itself a battleground where money and social standing are the criteria for success and where individuals rise and fall according to their skill in playing social games which are as amoral and arbitrary as the values of the Stock Exchange which determine the fortunes of the Osborne and Sedley families on which the novel centres. Though Thackerary focuses his interest on the newly emerging middle classes, his picture of society extends upwards into the metropolitan aristocracy and the landed gentry, and downwards to the working classes and Bohemia. What binds them all is the struggle for money and reputation in a cut-throat world where the clever can 'live well on nothing a year' and the weak go to the wall. It is a mark of Thackeray's originality that the character who most successfully exploits the possibilities of his social struggle is a woman, the intelligent and cynical Becky Sharp, whom as we have seen, for all her manifest faults, he can never bring himself thoroughly to condemn. The novel leaves a moral question mark over all its characters and in so doing forces its readers to engage actively in the process of questioning and judgement in a way calculated both to challenge and disturb.

Charles Dickens (1812–70), Thackeray's more successful rival for the affections of the novel-reading public, rarely leaves such moral openness, but develops more consistently towards a bleak view of society in which monolithic institutions (money and commerce in *Dombey and Son*, the law in *Bleak House*, the civil service in ▷ *Little Dorrit*) are potentially crushing to the strongly realized goodness of individuals. It was Dickens more than any other Victorian novelist who exploited the possibilities of the child as symbol of innocence amidst corruption, and this is one major factor which has led to accusations of sentimentality in his works. A catalogue of his maltreated but morally reformative children – Oliver Twist, David Copperfield, Paul and Florence Dombey, Jo the crossing sweeper, Little Nell, Sissy Jupe, Little Dorrit (amongst many others) – suggests a preoccupation with the innocence of childhood which could add weight to such an accusation, and it is largely true that Dickens's children are exempt from the barbs of humorous exposure with which he mercilessly illuminates the grotesque flaws in most of his characters' compositions. But his best portrayals of childhood – those in which the child ceases to be a simple symbolic force – uniquely capture the guilts and fears as well as the pathetic helplessness of juvenile innocence.

Modern mainstream humanist criticism tends to base its praise for Dickens on a perception of the development in his later novels of a thematically coherent critique of his society which works through imagery and symbolism rather than through the creation of psychologically convincing characters. One can point, for example, to the recurrent images of imprisonment in *Little Dorrit* (1855–57) or to the sustained exploration of legal ramifications in *Bleak House* (1852–53). His world is so richly animated, his descriptive powers so invigoratingly original, as to invest the inanimate objects of his world with a vitality and significance often assumed to compensate for the lack of realism in the people which inhabit it. His women are prime targets for criticism here, since it is generally female characters who, for obvious reasons, carry the sometimes crippling weight of his moral approval. Dickens, while anatomizing the evils of his society with unique imaginative power, had a characteristically Victorian belief in the possibility of unsullied goodness and it is generally the heroines of his novels who provide examples of its morally regenerative force. Sissy Jupe in *Hard Times* (1854) works a change in the harshly utilitarian Gradgrind household 'by mere love and gratitude' and it is her 'wisdom of the Heart' which effectively counteracts the mechanistic values that the novel attacks. Her passive goodness and sweetly self-sacrificing nature exemplify the qualities often taken to be regrettably typical of Dickens's portrayal of women. However, it could also be argued that the twentieth century's automatic suspicion of pure virtue blinds the modern reader to more subtle qualities in Dickens's heroines. His skill in depicting the psychological results of guilt and repression, often noted in his male characters, is present also in his portrayal of many of the women. There is a great deal more to such characters as Florence Dombey, Esther Summerson or Little Dorrit than is usually perceived by an eye habitually prejudiced against the stereotype of the good woman.

Whatever may be reclaimed for Dickens's reputation in the portrayal of women, though, he can never hope to rival the Brontës in this area. ▷ Anne Brontë (1820–49), perhaps less talented and original than her sisters, still writes movingly and perceptively about the loneliness of the governess in *Agnes Grey* (1847), and adds new dimensions to the depiction of marital misery in *The Tenant of Wildfell Hall* (1848). Emily Brontë's only novel, *Wuthering Heights*, is generally recognized to transcend normal moral and spiritual expectations. Though Charlotte Brontë (1817–55) felt it necessary in her Preface to apologize for what she felt 'must appear a rude and strange production', the novel is meticulously planned and structured. Its strangeness derives partly from its unaccustomed settings, more perhaps from its extremities of violence and passion, and the central portrayal in Cathy and Heathcliff of a relationship which cannot be assimilated into any conventional framework or concept of character. That Emily Brontë (1818–48) was aware of the difficulties of this structure is shown by the care with which she draws her readers into the story through narrators of familiar social and psychological backgrounds; as their limitations are exposed, so their conventional judgements are progressively rejected and the reader is invited to accept an entirely unfamiliar scheme of values. At the end of the novel, Lockwood's inability to imagine 'unquiet slumbers for the sleepers in that quiet earth' seems more a reflection of his own limitations than an assurance that the grave will provide a final peace for the spirits of Cathy and Heathcliff.

However, the radical nature of Emily Brontë's vision makes her less influenced by social realities. Her main characters, in being largely outside convention, make no direct comment upon it. Charlotte Brontë, on the other hand, in working more within the bounds of recognizable society, produces original depictions of women which are overtly hostile to contemporary ideals. The autobiographical elements in her work create repeated images of women struggling against a world whose expectations they are unable and indeed unwilling to fulfil. Jane Eyre, 'poor, plain and little', and Lucy Snowe, wracked with the pain of unrequited love, obviously call upon Charlotte Brontë's own experiences. Her heroines all struggle in a world whose standards of female behaviour are alien to their own, and their achievements are wrenched painfully from the creation of a personal morality which is frequently at odds with the conventions of their society. Though Lucy Snowe in ▷ *Villette* (1853), who in the novel's slightly ambiguous ending is shown as independent mistress of her own school, may seem the most obvious candidate for modern feminist approval, it is really Jane Eyre who is the more impressive figure. Jane's impassioned cry 'I will be myself' summarizes the novel's sustained plea for a morality in which the heroine has the right and indeed the duty to realize her individuality independent of expectations from more familiar moral systems. Both Charlotte and Emily Brontë participate in the Romantics' championing of the unique individual, the first within, the second largely outside, contemporary social realities. The poetic intensity of their writing, together with the patent influences of the Gothic and Byronic traditions, make their works most striking inheritors of Romanticism in the fiction of the period.

The mid-Victorian period: George Eliot

It is gratifying to reflect that arguably the first intellectual amongst major English novelists was a woman. In an age when female education was largely limited to the acquisition of 'accomplishments', George Eliot (1819–80) could read French, Italian, German, Latin and Greek. Deeply involved in and influenced by the philosophical and scientific movements of the time, she lost her religious faith in early womanhood but retained a profound sense of moral imperatives in a secular context. In common with many of her contemporaries, her interests focused on history and on modern attempts to arrive at systematic descriptions of social, religious and intellectual evolution. Her novels continually show her interest in the relationship between individual and historical change: as the individual is the product of social and historical forces, so society is formed and changed by the apparently inconsiderable lives of the individuals who compose it. Dorothea, who sets out at the beginning of ▷ *Middlemarch* (1871–2) in the view of the narrator as 'a modern Saint Theresa', may be defeated in her youthful objectives of effecting visible or dramatic change in her society but is convincingly displayed at the end as having an effect 'incalculably diffusive' on 'the growing good of the world'. The portrayal of the individual within a complex network of social and historical relationships forms a major part of George Eliot's fictional vision.

The past, and the extent to which her characters are determined by forces contained within it, form a continual theme in her fiction. 'Our deeds determine us, as much as we determine our deeds,' she wrote in ▷ *Adam Bede* (1859), and her novels repeatedly display what in *Middlemarch* she described as 'the slow preparation of effects from one life on another'. Seeing her characters as largely determined by a meticulously charted individual past, and a socially and historically realized present, she nevertheless insists upon the stern exercise of personal responsibility in moral decision-making. Her characters, or more particularly her narrators, are among the first in English fiction to be consistently portrayed in the process of rigorous *thought*, whether about personal choices or larger intellectual systems. However, George Eliot as narrator remains firmly in control of both her structures and her readers' responses. When in *Middlemarch* she comments on the unknowable significance of future developments in individual lives – 'destiny stands by sarcastic with our *dramatis personae* folded in her hand' – she could have legitimately substituted herself for destiny. George Eliot's authorial voice, omniscient, magisterial and tolerant, constantly controls our reactions and to some extent raises her readers to a level close to her own lofty overview. When ▷ Virginia Woolf described *Middlemarch* as 'one of the few English novels written for grown-up people', she was deftly defining the degree to which George Eliot's fiction makes demands of serious moral response in a readership which could previously have rested happily within the safe bounds of entertaining diversion.

Hardy and the late nineteenth century

Some contemporary reviewers of Thomas Hardy's early, anonymously published, work speculated that it might be by George Eliot. Presumably they were misled by the superficial similarities in the portrayal of rural communities and perhaps by Hardy's youthful pretensions to a command of contemporary intellectual issues, imperfectly assimilated. Indeed, an inability to judge his readers' tolerance of progressive moral and intellectual views was a continuing, and to modern eyes endearing, quality of Hardy's fiction, deriving as it did from his unusual combination of a countryman's pragmatism with a self-educated intellectualism. As the creator of the semi-fictional world of ▷ Wessex, Hardy (1840–1928) became the most significant regional novelist of the age and, with his unrivalled knowledge of the local customs and accents of his native land, was in a better position than any other writer to chart the changes in agricultural communities under the various dramatic shocks of nineteenth-century change. Hardy has, moreover, an eye for nature which is at once entirely unsentimental and supremely observant. When in *A Pair of Blue Eyes* (1873) Henry Knight clings desperately to a cliff with a fatal drop beneath him, Hardy notes that his torments are increased by the fact that rain driven against such an obstacle moves upwards not down: and, metaphorically staring death in the face, Knight's eyes actually meet the fossilized gaze of a trilobite embedded for millions of years in the rock before him. The vulnerable human in his extremity meets the indifferent but infinitely varied forces of nature, yet has contact over a gap of several million years with a fellow creature who has similarly suffered the pangs of life and death.

Such an incident is typical of the way in which Hardy's immense imaginative range and habitual preoccupation with the ironies of time are given solidity by observation of the precisely natural. It is also characteristic in that Knight's eventual rescue is effected by an incident at once stimulating and shocking to Victorian sexual tastes. The novel's heroine, Elfride, strips herself of all her undergarments in order to make a rope and, clad merely in a 'diaphanous exterior robe', hauls him to safety. Throughout his career Hardy found himself embroiled in battles against the prudish sensibilities of his readership and as his later novels began to engage more directly with contemporary questions of sexual morality, he was drawn, apparently protestingly, into fervent debates about women, sex and marriage. His views of the human condition, though, are more comprehensively tragic than would be suggested by confining him to immediate social criticism. Frequently accused of being irredeemably pessimistic, he described himself as a meliorist who portrayed the worst in order to point towards the better. But, despite the sharpness of their social criticism, there is little in his last novels – in *Tess of the D'Urbervilles* (1891) or *Jude the Obscure* (1895) – to suggest that possible future change could effectively alleviate their essentially tragic vision.

Fiction at the Fin de siècle

During the final years of the century, the debate about the relationship between romance and realism continued, with Gissing and ▷ George Moore as the prime realists vying with the exotic romances of, for example ▷ Robert Louis Stevenson and ▷ H. Rider Haggard. The approach of a new century (an event which generally prompts ideas of decadence, revolution and ending), combined with social changes such as the Married Woman's Property Act of 1882, the campaign for women's suffrage, and the emergence of male homosexuality as a defined (though persecuted) social identity contributed to a wave of novels (continuing into the early years of the twentieth century) which engaged in various ways with instabilities in gender identity and power relations between the sexes. One group of such novels was concerned with the idea of the New Woman – a contemporary term for women who refused to conform to conventional Victorian expectations of a woman's role, whether by seeking more education, like the heroine of ▷ H.G. Wells's *Ann Veronica* (1909), by leading an independent, single life, like the heroine of ▷ Annie Holdsworth's *Joanna Traill, Spinster* (1894), or by conducting a sexual relationship outside marriage, like the protagonist of ▷ Grant Allen's *The Woman who Did* (1895). Allen's novel, with its attack on the institution of marriage as a 'temple' where 'pitiable victims languish and die in ... sickening vaults' was something of a *succès de scandale*, a notoriety earlier attained by Henrik Ibsen's play *A Doll's House*, which was staged in England in 1889 and represented an important early statement of the theme of the New Woman. In fiction the theme received both sympathetic and hostile treatment: there were novels offering feminist critique and emancipated role models such as ▷ Sarah Grand's *The Heavenly Twins* (1893) and ▷ Ella Hepworth Dixon's *The Story of a Modern Woman* (1894), but there were also virulently anti-feminist works such as ▷ Walter Besant's anonymously published dystopia, *The Revolt of Man* (1882). More ambivalent presentations of the behaviour and fate of the New Woman are found in George Gissing's *The Odd Women* (1893), in Hardy's *Jude the Obscure* (in the character of Sue Brideshead) and in Henry James's *The Bostonians*, which, set in America, stages a contest for the mind and body of a young woman between a Boston feminist and a man committed to the reactionary social values of the old South. One of the most compelling and influential of nineteenth-century novels on the theme of the emancipation of women was ▷ Olive Schreiner's partly autobiographical work *The Story of an African Farm* (1883), about two female cousins and the son of a German overseer growing up together on a Boer farm in South Africa in the 1860s. The novel combines a tragi-comic satirical portrait of human weakness, kindness, deceit and cruelty in this isolated rural community with a mystical intensity in relation to the landscape. As the children approach adulthood, each takes a different route in search of happiness, and one of the cousins, Lyndall, resolutely refuses to conform with the constraints of conventional womanhood; a resolve which leads to a conclusion of sadness which joins with affirmation of hope.

In a curious and striking episode of Schreiner's novel, Gregory, a man who is in love with Lyndall, dresses as a woman in order to nurse her during her final illness. Although it is generally less explicit a theme than that of the New Woman, the calling into question of masculinity is similarly a potent element in the fiction of the *fin de siècle*. One form which this takes is the trope of the double: a symbolic splitting of a male character. In both Stevenson's *The Strange Case of Dr Jekyll and Mr Hyde* (1886) and ▷ Oscar Wilde's *The Picture of Dorian Gray* (1890) there is a division between two parts of the male self, one of which possesses a conscience (in the case of Jekyll) or symbolically exhibits the consequences of transgression (in the case of Dorian's portrait), while the other part is able to commit indulgences and atrocities with (temporary) impunity. Many of the forbidden acts committed remain unspecified, and both works evoke social worlds which are largely or exclusively male; this combination has been taken by some critics as a coded allusion to the 'open secret' of male homosexuality. Doubles are also found in a range of other texts such as Henry James's story 'The Jolly Corner' and Conrad's novella 'The Secret Sharer'. Furthermore, doubling in combination with unspecified transgression and a male grouping that marginalizes women is important for the symbolic structure of Conrad's *Heart of Darkness* (1902). Secret relations between men may, as in Oscar Wilde's work, have a clear relation to a socially marginalized homosexuality. On the other hand, they may imply the misogyny, homophobia and defence of privilege reflected in the social practices of the Victorian male club, officer's mess and imperial outpost. Furthermore these two possibilities exist in complex relationships of opposition and complementarity. The blurring or transgressing of boundaries of sexuality and gender is also implicit in ▷ Bram Stoker's *Dracula* (1897). The relentlessly male-oriented *She* (1887), by Rider Haggard, with its concern to master a threatening symbolic femininity, exhibits a preoccupation with relations between men, a fear of women and the unsettling of gender roles. *Dracula*, *She* and *Heart of Darkness* all involve journeys to foreign parts (Africa or Transylvania) which are invested with a feared but alluring otherness. These texts represent an intersection between the theme of gender instability and a preoccupation with racial difference: a congruence of imperial and sexual fantasies. These concerns were to be of considerable importance in the modernist novel of the early twentieth century.

5

Culture and Consciousness: the Twentieth-century Novel in English

Andrew Michael Roberts

PART I – 1900 to 1930

Between 1900 and 1930 revolutionary developments took place in the English novel. These developments involved new subject matter, style and technique, and led ultimately to a radical rethinking of the relationship between fiction and reality. This era in the history of the novel, like the corresponding periods in the history of drama, poetry and other arts, is now widely known as ▷ modernism. The roots of modernism are exceptionally diverse, the result of cross-fertilization between cultures, between art forms and between disciplines. Like most historical generalizations, however, the concept of modernism can generate exclusions and omissions. At one time there was a tendency for critics to neglect the role of women writers in modernism (with a few exceptions such as ▷ Virginia Woolf); now, however, there is a greater (though not universal) awareness of the role played by such novelists as ▷ Katherine Mansfield, ▷ Dorothy Richardson, ▷ May Sinclair, ▷ Rebecca West and ▷ Sylvia Townsend Warner. This in turn brings a wider conception of the nature and significance of modernism as a movement in the arts. However, it is also important to recognize the considerable body of fiction for which the term modernism is not appropriate. This includes fiction in the realist mode such as the novels of ▷ Arnold Bennett and ▷ John Galsworthy as well as ▷ H.G. Wells's comedies of lower-middle-class life. There was also a wide range of popular fictional genres which, without sharing the high cultural aspirations of modernist innovation, can be inventive, entertaining and revealing of early twentieth-century culture, such as the light comedies of ▷ P.G. Wodehouse, the fantasies and detective stories of ▷ G.K. Chesterton, writing for children by ▷ Kenneth Grahame and ▷ A.A. Milne, and H.G. Wells's ▷ science fiction.

Culture and reality: James, Conrad, Ford, West

▷ Joseph Conrad (1857–1924) and ▷ Henry James (1843–1916), both of whom first published in the nineteenth century, are the earliest of the great modernist novelists writing in English. One form of cross-fertilization is evident at once, in that James was born an American and Conrad a Pole. Each chose to settle in England and to become an English subject and for each the collision of different cultures was an important theme. The relation of America to Europe is a central concern of James's fiction: in major novels such as ▷ *The Portrait of a Lady* (1881) and ▷ *The Wings of the Dove* (1902), as well as ▷ novellas such as ▷ *Daisy Miller* (1879), the moral consequences of the meeting of American innocence and enthusiasm with a sophisticated but corrupt European culture are explored by means of irony, a sustained attention to the nuances of individual consciousness, and a prose style of increasing subtlety and complexity. It was not only in theme that James was cosmopolitan; influences on his work include ▷ Jane Austen ▷ George Eliot, Nathaniel Hawthorne, ▷ Balzac and Turgenev.

Conrad's life as a merchant seaman, and his upbringing in Poland and Russia, brought him into contact with a wide range of cultures. His prose style owes much to the influences of the nineteenth-century French writers Maupassant and ▷ Flaubert, and in a number of his works he explores what was to become a major concern of the twentieth-century English novel: the experience of the European in Asia, Africa or South America. In ▷ *Heart of Darkness* (1902) a supposedly enlightened colonial programme is revealed as ruthless commercial exploitation and a journey up the Congo becomes symbolic of an exploration of the darkness within man, the atrocities of history, the powerful forces of the unconscious, the mystery of evil.

This work epitomizes many features of modernist fiction: the need to confront violence, nihilism and despair; the fascination with, but fear of, the unconscious; the centrality of a dramatized narrator who is not omniscient but rather himself searching for understanding; a symbolic richness which invites multiple interpretations. The last two of these features reflect the influence on modernism of the French Symbolist (▷ symbolism) movement of the nineteenth century, one of whose exponents, Rémy de Gourmont, defined the writer's purpose as being 'to unveil to others the kind of world which he beholds in his own personal mirror'. Conrad's critique of the ideology of Empire also foreshadows the many later works of fiction which use colonial or post-colonial settings to explore the European mind through its contact with what is alien and with what is shared in other cultures, while protesting against bigotry and exploitation. Examples include ▷ E. M. Forster's ▷ *A Passage to India* (1924), ▷ George Orwell's *Burmese Days* (1934), ▷ Graham Greene's *The Heart of the Matter* (1948), and, more recently, the Indian novels of ▷ Ruth Prawer Jhabvala.

But it is in their technique that James and Conrad are most revolutionary. While novelists such as Arnold Bennett (1867–1931) and John Galsworthy (1867–1933) continued to write in the accepted realist mode, using an omniscient narrator, a chronologically sequential narrative and the accumulation of details of social and public life, modernist novelists sought radical redefinitions of the real. One such redefinition is based on the view that, since the individual always perceives reality through his or her own consciousness, the contents and structure of consciousness represent the only accessible reality. A number of philosophical influences are relevant here. William James, the brother of Henry James, was an American psychologist and philosopher. In *Essays in Radical Empiricism* (1912) he elaborated the notion of a world of 'pure experience', all reality being described in terms of subjective human experience (James is also the originator of the term ▷ 'stream of consciousness'). ▷ Sigmund Freud (1856–1939), whose work began to be known in Britain around 1912, has had an enormous influence on modern literature, though less through direct application of his ideas than as a result of his contribution to the assumptions and preoccupations of modern Western society. One of his most potent ideas is also one of the simplest: that all mental phenomena have meaning. This assumption helped to validate new ways of structuring narrative based on dreams, fantasies, and chains of association. ▷ Henri Bergson (1859–1941), the French philosopher of evolution, distinguished between scientific time (a mathematical, abstract, homogeneous medium) and 'real duration' (our direct experience of time as a flowing, irreversible succession of heterogeneous and concrete states). The former, he claimed, is essentially an illusion; it is our subjective experience of time which is 'real'.

The novel was a particularly suitable form for the exploration of such perceptions, because of the possibility of manipulating the reader's experience of time by means of disruption of narrative chronology, and the possibility of representing the nature of consciousness by describing events through the awareness of one or more characters.

In the opening chapters of Conrad's ▷ *Lord Jim* (1900) a sense of foreboding is created so that the reader's expectation and interest are engaged, but at precisely the point of crisis, when an accident occurs to the ship on which Jim is first mate, the narrative jumps forward to the subsequent inquiry. Conrad thus deliberately frustrates the desire for plot satisfaction, diverting our interest from what happens, to the moral and philosophical significance of events. The narrative is structured as an investigation; an attempt, largely on the part of Marlow, who befriends Jim, to understand Jim's life. However, Marlow himself obtains much of his information at second hand, through accounts of events given to him by other characters, so that the effect is one of an enigmatic reality seen through a series of consciousnesses.

But it was Henry James above all who, in practice in his novels and in theory in his prefaces, developed the use of an observing consciousness whose viewpoint shapes the narrative. Here we need to distinguish between the narrator (the narrating 'voice' which, if it refers to itself, must do so in the first person) and the focal character or 'reflector' (the character whose point of view orients the narrative perspective). In Conrad's *Heart of Darkness* Marlow is both narrator and focal character, but the two are not identical since they represent Marlow at different points in his life. One of the subtle pleasures of the story is our sense of Marlow the narrator (middle-aged, sitting on a boat on the Thames) reflecting on and reassessing the experience of Marlow the focal character (younger, more idealistic, in the Congo). James's most favoured device is the restriction of the narrative focalization to a reflector who is not the narrator but is referred to in the third person, a prime example being Strether in ▷ *The Ambassadors* (1903). Associated Jamesian techniques include a dominance of 'scene' (the highly detailed account of particular occasions) and long accounts of the nuances of the reflector's sense of events. These reflectors become centres of interest themselves. Viewing events through their eyes, we share the limitations of their knowledge and the distortions of their viewpoint, and this is realistic in the sense that our actual experience of life is always limited in this way; we do not have all the facts, nor access to the thoughts of others. We share in the progressive illumination of Marlow and Strether. Conrad and James inaugurated a form of realism which ▷ Malcolm Bradbury (b 1932) has aptly described as 'not so much a substantiation of reality as a questing for it'.

These various manipulations of narrator and reflector are fruitful sources of irony, a primary characteristic of much modern fiction. Irony can be generated when the reader perceives more, or understands better, than the narrator and/or reflector, and can occur even when our perspective is technically limited to that of this character. James's novella *The Aspern Papers* (1888) is entirely first-person narration, but we gradually realize, through his own words and thoughts, the moral and emotional limitations of the narrator. A different form of irony is developed by Conrad in ▷ *The Secret Agent* (1907) and ▷ *Under Western Eyes* (1911): a pervasive irony of tone and event. The former is produced by a portrayal of human activity as largely futile and human nature as inherently given to self-deception and illusory beliefs. The latter occurs as characters' actions consistently go awry and produce the opposite effect to that intended. The result is a blend of black comedy with a satirical and tragic view of humanity, its pretensions, and its ideals.

A special case of the dramatized central consciousness is the unreliable narrator or reflector. One of the most fascinating examples of the unreliable narrator is Dowell in ▷ Ford Madox Ford's novel *The Good Soldier* (1915). Our initial tendency to accept a first-person narrator as an accurate source of information is exploited so that the cruelty, deception and insanity lurking beneath the genteel surface of the lives of two couples emerges with a greater sense of shock. Dowell also reflects on the nature of story-telling and its relation to truth ('I don't know how it is best to put this thing down . . .') and this novel thus anticipates two recurrent features of the twentieth-century novel. The first is the use of narrators or reflectors who are unbalanced, malevolent, of limited understanding or otherwise in an abnormal state of mind. Examples include *The Collector* (1963) by ▷ John Fowles (parts 1 and 3), and *The Spire* (1964) by ▷ William Golding. The second feature is reflexive narrative, in which the nature and purpose of writing becomes a constant secondary theme, or even the primary interest of the work. Examples include ▷ Doris Lessing's *The Golden Notebook* (1962) and William Golding's *Rites of Passage* (1980).

Rebecca West had published a study of Henry James in 1916 and her first novel *The Return of the Soldier*, which followed two years later in 1918, has marked affinities with the work of James, Conrad and Ford. Like James, she uses the device of a narrator who is a sensitive, perceptive but not impartial observer: the story of Chris, a soldier who returns from the front during the First World War having lost his memory of the last fifteen years, is told by his cousin Jenny, whose account is coloured by her own adoration for Chris. Like Conrad in *Heart of Darkness* and other of his works, West employs a narrative within a narrative, but she introduces a distinctive form of displacement between the two narrative levels: in an inset account, Jenny narrates the story of Chris's first love (which she knows only at second hand) with an instability of pronoun (shifting from 'one' to 'they') which suggests her shifting emotional identifications. Like Ford's *The Good Soldier*, West's *The Return of the Soldier* uses the play of subjectivity and projection to study loss, alienation, jealousy and the subtleties of self-deception. However, West's novel ends in partial consolation rather than the desolation evoked by Ford. In *The Return of the Soldier* modernist narrative technique contributes to the celebration of an almost mystical power of nurturing which West sees in certain women.

History, Consciousness and Gender: Lawrence, Woolf, Richardson

The relationship of history and the novel may be formulated in two ways. On the one hand, we may regard history as an objective series of public events, and the novel as an art form which may represent, ignore or fictionalize them. On the other hand, we may regard history itself as a narrative, and its relation with the novel as more reciprocal, our sense of the nature and significance of narrative influencing our sense of historical pattern and meaning and vice versa. Modernism is sometimes accused of ignoring historical and social realities. But the sense of living in a period of historical crisis is an important aspect of much modernist fiction. The apocalyptic world view which the critic Frank Kermode has identified in the work of ▷ D. H. Lawrence (1885–1930) is at once a reaction to accelerating social change and an expression of a mystical or prophetic view of the role of the artist, influenced by the Bible, and especially the Book of Revelation. ▷ *The Rainbow* (1915) describes the life of three generations of the Brangwen family in the English Midlands, and ▷ *Women in Love* (1921) (originally planned as part of the same work), continues the story of the third generation. In neither novel is there extensive reference to historical events in the conventional sense, though the effect on rural life of progressive industrialization is powerfully felt. Rather, what Lawrence writes is a history of the development of human consciousness and the unconscious life, in which the individual's relation with partner, family, work and the natural and man-made environment reflects large-scale cultural changes. The harmony achieved by Tom and Lydia, the first-generation couple living at Marsh Farm, is symbolized by the biblical image of the rainbow; by the end of *The Rainbow*, when Ursula, the modern woman, rejects marriage with Skrebensky, the representative of the mechanistic modern society, the rainbow can be only a tentative hope for a future regeneration. Just as James's novels seem to take place in a theatre of consciousness which is his unique discovery, so a considerable part of Lawrence's achievement is his development of a wholly new way of writing about human experience. The aspect of life to which he attends does not fit any of our normal categories; it cannot be summarized as the realm of the instinctual, nor of the unconscious, not of the physical, nor of the emotional, though it touches all of these. It reflects Lawrence's radically new sense of the nature of the self and his rejection of what he called 'the old stable ego of the character', and is realized by techniques of symbolism, the repetition of imagery, and the use of sustained passages of highly poetic yet often abstract language to describe the development of the individual. In *Women in Love* contemporary society is unequivocally rejected as mechanistic and destructive, and regeneration is located in personal relations of mystical intensity.

In its apocalyptic view Lawrence's work may be said to subordinate the contingency of history to a typological pattern: that is to say, a pattern of 'types' (events or persons), analogous to, and in many cases based upon, the events and persons of the Old Testament which foreshadow the dispensation of the New Testament. It is a feature of modernist narratives to order their material by symbol, pattern or metaphor rather than by the linear sequence of history. If the patterns to which history conforms are for Lawrence apocalyptic and typological, for Virginia Woolf (1882–1941) they are the patterns of art and of human sensibility. ▷ *To The Lighthouse* (1927) was described by Leonard Woolf as a 'psychological poem', and this reflects the privileging of consciousness and the work of art as a made object over the chronological sequence of conventional fiction. The novel is in three sections, of which the first and third describe the life of a family in their holiday home in Scotland on two days, one before and one after the First World War. These sections use the stream of consciousness technique developed in the English novel by Woolf, ▷ James Joyce (1882–1941) and ▷ Dorothy Richardson (1873–1957).

So *To The Lighthouse* represents the thought sequences of the Ramsay family and their guests, moving freely in time and space. The middle section of the novel, entitled 'Time Passes', is concerned with the non-human, with change, with history and the ravages of time (the war takes place and several of the characters die; the house decays). An opposition is set up in the novel between, on the one hand, the destructive effect of history and of impersonal nature, and on the other the ordering power of art (represented by the painter, Lily Briscoe) and of human consciousness as a builder of social relationships (represented by Mrs Ramsay's drawing together of family and friends). The novel ends with Lily finishing her painting, completing a pattern in which the past and the dead are not lost, but reconciled in memory and in art. In so far as this painting is an analogue for the novel itself, history is mastered by art.

In Woolf's work the stream of consciousness technique moves towards a radical view of the nature of the self, which is of particular importance for ▷ feminist writing. In ▷ *The Waves* (1931) the lives of six characters are represented, and the close interaction of their consciousnesses is symbolically associated with a pattern of waves on the sea, separate yet part of a greater whole. From her first novel, *The Voyage Out* (1915), Woolf expressed a sense of the fluid nature of the self, its interdependence with the selves of others, and its relation to ▷ gender and class-based power structures. Feminists have increasingly seen the self as socially and politically constructed and have drawn inspiration from Woolf's moves towards ▷ deconstruction of the idea of immutable gender identity. Her interest in androgyny, her sense of the social protest which madness can represent and her satire on repressive psychiatric practices in ▷ *Mrs Dalloway* (1925) have also remained points of reference for feminist writers, although there is disagreement concerning her relationship to issues of class and privilege.

Woolf's ▷ *Orlando* places ideas of androgyny in a historical context through the fantasy of a single character who lives many lives, some male and some female, over four centuries. Conversely, Lawrence's wish to essentialize gender differences becomes even stronger in his later works, notably *The Plumed Serpent* (1926) and 'The Woman who Rode Away' (1928), in which his earlier vision of apocalyptic regeneration is converted into the misogynist and fascistic worship of a ritualized male sexual power. A writer who has much in common with Woolf is Dorothy Richardson, whose autobiographical novel in thirteen volumes, *Pilgrimage* (1915–67), employs a lightly-punctuated and highly poetic stream of consciousness to reveal the mind of a young woman struggling in a society where 'history, literature, the way of stating records, reports, stories, the whole method of statement of things from the beginning ... was on a false foundation'. She herself objected to the use of the stream metaphor for consciousness, preferring the organic stability suggested by the metaphor of a tree. The life of her heroine, Miriam Henderson, is a pilgrimage in search of an indefinable fulfilment, associated with the joy of perception itself. Woolf saw Richardson's prose style as 'the psychological sentence of the feminine gender' and Richardson herself argued that men and women used language differently. Both writers, together with such contemporaries as Katherine Mansfield, have been the focus of debate concerning the existence and nature of a style and use of language specific to women's writing; an ▷ *écriture féminine*. In terms of content, much women's writing of this period emphasizes the significance to be found in the texture of experience: May Sinclair commented on the presence, in *Pilgrimage*, of a mysticism which could embrace mundane conversations and the eating of bread and butter. Sinclair's own ▷ *Bildungsroman*, *Mary Olivier: a Life* (1919) and her novel *The Life and Death of Harriet Frean* (1922) each explore, through stream-of-consciousness techniques, the development of a woman's mind and sensibility, in such a way that the details of ordinary life are informed by Sinclair's mystical, feminist and psychoanalytical interests.

Phases of modernism: Forster and Joyce

It is possible to distinguish an early phase of modernism, ending around the beginning of the First World War. In the first decade of the century James's three last great novels appeared, together with most of Conrad's major fiction and the first two novels of E. M. Forster (1879–1970), whose work is frequently regarded as containing both modernist and Victorian elements. In Forster's novel ▷ *Howards End* (1910) English society is seen as divided between the business world of action and the refined world of culture and the emotions, and a symbolic reconciliation is suggested by the marriage of the chief representatives of each group, and the inheritance of a house (the Howards End of the title), which stands for a threatened continuity in English life. The sense of threat and change is distinctively modernist, as is the location of renewal and reconciliation in the realm of the symbolic and the imagination. But Forster's social comedy, his narrative technique and his ▷ humanism associate him with more traditional strains in the English novel.

A Passage To India is at once more symbolic and less schematic than *Howards End*, and, appearing in 1924, belongs to the later post-war phase of modernism. While its satire on the arrogance and narrow-mindedness of British officials in India reflects the same belief in tolerance and liberalism as Forster's earlier work, the novel also explores at a deeper level the philosophical issues arising from the meeting of cultures. This is achieved in part through a symbolic evocation of the Indian landscape, and in particular the mysterious Marabar Caves, which call into question the identity and beliefs of several of the characters by their immitigable otherness. The novel ends with the voice of the landscape itself, on a note of ambivalent hope. While Forster made a contribution to both phases of modernism, the main figures of this post-war phase are Lawrence, Joyce and Woolf. Joyce's ▷ *Dubliners* (1914) is a seminal influence on the modern ▷ short story in English. He described his intention as that of writing 'a chapter in the moral history of my culture', using 'a style of scrupulous meanness'. Drawing on French influences, Joyce does indeed inaugurate in English the oblique, laconic short story, later developed by American writer Ernest Hemingway (1899–1961) and *The New Yorker* magazine. But the use of symbol, Joyce's mimicking of the diction and speech patterns of his Dublin characters, and his idea of the epiphany – a sudden spiritual manifestation in the ordinary – point to a more poetic and symbolic strain which culminates in the powerful yet ironic Romanticism of the last story in the collection, 'The Dead'.

▷ *A Portrait of the Artist as a Young Man* (1916) is comparable to Lawrence's ▷ *Sons and Lovers* (1913) in its semi-autobiographical nature. In each the primary interest is in the psychological and intellectual development of a young man, with great concentration on the protagonist. This is most obvious in the *Portrait*, where the other characters remain shadowy and the language and structure of the novel seeks to render the contents of Stephen's mind, but it is important that in *Sons and Lovers* much of what we learn about the other characters is essentially their roles in Paul Morel's psychological economy. The protagonists of both novels seek independence, but whereas in Lawrence's work this is primarily emotional independence, in that of Joyce it is predominantly cultural and intellectual, involving Stephen's escape from the restrictions of Irish society and the Catholic Church.

Joyce's ▷ *Ulysses* (1922) is a central text of modernism. A novel of over 600 pages concerned with one day in Dublin, it has an amazing richness of texture, combining mythical and literary allusions, parody and pastiche, punning and humour, with a powerful sense of the infinite complexity and subtlety of the individual's emotional and intellectual life. It is structured around a loose correspondence to the episodes of Homer's *Odyssey*, so that the juxtaposition of the ordinary with the heroic generates irony and wit while at the same time drawing on an archetypal level of experience comparable to that which the Swiss psychoanalyst ▷ Carl Jung located in a collective unconscious. The symbolist aspiration to imitate musical form is evident in the use of repeated words, phrases and images as forms of leitmotif. The novel encountered virulent opposition at the time of publication, being banned in England until 1936 on grounds of obscenity. Its acceptance into the canon of major works of English literature, together with the successful defence of D. H. Lawrence's ▷ *Lady Chatterley's Lover* at a 1960 obscenity trial, signalled the public endorsement of the principle that all areas of human experience could be valid subjects for the serious artist. It is in part for its combination of mundane details with a vast inclusiveness of reference that *Ulysses* is valued so highly.

The realist tradition: Bennett, Galsworthy, Wells

Despite the genuinely innovative and radical nature of modernist fiction, we should be wary of too schematic an opposition between modernists and traditionalists. We are inheritors of a distinction made by writers such as Woolf and Lawrence in order to define their artistic identity and literary programme. As Frank Kermode has pointed out, modernist programmes have the habit of claiming that they have to 'get out from under something', and Arnold Bennett, John Galsworthy and H. G. Wells were cast in the role of that 'something'. Wells himself participated in this process in his well-known comment in a letter to Henry James (8 July 1915): 'To you literature like painting is an end, to me literature is a means, it has a use ... I had rather be called a journalist than an artist.' Nevertheless, there are some affinities between the realists and the modernists in terms of influences and subject matter: Bennett was influenced by French and Russian novelists, and Wells, in his scientific romances, shows a strong sense of the apocalyptic and of the impact of war and technology on twentieth-century society. These writers are also part of important continuities in English fiction. Wells's emphasis on ideas is continued by ▷ Aldous Huxley (1894–1963) and George Orwell (1903–50) in the 1930s and 40s, while Bennett's regional settings in the Potteries district connect him with the regional realists of the 1950s. Wells, in works such as *The War of the Worlds* (1898) and *The First Men in the Moon* (1901), was also a pioneer of science fiction, one of the most fruitful of the popular genres in the twentieth-century novel.

Bennett's best work, such as *The Old Wives' Tale* (1908) and *Riceyman Steps* (1923), contains telling studies of ordinary lives, with a strong sense of the rich detail of society, and of the passing of time. The limitations of his style include a liability to give information too directly, to 'telling' rather than 'showing'. Like Bennett, Galsworthy was extremely popular and successful during his lifetime, with works such as ▷ *The Forsyte Saga* (1906–21) which are primarily concerned with upper-class society. The most general criticism of his work is that his satire is often lacking in focus and rigour. Wells was an extremely versatile writer of fiction and journalism; his fiction included Dickensian social comedy such as *The History of Mr Polly* (1910) and studies of contemporary social issues such as *Ann Veronica* (1909), as well as his science fiction or scientific romances. George Orwell, who considered Wells's thinking to be outmoded by the 1940s, nevertheless asserted of his own generation that 'the minds of us all, and therefore the physical world, would be perceptibly different if Wells had never existed'.

1920s satire: Lewis, Huxley and Waugh

Alongside the modernist experimentation of the 1920s a vein of tragi-comic satire emerged in the English novel in the work of Aldous Huxley, ▷ Wyndham Lewis (1882–1957) and ▷ Evelyn Waugh (1903–66). These authors shared a sense of the absurdity of modern society, and one form which this takes in their novels is that of dehumanization and the dissolution of the self. Wyndham Lewis, an artist, philosopher and editor as well as a novelist, was a leading spirit of Vorticism, an anti-realist movement in art, based on jagged, rhythmical, mechanistic forms. Such principles are also reflected in the portrayal of character in Lewis's novels, such as *Tarr* (1918); he described men as comic because they were 'things, or physical bodies, behaving as persons'. Aldous Huxley's *Crome Yellow* (1921) is primarily a novel of ideas, similar in form to the novels of ▷ Thomas Love Peacock (1785–1866), in which characters carry on debates in the setting of a country house. It is based on a somewhat schematic antithesis between men of thought and men of action. The protagonist, Dennis Stone, an example of the former who wants to be the latter, is a characteristic satirical anti-hero of the period, weak and ineffectual, but both types are portrayed as inadequate. The hero of Evelyn Waugh's first novel, *Decline and Fall* (1928), is described as a shadow; passively enduring a series of outrageous injustices and misfortunes, he ends up precisely where he started. The book describes itself as 'an account of the mysterious disappearance of Paul Pennyfeather'. Paul's adventures, however, bring him up against a large number of eccentrics, so that his shadowiness only serves to emphasize the egregious personalities which surround him.

These works contain images of the modern world as manic, mechanized and incomprehensible; they are essentially about the problem of how to live in a society which seems meaningless. The stance of the implied author (the author as manifest in the text) varies: Huxley tends to include some equivalent for himself in the novel, thereby making his own intellectual approach part of the object of his satire; Waugh is detached and invisible; Lewis is outraged, polemical and assertive. Drawing on the tradition of such European writers as Voltaire, ▷ Gogol and ▷ Swift, they represent a powerful alternative vision of the modern condition.

PART II – 1930 to 1950

In the 1930s and 40s political events were felt in English prose writing with a particular directness. The impact of the First World War and the associated social changes on the modernist novel tended to take place primarily at the level of the author's general world view, and to filter through into the content of the novel transformed by some principle of artistic shaping. From around 1930, however, there arose in many writers a sense that historical events were of such overwhelming importance in their implications for society that they demanded forms of writing which would attempt to represent, with as much immediacy as possible, the feel of contemporary experience, while also explicitly taking sides in a political or moral debate. In general terms, then, the period was one in which social or documentary realism reasserted itself; that form of realism which is concerned with an outward fidelity to the experience of the mass of individuals and an engagement with public issues. Such a generalization is, however, necessarily an oversimplification. Individual authors continued or commenced their literary careers, responding in a variety of ways to their own experiences, influences and interests as well as to the temper of the times. New works by Joyce and Woolf were still appearing during the early part of the period; Woolf's last novel was ▷ *Between The Acts* (1941) while Joyce's final work, ▷ *Finnegans Wake*, was published in 1939. ▷ Ivy Compton-Burnett (1884–1969), whose first novel had appeared as early as 1911, elaborated further her vision of power, pain and obsession in wealthy families of late Victorian and early Edwardian England, rendered almost entirely through dialogue. Evelyn Waugh's novels of the 1930s, including the hilarious *Scoop* (1938), continued and developed the satirical vein begun with *Decline and Fall*. ▷ Elizabeth Bowen (1899–1973), in novels such as *The Heat of the Day* (1949) and short stories such as 'Mysterious Kôr' (from *The Demon Lover*, 1945), combined an evocation of the atmosphere of wartime London with a Jamesian attention to the nuances of personal relations. ▷ Samuel Beckett's unique exploration of man as an isolated being confronting existential despair began with his first novel, *Murphy*, in 1938, which had been preceded by a collection of Joycean stories, *More Pricks than Kicks* (1934).

The approach of war: Orwell and Isherwood

In the public sphere the 1930s were dominated by two factors. The first was the economic depression which, from the collapse of the Wall Street Stock Market in 1929, began to cause widespread unemployment and poverty. The second was the rise of ▷ fascism in Europe: Hitler seized power in Germany in 1933; in Italy Mussolini had ruled since 1922; in 1932 Sir Oswald Mosley founded the British Union of Fascists. The most coherent ideological response to both these developments came from the left wing, so that during the 1930s a considerable number of British writers and intellectuals became socialists or communists. The Left Book Club, founded in 1936, provided a focus for this tendency. It is primarily from a left-wing perspective that modernism has been rejected or criticized, both in the 1930s and since. George Orwell, a socialist, though a very independent one, described the 1920s as 'a period of irresponsibility such as the world has never before seen'. Georg Lukács, the Hungarian Marxist critic (▷ Marx, Karl), writing in 1955 from a more dogmatic perspective, attacked modernism on the grounds that it treated man as a solitary and asocial being, thus denying the reality of history.

Orwell's own writings seek to bring home to readers the human consequences of the economic and political situation: the soul-destroying nature of poverty in *Down and Out in London and Paris* (1933) and *The Road to Wigan Pier* (1937), the miseries of war and the distortions of the press in *Homage to Catalonia* (1938) and the oppressions of British imperialism in *Burmese Days* (1934). The first three of these works blend reportage and autobiography with an element of the fictional, and in each many facts are given, ranging from the minute details of daily life in the trenches of the Spanish Civil War to the income and itemized expenditure of a Yorkshire miner in 1935. This might be seen as a return to the 'materialism' which Woolf objected to in the work of Galsworthy and Bennett, but it gains new force both from Orwell's passionate indignation, and from his imaginative realization of the influence of material conditions on human consciousness and society. However, his individualism and his sometimes sentimental portrayal of the working classes have been criticized by socialist thinkers such as ▷ Raymond Williams.

Orwell's novel *Coming Up For Air* was published in 1939, on the eve of World War II, in the same year as a work by another writer of left-wing views, ▷ Christopher Isherwood's *Goodbye to Berlin*. In each there is a powerful sense of foreboding, of European civilization slipping into violence and chaos. The contrast of narrative techniques illustrates the range of 1930s realism. *Goodbye to Berlin* is a series of linked short episodes set in the decadent atmosphere of Berlin during the Nazi rise to power. The detached quality of the first-person narrator is defined on the first page: 'I am a camera with its shutter open, quite passive, recording, not thinking'; he says relatively little of his own feelings as he moves among a cast of largely manipulative, destructive or self-destructive characters. The narrator's very passivity and neutrality of stance come to epitomize the failure of the European mind to confront the rise of fascism. Orwell's narrator is George Bowling, a disillusioned insurance salesman approaching middle age who returns to the village of his childhood in an attempt to recapture something of what now seems to him to have been an idyllic Edwardian age. He is an egregiously personal dramatized narrator, who addresses the reader throughout in a conversational tone, masking a highly skilful rhetoric which persuades us to share his vision of an England of petty, narrow lives, a civilization of rubbish dumps and synthetic food, a people with fascist violence hanging over them, 'so terrified of the future that we're jumping straight into it like a rabbit diving down a boa constrictor's throat'. George's anticipation of 'the coloured shirts, the barbed wire, the rubber truncheons' looks forward to Orwell's post-war vision of totalitarianism *1984* (1949) and his political allegory *Animal Farm* (1945).

These post-war works reflect a general disillusionment with communism, resulting from the revelation of the Stalinist show trials, and the Nazi-Soviet pact of 1941. But during the 1930s many writers and intellectuals had become Marxists, and a considerable number fought for the Republicans in the Spanish Civil War. Many novels of the 1930s reflect this commitment, including ▷ Rex Warner's allegory *The Wild Goose Chase* (1937), and Edward Upward's *Journey to the Border* (1938). Both these novels have propagandist Marxist conclusions; in *Journey to the Border* the protagonist's hallucinations and fantasies are associated with a decadent society, and at the end of the novel he decides to regain reality by joining the workers' movement. Thus by the end of the 1930s 'reality' has become for many a politically defined concept, a matter of class commitment rather than of the nuances of consciousness. The experience of working-class life is perhaps most powerfully expressed in the work of writers who grew up in working-class regional communities. ▷ Lewis Grassic Gibbon in *A Scot's Quair* (1932–34) and Walter Greenwood in *Love on the Dole* (1933) use dialect to convey social cohesion and social deprivation in north-east Scotland and northern England respectively. Gibbon's trilogy is especially remarkable for its sense of community, history and the impact of the Scottish landscape on the consciousness of the characters.

The inner and outer worlds: Greene and Lowry

The dangers of oversimplification inherent in an antithesis between a modernist concentration on the individual inner world, and a politically committed attention to social relations becomes evident when we consider the work of Graham Greene (1904–91). His early work of the 1930s, such as *It's a Battlefield* (1934) and *Brighton Rock* (1938) has a sense of the oppressive squalor of areas of modern urban life, a sense which is later translated into the more exotic settings of late colonialism; visions of seediness and corruption in such settings as Africa (*The Heart of the Matter*; 1948), Vietnam (*The Quiet American*; 1955) and South America (*The Honorary Consul*; 1973). He had a long-standing, if moderate, left-wing commitment, evident not only in his novels, with their critique of the Western role in the Third World, but also in his active friendship and support for those resisting the right-wing dictatorships of Central America, recounted in his memoir *Getting to Know the General* (1984). Yet characters such as the whisky priest of *The Power and the Glory* (1940) confront their moral choices in a condition of existential isolation and Greene himself associated his use of journeys (he was an inveterate traveller) with the methods of psychoanalysis (▷ psychoanalytical criticism); in the introduction to *Journey Without Maps* (1936) he explains that he sought to give general significance to his travels in Liberia by using 'memories, dreams and word-associations' to suggest a parallel, inner journey. From the time of *Brighton Rock* his ▷ Catholicism became more apparent. Though he did not regard himself as a 'Catholic novelist', his work is informed by a powerful sense of good and evil, and of the sinfulness of human nature, combined with a somewhat determinist tragic irony. In these respects, as well as in his use of extreme situations which test human morality and endurance, he has links to Conrad and Dostoevsky as precursors, and to the post-war English novelist William Golding (b 1911) as a successor. Many of Greene's novels are narrated in the third person in a detached, unemotive style which serves to highlight violence, tragedy, the sordid and the grotesque. This style has affinities with American writers of the 1920s such as Ernest Hemingway and John Dos Passos.

▷ Malcolm Lowry's *Under the Volcano* (1947), like Greene's best work, endows a tragic story of human failure with metaphysical overtones. Set in Mexico, where the presence of fascist elements anticipates the approaching world war, the story of the alcoholic British Consul Geoffrey Firmin achieves a wide resonance by means of symbol, an intricate metaphorical structure and a stream of consciousness technique in which the beautiful but sinister Mexican landscape becomes an equivalent for inner turmoil. This novel belongs to the high modernist tradition in its formal experimentation and literary allusiveness, as well as in its somewhat Laurentian apocalyptic vision of political and cultural crisis. D. H. Lawrence had also previously engaged with a revolutionary Mexico in his much earlier novel *The Plumed Serpent* (1923), in his short stories, and in his travel essays, *Mornings in Mexico*. In *Under the Volcano*, however, Firmin's story is associated with that of Doctor Faustus, who sold his soul to the devil, while Mexico is presented as an archetype both of paradise and of hell. Firmin's inebriation, self-destructiveness and guilt are attributed to contemporary civilization as a whole. The novel, intended as part of a trilogy which was never completed, owes much to Joyce's *Ulysses* in its shifts of consciousness, its concentration on one day, with extended flashbacks, and its intricate, allusive structure.

The complex interplay of modernist experiment and the impulse towards social realism and political commitment was to contribute to a remarkable diversity of modes in fiction of the post-war era.

PART III – 1950 to the present

There has been a tendency among critics to see the post-war English novel as lacking in power and scope compared to the great age of modernism, and essays on the subject frequently begin by acknowledging the lack of either a great genius of the novelist's art or a single dominant movement with techniques and themes which are felt as central to contemporary culture. Gilbert Phelps, for example, in his essay 'The Post-War English Novel' (*New Pelican Guide to English Literature*, 1983), asserts that 'the trend of the English novel since the war has, on the whole, been . . . a turning aside from the mainstream of European literature and a tendency to retreat into parochialism and defeatism' and from time to time articles appear in the book pages of national newspapers, lamenting the state of the novel or predicting its demise. Several points need to be made about such views. There is the obvious but important fact that both literary achievement and cultural significance are more readily detected in retrospect. Furthermore, contemporary critical theory has made us increasingly aware that this retrospective detecting involves an element of construction. A sense of literary history, of the significance of particular works and authors, and of the existence of a canon of recognized major or serious works is necessarily a matter of a subjective, value-loaded and culturally specific process of consensus. This is not to say that such judgements are arbitrary, but only that they represent a characteristically human activity of creating patterns of meaning, of ordering and valuing cultural productions according to certain sets of values and assumptions. Post-colonial and feminist critics have questioned many of the assumptions by which the canon has been established, while theorists of post-modernism have claimed that late twentieth-century Western culture is marked by the displacement of value-laden hierarchies in favour of multiplicity, and the simultaneous availability of many forms, including imitation and pastiche of those of the past. It could therefore be argued that the diversity of contemporary fiction, by encouraging the reader to select from a huge range of available modes and styles, itself characterizes the prevailing *Zeitgeist* more effectively than could any dominant individual or group. The modernist claim to centrality depended, as we have seen, on a doctrine of experimentation and radical newness, according to which changes in novel technique accompanied changes in the nature of human experience. Works such as Joyce's *Finnegans Wake* (1939) pushed innovation along modernist lines close to the point where the coherence of the novel as a genre seemed in doubt. We have observed one form of reaction against modernism in the politically committed writings of the 1930s. Experimentation did not die out, but it increasingly came to seem one option among many, rather than an essential expression of the times. Furthermore, the shock to the idea of Western civilization administered by the Second World War, the death camps and the atomic bomb rendered the very idea of cultural centrality a dubious one. On the other hand, fictionality itself seemed an increasingly appropriate focus of attention in a culture where clear standards of truth and significance were felt to be elusive.

The awareness of fictionality

Samuel Beckett continued the Joycean line of experimentation, combining a fascination with words with an acute awareness of their limitations, and with a rich vein of parody, irony, imitation and pastiche. His vision is, however, a darker one, although humour is an essential aspect of it. In his trilogy of the 1950s, *Molloy* (1956), *Malone Dies* (1956) and *The Unnamable* (1959), isolated, aged and decrepit social outcasts of obscure identity narrate their own stories with a mixture of black humour and remorseless grimness. They are aware of themselves as story-tellers, making reference to the futility of this activity, yet continuing with the story in order to pass the time, as an act of defiance, or as an obsessive compulsion. As in Beckett's plays, there is a progressive minimalism, in which life is reduced to language, mundane and sordid physical details and the isolated human consciousness. In this respect his novels represent the ultimate breakdown of the classic realist novel, in which character is portrayed in a rich social context. In drawing attention to their own fictionality, and in playing games with language (including the game of teasing the critics by laying false clues) Beckett's narrators anticipate the contemporary fascination with the idea of fiction and of narration. This kind of metafiction is widely regarded as an aspect of ▷ post-modernism, although such concerns are not, of course, the prerogative of the twentieth century, being prominent in, for example, ▷ Laurence Sterne's ▷ Tristram Shandy (1759–67) and Cervantes's ▷ Don Quixote (1605–15). However, the current interest in this area reflects structuralist and ▷ post-structuralist scepticism about the ability of language to refer to a non-linguistic reality, and the sense that fictionality is an attribute of forms of discourse other than fiction, such as history and the social sciences. This has generated an increasing interest in narrative as a model for the structuring both of culture and of individual experience. Indeed, the philosopher of post-modernism ▷ Jean-Francois Lyotard argues for an abandonment of 'grand narratives' of history in favour of a multiplicity of small-scale narratives, while the pragmatist philosopher Richard Rorty has argued that the telling of stories is more effective than an appeal to reason as a way of overcoming prejudice and hatred.

A widespread form of self-awareness in post-modernist fiction is what the critic Linda Hutcheon terms historiographic metafiction: novels which 'are both intensely self-reflexive and yet paradoxically also lay claim to historical events and personages'. Contemporary novelists who explore this model include John Fowles (b 1926), whose book The French Lieutenant's Woman (1969) combines a pastiche of a Victorian novel with passages of social history and statistics about Victorian sexual habits. The author addresses the reader, discussing his own techniques and the reader's likely response, and later, appearing as a minor character, decides to abrogate his authorial power over his characters by providing two alternative endings, even going to the length of tossing a coin to decide their order. The effect is that of an intriguing, if scarcely subtle, consideration of issues of free will, determinism, power and meaning. A less earnest and more exuberant treatment of such issues is found in Salman Rushdie's Midnight's Children (1981). Saleem Sinai, the protagonist and narrator of the novel, is one of 1001 children endowed with magical powers because they are born at the precise moment of India's independence in 1947. With witty and extravagant detail, the novel weaves together Saleem's life and the political history of India and Pakistan, playfully questioning the coherence of the self and the causes and structure of history as both are subsumed in the rich instability of the narrative. Saleem's 'chutnification of history' involves elements of the fantastical and magical which make the novel a notable example of ▷ magic realism; a term which might also be applied to ▷ Jeanette Winterson's Sexing the Cherry (1989). Here fantasy and magic dominate to the extent that we might see the novel as creating an alternative world, a view which would accord with the critic Brian McHale's conception of post-modernist fiction as 'ontological' (concerned with multiple worlds) where modernist fiction had been 'epistemological' (concerned with ways of knowing the world). There are elements of 'real' history in Winterson's novel, but with its fantastical, Gothic, carnivalesque, farcical juggling with time and place, gender and identity, it defies categorization as much as it defies summary, although showing clearly the influence of ▷ Angela Carter.

Playing games with history and fiction can of course be dangerous and controversial, since the past is so crucial to our personal and collective identities, to political and ideological programmes and to ideas of justice, justification and retribution. Within the discourses of both history and fiction it has been the Holocaust which has most acutely focused these concerns. ▷ D.M. Thomas's novels, The White Hotel (1981) and Pictures at an Exhibition (1993), both appropriate documentary records of the appalling sufferings of Jews and others under the Nazis in order to construct narratives that blend historical events, literary allusions, erotic fantasies and pseudo-Freudian theories. Many readers have found this offensive, and while theoretical expositions in terms of post-modernist and post-structuralist conceptions are readily available to support Thomas's procedures, it is not clear that these adequately deal with the ethics of voyeuristic aestheticization of violence and suffering. Another novel which has engaged with the perception of the Holocaust is *Time's Arrow* (1991) by ▷ Martin Amis. Rather than allusion, intertextuality, parody, self-interpretation and the other common devices of post-modernist fiction, this novel uses the single device of describing a world which resembles ours except that time flows backward. Inverting rather than subverting the traditional structures of cause and effect, person and responsibility which make ethical judgements possible, it presents a mirror-image of human life which has moral force as well ·as imaginative power.

A rather different testing of the limits and nature of fiction is apparent in ▷ B. S. Johnson's 1969 novel, *The Unfortunates*, which has twenty-seven loose-leaf sections of which twenty-five may be read in any order, the randomness of the resulting structure serving as a metaphor for the circling and shifting of the mind. Johnson saw 'truth' and 'fiction' as antithetical terms, and his last work, *See the Old Lady Decently* (1975), employs documents and photographs in an attempt to create a non-fictional novel. This aspiration is paralleled in the documentary style of Alan Burns (b 1929), some of whose novels are structured around news items or press-cuttings. A number of novelists have developed the modernist interest in multiple and unstable perspectives. These include Doris Lessing, and also ▷ Lawrence Durrell (1912–90), who, in his sequence *The Alexandria Quartet* (1957–60) portrays an intricate series of relationships in a community by means of a diversity of narratives, including third-person and first-person narratives, letters, journals and parts of an inset novel by a character. The reader's understanding of both character and event is subject to revision in the light of new information and perspectives, creating a work that has been described as 'a game of mirrors'.

In a sense, experimental novels are particularly dependent upon the traditional qualities of a good novel, such as plot interest and imaginative power in the realization of social context. In the absence of such qualities the reader is unlikely to overcome the difficulties of coming to terms with an unfamiliar form. A novelist who combines imaginative power with a wittily expressed examination of the nature of the fictional is ▷ Dan Jacobson (b 1929). *The Rape of Tamar* (1970) is set in the time of the Old Testament King David, and narrated by Yonadab, who is intensely aware of the philosophical and moral dilemmas of his role as narrator. He has knowledge of our own time as well as that of the story, and shares with us his reflections on the resulting ironies. Thus the act of narrating is a source of interest throughout, generating insights into such issues as hypocrisy, self-deception, voyeurism, the function of art, the pleasures and vicissitudes of speaking, and the culturally specific nature of modes of interpretation. But these sophisticated intellectual concerns are matched and sustained by a powerful poetic evocation of the physical and cultural context, and above all by the sheer vitality of Yonadab's personality as he addresses us with engaging frankness in what he terms 'the simulacrum of time in which you and I have managed to meet'. Self-conscious narrative, which by various means draws attention to its own fictionality, serves to question the nature of reality, and of our understanding of it, and to highlight issues of freedom and control. It has therefore held a strong appeal for writers influenced by French ▷ existentialist thought, including ▷ Christine Brooke-Rose (b 1926) and ▷ David Caute (b 1936). In the post-modernist anti-novel, practised by writers such as ▷ Gabriel Josipovici (b 1940), structures based around repeated scenes or interwoven narratives create a radical uncertainty, and the world evoked by the text disintegrates in order to fulfil the author's aim of, in his own words, 'insisting that his book is a book and not the world' (from *The World and the Book, a Study of Modern Fiction*; 1971).

Morality and art

A feature of the work of several considerable post-war novelists is a renewed attempt to present a vision of the world as a battleground of forces of good and evil. William Golding has had outstanding success in the construction of moral fables, shaped by Christian archetypes of sin, guilt, purgation and the tentative but precious hope of redemption. His novels, of which the first was ▷ *Lord of the Flies* (1954), show a powerful interest in the primitive and the physical, particularly in the examination of extreme conditions or states of consciousness in which human experience is stripped to moral and physical essentials. This description does not, however, do justice to the range of his settings and techniques. *The Inheritors* (1955) attempts to realize the mind and culture of Neanderthal man. This relatively idyllic and innocent culture is used to make us see our own nature (as represented by the arrival of *homo sapiens*) in a new and largely unflattering light. *The Spire* (1964) renders the tormented consciousness of a fanatical medieval cleric, while *Rites of Passage* (1980) uses pastiche and the ironies arising from a self-confident but mistaken narrator to portray the moral awakening of a gentleman traveller in the early nineteenth century. The limitation of Golding's work is its explicitness. The thrust of his moral vision and his mythic patterning can sometimes seem overbearing, though many readers will feel that this is a small price to pay for its power and authority.

In contrast to Golding's historical and cultural range, most of the novels of ▷ Iris Murdoch (b 1919) are set in contemporary English middle-class society, but are informed by a range of philosophical concerns centring on moral responsibility, individual freedom, the nature of love, and the possibility of actively pursuing goodness. They combine a serious, and at times tragic, exploration of these concerns with exciting plots, and elements of the comic, supernatural, and fantastic. These features have been sustained through a prolific career since the appearance of her first novel *Under the Net* in 1954. Doubts about her work focus on a sense that characters are excessively manipulated in the interest of illustrating abstract ideas, and a dissatisfaction with her use of violence and accident as a plot device. Of her early novels, *The Bell* (1958) is notable for its complex symbolic structure. The moral significance of the lives of a group of characters, brought together in a rather bizarre religious community, is examined by a pattern of interaction centred around the symbol of a convent bell, but using also animal and water symbolism. *The Sea, The Sea* (1978), a Booker Prize-winner, and one of the most acclaimed of her works, is a typically dark comedy about obsession, guilt and egotism, but is remarkable for the richness of its symbols and characters. ▷ A. S. Byatt (b 1936) shows the influence of Murdoch in her use of symbolic structures and her portrayal of the inter-relations of a large group of central characters. The latter feature is particularly evident in the opening books of a projected tetralogy: *The Virgin in the Garden* (1979) and *Still Life* (1985). Moral concerns are evident, but less explicit than in Murdoch's work, more attention being given to correspondences between experience and mythic or aesthetic patterns, and to the process of cultural change. Byatt's most popular work to date, the Booker Prize-winning *Possession*, is a cleverly interwoven pastiche of Victorian poetry, the lives of its writers, and the lives of a network of twentieth-century literary critics. The inter-relations of characters are thus wittily carried out across time, as the lives of Victorian poets intersect with those of their modern readers. The process, in *Possession*, whereby discovery of the past is crucial to the development of character and the reshaping of relationships in the present is paralleled in ▷ Alan Hollinghurst's *The Swimming Pool Library* (1988). Here a young aristocrat, part of the gay scene in London in the early 1980s, is commissioned to write a biography. In so doing he discovers the involvement of his own grandfather in the persecution of gay men, a discovery which arouses in him a new sense of defiance and political commitment in the present. As in *Possession*, literary allusions (in this instance to writers such as Oscar Wilde and E. M. Forster) and the excitement of detective work are important elements in a gripping narrative. Byatt has returned to the Victorian period in the double narrative of *Angels and Insects* (1992).

In the work of ▷ Muriel Spark (b 1918), manipulation is less a risk for the author than an explicit theme and, as in Ford Madox Ford's *The Good Soldier* (1915), the manipulative aspects of the narrating activity are exploited as a source of irony in the rendering of patterns of social and psychological control. Thus in the novella *The Driver's Seat* (1970) the use of the present tense, and an entirely external focalization on one character (the narrative recounting events from her point of view, but with almost no revelation of her feelings, thoughts or intentions) creates a grim and enigmatic vision of a woman with a psychological compulsion and a violent destiny which seem fixed and unchangeable, yet not understood either by author or reader. In *The Prime of Miss Jean Brodie* (1961) humour is more in evidence, but dark shadows of fascism and personal betrayal, evoked particularly through prolepses (jumps forward to later events), lurk around the story of a teacher's charismatic influence on a group of pupils. Spark's Catholic sensibility emerges in her portrayal of diabolic figures, such as the charming, egregiously manipulative Dougal Douglas of *The Ballad of Peckham Rye* (1960).

While Spark is a convert to Catholicism, ▷ Anthony Burgess (b 1917) has a Catholic background, and though not a practising member of the Church, acknowledges the importance of Catholic modes of thought in his work. *A Clockwork Orange* (1962) is concerned with the relation of evil and free will. The protagonist makes a deliberate choice of a life of horrifying violence and sadistic cruelty, and attempts by a futuristic authoritarian society to reform him by brainwashing can only destroy his human identity. The novel is notable for its use of an invented teenage patois, Nadsat, reflecting Burgess's enthusiasm for Joycean linguistic multiplicity and invention. Burgess has stated that he sees the duality of good and evil as the ultimate reality, and in *Earthly Powers* (1980) the history of the twentieth century is portrayed in terms of such a moral struggle, seen through the memories of the narrator, a homosexual writer. As in Murdoch's work, a strong sense of moral patterning underlies and unifies a complexity of events. In the novels of ▷ Margaret Drabble (b 1939) moral concern is focused on social justice and the individual quest for identity, particularly on the part of women. Works such as *The Ice Age* (1977) reflect her admiration for Arnold Bennett in their realist portrayal of the state of contemporary British society.

Feminist writing

The question of what constitutes 'feminist' writing is a contentious issue, but what is certain is that novels concerned with women's experience represent a significant section of the contemporary fiction market, and make rich use of innovations in narrative technique and of a range of styles and genres. An important divide among feminist critics is between those, such as Elaine Showalter, who see the role of contemporary female writing as that of self-discovery, articulating the nature of women's personal experience within society and revealing structures of oppression, and those such as Toril Moi, who advocate rather the deconstruction of the idea of the unitary self, and the rejection of the male/female dichotomy in favour of some ideal of androgyny.

The project of articulating women's experience includes the rediscovery of the unrecorded or what has been omitted from the conventional histories and novels. Thus ▷ Eva Figes (b 1932), in *The Seven Ages* (1986), writes a fictional chronicle of the lives of seven generations of women, from pre-history up to the present, concentrating on their struggles with poverty and violence, and their experience of childbirth and child-rearing. An associative, free-floating narrative style suggests a collective female consciousness, transcending the individual self and linking women to natural forces of generation. ▷ Zoe Fairbairns's *Stand We At Last* (1983) also recounts the lives of successive generations of women, though with closer attention to the detailed historical context, while the Manawaka series of novels and stories by the Canadian writer ▷ Margaret Laurence (1926–87) are narrated by women of various ages and generations in such a way as to explore simultaneously the social history of Canada and the dilemmas and achievements of women in the context of a prairie town. ▷ Jean Rhys (1894–1979), in *Wide Sargasso Sea* (1966), writes a feminist complement to ▷ Charlotte Brontë's ▷ *Jane Eyre*, recounting the early life of the 'mad' first Mrs Rochester, from her childhood in the West Indies. Rhys gives consciousness to the character who, in the original novel, is an inarticulate symbolic location for a rejected violence of feeling. Madness is a recurrent theme of feminist writing, because, considered as a refusal to conform to an imposed social identity, it can become a potent symbol of revolt against oppression. Doris Lessing (b 1919) does not see herself as primarily a feminist writer, but her novel *The Golden Notebook* (1962) has become an important feminist text. It is built out of a skeleton narrative, entitled 'Free Women', plus four notebooks kept by Anna, one of the characters of 'Free Women'. This fragmentation reflects her fear of breakdown as she confronts political, literary and sexual problems as an independent woman, but in the fifth and final 'Golden Notebook' a new unity is achieved through a mental breakdown shared with a man, during which the collapse of divisions leads to 'formlessness with the end of fragmentation'.

A number of writers, without adopting an overtly feminist standpoint, attend particularly to women's experience of isolation, betrayal, loss or guilt within the limitations imposed on their lives by social convention or male attitudes and behaviour. They include ▷ Edna O'Brien (b 1932), whose popular and entertaining novels are concerned particularly with the vicissitudes of sexuality and passion, and ▷ Anita Brookner (b 1928), who portrays the disillusionment of her sensitive female characters with an elegant, detached attention to the nuances of human relationships. In one sense these writers are the opposite of feminist, since their work could be held to accept as a premise the view that women seek self-fulfilment largely through relations with men. Yet in representing the tragedy or frustration which may result from such dependence, their novels raise crucial feminist issues, and are part of the context for the debate about the fictional portrayal of women.

▷ Fay Weldon (b 1931) recounts the lives of her women characters with a sort of desperate black humour. In works such as *Down Among the Women* (1971) and *Praxis* (1978), a constant shifting of relationships and roles suggests a terrifying instability of identity; both men and women move between the role of victim and victimizer, but the women are consistently the more disadvantaged, both socially and biologically. Both novels end by suggesting that a new breed of emancipated woman is emerging, but offer little convincing evidence for this hope, and Weldon's work has gradually tended towards disillusion, with an element of biological determinism. Women's sexuality, and sexual politics, have been central feminist concerns. In contrast to Weldon's cynical realism, Angela Carter (1940–92) approached these issues through fantasy, myth and symbol, reworking elements of fairytale in the stories of *The Bloody Chamber* (1979), and in her novel *Nights at the Circus* (1984) using post-modernist techniques: the disruption of narrative consistency and the blending of fiction and history. Fantasy and dream can serve as forms of experience emancipated from rational modes of thought which are seen as essentially male, and ▷ Emma Tennant (b 1937), in *The Bad Sister* (1978), employs a split between realist and fantasy modes to develop this opposition, while ▷ Sara Maitland's *Three Times Table* (1990) explores the lives of three women in a mode which seems predominantly realist but which can find room for dragons in a London park. Radical perspectives on sexual relations are also a feature of the work of ▷ Maureen Duffy (b 1933), who explores particularly working-class and lesbian experience, and of novels by members of the Feminist Writers Group who share socialist as well as feminist commitment: including Sara Maitland and Michèle Roberts (both of whom are interested in the relations of religion and female sexuality) and Michelene Wandor, who co-wrote with Maitland *Arky Types* (1987), a post-modernist ▷ epistolary novel.

Realism, satire, social comedy

There is a continuing strain in the English novel which is concerned with the analysis of contemporary English culture by means of satire, humour, or irony, primarily within realistic modes. The satirical strain building on the earlier work of writers such as Waugh and Huxley, includes ▷ Angus Wilson (1913–91), whose novel, *Anglo-Saxon Attitudes* (1956), set in the late 1940s, is a portrait of academic and London life and the egotism and self-deception of a range of characters. These concerns, however, take on a broader historical and social resonance because of the novel's examination of the effect of the past on the present via the troubled personal life of an historian and the confusion arising out of an historical fraud committed in 1912. *The Old Men at the Zoo* (1961) continues the vein of satirical analysis, but moves into fantasy and allegory in its bizarre tale of the administration of the London Zoo during another war. Wilson is also a writer of short stories, which combine a sharp satirical edge with a considerable emotional charge in their exposure of cruelty, snobbishness and pretension.

During the 1950s a group of writers emerged whose work combined a realist portrayal of provincial communities with a strong sense of social injustice. Some of these writers became known by the label ▷ 'angry young men'; they include ▷ Alan Sillitoe (b 1928), ▷ Stan Barstow (b 1928), ▷ John Wain (b 1925), ▷ John Braine (b 1922) and ▷ David Storey (b 1933), and in their early novels the heroes are working-class, or in revolt against the demands of a middle-class background. Novels such as John Braine's *Room at the Top* (1957), John Wain's *Hurry on Down* (1953), Stan Barstow's *A Kind of Loving* (1960) and Alan Sillitoe's *Saturday Night and Sunday Morning* (1958) seemed to epitomize a post-war sense of futility, discontent and rebellion. Their subsequent careers have developed in various ways, as, for example, towards narrative innovation in the case of Storey, or to a reaction against radicalism in the case of Braine. They were brought up outside London, coming in most cases from working-class backgrounds, and their work continued the tradition of working-class regional writing found earlier in the novels of Walter Greenwood and Lewis Grassic Gibbon.

Of those originally seen as 'angry young men', it is perhaps ▷ Kingsley Amis (b 1922) who has most successfully sustained his popular appeal over the succeeding decades. Unlike Angus Wilson, who, influenced by Virginia Woolf, used a range of interior monologues in his sixth novel *No Laughing Matter* (1967), Amis eschews modernist experiment, though working with a number of sub-genres, such as the ghost-story (*The Green Man*; 1969) and the fantasy of an alternative world (*The Alteration*; 1976). His novels are characterised by sharp wit, inventiveness, and a considerable animus against whatever Amis sees as bogus or blameworthy. *Lucky Jim* (1954), his very entertaining first novel, inaugurated the genre of the humorous campus novel, since developed by Malcolm Bradbury (b 1932) in *Stepping Westward* (1965) and *The History Man* (1975), and ▷ David Lodge (b 1935) in *Changing Places* (1975) and *Small World* (1984). Amis specializes in dislikeable characters, with objectionable attitudes, such as the xenophobia of the protagonists of *I Like It Here* (1958) and *One Fat Englishman* (1963), or the misogyny of Stanley in *Stanley and the Women* (1984). While these attitudes are subjected to a degree of satirical censure, they are not altogether repudiated. Amis's position is now a conservative one, marked by a distrust of the cosmopolitan and the experimental.

The influence of Jane Austen is apparent in the work of ▷ Barbara Pym (1913–80), which enjoyed a revival in the late 1970s, and consists of subtle and ironical studies of middle-class life, combining a shrewd humour with an uncompromising sense of the commonness of frustration, isolation and ennui. The delicacy of her work might be contrasted with the satirical shock-tactics of Martin Amis (b 1949) who employs black humour to portray human fears, obsessions and desires. Surprisingly, Amis (who is Kingsley Amis's son) claims to be influenced by Jane Austen too; he shares with Pym the use of humour of some sort to reveal human weakness, but they stand at opposite ends of a spectrum stretching from gentle irony to vigorous satire.

Post-colonial fiction: Africa, the Caribbean, India

This essay started by referring to the cross-fertilization of cultures as essential to the modernist movement at the beginning of the century. Since that time Britain's political and cultural relations with the rest of the world have changed radically. The British Empire has ended; two world wars have brought enormous social changes; technological developments have transformed the world economic system, and therefore the manner in which cultural artefacts are circulated. The diversity and plurality which have been noted as aspects of post-modern society have a particular value insofar as they promote an attention to the radical otherness of different cultures. There is thus a new, post-modern form of cross-fertilization taking place. The difference between the two forms might be epitomized by the difference between reading E. M. Forster's *A Passage to India*, the reaction of a sensitive and perceptive Englishman to Indian society, and reading the novels of ▷ R. K. Narayan (b 1906) which, though using the English language, are written by an Indian who knows that society from within. The availability of works in translation is also a part of this openness; since the 1970s the British novel-reading public has been less likely to read British works which somehow attempt to incorporate world culture, and more likely to read works in translation, such as the Latin American novels of ▷ Jorge Luis Borges (1899–1987), Gabriel García Márquez (b 1928), ▷ Isabel Allende (b 1942), Carlos Fuentes (b 1928) or Mario Vargas Llosa (b 1936) and the Eastern European novels of Alexander Solzhenitsyn (b 1918), Josef Skvorecky (b 1924) or Milan Kundera (b 1929).

Since 1950 there has been an explosion of fiction-writing in English in those countries of Africa, the Caribbean and South Asia which were once part of the British Empire. Independence was gained by most of these countries over a period of thirty years, including India and Pakistan in 1947, Nigeria in 1960, Kenya in 1963, Barbados in 1966 and Trinidad in 1976, up to 1980 when Zimbabwe became independent. In many of these states English provides, to varying degrees, a common literarary language, existing alongside indigenous languages and literary traditions. Sometimes referred to as Commonwealth fiction (a term which now tends to seem politically outdated), this huge and diverse body of fiction may usefully be termed post-colonial fiction, although with certain cautions. The term designates a political and linguistic context for such writing, as well as suggesting the presence of common themes and concerns. The political context is that of nations recently freed from imperial rule but still contending in many respects with its consequences and with new forms of economic, military or political involvement on the part of the West. The linguistic context clearly has a special importance for writers. Many writers in Africa and South Asia face a decision whether to publish in the language which is a legacy of foreign domination of their countries, or in an indigenous language, or both. For example, the Kenyan novelist ▷ Ngugi wa Thiong'o, after publishing four widely acclaimed novels in English, published a fifth in the language of his people, Gikuyu, later translating it into English himself; since 1982 he has abandoned writing in English. For those who do write in English, the historical role of this language, together with the history of its use and development in diverse cultures, may significantly inflect matters of genre, style, technique and diction, responding and contributing to the continuing evolution of the many 'Englishes' of the world. Politically and linguistically, then, 'post-colonial' designates an ambivalent, conflictual situation, in which the after-effects of imperialism remain powerful and where 'post' implies a transformation rather than an absolute break. Thematically, many novels have directly addressed the period of colonial rule, the transition to independence and the continuing personal and social consequences. These concerns have generated a strong tradition of realist novels of historical analysis and political critique. However, it would be limiting to see all post-colonial fiction in such terms, since it ranges widely in both technique and subject-matter.

There are instances of African writing in English as early as the end of the eighteenth century, and earlier this century we find novelists such as Sol T. Plaatje, whose novel *Mhudi* (1930) was written before 1920, and ▷ Peter Abrahams, who published *Song of the City* in 1945. But the start of a period of rapid growth in African English writing can be identified with the publication of ▷ Amos Tutuola's *The Palm-wine Drinkard* (1952) and ▷ Chinua Achebe's *Things Fall Apart* (1958). Achebe's novels articulate the impact on Nigerian culture of white colonialism and its aftermath, from the first appearance of white missionaries in *Things Fall Apart*, to Lagos in the 1960s in *A Man of The People* (1966). *Anthills of the Savannah* (1987) updates this historical chronicle, showing injustice and resistance under the rule of a 1980s African military dictator. Writing in English, Achebe incorporates African proverbs and idioms in such a way as to make the cultural context vivid and compelling for both African and English readers. Characters such as Okonkwo (the village leader who is the principal character of *Things*

Fall Apart, 1958) or Christopher Oriko (the Commissioner for Information who, in *Anthills of the Savannah*, compromises with, but eventually revolts against, the one-time friend who has became a dictator) achieve psychological complexity, and a considerable tragic status. Other important West African novelists of Achebe's generation include ▷ Wole Soyinka, ▷ Flora Nwapa, ▷ Ayi Kwei Armah and ▷ Cyprian Ekwensi. In East Africa a chronicling of the modern history of Kenya, comparable to Achebe's portrayal of Nigeria, is achieved by Ngugi wa Thiong'o. His first novel, *Weep not, Child* (1964), is the story of an adolescent boy at the time of the Mau Mau rebellions, while *The River Between* (1965) goes back in time to the first nationalist rebellion of the 1920s, representing divisions in Kenyan society through the symbolic separation of two villages, on either bank of a river. *A Grain of Wheat* (1967) presents Kenyan life in the troubled period leading up to independence through the lives of four friends, and *Petals of Blood* (1977) is a powerful, realistic, but also symbolically vivid attack on the economic exploitation of the peasants in the 1970s. Ngugi's mature fiction is explicitly informed by Marxist political analysis and after writing *Petals of Blood* he was imprisoned. His work embraces both the expression of a collective social awareness and the exploration of moral uncertainty through the gradual evolution of introspective characters.

Ngugi's fifth novel, *Devil on the Cross* (1982), moves away from realism towards allegory and fantasy. A number of African writers have employed experimental techniques, often drawing on oral and folklore traditions; for example *Our Sister Killjoy* (1970), by the Ghanaian playwright, poet and novelist ▷ Ama Ata Aidoo, uses typographical effects (such as pages with a single word on them), interposed commentaries in verse, ironic interplay between the voices of character and narrator, and a mode of address to the reader which draws on oral story-telling. The novel confronts feminist issues as well as expressing resistance to European appropriation and assimilation of African culture and African people, symbolized in the transplant of an African man's heart into a white man's body. The symbol of the heart is also structurally important to the story, in which a woman who travels to the 'heart' of Europe and is subject to its sexual and material attractions, eventually rejects it in favour of her responsibility to her African homeland. This complex inversion/subversion of the Eurocentric myth of Conrad's *Heart of Darkness* illustrates the process which Salman Rushdie has described by the phrase 'the Empire writes back to the Centre', a process of resistance and reappropriation through literary ▷ intertextuality. Aidoo's criticism of aspects of the work of male African writers (in particular their use of images and ideas of motherhood) places her in a strong feminist dynamic among African women writers, who have portrayed the 'double yoke' of black women who suffer from both racism and sexism; a concern evident in works such as Flora Nwapa's *Women are Different* (1986) and ▷ Buchi Emecheta's *Double Yoke* (1983). ▷ Bessie Head, who was born in South Africa but lived in Botswana from 1963, writes in a style of great intensity about experiences of displacement and the resulting personal anguish and conflictual relationships; for example, *Maru* (1971) is the story of an orphan girl facing racial prejudice among African peoples.

The oppression of white rule in South Africa dominates the novels of ▷ Nadine Gordimer, but is addressed obliquely through its impact on private experience. Writing primarily about the white middle classes, she traces the decay resulting from their involvement in a brutal and segregated social system. Another white South African who has addressed such concerns is ▷ J.M. Coetzee, whose *Age of Iron* (1990) combines allegory and realism in its grim picture of violent confrontation between police and Africans and the agonized complicity of a liberal white woman. ▷ André Brink, in *The Wall of the Plague* (1984), uses a comparable double technique, with a realist story set in modern France combined with an implicit allegory in which the medieval plague represents the effects of racism.

A number of African writers have lived or settled in Europe, whether to escape political persecution, like Ngugi, or for other reasons. But the move to Britain is more common among writers from the Caribbean; those who made the journey as part of the large-scale emigration in the 1950s included ▷ V.S. Naipaul and ▷ Samuel Selvon from Trinidad, ▷ Wilson Harris from Guyana and ▷ George Lamming from Barbados. Many novels by Caribbean writers explore the personal and social consequences of this journey, including Naipaul's *The Enigma of Arrival* (1987), Lamming's *The Emigrants* (1954) and ▷ Joan Riley's *The Unbelonging* (1985). Since the ancestors of many of these writers were brought to the West Indies from Africa as slaves, it is not surprising that the theme of the journey and the sense of homelessness as a cultural condition are found in much Caribbean fiction. The return journey to the West Indies (a return made by some writers, such as Lamming) also figures in certain works, such as Lamming's *Of Age and Innocence* (1958) and ▷ Caryl Phillips's *The Final Passage* (1985), as a possibility, a quest for a greater sense of belonging after experiences of loss, alienation, deprivation and racism in Britain. Such experiences are portrayed with humour, compassion and satirical force in Samuel Selvon's novels about life in urban Britain, such as *The Lonely Londoners* (1956) and *The Housing Lark* (1965).

George Lamming has also written about earlier stages in the history of West Indian society. His first novel, *In the Castle of My Skin* – (1953), is autobiographical and written in the first person. It begins when the protagonist is nine with an evocation of a pre-war Barbados village dominated by the house of the white landlord and the ideology of 'little England'. A strong sense of community is implied, but also the presence of tension, violence and humiliation, and the style is poetic and symbolic; for example, a flood becomes an anticipation of chaos and disruption to come. The novel ends with the destruction of this community, with the protagonist's initiation into self-conscious black politics and with his departure from the island; the concluding scene is his symbolic parting from the 'Pa' of the village – its oldest inhabitant and the embodiment of its collective identity, who is about to be confined in an institution. The relation between identity, family, community and people forms a frequent concern in Caribbean fiction. In many works by women novelists the role of the mother, identified in some way with the 'motherland' of the home island or home place, is central, whether as a powerful bond and source of strength, as in Jamaica Kincaid's (b 1949) *Annie John* (1983), or as a tragic absence, creating a need for re-connection, as in Paule Marshall's (b 1929) *The Chosen Place, the Timeless People* (1989).

The best-known West Indian writer is probably V.S. Naipaul, who has written about the lives of Indian people in Trinidad, but has also published novels set in other parts of the world, such as England (*The Mimic Men*; 1967), Mauritius (*Guerillas*: 1975) and Africa (*A Bend in the River*; 1979). His early novels, such as *The Mystic Masseur* (1957), evoke the life of Trinidad with an elegant clarity which emphasizes both its sordid aspects and its vitality. *A House For Mr Biswas* (1961) deals with the hero's search for independence combined with the capacity to love and accept responsibility. This search is articulated by the metaphor of the building of a house, a focus of self-respect and growth in the face of the displacement which is the aftermath of colonialism. The novel is a work of considerable scope in the comic realist tradition. Naipaul's ancestors came to the West Indies from India, and in that sense he represents one of the many cultural links between different parts of what was once the British Empire.

Post-Partition Indian fiction in English includes a strong tradition of novels that explore the inner lives and personal struggles of sensitive characters in relation to their immediate context: family, local community, romantic attachments. The forces of change and the pressure of cultural conflict are present, but are often experienced in more subtle and less extreme forms than in West Indian fiction. The established master of this tradition is R.K. Narayan, who has built his work around the fictional South Indian town of Malgudi (based on Mysore). Writing mainly about Hindu middle-class society, Narayan takes as his main theme the development or transformation of the self. In an unobtrusive, lucid style Narayan's writing attends to the details of places, objects and habits and explores subtleties of feeling and consciousness. The result is a combination of comedy and sadness as his modest, anxious, often ineffectual but highly sympathetic protagonists strive to cope with the frustrations of daily life and the elusiveness of their ambitions and desires. Broader areas of social and cultural conflict are not absent: *The Painter of Signs* (1976), for example, juxtaposes Western and Indian conceptions of the role of women and sexual relations in an ironic tale about a sign painter, his aunt and an emancipated woman who is seeking to promote birth control.

Narayan's delicacy, comedy and melancholy have often led to his work being compared with that of ▷ Chekhov, and the same comparison is sometimes made in relation to ▷ Anita Desai. *Fire on the Mountain* (1977), set in the mountains of north India, meditates on the unfulfilled lives of a group of women characters and their quests for various forms of peace, consolation or liberation. Desai, whose father was Bengali and mother German, was educated in India. Her work shows the influence of European and American modernism; for example, *Clear Light of Day* (1980) has epigraphs from T.S. Eliot and Emily Dickinson and its opening scene, set in a garden, has qualities reminiscent of the novels of Virginia Woolf. Desai's concern with the position of women is again apparent in this story of the lives of a middle-class Hindu family from Partition to the 1970s, notably in the character of Bib, a woman who achieves an independence of spirit despite heavy domestic responsibilities. However, indigenous Indian literary traditions (in the form of Urdu poetry) and an interest in male experience are evident in her novel *In Custody* (1984). Similarly, while Narayan's fiction can be seen within the traditions of the European novel, it can also be read in terms of plot and character elements mirroring Hindu mythological narratives: *The Man-Eater of Malgudi* (1961), for example, has a protagonist named Natara, one of the avatars of the god Shiva.

More explicitly political themes are found in the novels written in the 1980s by ▷ Nayantara Sahgal, a member of one of the most prominent Indian political family. *Plans for Departure* (1986) and *Mistaken Identity* (1988) depict India in the 1910s and the 1930s respectively, while *Rich Like Us* (1985) shows Sahgal's concern for human rights, using a narration from two perspectives to explore the causes and consequences of violence during the state of emergency declared by Indira Ghandi in the late 1970s. Sahgal's earlier novels, such as *Storm in Chandigarh* (1969), focused more on sexual politics, a concern which is central to the work of ▷ Shashi Despande who, in *That Long Silence* (1988), portrays the tension for a married woman between a sense of responsibility and a need for autonomy, in a story that also explores the psychic consequences of an abortion.

The British Raj and its legacy have provided central themes for two Europeans living in India. ▷ Paul Scott's *Raj Quartet* (1966–75), a study of racial tension, corruption and violence at the time of Independence was made into a hugely popular television series. Ruth Prawar Jhabvala's novel *Heat and Dust* (1975) juxtaposes the 1920s and the 1970s in a parallel double narrative, a technique which Jhabvala (who is a highly successful screenplay writer) describes in filmic terms as 'splicing'. Revisiting the period of E.M. Forster's *A Passage to India* and reassessing many of its political and moral concerns, this novel represents one version of the rewriting of the texts of the colonial period which has been a major technique of the post-colonial novel.

Post-colonial writing: Canada, Australia, New Zealand

There is an obvious difference of historical situation between what John Thieme terms the 'disrupted Third World societies' of Africa and India and the 'transplanted New World societies' of Canada, Australia and New Zealand (▷ post-colonial literature), although, as Thieme points out, the distinction has its limitations: the Aborigine, Maori and native Canadian peoples are 'disrupted' societies within the 'New World' societies of the latter group, while Caribbean societies are both disrupted and transplanted. To consider the fiction of both types of society under the heading 'post-colonial' is not to imagine a homogeneity but to invoke a fascinating series of similarities, contrasts and tensions, as diverse historical and geographical circumstances inflect certain broad themes, such as marginalization (both literary and political) and a divided personal and cultural identity, together with strategies such as 'writing back' and narratives of re-imagined and re-told history.

In both Canada and Australia one might pick out a single novelist of the post-war period in terms of international reputation. In Canada, ▷ Margaret Atwood has played a key role, as novelist, poet, feminist and critic, in the renaissance of Canadian writing in English which has taken place since around 1960. Her work foregrounds questions of both national identity and sexual politics. Symbolic and surreal elements are evident in the first-person narratives of *The Edible Woman* (1969) and *Surfacing* (1972), which centre on the internal lives of their women narrators. In *The Edible Woman*, feminist issues are dominant; the metaphor of eating illuminates the narrator's reaction against both consumerism and the egotistical emotional cannibalism of men. In *Surfacing*, a journey to a remote cabin in a French-speaking part of Canada is combined with the metaphor of diving into the depths of the self (with the possibilities of drowning or resurfacing). These two elements focus questions of cultural as well as personal identity. Both novels reflect the resolution stated in the last chapter of *Surfacing*: 'This above all, to refuse to be a victim.' Atwood has used a variety of techniques and genres: *The Handmaid's Tale* (1985) is a feminist dystopia (▷ utopian fiction), set in the future.

Margaret Laurence uses her fictional prairie town of Manawaka to chart Canadian social history (somewhat as Narayan uses Malgudi in India). Laurence, who has lived in Somaliland and Ghana, set her early fiction, such as *This Side Jordan* (1960), in Africa and her work exemplifies a creative link between different post-colonial societies, as does that of ▷ Michael Ondaatje, who came to Canada from Sri Lanka. Ondaatje's *In the Skin of a Lion* (1987) blends fiction and history to focus attention on marginalized elements within Canadian life: remote rural communities and the situation of an urban multicultural working class. ▷ Faction, combined with an innovative narrative technique, is also a feature of *Coming through Slaughter* (1979), which uses transcripts of interviews, song lyrics, biographical summaries and intensely imagined subjective narration to document the life of the jazz cornet player Buddy Bolden. A comparable inventiveness is found in the less tragic but equally compelling novel by ▷ Carol Shields, *Mary Swann* (1987). This story of academics and others seeking to rediscover the life and work of an (imaginary) little-known Canadian poet contains an element of mystery, built up through four narratives: each has a different ▷ focal character, while one consists partly of letters. The novel's conclusion takes the form of a film script (including camera directions).

▷ Patrick White remains the most widely known post-war Australian novelist. His work draws on the stark polarities of Australian life: the polite social milieu of suburban Sydney, satirized by White with a dry wit, and the starkly primitive outback, which in *Voss* (1957) becomes a spiritual testing ground. The eponymous hero of this novel is a dedicated German explorer, with a compulsive though enigmatic sense of his own destiny, who leads an expedition into the Australian interior. In the early part of the novel the narrative shifts freely between realistic observation of social mores and poetic evocation of characters' inner worlds of memory, anticipation and desire. This blend is characteristic of White's idiosyncratic style, which startles by its immediacy and tonal range. Voss's journey, like those of Graham Greene's characters, is also an inner journey, and, as in the work of Conrad, the confrontation with a harsh and alien landscape is endowed with philosophical and spiritual resonance through the questioning of personal identity; external and internal landscapes function as mutual metaphors. Central to *Voss* is the duality of the physical world and the human imagination; the latter becomes concentrated in the intense and mystical relationship between Voss and a woman he has met in Sydney, a relationship carried on in their thoughts and letters. White was both a social satirist and a visionary, and the authority of his work was recognized by the award of the Nobel Prize for Literature in 1973.

▷ Randolph Stow, of a slightly later generation than White, has made comparable use of a symbolic journey (a recurrent motif of post-colonial fiction) in *To the Islands* (1958). The journey of an ageing Christian missionary, searching for the Aboriginal 'island of the dead' resembles the journey of the heroine of Margaret Atwood's *Surfacing* to the extent that it is a personal journey into the self but also a quest for sources of cultural identity – in this case Aboriginal myth. ▷ Janette Turner Hospital, an Australian who moved to Canada in

1971, employs another powerful metaphor of post-colonial experience, that of the border, in her novel *Borderline* (1985). This story about a Canadian couple and an illegal Central American immigrant explores questions of involvement, privilege and detachment with a post-modernist fictional self-consciousness. The work of ▷ Peter Carey also displays the techniques and preoccupations of post-modernism: black comedy and shock tactics in *Bliss* (1981), a self-confessed unreliable narrator in *Illywhacker* (1985) and historical pastiche in *Oscar And Lucinda* (1988).

Although much New Zealand fiction before the 1950s tended towards social realism and a male orientation, there was a strong if (until recently) inadequately recognized tradition of feminist fiction, including the work of Edith Searle Grossman at the start of the twentieth century and of Katherine Mansfield and Jane Mander in the 1920s. Since the 1950s this tradition has been continued in the novels, stories and autobiographical writing of ▷ Janet Frame, whose importance to the contemporary New Zealand novel is comparable to that of Atwood in Canada. Her three-volume autobiography, *To the Is-Land* (1983), *An Angel at My Table* (1984; filmed 1990) and *The Envoy from Mirror City* (1985), is closely related to her fiction, which describes, with symbolic intensity and a linguistic inventiveness reminiscent of James Joyce, experiences – such as those of isolation, medical incarceration, and self-creation and self-healing through fiction – which are features of her own life. The work of ▷ Keri Hulme, a New Zealand novelist of partly Kai Tahu descent, reacts against the consequences of colonialism, social and ecological; her novel *The Bone People* (1983) is another example of the mythical journey narrative.

Post-colonial fiction in English, broadly defined, represents a significant form of literary expression for many diverse cultures: the authors named here are some of the most influential and widely-read, but represent only a small proportion of those who merit attention. Furthermore, literature in English is found in other countries such as Pakistan, Malaysia, Singapore, Oceania (the Pacific region) and Sri Lanka. It may be appropriate to conclude by stressing the creative tension of cultural specificity and internationalism in post-colonial writing. Almost all the writers discussed here have been concerned in one way or another to define, rediscover or reform a specific cultural identity. Nevertheless, the links, which have already been mentioned, between post-colonial societies, combined with what the critic Bruce King has termed 'the New Internationalism' in British literature (exemplified by writers from post-colonial and other cultures educated in Britain such as Salman Rushdie, Buchi Emecheta and ▷ Kazuo Ishiguro) indicates that post-colonial fiction holds an assured place in contemporary world culture.

Conclusion

The field of contemporary fiction is large and expanding. This essay attempts to provide an introduction to twentieth-century fiction by examining some perspectives on the major work of the first half of the century, and by suggesting something of the range and variety of writing since 1950, in the hope that the reader will be encouraged to explore further. Traditional features of the novel, such as satire, the pleasure of narrative, the excitement of plot and the rendering of moral distinctions still find new and original exponents. Narrative experiment and the awareness of fictionality provide powerful means for exploring the particular philosophical preoccupations of our age, while genres such as science fiction, ▷ horror and the fantasy novel offer popular alternative modes of writing. At the same time both the language and the techniques of the novel are successfully adapted to various and changing cultures. The diversity of the contemporary novel in English is a sign of the vitality of the form and of the continuing ability of fiction to engage at many levels with both intellectual issues and cultural processes.

Reference section

Aaron

In the ▷ Bible, the founder of the Jewish priesthood; he assisted Moses in leading the Jews out of Egypt to the frontiers of Canaan, the 'Promised Land'. His rod was a sacred emblem which Moses and he held up above the battle when the Jews were fighting the Amalekites (*Exodus* 17). The novel *Aaron's Rod* (1922) by ▷ D. H. Lawrence, is about a coal-miner who transforms his life with the aid of his flute.

Abelard, Peter (1079–1142)

A philosopher in the University of Paris early in the 12th century. At the height of his fame he fell in love with a young girl, Heloise (Eloise), and became her tutor. She bore him a child and to appease the anger of her uncle, Abelard proposed that they should be secretly married; open marriage was out of the question as it would obstruct Abelard's career in the Church. The marriage took place against Heloise's wishes, for she did not want her lover to risk his future prospects for her sake, and she refused to admit to it when challenged to do so. She took refuge in a convent, and her uncle revenged himself on Abelard by causing him to be castrated. Thereafter a famous correspondence took place between them. Abelard continued his career as a teacher but, at the instigation of Bernard of Clairvaux, he was eventually condemned for heresy (1141). The trial broke his health, and he died; his remains were secretly conveyed to Heloise, who died in 1164 and was buried in the same grave. The remains of both are now interred together in Père Lachaise. Their love affair became legendary and the subject of imaginative literature. Alexander Pope's *Eloisa to Abelard* (1717) is a poem on the subject. ▷ George Moore's novel, *Héloïse and Abélard*, appeared in 1921. There is also a novel by Helen Waddell, *Peter Abelard* (1933).

Abrahams, Peter (b 1919)

Novelist. Born in South Africa, which he left in 1939. After two years working as a sailor he lived in England (1941–56) and in France (1948–50) before moving to Jamaica in 1956. He has worked as an editor, journalist and broadcaster. His novels are all set in Africa (with the exception of *This Island Now*, 1966, set in Jamaica), and are concerned with social and political issues, particularly racial oppression. *Wild Conquest* (1950) deals with the historical theme of the Great Trek. *Dark Testament* (1942) is a collection of stories. His other novels are: *Song of the City* (1945); *Mine Boy* (1946); *The Path of Thunder* (1948); *A Wreath for Udomo* (1956); *A Night of Their Own* (1965); *The View from Coyaba* (1985); *Pressure Drop* (1991); *Revolution, No 9* (1992). His non-fiction includes: *Tell Freedom: Memoires of Africa* (1954) and *Jamaica: an Island Mosaic* (1957).
Bib: Ensor, R., *The Novels of Peter Abrahams and the Rise of Nationalism in Africa*.

Achebe, Chinua (b 1930)

Nigerian novelist, poet and short-story writer. Born Albert Chinualumogu in Ogidi, East Central State, his mother tongue is Ibo, but he studied English from an early age and in 1953 graduated in English Literature from University College, Ibadan. He has worked in radio, publishing, journalism and as an academic, visiting universities in the U.S.A. In his five novels he has successfully incorporated African idioms and patterns of thought in a lucid English prose style. *Things Fall Apart* (1958), with its title drawn from W. B. Yeats's poem 'The Second Coming', explores a major African dilemma; the destruction of the indigenous culture by European influence. It concerns Okonkwo, a village leader whose inflexible adherence to tradition cannot withstand the influence of a white missionaries. *No Longer At Ease* (1960) continues the theme of the conflict of African and European values, but in the urban context of Lagos in the 1950s. *Arrow of God* (1964) returns to tribal society, but at an earlier stage of colonialism, in the 1920s, while *A Man of the People* (1966) is again set in Lagos, with direct reference to the turbulent political events following Nigerian independence in 1960. Another novel, *Anthills of the Savannah*, was published in 1987. He has published two volumes of short stories, *The Sacrificial Egg* (1962) and *Girls at War* (1972) and two volumes of poetry: *Beware Soul-Brother and Other Poems* (1971) and *Christmas in Biafra and Other Poems* (1973). He also writes children's stories.
Bib: Lindfors, B., and Innes, C. L. (ed.), *Achebe*; Wren, R. M., *Achebe's World*; Carroll, D., *Chinua Achebe: Novelist, Poet, Critic*, Innes, C. L., *Chinua Achebe*.

Ackerley, J.R. (1896–1967)

Novelist and literary editor of *The Listener* (1935–59). His novels are largely autobiographical: *My Dog Tulip* (1956) and *We Think the World of You* (1960) are notable for having an Alsatian dog as the main character. Like his friend ▷ E.M. Forster, Ackerley worked for some time as private secretary to an Indian maharajah, an experience which forms the basis of *Hindoo Holiday* (1932), while *My Father and Myself* concerns the double life of his father, a businessman who secretly had two families. J.R. Ackerley's diaries have been edited by F. King (1982).
Bib: Petre, D., *The Secret Garden of Roger Ackerley*.

Ackroyd, Peter (b 1949)

Novelist, poet and critic. Born in London and educated at Cambridge University, he has been literary editor of the ▷ *Spectator* and a reviewer of books, television and cinema for *The Times* and the *Sunday Times*. His first novel was *The Great Fire of London* (1982), followed by *The Last Testament of Oscar Wilde* (1983), which took the form of the fictional diaries of ▷ Wilde during his tragic last years in Paris, and won the Somerset Maugham award. *Hawksmoor* (1985) interweaves a police investigation in contemporary east London with a narrative set during the great plague of the 17th century, in which the architects Hawksmoor and Wren appear; the novel won both the Guardian Fiction Award and the Whitbread Prize for the best novel. *Chatterton* (1987) is in part literary detective-story (in which it resembles ▷ A.S. Byatt's *Possession*) and combines historical pastiche (also a notable feature of *Hawksmoor*) with black comedy and elements of the sentimental and grotesque. *First Light* (1989) stages a confrontation between science and magic through the story of an archaeological dig in Dorset. His most recent novel is *English Music* (1992), a novel about Englishness and artistic traditions. Ackroyd has published three volumes of poetry: *London Lickpenny* (1973); *Country Life* (1978) and *The Diversions of Purley* (1987). His non-fiction includes: *Notes for a New Culture: An Essay on Modernism* (1976); *Dressing Up: Transvestism and Drag: The History of an Obsession* (1979); *Ezra Pound and his World* (1980); *T.S. Eliot* (1984) (which won the Whitbread Prize for biography); *Dickens* (1990).

Adam Bede (1859)

A novel by ▷ George Eliot. The setting is a village in the English Midlands and the events take place at the beginning of the 19th century. Adam Bede is the village carpenter, a young man of stern morals and great strength of character; he is in love with Hetty Sorrel, the vain and frivolous niece of a farmer, Martin Poyser. She is seduced by the village squire. Another principal character is the young and beautiful Dinah Morris, a Methodist preacher whom Adam marries after Hetty has been transported for the murder of her child. The novel belongs to the early phase of George Eliot's art when her principal subject was the rural civilization which had been the background of her youth; the fine parts of the novel are those scenes, such as the Poyser household, which are directly concerned with this way of life.

Adventures of Captain Singleton
▷ *Captain Singleton, Adventures of.*

Adventures of Roderick Random, The
▷ *Roderick Random, The Adventures of*

Aeneid

An ▷ epic poem by the Roman poet Virgil (70–19 BC). The poem tells the story of Aeneas, from his flight from Troy during the confusion of its destruction by the Greeks to his establishment as king of the Latins in central Italy and his death in battle with the Etruscans. The poem thus begins at a point near where ▷ Homer left off in the ▷ *Iliad*, and its description of the wanderings of Aeneas is parallel to the description of the wanderings of Odysseus in Homer's ▷ *Odyssey*. It is divided into 12 books, of which the second, fourth and sixth are the most famous: the second describes the destruction of Troy; the fourth gives the tragedy of Queen Dido of Carthage, who dies for love of Aeneas; the sixth shows his descent to the underworld and the prophetic visions of those who are to build the greatness of Rome.

Virgil wished to relate the Rome he knew, a settled and luxurious civilization which threatened to degenerate into complacent mediocrity, to her heroic past, and to inspire her with a sense of her great destiny in world history. The *Aeneid* is thus a central document for Roman culture, and inasmuch as Roman culture is the basis of the culture of western Europe, it has remained a central document for European culture too.

The most notable English translations of the *Aeneid* are those by the Scottish poet Gavin Douglas (1553) and by John Dryden (1697). Henry Howard, Earl of Surrey translated Books II and III into the earliest example of English blank verse.

Aeolists

In ▷ Swift's satire ▷ *A Tale of a Tub* (1704), a fictional sect of believers in direct inspiration: 'The learned Aeolists maintain the original cause of all things to be wind . . .' Swift's satire is an attack on all pretentions to truth not in accord with right reason or properly constituted authority, and the Aeolists, in Section VIII, are a kind of climax to the work. He associates them particularly with the ▷ Dissenters, who based their religious faith on belief in direct intimations from the Holy Spirit to the individual soul; Jack, who represents Presbyterianism in the *Tale*, is a leader of the sect.

Aesop

A Greek composer of animal ▷ fables of the 6th century BC. He probably did not write them down, but fables purporting to be his were collected by later classical writers, and they and imitations of them have had a wide popularity in European literature. The most notable Aesopian fable in English literature is ▷ Chaucer's *Nun's Priest's Tale* of the Cock and the Fox in the ▷ *Canterbury Tales*.

Aestheticism

A movement of the late 19th century, influenced by the Pre-Raphaelites and ▷ John Ruskin, but its immediate inspiration was the writings of the Oxford don ▷ Walter Pater. His two most influential books were *Studies in the History of the Renaissance* (1873) and *Marius the Epicurean* (1885). These show him as a ritualistic moralist, laying emphasis on the value of ecstatic experience. Apart from Pater and his predecessors, the aesthetes owed much to the current French doctrine of '*L'Art pour l'Art*' (Art for Art's sake) but they retained, if sometimes not obviously, a typically English concern with moral values and issues. The outstanding aesthete was ▷ Oscar Wilde (1856–1900), and a characteristic aesthetic product was his novel *The Picture of Dorian Gray* (1891). As the movement lacked a programme, writers of very different character were influenced by it: the naturalistic novelist ▷ George Moore; the poet Lionel Johnson who was a Catholic convert; Swinburne, a main channel for the art for art's sake doctrine, W.B. Yeats, the Celtic revivalist. A characteristic aestheticist periodical was ▷ *The Yellow Book* (1894–7), so called because French novels, conventionally considered 'daring', were printed on yellow paper. Its main illustrator was ▷ Aubrey Beardsley, whose line drawings were notorious for their sensuality. The excesses and affectations of the movement's adherents were much ridiculed in ▷ *Punch*.

Bib: Aldington, R. (ed.), *The Religion of Beauty:
Selections from the Aesthetes*.

Agnosticism
The term was invented by the biologist ▷ Thomas
Huxley in 1869 to express towards religious faith
the attitude which is neither of belief nor of disbelief
(▷ atheism). In his own words, 'I neither affirm
nor deny the immortality of man. I see no reason
for believing it, but on the other hand I have no
means of disproving it.' Agnosticism was widespread
among writers between 1850 and 1914; it arose
from the scientific thought of the time, especially
that of Huxley himself, and that of another biologist,
▷ Charles Darwin. Although the term can seem
to carry a less polemical charge than atheism in
our own time, 19th-century agnostics were often
extremely aggressive in their attacks on what they saw
as unfounded beliefs.

Aidoo, Ama Ata (b 1942)
Ghanaian novelist, poet and playwright. Educated
at the University of Ghana, she was for a time
Secretary of Education for Ghana but has lived in
Zimbabwe since 1983, where she has worked for the
Ministry of Education and is chair of the Zimbabwe
Women Writers Group. Her first novel, *Our Sister
Killjoy or Reflections from a Black-Eyed Squint* (1978),
uses a range of narrative techniques, including
interpolated poetic commentary, the ironic use of
a range of narrative voices, typographical effects
and elements drawn from oral narration. The story
of a Ghanaian woman who travels to Europe to
encounter both racism and the appeal of affluence, it
is a critique of racism and sexism, and an appeal for
Africans to commit themselves to the development of
their own countries. Here, as elswhere in her work,
Aidoo challenges the portrayal of African women
and of 'mother Africa' in the work of male African
novelists such as ▷ Kofi Awoonor. *Changes: a Love
Story* (1991) is similarly technically inventive. Her
plays are *The Dilemma of a Ghost* (1965) and *Anowa*
(1970); *No Sweetness Here* (1970) is a collection of
short stories and *An Angry Letter in January* (1992) is
a volume of poems. She has also written a historical
study of the Asante kingdom.
Bib: James, A., *In Their Own Voices: Interviews with
African Woman Writers*.

Ainsworth, William Harrison (1805–82)
Novelist. His best novels are historical: *Jack Shepherd*
(1839), *The Tower of London* (1840), *Guy Fawkes*
(1841), *Old St Paul's* (1841), *Windsor Castle* (1843).
He tended to idealize the heroic criminal, *eg* ▷ Dick
Turpin in *Rookwood* (1834) and Jack Shepherd; this
was a literary fashion in the 1830s and 1840s and
censured by ▷ Thackeray in his early reviews under
the designation 'The ▷ Newgate School of novelists'.
He edited *Bentley's Magazine* 1840–2, *Ainsworth's
Magazine* 1842–53 and ▷ *New Monthly Magazine*
from 1853.
Bib: Ellis, S. M., *W. H. Ainsworth and his Friends*;
Worth, G. J., *William Harrison Ainsworth*.

Aldiss, Brian (b 1925)
  ▷ Science Fiction.

**Alexander, Mrs (Annie Hector, née French)
(1825–1902)**
Novelist, born in Dublin, who published over 45
novels, most of which revolve around young heroines
seeking to reconcile love and financial security.
They include: *Look Before You Leap* (1865), *Which
Shall it Be* (1866), *The Wooing O't* (1873), *Her Dearest
Foe* (1876), *The Freres* (1882), *The Admiral's Ward*
(1883). *Kitty Costello* (1904) is partly autobiographical.
Because of her husband's ill health and relatively
early death (in 1875), she supported herself and her
family by her writing.

*Alice's Adventures in Wonderland; Through the
Looking-Glass*
  ▷ Carroll, Lewis.

All the Year Round
A periodical published by ▷ Charles Dickens from
1859, in succession to ▷ *Household Words*, until
his death in 1870. Novels which appeared in it in
instalments included Dickens's own ▷ *A Tale of Two
Cities* and ▷ *Great Expectations*.

Allegory
From the Greek, meaning 'speaking in other terms'.
A way of representing thought and experience
through images, by means of which (1) complex
ideas may be simplified, or (2) abstract, spiritual,
or mysterious ideas and experiences may be
made immediate (but not necessarily simpler) by
dramatization in fiction.
  In both uses, allegory was most usual and natural
as a medium of expression in the Middle Ages, in
morality plays, notably *Everyman* (15th century),
and romances of sexual love, such as *The Romance
of the Rose* (14th century) in part translated from
the French by ▷ Chaucer. When Chaucer wrote
a romance in which there was no overt allegory,
eg ▷ *Troilus and Criseyde*, the allegorical spirit was
still implicit within it (see C. S. Lewis, *Allegory of
Love*). Such implicit allegory extended into much
Renaissance drama, when explicit allegory, though
still pervasive, was greatly complicated by the break-
up of the dominant Catholic framework; various
Christian doctrines competed with one another and
with non-Christian ones such as neo-Platonism,
and also with political theories. Thus in a work
like Spenser's *Faerie Queene* (1590–6) religious,
political and Platonic allegories are all employed, but
intermittently and not with artistic coherence.
  Since the 17th century deliberate and consistent
allegory has continued to decline; yet the greatest
of all English allegories, ▷ *The Pilgrim's Progress* by
▷ John Bunyan, is a 17th-century work. The paradox
is explained by Bunyan's contact with the literature
of the village sermon, which apparently continued
to be conducted by a simple allegorical method with
very little influence from the Reformation. Moreover
allegory has continued into modern times, partly
as an indispensable habit of explanation, partly in
a suppressed form (*eg* the names of characters in
▷ Dickens's novels), and partly as a resource in the
expression of mysterious psychological experience

incommunicable in direct terms; here allegory merges with ▷ symbolism, from which, however, it needs to be distinguished.
  ▷ Fable.

Allen, Charles Grant Blairfindie (1848–99)

Novelist, born in Canada, brought up there and in the USA and educated at Oxford. He is best-known for *The Woman Who Did* (1895), a ▷ New Woman novel in which the protagonist is opposed to marriage on principle, lives with the man she loves, but is left alone with a child after his death and meets a tragic end. In the 1870s he taught philosophy at the Government College in Jamaica, an experience which helped to promote his interest in questions of emancipation, a theme of many of his novels. A number of these have foreign settings, such as *In All Shades* (1886), set in Jamaica and *The Tents of Shem* (1891), an adventure story set in Algeria. He was influenced by the evolutionary theories of ▷ Herbert Spencer. His first novel was a satire, entitled *Philistia* (1884), and he wrote in a range of genres, including the detective story (*An African Millionaire*, 1897).

Allingham, Margery (1904–66)

Writer of detective fiction. One of the foremost women detective writers of the 20th century, Allingham's work is characteristic of the inter-war 'golden age' of ▷ detective fiction, along with the work of ▷ Agatha Christie, ▷ Ngaio Marsh and Dorothy L. Sayers. Like Christie's Poirot or Miss Marple, or Sayer's Lord Peter Wimsey, Allingham has a chief detective, Albert Campion (said to be modelled on Wimsey), who is however a rather enigmatic, mysterious character, working in a London full of atmosphere and populated by eccentrics. She began writing in the 1920s and continued until her death in 1966; her many novels include: *The Crime at Black Dudley* (1929); *Look to the Lady* (1931); *Police at the Funeral* (1931); *Sweet Danger* (1933); *Dancers in Mourning* (1937); *The Fashion in Shrouds* (1938); *The Case Book of Mr Campion* (1947); *The Tiger in the Smoke* (1952); *The Mind Readers* (1965).

Alliteration

  ▷ Figures of Speech.

Althusser, Louis (b 1918)

One of the most influential French ▷ Marxist philosophers of the 1960s, whose work began to appear in English translation from 1965 onwards: *For Marx* (1965, trans. 1969), *Reading Capital* (with Etienne Balibar, 1965, trans. 1969), and *Lenin and Philosophy* (1968, trans. 1971). Althusser's ideas have been influential in the area of cultural studies, where his particular brand of structural Marxism has led to a radical rethinking of all social institutions, and the place of the human subject within their structures. His essay 'Ideology and Ideological State Apparatuses' (*Lenin and Philosophy*) lays the foundation for a reconsideration of literature and its relationship to ▷ ideology, and has far-reaching effects also in the area of media studies.

Ambassadors, The (1903)

A novel by ▷ Henry James. It belongs to his last period, during which he returned to his earlier theme of the interaction of the European and American character.

Lambert Strether, a conscientious, middle-aged American, is engaged to the rich American widow, Mrs Newsome. She sends him over to Paris to bring back her son Chad to run the family business. He arrives to find Chad immersed in Parisian culture, and absorbed in a love affair with the Comtesse de Vionnet, a relationship which Strether mistakenly assumes is not a sexual one. Strether, instead of persuading Chad to return, finds his sensibilities released by the freedom and richness of Parisian life, and delays his own return. Chad's sister, Mrs Pocock, and her husband, Jim, are now sent over by Mrs Newsome. Strether urges upon Chad the duty of loyalty to the Comtesse, and Mrs Newsome breaks off her engagement to Strether. After discovering the true nature of Chad's relations with the Comtesse, Strether decides to go back, abandoning his friendship with the intelligent and sympathetic Maria Gostrey, an American expatriate. Chad, however, remains.

Mrs Newsome is an authoritarian American matron, full of rectitude and prejudice. Strether has the highly developed New England conscience (it is his conscience that forces him to return) and a hitherto starved imagination. He is the ▷ focal character of the narrative throughout, so that his progressive understanding and development is a rich source of interest and irony. The Pococks stand for American philistinism, without imagination or sensibility. Together with ▷ *The Golden Bowl* (1904) and ▷ *The Wings of the Dove* (1902), the novel shows James's art at its most highly wrought and difficult stage.

Amelia (1751)

A novel by ▷ Henry Fielding. Unlike ▷ *Joseph Andrews* and ▷ *Tom Jones*, *Amelia* deals with married love, and was Fielding's own favourite, although fiercely attacked by, among others, ▷ Johnson and ▷ Samuel Richardson.

Set against a background of squalor and poverty, the novel opens with the imprisonment of the innocent but careless husband Captain Booth. In prison Booth meets the courtesan Miss Matthews, an old admirer who invites him to share the clean cell she has been able to afford. Booth accepts, though feeling guilty about his virtuous wife Amelia, and the two characters exchange stories about their past lives.

An old friend Colonel Bath pays Booth's bail and takes Miss Matthews as his mistress. Once out of jail, Booth turns to a life of gambling while trying to curry favour with the great. An aristocratic acquaintance assures Amelia that Booth will get his commission, and invites her to accompany him to a masquerade. But 'My Lord' is a rake plotting to seduce Amelia, with the connivance of Colonel Bath and the Booths' landlady, Mrs Ellison.

Just as Amelia is about to set out to the masquerade, a fellow lodger, Mrs Bennet, warns her that 'My Lord' had ruined her own life and is now threatening to destroy Amelia's 'virtue'. After several complications, the plot ends happily; the Booths are rescued by their good friend Dr Harrison, and Amelia discovers that her virtue is rewarded, as she will inherit her mother's fortune.

Amis, Sir Kingsley (b 1922)

Novelist and poet. Associated at first with the ▷ 'angry young men' of the 1950s for his novels, and with the Movement for his poetry, he has long outgrown such labelling, achieving considerable popular success with a series of sharp, ironic novels notable for entertaining incident, vivid caricatures and the comic demolition of pretension. *Lucky Jim* (1954; filmed 1957) is a hugely enjoyable novel about a young English lecturer in a provincial university and his battles against the academic establishment and a range of comically infuriating characters. It is not really a subversive work; it ends with the hero being given a good job in London by a wealthy man as well as winning the best girl. Amis's later novels tend to be less good-humoured; the protagonist of *One Fat Englishman* (1963) retains some of Jim's methods, but is fully as unpleasant as his enemies. Although Amis has remained within the format of a well-crafted plot and largely conventional modes of narration, he has employed a wide range of genres such as the detective story (*The Riverside Villas Murder*, 1973), the spy-story (*The Anti Death League*, 1966) and the ghost-story (*The Green Man*; 1969). *The Alteration* (1976), one of his most inventive works, imagines a 20th-century society dominated by the Catholic Church.

Amis's other novels are: *That Uncertain Feeling* (1955); *I Like It Here* (1958); *Take A Girl Like You* (1960); *The Egyptologists* (1965); *I Want It Now* (1968); *Colonel Sun* (as Robert Markham; 1968); *Girl, 20* (1971); *Ending Up* (1974); *The Alteration* (1976); *Jake's Thing* (1978); *Russian Hide and Seek* (1980); *Stanley and the Women* (1984); *The Old Devils* (1986); *Difficulties With Girls* (1988); *The Russian Girl* (1992) Story collections include: *My Enemy's Enemy* (1962); *Dear Illusion* (1972); *The Darkwater Hall Mystery* (1978); *Collected Short Stories* (1980). Poetry: *Bright November* (1947); *A Frame of Mind* (1953); *A Case of Samples* (1956); *The Evans Country* (1962); *A Look Around The Estate: Poems 1957–1967* (1967); *Collected Poems 1944–1979* (1979). Essays and criticism include: *New Maps of Hell* (on ▷ science fiction; 1960); *The James Bond Dossier* (1965); *What Became of Jane Austen?* (1975); *Rudyard Kipling and His World* (1975). He has also published his *Memoirs* (1991). Amis was knighted in 1990.
Bib: Salwak, D., *Kingsley Amis, A Reference Guide*, and *Kingsley Amis: In Life and Letters*; McDermott, S., *Kingsley Amis: An English Moralist*.

Amis, Martin (b 1949)

Novelist. Son of ▷ Kingsley Amis, he was educated at schools in Britain, Spain and the U.S.A., and at Oxford University. He has worked for the *Times Literary Supplement*, the *New Statesman* (as literary editor) and the *Observer*. His early novels are characterized by black humour, concern with the sordid, violent and absurd, and an apparent

misogyny, features which he defends as satire. *The Rachel Papers* (1973) is an account of adolescence through flashbacks and memories; *Dead Babies* (1975) (paperback as *Dark Secrets*) is a tale of decadence and sadism; *Success* (1978) is closer to the hilarity of *The Rachel Papers*, while *Other People* (1981) is an experiment in ambiguity. With the linguistic wealth of *London Fields* (1989) and the experimental narrative technique of *Time's Arrow* (1991, shortlisted for the Booker Prize), Amis has emerged as a ▷ post-modernist novelist of considerable versatility. Other works: *Money* (novel; 1984); *The Moronic Inferno* (essays; 1986); *Einstein's Monsters* (stories; 1987).

Amos Barton, The Sad Fortunes of the Rev. (1857)

The first of the three tales composing ▷ *Scenes of Clerical Life* (1858) by ▷ George Eliot.

Amphibology, Amphiboly

A sentence having two possible meanings owing to the ambiguity of its construction.

Anacoluthon

▷ Figures of Speech.

Ancien Régime

A French phrase, commonly used in English, to signify the political and social order in France before the Revolution of 1789, and more loosely to indicate a former state of order.
▷ French Revolution.

Andersen, Hans Christian (1805–75)

Danish author known in Britain almost entirely for ▷ fairy tales of his own composition, such as 'The Tinder Box', and 'The Princess and the Pea'. They began to appear in Denmark in 1835 and were translated into English first in 1846. Their poetic quality has been much imitated by English writers, *eg* ▷ Oscar Wilde.
▷ Children's Books.

Anglo-Saxon

The name is practically identical with ▷ Old English in denoting the language, literature and culture of the English before the Norman-French conquest of 1066, and also after it until it becomes fused (Middle English) in the 13th century with the insular Norman-French; it was later occasionally used *eg* in Disraeli's ▷ *Coningsby* and ▷ *Sybil*, to differentiate the common people from the aristocracy of (supposedly) Norman-French descent, or to refer to supposed indigenous traits of the English *eg* in ▷ Angus Wilson's ironic title (taken from Lewis Carroll) *Anglo-Saxon Attitudes*.
▷ English language.

Angry young men

A term which was loosely applied to novelists and dramatists of the 1950s who expressed a sense of dissatisfaction and revolt against established social mores. John Osborne's play *Look Back In Anger* (1956) epitomized the mood. Other authors of whom

the term was used include ▷ John Braine, ▷ John Wain, ▷ Alan Sillitoe, and ▷ Kingsley Amis. ▷ Realism.
Bib: Allsop, K., *The Angry Decade*.

Anti-climax
▷ Figures of Speech.

Anti-industrialism
A tradition of writing identified initially by the work of ▷ Raymond Williams in *Culture and Society*. 19th-century observers, the foremost of whom was ▷ Thomas Carlyle, identified a number of threats to what they saw as constructive social living brought by industrialism. When the industrial system was being imposed it could be seen how its pressures obliged the workforce into working in mechanical unison and consequently altered their sense of themselves. The emphasis it brought on material production and material acquisition changed the conditions of life and sapped the individual's powers of resistance. ▷ D. H. Lawrence was its most impassioned 20th-century opponent.
▷ Capitalism.

Anti-novel
A novel which self-consciously transgresses the existing conventions of fiction, such as ▷ Sterne's ▷ *Tristram Shandy* or the French ▷ *nouveau roman*. The term dates from the 17th century, but became fashionable in the 1950s. As Frank Kermode has pointed out in *The Sense of an Ending*, many novels were anti-novels in their day, but helped to create new conventions which were then broken in their turn.

***Antiquary, The* (1816)**
A novel by ▷ Walter Scott, the third of his 'Waverley Novels', set in Scotland in the 18th century. The main story is an ordinary romance. A young officer, Major Neville, falls in love with Isabella Wardour, whose father rejects him on account of his supposed illegitimacy. Neville follows the father and daughter to Scotland, where the three have sundry adventures; Neville saves their lives and rescues Sir Arthur Wardour from impending ruin. He also turns out to be the son and heir of a Scottish nobleman. Thus the objections to the union between Neville and Isabella are removed. The distinction of the novel arises from the subsidiary characters: Jonathan Oldbuck, a learned antiquarian scholar (like Scott himself), and Edie Ochiltree, a wandering beggar who epitomizes the feelings and traditions of the Lowland Scottish peasantry. Scott states in his preface that he agrees with Wordsworth's opinion (expressed in the Preface to the *Lyrical Ballads*) that the peasantry have an eloquence in expressing the basic and most universal passions which is lost to the educated classes.

Antithesis
▷ Figures of Speech.

Aphasia
Generally used to designate language disorder. However, in literary criticism it has been given a more specific definition by the linguistician and supporter of the Russian ▷ Formalist movement, ▷ Roman Jakobson. Jakobson begins with the observation that language functions through the *selection* and *combination* of its elements into units such as words and sentences. *Combination* is a term used to designate the process whereby a linguistic ▷ sign can generate meaning only through its relationship with other signs which provide a context for it. *Selection* permits the substitution of one element for another from the total number of elements that make up the linguistic code as a whole, and which both speaker (addresser) and listener (addressee) share. The addresser encodes a particular message, and the addressee decodes or interprets it. Any interference with either the selection or combination of linguistic units which form an utterance, such as an unusual use in a literary work, is designated as aphasia, and this disordering serves, by contrast, to reveal the ways in which language operates normally.

Aphorism, apophthegm
A terse sentence, weighted with sense; with more weight of wisdom than an ▷ epigram need have, but less elegance.

Apocalypse
From Greek 'disclosure'. A kind of visionary literature, especially *Revelation* in the ▷ Bible. An apocalyptic mood (the expectation of the end of the world as we know it, or at least the anticipation of radical social transformation) is a feature of some ▷ modernist fiction, notably ▷ D.H. Lawrence's ▷ *The Rainbow* and ▷ *Women in Love*.
Bib: Kermode, F., *The Sense of an Ending: Studies in the Theory of Fiction*.

Apollo
▷ Classical mythology.

Apollyon
In the Bible, *Revelation* 9:11, Apollyon is 'the angel of the bottomless pit'. He is chiefly famous in English literature for his appearance in ▷ Bunyan's ▷ *Pilgrim's Progress*, where he is identifiable with Satan. Apollyon means 'destroying'.

Apologia, Apology
In ordinary speech, *apology* has the sense of an expression of regret for offensive conduct, but as a literary term it commonly has the older meaning still conveyed by *apologia*: defence, *eg* ▷ Sir Philip Sidney's ▷ *Apologie for Poetrie*, or explanation, vindication, *eg* ▷ Cardinal Newman's *Apologia pro Vita sua*.

Apologue
A little story, very often a ▷ fable, with a moral.

Apophthegm
▷ Aphorism.

Apostrophe
▷ Figures of Speech.

Arabian Nights Entertainments

Also known as *The Thousand and One Nights*, this collection of stories supposed to be told by Scheherazade was probably put together by an Egyptian story-teller around the 15th century. The stories became well-known and popular in Europe early in the 18th century. English translations have been made by Edward Lane in 1840 and, with greater literary merit, by Sir Richard Burton in 1885–88. They provided, with the Bible, the chief source of opulent and dramatic reading approved for and available to 19th-century children.

▷ Children's books.

Bib: Caracciolo, P., *The Arabian Nights in English Literature*.

Arbuthnot, Dr John (1667–1735)

Close friend of Alexander Pope, ▷ Jonathan Swift and John Gay, with whom he collaborated in the satiric sallies of the ▷ Scriblerus Club. Arbuthnot was physician in ordinary to Queen Anne and a Fellow of the Royal Society; he was widely admired for his medical science and for his genial wit. His most famous satire is 'The History of John Bull' (1712), a series of pamphlets advocating an end to the war with France which turned the arguments of Swift's *Conduct of the Allies* into a comic allegory. He also had a hand in such collaborative Scriblerian satires as *The Memoirs of Martin Scriblerus* (1741), *The Art of Sinking in Poetry* (1727) and *Three Hours after Marriage* (1717). Among his more important scientific writings are his *Essay on the Usefulness of Mathematical Learning* (1701) and his *Essay concerning the nature of Aliments* (1731).

Bib: Aitken, G. A. (ed.), *The Life and Works of Dr John Arbuthnot*; Beattie, L. M., *John Arbuthnot, mathematician and satirist*.

Arcadia, The (1578 and 1590)

▷ Phillip Sidney's pastoral ▷ romance, *The Arcadia* exists in two distinct versions. The 'old' *Arcadia* was begun c 1578, and circulated widely in manuscript form before Sidney undertook to revise it in 1584 – a task which was interrupted by his death in 1586. This revised (though incomplete) version – the 'new' *Arcadia* – was published in 1590. In 1593 Sidney's sister, Mary Herbert, Countess of Pembroke, to whom the work had been dedicated, undertook to publish a composite version of the text, which combined the two versions in existence together with her own (substantial) emendations. Thus *The Arcadia*, which enjoyed enormous popularity in the 16th and for much of the 17th century, was a curious hybrid.

In its original version the work was a mixture of love and intrigue, but in its revised form, Sidney broadened the scope of his undertaking. The episodic narrative of lovers, derived from Sidney's reading in late Greek romance, was transformed into what Sidney termed 'an absolute heroical poem' the purpose of which, in accordance with the critical precepts which had been established in *An Apologie for Poetrie*, was to instil 'delightful teaching'. From the first appearance of the work, critical opinion has been divided as to its seriousness. Some of Sidney's contemporaries understood *The Arcadia* as a profound meditation on morals and politics. For other writers, in particular John Milton, the work was no more than an exercise in escapist fantasy.

Bib: Editions include: Evans, M. (ed.), *The Countess of Pembroke's Arcadia*; Duncan Jones, K. (ed.), *The Old Arcadia*.

Archaeology

This term is commonly used to describe the scientific study of the remains of prehistoric times. However, in the 20th century the French philosopher ▷ Michel Foucault has sought to redefine it in such a way that the focus of attention becomes not objects, or documents, but the very ▷ discourses through which they come to have meaning. In other words, 'archaeology' does not designate the process of returning to some sort of 'origin' or basis which has an existence outside or beyond language (*ie* the bottom layer of a 'dig'); rather it concerns itself with what Foucault himself describes as 'the systematic description of a discourse-object' (*The Archaeology of Knowledge*, 1972). Foucault contends that knowledge is produced within social contexts where questions of power, politics, economics and morality intersect. It is the purpose of archaeology to rediscover discursive formations in all their complexity as indices of the ways in which society is organized and it is therefore interdisciplinary in its historical concerns. This form of analysis is to be distinguished from a more traditional 'history of ideas' which privileges evolution and development. From around 1970 Foucault abandoned the term in favour of 'genealogy' (borrowed from ▷ Nietzsche) or 'cartography', terms which he used to further emphasize the importance of power in the formation of knowledge.

Bib: Foucault, M. *The Archaeology of Knowledge* (1969; translated into English, 1972); Sheridan, A., *Michel Foucault: The Will to Truth*.

Aristotle (384–322 BC)

A Greek philosopher, born at Stageira, and so sometimes called the Stagirite. He was first a pupil of ▷ Plato, later developing his thought on principles opposed to those of his master. He was tutor to the young Alexander (the Great). His thought covered varied fields of knowledge, in most of which he has been influential. His best known works are his *Ethics*, *Politics*, and *Poetics*.

The difference between Aristotle and Plato has been described as follows: Plato makes us think in the first place of an ideal and supernatural world by turning our minds to ideal forms which are the truth in terms of which imperfect earthly things can be known and judged; Aristotle turns us towards the natural world where things are what they are, perfect or imperfect, so that knowledge comes through study and classification of them in the actual world. It can thus be seen that whilst Plato leads in the direction of mysticism, Aristotle leads towards science. Until the 13th century, Christian thought tended to be dominated by Plato, but medieval Christian thought, owing to the work of Thomas Aquinas (c 1225–74), found Aristotelianism more acceptable.

Armah, Ayi Kwei (b 1938)

Ghanaian novelist, educated at schools in Accra and Massachusetts and at Harvard and Columbia universities. He has worked as a translator, a television scriptwriter, an English teacher and an editor. His novels express nationalist feeling and a strong sense of anger, combined in *The Beautyful Ones Are Not Yet Born* (1968) and *Fragments* (1970) with elements of the comic, though the ironically-titled *Why Are We So Blest?* (1972) is a horrific and fragmented narrative of the sexual exploitation of an African man by a European woman and the violence that follows. He has drawn on Akan culture for organizing structures (generally cyclical): *Fragments* is shaped by its Akan chapter headings and *The Healers* (1978) uses the structure of Akan folk stories for an historical account of the fall of the Asante Empire; *Two Thousand Seasons* (1973) is also a historical novel.
Bib: Fraser, R. *The Novels of Ayi Kwei Armah: A Study in Polemical Fiction.*

Arnold, Matthew (1822–88)

Poet, critic and educationalist, son of ▷ Thomas Arnold. Most of Arnold's verse was published by the time he was 45: *The Strayed Reveller* (1849); *Empedocles on Etna* (1852); *Poems* (1853); *Poems, Second Series* (1855); *Merope, a Tragedy* (1858); *New Poems* (1867).

As Arnold began to abandon poetry writing, his essay and prose writing career took off; as a critic, he was strongly influential on early 20th-century thought, as a crucial figure in the development of English studies as a discipline in its own right. Mediated by the works of T. S. Elliot, I. A. Richards, Lionel Trilling, ▷ F. R. Leavis and the journal ▷ *Scrutiny*, his cultural criticism forms a lynch-pin of traditional English criticism. This influence does not come from his studies of individual writers but from his studies of contemporary culture and of the relationship, actual and potential, of literature to industrial civilization. His best known critical works are ▷ *Essays in Criticism*, First and Second Series, 1865 and 1888; *On Translating Homer*, 1861; and *Culture and Anarchy*, 1869.

Arnold's work as an inspector of schools and educationist was related to his most serious critical preoccupations, and the two worlds meet in such a work as *Culture and Anarchy*. His educational theories and absolute valuing of culture were pitted against the ▷ Utilitarianism of historical moment. Arnold posited a system of humane education under the headship of an ideal, liberal state, as the means of ensuring the triumph of culture over social and spiritual anarchy.
Bib: Trilling, L., *Matthew Arnold*; Jump, J. D., *Matthew Arnold*; Brown, E. K., *Arnold: a Study in Conflict*: Tinker, C. B. and Lowry, H. F., *The Poetry of Arnold*; Honan, P., *Matthew Arnold; a Life*; Carroll, J., *The Cultural Theory of Matthew Arnold*; Baldick, C., *The Social Mission of English Criticism*.

Arnold, Thomas (1795–1842)

Influential Broad Church liberal ▷ Protestant, headmaster of ▷ Rugby School, and an important figure in the development of the ▷ public school system and its values. The father of ▷ Matthew Arnold, he became professor of Modern History at Oxford University in 1841. Famously characterized in Thomas Hughes's *Tom Brown's Schooldays* (1857).

Arts Council of Great Britain

This body began as the Council for the Encouragement of Music and Art in 1940, to promote theatrical and musical entertainment during World War II. It now provides funding for a great variety of arts projects, including conferences, educational events and grants to writers, publishers and theatrical companies. Its purpose is 'to develop a greater knowledge, understanding, and practice of the Fine Arts, to increase their accessibility to the public, and to improve their standard of execution'. Although its distribution of funds has often been contentious, its existence has helped the proliferation of theatre companies during the last two decades.

Aspects of the Novel (1927)

A critical work on the novel by ▷ E.M. Forster, based on his Clark Lectures delivered in the University of Cambridge. Well known for its engaging conversational style, the book anticipates aspects of ▷ narratology in its consideration of point of view and ▷ flat and round characters, but is sharply distinguished from later narratology, as well as from the more earnest and prescriptive approach of ▷ Henry James's Prefaces, by Forster's jaunty scepticism about any pretensions to abstract rigour.

Assonance

▷ Figures of Speech.

Astell, Mary (1666–1731)

Now claimed as 'the first English feminist', Mary Astell was a writer and intellectual, who published influential tracts on the duties and injustices of marriage, the most famous being *A Serious Proposal to the Ladies for the Advancement of their true and greatest Interest* (1694), which appeared anonymously as the work of 'a Lover of Her Sex'. With the help of several patrons, most notably William Sancroft, the archbishop of Canterbury, Astell was able to live independently in London and make a career of writing. Her views on the equality of the sexes were, however, modified by her conservative politics and her religious commitment to the Anglican Church. A wife's status in relation to her husband was, she argued, in the nature of a voluntary contract, but: 'It may be any Man's Business and Duty to keep Hogs; he was not Made for this, but if he hires himself out to such and Employment, he ought conscientiously to perform it'.
Bib: Perry, Ruth, *The Celebrated Mary Astell.*

Atheism

Disbelief in God. In the Middle Ages and the 16th and 17th centuries, atheism was abhorrent; it was equivalent to a denial of conscience. There were some who adopted this position and effectively challenged the power of organized religion – Christopher Marlowe was charged with it in 1593.

Nevertheless atheism at this period was different from the systematic belief that man's reason suffices for his welfare. This belief grew in the 18th century and emerged in the ▷ French Revolution, influencing such English intellectuals as ▷ William Godwin and through him P. B. Shelley, whose atheism caused him to be expelled from Oxford, and for whom Platonism sufficed (▷ Plato). Different, but still 18th-century in its sources, was the atheism of ▷ Utilitarians such as James Mill (1773–1836) and ▷ John Stuart Mill, who were less naïve about Reason than Godwin but, as practical men, saw religion as unnecessary in their scheme for human betterment. The scientific ideas of the ▷ Victorian period, especially those of ▷ Charles Darwin and ▷ Thomas Huxley, were more productive of ▷ agnosticism than of atheism. Modern atheism is exemplified by the Rationalist Press, but it remains a minority attitude among writers, in contrast to agnosticism, which is rather commoner than professed faith.

Athenaeum, The

Founded in 1828, it was one of the most enlightened periodicals of the 19th century. It was honest and independent in literary criticism, and a leader of the movement to spread education among the working classes. In 1831 it reduced its price by half in order to reach this wider public, and in consequence increased its circulation six times. It was also very progressive in social reform. In 1921 it was incorporated in the *Nation and Athenaeum*, which in turn was merged in 1931 with the socialist weekly. ▷ *The New Statesman*.

Atwood, Margaret (b 1939)

Canadian novelist, poet and short-story writer. Born in Ottawa, she spent part of her early years in the wilds of northern Quebec, and her poetry makes considerable metaphorical use of the wilderness and its animals. Her first two novels are poetic accounts of the heroines' search for self-realization, and each has a dominant central metaphor: emotional cannibalism in *The Edible Woman* (1969) and drowning and surfacing in *Surfacing* (1972). *Lady Oracle* (1976) is a more comic and satirical work, portraying the limitations of middle-class Canadian life. Her poetry, which is unrhymed, shares many themes with her novels; *The Journals of Susanna Moodie: Poems* (1970) employs pioneering as a metaphor for contemporary feminist questioning of gender roles. Her more recent novels have broader social themes: *Bodily Harm* (1981) is a political satire set on a Caribbean island, while *The Handmaid's Tale* (1986) is a vision of a futuristic dystopia, influenced by ▷ George Orwell's *1984*. It focuses on the exploitation of women in a state ruled by religious fundamentalism, and the ambivalent, ironic conclusion promotes a complex sense of the novel's relevance to our own times. The novel *Cat's Eye* (1989) and the collection of short stories *Wilderness Tips* (1991) return to her Canadian background, evoking with acute irony the middle-class Canada of the 1950s, 1960s and 1970s. Atwood's interest in Canadian nationalism and in feminism have made

her an important figure in contemporary Canadian culture.

Other novels include: *Life Before Man* (1979). Story collections: *Dancing Girls* (1977); *Murder in the Dark* (1984); *Bluebeard's Egg* (1986). Volumes of poetry include: *Selected Poems* (1976); *Marsh, Hawk* (1977); *Two Headed Poems* (1978); *True Stories* (1981); *Notes Towards a Poem That Can Never Be Written* (1981); *Snake Poems* (1983); *Interlunar* (1984). Criticism: *Second Words: Selected Critical Prose* (1982).

▷ Post-colonial Literature.
Bib: Rigney, B. H., *Margaret Atwood*.

Aubrey, John (1626–97)

Biographer and antiquary. Aubrey was a man of endlessly fascinated speculation on every aspect of the world in which he found himself. Entirely without any form of method, he nevertheless produced (though never published) an invaluable record of people, events and happenings of the period in which he lived. Frequently the record of personalities preserved by Aubrey is highly untrustworthy in terms of its factual content, and yet his *Brief Lives* are still an important document not least because of their often penetrating assessment of his subjects' lives and works. If nothing else, Aubrey has preserved a running critical commentary on many of the figures from the 17th century whose works are read in the 20th century.

▷ Biography.
Bib: Dick, O. L. (ed.), *Aubrey's Brief Lives*.

Austen, Jane (1775–1817)

Novelist. Her novels in order of publication are as follows: ▷ *Sense and Sensibility* (1811), ▷ *Pride and Prejudice* (1813), ▷ *Mansfield Park* (1814), ▷ *Emma* (1816), ▷ *Northanger Abbey* and ▷ *Persuasion* (1818). The last two, published posthumously, are her first and last work respectively in order of composition. Fragments and early drafts include: *Lady Susan* (pub 1871), *The Watsons* (1871) and *Sanditon*, on which she was working when she died, published in 1925.

She restricted her material to a narrow range of society and events: a prosperous, middle-class circle in provincial surroundings. However, she treated this material with such subtlety of observation and depth of penetration that she is ranked among the best of English novelists. A French critic, Louis Cazamian, writes of her method that it is 'so classical, so delicately shaded . . . that we are strongly reminded of the great French analysts'. Her classicism arises from respect for the sane, clear-sighted judgement of the Augustan age that had preceded her, but its vitality is enhanced by the Romanticism of her own period, so that her heroines acquire wisdom by a counter-balancing of the two. She brought the English novel, as an art form, to its maturity, and the wide range which that form covered later in the 19th century owed much to the imaginative assurance which she had given it.

Her life as a clergyman's daughter was outwardly uneventful but it is probably not true that this accounts for the absence of sensationalism in her novels; her circle of relatives and friends was such as could have given her a wide experience of contemporary society. The restriction of the subject matter of her fiction seems to have been dictated by artistic considerations. D. W. Harding's essay 'Regulated Hatred: An Aspect of the Work of Jane Austen' (*Scrutiny*, 1940) credits her with being a caustic satirist and critic of society.

Bib: Austen-Leigh, J. E., *A Memoir of Jane Austen*; Lascelles, M., *Jane Austen and her Art*; Mudrick, M., *Jane Austen: Irony as Defence and Discovery*; Trilling, L., 'Mansfield Park' in *The Opposing Self*; Leavis, Q. D., *A Critical Theory of Jane Austen's Writings* (*Scrutiny* x, xiii); Southam, B. C. (ed.), *Jane Austen: The Critical Heritage*; Cecil, D., *A Portrait of Jane Austen*; Tanner, T., *Jane Austen*; Butler, M., *Jane Austen and the War of Ideas*.

Authorized Version of the Bible
▷ Bible in England.

Autobiography
The word came into English at the very end of the 18th century. In the 19th and 20th centuries the writing of the story of one's own life has become a common literary activity. However, the practice already had an ancient history, and English autobiography may be divided into three overlapping historical segments: 1 the spiritual confession; 2 the memoir; 3 the autobiographical novel.

1 The spiritual confession has as its basic type the Confessions of St Augustine of Hippo (345–430) who described his conversion to Christianity. Such records of the inner life existed in the English Middle Ages. *eg* the *Book of Margery Kempe* (15th century), but the great age for them was the 17th century, when the ▷ Puritans, depending on the Word of God in the Bible and the inner light of their own consciences, made a practice of intensive self-examination. By far the best known of these records is ▷ Bunyan's ▷ *Grace Abounding to the Chief of Sinners* (1666). It is characteristic of such works that they contain detailed accounts of the emotional life, but little factual description of events.

2 The memoir, on the other hand, of French derivation, originates largely in the 17th century and owes much to the practice of extensive letter-writing which then developed, *eg* the letters of Madame de Sévigné (1626–96). An unusual early example of this class is the autobiography of the musician Thomas Whythorne (1528–96), published in 1964 and entitled *A Book of Songs and Sonetts*. An example from 18th-century England is the fragmentary *Memoirs* (pub. 1796) by the historian ▷ Edward Gibbon. But the objective memoir and the subjective confessions came together in the *Confessions* of the French-Swiss ▷ Jean-Jacques Rousseau, and this is the most prevalent form of the outstanding English autobiographies of the 19th century. The varieties of this form are extensive: they may be a record of emotional struggles and experiences, *eg* ▷ *The Confessions of an English Opium Eater* by ▷ Thomas de Quincey; ▷ *Sartor Resartus* by ▷ Thomas Carlyle. They may be essentially a history of the growth of ideas, convictions, and the strengthening of vocation, in the life of the writer, *eg Autobiography* (1873) by ▷ John Stuart Mill; *My Apprenticeship* (1926) by ▷

Beatrice Webb; *Apologia pro Vita Sua* (1864) by ▷ Cardinal Newman. In any case, an autobiographical element becomes prominent in works which are not strictly autobiographies from the early 19th century on; *eg* ▷ Wordsworth's *Prelude, or Growth of a Poet's Mind* (first version 1805); the periodical essays of ▷ Charles Lamb in *Essays of Elia* (1820–3) ▷ Coleridge's mixture of autobiography with philosophy and literary criticism in ▷ *Biographia Literaria* (1817). It may be said that from 1800 on it becomes the instinct of writers of many kinds to use autobiographical material, or to adopt from time to time an autobiographical standpoint.

3 Thus we come to the autobiographical novel: this begins with the novels of ▷ Charlotte Brontë (▷ *Jane Eyre*, 1847, and ▷ *Villette*, 1853), and ▷ Charles Dickens's ▷ *David Copperfield* (1849–50). This method of writing a novel really came into its own however, with ▷ Samuel Butler's ▷ *Way of all Flesh* (1903), which led to many successors in the 20th century, notably ▷ James Joyce's ▷ *Portrait of the Artist as a Young Man* (1916), and ▷ D. H. Lawrence's ▷ *Sons and Lovers* (1913). The links between identity, culture and politics have made the autobiographical novel an important form of ▷ post- colonial and feminist fiction, *eg* ▷ George Lamming, *In the Castle of My Skin* (1953), ▷ Bessie Head, *A Question of Power* (1973).

Awkward Age, The (1899)
A novel by ▷ Henry James. Nanda Brookenham is a young girl brought up in a smart but corrupt section of London society; her mother and her mother's circle are willing to carry on immoral intrigues so long as respectable appearances are scrupulously protected. Nanda is in love with Vanderbank, who, as she learns later, is her mother's lover, and she feels some affection for Mitchett, a young man of less charm than Vanderbank, but with an attractive simplicity of heart. Unlike the other members of her mother's circle, she is free and candid in her feelings and open in her conduct; this alarms Vanderbank and inhibits him from declaring his love for her. Her elderly friend, Mr Longdon, an admirer of her dead grandmother, gives Nanda a dowry to attract Vanderbank, but this only increases the latter's fastidious reluctance to declare himself. Meanwhile, the Duchess, Mrs Brookenham's friend and rival, conspires to capture Mitchett for her own daughter, Aggie, whose appearance of immaculate innocence immediately breaks down when it has served its purpose of qualifying her for the marriage market. Vanderbank's mixture of scrupulousness and timidity remains a permanent barrier between himself and Nanda. Mr Longdon adopts her, and they remain together in their love of truthful feeling, isolated from the sophisticated but essentially trivial society which has hitherto constituted Nanda's environment.

The novel is an example of James's interest in the survival of integrity in a materialistic society blinded by its own carefully cultivated artificiality.

Awoonor, Kofi (b 1935)
Ghanaian novelist and poet, educated at University College of Ghana, University College London and

the State University of New York. He has worked as a university lecturer and professor in Ghana and the USA, as a film director and for the Ghana Ministry of Information. He was imprisoned in Ghana during 1975–76 for alleged subversion; in 1983 he was appointed as Ghana's ambassador to Brazil. His first novel, *This Earth, My Brother* (1971) consists of prose chapters interspersed with poetic fragments; a dead girl, cousin of the novel's hero, is symbolically identified with the Ghanaian nation and with the figure of 'Manny Watta', a mythical water spirit. His other works include: *Night of My Blood* (1971); *Ride Me Memory* (1973); *Guardians of the Sacred Wand* (1794); *The Breast of the Earth* (1975); *Comes the Voyager at Last: A Tale of Return to Africa* (1992). Volumes of poetry: *Rediscovery and Poems* (1964); *The House by the Sea* (1978); *The Morning After: Selected Poems 1963–85* (1985).

Bib: Morell, K. (ed.), *In Person*.

B

Babes in the Wood
▷ Children in the Wood.

Badman, The Life and Death of Mr (1680)
A moral ▷allegory by ▷John Bunyan, author of
▷The Pilgrim's Progress, and, apart from the more
famous work, the only one of Bunyan's fictions
to remain widely known. It is the biography of a
wicked man told by Mr Wiseman, and contains
vivid and dramatic detail. Its realism of detail and
its psychology make it one of the forerunners of
the novel.

Baedeker, Karl (1801–59)
The author of famous guide-books, which were
carried on by his son and eventually covered most
of the civilized world. Their frequent mention in
English 19th- and 20th-century fiction shows how
indispensable they were to English middle- and
upper-class tourists of the last 100 years, especially in
visits to countries in which monuments and works of
art are plentiful, such as Italy. He wrote in German
but English editions were produced after his death,
from 1861 onwards.
Bib: Pemble, J., *The Mediterranean Passion*.

Bagehot, Walter (1826–77)
A writer on political and economic affairs, best known
for his book *The English Constitution* (1867) which,
despite historical change, is still a classic study of the
spirit of English politics and notably of the function
of monarchy in providing the imaginative appeal
of the state and ensuring the dignity of government
without hindering desirable conflict of opinion.

Bagehot was also the author of a number of critical
essays, the best known of which is *Wordsworth,
Tennyson, and Browning or Pure, Ornate, and Grotesque
Art in English Poetry* (1864). It is republished in
English Critical Essays ed. by E. D. Jones (World's
Classics).
Bib: Stephen, Leslie in *Studies of a Biographer*,
Buchan, A., *The Spare Chancellor*, St John-Stevas, N.
A. F., *Life*.

Bainbridge, Beryl (b 1933)
Novelist. Brought up near Liverpool, she worked as
an actress before writing her first novel (though not
the first to be published), *Harriet Said* (1972), which
concerns two girls involved in a murder. Initially
seen as a writer of macabre thrillers, she has gained
an increasing following and has gradually attracted
more serious critical attention. Her novels are
characterized by black humour, economy of style and
portraits of lower-middle-class manners with a strong
element of the ▷ Gothic and grotesque. *The Bottle
Factory Outing* (1974) centres on the relationship
of two women on an increasingly sinister works
outing which leads to the death of one of them.
Confused and sordid lives are observed in a detached
and ironic manner. *A Quiet Life* (1976) is a partly
autobiographical tale of family eccentricities and the
tragic precariousness of love, while *Winter Garden*
(1980) draws on a visit Bainbridge made to the Soviet
Union to create a chilling though comic account of
confusion and intrigue on a tour of that country.

Other novels are: *A Weekend with Claude* (1967);
Another Part of the Wood (1968); *The Dressmaker*
(1973); *Sweet William* (1975); *Injury Time* (1977);
Young Adolf (1978); *Watson's Apology* (1984); *Filthy
Lucre* (1986); *An Awfully Big Adventure* (1989); *The
Birthday Boys* (1991).

Bakhtin, Mikhail (1895–1975)
Bakhtin's first major work was *Problems in Dostoevsky's
Poetics* (1929), but his most famous work, *Rabelais and
His World*, did not appear until 1965. Two books,
Freudianism: a Marxist Critique (1927), and *Marxism
and the Philosophy of Language* (1930) were published
under the name of V. N. Volosinov, and a third, *The
Formal Method in Literary Scholarship* (1928) appeared
under the name of his colleague P. N. Medvedev.
Bakhtin's concern throughout is to show how ▷
ideology functions in the process of the production of
the linguistic ▷ sign and to develop and identify the
concept of 'dialogism' as it operates in literary texts.
In Bakhtin's words 'In dialogue a person not only
shows himself outwardly, but he becomes for the first
time that which he is, not only for others but himself
as well. To be means to communicate dialogically.'
The dialogic is contrasted to the monologic, which
speaks with a single voice. Bakhtin argued that
the novel was a form of literature uniquely open to
historical change and to the future. His work has
in recent years enjoyed a revival, particularly among
critics. Especially important is the way in which he
theorizes and politicizes the concepts of festivity and
▷ carnival. Also one of his concerns is to identify the
dialectical relationship between those various 'texts'
of which any one literary work is comprised. This
notion of ▷ 'intertextuality' is currently used within
areas such as ▷ feminism and ▷ deconstruction.
Much of Bakhtin's work was suppressed during his
life-time and not published until his death.
Bib: Holquist, M. (ed.), *The Dialogic Imagination:
Four Essays by M. M. Bakhtin*.

Ballantyne R.M. (1825–94)
Writer of adventure stories, aimed primarily
at boys, the most famous being *The Coral island*
(1858), probably the most popular such work of the
Victorian era. This story, in which a trio of boys
are shipwrecked on a Pacific island, is implicitly
a colonial fable (▷ colonialism), full of bloody and
masculine resourcefulness. Ballantyne's life was
suitably adventurous: born in Edinburgh, he received
little formal education but worked as a fur trader
in northern Canada from the age of 16. This
experience produced *Hudson's Bay* (1848) and *The
Young Fur Traders* (1856). After establishing himself
as an author he continued to travel to research the
background to his novels, which included: *Martin
Rattler, Or A Boy's Adventure in the Forests of Brazil*
(1858), *Pirate City* (1874), set in Algiers, and *A Tale
of the London Fire Brigade* (1867).

Ballard, J.G. (James Graham) (b 1930)
Novelist and short-story writer. Ballard is closely
identified with the ▷ science fiction genre, primarily
because his more widely read novels and short
stories, though essentially uncategorizable, fit most

readily into the sci-fi/fantasy bracket. However, whilst his obsessions with mental decay, violence and its imagery, and the fragmentation of contemporary culture are filtered through the landscapes of more conventional fantasy writing, his allegiance with mainstream fantasy or science fiction is uneasy, and his later writing, particularly the Booker Prize shortlisted *Empire of the Sun* (1984), has moved nearer to realism, drawing upon Ballard's own childhood experiences. His works include: *The Drowned World* (1962); *The Terminal Beach* (1964); *The Drought* (1965); *The Crystal World* (1966); *The Atrocity Exhibition* (1970); *Crash* (1973); *The Unlimited Dream Company* (1979); *The Day of Creation* (1987); *The Kindness of Women* (1991).

Balzac, Honoré de (1799–1850)

French novelist. His *La Comédie humaine* is a panorama of French society from the ▷ Revolution to the July Monarchy (1830). It is bound together by the use of recurrent characters (Vautrin is one notable instance, Rastignac another) and recurrent motifs (notably the necessity of moral and social order contrasted with the pressures of the individual ego). Among the one hundred novels which Balzac completed, drafted or projected are *Eugénie Grandet* (1833), *Illusions perdues* (1837–43), *La Cousine Bette* (1846), *Le Cousin Pons* (1847), *Le Père Goriot* (1835), *Splendeurs et misères des courtisanes* (1847).

French society was to be the historian,' Balzac wrote, 'I had only to be the scribe'. His ways of depicting French society are geographical, historical, political and even geological insofar as all social strata find a place. These different representations, taken individually or in combination, bring into play a dynamic explained in *La Peau de chagrin* (1831) as the product of desire and power, with knowledge enlisted to restrain them. But such a restraint is rare or non-existent, and society in the *Comédie humaine* is driven by a restlessness which tends to exhaustion as it competes for the fulfilment of desire. Like society, character too is open to multiple descriptions, as a machine driven by abstracts (passion, ambition, penury, for instance) or as a representative of a human or social type. In that respect, character has a potential for expansion. It is always ready to merge into symbol (more than just the performance of symbolic actions) or be exaggerated into ▷ melodrama. Indeed, melodrama is a central Balzacian ingredient and, just as characters are actors, buildings and places too are subject to mutation into a theatre or a scene in which the novelistic events unfold. In its liking for myth and melodrama, Balzac's social realism is correspondingly more than the accumulation of surface detail, since the detail acts as an indicator of underlying causes. In turn, understanding of these causes is open only to the novelist defined by his capacity for 'second sight', the capacity to perceive pattern as well as pattern destroyed. And it is considerations of this kind which distinguish Balzac from other ▷ *feuilleton* novelists such as Eugène Sue (1804–57) and help account for his pervasive influence on 19th-century fiction, particularly in England where Balzac shaped the already strong vein of social ▷ realism.

Bib: Prendergast, C., *Balzac: Fiction and Melodrama*; Bellos, D., *Balzac: Le Père Goriot*.

Baptists

An important sect of Nonconformist Protestants; originally one of the three principal branches of English ▷ Puritanism, the other two being the Independents (Congregationalists), and the Presbyterians (Calvinists). Their especial doctrine is to maintain that the rite of baptism must be administered to adults, and not to infants. They began as an offshoot of the Independents in the first decade of the 17th century, and made rapid progress between 1640 and 1660 – the period of the Civil War and the Interregnum, when the Puritans usurped the position of the ▷ Church of England. One of the foremost exponents of the Baptist Church in the second half of the 17th century was ▷ John Bunyan (1628–88).

Barbauld, Mrs Anna Laetitia (1743–1824)

Best known as the editor of ▷ Samuel Richardson's correspondence, Mrs Barbauld also published several volumes of tales for children. After the suicide of her husband in 1808, she embarked on a major series of literary editions, bringing out *The British Novelists* in 50 volumes. She was also a prominent member of the ▷ Bluestocking circle.

Barker, Clive (b 1952)

Novelist, playwright, painter, screenwriter and director. Born, raised and educated in Liverpool, Barker wrote a number of plays (*The Magician*, *The History of the Devil*) before achieving fame as a leading light of Britain's 'new wave' of horror writers (▷ horror fiction). In 1987, *Hellraiser* established Barker as a maverick directorial talent; he currently lives in Hollywood where he continues to write and direct. Barker's early short stories (collected in *The Books of Blood* volumes 1 to 6, 1984–5) celebrate cultural multiplicity and sexual perversity, inverting the traditional conservatism of the horror genre. Describing himself as 'a proselytizer on behalf of horror', Barker has sought both on the page and screen to subvert concepts of 'monstrousness'. Most ambitiously, his lengthy novel *Cabal* (1988, filmed as *Nightbreed*, 1990) posits a tribe of variegated shape-shifters in whose bizarre disfigurement the reader is encouraged to delight. Barker's later works (*Weaveworld*, 1987; *Imajica*, 1991) have eschewed the visceral revelry which characterized his short stories, and explored the worlds of mythology and fantasy. Despite his huge success as a writer/film-maker, Barker maintains that painting is his first love.
Bib: Jones, S. (ed.), *Shadows in Eden*.

Barnaby Rudge (1841)

A novel by ▷ Charles Dickens, published as part of ▷ *Master Humphrey's Clock*. The only other novel that he published in this proposed series was ▷ *The Old Curiosity Shop*; Dickens then abandoned it.

It is set in the 18th century and its central episodes are descriptions of the fierce anti-Catholic disorders called 'the Gordon Riots', which terrorized London for several days in 1780. These vivid scenes, and the

characters directly concerned in the riots (such as
the half-wit Barnaby Rudge, the locksmith Gabriel
Varden and his apprentice Simon Tappertit),
constitute the part of the book which is most
memorable and most representative of Dickens's
style. The main story is a romantic one about the
love affair of Emma Haredale, whose father has been
mysteriously murdered, and Edward Chester, the
son of Sir John Chester, a suave villain who helps
to instigate the Riots. Sir John and Emma's uncle,
Geoffrey Haredale, a Catholic, are enemies, but they
unite in opposition to the marriage of Edward and
Emma. During the riots, Geoffrey Haredale's house
is burnt down but Edward saves the lives of both
Emma and her uncle, and thus wins his approval of
the match. The murderer of Emma's father turns out
to be the father of Barnaby.

Barnaby Rudge is one of Dicken's two historical
novels, the other being ▷ *A Tale of Two Cities*.

Barnes, Julian (b 1946)

Novelist. Born in Leicester and educated in London
and Oxford, Barnes has worked as a lexicographer
on the O.E.D. Supplement (1969–1972), and
in journalism, writing for the *New Statesman*, *The
Sunday Times*, *The Observer*, and as the notorious
gossip columnist 'Edward Pygge' in the journal of
modern literature, the *New Review*, which ran from
1974 to 1979 under poet and critic Ian Hamilton's
editorship. Barnes's work is greatly influenced by
French 19th-century novelist ▷ Gustave Flaubert,
the ostensible subject of the playful and very
successful 1984 novel *Flaubert's Parrot*, which was
shortlisted for the 1985 Booker Prize and won
the Geoffrey Faber Memorial Prize. Barnes's
work is typically witty and parodic: *A History of
the World in 10½ Chapters* (1989), an example of
▷ post-modernist ▷ historiographic ▷ metafiction,
consists of a series of episodes, some comic, but
with a satirical and even tragic edge. Other novels:
Metroland (1981); *Before She Met Me* (1982); *Staring at
the Sun* (1986); *Talking It Over* (1991); *The Porcupine*
(1992). Barnes also writes crime fiction, and under
the pseudonym Dan Kavanagh published *Duffy*
(1980); *Fiddle City* (1983) and *Putting Jack In*
(1985). In 1986 he won the E. M. Forster Award
from the American Academy of Arts and Letters.

Barrie, Sir J. M. (1860–1937)

Best known for his fantasy drama for children *Peter
Pan, or the Boy who wouldn't grow up* (1904), and for
plays such as *The Admirable Crichton* (1902), Barrie
had earlier written a number of works of fiction,
including *Sentimental Tommy* (1896), about the youth
of a working-class boy, *A Window in Thrums* (1889)
and *The Little Minister* (1891), a love story about a
Presbyterian minister. He also wrote a biography of
his mother, *Margaret Ogilvy* (1896). He was seen as
the most prominent of the 'Kailyard School', Scottish
writers of romantic fiction using vernacular language
and working-class settings.

Barsetshire

An imaginary English county invented by ▷ Anthony
Trollope for a series of novels, some of which centre

on an imaginary town in it, the cathedral city of
Barchester. It is a characteristic southern English
setting. The novels are the best known of his works.
Titles: ▷ *The Warden*, *Barchester Towers*, *Doctor
Thorne*, *Framley Parsonage*, *The Small House at
Allington*, *The Last Chronicle of Barset*.

Barstow, Stan (b 1928)

Novelist and short-story writer. His best-known
work is his first novel, *A Kind of Loving* (1960),
a first-person, present-tense narrative of a young
man forced to marry his pregnant girlfriend.
Barstow came to prominence as one of a group of
novelists from northern, working-class backgrounds,
including ▷ John Braine, ▷ Alan Sillitoe and Keith
Waterhouse. He has retained his commitment to
the realist novel (▷ realism) with a regional setting
and his suspicion of metropolitan and international
culture. *The Watcher on the Shore* (1966) and *The True
Right End* (1976) form a trilogy with *A Kind of Loving*.
Other novels are: *Ask Me Tomorrow* (1962); *Joby*
(1964); *A Raging Calm* (1968); *A Brother's Tale* (1980);
Just You Wait and See (1986); *B Movie* (1987). Story
collections include: *The Desperadoes* (1961); *A Season
with Eros* (1971); *A Casual Acquaintance* (1976); *The
Glad Eye* (1984).

Barthes, Roland (1915–80)

Probably the best known and most influential of all
the ▷ structuralist and ▷ post-structuralist critics. In
books such as *Writing Degree Zero* (1953), *Mythologies*
(1957), and *S/Z* (1970), Barthes undertook to expose
how language functioned, and its relationship with
▷ ideology. Moreover, he was also concerned
to uncover the distinctions between literary texts
which operated on the basis of a stable relationship
between signifier and signified (▷ sign), and those
for whom the act of signification (establishing
meaning) itself was of primary importance. The
terms he uses to distinguish between the two types
of text are 'readerly' (*lisible*) and 'writerly' (*scriptible*).
In later works, such as *The Pleasure of the Text*
(1975), he went on to investigate the sources of
pleasure which the text affords to the reader, and
distinguished between 'the text of pleasure' which
does not challenge the cultural assumptions of
the reader and which is therefore comforting, and
'the text of bliss' where the reader experiences a
'*jouissance*' from the unsettling effect elicited from
the text's representation of the crisis of language. In
addition to offering penetrating analyses of literary
texts, Barthes concerned himself with the structural
analysis of all cultural representations, including
topics such as advertising, film, photography, music
and wrestling.
Bib: Heath, S. (ed), *Image-Music-Text*; Lavers, A.,
Roland Barthes: Structuralism and After.

Bath

A city in the west of England with hot springs with
certain mineral properties which afford relief to
those with rheumatic diseases. In the 18th century,
largely owing to the energies of Richard (Beau) Nash
(1674–1762), the city became a brilliant social centre;

nearly everyone of eminence in politics, literature or the arts at some time visited or lived there. Hence its prominence in the literature of the time. Nash, who virtually ruled Bath, was a civilizing influence on fashionable society: by his discipline he improved the manners of the rich but ill-bred country gentry, and by refusing to allow the wearing of swords in public assemblies he helped to reduce the practice of duelling.

▷ Austen, Jane.

Bathos

▷ Figures of Speech.

Battle of the Books, The (1697, published 1704)

(A Full and True Account of the Battel Fought last Friday, Between the Ancient and the Modern Books in St James's Library.) A prose satire by ▷ Jonathan Swift, written while he was staying with ▷ Sir William Temple. Temple's essay on 'Ancient and Modern Learning', with its praise of the Epistles of Phalaris, had been attacked by the critics Wotton and Bentley, the latter proving that the Epistles were false. Swift's *Battle of the Books* satirizes the whole dispute, parodying the scholars' concern with minutiae. The ancients (*ie* the classical writers) are given the stronger claims, but overall the satire leaves the issue undecided.

Baxter, Richard (1615–91)

Theologian, religious writer and autobiographer. Baxter was one of the dominating figures in the period of the English Civil War. A chaplain to Oliver Cromwell's army, Baxter served after the Restoration as chaplain to Charles II, but he soon fell out with the king on religio-political grounds. Though an initial supporter of the Parliamentarian cause in the Civil War, Baxter's experiences in the New Model Army, in particular his exposure to the thinking of the Levellers, Seekers, ▷ Quakers and Behmenists, led him to adopt rather more conservative postures. In the 1650s his position changed once more and he emerged as a strong supporter of the Protectorate, dedicating his *Key for Catholics* (1659) to Richard Cromwell. Baxter's stance on religious issues has been defined as one of the earliest examples of ecumenicism. He composed over 100 works on religious topics, but his major work has come to be recognized as his spiritual autobiography *Reliquiae Baxterianae* (1696). This 800-page folio volume is one of the most important of 17th-century ▷ autobiographies.
Bib: Keeble, N. H. (ed.), *The Autobiography of Richard Baxter*; Webber, Joan, *The Eloquent 'I': Style and Self in Seventeenth-century Prose*.

Beaconsfield, Lord

▷ Disraeli, Benjamin.

Beardsley, Aubrey (1872–98)

An artist famous in the 1890s for his black and white illustrations to writers such as ▷ Oscar Wilde and Ernest Dowson. He contributed to the periodicals ▷ *The Yellow Book* (the first four covers of which he designed) and *The Savoy* (including his tale, *Under the Hill*), which were regarded as organs of the aesthetic movement. The flowing lines and sumptuous compositions of his illustrations expressed what was considered most bold and most daring in the movement.

▷ Aestheticism.

Beauclerc, Amelia (fl 1810–20)

Novelist. At present very little is known of Amelia Beauclerc's life and even her novels have occasionally been wrongly ascribed to another author. However, of her eight extant novels, *Alinda, or The Child of Mystery* (1812) includes carefully balanced scenes of transvestism and homoerotic encounters between women. Her female characters often triumph over difficulties encountered in their dealings with men and, as such, she could be considered proto-feminist. However, much of her work is conventional and uninspired, as, for example, her ▷ Gothic novel *Husband Hunters* (1816).

▷ Feminism.

Beauty and the Beast

A fairy story, best known in the French version of Madame de Villeneuve (1744). The theme is that of a young girl who learns to love a monster who holds her in his power; her freely given love transforms him into a young prince. Before she can go through this experience, however, she has to surrender her safe, tender relationship with the father who dotes on her.

▷ Fairy tales.

Beauvoir, Simone de

▷ De Beauvoir, Simone.

Beckett, Samuel (1906–89)

Dramatist and novelist. Born in Dublin of Jewish parents, he was educated at Trinity College there. He became a lecturer in English at the Ecole Normale Supérieure in Paris (1928–30) and was then a lecturer in French at Trinity College. Since 1932 he has lived chiefly in France, and has written in both French and English. In Paris he became the friend and associate of the expatriate Irish novelist ▷ James Joyce (1882–1941), whose ▷ stream of consciousness subjective method of narrative has strongly influenced Beckett's own novels; another important influence upon him has been the French novelist ▷ Marcel Proust (1871–1922).

Poems include: *Whoroscope* (1930); *Echo's Bones* (1935).

Novels and stories include: *More Pricks than Kicks* (1934); *Murphy* (1938); *Watt* (1944); *Molloy* (1951; English. 1956); *Malone Meurt* (1952; trans. *Malone Dies*, 1956); *L'Innommable* (1953; trans. *The Unnamable*, 1960); *Comment C'est* (1961; English, 1964); *Imagination Dead Imagine* (1966, from French); *Nouvelles et Textes Pour Rien* (1955); *Le Depeupleur* (1971; trans. *The Lost Ones*. 1972); *First Love* (1973); *Mercier et Camier* (1974).

Plays include: *En Attendant Godot*, (1952; trans. *Waiting for Godot*, 1954); *Fin de Partie* (1957; trans. *End Game*, 1958); *Krapp's Last Tape* (1959); *Happy Days* (1961); *Play* (1963); *Eh Joe* (1966); *Breath and Other Short Plays* (1972); *Not I* (1973); *That Time*

(1976); *Footfalls* (1976); *Ghost Trio* (1976); ... *But the Clouds* ... (1977); *Rockaby* (1980); *Ohio Impromptu* (1981); *Quaa* (1982); *Catastrophe* (1982); *Nacht und Träume* (1983); *What Where* (1983). Plays for radio include: *All that Fall* (1957); *Embers* (1959); *Cascando* (1964).

Beckett is one of the most singular and original writers to appear in English, or possibly in French, since 1945. Like Joyce an Irish expatriate, he seems to belong to Ireland and to Europe; his characters are commonly Irish, and his cultural background the desolation of European culture. In both narrative and drama his method has been to create art out of increasingly simplified material, reducing his images of humanity to the sparest elements. His particular view of life's absurdity is often expressed through striking images which reveal a vision of life which is both bleak and grotesquely comic. Thus, in *Happy Days*, Winnie appears on stage buried up to her waist in a mound of earth, while in *Molloy*, a character on a journey progressively loses the use of his limbs, until he travels by rolling along the ground. In so far as he is related to an English literary tradition, it is to the generation between the wars of 1914–18 and 1939–45 when, most notably in the work of James Joyce, communication with an audience was often secondary to experiments in the medium of language. His novels, with their black humour, obsessive lists and narrative instability, now seem in certain respects to anticipate ▷ post-modernist fiction: *Molloy* concludes: 'Then I went back into the house and wrote, It is midnight. The rain is beating on the windows. It was not midnight. It was not raining.' His plays, especially *Waiting for Godot* and the plays for radio, have shown new possibilities in the handling of dialogue, by which speech is used less for communication than for the expression of minds that feel themselves in isolation, or on the point of sinking into it.

▷ Irish fiction in English.
Bib: Kenner, H., *Samuel Beckett, a Critical Study*; Jacobsen, J. and Mueller, W.R., *The Testament of Beckett*; Bair, D., *Beckett: A Biography*; Connor, S., *Samuel Beckett: Repetition, Theory and Text.*

Beckford, William (1759–1844)

Chiefly remembered for his ▷ Gothic novel *Vathek*, Beckford also wrote travel books, and was an extravagant collector of Gothic curiosities. Son of a Lord Mayor of London, Beckford's substantial family wealth enabled him to create Fonthill Abbey, where he lived in eccentric and scandalous seclusion.

Bedlam

A famous lunatic asylum. Originally it was a priory, founded in 1247, for members of the religious order of the Star of Bethlehem. Lunatics were admitted to it in the 14th century, and in 1547, after the dissolution of the monasteries, it was handed over to the City of London as a hospital for lunatics. Antonia White's novel, *Beyond the Glass* (1954) gives an account of being ill there and of the primitive treatment used in this century to women in a state of breakdown. The name became shortened to Bedlam, and a Bedlamite, Tom o'Bedlam, Bess o'Bedlam,

became synonyms for lunatic asylum. In modern English, 'bedlam' is a scene of uproar and confusion.
Bib: Showalter, E., *The Female Malady.*

Beerbohm, Max (1872–1956)

Essayist, cartoonist, writer of fiction. When he began his career Beerbohm belonged to the so-called 'decadent' generation of the aesthetic school in the 1890s; this included ▷ W. B. Yeats in his ▷ Celtic Twilight phase, ▷ Oscar Wilde, ▷ Aubrey Beardsley, and the poets Lionel Johnson and Ernest Dowson. He showed his affiliation to this school by the playful fastidiousness of his wit, especially in his cartoons and parodies. *A Christmas Garland* (1912) contains parodies of contemporary writers including ▷ H. G. Wells, ▷ Arnold Bennett, and ▷ Joseph Conrad. But it is in his cartoons that his satirical wit is displayed with most pungency and originality, *eg Caricature of Twenty-five Gentlemen* (1896), *The Poet's Corner* (1904), *Rossetti and his Circle* (1922). As a writer he was above all an essayist; he entitled his first slim volume with humorous impertinence *The Works of Max Beerbaum* (1896), to which he added *More* (1899), *Yet Again* (1909), *And Even Now* (1920). He also wrote stories (*Seven Men*; 1919), and he is probably now most read for his burlesque romance *Zuleika Dobson* (1911), about the visit of a dazzling beauty to the University of Oxford where she is responsible for a mass suicide among the students.

Beerbohm was educated at Charterhouse and Merton College Oxford. He contributed to the ▷ *Yellow Book*, and in 1898 succeeded ▷ George Bernard Shaw as dramatic critic on the *Saturday Review*. From 1910 he lived in Italy, except during the two world wars. He was knighted in 1939. His personal and literary fastidiousness caused him to be known as 'the Incomparable Max', and as such ▷ Ezra Pound commemorates him as 'Brennbaum the Impeccable' in section 8 of *Hugh Selwyn Mauberley*.
Bib: Cecil, D., *Max: A Biography*; Riewald, J. G., *Beerbohm: A Critical Analysis with a Brief Life and a Bibliography.*

Beeton, Mrs (1836–65)

The author of a book on cooking and household management, published serially in *The Englishwoman's Domestic Magazine* (1859–61). The book met the needs of the rapidly broadening Victorian middle class, which was strongly attached to the domestic virtues and satisfactions. It was soon regarded as an indispensable handbook.

Behn, Aphra (1640–89)

Probably born Aphra (or Afra) Johnson, Behn changed her surname on marriage in 1664. Her husband, who died within two years of the marriage, appears to have been a city merchant, probably of Dutch origins. Behn had already travelled as far as Surinam before her marriage, and in 1666 Charles II recruited her to act as a spy in Antwerp during the Dutch war.

Her first play, *The Forced Marriage*, was staged in 1670, and among the best known of her works is *The Rover*. Her plays are characterized by sharp social satire focussed on sexual relationships.

Behn also produced poems and novels. Her novel *Oroonoko, or the History of the Royal Slave* (c 1688), challenges the hypocrisy of Christian slave traders, and was influenced by her experiences in the British colony of Surinam. Her fictional *Love Letters Between a Nobleman and His Sister* (1684–87) is an early example of the ▷ epistolary novel.

As a woman writer Behn was attacked for her lewd language and daring themes, and her own unconventional lifestyle has tended to obscure criticism of her work by moral condemnation. In *A Room of One's Own*, Virginia Woolf praised Behn as the first professional woman writer.

Bib: Spender, D., *Women of Ideas*; Spender, D., *Mothers of the Novel*; Spender, J., *The Rise of the Woman Novelist*; Duffy, M., *The Passionate Shepherdess: Aphra Behn, 1640–89*; Ballastor, R., *Seductive Forms: Women's Amatory Fiction from 1684 to 1740*.

Belloc, Hilaire (1870–1953)

A versatile writer (novelist, poet, essayist, biographer, historian) now especially remembered for his association with ▷ G.K. Chesterton in Roman Catholic propaganda. The most important phase of his career was before 1914, when he was one of a generation of popular, vivid, witty propagandists; George Bernard Shaw, ▷ H.G. Wells and Chesterton were his equals, and the first two (as agnostic socialists) his opponents. With Chesterton, he maintained the doctrine of Distributism – an alternative scheme to socialism for equalizing property ownership. Among his best works is his earliest: *The Path to Rome* (1902), a discursive account of a journey through France, Switzerland and Northern Italy. He is now chiefly read for his light verse, *eg Cautionary Tales* (1907), *A Bad Child's Book of Beasts*. (1896)

▷ Catholicism in English literature; Children's books.

Bib: Hamilton, R., *Belloc: An Introduction to his Spirit and Work*; Speaight, R., *The Life of Hilaire Belloc*.

Bennett, Anna Maria (c 1750–1808)

Novelist. Anna Bennett (she is sometimes mistakenly known as Agnes Bennett) was a Welsh writer about whose early life little is certain – mainly because she herself offered so many variations. In 1785 two verifiable events occurred: first, the death of her lover Admiral Sir Thomas Pye, father to two of her children, and secondly the publication of her first novel, *Anna, or memoirs of a Welch Heiress*, whose success made her economically independent. The novel's bawdy satire set the tone for her other five works, making her a ▷ Minerva best-selling author. Her most interesting work is *The Beggar Girl and Her Benefactors* (1797), which ▷ Coleridge described as 'the best novel since Fielding'. She was influenced more by the Augustan writers ▷ Samuel Richardson and ▷ Henry Fielding than by her own period's Romantic authors, and she often mocks the ▷ Gothic writings of her contemporaries. Perhaps as a result of these allegiances her popularity waned quite quickly, although she was much admired by Coleridge and ▷ Scott.

Bib: Blakey, D., *The Minerva Press 1790–1820*; Rodgers, K. M., *Feminism in Eighteenth-century England*; Todd, J., *Dictionary of British Women Writers*.

Bennett, Arnold (1867–1931)

Novelist. His principal novels are: *The Old Wives' Tale* (1908); the Clayhanger trilogy – *Clayhanger* (1910), *Hilda Lessways* (1911), and *These Twain* (1916) – all three reprinted as *The Clayhanger Family* (1925); *Riceyman Steps* (1923); *The Grand Babylon Hotel* (1902). His distinctive characteristics as a novelist are his regionalism and his ▷ naturalism. His books mainly concern life in the industrial Five Towns of the north-west Midlands (the Potteries), the particular characteristics of which differentiate his fiction considered as an image of English society. Secondly, he was strongly influenced by the naturalism of French fiction-writers such as ▷ Zola and Maupassant. This led him to emphasize the influence of environment on character, and to build his artistic wholes by means of a pattern of mundane details. This importance that he attached to environment caused a reaction against his artistic methods on the part of novelists like ▷ Virginia Woolf (see her essay 'Modern Fiction' in *The Common Reader, First Series*; 1925) and ▷ D. H. Lawrence, who found Bennett too rigid in his notions of form and too passive in the face of environmental influence. Nonetheless, Bennett lacked the ruthlessness of the French naturalists, and softened his determinism with a sentimentality that recalls ▷ Dickens.

Bib: Drabble, M., *Arnold Bennett, a Biography*; Hepburn, J., *The Art of Arnold Bennett*; Lucas, J., *Arnold Bennett: A Study of His Fiction*.

Bentham, Jeremy (1748–1832)

An extremely influential thinker, founder of the school of thought called ▷ Utilitarianism. The basis of his thought was: 1 that human motives are governed by the pursuit of pleasure and avoidance of pain; 2 that the guiding rule for society should be the greatest happiness of the greatest number; 3 that the test of value for human laws and institutions should be no other than that of usefulness. These views he expounded in *Fragment on Government* (1776) and *Introduction to Principles of Morals and Legislation* (1780). His principal associates were James Mill (1773–1836) and ▷ John Stuart Mill (1806–73); collectively they were known as the Philosophical Radicals, and together they established a practical philosophy of reform of great consequence in 19th-century Britain. But their excessive rationalism frustrated sympathy and imagination in education and the relief of poverty – see ▷ Dickens's novel ▷ *Hard Times* (1854). Bentham's thought derived from the sceptical 18th-century French 'philosophes' such as Helvetius and 18th-century English ▷ rationalists such as David Hartley (1705–57) and Joseph Priestley (1733–1804). It was, in fact, the outstanding line of continuity between 18th-century and 19th-century thinking.

Bib: Stephen, L., *The English Utilitarians*; Pringle-Patterson, A. S., *The Philosophical Radicals and other essays*; Atkinson, C. M., *Life*.

Bentley, E. C. (Edmund Clerihew) (1875–1956)
Journalist and writer of detective fiction and light
verse. E. C. Bentley's famous detective novel *Trent's
Last Case* (1903), dedicated to his friend ▷ G. K.
Chesterton, was originally written as an 'exposure of
detective stories', but it was soon received as a classic
of the genre (▷ detective fiction). In the same spirit,
he published a brilliant parody of Dorothy L. Sayers,
'Greedy Night', in 1939. Bentley is also known as
the originator of the humorous, aphoristic verse
form 'clerihew' (from his middle name), which aims
to capture the subject of the poem in two rhyming
couplets, a well-known example being,

> The art of Biography
>   Is different from Geography
> Geography is about maps,
>   But Biography is about chaps.

Bentley worked as a journalist for *The Daily News*
and *The Daily Telegraph*, and his other books include
Trent's Own Case (1936), *Trent Intervenes* (1938) and
Elephant's Work: An Enigma (1950).

Beowulf
The single extant text of this important Old English
heroic narrative was copied about the year 1000 but
there are linguistic traces of an earlier written version
dating from the 8th-century in the text, and the
story material may derive from earlier narratives still.
It deals with key events in the life of a 6th-century
warrior, Beowulf, from Geatland in south Sweden,
who first kills the monster Grendel, which had been
ravaging the great hall of Heorot, built by Hrothgar,
king of the Danes. Beowulf, nephew of the king
of the Geats, slays the monster by wrestling with it
and wrenching out its arm. Grendel's mother then
seeks vengeance by carrying off one of the Danish
nobles, but Beowulf enters the mere beneath which
she lives and kills her too. Beowulf returns home
and in due course becomes king of the Geats. When
he has reigned 50 years, his kingdom is invaded by
a fiery dragon which he manages to kill with the
aid of a young nobleman, Wiglaf, when all the rest
of his followers have fled. However, he receives his
own death wound in the fight and as he dies, he
pronounces Wiglaf his successor. His body is burnt
on a great funeral pyre and the dragon's treasure is
buried with his ashes; 12 of his followers ride round
the funeral mound celebrating his greatness. This
narrative is interlaced with digressions on historical
analogues to the action, and asides concerning
retrospective and prospective events, which give the
poem a dense and complex narrative texture.
Bib: Swanton, M (ed.), *Beowulf*.

Berger, John (b 1926)
Novelist, painter and art critic. His novels reflect
both his Marxism (▷ Marx, Karl), in their attention
to the oppressive structures of society, and his
painting, in their vivid realization of sensual detail.
A Painter Of Our Time (1958) through the story of
an emigré Hungarian painter, explores the role of
the artist in a consumer society and the relationship
of art to experience. His best-known work is
G (1972), in which authorial self-consciousness,
open-ended, fragmentary narrative and documentary
elements serve to resist the imposition of order on
political events.

He has collaborated with the photographer Jean
Mohr on a number of works which address political
and social issues by combining various media and
genres, including photographs, political and social
analysis, poems and fictionalized case studies; these
are *Ways of Seeing* (1972); *A Fortunate Man* (1967);
A Seventh Man (1981); *Another Way of Telling* (1982).
Berger has also published two volumes of a trilogy
entitled *Into Their Labours*; these are *Pig Earth* (1979),
which comprises short stories and poems, and *Once
In Europa* (1987). Other novels include: *The Foot
of Clive* (1962); *Corker's Freedom* (1964). Drama:
A Question of Geography (1987; with Nella Bielski).
Volumes of essays include: *Permanent Red* (1960);
The White Bird (1985); *Keeping a Rendezvous* (1992).
Art criticism includes; *The Success and Failure of
Picasso* (1965).
Bib: Dyer, G., *Ways of Telling: The Work of
John Berger*.

Bergson Henri (1859–1941)
French philosopher. Bergson's work on time and
consciousness had a great influence on 20th-century
novelists, particularly ▷ modernist writers engaged
in so-called ▷ 'stream of consciousness' work such
as ▷ James Joyce, ▷ Dorothy Richardson and
▷ Virginia Woolf. His text of 1889, which was
published in English in 1910 as *Time and Free Will:
An Essay on the Immediate data of Consciousness*, was
particularly important. Bergson is also known as one
of the key theorists of vitalism, the belief that the
material progress of the world is not underpinned by
determining biological or physical mechanisms but
by the movements of living energy; Bergson's theory
of an essential *élan vital* or *life force*, which animates
material progress through its constant process of
change and becoming, was taken up by George
Bernard Shaw in his plays. Bergson was awarded the
Nobel Prize for literature in 1928, and was married
to a cousin of French novelist Marcel Proust, whose
work he also greatly influenced.
Bib: Humphrey, R., *Stream of Consciousness in the
Modern Novel*; Sokel, W. H., *The Writer in Extremis*;
Hanna, T. (ed.), *The Bergson Heritage*.

Berkeley, George (1685–1753)
Irish churchman and a philosopher in the tradition
of ▷ Descartes (1590–1650) of France and ▷ John
Locke (1632–1704), but the opponent of the latter.
Locke had affirmed the independence of matter
and mind; Berkeley held that the reality of anything
depended on its being perceived by a conscious
mind; thus mind (and spirit) had primacy over
matter. Nature is the experience of consciousness,
and the evidence of Universal Mind, or God. He
considered that Locke's insistence on external matter
and physical causes led to ▷ atheism; but his own
lucid and precise prose is as much the vehicle of
reason as Locke's. While Locke led towards scientific
scepticism, Berkeley's faith, combined with reason,

maintained the religious vision in an essentially
rational century. His philosophy is expressed in *A
New Theory of Vision* (1709), and in *Principles of
Human Knowledge* (1710). His *Dialogues of Alciphron*
(1732) are distinguished for their grace of style.
Bib: Wild, J., *Berkeley: a study of his life and
philosophy*; Luce, A. A., *The Life of Berkeley*; Warnock,
G. J., *Berkeley*.

Besant, Walter (1836–1901)

Novelist, philanthropost and journalist, born in
Portsea and educated at King's College London
and Christ's College Cambridge. Many of his novels
were set in east London; for example *All Sorts and
Conditions of Men* (1882) is an idealistic story about
an heiress and a cabinet maker who combined to
bring about the dream of a 'People's Palace of
Delight' in the East End (a project which Besant
contributed to in real life). His novel *The Revolt of
Man* (1882) is an anti-feminist dystopia, part of the
debate over the ▷ New Woman.

Best-sellers

A transformation of the means of production in the
early years of the 19th century made it possible for a
single text to be printed, advertised, distributed and
sold in numbers hitherto inconceivable. ▷Charles
Dickens's ▷*Pickwick Papers* was the first work of
fiction to exploit these new conditions. The financial
return on this new mode of production was highly
profitable, and a wide market for the commodity
was opened up. In our own day the best-seller is
associated not only with high sales, however, but also
with quick ones. Though there is no agreement on
the sales figures which define a text as a best-seller,
national newspapers carry weekly charts, showing
the titles which are selling most strongly in fiction
and non-fiction. This may be seen as a form of
advertisement, encouraging further sales of what
has been guaranteed as an acceptable product by
market success. Writing a best-seller may make a
large sum of money for the author and some make it
clear (Jeffrey Archer or Shirley Conran for instance)
that they gear their fiction to the market with that
intention. Recent moves, by publishers as well as
authors, to aim writing and publication towards
the best-seller lists inevitably threaten to narrow
the range of what is published and to discourage
publishers from taking chances with new authors and
new kinds of writing.
　▷Detective Fiction; Horror Fiction; Science
Fiction.

Between the Acts (1941)

▷ Virginia Woolf's last novel, published posthumously.
The story concerns the staging of a pageant of English
history in the grounds of a country house on the eve
of World War Two. Miss La Trobe, who creates and
organizes the performance, is, like Lily Briscoe in
▷ *To The Lighthouse*, a representative of the woman
artist. Her pageant serves to explore issues of truth
and illusion, art and reality, community and isolation,
self-knowledge and deception; it briefly unites the
lives of a disparate group of characters.

Beulah, The Land of

In the ▷ Bible, *Isaiah* 62:4. A Hebrew word =
'married'. In Bunyan's ▷ *Pilgrim's Progress* it lies in
sight of the Heavenly City and beyond the reach of
Giant Despair. It signifies the state in which the soul
is 'married' to God.

Bible in England

The Bible falls into two parts.
1 Old Testament
The first and larger part of the Bible, consisting
of the sacred writings of the Jews. It concerns the
peculiar, divinely ordained destiny of the Jewish race
from earliest times, and it is considered by Christians
to expound the divine promise which the New
Testament fulfils not merely for the Jews but for the
whole of mankind. The Old Testament is divided
into books which are grouped by Jews into three
main sections, as follows:
　1 The Torah ('Law', otherwise called the
Pentateuch), consisting of five books as follows: *Genesis*,
Exodus, *Leviticus*, *Numbers*, *Deuteronomy*. They are
called 'the five books of Moses'. The first two are
narrative and descriptive, and move from the creation
of the world to the escape of the Jews from slavery in
Egypt. The remainder contain laws and discourses.
　2 The Prophets. This section is divided into two in
the Hebrew Bible: the 'Former Prophets', consisting
of *Joshua*, *Judges*, the two books of *Samuel* and
the two books of *Kings*; and the 'Latter Prophets',
consisting of *Isaiah*, *Jeremiah*, *Ezekiel*, and the Minor
Prophets. The books of the Former Prophets tell the
story of the establishment of the Jews in the kingdom
of Israel, and their subsequent history. The Latter
Prophets contain history together with prophetic
discourses.
　3 The Sacred Writings, or Hagiographa,
which are divided into three sections: (i) the
Poetical books, consisting of *Psalms*, *Proverbs*,
Job; (ii) the five 'Rolls', which are read at special
seasons in the Jewish year: *Song of Songs*, *Ruth*,
Lamentations, *Ecclesiastes*, *Esther* – of these *Esther*
and *Ruth* are narratives; the other three are
poetic meditations; (iii) *Daniel*, *Ezra*, *Nehemiah*,
and *Chronicles*, all consisting mainly of historical
narrative.
2 New Testament
The second and shorter part of the Bible, containing
the sacred books of the Christians. It is divided into
books, on the pattern of the Old Testament, and
dates as a whole collection from the end of the 2nd
century AD. It is customary to divide the books into
four groups.
　1 The three Synoptic (*ie* 'summary narrative')
Gospels of Saints Matthew, Mark and Luke, and
the *Acts of the Apostles*. The Gospels are narratives
about Jesus Christ, and *Acts* is the narrative of the
missionary careers of the apostles (including St Paul)
after Christ's death.
　2 The Epistles (letters) of St Paul. The four
shortest of these are addressed to individuals: two
to Timothy, and one each to Titus and to Philemon.
The remainder are addressed to various early
Christian communities. These are the Epistles to
the Romans, Galatians, Ephesians, Philippians,

Colossians, two to the Corinthians, and two to the Thessalonians. The Epistle to the Hebrews has been ascribed to Paul, but is nowadays considered to be by a disciple of his.

3 The Catholic Epistles, so called because they were directed to Christians generally. Two of these are ascribed to St Peter, and one each to James and Jude.

4 The Johannine writings, ascribed to the Apostle John. These are the Gospel of St John, distinguished from the Synoptic Gospels as probably not intended as a historical narrative, the Epistles of John, and the poetic, visionary narrative called the *Apocalypse*, or *Revelation*.

In the Middle Ages the only version of the Bible authorized by the Church was the Vulgate, *ie* the translation into Latin by St Jerome, completed in 405. Partial translations were made into Old English before the 11th century. From the 14th century translations were made by reformers, who believed that men without Latin should have the means of seeking guidance from divine scripture without dependence on Church authority. The main translators were: Wycliffe (14th century); ▷ Tyndale, and Coverdale (16th century). The last-named was the producer of the *Great Bible* (also called Cranmer's Bible after the archbishop of the time), but Henry VIII, concerned for his intermediate position between Catholics and Protestants, ended by restricting its use. Under the Catholic Mary I (1533–8) English reformers produced the *Geneva Bible* abroad, with annotations suited to ▷ Puritan Calvinist opinion; and in 1568 the so-called *Bishops' Bible* was issued by the restored Anglicans to counteract Puritan influence. Finally, in 1611 the Authorized Version was produced with the approval of James I (1603–25). For three centuries it was to be the only one in general use, and it is still the prevailing version. In the 19th century it was revised (Revised Version) and recently a new translation has been authorized and produced (New Testament 1961; Old Testament 1961; Old Testament Apocrypha 1970). A Catholic translation the (Douai Bible) was issued at about the same time as the Authorized Version.

In spite of various other translations. Catholic and Protestant, in the 19th and 20th centuries the Authorized Version is by far the most important for its literary and social influence. It was based on previous translations, especially that of Tyndale, so that the cast of its prose is characteristically more 16th than early 17th-century in style. Nonetheless much of it is of supreme eloquence, *eg* the Book of *Job*, and last 15 chapters of *Isaiah*. It was for many people in the 17th and 18th centuries the only book that was constantly read, and it was familiar to all from its use in church and education. The musical cadence of Authorized Version prose can be often heard in the prose of English writers, whether or not professing Christians. It is conspicuous in John Bunyan's ▷ *Pilgrim's Progress* but it can also be heard in the prose of 20th-century novelists ▷ T. F. Powys, *eg Mr Weston's Good Wine* (1927).

Bib: Daches, D., *The King James' Version of the Bible*.

Bildungsroman

A novel which describes the youthful development of the central character. Prominent examples in English include ▷ James Joyce's ▷ *A Portrait of the Artist as a Young Man* (1916), ▷ Samuel Butler's ▷ *The Way of All Flesh* (1902) and ▷ D. H. Lawrence's ▷ *Sons and Lovers* (1913).

Biographia Literaria (1817)

A miscellaneous work of ▷ autobiography, philosophy, and literary criticism, by ▷ Samuel Taylor Coleridge. Its psychological approach to creativity, influenced by the German philosophers Schlegel and ▷ Kant, foreshadows the ▷ Freudian concept of the unconscious, and its theory of imagination is central to the development of literary critical theory. The famous distinction between primary imagination, secondary imagination and fancy occurs in Chapter XIII. Primary imagination is seen as 'the living power and prime agent of all human perception'. Secondary imagination is the creative power to synthesize and re-express experience in new forms: 'It dissolves, diffuses, dissipates, in order to recreate; or where this process is rendered impossible, yet still, at all events, it struggles to idealize and to unify.' Fancy, on the other hand, simply juxtaposes memories and impressions and 'has no other counters to play with but fixities and definites'. Primary perception is thus not the mere passive holding of a mirror up to nature of classical literary theory, but involves an interaction between subjectivity and objective reality.

Much of the literary criticism in the book is devoted to detailed analysis and appreciation of William Wordsworth's artifice, and to pointing out that his language is not simply, as he asserted in the Preface to the *Lyrical Ballads*, 'the real language of men', but a highly individual artistic construct of his own. The 'critical analysis' of poems by Shakespeare and Wordsworth which occupies much of the second volume, displays a very modern sophistication in its treatment of metre and diction.

Biography

The chief source of inspiration for English biographers was the Greek, Plutarch (1st century AD), whose *Parallel Lives* of Greek and Roman great men was translated into English by ▷ Sir Thomas North in 1579 and was widely read. Biography had been practised before in England; there had been the lives of the saints in the Middle Ages, and in the 16th century Cavendish's life of the statesman Cardinal Wolsey had appeared. The regular practice of biography, however, starts with the 17th century, not merely owing to the influence of North's translation of Plutarch, but as part of the outward-turning, increasingly scientific interest in many kinds of people (not merely saints and rulers) which in the 18th century was to give rise to the novel. Biography is a branch of history, and the art of historical writing advanced with biography: Edward Hyde, ▷ Earl of Clarendon, included fine biographical portraits in his history of the Great Rebellion, written between 1646 and 1670. ▷ Izaak Walton's lives of John Donne (1640), Sir Henry Wotton (1651), Richard

Hooker (1665), George Herbert (1670) and Bishop Sanderson (1678) are closer to our modern idea of biography, and they are landmarks, if not originals, in the form inasmuch as the subjects, though eminent men, were humble enough to lead ordinary lives in touch with usual experience. In the 18th century the writing of biographies became habitual; and also biography, or autobiography, became a way of disguising pure fiction, *eg* in the novels of ▷ Defoe. ▷ Samuel Johnson was a master of biography in his ▷ *Lives of the Poets* (1779–81), most notable among which is his *Life of Mr Richard Savage*, previously published in 1744. The outstanding biography of the century, however, is the life of Johnson himself by ▷ James Boswell (1791), an intimate and vivid account of a great man. ▷ William Godwin wrote a biography of his wife ▷ Mary Wollstonecraft, entitled *Memoirs of the author of a Vindication of the Rights of Women* (1798), which contributed to her notoriety. Of the many 19th-century biographies, perhaps the most pre-eminent was ▷ Elizabeth Gaskell's life of her friend ▷ Charlotte Brontë (1857). The 19th century was, however, more outstanding for its achievements in the largely new form, ▷ autobiography. The 20th century saw a new approach to the art in the work of ▷ Lytton Strachey (1880–1932). His *Eminent Victorians* (1918) sought for the truth in the lives of its subjects in unexpected details, and instead of expounding their greatness exposed the weakness of their mere humanity. The psychological approach and the revolutionary tone of biography has made it one of the fastest growth areas in publishing. Michael Holroyd, Victoria Glendinning and Richard Ellman are among the important biographers of the late 20th century. Biographies of women writers have played a major role in ▷ feminist analyses of the conditions and achievements of women's writing.
Bid: Gittings, R., *The Nature of Biography*.

Blackmore, R.D. (Richard Dodderidge) (1825–1900)

Novelist and poet. Born in Berkshire, the son of a clergyman, Blackmore was educated at school in Tiverton, where he was head boy, and at Exeter College, Oxford. His mother had died when he was a baby and he spent much of his youth with an uncle in Glamorgan. A career as a barrister was cut short by epileptic fits and after an unsuccessful period as a schoolteacher, Blackmore built a house in Teddington where he lived a retired life, dividing his time between writing, and growing and selling fruit and flowers. He married Lucy Maguire in 1852; there were no children and after her death in 1888 he continued to mourn her and keep the house unchanged. He was a shy man, kind but self-centred and determined. He was fond of animals, especially dogs, and deeply absorbed in his gardening enterprise.

He published volumes of poetry, including translations of Theocritus and Virgil. His 14 novels include *Lorna Doone* (1869), which was rejected by 18 publishers and is now his most famous novel, *Cradock Nowell* (1866), *The Maid of Sker* (1872), his first attempt at fiction only later finished, *Alice Lorraine* (1875) and *Springhaven* (1887). *Lorna Doone* is said to

have done for Devonshire what ▷ Sir Walter Scott did for the Highlands and in general Blackmore's novels abound with carefully observed and detailed descriptions of locations, wildlife and the weather along with exciting incidents, all somewhat loosely structured.
Bid: Burris, Q. G., *R. D. Blackmore: His life and Novels*; Dunn, W. H., *R. D. Blackmore, The Author of Lorna Doone: A Biography*; Budd, K. G., *The Last Victorian: R. D. Blackmore and his Novels*.

Blackwood's Magazine

Founded in 1817 by the publisher William Blackwood as the *Edinburgh Monthly Magazine*, it was particularly influential in the first 15 years of its existence. Like the ▷ *Quarterly* it was intended as a Tory rival to the liberal ▷ *Edinburgh Review*, but called itself a 'magazine' to indicate a lighter tone than that of the 'Reviews'. It attacked Lord Byron and Percy Bysshe Shelley on political grounds, and was, like the *Quarterly*, particularly hostile to John Keats, because of his association with the radical journalist Leigh Hunt. Hunt, Keats, ▷ Charles Lamb and William Hazlitt were stigmatized as the 'Cockney School' of literature. *Blackwood's Magazine* began with a brilliant group of contributors, especially ▷ Sir Walter Scott, John G. Lockhart (known because of his fierce criticism as 'the Scorpion'), ▷ James Hogg, and John Wilson, who wrote under the pen-name of Christopher North. Between 1822 and 1835 the magazine ran a series of brilliant dialogues, *Noctes Ambrosianae*, 'Nights at Ambrose's' (a well-known inn). In 1857 it published ▷ George Eliot's *Scenes from Clerical Life*.

Bleak House (1852-3)

A novel by ▷ Charles Dickens, published, like most of his novels, in monthly parts. It opens with an attack on the part of the legal system called the High Court of Chancery. The rest of the novel expands this opening into a dramatization, through a wide range of characters, of the various forms of parasitism that society lends itself to, and of the ways in which institutions (especially legal ones) falsify relationships and degrade human beings. Most of the story takes place in London. The telling of the story is shared by two contrasted narrators: the savagely sardonic but impersonal author who uses the present tense, and the ingenuous, saccharine, unresentful girl, Esther Summerson, who is ignorant of her parentage, though she knows that she is illegitimate. She is adopted by a philanthropist, John Jarndyce, who also adopts two young orphan relatives, Richard Carstone and Ada Clare, who are 'wards in Chancery' (*ie* legally under the care of the Lord Chancellor) while the distribution of an estate to which they have claims is endlessly disputed in the Court of Chancery (the case of 'Jarndyce and Jarndyce'). Through Richard, Ada and Mr Jarndyce, Esther becomes acquainted with a large number of characters, some of whom are also despairing participants in Chancery Suits, and others (such as Skimpole, the parasitic man of letters, Mrs Jellyby, a well-meaning but incompetent philanthropist, and Turveydrop, the self-styled model of fashionable

deportment) who live off society without giving
anything substantial in return. Another focus in the
novel is Sir Leicester Dedlock, a simple-minded but
self-important land-owner, whose one redeeming
feature is his devotion to his wife, the beautiful and
silent Lady Dedlock. Lady Dedlock is in fact the
mother of Esther Summerson, a fact known to the
family lawyer, Tulkinghorn, who blackmails her.
Her former lover, Captain Hawdon, is still alive, but
lives in destitution and misery. His only friend is the
crossing-sweeper, Jo, who resembles Sir Leicester
in that they are equally simple-minded and equally
capable of one great love for another person. In
social respects they are so differentiated, by the lack
of any advantages in the one case and by excess of
privilege in the other, that it is hard to think of them
as belonging to the same species. A large number of
other characters contribute to Dickens's panorama
of society as mainly constituted by parasites and the
victims of parasites. The theme is conveyed partly
through the atmosphere of contrasted houses: Bleak
House, which is in fact the cordial and life-giving
home of Mr Jarndyce; Chesney Wold, the vast but
empty mansion of Sir Leicester; Tom-all-alone's,
the slum dwelling where Jo finds his sole refuge;
the clean and orderly household of the retired
soldier, Bagnet; the squalid one of the money-lender,
Smallweed, and so forth. For the main characters,
the story ends with the corruption of Richard
Carstone, the death in despair of Lady Dedlock, the
murder of Tulkinghorn and Esther's marriage to the
young doctor, Woodcourt. The case of 'Jarndyce and
Jarndyce' was based on an actual case centring on
a Birmingham millionaire, William Jennings. The
character of Skimpole is partly based on Leigh Hunt
(1784–1859), and another character, Boythorn, on
Walter Landor (1775–1864).

Blixen, Karen Christentze (née Dinesen) (1885–1962)

Danish novelist and short-story writer, who wrote
mainly in English, using the pen-names Isak
Dinesen and Pierre Andrezel. Born in Rungsted,
Denmark, she studied art in Copenhagen, Paris
and Rome before marrying her cousin, Baron Bror
Blixen-Finecke, in 1914, and settling in Kenya where
they ran a coffee-plantation (work which Blixen
continued after their divorce until 1931). Her novel
Out of Africa (1937) is based on her experiences in
Africa. A number of her short stories use elements
of the fantastic, the symbolic, and the ▷ Gothic: the
volumes include: *Seven Gothic Tales* (1934); *Winter's
Tales* (1942); *Angelic Avengers* (1944); *Last Tales*
(1957); *Anecdotes of Destiny* (1958); *Shadows on the
Grass* (1960); *Carnival: Entertainments and Posthumous
Tales* (1979). She also published essays, some of
which are collected in *Daguerreotypes and Other
Essays* (1984) and *On Modern Marriage and Other
Observations* (1987).
Bib: Thurman, Judith, *Isak Dinesen: The Life of a
Storyteller.*

Bloom, Harold (b 1930)

One of the leading members of the so-called Yale
school of literary criticism, along with the late

▷ Paul De Man, Geoffrey Hartman, and J. Hillis
Miller. In books such as *The Anxiety of Influence*
(1973), *A Map of Misreading* (1975), and *Poetry and
Repression* (1976) Bloom seeks to offer a revisionary
account of poetry, based especially on a ▷ Freudian
model of the relationship between the aspiring
poet and his literary predecessor. In this way
Bloom moves away from the tenets of American
▷ New Criticism in his suggestion that all poetry
seeks, but fails, to exclude 'precursors' texts, with
which it enters into a struggle, both destructive
and creative, in order to achieve its particular
identity.

Bloomsbury Group, The

An exclusive intellectual circle that centred on the
house of the publisher, Leonard Woolf, and his
wife, the novelist, ▷ Virginia Woolf, in the district
of London round the British Museum, known as
Bloomsbury. It flourished notably in the 1920s,
and included, besides the Woolfs, the economist
Lord Keynes, the biographer ▷ Lytton Strachey,
the art critics Roger Fry and Clive Bell, and the
painters Venessa Bell and Duncan Grant, as well as
others. The group owed much to the Cambridge
philosopher ▷ G.E. Moore and the importance he
attached to the value of friendship and aesthetic
appreciation. Their close relationship which
resulted from this, in addition to the fastidiousness
which arose from their critical attitude to the
prevailing culture of English society, gave them an
apparent exclusiveness which made them many
enemies. Moore's influence also contributed to
their scepticism about religious tradition and
social and political conventions; they tended to be
moderately left-wing and agnostic. Positively, they
were innovators in art and represented an important
section of the English avant-garde. Their opponents
attacked them for excessive self-centredness and
an aestheticism which, it was claimed, was too
individualistic and self-regarding to be really creative
in social terms.

Bluestocking

The 'Blue Stocking Ladies' were a group of
intelligent, literary women in the mid-18th century
who held evening receptions for serious conversation.
As a setting for discussions in which both sexes were
included, the evenings were a deliberate attempt
to challenge the social stereotypes which confined
intellectual debate to male gatherings and relegated
the female sex to trivial topics. By bringing men and
women together in this atmosphere, it was hoped that
the 'polite' codes of gallantry could be disposed of.
The chief hostesses included ▷ Elizabeth Montagu,
Elizabeth Carter, ▷ Mary Delany, and later, ▷
Hannah More.

The name 'bluestocking' is thought to derive from
the stockings of Benjamin Stillingfleet, who, too
poor to buy evening dress, attended in his daytime
blue worsteds. ▷ Hannah More's poem *Bas Bleu*
(1786) helped to establish to the use of the term
referring to the society women, although Admiral
Boscawen is traditionally credited with coining the
collective noun.

Blyton, Enid (1897–1968)
Writer for children. Blyton is one of the most famous and maligned children's novelists of the 20th century. She was phenomenally prolific, beginning with *The Enid Blyton Book of Fairies* (1924), writing school stories and the Famous Five sequence in the 1940s and 1950s, the Noddy stories in the 1950s and 1960s, as well as adaptations of classical and Uncle Remus stories, and non-fiction for children. Blyton's works are severely chastised by contemporary critics both on educational grounds (her works do not tax their young readers, their vocabulary is limited, their characters thin, and their plots simple-minded) and on political grounds (her writing is sexist, racist and nostalgic for a pre-war middle-class idyll). Despite this her novels continue to sell and most are still in print. Other works include: *Naughty Amelia Jane!* (1939); *The Naughtiest Girl in School* (1940); *Five on a Treasure Island* (1942); *First Term at Malory Towers* (1946); *Noddy and His Car* (1951) and *Noddy in Toyland* (1955).
Bib: Ray, S.G., *The Blyton Phenomenon*; Stoney, B., *Enid Blyton: A Bibliography*.

Boccaccio, Giovanni (?1313–75)
Italian humanist scholar and writer, born near Florence. His literary studies began in Naples where he wrote his first works but he later returned to Florence and was employed on diplomatic missions for the Florentine state. He publicly lectured on ▷ Dante's ▷ *Divine Comedy*, was a friend of the poet Petrarch (1304–74) and the centre of a circle of humanist learning and literary activity. His works included a wide range of courtly narratives, a vernacular imitation of classical epic and a number of important encyclopaedic works in Latin which occupied the last years of his life. ▷ Chaucer made extensive use of his work, drawing, for example, on the *Filocolo* (for the *Franklin's Tale*), the *Filostrato* (for ▷ *Troilus and Criseyde*), the *Teseida* (for the *Knight's Tale*) and in all likelihood, on the ▷ *Decameron* (for a number of the ▷ *Canterbury Tales*). The *Decameron*, like the *Canterbury Tales*, is a story-collection but it has a rather different setting. In Boccaccio's collection, the stories are narrated by a group of ten nobles who take refuge in the country as the plague rages in Florence. The company of noble women and men amuse themselves for two weeks by telling stories loosely based on a love theme of some kind, chosen by the leader of the day. However, the narrators of the resulting 100 stories are far less memorable than those of the *Canterbury Tales* and Chaucer's story-collection, though shorter than Boccaccio's has a far greater tonal range too.
  Boccaccio's collection of brief tragic-narratives in Latin (*De Casibus Virorum Illustrium*) was reworked in English by John Lydgate in the 15th century and it provided much material for the Elizabethan compilation of short tragic-narratives, the *Mirror for Magistrates* (1559). Tales from the *Decameron* were included in William Painter's anthology, *The Palace of Pleasure*, and many Elizabethan dramatists, including Shakespeare, quarried plots from either Painter's collection or from the *Decameron* itself. Boccaccio's vast narrative compilations in Latin and in the vernacular continued to provide narrative sources for many later English writers, including Dryden, Keats and Tennyson.

Boethius, Ancius Manlius Torquatus Severinus (475–524)
Philosopher, scholar and statesman, born in Rome and educated at Athens and Alexandria. He wrote textbooks on logic and music, and was made consul in 510. His illustrious political career, as advisor to the Ostrogothic Emperor Theodoric, ended when he was accused of treason, imprisoned and executed in 524. While imprisoned, he composed his most famous and influential work, the (*Consolation of Philosophy*), *De Consolatione Philosophiae*. Written in prose and verse sections in the voice of a first-person speaker, it recounts how the speaker was tutored by Lady Philosophy to view his imprisonment philosophically and to see his place within a broader universal scheme. It deals with complex issues such as the relationship between divine foreknowledge and individual free will and was one of the most influential philosophical works of the medieval period, being translated into Old English by Alfred and later by ▷ Chaucer. The influence of Boethius pervades Chaucer's narratives. Another English translation from the Elizabethan period has been attributed to Elizabeth I.
Bib: Watts, V. (trans.), *The Consolation of Philosophy*.

Bohemian
Applied to artists and those who live a life supposedly dedicated to the spirit of the imaginative arts, it means living freely, refusing to observe social conventions, especially when they depend on mere habit, snobbery or fear of 'seeming different'. Recently it often carries a slightly mocking tone and is rarely used now without irony. Literally, Bohemian means native to Bohemia, now the western part of Czechoslovakia. In the 15th century ▷ gipsies were supposed to have come from there; in the 19th century, French students were supposed to live like the gipsies and hence to be 'Bohemian'. The word was then introduced into English with this meaning by the novelist ▷ William Makepeace Thackeray. His novel ▷ *The Newcomers* is one of the first studies in English of Bohemianism.

Bonhote, Elizabeth (1744–1818)
Novelist and poet. One of ▷ Minerva's best-selling authors, Bonhote was an unadventurous and conservative novelist; her settings are often rural and, in *Bungay Castle* (1796), historicized, and she employed strong moral didacticism. Her unquestioning acceptance of traditional values is emphasized in her collection of essays, *The Parental Monitor* (1788), which contains advice for her children. Interestingly, however, while she advocates that women should stay at home and look after their families, she encourages them to write and not to be diverted from literary pursuits.
Bib: Todd, J., *Dictionary of British Women Writers*.

Borges, Jorge Luis (1899–1986)
Argentinian short-story writer, poet and essayist, born in Buenos Aires and educated in Geneva.

His paradoxical, metaphysical, metafictional stories, which employ elements of the ▷ detective story, of ▷ science fiction, of fantasy and of philosophical speculation, helped to define the genre of ▷ magic realism, although this was not a term he himself favoured. Notable collections are: *A Universal History of Infamy* (1935), *Fictions* (1945), *Labyrinths* (1953) and *Doctor Brodie's Report* (1971). Stories such as 'The Library of Babel' (in *Fictions*), which imagines the universe as a vast library, amount to existential fables, while others, such as 'The Garden of Forking Paths' (in the same collection) are more like puzzles.

Borrow, George Henry (1803–81)
Born in Norfolk, Borrow was educated in Edinburgh and Norwich as his father, a recruiting officer in the militia, moved around. Borrow was articled to solicitors in Norfolk 1818–23, then when his father died he moved to London and worked for a publisher. He travelled in France, Germany, Russia, the East and Spain 1833–9, sending letters to the *Morning Herald* 1837–9, blazing a trail as effectively the first newspaper correspondent. In 1835 he published in St Petersburg *Targum*, translations from 30 different languages and dialects. In Russia and Spain he was an agent for the British and Foreign Bible Society. In 1840 he married Mary Clarke, the widow of a naval officer he met in Spain, and bought an estate on Oulton Broad in Norfolk, in which he had already inherited a share. There he allowed gipsies to pitch tents and live, and became friends with them. His books are in part based on his life. *The Bible in Spain* (1834) and *The Zincali or an account of the Gypsies in Spain* (1841) owed as much of their success to public interest in Borrow the man as Borrow the writer. *Lavengro* followed in 1851, losing Borrow much of his popularity due to its strong 'anti-gentility' tone. *The Romany Rye* (1857) and *Wild Wales* (1862) continued the mixture of fact with fiction, vivid portraits and revelations of the personality of the writer. He died largely unknown and little read.
Bib: Knapp, W. I., *Life, Writings, and Correspondence of George Borrow*; Collie, M., *George Borrow, Eccentric*; Williams, D., *A World of His Own: The Double Life of George Borrow*.

Boswell, James (1740–95)
Best known for his *Life of Samuel Johnson*, whom he met in 1763, Boswell was also a copious diarist. Eldest son of Alexander Boswell, Lord Auchinleck, Boswell studied law at Edinburgh, Glasgow and Utrecht, and reluctantly entered the legal profession.

From 1760 onwards. Boswell published many pamphlets, often anonymously. After meeting ▷ Johnson, he travelled in Europe, where he met ▷ Rousseau and ▷ Voltaire. Rousseau fired him with enthusiasm for the cause of Corsican liberty, and he cultivated a lifelong friendship with General Paoli; in 1768 he published an *Account of Corsica*, which attracted considerable international recognition.

In 1769 Boswell, by now a Scottish Advocate, married his cousin Margaret Montgomerie. But Boswell longed to be part of London literary culture, and made journeys to the capital as frequently as he could. Here he was elected a member of The Club (later the Literary Club), though his habit of 'scribbling' memoranda of conversations, with the aim of writing Johnson's *Life*, irritated some of its members.

In 1773, Boswell and Johnson made their tour of the Hebrides (see ▷ *The Journal of a Tour to the Hebrides*). From 1777 to 1783 Boswell wrote a series of articles for the *London Magazine* under the pen-name of 'The Hypochondriack'. In 1782 he inherited the Scottish estate on his father's death, and his last meeting with Johnson was in 1784.

Boswell attempted, unsuccessfully, to make a career in politics, while working on the *Life of Samuel Johnson*, which appeared in 1791.
Bib: Pottle, F. A. (ed.), *Boswell's London Journal, 1762–63*; Hill, G. B. (ed.), revised Powell, L. F., *Life of Johnson and Journal of a Tour to the Hebrides*.

Botany Bay
In New South Wales, Australia, near Sydney. Captain Cook landed there in 1770 and took possession of it for the British Crown. From 1787 Australia was used for convict settlements, ie convicted criminals sentenced to transportation were sent there. They were not in fact sent to Botany Bay, but the name was used in common speech to cover convict settlements in Australia generally. The bay received its name from Joseph Banks, a botanist accompanying Cook, because of its rich plant life. The brutality of this system and the suffering it imposed is only now being traced by scholarship and reflected in public opinion. It involved injury not only to the transportees and their families but also to the native peoples whose lands were invaded and appropriated.
Bib: Keneally, T., *The Fatal Shore*.

Bowdler, Thomas (1754–1825)
Famous for *The Family Shakespeare*, 1818; an edition in which 'those words and expressions are omitted which cannot with propriety be read aloud in a family'. He later published an edition of ▷ Gibbon's ▷ *Decline and Fall of the Roman Empire* similarly expurgated. From these we get the word 'bowdlerize' = to expurgate.

Bowen, Elizabeth (1899–1973)
Novelist and short-story writer. Born in Dublin and educated in England, she worked in a Dublin hospital during World War I, and for the Ministry of Information in London during World War II. Her novels are concerned with themes of innocence and sophistication, the effect of guilt and of the past on present relationships, and the damaging consequences of coldness and deceit. Her portrayal of the inner life of female characters and her symbolic use of atmosphere and environment show the influence of ▷ Virginia Woolf, as does the structure of her first novel. *The House in Paris* (1935). Her treatment of childhood and youthful innocence owes something to the work of ▷ Henry James, especially in *The Death of the Heart* (1938), where Bowen narrates the story partly through the consciousness of a young girl. Bowen powerfully

conveyed the atmosphere of World War II London during the Blitz, and the emotional dislocation resulting from the war, both in *The Heat of the Day* (1949) and in short stories such as 'In The Square' and 'Mysterious Kôr' (in *The Demon Lover*, 1945). Her other novels are: *The Hotel* (1927); *The Last September* (1929); *A World of Love* (1955); *Eva Trout* (1969). Other story collections include: *The Cat Jumps* (1934); *Look at all those Roses* (1941); *A Day in the Dark* (1965).
Bib: Glendinning, V., *Elizabeth Bowen: Portrait of a Writer*; Craig, P., *Elizabeth Bowen*.

Boys Own Paper
A weekly magazine for boys, founded in 1879 and published by the Religious Tract Society. It ran until 1967, reached a circulation of around 250,000 and published adventure stories, often with imperialist themes, as well as essays, letters, puzzles, and competitions.
Bib: Bristow, J., *Empire Boys: Adventures in a Man's World*.

Bradbury, Malcolm (b 1932)
Novelist and critic. His novels are: *Eating People Is Wrong* (1959); *Stepping Westward* (1963); *The History Man* (1975); *Rates Of Exchange* (1983); *Cuts* (1987). These are witty, satirical portraits of the period since 1950; the first three use university settings to epitomize the changing social and political situation of Western liberalism, while *Doctor Criminale* (1992) revolves around a journalist's pursuit of an enigmatic philosopher around the Europe of the early 1990s. He is often compared to ▷ Kingsley Amis for his hilarious send-ups of academic habits and pretensions, but Bradbury also has a fascination with the idea of fictionality, which he sees as central to the contemporary understanding of reality. His works are therefore informed by current critical theory (a feature which they share with the novels of ▷ David Lodge). *Rates of Exchange* draws on ▷ structuralist theories, has an eastern European setting, and a somewhat harsher tone than Bradbury's earlier work, in an attempt to register the atmosphere of the 1980s. The title of *Cuts* refers to both cuts in funding and film cutting, and the novel portrays Tory Britain in the mid-1980s through the story of a collision between an academic and a woman television executive. Bradbury teaches on the successful creative writing postgraduate course at the University of East Anglia, which has included among its graduates ▷ Ian McEwan and ▷ Kazuo Ishiguro.
Bib: Morace, R. A., *The Dialogic Novels of Malcolm Bradbury and David Lodge*.

Braddon, Mary Elizabeth (1835–1915)
Novelist. Daughter of a solicitor, educated privately, Braddon became an actress for three years to support her mother, before beginning to write. She met publisher John Maxwell in 1860 and lived with him and his five children, producing six more of their own. They married in 1874 on the death of Maxwell's first wife, who was in a lunatic asylum. She wrote more than 80 ▷ sensation novels; her publisher called her the 'Queen of the Circulating

Libraries'. *Lady Audley's Secret* (1862) was first serialized in *Robin Goodfellow* and *The Sixpenny Magazine*, and was immediately successful. Other novels include *Aurora Floyd* (1863), *The Doctor's Wife* (1864), *Henry Dunbar* (1864), *Ishmael* (1884) and *The Infidel* (1900).

Bradley, F. H. (Francis Herbert) (1846–1924)
Brother of A. C. Bradley, the literary critic. He was himself an eminent philosopher, author of *Ethical Studies* (1876); *Principles of Logic* (1883); *Appearance and Reality* (1893), and *Essay on Truth and Reality* (1914). His position philosophically was an idealist one, and in this he has been opposed by most British philosophers ever since, beginning with ▷ G. E. Moore. Bradley, however, had a strong influence on T. S. Eliot, the poet and former philosophy student, whose early thesis on him has recently been published.
▷ Idealism; Realism.

Braine, John (b 1922)
Novelist. His most famous novels are *Room at the Top* (1957; filmed 1958) and *Life at the Top* (1962; filmed 1965). Both of these deal with the new kinds of social mobility and anxiety, characteristic of Britain since World War II, and led to him being thought of as one of the ▷ 'angry young men' of the 1950s. Like the heroes of his novels, however, he has become progressively more conservative in his attitudes. Other novels are: *The Vodi* (1959); *The Jealous God* (1964); *The Crying Game* (1968); *Stay with me till Morning* (1970); *The Queen of a Distant Country* (1972); *The Pious Agent* (1975); *Waiting For Sheila* (1976); *The Only Game in Town* (1976); *Finger of Fire* (1977); *One and Last Love* (1981); *The Two of Us* (1984); *These Golden Days* (1985).
▷ Realism.
Bib: Salwak, D., *John Braine and John Wain: A Reference Guide*.

Brathwaite, E. R. (b 1912)
Novelist and autobiographer. Born in Guyana, most of Brathwaite's writing is concerned with his working life in Britain in the 1950s and 1960s. His most successful work (which was turned into a popular film), *To Sir, With Love* (1959), is concerned with his experiences as a black teacher in London, and other semi-autobiographical novels have discussed his social work and time in the RAF. He is the author of: *Paid Servant* (1962); *Reluctant Neighbours* (1972); *A Kind of Homecoming* (1962) and *A Choice of Straws* (1967).

Breton, André (1896–1966)
French poet, founder of ▷ Surrealism, which he launched in 1924 with the first *Surrealist Manifesto*. Prior to this, Breton had met both the poet Guillaume Apollinaire (during 1917–18) and ▷ Sigmund Freud (in 1921), both of whom provided inspiration for the movement. In 1919, he published his first collection of poems, *Mont de piété*, and in the same year he collaborated with Philippe Soupault (b 1897) on his first properly Surrealist text, *Les Champs magnétiques*, which preceded the official

launch of Surrealism. Between 1919 and 1921, he participated in the ▷ Dadaist movement, although it was his initiative to hold in Paris the international congress which led to the break-up of Dada. Believing firmly in the radicalism of Surrealism, Breton resisted any attempt to make the movement subservient to an established political creed. In *Légitime Défense* (1926), he rejected any form of control, even Marxist control, of the psychic life and, by contrast with other members of the movement, this was to lead to his break with communism in 1935. After the war, Breton continued to campaign vigorously on behalf of Surrealist radicalism. He opposed Albert Camus's (1913–60) thesis, as expounded in *L'Homme révolté* (1952) that revolt has its limitations, and a year before his death organized a final Surrealist exhibition, *L'Ecart absolu*, which aimed to challenge the consumer society. Breton contributed to Surrealist writing not only by the three manifestos (1924, 1930, 1934) and other polemical writing, but also by numerous collections of poetry and prose, the original editions of which were usually illustrated by leading artists connected with Surrealism.

Bib: Bozo, D., *André Breton: La beauté convulsive.*

Brighton Rock (1938)

One of the best-known novels by ▷ Graham Greene. Set in Brighton, it combines elements of the thriller with the moral and religious themes prominent in Greene's later work. The story of murder, innocence and corruption set in the criminal underworld is centred on Pinkie, a 17-year-old Catholic gangster obsessed with evil, whose murder of a journalist sets him on a path to damnation. He marries Rose, a 16-year-old girl, in order to protect himself from the law but Ida, an acquaintance of the murdered man, pursues Pinkie, leading eventually to his death.

Brink, André (b 1935)

South African novelist, playwright and critic, educated at Potchefstroom and Rhodes universities in South Africa and at the Sorbonne in Paris. He teaches Afrikaans and Dutch literature and is now professor at Rhodes University. His novels are concerned with the history, sources and consequences of racism and apartheid in South Africa. *Looking on Darkness* (1974) and *An Instant in the Wind* (1976) are both stories about sexual relationships between people of different races, though the former is set in the 20th century and the latter in the 18th. *A Chain of Voices* (1982) uses multiple narrators to recount the story of a slave revolt in Cape Colony in the early 19th century and *Rumours of Rain* (1978) is about the Soweto riots of 1976. *The Wall of the Plague* (1984), set in France, establishes parallels between apartheid and the Great Plague of the 14th century in Europe. His other novels are: *File on a Diplomat* (1965); *A Portrait of Woman as a Young Girl* (1973); *A Dry White Season* (1979); *An Act of Terror: A Novel* (1991). Brink's novels have been published in both Afrikaans and English; he moves back and forth between the two languages in the process of writing. Several of his novels were intially banned in South Africa. He has

three times won the CNA award (a South African literary prize). *Mapmakers: Writing in a State of Siege* (1983) is a collection of essays on politics and literature, and he has edited, with ▷ J.M. Coetzee, *A Land Apart: A South African Reader* (1986).

British Academy

Founded in 1901 it was intended to complement the function of the Royal Society by representing 'literary science', which was defined as 'the sciences of language, history, philosophy and antiquities, and other subjects the study of which is based on scientific principles but which are not included under the term "natural science"'. It derived its authority from the backing of the Royal Society, the grant of a Royal Charter (1902) and the addition of bye-laws by Order in Council (1903). The British Academy elects its own Fellows, up to a total of 200; candidates have to be nominated by not fewer than three and not more than six existing Fellows. The British Academy publishes its *Proceedings* and certain lectures; research awards are annually made available for competition.

British Council

Established in 1934, its brief is to promote an enduring understanding and appreciation of Britain overseas through cultural, technical and educational exchange. The Council has staff in over 80 countries and is responsible for the implementation of more than 30 cultural agreements with other countries. It has 116 libraries world-wide and its activities include the recruitment of teachers for posts overseas, fostering personal contacts between British and overseas academics, and the placing and welfare of overseas students in Britain. It is exceptionally powerful in determining how Britain represents itself abroad in that the Council decides what is to be presented overseas as 'the best of British arts and culture' ▷ Graham Greene, ▷ Lawrence Durrell and ▷ Olivia Manning in various novels offer a view of the early years of the Council's work.

Brittain, Vera (1893–1970)

Autobiographer, poet, novelist and journalist. Vera Brittain is best known for her autobiographical books, *Testament of Youth* (1933) and *Testament of Experience* (1957), the first detailing with great feeling her life as a nurse in France during World War I, and particularly the loss of her fiancé to the war itself, whilst the second recounts the period from 1925–1950, including an account of the therapeutic experience of writing the first book itself. She is also something of a war poet, offering a perspective on the conflict not represented by those usually characterized as War Poets, in *Poems of the War and After* (1934). Her other novels and non-fiction writing include: *The Dark Tide* (1923); *Account Rendered* (1945); *Born 1925* (1948); *Lady into Woman: A History of Women from Victoria to Elizabeth II* (1953); *The Women at Oxford: A Fragment of History* (1960).

Her friendship with fellow-novelist ▷ Winifred Holtby, whom she had met at Oxford after the war where the two were students, and with whom she set up house after the two graduated, was an important factor in her early life, and their friendship

is represented in *Selected Letters of Winifred Holtby and Vera Brittain* (1960), and in Brittain's *Testament of Friendship* (1940), a memorial to Holtby written on her death. Brittain was also deeply committed to Labour Party politics (one of her daughters, Shirley Williams, became a prominent Labour, and then SDP, politician), and she was an important founder-member of CND, writing in support of the peace movement (see particularly *The Rebel Passion: A Short History of Some Pioneer Peace-Makers*; 1964).
Bib: Bailey, H., *Vera Brittain*.

Bromley, Eliza (d 1807)
Novelist. An early colonialist writer whose childhood in the West Indies provided her with a genuine love for the vigour and mysteries of the place, though Bromley often presents a stereotypical and patronizing view of the indigenous Indians and negro slaves. Her *Louisa and Augustus, An Authentic Story in a Series of Letters* (1784) was mocked by ▷ Jane Austen in *Love and Friendship*.

Brontë, Anne (1820–49)
Novelist and poet. The younger sister of ▷ Charlotte and ▷ Emily Brontë. She was very close to Emily as a child and together they invented the imaginary world of Gondal, the setting for several poems and a prominent feature in their lives. She wrote under the name of Acton Bell, contributing to the volume of poems by all three sisters. Her two novels are *Agnes Grey* (1847), an autobiographical account of the trials and hopes of a young governess, and *The Tenant of Wildfell Hall* (1848), the story of a man who falls in love with a young widow (as he supposes), only to discover that her alcoholic and unfaithful husband is still alive. Both novels have happy endings, although the second of them was regarded by many critics at the time as morbid in its preoccupations.
Bib: Gérin, W., *Anne Brontë*.

Brontë, Charlotte (1816–55)
Novelist; the third among five daughters of Patrick Brontë, a Yorkshire clergyman of Irish origin. All the daughters seem to have been gifted, and all died with their single brother before their father; their mother died in 1821.
In 1846 Charlotte, with ▷ Emily and ▷ Anne Brontë, published a volume of poetry under the pen-names of Currer, Ellis and Acton Bell: only Emily's verse is particularly noteworthy. Charlotte's first novel, ▷ *The Professor*, was not published until after her death; her second, ▷ *Jane Eyre* (1847), was immediately successful. Her third novel, ▷ *Shirley*, came out in 1849, ▷ *Villette*, based on her period of teaching in Brussels, in 1853. *Villette* is her most mature. The impressiveness of her writing comes from the struggle – experienced by herself, related through her heroines in *Jane Eyre* and *Villette* – to preserve her independence of spirit in circumstances which are overwhelmingly adverse. Her novels are often seen to be autobiographical ones. *Jane Eyre* continues to be successful, and *Villette* is increasingly esteemed. *The Professor* is really *Villette* in an earlier and more imperfect form; and *Shirley*, the only one not to have autobiographical form, is less admired.

Like Anne and Emily, Charlotte has been the focus of attention for modern ▷ feminist critics and the confined and restless imagery of their novels is often seen as representative of the anger of suppressed and misrepresented women.
Bib: Gaskell, E., *Life*; Cecil, D., *Early Victorian Novelists*; Ratchford, F., *The Brontës' Web of Childhood*; Hanson, L. and E.M., *The Four Brontës*; Gérin, W., *Charlotte Brontë: The Evolution of Genius*; Peters, M., *Unquiet Soul: A Biography of Charlotte Brontë*; Gilbert, S. and Gubar, S., *The Madwoman on the Attic*.

Brontë, Emily (1818–48)
Novelist and poet. She has been described as the finest woman poet in English literature. It is, however, for her only novel, ▷ *Wuthering Heights* (1847), that she is chiefly famous. The novel is unique in its structure and its vision; the former is so devised that the story comes through several independent narrators. Her vision is such that she brings human passions (through her characters Heathcliff and Catherine Earnshaw) against society (represented by the households of Wuthering Heights and Thrushcross Grange) with extraordinary violence, while at the same time retaining a cool artistic control. This enables the reader to experience a highly intelligent criticism of society's implicit claim to absorb all the energies of the individual, who potentially is larger in spirit than society ever can be. Initially received as morbid and too violent, it has grown in critical stature, particularly with regard to its structure.
Bib: Kavanagh, C., *The Symbolism of Wuthering Heights*; Sanger, C. P., *The Structure of Wuthering Heights*; Gérin, W., *Emily Brontë: A Biography*.

Brooke, Henry (1703–83)
Novelist, poet and playwright. Brooke's novels *The Fool of Quality* (1765–70) and *Juliet Grenville* (1774) contributed to the late 18th-century fashion for ▷ sensibility. He also published a poem, *Universal Beauty* (1735), and a tragedy, *Gustavus Vasa* (1739).

Brooke-Rose, Christine (b 1926)
Novelist and critic. Born in Geneva, of an English father and a Swiss/American mother, she is bilingual, and her best-known works are influenced by the French ▷ *nouveau roman* of Alain Robbe-Grillet and Nathalie Sarraute. *Out* (1964) uses Robbe-Grillet's technique of exhaustive description of inanimate objects. In *Such* (1966) a scientist recalls his past during the three minutes taken to bring him back to consciousness after heart failure, while *Thru* (1975) is a multilingual, playful, Joycean novel, employing typographical patterns and self-referential discussion of its own narrative technique. More recently, *Xorander* (1986) is a work of ▷ science fiction, exploring the possibilities of a computer-dominated society, while *Textermination* (1991) presents an image of the post-modern (▷ post-modernism) condition in the form of a convention of characters from fiction held in the San Francisco Hilton. Brooke-Rose lives in France, where she is a

professor at the University of Paris, and her resolute commitment to modernist (▷ modernism) and post-modernist experimental techniques has led to her relative neglect by English-speaking readers.

Brookner, Anita (b 1928)

Novelist. Since her first novel, *A Start In Life*, was published in 1981 she has rapidly achieved popular success, confirmed by the award of the Booker Prize to her fourth novel, *Hôtel Du Lac* (1984). Her novels have an autobiographical element and somewhat similar heroines: sensitive, intelligent, but not glamorous, their search for love and fulfilment leads to disillusionment and betrayal by attractive but selfish men. Brookner's prose style is careful, elegant, lucid and mannered in a way somewhat reminiscent of ▷ Henry James. She lectures and writes on the subject of art history.

Her other novels are: *Providence* (1982); *Look At Me* (1983); *Family And Friends* (1985); *A Misalliance* (1986); *A Friend From England* (1987); *Latecomers* (1988); *A Closed Eye* (1991); *Fraud* (1992).
Bib: Skinner, J., *The Fictions of Anita Brookner*.

Brophy, Brigid (b 1929)

Novelist and critic. The daughter of the novelist John Brophy, she won immediate acclaim with her first novel, *Hackenfeller's Ape* (1953), a fable about imprisonment, rationality and the instinctive life. During the 1960s she acquired a reputation as a polemical and aggressive writer, with controversial libertarian views on sex and marriage. She campaigned for animal rights, defended ▷ pornography, and, with ▷ Maureen Duffy, set up a writers' action group in the 1970s to campaign for Public Lending Right (the Public Lending Right Bill, which provides payments to authors out of a central fund on the basis of library lending, was passed in 1979). Her novels reflect her adherence to ▷ Freudian ideas, and to the evolutionism of George Bernard Shaw. *Flesh* (1962) is a detached yet poetic study of sexual awakening; *The Finishing Touch* (1963), described as 'a lesbian fantasy', is stylistically inspired by the work of ▷ Ronald Firbank; *The Snow Ball* (1964) is an artificial, baroque black comedy of seduction; *In Transit* (1969) uses a bizarre combination of styles and characters and is set in an airport. Her works of criticism include psychological studies of creative artists: *Mozart the Dramatist* (1964); *In Black and White: A Portrait of Aubrey Beardsley* (1968); *Prancing Novelist* (on Ronald Firbank; 1973); *Beardsley and his World* (1976). Her other works of non-fiction include: *Black Ship to Hell* (1962), a Freudian account of the nature of hate; *Don't Never Forget* (1966) and *Baroque and Roll* (1987), collections of her journalism on a wide range of subjects. Other novels include: *The King of a Rainy Country* (1956); *Pussy Owl: Super Beast* (1976); *Palace Without Chairs* (1978). *The Adventures of God in His Search for the Black Girl* (1973) is a series of fables. *The Burglar* (1968) is a play.

Broughton, Rhoda (1840–1920)

Novelist. Broughton grew up in Staffordshire where she set many of her ▷ best-sellers. She was a prolific and financially successful writer, producing novels of sexual intrigue and pathos, such as *Not Wisely But Too Well* (1867) and *Goodbye Sweetheart* (1872).

Browne, Sir Thomas (1605–82)

Physician and author. Sir Thomas Browne studied medicine at Montpellier, Padua and Leiden, and began practising medicine in 1633, before moving in 1637 to Norwich, where he was to spend the rest of his life. Browne's most influential work was *Religio Medici* (1642, re-issued in an authorized edition in 1643), a title which can be translated as *The Religion of a Physician*. The conjunction between religious meditation and an enduring fascination with observation of the most minute details of the physical world informs the *Religio*, which stands as both a determined act of creation of an authorial persona, and as a disquisition which attempts to reconcile scepticism and belief.

In some ways, Browne can be thought of as a Baconian in his adherence to the principles of observation, and his determination to refute ideas commonly entertained by the credulous. But his Baconianism is tempered with a vein of mysticism. The two tendencies in his thought are displayed in his later works – *Pseudodoxica Epidemica*, or *Vulgar Errors* (1646); *Hydriotaphia*, or *Urn Burial* (1658); and *The Garden of Cyrus* (1658).
Bib: Keynes, Sir G. (ed.), *Works*, 4 vols.; Bennett, J., *Sir Thomas Browne*.

Brunton, Mary (1778–1818)

Novelist. She married Rev Alexander Brunton in 1798 and, although she had only a meagre education, they set about studying history and philosophy together. Her first novel, *Self-Control*, was published anonymous in 1811. Brunton was particularly keen to show how romantic stereotypes often acted to the detriment of women; for example, at the beginning of *Self-Control* she states that her purpose is: 'to shew the power of the religious principle in bestowing self-command; and to bear testimony against a maxim as immoral as indelicate, that a reformed rake makes the best husband.' She only completed one more work, *Discipline* (1814), before dying in childbirth, although she did leave the unfinished *Emmeline*. The novels focus upon the psychological development of central female characters, who are in some way made to rethink their presuppositions because of outside forces. The quality and influence of Brunton's work (on ▷ Jane Austen particularly) have only recently been acknowledged.
Bib: Moers, E., *Literary Women*; Springer, M., *What Manner of Woman?*

Bryher (1894–1983)

Novelist. Bryher's historical novels, always published under the single name she legally took on (after one of the Scilly Isles) so as not to be identified with her influential industrialist father, are serious and meticulously researched works on the Greek and Roman Empires (particularly *Roman Wall*, 1954, *Gate to the Sea*, 1958, and *The Coin of Carthage*, 1963) and on the connections between early British history and

contemporary life (*The Fourteenth of October* 1951, *The January Tale*, and *Beowulf*, 1956). Bryher lived with the poet ▷ H.D. for much of her life, and wrote two autobiographies, *The Heart of Artemis* (1962) and *The Days of Mars* (1972). She also wrote literary critism (a book, in 1918, on the poet Amy Lowell), and on film, setting up the film journal *Close-Up*.
Bib: Hanscombe, G. and Smyers, V.L., *Writing For Their Lives*.

Buchan, John, 1st Baron Tweedsmuir (1875–1940)
Novelist. Buchan was born in Scotland and educated at Glasgow and Oxford; he contributed to the ▷ *Yellow Book* while still a student. He is best known for his adventure stories involving the character of Richard Hannay, notably *The Thirty-nine Steps* (1915), filmed by Hitchcock in 1935. Other novels include: *Scholar Gypsies* (1896); *A Lost Lady* (1899); *The Half-Hearted* (1900); *Greenmantle* (1916); *Mr Steadfast* (1918); *Sick Heart River* (1941). He had a distinguished political career and was Governor-General of Canada 1935–1940.

Bunyan, John (1628–88)
Born at Elstow, near Bedford, Bunyan was the son of a tinsmith, educated at the village school. Of Baptist sympathies, he fought in the Civil War, although little is known of his military activities. With the persecution of the ▷ Puritans which followed the Restoration of Charles II, Bunyan's non-conformist beliefs came under severe censure, and in 1660 he was arrested for preaching without a licence.

For most of the next twelve years Bunyan was imprisoned in Bedford jail, where he began to write. His spiritual autobiography, ▷ *Grace Abounding to the Chief of Sinners*, appeared in 1666, and the first part of his major work, ▷ *The Pilgrim's Progress* was largely written during this period of imprisonment, though it is probable that Bunyan completed Part I during a second spell in jail in 1676; the full text, with the addition of Part II, was published in 1684. A spiritual allegory strongly in the ▷ Puritan tradition, it tells of the pilgrimage of Christian to reach the state of grace. Bunyan's other major works, ▷ *The Life and Death of Mr Badman* (1680) and ▷ *The Holy War* (1682) are also spiritual allegories.
Bib: Sharrock R., *John Bunyan*.

Burgess, Anthony (b 1917)
Novelist and critic. Born John Anthony Burgess Wilson of a Roman Catholic Lancashire family, he was educated at Manchester University. After military service during World War II he worked as a schoolmaster in Oxfordshire, Malaya and Borneo. His experiences in Malaya inspired his *Malayan Trilogy* (1956–9), a rich portrait of the Malayan culture and people, employing words and expressions from Malay, Urdu, Arabic, Tamil and Chinese. A fascination with the textures of language and a Joycean inventiveness (▷ Joyce, James) and multilingual playfulness have characterized much of·Burgess's work. In 1959 Burgess returned to England with a brain tumour, expecting to survive only a year, yet in that year wrote five novels: *The*

Doctor is Sick (1960), *One Hand Clapping* (1961), *The Worm and the Ring* (1961), *The Wanting Seed* (1962) and *Inside Mr Enderby* (1963). During the 1960s he worked as a music and drama critic, and produced plays, T.V. scripts, short stories and numerous book reviews. He has since done a considerable amount of university teaching, and lived in Malta, Rome and Monaco. *A Clockwork Orange* (1962), filmed in 1971 by Stanley Kubrick, is an anti-utopian vision with an appalling vicious protagonist who deliberately chooses evil, and who is brainwashed by penal techniques based on behaviourist psychology. Its most striking feature is the use of Nadsat, an invented teenage underworld slang largely based on Russian words and English colloquialisms. *Nothing Like The Sun* (1964) is a fictional account of ▷ Shakespeare's love life, told as the parting lecture of a schoolmaster in the Far East, who progressively identifies himself with his subject. An impression of Elizabethan life is conveyed through descriptive detail and imitation of contemporary idiom. *Earthly Powers* (1980) is a large-scale consideration of the nature of evil, with extensive reference to 20th-century literary and political history. Other novels include: *1985* (1978); *The Piano Players* (1986); *Any Old Iron* (1989); *The Devil's Mode* (1989); and *Mozart and the Wolf Gang* (1991). Non-fiction includes: *The Novel Today* (1963); *Language Made Plain* (1964); *Ernest Hemingway and his World* (1978); *Flame into Being: the Life and Work of D. H. Lawrence* (1985).
Bib: Aggeler, G., *Anthony Burgess, the Artist as Novelist*.

Burke, Edmund (1729–97)
Statesman and political philosopher; described by ▷ Matthew Arnold as 'our greatest English prose-writer'. Born in Dublin, he pursued his political career in England, and was a Member of Parliament for much of his life. Although never attaining high office, his political status was considerable, due mainly to his formidable powers of oratory and polemical argument. His early work *A Philosophical Inquiry into the Origin of our Ideas of the Sublime and the Beautiful* (1756) marks a transition in aesthetic theory from the neo-classicism of John Dryden (1631–1700) and Alexander Pope (1688–1744). Influenced by Longinus and Milton, it emphasizes the sense of awe inspired by both art and nature. His most celebrated work, ▷ *Reflections on the Revolution in France* (1790), argues for the organic, evolutionary development of society, as opposed to the brutal surgery and doctrinaire theories of the French revolutionaries.

Burke's character reveals a number of paradoxes. His writings combine the cautious, pragmatic instincts of a conservative politician with a passionate rhetorical style. He regarded all forms of political innovation with suspicion, yet defended the cause of the American rebels in *On Conciliation with the Colonies* (1775). He attacked the corrupt practice of court patronage and the exploitative activities of the East India Company, yet retained for himself many benefits of the systems he deplored.
Bib: Cone, C. B., *Burke and the Nature of Politics* (2 volumes); Stanlis, P. J. (ed.), *Edmund Burke: The*

Enlightenment and the Modern World; Wilkins, B. T., *The Problem of Burke's Political Philosophy*.

Burnett, Frances Eliza (née Hodgson) (1849–1924)
Novelist. Burnett is known for her best-selling children's stories: *Little Lord Fauntleroy* (1886) about a boy living in New York who turns out to be the heir of an English aristocratic family, and *The Secret Garden* (1911). Burnett also wrote accomplished novels for adults: some, like *Haworth's* (1879), are set in an industrial environment in the north of England while others, like *Through One Administration* (1883), deal with American society.

Burney, Dr Charles (1726–1814)
Father of novelist ▷ Fanny Burney, Charles Burney was the friend of ▷ Samuel Johnson, the actor David Garrick and the painter Sir Joshua Reynolds. An organist and musical historian, he also wrote travelogues of France, Italy, Germany and the Low Countries – journeys he made to collect material for his *History of Music* (published 1776–89).

Burney, Fanny (Frances, Madame D'Arblay) (1752–1840)
Daughter of ▷ Dr Charles Burney, Fanny grew up in the distinguished company of ▷ Johnson, Sir Joshua Reynolds, Garrick and the ▷ Bluestockings. In 1786 she was appointed as an attendant upon Queen Charlotte, wife of George III, and in 1793 she married a French exile, General D'Arblay. From 1802–12, interned by Napoleon, she and her husband lived in France.

Burney's major novels are ▷ *Evelina* (1778), *Cecilia* (1782) and *Camilla* (1796). Their common theme is the entry into society of a young girl, beautiful and intelligent but lacking experience of the world; during subsequent adventures the girl's character is moulded. Burney was a great admirer of ▷ Richardson, and his influence is apparent in her use, in her first novel, of the epistolary (*ie* letter-writing) form.

Burney was also well known for her diaries and letters. Her *Early Diary* (1889) covers the years 1768–78, and contains many sketches of Johnson and Garrick; her *Diary and Letters . . . 1778–1840* (published 1842–6) is a lively account of life at court. Amongst her admirers, ▷ Jane Austen shows Burney's influence.
Bib: Simons, J., *Fanny Burney*.

Burney, Sarah (1772–1844)
Novelist. Overshadowed by her half-sister ▷ Fanny Burney, Sarah was a successful novelist in her own right, earning her living mainly from her writing. Her life seems to have been conventional (for example she accepted jobs as a governess and paid companion), with the exception of a five-year interlude when, as a young adult, she and her married half-brother left their respective homes to live together. Her first novel, *Clarentine* (1796), although published anonymously, received great acclaim, and a number of others followed, the most noteworthy being: *Geraldine Fauconberg* (1808), *The Shipwreck* and *Country Neighbours* (1816–20),

and *The Renunciation* (1839). These focus upon the psychological reactions of their young heroines when confronted by some calamitous occurrence or mysterious revelation.
Bib: Hemlow, J., *The History of Fanny Burney*; Kirkpatrick, S., *Fanny Burney*.

Burton, Sir Richard Francis (1821–90)
Explorer and travel writer. His works include: *Scinde, or the Unhappy Valley* (1851); *First Footsteps in East Africa* (1856); *The Lake Region of Central Africa* (1860); *The Pilgrimage to Al-Medina and Meccah* (1855). He also translated the ▷ *Arabian Nights* (*The Thousand Nights and a Night* – 1885–8) and *The Lusiads of Camoens* (1880). For the last 14 years of his life he worked on a translation of *The Perfumed Garden*, which his widow burned after his death.
Bib: Lady Burton, *Life*; Schonfield, A. L., *Richard Burton Explorer*, Wilson, A. T., *Richard Burton*.

Butler, Samuel (1835–1902)
Satirist, scientific writer, author of an autobiographical novel ▷ *The Way of All Flesh* (1903) in a form which became a model for a number of 20th-century writers. His satires ▷ *Erewhon* (*Nowhere* reversed) and *Erewhon Revisited* (1872 and 1901) are anti-utopias, *ie* instead of exhibiting an imaginary country with ideal customs and institutions in the manner of Sir Thomas More's ▷ *Utopia* (1516). Butler describes a country where the faults of his own country are caricatured, in the tradition of Jonathan Swift's Lilliput (▷ *Gulliver's Travels*). He attacks ecclesiastical and family institutions; in Erewhon, machines have to be abolished because their evolution threatens the human race – a blow at Darwinism.

His scientific work concerned ▷ Charles Darwin's theory of evolution, to which he was opposed because he considered that it left no room for mind in the universe; he favoured the theory of Lamarck (1744–1829) with its doctrine of the inheritability of acquired characteristics. His disagreements and his own theories are expounded in *Life and Habit* (1877), *Evolution Old and New* (1879), *Unconscious Memory* (1880) and *Luck or Cunning?* (1886).

The Way of All Flesh attacks the parental tyranny which Butler saw as the constant feature of Victorian family life (despite much evidence to the contrary); so close did he keep to his own experience that he could not bring himself to publish the book in his own lifetime.

George Bernard Shaw admitted a great debt to Butler's evolutionary theories and to Butler's stand against mental muddle, self-deception and false compromise in society. Writers as different from Butler and from each other as ▷ D. H. Lawrence and ▷ James Joyce wrote autobiographical novels after him in which the facts were often as close to their own experience.
Bib: Cole, G. D. H., *Butler and The Way of All Flesh*; Henderson, P., *The Incarnate Bachelor*; Furbank, P. N., *Samuel Butler*; Jeffers, T. L., *Samuel Butler Revalued*; Joad, C. E. M., *Samuel Butler*; Muggeridge, M., *Earnest Atheist*; Pritchett, V. S., 'A Victorian Son' in *The Living Novel*.

Byatt, A. S. (Antonia Susan) (b 1936)
Novelist, critic and reviewer. Born in Sheffield
and educated at the universities of Cambridge and
Oxford, she has worked as a teacher and lecturer
in English. The novelist ▷ Margaret Drabble is
her sister. Her novels are influenced by the work
of ▷ Proust and of ▷ Iris Murdoch (Byatt has
published two books on Murdoch), and combine a
realistic portrayal of English manners with symbolic
structures and a wide range of reference to history,
myth and art. *The Shadow of a Sun* (1964) is a
feminist ▷ *Bildungsroman* about a girl seeking to
escape from a dominating novelist father, while *The
Game* (1967), a story of the tragic rivalry between two
sisters, has overtones of the Fall of Man. *The Virgin
in the Garden* (1979) and *Still Life* (1985) are the first
two volumes of a projected tetralogy, intended

to trace the lives of a group of characters from the
accession of Queen Elizabeth II in 1952 up to the
1980 Post-Impressionist Exhibition in London.
Byatt's later style includes quotation, allusion,
narrative prolepses (anticipations of later events)
and metafictional reflections on novel writing. Story
collection: *Sugar* (1987). Her 1990 novel *Possession*
is an academic ▷ detective story which splices the
tale of two young scholars' researches into the love
between a male and female poet in the 19th century
with the story of the romance itself. It became a ▷
best-seller and won the Booker Prize in 1990. *Angels
and Insects* (1992), which consists of two ▷ novellas,
also combines 19th-century settings with literary
concerns. *Passions of the Mind* (1991) is a volume
of essays.

C

Campbell, Ramsey (b 1946)

Novelist and journalist. Born and raised in Liverpool, Campbell is a leading light of Britain's 'new wave' of horror writers, described by Robert Hadji as 'the finest living exponent of the British weird fiction tradition'. Has published pseudonymously under the names Carl Dreadstone and Jay Ramsay. Campbell was a young devotee of H. P. Lovecraft whose style he mimicked in his early short stories, collected in *The Inhabitant of the Lake and Less Welcome Tenants* (1964). Although his first novel *The Doll Who Ate His Mother* (1976) was a minor success, Campbell came of age with *The Face That Must Die*, (1979, revised 1983) which presents a coherently grim portrait of the world through the eyes of a psychotic. His subsequent novels successfully transpose the terrors of writers such as Lovecraft, M. R. James, Robert Aickmen and Arthur Machen into starkly realistic situations of modern urban collapse. A fierce defender of the honourable tradition of horror fiction, Campbell describes himself as 'working against the innate prejudices and conservatisms of the field', using visceral horror to make people look again at things they may have taken for granted'. Campbell has also edited a number of horror anthologies and critical works. Works include *Demons by Daylight* (1973); *The Parasite* aka *To Wake The Dead* (1980); *Incarnate* (1983); *Obsession* (1985); *Scared Stiff* (1987); *Ancient Images* (1989); *Count of Eleven* (1991); and *Waking Nightmares* (1992).
▷ Horror fiction.

Canterbury Tales, The

A famed story-collection by ▷ Geoffrey Chaucer, begun sometime in the later 1380s. The General Prologue gives details of the occasion for the story-telling, relating how a group of pilgrims, bound for the shrine of St Thomas Becket at Canterbury, meet up at the Tabard Inn in Southwark. The pilgrims are introduced in a sequence of portraits which focus on the professional activities of the company (who number 31 in all). The material for these portraits derives partly from a long-standing literary tradition of social analysis and satire, but Chaucer enlarges the scope of the cross-section of society on the pilgrimage by including a broader range of bourgeois professionals in the group. The varied format and style of the descriptive cameos (in which details of dress, character or professional habits are mentioned seemingly at random) enhances the impression of the individuality of the pilgrims, who are introduced by a pilgrim-narrator whose stance is that of a reporter of events.

The list of portraits begins with that of the Knight, a representative of the higher levels of the social élite, who is travelling with his son, the Squire, and their Yeoman. The focus then shifts to the description of members of the clerical elite on the trip, including a Prioress, a Monk and a Friar. There is no clear-cut ordering principle in the sequence of portraits which follows (other than perhaps a broad downward movement through the social scale), describing a Merchant, a Clerk of Oxford, a Lawyer, a Franklin, a group of five Guild members, their wives and their Cook, a Shipman, a Physician, a Wife of Bath, a Parson and his brother, a Ploughman, a Miller, a Manciple, a Reeve and, finally, a Summoner and a Pardoner who pair up as travelling companions. The pilgrim-narrator is described in more detail by the Host, later on the journey. The General Prologue concludes with an account of how the Host of the Tabard Inn, Harry Bailey, devises a story-telling competition to take place on the round trip to Canterbury. The pilgrims agree to tell two stories each on the forward and return journeys; Harry Bailey plans to accompany the pilgrims, act as games-master and reward the pilgrim providing the best story with a meal on return to Southwark.

Diversity seems to be the organizing principle of the collection. The *Canterbury Tales* includes an extraordinarily wide range of material in verse (in rhymed decasyllabic couplets, rhyme royal verse) and prose, covering a wide range of literary genres and forms: ▷ romances, fabliaux, an animal fable, saints' lives, examplary narratives, a moral treatise, a prose treatise on the process of penitence (which concludes the game). The relationship between 'earnest' and 'game', between serious and playful literary material, is one of the running topics of debate within and between the tales.

Judging from the condition of the extant manuscript copies of the *Canterbury Tales*, the project outlined by Harry Bailey in the General Prologue was never completed by Chaucer. The *Canterbury Tales* has the status of a 'work in progress', comprising a series of fragmentary tale-telling sequences, some of which are linked by dramatic interactions between the pilgrims and Harry Bailey, some of which begin and end without any contextual framing, and some of which show signs of being linked to other tellers at an earlier stage in the process of compilation. However, the opening and closing sequences of the *Tales* are provided and from these it seems that the literary plan was designed to change *en route* from a round journey to a one-way trip. The last tale of the sequence, the Parson's prose treatise on penitence, signals not only the end of the journey to Canterbury, but also the end of story-telling altogether, and is followed in most manuscripts by Chaucer's literary Retraction.

None of the 82 manuscripts of the *Tales* was copied during Chaucer's lifetime, and variations in form, style and tale-teller linkage are apparent. Some of the variation seem to reflect the attempts of later scribes and editors to tidy up some of the loose ends of the story-collection and provide more cohesive links for the series of fragmentary sequences left by Chaucer. Modern editions of the *Canterbury Tales* are based on two important early 15th-century manuscripts: the Ellesmere manuscript (E) and the Hengwrt manuscript (H). The form and arrangement of the text in E have provided the basis for the most accessible editions of the *Tales* (by F. N. Robinson, revised and updated by Larry Benson et al.). In E, 22 of the pilgrims mentioned in the Prologue produce a tale, beginning with the Knight, followed by the Miller, the Reeve, the Cook, the Man of Law, the Wife of Bath, the Friar, the Summoner, the Clerk, the Merchant, the Squire, the Franklin, the Physician, the Pardoner, the Shipman, the Prioress, the pilgrim/narrator (who tells two tales, *Sir Thopas*, which is rejected by the Host, and *Melibeus*), the Monk, the Nun's Priest, the Second Nun, the Canon's Yeoman (who joins the pilgrimage *en route*), the Manciple and finally the Parson. It is now generally accepted that the E text has been quite extensively edited by Chaucer's literary executors and represents a later, tidied-up version of the text represented in H, and more recently the Hengwrt manuscript has been used as the basis for new editions of the *Canterbury Tales* (by N. Blake, by Paul Ruggiers and David Baker). The differences between the two versions are mainly in the ordering and linking of the tales: the E text has more connected sequences of stories and contains the *Canon's Yeoman's Prologue and Tale*, which is not in H.

Since its publication by Chaucer's literary executors, the *Canterbury Tales* has had an active 'afterlife'. Some new tales were added to the collection by 15th-century editors (notably Gamelyn), an attempt was made to continue the narrative after the arrival at Canterbury (in the *Tale of Beryn*) and John Lydgate, the prolific court writer of the 15th century, wrote himself into the literary event of the *Tales* in his work *The Siege of Thebes*, which opens with a description of Lydgate himself joining the pilgrimage and then contributing his Theban story to the competition. Translations of selected tales were made by John Dryden (1631–1700) and Alexander Pope (1688–1744). The attention given to the *Canterbury Tales*, in relation to the rest of the Chaucerian canon, has varied according to the critical temper and tastes of the time, but the enormous attention given by modern scholars and critics to the phenomenon of the *Tales* is only the most recent stage in the long history of their critical reception. The *Canterbury Tales* continues to be a work in progress.
Bib: Benson, L., et al. (eds.), *The Riverside Chaucer*; Boitani, P., and Mann, J. (eds.), *The Cambridge Chaucer Companion*; Cooper, H., *The Structure of the Canterbury Tales*; Howard, D. D. R., *The Idea of the Canterbury Tales*; Pearsall, D., *The Canterbury Tales*.

Capitalism
The system by which the means of production is owned privately. Production is for private profit and productive enterprise is made possible by large-scale loans of money rewarded by the payment of interest.

Before about 1350, in England as in much of the rest of Europe, there was little opportunity for capitalism. On the land, the economic unit was the manor (corresponding approximately to a village) which consumed its own produce and had little left over for sale; the economic relations were feudal, *ie* the landlords provided protection to the peasants in return for economic services, and the peasants were mostly serfs, *ie* they were bound to the land they worked on and were unable to sell their labour freely. The towns were small and manufacture was by master craftsmen, who worked with their own hands, and employed apprentices and journeymen only in small numbers. The masters combined in craft guilds which regulated trade and limited profits to a communally arranged 'just price'. Moreover,

commerce, except for the export of wool, was mainly limited to the districts round the towns. Finally, it was difficult to borrow money for capital investment, partly because the Church disapproved of the taking of interest on money loans, since it regarded this as the sin of usury. The economic bond was not, in fact, a money relationship but a personal one, bound up with an elaborate system of rights and duties; these divided society into something more like castes than the modern social classes, which are differentiated chiefly by wealth.

But already by the lifetime of the poet ▷ Chaucer capitalism was making beginnings. Towns were growing, and they now contained a substantial middle class, as the *Prologue* to ▷ *The Canterbury Tales* illustrates. Master craftsmen were gradually becoming employers of labour rather than workers themselves; this was particularly true in the manufacture of cloth, which required a variety of processes impossible for one man, or even one guild, to undertake alone. The craft guilds were becoming supplemented by the merchant companies, such as the Merchants of the Staple, who had a monopoly of the export of wool to the cloth manufacturers of Flanders, and later (15th and 16th centuries) the Merchant Adventurers, whose export of cloth became even more important than the older commerce of the export of wool. The economic cause of the Hundred Years' War (1338–1453) was Edward III's determination to protect the English wool staple towns – *ie* those through which the export of wool was channelled into Flanders – from the threat of France. To sustain the war, Edward III and Henry V had to borrow extensively from foreign bankers, who were finding methods of escaping the Church's prohibition of usury. Meanwhile, on the land the serfs were becoming independent wage-earners, able to sell their labour freely and where they pleased; this was thanks to the shortage of labour that resulted from the Black Death epidemics (about 1350). Lack of labour caused many landowners to turn their arable land into pasture and to enclose open land with hedges. This process continued in Tudor times for economic reasons, despite a labour surplus. It weakened the landowners' ties with the peasantry and encouraged the 'drift to the towns' which drained the countryside in the 18th–19th centuries.

The rapid growth of capitalism in the 17th and 18th centuries was aided by the Reformation, since certain of the ▷ Puritan sects – notably the Calvinist Presbyterians – found that religious individualism gave support to and was supported by economic individualism. The dramatists of the period of English drama 1580–1640 found the Puritans to be against them, and they (*eg* Ben Jonson, Thomas Middleton, Philip Massinger) tended to satirize the money-loving, socially ambitious middle classes, among whom the Puritans had their main strength. By the end of the 17th century, however, Puritanism was losing its ferocity; the traditional non-economic bonds of community were by then gravely weakened, and the novels of ▷ Daniel Defoe depict the loneliness of men guided predominantly by economically individualistic motives.

The full triumph of capitalism came only with

the fulfilment of the ▷ Industrial Revolution in the 19th century. Workers were, for the first time on a large scale, employed in the mass, in factories. The employers (backed by a number of gifted theorists, such as ▷ Adam Smith, ▷ Jeremy Bentham, ▷ Malthus, Ricardo) developed a ruthless philosophy, according to which their relationship with their workers should be governed entirely by the economic laws of supply and demand, with which the state interfered, in their opinion, only at the cost of wrecking national prosperity, even if the interference were dictated by the need to save the workers from intolerable misery. This stream of opinion among the industrialist employers was, however, progressively opposed by Evangelical Christians among the politicians (*eg* ▷ Lord Shaftesbury), by socialists of the school of ▷ Robert Owen and by the very popular novelists between 1830 and 1860, such as ▷ Elizabeth Gaskell, ▷ Benjamin Disraeli and ▷ Charles Dickens. The most cogent and revolutionary opposition, however, was formulated in the work of Friedrich Engels, *The Condition of the Working Class* (1845) and of ▷ Karl Marx, *Das Kapital* (1867). The two men collaborated, in London, on the *Communist Manifesto* (1848). Gradually industrial capitalism became less inhumane, and in the last twenty years of the 19th century, socialist opinion grew, aided by the leadership of intellectuals such as George Bernard Shaw and ▷ Beatrice Webb. The principal issue now dividing the main political parties is how much economic activity should be left in private hands and how much freedom this 'free enterprise' should be allowed: the Conservatives support capitalist enterprise and the Labour Party emphasizes the value of state control. This compromise between capitalism and socialism since the Second World War produced the ▷ Welfare State, where nobody should starve and nobody is supposed to suffer social injustice, though many still do. (One of the projects of the Thatcher administration in Britain from 1979–1990 was the erosion of the Welfare State.) The Welfare State combined with better education since the war to produce a more articulate working class than has ever been seen in England before; one result of this has been a much larger production of novels, plays and films exploring the experience of social mobility, *eg* the plays of Arnold Wesker and the novels of ▷ Alan Sillitoe.
▷ Anti-industrialism.

Captain Singleton, Adventures of (1720)
A novel by ▷ Daniel Defoe. Like the heroes and heroines of Defoe's other novels, the hero has at first no morality and takes to a life of wandering adventure; some of this takes place in Africa (which Defoe knew only from reading and hearsay). Later he becomes a pirate in the Indian Ocean and further east; finally he settles down in England, a respectable married man, converted to a religious life. The story is told in the first person.

Carew, Jan (b 1925)
Guyanese novelist, poet and playwright. He has worked as a writer, actor, lecturer (University of London extra-mural department), radio editor (BBC Overseas Service) and broadcaster. He is now a professor of English in the USA. His novels include: *Black Midas* (1958); *The Wild Coast* (1958); *The Last Barbarian* (1961); *Moscow is Not My Mecca* (1964). His plays include *University of Hunger* (1966) and *Black Horse, Pale Rider* (1970). *Streets of Eternity* (1952) and *Sea Drums in My Blood* (1981) are volumes of poetry, and he has also published books for children, television and radio plays and historical works.

Carey, Peter (b 1943)
Australian novelist and short-story writer. Born in Victoria and educated in science at Monash University, Carey now works part-time in advertising in Sydney. He has published two volumes of short stories: *The Fat Man in History* (1974) and *War Crimes* (1979) (combined in the UK as *Exotic Pleasures*, 1981). His first two novels were: *Bliss* (1981), a bleak black comedy of the Australian suburbs about a man who believes himself to be dead and in Hell; and *Illywhacker* (1985), which combines realist elements with an outrageously unreliable narrator, who announces on the first page that he is a 'terrible liar'. These were followed by: *Oscar and Lucinda* (1988), which won the Booker Prize, and *The Tax Inspector* (1991), a sinister and violent story about abuse within a family over several generations in a suburb of Sydney. Carey is often described as a fabulist, and has acknowledged the influence on his work of the ▷ magic realism of Gabriel García Márquez.
▷ Post-colonial fiction.

Carlyle, Thomas (1795–1881)
Scottish essayist, historian, philosopher. The term 'philosopher' is inappropriate to him if it implies the use of the reason for the logical investigation of truth; his friend ▷ John Stuart Mill, who was a philosopher in this sense, called Carlyle a poet, meaning that he reached his conclusions by imaginative intuition. In his old age he became known as 'the sage of Chelsea'; this is the kind of admiration that he received in England between 1840 and his death. He hated spiritual mediocrity, mere contentment with material prosperity, moral lassitude and the surrender to scientific scepticism and analytic reasoning. All these he regarded as characteristic of British civilization in the mid-19th century. Part of their cause was the overwhelming technical advances resulting from the ▷ Industrial Revolution; he also considered the immense popularity of the poet Byron (1788–1824) had helped to disintegrate spiritual wholeness because of the cynicism and pessimism of his poetry, and he distrusted equally the influence on the English mind of the coldly logical French philosophers. To counter Byron, he pointed to the spiritual health which he found in Goethe (1749–1832), and to counter the French he advocated the more emotional and intuitive 18th and 19th-century German thinkers like Richter and Goethe.
Carlyle's influence derives even more, however, from his own character and the environment from which he sprang. His father had been a Scottish stonemason, with the moral energy and intellectual

interests which come partly from the influence
of Scottish Calvinism. This religious tradition in
Scotland had much in common with 17th-century
▷ Puritanism which had left such a strong mark on
the English character; the resemblance between the
two traditions helps to account for the hold which
Carlyle established on the English imagination.
His own personality was strong and individualistic;
this, combined with his intention of counteracting
the abstract intellectual thought of writers like ▷
Bentham, caused him to write in an eccentric prose
style, distorting natural word order and using archaic
language. His ▷ *Sartor Resartus* ('Tailor Repatched',
1833–4) is a disguised spiritual ▷ autobiography
in which he faces the tendencies to intellectual
scepticism and spiritual denial in himself, and
dedicates himself to a life of spiritual affirmation.
He is unable to base this affirmative spirit on the
traditional religious beliefs that had supported his
father, so that he has to base it on his own will, his
imaginative response to nature and the inspiration
provided by the lives of great men.

History was for Carlyle the storehouse of example
of these great men, his 'Heroes' – and it is in this
spirit that we have to approach his historical works:
French Revolution (1837), *On Heroes and Hero Worship*
(1841), *Oliver Cromwell's Letters and Speeches* (1845)
and *Frederick II of Prussia* (1858–65). In *Signs of the
Times* (1829), *Chartism* (1839) and *Past and Present*
(1843) he criticized the mechanistic philosophy which
he saw underlying contemporary industrial society,
and in *Latter-Day Pamphlets* (1850) he attacked the
quasi-scientific treatment of social questions by the
rationalist political economists. In 1867 *Shooting
Niagara – and After?*, written at the time of the
Second Parliamentary Reform Bill, reflects his total
disbelief in the efficacy of mere political reform.

As a historian, Carlyle wanted history to be related
to the life of the ordinary human being; as a social
thinker, his advocacy of the imaginative approach
to man in society relates him to the thought of ▷
Coleridge, whom he knew through his friend John
Sterling (*Life of John Sterling*, 1851), and also to his
own disciple, ▷ John Ruskin.
▷ Utilitarianism; Scottish literature in English.
Bib: Trevelyan, G. M., *Carlyle Anthology*; Froude,
J. A., *Life*; Neff, E., *Carlyle and Mill*; Harold, C. F.,
Carlyle and German Thought, 1819–34; Symons, J.,
Carlyle: the Life and Idea of a Prophet; Sanders, C.
R. and Fielding, K. J.(eds.), *The Collected Letters of
Thomas and Jane Carlyle*.

Carnival
The literal meaning of this term is the 'saying goodbye' to meat at the start of Lent. Traditionally it was
a period of feasting during the Christian calendar
which reached its climax on Shrove Tuesday, and
included many forms of festive inversion of normal
behaviour, often comic and mocking of authority.
To this extent it signifies a spontaneous eruption of
those social forces shortly to be restrained by Lent.
This sense of disruption of the norm has brought
the term 'carnival' into the language of contemporary
critical theory. ▷ Mikhail Bakhtin first used the
term to describe a form of festive language which

threatens disruption and challenges the social order.
The association of carnival with popular energies
highlights the political tension between official
▷ ideology and potentially subversive energies. In
contemporary critical theory, the carnivalesque points
to the polyphonic nature of literary texts, identifying
in them a series of different and frequently opposing
'voices'.
▷ Deconstruction; discourse.
Bib: Bakhtin, M., *Rabelais and His World*.

Carr, J.L. (b 1912)
Novelist. Carr runs his own publishing company
from his home in Kettering, Northamptonshire,
England, producing also children's writing, reference
works and anthologies of poetry. His novel *A Month
in the Country* (1980) won the *Guardian* fiction prize
and was adapted for television; its several strands
of plot revolve around the uncovering of mysteries
from the past, and it makes characteristic use of a
first-person narrative by an observing character. *The
Harpole Report* (1972) is a satirical comedy about a
modern primary school, which makes use of letters
and journals as part of the narrative. His other
novels are: *A Day in Summer* (1964); *A Season in
Sinji* (1967); *How Steeple Sinderby won the F.A. Cup*
(1975); *The Battle of Pollock's Crossing* (1985); *What
Hetty Did* (1988); *Harpole and Foxberrow, General
Publishers* (1992).

Carrington (1893–1932)
Carrington (who did not use her first name) was
a central figure in the ▷ Bloomsbury Group,
and the live-in companion of ▷ Lytton Strachey
(whose homosexuality prevented her passion for
him from being expressed in marriage or any sexual
connection). She is best known for her letters and
diaries (published as *Carrington: Letters and Extracts
from her Diaries*, edited by David Garnett, 1970).
Carrington studied art at the Slade School with many
of the more well-known artists of the day, and was
herself a gifted painter.
Bib: Carrington, N., *Carrington: Paintings, Drawings
and Decorations*.

**Carroll, Lewis (Charles Lutwidge Dodgson)
(1832–98)**
Writer for children; author of *Alice's Adventures in
Wonderland* (1865) and *Through the Looking-Glass*
(1872). By profession, a mathematics lecturer at
Oxford University. The 'Alice' books describe the
adventures of a child in dreams, and owe their
distinctiveness to the combination of childlike naivety
and an authentic dream atmosphere, so that events
succeed and language is used with dream logic
instead of daylight logic. Thus these two books
mark an epoch in the history of dream literature;
the dream state is not merely a pretext for fantasy,
but is shown to follow its own laws. Consequently
Carroll's two masterpieces have had as much appeal
for adults as for children. Dodgson was also a
master of ▷ 'nonsense' verse which shows the same
characteristics; his most famous poem is *The Hunting
of the Snark* (1876). His other book for children,
Sylvie and Bruno (1889), is less memorable.

▷ Children's books.
Bib: Gardner, M., *The Annotated Alice*; Collingwood, S. D., *The Life and Letters of Lewis Carroll*; Empson, W., 'Alice in Wonderland' in his *Some Versions of Pastoral*; Green, R. L., *The Story of Lewis Carroll*; Sewell, E., in *The Field of Nonsense*; Hudson, D., *Lewis Carroll*.

Carswell, Catherine (1879–1946)
Novelist and critic. Catherine Carswell was a member of the 'Other Bloomsbury' – the circle centred on ▷ D. H. Lawrence which strove to distinguish itself from ▷ Virginia Woolf's more cerebral and self-consciously bohemian group (▷ Bloomsbury). One of the first favourable critics of Lawrence's ▷ *The Rainbow* (her review of the book lost her her job at the *Glasgow Herald* in 1915), Carswell's famous *The Savage Pilgrimage* (1932) is a vindication of Lawrence against ▷ John Middleton Murry's pseudo-Freudian attack on his former friend, *Son of Woman* (1931). Lawrence encouraged Carswell in her novelistic endeavours, including *Open the Door* (1920), *The Camomile* (1922). Her autobiography appeared posthumously in 1952 as *Lying Awake*.
Bib: Delaney, P., *D. H. Lawrence's Nightmare: The Writer and His Circle in the Years of the Great War*.

Carter, Angela (1940–92)
Novelist and short-story writer. From her first novel. *Shadow Dance* (1966), her work was notable for a strain of ▷ surrealist ▷ Gothic fantasy, a fascination with the erotic and the violent, and a blending of comedy and horror. *The Magic Toyshop* (1967) is a ▷ Freudian fairy-tale seen through the eyes of an orphaned 15-year-old girl, sent, with her brother and baby sister, to live in the claustrophobic and sinister home of her uncle, a sadistic toymaker. Her new family are examples of Carter's ability to create vivid Dickensian caricatures. After *Several Perceptions* (1968) her work became unequivocally Gothic and anti-realist, centring on the reworking of myth and fairytale, and the exploration of aggressive and sexual fantasies. *Heroes and Villains* (1969), *The Infernal Desire Machines of Doctor Hoffman* (1972) and *The Passion of New Eve* (1977) are macabre visions of imaginary worlds, projections of the 'subterranean areas behind everyday experience', with ▷ picaresque and pastiche elements. One of her collections of short stories, *The Bloody Chamber* (1979), is a feminist re-working of traditional European fairy-tales; one of these stories, 'The Company of Wolves', was filmed by Neil Jordan in 1984, with a screenplay by Angela Carter. Her interest in the politics of sexuality is reflected in her non-fiction work *The Sadeian Woman* (1979), an analysis of the codes of ▷ pornography. Her other novels are: *Love* (1971); *Nights at the Circus* (1984). Story collections are: *Fireworks* (1974); *Black Venus's Tale* (1980); *Black Venus* (1985); *American Ghosts and Old World Wonders* (1993). Radio Drama: *Come Unto These Yellow Sands* (1985) Her last novel was *Wise Children* (1991), a pastiche of family life in theatrical and vaudeville circles, and perhaps Carter's most comic and accessible text. *Expletives Deleted: Selected Writings* was published in 1992.

Bib: Harrenden, J., *Novelists in Interview*; Punter, D., *The Hidden Script: Writing and the Unconscious*.

Cartesianism
The philosophy of ▷ Descartes.

Cartland, Barbara (b 1901)
Romantic novelist. According to the *Guinness Book of Records*, Barbara Cartland holds the record as the most prolific living author. She has written over 300 books, including twenty-seven in 1977 alone, and she has a deeply loyal, overwhelmingly female, readership. Her novels are remarkable for their sheer numbers and similarity of plot and theme: although she has written drama, biography and other non-fiction, she is known to many as the ▷ best-selling author of a conservative brand of romantic fiction which champions the escapist delights of marriage, monogamy and the absolutes of sexual difference. Her heroines are nothing if not feminine, and Cartland's preference for pink is legendary. Whilst she could by no stretch of the imagination be deemed a feminist writer, she has been writing constantly since the 1920s (her first novel was published in 1925), and is something of a figurehead for older women in her fierce commitment to her writing career (despite her obvious wealth and connections to the British aristocracy, and despite the doctrine of her own books which suggest that a woman's identity should be found in her husband rather than in her own work), and in her active attitude to health and fitness (she has recently set up a successful health-food business, and in 1971 published her *Health Food Cookery Book*). Her books include: *Jig-Saw* (1925); *Touch the Stars* (1935); *Love is an Eagle* (1951); *Love Under Fire* (1960); *Men Are Wonderful* (1973); *A Shaft of Sunlight* (1982); *Tempted to Love* (1983); and *A Runaway Star* (1987).
Bib: Cloud, H., *Barbara Cartland: Crusader in Pink*; Radford, J., *The Progress of Romance: The Politics of Popular Fiction*; Anderson, R., *The Purple Heart Throbs*.

Cary, Arthur Joyce Lunel (1888–1957)
Novelist. He was born in Northern Ireland, where there is a strong tradition of ▷ Protestantism; he was brought up against a background of devout Anglicanism, lost his faith, and later constructed an unorthodox but strongly ethical faith of his own along Protestant lines. He came late to the writing of novels. He studied as an art student in Edinburgh and Paris before going to Oxford University. In 1912–13 he fought, and served in the Red Cross, in the Balkan War. In 1913 he joined the Nigerian political service, fought against the Germans in West Africa in World War I, and returned to the political service after it. His first novel, *Aissa Saved*, appeared in 1932. His subsequent works were: *An American Visitor* (1933); *The African Witch* (1936); *Castle Corner* (1938); *Mister Johnson* (1939); *Charley is my Darling* (1940); *A House of Children* (1941); the trilogy *Herself Surprised* (1941), *To Be a Pilgrim* (1942) and *The Horse's Mouth* (1944); *The Moonlight* (1946); *A Fearful Joy* (1949); another trilogy, *Prisoner of Grace*

(1952), *Except the Lord* (1953), and *Not Honour More* (1955); *The Captive and the Free* (1959). *Spring Song* (1960) is a collection of stories. He also produced three volumes of verse, *Verse* (1908), *Marching Soldier* (1945) and *The Drunken Sailor* (1947), and a number of political tracts – *Power in Men* (1939), *The Case for African Freedom* (1941; revised 1944), *Process of Real Freedom* (1943), and *Britain and West Africa* (1946).

In the first 30 years of the 20th century novelists tended to be open to foreign influences and experimental in expression; Cary was among the first distinguished novelists to return to English traditions and direct narrative, although he here and there uses the ▷ stream of consciousness technique of narration evolved by novelists of the 1920s, notably ▷ James Joyce. He is one of the most eclectic of modern novelists, both in method and in subject. In his comedy and his loose, vigorous narrative he has been compared to the 18th-century novelists ▷ Smollett and ▷ Defoe; in his characterization, to ▷ Dickens; in his attitude to human nature, to ▷ D. H. Lawrence; in his concern with heroic morality, to ▷ Joseph Conrad; in his endeavour to present experience with immediacy, to ▷ Virginia Woolf and Joyce; in his interlocking of human destiny and social patterns he might be compared with ▷ George Eliot. His first three novels and *Mister Johnson* are products of his African experience; *Charley is my Darling* and *A House of Children* are novels of childhood, and his two trilogies – thought by some to be his major work – are attempts, in his words, to see 'English history, through English eyes, for the last 60 years'.
Bib: Wright, A., *Joyce Cary: a Preface to his Novels*; Mahood, M. M., *Joyce Cary's Africa*: Fisher, B., *Joyce Cary, the Writer and his Theme*.

Castle of Otranto, The (1764)
One of the first so-called ▷ Gothic novels, by ▷ Horace Walpole. The fantastic events are set in the Middle Ages, and the story is full of supernatural sensationalism. The story concerns an evil usurper, a fateful prophecy about his downfall, a mysterious prince disguised as a peasant, and his eventual marriage to the beautiful heroine whom the usurper had intended as his own bride.

Catholicism (Roman) in English literature
Until the Act of Supremacy (1534) by which King Henry VIII seperated the English Church from Roman authority, and the more violent revolution in Scotland a little later, both countries had belonged to the European community of Catholic Christendom. This community was a genuine culture, allowing great unity of belief and feeling together with great variety of attitude. In the 16th century this community of cultures broke up, owing not only to the ▷ Protestant rebellions but also to the increase of national self-consciousness, the influence of non-Christian currents (especially Platonism), and the gradual release of various fields of activity – political, commercial, philosophical – from religious doctrine. The Counter-Reformation after the Catholic Council of Trent (1545–63), even more than the Reformation, tended to define Roman Catholicism in contrast to Protestantism. Thus, although the

dramatists and lyric poets in England from 1560 to 1640 show a plentiful survival of medieval assumptions about the nature of man and his place in the universe, in conflict with newer tendencies of thought and feeling, the Roman Catholic writer in the same period begins to show himself as something distinct from his non-Catholic colleagues. The clearest example in the 17th century is the poet Richard Crashaw. Milton's epic of the creation of the world, *Paradise Lost* (1667 and 1647), is in many ways highly traditional, but the feeling that inspires it is entirely post-Reformation. By the 18th century, however, religion of all kinds was becoming a mere department of life, no longer dictating ideas and emotions in all fields, even when sincerely believed; it is thus seldom easy to remember that the poet Alexander Pope (1688–1744) was a Roman Catholic. By the 19th century, writers of strong religious conviction were increasingly feeling themselves in a minority in an indifferent and even sceptical world. They therefore tended to impress their work once more with their faith, and this was especially true of the few Catholic writers, since Catholic faith was dogmatically so strongly defined, *eg* the poet Gerard Manley Hopkins (1844–89). The century also saw a revival of Anglo-Catholicism. From the time of the Reformation there had been a school of opinion which sought to remain as close to Roman Catholicism as Anglican independence allowed. This wing of the Church was important under Charles I, but lost prestige until it was revived by the ▷ Oxford Movement. Since then it has remained important in the strength of its imprint on literature. Thus in the 20th century the Anglo-Catholicism of the poet T. S. Eliot is as conspicuous as and more profound than the Roman Catholicism of the novelists ▷ Evelyn Waugh and ▷ Graham Greene. Amongst writers later in the 20th century, Catholicism is noticeable in the work of ▷ Anthony Burgess ▷ David Lodge and ▷ Muriel Spark.

Caute, David (b 1936)
Novelist and dramatist. Caute is one of a group of English writers, including ▷ Andrew Sinclair and Julian Mitchell, interested in formal experiment, self-referential narrative strategies and the blending of ▷ realism with elements of fantasy. He admires the work of ▷ Christine Brooke-Rose, and is strongly influenced by ▷ Jean-Paul Sartre. *The Confrontation* is a trilogy consisting of a play, *The Demonstration* (produced 1969), a critical essay supposedly by one of the characters in the play, *The Illusion* (1970) and a novel, *The Occupation* (1971). The questioning of the borders of fiction with other discourses is sustained by the competing narrators and narrative strategies within *The Occupation*. Caute's works reflect his commitment to Marxism (▷ Marx, Karl) in their analysis of society and history, and his novel *The Decline of the West* (1966) has been criticized as being over-didactic. He has worked as a lecturer, and as literary and arts editor of the ▷ *New Statesman*. Later novels include *News from Nowhere* (1986) and *The Woman's Hour* (1991).

Cavendish, Margaret, Duchess of Newcastle (1623–73)

A prolific author, Margaret Cavendish wrote poetry, drama, natural philosophy, ▷ biography, letters, science fiction and ▷ autobiography. She was both admired and ridiculed in her lifetime, but seems not to have paid much heed to her critics. While appearing modest in her writings, she simultaneously reveals an overwhelming desire for earthly fame. A woman of contradictions and controversy, Cavendish had begun her life as a lady-in-waiting to ▷ Henrietta Maria, whom she followed into exile in France. There she met her husband, William Cavendish, whose biography she was later to write. During the Interregnum (1649–60) Newcastle's estates had been sequestered by Parliament and Margaret was forced to visit Britain in an attempt to raise finances. It was during this stay that she wrote her first book, *Poems and Fancies* (1653), which already showed signs of her later scientific interests; for example, there is a poem on the theory of atoms. After the Restoration, Margaret returned with her husband to Britain, where she continued to write in several genres, covering issues such as women's oppression. Though she was lavishly entertained by the Royal Society in 1667, it was never suggested that she be elected to a Fellowship. Her autobiography, *A True Relation of My Birth Breeding and Life*, was published with *Natures Pictures* in 1656. Despite the fact that she was considered eccentric her tombstone at Westminster Abbey provides a fitting epitaph, 'wise, witty and learned lady'.

Celestial City

The name by which Heaven is denoted in ▷ John Bunyan's ▷ *Pilgrim's Progress*. It is contrasted with the ▷ City of Destruction, a typical earthly town standing for worldliness, from which Christian flees on hearing that it is doomed.

Celtic Twilight, The

Originally *The Celtic Twilight* was a book of short stories by the poet W.B. Yeats (1865–1939), published in 1893. The book dealt with the widespread beliefs in magic and the supernatural which were current among Irish peasants. Since then, the term Celtic Twilight has been widely used to describe the idea that the Celts, especially in Ireland, preserve a mystical, imaginative, poetic vision which the practical and materialistic ▷ Anglo-Saxons (both in England and in southern Scotland) have lost. At the end of the 19th century and beginning of the 20th century Yeats and other Irish poets used this conception of the Celtic character as a weapon in the cause of Irish nationalism, and they cultivated ancient Irish legends about heroes such as Cuchulain and heroines such as Queen Deirdre so as to build up a distinctively Irish literary consciousness to replace the dominant English culture.
▷ Irish fiction in English.

Censorship

Systematic censorship has never been an important restriction on English writing except in times of war; but English writers have certainly not always been entirely free.

Until 1640 the monarch exercised undefined powers by the Royal Prerogative. Early in her reign, Elizabeth I ordered dramatists not to meddle with politics and in the reign of Charles I the term Crop-ears was used for opponents of the king who lost their ears as a penalty for criticizing the political or religious authorities. Moreover, printing was monopolized by the Stationer's Company, whose charter might be withdrawn by the Crown, so that the monopoly would cease.

In the Civil War, Parliament was in control of London, and issued an edict that the publication of any book had to be licensed. The edict provoked John Milton's *Areopagitica*, an appeal for freedom of expression. Its influence was not immediate; after the Restoration of the Monarchy, Parliament issued a similar edict in the Licensing Act of 1663. The Act was only for a period, however, and in 1696 it was not renewed. The lapsing of the Licensing Act was the starting point of British freedom of the press except for emergency edicts in times of war in the 20th century, although in the early 19th century the government attempted a form of indirect censorship by imposing a tax on periodicals which restricted their sale amongst the poor. Nonetheless there are still laws extant which restrict freedom of political expression beyond certain limits.

Also serious are the English laws of libel and of obscene libel. The first exists to punish attacks on private reputation, and the second concerns the defence of sexual morals. The restrictions are serious restraints on opinion because they are vaguely defined, so that it is difficult for a publisher or writer to know when they are being infringed. Moreover, prohibition under obscenity law is frequently reversed, *eg* ▷ D. H. Lawrence's ▷ *The Rainbow* was suppressed for obscenity, but by 1965 it was a prescribed text for study in schools. One of the most celebrated challenges to public morality was the test which Penguin Books' publication of D. H. Lawrence's ▷ *Lady Chatterley's Lover* gave to the 1959 Obscene Publications Act; the 1960 'Trial of Lady Chatterley' altered the way in which the Act could be interpreted, and after it the censorship of writing on sexual grounds became much more difficult. Organizations such as Mary Whitehouse's National Viewers and Listeners Association have thus channelled their pro-censorship energies into images of violence and sexual explicitness on television and in films. The 1984 Video Recordings Act in effect raised the British Board of Film Classification 'from an industrial advisory body to legally empowered censors' (Mandy Merck).

Censorship in the theatre has been a special case since the 18th century. Henry Fielding's comedies attacking the Prime Minister, Robert Walpole, led in 1737 to the restriction of London theatres to two 'patented' ones – Covent Garden and Drury Lane – and the Court official, the Lord Chamberlain, had to license plays. In 1843 the Theatres Act removed the restriction on the theatres and defined the Lord Chamberlain's powers to the restraint of indecency. The Lord

Chamberlain's censorship came to an end in 1968.

Since 1979 there has been a gradual return to the censorship of literature and this has been extended to cover the media. The Official Secrets Act is in the process of being rewritten so as to prevent both former Crown servants from revealing information – especially in autobiographies – as well as the media from printing or broadcasting, sometimes in dramatic form, any of this material. A directive was issued in November 1988 to prevent the broadcasting of statements from people of named organizations; again this may have an effect on drama. Also in 1988, the government emended the 1986 Local Government Act to forbid any Local Authority promoting homosexuality through educational means, printed material or support of 'gay writers. The Broadcasting Standards Council was established in 1988 in order to monitor taste and decency in the media. Finally, a non-governmental form of censorship may be found in the effects of the concentration of ownership in publishing houses and the press, which severely limit the range of writing that is commercially encouraged.

Two organizations attempt to alert people to the extent and dangers of these new censorship laws: the Campaign for Press and Broadcasting Freedom and the Writers' Guild of Great Britain.
Bib: Findlater, R., *Banned: A Review of Theatrical Censorship in Britain*; Barker, M., *The Video Nasties: Freedom and Censorship in the Media*; Chester and Dickey (eds.), *Feminism and Censorship*.

Cervantes Saavedra, Miguel de (1547–1616)

Spanish novelist and dramatist, author of ▷ *Don Quixote* (1605, 1616), a satirical romance which is widely regarded as one of the first European novels and which has had a great influence on European literature. Cervantes was born at Alcalá in Spain, was injured at the battle of Lepanto (1571), and spent five years as a prisoner in Algiers after being captured by pirates. Apart from his most famous book, he wrote a pastoral novel, *La Galatea* (1585), a collection of short stories, an adventure tale, *Persiles and Sigismunda*, and a number of plays.

Chapbooks

The name for a kind of cheap literature which flourished from the 16th to the 18th century, after which they were replaced by other forms. They were so called because they were sold by 'chapmen' or travelling dealers. Their contents consisted commonly of traditional romances retold, often from the French, in crude form: *Bevis of Hampton*, *Guy of Warwick*, *Till Eulenspiegel*, *Doctor Faustus*, are examples. Some of them, such as *Dick Whittington*, about the poor boy who ended up as Lord Mayor of London, have survived as children's stories to the present day, and are often the theme of Christmas pantomines.

Characters, Theophrastian

In the early 17th century a form of ▷ essay devoted to the description of human and social types grew up, and collections of such essays were known as 'Characters'. The origin of the fashion is in the brief sketches by one character of another in the comedies of the time – *eg* those of Thomas Dekker and Ben Jonson – and in the verse satires of such poets as John Donne and Joseph Hall. The tone was always light and often satirical; as a literary form, Characters displaced the satirical ▷ pamphlet popular in the last decade of the 16th century written by such men as ▷ Greene and ▷ Nashe. The basic pattern of the form was the *Characters* of the ancient Greek writer Theophrastus (3rd century BC); hence the designation 'Theophrastian'.

The two most famous collections were that of Sir Thomas Overbury – partly by other hands – published in 1614, and *Microcosmographie* by John Earle, published in 1628. The fashion continued, though it became less popular, throughout the 17th century and into the 18th. It was eventually superseded by the more elaborate and individualized studies by Joseph Addison and ▷ Steele in the *Spectator*, especially the ▷ De Coverley papers, and by the growth of the 18th-century novel.

Charke, Charlotte (1713–60)

Actress, manager, puppeteer, dramatist, novelist. Youngest child of the actor, manager, and dramatist Colley Cibber, and his wife, the former actress Katherine Shore. By the time she was four, Charlotte expressed a preference for masculine clothing, which she resumed at intervals throughout her later career. In 1730 she married Richard Charke, a musician and actor employed at Drury Lane. She worked as an actress and dancer at Drury Lane and joined her brother Theophilus Cibber among a group of performers who deserted to the Haymarket Theatre in 1733. There she added more than a dozen male roles to her repertory of female ones, including Macheath in *The Beggar's Opera* and George Barnwell in *The London Merchant*. Later she acted Polly in *The Beggar's Opera*, and Millwood in *The London Merchant*. In 1736 Charke joined Henry Giffard's company at Lincoln's Inn Fields. From 1737 she managed a succession of businesses, including a puppet theatre. In 1745 she was married again, clandestinely, to John Sacheverell. He died soon afterwards, leaving her penniless, and her subsequent series of odd jobs in London and the provinces did nothing to alleviate her distresses. Estranged from her father for many years, she attempted unsuccessfully to heal the rift in 1755. Her memoirs, *A Narrative of the Life of Mrs Charlotte Charke* were published in eight instalments, in 1755, and again posthumously, in 1775. Her published works also include a play, *The Art of Management* (1735), the novel, *The History of Henry Dumont, Esq., and Miss Charlotte Evelyn* (1756), and two short novels, *The Mercer: Or Fatal Extravagance* (1755), and *The Lover's Treat; Or Unnatural Hatred* (1758).
Bib: Charke, C., *A Narrative of the Life of Mrs Charlotte Charke*.

Chartist movement

A working class political movement which flourished between 1837 and 1848. It arose because the ▷ Reform Bill of 1832 had reformed Parliament in favour of middle-class political rights but had left the working class without them. The Chartists wanted Parliament to be closely responsible to the nation as a whole and to reform an electoral system according to which the poor were excluded from membership of Parliament and denied the right to vote others into membership by their lack of the necessary property qualification. Some regions were more heavily represented in Parliament than others and all voting was subject to bribery or intimidation because votes had to be declared publicly. Consequently they put forward their Charter containing Six Points: 1 votes for all males; 2 annually elected Parliaments (instead of general elections every seven years); 3 payment of Members of Parliament (so that poor men could have political careers); 4 secret voting (voting 'by ballot'); 5 abolition of the property qualification for candidates seeking election; 6 electoral districts equal in population. The movement seemed to be a complete failure, but all these points became law between 1860 and 1914 except the demand for annually elected parliaments. The Chartists attracted an ardent following but they were badly led. Allusions are made to them in those novels between 1840 and 1860 which were concerned with 'the Condition-of-the-People Question', eg ▷ *Sybil* by ▷ Benjamin Disraeli. This serious discussion of the social crisis of the second quarter of the 19th century was greatly stimulated by ▷ Thomas Carlyle's essay *Chartism* (1839), one of his fiercest and most influential writings.

Chatwin, Bruce (1940–1989)

Novelist and travel writer. Chatwin was born in Sheffield and worked as an art consultant and journalist. His first publication, *In Pantagonia* (1977), was a travel book and won the Hawthornden Prize; it was followed by *The Songlines* (1981). His novel *On the Black Hill* (1982) is about a rural community on the Welsh borders and the story is centred on two farmers who are identical twins. His other novels are *The Viceroy and Ouidah* (1980), *Utz* (1988), *What Am I Doing Here* (1990). Also: *Nowhere is a Place: Travels in Pantagonia* (with Paul Theroux, 1992).

Chaucer, Geoffrey (c 1340–1400)

Influential poet of the 14th century who occupies a privileged place in the history of English literary traditions because his work has been continuously transcribed, published, read and commented upon since his death.

He was the son of a London vintner, John Chaucer (1312–68), and served in the court of Edward III's son Lionel (later Duke of Clarence). In 1359 he was taken prisoner while fighting in France with Edward III, and ransomed. His wife, Phillipa de Roet, whom he married perhaps in 1366, was the sister of John of Gaunt's third wife, Katherine Swynford. Substantial records exist of Chaucer's career in royal service, as a member of the court and diplomat. He is first recorded as a member of the royal household in 1367 and he made several diplomatic journeys in France and Italy, which perhaps gave him the opportunity to gain access to the work of important 14th-century Italian writers (▷

Dante, Petrarch, ▷ Boccaccio). He was appointed controller of customs in the Port of London in 1374, was 'knight of the shire' of Kent in 1386 (ie, represented Kent in the House of Commons), and was appointed clerk of the king's works in 1389 and then deputy forester of the king's forest at Petherton in Somerset in 1391. He returned to London for the last years of his life and was buried in Westminster Abbey. His tomb, erected some time later (1555?) gives the date of his death as 25 October 1400.

The upward mobility of Chaucer's family is clear not only from the professional life of Chaucer himself but also from that of his son Thomas, who married into the nobility and became one of the richest men in England at the time. Thomas's daughter, Alice, married William de la Pole, Duke of Suffolk, and their grandson, John, Earl of Lincoln, was heir designate to the throne of Richard III. We may only speculate about the part Chaucer's literary activities played in advancing his social status and that of his family. Although more records survive of Chaucer's professional life than any other English writer of the time, the records do not contain any references to his literary labours. Thus dating Chaucer's literary works is an exercise in hypothesis and depends largely on information provided in Chaucer's own list of works, notably in the prologue to the *Legend of Good Women*, and in the prologue to the *Man of Law's Tale*.

Chaucer's literary work is notable for its range and diversity. It explores the possibilities of a number of different literary genres, and includes dream-vision poems (the *Book of the Duchess*, the *House of Fame*, the *Parliament of Foulys*, the *Legend of Good Women*), a classical love-tragedy (▷ *Troilus and Criseyde*), story-collections (the *Legend of Good Women*, and the ▷ *Canterbury Tales*, which itself encompasses a great range and variety of genres), as well as shorter lyrical texts, translations (of ▷ Boethius's *Consolation of Philosophy* and probably the first part of the English translation of the *Roman de la Rose*) and scientific treatises (on the Astrolabe, and the *Equatorie of the Planets*, which is now generally accepted as Chaucer's work).

A distinctive feature of Chaucer's literary work is that it engages not only with French and Latin literary traditions but also with the work of earlier and contemporary Italian writers (notably Boccaccio). His work became a reference point for later poets in English, and is frequently discussed in terms which suggest it played a founding role in the establishment of an English literary tradition – a point neatly underlined by the subsequent establishment of Poet's Corner in Westminster Abbey, around Chaucer's tomb.

Bib: Benson, L., et al. (eds.), *The Riverside Chaucer*; Boitani, P. and Mann, J. (eds.), *The Cambridge Chaucer Companion*; Crow, M. C. and Olsen, C. C. (eds.), *Chaucer Life Records*.

Chekhov, Anton Pavlovich (1860–1904)

Russian dramatist and short-story writer. In his last four plays (*Seagull, Uncle Vanya, Three Sisters, The Cherry Orchard*) he evolved a dramatic form and idiom of dialogue which were highly original and

had a great influence on 20th-century drama. His originality lay in his combination of faithfulness to the surface of life with poetic evocation of underlying experience. This he achieved partly by exploiting the character of human conversation when it seems to be engaged in communication, but is actually concerned with the incommunicable. This leads on to the non-communicating dialogue in the work of playwrights such as ▷ Beckett and Harold Pinter (b 1930), when the characters on the stage alternately baffle and enlighten the audience by the undercurrents implicit in their words. The realism of Chekhov's stories is similarly subtle and original; they have similar faithfulness to surface combined with delicate artistic pattern, giving significance to seeming irrelevance and slightness of incident. An outstanding exponent of the method in English is the New Zealand writer ▷ Katherine Mansfield.
Bib: Magarshack, D., *The Plays of Anton Chekhov*; Styan, J. L., *Chekhov in Performance*.

Chesterton, G. K. (Gilbert Keith) (1874–1930)
An extremely versatile writer of essays, stories, novels, poems; Chesterton is best described as a polemicist, since polemics entered into everything he wrote, whether it was detective stories (the Father Brown series; 1911, 1914, 1926, 1927), fantasy (*The Man who was Thursday*, 1908), comic verse, or religious studies such as *St Francis of Assisi* (1923) or *St Thomas Aquinas* (1933). He wrote against life-denial, whether this manifested in the denial of humanity in the Victorian political economy, or the sceptical withdrawal into ▷ aestheticism of the 1890s. His basis of attack was a conviction that life is to be enjoyed with all the faculties; he also had the belief that such fullness of life required a religion large enough to comprehend all the spiritual and moral potentialities in man, and he found this religion in Roman Catholicism. He was not received into the Catholic Church until 1922, but from *The Napoleon of Notting Hill* (1904) – a fantasy about a war between London boroughs – he shows the romantic medievalism which for him was a large part of the appeal of Catholicism. The period of his greatest influence was probably between 1900 and 1914, when he belonged to a group of vigorous witty polemicists, including George Bernard Shaw (1856–1950), ▷ H. G. Wells, ▷ Hilaire Belloc. He was from the first an ally of the Catholic Belloc against the agnostic socialists, Wells and Shaw. He had in common with both his antagonists a genius for vivid particularity strongly reminiscent of the Victorian novelist, ▷ Charles Dickens; with Shaw he shared a delight in witty and disturbing paradox, which he used as Shaw did, to startle his readers out of the acceptance of platitudes into genuine thinking. In spite of his homely, zestful humanity, one notices nowadays a journalistic superficiality about Chesterton's work, as though he felt that his audience demanded entertainment as the indispensable reward for receiving enlightenment, and this may account for the neglect of his work since his death.
Politically, with Belloc, he preached an alternative to socialism in Distributism, a vision of a society of small proprietors. His critical work perhaps survives better than his other work; it included studies of Browning (1903), Dickens (1906), ▷ Thackeray (1909), ▷ Chaucer (1932), and *The Victorian Age in Literature* (1913). He is otherwise perhaps best read in selection, for instance in *Selected Stories* (ed. K. Amis) and *G. K. Chesterton: A Selection from his Non-fictional Prose* (selected by W. H. Auden).
▷ Catholicism in English literature; Detective fiction.
Bib: Belloc, H., *The Place of Chesterton in English Letters*; Canovan, H., *Chesterton, Radical Populist*; Hollis, C., *The Mind of Chesterton*.

Child labour
The use of children in agricultural labour was widespread, and not necessarily pernicious, up till the 19th century, but their use in factories and mines after 1800 and during the ▷ Industrial Revolution aroused widespread indignation and led to reform. The Factory Act of 1833 limited their working hours in factories and in 1847 their hours were restricted to ten. In 1842 the Mines Act forbade the employment of women and children under ten underground; this evil was very old, but had become much severer with the expansion of the coal industry in the 18th century after the invention of steam-powered machinery. An old abuse, too, was the employment of little boys to clean chimneys; the boys were made to climb inside the chimneys. Public indignation against the practice was aroused by ▷ Charles Kingsley's ▷ *Water Babies* (1863), but it was only effectively prohibited in 1875. The Victorian age saw the abolition of the worst abuses of children, as well as the establishment of the first universal system of education in England. Since 1939 it has been illegal to employ children under 15.

Children in the Wood (Babes in the Wood)
A ballad (1593) well-known for its story, which is often retold in books of children's fairy tales (▷ Children's books). It concerns the plot of a wicked uncle to murder his little nephew and niece, whose property he means to seize. The hired murderers abandon the children in the forest, where they perish and the birds cover them over with leaves. The wicked uncle is then punished by God, with the loss of his son, his wealth and eventually his life.

Children's books
Until the 19th century, children were not regarded as beings with their own kind of experience and values, and therefore did not have books written specifically for their entertainment. The literature available to them included popular versions of old romances, such as *Bevis of Hampton*, and magical folk-tales, such as *Jack the Giant-Killer*, which appeared in ▷ chapbooks. Children also read such works as ▷ John Bunyan's ▷ *Pilgrim's Progress*, ▷ Daniel Defoe's ▷ *Robinson Crusoe* (1719), and ▷ Jonathan Swift's ▷ *Gulliver's Travels* (1726); ▷ Perrault's collection of French ▷ fairy-tales appeared in English as *Mother Goose's Fairy Tales* in 1729.
During the Romantic period it was recognized

that childhood experience was a world of its own and, influenced, in many cases, by Rousseau's ideas on education, books began to be written especially to appeal to children. Such works as Thomas Day's *Merton and Sandford* (1783–9), ▷ Maria Edgeworth's *Moral Tales* (1801) and Mrs Sherwood's *The Fairchild Family* (1818) usually had a serious moral tone, but showed an understanding of a child's mind that was lacking from Anne and Jane Taylor's cautionary tales in verse (later to be parodied by ▷ Hilaire Belloc in *The Bad Child's Book of Beasts* etc.).

It was not until the Victorian period that writers began extensively to try to please children, without attempting to improve them at the same time. Edward Lear's *Book of Nonsense* (1846) and ▷ Lewis Carroll's *Alice* books combine fantasy with humour. Romance and magic had a strong appeal to the Victorians, and fairy stories from all over the world were presented in versions for children. The collection of the brothers ▷ Grimm had appeared in 1824 as *German Popular Stories* and ▷ Hans Christian Andersen's original compositions were translated into English in 1846. Andrew Lang's *Fairy Books* were published later in the century. Adventure stories for boys, such as ▷ Captain Frederick Marryat's *Masterman Ready* (1841) and ▷ Robert Louis Stevenson's ▷ *Treasure Island* (1883) became a flourishing genre, but the tradition of moral improvement persisted in such books as ▷ Charles Kingsley's ▷ *Water Babies* (1863). Children's literature is a field to which women writers have made a notable contribution; in the latter half of the 19th century enduring classics were written by Mrs Molesworth (*The Tapestry Room*, 1879), Louisa May Alcott (*Little Women*, 1868), Anna Sewell (*Black Beauty*, 1877) and E. Nesbit (*The Story of the Treasure-Seekers*, 1899, etc.).

Animals have loomed large in children's books. Beatrix Potter's *Peter Rabbit* appeared in 1902 (doing much to establish the book where text and illustrations were of equal importance), Kenneth Grahame's *The Wind in the Willows* in 1908, the first of Hugh Lofting's *Dr Dolittle* books in 1920, ▷ A. A. Milne's *Winnie the Pooh* in 1926 and the first of Alison Uttley's *Little Grey Rabbit* books in 1929. Charges of anthropomorphism seem to have had little effect on the popularity of these books, and another writer whose lack of critical acclaim has hardly diminished her sales is ▷ Enid Blyton. Recently, allegations of racism and sexism have been laid against old favourites, and there have been efforts to bring children's literature into touch with 20th-century problems, such as single-parent families and racial prejudice. As well as writers (*eg* Noel Streatfeild and Nina Bawden) who have concerned themselves with stories about everyday life, there have been others who have continued the tradition of magical fantasy. ▷ Tolkien's *The Hobbit*, Philippa Pierce's *Tom's Midnight Garden*, ▷ C. S. Lewis's *Tales of Narnia*, Ursula Le Guin's stories about *Earthsea* and the work of Alan Garner all fall into this category. In a rather different field, Rosemary Sutcliff has won recognition for the careful research underlying her historical novels. Mention should also be made of Ladybird books,

which, in addition to their fiction publications, have done much to introduce children to a wide variety of topics, from music to magnetism. Following Robert Louis Stevenson's *A Child's Garden of Verses* (1885), children's verse has been written by Belloc, ▷ De la Mare, A. A. Milne, Ted Hughes and Charles Causley.

Christie, Agatha (1890–1976)

▷ Detective fiction writer (who also wrote romantic novels as Mary Westmacott), Agatha Christie is one of the most well-known, and certainly the most widely translated, of British writers this century. Her large range of intricate but formulaic novels gained her a vast readership, and they have been widely filmed, televised and staged (*The Mousetrap*, 1952, is the longest-running stage play, still showing in London's West End). Even though she continued to write from the 1920s until her death, most of her work evidences a nostalgia for the pre-war England of the prosperous classes with which she is aptly identified, the calm setting for novels populated by abnormal, criminal psyches (crime is never, for Christie, socially justifiable) and brilliant, sexless sleuths (Hercule Poirot and Miss Marple being the most famous). Her books include: *The Mysterious Affair at Styles: A Detective Story* (1920); *The Murder of Roger Ackroyd* (1926); *Murder on the Orient Express* (1934); *Death on the Nile* (1937); *Ten Little Niggers* (1939); *Sparkling Cyanide* (1945); *Ordeal by Innocence* (1958) and *Endless Night* (1967).
Bib: Keating, H. (ed.), *Christie: The First Lady of Crime*; Sanders, D. and Lovallo, L. (eds), *The Agatha Christie Companion*; Shaw, M. and Vanacker, S., *Reflecting on Miss Marple*.

Christmas Carol, A (1843)

A story by ▷ Charles Dickens, about a miser, Scrooge, who is converted by a series of visions from a condition of mercantile avarice and misanthropy into an embodiment of the Christmas spirit, with its generosity and good will to humankind in general. By no means one of the best of Dickens's works, it nonetheless represents entertainingly his celebration of the virtues associated with Christmas (especially characteristic of his early work). He represented these virtues as the cure for the puritan narrowness of feeling and inhumanity of outlook which were the dark side of Victorian commerce. Compare the Christmas scenes in his ▷ *Pickwick Papers* (1837) and the comments of Sleary in ▷ *Hard Times*.

Church of England

The history of the Church of England is closely bound up with the political and social history of England. In the Middle Ages the Church of England was a division of the Catholic Church of Western Europe. Ultimate authority over it, as over the rest of the Catholic Church, was vested in the Pope in Rome. The clergy consisted of an order of priests who, at the humblest level, had in their charge the village churches and the parishes (each more or less coincident with a village) that surrounded them. The parishes were grouped into regions known as 'sees', each of which was governed by a bishop, and the sees.(bishoprics) were grouped into two provinces under two archbishops, those of Canterbury and York, the Archbishop of Canterbury being the senior. The bishops and the archbishops attended Parliament, and the Church had its own assemblies or convocations, attended by the senior clergy and representatives of the lower clergy, *ie* the parish priests. This organization of the Church has survived to the present day, with the important difference that since the 16th century the Pope has ceased to be the Church's supreme authority.

The Church of England became independent in 1534, when Henry VIII caused Parliament to pass the Act of Supremacy which declared him to be the 'Supreme Head of the English Church and Clergy'. This action was political rather than religious; Henry was conservative in his religious beliefs, and reaffirmed the traditional Catholic doctrines by his Act of the Six Articles (1539). However, a ▷ Protestant party, influenced by the German reformer Martin Luther, had long been growing in England and was favoured by the Archbishop of Canterbury, Thomas Cranmer. Under the boy King Edward VI, the Protestants seized power, and Catholic doctrine was modified by Cranmer's two Books of Common Prayer. These changes were accompanied by the destruction of images and the covering up of holy wall-paintings in village churches; such actions, combined with the rapacity of the nobles who seized church money, were unpopular, and partly reconciled the nation to a return to the Catholic Church under Mary I. She too became unpopular owing to her persecution of Protestants, and her successor, Elizabeth I, attempted a compromise Settlement, by means of which she hoped to keep in the Church of England both the Catholics and the extremer Protestants. She succeeded, in so far as her Settlement prevented religious conflict breaking into civil war during her reign.

The Roman Catholics were and remained a small minority, but during the first half of the 17th century the extreme Protestants (now known as ▷ Puritans) grew in strength, especially in London and in the south and east. Their hostility to the monarchy and their dislike of religious direction by bishops led in the end to the Civil War and the overthrow of Charles I. Under the Protectorship of the Puritan Oliver Cromwell, the Church of England ceased to exist as a state religious organization, but in 1660 the monarchy and the Church of England were restored, and Puritans were excluded from the Church, from political rights and from attendance at the universities of Oxford and Cambridge. From this time, the Puritans (increasingly called Dissenters of Nonconformists) set up their own Churches. Within the Church, religious differences remained and were the basis of the newly emerging political parties, the ▷ Whigs being more in sympathy with the Puritans and the Tories being closer to, though never identified with, the Roman Catholics.

During the 18th century the apathy into which the Church of England had fallen was shaken by the religious revival led by John Wesley, who worked mainly among the poorer classes. Although

Wesley was forced to form a separate Methodist Church, his example inspired the Evangelical Movement within the Church of England, which by the 19th century was an important force towards social reform. A different sort of revival was led by a group of Anglicans at Oxford University, of whom ▷ John Henry Newman was the most active. The resulting ▷ Oxford (or Tractarian) Movement affirmed the spiritual independence of the Church and its continuity with the medieval Catholic Church. Newman eventually became a Roman Catholic, and the Oxford Movement lost in him its main inspiration. He left behind him, however, divisions of opinion within the Church that exist today: the High Church is composed of Anglicans who are essentially Catholic in belief, though they reject the authority of the Pope; they can be said to be descendants from Henry VIII's Reformation. The Low Church feels itself to be Protestant, and can be said to favour the Reformation of Edward VI. A third group, prominent in the mid-19th century but not to be distinguished now, was the Broad Church; it developed from the Evangelical Movement and was especially active in social and political reform. These have all existed under the common organization of the Church.

Today, the Church of England is the state Church, under the Crown, only in England; in Scotland and Wales, the Commonwealth, and the U.S.A., members of churches originally derived from the Church of England are known as Episcopalians.

Cinderella
A widespread ▷ fairy tale, known in English from its version by the French collector of fairy tales, ▷ Charles Perrault, whose work was translated into English in about 1729. Cinderella means the 'little cinder girl', because in the story she is made to do all the hard work of the house by her cruel elder step-sisters, and is dirty with the ashes of the fire. Aided by her fairy godmother, she wins a prince in marriage. Recent interpretations of this story focus on the sexual jealousies and competition it implies.

Circulating libraries
A library from which books may be borrowed. Such libraries were in private hands in the 18th century and subsisted on subscriptions from clients. The first circulating library started in 1740 and as the institution spread so the reading habit greatly increased. It was the more important since, apart from ▷ chapbooks, books were very expensive in the 18th century.
▷ Mudie, Charles.
Bib: Leavis, Q. D., *Fiction and the Reading Public.*

City of Destruction, The
In ▷Bunyan's ▷*Pilgrim's Progress* the town from which the pilgrim, Christian, flees to the ▷ Celestial City, *ie* Heaven. The City of Destruction stands for the world divorced from spiritual values, doomed to the destruction that is to overcome all the merely material creation.

Cixous, Hélène (b 1937)
French writer. Hélène Cixous's work has been most influential when it has actively attempted to

challenge the categories of writing, and her work encompasses poetry and poetic prose, ▷ feminist théory, philosophy and psychoanalysis. She is a key player in the French feminist ▷ *écriture féminine* movement, and has written some forty influential texts (only a few of which have been translated into English), beginning with her PhD thesis on ▷ James Joyce (published in English as *The Exile of James Joyce or the Art of Replacement* in 1972), and including *The Newly Born Woman* (with Catherine Clément), the seminal essay on women and writing 'The Laugh of the Medusa' ('*Le Rire de la Meduse*') (published in English in 1976), dramas and fiction (including *Portrait de Dora*, Cixous's vindication of ▷ Freud's famous patient, the central figure in one of his most important case histories and latter-day feminist heroine), and literary-critical works (*To Live the Orange* is a celebration of the work of Brazilian writer Clarice Lispector). Cixous is Professor of Literature at the experimental University of Paris – VIII which she co-founded in 1968, and director of the *Centre d'Etudes Feminine*.

▷ Psychoanalytical criticism.
Bib: Marks, E. and de Coutivron, I. (eds.), *New French Feminisms*; Conley, V. A., *Hélène Cixous: Writing the feminine*; Sellers, S. (ed.), *Writing Differences: Readings from the seminar of Hélène Cixous*; Wilcox, H. et al, *The Body and the Text*; Moi, T. *Sexual/Textual Politics*.

Clarendon, Edward Hyde, Earl of (1609–74)
Statesman and historian; author of *The True Historical Narrative of the Rebellion and Civil Wars in England* about the Civil War during which he had supported King Charles I. The published history combines two separate manuscripts: a history written 1646-8 while the events were fresh in his mind, and an ▷ autobiography written between 1668 and 1670 in exile and without the aid of documents. In consequence, Books I-VII are superior in accuracy to Books VIII-XV, with the exception of Book IX, containing material written in 1646. Clarendon's history is a literary classic because of its series of portraits of the participants in the war. His book is a notable contribution to the rise of the arts of biography and autobiography in England in the 17th century and contributed to the development which in the 18th century produced the first English novels.

As a statesman, Hyde was at first a leading opponent of Charles I, but his strongly Anglican faith led him to take the Royalist side shortly before the war. He became one of the king's chief advisers. He followed the royal court into exile, and was Lord Chancellor and Charles II's chief minister at the Restoration (1660). The king's brother, the future James II, married his daughter, so that he became grandfather of Queen Mary II and Queen Anne. He was made the scapegoat for the unpopularity of Charles II's government in its early years, however, and was driven into exile in 1667. He lived the remainder of his life in France.

▷ Histories and Chronicles.
Bid: Huehns, G., *Selections from the History of the Rebellion and the Life*; Wormald, B. H. G., *Clarendon,*

Politics, History and Rebellion; Firth, C., *Essays, Historical and Literary*.

Clarissa (1747–8)
An epistolary novel by ▷ Samuel Richardson. The central characters are Clarissa Harlowe, Anna Howe, Lovelace and John Belford. Clarissa's family wish her to marry the odious suitor, Solmes, a wealthy man whom she abhors. The marriage is proposed to elevate the Harlowes socially, yet in the motives of Clarissa's brother and sister there is also a disturbing undertone of sadistic sexuality. As she refuses to accept Solmes the family ostracize her within their home.

Lovelace, a handsome rake, is initially the suitor of the elder sister Arabella, but his real interest is in Clarissa. When the family ill treat her he poses as her deliverer and persuades her to escape with him to London, promising that he will restore her in the esteem of her relatives. But the apparently respectable house where they stay is in reality a brothel.

Lovelace's attempts at seducing Clarissa are unsuccessful, and he eventually resorts to drugging her and then rapes her. Through this theme Richardson explores the hypocrisy of a society which equates 'honour' with virginity. Clarissa dies after the rape, not from shame but from a spiritual integrity which cannot be corrupted. In the self-martyrdom of the heroine, Richardson achieves a psychological complexity which transcends the limitations of her purported morality.
Bib: Flynn, C., *Samuel Richardson: A Man of Letters*. Eagleton, T., *The Rape of Clarissa*; Keymer, T., *Richardson's 'Clarissa' and the Eighteenth-Century Reader*.

Clarke, Arthur C. (b 1917)
Science-fiction writer, educated at King's College, University of London. He worked as an auditor, served in the RAF 1941–46 and since then has been a scientific editor, underwater explorer and photographer, company director and television and radio presenter, as well as writing numerous novels, short stories, books for children and works of popular science. He is a Fellow of the Royal Astronomical Society and has won many prizes for his work. His science fiction draws on his wide scientific knowledge, combining exciting narrative and philosophical concerns with detailed explanations of the imagined technology of the future. Many of his fictions involve narratives of exploration and discovery, carried out by romantic individualists. His best-known work remains *2001: A Space Odyssey* (1968), the script of a hugely popular film which he subsequently turned into a novel. His other novels include: *Prelude to Space* (1951); *The Sands of Mars* (1951); *Against the Fall of Night* (1953); *Earthlight* (1955); *A Fall of Moondust* (1961); *Rendezvous with Rama* (1973); *The Fountains of Paradise* (1979); *The Songs of Distant Earth* (1986); *The Ghost from the Grand Banks* (1990). Among his many volumes of short stories are: *The Nine Billion Names of God: The Best Short Stories of Arthur C. Clarke* (1967) and *Tales from Planet Earth* (1989).

Clarke, Marcus (1846–81)
Novelist. The son of a wealthy lawyer, Clarke
emigrated to Australia in 1863, where he worked
on a sheep station and then as a journalist. His
first novel, *Long Odds* (1869), is an unremarkable ▷
sensation novel, but this was followed by *His Natural
Life* (serialized 1870–2; published in a three-volume
abridged form 1875), which, despite a convoluted
plot concerning inheritances and impersonation,
contains powerful accounts of convict life in
1840s Australia, and has become the most famous
19th-century Australian novel.
Bib: Wilding, M., *Marcus Clarke*.

Classic, Classics, Classical
These words are apt to cause confusion. The term
'classic' has been used to denote a work about whose
value it is assumed there can be no argument, *eg* ▷
David Copperfield is a classic. The word particularly
implies a supposedly changeless and immutable
quality; it has sometimes been used to deny the
need for reassessment, reinterpretation and change
and may imply an ahistorical approach to literature.
Because only a few works can be classics, it may be
argued that the term is synonymous with the best.
This is not necessarily the case, especially with
regard to changes in literary taste and a constantly
moving canon of texts. The term is derived from a
Roman taxation category and its usage has retained
links to social hierarchies.
'Classics' is the study of ancient Greek and
Latin literature. 'Classic' is used as an adjective as
well as a noun, *eg* ▷ Dickens wrote many classic
novels. 'Classical' is mainly used as the adjective for
'classics', *eg* classical scholarship.

Classical mythology
Ancient Greek mythology can be divided between the
'Divine Myths' and the 'Heroic Myths'.
The divine myths are known in differing versions
from the works of various Greek poets, of whom
the most notable are ▷ Homer and Hesiod.
Hesiod explained the origin of the world in terms
of a marriage between Earth (Ge or Gaea) and
Sky (Uranus). Their children were the 12 Titans:
Oceanus, Crius, Iapetus, Theia, Rhea, Mnemosyne,
Phoebe, Tethys, Themis, Coeus, Hyperion, and
Cronos. Cronos overthrew his father, and he
and Rhea (or Cybele) became the parents of the
'Olympian gods', so called from their association with
the sacred mountain Olympus. The Olympians, in
their turn, overthrew Cronos and the other Titans.
The chief Olympians were Zeus and his queen
Hera. The other gods and goddesses were the
offspring of either, but as Zeus was usually at war
with Hera, they were not the joint parents. They
seem to have been seen as male and female aspects
of the sky; their quarrels were the causes of bad
weather and cosmic disturbances. The principal
offspring of Zeus were Apollo, (the sun god)
Artemis, Athene (goddess of wisdom), Aphrodite
(sometimes represented as a daughter of Uranus out
of the sea), Dionysus (a vegetation god associated
with wine), Hermes (the messenger of the gods),
and Ares. Zeus had three sisters, Hestia, Demeter

(the corn goddess) and Hera (also his wife), and two
brothers, Poseidon who ruled the sea, and Hades
who ruled the underworld. In the 3rd century BC
the Olympian gods were adopted by the Romans,
who used the Latin names more commonly known
to later European writers. Uranus, Apollo, and some
others remained the same. Gaea became Tellus:
Cronos = Saturn; Zeus = Jupiter (or Jove): Hera
= Juno; Athene = Minerva; Artemis = Diana;
Hermes = Mercury; Ares = Mars; Hephaestus =
Vulcan; Aphrodite = Venus (and her son Eros =
Cupid); Demeter = Ceres: Poseidon = Neptune.
There were numerous minor deities such as nymphs
and satyrs in both Greek and Roman pantheons.
Dionysus is sometimes contrasted with Apollo:
'Dionysiac' writing is passionate and explosive;
'Apolline' writing is contemplative and serene.
The Olympian deities mingled with men, and
rivalled one another in deciding human destinies.
They concerned themselves particularly with the
destinies of the heroes, *ie* those men, sometimes
partly divine by parentage, who were remarkable for
the kinds of excellence which are especially valued
in early societies, such as strength (Heracles),
or cunning (Odysseus). Each region of Greece
had its native heroes, though the greatest heroes
were famous in legend all over Greece. The most
famous of all was Heracles (in Latin, Hercules)
who originated in Thebes. Other leading examples
of the hero are: Theseus (Athens); Sisyphus and
Bellerophon (Corinth); Perseus (Argolis); the
Dioscuri, *ie* Castor and Pollux (Laconia); ▷ Oedipus
(Thebes); Achilles (Thessaly); Jason (Thessaly);
Orpheus (Thrace). Like the Greek gods and
goddesses, the Greek heroes were adopted by Roman
legend, sometimes with a change of name. The
minor hero of Greek legend, Aeneas, was raised to
be the great ancestral hero of the Romans, and they
had other heroes of their own, such as Romulus, the
founder of Rome, and his brother Remus.
After the downfall of the Roman Empire of the
west, classical deities and heroes achieved a kind of
popular reality through the planets and zodiacal signs
which are named after them, and which, according
to astrologers, influence human fates. Thus in ▷
Chaucer's *The Knight's Tale*, Mars, Venus, Diana
and Saturn occur, and owe their force in the poem
as much to medieval astrology as to classical legend.
Otherwise their survival has depended chiefly on
their importance in the works of the classical poets,
such as Homer, Hesiod, Virgil and Ovid, who have
meant so much to European culture. In Britain,
important poets translated and thus helped to
'naturalize' the Greek and Latin poems; *eg* Gavin
Douglas in the 16th century and Dryden in the 17th
century translated Virgil's ▷ *Aeneid*; Chapman in the
16th century and Pope in the 18th century translated
Homer's epics. In the 16th and 17th centuries, poets
used major and minor classical deities to adorn
and elevate poems intended chiefly as gracious
entertainment, and occasionally they added deities of
their own invention.
While European culture was understood as a
more or less distinct system of values, the poets
used classical deities and heroes deliberately and

objectively. In the 19th century, however, the deep disturbance of European beliefs and values caused European writers to use classical myth more subjectively, as symbols through which they tried to express their personal doubts, struggles, and beliefs. Thus John Keats in his unfinished epic *Hyperion* tried to emulate Milton's great Christian epic, *Paradise Lost*, but instead of Christian myth he used the war of the Olympian gods and the Titans to embody his sense of the tragedy of human experience. Tennyson wrote dramatic monologues in which personifications of Greek heroes (*eg* Ulysses, Tithonus, Tiresias in eponymous poems) recounted the experiences associated with them in classical (or, in the case of Ulysses, medieval) legend, in such a way as to express the emotional conflicts of a man from the ▷ Victorian age like Tennyson himself. In the 20th century, writers have used figures from the classical myths differently again; they are introduced to establish the continuity of the emotions and attitudes characteristic of modern men and women with emotions and attitudes of those from the past. It is thus that T. S. Eliot uses Tiresias in his poem *The Waste Land*, and ▷ James Joyce uses the Odysseus myth in his novel ▷ *Ulysses*. In a comparable way, modern psychologists have used the Greek myths as symbolic expressions of basic psychological conflicts in human beings in all periods. ▷ Freud's theory of the Oedipus complex is the most famous of these reinterpretations.

▷ *Odyssey, Iliad.*

Claudius

1 The Roman Emperor (AD 41–54) who began the systematic conquest of Britain. Subject of the novels by ▷ Robert Graves, *I, Claudius* and *Claudius the God*.

2 King of Denmark in Shakespeare's *Hamlet*.

Cleland, John (1709–89)

Novelist and journalist, most famous for his novel *Fanny Hill: Memoirs of a Woman of Pleasure*, published in two volumes in 1748 and 1749 and immediately suppressed as pornography. An unexpurgated edition of the book published in England in 1963 was seized by police and became the subject of a trial. Cleland also wrote *Memoirs of a Coxcomb* (1751) and several other novels and dramatic pieces.

Cliché

A word borrowed from the French, used to denote a phrase or idiom employed by habit instead of meaningfully, eg 'her skin was *as white as snow*'. It is a stock phrase, employed without thought and heard (or read) without visualization.

Climax

▷ Figures of Speech.

Clive, Caroline (1801–73)

Novelist and poet. Born Caroline Meysey-Wigley, her father was an MP. She published her poems in 1840 (as 'V'), though more interest was aroused by her first (and anonymous) novel, *Paul Ferroll* (1855), whose hero murders his first wife and is able to

keep his secret for eighteen years through a happy and prosperous second marriage. The novel entered into the wider debate about divorce (leading up to the 1857 Divorce Act), while the moral ambiguities arising from the author's apparent unwillingness to condemn her hero, combined with the novel's interest in secrecy, make *Paul Ferroll* an important forerunner of the ▷ sensation novel of the 1860s. In the sequel, *Why Paul Ferroll Killed His Wife* (1860), Clive adopts a more conventionally moralistic tone.

Cloud of Unknowing, The

One of the most admired texts of the medieval English mystical tradition. This spiritual treatise was produced some time in the second half of the 14th century in the north-east Midlands area. The text, which explores the active and contemplative ways of living, is addressed to a young contemplative and is partly presented in dialogue form. The tutor counsels that it is only by experiencing the cloud of unknowing that God will be felt and seen. Several other spiritual treatises have been attributed to the author of *The Cloud of Unknowing* (who is otherwise unknown).
Bib: Hodgson, P. (ed.), *The Cloud of Unknowing and the Book of Privy Counselling*; Wolters, C. (trans.), *The Cloud of Unknowing.*

Cobbett, William (1762–1835)

Journalist and political leader of the working class, especially of the rural labourer. The son of a small farmer and self-educated, he remained identified with country pursuits and interests; he was always a peasant, but a fully articulate one. The work by which he is especially known is ▷ *Rural Rides*, an account of tours through England on horseback, written for the enlightenment of a working-class public, and published between 1820 and 1830 in his periodical ▷ *Political Register*, which he edited from 1802 until his death. The *Rides* are famous for their racy, vigorous description of the countryside. His language is always clear, plain and lively; in an autobiographical fragment he declares that his first inspiration in the writing of prose was the work of ▷ Jonathan Swift, though he is completely without Swift's ironical suavity. His next most famous work is his *Advice to Young Men* (1829); his *Grammar of the English Language* (1818) is an outstanding guide to the writing of vigorous English.

Apart from the still appreciated vividness of his writings, Cobbett has remained a hero of forthright, independent political journalism. When he was in America (1792–1800) his *Porcupine's Gazette* and various pamphlets were in defence of Britain against the prejudices of the newly independent Americans; once back in England, he refused offers of government patronage, and though he started his *Political Register* in support of the Tories, then in power, in a few years he moved over to radical opposition, and spent two years in prison. In 1832 he was elected Member of Parliament in spite of his refusal to use the corrupt methods for influencing electors common at the time; in Parliament he went into opposition to the Whig government as an extreme left radical. He was excessively quarrelsome and prejudiced, but also exceedingly brave and eloquent in support of the cause of justice as, at any given time, he saw it.

▷ Whig and Tory.

Bib: Cole, G. D. H., *Life*; *Opinions of William Cobbett*; Lobban, J. H. (ed.), *Rural Rides*; Hughes, A. M. D., *Selections*; Hazlitt, W., in *Spirit of the Age*; Carlyle, E. I., *Cobbett*.

Coetzee, John Michael (b 1940)
South African novelist, translator and critic. Educated at the University of Cape Town, where he has taught literature and linguistics since 1972, having previously worked in computing in England and held an academic job at the State University of New York. Since 1984 he has been Professor of General Literature at Cape Town, and has held visiting professorships at various universities in the USA. His fiction includes *Dusklands* (two novellas, 1974); *In the Heart of the Country* (1977; published in the USA as *From the Heart of the Country*); *Waiting for the Barbarians* (1980); *Life and Times of Michael K* (1983); *Foe* (1986); *Age of Iron* (1990). Together with the novelist ▷ André Brink, he edited *A Land Apart: A South African Reader* (1986). His translations include: *A Posthumous Confession*, by Marcellus Emants (1976); *The Expedition to the Baobab Tree*, by Wilma Stockenstrom (1983). Critical writing: *White Writing: On the Culture of Letters in South Africa* (1988). His fiction frequently works through the self-conscious transformation of established genres, such as the 18th-century novel of travel and exploration (in *Foe*, which takes as its point of departure Daniel Defoe's *Robinson Crusoe*). Coetzee's most persistent concern has been the impact on the self of colonial power-structures; many of his protagonists are compromised by their privileged position within such structures.

Bib: Dovey, T., *The Novels of J. M. Coetzee: Lacanian Allegories*; Penner, A. R., *Countries of the Mind: The Fiction of J. M. Coetzee*; Atwell, D. (ed.), *Doubling the Point: Essays and Interviews*.

Coleridge, Samuel Taylor (1772–1834)
Poet and critic. Son of a Devon clergyman, he was educated in London and at Jesus College Cambridge. He left Cambridge to enlist in the Dragoons under the pseudonym Silas Tomkyn Comberbache, and although he returned after a matter of months he never completed his degree. His early religious leanings were towards Unitarianism. In 1794 he made the acquaintance of Robert Southey (1774–1843), with whom, under the influence of ▷ French Revolution, he evolved a communistic scheme which they called 'Pantisocracy', and together they wrote the tragedy. *The Fall of Robespierre*. In 1795 he married Sara Fricker, Southey marrying her sister. His *Poems on Various Subjects* were published in 1796, at about the time he met William Wordsworth. The two poets became friends, and lived close to each other for a time in Somerset. *Kubla Khan* and the first part of *Christabel* were written in this period, though they were not published until later. The joint publication, *Lyrical Ballads*, which included Coleridge's *The Rime*

of the Ancient Mariner, appeared in 1798. Coleridge expressed his loss of faith in the French Revolution in *France, An Ode* (1798).

In 1798–9 he travelled in Germany and came under the influence of the transcendental philosophy of Schlegel and ▷ Kant, which dominates his later theoretical writing. During 1800–4 he moved near to Wordsworth in Keswick, and fell unhappily in love with his sister-in-law, Sarah Hutchinson, a relationship referred to in *Dejection: An Ode* (1802). Early in his life he had become reliant on opium and never succeeded in fully controlling the addiction. He began to give public lectures and became famous for his table talk. In 1809 he founded a periodical, *The Friend*, which was later published as a book (1818). In 1817 appeared ▷ *Biographia Literaria*, his autobiographical apologia and a landmark in literary theory and criticism. He quarrelled with Wordsworth in 1810, and in later life he lived in the homes of various benefactors, including the surgeon, James Gillman, who helped him to cope with his addiction. He became increasingly Tory in politics and Anglican in religion, developing an emotionalist conservatism in the tradition of Burke.

Coleridge's poetic output is small, diverse, but of great importance. His 'conversation poems', such as *Frost at Midnight* (1798), *The Lime-Tree Bower and My Prison* (1800), continue and deepen the reflective tradition of Gray and Cowper, culminating in the poignant *Dejection: An Ode* (1802). On the other hand his major symbolic works, such as *The Rime of the Ancient Mariner* (1798), *Kubla Khan* (1816) and *Christabel* (1816), plumb new psychological and emotional depths, and can be seen to develop along similar lines as his famous theoretical definition of imagination in *Biographia Literaria*, Chapter XIII. His perspectives are consistently more intellectually alert than those of his friend Wordsworth, though the expression of his philosophical ideas is sometimes confused. His sympathetic but discriminating analysis of Wordsworth's work in *Biographia Literaria* is a model of unfussy analytical method. As both practitioner and theorist, Coleridge is central to Romanticism.

Bib: House, H., *Coleridge*; Lowes, J., L., *The Road to Xanadu*; Coburn, K., *In Pursuit of Coleridge*; Holmes, R., *Coleridge*; Jackson, J. R. de J. (ed.), *Coleridge: The Critical Heritage*; Jones, A. R., and Tydeman, W., *Coleridge: The Ancient Mariner and Other Poems* (Macmillan Casebook); Fruman, N., *Coleridge: The Damaged Archangel*; Cooke, K., *Coleridge*; Hamilton, P., *Coleridge's Poetics*; Wheeler, K. M., *The Creative Mind in Coleridge's Poetry*; Sultana, D. (ed.), *New Approaches to Coleridge*; Magnuson, P., *Coleridge's Nightmare Poetry*.

Collins, Merle
Caribbean poet and novelist. Collins was born and educated in Grenada, where she worked as a teacher until the US invasion in 1983. She is now a lecturer at the University of North London. Her first novel was *Angel* (1987); *Rain Darling* (1990) is a collection of stories and she edited, with Rhonda Cobham, *Watchers and Seekers: Creative Writing by Black Women in Britain* (1987). As well as poems in anthologies,

she has published a collection, *Because the Dawn Breaks, Poems Dedicated to the Grenadian People* (1985).

Collins, Wilkie (1824–89)

Novelist; the first ▷ detective novelist in English. His two famous novels are *The Woman in White* (1860), first published in ▷ *Household Words*, a magazine edited by ▷ Charles Dickens, and ▷ *The Moonstone* (1868). These novels of ▷ sensation established a pattern for English detective fiction. His mastery was especially over plot-construction in which he influenced Dickens. His characterization is less distinguished but in *The Woman in White* he excels in this, too, and in the creation of disturbing atmosphere. He collaborated with Dickens in a few stories in *Households Words* and in ▷ *All the Year Round: The Wreck of the Golden Mary, A Message from the Sea, No Thoroughfare*. Collins's other novels include *No Name* (1862) and *Armadale* (1866), which has been praised for its melodrama.
Bib: Robinson, K., *Life*; Phillips, W. C., *Dickens, Reade and Collins: Sensation Novelists*; Ashley, R., *Wilkie Collins*; Eliot, T. S., Preface to *The Moonstone*, World's Classics edition; Lonoff, S., *Wilkie Collins and His Victorian Readers*; Peters, C., *The King of Inventors*.

Colonel Jack (1722)

The History and Remarkable Life of Colonel Jacque, a novel by ▷ Daniel Defoe. Jack is abandoned by his parents, becomes a thief, a soldier, a slave on an American plantation, a planter, and eventually a rich and repentant man back in England. The sequence through crime, suffering and repentance, and from poverty to prosperity, is typical of Defoe's novels.

Colonialism

Although it is known that colonies were established in early history, the term is now taken to refer to nationalistic appropriation of land dating from the Renaissance period in the West, and is usually understood as prepetrated on black or coloured non-Europeans in Asia, Africa, Australasia, the Americas or the Caribbean by the white western European powers. Colonialism does not have to imply formal annexation, however. Colonial status involves the imposition of decisions by one people upon another, where the economy or political structure has been brought under the overwhelming influence of another country. Western colonialism had its heyday from 1450 to 1900. It began in the Renaissance with the voyages of discovery; the new territories were annexed for their material resources and for the scope they offered to missionary efforts to extend the power of the Church. The last independent non-Western territories were parcelled out in 1900. After World War I the growth of nationalism in Africa and Asia started to reverse the process. The establishment of the United Nations (1945), which declared colonial policy a matter of interest to the entire world, helped to spur the relinquishing of former colonies.
Works from Shakespeare's *The Tempest* to ▷ Joseph Conrad's ▷ *Heart of Darkness* demonstrate the struggle to determine the meaning of colonial

power, though there was a strong tradition, founded on the imperialist myth of the Victorian era, of which ▷ Rudyard Kipling and ▷ Rider Haggard were the most famous exponents, that white intervention was made in the interests of the native inhabitants.
▷ Post-colonial fiction.
Bib: Memmi, A., *The Colonizer and the Colonized*; Said, E., *Orientalism*; Spivak, G. C. *In Other Worlds*.

Commonwealth fiction

▷ Post-colonial fiction.

Communism

Communism may be interpreted in two ways: 1 the older, imprecise sense covering various philosophies of the common ownership of property; 2 the relatively precise interpretation understood by the remaining Marxist-Leninist Communist Parties of the world.
  1 The older philosophies derive especially from the Greek philosopher ▷ Plato. His *Republic* proposes that society should be divided into classes according to differences of ability instead of differences of wealth and birth; the state is to provide for the needs of all, and thus to abolish rivalries and inequalities between rich and poor; children are to be educated by the state, and women are to have equal rights, opportunities and training with men. In England, one of the most famous disciples of Plato is ▷ Sir Thomas More in his ▷ *Utopia* (1516). More's prescriptions are similar to Plato's in many respects, but though he also requires equal opportunity and training for men, he goes against Plato in keeping the monogamous family intact, whereas Plato wanted a community of wives and children to be brought up by the state. Both Plato and More require for their schemes an all-powerful state in the charge of an intellectual aristocracy; what we should call 'enlightened totalitarianism'. With the growth of the power of the state in the 20th century, however, all forms of totalitarianism were regarded with abhorrence by liberal intellectuals, and so arose the 'anti-utopian' class of literature, for example ▷ Aldous Huxley's *Brave New World* (1932) and ▷ George Orwell's *Animal Farm* (1945) and *1984* (1948), vehemently satirizing totalitarian communism.
  In practical experiment, the vows of poverty taken by members of orders of monks and friars and the communal ownership of property in such communities may have kept alight for people in general the ideal of the freedom of the spirit attainable by the renunciation of selfish material ambitions and competition. Protestant sectarian beliefs emphasizing the equality of souls led to such an abortive communistic enterprise as that of the Levellers in the Interregnum (1649–1660). In America, a number of experiments were undertaken by immigrant sects such as the Amana community, and under the influence of the English socialist ▷ Robert Owen and the French socialists Fourier and Cabet, but few of them lasted long.
  2 Modern so-called scientific communism, based mainly on ▷ Karl Marx and Lenin, differs from certain forms of modern socialism by affirming the necessity for revolutionary, as distinct from

evolutionary, method, to be followed by a period of dictatorship. This form of communism is supported in Britain by a small but fairly influential political party which is active in the ▷ trade unions but has no place in Parliament or in local government. Lenin attempted to implement the communist programme defined by Marx. Between the Revolution of 1917 and 1924, when he was killed, he tried to guide the newly inaugurated 'dictatorship of the proletariat' in Russia. Not all communism is revolutionary, however: the Italian communist party has adopted the parliamentary route to socialism.

In a series of dramatic, though in some cases initially or relatively peaceful revolutions, from 1989–91, communism was largely abandoned by the rapidly fragmenting former Eastern bloc. This has prompted reassessment, and in some cases a change of name among Western communist parties.

Compleat Angler, The (1653)
A discourse on the sport of fishing (in full, *The Compleat Angler, or the Contemplative Man's Recreation*) by ▷ Isaak Walton, first published in 1653; its 5th edition has a continuation by Charles Cotton (1630–87) and came out in 1676. The book has been described as perhaps the only handbook of art and craft to rank as literature. This is because Walton combines his practical instruction with digressions about his personal tastes and opinions, and sets it in direct, fresh description of the English countryside which may be contrasted with the artificial pastoralism which had hitherto been characteristic of natural description. The book has the form of a dialogue mainly between Piscator (Fisherman) and Venator (Hunter), which takes place on the banks of the river Lea near London. Cotton's continuation is transferred to the banks of the river Dove between Derbyshire and Staffordshire.

Compton-Burnett, Ivy (1884–1969)
Novelist. Her first novel, *Dolores* (1911) is distinguished from all her others by an approach to the method of novel-writing similar to that of the 19th century, in particular that of ▷ George Eliot, and a disposition to accept usual conceptions of moral retribution. From *Pastors and Masters* (1925) both the method and the moral vision change radically. The novels are narrated almost wholly through dialogue; the manner derives from ▷ Jane Austen, but with even less attempt to present visualized environments. In treating occurrences such as matricide, bigamy, betrayal and incest they show affinities with Greek tragic drama, while the novels of ▷ Samuel Butler are another important influence. The period is always 1890–1914; the setting, a prosperous household of the period; the characters include some who are arrogant to the point of evil, and are able, without retribution, to dominate those who are selfless or weak; the plots are melodramatic but never break up the surface of respectability. The dialogue is epigrammatic and pungent, with the consequence that the novels are all exceptionally concentrated structures. The effect is commonly of sardonic comedy with tragic conclusion, although the comic side tends to dominate.

After 1925 the novels are as follows: *Brothers and Sisters* (1929); *Men and Wives* (1931); *More Women than Men* (1933); *A House and its Head* (1935); *Daughters and Sons* (1937); *A Family and a Fortune* (1939); *Parents and Children* (1941); *Elders and Betters* (1944); *Manservant and Maidservant* (1947); *Two Worlds and Their Ways* (1949); *Darkness and Day* (1951); *The Present and the Past* (1953); *Mother and Son* (1955); *A Father and his Fate* (1957); *A Heritage and its History* (1959); *The Mighty and their Fall* (1961); *A God and his Gifts* (1963); *The Last and the First* (1971). Few distinguished novelists have shown such uniformity of treatment and lack of development throughout their career. Probably *A House and its Head* and *A Family and a Fortune* are her two outstanding achievements.
Bib: Hansford Johnson, P., *Ivy Compton-Burnett*; Liddell, R., *The Novels of Ivy Compton-Burnett*; Spurling. H., *Ivy When Young* and *Secrets of a Woman's Heart*.

Comte, Auguste (1798–1857)
French philosopher. He sought to expound a scientifically based philosophy for human progress, called Positivism which deduced laws of development from the facts of history and excluded metaphysics and religion. His chief works were translated into English. In them he sought to establish a system that would be the scientific equivalent of the Catholic system of philosophy. In this he failed, but his work led to the modern science of sociology. In England, his chief disciple was Frederick Harrison (1831–1923), but he also deeply interested the philosopher ▷ John Stuart Mill and the novelist ▷ George Eliot. The character of his beliefs suited radically reformist and religiously sceptical English intellectuals such as these; on the other hand, his systematization of ideas was alien to English habits of mind, and was criticized by the philosopher ▷ Herbert Spencer.

Condensation
This term is used by ▷ Freud in *The Interpretation of Dreams* (1900) to describe the compression and selection that takes place during the process of dreaming. When subjected to analysis the details of the dream can be shown to relate to a series of deeper, more extensive psychic connections. Freud distinguishes between the 'manifest content' of the dream, which is what is remembered, and the 'latent content' which can only be arrived at retrospectively through the analytical business of interpretation. Interpretation seeks to reverse the process of condensation and to investigate 'the relation between the manifest content of dreams and the latent dream-thoughts' and to trace out 'the processes by which the latter have been changed into the former' (*The Interpretation of Dreams*). The term has also become part of the language of critical theory. Applied to a literary text was first used to afford a partial explanation of the energies which bring the text into existence, or to give an account of the unconscious motivations of represented 'characters'. More recently, the analogy between the interpretation of dreams and of texts has been used to suggest

the impossibility of arriving at an original 'core' of
meaning, prior to ▷ displacement or condensation.
Freud speaks of the dream's 'navel' – that knotted
point of enigma which indicated that there is always
something unresolved, unanalysed.
  ▷ Psychoanalytical criticism.

Confessions of an English Opium-Eater (1822: enlarged ed. 1856)

An autobiography, and the most famous work of ▷
Thomas De Quincey. Like ▷ Coleridge, De Quincey
began taking opium to ease physical suffering, and
eventually increased the dose until he became an
addict. The book contains eloquent, prose-poetic
accounts of his opium dreams and also graphic
descriptions of his life of poverty in London. In the
former aspect the prose evokes the high musical
rhetoric of the 17th-century masters – Thomas
Browne, John Milton, Jeremy Taylor; in the latter,
it is typical of the 19th-century mode of transmitting
intimate, minute personal experience, resembling the
increasingly close-textured psychology of the novel.
In his tenderness for and understanding of childish
suffering, De Quincey represents a development
that was new in the history of literature, and came to
fruition in the Victorian novelists, notably ▷ Charles
Dickens.

Congreve, William (1670–1729)

Well-known as a Restoration dramatist for such
works as *The Double Dealer* (1694) and *The Way of
the World* (1700), Congreve also wrote *Incognita: or,
Love and Duty Reconciled* (1691), his first work and an
early example of a novel in English which the author
termed as such: in his Preface Congreve identifies it
as a novel, a form which he distinguishes from the ▷
romance as being 'of a more familiar Nature'.

Coningsby, or The New Generation (1844)

A political novel by ▷ Benjamin Disraeli. By means
of it, the rising politician, Disraeli, expresses his
contempt for the lack of principle behind the
contemporary Tory (right-wing) party (▷ Whig and
Tory), whose side he nonetheless took against the
expediency and materialism of the Whigs and ▷
Utilitarians. Against them he advocates a revived,
platonically idealized aristocracy with the interests of
the people at heart and respected by them as their
natural leaders. Such a new aristocrat is the hero of
the novel, Coningsby, and he and his friends form
a group comparable to the Young England group
which Disraeli himself led in Parliament Coningsby
is the grandson of Lord Monmouth, type of the old,
unprincipled, predatory aristocracy, whose inveterate
enemy is the industrialist Millbank, representing
the new and vital middle class. Coningsby falls in
love with Millbank's daughter, is disinherited by his
grandfather and eventually is elected to Parliament
with Millbank's support. The novel is essentially one
of propaganda of ideas, but written with great feeling,
liveliness and intelligence. Lord Monmouth was
based on the actual Lord Hertford, also used as the
basis of Lord Steyne in ▷ Thackeray's ▷ *Vanity Fair*.
Another excellently drawn character is the detestable
Rigby, based on John Wilson Croker, politician and
journalist, and author of the notoriously abusive
review of Keats's *Endymion*.

Conrad, Joseph (1857–1924)

Novelist. His name in full was Józef Teodor Konrad
Korzeniowski. He knew hardly any English when he
was 20; yet before he was 40 he had completed his
first English novel, *Almayer's Folly* (1895), and ten
years later he had published one of the masterpieces
of the novel in English: ▷ *Nostromo* (1904). The
background to Conrad as a novelist is complicated
and important for understanding the richness of his
art. 1 Early life. His father was a Polish patriot and
man of letters, exiled from the Polish Ukraine by
the Russian government, which then ruled it, for
his political activity. His mother died when he was
seven, and his father when he was 11, and his uncle
subsequently became the main family influence in
his life. 2 Life at sea. From the tales of sea life (in
translation) by the English writer ▷ Captain Marryat,
the American Fenimore Cooper, and the Frenchman
▷ Victor Hugo, he became fascinated by the sea
and joined the crew of a French ship in 1874, and
of an English one in 1878. By 1884 he was a British
subject and had qualified as a master (ship's captain).
In his voyages Conrad had visited the Mediterranean,
South American, the Far East, and Central Africa. 3
Writing life. He began writing in about 1886 with at
least as good an acquaintance with French language
and literature as English. He brought to the English
novel an admiration for the French ▷ realists, ▷
Flaubert and Maupassant. He also had a knowledge
of many peoples, and a profound feeling of the
contrast between the tightly enclosed communities of
ships' crews and the loose egocentric individualism
characterizing land societies. In addition, he knew,
from his childhood experience in Russian Poland
and Russia itself, the tragic impingement of political
pressures on personal life, in a way that was unusual
in the West until after the outbreak of World War I
in 1914. In his preoccupation with the exploration of
moral issues he was in the English tradition.

His major work is represented by the novels ▷
Lord Jim (1900), *Nostromo*, ▷ *The Secret Agent* (1907)
and *Under Western Eyes* (1911) and the novellas *The
Nigger of the Narcissus* (1898); *Youth* (1902); ▷ *Heart
of Darkness* (1902); *Typhoon* (1903); and *The Shadow
Line* (1917). *Lord Jim* and *The Nigger of the Narcissus*
are concerned with honour, courage and solidarity,
ideals for which the merchant service provided
a framework. *The Secret Agent* and *Under Western
Eyes* deal with political extremism, the contrast
between eastern and western Europe, and human
folly, cruelty, fear and betrayal. *Nostromo*, set in an
imaginary South American state, shares some of the
themes of the other work, but is notable for its sense
of history and the power of economic forces. *Heart
of Darkness* is famous for its ambiguous and resonant
portrayal of evil. Conrad's earlier novels, *Almayer's
Folly* and *An Outcast of the Islands* (1896) have Far
Eastern settings, and a less developed prose style.
His later work includes *Chance* (1914), the first to
bring him a big public; *Victory* (1915); *The Arrow of
Gold* (1919); *The Rescue* (1920); *The Rover* (1923);
and *Suspense*, which he was working on when he

died. Conrad is one of the most important modern. English novelists, both for his concerns and for his techniques. He addressed issues which have come to seem central to the 20th-century mind: the problem of identity; the terror of the unknown within and without; the difficulty of finding a secure moral base; political violence and economic oppression; isolation and existential dread. His technical innovations were particularly in the use of narrators, the disruption of narrative chronology and the employment of a powerful irony of tone.

His other works are: a number of volumes of short stories and essays, including *Tales of Unrest* (1898) and *Notes on Life and Letters* (1921). *The Mirror of the Sea* (1906) and *A Personal Record* (1912) are autobiographical. Conrad co-operated with ▷ Ford Madox Ford in the writing of two novels: *The Inheritors* (1901) and *Romance* (1903). The first three volumes of his *Collected Letters* were published in 1983, 1986 and 1988.
Bib: Baines, J., *Joseph Conrad: A Critical Biography*; Berthoud, J., *Joseph Conrad: the Major Phase*; Guerard, A. J., *Conrad the Novelist*; Najder, Z., *Joseph Conrad: A Chronicle*; Watt, I., *Conrad in the Nineteenth Century*; Hewitt, D., *Conrad: A Reassessment*; Erdinast-Vulcan, D., *Joseph Conrad and the Modern Temper*; Hawthorn, J., *Joseph Conrad: Narrative Technique and Ideological Commitment*; Hampson, R., *Joseph Conrad: Betrayal and Identity*; Roberts, A. M. (ed.), *Conrad and Gender*.

Consciousness
In its most general sense consciousness is synonymous with 'awareness'. In a more specifically ▷ Freudian context it is associated with the individual's perception of reality. For Freud, of course, the impression which an individual has of his or her experience is partial, since awareness is controlled by the processes of the unconscious, which are never recognized in their true form. More recently 'consciousness' has been associated with the ▷ Enlightenment view of individualism, in which the individual is conceived of as being distinct from society, and is also held to be the centre and origin of meaning. Following from this, what distinguishes humanity is its alleged capacity for autonomy, and hence freedom of action. The Romantic equivalent of this philosophical position is that literature is the expression of the pre-existent 'self' of the writer, and that the greatest literature is that which manifests the writer's consciousness most fully. These views of consciousness should further be distinguished from the Marxist version (▷ Marx, Karl), in which the self is 'produced' through 'material practices', by means of which social relations are generated. Theories of consciousness affect notions of the relationships between writer and reader, and it is in working out such relationships that the concept of 'consciousness' is important in current literary critical debate.

Contemporary Review, The
It was founded in 1866 and has Sir Percy Bunting as its most famous editor. It covered a variety of subjects and in 1955 incorporated ▷ *The Fortnightly Review*.

Contradiction
Used in literary criticism to identify the incoherences in a literary text. Derived from Hegel, Engels and ▷ Marx, contradiction, as applied to literature, implies that artistic representation is not the product of a unifying aesthetic impulse. Contradiction describes patterns of dominance and subordination and thus, in literary terms, points towards divisions within the work which challenge notions of aesthetic coherence.

Cookson, Catherine (b 1906)
Romantic novelist. Cookson is one of the ▷ best-selling writers currently working in Britain, whose stories have much in common with classic Mills and Boon romantic plots but which also deploy historical motifs and display richer characterization. Her native Northumberland, in which most of her novels are set, has become immortalized as 'Cookson Country' by the local tourist board, which at least is testament to the rich evocations of landscape and regional feeling which her primarily romantic fiction offers.

Her wide range of novels, all written since she was in her early forties, include: *Fanny McBride* (1977); *Pure as the Lily* (1978); *The Mallen Novels* (1979); *Tilly Trotter* (1980) and *Marriage and Mary Ann* (1984).
Bid: Radford, J. (ed.), *The Progress of Romance: The Politics of Popular Fiction*; Radway, J., *Reading the Romance*.

Cooper, William (b 1910)
Pen name of H. S. Hoff, novelist. Having already published four novels under his real name, Cooper came to prominence in 1950 with *Scenes from Provincial Life*, the story of an unconventional and sceptical schoolteacher living in a Midlands town around the outbreak of World War II. In reacting against the experimental tradition of the ▷ Bloomsbury Group and of ▷ modernism, Cooper's novel initiated the 1950s school of dissentient ▷ realism, which included such writers as ▷ John Braine, ▷ David Storey, ▷ Stan Barstow and ▷ John Wain. *Scenes from Metropolitan Life* (written in the 1950s but not published until 1982) and *Scenes from Married Life* (1961) complete a trilogy. Other novels include: *You Want the Right Frame of Reference* (1971), *Love on the Coast* (1973) and *Scenes from Later Life* (1983).

Coppard, A. E. (1878–1957)
Writer of short stories. He was largely self-educated, and began serving in a shop at the age of nine. Later he began writing while working as an accountant, and his literary interests were nourished when he obtained a post at Oxford where he met and made friends with the intelligentsia. The best of his stories are chiefly in the earlier volumes: *Adam and Eve and Pinch Me* (1921); *Clorinda Walks in Heaven* (1922); *Fishmonger's Fiddle* (1925); and *The Field of Mustard* (1926). Later volumes include: *Pink Furniture* (1930); *Tapster's Tapestry* (1938); *You Never Know Do You?* (1939); and *The Dark-Eyed Lady* (1947). He also wrote poems: *Collected Poems* (1928); *Easter Day* (1931); and *Cherry Ripe* (1935), and an autobiography, *It's Me, O Lord* (1957).

Coppard had a remarkably acute ear for the spoken word, and his best tales have the freshness and simplicity of oral folk-tales. Although his subject matter was often more sophisticated than this suggests, many of his finest stories are about the life of the countryside. He was influenced by ▷ Thomas Hardy's short stories, and he often shows a stoically resigned attitude to human destiny which is similar to Hardy's outlook, but he combined this with a remarkable talent for sharp comedy, again reminiscent of peasant folk-tales.

Copyright, The law of
The right of writers, artists and musicians to refuse reproduction of their works. The right is now established law in every civilized country. The first copyright law in England was passed under Queen Anne in 1709. Before this, it was possible for publishers to publish books without the author's permission, and without allowing him or her any profits from sale, a practice very common during the lifetime of Shakespeare. Until 1909, the laws of the United States did not adequately safeguard British authors against having their works 'pirated' there, *ie* published without their permission and without giving them suitable financial return. ▷ Dickens was a main sufferer from this state of affairs, which greatly angered him.

Corelli, Marie (1855–1924)
Novelist. Born Mary Mackay, illegitimate daughter (though she claimed to be adopted, and born in 1864) of Scottish songwriter Charles Mackay and his second wife. She was educated by governesses and for a while at a convent, and was a gifted pianist, intending to take up a musical career, for which she adopted the name Corelli. In 1885 a psychic experience led her to start writing and her novels are sensational, full of trances, swoons, religious conversions and visions etc. She was very successful around the turn of the century, but her popularity declined into ridicule before her death. Her first novel was *A Romance of Two Worlds* (1886) but her great popularity occurred with *Barabbas: A Dream of the World's Tragedy* (1893), despite unfavourable reviews, *The Sorrows of Satan* (1895) had a greater initial sale than any previous English novel. Other novels include *The Mighty Atom* (1896) and *Boy* (1900).
Bib: Bigland, E., *Marie Corelli: The Woman and the Legend*; Masters, B., *Now Barabbas Was a Rotter: The Extraordinary Life of Marie Corelli*.

Corn Laws, Repeal of the, 1846
The Corn Laws existed to protect English home-grown corn from competition from imported foreign corn. Their existence made for higher food prices and assumed the superior importance of agricultural interest over urban industrial interests. In the first half of the 19th century the Tory party derived its main support from landowners, whereas the Whigs owed much of their support to the new industrialists of the rapidly growing industrial towns. The Whig Anti-Corn Law League consequently represented not merely opposition to a particular measure but

rivalry between main segments of society; moreover, the workers, anxious above all for cheap food, supported the urban middle class and the Whigs. It was nonetheless a Tory Prime Minister, Robert Peel, who repealed the Corn Laws under pressure of a severe famine in Ireland. The abolition of the Corn Laws was of historic importance in several ways: 1 it divided the Tory party, sending its younger leader, ▷ Benjamin Disraeli, into opposition, with his supporters, against Peel; 2 it began the era of ▷ free trade (*ie* trade unrestricted by import or export taxes); 3 it acknowledged implicitly that industrial interests were henceforth to be regarded as more important than agricultural interests; 4 it relieved the almost revolutionary restlessness of the working class, so that England was one of the few countries in Europe not to undergo upheaval or serious threat of upheaval in the Year of Revolutions, 1848.
▷ Whig and Tory.

Cornhill Magazine, The
A monthly periodical, at the height of its fame soon after its foundation by ▷ William Thackeray, the novelist, in 1860. Contributors included ▷ John Ruskin, ▷ Matthew Arnold, ▷ Mrs Gaskell, ▷ Anthony Trollope and ▷ Leslie Stephen, besides Thackeray himself. It continued this century to publish the work of many writers.

Court of Chancery
A Court of law under the Lord Chancellor, head of the English judicial system. The Court grew up in the 15th century to deal with cases which for any reason could not be dealt with efficiently by the established law courts administering Common Law. The practice developed a system of law supplementary to Common Law, known as Equity. Few things so neatly demonstrate the disadvantage of women in English law as the fact that they are treated as the legal equivalents of orphans and lunatics, through one of the special fields of jurisdiction Equity was created to cover. There have been recent attempts, by means of 'equal opportunities' legislation, for instance, to remedy this long-standing disability. By the 19th century Chancery procedure became excessively complex, its relationship with other courts of law was ill-defined, and judgements were often delayed for years – hence the satire to which ▷ Charles Dickens subjected the Court in his novel, ▷ *Bleak House*. The system was reformed by the Judicature Act, 1873. (The idiom 'in chancery' means 'remaining undecided indefinitely'; a 'ward in Chancery' is an orphan whose interests are in the care of Chancery.)

Coverley, Sir Roger de
A fictional character invented by the essayist ▷ Sir Richard Steele for the pages of ▷ *The Spectator*, and developed by his colleague Joseph Addison. The name was taken from a north country dance, Roger of Coverley. Sir Roger was at first a member of an imaginary club, the Spectator Club, where Steele in his journalist guise of the 'Spectator' purported to be studying human nature. In the hands of Addison, Sir Roger came to take up much more space than

the other members; the papers devoted to describing his life (20 by Addison, eight by Steele, and two by Budgell) are much the best known parts of *The Spectator*. In his conservatism, his devotion to the Church of England, and his kindly but despotic control of his tenants, he is a typical squire of the time, but in his civilized manners he is deliberately made superior to the general run of country squires (compare Squire Western in ▷ Fielding's ▷ *Tom Jones*). In his simplicity and idiosyncrasies he was individual, with a literary relationship to ▷ Don Quixote. Though the 'Coverley Papers' are not a novel, the envisioning of the character is distinctly novelistic, so that they rank among the precursors of the English novel. Addison's especial aim, beyond entertainment, was to civilize the country squire; a secondary aim was the political one of making fun of the Tory English gentry.

Craik, Mrs Dinah Maria Mulock (1826–87)
Born in Stoke-on-Trent, the daughter of a Nonconformist clergyman, she wrote novels, plays, poetry, ▷ biography, ▷ travel books, didactic essays and children's stories (▷ children's books). After an unsettled childhood, she lived with her brother in London, becoming well-known in literary society and marrying a partner in Macmillans in 1865. She was a shrewd negotiator and businesswoman, but a generous woman, using a pension granted to her in 1864 to help needy authors. Her novels include *The Ogilvies* (1849), *Olive* (1850), *The Head of the Family* (1851) and *John Halifax, Gentleman* (1856), on which her fame largely rests.

Craik, Helen (c 1750–1825)
Poet and novelist. A Scottish writer who was encouraged by Robert Burns, Craik's poetry is now rarely read; recent criticism has focused on her ▷ Minerva novels. Her prose writing tends towards the gloomy and fantastic, but her characters introduce a realistic element into the otherwise far-fetched narrative. Among her novels are: *Julia de Saint Pierre* (1796), *Henry of Northumberland, or The Hermit's Cell* (1800) and *The Nun and Her Daughter* (1805).

Cranford (1853)
A novel by ▷ Elizabeth Gaskell (1810–65), first published in ▷ *Household Words* (ed. ▷ Charles Dickens) 1851–3. It is the best known of her novels. The town of Cranford is actually based on Knutsford, some 17 miles from Manchester. The book describes the life of the predominantly feminine genteel society of the place. Though apparently very slight, it contains graphic description, subtle, ironic humour resembling ▷ Jane Austen's, and acute discernment in discriminating between the vulgar arrogance of the merely rich and the sensitive, humane pride of the gentility. Its most famous characters are the blatant and ostentatious Honourable Mrs Jamieson and, in contrast, the timid, retiring, yet distinguished Miss Matty.

Creoles
British, French and Spanish settlers in South and Central America, Louisiana and the West Indies, and their descendants of any colour. In English literature it applies especially to British sugar planters in the West Indies, who were very prosperous in the 18th century. Because it was unclear whether place of origin or race was being indicated, the term could be used to hint at or to mask blackness.

Cricket on the Hearth, The (1846)
A Christmas book by ▷ Charles Dickens, one of a series started by ▷ *A Christmas Carol* (1843). It is a tale in which the evil schemes of old Tackleton to injure the married love of Peerybingle and his young wife, Dot, and to marry May Fielding are frustrated by the magic of the Cricket and by a mysterious stranger.

Critique
A term used in critical theory. Traditional conceptions of 'criticism' have privileged the acts of judgement and comparison but have often anchored them in the unspecified sensitivity of the reader. Criticism presupposes a direct relationship between reader and literary text; the reader responds to the stimulus of particular verbal forms which are evaluated according to their appeal to a universal human condition. The practice of 'critique', in a literary context, however, concerns itself not just with producing readings of primary texts and accounting for those social, cultural, or psychological motivations which are responsible for its appearance in a particular form, but also with appraising critical readings of those texts. Critique addresses itself to questions of why individual texts should be accorded importance at particular historical moments, and implicates 'criticism' in its more traditional guise as a process whereby meanings are constructed, as opposed to being passively discovered.

Crotchet Castle (1831)
A novel by ▷ Thomas Love Peacock. The plot is unimportant, and the novel consists mainly of witty talk, burlesquing and satirizing contemporary attitudes and ideas. A crotchet is an eccentric and frivolous notion or prejudice. Some of the characters are representatives of intellectual tendencies, *eg* MacQuedy, a Scots economist whose name suggests 'Q.E.D.' (*quod erat demonstrandum*), stands for the excessive rationalism of the political economists and utilitarians of the age. On the other hand, Mr Skionar stands for the poet, critic and philosopher, ▷ S. T. Coleridge, and burlesques his transcendental mysticism. Mr Chainmail stands for the sentimental cult of the 'Gothic', *ie* the romance and sensationalism of the cult of the Middle Ages, familiar from the historical novels of ▷ Walter Scott and from the ▷ Gothic novels of the previous generation. Sanity is represented by Dr Folliott, a clergyman, a character of robust and cheerful common sense.

Cruikshank, George (1792–1878)
Illustrator, with a strong satirical and moralistic bent: famous especially for his illustrations to ▷ Charles Dickens's novel ▷ *Oliver Twist*.

Culler, Jonathan (b 1944)

Academic and critic whose works have done much to introduce English-speaking audiences to the works of ▷ structuralist and ▷ post-structuralist critics. His major studies include *Structuralist Poetics* (1975), *The Pursuit of Signs* (1981) and *On Deconstruction* (1983). He is Professor of English and Comparative Literature at Cornell University.

Cultural materialism

The foreword to Jonathan Dollimore and Alan Sinfield's collection of essays *Political Shakespeare* (1985) acts as a manifesto for this new radical Marxist criticism. The authors themselves trace the origins of the theory to general dissatisfaction in the British academic world with the traditional essentialist humanism of existing criticism and the rise of numerous approaches (▷ feminism, ▷ structuralism, ▷ psychoanalytic criticism) which challenged this premise. Apart from a debt to the political commitment to change, derived from Marxism, cultural materialism also draws upon ▷ Raymond Williams's cultural analysis which, as Dollimore and Sinfield put it, 'seeks to describe the whole system of significations by which a society or a section of it understands itself and its relations with the world'. Thus, cultural materialism rejects any notion of 'high culture', and sets material values in the place of the idealism of conventional criticism, looking instead at texts in history. Cultural materialism also has links with ▷ new historicism (particularly the work of Stephen Greenblatt) in its emphasis upon the nature of subjectivity and the decentring of man, and with feminism, where the exploration of the gendered human subject is an overlapping interest.

   ▷ Post-structuralism; Marx, Karl.

Cumberland, Richard (1732–1811)

Dramatist, poet, novelist, translator, essayist, associated with the rise of sentimental domestic comedy on the English stage. He began writing poetry while still a pupil at school in Bury St Edmunds. After further education at Westminster School and Cambridge University he published his first play, *The Banishment*

of *Cicero* in 1761. Disappointed in his career aspirations in government, he turned to writing for the stage in earnest. He continued this activity even after his political fortunes improved, eventually completing over 50 plays, operas, and adaptations of plays. His first success of any consequence was with the comedy, *The Brothers*, in 1769. In 1770 he wrote his most famous play, generally considered his best, *The West Indian*, which the actor David Garrick (1717–79) staged in the following year. Even so his work was often under attack for its supposed sentimentality, and Sheridan satirized him as the vain and defensive Sir Fretful Plagiary in *The Critic* (1779). However, Cumberland was sympathetic to the causes of others, especially outcast and vilified groups. He defended the Jews in *The Jew* (1794), which was translated into several languages, including Yiddish and Hebrew, and remained popular well into the 19th century. *The Jew of Mogadore* (1808) again portrays a Jew in a kindly light, and Cumberland also defended Jews in articles in *The Observer*, written under a Jewish pseudonym. His efforts did much to rescue Jews from the villainous anti-Semitic image hitherto afforded them on the stage. In addition to plays, he wrote two novels, translations of Greek plays, ▷ epic poetry, and pamphlets expressing his views on controversial topics of the day.

Bib: Borkat, R. F. S. (ed.), *The Plays of Richard Cumberland*.

Cynics, The

A school of ancient Greek philosophers founded by Antisthenes in the 4th century BC. Their belief, that the only realizable aim in life was the fulfilment of the individual by the strict application of reason to practical issues, led them to an extreme individualism, according to which social considerations were irrelevant, ambition was a distraction, pleasure a corruption, and poverty and disrepute were of active assistance in promoting self-reliance. The word 'cynic' seems to derive from the Greek word for 'dog', and they agreed in taking this animal as their emblem. The word has degenerated to imply an attitude of disbelief in the goodness of human motives and in the reality of human values.

Dabydeen, David (b 1955)
Guyanese novelist and poet. Dabydeen came to
Britain in 1969 and studied at the universities of
Cambridge, London and Oxford. During the 1980s
he worked as a community education officer and as
a lecturer in Caribbean Studies at the University of
Warwick. His first novel was *The Intended* (1991) and
his collection of poems, *Slave Song* (1984) won the
Commonwealth Poetry Prize. He has also published
critical works on the 18th-century painter Hogarth
and on black writing in Britain.

Dacre, Charlotte (c 1782–?)
Novelist and poet. Dacre and her sister, the writer
▷ Sophia King, dedicated their first work, *Trifles
From Helicon* (1798) to their notorious father, John
King, who had just been arrested for bankruptcy.
Her first solo novel, *The Confessions of the Nun of
St Omer* (1805; published under the name 'Rosa
Matilda'), was dedicated to ▷ Matthew Lewis, and
later ridiculed by Lord Byron. Her most famous
work is *Zofloya, or the Moor* (1806), a ▷ Gothic novel
indebted to Lewis's *The Monk*; it ostensibly warns
against the dangers of lust and passion, but Dacre's
obvious fascination in depicting these belies the
explicit didactic purpose. The final scene is a *tour de
force* of Gothicism, in which the heroine is thrown to
her death from a cliff by the devil. *Zofloya* influenced
P. B. Shelley's *Zastrozzi* and was published in ▷
chapbook format as *The Daemon of Venice* (1810).
Dacre wrote several other novels, poetry, and the
lyrics for popular stage songs, though little is known
of her later life.

Dada
Artistic and literary movement. It arose in two
distinct places at about the same time. One group
was formed in Zurich in 1916 by three refugees,
Tristan Tzara (1887–1968), Hans Arp (1887–1966)
and Hugo Ball (1886–1927); another group was
formed in New York in the years 1916–19 by Marcel
Duchamp (1887–1968), Man Ray (1890–1976) and
Francis Picabia (1879–1953). By 1920, both groups
had united and made their headquarters in Paris
where their journal was *Litterature* (1919–21). The
Dada emphasis was on instinctual expression free
from constraints and the consequent cultivation
of destructiveness, randomness and incoherence;
indeed, the very name 'Dada' (= hobby horse) was a
random selection from the dictionary. The movement
lasted until the mid-1920s. A number of its adherents
joined the ▷ Surrealists, a movement which in part
evolved out of Dada.

Daedalus
In Greek myth, an artist of wonderful powers. He
made wings for himself and his son Icarus, and flew
from Crete to Sicily to escape the wrath of King
Minos, for whom he had built the labyrinth. The fact
that he was an artist explains the use of a form of the
name by ▷ James Joyce – Dedalus – in ▷ *Portrait of
the Artist as a Young Man.*

Daisy Miller (1879)
A story by ▷ Henry James. It concerns the visit
of an American girl to Europe, and is one of the
stories in which James contrasts American freshness
of impulse, moral integrity, and naivety with the
complexity and deviousness of the European
mentality. The girl's innocence and candour is
misinterpreted as moral turpitude by the Americans
who are long settled in Europe, including the young
man who acts as focal character for the narrative.

Dane, Clemence (1887–1965)
Playwright and novelist. Clemence Dane is the
pseudonym of Winifred Ashton, a highly prolific
playwright and novelist whose work was extremely
successful in her lifetime, but who has to some extent
been neglected by critical history. Her career was
a long one – Dane published her first novel (which
deals with power and lesbianism in a girls' public
school) *Regiment of Women*, in 1917, and continued
writing until her death – some of her later works
were dramas for BBC television. She also wrote
essays, and was awarded the CBE in 1953. Her
plays include: *A Bill of Divorcement* (1921); *Naboth's
Vineyard* (1925); *Manners* (1927); *The Saviours* (1942);
and *Call Home the Heart* (1947). Her novels include
Enter Sir John (1930); *The Moon is Feminine* (1938);
and *He Brings Great News* (1939).

Dangarembga, Tsitsi (b 1958)
Novelist and playwright, born and brought up in
Rhodesia (now Zimbabwe). She was educated in
Harare (at that time called Salisbury) before going on
to study medicine and psychology at the University of
Oxford and film at the Berlin film school. Her novel
Dangerous Conditions (1988) won the Commonwealth
Prize and reveals some of the psychological effects
of colonialism through the lives of two young girls in
pre-independence Rhodesia.

Daniel Deronda (1876)
A novel by ▷ George Eliot (Mary Ann Evans). It
contains a double story: that of the hero, Daniel
Deronda, and that of the heroine Gwendolen
Harleth. Daniel is the adopted son of an aristocratic
Englishman, and a young man of gracious personality
and positive values; he discovers that he is of
Jewish parentage, and ends by marrying a Jewish
girl, Mirah and devoting himself to the cause of
establishing a Jewish homeland. Gwendolen belongs
to an impoverished upper-class family and marries
(under pressure from her clergyman uncle) a
rich and entirely self-centred aristocrat, Henleigh
Grandcourt, to redeem their fortunes. Her story is
the discovery of the truth of her own nature, just
as Deronda's story is the discovery of his origin
and vocation. Their stories are linked by the almost
casual but entirely beneficent influence of Deronda
over Gwendolen, whom he saves from despair after
the death of her husband in circumstances that
compromise her conscience. (The theme of artistic
dedication is central.) Critics have observed that
the story of Gwendolen is one of the masterpieces
of English fiction, but that that of Daniel is
comparatively flat and unconvincing.

Dante Alighieri (1265–1321)
Poet and philosopher. Very little is known about
the early life of Dante. He was born in Florence, a

member of the Guelf family, and married Gemma Donati in 1285. His involvement in Florentine politics from 1295 led in 1300 to his exile from Florence, to which he never returned. He died at Ravenna in 1321. According to his own report, he was inspired throughout his life by his love for Beatrice, a woman who has been identified as Bice Portinari (d 1290).

It is difficult to date Dante's work with any degree of precision. The *Vita Nuova* (1290–4) is a lyric sequence celebrating his inspirational love for Beatrice, linked by prose narrative and commentary sections. His Latin treatise *De Vulgari Eloquentia*, perhaps begun in 1303–4 but left unfinished, is a pioneering work of literacy and linguistic commentary. Here Dante considers the state and status of Italian as a literary language, and assesses the achievements of earlier French and Provençal poets in elevating the status of their vernacular media. The *Convivio* (1304–7) is an unfinished philosophical work, a 'banquet of knowledge', composed of prose commentaries on allegorical poetic sequences. Dante's political ideas, specifically the relationship between the Pope, Emperor, and the universal Empire, are explored in *De Monarchia* (c 1310). Dante may not have begun his principal work, the ▷ *Divina Commedia*, until as late as 1314. This supremely encyclopaedic work, which encompasses a discussion of every aspect of human experience, knowledge and belief, recounts the poet's journey, with Virgil as his guide, through Hell (▷ *Inferno*) and Purgatory (▷ *Purgatorio*) and finally, through the agency of Beatrice herself, to Paradise (▷ *Paradiso*).

▷ Boccaccio (1313–75) composed an account of Dante's life and was the first to deliver a series of public lectures on the text of the *Divina Commedia* (1313–14), thus confirming the literary authority, prestige and influence of the work and its author. ▷ Chaucer, the first English poet to name Dante in his work, undoubtedly knew the *Divina Commedia*; quotations from it are scattered through his later work. Dante was read and admired by English poets in the 16th and 17th centuries (including Milton, and one of the earliest English translations (of part of the *Inferno*) appeared in 1719. 19th-century poets, especially Byron, Shelley and ▷ Thomas Carlyle much admired Dante's work and thus revived interest in the medieval poet. Of 20th-century writers, T. S. Eliot in particular was profoundly influenced by Dante's work. According to Eliot, Dante has the power to make the 'spiritual visible'. Bib: Holmes, G., *Dante*.

D'Arblay, Madame
▷ Burney, Fanny.

Darwin, Charles Robert (1809–82)
Biologist. His book *On the Origin of Species by means of Natural Selection* (1859) not only expounded the theory of the evolution of natural organisms (which in itself was not new, for it had been held by, among others, Darwin's grandfather, the poet Erasmus Darwin) but presented persuasive evidence for the theory. In brief, this was that species naturally tend to produce variations and that some of these

variations have better capacity for survival than others, which in consequence tend to become extinct. Darwin's conviction partly began with his study of ▷ Malthus on population, and it thus belongs to the rationalistic tradition which the 19th century inherited from the 18th. The book greatly disturbed many religious people, since it apparently contradicted the account of the creation of the world of *Genesis* in the Bible; it also raised serious doubts about the existence of the soul and its survival after the death of the body. However, it is possible to exaggerate the importance of the Darwinian theory as a cause of religious disbelief: on the one hand, ▷ Charles Lyell's *Principles of Geology* (1830–3) had already done much to upset traditional beliefs (those, for instance, of the poet Tennyson) and so had scientific scholarship on biblical texts by men like Charles Hennell (as in the case of the novelist ▷ George Eliot): on the other hand, intelligent believers such as ▷ Coleridge had long ceased to accept the Bible as a sacred record of fact in all its books. The effect of Darwin's ideas was probably rather to extend religious doubt from the intelligentsia (who were already deeply permeated by it) to wider circles. Another kind of effect was to produce in the popular mind a naïve optimism that man was subject to a general law of progress; it thus encouraged an uncritical view of history and society.

Darwin wrote a number of other scientific works, including *The Descent of Man* (1871). His *Journal of Researches into the Geology and Natural History of the various countries visited by H.M.S. 'Beagle'*, a report of his first important scientific expedition (1831–6), is a fascinating travel book. He also wrote a brief but interesting *Autobiography* (edited with additions by Nora Barlow, 1958).
▷ Agnosticism.
Bib: Huxley, L., *Charles Darwin*; Stevenson, L., *Darwin among the Poets*; West, G., *Darwin: the Fragmentary Man*; Darwin, F., *Life and Letters*; Beer, G., *Darwin's Plots*.

Dathorne, O.R. (b 1934)
Novelist, poet and critic. Dathorne was born in Guyana and educated at the universities of Sheffield, London and Miami. He has taught at universities in Zaire, Nigeria, Sierra Leone and the USA, where he is now professor at the University of Kentucky. His novels are: *Dumplings in the Soup* (1963), set in London, *The Scholar-Man* (1964), set in Africa and *Dele's Child* (1986). *Kelly's Poems* (1977) and *Songs for a New World* (1988) are collections of poems. He has published a number of short stories and several critical works on African and Caribbean literature as well as editing collections of poetry, stories and essays. His novels present cultural displacement and the search for a sense of identity and history.

David Copperfield (1849–50)
A novel in autobiographical form by ▷ Charles Dickens. 'Of all my books I like this the best; like many fond parents I have a favourite child and his name is David Copperfield.' Some commentators have thought that the hero is representative of Dickens himself, and point to the resemblance of

initials: C.D. and D.C. It is true that in outline Copperfield's experiences – his sense of early rejection, child labour in a warehouse, experience as a journalist and final success as a novelist – are similar to Dickens's own. But Dickens's purpose was to present an imaginative picture of growth from childhood to manhood in his own period of history, using his own experience as some of its material but without intending a biographical record. The social landscape of this novel is broader than an autobiography would be likely to achieve. It includes the moralistic and sadistic oppressiveness of Copperfield's mercantile step-father, Murdstone, and the intimate study of selfish hedonism in Copperfield's aristocratic friend, Steerforth; the spontaneous cordiality of the humble Yarmouth boatman, Peggotty, and his sister, and the cunning deviousness of Uriah Heep, whose servile humility is a disguise for his total ruthlessness in making his way from bleak beginnings to a position of power. The novel is strong in dramatic contrast, and particularly interesting in the counterbalancing of the women characters in a series of feminine archetypes. Copperfield is fatherless, and his gentle, guileless mother (who becomes victim in matrimony to Murdstone) is like an elder sister to the child; both are children to the motherly, protective servant, Clara Peggotty. She is replaced by the harsh and loveless Miss Murdstone who plays the role of cruel stepmother. Copperfield runs away and takes refuge with his idiosyncratic aunt, Betsey Trotwood, who has shaped for herself an eccentric independence of men, retaining for a harmless lunatic (Mr Dick) a compassionate tenderness which she now extends to her nephew, in spite of having rejected him at birth because he was a boy. Copperfield's first wife, Dora Spenlow, is a simulacrum of his mother – a child wife, on whom Ibsen seems to have based Nora in *A Doll's House*. Two other representatives of Victorian womanhood are Agnes Wickfield (whom he eventually marries), the stereotype of defenceless womanly sanctity and nearly a victim of Heep's rapacity, and Little Em'ly who is first under the protection of Peggotty and then becomes 'the fallen woman' when she is seduced by Steerforth. Another very striking portrait is Rosa Dartle, companion to Steerforth's mother and poisoned by vindictive hatred of him because of his cool assumption of social and masculine privilege. Though not the richest and deepest of Dickens's novels, it is perhaps psychologically the most revealing, both of Dickens himself and of the society of his time.

Davies, (William) Robertson (b 1913)

Canadian novelist, playwright and critic. Born in Thamesville, Ontario, and educated at the universities of Queen's (Kingston) and Oxford, Davies has worked as an actor, journalist, and newspaper editor. From 1963 to 1981 he was Professor of English at the University of Toronto. His plays include: *Fortune, My Foe* (1948); *A Masque of Aesop* (1952); *A Masque of Mr Punch* (1963); *Question Time* (1975). Davies is primarily known as a novelist, however, particularly for his three trilogies: the 'Salterton' – *Tempest-Tost* (1951); *Leaven of Malice*

(1954); *A Mixture of Frailties* (1958) – the 'Deptford' – *Fifth Business* (1970); *The Manticore* (1972); *World of Wonders* (1975) – and the 'Cornish' – *The Rebel Angels* (1981); *What's Bred in the Bone* (1985); *The Lyre of Orpheus*. These novels are essentially satirical comedies of manners, characterized by an often recondite allusiveness (for example, to the arcane lores of alchemy, saints, vaudeville, and fortune-telling). Despite this ▷ post-modern playfulness, Davies writes in the 19th-century moralist tradition, employing tightly constructed and interweaving plots. His most recent novel is *Murther and Walking Spirits* (1991), in which the ghost of a murdered man watches films of his ancestors, which together constitute a personalized history of Canada. Other books include a collection of ghost stories, *High Spirits* (1982), and *The Papers of Samuel Marchbanks* (1985), a collection of newspaper pieces.
▷ Post-colonial fiction.
Bib: Lawrence, R. G. and Macey, S. L., *Studies in Robertson Davies' Deptford Trilogy*.

De Beauvoir, Simone (1908–86)

French novelist and one of the founding 'mothers' of 20th-century ▷ feminism, long associated with ▷ Sartre and the ▷ Existentialist movement, whose views she promoted in a series of novels: *L'Invitée* (1943); *Le Sang des autres* (1944); *Les Mandarins* (1954). Her uncensored *Letters to Sartre* (1991) reveal the intensity and passion of their relationship. A play, *Les Bouches inutiles* was performed in 1945. She contributed greatly to the genre of autobiography: *Mémoires d'une jeune fille rangée* (1958); *La Force de l'âge* (1960); *La Force des choses* (1965); *Tout compte fait* (1974) (all translated). Her two-volume study of femininity and the condition of women, *The Second Sex* (*Le Deuxième Sexe*; 1949) is one of the most important feminist texts of this century, and her influence on subsequent thinkers is now eclipsing Sartre's. Contemporary feminist writers who have taken up her ideas in particular include Kate Millett (in *Sexual Politics*, 1970), ▷ Germaine Greer, Mary Ellman (in *Thinking About Women*; 1968) and Betty Friedan (*The Feminine Mystique*; 1963).
Bib: Moi, T., *Sexual/Textual Politics*; Moi, T., *French Feminist Thought: A Reader*.

De la Mare, Walter (1873–1956)

Poet, novelist, writer of short stories. He was born in Kent, and educated at St Paul's Cathedral Choir School. From 1890 to 1908 he was a clerk in the offices of the Anglo-American Oil Company: he was then given a government ('Civil List') pension to enable him to devote himself to writing. Many of his poems and his stories were addressed to children. Books of verse of this sort were: *Songs of Childhood* (1902); *A Child's Day* (1912); *Peacock Pie* (1913). ▷ Children's stories: *The Three Mulla-mulgars* (1910); *The Riddle* (1923); *The Magic Jacket* (1943); *The Dutch Cheese* (1946). He had conspicuous talent for retelling traditional ▷ fairy tales: *Told Again* (1927); and compiled two unusual anthologies: *Come Hither* (for children, 1923) and *Love* (for adults, 1943). His most remarkable prose fiction for adults is probably *On the Edge* (stories, 1926) and *Memoirs of a Midget* (stories, 1921). His books of verse for adults include: *The Listeners* (1912); *The Veil* (1921); *Memory and other poems* (1938); *The Burning-glass and other poems* (1945); *The Traveller* (1946); *Inward Companion* (1950); *Winged Chariot* (1951); *O Lovely England and other poems* (1953); *Collected Poems* (1979). See also ▷ W. H. Auden's collection, *A Choice of De La Mare's Verse* (1963).

His poems are conservative in technique, with the melody and delicacy of diction characteristic of the poetry of the late 19th and early 20th century, but are unusual in the quiet intensity with which they express evanescent, elusive and mysterious experience. His stories have a singular quietness of tone and are written in an unassuming style, conveying material which is on the borderline of conscious experience. *The Three Mulla-mulgars*, also published under the title of *The Three Royal Monkeys*, is one of the most original stories for children in English literature. De la Mare's unusual combination of intensity and innocence makes the border line between his work for children and for adults an almost imperceptible one.

Bib: Mégroz, R. L., *De la Mare: A Biographical and Critical Study*; Reid, Forrest, *De la Mare: A Critical Study*.

De Man, Paul (1919–83)

Arguably the most rigorous of the so-called Yale School of criticism, and by the time of his death had become the foremost exponent in the USA of Derridian ▷ deconstruction (▷ Jacques Derrida) in its most unsettling of forms. As Sterling Professor of Comparative Literature at Yale, he was responsible for the first major application of deconstruction to a variety of primary and critical texts, for example in his book *Blindness and Insight* (1971). His approach was extended in books such as *Allegories of Reading* (1980) and *The Rhetoric of Romanticism* (1984). De Man reflected on the whole of this process, and upon the resistance to certain sorts of theorical enquiry in a collection of essays, *The Resistance to Theory* published posthumously in 1986. His reputation has suffered following the rediscovery of collaborationist journalism written by de Man during World War II.

▷ Rhetoric.

De Quincey, Thomas (1785–1859)

Essayist and critic Most famous for his autobiography ▷ *Confessions of an English Opium-Eater*. His work was mostly for periodicals and is voluminous, but only a few pieces are now much read. His strong points as a writer were his exceptionally sensitive, inward-turning imagination and his breadth of understanding. The first produced not only his autobiography but a fragment of exceptional literary criticism, *Knocking at the Gate in Macbeth*. *The English Mail Coach* (1849) and *Murder Considered as One of the Fine Arts* (1827) show the quality of an exceptional psychological novelist. His second gift produced studies of German philosophy (▷ Kant, Lessing, Richter) and able translations of German tales, besides some original historical criticism. He was very much a representative of the first generation of English

Romanticism and as the poets of that generation found new ranges of expression for their medium, so De Quincey expanded the poetic range of prose, partly by recapturing some of the quality of the early 17th-century prose writers.

Bib: Eaton, H. A., *Life*; Abrams, M. H., *The Milk of Paradise*; Clapton, G. T., *Baudelaire et De Quincey*; Jordan, J. E., *Thomas De Quincey, Literary Critic*; Saintsbury, G., in *Essays in English Literature*, Sackville-West, E., *A Flame in Sunlight*.

Decameron, The

A collection of 100 stories in prose, compiled by ▷ Boccaccio in the years 1349–51. The fictional framework of the collection describes how the stories were told by a company of ten gentle-ladies and gentlemen who decide to retreat from plague-ridden Florence and spend two weeks in the country. They spend their weekdays telling short stories to pass the time, and the proceedings are organized by one member of the company who is elected anew every day Many of the stories concern heterosexual relations of some kind, usually set in the contemporary world, and treated in a variety of serious and comic ways. Many of the short stories have fabliau-type plots. It seems likely that ▷ Chaucer knew and used the *Decameron* as a resource for the ▷ *Canterbury Tales* (though the connection has not been definitely proved and remains a controversial issue). Boccaccio's work undoubtedly provided many later writers and dramatists (including Shakespeare) with an important source of narratives. Many of Boccaccio's stories were incorporated into William Painter's *Palace of Pleasure* (1566–7), and the first English translation of the *Decameron* itself appeared in 1621.

Bib: McWilliam, G. H. (trans.), *The Decameron*.

Decline and Fall of the Roman Empire, The (1776–88)

By ▷ Edward Gibbon; the most eloquent and imposing historical work in the English language. It begins at the height of the Roman Empire in the 1st and 2nd centuries AD – an age with which Gibbon's own era, so deeply imbued with Latin scholarship, felt strong kinship. He then proceeds to record the successive stages of Roman decline, the rise of Christianity, the struggle with the Eastern Roman Empire (the Byzantine) centred on Constantinople (Byzantium), and that empire's eventual extinction by the capture of Constantinople in 1453. As an account, it has of course been somewhat outdated in consequence of later research, but as an imaginative epic (still regarded as substantially true) and an expression of the background to modern Europe as understood in the 18th century, it remains a much read and very important work. Its structure is as spacious as the subject, and is sustained by the energy of Gibbon's style. The attitude is one of 18th-century truth-seeking, and of urbane irony towards the Christian religion, whose growth he sees as one of the agents of destruction of classical civilization. Gibbon's sceptical mind is at the same time constantly critical of human pretensions to self-sufficiency, the attainment of wisdom, and integrity of motive; in such respects he is in the tradition of the great satirists of his century – Alexander Pope (1688–1744) and ▷ Jonathan Swift.

Deconstruction

A concept used in critical theory. It has a long philosophical pedigree, but is usually associated with the work of the French philosopher ▷ Jacques Derrida. It is a strategy applied to writing generally, and to literature in particular, whereby systems of thought and concepts are dismantled in such a way as to expose the divisions which lie at the heart of meaning itself. If interpretation is a process designed to reduce a text to some sort of 'order', deconstruction seeks to undermine the basis upon which that order rests. Deconstruction challenges the notion that all forms of mental and linguistic activity are generated from within an autonomous 'centre', advancing the more disturbing proposition that such centres are themselves to be grasped textually only as rhetorical constructions.

▷ De Man, Paul; Difference; Post-structuralism, Grammatology.
Bib: Derrida. J., *Speech and Phenomena*; *Writing and Difference*; *Of Grammatology*; *Positions*; Norris, C., *Deconstruction: Theory and Practice*; Descombes, V., *Modern French Philosophy*.

Dedalus, Stephen

Principal character in ▷ James Joyce's novel ▷ *Portrait of the Artist as a Young Man*; he is also a main character in Joyce's ▷ *Ulysses*. The surname derives from the mythical artist of ancient Greece, ▷ Daedalus.

Defamiliarization

In the context of critical theory this term has its origins in Russian ▷ Formalism and in the desire to distinguish between the Aristotelian (▷ Aristotle) view of writing as an image of reality (▷ mimesis) and imaginative literature as a form of writing which deploys images rhetorically. The Russian term '*ostranenie*' means literally, 'making strange', rendering unfamiliar that which has hitherto been regarded as familiar. It draws attention to the fact that 'reality' is never depicted in literature in an unprocessed, or unmediated way. Indeed, what literature exposes is the formal means whereby what is commonly taken to be reality itself is, in fact, a construction. In many ways, 'defamiliarization' is a form of ▷ deconstruction, although its objective is to replace one set of epistemological principles (those upon which ▷ capitalism as a particular kind of social formation rests), with other ways of organizing reality. By contrast, deconstruction has the effect of undermining all assumptions and certainties about what we know.

Defoe, Daniel (1660–1731)

Son of a London tallow-chandler, James Foe, Defoe changed his name in about 1695 to suggest a higher social status. His writings reflect his ▷ Puritan background: Defoe was educated at Morton's academy for Dissenters at Newington Green, and his pamphlet of 1702, *The Shortest Way with Dissenters*, landed him in the pillory when its ironic attack on Dissenters was taken seriously.

Defoe's attempts to make a living form a colourful picture. Various business enterprises failed dramatically, including the unfortunately timed scheme of marine insurance in wartime, and a disastrous project to breed civet cats. Between 1703 and 1714 he worked as a secret agent for the Tory government of Robert Harley, writing many political (and anti-Jacobite) pamphlets.

Defoe produced some 560 journals, tracts and books, many of them published anonymously or pseudonymously. His reputation today rests on his novels, a genre to which he turned with great success late in his life.

▷ *The Life and strange surprising Adventures of Robinson Crusoe* appeared in 1719, and its sequel, *The Farther Adventures of Robinson Crusoe*, was published some months later. 1720 saw the publication of the *Life and Adventures of Mr Duncan Campbell*, and *Captain Singleton*; 1722, ▷ *Moll Flanders*, ▷ *A Journal of the Plague Year*, *The History of Peter the Great*, and *Colonel Jack*; 1724 ▷ *Roxana*, the *Memoirs of a Cavalier*, and *A New Voyage round the World*; and 1726, *The Four Voyages of Capt. George Roberts*. His guide-book, *A Tour through the Whole Island of Great Britain*, appeared in three volumes, 1724–6.

Among Defoe's later works are *The Complete English Tradesman* (1726), *A Plan of the English Commerce* and *Augusta Triumphans* (1728), and *The Complete English Gentleman*, not published until 1890. Defoe died in Moorfields, and was buried in the area now called Bunhill Fields.
Bib: Moore, J. R., *Daniel Defoe: Citizen of the Modern World*; Richetti, J., *Defoe's Narratives: Situations and Structures*; Bell, A., *Defoe's Fiction*.

Deism

A form of religious belief which developed in the 17th century as an outcome of the Reformation. Edward Herbert evolved the idea that, while the religion revealed in the Gospels was true, it was preceded by ▷ 'natural' religion, according to which by his own inner light a man could perceive all the essentials of religious truth. Herbert's deism was further expounded in the 18th century by others (often in such a way as to suggest that the Christian revelation as presented in the Gospels was redundant), and it suited the 18th-century cool and rational habit of mind which tended to see God as abstract and remote. Bishop Butler among the theologians and ▷ Hume and ▷ Kant among the philosophers, exposed the unsoundness of deistic arguments in the 18th century, and in the 19th century the growth of the genetic sciences demolished the basic assumptions of deism, *ie* that human nature and human reason have always been constant, in a constant environment.

Delany, Mrs Mary (1700–88)

One of the famous letter writers of the 18th century. She had a wide circle of friends among the famous people of her day, and her letters give a vivid picture of contemporary life.

Deloney, Thomas (?1560–1600)
Author of four works of prose fiction about the
lives, work, social activities and ambitions of London
craftsmen and working people: *Jack of Newbury*;
Thomas of Reading; *The Gentle Craft*; *The Gentle
Craft: the Second Part* (all published between 1597
and 1600). Little is known about his life; he was a
silk-weaver, and celebrates the values of his craft in
his works, which anticipate the kind of novel that
▷ Daniel Defoe was later to write. He also wrote
ballads, ▷ pamphlets, translation and anthologies,
including *Strange Histories of Kings* (1600).
Bib: Lawless, M.E., *Apology for the Middle Ages: The
Dramatic Novels of Thomas Deloney*.

Demosthenes (4th century BC)
In ancient Greece, a great Athenian orator; he is
often referred to in English literature as the pattern
and ideal of all orators. He is especially famous for
his speeches warning the Athenians of the danger
from the growing empire of Philip of Macedon,
father of Alexander the Great. Hence the word
'philippic' for an aggressive political speech.

Dennis, Nigel (b 1912)
Novelist. He is best known for *Cards of Identity*
(1955), a satirical fantasy about the nature of
individual and cultural identity, influenced by the
▷ existentialism of ▷ Jean-Paul Sartre. It reflects
the atmosphere of British life in the early 1950s, but
combines this with a self-referential concern with the
nature of fiction. His other novels are: *Boys and Girls
Come Out to Play* (1949); *A House in Order* (1966).

Depression, The
A 'depression' signifies the slowing of economic
activity so that it is at a lower rate than it could
be for a considerable period of time. High
unemployment and poverty usually accompany
economic depression. The most significant such
period in Britain was the 1930s, which is currently
called 'The Depression'.

Derrida, Jacques (b 1930)
Although he is primarily a philosopher, the influence
of Derrida's work on the study of literature has been
immense. He is the originator of a mode of reading
known as ▷ 'deconstruction', the major strand
in what is now regarded as the general area of ▷
post-structuralism. His main works are *Speech and
Phenomena* (trans. 1973), *Of Grammatology* (trans.
1974), and *Writing and Difference* (trans. 1978). For
Derrida, as for ▷ Saussure, language is composed of
differences, that is, a series of non-identical elements
which combine with each other to produce linguistic
▷ signs which are accorded meaning. Traditionally,
this process is anchored to an organizing principle,
a centre, but Derrida questions this concept and
rejects the idea of a 'presence' in which authority
resides, thereby lifting all restrictions upon the
'play' of differences. But, in addition to the idea that
language is composed of 'differences', Derrida also
deploys the term '*différance*' to indicate the continual
postponement of 'presence' which is located in
all signifiers. Thus, signs are produced through a

relatively free play of linguistic elements (difference),
but what they signify can never be fully present since
meaning is constantly 'deferred' (*différance*). Derrida's
influence has been greatest in the U.S.A. where
after his visit to Johns Hopkins and his teaching at
Yale, deconstruction has become the successor to
American new criticism.
▷ Grammatology; De Man, Paul; Difference.

Desai, Anita (b 1937)
Indian novelist and short-story writer. Her novels
offer a satirical view of social change in India since
Independence, with a powerful sense of waste,
limitation, self-deception and failure. *Where Shall
We Go This Summer* (1975) and *Clear Light of Day*
(1980) are particularly concerned with the problems
of Indian women to whom Westernization offers
an apparent freedom. She uses visual detail and an
impressionistic style in an attempt to convey a sense
of the meaning underlying everyday behaviour and
objects. Her other novels include: *Cry the Peacock*
(1063): *Voices in the City* (1965); *Bye-Bye Blackbird*
(1971); *Fire on the Mountain* (1977); *In Custody*
(1984). Story collections: *Games at Twilight* (1978).
She has also written works for children, including
The Village by the Sea (1982).

Descartes, René (1596–1650)
French philosopher, mathematician. In ethics
and religious doctrine he was traditional, but in
method of thought he was the starting point of the
total reliance on reason – ▷ rationalism – that was
pre-eminent in the later 17th and 18th centuries.
In his *Discours de la Méthode* (1637) he reduced
knowledge to the basic principle of *Cogito, ergo sum*
(I think, therefore I am), from which intuition he
deduced the existence of God and thence the reality
of the external world. He also distinguished mind
and matter, finding their source of combination again
in God. It was the influence of Descartes's writings
that drew the English philosopher ▷ John Locke, the
dominant figure in English rationalism, to the study
of philosophy.

Deshpande, Shashi (b 1938)
Novelist and short-story writer. Deshpande was
born in Dharwad, south India and educated at
the universities of Bombay and Bangalore (where
she took degrees in economics and law) and the
University of Mysore. Much of her fiction deals
with feminist issues: the struggle of a daughter to
be allowed to study medicine in *The Dark Holds No
Terrors* (1983); questions of autonomy, responsibility
and power within marriage in *That Long Silence*
(1988). Her feminism is informed by Hindu thought
and myth and by her knowledge of Sanskrit texts, as
well as showing some influence of Buddhist ideas.
Her other novels are: *Roots and Shadows* (1983); *Come
up and be Dead* (1983); *It was the Nightingale* (1986).
Volumes of short stories: *The Legacy* (1971), *The
Miracle* (1986), *It was Dark* (1986).

Detective fiction
This branch of literature is usually easy to distinguish
from the much wider literature of crime and

retribution in drama and in the novel. Unlike the latter, detective fiction seldom relies on the presentation of deep emotions or on subtle and profound character creation. Character, emotion, psychological analysis of states of mind, social reflections, will all be present as flavouring, and may even be conspicuous, but the indispensable elements are always a mysterious – but not necessarily horrible – crime, and a detective, who is commonly not a professional policeman, but who has highly developed powers of scientific deduction. It is essential that the surface details should be convincing, and that the author should keep no clues from the reader, who may thus have the satisfaction of competing with the detective at his game. In the detective story proper, as opposed to the crime novel, the criminal's identity is not revealed until the end, and provides the focus of attention. Precursors of the form are ▷ Wilkie Collins's novel *The Moonstone* (1868) and the stories of the American writer Edgar Allan Poe (1809–49), featuring the French detective Dupin. But the widespread popularity of detective fiction began with ▷ Arthur Conan Doyle's Sherlock Holmes stories, of which the first was *A Study in Starlet* (1887). The staggering perspicuity of the amateur detective from Baker Street, and his superiority to the police and to his companion and foil, Dr Watson, won him a world-wide audience. Another early exponent of the detective short story was ▷ G. K. Chesterton, whose detective, Father Brown, is a modest and intuitive Roman Catholic priest who first appeared in *The Innocence of Father Brown* (1911). From the time of E. C. Bentley's classic work *Trent's Last Case* (1912) the full-length novel became the most popular form. After Conan Doyle, the dominant figure of detective fiction is Dorothy L. Sayers, whose aristocratic amateur detective, Lord Peter Wimsey, appears in works such as *Murder Must Advertise* (1933) and *The Nine Tailors* (1934); she also published a history of crime fiction in 1928 and wrote critical essays on the genre. Other prominent authors of detective fiction include ▷ Agatha Christie (the creator of Hercule Poirot and Miss Marple), Michael Innes (pseudonym of the novelist and critic J. I. M. Stewart), H. C. Bailey, ▷ P. D. James and H. R. F. Keating. The American school of tough detective fiction is exemplified by Raymond Chandler (1888–1959) and Dashiell Hammett (1894–1961).

▷ Allingham, Margery; Marsh, Ngaio.

Determination

A Marxist term used in critical theory, it is often confused with 'determinism' whereby a particular action or event is wholly caused by some external agency, and must therefore be assumed to be inevitable. In 'determination', the traditional fatalistic implications of the term 'determinism' are softened considerably, to draw attention to those constraints and pressures which mould human action. Thus a distinction is to be made between a tendency which attributes all movement in the social formation to economic factors, and one which seeks to account structurally for the patterns of dominance and subordination (▷ contradictions) operating at any one moment in history. The concept of determination can also be used to ask questions about particular literary ▷ genres and their historical significance, as well as helping to account for particular elements of the rhetorical structures of texts. Determination helps in seeing texts as part of a larger social context rather than as isolated verbal constructs, and it helps also to raise a number of questions concerning the inter-relationship between literature and the ways in which it represents 'reality'.

Dhondy, Farouk (b 1944)

Novelist and playwright. Dhondy was born in Poona, Bombay, India and educated at Cambridge University, Bombay Engineering College and Leicester University. He has taught English in schools in London. His work includes the novel *Vigilantes* (1988) and the plays, *Mama Dragon* (1980), *Trojans* (an adaptation of the plays of Euripides) and *Kipling Sahib* (1982). He has also written television plays and fiction for children.

Diachronic

▷ Synchronic.

Dialectic

Originally used to refer to the nature of logical argument, but in the 19th century this term underwent something of a revaluation, and came to be associated with the work of the German philosophers Kant and Hegel. 'Dialectic' referred to the process whereby the 'idea' (*thesis*) was self-divided, and its internal oppositions (*antithesis*) were resolved in a *synthesis* which opened the way to a higher truth. In Marxist thinking 'dialectic' refers to the ▷ contradictions present in any one phenomenon, and to their resolution through conflict. It is the nature of that opposition and that conflict which determines movement and change.

▷ Marx, Karl.

Dialogic

▷ Bakhtin, Mikhail.

Diaries

As a form of literature in English, diaries begin to be significant in the 17th century. The spirit of criticism from the Renaissance and the stress on the individual conscience from the Reformation combined with the political and social turbulence of the 17th century to awaken people to a new awareness of personal experience and its possible interest for general readers. The private nature of the diary form also led to many women taking up this form of writing. Thus the art of the diary arose with the art of ▷ autobiography. Diaries may first be divided into the two classes of those clearly meant to be strictly private and those written more or less with an eye to eventual publication. A further division may be made between those which are interesting chiefly as a record of the time in which the writer lived and those which are mainly a record of his personality.

The best known of the English diaries is that of ▷ Samual Pepys (1633–1703), which was both purely private (written in code) and entirely un-self-conscious, as well as an excellent record of the time. His contemporary, ▷ John Evelyn (1620–1706), is less famous partly because his diary is a more studied, self-conscious work. ▷ Jonathan Swift's *Journal to Stella* (covering the years 1710–13) is a personal revelation but unusual in that it was addressed to the woman Swift loved. The diary of the ▷ Quaker, ▷ George Fox (1624–91), is a record of his spiritual experience for the education of his followers. In the 18th and early 19th century the most famous is that of the novelist ▷ Fanny Burney (Madame D'Arblay, 1752–1840), considered as a record of the time ingenuously imbued with her own personality. The diary of the great religious reformer, John Wesley (1703–91), is comparable to that of Fox as a spiritual record, with a wider outlook on his time. In the 19th century the diaries of Thomas Creevey (1768–1838) and Charles Greville (1794–1865) are famous as records of public affairs, and that of Henry Crabb Robinson (1775–1867) for impressions of the leading writers who were his friends. In the 20th century the *Journal* of ▷ Katherine Mansfield is an intimate and vivid record of personal experience, and that of ▷ Virginia Woolf is an extremely interesting record of a writer's experience of artistic creation.

Dickens, Charles (1812–70)

The most popular and internationally known of English novelists. His father was a government clerk who liked to live prosperously, and his sudden impoverishment and imprisonment for debt in the Marshalsea debtor's prison was a drastic shock to the boy Dickens; prisons recur literally and symbolically in many of his novels, which are also filled with attacks on the injustice of social institutions and the inequalities between the rich and the poor. He began his writing career as a journalist, and all his novels were published serially in periodicals, especially in two edited by himself – ▷ *Household Words* started in 1850, and ▷ *All the Year Round*, started in 1859, both of them weeklies.

His first book, ▷ *Sketches by Boz* (1836), was a collection of stories and descriptive pieces written for various papers in the tradition of the essayists – ▷ Charles Lamb, William Hazlitt, Leigh Hunt – of the previous generation, with the especial difference that Dickens wrote about the hitherto neglected lower middle class. ▷ *The Pickwick Papers* (1836–7), at first loosely connected but gathering unity as it proceeded, was immensely successful. There followed: ▷ *Oliver Twist* (1837–8), ▷ *Nicholas Nickleby* (1838–9), ▷ *The Old Curiosity Shop* and ▷ *Barnaby Rudge* (1840–1). This concludes the first, comparatively light-hearted phase of Dickens's writing, in which he developed his characteristic comedy and melodrama. ▷ *Martin Chuzzlewit* (1843–4) begins a more impressive style of writing in which the comedy and melodrama deepen into new intensity, though critics observe that the beginning of the novel is still in the earlier manner. In 1843 begins his series of Christmas Books, including ▷ *A Christmas Carol* and ▷ *The Cricket on the Hearth*. Thereafter come his mature masterpieces: ▷ *Dombey and Son* (1846–8); ▷ *David Copperfield* (1849–50); ▷ *Bleak House* (1852–3); ▷ *Hard Times* (1854); ▷ *Little Dorrit* (1855–7); ▷ *A Tale of Two Cities* (1859); ▷ *Great Expectations* (1860–1): ▷ *Our Mutual Friend* (1864–5). Dickens was writing ▷ *Edwin Drood* when he died.

Bib: Forster. J., *Life*, Johnson. E., *Life*; Wilson, E., in *The Wound and the Bow*; Chesterton, G. K., *Charles Dickens;* Gissing, G., *Charles Dickens: A Crucial Study*; House, H., *The Dickens World;* Leavis, F. R., in *The Great Tradition;* Collins, P., *Dickens and Crime; Dickens and Education;* Gross J., *Dickens and the Twentieth Century;* Leavis, F.R. and Q.D., *Dickens the Novelist;* Wilson, A., *The World of Charles Dickens;* Carey, J., *The Violent Effigy: A Study of Dickens' Imagination:* Kaplan. F., *Dickens: a biography;* Ackroyd, P., *Dickens;* Tomalin, C., *The Invisible Woman: The Story of Nelly Ternan and Charles Dickens.*

Dickens, Monica (b 1915)

Novelist, children's writer and journalist. Monica Dickens is best known as the author of the popular *Follyfoot* series of books written in the 1970s (and subsequently televised), but she only began writing for children in 1970, by which time she had already published a range of (often semi-autobiographical) novels, beginning with *One Pair of Hands* in 1939. The inspiration for Dickens's writing has often come from her working life, as a nurse (*One pair of Feet*; 1942), as a journalist (*My Turn to Make the Tea*; 1951), with the Samaritans (*The Listeners*; 1970) and more generally in her life in the countryside (*The House at World's End*; 1970, and the *Follyfoot* books). Dickens was a columnist for the *Woman's Own* magazine from 1946 to 1965, and is the great-granddaughter of the Victorian novelist ▷ Charles Dickens. Other works include: *Mariana* (1940); *The Fancy* (1943); *Flowers on the Grass* (1949); *The Winds of Heaven* (1955); *The Room Upstairs* (1966); *Follyfoot* (1971); *World's End in Winter* (1972); *Follyfoot Farm* (1973); *Stranger at Follyfoot* (1976); *The Ballad of Favour* (1985).

Dictionary of the English Language, A (1755)

Usually known as *Johnson's Dictionary*, it was compiled by ▷ Samuel Johnson, published in 1755, and was accepted as authoritative for about a hundred years. The excellence of the work is not so much its scholarship as its literary intelligence. It is weak in etymology, as this was still an undeveloped science, but it is strong in understanding of language, and in particular the English language. In the Preface, Johnson writes a short grammar, but he points out that English simplicity of forms and freedom from inflexions make an elaborate one (as grammar was then understood) unnecessary. He makes clear that the spirit of the English language had been unduly influenced by the spirit of French, and he rejects the idea that correctness should be fixed by the authority of an Academy, since the inherent mutability of language will always cause it to follow its own laws. Johnson thus began the English habit of relying upon current English dictionaries and manuals of usage to discover the best existent expression: Fowler's *Modern English Usage* and the Oxford *New English Dictionary* are 20th-century equivalents of *Johnson's Dictionary.*

Didactic literature

Literature designed to teach, or to propound in direct terms a doctrine or system of ideas. In practice, it is not always easy to identify; so much literature is didactic in intention but not in form; sometimes writers renounce didactic intentions but in practice use didactic forms. Thus Edmund Spenser declared that *The Faerie Queene* (1590–6) was meant to 'fashion a gentleman . . . in vertuous and gentle discipline', but the poem may be enjoyed for its imaginative vision without much regard to its didacticism, and the same is true of ▷ Bunyan's ▷ *Pilgrim's Progress*. Some 18th-century novelists, such as ▷ Richardson and ▷ Defoe, made didactic claims, often as a way of defending themselves against accusations that their subject-matter was not respectable.

The 19th-century novelists, especially ▷ Dickens and ▷ George Eliot, used didactic digressions, but in the former such passages are especially of passionate social invective, and in the latter they are usually more integrated into the imaginative art than may be apparent. In general, the view now is that novelists may be didactic if they choose, but didacticism is not much in fashion.

Diderot, Denis (1713–84)

French novelist, philosopher, dramatist and critic. His novel *Jacques the Fatalist and His Master* (1773) is a self-conscious and digressive narrative, influence by ▷ Sterne's ▷ *Tristram Shandy*; it reflects on questions of truth, communication and understanding. *Rameau's Nephew* (1761) is similarly playful. Diderot was a founder and director of ▷ *L'Encyclopédie*, and wrote philosophical and critical works as well as the sentimental plays *The Natural Son* (1757) and *The Father* (1758).

Difference

A term introduced by ▷ Ferdinand de Saussure in his study of linguistics and used in literary theory. It is the means whereby value is established in any system of linguistic signs whether it be spoken or written. Saussure's *Course in General Linguistics* (1915) argues that in speech it is 'the phonetic contrasts' which permit us to distinguish between one word and another that constitute meaning. In writing the letters used to form words are arbitrary ▷ signs, and their values are therefore 'purely negative and differential' (Saussure). The result is that the written sign becomes important only in so far as it is different from other signs within the overall system of language. The notion of difference as a principle of opposition has been extended beyond the limits of Structuralist thinking laid down by Saussure. For example, the critic and philosopher ▷ Mikhail Bakhtin in a critique of Saussurean ▷ Structuralism argued that 'the forms of signs are conditioned above all by the social organization of the participants involved and also by the immediate conditions of their interaction' (*Marxism and The Philosophy of Language*; 1930). Thus the clash of opposites through which meaning and value emerge is determined by the social positions of those who use the language. This means that secreted at the very heart of the

form of the linguistic sign is a series of dialectical opposites whose interaction refracts the struggle taking place within the larger framework of society itself. For Bakhtin these oppositions can be defined in terms of the struggle between social classes, but the dialectical structure of these conflicts makes the notion of difference suitable for any situation which can be analysed in terms of binary opposites. For example, for ▷ feminism this would be an opposition between 'masculine' and 'feminine' as the basis upon which sexual identity is constructed. ▷ Jacques Derrida has adapted the term to form the neologism '*différance*', which denotes the deferral of meaning whereby no sign can ever be brought into direct alignment with the object that it purports to recall. This means that meaning is always *deferred*, and can never be final.

Dineson, Isak

▷ Blixen, Karen.

Dionysus

▷ Classical Mythology.

Discourse

A term used in critical theory. Especially in the writings of ▷ Michel Foucault, 'discourse' is the name given to the systems of linguistic representations through which power sustains itself. For Foucault discourse manifests itself only through concrete examples operating within specific areas of social and institutional practice. He argues that within individual discourses a series of mechanisms are used as means of controlling desire and power, which facilitate 'classification . . . ordering [and] distribution' (Foucault). In this way a mastery is exerted over what appears to be the randomness of everyday reality. It is thus possible to investigate those discourses which have been used to master reality in the past *eg* discourses concerned with questions of 'sexuality', criminality and judicial systems of punishment, or madness, as Foucault's own work demonstrates.
Bib: Foucault, M., *The Order of Things; Power/ Knowledge: Selected Interviews and Other Writings* (ed. C. Gordon).

Dismal science, The

Political economy; so called by ▷ Thomas Carlyle because the social thought of such writers as ▷ Adam Smith, ▷ Jeremy Bentham, ▷ Thomas Malthus and David Ricardo tended to be pessimistic about the alleviation of poverty and inhumanly indifferent to the consequences of economic laws as they saw them.

Displacement

For ▷ psychoanalytical usage 'displacement' is associated by ▷ Freud (along with ▷ 'condensation') with the mechanisms whereby the conscious mind processes the unconscious in dreams. 'Displacement' is a form of censorship which effectively distorts the ideas which act as the controlling forces of the dream, (what Freud calls 'the latent dream-thoughts') and attaches them to other, more acceptable thoughts or ideas. This complex process is one which involves the omission or re-arrangement of detail, and modification of the dream thoughts. In order to reach the unconscious the 'manifest dream' must be interpreted as a symbolic expression of another text which lies beneath its surface and which is not readily accessible to the conscious mind. This whole mechanism rests on the assumption that psychic energy can attach itself to particular ideas, or objects (cathexis); those ideas or objects are related to the 'latent dream-thoughts', but derive their new-found significance by a process of association. Literature habitually invests objects and ideas with value, and psychic intensity, and the manner in which it does so can be read psychoanalytically as a manifestation of deeper, more disturbing activities going on in the mind of the writer, or – by analogy – in the 'unconscious' of the society of which the writer is a part.

Disraeli, Benjamin (Lord Beaconsfield) (1804–81)
Statesman and novelist. He was of Spanish-Jewish descent; his grandfather settled in England in 1748. His political career was brilliant; he entered Parliament in 1837; in the 1840s he was the leader in the House of Commons of a small number of Tory (▷ Whig and Tory) politicians who, as the 'Young England' group, wanted a revival of the party and of the national spirit in an alliance between a spiritually reborn aristocracy and the common people; by 1848 he was leading the Conservatives in the House of Commons; in 1868 and in 1874–80 he had his two periods as one of the most brilliant of English Prime Ministers. Both politically (he secured the vote for the urban working class) and socially (eg his trade union legislation) he at least partly succeeded in securing support for his party from the working class. He was made Earl of Beaconsfield in 1876.

The novels which now chiefly hold attention are his 'Young England Trilogy': ▷ *Coningsby* (1844); ▷ *Sybil* (1845) and *Tancred* (1847). All were written to promulgate his doctrine of Tory Democracy and they all have imperfections, partly because for Disraeli literature was second to politics. On the other hand they have great liveliness of characterization and show keen insight into the structure of society with its cleavage between rich and poor, which Disraeli called 'the two nations'. His other novels are: *Vivian Grey* (1826); *The Young Duke* (1831); *Alroy and Ixion in Heaven* (1833); *The Infernal Marriage* and *The Rise of Iskander* (1834); *Henrietta Temple and Venetia* (1837); *Lothair* (1870) and *Endymion* (1880).
Bib: Blake, R., *Life*; Moneypenny, W. F. and Buckle, G. E., *Life*. Jerman, B. R., *The Young Disraeli*; Holloway, J., in *Victorian Sage*; Dahl, C., in *Victorian Fiction* (ed. L. Stevenson); Pritchett, V. S., in *The Living Novel*; Schwartz, D. R., *Disraeli's Fiction*; Brava, T., *Disraeli the Novelist*.

Dissenters
A term used for those ▷ Puritans who, owing to their 'dissent' from the established ▷ Church of England, were refused certain political, educational, and (at first) religious rights from the second half of the 17th century. That is to say, they could not

enter Parliament, they could not enter a university, and, until 1688, they could not join together in worship. Puritans were not thus formally restricted before 1660. They were released from their political restraints in 1828. In the 19th century it became more usual to call them ▷ Nonconformists or Free Churchmen. The term does not apply to Scotland, where the established Church is ▷ Presbyterian, not the ▷ episcopalian Church of England.

Divina Commedia (Divine Comedy)
The principal work of the Italian poet ▷ Dante (1265–1321). For an account of its contents, see the entries under its major sections: ▷ *Inferno*, ▷ *Purgatorio*, ▷ *Paradiso*.
Bib: Cunningham, G.F., *The Divine Comedy in English, 1290–1966*; Sinclair, J.N. (trans.), *The Divine Comedy*.

Divorce
Until 1857 divorce was possible only through Church courts which had kept their authority over matrimonial relations since before the Reformation, while losing it in nearly all other private affairs of laymen. Even after a marriage had been dissolved by a Church court, a special ('private') act of Parliament was necessary before the divorce was legalized. In consequence, divorces were rare and only occurred among the rich and influential. Adultery and cruelty were the accepted grounds, and the wife was commonly in an unfavourable position, so that no divorce was granted on account of a husband's adultery until 1801. The law of 1857 added desertion as a ground for divorce, and proceedings were taken out of the hands of the Church courts and put under the courts of the realm. Since 1938, unsoundness of mind may also be pleaded as a cause of divorce, and it has been further facilitated in other ways, perhaps the most important of which is the concept of 'marital breakdown'. This abolishes the idea of one of the partners being 'guilty' and the other, 'injured'.
▷ Marriage; Women, Status of.

Dixon, Ella Hepworth (1855–1932)
Journalist, short-story writer and feminist. Dixon's one novel, *The Story of a Modern Woman* (1894), is an autobiographical account of the loneliness suffered by a woman who leads an independent life as a journalist. It is one of the most moving of the ▷ New Woman novels.

Dombey and Son (1847–8)
One of the earliest of the mature novels by ▷ Charles Dickens. Dombey is a proud and heartless London merchant whose sole interest in life is the perpetuation of his name in connection with his firm. For this reason he neglects his deeply affectionate daughter Florence for the sake of his little son, Paul, whom, however, he values not for himself but as the future embodiment of his firm. The boy is motherless, deprived of affection and physically delicate – he dies in childhood. To prevent Florence from marrying a mere clerk in his firm, Dombey sends her lover – Walter Gay – on business to an unhealthy colony in the West Indies. Dombey's

pride makes him susceptible to flattery; he is preyed upon by Carker, his manager, one of Dickens's most notable villains, and by Major Joe Bagstock. He is led into marriage with a cold, disillusioned girl, Edith Granger, who runs away from him with Carker. Both his pride and his wealth are eventually taken from him and he finds himself in the end dependent on the forgiving Florence and Walter Gay. A particular interest of the book is that railways play an important part in it just at the time when they were transforming English life. The sombreness of Dombey's mansion is opposed to the warm-hearted if unbusinesslike environment of the shop of Solomon Gills, Gay's uncle.

Don Juan (1819–24)

Lord Byron's unfinished satirical epic in *ottava rima*, based very freely on the legendary figure of Don Juan. After a love affair in Spain (Canto I), Juan is sent abroad by his mother, but is shipwrecked and washed ashore on a Greek island where he is cared for by a Greek maiden, Haidee. Cantos III and IV describe their love and the destruction of their relationship by Haidee's pirate father, Lambro. In Canto V Juan has been sold as a slave to a Turkish princess who loves him; and in Cantos VI, VII and VIII he escapes and serves the Russian army against the Turks in the siege of Ismail. In Canto IX he attracts the attention of the Russian Empress, Catherine the Great, who in Canto X sends him on a mission to England, the setting for Cantos XI-XIII. Juan's affair with a duchess, and his deeper emotion for an English Catholic girl, are used as foci for a free-ranging satire on contemporary society. Juan has fewer mistresses in Byron's poem than in earlier versions of the legend, and is portrayed essentially as an *ingénu*, more often seduced by women than the seducer. The story-line is however subordinated to the philosophizing commentary of the poet himself, which ranges from flippant witticism ('What men call gallantry, and gods adultery,/ Is much more common where the climate's sultry'), through the moving rhetoric of the inserted lyric 'The isles of Greece', to harsh satire on 'the best of cutthroats', the Duke of Wellington ('and I shall be delighted to learn who, / Save you and yours, have gain'd by Waterloo?'). The greatness of the poem derives from its flexible and informal metrical form, which, unlike the Spenserian stanzas of *Childe Harold's Pilgrimage* (1812–18) and the couplets of his verse tales, allows Byron to give full expression to his complex and contradictory personality. *Don Juan* is an example of a narrative poem which might also be termed a ▷ novel in verse.

Don Quixote de la Mancha (1605–15)

A satirical romance by the Spanish writer Miguel de Cervantes (1547–1616). It begins as a satire on the medieval and Renaissance style of romance about wandering knights and their adventures in the pursuit of the rectification of injustices. It deepens into an image of idealism perpetually at odds with the pettiness, vulgarity and meanness of the real world. Don Quixote is an impecunious gentleman whose mind has been turned by reading too many romances. He sets out on his wanderings accompanied by his servant, Sancho Panza, the embodiment of commonplace credulity and a shrewd sense of personal advantage. He takes as his patroness a peasant girl, Dulcinea del Toboso, whom he transfigures in his imagination and who is quite unaware of his devotion. The book was translated into English in 1612–20, and again a hundred years later in a more famous version by Peter Motteux. Its influence on our literature has been extensive. In the 17th century the burlesque element is emulated by Francis Beaumont in his play *The Knight of the Burning Pestle* (1607) and by Samuel Butler in his mock epic *Hudibras* (1663–78). In the 18th century the theme of idealists misunderstanding and misunderstood is followed in ▷ Henry Fielding's ▷ *Joseph Andrews* and ▷ Oliver Goldsmith's ▷ *Vicar of Wakefield*. The influence can likewise be traced in ▷ Lawrence Sterne and ▷ Tobias Smollett, and, in the 19th century, in ▷ Charles Dickens (especially in ▷ *Pickwick Papers*).

Doolittle, Hilda

▷ H. D.

Dostoevsky, Fyodor Mikhailovich (1821–81).

Russian novelist. Born in Moscow and educated at the St Petersburg Engineering Academy, he was arrested in 1849 for his socialist activities and spent eight years in a penal colony and in the army, during which period he experienced a religious conversion (to the Russian Orthodox Church), an experience which informs his major works. These include *Notes from the House of the Dead* (1869–61), *The Insulted and the Injured* (1861), *Notes from the Underground* (1864), *Crime and Punishment* (1866), *The Idiot* (1868), *The Devils* (1872) and *The Brothers Karamazov* (1880). Dostoevsky's moral and religious intensity, the compelling momentum of his narrative and his insight into extreme and disturbed states of mind have made his work highly influential in England, especially during the 20th century (much of his work was translated into English during the 1880s).

Doubting Castle

In Part I of ▷ John Bunyan's ▷ *Pilgrim's Progress*, the castle belonging to the Giant Despair, where Christian and Hopeful lie prisoners. In Part II the Castle is destroyed by the champion Greatheart.

Doyle, Sir Arthur Conan (1859–1930)

Novelist; chiefly noted for his series of stories and novels about the amateur detective, Sherlock Holmes, a genius in minute deduction and acute observations. His friend, Dr Watson, is represented as the ordinary, ingenuous man, who needs to have everything pointed out to him and explained; and this offsets the ingenuity of the detective. The combination of acute detective. The combination of acute detective and obtuse colleague has been imitated in many detective stories ever since. The stories include: *A Study in Scarlet* (1887); *The Adventures of Sherlock Holmes* (1891); *The Memoirs of Sherlock Holmes* (1893); *The Hound of the Baskervilles* (1902); *The Return of Sherlock Holmes* (1905). Conan Doyle also wrote historical novels of merit: *eg Micah*

Clarke (1888), *The White Company* (1891), and *Rodney Stone* (1896).

  ▷ Detective fiction.
Bib: Lamond, J., *Conan Doyle: a Memoir*; Conan Doyle, A., *The True Conan Doyle*; Carr, J. D., *The Life of Conan Doyle*; Roberts, S. C., *Holmes and Watson*; Pearsall, R; *Conan Doyle: A Biographical Solution*.

Drabble, Margaret (b 1939)

Novelist and short-story writer. Born in Sheffield and educated at Cambridge University. The novelist ▷ A.S. Byatt is her sister. She achieved considerable popular success with her novels of the 1960s, which dealt with the personal dilemmas of intelligent and educated heroines. In *The Millstone* (1965) Rosamund struggles for independence, and achieves relative stability and a sense of moral responsibility through her love for her baby daughter, the result of a casual liaison. Drabble's later novels broaden their scope, subsuming feminist issues in a general concern for equality and justice, and addressing wider national and international issues. *The Needle's Eye* (1972) established her as a major writer by the moral intensity of its concern with social justice. *The Ice Age* (1977) is a sombre picture of the corrupt and sterile condition of Britain in the mid-1970s. Drabble sees herself as a social historian, and admires the novelist ▷ Arnold Bennett, a biography of whom she published in 1974. The literary allusion which has been a feature of her work becomes more marked in the 1970s, and her narrative techniques become more adventurous, as in the three points of view, alterations of style and self-conscious authorial voice of *The Realms of Gold* (1975). Her other novels are: *A Summer Bird-Cage* (1962); *The Garrick Year* (1964); *Jerusalem the Golden* (1967); *The Waterfall* (1969); *The Middle Ground* (1980); *The Radiant Way* (1987); *A Natural Curiosity* and *Gates of Ivory* (1991). Story collections: *Penguin Modern Stories 3* (with others) (1969); *Hassam's Tower* (1980). She also edited *The Oxford Companion to English Literature* (1985).
Bib: Creighton, J. V., *Margaret Drabble*.

Dramatic monologue

A poetic form in which the poet invents a character or, more commonly, uses one from history or legend, and reflects on life from the character's standpoint. The dramatic monologue is a development from the conversation poem of ▷ Coleridge and Wordsworth, in which the poet reflects on life in his own person.

  Tennyson (1809–92) was the first to use the form, *eg The Lotus-Eaters* (1833), *Ulysses* (1842) and *Tithonus* (pub. 1860). In these poems, he takes the standpoint of characters in Greek myth and causes them to express emotions relevant to their predicaments. The emotions, however, are really more relevant to those of Tennyson's own age, but the disguise enables him to express himself without inhibition, and particularly without involving himself in the responsibility of having to defend the attitudes that he is expressing. His most ambitious poem in this form is the monodrama *Maud* (1855).

  However it was Robert Browning (1812–89) who used the form most profusely, and with whom it is

most associated, *eg My Last Duchess* (1845); *Fra Lippo Lippi, Andrea del Sarto, The Bishop Orders His Tomb, Bishop Blougram's Apology*, all in *Men and Women* (1855); *Mr Sludge the Medium* in *Dramatis Personae* (1864); and *The Ring and the Book* (1869). Browning used it differently from Tennyson: his characters are more detached from his own personality; the poems are attempts to explore a wide variety of attitudes to art and life. His monologues have little to do with drama, though superficially they resemble soliloquies in plays of the age of Shakespeare. They have an even closer resemblance, though still a rather superficial one, to the medieval convention of public confession by characters such as the Wife of Bath and the Pardoner in ▷ Chaucer's ▷ *Canterbury Tales*. Most of all, however, they emulate the exploration of character and society in the novel of Browning's own day, and his *The Ring and the Book* is really an experiment in the novel; the tale unfolds through monologues by the various participators in and spectators of the events. Still another use for the dramatic monologue is that to which ▷ Arthur Clough (1819–61) puts it in his poem *Dipsychus* (*Divided Mind*, 1850). This poem is in the form of a dialogue, but it is a dialogue between the two parts of a man's mind: that which tries to sustain moral principle, and that which is sceptical of principle, seeking only pleasure and material well-being.

  A more searching irony was brought to the dramatic monologue by T. S. Eliot in *The Love Song of J. Alfred Prufrock* (1915) and *Gerontion* (1920).

  The dramatic monologue has certain affinities with first-person ▷ narration and ▷ stream of consciousness in the novel.

Drapier's Letters (1724)

A series of pamphlets by ▷ Jonathan Swift against a monopoly to issue copper coins in Ireland, granted by the English Government to the Duchess of Kendal (George I's mistress) and sold by her to William Wood ('Wood's halfpence'). The Irish considered that the monopoly would be economically harmful to them. Swift wrote in their support in the semblance of a Dublin 'drapier' (= draper), *ie* an ordinary shopman. The pamphlets are an example of his apparently moderate, plain style carrying an immense force of irony; they were so effective that the Government had to withdraw the monopoly.

Du Maurier, Daphne (1907–1989)

Novelist and short-story writer. Daphne Du Maurier began publishing in 1928, and her long career spanned and mastered a wide range of ▷ genres. She is a skilled writer of psychological suspense and supernatural tales, as well as the author of the classic romantic thriller, *Rebecca* (1938), which was filmed by Alfred Hitchcock in 1940, and has run to many editions in many different languages. Hitchcock also filmed Du Maurier's famous short story 'The Birds' in 1963, and the Hitchcock connection underlines what is perhaps most remarkable about Du Maurier's work: its concern with neo-Gothic motifs and the thin line which divides psychological obsession from supernatural possibilities. Du Maurier is also interested in exploring concepts of time in her fiction, both in the sense of how history is lived in the present (one of the concerns of her Cornish historical romances) and in concepts of non-linear time, and parallel time-scales, as the framework for her psychological thrillers. This last interest is best illustrated by the 1971 story *Don't Look Now*, which, again, was filmed, this time by Nicholas Roeg in 1973. Du Maurier's success as the originator of a number of classic modern horror films is important. She is also one of Cornwall's most famous inhabitants, and four famous Cornish historical romances, *Jamaica Inn* (1936), *Frenchman's Creek* (1941); *My Cousin Rachel* (1951) and *Rebecca* itself have become key props for the Cornish tourist industry. Du Maurier's passion for her county is also evident in her non-fictional writing, particularly *Vanishing Cornwall*.

Other works include: *The Loving Spirit* (1931); *The Apple Tree* (1952); *The Breaking Point* (1959); *The Birds and Other Stories* (1963); *The House on the Strand* (1969); *Echoes from the Macabre: Selected Stories* (1976); *The Blue Lenses and Other Stories* (1970). Autobiographical works include: *Growing Pains: The Shaping of a Writer* (1977) and *The Rebecca Notebook and Other Memories* (1980).

▷ Horror fiction; Detective fiction.
Bib: Light, A., 'Rebecca' in *Feminist Review* (1984); Radcliffe, E. J., *Gothic Novels of the 20th Century: An Annotated Bibliography*.

Du Maurier, George (1834–96)

Graphic artist and novelist; born in Paris. His grandparents had been refugees in England from the ▷ French Revolution; his father was a naturalized British subject; his mother was English. In 1865 he joined the staff of ▷ *Punch* and became one of the best known British humorous artists, satirizing the upper classes rather in the style of ▷ William Thackeray. He wrote three novels: *Peter Ibbetson* (1891), ▷ *Trilby* (1894) and *The Martian* (posthumous, 1896). The first two were extremely popular, but their sentimentality has put them out of fashion.
Bib: Ormond, L., *George du Maurier*.

Dubliners (1914)

A volume of short stories by ▷ James Joyce. Joyce later wrote: 'My intention was to write a chapter of the moral history of my country and I chose Dublin for the scene because that city seemed to me the centre of paralysis. I have tried to present it . . . under four of its aspects: childhood, adolescence, maturity and public life. The stories are arranged in this order.' He adds that he has used in them 'a style of scrupulous meanness', but, in fact, the apparent bare realism of the stories conceals subtle mimetic and symbolic effects which render the spiritual poverty and domestic tragedy of Dublin life through its characteristic colloquial idioms. The stories are based on Joyce's theory of the 'epiphanies', by which he meant that deep insights might be gained through incidents and circumstances which seem outwardly insignificant. Their effect is thus often through delicate implication, like the stories of ▷ Chekhov. However, some of them contain sharp humour,

notably 'Grace', and more have very sensitive poignancy, especially the last and longest, 'The Dead'. This story, which moves from ironical satire to a highly poetic conclusion, is often regarded as a masterpiece; it was filmed in 1987 by John Huston.

Duffy, Maureen (b 1933)

Novelist, poet and dramatist. Her auto-biographical first novel, *That's How It Was* (1962) is the account of a childhood of material insecurity and social isolation illuminated by a living relationship between mother and daughter. The themes of her fiction have been the outsider, the oppressions of poverty and class, the varieties of sexual experience and the power of love to transform and redeem. Her work reflects her socialism, lesbianism and commitment to animal rights. *The Microcosm* (1966) is a study of lesbian society using various modes of narration, including pastiche and ▷ stream of consciousness; it shows the distance between sexual creativity and ordinary life imposed by society. Duffy has lived in London for most of her adult life, and celebrates that city in *Capital* (1975). She employs colloquial language, and a laconic but vivid style. Her play *Rites*, a black farce set in a ladies' public lavatory, was produced at the National Theatre in 1969. *Rites*, *Solo* (1970) and *Old Tyme* (1970) rework the Greek myths of the Bacchae, Narcissus and Uranus respectively in terms of modern sexual and public life (▷ Classical Mythology). Her other plays are: *The Lay Off* (1962); *The Silk Room* (1966) and *A Nightingale in Bloomsbury Square* (1973). Other novels are: *The Single Eye* (1964); *The Paradox Players* (1967); *Wounds* (1969); *Love Child* (1971); *I Want to Go to Moscow* (1973); *Housespy* (1978); *Gor Saga* (1981); *Scarborough Fear* (as D. M. Layer, 1982); *Londoners: An Elegy* (1983); *Change* (1987); *Occam's Razor* (1993). Poetry: *Collected Poems* (1985).

Duration

One of the five categories in which ▷ Genette analyses narrative discourse, duration is concerned with the relationship between how long a fictional event would notionally last and how much of the text is devoted to telling of it (*eg* in Virginia Woolf's ▷ *To the Lighthouse*, the long first section of the novel tells the events of one day; the shorter second section tells the events of ten years). Duration, ▷ order and ▷ frequency are matters of temporal arrangement or 'tense'; the other two categories are ▷ mood and ▷ voice.

Durrell, Lawrence (b 1912–90)

Novelist and poet. He began writing before the war, and published an experimental novel, *The Black Book* (1938) in France. His present high international reputation is based in particular on the sequence *The Alexandria Quartet* comprising *Justine* (1957); *Balthazar* (1958); *Mountolive* (1958) and *Clea* (1960). *The Alexandria Quartet* has achieved fame partly through its lavishly exotic appeal, and partly through Durrell's experimental technique: a wide range of narrative forms are employed, and the same events are seen, and interpreted quite differently, by the different characters participating in them. *Tunc* (1968) and *Nunquam* (1970) together form *The Revolt of Aphrodite*, which explores the destruction of love and creativity by social pressures, embodied in the 'Firm', a vast and dehumanizing multi-national enterprise. Durrell has followed up the success of *The Alexandria Quartet* with a five-volume novel, *The Avignon Quincunx*, which also uses exotic settings and multiple narratives and, combining elements of myth with philosophical speculation, satirizes the values of Western society. It is made up of the following volumes: *Monsieur; or, The Prince of Darkness* (1974); *Livia; or, Buried Alive* (1978); *Constance: or, Solitary Practices* (1982); *Sebastian; or, Ruling Passions* (1983); *Quinx; or, The Ripper's Tale* (1985).

As the titles of his two major sequences suggest, the spirit of particular places has always been of importance to Durrell; he has said that in *The Alexandria Quartet* he 'tried to see people as a function of place'. He has published many volumes of travel writing, particularly about the islands of the Mediterranean, including: *Prospero's Cell* (about Corcyra; 1945); *Reflections on a Marine Venus* (about Rhodes; 1957): *The Greek Islands* (1978). Durell has also published collections of short stories, including: *Sauve Qui Peut* (1966); *The Best of Antrobus* (1974); *Antrobus Complete* (1985); a number of plays, including: *Sappho* (1959); *Acto* (1961); *An Irish Faustus* (1963) and many volumes of poetry: *Collected Poems* (1960; revised 1968) and *Collected Poems 1931–74* (1980). But his greatest achievement has been to express the indeterminate and multi-faceted nature of experience through the techniques of experimental fiction.

Bib: Fraser, G. S., *Lawrence Durrell: A Critical Study;* Friedman, A. W., *Lawrence Durrell and The Alexandria Quartet.*

Dystopia
  ▷ Utopian fiction.

Eagleton, Terry (b 1943)

The foremost Marxist critic writing in Britain today. Currently a professor of English at Oxford, he has for some time been a leading force in Marxism's encounter with a range of intellectual movements from ▷ structuralism onwards. His book *Criticism and Ideology* (1976) laid the foundation for the introduction into British literary criticism of the work of the French critic Pierre Macherey, and is a clear development of ▷ Louis Althusser's understanding of culture. In later works, such as *Walter Benjamin or Towards a Revolutionary Criticism* (1981), *The Rape of Clarissa* (1982), *The Function of Criticism* (1984), and *William Shakespeare* (1986), he has sought to develop a sophisticated ▷ materialist criticism which is prepared to engage with, but which refuses to be overawed by ▷ post-structuralism.

▷ Marx, Karl.

Earle, John

▷ Characters, Theophrastian.

Eclecticism

In ancient Greece, a term for the kind of philosophy that did not follow any one school of thought (eg ▷ Platonism) but selected its doctrines from a number of schools. The term is now applied to thinkers, artists and writers who follow this principle in the formation of their thought or artistic methods.

Écriture féminine

A term usually reserved for a particular kind of critical writing by women, emanating from the radical ▷ feminism of contemporary French critics such as Luce Irigaray, ▷ Hélène Cixous and ▷ Julia Kristeva. What unites this form of feminist criticism is the belief that there is an area of textual production that can be called 'feminine', that it exists beneath the surface of masculine discourse, and only occasionally comes to the fore in the form of disruptions of 'masculine' language. A further assumption is that woman is given a specific identity within the masculine structures of language and power, and that she must strive to challenge it. This particular brand of radical feminism takes the view that there is an 'essential' femininity that can be recovered, and that it is also possible to distinguish between a genuine feminine 'writing' and other forms of language. Cixous sees the Brazilian novelist Clarice Lispector (1925–77) as exemplifying a form of *écriture féminine*.

Bib: Kristeva, J., *Desire in Language*; Moi, T., (ed.), *The Kristeva Reader*; Moi, T., *Sexual / Textual Politics*; Marks, E. and De Courtivon, I., *New French Feminisms*; Newton, J. and Rosenfelt, D., *Feminist Criticism and Social Change*; Greene, G. and Kahn, C, *Making the Difference: Feminist Literary Criticism*; Wilcox, H. et al., *The Body and the Text: Hélène Cixous, Reading and Teaching*.

Eden, Emily (1797–1869)

The daughter of William Eden, the first Baron Auckland, Emily Eden was born in Westminster. She was a close friend of Prime Minister Melbourne, who appointed her brother George governor general of India in 1835. She went with him and her sister Frances, and acted as his hostess until their return in 1842, and in London till 1849. She was a member of the highest social circles and many celebrities visited her house where she held morning gatherings due to ill health. In 1844 she published *Portraits of the People and Princes of India*, and then in 1866 and 1872, *Up the Country: Letters Written from the Upper Provinces of India*. In 1919 her great-niece edited a further selection of her letters. Her novels, *The Semi-detached House* (1859), published anonymously, and *The Semi-attached Couple* (1860), by 'E. E.', were written some 30 years previously. They portray fashionable society with good-humoured wit and owe something to ▷ Jane Austen whom Eden much admired.

Edgeworth, Maria (1767–1849)

Novelist. Her tales are commonly set in Ireland. Her work is minor but still read for its vivacity, good sense and realism. *Castle Rackrent* (1800) and *The Absentee* (1812) are two of her works still in print. She was also an excellent writer for children (see *Tales* ed. by Austin Dobson). She collaborated with her father, a noted educationist, in *Practical Education* (1798), influenced by the French-Swiss thinker ▷ Rousseau. She was admired by ▷ Jane Austen ▷ William Thackeray, ▷ John Ruskin, ▷ Turgenev and ▷ Walter Scott, whom she influenced. She has recently been re-evaluated by ▷ feminist critics as a liberal contributor to women's social history.

Bib: Clarke, I. C., *Life*; Newby, P. H., *Maria Edgeworth*; Butler, M. S., *Maria Edgeworth*.

Edinburgh Review

A quarterly periodical founded by Sydney Smith and Henry Brougham in 1802. It introduced a new seriousness into literary criticism and generally took a moderate ▷ Whig position in politics. Jeffrey's literary taste was rigidly classicist and he had little sympathy with the 'Lake Poets', William Wordsworth, ▷ Samuel Taylor Coleridge and Robert Southey. The term originates in the *Edinburgh Review*, Oct. 1807. Later contributors were ▷ Thomas Babington Macaulay, William Hazlitt, ▷ Thomas Carlyle and ▷ Matthew Arnold.

▷ *Blackwood's Magazine*; *The Spectator*.

Edwardian

A term descriptive of the political, social and cultural characteristics of the early years of the 20th century, roughly corresponding to the reign of King Edward VII (1901–1910). The period is often remembered nostalgically for its luxury and brilliance, soon to be darkened by the horror of World War I (1914–18) and obliterated by the relative austerity of the post-war years. This life of luxury, easy foreign travel, low taxation, etc. is also thought of as being relatively free from the close moral restraint commonly associated with the preceding ▷ Victorian period. It is sometimes remembered, however, that such brilliance was restricted to the upper class and the wealthier members of the middle class, and that life for four-fifths of the population was at best dull and at worst

squalid and impoverished. This darker aspect of
the time was responsible for the rise of the socialist
Labour party and the prominence of polemical
writers like George Bernard Shaw (1856–1950) and
▷ H. G. Wells. Such writers attacked the social
injustice and selfishness of the upper classes in an
idiom designed to reach wide audiences. Another
critic of the dominant materialism was the novelist
▷ E. M. Forster. ▷ Arnold Bennett was a more
representative novelist: his novels were not polemical
and convey a materialistic vigour and excitement
which were important elements in the harsh but
inspiring environments of the more prosperous
provincial towns. Thus some aspect of materialism
is generally associated with Edwardianism, whether
it is being enjoyed, suffered or criticized. Politically,
the period was one of disturbance and rapid
development: ▷ trade unionism was militant, women
fought for politcal rights (▷ Suffragette Movement),
and the social conscience inspired legislation which
was later to mature into the ▷ Welfare State of
the 1940s.

Edwin Drood, The Mystery of (1870)

A novel by ▷ Charles Dickens, unfinished at his
death. The novel begins in a cathedral town (based
on Rochester); the plot turns on the engagement of
Edwin and Rosa Bud, who do not really love each
other, and the rivalry for Rosa's love of Edwin's
sinister uncle, John Jasper, and an exotic newcomer
to the town, Neville Landless. Edwin disappears
and Neville is arrested for his murder; Rosa flees to
London to escape Jasper; on her behalf the forces
for good are rallying in the shape of Rosa's guardian,
Mr Grewgious, a clergyman called Crisparkle and
a mysterious stranger, Mr Datchery, when the
story breaks off. The fragment is quite sufficient to
show that Dickens was not losing his powers. The
sombreness and the grotesque comedy are equal
to the best in his previous works. There have been
numerous attempts to end the novel but none of any
particular note.

Egdon Heath

A gloomy tract of country which is the Dorsetshire
setting for ▷ Thomas Hardy's novel ▷ *The Return
of the Native*. As often in Hardy's novels, the place is
not merely a background to the events but exercises
an active influence upon them.

Egerton, George (1859–1945)

The pseudonym of Mary Chavelita Dunne, a
short-story writer and later literary agent. Born in
Australia, Egerton eloped with a married man in
1888 and lived for a short time in Norway, where was
influenced by the work of Ibsen. The relationship
was short-lived and she moved to England, where
she married George Egerton Clairemonte (they
divorced in 1901). She spent some period living in
Ireland. Her first volume of short stories was *Keynotes*
(1893), a series of psychological sketches focusing
on the trials and struggles of the ▷ New Woman.
The volume sold well and she wrote a series of
similar works: *Discords* (1894), *Symphonies* (1897)

and *Fantasies* (1898). *The Wheel of God* (1898) is an
autobiographical novel.

Egoist, The (1879)

One of the most admired novels by ▷ George
Meredith. The 'egoist' is the rich and fashionable
Sir Willoughby Patterne, who is intolerably
self-centred and conceited. The story concerns
his courting of Clara Middleton and her fight for
independence from his assertiveness. Willoughby
is opposed by Vernon Whitford, who is austere,
honest and discerning, the tutor of Willoughby's
poor relation, Crossjay, a boy whose vigorous animal
spirits are accompanied by deep and spontaneous
feeling. Partly owing to Crossjay, Clara is eventually
enabled to evade Willoughby's advances, which
have been backed by her father whose luxurious
tastes Willoughby had indulged. She marries
Whitford, a conclusion which is a victory for integrity
over deceitful subtlety. The story is told with the
brilliance of Meredith's rather mannered wit and
is interspersed with exuberant passages of natural
description symbolically related to the theme.
Though Meredith's mannerism has lost the book
some of its former prestige, his analysis of self-deceit
and his understanding of the physical components
of strong feeling make *The Egoist* an anticipation
of kinds of fiction more characteristic of the 20th
century.

Ekwensi, Cyprian (b 1921)

Nigerian, novelist and short-story writer. Ekwensi's
fiction, widely read in Nigeria, depicts in many
cases the experience of modern urban life in Lagos.
For example, *Jagua Nana* (1961) is about the life
of a prostitute (its title refers to the famous novel
by ▷ Zola, *Nana*) and *People of the City* (1954) is a
story of journalists and jazz musicians. Ekwensi's
work stresses storytelling and uses a rich variety of
language and styles. His other novels include: *When
Love Whispers* (1947); *Burning Grass* (1962); *Beautiful
Feathers* (1963); *Iska* (1966); *Survive the Peace* (1976);
For a Roll of Parchment (1987); *Divided We Stand*
(1980); *Jagua Nana's Daughter* (1986). Volumes of
short stories: *Locotown* (1966); *Restless City* (1975).
He has also written fiction for children and edited an
anthology of Nigerian writing.
Bib: Emenyonu, E.N. (ed.), *The Essential Ekwensi:
A Literary Celebration of Cyprian Ekwensi's Sixty-Fifth
Birthday*.

Eliot, George (1819–80)

Pen-name of the novelist, Mary Ann Evans (at
different times of her life she also spelt the name
Mary Anne, Marian and Marianne). She was the
daughter of a land-agent in the rural midlands
(Warwickshire); her father's work (the management
of estates) gave her wide experience of country
society and this was greatly to enrich her insight
and the scope of her novels. Brought up in a narrow
religious tradition, in her early twenties she adopted
▷ agnostic opinions about Christian doctrine but
she remained steadfast in the ethical teachings
associated with it. She began her literary career

with translations from the German of two works of religious speculation (▷ German influence); in 1851 she became assistant editor of the ▷ *Westminster Review*, a journal of great intellectual prestige in London. Her friendship with ▷ George Lewes led to a union between them which they both regarded as amounting to marriage; this was a bold decision in view of the rigid opposition in the English society of the time to open unions not legalized by the marriage ceremony.

Her first fiction consisted of tales later collected together as ▷ *Scenes of Clerical Life*. Then came her series of full-length novels: ▷ *Adam Bede* (1859), ▷ *The Mill on the Floss* (1860), ▷ *Silas Marner* (1861), ▷ *Romola* (1862–3), ▷ *Felix Holt* (1866), ▷ *Middlemarch* (1871–2) and ▷ *Daniel Deronda* (1876). Up till *Romola* the novels and tales deal with life in the countryside in which she was brought up; the society is depicted as a strong and stable one, and the novelist combines in an unusual degree sharp, humorous observation and intelligent imaginative sympathy. *Romola* marks a dividing point; it is a historical novel about the society of the Italian city of Florence in the 15th century. As a work of imaginative literature it is usually regarded as scholarly but dead; however, it seems to have opened the way to the more comprehensive treatment of English society in her last three novels, in which the relationship of the individual to society is interpreted with an intelligence outstanding in the history of the English novel and often compared with the genius of the Russian novelist, ▷ Leo Tolstoy. Her critical reputation has varied; it declined somewhat after her death, her powerful intellect being considered to damage her creativity. She was defended by ▷ Virginia Woolf in an essay in 1919, but was really re-established by inclusion in ▷ F.R. Leavis's *The Great Tradition* (1948). With the rapid strides in ▷ feminist criticism in the 1980s, however, Eliot has been reclaimed as a major influence on women's writing and her works have been the focus of numerous feminist critiques, *eg* S. Gilbert and S. Gubar, *The Madwoman in the Attic* (1979).

George Eliot's poetry (*The Spanish Gipsy*, 1868, and *The Legend of Jubal*, 1870) is now little regarded but her essays for the *Westminster Review* include work of distinction and she published a collection, *The Impressions of Theophrasius Such*, in 1879.

In 1880, George Lewes having died, she married John Walter Cross, but she died in the same year.

Bib: Haight, G.S., *Life*; Leavis, F.R., in *The Great Tradition*, Bennett, J., *George Eliot: Her Mind and her Art*; Harvey, W.J., *The Art of George Eliot*; Pond, E.J., *Les Idées Morales et Religieuses de George Eliot*; Hardy, B., *The Art of George Eliot*; Roberts, N., *George Eliot: Her Beliefs and Her Art*.

Elizabethan novels

The events in a novel or novella are not drawn directly from traditional or legendary sources but are invented by the writer, so that they are new (or 'novel') to the reader. The 'novels' of the Elizabethan period are distinguishable from the long prose romances, such as Sir Philip Sidney's ▷ *Arcadia*, by their comparative brevity, but *Arcadia* is sometimes included among them.

The Italian novella began its history in the 13th century, and one of its best practitioners, ▷ Giovanni Boccaccio, was already well known in England, especially from ▷ Chaucer's adaptation of his work. In the first 20 years of Elizabeth I's reign, various Italian 'novelle', especially those of Bandello (?1480–1562), were translated into English, notably by William Painter in his collection *The Palace of Pleasure* (1566–7). These translations created a taste for the form, and led to the production of native English 'novels'. John Lyly's ▷ *Euphues* (1578) was the first of these. Best known among those that followed are: Lyly's *Euphues and his England* (1580), Barnabe Rich's (1542–1617) collection *Farewell to the Military Profession* (1581), Robert Greene's ▷ *Pandosto* (1588) and *Menaphon* (1589), ▷ Thomas Lodge's *Rosalynde* (1590), ▷ Thomas Nashe's ▷ *Unfortunate Traveller* (1594), and Thomas Deloney's *Thomas of Reading, Jack of Newbury*, and *The Gentle Craft* (all between 1596 and 1600). The style of these works varies greatly. Rich, Greene and Lodge wrote mannered and courtly tales in imitation of Lyly; Nashe's rambling narrative is sometimes strongly realistic, and his style parodies a wide range of contemporary prose styles; Deloney addressed a middle-class public and at his best (in *Thomas of Reading*) anticipates the sober vividness of ▷ Daniel Defoe. The taste for the form lapsed in the early 17th century. There is no continuous development between the Elizabethan novel and the novel form as we know it today: the latter has its beginnings in the work of Defoe in the early 18th century, though it had late 17th-century forerunners.

Both the Italian and the English novels were used as sources for plots by contemporary English dramatists. Shakespeare's *Twelfth Night* is drawn from *Apolonius and Silla* in Rich's collection, adapted from an Italian original; his *As You Like It* is based on Lodge's *Rosalynde*; his *Winter's Tale* draws on Greene's *Pandosto*.

Ellis, Alice Thomas (b before 1939)

Novelist. Alice Thomas Ellis's work has much in common with that of ▷ Beryl Bainbridge, Patrice Chaplin and Caroline Blackwood (with whom Ellis wrote *Darling, You Shouldn't Have Gone to So Much Trouble* in 1980), who have all been collectively termed 'the Duckworth gang' for the similarity of their concerns and plot: most of their novels deal (with varying degrees of irony and biting wit) with modern women negotiating their own obsessions and a bizarre range of domestic situations, often stemming from sexual and romantic traumas. Thomas Ellis's works are psychologically astute black comedies of contemporary moral dilemmas, which map the terrain between modern sexual codes and (Ellis's strongly Catholic) religious background. She is married to the director of Duckworth publishers (hence 'the Duckworth gang'), and her works include: *The Sin Eater* (1977); *The 27th Kingdom* (1982, nominated for the Booker Prize); *Unexplained Laughter* (1985); *Home Life* (1986); *Secrets of Strangers*

(1986 with Tom Pitt-Atkins); *The Skeleton in the Cupboard* (1988); and *Pillars of Gold* (1992).

Ellis, Henry Havelock (1859–1939)
Psychologist and essayist. Part of his work was scientific: *Man and Woman* (1894); *Studies in the Psychology of Sex* (1897–1910). Part of it was literary and expressed in reflective essays: *Little Essays in Love and Virtue* (1922); *Impressions and Comments* (1914–23); *The Dance of Life* (1923). In the latter work he exemplified the revival of the ▷ essay as a reflective form early in this century. He was a friend of the novelist ▷ Olive Schreiner.
Bib: Calder Marshall, A., *Life*; Collis, J. S., *An Artist of Life*.

Ellmann, Lucy (b 1956)
Novelist. Daughter of the American writers Richard and Mary Ellmann, she was educated at Essex University and the Courtauld Institute and lives in Britain. *Sweet Desserts* (1988), which won the *Guardian* fiction prize, concerns the destructiveness of consumerism and the life of a young woman overshadowed by a successful academic father. Her second novel is *Varying Degrees of Hopelessness* (1991).

Emecheta, Florence Onye Buchi (b 1944)
Novelist, short-story writer, radio and television playwright. Born near Lagos, Nigeria of Ibuza parents, she moved to England in 1962 and took a sociology degree at London University. She has worked in the Library Office at the British Museum and as a youth and community worker, and, since 1972, as a writer and lecturer. She has also served on the Advisory Council to the British Home Secretary on race and equality, and on the Arts Council of Great Britain. In 1980–81 she was Senior Research Fellow in the Department of English and Literary Studies at the University of Calabar, Nigeria and she has held various visiting professorships in the United States. Her novels are: *In the Ditch* (1972); *Second Class Citizen* (1974); *The Bride Price* (1976); *The Slave Girl* (1977); *The Joys of Motherhood* (1979); *Nowhere to Play* (1980); *Destination Biafra* (1982); *Naira Power* (1982); *Double Yoke* (1982); *The Rape of Shavi* (1983); *Adah's Story: A Novel* (1983); *A Kind of Marriage* (a novella, 1986; also as a teleplay, 1987); *Gwendolen* (1989); *The Family* (1990). She has written several teleplays, including *Tanya: A Black Woman* and *The Juju Landlord* and four works for children: *Titch the Cat* (1979); *Nowhere To Play* (1980); *The Wrestling Match* (1980); *The Moonlight Bride* (1981). *Head Above Water* (1988) is an autobiography. Much of her work contains a strong autobiographical element and deals with the situation of women confronting oppression in both African and Western value-systems and social practices, while a number of her novels are historical, set in Nigeria before and after independence.

Emma (1816)
A novel by ▷ Jane Austen. The heroine, Emma Woodhouse, has wealth, social prestige, good looks and intelligence. But her good fortune and the admiration she elicits are in reality her greatest disadvantage: they blind her to the need for self-knowledge and self-criticism. In what she imagines to be pure generosity of heart, she sets about trying to control the fate of her orphan friend of illegitimate birth and insignificant character, Harriet Smith, imagining her to be the daughter of an aristocrat and deserving a marriage socially worthy of her paternity. Later she also becomes involved with a young man, Frank Churchill, who unknown to her is secretly engaged to a girl, Jane Fairfax, who is superior to Emma in talent but much inferior in worldly fortune. Jane Austen is in fact expanding the theme of the way in which romantic fantasy can blind a character to the realities of experience, more overtly used in earlier novels, ▷ *Northanger Abbey* and ▷ *Sense and Sensibility*. Emma, who has imagination and ability but nothing on which to employ them, is first trying to make a real-life novel with Harriet Smith as heroine and then participating in a mysterious drama, which she misconceives as her own fantasy wants it to be, with Jane Fairfax as main protagonist. But Harriet decides that she is to marry the man, George Knightley, with whom Emma herself has long been unconsciously in love; Emma also discovers that Churchill, with whom she has been conducting a flirtation, has merely been using her as a tool to mask his secret engagement. She realizes, in fact, that she has caused herself to be a victim of the first of her romances and has been made to play an ignominious and unworthy role in the second. Duly repentant, Emma is ultimately rewarded by Mr Knightley's proposal of marriage. The novel is perhaps Jane Austen's finest, displaying her irony at its most subtle.

Empiricism
A philosophical theory, according to which ideas are derived from experience, and the verification of knowledge must depend upon experience.

Encounter
Political and literary magazine, founded in 1953 and initially edited by the poet Stephen Spender and Irving Kirstol. During the 1950s and early 1960s it provided a prominent forum for the discussion of cultural issues, especially the condition and future of British society. Politically it was anti-communist and claimed to advocate reform on the basis of a post-ideological consensus in the West.

Encyclopaedists
The collaborators in the production of the great French encyclopaedia (▷ *L'Encyclopédie*) of the 18th century. The enterprise began with a translation of the English *Cyclopaedia* by Ephraim Chambers but the French version was intellectually altogether more impressive. Its editors were two leaders of the 'philosophers' – D'Alembert and ▷ Diderot – and its contributors were the leading male minds of France, such men as Voltaire and ▷ Rousseau. The inspiration was faith in reason and the desire to destroy superstition and beliefs thought to arise from it. The movement contributed to the influences which later led to the ▷ French Revolution, and

it reinforced ▷ rationalism throughout Europe. In England the movement influenced ▷ Jeremy Bentham and through him the ▷ Utilitarians of the 19th century.

▷ French influence on English fiction.

Encyclopédie, L'

An encyclopaedia published in 35 volumes between 1751 and 1776, under the editorship of ▷ Diderot and (until 1758) the mathematician D'Alembert (1717–83). Its contributors included Voltaire (1694–1778), ▷ Rousseau, Montesquieu (1689–1755), Buffon (1707–88) and Turgot (1727–81). The work originated in a translation of the English *Cyclopaedia* (1728) of Ephraim Chambers (d 1740), but the French version was intellectually more ambitious and more impressive. It was guided by a trust in reason and rationalistic explanation, and the desire to destroy superstition and the beliefs thought to arise from it. The work's fierce attacks on Church and state proved potent criticism of the ▷ ancien régime (it was suppressed at various stages of its composition) and heralded the overthrow of the monarchy in the ▷ French Revolution. It reinforced European rationalism and in England influenced ▷ Jeremy Bentham and through him the 19th-century Utilitarians (▷ Utilitarianism).

English language

Historically, the language was categorized into three periods: Old English extending to the 12th century; Middle English, from the 12th to the 16th centuries; and Modern English.

Old English consisted of ▷ Anglo-Saxon and Jutish dialects, and was called English because the language of the Angles was the earliest discoverable in writing. Old English was strongly modified by Scandinavian elements in consequence of the Danish invasions, and Middle English by an extensive infusion of French vocabulary.

Middle English was divided into a variety of dialects: William Langland (1330–?81), for instance, the author of *Piers Plowman*, wrote in the West Midland dialect; the author or authors of *Sir Gawain and the Green Knight* and *Pearl* wrote in a dialect from farther north, and ▷ Chaucer in the East Midland dialect. Because London was the chief city of England and the seat of the royal court, and because William Caxton (1422–91), established his printing press there in the 15th century, East Midland became the forebear of Modern English. Since the 15th century English has not undergone important structural changes; social differences of speech as between the classes have been of greater importance, at least for literary purposes, than regional ones.

Exceptions to this statement have to be made, however, for the form of English spoken and written in southern Scotland, and for those regions of the British Isles where until comparatively recent times Celtic languages were predominant: north-west Scotland, Wales and Ireland. In Ireland especially, a variety of spoken language known as Hiberno-English tends to follow the substratum of Irish Gaelic. This non-standard idiom of English was exploited by Irish writers such as the dramatist J.M. Syngne

(1871–1909) and the poet W.B. Yeats (1865–1939). Irish or Welsh writers may use standard English if they do not adhere to the surviving Celtic languages. In different ways Southern Scots is also important; it is a highly codified variety of non-standard English and has been unusual in that it has enjoyed a long-established written form. The literature in Scots (known in the Middle Ages as Inglis and today sometimes as Lallans, *ie* Lowlands) is considerable, whether one thinks of the late medieval poets such as Dunbar, Douglas, or Henryson; an 18th-century poet such as Burns, or a 20th-century one like Hugh MacDiarmid. However, from the 17th century eminent Scottish writers took to writing in standard English, and this became universal amongst prose writers of the 18th century (▷ Hume, Robertson, ▷ Adam Smith).

'The Queen's English' is the term used for the language spoken by the educated classes in England; linguists, however, prefer the term 'Standard English'. The pronunciation most in use among educated people is known as 'Received Pronunciation'.

English vocabulary is basically Germanic, but it also contains a very large number of Latin words. French, of course, developed from Latin, and many of these Latin words entered English in their French form after the Norman Conquest in the 11th century. For about two and a half centuries the upper classes were French-speaking. Vestiges of this social difference survive in such distinctions as the word 'sheep' used for the live animal, and 'mutton' for the same animal when it is eaten at table; the English shepherds who cared for the sheep ate very little meat, whereas their Norman-French masters were chiefly concerned with the animal when it had been transformed into food. Even after the aristocracy became English-speaking in the 14th century, the adoption of French words continued to be frequent owing to the strong influence of French culture and ways of life on the English educated classes. Latin words, however, have also entered English independently of their French forms; the 'clerks', *ie* the literate class of the earlier Middle Ages, used Latin as a living language in their writings; they were churchmen, and Latin was the language of the Church all over western Europe. In the 16th century, there was a new and different kind of influx from Latin owing to the fresh interest taken by scholars in ancient Latin culture.

The Latin contribution to the basically Germanic English vocabulary has resulted in a large number of Latin and Germanic synonyms, with important consequences for subtleties of English expression. The associations of Latin with the medieval Church and with ancient Roman literature cause the words of Latin origin to have suggestions of grandeur which the words of Germanic origin do not possess; thus we use 'serpent' in connection with religious and mythological ideas, *eg* the story of the Garden of Eden, but 'snake' will do in reference to the ordinary reptile. On the other hand, the Latinate word is emotionally less intimate than its Germanic synonym; when we wish to lessen the painfulness of death, we say that a man is 'deceased', instead of saying that

he has 'died'. This kind of differentiation clearly
carries important pragmatic consequences, yielding
differences in tone and register. Thus, socially,
it is often considered vulgar to use the synonym
of French or Latin construction, as suggesting a
disposition to speak stylishly rather than truly: many
people consider it vulgar to use the French 'serviette'
instead of the older 'napkin', the latter is also of
French origin, but is more fully anglicized.

Some English writers, eg John Milton (1605–74)
and Samuel Johnson, and some periods of literature,
especially the 18th century, are often singled
out for their preference for the Latin part of the
vocabulary, and in the 19th century the preference
was sometimes regarded as a fault. Correspondingly,
some literature is admired for its reliance on mainly
Germanic vocabulary, eg the ballads and the poems
of John Clare (1793–1804) and Christina Rossetti
(1830–94), but in this kind of judgement Latin
and French words adopted long ago and grown
fully familiar are allowed to have the same merit as
words of Germanic descent. Language which shows
sensitiveness to the value of contrasting Latinate
and Germanic vocabulary is always allowed peculiar
merit; such is the case with Shakespeare.

English has borrowed words from many other
languages: the chief of these is ancient Greek which
contributed extensively during the 16th century
Renaissance, and coloured the language similarly to
the Latin contribution at the same time. Borrowings
from other languages are more miscellaneous and
less distinctive; the most distinctive are the modern
borrowings from colloquial american diction.

English has not only borrowed more freely than
most languages; it has been spread abroad more
than any other world language. It is not only the
first language of the larger parts of North America
and Australasia, but it is spoken widely, sometimes
as a first language, in Africa and Asia (especially
India), where it is a *lingua franca* in countries which
have a variety of indigenous languages. This has
complicated the study of literature in English; as
the various territories of the former British Empire
have acquired independence. so they have developed
their own literature, which, although in the English
language, have distinctive styles and directions
(▷ Post-colonial fiction). Only a few 20th-century
American writers, for instance, can be included in
the truly English tradition; it is now necessary to
talk of 'American literature'. It is similarly difficult to
think of the Australian ▷ Patrick White or the West
Indian ▷ V.S. Naipaul as English writers, in the
sense of belonging to the English literary tradition.

In the 20th century the relationship between
English language and literature has become
theoretical, that is based upon the developments
in linguistic techniques as related to the *language* of
literature. Today, the teaching of English language
with literature is founded on the discipline of
literary stylistics and rejects an impressionistic
approach to literature, preferring to concentrate on
the rigorous analysis of the language texts use. It is
the theoretical framework, as for example with the
works of ▷ Bakhtin, that form the unifying basis
for stylisticians, semioticians, literary theoreticians

and linguists, as well as for the simple educational
processes of teaching English language and literature.
Bib: Carter, R. (ed.), *Language and Literature: An
Introductory Reader in Stylistics*; Fowler, R., *Linguistic
Criticism*; Carter, R. and Simpson, D. (eds.),
*Language, Discourse and Literature: An Introductory
Reader in Discourse Stylistics*.

Enlightenment

The term was originally borrowed into English in
the 1860s from German (*Aufklärung*), to designate
the spirit and aims of the French philosophers of the
18th century, such as ▷ Diderot and Voltaire. But
as historical perspectives have changed the word has
come to be used in a much wider sense, to denote
the whole period following the Renaissance, during
which scepticism and scientific rationalism came to
dominate European thinking. Enlightenment grew
out of Renaissance at different times in different
countries. In Britain, the empiricism of Francis
Bacon (1561–1626) and the secular pragmatism of
Thomas Hobbes (1588–1679) mark its early stages.
Its golden age began however with ▷ John Locke
(1632–1704) in philosophy, and Sir Isaac Newton
(1642–1727) in science, and it reached its height
in the first half of the 18th century. Locke argued
that 'Reason must be our last judge and guide in
everything', and rejected medieval philosophy as
superstition. Newton's theory of gravitation seemed
to explain the mysteries of the solar system. The
fact that Newton had also worked on optics was
ingeniously alluded to in Alexander Pope's couplet:
'Nature, and Nature's Laws lay hid in Night / God
said, *Let Newton be!* and All was *Light*'.

The onset of Enlightenment in Britain coincided
with the bourgeois revolution and many of its
values reflect the optimistic temper of the newly
dominant class, as much as any abstract philosophical
system. In contrast to the previous ideology of static
hierarchy, appropriate to a landowning aristocracy
and its peasant underclass, the new ideology of
merchants and professional men places its emphasis
on understanding and dominating the environment.
God loses his numinousness, becoming a kind of
divine mathematician, and the Deist thinkers of the
time rejected the dogmas of the scriptures in favour
of 'natural religion' based on an understanding of
God's laws through science. Pope expresses this
idea in classic form in his *Essay on Man* (1733–4),
cleverly blending it with the older hierarchical idea
of the Great Chain of Being. Pope's *Essay* stands
as a compendium of popular Enlightenment ideas,
expressing the expansive confidence of the middle
class that 'Whatever *is*, is *right*'. It was easy for the
middle-class reader of the day to feel that British
philosophy, science, trade, and imperialism were all
working together to advance civilization throughout
the world. It is a myth projected in many of the
works of Pope, James Thomson and other writers of
the time.

As the 18th century developed, the bourgeoisie's
confidence in its progressive destiny faltered,
reaching a crisis after the ▷ French Revolution
in what we now call the Romantic movement.
William Blake (1757–1827) attempted to restore

the pre-Enlightenment numinousness of God and nature, rejecting Newton's 'particles of light', and the idea of inert matter or empty space. Imagination, not science, was for him the key to nature: 'Every thing possible to be believ'd is an image of truth.' ▷ Percy Bysshe Shelley (1792–1822), using politically resonant imagery, asserted that 'man, having enslaved the elements, remains himself a slave' and warned of the dangers of 'an unmitigated exercise of the calculating faculty' (one of the characteristic institutions of the Enlightenment period was, of course, the slave trade).

More recently 'Enlightenment' has been given a yet wider historical application by the German philosophers Theodor Adorno and Max Horkheimer, whose book, *Dialectic of Enlightenment* (1944) sees the manipulative, calculating spirit of Enlightenment as the identifying characteristic of Western civilization. They trace its manifestations from Odysseus's tricking of the primitive bumpkin Polyphemus, to the treatment of people as means rather than ends which characterizes both modern totalitarian politics and consumer capitalism. Recent ecological movements, which advocate a respect for nature, rather than an exploitation of it, continue the same dialectic.
Bib: Willey, B., *The Eighteenth-Century Background*; Redwood, J., *Reason, Ridicule and Religion: The Age of Enlightenment in England*.

Epic

1 A narrative of heroic actions, often with a principal hero, usually mythical in its content, offering inspiration and ennoblement within a particular cultural or national tradition.

2 The word denotes qualities of heroism and grandeur, appropriate to epic but present in other literary or even non-literary forms.

Epics occur in almost all national cultures, and commonly give an account of national origins, or enshrine ancient, heroic myths central to the culture. For European culture at large, much the most influential epics are the ▷ *Iliad* and the ▷ *Odyssey* of ▷ Homer and the ▷ *Aeneid* by Virgil. ▷ C. S. Lewis in *Preface to Paradise Lost* makes a helpful distinction between primary and secondary epics: primary ones, such as Homer's, are composed for a society which is still fairly close to the conditions of society described in the narrative; secondary epics are based on the pattern of primary epics but written for a materially developed society more or less remote from the conditions described, *eg* Virgil's *Aeneid*. In English literature the Old English *Beowulf* may be counted as a primary epic. A number of attempts at secondary epic have been made since the 16th century, but John Milton's *Paradise Lost* (1667) is unique in its acknowledged greatness and its closeness to the Virgilian structure. Edmund Spenser's *The Faerie Queene* (1590–6) has many epic characteristics, but, in spite of the important classical influences upon it, the poem's structure is derived from the 'romantic epic' of the 16th-century Italian poets, Ariosto and Tasso; moreover, though allegory often plays a part in epics, the allegorical elements in *The Faerie Queene* are so pervasive as to present a different kind of imaginative vision from that normally found in them.

Many other works in English literature have epic qualities without being definable as epics. For example, ▷ Fielding described ▷ *Tom Jones* as a comic epic, and it is this as much as it is a novel: a series of adventures of which Tom is the hero, but of which the consequences are loss of dignity rather than enhancement of dignity. Melville's prose romance *Moby Dick* (1851) has true epic scale, seriousness of treatment and relevance to the human condition. ▷ James Joyce's ▷ *Ulysses* uses the *Odyssey* as the ground plan for a narrative about a day in the life of a Dublin citizen, and though the intention of this and of Joyce's succeeding work ▷ *Finnegans Wake* is in part comic, there is also in both books deep seriousness, such as derives from the authentic epic tradition. In fact, this tradition, in the last three hundred years, has mingled with other literary forms, such as the romance, the comic romance (*eg* ▷ *Don Quixote*), and the novel, and it is in this mixed rather than in its original pure form that it has proved most productive.

Epicurean
▷ Epicurus.

Epicurus (342–270 BC)
Greek philosopher and founder of the Epicurean school of philosophers. He is best known for his principle that pleasure is the beginning and end of the blessed life. This has commonly been misunderstood to mean that the purpose of life is pleasure-seeking; in fact Epicurus meant by pleasure the acquisition of a mind at peace and this implied, for him, the pursuit of virtue and hence a life of asceticism rather than excess. His best-known disciple is the Latin poet Lucretius, who expounded the philosophy in his poem *De Rerum Natura* (*Concerning the Nature of Things*). The Epicureans were rivals of the ▷ Stoics, who taught that the end of life was fortitude and liberation from the passions.

Epigram
For the ancient Greeks the word meant 'inscription'. From this, the meaning extended to include very short poems notable for the terseness and elegance of their expression and the weight and wit of their meaning. The richest of the ancient Greek collections is the Greek *Anthology*; the greatest Latin masters were Catullus and Martial. Ben Jonson's *Underwoods* contains epigrams in their tradition. After him, epigrams became shorter and most commonly had satirical content; Alexander Pope (1688–1744) was the greatest master of this style, and his poems include many epigrams.
▷Aphorism.

Epiphany
A Church festival celebrating the showing ('epiphany' means manifestation) of the Christ child to the Magi, otherwise known as the Three Wise Men or the Three Kings (*Matthew* II). The festival is twelve days after Christmas Day, so it is also called Twelfth Night. It concludes the season of Christmas festivities.

The novelist ▷ James Joyce began his career by

writing what he called 'epiphanies', *ie* sketches in
which the incident, though often in itself slight,
manifests or reveals the inner truth of a character.
This is the method he pursues in ▷ *Dubliners*.

Episteme

The traditional meaning of the term 'epistemology'
is 'the theory or science of the method or grounds
of knowledge' (Oxford English Dictionary). In the
work of the French philosopher ▷ Michel Foucault,
'episteme' has come to mean something more
specific. He uses the term to describe 'the total
set of relations that unite, at a given period, the
discursive practices that give rise to epistemological
figures, sciences, and possibly formalized systems,'
(*The Archaeology of Knowledge*; 1972). In short, the
episteme is historicized as the basic unit used to
describe the manner in which a society represents
knowledge to itself. Foucault conceives of the
episteme in dynamic rather than static terms, since
knowledge is always a matter of the ways in which
'desire' and 'power' negotiate their way through
the complex ▷ discourses of society. Foucault is
at pains to point out, however, that the episteme
does not establish a transcendental authority which
guarantees the existence of scientific knowledge, but
rather points towards the fact that different kinds
of knowledge are inscribed in 'the processes of a
historical practice'.
   ▷ Archaeology.

Epistolary novel

A novel which takes the form of letters written
by one or more of the characters. One of the
best-known examples in English is ▷ Samuel
Richardson's ▷ *Pamela* (1740–1).

Erasmus, Desiderius (?1466–1536)

Dutch-born Augustinian monk, translator, ▷
humanist, educationalist, biblical scholar and linguist.
Erasmus was one of the most important northern
European scholars of the Renaissance period.
The diversity of his interests, the range of his
accomplishments, and the weight of his influence on
European thought in the 16th century and later are
almost impossible to quantify.
   Erasmus's chief works are: *the Adages* (first
published in 1500), the *Enchiridion* (1503), the *Praise
of Folly* (1509) and the *Colloquies* (first published in
1516). But to these popular successes can be added
his editions of the Church Fathers, paraphrases,
commentaries on the scripture, editions of the
classics and a huge correspondence with other
European scholars and thinkers, the most important
of whom, in England, was his close friend ▷ Sir
Thomas More. The *Praise of Folly*, a satirical work
which ranges widely over all aspects of public life
in the period, was conceived while Erasmus was
travelling to England to see More – a circumstance
preserved in the work's punning Latin title:
Encomium Moriae.
   The *Enchiridion*, on the other hand, is a manual
of the Christian life which encourages knowledge of
pagan (that is ▷ classical) literature as a preparative

towards attaining Christian scriptural understanding.
The *Adages* – a work which grew from some 800
'adages' or classical sayings into over 4,000 short
essays by the time Erasmus died – provided an
entry into classical literature, and into humanistic
thought generally, for the public at large. Similarly,
the *Colloquies* expanded as Erasmus worked at the
project until they eventually formed a wide-ranging
series of dialogues on a huge variety of topics, which
were to include education, games, travel, parenthood,
punishment, and social and religious questions.
Bib: *The Collected Works of Erasmus*: Huizinga, J.,
Erasmus of Rotterdam.

Erewhon (1872) and Erewhon Revisited (1901)

Satirical anti-utopias by ▷ Samuel Butler. ▷ Sir
Thomas More's ▷ *Utopia* is a description of an
ideal country as different as possible from England.
Erewhon (an anagram of 'Nowhere') represents a
country many of whose characteristics are analogous
to English ones, caricatured and satirized. Thus
Butler satirizes ecclesiastical institutions through
the Musical Banks and parental tyranny through
the Birth Formulae; machinery has to be abolished
before it takes over from human beings. In *Erewhon
Revisited*, Higgs, the English discoverer of Erewhon,
finds that his previous departure by balloon has been
used by Professors Hanky and Panky ('hanky-panky'
is deceitful practice) to impose a new religion,
according to which Higgs is worshipped as a child of
the sun. Butler's method in these satires resembles ▷
Jonathan Swift's satirical technique in the Lilliput of
▷ *Gulliver's Travels*.

Essay, The

'Essay' derives from the French *essai*, meaning
'experiment', 'attempt'. As a literary term it is
used to cover an enormous range of composition,
from schoolboy exercises to thorough scientific and
philosophical works, the only quality in common
being the implied desire of the writer to reserve to
himself some freedom of treatment. But the essay
is also a recognized literary form in a more defined
sense: it is understood to be a fairly short prose
composition, in style often familiarly conversational
and in subject either self-revelatory or illustrative
(more or less humorously) of social manners and
types. The originator of the form was the great
French writer ▷ Montaigne.
   Montaigne's essays were published in completed
form in 1595, and translated by John Florio into
English (1603). His starting-point is *'Que sais-je?'*
('What do I know?') and it leads him into a serious
inquiry into his own nature as he feels it, and
into investigations of facts, ideas, and experiences
as he responds to them. In 1597 the first great
English essayist, Francis Bacon, published his first
collection of essays, of a very different kind: they
are impersonal and aphoristic, weightily sententious.
The character writers, ▷ Sir Thomas Overbury
and John Earle (?1601–65) use the classical model
of the Greek writer Theophrastus (▷ Characters,
Theophrastian), reminding one that with so
indefinite a form it is impossible to be too precise
about the dating of starting-points. Abraham Cowley

(1618–67) published the first essays in English closely corresponding to what it now understood by the form, and perhaps shows the first sign of its degeneracy: easiness of tone, which in Montaigne is a graciousness of manner introducing a serious and interesting personality, but which in less interesting writers may be an agreeable cover for saying nothing in particular.

In the early years of the 18th century Addison and ▷ Steele firmly established what is now known as the 'periodical essay' – a kind of higher journalism, intended often to please rather than instruct, but in their case to instruct through pleasure. In creations such as ▷ Sir Roger de Coverley, they developed the Theophrastian character into a personal, idiosyncratic portrait anticipating the characterization of the novelists a little later in the century. Their graciousness and lightness of tone take point and interest from their serious and conscious social purpose. ▷ Dr Johnson in *The Rambler* and in his essays as ▷ 'The Idler' used the weighty, impressive style soon to be regarded as unsuitable for the medium. ▷ Oliver Goldsmith in *The Citizen of the World* (1762) perfected the graceful, witty manner which came to be considered ideal for it.

If the 18th century was what may be called the golden age of the English essay, the early 19th, in the work of ▷ Charles Lamb, William Hazlitt, Leigh Hunt and ▷ De Quincey, was perhaps its silver age. In these writers, social comment combines with a confessional, autobiographical element which had never been so prominent in the English essay before. This was true to the autobiographical spirit of so much 19th-century literature. These essayists were links between the early Romantic poets – especially Wordsworth – and the mid-Victorian novelists; they shared the close interest in material surroundings characteristic of those poets, and their essays often contained character delineations related to such environmental settings. The earliest work of ▷ Charles Dickens, ▷ *Sketches by Boz*, is in the essayists' tradition.

After 1830, the periodical essay in the tradition of Addison, Goldsmith, Hazlitt and Lamb dissolved into the morass of constantly increasing journalism; though they had emulators in the 20th century, the form was increasingly despised by serious writers, and the famous essayists of the later 19th century were the more specialized sort, such as ▷ Matthew Arnold and ▷ John Stuart Mill. Yet it is not true to say that the informal essay of serious literary interest has disappeared. In the later 19th and 20th century, essays of natural description of remarkable intensity were produced by ▷ Richard Jefferies and Edward Thomas (1878–1917). More important still is the use of the essay for unspecialized but serious social and cultural comment by – to take leading examples ▷ Virginia Woolf ▷ D. H. Lawrence, ▷ George Orwell, and ▷ Aldous Huxley. With the growth in popularity of serious ▷ magazines and the extended articles in the Sunday newspapers, the essay is today having a considerable revival. These informal arguments and 'personality pieces', such as those by Bernard Levin in *The Times*, are very far, however, from the formal essay genre.

Essay concerning Human Understanding (1690)
A philosophical treatise by ▷ John Locke. Locke emphasizes reason as the dominant faculty of man. All knowledge is acquired through experience based on sense impressions; there are no 'innate ideas', *ie* no knowledge arises in the mind independently of impressions received from the outside world. These impressions divide into primary qualities, *ie* the measurable ones such as size, number, form, etc., and secondary ones, such as colour, sound and scent, which are not demonstrably part of the object, but dependent on the observer. Knowledge begins with perception of agreement or disagreement in the qualities observed in the objects or, as Locke calls them, 'ideas'. He distinguishes between rational judgement, which identifies and analyses ideas, and 'wit', which relates them by their resemblances; the distinction is practically one between reason and imagination and gives advantage to reason. Faith, *eg* in religious doctrine, is not distinct from reason, but the assent of the mind to a belief that accords with reason. Thus Locke appeals to clear definition in language and expression; he depreciates the intuitive and imaginative faculties of the mind and elevates the rational ones. His thesis accords with the reaction at the end of the 17th century against the intolerance and fanaticism of the religious conflicts which had prevailed during the first half of it. The influence of his philosophy is impressed on the imaginative prose literature of the first thirty years of the 18th century, for instance in the realism of ▷ Daniel Defoe. Later in the century, the novelist ▷ Laurence Sterne makes ingenious use of Locke's theory of the association of ideas in ▷ *Tristram Shandy*.

Essays in Criticism (1865, 1888)
The two volumes (First Series 1865; Second Series 1888) that contain much of the most important of ▷ Matthew Arnold's literary critical work. The first volume opens with 'The Function of Critism at the Present Time', a discussion of the relevance of criticism both to creative literature and to society and civilization; it is an example of what T. S. Eliot was later to call Arnold's 'propaganda for criticism', and it has been influential among 20th-century critics. The second essay, 'The Literary Influence of Academies', makes a case for authoritative standards in culture, and constitutes an implicit criticism of the habits of English culture, again in a way that is still relevant. The remainder of the first volume comprises essays on foreign writers and literature. The Second Series opens with a striking essay on 'The Study of Poetry', in which Arnold puts his view that poetry will supply to the modern world the kind of inspiration that was afforded by great religions in the past – a view which has also been put forward in the 20th century, notably by I. A. Richards in *The Principles of Literary Criticism* (1924), though he expresses the view in other terms. The remainder of the Second Series consists principally of studies of English poets of the 18th and 19th centuries. On the whole, Arnold's fame rests more on the broad themes of the relationships of literature and society than on his particular studies, though some of these,

eg on the German poet Heinrich Heine in the First Series, are of great interest.

Essentialism

Philosophically, the notion of 'essence' refers to the proposition that the physical world embodies in it a range of fixed and timeless essences which precede existence. In Christianity this is exemplified in the division between the soul and the body, where the latter is relegated to the realm of temporal existence. In ▷ materialist accounts essentialism has come to be associated with attempts to deny the primacy of history as a formative influence on human affairs and human personality. Materialism also challenges the emphasis upon the autonomy of the individual as a theoretically 'free' agent who is the centre of meaning. Any questioning of the notion that essence precedes existence deeply affects the issue of what is assumed to be the coherent nature of human identity, and resists the essentializing attempt to reduce material reality to a set of mental images. To remove the human subject from the centre and to reinscribe him or her in a series of complex historical relations is to challenge, at a theoretical level, human autonomy. It also suggests that those philosophical arguments which place the individual at the centre of meaning and authority are restrictive in that they propose a view of the world which masks the connection between knowledge and particular human interests.
▷ Archaeology.

Establishment

A term which has come into use since World War II to describe the institutions which by long tradition have prestige and authority in Britain. It probably originates in the official description of the ▷ Church of England as 'the Established Church' – ie the official state Church, having the Queen at its head. The monarchy itself, and Parliament, are obviously part of the Establishment, and so is the government bureaucracy loosely known as 'Whitehall'. Beyond this nucleus, the constituents of the Establishment vary according to the point of view of any particular user of the term, but it nearly always includes the following items: the fashionable men's clubs in London, especially those with long-established intellectual or political prestige, such as the Athenaeum and the Carlton; the older members and leaders of the older political parties – the Conservatives and Liberals, and sometimes also of the Labour party; the 'ancient universities' of Oxford and Cambridge, and within them, certain colleges of special prestige, such as All Souls and Christ Church at Oxford and King's and Trinity at Cambridge; the ▷ public schools, especially the older and more fashionable ones, such as Winchester, Eton, Harrow, Westminster and ▷ Rugby; ▷ *The Times* newspaper, with its special prestige (formerly at least); and the officer corps of the fighting services, especially the Navy. Apart from these, the term may be made to include almost anyone or anything that has prestige from tradition or happens to occupy or constitute a position of authority.

The term 'Establishment' is generally used by those who are at least fairly young and by such as are opposed to, or at least critical of, the traditions of existing authority. The war left Britain with reduced importance in the world but without an urgent crisis to absorb social energies. The result was a feeling of restless discontent among the young, who felt – and to some extent still feel – the nation to have become static and dissatisfying. This mood produced the ▷ 'Angry Young Men' of the 1950s who dissented from the traditions of the nation as represented by the 'Establishment'. The playwright John Osborne (b 1929) and the novelists ▷ Kingsley Amis and ▷ John Braine were prominent among these writers. In the 1980s the term has come to imply a political bias, and one which is particularly Conservative.

Ettrick Shepherd, The
▷ Hogg, James.

Euphemism
▷ Figures of Speech.

Euphues (1578–80)

A prose romance by John Lyly (1554–1606), in two parts; the first, *Euphues, or the Anatomy of Wit* was published in 1578; the second, *Euphues and his England*, in 1580. The tales have very little story; they have been described as 'pattern books' for courtly behaviour, especially in love. Their most striking quality is their elaborate style: long sentences balance clause against clause and image against image, so as to produce an effect of ornament taking priority a long way over sense. Falstaff in *Henry IV Part I* (II.iv) parodies *Euphues* when he is burlesquing the king, *eg* 'for though the camomile, the more it is trodden on, the faster it grows, yet youth, the more it is wasted, the sooner it wears'. Though often parodied as the language of fops, the style was much imitated especially by Elizabethan romance writers such as ▷ Robert Greene in *Menaphon* (1589), and ▷ Thomas Lodge in *Rosalynde* (1590). The name 'Euphues' is from Greek, and means, generally, 'well-endowed by nature'. Roger Ascham in *The Schoolmaster* had already used it to designate a man well endowed for learning and able to put it to good use. Ascham was an admirer of Castiglione's *The Courtier,* (1528; trans. 1561), and Lyly's cult of the courtly virtues is in the same tradition. Basic to it is the conception that nature is not to be imitated but to be improved upon.

Euphuism
▷ Figures of Speech.

Evangelical Movement

A movement for ▷ Protestant revival in the Church of England in the late 18th and early 19th century. It was stimulated partly by John Wesley's Methodist revival and the activities of other sects (especially among the lower classes) outside the Church of England; it was also a reaction against the ▷ rationalism and scepticism of the 18th-century aristocracy, and against the ▷ atheism of the ▷ French Revolution. Politically, the movement tended to be conservative and was therefore strong among the Tories, whereas the ▷ Whigs (especially their aristocratic leaders such as Charles James Fox) retained more of the 18th-century worldliness and scepticism. In doctrine the Evangelicals were inclined to be austere, to attach importance to strength of faith and biblical guidance, and to oppose ceremony and ritual. Socially they developed a strong sense of responsibility to their fellow human beings, so that one of their leaders, William Wilberforce, devoted his life to the cause of abolishing slavery and the slave trade in British dominions, and later Lord Shaftesbury (1801–85) made it his life-work to alleviate the social and working conditions of the working classes. The leaders of the movement were laymen rather than clergy, and upper class rather than lower class, amongst whom the Nonconformist sects were more actively influential. As the Nonconformists were to contribute to English socialism later in the century a religious rather than a ▷ Marxist inspiration, so the Evangelicals later led to generations of highly responsible, independent-minded intellectuals such as the historians Thomas Babington ▷ Macaulay and Trevelyan, and the novelist ▷ Virginia Woolf.

Evelina (1778)
A novel in letters by ▷ Fanny Burney. Evelina has been abandoned by her aristocratic father, and her socially much humbler mother is dead. She has been brought up by her guardian, a solitary clergyman. As a beautiful, well-bred, and intelligent young girl, she pays a visit to a friend in London, where she falls in love with a handsome aristocrat, Lord Orville, is pursued by an unscrupulous rake, Sir Clement Willoughby, and is much embarrassed by vulgar relatives, especially her grandmother, Madame Duval. The convincing and delightful part of the novel consists in its acute and lively social observation, in many ways superior to anything of the sort yet accomplished in the 18th-century novel, and anticipating the maturer art of ▷ Jane Austen in the early 19th century.

Evelyn, John (1620–1706)
Chiefly remembered as a diarist. His diary, published in 1818, covers the years 1641–97, and includes impressions of distinguished contemporaries, customs and manners, and accounts of his travels. He published translations from Greek, Latin and French, as well as essays on the practical arts (gardening, the cultivation of trees, engraving, architecture). He also wrote an interesting ▷ biography of a court lady (*The Life of Mrs Godolphin*, unpublished until 1847).
▷ Diaries.
Bib: *Diary*, ed. E. S. de Beer; Ponsonby, A., *Life*; Hiscock, W. G., *John Evelyn and his Family Circle*; Marburg, C., *Mr Pepys and Mr Evelyn*.

Examiner, The
1 A right-wing (Tory) journal, started by Lord Bolingbroke and continued by ▷ Jonathan Swift. Engaged in controversy with the left-wing (▷ Whig) writers, Joseph Addison and ▷ Sir Richard Steele.
2 A weekly periodical founded by John and Leigh Hunt in 1808, famous for its radical politics. It had no political allegiance, but criticized public affairs, in the words of Leigh Hunt's friend John Keats, 'from a principle of taste'. In 1813 the Hunts were sent to prison for two years for exposing the gross flattery of the Prince Regent (later George IV) in another paper.

Exhibition, The Great
Held in 1851, in Hyde Park in London, it was the first international exhibition of the products of industry and celebrated the peak of the British ▷ industrial revolution. It was regarded as a triumph for British prosperity and enlightenment, though by some critics, eg the philanthropist ▷ Lord Shaftesbury, as concealing the scandal of immense urban slums. Its principal building, the Crystal Palace, was a pioneer construction in the materials of glass and cast-iron. The architect was Joseph Paxton.

Existentialism
A modern school of philosophy which has had great influence on European literature since World War II. The doctrines to which the term has been applied are in fact very various, but a number of common themes may be identified. The first is the primacy of the individual, and of individual choice, over systems and concepts which attempt to explain him or her. The second is the absurdity of the universe; reality, it is claimed, always evades adequate explanation, and remains radically contingent and disordered. This absurdity causes anxiety, but also makes freedom possible, since our actions also cannot be causally explained or predicted. Neither the behaviour nor the nature of others can be understood by observation. Existentialism sees freedom of choice as the most important fact of human existence. According to ▷ Jean-Paul Sartre, consciousness of our own freedom is the sign of 'authentic experience', as opposed to the 'bad faith' of believing oneself bound. Investigation of this freedom involves investigation of the nature of being, and this has caused existentialism to form two main streams, the first atheistic, which interprets individual existence as dependent on transcendent Being. The best-known leaders of existentialism have been the philosophers Martin Heidegger (1889–1976) and Karl Jaspers (1883–1969) in Germany, and Sartre (1905–80) and the philosopher and dramatist Gabriel Marcel (1889–1973) in France. Marcel represents the religious stream whose progenitor was the 19th-century Danish thinker Sören Kierkegaard (1813–55).

Existentialism has had relatively little influence on British philosophy, because of the strong empirical tradition in Britain, although the novelist and philosopher ▷ Iris Murdoch has termed modern British empiricists existentialist in her essay *The Sovereignty of Good*. Correspondingly, existentialism has had a less powerful influence on literature than in France, where authors like Sartre, ▷ Simone de Beauvoir, and Albert Camus have expounded its doctrines in, for example, such works as Sartre's trilogy of novels, *Roads to Freedom* (1947–9) and his play *No Exit* (1944), or Camus's novel *The Outsider* (1942). Nevertheless, these doctrines have been important in two ways. First, they have directly influenced a number of experimental novelists with Continental affinities, such as ▷ David Caute, ▷ Nigel Dennis, ▷ Andrew Sinclair, ▷ Colin Wilson and ▷ Christine Brooke-Rose. The most important writer in this category is ▷ Samuel Beckett in whose plays and novels the isolation and anxiety of the characters combine with an awareness of the issues of manipulation and choice implicit in the narrative and dramatic modes, to present existential dilemmas with unrivalled power. Second, existentialist doctrines have contributed much to the general ethos of ▷ post-modernism, and affected a number of major writers, prompting either admiration or resistance. Thus the post-modern concern with the nature of fictionality arises in part from the sense that neither individuals nor reality as a whole can be adequately conceptualized. The author's manipulation of his or her characters has provided a fruitful metaphor for the exploration of issues of freedom, as for example in the work of ▷ John Fowles, Iris Murdoch and ▷ Muriel Spark. Existentialism speaks powerfully to the sense of the 20th century as a chaotic and even catastrophic era, in which certainties have been lost and man is faced with the abyss of nothingness, or of his own capability for evil. It lays stress on extreme situations, which produce dread, arising from awareness of freedom of choice (according to Sartre) or awareness of original sin (according to Kierkegaard). Extremity and existential dread are important in the work of ▷ William Golding and ▷ Patrick White, and, earlier in the century, ▷ Joseph Conrad, who in this respect as in others anticipates the 20th-century *Zeitgeist*.

Expedition of Humphry Clinker, The
▷ *Humphry Clinker, The Expedition of.*

Expressionism
Expressionism was originally intended to define an artistic movement which flourished at the beginning of the 20th century in Europe, especially in Germany. The expressionist painters, such as Edvard Munch and Vasili Kandinsky, built upon the

departure from realism of Vincent Van Gogh and Henri Matisse, and developed towards the expression of feeling through colour and form. This often led to exaggeration and distortion, which induced unease in the viewing public. Similar haunting and irrational imagery were used in German expressionist cinema, such as Robert Wiene's *The Cabinet of Dr Caligari* (1919) and F. W. Murnau's *Nosferatu* (1922).

The origins of expressionism as a theatrical movement are to be found in the work of a number of German dramatists who wrote between 1907 and the early 1920s. These include Ernst Barlach, Reinhard Goering, Walter Hasenclever, Carl Hauptmann, Franz Kafka, Georg Kaiser, Oscar Kokoschka, Carl Sternheim and Ernst Toller. Even Bertolt Brecht was influenced by the movement in his early days. Although their individual styles differ greatly the expressionist playwrights rejected the 'objective' approach of naturalism and developed a highly emotional and subjective form of dramatic expression which aimed to explore the 'essence' of human experience. In their view this could be revealed only by getting beyond the surface appearances of ordinary life and exploring man's subconscious desires and visions. The impulse for this was revolutionary, if politically unclear. Strindberg, Wedekind, ▷ Freud and ▷ Nietzsche were the idols of the movement. Bourgeois ideology was the enemy, and the uniting vision ubiquitously advocated was the rebirth of man (with the emphasis very much on the male) in touch with his spirit and free from petty social restraints. The use of exaggerated gesture, disturbing sound, colour and movement was a vital part of the dramatists' technique of shocking the audience and conveying ecstatic or *Angst*-ridden states of being. Short disconnected scenes replaced carefully constructed plots, and scenery was distorted and hallucinatory rather than realistic. Later dramatists, such as Eugene O'Neill, Elmer Rice and Sean O'Casey, have tended to borrow from the dramatic language of expressionism without necessarily sharing the fervour of their German predecessors.

Fabian Society

A large society of socialistic intellectuals, closely bound up with the British Labour Party. It was founded in 1884 and named after the Roman general Fabius Cunctator – 'Fabius the Delayer' – who in the 3rd century BC saved Rome from the Carthaginian army under Hannibal, by using a policy of attrition instead of open battle, *ie* he destroyed the army by small attacks on isolated sections of it, instead of risking total defeat by confronting Hannibal with the entire Roman army. The Fabian Society similarly advocates socialism by piecemeal action through parliamentary reform instead of risking disaster by total revolution; this policy has been summarized in the phrase 'the inevitability of gradualness'. The Fabians were among the principal influences leading to the foundation of the Labour Party in 1900. The years between 1884 and 1900 were those of its greatest distinction; they were led by George Bernard Shaw and Sidney and ▷ Beatrice Webb, and made their impact through the Fabian Essays on social and economic problems. They always advocated substantial thinking on solid evidence, in contrast to the more idealistic and 'utopian' socialism of such writers as ▷ William Morris.

Fable

In its narrower, conventional definition, a fable is a short story, often but not necessarily about animals, illustrating a piece of popular wisdom, or explaining unscientifically a fact of nature. Animals are commonly used as characters because they are readily identified with simplified human qualities, as the fox with cunning, the lamb with meekness, the wolf with greed, the ass with stupidity. In primitive folklore, fables are worldwide. The tales in ▷ Rudyard Kipling's *Just So Stories* (1902) for children resemble the kind of primitive fable which seeks to explain facts of nature (such as how the leopard got its spots) without the aid of science. Sophisticated literatures favour the moral fable, the leading European tradition for which was established by the Greek fabulist ▷ Aesop. To this tradition belongs the medieval Latin and German beast satire of Reynard the Fox, from which is derived the best strict fable in English – ▷ Chaucer's *Nun's Priest's Tale* of the Cock and the Fox in the ▷ *Canterbury Tales*. However, though fables are plentiful in English as in every literature, used illustratively and ornamentally amongst other matter, English literature is comparatively poor in strict fabulists. John Gay's *Fables* are usually regarded as pleasant minor works; John Dryden's *Fables Ancient and Modern* (1699) are mostly not fables. Rudyard Kipling's *Jungle Books* (1894–5), like his *Just So Stories*, are minor children's classics. ▷ T. F. Powys's *Fables* (1929) are original and beautiful, and ▷ George Orwell's *Animal Farm* (1945) is very well known.

A broader interpretation of the term 'fable' allows a wider range of depiction: a tale which is a comment in metaphor on human nature, less directly figurative than allegory, and less roundabout in reaching its point than parable. In this broader meaning, English literature perhaps produced the greatest of all fables, Swift's ▷ *Gulliver's Travels*. But this broader interpretation admits an aspect of fable into almost any serious fiction; thus critics sometimes speak of a novelist's 'fable' in trying to express the underlying intention implicit in a novel. A modern view of this broader interpretation of the fable is expressed by ▷ William Golding in his essay 'Fable' in *The Hot Gates*, and its practice is exemplified in his own novels.

▷ Allegory.

Fabliau

Derived from 'fable', the term is applied to a medieval genre of short, humorous narratives, particularly popular in Old French poetry of the 13th century, which are usually structured around a battle of wits of some kind. Wit and ingenuity are celebrated in these stories; their outcomes may not conform to the dictates of a Christian morality. Characteristically, fabliaux are located in contemporary settings and many, though not all, have plots centred an adulterous situations. Explicitly sexual, scatological and bawdy terms are frequently employed in these narratives as befits the kind of action they depict. ▷ Chaucer is one of the first English writers to work in this genre (in the *Miller's Tale*, the *Reeve's Tale*, the *Shipman's Tale*, for example, from ▷ *The Canterbury Tales*), but it is clear that fabliaux were circulating in England before the composition of *The Canterbury Tales*. Many of the narratives in ▷ Boccaccio's ▷ *Decameron* are reworkings of fabliaux plots.

Fabula, Sjuzet/Syuzhet

The Russian ▷ Formalist critics made a distinction between the *fabula* (the chronological series of events that are represented or implied in a fiction) and the *sjuzet* or *syuzhet* (the order, manner and techniques of their presentation in the narrative). The distinction closely resembles that made in more recent ▷ narratology between ▷ story and ▷ narrative or text; but a third category, that of the act of ▷ narrating has now been added.

Fabulation

A form of writing which playfully flaunts its own fictionality and narrative artifice. The term has been applied in particular to American novelists such as John Barth and South American writers such as ▷ Jorge Luis Borges.

Faction

A form of writing in which real persons and events are portrayed, but the detail and presentation are fictional. The form has similarities to the dramatized television documentary. The term was coined by the American novelist Truman Capote, for his book *In Cold Blood*. An example is *Coming through Slaughter* by ▷ Michael Ondaatje, which is about the life of the jazz cornet player Buddy Bolden.

Factories

In the sense of industrial buildings in which large numbers of men were at work under one roof, as opposed to domestic industry with the workers in their own homes, factories existed to some extent in the 16th century. It was in the 18th century, however, with the invention of labour-saving machines and then of steam power to drive them, that the factory system became general. Pockets of domestic industry continued well into the 19th century, but it became increasingly the exception. Large industrial towns grew up haphazardly to accommodate the new factories; there is a vivid description of an extreme example in ▷ Benjamin Disraeli's novel ▷ *Sybil*. The employment of masses of labour tended to dehumanize relations between employer and employees, and instigated a new kind of class war; ▷ Elizabeth Gaskell's novels ▷ *North and South* and ▷ *Mary Barton*, and ▷ Charles Dickens's ▷ *Hard Times* illustrate this. The first Factory Act to have an important effect in the improving of conditions was that of 1833; by then the public conscience was truly aroused and the Ten Hours Act of 1847 restricted hours of labour. The main intention of the early Factory Acts was to prevent the employment of young children and to limit the hours of employment of women; they were made effective by the use of Factory Inspectors. Later Factory Acts have sought to prevent the use of dangerous machinery and to ensure that factories are healthy places to work in. Some employers came to see that it was in their own interests to make factory conditions as healthy and pleasant as possible: Andrew Undershaft in George Bernard Shaw's play *Major Barbara* (1905) is an example of an enlightened factory owner of the 20th-century sort.

Another use of the word 'factory' is to denote a centre for 'factors', *ie* men of commerce who transact trade on behalf of their employers. In the 18th century the East India Company established such factories in India, *eg* at Madras.

▷ Anti-industrialism; Industrial Revolution.

Fairbairns, Zoë (b 1948)

Novelist. Her novels are: *Live as Family* (1968); *Down: An Exploration* (1969); *Benefits* (1982); *Stand We At Last* (1983); *Here Today* (1984); *Closing* (1987). She uses a range of genres, such as ▷ science fiction (*Benefits*) or the crime thriller (*Here Today*) to explore the development of the ▷ feminist consciousness. *Stand We At Last* recounts the lives of a succession of women from the middle of the 19th century up to the 1970s, and may be compared with *The Seven Ages* by ▷ Eva Figes in its project of rediscovering the unwritten history of women's experience.

Fairies

Supernatural beings such as provide material for folk-tales all over the world. In Britain, as in many other countries, fairies have been regarded as neither good nor evil, but sometimes mischievous and sometimes beneficent, as human behaviour has given opportunity and invitation (see for instance Mercutio's speech on Queen Mab in Shakespeare's *Romeo and Juliet*, I.iv). Belief in them has been thought to be a vestige of pre-Christian beliefs in nature-spirits. Stories about them sometimes include elements of medieval romance and classical myth; thus in Shakespeare's *Midsummer Night's Dream*, Oberon derives from a 13th-century French romance, *Huon de Bordeaux*, Titania is used as a version of Diana the huntress in Ovid's *Metamorphoses* and Puck, also called Robin Goodfellow, is from English folklore. Spenser's Faerie Queen Gloriana gives Queen Elizabeth I the allure of romance at the same time as identifying her with the Platonic ideal of Glory. Although witches play a part in fairy stories, witchcraft, as exemplified by 16th- and 17th-century belief and manifested in Shakespeare's *Macbeth*, is altogether more serious and sinister, and requires separate treatment.

Belief in fairies – or half-belief – may have been widespread among all classes in England until the 17th century, but since then it has steadily shrunk even among country folk. It has persisted longest in Wales, north-west Scotland, south-west England and especially in Ireland; hence the comparatively serious use to which fairies are put in the verse of the Irish poet W. B. Yeats, *eg The Man Who Saw the Fairies*.

Among popular beliefs about fairies have been these: that they are small, hence sometimes called 'the little people'; they are used to explain natural phenomena such as 'fairy rings' on grass, said to be the traces of their midnight dances; they foretell the fortunes of children (fairy godmothers); they are supposed to steal human babies and leave fairy children ('changelings') in their stead. Many subdivisions of fairy exist, such as elves, pixies, gnomes, brownies, goblins.

▷ Fairy tales.

Fairy tales

Fairy tales have often been seen as simple narratives to amuse children, but their more pervasive significance was noted as early as the 17th century when writers used the stories for a didactic purpose. In the 19th century there was an emphasis on the moral role and related psychological impact of the tales. The major development in the theoretical treatment of fairy tales occurred, however, with ▷ Freud and ▷ Jung: the former saw the narratives as a way in which the subjects could work out their psychic problems, while the latter looked for universal and archetypal patterns. More recently the stories have been linked to a process of socialization as well as the imposition on girls of patriarchal value judgements.

▷ Women, Status of.
Bib: Zipes, J., *Don't Bet on the Prince*.

Family

Family has been in most societies the route by which property, wealth and status or their lack have been transmitted. ▷ Marriage, in any formalized sense, according to some authorities did not become established in England until after the 11th century, before which polygamy was practised. The household, which included others beside members related by ties of kin, was the domestic unit of significance and the economically productive unit. Only at the Reformation did a new ideology of marriage and of the parental role develop, which gave dignity to the wife as her husband's helpmeet and emphasis to the duty of father and mother to raise their children in the fear and knowledge of God. In the 18th century this ideal grew, with an emphasis on the importance of maternal intimacy: suckling her own children, instead of sending them out to nurse, playing with them and instructing them were construed as the proper activities of the mother. The male role throughout was defined in relation to positions held outside the home with which his greater authority inside it was associated. The following century marked the refinement of the concept of 'separate spheres': public life was stringently demarcated from the private world of home, in which children were reared and the wife secluded. Ideas of 'the child' are similarly period-specific.

Bib: Stone, L., *The Family, Sex and Marriage*; Davidoff, L. and Hall, C., *Family Fortunes*.

Fantastic

As used by the critics Tzvetan Todorov and ▷ Christine Brooke-Rose, the term fantastic denotes a situation in which the reader of a fiction cannot be sure whether an event (or a set of events) has a natural or a supernatural explanation. The classic example is ▷ Henry James's ▷ novella ▷ *The Turn of the Screw*, where the reader may remain uncertain, even after reaching the end, as to whether the ghosts were 'real' or a figment of the governess's imagination. If a natural explanation is forthcoming, the fantastic gives way to the uncanny; if supernatural explanations are explicitly required, then we are in the realm of the marvellous.

Far from the Madding Crowd (1874)

A novel by ▷ Thomas Hardy. The title is a quotation from *Elegy Written in a Country Churchyard* by Thomas Gray. It is one of Hardy's ▷ Wessex novels, and the first of real substance, following the comparatively slight ▷ *Under the Greenwood Tree*. The central character is Bathsheba Everdene, who is loved by three men: Farmer Boldwood, a solid but passionate squire; Gabriel Oak, a shepherd, who loves her with quiet constancy and wins her in the end, and the glamorous soldier, Sergeant Troy, whom she marries first. Troy combines fascinating gallantry with ruthless egoism; he allows his wife-to-be, Fanny Robin, to die in a workhouse, and is capricious and cruel to Bathsheba; he is eventually murdered by Boldwood. A crude outline such as this brings out the ballad-like quality of the story, characteristic of all Hardy's novels but more subtly rendered in later ones. Its distinction of substance is in Hardy's intimate understanding and presentation of the rural surroundings of the characters, and in the contrast between the urbane attractions of Troy and the rough but environmentally vigorous qualities of Boldwood and Oak. Bathsheba herself is a capricious and colourful heroine, not presented with psychological depth but with confident assertiveness which makes her convincing.

Farah, Nuruddin (b 1945)

Novelist and playwright. Farah was born in Somalia and educated in Ogaden (which is now in Ethiopia), at Panjab University in India and at the universities of London and Essex. The main theme of his work has been social and political change in East Africa but he chose to write in English, partly to circumvent censorship in Somalia and partly to gain an international readership. He was obliged to flee from Somalia in 1973 and subsequently lived in many parts of the world, including Nigeria, Gambia, Sudan, France, Germany, Italy and the United States. Since 1990 he has been Professor at Makere University, Kampala, Uganda. His novels have satirized the rule of dictators and the regime in Somalia as well as exploring the dilemmas of independent women living in a society where traditional gender roles are dominant. Stylistically, his fiction draws on the complex and elegant traditions of Somali poetry as well as alluding to a range of modern European writers. His novels are: *From a Crooked Rib* (1970); *A Naked Needle* (1976); *Sweet and Sour Milk* (1979); *Sardines* (1981); *Close Sesame* (1983); *Maps* (1986); and *Gifts* (1993), a novel set in Mogadishu before the civil war, which deals with the political and moral issues surrounding foreign aid through the story of a nurse who wishes to resist dehumanizing dependence. Plays include *The Offering* (1975) and *Yussuf and his Brothers* (1982). He has also written for radio.

Farrell, J. G. (James Gordon) (1935–79)

Novelist. His best work consisted of carefully researched, and powerfully imagined historical novels. *The Siege of Krishnapur* (1973), a fictitious account of the Indian mutiny, won the Booker Prize; *The Singapore Grip* (1978) recounts the collapse of British power in Malaya, culminating in the Japanese capture of Singapore in 1942; *Troubles* (1970) is set in Ireland in 1919. These three novels, which form a kind of trilogy concerned with the long demise of the British Empire, represent an ambitious attempt at historical novel-writing. His career was ended by his early death on a fishing expedition in Ireland. Other novels are: *A Man From Elsewhere* (1963); *The Lung* (1965); *A Girl in the Head* (1967); *The Hill Station* (unfinished, 1981).

Fascist

The fasces, a bundle of rods bound round an axe, were the symbol of the civil power of ancient Rome. The symbol was adopted by Mussolini's Fascist party which ruled Italy from 1922 to 1945. It was right-wing and anti-communist. The National Socialist Party in Germany (1933–45) and the Falangist Party that helped to bring Franco to power in Spain in 1938 were akin to the Italian Fascist party, and to some extent modelled on it. This is also true of the smaller Fascist parties in other countries, though Oswald Mosley's British Union of Fascists was never politically significant. All such parties favoured strong nationalism, political dictatorship, the suppression of ▷ communism and socialism; under German influence, they were usually marked by racial prejudice.

English writers, especially between 1930 and 1945, were predominantly left-wing in sympathy, and used the term 'Fascist' in the sense of right-wing,

despot, reactionary, brutal, etc. and applied it to
any person or body of people whose politics they
disliked. This abusive use of 'Fascist', though
misleading, is not due merely to political prejudice:
few political ideas of historical importance have
been so closely associated with brutality as Fascism,
and few have contributed so little of significance to
political thinking. Nonetheless, Fascists' emphasis
on leadership and (implicitly) on aristocracy of the
sort that requires a trained élite and not hereditary
privilege, appealed in varying degree to some leading
British and American writers of the period 1920–40,
such as W. B Yeats and Ezra Pound. T. S. Eliot,
▷ Wyndham Lewis and ▷ D. H. Lawrence have
also been accused of Fascist leanings. All these
writers had right-wing tendencies because they
reacted strongly against the simplifications of social
theory resulting from the traditions of 19th-century
liberalism and from Marxist Socialism (▷ Marx,
Karl); only Pound became deeply identified with
Fascism.
Bib: Carey, J., The Intellectuals and the Masses.

Feinstein, Elaine (b 1930)

Poet, novelist and translator. Born in Lancashire
and educated at Cambridge, Feinstein has taught
literature at Essex University as well as working
in publishing. Her poetry is written closely from
personal situations, and is deeply experiential. Her
volumes of verse include: In a Green Eye (1966) (her
first collection); The Magic Apple Tree (1971); The
Celebrants (1973); Some Unease and Angels: Selected
Poems (1977) and The Feast of Eurydice (1980). She
has also edited an edition of Marina Tsvetayeva's
poetry and written her biography. Her novels include
Children of the Rose (1975), The Ecstasy of Dr Miriam
Garner (1976) and The Border (1984).

Felix Holt the Radical (1866)

A novel by ▷ George Eliot. The hero is a talented
young working man who makes it his vocation
to educate the political intelligence of his fellow-
workers. His rival for the love of Esther Lyon,
the daughter of a Nonconformist minister, is the
local landowner, Harold Transome, also a radical
politician though pursuing a more conventional
political career. George Eliot makes Holt utter
high-minded speeches which weaken the reality he is
supposed to possess. On the other hand, a subsidiary
theme which concerns Harold Transome's mother,
the secret of Harold's illegitimacy, and his hostility to
the lawyer, Jermyn, who is really his father, is treated
so well that it is among the best examples of George
Eliot's art.

Fell, Alison (b 1942)

Poet, journalist and fiction writer. Born in Dumfries,
Fell has worked as a sculptor, with women's theatre
and for the feminist journal Spare Rib, for whom she
edited the fiction ▷ anthology, Hard Feelings. Her
novels are the autographical Every Move You Make
(1984) and The Bad Box (1987). The Grey Dancer
(1981) is a novel for children and her collections of
poetry include: At the edge of Ice (1983) and Kisses For
Mayakovsky (1984).

Feminism

In literary criticism this term is used to describe
a range of critical positions which argues that the
distinction between 'masculine' and 'feminine'
(▷ gender) is formative in the generation of all
discursive practices. In its concern to bring to the
fore the particular situation of women in society
'feminism' as a focus for the raising of consciousness
has a long history, and can be taken to embrace an
interest in all forms of women's writing throughout
history. In its essentialist (▷ essentialism) guise,
feminism proposes a range of experiences peculiar
to women, which are, by definition, denied to
men, and which it seeks to emphasize in order to
compensate for the oppressive nature of a society
rooted in what it takes to be patriarchal authority.
A more materialist (▷ materialism) account would
emphasize the extent to which gender difference is
a cultural construction, and therefore amenable to
change by concerned political action. Traditional
materialist accounts, especially those of ▷ Marx,
have placed the issue of 'class' above that of
'gender', but contemporary feminism regards the
issue of 'gender' as frequently cutting across 'class'
divisions, and raising fundamental questions about
the social role of women in relations of production
and exchange. Insofar as all literature is 'gendered',
then feminist literary criticism is concerned with the
analysis of the social construction of 'femininity' and
'masculinity' in particular texts. One of its major
objectives is to expose how hitherto 'masculine'
criticism has sought to represent itself as a universal
experience. Similarly, the focus is adjusted in order
to enable literary works themselves to disclose the
ways in which the experiences they communicate
are determined by wider social assumptions about
gender difference, which move beyond the formal
boundaries of the text. To this extent feminism is
necessarily the focus of an interdisciplinary approach
to literature, psychology, sociology and philosophy.
   Psychoanalytic feminism, for example, often
overlaps with socialist feminism. It approaches the
concept of gender as a problem rather than a given,
and draws on ▷ Freud's emphasis on the instability
of sexual identities. The fact that femininity – and
masculinity – are never fully acquired, once and
for all, suggests a relative openness allowing for
changes in the ways they are distributed. Literature's
disturbance and exploration of ways of thinking
about sexual difference have proved a rich source for
feminist critics.
   ▷ Women's movement; Écriture Féminine.
Bib: De Beauvoir, S., The Second Sex; Greene, G.
and Kahn, C. (eds.), Making a Difference: Feminist
Literary Criticism; Millett, K., Sexual Politics;
Spender. D., Feminist Theorists; Wollstonecraft, M.,
Vindication of the Rights of Women.

Fenwick, Eliza (c 1760–c 1840)

Novelist and children's author. Fenwick may be
associated with the development of radical women's
writing at the end of the 18th century. She was
friendly with ▷ Mary Wollstonecraft and ▷ Mary
Lamb, and she left her alcoholic husband in 1800,
supporting herself, without regrets, for the remaining

forty years of her life. Fenwick's most important and compelling piece of work is her novel, *Secresy, or The Ruin on the Rock* (1795), which focuses on the lives of two women, Sibella and Caroline, who grow in self-awareness and recognize the ills of their society. The ending is tragic, with both women losing what they love, but the sexual openness of the work, together with its praise of female friendship, ensure that the overall tone of the book remains challenging rather than acquiescent (▷ Feminism). Fenwick believed that education and the erosion of ignorance were the answers to social problems, a theme which she takes up in her didactic children's book, *Visits to the Juvenile Library* (1805). Her last years were spent running ▷ Godwin's library and travelling the world as a governess.

Bib: Wedd, A. F., *The Fate of the Fenwicks*.

Ferrier, Susan Edmonstone (1782–1854)

Novelist. The youngest of ten children, Susan Ferrier was born in Edinburgh. Her father was a lawyer, a principal clerk of session along with ▷ Sir Walter Scott, so Ferrier was early introduced to literary society. Through visits to Inverary Castle she also became acquainted with the fashionable world. After her mother died in 1797 her three sisters married and she kept house for her father who died in 1829. She later insisted on the destruction of correspondence with a sister, thus destroying much biographical material. Her novels of Scottish life included portraits of known people. *Marriage* (1818) was written in 1810 with a minimal contribution from her friend Miss Clavering, *The Inheritance* in 1824 and *Destiny, or the chief's daughter* in 1831. Her aim was didactic and her method keen observation, comedy and clear writing.

Feuilleton

In French, a leaflet. Also used in French for that part of a newspaper devoted to literature, non-political news and gossip. In English the term was once used for the instalment of a serial story: it was the French newspaper *Le Siècle* it was the first to commission a serial novel specifically for part publication, in 1836. They were called *romans feuilletons*.

Fielding, Henry (1707–54)

Born at Sharpham Park in Somerset, the son of a lieutenant. After the death of his mother when he was 11, Fielding was sent to Eton. At the age of 19, after an unsuccessful attempt to elope with an heiress, Fielding tried to make a living in London as a dramatist.

In 1728 his play *Love in Several Masques* was successfully performed at Drury Lane, and Fielding departed for university at Leyden, where he studied classical literature for about 18 months. On his return to London he continued his career as a dramatist, writing some 25 plays in the period 1729–37. His dramatic works are largely satirical, the most successful being *Tom Thumb* (performed in 1730). Fielding also edited four periodicals, *The Champion* (1739–41), *The Covent Garden Journal* (under the pseudonym Sir Alexander Drawcansir, 1752), *The True Patriot* (1745–6) and *Jacobite's Journal*

(1747–8), but his major achievement is as a novelist.

▷ *Shamela*, a parody of ▷ Richardson's ▷ *Pamela*, published in 1741, was developed into the theme of ▷ *Joseph Andrews* (1742), an original and comic creation. In 1743 Fielding published ▷ *The Life of Jonathan Wild the Great*, a satire on the criminal class comparable in its inversion of values to John Gay's *Beggar's Opera* (1728). In the same year his lesser-known satire, *A Journey From This World to the Next*, also appeared. ▷ *Tom Jones*, his greatest work, was published in 1749, and ▷ *Amelia* in 1751.

In 1748 Fielding was made Justice of the Peace for Westminster, and pursued a successful career of social reform. In 1754, his health failing, he embarked on a journey to Lisbon in search of a better climate, but died on the way. *A Journal of a Voyage to Lisbon*, his final achievement, was published posthumously the following year.

▷ Fielding, Sarah.

Bib: Alter, R., *Fielding and the Nature of the Novel*; Rogers, P., *Henry Fielding*; Rawson, C. J., *Henry Fielding and the Augustan Ideal under Stress*.

Fielding, Sarah (1710–68)

Sarah Fielding, sister of the novelist ▷ Henry Fielding, was highly praised by ▷ Samuel Richardson, who rated her achievements more highly than her brother's: 'his was but a knowledge of the outside of a clockwork machine, while yours was that of the finer springs and movements of the inside'. Her first appearance in print consisted of contributions to her brother's works (see Jill Grey, 'Introduction' to *The Governess*, OUP; 1968).

Sarah Fielding's first novel, *The Adventures of David Simple*, began to appear in 1744, and proved a great success. In its interpretation of social conventions from a female point of view, it provides a revealing contrast with the attitudes expressed by male writers; the heroine, Cynthia, is subjected to constant sexual harassment condoned as socially acceptable behaviour. The second volume of *David Simple* appeared in 1747, and the final volume in 1753.

Sarah Fielding's concern for female education is evident in *The Governess or The Little Female Academy* (1749). Its success as a (somewhat pious) moral novel for young people ensured that it stayed in print for over 150 years.

In 1754, Sarah Fielding published *The Cry*, a dramatic fable co-written with her friend Jane Collier. In this allegorical framework the heroine tells her story to representatives of truth and justice, malice and exploitation.

Samuel Richardson was the publisher of Sarah Fielding's next work, *The Lives of Cleopatra and Octavia*, in which the two characters give different versions of their lives. In 1759 Richardson again helped with the printing of *The History of The Countess of Dellwyn*, a further critique of male-dominated society. Her later works include *The History of Ophelia* (1760) and a translation of Xenophon's *Memoirs of Socrates* (1762).

Figes, Eva (b 1932)

Novelist and ▷ feminist writer. Born Eva Unger to a German Jewish family who escaped to England

in 1939 after the imprisonment of her father by
the Nazis. Educated at London University, she
worked in publishing before writing her first novel,
Equinox (1966), a partly autobiographical and largely
pessimistic account of a woman's search for meaning
and human relationships. The influence of ▷
Virginia Woolf is apparent in her exploration of the
inner world of the self and her lyrical sense of the
flux of experience and the continuity of memories.
Days (1974) and *The Seven Ages* (1986) seek to
establish an unrecorded female history, linking
many generations of women, while *Waking* (1981)
is structured around seven waking moments of a
woman or women. These ▷ modernist techniques
combine with the influence of ▷ Samuel Beckett in
Winter Journey (1967), which represents the inner
world of an old man dying alone. Figes has a sense
of herself as a European, and an awareness of the
Holocaust which is a part of her family history, and
draws on the work of one of the great European
modernists, Franz Kafka. *Konek Landing* (1969) is
a Kafkaesque story of victims and executioners in a
nameless country. Figes's work rejects the English
realist tradition in favour of a ▷ post-modernist
commitment to experiment, apparent especially in
B (1972), a self-reflexive novel about the nature of
creativity, and the problematic relations of reality
and fiction. She has written short stories, radio plays,
children's fiction, criticism, and a classic text of the
feminist movement, *Patriarchal Attitudes: Women in
Society* (1970). *Little Eden: A Child at War* (1978) is
autobiography. Her other novels are: *Nelly's Version*
(1977); *Light* (1983); *Ghosts* (1988).

Figures of Speech

Alliteration The beginning of accented syllables near
to each other with the same consonantal sound, as in
many idiomatic phrases: 'safe and sound': 'thick and
thin'; 'right as rain'. Alliteration is thus the opposite
of rhyme, by which the similar sounds occur at the
ends of the syllables: 'near and dear'; 'health and
wealth'.

Anacoluthon From the Greek: 'not following on'.
Strictly speaking, this is not a figure of speech, but
a grammatical term for a sentence which does not
continue the syntactical pattern with which it starts.
However, it may be used deliberately with the virtue
of intensifying the force of a sentence *eg* by the
sudden change from indirect to direct speech.

Anti-climax
See *Bathos* (below).

Antithesis A method of emphasis by the placing
of opposed ideas or characteristics in direct contrast
with each other.

Apostrophe A form of direct address often used by a
narrator in the middle of his narrative as a means of
emphasizing a moral lesson.

Assonance The rhyming of vowel sounds without
the rhyming of consonants.

Bathos From the Greek: 'death'. The descent from
the sublime to the ridiculous. This may be the result

of incompetence in the writer, but Alexander Pope
(1688–1744) used it skillfully as a method of ridicule:

> *Here thou, great ANNA! whom three realms
>   obey
> Dost sometimes counsel take – and sometimes
>   tea.*
>
>   (*The Rape of the Lock*)

Pope wrote an essay *Bathos, the Art of Sinking in
Poetry*, as a travesty of the essay by the Greek critic
Longinus, *On the Sublime* (1st century AD). Longinus
had great prestige as a critic in Pope's time.

Climax From the Greek: 'a ladder'. The climb
from lower matters to higher, with the consequent
satisfying of raised expectations.

Euphemism A mild or vague expression used to
conceal a painful or disagreeable truth, *eg* 'he passed
on' for 'he died'. It is sometimes used ironically.

Euphuism A highly artificial quality of style
resembling that of John Lyly's ▷ *Euphues*.

Hyperbole Expression in extreme language so as to
achieve intensity.

Innuendo A way of expressing dislike or criticism
indirectly, or by a hint; an insinuation.

Irony From the Greek: 'dissimulation'. A form of
expression by which the writer intends his meaning
to be understood differently and less favourably, in
contrast to his overt statement:

> *It is a truth universally acknowledged, that a single
> man in possession of a good fortune must be in want
> of a wife.*

This opening sentence of ▷ Jane Austen's *Pride and
Prejudice* is to be understood as meaning that the
appearance of such a young man in a neighbourhood
inspires very strong wishes in the hearts of mothers
of unmarried daughters, and that these wishes cause
the mothers to behave as though the statement were
indeed a fact.

Dramatic irony occurs when a character in a play
makes a statement in innocent assurance of its truth,
while the audience is well aware that he or she is
deceived.

Litotes Emphatic expression through an ironical
negative, *eg* 'She's no beauty', meaning that the
woman is ugly.

Malapropism A comic misuse of language, usually
by a person who is both pretentious and ignorant.
The term derives from the character Mrs Malaprop
in Sheridan's play *The Rivals* (1775). This comic
device had in fact been used by earlier writers, such
as Shakespeare in the portrayal of Dogberry in *Much
Ado About Nothing*.

Meiosis Understatement, used as a deliberate
method of emphasis by irony, *eg* 'Would you like to
be rich?' – 'I should rather think so!'

Metaphor A figure of speech by which unlike
objects are identified with each other for the purpose

of emphasizing one or more aspects of resemblance between them. A simple example: 'the camel is the ship of the desert'.

Mixed metaphor is a confused image in which the successive parts are inconsistent, so that (usually) absurdity results: 'I smell a rat, I see it floating in the air, but I will nip it in the bud', *ie* 'I suspect an evil, and I can already see the beginnings of it, but I will take action to suppress it.' However, mixed metaphor is sometimes used deliberately to express a state of confusion.

Dead metaphor is one in which the image has become so familiar that it is no longer thought of as figurative, *eg* the phrase 'to take steps', meaning 'to take action'.

Metonymy The naming of a person, institution or human characteristic by some object or attribute with which it is clearly associated, as when a king or queen may be referred to as 'the Crown'. Metonymy has taken on additional meanings since the advent of ▷ structuralism. One of the originators of Russian ▷ Formalism, ▷ Roman Jakobson, draws a distinction between 'metaphor' – the linguistic relationship between two different objects on the grounds of their similarity – and 'metonymy' as a means of establishing a relationship between two objects in terms of their contiguity. Where metaphor is regarded as a major rhetorical device in *poetry*, metonymy is more usually associated with *prose*. The critic and novelist ▷ David Lodge takes up this distinction in his book *The Modes of Modern Writing* (1977), and suggests that 'metaphor' and 'metonymy' constitute a structurally significant binary opposition that enables the distinction to be made between poetry and drama on the one hand, and prose on the other. Lodge emphasizes, however, that these terms are not mutually exclusive, but rather contribute to 'a theory of dominance of one quality over another'. Hence it is possible for a novel to contain 'poetic' effects and vice versa.

Oxymoron A figure of speech formed by the conjunction of contrasting terms; it derives from two Greek words meaning 'sharp and dull'.

Palindrome A word or sentence that reads the same backwards or forwards, *eg*

> *Lewd did I live; evil I did dwel*
> (Phillips, 1706)

Paradox A statement that challenges the mind by appearing to be self-contradictory.

Pathetic fallacy A term invented by the critic ▷ John Ruskin (*Modern Painters*, Vol. III, Pt. iv, Ch. 12) to denote the tendency common especially among poets to ascribe human emotions or qualities to inanimate objects, *eg* 'an angry sea'. Ruskin describes it by dividing writers into four classes: those who do not see it merely because they are insensitive; superior writers in whom it is a mark of sensitivity; writers who are better still and do not need it because they 'feel strongly, think strongly, and see truly'; and writers of the best sort who use it because in some instances they 'see in a sort untruly,

because what they see is inconceivably above them'. In general, he considers that the pathetic fallacy is justified when the feeling it expresses is a true one.

Personification A kind of metaphor, by which an abstraction or inanimate object is endowed with personality.

Play on words A use of a word with more than one meaning or of two words which sound the same in such a way that both meanings are called to mind. In its simplest form, as the modern pun, this is merely a joke. In the 16th and 17th centuries poets frequently played upon words seriously; this is especially true of Shakespeare and dramatists contemporary with him, and of the Metaphysical poets, such as John Donne and George Herbert.

This very serious use of puns or plays upon words decreased in the 18th century, when ▷ Samuel Johnson censured Shakespeare's fondness for puns (or, as Johnson called them, 'quibbles'). The reason for this disappearance of the serious 'play upon words' was the admiration of educated men for what Bishop Sprat in his *History of the Royal Society* (1667) called 'mathematical plainness of meaning', a criterion emulated by poets as well as by prose writers. In the 19th century, the play on words was revived by humorous writers and writers for children, such as Thomas Hood, Edward Lear and ▷ Lewis Carroll (▷ Children's books). Although their use of the pun was ostensibly comic, its effect in their writings is often unexpectedly poignant or even profound, especially in Carroll's 'Alice' books. Puns continued to be despised by the adult world of reason, but they could freely and revealingly be used in what was regarded as the childish world of nonsense and fantasy.

Modern poets and critics have recovered the older, serious use of the play on words. Ambiguity of meaning which in the 18th century was considered a vice of expression, is now seen as a quality of rich texture of expression, though of course 'good' and 'bad' types of ambiguity have to be distinguished. ▷ James Joyce used the technique with unprecedented elaboration in ▷ *Finnegans Wake*; William Empson revived the serious punning of Donne and Marvell in his poems, and investigated the whole problem in *Seven Types of Ambiguity* (1930). Just as admiration for mathematics and the physical sciences caused the decline of the play on words, so the revival of it has been partly due to the rise of another science, that of psychoanalysis, especially the school of ▷ Freud, with its emphasis on the interplay of conscious and unconscious meanings in the use of language.

Pun
See *Play on words* (above).

Simile Similar to metaphor, but in similes the comparison is made explicit by the use of a word such as 'like' or 'as'.

Syllepsis A figure of speech by which a word is used in a literal and a metaphorical sense at the same time, *eg* 'You have broken my heart and my best china vase'.

Synecdoche A figure of speech by which a part

is used to express a whole, or a whole is used to express a part, *eg* 'fifty sail' is used for fifty ships, or the 'smiling year' is used for the spring. In practice, synecdoche is indistinguishable from metonymy (see above). Like metonymy this figure depends upon a relationship of contiguity, and is regarded as one side of the opposition between 'poetry' and 'non-poetry'. Both metonymy and synecdoche operate by combining attributes of particular objects, therefore they are crucial rhetorical devices for the representation of reality, and are closely related to ▷ realism as a literary style insofar as they function referentially.

Transferred epithet The transference of an adjective from the noun to which it applies grammatically to some other word in the sentence, usually in such a way as to express the quality of an action or of behaviour, *eg* 'My host handed me a hospitable glass of wine', instead of 'My hospitable host handed me . . .'

Zeugma A figure similar to syllepsis (see above); one word used with two others, to only one of which it is grammatically or logically applicable.

Finnegans Wake (1939)
A novel by ▷ James Joyce. It is one of the most original experiments ever undertaken in the novel form, and the most difficult of his works to read. It purports to be one night in the life of a Dublin public-house keeper, H. C. Earwicker, and as he is asleep from the beginning to the end of the book, his experiences are all those of dream. The advantage of dream experience is that it is unrestricted by self-conscious logic, and operates by free association unrestrained by inhibitions. The basis of the 'story' is his relationships with his wife, Anna Livia Plurabelle, his daughter, Isobel, and his twin sons Shem and Shaun; it reaches out, however, into Irish and European myths as these are suggested to his sleeping consciousness by objects in his mean little house and neighbourhood. Joyce intends in fact to make Earwicker a type of 'Everyman'. The language is made by fusing together words so as to cause them – as in dreams – to suggest several levels of significance simultaneously; this is a device which had already been used playfully by ▷ Lewis Carroll in his poem 'Jabberwocky' in the dream story for children *Through the Looking-Glass* (1872). Joyce, however, in his desire to universalize Earwicker, freely combines words from foreign languages with English ones, so that Earwicker's mind becomes representatively European while remaining his own. The movement of the narrative is based on the ideas of the 18th-century Italian philosopher Vico, who believed that ages succeed each other – gods, heroes, men – and then recommence; this is followed out in Earwicker's successive identifications (as Adam, Humpty Dumpty, Christ, Cromwell, Noah, The Duke of Wellington etc.), until at the end of the book the final sentence is completed by the first sentence at its beginning. The Christian pattern of fall and resurrection also contributes to the structure of the work. Another important influence on Joyce was the psychological ideas of ▷ Sigmund Freud on the mechanism of repression and the characteristics of dream association. Study necessitates the assistance of such a work as *A Reader's Guide to Finnegans Wake* by W. Y. Tindall.

Firbank, Ronald (1886–1926)
Writer of witty fantasies whose extravagant humour derives from the subtly calculated and highly-wrought style. His best-known tales are probably *Vainglory* (1915); *Valmouth* (1919); *The Flower Beneath the Foot* (1923); *The Artificial Princess* (1934). His stylistic innovations, including his highly condensed imagery, are regarded by some critics as a major contribution to ▷ modernism.
Bib: Fletcher, I. K., *Memoir*; Forster, F. M., in *Abinger Harvest*; Brooke, J., *Firbank*.

Fire of London, The Great
In 1666 over 13,000 houses, 87 churches and the old St Paul's Cathedral were destroyed. Celebrated accounts of it occur in the contemporary diaries of ▷ John Evelyn and ▷ Samuel Pepys. Owing to disagreements among the citizens, the original and independent architect Christopher Wren (1632–1723) was not allowed to carry out his great plan for rebuilding the City, whose streets accordingly still follow the twisting lines of the old City; but he rebuilt St Paul's and many other churches. A beneficial consequence of the fire was that it ended the terrible epidemic of plague which had devastated London in 1665.

Fitz-Boodle, George Savage
The pen-name assumed by the novelist ▷ William Makepeace Thackeray for the 'Fitz-Boodle Papers' contributed to ▷ *Fraser's Magazine*, 1842–3.

Flat and Round Characters
A categorization of characters, proposed by ▷ E.M. Forster in his influential study, ▷ *Aspects of the Novel*. Flat characters are 'constructed round a single idea or quality'; they are types or caricatures (such as Mrs Micawber in ▷ Dickens's ▷ *David Copperfield*). Round characters (such as ▷ Defoe's ▷ *Moll Flanders*) are 'capable of surprising [the reader] in a convincing way'. The idea of the flat character has passed into general use in the derogatory form of the 'two-dimensional character', but Forster himself recognized the virtues as well as the limitations of the flat character.

Flaubert, Gustave (1821–80)
French novelist. His first novel, *Madame Bovary*, involved him in a court action for immorality on its publication in 1857. The story of the adultery of a doctor's wife in Normandy, it ironizes not only the Romanticism of the principal character, but also the unappealing bourgeois values of the characters around her and the parochial milieu from which she attempts to escape. The book is equally notable for its contribution to psychological realism in the form of *style indirect libre* (▷ free indirect discourse), a version of the ▷ 'stream of consciousness' technique regularly employed by ▷ Virginia Woolf and ▷ James Joyce. Flaubert's 1869 novel, *L'Education sentimentale*,

intended as the moral history of his generation, portrays the fruitless love of Frédéric Moreau for Mme Arnoux, against the background of 1840s Paris and the 1848 Revolution; love and politics prove comparable in misdirected and misrecognized opportunities, which defuse both the dynamism of character and the fulfilment of plot. History, together with religion, comes under renewed investigation in *Salammbô* (1862), *La Tentation de Saint Antoine* (1874) and *Trois Contes* (1877). These end in further equivocation, with the reader left uncertain about what values are to be derived from works so pervaded by irony and authorial impersonality. In the unfinished *Bouvard et Pécuchet* (1881), the work's eponymous protagonists are composed of the novels, guide books and folk-lore they avidly read, and conversely they take for reality what are only representations of it. In addition to foregrounding fictive processes, this novel also dwells on the stupidity of bourgeois society and the received ideas on which this society feeds, a Flaubertian theme since *Madame Bovary*.

In the 19th century, Flaubert was prized for his ▷ realism (he was also claimed by ▷ naturalism and rejected both labels), understood as psychological representation or the accumulation of circumstantial detail (called the 'reality effect' by ▷ Roland Barthes). Yet such detail in Flaubert tends to overwhelm rather than sharply define the character. Accordingly, the 20th century has valued him for his challenges to ▷ mimesis, including the traditional privileged ties between author and reader, writer and character, individual and society.

Focal character

The character within a narrative 'whose point of view orients the narrative perspective' (▷ Genette). Where there is a focal character, his or her sense impressions and/or perceptions are what the narrative presents to the reader. The focal character is distinguished from the ▷ narrator, since the latter may be a different person. For example, there may be an impersonal, extradiegetic (▷ frame narrative) narrator, focalizing through a character in the third person, as in ▷ Henry James's ▷ *The Ambassadors*, or the narrator and focal character may be the same person, but at different points in time, as in ▷ Charles Dickens's ▷ *David Copperfield*.

▷ Narratology; Focalization

Focalization

In ▷ narratology, focalization is an aspect of ▷ mood, and is adopted by ▷ Genette as a more precise term than 'point of view' to indicate the focus of a narrative. Internal focalization views events through the mind of a particular ▷ focal character, external focalization follows the experiences of a character without revealing his or her thoughts, while non-focalized narration is told by an impersonal narrator without restriction.

Ford, Ford Madox (Ford Hermann Hueffer) (1873–1939)

Novelist, critic, poet. His father was of German origin, and became music critic for ▷ *The Times*;

his mother was daughter of the Pre-Raphaelite painter Ford Madox Brown. Ford was first known as an aesthetic writer of fairy stories, but he became deeply interested in contemporary French writing and culture, and became a propagandist for the rigorous discipline of French art, exercising a strong personal influence on ▷ Joseph Conrad and Ezra Pound. He co-operated with Conrad on two novels, *The Inheritors* (1901) and *Romance* (1903). He was a prolific writer, but is now chiefly remembered for *The Good Soldier* (1915) and for the four novels known in Britain as *The Tietjens Tetralogy* (after the name of its hero), and in America as *Parade's End: Some Do Not* (1924), *No More Parades* (1925), *A Man Could Stand Up* (1926), and *Last Post* (1928). The tetralogy is regarded by some critics as the most memorable fiction about the war of 1914–18 (in which Ford served, although he was 40 on enlistment), and as the most remarkable account of the upheaval in English social values in the decade 1910–20. *The Good Soldier* is a subtle and ambiguous study of the cruelty, infidelity and madness below the respectable surface of the lives of two couples, and is notable for its use of an unreliable narrator.

Ford has an undoubted importance in literary history because of his personal influence. As a poet, he played a significant part in the founding of Imagism. In 1908–9 he was editor of the brilliant but short-lived *English Review*, to which ▷ Thomas Hardy, ▷ Henry James, ▷ H. G. Wells, ▷ Joseph Conrad and the Russian novelist ▷ Leo Tolstoy all contributed. He was an early encourager of ▷ D. H. Lawrence. Brought up in the relatively narrow Pre-Raphaelite and ▷ aesthetic movements, in the 1900s he was a central figure among the writers who were thinking radically about problems of artistic form, especially in novel-writing. He regarded the 19th-century English novel as too much a product of the accident of genius, and, aligning himself with James and Conrad, was in opposition to H. G. Wells who preferred the title of journalist to that of artist. After World War I he moved to Paris and became part of a circle of expatriate writers, including ▷ James Joyce, Ernest Hemingway and Gertrude Stein. He also founded the *Transatlantic Review*.

After 1930 his imaginative writing was somewhat neglected but he is now recognized as an important figure of the modernist movement. Of present-day novelists, he has perhaps had most effect on ▷ Graham Greene. Apart from *The Tietjens Tetralogy* and *The Good Soldier*, novels selected for praise include the historical trilogy about Tudor England (*The Fifth Queen*, 1906; *Privy Seal*, 1907; *The Fifth Queen Crowned*, 1908). His *Collected Poems* were published in 1936.

Bib: Cassell, R. A. (ed.), *Ford Madox Ford: Modern Judgements*; Green, R., *Ford Madox Ford, Prose and Politics*; Meixner, J. A., *Ford Madox Ford's Novels: A Critical Study*; Mizener, A., *The Saddest Story* (biography); Ohmann, C., *Ford Madox Ford: From Apprentice to Craftsman*.

Formalism

School of literary thought which flourished in Russia after 1917. Its main exponents, particularly

▷ Roman Jakobson, focused on the differentiation between literary language and other forms of written expression. The insights of the Formalists have influenced later critics.

  ▷ Defamiliarization; Deconstruction.

Forster, E. M. (Edward Morgan) (1879–1970)
Novelist. His work is primarily in a realistic mode, and his ideas in the liberal tradition; indeed, much of his work is concerned with the legacy of Victorian middle-class liberalism. He was educated at Tonbridge School (a public school whose ethos is characterized by Sawston in the first two novels) and then at King's College, Cambridge, of which he was later made an honorary fellow. Through contacts made at Cambridge he came to be associated with the ▷ Bloomsbury Group. He travelled in Europe, lived in Italy and Egypt, and spent some years in India, where he was for a time secretary to a rajah after World War I.

  Forster's novels are: *Where Angels Fear to Tread* (1905); *The Longest Journey* (1907); *A Room with a View* (1908); ▷ *Howards End* (1910); ▷ *A Passage to India* (1924); and *Maurice* (1971). The last of these, which has a homosexual theme, was published posthumously, as was *The Life to Come* (1972), a collection of stories, many of which treat the same theme. His other two collections of short stories are: *The Celestial Omnibus* (1914) and *The Eternal Moment* (1928). These are mainly early work; they were published in a collected edition in 1947. His high reputation rests mainly on his fiction, but he has also written biographies and essays which are important for understanding his outlook as an imaginative writer. The biography of his friend Goldsworthy Lowes Dickinson (1934) is about a Cambridge scholar who was an important leader of liberal political opinion; that of his great-aunt. Marianne Thornton (1956), is enlightening about Forster's background. *The Hill of Devi* (1953) is an account of his experiences in India. The essays in *Abinger Harvest* (1936) and *Two Cheers for Democracy* (1951) include expressions of his opinions about politics, literature and society. *Aspects of the Novel* (1927) is one of the best-known critical works on the novel form. He co-operated with Eric Crozier on the libretto for Benjamin Britten's opera *Billy Budd* (1951).

  Forster's dominant theme is the habitual conformity of people to unexamined social standards and conventions, and the ways in which this conformity blinds individuals to recognition of what is true in what is unexpected, to the proper uses of the intelligence, and to their own resources of spontaneous life. Spontaneous life and free intelligence also draw on traditions, and Forster shows how English traditions have on the one hand nourished complacency, hypocrisy, and insular philistinism, and on the other hand, humility, honesty, and sceptical curiosity. In several of the novels, and especially in *A Passage to India*, British culture is contrasted with a foreign tradition which has virtues that the British way of life is without. His style is consistently light and witty, with a use of irony which recalls ▷ Jane Austen and a use

of comedy of situation which recalls ▷ George Meredith. *A Passage to India* stands out from his work for the subtlety and resonance of its symbolism.
Bib: Trilling, L., *E. M. Forster*; McConkey, J., *The Novels of Forster*; Bradbury, M. (ed.), *E. M. Forster: A Collection of Critical Essays*; Stone, W., *The Cave and the Mountain*; Furbank, P.N., *E. M. Forster: A Life* (2 vols).

Forster, Margaret (b 1938)
Novelist. Forster has produced a steady stream of writings since the early 1960s, as well as the screenplay (from her own novel) for one of the classic films of 'Swinging Sixties' London, *Georgy Girl* (1966, directed by Silvio Narizzano). Her works are broadly feminist, and often centre on a female protagonist or on relationships between women. Her other works include: *Dames' Delight* (1964); *The Bogeyman* (1966); *The Seduction of Mrs Pendlebury* (1974); *Mother Can You Hear Me?* (1979) and *Marital Rites* (1982). She has also written a biography of Victorian poet Elizabeth Barrett Browning, and published *Significant Sisters: The Grassroots of Active Feminism 1839–1939*.

Forsyte Saga, The
A sequence of novels constituting a study of ▷ Victorian and ▷ Edwardian society by ▷ John Galsworthy. They comprise: *The Man of Property* (1906); *The Indian Summer of a Forsyte* (1918); *In Chancery* (1920). *Awakening* (1920); *To Let* (1921). A television serialization of the work in 1967 was extremely popular.

Forties, The Hungry
The decade 1840–50, so called because bad harvests caused serious food shortages, leading to mass agitation for abolition of the tax on imported corn (Anti-Corn Law League) and for a more democratic political system (the ▷ Chartist Movement). It was in the years 1845–51 that the Irish Famine took place: about 10 per cent of the population died from hunger and disease, and mass emigration ensued from those remaining.

  ▷ Corn Laws; Free Trade.

Fortnightly Review, The
The Fortnightly Review was founded in 1865 by, among others, the novelist ▷ Anthony Trollope. It was a vehicle of advanced liberal opinion, and included amongst its contributors the scientist ▷ Walter Bagehot, the positivist philosopher Frederic Harrison, the critics ▷ Matthew Arnold and Leslie Stephen, the novelists ▷ George Eliot and ▷ George Meredith, the poets D. G. Rossetti and Algernon Swinburne, and ▷ Walter Pater and ▷ William Morris, both of them leaders of social and critical thought.

Foucault, Michel (1926–84)
Along with ▷ Louis Althusser and ▷ Jacques Derrida, Foucault is one of the most influential of French philosophers whose work has been taken up by the practitioners of other disciplines. Foucault rejects the totalizing explanations of

human development in favour of a more detailed analysis of how power functions within particular ▷ discourses. In *Madness and Civilization* (1965) he explored the historical opposition between 'madness' and 'civilization', applying ▷ Saussure's notion of differentials (▷ difference) to the various ways in which society excludes the behaviour which threatens it. He later took this issue up in *Discipline and Punish* (1977), and *I Pierre Riviere* (1978). In *The Order of Things* (1971) and *The Archaeology of Knowledge* (1972) he investigated the ways in which human knowledge is organized, and the transition from discourses which rely upon a notion of 'self-presence', to those which operate differentially to produce the kind of linguistic self-consciousness characteristic of ▷ post-modernism. In essays such as those translated in *Language, Counter-memory, Practice* (1977), he sought to clarify specific areas of opposition through which discourse is constructed. At the time of his death he had embarked on an investigation of the discourses of sexuality through the ages, and the three volumes of *The History of Sexuality* (1978–87) have now been published.

▷ Archaeology.

Fourth Estate, The

Traditionally, and for political purposes, English society was thought until the 20th century to have three estates: the lords spiritual, the lords temporal, the commons. ▷ Carlyle alludes to a Fourth Estate, *ie* the press, implying that the newspapers have an essential role in the political functions of society. He attributed the phrase to the 18th-century statesman ▷ Edmund Burke.

Fowles, John (b 1926)

Novelist. Born in Essex and educated at Oxford University. His novels are: *The Collector* (1963); *The Magus* (1965; revised edition 1977); *The French Lieutenant's Woman* (1969); *Daniel Martin* (1977); *Mantissa* (1982); *A Maggot* (1985). He is an experimental writer, interested in the nature of fiction and its interaction with history and reality, but he combines this with a skill in story-telling and an ability to create compelling characters and a vivid sense of social context. Several of his novels have been best-sellers, and three: *The Collector, The Magus* and *The French Lieutenant's Woman* have been filmed. His reception by the critics had tended to be more enthusiastic in the U.S.A. than in Britain. The recurrent concerns of his novels are the power of repressive convention and social conformity, the enigmatic nature of sexual relations, the desire to manipulate and control and the problem of individual freedom. The last of these concerns reflects the influence of ▷ existentialism.

The Collector, the story of the kidnapping of an attractive and wealthy girl by an introverted clerk, is in part a study of a pathological desire for possession, and in part a fable about social deprivation. It is in three parts, the first and last narrated by the man, and the second by the girl. Fowles's novels are highly allusive: *The Magus*, like *The Collector*, employs parallels with Shakespeare's *The Tempest*. It also draws on the literary archetype of the quest in its

story of a young man who travels to a Greek island where he is lured by a series of magical illusions into a confrontation with existential uncertainty and freedom of choice. *The French Lieutenant's Woman* employs parody of 19th-century novelistic style, quotations from sociological reports, from ▷ Darwin, ▷ Marx, ▷ Arnold and Tennyson, and authorial interruptions. Fowles's belief in the fundamental uncertainty of existence is reflected in his use of open endings; in *The Magus* the future of the main characters is 'another mystery' and *The French Lieutenant's Woman* has a choice of endings. *Daniel Martin* is more realist than his earlier work, exploiting his descriptive skill in a range of settings: it has less of the element of mystery and a more clearly affirmative ending. He has also written a volume of short stories, *The Ebony Tower* (1974) and works of non-fiction, including: *Islands* (1978); *The Tree* (1979); *The Enigma of Stonehenge* (1980) and *Land* (1985).
Bib: Conradi, P., *John Fowles*; Loveday, S., *The Romances of John Fowles*.

Fox George (1624–91)

Religious leader. He founded the Society of Friends (▷ Quakers), and left a journal of his spiritual experience, published in 1694. Apart from its religious importance, Fox's Journal is one of the classics amongst the English ▷ diaries.

Frame, Janet (b 1924)

New Zealand novelist and short-story writer, a major figure in contemporary New Zealand fiction. Her collection of stories, *The Lagoon* (1951) and her trilogy of novels *Owls Do Cry* (1957), *Faces in the Water* (1961) and *The Edge of the Alphabet* (1962) are about childhood innocence and the imagination, both threatened by bereavement and a repressive society. *Scented Gardens for the Blind* (1963) and *The Adaptable Man* (1965) explore the limitations and potentialities of language. Of her later work, *Intensive Care* (1970), written while Frame was in the U.S.A., draws on the horrors of the Vietnam War for a visionary satire on the place of war in the New Zealand consciousness. Her other novels are: *Living in the Maniototo* (1979); *A State of Siege* (1982); *The Carpathians* (1988). Other story collections: *You Are Now Entering the Human Heart* (1983). She has also written three volumes of autobiography: *To the Is-Land* (1983); *An Angel at My Table* (1984); *The Envoy from Mirror City* (1985). The 1990 film, *An Angel at My Table*, was based on these volumes.

Frame narrative, first-order narrative, extradiegetic narrative

Terms used for the outside or first narrative in a fiction, where this encloses a second-order narrative. For example, ▷ Conrad's ▷ *Heart of Darkness* has a frame narrative of a group of men sitting on a boat on the Thames; one of them, Marlow, narrates a second-order narrative about his experiences in Africa.

Frankenstein, or the Modern Prometheus (1817)

A philosophical romance which is also a tale of terror, by ▷ Mary Shelley. It belongs in part to

the 'Gothic' tradition of tales of terror popular at the time and partly to a philosophical tradition going back to ▷ Rousseau, concerned with themes of isolation, suffering and social injustice. Mary Shelley originally wrote it to compete with the tales of terror being composed for their own amusement by her lover and later husband, P. B. Shelley and their friend, the poet Lord Byron. Frankenstein is a Swiss student of natural philosophy who constructs a monster and endows it with life. Its impulses are benevolent, but it is everywhere regarded with loathing and fear; its benevolence turns to hatred, and it destroys its creator and his bride.
   ▷ Gothic Novels.

Fraser's Magazine
It started in 1830 as an imitator of ▷ *Blackwood's*, but after the mid-19th century it became Liberal. It published Carlyle's ▷ *Sartor Resartus* in 1833–4; at this time it was under the influence of ▷ Coleridge's Conservative philosophy. In 1848 it was publishing ▷ Charles Kingsley's novel of idealistic reform, *Yeast*. The historian J. A. Froude was its editor 1861–74, and tried to publish ▷ Ruskin's radical treatise on the nature of wealth, *Munera Pulveris* (1862–3), but this proved unpopular with the public, and the treatise was left unfinished. The magazine folded in 1882.

Frayn, Michael (b 1933)
British dramatist and novelist. His first plays, *Jamie* (1968) and *Birthday* (1969) were written for television. Since then he has acquired a reputation both as a leading comic writer for the stage, particularly with his production of *Noises Off* (1982), and an important translator of ▷ Chekhov's plays. Other plays include: *The Two of Us* (1970); *The Sandboy* (1971); *Alphabetical Order* (1975); *Donkeys' Years* (1976); *Clouds* (1976); *Liberty Hall* (1980); *Make and Break* (1980); *Benefactors* (1984). Translations: *The Cherry Orchard* (1978); *The Fruits of Enlightenment* (1979); *Three Sisters* (1983); *Number One* (1984); *Wild Honey* (1984); *The Seagull* (1986); *Uncle Vanya* (1988). Novels include: *The Tin Men* (1965); *The Russian Interpreter* (1966); *Towards the End of the Morning* (1967); *A Very Private Life* (1968); *Sweet Dreams* (1973); *A Landing on the Sun* (1991); *Now You Know* (1992)

Frazer, Sir James G. (1854–1941)
Anthropologist. His *Golden Bough* (1890–1915) is a vast study of ancient mythology; it has influenced 20th-century poetry such as T. S. Eliot's *The Waste Land*. An abridged edition was published in 1922. Other publications include: *Totemism* (1887); *Adonis, Attis, Osiris, Studies in the History of Oriental Religion* (1906); *Totemism and Exogamy* (1910); *Folklore in the Old Testament* (1918). Frazer was a major influence on the development of 20th-century anthropology and psychology, and in addition edited works by William Cowper and Joseph Addison.

Free indirect discourse
A technique whereby a narrative reports the speech or thoughts of a character, referring to that character in the third person but adopting the character's own idiom. Free indirect discourse thus falls between direct speech (or thought), which quotes a character's words verbatim, and reported speech (or thought), which paraphrases the speech or thoughts of the character in the idiom of the ▷ narrator. When free indirect discourse is used there is often a productive ambiguity as to which judgements are attributable to the character and which to the narrator and/or ▷ implied author. Also known as free indirect speech and (using the French term) as *style indirect libre*.

Free trade
Nowadays the term is understood to mean trade between nations without restrictions either in the form of the prohibition of certain commodities or in duties (taxes) on their importation. The view that trade should be so conducted was expressed most influentially in ▷ Adam Smith's *Wealth of Nations* (1776). In the 19th century free trade particularly suited English industrialists and it became a leading issue between the ▷ Whigs who represented industrial interests and the Tories who wished to protect agricultural ones. The repeal of the ▷ Corn Laws, which had imposed taxes on imported corn, was a decisive victory for the free-traders, though the policy of governments has always fluctuated, and trade has never been entirely free. Although most countries practise certain trade restrictions, the British Conservative government of the 1980s has encouraged a greater freedom than most.
   In the early 17th century the term was used for trade unrestricted by the monopolies granted (for a price) by the Crown to certain individuals. In the 18th century the term was a euphemism for smuggling.

French influence on English fiction
Invasion – the Norman invasion of England – may seem a suitably arresting way of establishing a starting point for the initial impact of France upon England. However, in all important senses this is too dramatic and too imprecise. It severely underestimates the degree of contact between Britain and the Continent before and after the Norman Conquest with Latin as the *lingua franca*.
   Later, in the 12th century Chrétien de Troyes's romances, as well as Marie de France's *Lais*, jointly suppose a sophisticated readership acquainted with Arthurian background and named settings, usually in southern England and Wales. This period was one of intense literary activity which benefited England through the marriage of Henry II with Eleanor of Aquitaine. The civilization of the southern French courts became available throughout England and elsewhere in Europe fuelled the revolution in courtly attitudes which was to affect the Italian poets ▷ Dante and Petrarch (1304–74). The English vernacular itself resorted to imitation as a means of securing its own achievements. Such imitative activity reaches an apogee with ▷ Chaucer. If his prioress spoke her French 'after the scole of Stratford atte Bowe', Chaucer himself was more fully conversant, as is attested by *The Book of the Duchess*, *The House of Fame* and *The Merchant's Tale*,

the last itself stimulated by the popularity of the *lai* (lay). Similar observations could be made about Sir Thomas Malory's contacts with France. At the same time, Chaucer translated Guillaume de Lorris's *Le Roman de la Rose* and in the later Middle Ages there are also adaptations and translations of earlier epic and romance works. Thus the history of the cross-Channel literary flow from France to England is to no small degree the history of the translations and adaptations undergone by French literature.

The influence of Petrarch, felt early on both sides of the Channel, was prolonged by the Italian vogue prevalent in France in the 1550s–70s. It is noticeable that poetry is the favoured genre for imitation, possibly because in France itself it is at once the most deeply exploited and the most cohesively organized. Of French drama there is no trace in England; and the fortunes of prose are the fortunes of translation, as represented most momentously in Shakespeare's recourse to John Florio for ▷ Montaigne's essay *Des Cannibales* for *The Tempest*. Yet while Montaigne can unquestionably be said to have had a hand in shaping the English essay form, ▷ Rabelais leaves more elusive traces and to discern his equivalent in English literature, one has to look as close to the Renaissance as Sir John Harington (?1560–1612), ▷ Thomas Nashe and Samuel Butler (1612–80), and as far forward as ▷ Laurence Sterne and ▷ James Joyce.

Florio and Sir Thomas Urquhart (1611–60) – Rabelais's 17th-century translator – are authors in their own right. At the same period, Joshua Sylvester's (c 1563–1618) translation of Guillaume de Salluste Du Bartas was no less influential. With the rise of the novel, Sterne can be found looking back to Rabelais rather than to contemporary French influence. But the important French work in the 18th century was the result of a collective enterprise rather than an individual piece: the ▷ *Encyclopédie*. It provided a focus for the *philosophes*, ▷ Diderot, Voltaire (1694–1778) and ▷ Rousseau, a forum larger than that which Voltaire, for example, enjoyed with ▷ John Locke. More famously, its criticisms of the ▷ Ancien Régime prefigured the French Revolution. It might be possible to see Wordsworth's *Prelude* as a transposed re-enactment of this yoking of *Encyclopédie* and revolution.

Throughout the 19th century, French and English prose entertained constant rapport, beginning with ▷ Stendhal whose *Chroniques pour l'Angleterre* were journalistic pieces aimed at a broad literate public. As a novelist, Stendhal beheads (*Le Rouge et Le Noir*) or cloisters away (*La Chartreuse de Parme*) those romantic heroes he had absorbed from a reading of Byron and English Romantics. By contrast, ▷ Balzac could stand for a more fully socialized version of the novelist's enterprise. If Stendhal is closer to the romance, Balzac is closer to epic; his individuals are bonded to large-scale social change and evolution, Empire to Restoration, aristocracy to bourgeoisie. The vigour or decay of the individual is analogous to the vigour or decay of the social unit. The individual is not part of, a token for, society and made or unmade by it. He or she absorbs society and seeks to act upon it according to his or her will. Balzac's

characters are accordingly all larger than the ▷ realism of which they are taken to be the accredited representatives. As with ▷ Dickens's characters, their fictional representation is constantly extended beyond the terms set for ▷ mimesis alone.

Another version of the social story is followed in ▷ Flaubert. His task was, he said, to demoralize us; and he commences his career as a novelist by poisoning his romantic heroine, Emma Bovary. Flaubert progressively narrates the interwoven failures of individual and society, which are simultaneously a vitiation of historical and emotional plots (*L'Education sentimentale*) and the liquidation of character into cliché (*Bouvard et Pécuchet*) Flaubert's use of irony and his quasi-deconstructionist approach moves him closer to Stendhal than to Balzac, and it may be argued that no English novelist of the period exploited irony to so refined a degree as Stendhal and Flaubert.

Despite Champfleury's (Jules Fleury, 1821–69) manifesto of 1857, realism was never a fixed body of doctrine consciously adhered to by all its supposed exponents. Nonetheless, it was as a realist that Flaubert was most admired in Britain, and the position of French realism was secured when ▷ Emile Zola experimented with veins of psychological determinism traced throughout several generations and several members of two families. Human beings in Zola may seem to be weasels fighting in a hole, yet as the advocate of ▷ naturalism (realism's more exact and scientific successor) Zola helped give impetus to British social and psychological realism explored by ▷ George Gissing and Arthur Morrison (1863–1945), ▷ George Moore and ▷ Arnold Bennett (the latter's *Journal* is based on the brothers ▷ Goncourt, also exponents of naturalism). Arguably, this vein proved consistently richer for the development of the English novel than the experimentation associated in France with the names of ▷ Proust and ▷ André Gide and reflected in the Anglo-Saxon world in the work of ▷ Henry James, ▷ Virginia Woolf and James Joyce. Unreliable protagonists narrating from a restricted angle of vision, disjointed temporal sequences, endings without full resolution – these became familiar devices in the first three decades of this century, but they had their counterparts principally in America rather than in Britain.

In France, this early opening up of the novel proved indispensable to the post-World War II developments – the overlapping of criticism and literature gravitating around the French ▷ *nouveau roman* (new novel). The trajectory between the two points is admittedly not unilinear, and ▷ existentialist writing – which dominated the war years and through into the 1950s – projected a more traditional use of the novel (and for theatre) as dramatizing, faced with the absurd, the urgent choices of 'the human condition' (this was Montaigne's term before it became André Malraux's). The existentialist idiom caught a public mood and proved popular in Britain. If for existentialism the world existed to be acted upon and in, for the *nouveau roman* the world simply is. It cannot be colonized by mere human presence or behaviour nor is it open to shaping by intellectual speculation. In the circumstances, the unresponsiveness of things to words throws the attention back on to language itself. The caterpillar which the narrator insistently describes in Alain Robbe-Grillet's *La Jalousie* (1957) yields a plurality of meanings. Thus the *nouveau roman* anticipates and nurtures as well as illustrates ▷ Roland Barthes's encoded narratives, ▷ Mikhail Bakhtin's carnival, ▷ Jacques Lacan's dispossessed human subject, and ▷ post-structuralism's play of the signifier. As a movement, the *nouveau roman* was a formidable alliance of literature with psychology, philosophy, the human sciences in general.

One crucial result of this activity in France has been the revision of the literary canon: ▷ Marquis de Sade, ▷ Comte de Lautréamont and Mallarmé have long since taken their place alongside ▷ Samuel Beckett, Georges Bataille (1897–1962) and Maurice Blanchot (b 1907) to provide the instrumental forces of disruption which unsettle rather than confirm assumptions about the world (narrative or real). Thus current French objections to realism are not simply objections to a world view taken as paradigmatic for literature, they are equally objections to a type of critical view which sponsors such a world view as natural, co-extensive with the order of things. There is no immediate parallel in Britain for this overall reassessment in theory as well as literature. There are nonetheless equivalents and adaptations. In the novel, these include ▷ John Fowles's experiments, most notably in *The Magus* (1966) and *The French Lieutenant's Woman* (1969), William Boyd's (b 1952) splicing of Rousseau and cinema in *The New Confessions* (1987), ▷ Julian Barnes's witty and humorously ironical recreation of Flaubert in *Flaubert's Parrot* (1984). All of these tend to question realism of character psychology, plot motivation and narrative expectation. Contemporary British ▷ feminism mirrors the coherence of the French position and its iconoclastic thrust, blending theoretical reflection with literary production. It has undoubtedly been stimulated by the work of ▷ Julia Kristeva and ▷ Hélène Cixous amongst others, and has drawn on the theoretical investigations of Jacques Lacan and ▷ Jacques Derrida.

French Revolution (1789–94)

The immediate effect of the French Revolution was to abolish the French monarchy, to reduce forever the rigid class division of French society, and to begin wars (lasting till 1815) which for the time being extensively altered the map of Europe. Its lasting effect was to inspire the European mind with the belief that change is historically inevitable and static order unnatural, and to imbue it with modern ideas of democracy, nationalism and equality, at least of opportunity.

The immediate effect on England was confusing, for many of the changes being brought about in France had already occurred here in the 17th century, especially the establishment of the sovereignty of the elected representatives of the people in Parliament in 1688. Such changes had occurred here, however, without the same upheavals, partly because English society and politics had always been more fluid than in the other larger states of Europe, and though unjustified privileges and inequalities existed, there were few definable between the ▷ Whigs on the left who were neutral or sympathetic to the Revolution, and the Tories on the right who feared it from the start. Only when General Bonaparte took increasing charge of France and became Emperor Napoleon I in 1804 did Britain become united in fear of French aggression. However, ▷ Edmund Burke published in 1790 his ▷ *Reflections on the Revolution in France*, one of the most eloquent documents of English political thinking, foretelling the disasters which the Revolution was to bring, and condemning it as ruthless surgery on the living organism of society. His opponent ▷ Tom Paine answered him with *The Rights of Man* (1791),and the younger intellectuals agreed with Paine. Wordsworth wrote later in *The Prelude* 'Bliss was it in that dawn to be alive', and William Blake wore a revolutionary cockade in the streets; Robert Southey and ▷ Coleridge planned the ideal communist society, Pantisocracy; the philosophic novelist ▷ William Godwin published *Political Justice* and *Caleb Williams* to prove that reason was the only guide to conduct and society needed by man. Later Wordsworth and Coleridge came round to a view closer to Burke's, and the younger generation, Byron and Shelley, saw them as traitors; the more so because the defeat of Napoleon at Waterloo introduced a phase of political and social repression everywhere. But the older generation (except perhaps Southey) did not so much go back on their earlier enthusiasms as think them out more deeply; the philosophical conservatism of the older Coleridge was as radical in its thinking as the ▷ Utilitarianism of the philosophical radicals, ▷ Bentham and James and ▷ John Stuart Mill. Fear of revolution, prompted by the French model, is evident in ▷ Dickens's novel ▷ *A Tale of Two Cities*.

Frequency

One of the five categories in which ▷ Genette analyses narrative discourse, frequency is concerned with the relationship between how many times a fictional event took place, and how many times it is narrated. Frequency, ▷ duration and ▷ order are matters of temporal arrangement or 'tense'; the other two categories are ▷ mood ▷ voice.

Freud, Sigmund (1856–1939)

The founder of psychoanalysis, and one of the seminal figures of 20th-century thought. Born in Moravia, then part of the Austro-Hungarian Empire, he settled in Vienna. He began his career as a doctor specializing in the physiology of the nervous system and, after experimenting briefly with hypnosis, developed the technique of free association for the treatment of hysteria and neurosis. His work is based on a number of principles. The first is psychic determinism, the principle that all mental events, including dreams, fantasies, errors and neurotic symptoms, have meaning. The second is the primacy of the unconscious mind in mental life, the unconscious being regarded as a dynamic force drawing on the energy of instinctual drives, and as the location of desires which are repressed because they are socially unacceptable or a threat to the ego. The third is a developmental view of human life, which stresses the importance of infantile experience and accounts for personality in terms of the progressive channelling of an initially undifferentiated energy or libido. Important aspects of ▷ psychoanalytical theory and practice arising from these principles include the theory of infantile sexuality and its development, centred on the ▷ Oedipus Complex, the techniques of free association and dream interpretation as means of analysing repressed material, and the beliefs that much behaviour is unconsciously motivated, that sexuality plays a major role in the personality, and that civilization has been created by the direction of libidinous impulses to symbolic ends (including the creation of art). Freud regarded neurotic and normal behaviour as differing in degree rather than kind.

Despite his scientific orientation, Freud's thought had affinities with that of the Romantic poets, and several features of modern literature which show his influence also have Romantic antecedents. These include a particular interest in the quality and significance of childhood experience, a fascination with memory and with what is buried in the adult personality, and a concern with disturbed states of consciousness. Such features are found in the work of ▷ James Joyce and ▷ Virginia Woolf, as well as many later writers. The ▷ stream of consciousness technique and other experimental narrative techniques which abandon external realism in favour of the rendering of consciousness, of dreams or of fantasies, owe much to Freud's belief in the significance of these areas of experience, which had been relatively neglected by scientific thought. Furthermore, the technique of free association revealed a tendency of the mind, when rational constraints were lessened, to move towards points of psychic conflict, and this discovery helped to validate new means of structuring literary works,

through association, symbol, and other forms of non-rationalistic patterning (for example in the work of T. S. Eliot). The view that the individual's unconscious life is as important as his or her public and social self is crucial to much 20th-century literature a notable example being the work of ▷ D. H. Lawrence, which rests on the assumptions that human beings live through their unconscious, and that sexuality is central to the personality. The Freudian unconscious is in particular the realm of fantasy, and Freudian thought has encouraged the belief that fantasy is of profound significance in our lives, with considerable consequences for literary forms and modes.

Psychoanalysis has developed very considerably since Freud, and continues to interact with literary practice and theory. In the field of theory, those who have studied but radically revised Freud's ideas, such as ▷ Jacques Lacan and ▷ feminist theorists, have been especially important.

Bib: Brown, J. A. C., *Freud and the Post-Freudians*; Freud, S., *Introductory Lectures on Psychoanalysis*.

Fuller, Roy (b 1912)

Poet and novelist. Fuller was born in Lancashire, and trained and worked as a solicitor. He began writing in the 1930, and published two volumes of poetry whilst he was in the Royal Navy during World War II: *The Middle of a War* (1942) and *A Lost Season* (1944) (his first volume appeared in 1939). His more recent publications include: *Counterparts* (1954); *Collected Poems* (1962) and *From the Joke Shop* (1975). His novels are restrained in tone and style but frequently express an underlying psychological tension as well as a sharp, though understated, critique of social practices. They include: *With My Little Eye* (1948); *The Second Curtain* (1953), *Fantasy and Fugue* (1954); *Image of a Society* (1956); *The Ruined Boys* (1959); *The Father's Comedy* (1961); *The Perfect Fool* (1963); *My Child, My Sister* (1965); *The Carnal Island* (1970); *Stares* (1990).

G

Gael, Gaelic
The Scottish Highland branch of the Celtic race and its language. The words are sometimes used for the Scottish and Irish Celts together.

Galloway, Janice (b 1956)
Novelist. Galloway is one of a group of Glasgow writers that has emerged since the 1980s (▷ Gray, Alasdair; ▷ Kelman, James). She has also worked as a teacher. *Blood* (1991) is a collection of stories which explore feminist issues of identity and autonomy through a mixture of realism and fantasy and an inventive use of language.

Galsworthy, John (1867–1933)
Novelist and dramatist. As a novelist, his reputation was high in the first quarter of this century for his surveys of upper-class English life, especially the ▷ *Forsyte Saga* sequence (1906–21) and *A Modern Comedy* (*The White Monkey*, 1924; *The Silver Spoon*, 1926; *Swan Song*, 1928). After World War I, Galsworthy underwent severe criticism by novelists of the new generation as different as ▷ Virginia Woolf ('Modern Fiction' in *The Common Reader*, 1925) and ▷ D. H. Lawrence ('John Galsworthy', in *Phoenix*, 1927). These novelist-critics were writing in a period of rich experiment in rendering the inwardness of human experience and in testing and renewing humane values in the social context; to them, Galsworthy was artistically an obstructive conservative, severely limited to a vision of the outside of social phenomena and to a merely social definition of human beings. From such attacks, Galsworthy's reputation has never recovered among the intelligentsia; however, the popularity of a televised serial version of the *Forsyte Saga* in 1967 suggests that he may still be favoured by at least the older generation of the general public. His other novels are: *Jocelyn* (1898); *The Country House* (1907); *Fraternity* (1909); *The Patrician* (1911); *The Freelands* (1915); *Maid in Waiting* (1931); *Flowering Wildness* (1932).

As a dramatist, Galsworthy was one of those in the first decade of the century who restored to the English theatre a substantiality of subject-matter which had long been missing from it. His plays dramatized ethical problems arising from social issues. These too, however, have lost prestige, partly because of weaknesses similar to those that his novels are supposed to suffer from. Another criticism of the plays is that he brought to the theatre a novelist's vision rather than a dramatist's: during the last 50 years, British dramatists have believed that the drama requires an approach to the depiction of character and to the use of dialogue which is different to the vision of the novelist. Plays: *The Silver Box* (1906); *Joy* (1907); *Strife* (1909); *Justice* (1910); *The Pigeon* (1912); *The Eldest Son* (1912); *The Fugitive* (1913); *The Skin Game* (1920); *Loyalties* (1922); *The Forest* (1924).
▷ Realism.
Bib: Barker, D., *A Man of Principle*; Marrot, H. V., *The Life and Letters of John Galsworthy*; Fréchet, A., *John Galsworthy, A Reassessment*.

Galt John (1779–1839)
Scottish writer of poems, travels, dramas and novels. He is chiefly remembered for his novels, especially *The Ayrshire Legatees* (1821), *Annals of the Parish* (1821), *The Provost* (1822) and *The Entail* (1823). These are vivid, realistic, humorous accounts of Scottish provincial society.
Bib: Gordon, R. K., *John Galt*; Aberdein, J. W., *John Galt*; Parker, W. M., *Susan Ferrier and John Galt* (British Council).

Gargantua
A giant, chiefly known as the hero of ▷ François Rabelais's romances *Gargantua* and *Pantagruel*, though he had a previous existence in French folk-lore connected with the Arthurian legends. He is mentioned in Shakespeare's *As You Like It* II. 2 before Rabelais had been translated into English (1653), though Shakespeare may have read Rabelais in French.

Garner, Alan (b 1934)
Novelist and writer for children. Many of Garner's works are set in his home territory of Cheshire, and the south Manchester landmark Alderley Edge figures particularly prominently as the setting for a series of fantasy plots which mingle contemporary reality with an uncanny sense of the mythic past, which cause alternative values and belief systems to erupt into the present. Garner draws particularly on Celtic mythology and the beliefs of pre-Christian religions (especially in his first novels, *The Weidtone of Brisingamen*, 1960, *Elidor*, 1965, and *The Owl Service*, 1967), and is also interested in the fictional possibilities of parallel time scales and relativity, which he explores in the more adult novel, *Red Shift* (1973). More recent works include *The Stone Book Quartet* (1976–8).
▷ Children's books.

Gaskell, Elizabeth Cleghorn (1810–65)
Novelist and biographer. She spent her married life in Manchester. She and her husband, who was a ▷ Unitarian minister, first intended to write the annals of the Manchester poor, in the manner of the poet George Crabbe (1754–1832) and her first novel, ▷ *Mary Barton* (1848), presented the outlook of the industrial workers with justice and sympathy sufficient to anger some of the employers. The novel appealed to ▷ Charles Dickens and she published her best known work ▷ *Cranford* (1851–3) in his periodical, ▷ *Household Words*. *Cranford* has been compared with the work of ▷ Jane Austen; it is slighter but has some of Jane Austen's ability to endow smallness of circumstance with large implications. It is a study of a small circle in a small town, modelled on Knutsford, Cheshire. *Ruth* (1853) is based on the same place. ▷ *North and South* (1854–5) is another study of industrial relations, centred this time on a south English heroine who comes to the north as to a foreign country. *Sylvia's Lovers* (1863) is more romantic than her previous work; in the same year appeared *A Dark Night's Work*; *Cousin Phyllis and other Tales*. Her masterpiece, ▷ *Wives and Daughters*, was not quite completed

at her death. It belongs to the *Cranford* strain in her work but has greater richness, substance and variety. Her novels are an interesting connecting link between those of Jane Austen and those of ▷ George Eliot. She lacks the greatness of either and her reputation has unfairly suffered by comparison with them, but her achievement is substantial and enduring.

Her biography of her friend ▷ Charlotte Brontë, published in 1857, is accounted one of the best in English.
Bib: Hopkins, A. B., *Life*; Cecil, D., *Early Victorian Novelists*; Haldane, E., *Mrs Gaskell and her Friends*; Tillotson, K. (on *Mary Barton*) in *Novels of the Eighteen-Forties*; Gérin, W., *Elizabeth Gaskell: A Biography*; Easson, A., *Elizabeth Gaskell*.

Gawain and the Green Knight
One of the four later 14th-century alliterative (▷ Figures of speech) narratives attributed to the Gawain poet, which survives, along with *Patience*, *Cleanness* and *Pearl*, in a single manuscript. While the other poems address explicitly Christian topics and material, *Gawain and the Green Knight* tackles the traditions and conventions of Arthurian romance in a brilliant and complex narrative, structured around a series of interlocking games which have potentially very serious outcomes.

The story tells how a mysterious Green Knight visits King Arthur's court on New Year's Eve, offering a game. He offers any knight the opportunity to strike his head with an enormous axe if, in return, the knight agrees to submit to a return blow the following year. Gawain accepts the challenge on behalf of the court, and beheads the Green Knight, who proceeds to pick up his head and leave Arthur's court, reminding Gawain of his promise to come to his Green Chapel in a year for a return blow. The following year Gawain embarks on his quest for the Green Chapel, and takes refuge over the Christmas period in the castle of one Sir Bertilak. There Gawain gets involved in another game: for three days Bertilak is to go hunting and present Gawain with his winnings every evening. In return Gawain is to give Bertilak whatever he has won during the day at the castle. Over the next three days Gawain is subject to the attentions of Bertilak's beautiful wife as he rests in bed. His chastity, loyalty to his host, and courtesy are tested, for in defending himself against the lady's advances, Gawain has to avoid any offence to her. At the end of every one of the three days Gawain has kisses to exchange for the spoils of Bertilak's hunting expeditions. However, on the final day Gawain does not hand over the green girdle he has accepted from the wife (she has claimed it has magic qualities and will protect Gawain's life against any threat). Gawain, wearing the green girdle, leaves Bertilak's court, and eventually finds the Green Chapel and the Green Knight. There Gawain is made to submit to three feints from the axe of the Green Knight, the last just cutting the flesh of his neck. Although Gawain is overjoyed at having survived his ordeal, his mood changes as the Green Knight reveals his identity and the mechanics of the games which Gawain has played. The Green Knight and Sir Bertilak are the same figure: the outcome of Gawain's experience at the Green Chapel has depended on how honestly he has played the exchange of winnings game at the castle. Gawain's slight wound repays his retention of the girdle, which the Green Knight now excuses. Gawain is mortified, and vows to wear the girdle as a sign of his shame and failure, but is feted as a great hero on his return to Arthur's court. Henceforth all the members of Arthur's court decide to wear a green girdle.

There are analogues in earlier French romances and Welsh narrative for the beheading game and the exchange of winnings game, but not for their combination. The power and skill of the narrative technique of *Gawain* is reflected in the enormous amount of modern critical interest in the poem, but there is hardly any evidence at all which illuminates its contemporary reception.
Bib: Burrow, J. A., *A Reading of Gawain and the Green Knight*; Tolkien, J. R. R., Gordon, E. V. and Davis, N (eds.), *Gawain and the Green Knight*.

Gender
Originally used to distinguish between the categories of 'masculine' and 'feminine'. In modern ▷ feminist criticism it denotes something more than the different physical characteristics of both sexes. Feminist criticism regards 'masculinity' and 'femininity' as primary social constructions, supported by a range of cultural phenomena. The relationship between men and women is seen in material terms as a process of domination and subordination which functions objectively in material relations, but also subjectively in the ways in which men and women think of themselves. The concept of gender draws attention to the objective and subjective constructions of sexual difference, making possible an understanding of the mechanisms by which they operate, and offering the possibility of change.

There is a difference between the more sociological accounts and those – sometimes psychoanalytically based – which suggest there is something irreducible and specific in the nature of sexual difference. Here 'gender' is not one cultural label among others, but a firmly established basis for identity, as masculine or feminine (and not necessarily according to biological sex).
▷ *Écriture féminine*.

Genealogy
▷ Archaeology.

Genette, Gérard (b 1930)
French critic. His book *Narrative Discourse* (1980, translated by Jane E. Lewin) provides one of the most systematic and thorough categorizations of forms and modes of narrative.
▷ Narratology; Structuralism.

Genre
In its use in the language of literary criticism the concept of 'genre' proposes that particular groups of texts can be seen as parts of a system of representations agreed between writer and reader. For example, a work such as ▷ Aristotle's

Poetics isolates those characteristics which are to be found in a group of dramatic texts which are given the generic label 'tragedy'. The pleasure which an audience derives from watching a particular tragedy emanates in part from its fulfilling certain requirements stimulated by expectations arising from within the form itself. But each particular tragedy cannot be reduced simply to the sum of its generic parts. It is possible to distinguish between a tragedy by Sophocles, another by Shakespeare, or another by Edward Bond, yet at the same time to acknowledge that they all conform in certain respects to the narrative and dramatic rules laid down by the category 'tragedy'. Each example, therefore, repeats certain characteristics which have come to be recognized as indispensable features of the genre, but each one also exists in a relationship of difference from the general rule. The same kind of argument may be advanced in relation to particular sorts of poetry, or novel. The concept of genre helps to account for the particular pleasures which readers/spectators experience when confronted with a specific text. It also offers an insight into one of the many determining factors which contribute to the formation of the structure and coherence of any individual text.

Gentleman

The French '*gentil homme*' meant 'nobleman', man of aristocratic descent. The tradition of courtly love required, however, that a gentleman's behaviour should correspond to his birth, *eg* in ▷ Chaucer's 14th-century translation of the *Roman de la Rose*: 'he is gentil bycause he doth as longeth to a gentylman'. By the 15th century, a gentleman did not necessarily own land, and at no time in the Middle Ages was a coat of arms considered a necessary adjunct to the rank. By the 16th century, however, the connection between the gentleman and the fighting man was established, and coats of arms, whose original function had been to distinguish a man for his followers and friends in battle, were regarded as indispensable. They could be obtained for money from the Heralds' College (as Shakespeare's father obtained his in 1596), and as soldiering was not a profession for which there was much opportunity in a peaceful country, they were freely granted. English society was anyway very mixed and the sons of long-established gentlemen became apprentices in the City. By the 17th century the feeling that a gentleman was known by his behaviour more than by his birth was thus more firmly established and James II is said to have remarked that he could turn a man into a nobleman but God Almighty could not turn him into a gentleman.

By the 19th century the title was allowed to all men of the educated classes, though being occupied in trade was still regarded as a barrier; in this respect the 19th century was perhaps less liberal than the 16th. Frequent explorations of the term in ▷ Anthony Trollope's novels show it as a site of contest: everyone wanted to claim they were a gentleman and its moral connotations were quite unstable. Though in theory it was behaviour that counted, appearances for most people counted

still more, as is shown in Magwitch's notions of a gentleman in ▷ Charles Dickens's novel ▷ *Great Expectations* Chap. 39. The ▷ public schools, at least since the 17th century, had associated the idea of gentleman with education, especially a classical education in Greek and Latin literature; in the 19th century the public schools were greatly increased in numbers.

Gentleman's Magazine, The

Founded in 1731, it was the first to call itself a 'magazine'. It included, as later magazines were to do, a wider variety of material than the Reviews, including political reports which, in 1739–44, were contributed by ▷ Samuel Johnson.

Geoffrey of Monmouth (d 1155)

Author of the highly influential account of British history, in Latin prose, the *Historia Regum Britanniae* (*History of the Kings of Britain*), completed c 1138, which opened up a new vision of insular history, revealing Britain to be a formerly great European power. Little is known for certain about Geoffrey of Monmouth himself. He was probably born in Monmouth, of Welsh or Breton extraction, and seems to have been a resident of Oxford, probably a canon of the college of St George's, for many years of his life (?1129–51). In 1151 he became Bishop Elect of St Asaph. Before finishing his history of Britain, he produced a version of Merlin's prophecies, which were then incorporated into the history itself. At a later stage he returned to the subject of Merlin and around 1150 produced a Latin poem, the *Vita Merlini* (*The Life of Merlin*).

His history of Britain is an accomplished and complex exercise in history writing. He claims to have access to a source of British history, 'an ancient book in the British language', which has not been used by his contemporary historiographers, nor their predecessors. His narrative seems less likely to be the product of a single unidentified source, and much more the result of a careful act of compilation (using the work of contemporaries such as William of Malmesbury and earlier authorities on the history of the island, notably Gildas, Bede, and Nennius), and fabrication. In Geoffrey's narrative, a shadowy period of the island's past, covering the period before and after the Roman conquest, up to the beginnings of Saxon control in the 6th century, was given relatively detailed documentation, and a rather startling revision of Roman/British and British/Saxon power relations was advanced which disrupted some of the accepted facts of insular history. Geoffrey not only suggested that at certain stages of British history the power of Britain was a major threat to that of Rome, but that Britain was a unified realm well into the 6th century. His history also presented a picture of Britain as a world-famous chivalric centre during the reign of King Arthur. A powerful argument for unified rule emerges from the history, which is a point of some relevance to the turbulent political context in which Geoffrey was writing.

The historical value of the *History of the Kings of Britain* was a controversial issue, debated and disputed by some historians of the 12th and later centuries. But Geoffrey's formulation of British history was widely used in chronicle histories of the island up to the 16th century and provided a historic foundation for the development of Arthurian narrative during the medieval period. Approximately 200 manuscripts survive of the history, and in addition there are numerous vernacular translations and adaptations extant. Poetic and dramatic versions of early British history, such as *Gorboduc* (1565), Spenser's *Faerie Queene*, Shakespeare's *King Lear* and *Cymbeline*, all use material which derives ultimately from Geoffrey of Monmouth's *History of Britain*.

▷ Histories and Chronicles.

Bib: Thorpe, L. (trans.), *Geoffrey of Monmouth: The History of the Kings of Britain*.

German influence on English fiction

Unlike other European literatures, such as French or Italian, the literature of the German-speaking world did not begin to make itself felt in Britain to any great extent until relatively recent times. There are two reasons for this. The first is that the great flowering of a literature written in the *modern* form of the German language did not take place until the second half of the 18th century; the second is that German did not begin to assume the status of a major foreign language for the English until the second decade of the following century and even then it remained far behind French in importance. However, there are isolated examples of such influence before the late 18th century.

In the cultural interchange between the two literatures Britain has on balance been the dominant partner. German men and women of letters during the 18th century were far more likely to have a lively awareness of current developments in English literature than were their English counterparts of developments in Germany. Goethe's epistolary novel *Die Leiden des jungen Werthers* (*The Sorrows of Young Werther*) (1774) was a landmark for it was the first work of German literature to achieve European recognition. It was translated into most European languages and reached Britain in 1799, significantly via a French version. The novel's apparent defence of suicide caused a storm of righteous indignation, but the huge popularity of the novel, here as elsewhere, had much to do with the fact that it appealed to a taste for 'sentimental' literature which had already been established in Germany and Britain by, among others, ▷ Samuel Richardson.

This discovery of German literature by an English audience unfortunately soon met an insurmountable obstacle in the form of war. In the wake of the ▷ French Revolution a climate of opinion was created which was deeply and indiscriminately suspicious of all mainland European influence as ▷ Jacobin, subversive and unpatriotic. The fashion for German plays was snuffed out almost instantly, and it was not until the ending of the Napoleonic wars, with England and Prussia as victorious allies, that a new climate favourable to the reception of German writers could be created. The publication of Madame de Staël's *De l'Allemagne* (1813) is rightly regarded as a crucial event in this process.

▷ Thomas Carlyle was the single most important

conduit of German literature and thought in the 19th century. He had already published his translation of Goethe's *Wilhelm Meister* when, in 1839, his *Critical and Miscellaneous Essays* appeared, containing the many articles on German literature which he had written for the journals of the day. The work was seminal, and inaugurated what was the great age of German influence in Britain. Probably inspired by Carlyle, ▷ Matthew Arnold immersed himself in the works of Goethe and was deeply influenced by him. His discovery and admiration of Heinrich Heine (1797–1856) on the other hand was quite independent and an appreciative essay on the later poet is included in *Essays in Criticism* (1865). For Arnold, Goethe and Heine were great modern spirits in comparison with whom the English Romantics were insular and intellectually deficient. Arnold's German culture extends far beyond these two authors however, and, in scope at least, he is like ▷ George Eliot in this regard. It is now appreciated that the profound influence of the so-called 'Higher Criticism' in Britain does not commence with the publication in 1846 of her translation of Strauss's *Das Leben Jesu* (1835) but has roots which reach back into the last quarter of the 18th century, and that Coleridge was ahead of his time in his appreciation of the significance to religion and philosophy of the German school of biblical criticism. George Eliot is less a beginning than a culmination. Arnold had recognized in Goethe a figure who was working to 'dissolve' the dogmatic Christianity which had once been the bedrock of European civilization. It is now clear, however, that it was the Higher Criticism which, by mythologizing Christianity, undermined its claims more surely even than ▷ Charles Darwin, the geologists and positivist science. From this it is clear that when considering the massive response of English writers to German literature at this time, no sharp line can be drawn between works of imagination on the one hand and works of historical scholarship, cultural history and philosophy on the other. If a novel of ideas such as ▷ *Daniel Deronda* could hardly have been written without Strauss (1808–74) and Feuerbach (1804–72), then Goethe's *Wilhelm Meister* is scarcely less crucial. The relevance here of ▷ G. H. Lewes, whose *Life of Goethe* appeared in 1855, is obvious. In the last decade of the century another admirer of Goethe, ▷ Oscar Wilde, with inspired flippancy, could show young Cecily earnestly studying her German grammar under the eyes of Miss Prism and the Reverend Chasuble, but for many the loss of religious faith which followed the encounter with German thought brought great anguish before it brought serenity.

It is one of the paradoxes of the Victorian era that, while a series such as Bohn's Standard Library made available to a reading public a large number of German classic texts in translation, there were still many gaps and absences. The imaginative literature of the middle and second half of the century, represented by writers such as the Austrian Franz Grillparzer (1791–1872), E. Mörike (1804–75), A. Stifter (1805–68), Friedrich Hebbel (1813–63), T. Storm (1817–88), Theodor Fontane (1819–98), and the Swiss writers G. Keller (1819–90) and C. F.

Meyer (1825–98) did not reach the wider audience it deserved. Because this literature is in a sense provincial, its failure to make much impression in Britain is less surprising than the British blindness to the considerable achievements of important earlier figures such as Heinrich von Kleist (1777–1811) or E. T. A. Hoffmann (1776–1822), though the latter was not unknown and certainly influenced Edgar Allen Poe. Of this generation it was perhaps the figure of Richard Wagner (1813–83), more associated with music than literature, whose work has had most influence on English literature. In some ways he was an important precursor of the Celtic revival, and his aesthetic theories as much as his use of the leitmotif influenced subsequent writers throughout Europe, including ▷ James Joyce.

During the 19th century the figures of ▷ Walter Scott, ▷ William Thackeray and ▷ Charles Dickens exercised a profound influence on the development of ▷ realist fiction in Germany. Thomas Mann (1875–1955) was closest to this tradition in his novel of the decline of a bourgeois family, *Buddenbrooks* (1901), and for many years was held in high esteem, but, perhaps his later fiction took a rather different and more philosophical direction, his reputation has waned in recent years. Hermann Hesse (1877–1962), after a period of considerable popularity, has suffered a similar fate, but the fascination of the Czech Franz Kafka (1883–1924) is undiminished. All his writings are fables of alienation and his name has become a byword for the bizarre and nightmarish. His unique vision is too personal for imitation, but it is hard to imagine how Joseph Heller's *Catch 22* (1961) and *Something Happened* (1974) could have been written without Kafka. A very different kind of fantastic realism characterizes the work of Günther Grass (b 1917) and, together with Heinrich Böll (b 1917), he stands out among the writers of the post-war generation as one whose work has spoken most immediately to his English-speaking contemporaries.

There can be little doubt that the profoundest influence on English literature and the literatures of most other countries in the 20th century stems not from the imaginative literature of Germany but from the philosophical. Probably this should not surprise us, since a philosophical tradition from which emerged in the 19th century the towering figures of Hegel, Schopenhauer and ▷ Nietzsche had already left its mark. In ▷ Karl Marx and ▷ Sigmund Freud, however, the German-speaking world produced two thinkers who have as decisively and permanently transformed the whole framework of terms within and by which we conceive society and the human mind, as Darwin and Einstein have transformed our understanding of the physical world. This is no less true for a writer like Vladimir Nabokov (1899–1977), who dismisses Freud as the Viennese witch-doctor, than for ▷ D. M. Thomas. For the British there is, of course, a special poignancy in this, as both these radical thinkers were driven by political circumstances from their native countries and found refuge in Britain.

Goethe foresaw a time when, with the help of translations, national literatures would give way to a *Weltliteratur*. In the bookshops of Germany, where translations from English abound, one is inclined to feel that the day has arrived, but a visitor to a British bookshop in search of translations from the German is likely to reflect that here at least this consummation has still to come.

Ghose, Zulfikar (b 1935)

Novelist and poet. Ghose was born in Pakistan and educated at the University of Keele. During the 1960s he worked as cricket correspondent for the *Observer* before becoming a teacher in London and then Professor of English at the University of Texas. His trilogy, entitled *The Incredible Brazilian* and comprising *The Native* (1972), *A Beautiful Empire* (1975) and *A Different World* (1985), uses elements of ▷ magic realism to portray the cultural history of Brazil through the reincarnations of a single character named Gregório. His other novels are: *The Contradictions* (1966); *The Murder of Aziz Khan* (1967); *Crump's Terms* (1975); *The Texas Inheritance* (1980, published under the name William Strang); *Hulme's Investigations into the Bogart Script* (1981); *A New History of Torments* (1982); *Don Bueno* (1983); *Figures of Enchantment* (1986); *The Triple Mirror of the Self* (1991). Short stories: (with ▷ B.S. Johnson) *Statement Against Corpses* (1964). Poetry: *The Loss of India* (1964); *Jets from Orange* (1967); *The Violet West* (1972); *A Memory of Asia* (1984); *Selected Poems* (1991). He has also published critical works, and an autobiographical piece, *Confessions of a Native-Alien* (1965).

Gibbon, Edward (1737–94)

One of the greatest English historians, author of ▷ *The Decline and Fall of the Roman Empire* (1776–88). His reputation rests almost entirely on this work, but his *Memoirs* (1796), put together from fragments after his death, are one of the most interesting biographies of the 18th century. In 1761 he published in French his *Essai sur l'Etude de la Littérature*, translated into English in 1764; it was more successful abroad than at home. He was also a Member of Parliament, 1774–81.
Bib: Low, D.M., *Edward Gibbon*; Young, G. M., *Gibbon*; Sainte-Beuve, C.-A., in *Causeries dy Lundi* vol viii.

Gibbon, Lewis Grassic (1901–1935)

Novelist. Lewis Grassic Gibbon was the pen name of James Leslie Mitchell, a Scots writer whose most famous work, the trilogy of novels, *A Scots Quair* (*Sunset Song*, 1932, *Cloud Howe*, 1933, and *Grey Granite*, 1934) dramatizes working life in the early part of the 20th century in rural Scotland. Gibbon's work is characterized by his formally innovative combination of north-eastern Scottish dialogue and speech-rhythms, mixed with a burning belief in a rural form of socialism and feminism. Gibbon also wrote seven other novels under his own name, collaborated with poet ▷ Hugh MacDiarmid on *Scottish Scene, or, The Intelligent Man's Guide to Albyn* (1934), and, again under his own name, wrote three anthropological/archaeological texts. He died young, having produced a large body of wide-ranging work.

▷ Scottish fiction in English.

Gibbons, Stella (1902–1989)
Novelist. Gibbon's most famous work (perhaps more famous than its author), the novel *Cold Comfort Farm* (1932), was the first in a long series of astute, witty comedies of manners, a ▷ parody of both Lawrentian primitivism (▷ D. H. Lawrence) and rural fiction (popularized by writers such as Mary Webb, 1881–1927) which became a best-seller and has since been serialized for radio. Gibbons has also written short stories, poetry and many other novels; her works include *The Mountain Beast and Other Poems* (1930); *The Untidy Gnome* (1935); *Roaring Tower and Other Short Stories* (1937); *Nightingalewood* (1938); *Christmas at Cold Comfort Farm and Other Stories* (1940); *Westwood* (1946); *Conference at Cold Comfort Farm* (1949); *Collected Poems* (1951); *The Shadow of a Sorcerer* (1955); *The Pink Front Door* (1959); *The Charmers* (1965); *The Woods in Winter* (1970).

Gide, André (1869–1951)
French novelist. He developed an early preference for the *sotie* or *récit* (short prose piece) and in this form produced *L'Immoraliste* (1902), *La Porte étroite* (1909) and *La Symphonie pastorale* (1919). These are short, tightly-organized stories which exploit the characteristic weakness of first-person narration, in that their narrator-protagonists are without exception blind to the consequences of their words and actions. In all cases, this narrator is sharply distinguished from the author, who distances himself from his characters through irony (the title *sotie* denotes strong mockery). *Les Caves du Vatican* (1914) is a longer *récit* which develops the notion of the 'gratuitous act', an unmotivated and unpremediated act which would constitute an effect without a cause and novelistically represent an unpredictable element altering the course of the narration. The work also portrays the stifling, hidebound world of marriage, the family and religion, all objects of Gidean criticism. These concerns surface again in the only work which Gide called a novel, *Les Faux-Monnayeurs*, published in 1925. Its theme is moral and literary counterfeiting and the contrasting search for authenticity and openness (*disponibilité*) to experience. The experimental aspect of the novel is striking. Narrative orderliness and momentum are broken up by the plurality of angles of vision and the constant switching from one sub-plot to the next. Moreover, the author himself intervenes in the narrative to rupture any suspension of disbelief by declaring his own lack of control over characters and events. Above all, Gide makes crucial use of what he named the *mise en abyme* technique, a procedure by which the novel debates its own problems. In Gide's novel, this technique is exemplified in the character Edouard. Edouard is a novelist whose diary, 'quoted' by Gide, records his difficulties in writing his own novel, itself called *Les Faux-Monnayeurs*. This self-consciousness, highlighting the literariness of literature, has proved influential in the subsequent development of the novel in France.

Gide also helped found the literary magazine *La Nouvelle Revue française* and certain of his own works

first appeared in its pages (*La Porte étroite*, *Les Caves du Vatican*, *Les Faux-Monnayeurs*).
▷ French influence on English fiction.

Gilfil's Love-Story, Mr
One of ▷ George Eliot's ▷ *Scenes of Clerical Life*.

Gilroy, Beryl (b 1924)
Novelist. Born and brought up in Guyana, Gilroy trained as a teacher and worked for UNICEF. In 1951 she moved to Britain where she studied at the universities of London and Sussex. She has worked as a journalist and teacher in London. Her novels are *Frangipani House* (1986), about the indignities suffered by an old and infirm woman in Guyana, and *Boy-Sandwich* (1989). She has also published fiction for children and *Black Teacher* (1970), which is autobiographical.

Gipsies
A nomadic race, dark-skinned, speaking their own language related to the Indian Hindi. They spread across Europe in the 15th century and seem to have reached Britain about 1500. Owing to a belief that they came from Egypt, they were known as Egyptians, corrupted to Gipsies (Gypsies), but they called themselves Romanies. They commonly lived in caravans and moved from place to place, making a living (in the English countryside) as tinkers and by begging. Among country people they had a bad reputation for lawlessness and stealing, including the kidnapping of children; but their exoticism caused them to be romanticized in the 10th century, *eg* the gipsies in the novel ▷ *Guy Mannering* (1815) by ▷ Walter Scott. ▷ George Borrow is the most notable romanticizer of gipsies (of whom he made almost a life study) in his rambling, often vivid semi-fictional autobiographical and travel books, such as *Lavengro* (1851), *The Romany Rye* (1857). In modern Britain, so-called gipsies are often travellers with no gipsy ancestry. Centuries of intermittent persecution have done less than the modern ▷ Welfare State has done to make the gipsy existence difficult. They have, however, in 1988 been officially recognized as a racial group by the Commission for Racial Equality. For a 20th-century tale of a gipsy see *The Virgin and the Gypsy* by ▷ D. H. Lawrence.

Gissing, George Robert (1857–1903)
Novelist; author of: *Workers in the Dawn* (1880); *The Unclassed* (1884); *Demos* (1886); *A Life's Morning* (1888); *The Nether World* (1889); *The Emancipated* (1890); ▷ *New Grub Street* (1891); *Born in Exile* (1892); *The Odd Women* (1893); *The Town Traveller* (1898); *The Crown of Life* (1899); *Our Friend the Charlatan* (1901); *By the Ionian Sea* (1901); *The Private Papers of Henry Ryecroft* (1903). Posthumous: the historical novel *Veranilda* (1904) and *Will Warburton* (1905). Of these, much the best known is *New Grub Street*, a study of literary life in late 19th-century London. Gissing saw with deep foreboding the spread of a commercialized culture which would so oppress the disinterested artist and so encourage the charlatan that, in his view, national culture was bound to deteriorate, with concomitant effects on

the quality of civilization as a whole. The partial fulfilment of his predictions has given this novel in particular a greatly revived prestige. His vision was serious and sombre, and he depicted the enclosed, deprived world of the poor of his time in *Demos* and *The Nether World*. *Thyrza* and *Henry Ryecroft* are other novels which are singled out from his work. He was deeply interested in ▷ Charles Dickens and his study of that novelist (1898) is among the best on the subject; but he had also been affected by the austere, scrupulous artistry of the French 19th-century novelists ▷ Flaubert and ▷ Zola. His best work often has a strong autobiographical content, characteristic of some of his contemporaries, such as ▷ William Hale White and ▷ Samuel Butler.

▷ New Woman.

Bid: Donnelly, M., *Gissing, Grave Comedian*; Korg, J., *Gissing*; Roberts, M., *The Private Life of Henry Maitland* (novel based on Gissing's life); Poole, A., *Gissing in Context*; Collie, M., *The Alien Art: A Critical Study of George Gissing's Novels*.

Godwin, William (1756–1836)

Philosopher and novelist. His central belief was that reason was sufficient to guide the conduct, not merely of individuals but also of all society. His principal work was *The Inquiry concerning Political Justice* (1793). Man he believed to be innately good and, under guidance of reason, capable of living without laws or control. Punishments he declared (at a time when the English penal system was one of the severest in Europe) to be unjust; as were the accumulation of property and the institution of marriage. The Prime Minister, William Pitt (the Younger), decided that the book was too expensive to be dangerous. Godwin's best-known novel came out in 1794: *Caleb Williams* was written to demonstrate the power for injustice accessible to the privileged classes. Godwin was a brave man, not merely with the pen; but his naivety as a thinker would have left him without influence if his opinions had not agreed so well with the more extreme currents of feeling provoked by the contemporary ▷ French Revolution. As it was, he influenced a number of better minds, including, for a very short time, the poet ▷ Coleridge and, for a much longer period, Shelley, who became his son-in-law. Godwin's wife was ▷ Mary Wollstonecraft, an early propagandist for the rights of women and authoress of *A Vindication of the Rights of Woman* (1792).

Goethe, Johann Wolfgang von (1749–1832)

German poet; the greatest European man of letters of his time. His fame was due not only to the wide scope of his imaginative creation, but to the many-sidedness and massive independence of his personality. From 1770 to 1788 he was an inaugurator and leader of the passionate outbreak known in German as the *Sturm und Drang* – 'storm and stress' – movement, but from 1788 (after his visit to Italy) he represented to the world a balanced harmony inspired by the classicism he had found there. But he did not lose his sense that the spirit is free to find its own fulfilment according to its own principle of growth. At the same time, from 1775 he was prominent in the affairs of the German principality of Weimar (whose prince was his friend), concerning himself with practical sciences useful to the state, and thence with a serious study of botany and other natural and physical sciences to the point of making significant contributions to scientific thought. His commanding mind was admired in France, England, and Italy, with whose literatures Goethe was in touch; he corresponded with Byron; ▷ Walter Scott translated his *Goetz von Berlichingen*, which dated from the Romantic phase of Goethe's career; he encouraged the young ▷ Thomas Carlyle. For Carlyle (▷ *Sartor Resartus*) Goethe was the spirit of affirmation that the age needed, to be set against the spirit of denial and withdrawal which he saw manifested in Byron. For ▷ Matthew Arnold, one of the most influential critics of the mid-19th century, Goethe's serene and responsible detachment represented the needed outlook for the practice of criticism.

Goethe is most famous for his double drama of *Faust* (1808 and 1832), but other works that became famous in England include the Romantic drama already mentioned; the epic *Hermann and Dorothea*; a study in Romantic sensibility *The Sorrows of Young Werther*; the novel *Wilhelm Meister*, an example of the ▷ *Bildungsroman*, and a large body of lyrical verse.

▷ German influence on English fiction.

Gogol, Nikolai Vasilyevich (1809–52)

Playwright, novelist and short story writer, Gogol was born in the Ukraine. He worked as a civil service clerk in St Petersburg, which he hated but made notes for future use in the portrayal of characters. He was a brilliant but unbalanced man, suffering hallucinations and prone to religious extremism. At one stage he walked everywhere sideways, keeping his back to the wall for fear of being stabbed, and he had a pathological fear of eternal damnation. He admired Shakespeare, ▷ Henry Fielding and ▷ Laurence Sterne among others, and is thought to have greatly influenced Dostoevsky. His first collection of stories was *Evenings at a Farmhouse Near Dikana* (1831–2) which describe Ukranian country life. *Taras Bulba* (1834) has a Cossack tale as its title story, and *Mirgorod* and *Arabeski* followed in 1835. The play, *The Government Inspector* (1836) is a savage satire of civil servants and bureaucracy. His St Petersburg stories, including 'Nevsky Prospekt', 'Notes of a Madman' and 'The Portrait' (1835), 'The Nose' (1836) and 'The Greatcoat' (1842), have a surreal quality. The farce *Marriage* (1842) was successful. *Dead Souls* (1842), begun in Italy, combines satire, humour and brilliant characterization, but during increasing bouts of religious fervour, Gogol burnt the manuscript of the second part, along with further manuscripts. *Selected Passages from Correspondance with Friends* (1847), for which he was rebuked, was an attempt to convey his moral scruples. His work is remarkable for the power of his language and imagination.

Golden Bowl, The (1904)

A novel by ▷ Henry James. The theme is the relationship of four people: the American millionaire collector, Adam Verver; his daughter, Maggie; the Italian prince, Amerigo, whom Verver acquires as a husband for his daughter; and Charlotte Stant, whom Maggie acquires as a wife for her widowed father. To the grief of the father and the daughter, Charlotte seduces the prince into becoming her lover; the story is about the defeat of Charlotte, and Maggie's recovery of the prince's affections.

The novel belongs to James's last phase, which some critics consider to be his best, and others consider to show an excessive obliquity of style. The language of the characters is charged with feeling and yet disciplined by their civilized restraint and their fear of degrading themselves and one another by damaging explicitness. It is a measure of their indirectness that the affair between the prince and Charlotte is never actually mentioned between the father and the daughter. Behind the conflict of personalities there is the theme of the clash between European and American kinds of value and consciousness; this theme is conspicuous in James's early novels, and the returned to it in his last period after a middle phase in which he was chiefly concerned with the European, and particularly the English, scene.

Golden Notebook, The (1962)

Novel by ▷ Doris Lessing, an important ▷ feminist text despite its author's reservations about such a categorization. The novel is a relatively early example of the multiple narratives, indeterminacy and paradox which characterize ▷ post-modernist fiction. A series of realist episodes (entitled 'free women') from the lives of two women friends, Anna and Molly, are interspersed with excerpts from the four notebooks – red, yellow, blue and black – in which Anna records different aspects of her life and thought, including a novel that she is writing. The book culminates in a transformation of the self through traumatic mental breakdown, recorded in the final golden notebook: an important example of the feminist theme of mental disturbance as a reaction against social constraint or the oppression of a given feminine role. The conclusion of *The Golden Notebook* involves a ▷ *mise en abyme*, as different narrative levels seem to contradict each other.

Golding, William (b 1911)

Novelist. His novels are: *Lord of the Flies* (1954; filmed 1963); *The Inheritors* (1955); *Pincher Martin* (1956); *The Spire* (1964); *The Pyramid* (1967); *Darkness Visible* (1979); *Rites of Passage* (1980); *The Paper Men* (1984); *Close Quarters* (1987); *Fire Down Below* (1989). *Sometime, Never* (1956) and *The Scorpion God* (1971) are collections of novellas. He has also written a play, *The Brass Butterfly* (1958), and published two collections of essays, *The Hot Gates* (1965) and *A Moving Target* (1982).

No novelist who started his career since 1945 has achieved more prestige, and this was acquired very quickly on the publication of his first book, *Lord of the Flies*. Its fame has no doubt been in part due to its pessimistic vision of human nature as inherently violent, reflecting the mood of the post-war and post-Hitler years; it also epitomizes

mid-20th-century disillusionment with 19th-century optimism about human nature. Golding's father (see 'The Ladder and the Tree' in *The Hot Gates*) was a schoolmaster with radical convictions in politics, a belief that religion is outmoded superstition, and a strong faith in science. Golding's own work is strongly, but not explicitly, religious, in the Puritan tradition which emphasizes Original Sin. In 'Fable' (*The Hot Gates*) he explains how his first novel arose from his insights in the last war: 'Anyone who moved through those years without understanding that man produces evil as a bee produces honey, must have been blind or wrong in the head.' The book is also meant to counteract what may be called 'the desert island myth' in English literature, deriving from ▷ Daniel Defoe's ▷ *Robinson Crusoe*, and particularly evident in a famous book for boys, *The Coral Island* (1857) by R. M. Ballantyne. This myth nourished the belief that human beings in isolation from civilized restraints will sustain their humanity by innate virtues. Most of the boys in *Lord of the Flies* quickly degenerate into savages, and the process is made more horrifying by the convincing delineation of the characters: Golding, like his father, has been a schoolmaster. His later novels have shown variety of theme and treatment, but similar preoccupation with fundamental corruption and contradiction in human nature. They show, likewise, Golding's most conspicuous literary qualities: great inventiveness in realistic fantasy, and a disposition to use the novel form as fable. For instance, *The Inheritors* is ▷ science fiction about the remote human past: the elimination of innocent Neanderthal Man by the arrival of rapacious Homo Sapiens – a new version of the myth of the Fall. *Pincher Martin* is a dramatization of this rapacity in an individual, and a spectacular example of fantasy presented within the conventions of realism. *The Spire* shows comparable ingenuity used quite differently: it describes the building of the spire of Salisbury Cathedral and dramatizes the conflict between faith and reason. *Rites of Passage* employs a characteristic shift of perspective: the narrow viewpoint of the narrator, a snobbish young aristocrat on a voyage to Australia in the early 19th century, is undermined by his gradual understanding of the devastating experiences of an awkward but sincere clergyman. The story of the voyage is continued in *Close Quarters* and *Fire Down Below*.

Bib: Gregor, I., and Kinkead-Weekes, M., *William Golding: a Critical Study*; Johnston, A., *Of Earth and Darkness*; Medcalf, S., *William Golding*.

Goldsmith, Oliver (1730–74)

Dramatist, novelist, essayist, and poet. Born in Ireland, he studied at Trinity College, Dublin, but ran away to Cork after being disciplined by his tutor. He returned, however, and graduated in 1749. He applied for ordination, but was rejected, then was given £50 to study for the law, but gambled it away. After this, he studied medicine at Edinburgh and at Leyden but it is unclear whether he obtained the medical degree to which he later laid claim. In 1756 he came to London, penniless, and supported himself with a variety of occupations, including messenger, teacher, apothecary's assistant, usher, and hack writer for a periodical.

In 1758 he translated Marteilhe's *Memoirs of a Protestant, Condemned to the Galleys of France for His Religion*, and in 1759 his *Enquiry into the Present State of Polite Learning in Europe*. His 'Chinese Letters', written for John Newbery's *The Public Ledger* (1760–1) were reissued in 1762 as *The Citizen of the World*, a satiric view of England written from the supposed viewpoint of a Chinaman. His first real success as a writer was with the poem, 'The Traveller', published in 1764. A number of his works are now highly valued, including *The Citizen of the World*; his life of Beau Nash (1762); his novel, ▷ *The Vicar of Wakefield*; a poem, *The Deserted Village*; and the plays, *The Good Natur'd Man* (1768) and *She Stoops to Conquer* (1773) written, like the plays of Richard Brinsley Sheridan, in reaction to the sentiment of many plays of the period, and with the intention to revive the spirit of Restoration comedy. He wrote much else, including histories of England, Greece and Rome, and biographies of Voltaire, Bolingbroke and Parnell.

Goldsmith was a friend of the actor David Garrick, and ▷ Samuel Johnson, and figures largely in ▷ James Boswell's *Life of Johnson* (1791). Johnson praised his writing for its 'clarity and elegance', and later generations have repeatedly praised his literary 'charm', a quality made up of humour, modesty, vitality, and graceful lucidity. These he combined with the Augustan properties of balance and proportion. He died of a fever, deeply in debt, and the Literary Club which he had helped to found in 1764 erected a monument to him in Westminster Abbey. Garrick wrote an epitaph to comment on his greatness as an author and reputed failings in other areas: 'Here lies Nolly Goldsmith, for shortness called Noll, Who wrote like an angel, but talked like poor Poll'.
Bib: Forster, J., and Wardle, R. M., *Lives*; Balderston, K. B. (ed.), *Letters*; Ginger, J., *The Notable Man*; Danziger, M. K., *Oliver Goldsmith and Richard Brinsley Sheridan*; Swarbrick, A. (ed.), *The Art of Oliver Goldsmith*.

Goncourt, Edmond Louis Antonine Huot de (1822–96) and Jules Alfred Huot de (1830–70)
The brothers, novelists, historians and art critics, of an old Lorraine family, collected books, pictures, manuscripts and furnishings, collaborating on several books of history and art criticism. They wrote novels which are now not much read but helped make literary history, originating the '*roman documentaire*' with its painstaking naturalistic detail, believing novelists should write 'history which might have happened'. After Jules's death, Edmond wrote some further novels and the famous *Journal des Goncourt* which portrayed literary life in Paris 1851–96. The Académie Goncourt was founded under the terms of Edmond's will; it awards the annual Prix Goncourt for imaginative prose. *Germinie Lacerteux* (1864) details the history of their maid, faithfully serving while living a life of vice and debauchery. Other novels include *Soeur Philomène* (1861) and *Madam Gervaisais* (1869). Non-fiction includes *L'Art du*

dix-huitième siècle (1859–75) and *Portraits intimes du dix-huitième siècle* (1857). Novels written by Edmond alone include *Les Frères Zemganno* (1879), *La Faustin* (1882) and *Chérie* (1884).

Gooch, Elizabeth Sarah (1756–?)
Novelist, poet and autobiographer. Elizabeth Gooch's most fascinating work is her ▷ autobiography, *Life* (1792), partly because of the difficulties she encountered and the sordid world she was forced to live in, but mainly because of the rapid-paced narrative and her penchant for vivid sensationalism. She was the daughter of a Portuguese Jewish father who died when she was three; her stepfather never really accepted her into his family. She was sent to school at Fountains Abbey where she entered into a romance, which was thwarted. Following this she was 'married off' to William Gooch who was more interested in her dowry than in showing her any real affection. It was not long before Gooch accused her of adultery and sent her to France, where she became a prostitute. The subsequent years saw a series of escapades in which she acted on stage, fled from debtors, disguised herself as a man so as to follow her lover into battle, and persistently tried to wring money out of her embarrassed family. By 1788 she was in prison, from where she wrote *Appeal to the Public*. Gooch's later life is obscure, but several novels and a biography of Thomas Bellamy, all written between 1795 and 1800, remain.

Gordimer, Nadine (b 1923)
South African novelist and short-story writer living in Johannesburg. She has won an international reputation and numerous prizes, including the Booker Prize for *The Conservationist* (1974). Much of her work is concerned with the situation of white middle-class liberals in South Africa, privileged by a system to which they are opposed, the relation of the private self to the political, and the failure of liberal compromise. Her work has become progressively bleaker and more disillusioned. In *A World of Strangers* (1958) she uses the perspective of an outsider coming to South Africa, while *The Conservationist* is written from the viewpoint of a rich and conservative capitalist, and employs symbolic elements in its treatment of the struggle for the control of the land. In 1991 she won the Nobel Prize for literature. Her other novels are: *The Lying Days* (1953); *Occasion for Loving* (1963); *The Late Bourgeois World* (1966); *A Guest of Honour* (1970); *Burger's Daughter* (1979); *July's People* (1981); *A Sport of Nature* (1987); *My Son's Story* (1990). Story collections include: *Selected Stories* (1975); *Some Monday For Sure* (1976); *A Soldier's Embrace* (1980); *Town and Country Lovers* (1980); *Something Out There* (1984); *Jump* (1991).
Bib: Heywood, C., *Nadine Gordimer*; Cligman, S., *The Novels of Nadine Gordimer: History from the Inside*.

Gore, Catherine Grace Frances (1799–1861)
Born Moody, the daughter of a wine merchant in East Retford, Nottinghamshire, Catherine Gore showed literary ability at an early age and was

nicknamed 'the Poetess' by her peers. She wrote some 70 novels between 1824 and 1862, of the ▷ 'silver-fork school': novels of fashionable and wealthy life. They include *Theresa Marchmont or the Maid of Honour* (1824), *Manners of the day, or Woman as the game* (1830), which was praised by George IV, *Mothers and Daughters* (1830), *Mrs Armytage: or female domination* (1836), possibly her best, *Cecil, or the adventures of a coxcomb* (1841) and *The banker's wife, or court and city* (1843), which was dedicated to Sir John Dean Paul, portrayed as a swindler, as he in fact turned out to be in 1855 when Gore lost £20,000. She also wrote poems, plays – *The School for Coquettes* (1831), *Quid pro Quo or the Days of Dupes* (1844) – and short stories, and composed music. Her writing is characterized by shrewd observation and perceptive insight, together with satire and invention, and gives an interesting portrait of life in a certain class and time, particularly of the life of women.
Bib: Moers, E., *Literary Women*; Rosa M. W., *The Silver-fork School*.

Gosse, Edmund (1849–1928)

Critic, biographer and poet. He is especially known for his ▷ autobiography *Father and Son* (1907) – one of the classic works for interpreting the Victorian age. As a critic, he was one of the first to introduce the Norwegian dramatist Ibsen to the British public. He also wrote a number of studies of 17th-century literature and a life (1917) of his friend and contemporary, the poet A. C. Swinburne (1837–1909).

Gothic novels

A genre of novels dealing with tales of the macabre and supernatural, which reached a height of popularity in the 1790s. The term 'Gothic' originally implied 'medieval', or rather a fantasized version of what was seen to be medieval. Later, 'Gothic' came to cover all areas of the fantastic and supernatural, and the characteristics of the genre are graveyards and ghosts.

▷ Walpole's ▷ *The Castle of Otranto* is generally seen as the earliest Gothic novel. ▷ Matthew 'Monk' Lewis, ▷ William Beckford and ▷ Ann Radcliffe are notable exploiters of the genre. The vogue for Gothic novels soon produced parodies; ▷ Thomas Love Peacock's ▷ *Nightmare Abbey* and ▷ Jane Austen's ▷ *Northanger Abbey* are among the best examples.

In the 19th century, ▷ Mary Shelley, the ▷ Brontës and ▷ Dickens show the influence of the tradition and the novels of such modern writers as ▷ Emma Tennant and ▷ Angela Carter suggest that tales of the supernatural have undying appeal.

Grace Abounding to the Chief of Sinners (1666)

The spiritual autobiography of ▷ John Bunyan, author of ▷ *The Pilgrim's Progress*. The torments undergone by Christian in the latter book are substantially those of Bunyan in the earlier one. Bunyan had a similar spiritual awakening to Christian's, being aroused by a book; he suffers the terrible convinction of sin, like Christian's; he believes himself to commit the sin of blasphemy as Christian thinks he does in the Valley of the Shadow

of Death; at last he achieves confidence in God's mercy. Much of the narrative is an account of painful mental conflict; but Bunyan never lost the sanity of perception into the fanaticism and mental morbidity of others, such as the old man who told him that he had certainly committed the sin against the Holy Ghost (for which there is no forgiveness). The book records how he developed that compassionate understanding of other men's spiritual conflicts which makes *The Pilgrim's Progress* the antecedent of the great English novels.

Grahame, Kenneth (1859–1932)

Children's writer and essayist. Grahame is remembered for his animal fable *The Wind in the Willows* (1908), which was based on stories made up for his son and which, after receiving little attention when first published, subsequently became a classic of ▷ children's fiction. Previously Grahame had contributed to ▷ *The Yellow Book* and had published several works primarily concerned with childhood experience: *Pagan Papers* (1893), *The Golden Age* (1895) and *Dream Days* (1898). He was born in Edinburgh, went to school in Oxford and worked in the Bank of England until 1908 when he retired because of ill-health.

Grammatology

This term is used by the French philosopher ▷ Jacques Derrida to denote 'a general science of writing'. As a scientific practice, its objective is to disturb the traditional hierarchical relationship between 'speech' and 'writing' where the latter is regarded as an instrument of the former. Derrida's 'science of writing' is an attempt to deconstruct (▷ deconstruction) the metaphysical assumptions upon which the hierarchical relationship between speech and writing is based. He takes to the limit the Saussurean (▷ Saussure) notion of the arbitrariness of the linguistic ▷ sign, arguing against a natural relationship between the spoken word and what it signifies.

Grand guignol

A term denoting an entertainment relying merely on sensational horror for its effect; after an old French puppet show.

Grand, Sarah (1854–1943)

Novelist. Grand was a feminist who dealt effectively with the issues surrounding the ▷ New Woman in such works as *Ideala* (1888) and *A Domestic Experiment* (1891), both of which polemically justify the breaking of the sexual taboos surrounding the 'respectable' woman.

Graves, Richard (1715–1804)

Novelist. Graves was the rector of Claverton and a well-known figure in Bath society. His novel *The Spiritual Quixote, or the Summer Rambles of Mr Geoffrey Wildgoose* (1773) recounts the comic journeys of a Methodist preacher. The figure of Wildgoose satirizes the real life Methodist, George Whitefield (1717–70), who Graves had met as a student at Oxford.

Bib: Hill, C.J., *The Literary Career of Graves*.

Graves, Robert (1895–1985)

Poet, critic, novelist. His poetry belongs to a
distinctively English strain of lyrical verse which has
been overshadowed by the more ambitious and more
massive work of the Anglo-Irish W. B. Yeats and the
American-born T. S. Eliot. Earlier representatives of
this kind of verse were ▷ Thomas Hardy, Edward
Thomas and the war poets such as Wilfred Owen,
Siegfried Sassoon and Issac Rosenburg. The
development of Graves's work was decisively affected
by his experiences as an officer in World War I,
and understanding of it is helped by a reading of
Owen and Sassoon. Such poetry was partly a means
of preserving sanity in the face of extreme horror,
partly a desire to awaken in the reader a distrust of
attitudes imposed on him by convention, or adopted
by himself to help him preserve his own illusions.
Graves published his first poems during World
War I, but he is not primarily one of the war poets;
he extended the vision aroused by the war into
the post-war world of human relations, especially
those between the sexes, and into the impulses
to self-deceive and to escape the realities of inner
experience, especially by choosing to dull its image.
He always wrote lyrics with skilful and precise
rhythm and often poignant or pungent rhymes, and
an austere yet lively, colloquial diction. A collected
edition of his works was published in 1975.

As a critic he was at first a self-conscious ▷
modernist; *A Survey of Modernist Poetry* (1927),
written with the poet Laura Riding, educated
the public in new kinds of poetic expression by
a pioneering critical interest in subtleties and
ambiguities of language. His later criticism has been
less influential; it includes *The Common Asphodel*
(1949), *The Crowning Privilege* (1955).

Graves engaged extensively in historical and
anthropological enquiry; this resulted in work on
poetry and primitive religion, *eg The White Goddess*
(1948), which aroused controversy but was taken up
by some ▷ feminists in the 1960s and 70s, and in
historical fiction of great popularity, *eg I, Claudius*
and *Claudius the God* (1934). By far the most
important of his prose works, however, was his ▷
autobiography recounting his experiences in World
War I – *Good-bye to All That* (1929).
Bib: Seymour Smith, M., *Swifter than Reason*;
Graves, R. P., *Robert Graves*.

Gray, Alasdair (b 1934)

Scottish novelist and short-story writer. Gray was
educated at Glasgow Art School and works as
an art teacher, painter and writer. His fiction is
exuberant in style although often bleak in content,
employing fantasy, myth, parable, allusion (certain
of his texts include an index of plagiarisms),
typographical effects, illustrations (by the author),
arcane vocabulary, pseudo-historical texts and many
other post-modernist devices. His work also has
considerable political impact; for example *Something
Leather* (1990), an erotic fantasy, also contains a
biting satire on Glasgow's role as 1990 'European
City of Culture'. He has been seen as a major figure

of 'the new Glasgow writing', a movement involving
such fiction writers as ▷ James Kelman and ▷ Janice
Galloway, as well as poets such as Tom Leonard.
His first novel, *Lanark: A Life in Four Books* (1981),
takes its narrator from a bleak contemporary urban
landscape (Glasgow is suggested but not identified)
to an imaginary realm named 'unthank', while his
most recent, *Poor Things* (1992), evokes late-Victorian
Glasgow as a setting for the Frankenstein-like story
of a doctor who tries to create his 'ideal woman'
by a brain transplant. His other novels are: *1982,
Janine* (1984); *The Fall of Kelvin Walker: A Fable
of the Sixties* (1985, adapted from a 1968 television
play); *McGrotty and Ludmilla: or, The Harbinger Report*
(1990). Volumes of stories: *The Comedy of the White
Dog* (1979); *Unlikely Stories, Mostly* (1983); *Lean Tales*
(1985), with James Kelman and Agnes Owens; *Ten
Tales Tall and True* (1993). Poetry: *Old Negatives: Four
Verse Sequences* (1989). Autobiography: *Self-Portrait*
(1988). He has also written plays and documentaries
for radio and television and a work entitled
Independence: Why Scots Should Rule Scotland (1992).

Great Expectations (1860–1)

A novel by ▷ Charles Dickens. Its title refers to
expectations resulting from wealth anonymously
donated to Philip Pirrip (shortened to Pip) who
has been brought up in humble obscurity by his
half-sister and her husband, the village blacksmith,
Joe Gargery. His 'expectations' are to be made a ▷
'gentleman' – understood in social terms as holding
privilege without responsibility. He supposes his
money to be the gift of the rich and lonely Miss
Havisham, who has in fact merely used him as an
experimental victim on whom her ward, Estella, is to
exert her charm with the aim of breaking his heart.
Pip's great crisis comes when he discovers his real
benefactor to be the convict Magwitch, whom he had
helped in an attempted escape when he was a child.
Magwitch, who had been made into a criminal by the
callousness of society in his own childhood, has built
up a fortune in Australia (to which he was deported)
and has tried the experiment of 'making a gentleman'
out of another child. His assumption is essentially
that of society as a whole, that appearances, and the
money that makes them, are what matters. Magwitch
returns to England illegally to see the fruit of his
ambition, and Pip has to decide whether he will be
responsible for his unwanted benefactor or escape
from him. His decision to protect Magwitch and
help him to escape again produces a revolution in
Pip's nature: instead of assuming privilege without
responsibility he now undertakes responsibility
without reward, since he will also divest himself of
his money. 'Expectations' are important in other
senses for other characters: Estella expects to
become a rich lady dominating humiliated admirers,
but she becomes enslaved to a brutal husband;
Pip's friend, Herbert Pocket, dreams of becoming
a powerful industrialist, but he has no capital until
Pip (anonymously) provides it; Wopsle, the parish
clerk in Pip's village, imagines himself a great
actor and becomes a stage hack; Miss Havisham is
surrounded by relatives whom she despises and who
nonetheless live in expectation of legacies after her

death; Miss Havisham herself, and Magwitch also, live for expectations (in Estella and Pip) which are frustrated – in these instances fortunately. In its largest implications, *Great Expectations* is concerned with the futility of a society in which individuals live by desires powered by illusion. This view of the novel gives emphasis to those characters who are free of illusion: the lawyer Jaggers who exerts power by his cynical expectation of human folly; his clerk, Wemmick, who divides his life sharply between the harshness demanded by his profession and the tenderness of his domestic affections; Joe Gargery and his second wife Biddy, survivors from an older social tradition, who remain content with their own naïve wisdom of the heart. Dickens was persuaded by his friend ▷ Bulwer Lytton to change the end of the novel: in the first version Pip and Estella, older and wiser, meet again only to separate permanently; in the revised one, Dickens leaves it open to the reader to believe whether they will be permanently united, or not.

Green, Henry (1905–73)

Pen-name of the novelist H. V. Yorke. His novels are: *Blindness* (1926); *Living* (1929); *Party-Going* (1939); *Pack My Bag* (1940); *Caught* (1943); *Loving* (1945); *Back* (1946); *Concluding* (1948); *Nothing* (1950); *Doting* (1952). Of these, possibly the most distinguished are: *Living*, with an industrial working-class setting; *Loving*, about servants in an anachronistic great house in Ireland during World War II; *Concluding*, set in the future, about an institution for educating women civil servants, and *Party-Going*, a novel in which the events have only a few hours' duration and take place in a fog-bound London railway station. His style is condensed and poetically expressive; events are caught in movement, with a cinematic use of flash-backs to bring the past into relationship with the present. In the autobiographical *Pack my Bag* he wrote: 'Prose should be a long intimacy between strangers with no direct appeal to what both may have known. It should slowly appeal to feelings unexpressed, it should in the end draw tears out of the stone.' Green is set aside from the ▷ modernist interest in the rendering of consciousness by a belief that the novelist should not attempt to portray the inner depths of characters, but should use their spoken words to capture the opaque and shifting surface of social relations. The later novels show increasing reliance on dialogue, following the example of the novels of ▷ Ivy Compton-Burnett. Green also professed admiration for the work of the French writer, Céline. He wrote no novels in the last 20 years of his life.
Bib: Stokes, E., *The Novels of Henry Green*; Russell, J., *Henry Green*; Bassoff, B., *Towards Loving*; Sarraute, N., in *The Age of Suspicion*.

Green, Sarah (c 1790–1825)

Novelist and prose writer. Little is known about Sarah Green's personal life, but it is possible to trace through her novels a development from quiet docility to sharp ▷ feminist satire. Her *Mental Improvement for a Young Lady* (1793) is a ▷ didactic text aimed at teaching her niece correct feminine behaviour which, unsurprisingly, amounts to being chaste and obedient. Interestingly, novels are forbidden reading for the well brought-up young lady. *The Private History of the Court of England* (1808), however, describes the scandals of contemporary court life, especially the notorious affairs of the Prince of Wales, under the veil of an historical setting. The actress and novelist ▷ Mary Robinson, who was one of the Prince's many mistresses, is depicted in the novel as an intelligent woman oppressed by a misogynistic husband. Green took up this last theme again in her novel *Gretna Green Weddings, or The Nieces* (1823) which attempts to show that the abuse of women is true villainy, rather than an acceptable, although repugnant, social trait. The other butt of her satiric wit was the romance, which she attacked ruthlessly in *Romance Readers and Romance Writers* (1810–11), and which she fictionalized in the hilarious *Scotch Novel Reading, or Modern Quackery* (1824). In this latter book a father tries to save his two daughters from mental instability which has been brought on by reading Byron and ▷ Sir Walter Scott. Their madness takes the form of attempting to live out fiction in their own lives: the younger daughter who is obsessed with Scott is saved, but the Byronic daughter dies tragically.

Greene, Henry Graham (1904–91)

Novelist. The son of a schoolmaster. He went to Balliol College, Oxford, and then became a journalist (1926–30) on ▷ *The Times*. He was converted to Catholicism in 1926. His first novel, *The Man Within*, appeared in 1929. It was followed by a steady succession of novels, of which the fourth, *Stamboul Train* (1932) made him well known. It was nonetheless one of the books he called 'entertainments', meaning that they were among his less serious works; this group also includes *A Gun for Sale* (1936), *The Confidential Agent* (1939), *The Ministry of Fear* (1943), and *Our Man in Havana* (1958). In 1934 he published *It's a Battlefield*, and in 1935 a volume of stories the title story of which, *The Basement Room*, was later adapted into the film, *The Fallen Idol* (1950). In 1935 came *England Made Me*. In the same year he travelled in Liberia, on which he based his travel book *Journey Without Maps* (1936). He then became film critic for the weekly journal ▷ *The Spectator* (of which he was made literary editor in 1940). His next novel, *Brighton Rock* (1938) was the first in which there was clear evidence of Catholicism. In the same year he was commissioned to visit Mexico and report on the religious persecution there; the result was another travel book, *The Lawless Roads* (1939) and one of his most famous novels, *The Power and the Glory* (1940). During World War II he worked for the Foreign Office, and again visited West Africa. After the war he became a publisher. Later fiction: *Nineteen Stories* (1947; including eight in *The Basement Room* volume); *The Heart of the Matter* (1948); *The Third Man* (1950; also made into a film); *The End of the Affair* (1951); *The Quiet American* (1955); *A Burnt-Out Case* (1961); *A Sense of Reality* (four stories, 1963); *The Comedians* (1966); *Travels with My Aunt* (1969); *A Sort of Life* (1971); *The Honorary Consul* (1973); *Lord Rochester's*

Monkey (1974); *The Human Factor* (1978); *Dr Fischer of Geneva, or the Bomb Party* (1980); *Monsignior Quixote* (1982); *The Tenth Man* (1985); *The Captain and the Enemy* (1988).

He has also written plays: *The Living Room* (1953); *The Potting Shed* (1957); *The Complaisant Lover* (1959); *The Return of A. J. Raffles* (1975), and books of critical essays, *The Lost Childhood* (1951) and *The Pleasure Dome* (film criticism, 1972). His *Collected Essays* were published in 1969 and his *Collected Plays* in 1985. His autobiographical works include *A Sort of Life* (1971), *Ways of Escape* (1981) and *Getting to Know the General* (1984).

Graham Greene's high reputation is partly due to his exploration of emotions that were particularly strong from the middle of the 20th century: the sense of guilt and frustration, impulses to violence and fear of it, pity, including self-pity. He had strong gifts for narrative and for the evocation of atmosphere, especially the atmosphere of squalid surroundings which convey deprivation and despair. His Catholicism counteracts the misery in his books by its implications of spiritual dignity remaining intact even amid degradation and abject suffering.

▷ Catholicism in English literature.
Bib: Allott, K., and Farris, M., *The Art of Graham Greene*; Lodge, D., *Graham Greene*; Pryce-Jones, D., *Graham Greene*; Sharrock, R., *Saints, Sinners and Comedians: the Novels of Graham Greene*; Smith, G., *The Achievement of Graham Greene*.

Greene, Robert (1558–92)

Dramatist and pamphleteer. He was one of the University Wits, having himself been at Cambridge. Four plays by Greene, apart from collaborations, have survived: *Alphonsus, King of Aragon* (?1587); *Friar Bacon and Friar Bungay* (1589); *History of Orlando Furioso* (acted 1592); *The Scottish History of James IV* (acted 1594). Of these the best known are the second and the fourth, and in them both the melodious and fluent handling of the blank verse and the appealing portrayal of the heroines anticipate Shakespeare's romantic comedies of the 1590s.

Greene is more notable for his prose. This includes romances written in emulation of Lyly's ▷ *Euphues* and ▷ Sidney's ▷ *Arcadia*, including *Pandosto, or The Triumph of Time* from which Shakespeare derived *The Winter's Tale* (1610). More distinctive and very lively reading are his 'cony-catching pamphlets' (*ie* booklets about criminal practices in the London underworld), *A Notable Discovery of Cosenage* (*ie* 'cozenage' or criminal fraud, 1591) and *The Blacke Booke's Messenger* (1591) – both excellent examples of Elizabethan popular prose. A semi-fictional autobiography, *Greene's Groatsworth of Wit bought with a Million of Repentance* (1592) is notorious for containing the earliest reference to Shakespeare as a dramatist and actor, though it is an oblique one. The object of the pamphlet is ostensibly a warning to three others of the University Wits – probably George Peele (1556–96), Christopher Marlowe (1564–93) and ▷ Nashe – to amend their lives. The allusion to Shakespeare – 'an upstart crow beautified with our feathers . . . in his owne conceyt the onely shake-scene in a countrey' – comes by way of a

charge of plagiarism. 35 prose works, most of them short, and many containing lyrics of great charm, are ascribed to Greene.

Greenwood, Walter (1903–74)

Novelist. Born in Salford, Greenwood worked as an office boy, cab driver and salesman (among other things) before the success of his first novel *Love on the Dole* (1933). Describing the misery, poverty and squalor of life in a northern town during the Depression, the book became a *cause célèbre*, even discussed in Parliament; it was dramatized in 1934 and made into a film in 1941. His other novels include: *His Worship the Mayor* (1934); *Standing Room Only* (1936); *The Secret Kingdom* (1938); *Down by the Sea* (1951); and the autobiography *There was a Time* (1967).

Greer, Germaine (b 1939)

Feminist theorist and critic. Germaine Greer is one of the most influential writers of her generation. Her groundbreaking feminist work of 1971, *The Female Eunuch*, was a brilliantly timed and characteristically outrageous critique of traditional images of feminity and women's role in Western society, as well as being a celebration of more radical female powers and talents hitherto suppressed and repressed. Greer is an incisive writer and considerable scholar, who nevertheless always exudes an intoxicating energy in her writing. She has had an enormously varied career, and is one of the foremost spokeswomen of British ▷ feminism (although she was born in Australia and continues to explore this identity in her more autobiographical writings). Greer has held university lecturing posts (at Warwick University in the early 1970s, and more recently in Cambridge and the USA), has written for the underground press (the cult journal *Oz* in the late 1960s), has edited a collection of 17th-century women's poetry (*Kissing the Rod*, 1988), has written on women's role in art history (*The Obstacle Race*, 1979), on fertility and maternity (*Sex and Destiny*, 1984), on Shakespeare (1986), and on the menopause *The Change* (1991).
Bib: Plante, D., *Three Difficult Women*.

Grimm's Fairy Tales

German folk-tales collected by the brothers Jacob (1785–1863) and Wilhelm (1786–1859) Grimm, and published 1812–15. They first appeared in English in a volume illustrated by ▷ George Cruickshank and containing such stories as 'Snow White', 'Hansel and Gretel' and 'Rumpelstilskin'. They were the first collectors to write down the stories just as they heard them, without attempting to improve them.

▷ Children's books; Fairy tales.

Grossmith, George (1847–1912) and Weedon (1852–1919)

The brothers were both involved with the theatre, coming from a theatrical family, friends of the Terrys and Henry Irving. They are remembered, however, for *The Diary of a Nobody* (1892), initially serialized in ▷ *Punch*, written by both brothers and illustrated by Weedon. The nobody in question, Mr Pooter, sensitive to the slightest humiliation, conveys the events and contemporary background detail in a life striving for gentility. The book was immediately successful, with a wide readership, and has remained popular.

Grub Street

A street in London frequented in the 18th century by hack writers. Hence 'Grub Street' (adjective or noun) indicates literature or journalism of a low order. In the 19th century it was renamed Milton Street.
    ▷ *New Grub Street.*

Grundy, Mrs

A symbol of narrow-minded, intolerant, out-of-date moral censoriousness. The symbol derives from a character in an otherwise forgotten play, *Speed the Plough* (1798) by Thomas Morton. Mrs Grundy herself never appears, but her neighbour, Mrs Ashfield, is constantly worried about what Mrs Grundy's opinion will be about this or that incident or piece of behaviour.

Gulliver's Travels (1726)

A satirical fable by ▷ Jonathan Swift. It exploits the contemporary interest in accounts of voyages *eg* William Dampier's *New Voyage* (1697). ▷ Daniel Defoe's fictional account of Robinson Crusoe's voyages had been published in 1719, and had achieved great popularity; this was partly due to Defoe's strictly factual presentation, such that his book could quite well pass for a true account. Swift makes his hero, Lemuel Gulliver, recount his adventures with the same sober precision for the effect of accuracy, causing him, as Defoe caused Crusoe, to follow the philosopher ▷ John Locke in describing only the primary qualities of his strange environments – *ie* the objective, measurable ones – ignoring the secondary qualities of colour, beauty, etc. which are more subjective, less verifiable, and so more likely to arouse a reader's disbelief. Swift's intention in doing this was of course not to deceive his readers into supposing that Gulliver's fantastic adventures were true, but to make them realize the absurdity, and worse, of accepted human characteristics when they are looked at from an unfamiliar point of view. Thus in Part I, ▷ *Lilliput*, Gulliver is wrecked on an island where human beings are little bigger than insects, and their self-importance is clearly laughable, but in Part II, *Brobdingnag*, he is himself an insect in a land of giants, and made to feel his own pettiness. In Part III, contemporary scientists of the Royal Society are held up for ridicule: science is shown to be futile unless it is applicable to human betterment – the science of Swift's day had not yet reached the stage of technology. Part IV is about the land of the ▷

Houyhnhnms, where horses are endowed with reason but human beings are not; the point here is that the horses recognize that Gulliver has reason, unlike the Yahoos of the island which he so much resembles, but they succeed in demonstrating to him that human reason is woefully inadequate for the conduct of life because of the mischievousness of the human mind. Swift was, after all, a Christian, and believed that Man would destroy himself without divine aid.

Swift was such a good story-teller that his fable became popular for the sake of the narrative, and though it was in no ordinary sense a novel, his close attention to factual detail (the way in which, especially in Parts I and II, Gulliver is continuously under the pressure of his environment) takes a long stride in the advance of novelistic art.
    ▷ Lagado; Luggnagg.

Gunning, Elizabeth (1769–1823)

Novelist and translator. Daughter of the Augustan novelist Susannah Gunning, the sensational nature of Elizabeth's family life led ▷ Walpole to entitle them the 'Gunningiad'. Elizabeth herself rejected the husband her father chose for her, instead pursuing a relationship with a somewhat reluctant suitor. However, it was when she was accused of forging letters that her father disowned her and she was left dependent upon the bounty of her mother, which she also came close to losing. Her novels are reminiscent of her mother's writing, following the traditions of sentiment and melodrama, with aristocratic settings and sensational plots, and include *The Orphans of Snowdon* (1797) and *The Gipsy Countess* (1799). *Family Stories* (1802) purports to be a collection of magic tales for children, but retells the traditional material from a darker and more adult perspective.

Guy Mannering (1815)

A novel by ▷ Sir Walter Scott. It is set in the south of Scotland near the English border during the 18th century. The plot concerns the attempt of a criminal lawyer, Glossin, to deprive Harry Bertram, the heir to the Scottish estate of Ellangowan, of his property. Bertram is kidnapped as a child by smugglers in Glossin's pay, and carried abroad. He returns to Scotland as a young man and recovers his estate with the help of a gipsy who lives on it, Meg Merrilies. Mannering is an English officer under whom Bertram has served in the army, and with whose daughter Julia he is in love. The novel is notable partly for its romantic scene-painting, and partly for the characterization which is markedly more vivid in the lower social orders – the ▷ gipsies, the farmer Dandy Dinmont, the tutor Dominie Sampson – than in its ladies and gentlemen. There are also very good descriptions of Edinburgh.

H

Haggard, Sir H. (Henry) Rider (1856–1925)
Son of a Norfolk squire, he spent several years
in South Africa as a young man, writing books
on its history and farming, but he is famous for
his numerous adventure novels set in such exotic
locations as Iceland, Mexico and ancient Egypt. They
are characterized by gripping narrative and strange
events, as well as evocative descriptions of landscape,
wildlife and tribal society, particularly in Africa. He
has had a world-wide readership and some of his
stories have been filmed. *King Solomon's Mines* (1886)
and *She* (1887) are the most famous novels. *The Days
of My Life: an Autobiography* appeared in 1926.
Bib: Haggard, L. R., *The Cloak that I Left*; Ellis,
P. B., *H. Rider Haggard: A voice from the Infinite*;
Higgins, D. S., *Rider Haggard: The Great Storyteller*.

Hakluyt, Richard (?1553–1616)
Geographer. In 1589 and 1598 he published
his *Principal Navigations, Voyages and Discoveries
of the English Nation*, being a record of English
explorations, which had lagged behind those of the
French, Spanish, Portuguese and Dutch until the
middle of the century, and then made prodigious
progress with the nationalistic energy characteristic of
England in the reign of Elizabeth I.

Hall, Edward (?1498–1547)
Chronicler; author of *The Union of the Noble and
Illustrious Families of Lancaster and York* (1542;
enlarged 1548, 1550). This tells of the bitter rivalries
of the two branches of the House of Anjou from
the death of the childless Richard II in 1400, and
the accession of Henry IV, first of the House of
Lancaster, to the death of the last of the House of
York, Richard III, in 1485, and the accession of
Henry Tudor as Henry VII. He idealizes Henry VII
and Henry VIII, partly because they re-established
dynastic harmony, and partly because, as a ▷
Protestant, Hall was strongly sympathetic to Henry
VIII's reform of the Church. The Chronicle was
one of Shakespeare's two main source-books for his
English history plays, the other being ▷ Holinshed.
▷ Histories and Chronicles.

Hall, Joseph (1574–1656)
Satirist; 'character' (▷ Characters, Theophrastian)
writer; religious controversialist; bishop, 1627–47.
He published his *Virgidemiae* (or *Harvest of Rods*,
ie for chastisement) in 1597–8; he claimed to
be the first English satirist, but John Donne and
John Marston were writing at the same time, not
to mention Edmund Spenser's *Mother Hubberd's
Tale*. He may have considered himself more truly
a satirist than his rivals inasmuch as he was stricter
in following classical Latin models, notably of
Juvenal. Like Juvenal, he attacked what he saw as
contemporary vices. His *Characters of Virtues and
Vices* (1608) was likewise in classical tradition, this
time modelled on the Greek Theophrastus, and
was also intended for the moral improvement of
the age.
Bib: Davenport, A., *The Poems of Joseph Hall*;
Huntley, F. L., *Bishop Joseph Hall*.

Hall, Marguerite Radclyffe (1883–1943)
Novelist, poet and short-story writer. Her novel *The
Well of Loneliness* (1928) is perhaps the most famous
lesbian novel ever published; it concerns the lesbian
relationship of a writer, who eventually loses her
partner to a male rival, but, having acknowledged her
own sexuality, is enabled to write a successful novel.
The book was banned on first appearance, despite
the support of writers such as ▷ Virginia Woolf and
▷ E. M. Forster; it was republished in 1949. Born in
Hampshire, England, Hall wrote poetry from an early
age, and began to publish with *Twixt Earth and Stars*
(1906), followed by *A Sheaf of Verses* (1908), in which
she started to represent and explore her lesbianism
in the poems 'The Scar' and 'Ode to Sappho'. She
won the Prix Femina and the James Tait Black
Memorial Prize for the novel *Adam's Breed* (1926),
before the notoriety caused by *The Well of Loneliness*.
Her other novels are: *The Unlit Lamp* (1924), about
a destructive mother–daughter relationship; *The
Forge* (1924); *A Saturday Life* (1925); *The Master of the
House* (1932); *The Sixth Beatitude* (1936). *Miss Ogilvy
Finds Herself* (1934) is a collection of stories.
▷ Feminism; Lesbian and Gay Writing.
Bib: Dickson, L., *Radclyffe Hall and the Well of
Loneliness*; Franks, C.S., *Beyond the Well of Loneliness:
The Fiction of Radclyffe Hall*; Baker, M., *Our Three
Selves: A Life of Radclyffe Hall*; Troutbridge, U.B., *The
Life and Death of Radclyffe Hall*.

Hamilton, Elizabeth (1758–1816)
Essayist and satirist. Elizabeth Hamilton is known
to have predicted her fate as 'one cheerful, pleased,
old maid', and although she became ill during the
last years of her life, this proved to be a very apt
prophecy. Her many publications include *Translation
of the Letters of a Hindoo Rajah* (1796), which is not
a translation but a satire of contemporary British
society through the eyes of the fictional character of
an Indian Rajah, and *Memoirs of Modern Philosophers*
(1800), which attacks contemporary society for its
treatment of women, but simultaneously exposes the
ludicrousness of women who believe they can alter
anything. For example, she attacked contemporary
philosophers as, 'men who, without much knowledge,
either moral or natural, entertain a high idea of their
own superiority from having the temerity to reject
whatever has the sanction of experience and common
sense'. She also wrote on education and undertook
historical character sketches.
Bib: Butler, M., *Jane Austen and the War of Ideas*.

Hamilton, Patrick (1904–1962)
Novelist and playwright. His trilogy *Twenty Thousand
Streets Under the Sky* (1935), comprising *The Midnight
Bell* (1929), *The Siege of Pleasure* (1932) and *The
Plains of Cement* (1934), revolves around the lives of
a prostitute, a barmaid and a waiter in London, and
portrays a characteristically seedy world of streets
and bars. He also wrote thrillers, both in the form of
novels, such as *Hangover Square* (1941), and in the
form of plays, most notably *Rope* (1929) and *Gaslight*
(1939). His other novels include *Craven House* (1926)
and *The Slaves of Solitude* (1947), both of which are
set in London boarding-houses.

Hammett, Dashiell (1984–1961)
▷ Detective fiction.

Hanway, Mary Ann (c 1775–1815)
Novelist. Little is known about Hanway's life, and she is memorable mainly for her ▷ Minerva novels. The plots of her works are predictable – beautiful, orphaned heroines discover their long-lost parents and marry happily – and the didacticism advocating unadulterated moral virtue is cloying and repetitive. But Hanway's figurative language, although unsophisticated, is passionate and ornate, and some of the descriptive passages appear darkly obsessive. These preoccupations are coupled with an odd, but clearly stated, intention of writing so that her female readers could expunge their own emotional and bodily disorders through the process of reading the texts. As well as seeing novels as a form of therapy, Hanway held other ideas in advance of her time: she attacked contemporary society for the way in which it treated black people, and perceived that the education system was biased towards men (▷ Women, Education of).
Bib: Schlueter, P. and J., *An Encyclopedia of British Women Writers*.

Hard Times (1854)
A novel by ▷ Charles Dickens. It is the only one by him not at least partly set in London. The scene is an imaginary industrial town called Coketown. One of the main characters, Thomas Gradgrind, is based on the ▷ Utilitarian leader James Mill (1773–1836); as such, he is an educationist who believes that education should be merely practical and hence factual, allowing no place for imagination or emotion. He marries his daughter Louisa to a ruthless manufacturer, Josiah Bounderby, who puts Gradgrind's philosophy into practice in that he has no place for humane feeling in the conduct of his business. Louisa accepts him in order to be in a position to help her brother Tom who becomes, under the influence of his upbringing, callous, unscrupulous and meanly calculating. Louisa is nearly seduced by a visiting politician, James Harthouse, who is cynically concerned only to find amusement in a place with no other charms. The opposition to this world of calculating selfishness is a travelling circus called 'the horse-riding' owned by Sleary. Sissy Jupe, a product of the circus and the human fellowship that it engenders, is found ineducable by Gradgrind, whose dependant she becomes, but she has the inner assurance required to face Harthouse and compel him to leave the town. Gradgrind's world falls apart when he discovers that he has ruined his daughter's happiness and turned his son into a criminal. A subplot concerns a working-man, Stephen Blackpool, a victim of the Gradgrind-Bounderby system, and of young Gradgrind's heartless criminality.

Hardy, Thomas (1840–1928)
Novelist and poet, and former architect. He was the son of a village stonemason in Dorset; thus he was close to the country life by his origins, and he never lost feeling for it. As he grew up, he underwent the painful loss of faith so common among intellectuals in England in the second half of the 19th century; this led him to a tragic philosophy that human beings are the victims of indifferent forces. At the same time he witnessed the steady weakening from within and erosion from without of the part of rural England with which he was so much indentified. This region is the six south-western counties of England, approximately coterminous with the 6th-century Saxon kingdom of ▷ Wessex, by which name he calls them in his 'Novels of Character and Environment'. These novels are by far his best known: ▷ *Under the Greenwood Tree* (1872); ▷ *Far from the Madding Crowd* (1874); ▷ *The Return of the Native* (1878); ▷ *The Mayor of Casterbridge* (1886); ▷ *The Woodlanders* (1887); ▷ *Tess of the D'Urbervilles* (1891); ▷ *Jude the Obscure* (1895). Two volumes of stories are *Wessex Tales* (1888) and *Life's Little Ironies* (1894). Hardy's originality was his discernment of the intimate relationship of character and environment, and his characters nearly always became less convincing when this relationship loses closeness, *ie* in his socially higher, more sophisticated characters. This may account for the fact that the other two groups of his novels have much less prestige. He called them 'Romances and Fantasies' (*A Pair of Blue Eyes*, 1873; *The Trumpet-Major*, 1880; *Two on a Tower*, 1882; *A Group of Noble Dames*, 1891; *The Well-Beloved*, 1897) and 'Novels of Ingenuity' (*Desperate Remedies*, 1871; *The Hand of Ethelberta*, 1876; *A Laodicean*, 1881).

Hardy's poetry is as distinguished as his novels; indeed he regarded himself as primarily a poet. Though he wrote poetry from the beginning of his career, his best verse was chiefly the fruit of his later years when he had abandoned novels. It is in some respects very traditional – ballads such as *The Trampwoman's Tragedy* and tuneful, rhyming lyrics. But though traditional – in touch with folksong and ballad – Hardy was never conventional. His diction is distinctive; he experimented constantly with form and stresses, and the singing rhythms subtly respond to the movement of his intense feelings; the consequent poignance and sincerity has brought him the admiration of poets since 1945, who seem especially sensitive to dishonesty of feeling. His lyrics have the peculiarity that they nearly always centre on incident, in a way that gives them dramatic sharpness. Amongst the most admired are some that he wrote to his dead first wife, included in *Satires of Circumstance* (1914).
Bib: Hardy, E., *Life*; Brown, D., *Thomas Hardy*; Weber, C. J., *Hardy of Wessex*; Stewart, J. I. M., *Thomas Hardy: A Critical Biography*; Gittings, R., *Young Thomas Hardy*; *The Older Hardy*; Millgate, M., *Thomas Hardy: A Biography*; *Thomas Hardy, His Career as a Novelist*; Bayley, J., *An Essay on Hardy*; Boumelha, P., *Thomas Hardy and Women*.

Harris, Wilson (b 1921)
Guyanese novelist and short-story writer. The landscape and history of Guyana play an important part in his work, which is concerned with such issues as the legacy of the colonial past and the destruction and recreation of individual and collective identity. His novels are visionary, experimental,

anti-realist explorations of consciousness, employing multiple and fragmentary narrative structures, and symbolic correspondences between inner and outer landscapes. The later novels use a wider range of geographical settings, including England, Mexico and South America. His volumes of short stories, *The Sleepers of Roraima* (1970) and *The Age of the Rainmakers* (1971) locate a redemptive power in Amerindian myth. His novels are: *The Guyana Quartet: Palace of the Peacock* (1960); *The Far Journey of Oudu* (1961); *The Whole Armour* (1962) and *The Secret Ladder* (1963); *Heartland* (1964); *The Eye of the Scarecrow* (1965); *The Waiting Room* (1967); *Tutamari* (1968); *Ascent to Omai* (1970); *Black Marsden* (1972); *Companions of the Day and Night* (1975); *Da Silva da Silva's Cultivated Wilderness, and the Genesis of the Clowns* (1977); *The Tree of the Sun* (1978); *The Angel at the Gate* (1982); and a trilogy consisting of: *Carnival* (1985), *The Infinite Rehearsal* (1987) and *The Far Banks of the River of Space* (1990).

▷ Post-colonial fiction.
Bib: Gilkes, M., *Wilson Harris and the Caribbean Novel*.

Hartley, L. P. (Leslie Poles) (1895–1972)

Novelist. His novels and stories are: *Night Fears* (1924); *Simonetta Perkins* (1925); *The Killing Bottle* (1932); a trilogy – *The Shrimp and the Anemone* (1944), *The Sixth Heaven* (1946) and *Eustace and Hilda* (1947); *The Travelling Grave* (1948); *The Boat* (1949); *My Fellow Devils* (1951); *The Go-Between* (1953); *The White Wand* (1954) *A Perfect Woman* (1955); *The Hireling* (1957); *Facial Justice* (1960); *Two for the River* (1961); *The Brickfield* (1964); *The Betrayal* (1966); *Poor Clare* (1968); *The Love Adept* (1968); *My Sister's Keeper* (1970); *The Harness Room* (1971); *The Collections* (1972); *The Will and the Way* (1973). His reputation rests chiefly on the trilogy (especially *The Shrimp and the Anemone*) and *The Go-Between*. These both contain very sensitive child studies, and relate the influence of childhood experiences on the development of the adult. Hartley wrote in the tradition of ▷ Henry James, whom he resembles in his presentation of delicate but crucial personal inter-relationships; the influence of ▷ Sigmund Freud intervened to give Hartley a different kind of psychological depth, more concerned with the recovery of the self buried in the forgotten experiences of the past than with the self buried under the false assumptions of society.
Bib: Bien, P., *Hartley*; Mulkeen, A., *Wild Thyme, Winter Lightning*.

Hawkins, Laetitia-Matilda (1759–1835)

'Novelist, autobiographer and travel writer. Her father was the scholar John Hawkins, who produced one of the first histories of music as well as a life of ▷ Dr Johnson. Johnson, who appointed Hawkins as his executor, found him difficult, and this is certainly also the experience of his daughter, who felt that her spirit had been broken by his incessant condemnation and criticism. Her first works were published anonymously, but she used her own name for *The Countess and Gertrude, or Modes of Discipline* (1811). Her narratives often depict a repressed and

self-deprecating heroine, who battles to assert herself over her male relatives. She produced a somewhat amorphous ▷ autobiography with general comments, *Anecdotes, Biographical Sketches and memoirs* (1823), which was mocked by ▷ De Quincey. Her novels, however, were admired by ▷ Jane Austen. Her ▷ travel writings remain in manuscript form.
Bib: Todd, J., *Dictionary of British Women Writers*.

Haywood, Eliza (?1693–1756)

Haywood's literary career spanned some 30 years, from the publication of *Love in Excess or The Fatal Enquiry* (1719) to *Jemmy and Jenny Jessamy* (1753). Haywood was a prolific and highly successful writer: works known to be by her amount to almost a hundred, and she may also have published anonymously.

Like ▷ Delarivière Manley and ▷ Aphra Behn, Haywood's literary reputation has been obscured by the notoriety of her personal life. Alexander Pope (1688–1744) satirized her in *The Dunciad*, as a 'Juno of majestic size/ With cow-like udders, and with ox-like eyes', her sexual favours offered as the prize in a urinating contest. Yet Pope's vituperative attack, which has been regarded as evidence of misogyny, should be read in the context of the satire on literary hacks; the rival contestants Curll and Chetwood are no less damningly portrayed.

Haywood's novels were widely acclaimed, bringing her something of the status of a 'best-seller'. Their great diversity in tone and scope reflects a period of considerable change in novelistic fashions; the earliest works use romantic names, while the later employ 'character' types such as Trueworth, Saving and Gaylord, and there is an increasing emphasis on the female experience and the heroine as central character.

Haywood was also a prolific journalist, founding, amongst other periodicals, *The Female Spectator*, a women's equivalent to the periodicals of Joseph Addison and ▷ Steele. The articles generally deal with issues of social conduct and moral behaviour, and show an advanced attitude to sexual politics. Haywood also had a brief theatrical career in both writing and acting; her play, *A Wife to Be Let* (1724), was staged at Drury Lane with the author herself as a leading actress, and in the 1730s her frequent stage appearances included roles in *Arden of Faversham* and *The Opera of Operas* (1733), her own operatic version of *Tom Thumb*.

H. D. (Hilda Doolittle) (1886–1961)

Poet. H. D. was born in Bethlehem, Pennsylvania, educated at Bryn Mawr, where she was a contemporary of American poet Marianne Moore, and moved to Britain in 1911. She was an important figure in the Imagist group, signing her first poems, published in Harriet Monroe's *Poetry* in 1913, 'H. D. Imagiste'. She was a close associate of Ezra Pound, to whom she was briefly engaged in 1907. The 'Hellenic hardness' of her work epitomized Imagism. She married fellow writer Richard Aldington in 1913, becoming part of the network sometimes known as the 'Other ▷ Bloomsbury' which was dominated by ▷ D. H. Lawrence, who is characterized in H. D.'s

novel *Bid Me To Live* (published 1960). From 1916
she co-edited, with T. S. Eliot, *The Egoist*, Dora
Marsden's originally ▷ feminist journal which had
published amongst other texts ▷ James Joyce's ▷
Portrait of the Artist as a Young Man in serial form in
1914–15. In 1917 H. D. separated from Aldington,
gave birth to her daughter Perdita, and began to
travel with her friend ▷ Bryher (Winifred Ellerman),
with whom she spent much of the rest of her life.
Her first collection, *Sea Garden*, was published in
1916, followed by *Hymen* (1921), *Heliodora and Other
Poems* (1924), and *Red Roses for Bronze* (1929). The
trilogy, *The Walls Do Not Fall* (1944–6) and *Helen in
Egypt* (1961), perhaps H. D.'s most important works,
have only recently received the critical attention
they deserve. Her poetry is intense, difficult, and
infused with her passion for classical Greek culture.
Although primarily known as a poet, H. D. wrote
novels, and having undergone psychoanalysis with ▷
Freud in Vienna 1933–4, published an account of the
process. *Tribute to Freud* is important both as a poetic
and visionary text and as a key text in debates about
psychoanalysis and feminism.
Bib: Duplessis, R. B., *H. D. The Career of That
Struggle*; Buck, C., *H. D. and Freud: Bisexuality and a
Feminine Discourse*.

Head, Bessie Emery (1937–86)
African novelist and short-story writer. Born in
South Africa in a mental hospital, where her
Scottish mother had been confined as a result of her
relationship with her Zulu father, she was brought
up by a foster family until the age of thirteen, then
attended a mission school in Durban and trained
as a teacher. She taught in South Africa, worked
as a journalist for *Drum* magazine and became
involved in African nationalist circles, but in 1963
went into exile in Botswana, where she worked,
with other political refugees, in a village garden
co-operative at Serowe, commemorated in her book
Serowe: Village of the Rain Wind (1981), which is built
around interviews. She took Botswanan citizenship in
1979. Her first three novels contain a considerable
element of autobiography, most notably *A Question
of Power* (1974), which is based directly on her own
experience of mental breakdown, but also *When Rain
Clouds Gather* (1969), about a Botswana agrarian
community, and *Maru* (1971), which deals with
racial prejudice through the story of an orphaned
Masarwa woman, teaching in a Botswanan village
where her people are regarded as outcasts. *The
Collector of Treasures and Other Botswana Village Tales*
(1977) is a volume of short stories, while *A Bewitched
Crossroad: An African Saga* (1984) is a history of the
Bamangwato tribe. *Tales of Tenderness and Power*,
published posthumously in 1989, is a collection of
stories, personal observations and legends, while
A Woman Alone, published posthumously in 1990,
consists of autobiographical fragments.
Bib: Vigne, R., (ed.), *A Gesture of Belonging: Letters
from Bessie Head 1965–1979*; MacKenzie, C.,
Bessie Head: An Introduction; MacKenzie, C., and
Clayton, C., *Between the Lines: Interviews with Bessie
Head*; Abrahams, C., *Bessie Head and Literature in
South Africa*.

Headlong Hall (1816)
A novel by ▷ Thomas Love Peacock. It is his
first and shows the main characteristics of his
maturer work: witty, burlesque conversations
and, innovatively, very little plot. The narrative is
interspersed with attractive lyrics and songs. As in
his other novels, the characters are caricatures of
contemporary types.

Heart of Darkness (1902)
A ▷ novella by ▷ Joseph Conrad. It is narrated by
Marlow, an officer in the Merchant Navy who also
appears in Conrad's other works ▷ *Lord Jim*, *Youth*
and *Chance*. Sitting on board a ship anchored in the
lower reaches of the River Thames, he tells a group
of friends the story of his journey up the Congo
River in Africa, in the employment of a Belgian
trading company. This supposedly benevolent
organization is in fact ruthlessly enslaving the
Africans and stripping the area of ivory, and what
Marlow sees on his arrival in Africa disgusts him. At
the company's Central Station he hears much about
Kurtz, their most successful agent, who is apparently
lying ill at the Inner Station upriver. Marlow's
attempts to set out to reach him are delayed by the
machinations of the manager and other agents, who
are jealous of Kurtz's success. When the steamer
which Marlow is to captain is finally repaired, and
the party sets off, Marlow experiences a powerful
sense of dread as the boat carries them deeper
into the primitive world of the jungle, but this is
combined with a strong desire to meet Kurtz. After
being attacked by natives from the bank, they reach
the Inner Station, where an eccentric young Russian
adventurer who idolizes Kurtz tells Marlow of his
power over the local inhabitants, and the fluency
and fascination of his ideas. But Kurtz's hut is
surrounded by heads on poles, and it becomes
apparent that, in addition to writing a report on the
'Suppression of Savage Customs', ending with the
words 'exterminate all the brutes!', he has become
compulsively addicted to unspecified barbaric
practices, presumably involving human sacrifice.
He has also acquired an African mistress. Marlow
tries to get Kurtz away down river, but he dies, his
last words being 'The horror! The horror!'. Back in
Europe, Marlow tells Kurtz's fiancée that he died
with her name on his lips.
   The story has come to be regarded as a classic of
20th-century literature, and its ambiguity has made
it the subject of numerous interpretations. It has
also been criticized by some, notably by the Nigerian
novelist ▷ Chinua Achebe, for containing racist
assumptions.

Heart of Midlothian, The (1818)
A novel by ▷ Sir Walter Scott. Midlothian is a
county in Scotland in which Edinburgh, the Scottish
capital, is situated. The title refers to the old
Tolbooth prison in Edinburgh, so nicknamed. The
central part of the story is Jeanie Deans's journey
on foot to London in order to appeal to the Duke of
Argyle – a Scottish nobleman high in royal favour –
on behalf of her sister Effie who has been wrongfully
charged with child murder. Argyle was a historical

character, and the events are linked up with the attack on the Tolbooth – known as the Porteous Riot – which actually took place in 1736. As in other novels by Scott about 18th-century Scotland, the characterization is vigorous, *eg* of Madge Wildfire who has abducted the child whom Effie is supposed to have murdered, and Dumbiedikes, the silent suitor of Jeanie. It is often regarded as the best of Scott's novels.

Heath, Roy (b 1926)
Novelist. Heath was born in Guyana, and educated at the University of London. He worked as a clerk and then as a primary school teacher in London before being called to the Bar at Lincoln's Inn in 1964; since 1968 he has taught French and German in London. His novels combine realism and mythic patterns to portray Guyanese life in the 20th century, focusing in particular on stories of personal struggle and tragic family relations among the poor and lower middle class of Georgetown. For example his *Georgetown Trilogy*, comprising *From the Heat of the Day* (1979), *One Generation* (1981) and *Genetha* (1981), chronicles the life of a single family. His other novels are: *A Man Came Home* (1974); *The Murderer* (1978); *Kwaku: or, the Man Who Could Not Keep His Mouth Shut* (1982); *Orealla* (1984); *The Shadow Bride* (1988). He has also published short stories, a play and an autobiographical work, *Shadow Round the Moon: Caribbean Memoirs* (1990).

Hegemony
Originally used to denote political domination. In its more modern meaning and its use in literary criticism it has come to refer to that process of political control whereby the interests of a dominant class in society are shared by those subordinated to it. Hegemony depends upon the consent of subordinate classes to their social positions, but the constraints within which that consent operates, and the ways in which it is experienced, are determined by the dominant class. This concept also offers ways of understanding the different kinds of social and personal relationships represented in literary texts. Along with a number of other concepts, it opens the way for an analysis of the different forms of negotiation that take place within texts, and between text and reader, and serves to emphasize the social context of experience, ▷ consciousness and human interaction.

Henry Esmond, The History of (1852)
A historical novel by ▷ William Makepeace Thackeray. It is a very careful reconstruction of early 18th-century English aristocratic and literary society. The hero's father has been killed fighting for James II, *ie* he was a Jacobite. The politics of the book are involved with Jacobite plotting by the Roman Catholic branch of the House of Stuart to recover the throne of Britain from the Protestant branch. There are portraits of some of the distinguished personalities of the time – the Duke and Duchess of Marlborough, and the writers ▷ Sir Richard Steele, Joseph Addison and ▷ Jonathan Swift. The style

emulates that of Addison himself. The theme is the devotion of the young Henry Esmond to his relatives, Lady Castlewood, eight years older than himself, and her proud and ambitious daughter, Beatrix. These relationships are complicated by political intrigues and by family mysteries – Esmond is in reality himself the heir to the title and properties inherited by Lady Castlewood's husband. In the end, Esmond marries the widowed Lady Castlewood and emigrates to Virginia; his story continues in *The Virginians* (1857–9).

Heptarchy
From the 5th to 9th centuries England was divided into a number of kingdoms, considered by 16th-century historians to have been seven (hence heptarchy, for seven kingdoms). These were: Northumbria in the north, Mercia in the midlands, East Anglia and Essex in the east, Kent in the south-east, Sussex and ▷ Wessex in the south and south-west. Such kingdoms certainly existed but in fact the number was sometimes larger than seven, sometimes smaller. Essex (=East Saxons), Sussex (= South Saxons) and Kent have survived into modern England as counties. Wessex was a geographical term revived by ▷ Thomas Hardy in his regional novels. East Anglia is still used for the counties of Norfolk (= North folk) and Suffolk (= South folk) together. Northumberland remains as the nucleus of the former much larger Northumbria. The term Mercia is rarely used, Midlands having replaced it.

Heraclitus (6th century BC)
Greek philosopher. He taught that the primary element is fire and that all being is, despite appearances, the process of 'becoming', by the harmonious interaction of opposites (hot, cold; dark, light; good, evil; etc.). 'The law of things is a law of Reason universal; but most men behave as though they had a wisdom of their own.' His mysticism and his sombre view of human nature caused him to be designated 'the dark philosopher'. Gerard Manley Hopkins' poem 'That Nature is a Heraclitean fire . . .' is an interesting example of the 19th century's attempt to found its beliefs in classical antecedents.

Herbert, James (b 1943)
Britain's best-selling ▷ horror novelist, Herbert rose to notoriety in the 1970s as a purveyor of unabashed visceral gore set in grimy, modern urban surroundings. His first novel *The Rats* (1974) was a huge paperback hit, earning Herbert the title 'King of the Nasties'; described by the author as a metaphor for urban collapse in which 'the rats are the establishment', the novel set new standards of gruesome violence for popular horror fiction. Although subsequent works such as *The Fog*, *Lair* and *Domain* have continued this penchant for dismemberment, Herbert has also explored more subtle territory; *Fluke* (1977) is a satirical reincarnation fantasy notable for its restrained tone, while *Shrine* (1983) takes a bold swipe at organized

religion and fraudulent 'miracles'. Having worked as an advertising art director before turning to writing, Herbert is unique in retaining total control of his book covers, which he designs himself. Works include: *The Survivor* (1976); *The Spear* (1978); *The Dark* (1980); *The Jonah* (1981); *Domain* (1984); *Moon* (1985); *The Magic Cottage* (1987).

Hermeneutics

Used in literary criticism to denote the science of interpretation as opposed to commentary. Hermeneutics is concerned primarily with the question of determining meaning, and is based upon the presupposition of a transcendental notion of understanding, and a conception of truth as being in some sense beyond language. Hermeneutics also postulates that there is one truth, and is therefore opposed on principle to the notion of 'pluralism' that is associated with ▷ deconstruction and materialist readings.

Heroic, Mock

A literary mode in which large and important events are juxtaposed with small and insignificant ones for a variety of comic, satirical or more profoundly ironic effects. In its narrow sense mock heroic is the product of the Augustan, neo-classical age. As the bourgeoisie wrested cultural hegemony from the aristocracy in the late 17th century, a new, more complex attitude to the ancient aristocratic ideals of honour and nobility developed. A new irony infused their literary expression in the ▷ classical forms of ▷ epic and tragedy. Epic retained the respect of the reading public, but it was too archaic and primitive to satisfy the modern imagination in its traditional form. John Milton's *Paradise Lost* (1667), the only significant literary epic in English (*Beowulf* being an oral poem) has about it much of the complexity of the novel, and its more atavistic heroic elements (the war in heaven, the vision of future history) seem mechanical. In the generations following Milton, the major poets, John Dryden (1631–1700) and Alexander Pope (1688–1744) translated the ancient epics, but their own original work took the more complex form of mock epic.

Although mock heroic is most closely associated with the age of Dryden, ▷ Jonathan Swift and Pope, it is found in all periods. An early example is ▷ Chaucer's *Nun's Priest's Tale* in which the cock behaves like a prince, although he is merely the property of a poor widow. The 'most Lamentable Comedy' of Pyramus and Thisby, performed by Bottom and the 'mechanicals' in *A Midsummer Night's Dream*, is a particularly complex example. In the Victorian period, mock heroic can be seen in simple form in the endearing pomposity of ▷ Charles Dickens's Pickwick, and also in the more earnest social satire of such characters as Pecksniff and Dombey. In the 20th century the full complexity of 18th-century mock heroic is again achieved in ▷ James Joyce's ▷ *Ulysses*, whose carefully worked-out parallels with ▷ Homer's ▷ *Odyssey* are designed to demonstrate the comic irrelevance to human existence of any pretension to order, hierarchy, or even meaning.

Hervey, Elizabeth (c 1748–c 1820)

Novelist. Hervey was the half-sister of ▷ William Beckford, who is thought to have attacked her in *Modern Novel Writing* for writing sentimental novels, although his attack could equally well be directed at ▷ Hannah More or ▷ Mary Robinson. Whoever the target, Hervey appears to have been genuinely upset, partly because the accusation was not particularly just. Her works exhibit some of the plot characteristics of sentimental novels – for example in *Louisa* (1789) the heroine is selflessly devoted to the illegitimate child of her betrothed – but her character sketches and descriptive passages are sharper and more self-consciously witty than Beckford's summation suggests.

Heyer, Georgette (1902–1974)

Novelist. Goergette Heyer was a phenomenally prolific and popular writer of detective stories and historical romances, the latter populated with a mixture of fictional characters and real historical figures, and often set in the Regency period. Whilst her writing has traditionally been criticized for its predictably escapist plots, recent feminist work on romantic fiction has emphasized its interest as fantasy and the important role that her books play in many ordinary women's lives. Her works include: *The Black Moth* (1921); *Simon the Coldheart* (1925); *The Barren Court* (1930); *The Convenient Marriage* (1934); *Regency Buck* (1935); *Royal Escape* (1937); *Beau Wyndham* (1941); *Arabella* (1949); *Bath Tangle* (1955); *April Lady* (1957); *Freedom* (1965); *Lady of Quality* (1972). ▷ Detective fiction.
Bib: Radway, J., *Reading the Romance*.

Hill, Susan (b 1942)

Novelist, short-story writer and radio dramatist. Since graduating from London University, she has worked as a literary journalist and broadcaster. Her novels are sensitive, formal and conventionally structured, and tend to explore loss, isolation and grief. *In The Springtime of the Year* (1974) recounts the gradual adjustment to bereavement of a young widow. She has written effectively of the experience of children (*I'm The King of The Castle*; 1970) and the elderly (*Gentlemen and Ladies*; 1968). Two of the novels deal with intense male friendships; these are *The Bird of the Night* (1972) and, probably her best-known work, *Strange Meeting* (1971). The latter takes its title from a poem by Wilfred Owen, and is set in the trenches of Flanders during World War I. Other novels: *The Enclosure* (1961); *Do Me A Favour* (1963); *A Change for the Better* (1969); *The Woman in Black: A Ghost Story* (1983). Story collections are: *The Albatross* (1971); *The Custodian* (1972); *A Bit of Singing and Dancing* (1973).

Historical novel

A novel set in a well-defined historical context, generally before the author's own life (and therefore, in that sense at least, not based on the author's own experience, but on other sources, whether literary or historical). Historical novels often include versions of real events and persons and descriptions of social customs, clothing, buildings etc. to give an effect of verisimilitude. However, there are also more fantastical versions of the form, such as the ▷ Gothic novel (often though not always historical). Contemporary best-selling historical romances, such as those of ▷ Georgette Heyer, have a certain limited verisimilitude of detail, but a strong fantasy element as regards plot. An early example of the European historical novel is *The Princess of Clèves* by ▷ Madame de La Fayette, while later distinguished practitioners of the form include ▷ Balzac, ▷ Tolstoy, ▷ Stendhal and the German novelist Thomas Mann. In Britain it was ▷ Sir Walter Scott who established the popularity of the form, but there are examples by such novelists as ▷ Charles Dickens, ▷ George Eliot and ▷ Thomas Hardy and, more recently, ▷ William Golding and ▷ J.G. Farrell. There are also many historical novels by post-colonial writers about the colonial period, such as ▷ Patrick White's *Voss* and ▷ Chinua Achebe's *Arrow of God*. ▷ Historiographic metafiction represents a distinctively ▷ post-modernist version of the historical novel. **Bib:** Lukács, Georg, *The Historical Novel*.

Histories and Chronicles

Histories and chronicles are important in the study of literature in two ways: as sources for imaginative material and as literature in their own right. However, with the exception of the Venerable Bede, it was not until the 17th century that English historians began to achieve the status of major writers.

▷ Geoffrey of Monmouth (d 1154) is the most important amongst a number of medieval historians for originating two national myths in his *Historia Regum Britanniae*; the myth that Brutus, great-grandson of Aeneas, was the founder of the British race, and the myth of King Arthur as the great defender of British Christianity. Both had importance in nourishing nascent English patriotism. When England became a centralized state under the Tudor monarchs, Henry VII chose the name Arthur for his eldest son. It was the main task of Tudor chroniclers both to heighten patriotism and to identify it with loyalty to the ruling family. This was the purpose of the Latin history of England by the Italian Polydore Vergil, in the service of Henry VII and Henry VIII. More important was ▷ Edward Hall's *The Union of the two Noble and Illustrious Families of Lancaster and York* (1548), which showed the House of Tudor to be the saviour of the nation after the civil Wars of the Roses in the 15th century. ▷ Raphael Holinshed's *Chronicles of England, Scotland and Ireland* (1578) was a compilation from various sources, including Geoffrey of Monmouth, and begins in ancient biblical times. The belief of the time was that history was useful as the means by which the present could learn from the past as a source of warnings, precepts and examples. The imaginative writers used the material of the chronicles in this spirit. Geoffrey of Monmouth, Hall and Holinshed were sources for many of the historical dramas of the reign of Elizabeth including those of Shakespeare, and also for narrative poets such as those who contributed to *A Mirror for Magistrates* (1559), Samuel Daniel (*Civil Wars*, 1595–1609) and Michael Drayton (*The*

Barons' Wars, 1603). Much of this new interest in history arose from the Renaissance transference of attention from heavenly destinies to earthly ones; thus the period 1500–1650 also produced the first eminent antiquarians, notably William Camden (1551–1623), and the first historical ▷ biographies: ▷ Thomas More's *Richard III* (written 1513), George Cavendish's life of Cardinal Wolsey (written shortly after the Cardinal's death but not published in full until 1667), Francis Bacon's life of Henry VII (1622) and Lord Herbert's life of Henry VIII (1648).

The True Historical Narrative of the Rebellion and Civil Wars in England by ▷ Edward Hyde, Earl of Clarendon, is the first major historical work to rank as distinguished literature in English. Clarendon began it in 1646 but it was not published until 1702–4. It is told from the point of view of an important participator in the events and is notable especially for its portraits of other participators. Clarendon was a royalist; his younger contemporary, Gilbert Burnet (1643–1715), told the story of the second half of the century from the opposing political viewpoint in his most important work, *The History of My Own Time*. Burnet was more of a professional historian than Clarendon (who was primarily a statesman who took to history partly in self-justification) and he initiated historical writing as a major branch of literary activity and scholarship. The distinguished historical writing of William Robertson (*History of Scotland during the Reigns of Queen Mary and James VI*, 1759, and *Charles V*, 1769), of ▷ David Hume the philosopher (*History of Great Britain*, pub. 1754–61) and the lighter histories of England by the novelist ▷ Tobias Smollett (1756) and by ▷ Oliver Goldsmith (1764) have been superseded by later work, but ▷ Edward Gibbon's ▷ *Decline and Fall of the Roman Empire* (1776–88) is a work not only of history but of English literature and, in the quality of its outlook on civilization, an 18th-century monument.

The 18th century was the one in which antiquarian scholarship became thoroughly established; the antiquarians were interested by the nature of their studies in the detailed life of the past. ▷ Walter Scott was one of them and his historical novels, though very uneven in quality, are important as a new kind of history as well as a new kind of imaginative literature. It was his re-creation of the daily life of the past that was one of the influences upon ▷ Thomas Carlyle, whose historical works (the most notable of which is his *French Revolution*, 1837) are more imaginative than factual. ▷ T.B. Macaulay was a better historian and not inferior as an imaginative writer; ▷ *Macaulay's History of England* is the only historical work which comes near Gibbon's *Decline and Fall* in reputation, and Macaulay was responsible for the so-called 'Whig view of history' as steady progress in material welfare and political advance. Other eminent 19th-century English historians were J.A. Froude, who is, however, notorious for his prejudices in *A History of England from the Fall of Wolsey to the Spanish Armada* (1856–70), and J.R. Green whose *Short History of the English People* (1874) was for some time a popular classic owing to the breadth of Green's social sympathies. It was, however, in the 19th century that the controversy about history as an art or as a science developed, and other distinguished historians of the period tended to become comparatively specialized scholars without the breadth of appeal of such men as Gibbon and Macaulay. The latter's great-nephew, G.M. Trevelyan (1876–1962), continued the broader humane tradition of historical writing, as did Arnold Toynbee's *A Study of History* (1934–61). Recent theoretical developments have led to renewed questioning of the terms of historical knowledge: see for example the work of Hayden White.

Historiographic metafiction

Term coined by the critic Linda Hutcheon to refer to 'novels which are both intensely self-reflexive and yet paradoxically also lay claim to historical events and personages' (*A Poetics of Postmodernism: History, Theory, Fiction*). Examples are *The French Lieutenant's Woman* by ▷ John Fowles, and *Midnight's Children* by ▷ Salman Rushdie.

History of Rasselas, Prince of Abyssinia, The
   ▷ *Rasselas, Prince of Abyssinia, The History of.*

History of Sir Charles Grandison, The
   ▷ *Sir Charles Grandison, The History of*

Hoban, Russell (b 1925)

American novelist who has lived in London since 1969. After serving in the US army during World War II, he worked as a magazine and advertising artist and an advertising copywriter before becoming a full-time writer in 1967. His best-known work is *Ridley Walker* (1980), set 2,000 years after a nuclear war and written in an invented argot combining elements of cockney and technical language. His other novels are: *The Lion of Boaz-Jachim and Jachim-Boaz* (1973); *Kleinzeit* (1974); *Turtle Diary* (1976); *Pilgermann* (1983); *The Medusa Frequency* (1987). He has also published much fiction and verse for children, a play and a television play. He won the Whitbread Award in 1974.

Hobbes, John Oliver (1867–1906)

Pseudonym of Mrs Pearl (Mary Teresa) Craigie, Hobbes was born near Boston, Massachusetts, the daughter of a New York merchant. She moved with her family to London as a baby, and was educated in Berkshire and Paris. She read widely and published stories from the age of nine, later writing articles and criticism for journals. She married at 19, but the marriage was unhappy and she left her husband after the birth of their son, of whom she gained custody after a public trial. She became a Roman Catholic and added Mary Teresa to her name. Her first novel, *Some Emotions and A Moral* (1891), established her reputation. Others include *The Sinner's Comedy* (1892), *The Gods, Some Mortals and Lord Wickenham* (1895), *The Scheme for Saints* (1897), *Robert Orange* (1899) and *The Serious Wooing* (1901). Her several plays include *The Ambassador* (1898) and she wrote critical essays on ▷ George Eliot (1901) and ▷ George Sand (1902). She was a figure in London's

literary life and entertained at her father's house, was President of the Society of Women Journalists in 1895, but also a member of the Anti-Suffrage League, saying 'I have no confidence in the average woman or her brains.'

Hobbes, Thomas (1588–1679)

Philosopher. Together with the writings of Francis Bacon (1561–1626) and René Descartes (1596–1650), the political and philosophical theories of Thomas Hobbes dominated thought in late 17th-century England. Yet, unlike Bacon's boundless optimism, Hobbes's philosophy appeared to be determined by an almost cynical view of human nature and society. In his great analysis of the individual and the individual's place in society, *Leviathan* (1651), Hobbes argued that human society was governed by two overwhelming individual concerns: fear (of death, other individuals, etc) and the desire for power. For Hobbes society is organized according to these two principles, and can be rationally analysed as a 'mechanism' (an important Hobbesian concept) governed by these two concerns.

Leviathan itself emerged out of the turmoil of revolutionary upheaval in England during the Civil War (1642–51), and the figure of the 'Leviathan' – the sovereign power, though not necessarily the monarch – expresses a desire for stable government. But in addition to *Leviathan* Hobbes published in various fields of philosophical and social enquiry. His interest in language and the uses of ▷ rhetoric was to be influential amongst post-Restoration thinkers. But it was his analysis of the mechanical laws (as he saw them) of production, distribution and exchange which was to be of profound importance in British economic and philosophical thought in the 18th century and later.

Hobbes's chief works include: *The Elements of Law* (written by 1640, but published ten years later); *De Cive* (1642, translated into English in 1651); *De Corpore* (1655, translated in 1656); and *De Homine* (1658). Hobbes also undertook an analysis of the causes of the English Civil War in composing *Behemoth* (1682), as well as critical work – in particular his *Answer* to Sir William D'Avenant's *Preface to Gondibert* (1650).
Bib: Molesworth, Sir W. (ed.), *The English Works of Thomas Hobbes*, (11 vols.); Mintz, S. I., *The Hunting of Leviathan*.

Hogan, Desmond (b 1950)

Irish novelist, short-story writer and playwright. Born in County Galway and educated at University College Dublin, Hogan has worked as an actor, writer and teacher. His fiction, set in Ireland, has primarily been concerned with the tragic stories of vulnerable, isolated individuals. Novels: *The Ikon Maker* (1976); *The Leaves on Grey* (1980); *A Curious Street* (1984); *A New Shirt* (1986); *A Link with the River* (1989). Volumes of short stories: *The Diamonds at the Bottom of the Sea* (1979); *Children of Lir: Stories of Ireland* (1981); *Stories* (1982); *The Mourning Thief* (1987); *Lebanon Lodge* (1988). He has also written plays for the stage, for radio and for television.

Hogarth, William (1697–1764)

Painter. He excelled in the depiction of social life, especially the heartlessness of the richer classes permeated by social arrogance and commercial greed, with the consequent neglect of the poor. He painted sequences, each following a theme, a technique which is a pictorial equivalent of a stage drama. His art became an extremely popular one, because he made engravings of his oil paintings, and they were to be found on the walls of inns and cottages, not merely in great country houses. In his breadth of appeal and his realism, he is in strong contrast to the fashionable portrait painters of the 18th century, Joshua Reynolds and Gainsborough, and in the quality of his social indignation and his concern with unprivileged humanity he anticipates the poet-engraver William Blake. Some of his series of what he called 'pictur'd Morals' are: *A Harlot's Progress* (1731); *A Rake's Progress* (1735); *Marriage à la Mode* (1743–5); *The Four Stages of Cruelty, Beer Street* and *Gin Lane* (1751) (2.2.3) and *Election* (1754–66).

Hogarth's literary connections were close. ▷ Jonathan Swift invokes him as natural collaborator in his own kind of savage satire in his poem *The Legion Club* (1736), and his friendship with the novelists ▷ Samuel Richardson and ▷ Henry Fielding influenced the visual element which gives their novels an advantage over those of ▷ Daniel Defoe (*see* R. E. Moore, *Hogarth's Literary Relationships*). The ordinary people who enjoyed owning and interpreting his engravings, with their satirical edge, were the foundation of the market for later cheap serial fiction, with its engraved illustrations. The importance of the visual element in serials from ▷ Charles Dickens's ▷ *Pickwick Papers* onwards owes a debt to Hogarth and his successors.

Hogg, James (1770–1835)

Poet and novelist. Hogg was nicknamed 'the Ettrick Shepherd' because he had been a shepherd in Ettrick Forest in southern Scotland until his poetic talent was discovered by Sir Walter Scott. He is now best known for his powerful work of Calvinist guilt and ▷ Gothic supernaturalism, *The Private Memoirs and Confessions of a Justified Sinner* (1824).

Holcroft Thomas (1745–1809)

Dramatist, novelist, actor, translator, largely associated with the introduction of Continental melodrama to the English stage. In 1770 Holcroft obtained a post as prompter in the Dublin theatre and this was followed by a period of acting with strolling companies in England, and in 1778 an engagement at the Drury Lane Theatre, where his first play was performed. In 1780 his first novel, *Alwyn or the Gentleman Comedian* was published, drawing on his experiences as a strolling actor. His first comedy, *Duplicity*, was staged at Covent Garden in 1781. In 1784, on a visit to Paris, Holcroft was impressed by a production of Beaumarchais's *Le Mariage de Figaro* and, being unable to obtain a copy, he committed the entire play to memory. On his return, his translation was mounted at Covent Garden, under the title, *The Follies of the Day*. In 1792 Holcroft's most successful play, *The Road to Ruin*, was produced, again at Covent Garden.

An ardent supporter of the French Revolution, Holcroft became active on its behalf in England, and was imprisoned briefly for alleged treason. In 1799 he moved to Paris, where he lived for four years. In his absence his *A Tale of Mystery*, a translation from a play by Pixérécourt, was produced in London. His novels include *Anna St Ives* (1792) and *The Adventures of Hugh Trevor* (1794). He also published several translations of novels and wrote operas, afterpieces, polemical essays, and an ▷ autobiography, *Memoirs of the Late Thomas Holcroft* (1816), edited by his friend the critic William Hazlitt.
Bib: Rosenblum, J. (ed.), *The Plays of Thomas Holcroft*.

Holdsworth, Annie (d ?1910)

Novelist, feminist and editor. Born in Jamaica, Holdsworth's book *Joanna Traill, Spinster* (1894) addresses the ▷ New Woman theme of female independence. She was co-editor of *The Woman's Signal*. Her later novels include: *The Years That the Locust Hath Eaten* (1896) and *The Gods Arrive* (1897).

Holinshed, Raphael (d ?1580)

Chronicler: *Chronicles of England, Scotland, and Ireland* (1578). The history of England was written by Holinshed himself but a vivid *Description of England* added to the history is by William Harrison. The history of Scotland is a translation of a Scottish work written in Latin – *Scotorum historiae* (1527) by Hector Boece, and the account of Ireland is by Richard Stanyhurst and Edward Campion, and others. Shakespeare and other Elizabethan dramatists used the *Chronicles* as a source book.
▷ Histories and Chronicles.

Hollinghurst, Alan (b 1954)

Novelist. Educated at Magdalen College Oxford, Hollinghurst lectured at Oxford and at London University, was assistant editor of the *Times Literary Supplement* (1982–90) and poetry editor from 1990. *The Swimming-Pool Library* (1988) depicts both contemporary gay life in London and, through the researches carried out by the protagonist, who is commissioned to write a biography, the persecution of homosexual men in 1950s Britain. *Confidential Chats with Boys* (1982) is a volume of verse.

Holmes, Sherlock

▷ Detective fiction; Doyle, Sir Arthur Conan.

Holtby, Winifred (1898–1935)

Novelist and journalist. Winifred Holtby's short career was extremely prolific. She is best known as the writer of *South Riding* (1936), a study of life and rural politics in her native Yorkshire, but Holtby's career is much more varied than this suggests. She was a farmer's daughter whose first book of poetry was published when she was only 13 (*My Garden and Other Poems*), who then went on to study at Oxford (where she met and befriended ▷ Vera Brittain), worked as a nurse in the First World War, and wrote the first full-length critical study of ▷ Virginia Woolf

(1932). She also lectured, and had a distinguished journalistic career (writing for, amongst others, the *Manchester Guardian* and the *News Chronicle*). Her other works include: *Anderby Wold* (1923); *The Land of Green Ginger* (1927); *Poor Caroline* (1931); *Mandoa! Mandoa!* (1933); *Women and a Changing Civilisation* (1934); *Letters to a Friend* (1937).
Bib: Brittain, V., *Testament of a Friendship*; Handley-Taylor, G., *Winifred Holtby: A Concise and Selected Bibliography with Some Letters*.

Holy War, The (1682)

An ▷ allegory by ▷ John Bunyan. Its subject is the fall and redemption of man. The city of Mansoul has fallen into the hands of Diabolus (the Devil) and has to be recaptured by Emmanuel (Jesus Christ), who besieges it.

Homer

Ancient Greek epic poet, author of the ▷ *Iliad* and the ▷ *Odyssey*, basic works for Greek literature. Ancient traditions exist about Homer, for instance that latterly he was blind and that seven cities claimed to be his birthplace, but nothing is conclusively known about him. Archaeological investigation has disclosed that the destruction of Troy, following the siege described in the *Iliad*, took place in the 12th century BC; linguistic, historical and literary analysis of the poems show them to date as artistic wholes from perhaps the 8th century BC. That they are artistic wholes is in fact the only evidence for the existence of Homer; efforts to show that they are compilations by a number of poets have proved unconvincing, though it is clear that Homer himself was using the work of other poets between the Trojan war and his own time. The critic ▷ Matthew Arnold in his essay *On Translating Homer* (1861) says that Homer is rapid in movement, plain in diction, simple in ideas and noble in manner; and that the translations of three eminent English poets, George Chapman (16th century), Alexander Pope and William Cowper (18th century), all fail in one or more of these qualities, however fine their verse is in other respects.

The most notable use of Homeric myth in the novel is ▷ James Joyce's ▷ *Ulysses*.

Homosexuality

▷ Lesbian and Gay Writing.

Hope, Christopher (b 1944)

Novelist, short-story writer and poet. Born in South Africa of an Irish Catholic family and educated at the universities of Witwatersrand and Natal, he moved to Europe in 1975. He served in the South African navy in 1962 and has worked as an underwriter, in publishing, as a reviewer and as an English teacher in England. His first two novels, *A Separate Development* (1980, banned in South Africa) and *Kruger's Alp* (1984) both deal with apartheid, the second in allegorical terms. His fiction has a satirical edge and contains strong elements of the surreal and the bizarre as well as some sinister humour. His other novels include: *The Hottentot Room* (1986); *My Chocolate Redeemer* (1989); *Serenity House* (1992).

Private Parts (1981) is a volume of short stories and *Black Swan* (1987) a ▷ novella. His volumes of poetry include: *Cape Drives* (1974); *In the Country of the Black Pig* (1981); *Englishmen* (1985).

Horror Fiction

Although horror fiction has undergone astonishing changes since the earliest of ▷ 'Gothic' novels, the themes of transgression with which the genre deals have remained largely unchanged. Returning obsessively to taboo subjects (death, sex, incest, decay, bodily corruption, psychosis) horror novels have been described both by critics and champions as an 'undergrowth of literature' whose function is to speak the unspeakable. In his critical work, *Supernatural Horror in Literature*, H. P. Lovecraft declares: 'The oldest and strongest emotion of mankind is fear, and the oldest and strongest kind of fear is of the unknown. These facts few psychologists will dispute, and their admittedness must establish for all time the genuineness and dignity of the weirdly horrible tales.' Sixty years later leading contemporary horror novelist Stephen King writes: 'Horror appeals to us because it says, in a symbolic way, things we would be afraid to say . . . It offers us a chance to exercise (not exorcise) . . . emotions which society demands we keep closely in hand' (*Danse Macabre*, 1981). Similarly, British horror novelist Ramsey Campbell has described the genre as 'the branch of literature most often concerned with going too far. It is the least escapist form of fantasy. It shows us sights we would ordinarily look away from or reminds us of insights we might prefer not to admit we have.'

Whilst much early Gothic fiction is rooted in American literature (Edgar Allen Poe is frequently cited as the godfather of modern Gothic), Britain has produced a number of key texts. ▷ Bram Stoker's *Dracula* (1897) set the tone for future tales of vampirism, while ▷ Mary Shelley's ▷ *Frankenstein* (1817) has become the genre's single most reworked (and indeed abused) text, both on page and later screen. Of the longevity of these horror icons David Punter writes: '*Frankenstein* and *Dracula* are still granted fresh embodiments [because of] both their own imagistic flexibility and . . . the essential continuity under capitalism of the anxieties about class and gender warfare from which they sprang.' The question of whether classic horror fiction alludes to contemporary rather than timeless fears has been of central import in recent years. Following a slump in the 1960s, horror fiction was revitalized in 1971 by the extraordinary success of William Peter Blatty's occult chiller *The Exorcist*. Described by the author as 'a 350 page thankyou note to the Jesuits' for his education, *The Exorcist* rekindled modern popular religious debate, but its success was attributed by some to a contemporary fear of adolescent rebellion which the novel appeared to reflect. In the wake of Blatty's success, American short story writer Stephen King published his first novel *Carrie*, which also dealt with aggressive adolescence. In Britain, ▷ James Herbert rapidly became the leading light of modern pulp horror fiction, producing viscerally gory tales set against a backdrop of modern urban decay.

'The rats are the establishment,' explained Herbert of the subtexts of his first best-seller *The Rats*. Although Herbert's later work became more discreet, he opened the flood-gates for a slew of writers specializing in sensationally violent fantasy; most notable is Shaun Hutson (*Spawn, Slugs, Assassin*), a connoisseur of outlandish mutilation with a recurrent sexual bent, while Guy N. Smith (*Crabs, The Sucking Pit, Crabs on the Rampage*) deserves mention for his prolific output. In the early 1980s, ▷ Clive Barker and ▷ Ramsey Campbell rose to the forefront of the British 'new wave' of horror writers. Challenging the 'innate conservatisms and prejudices of the field', Barker and Campbell forged a new brand of horror which sought to demystify taboo subjects rather than merely revel in them. In America, Stephen King's popularity remains unchallenged, but he is outstripped in terms of invention by Peter Straub, author of *Ghost Story* (1979), and with whom King collaborated on *The Talisman* (1984). Current upcoming authors include K. W. Jeter, Kim Newman, Thomas Ligotti, Michael Marshall Smith, Nicholas Royle, Ian R. MacLeod, D. F. Lewis and Joel Lane. Recent short story collections are: *Best New Horror* (Steven Jones and Ramsey Cambell, eds.) and *Dark Voices* (edited by Steven Jones et al.). Bib: King, S., *Danse Macabre* (1981); Campbell, R., and Jones, S., *Horror: 100 Best Books*; Sullivan, J., (ed.), *The Penguin Encyclopaedia of Horror and the Supernatural*.

Hosain, Attia (b 1913)
Novelist and short-story writer. She was born in Lucknow to an aristocratic family and educated at schools in Lucknow and at home (where she studied Arabic, Persian and Urdu). She moved to London when India was partitioned in 1947, working as a BBC presenter, an actress and a journalist. *Phoenix Fled* (1951) is a collection of short stories and *Sunlight on a Broken Column* (1961) a novel.

Hospital, Janette Turner (b 1942)
Novelist and short-story writer. Born in Australia and educated at the University of Queensland and at Queens University in Canada, Hospital settled in Canada in 1971 but has also lived in India, England and the USA. She has worked as a teacher, a librarian (at Harvard University), a writer-in-residence and a lecturer. The title of one of her volumes of short stories, *Dislocations* (1986), sums up a principal theme of her fiction, whether set in India, like *The Ivory Swing* (1982), or in Canada, like *Borderline* (1985), a novel of ▷ post-modernist self-consciousness in which a couple's encounter with an illegal immigrant to Canada poses issues of commitment and responsibility. *The Tiger in the Tiger Pit* (1983) is a drama of family conflict set in the USA and Australia. Her other works are: *Isobars* (short stories, 1990); *Charades* (a novel, 1989); *The Last Magician* (1992).

Household Words
A weekly periodical edited by ▷ Charles Dickens from 1850 to 1859. It emulated the magazine tradition of ▷ *Blackwood's* (started 1817) but aimed at a wider public. Among works published in it were Dickens's novel ▷ *Hard Times* and ▷ Mrs Gaskell's ▷ *North and South*. It was followed by ▷ *All the Year Round*.
▷ Reviews and Periodicals.

Houyhnhnms, The
The horses endowed with reason in Part IV of ▷ Swift's ▷ *Gulliver's Travels*. The word imitates the whinnying of a horse. The enlightened horses are a purely reasonable aristocracy, inhabiting an island which also contains a race called Yahoos, who, not endowed with reason, typify brutish and degraded behaviour. Gulliver's Houyhnhnm host recognizes that Gulliver is unlike the Yahoos in his possession of the faculty of reason, but proves to him that owing to his other qualities, which are Yahoo-like, he can only use his reason destructively.

Howards End (1910)
A novel by ▷ E. M. Forster. The theme is the relationship between the Schlegel family (Margaret, Helen, and their brother Tibby) who live on an unearned income and are liberal, enlightened, and cultivated, and the Wilcoxes, who work in the commercial world which the Schlegels are inclined to despise but from which they draw their income. The Wilcoxes are snobbish, prejudiced, insensitive, and philistine; in fact they have much in common with the middle classes as described by ▷ Matthew Arnold in his critique of English culture – *Culture and Anarchy* (1869). Mrs Wilcox, however, who has bought her husband the old house, Howards End, belongs to the older, aristocratic continuity of English culture; never understood by her husband and children, on her death she bequeaths the house unexpectedly to Margaret Schlegel. Margaret comes into the inheritance at the end of the book, but only after she has married and subdued to her values Mrs Wilcox's former husband. Meanwhile Helen, moved by sympathy and indignation, has become pregnant by Leonard Bast, a poor bank-clerk who has been the victim of both the Schlegel and the Wilcox social illusions and mishandling. Bast dies after being beaten by one of the Wilcox sons, and Helen and her child come to live at Howards End with Margaret and Mr Wilcox. The house remains a tentative symbol of hope for the future of English society.

Hughes, Richard (1900–76)
Novelist, dramatist and poet. He published four novels: *A High Wind in Jamaica* (1929); *In Hazard* (1938); *The Fox in the Attic* (1961) and *The Wooden Shepherdess* (1971). He was educated at Charterhouse School, and at Oxford University, where he met W. B. Yeats, A. E. Coppard, ▷ T. E. Lawrence and ▷ Robert Graves. As an undergraduate he wrote a one-act play, *The Sister's Tragedy*, which was staged in 1922 and enthusiastically received, and a volume of poems entitled *Gipsy Night* (1922). In 1924 he wrote the first original radio play, *Danger* and a stage play, *A Comedy of Good and Evil*. Born in Surrey but of Welsh descent, he adopted Wales as his home, but travelled extensively around the world. His

travels are reflected in his book of short stories, *In the Lap of Atlas: Stories of Morocco* (1979), as well as in his first two novels, which are set mainly at sea and are intense studies of moral issues in the context of human crisis. *A High Wind in Jamaica*, his best-known work, is the story of a group of children captured by pirates. It deals with violence, the relation of innocence and evil, and the fallibility of human justice, and takes an unsentimental view of childhood. *In Hazard* describes in great detail the events on board a cargo ship at sea during a hurricane, and has affinities with the work of ▷ Joseph Conrad. After an administrative post in the Admiralty during World War II, Hughes worked as a book reviewer and teacher. His last two novels are part of a projected historical sequence entitled *The Human Predicament*, recounting the events leading up to World War II. Other publications include: *The Man Born to be Hanged* (1923) (stage play); *A Moment of Time* (1926) (short stories); *The Spider's Palace* (1931) and *Don't Blame Me* (1940) (short stories for children); *Confessio Juvenis* (1926) (collected poems). Bib: Thomas, P., *Richard Hughes*.

Hughes, Thomas (1822–96)

In his time a prominent public figure as a lawyer, leading Christian Socialist and Radical MP, Hughes is now remembered for his *Tom Brown's Schooldays* (1857), which launched a whole genre of boys' school tales. The novel records how Tom Brown triumphs over various schoolboy trials (including the archetypal bully, Flashman) finally to captain the school cricket team and become a solid citizen. As well as spinning a good yarn, the book is also interesting for its first-hand (if fictionalized) account of ▷ Thomas Arnold's reform of the ▷ public school system at ▷ Rugby. The sequel, *Tom Brown at Oxford* (1861), is of interest for its evocation of the ▷ Oxford Movement.
▷ Lawrence, G.A.

Hugo, Victor(-Marie) (1802–85)

French poet, playwright and novelist. Born in Besançon, he lived in Spain and Italy as a child, where his father, a General, followed Napoleon. Despite nostalgia for the Napoleonic age, Hugo was a confirmed democrat and was elected to the Assembly in 1848 and again in 1870. He lived in exile in the Channel Isles between 1851 and 1870 after the *coup d'état* of Louis Napoleon. As a young man he refused a military career in favour of literature; he gained favour through poetry and was made Chevalier de la Legion d'Honeur by 1825. He read and admired Chateaubriand, a proto-Romantic influence, and after the publication of his play *Cromwell* (1827) with its famous Preface, became a spearhead of the French Romantic movement. He married Adèle Foucher, and was much affected by the death of his daughter in 1845. He was made a peer and became an important figure, being buried with great ceremony in the Panthéon. His plays have lasted less well than the novels and poetry which are remarkable not for intellectual content so much as beauty, faith and feeling. Hugo's output was prolific: the plays include *Hernani* (1830) and *Ruy Blas* (1838); the novels *Notre Dame de Paris* (1831), the celebrated

Les Misérables (1862), *Les Travailleurs de la Mer* (1866), *L'Homme qui Rit* (1869). His many collections of poems include *Les Odes* (1822), *Odes et Ballades* (1826), *Les Orientales* (1829), *Les Feuilles d'Automne* (1831), *Les Chants du Crépuscule* (1835), *Les Voix Intérieures* (1837), *Les Rayons et les Ombres* (1840), *Les Châtiments* (1853), *Les Contemplations* (1856) and *La Légende des Siècles* (1859, 1877, 1883).
▷ French influence on English fiction.

Hulme, Keri (b 1947)

Novelist and short-story writer. Hulme was born in Christchurch and educated at Canterbury University, New Zealand. She has worked as a postwoman, television director and writer, as well as engaging in fishing and various forms of seasonal work on New Zealand's South Island, where she now lives in Okarito, Westland. Her family heritage includes not only Maori (the Kai Tahu tribe) but Scots and English. Maori cultural identity, language and history have been central to her work, together with environmental and feminist concerns. Her novel *The Bone People* (1983), which won the Booker Prize, is a mythic narrative of national regeneration based on Maori religious beliefs. *Lost Possessions* (1985) is a novella, *Te Kaihu/The Windeater* (1986) a collection of short stories and *The Silences Between [Moeraki Conversations]* (1982) and *Strands* are volumes of poetry.

Humanism

The word has two distinct uses: 1 the intellectually liberating movements in western Europe in the 15th and 16th centuries, associated with new attitudes to ancient Greek and Latin literature; 2 a modern movement for the advancement of humanity without reliance on supernatural religious beliefs.

1 Humanism in its first sense had its beginnings in Italy as early as the 14th century, when its pioneer was the poet and scholar Petrarch (1304–74), and reached its height (greatly stimulated by the recovery of lost manuscripts after the fall of Constantinople in 1453) throughout western Europe in the 16th century, when it first reached England. Its outstanding characteristic was a new kind of critical power. In the previous thousand years European civilization had above all been dominated – even created – by the Church, which had put the literatures of the preceding Latin and Greek cultures to its own uses and had directed movements in thought and art through its authority over the religious orders and the universities. The humanists began by criticizing and evaluating the Latin and Greek authors in the light of what they believed to be Roman and Greek standards of civilization. Some of the important consequences of humanism were these: the rediscovery of many ancient Greek and Latin works; the establishment of new standards in Greek and Latin scholarship; the assumption, which was to dominate English education until the present century, that a thorough basis in at least Latin literature was indispensable to the civilized man; the beginnings of what we nowadays regard as 'scientific thinking'; the introduction of the term Middle Ages for the period between the fall of the Roman Empire

of the West (5th century AD) and the Renaissance, meaning by it a period of partial and inferior civilization. The most prominent of the European humanists was the Dutchman Erasmus, and the most prominent of the earlier English humanists was his friend ▷ Sir Thomas More. The Church was not at first hostile to humanism; indeed such a pope as Leo X (reigned 1513–21) was himself a humanist. When, in the second 30 years of the 16th century, the critical spirit became an increasingly aggressive weapon in the hands of the religious reformers – the Renaissance branching into the Reformation – the attitude of the Church hardened, and humanists in the later 16th century found themselves restricted by the religious quarrels of ▷ Protestants and Catholics, or obliged (like ▷ Montaigne) to adopt a retiring and circumspect policy. In the 17th and 18th centuries, humanism hardened into neo-classicism.

2 Modern humanism assumes that man's command of scientific knowledge has rendered religion largely redundant. Its central principle is that 'man is the measure of all things', and elsewhere in Europe it is sometimes called 'hominism' (Lat. *homo* = man).

'Humanism' is also used as a general expression for any philosophy that proposes the full development of human potentiality. In this sense, 'Christian humanism', since the 16th century, has stood for the marriage of the humanist value attached to a conception of humanity, based on reason with the Christian value based on Divine Revelation. An example of a Christian humanist movement is that of the Cambridge Platonists (▷ Plato) in the 17th century. 'Liberal humanism' values the dignity of the individual and their inalienable right to justice, liberty, freedom of thought and the pursuit of happiness; its weakness lies in its concentration on the single subject and its failure to recognize the power of institutions in determining the conditions of life.

Hume, David (1711–76)

Philosopher. His first major work, *Treatise of Human Nature* (1739–40) did not arouse much interest. His *Enquiry concerning Human Understanding* (1748) and *Enquiry concerning the Principles of Morals* (1751) are revisions and developments of the first work. His theory of knowledge was distinct from those of ▷ John Locke and ▷ George Berkeley. Locke had said that ideas proceeded from sensations, *ie* from experience received through the senses, implying that we know mind only through matter; Berkeley that on the contrary we know matter only through our mental conceptions of it and that this proves the primacy of mind. Hume said that we cannot know of the existence of mind, except as a collective term covering memories, perceptions and ideas. He further argued that there was no necessity in the law of cause and effect, except in mathematics; what we call that law is inferred but not observed, a customary association confirmed by experience but with no provable necessity in it. Thus if Locke had seemed to validate science at the expense of religion and Berkeley the reverse, Hume seemed to drive at the roots of both. The graceful lucidity with which he

expounded this extreme scepticism caused a wit to summarize his philosophy in the epigram; 'No mind! – It doesn't matter. No matter! – Never mind.' In his ethics, Hume held that virtue is what makes for happiness, both in ourselves and others, and that the two kinds of happiness are in accord with each other.

Hume also wrote the first systematic history of England, beginning, at first, with the reign of James I, when, as he considered with reasonable justice, the political differences of his own day had their start. His historical view is, however, marked by his political prejudices and, since he was a Scotsman, by his suspicion of English motives towards Scotland. His *Essays Moral and Political* (1741), and later volumes, contain acute comments on contemporary society. He differed from ▷ Rousseau by arguing against the long-established hypothesis that society is based on a 'social contract'. His economic writings were a stimulus to ▷ Adam Smith.

Bib: Mossner, E.C., *The Life of Hume*; Willey, B., *The Eighteenth Century Background*; Smith, N. K., *The Philosophy of David Hume*, Pears, D. F. (ed.), *Hume: A Symposium*.

Humphry Clinker, The Expedition of (1771)

A ▷ picaresque novel by ▷ Tobias Smollett, written in letters. It describes a tour of England and Scotland made by Mr Matthew Bramble and his family party – his sister Tabitha, his nephew and niece Jerry and Lydia, and the maid Winifred Jenkins. Humphry Clinker is a coachman who joins the party on the way, turns out to be Mr Bramble's illegitimate son, and marries Winifred. Characterization is strongly marked but superficial, the chief object being to characterize the society of the time realistically and with an often coarse humour. This is usually held to be the most successful of Smollett's novels, and shows something of the humane sympathies of the 16th-century Spanish novelist Cervantes, whose ▷ *Don Quixote* Smollett had himself translated in 1755.

Hunter, Rachel (1754–1813)

Novelist. Hunter became a novelist in her forties, and at the time her novels appeared to be somewhat self-conscious of their narrative form, and were mocked by ▷ Jane Austen. Today, however, we would call them ▷ 'metafictional', that is, writing which deliberately questions the relationship between fiction and reality by drawing attention to its own status as a linguistic construct. For example, in *The Unexpected Legacy* (1804), the Preface is written by an author who quotes an attack on novels by a friend; both characters are fictitious, although appearing in the Preface the reader expects them to be real. Similarly, in *Lady Maclairn, The Victim of Villainy* (1806), the author is supposedly only the editor of the letters, but also places herself within the novel as a character, ending up as a governess to the heroine's family. In addition to the adoption of multiple authorial voices, Hunter also layers plot and time to create a complex interweaving of stories, each creating a different relationship between 'fiction' and 'reality'. Thematically, she seems to have been fascinated by the idea of mixed racial marriages;

this is the concern of *Lady Maclairn* and her first published novel, *Letitia, or The Castle without a Spectre* (1801), the latter of which may also be classed as a ▷ Gothic novel.

Huxley, Aldous (1894–1963)
Novelist and essayist. His novels are 'novels of ideas', involving conversations which disclose viewpoints rather than establish characters, and having a polemical rather than an imaginative theme. An early practitioner of the form was ▷ Thomas Love Peacock, and it is his novels that Huxley's earlier ones recall: *Crome Yellow* (1921); *Antic Hay* (1923); *Those Barren Leaves* (1925). *Point Counter Point* (1928) is his best-known novel and is an attempt to convey a social image of the age with more imaginative depth and substance, but his polemical and inquisitorial mind was better suited to *Brave New World* (1932), in which a future society is presented so as to bring out the tendencies working in contemporary civilization and to show their disastrous consequences. Fastidious, abhorring what he saw to be the probable obliteration of human culture by 20th-century addiction to technology, but sceptical of religious solutions – he was the grandson of the great 19th-century agnostic biologist ▷ Thomas Huxley – he turned in the 1930s to Eastern religions such as Buddhism for spiritual support. This is shown in *Eyeless in Gaza* (1936). This and his last books – *After Many a Summer* (1939), *Ape and Essence* (1948), *Brave New World Revisited* (1958) – return to the discursive form of his earlier work. His novels and his essays (Collected Edition; 1959) are all concerned with how to resist the debasement of 'mass culture' and to sustain the identity of the human spirit without the aid of faith in supernatural religion of the Christian kind.
Bib: Bowering, P., *Aldous Huxley*; Ferns, C. S., *Aldous Huxley, Novelist*; Woodcock, G., *Dawn and the Darkest Hour*.

Huxley, Thomas Henry (1825–95)
Biologist. He was a supporter of ▷ Darwin's theory of evolution and combined philosophical speculation with technical exposition. His many works, essays, lectures and articles included the influential publications: *Man's Place in Nature* (1863), *The Physical Basis of Life* (1868), *Science and Culture* (1881) and *Science and Morals* (1886). He held that scientific discoveries had neither given support to nor discredited religious faith, and he invented the term ▷ agnosticism for this attitude to religion.

Hyperbole
▷ Figures of Speech.

I

Idealism

In philosophy, any form of thought which finds reality not in the mind of the perceiver (the subject), nor in the thing experienced (the object) but in the idea in which they meet. In its earliest form idealism was developed by Socrates and his disciple ▷ Plato. Their influence was important in the 16th-century Europe of the Renaissance, *eg* on Edmund Spenser. A modern idealist, ▷ F. H. Bradley, had as strong an influence on the poet T. S. Eliot.

In ordinary usage, idealism means the ability to conceive perfection as a standard by which ordinary behaviour and achievement is to be judged. This view is really an inheritance from Plato, who believed that earthly realities were imperfect derivatives of heavenly perfections. To 'idealize' a thing or person is to present the image of what ought to be, rather than what experience knows in ordinary life. In imaginative art we have come to consider this as a fault, but to a 16th-century critic such as ▷ Sir Philip Sidney poetry existed for just such a purpose. This is not, however, the kind of influence which Bradley had on Eliot; Bradley maintained that no reality existed outside the spirit, and he influenced Eliot towards interpreting the phenomena and dilemmas of his age in religious terms.

In modern critical theory idealism is associated with the anti-materialist impulse to denigrate history and social context. The meaning of this term is complicated by its history within the discipline of philosophy, and by its common usage as a description of human behaviour not susceptible to the 'realistic' impulses of self-interest. The term is sometimes used in critical theory to denote the primacy of thought, and to indicate a particular kind of relationship between writer and text where it is a sequence of ideas that act as the deep structure for events and relationships.

Ideology

This term is defined by ▷ Karl Marx and Friedrich Engels (1800–95) in *The German Ideology* as 'false consciousness'. A further meaning, which ▷ Raymond Williams traces to the usage initiated by Napoleon Bonaparte, denotes a fanatical commitment to a particular set of ideas, and this has remained a dominant meaning in the sphere of modern right-wing politics, especially in relation to the question of dogmatism. The term has come to the fore again in the ▷ post-structuralist Marxism of ▷ Louis Althusser, where it is distinguished from 'science'. Ideology here is defined as the means whereby, at the level of ideas, every social group produces and reproduces the conditions of its own existence. Althusser argues that 'Ideology is a "representation" of the imaginary relationship of individuals to their real conditions of existence' (*Lenin and Philosophy*; 1971). In order to ensure that political power remains the preserve of a dominant class, individual 'subjects' are assigned particular positions in society. A full range of social institutions, such as the Church, the family and the education system, are the means through which a particular hierarchy of values is disseminated. The point to emphasize, however, is that ideology disguises the real material

relations between the different social classes, and this knowledge can only be retrieved through a theoretically aware analysis of the interrelationships that prevail within society at any one time. A ruling class sustains itself in power, partly by coercion (repressive apparatuses), but also by negotiation with other subordinate classes (▷ hegemony; Althusser's ideological state of apparatuses).

Social change occurs when the ideology of the dominant class is no longer able to contain the contradictions existing in real social relations. The function of literary texts in this process is complex. In one sense they reproduce ideology, but also they may offer a critique of it by 'distancing' themselves from the ideology with which they are historically implicated. Since all language is by definition 'ideological', insofar as it is motivated by particular sorts of social relationship, the language of a literary text can very often be implicated in an ideology of which it is not aware. The text's implication in ideology can only be excavated through a critical process which seeks to uncover the assumptions upon which it is based. Other helpful definitions of the term include those offered by Jerome McGann – 'A coherent or loosely organized set of ideas which is the expression of the special interests of some class or social group' (*The Romantic Ideology*) – and by Judith Williamson: 'the meaning made necessary by the conditions of society while helping to perpetuate those conditions' (*Decoding Advertisements*)

▷ Archaeology.

Bib: Althusser, L., *For Marx*; Thompson, J. B., *Studies in The Theory of Ideology*; Jameson, F., *The Political Unconscious*.

Idler, The

Essays contributed weekly by ▷ Samuel Johnson to the *Universal Chronicle*, or *Weekly Gazette* from April 1758 to April 1760. As compared to his ▷ *Rambler* papers, they contain more humour, and more flexible treatment of the fictional characters such as Dick Minim, but they have the same kind of emotional force and moral gravity which distinguish Johnson as a periodical essayist.

Iliad

An ▷ epic by the ancient Greek poet ▷ Homer. Its subject is the siege of Troy by an alliance of Greek states; the occasion of the war is the elopement of Helen, wife of Menelaus, king of the Greek state of Sparta, with Paris, a son of Priam, king of Troy. The poem is in 24 books; it begins with the Greeks already besieging Troy. In Book I the chief Greek hero, Achilles, quarrels with the Greek commander-in-chief, Agamemnon, king of Argos and brother to Menelaus. Achilles withdraws from the fighting, and returns to it only in Book XIX after the killing of his friend Patroclus by the chief Trojan hero, Hector. Achilles kills Hector in XXII, and the poem ends with Hector's funeral in Troy. Hector is the principal hero of the epic, much of which is taken up with his exploits, as well as with those of other Greek and Trojan heroes and with the intervention of the gods on either side. There is much speculation about the date of the historical events and that of the poem respectively. Present opinion seems to be that the historical city of Troy fell early in the 12th century BC and that the poem was written about 300 years later. The surviving text dates from the 2nd century BC.

The *Iliad* has had an enormous influence on the literature of Europe. With Homer's ▷ *Odyssey*, it set the standard for epic poetry, which until the 19th century was considered the noblest poetic form. Its first successor was the ▷ *Aeneid* (1st century BC) by the Roman poet Virgil. The poem has been several times translated into English verse; the most notable versions are those by George Chapman (1611) and Alexander Pope (1720).

▷ Classical Mythology.

Imaginary

When used in contemporary literary theory, this term originates in ▷ Jacques Lacan's re-reading of ▷ Freud, where it refers generally to the perceived or *imagined* world of which the infant sees itself as the centre. In other words, this is the first opportunity that the child has to construct a coherent identity for itself. But in Lacan's view this image is a myth; it is an imaginary subjectivity that allows the ego to speak of itself as 'I', but which represses those fragmentary energies which constitute the unconscious. ▷ Louis Althusser uses the term 'imaginary', which he takes from Lacan, in a very different way, while retaining the concept of a constellation of forces which contribute to the formation of the human subject. In Althusser the subject *misrecognizes* his or her place in the social order through an ideology which posits as 'natural' a fixed relationship between social classes. What is at issue for both Lacan and Althusser is the way in which individual human subjects are constituted by an order which extends beyond the images through which that order is represented to them. In Lacan's psychoanalytical theory the realm of the 'imaginary' is contained within that of the ▷ 'symbolic order', and it is the function of psychoanalysis to uncover the 'real' relations which exist beneath this series of representations. In Althusser, the 'mirror' phase can be equated with 'ideology' in that this is the means through which individual human subjects *misrecognize* themselves and their position in the social order.

▷ Psychoanalytical criticism.

Imperialism

A desire to build up an empire, that is, to dominate politically and assimilate other countries. It has a long history, from Rome to the present day, although the main period of imperialism began with the 17th-century conquests of the Americas and reached its height in the 1880s and 90s. The British Empire has this century developed into the Commonwealth, and new forms of imperialism can be seen in the pervasive economic and political influence of the USA in many parts of the world and, until the late 1980s, the comparable influence of the USSR.

▷ Post-colonial fiction; Kipling, Rudyard.

Implied author

The notional possessor of the set of attitudes and beliefs implied by the totality of a text; distinguished from the 'real' or biographical author. The distinction is necessary because a text may imply a set of beliefs (and perhaps a personality) which the author does not, in life, possess, and because different texts by the same author often imply different values.

Implied reader

A term developed on analogy with the ▷ implied author and used especially in reader-response and ▷ reception theory. It refers to the sort of reader which a novel (or other text) seems to expect or demand; the implied reader often corresponds roughly to some actual group of readers, though it is also quite possible to have an implied reader who does not correspond even to a single actual reader. There are a range of related terms which differ in meaning to various degrees, including the ideal reader, the intended reader, the postulated reader and the inscribed reader.

Bib: Freund, E., *The Return of the Reader: Reader-Response Criticism*.

Inchbald, Mrs Elizabeth (1753–1821)

Novelist, dramatist and actress. Among other plays she translated Kotzbue's *Lovers' Vows* from the German, and this is the play rehearsed in ▷ Jane Austen's ▷ *Mansfield Park*. This, and some of the other 19 plays she wrote or adapted, were popular successes: Jane Austen assumes knowledge of it by the reader. However, her best works are her two novels: *A Simple Story* (1791) and *Nature and Art* (1796).

Bib: Littlewood, S. R., *Elizabeth Inchbald and her Circle*.

Independent, The

A daily newspaper, founded in 1985 and aimed at a serious readership. As its name suggests, it aims for a relative independence of political viewpoint, which in practice means a centre position.

Industrial Revolution, The

An industrial revolution has been defined as 'the change that transforms a people with peasant occupations and local markets into an industrial society with world-wide connections' (*Encyclopaedia Britannica*). Clearly then many countries have industrial revolutions, and more than one; for example it is currently said that Britain is undergoing a new industrial revolution in high-technology processes. However, we understand *the* industrial revolution to mean the succession of changes which transformed England from a predominantly rural and agricultural country into a predominantly urban and manufacturing one in the 18th and 19th centuries, and especially between 1750 and 1850. It was, moreover, the first such revolution in the modern world.

1 *Causes*. Although not, apart from London, a country of great towns, England at the beginning of

the 18th century was already a great trading nation, with much private capital ready for investment. Not only was trade free to move throughout the British Isles but there was considerable freedom of movement between the social classes, which were not rigidly defined almost into caste systems as in other European countries, *eg* France. English middle-class religion had emphasis on the individual conscience as the guide to conduct and also on the moral excellence of sober, industrious employment; these values encouraged self-reliance and enterprising initiative. Although some of this middle class (the Nonconformist or Dissenting sects which rejected the Church of England) were barred from political rights, and Parliament, controlled by the aristocracy, was far from truly representative, the political leaders of the country were extremely interested in commerce, which they were ready to participate in and profit from. The steadily growing population provided a market which invited exploitation by various methods of improved production. Once the process started, it gathered its own momentum, which was increased by the existence of large supplies of convenient fuel in the country's coalfields. Agriculture also contributed to industrial growth: the landowners were zealous farmers and their improved methods of cultivation not only freed much labour which then became available for employment in the town factories, but increased the food supplies available for the towns. Finally, the 18th century (in contrast to 17th) was a time of peace and stability in Britain, undisturbed by the wars in which her armies and money were engaged across the sea.

2 *Process*. In the textile industry, already established since the 15th century as the principal industry, a number of machines were invented which increased production and reduced labour but were too large for the cottages where the processes had hitherto been carried out. They therefore had to be housed in factories and mills where large numbers of employees worked together. These machines were at first operated by water power. In the iron industry, the principal fuel used hitherto had been charcoal, the supply of which was becoming exhausted. However, improved methods of smelting by coal were discovered and ironmasters set up their blast furnaces in the neighbourhood of the coalfields in the north midlands and north of England.

Most important of all, in 1769 James Watt patented an adaptation of his steam-engine to the machines used in the textile industry; this consequently ceased to depend on water power and concentrated itself in the north of England to be near the coalfields. An important result was the immense expansion in manufacture of cotton cloth. An extensive system of canals was constructed in the 18th century for the transport of goods and fuel, and the modern methods of road and bridge building were introduced, but the decisive advance in communications was the invention of the steam rail locomotive by George Stephenson (1814); by 1850 a railway system covered the country. We cannot understand the process of the British Industrial Revolution if we do not appreciate that it was a period of epic excitement, especially in the development of rail transport. It produced inventors and engineers such as Isambard Brunel (1806–59) who had to force their projects against established prejudice and ignorance. The other side of the epic story was the meteoric emergence of great financial speculators such as George Hudson (1800–71), the 'Railway King', who rose from being a York draper to control of a third of the railway system, and ended in disgrace. The social changes were unprecedentedly dramatic, in the rapid growth of the midland and northern industrial towns and the opening of new opportunities for wealth among humble but ambitious men. This heroic and fantastic aspect of industrialism has to be remembered as a great motive power in Victorian culture.

3 *Consequences*. Britain was by 1850 the 'work-shop of the world'; no other country was yet ready to compete with her in industrial production. The towns were the source of her wealth, though the landowners retained their social prestige and often became much richer by ownership of coalfields, The north of England, until the 18th century a backward region, was now the most advanced in Britain; its towns grew rapidly, unplanned, in ugliness and dirt. The economic motives outran the social conscience and the new urban proletariat worked and lived in evil conditions under employers who had often risen themselves from poverty and had the ruthlessness which was a consequence of the severity of their struggle. England was divided as never before; the industrial north from the agricultural south, the industrial working class from (sometimes) pitiless employers, and both from the long-established gentry, particularly of the south. Victorian novels are eloquent testimony to the social conditions; the title of ▷ Elizabeth Gaskell's novel ▷ *North and South*, and the subtitle of ▷ Benjamin Disraeli's ▷ *Sybil, or The Two Nations* are evidence in themselves. Josiah Bounderby in ▷ Charles Dickens's ▷ *Hard Times* is a portrait of the unprincipled kind of industrial employer; Sir Leicester Dedlock and Rouncewell the ironmaster in ▷ *Bleak House* exemplify the old order's failure to understand the new.

▷ Anti-industrialism.

Inferno, The

The first part of ▷ Dante's great poem, the ▷ *Divina Commedia*, which describes the poet's journey through Hell, under the guidance of ▷ Virgil, where he speaks to various former friends and enemies. Hell is conceived of as a conical funnel, reaching to the centre of the earth. Various categories of sinners are assigned to the nine gradated circles, where they receive appropriate punishments. The first circle is reserved for pre-Christian pagans who have not had the chance of knowing the true faith. Virgil belongs to these, whose only punishment is the hopeless desire for God. At the very bottom is Satan (Lucifer) himself, and from him Dante and Virgil pass through the earth to its opposite surface, where they arrive at the foot of the Mount of Purgatory (▷ *Purgatorio*).

Inns of Court

Institutions belonging to the legal profession, in London. There are now four, all dating from the

Middle Ages: Lincoln's Inn, Gray's Inn, the Inner Temple and the Middle Temple. The buildings resemble those of Oxford and Cambridge colleges, and their function is to be responsible for the education of those students of the law who intend to become barristers, with the right to plead in the senior courts of law and – in the senior rank – the qualifications to be appointed judges. Each Inn is a separate society, governed by its senior members, called Benchers. The buildings are not exclusively occupied by barristers or their students, however; thus Furnivall's Inn (now pulled down) was for a time the home of ▷ Charles Dickens, and one of his characters, Pip of ▷ *Great Expectations*, had rooms in Barnard's Inn, now part of a school.

Innuendo
▷ Figures of Speech.

Interpellation
A term used by the Marxist philosopher ▷ Louis Althusser to describe the process by which ▷ ideologies present us with a version of our own ▷ subjectivity, which we are induced to (mis)recognize as our self or innate identity. The term is borrowed from the technical vocabulary of French government procedures, and should not be confused with 'interpolation', which means insertion. The concept of interpellation has been applied to literature; for example Catherine Belsey argues that 'classic realism constitutes an ideological practice in addressing itself to readers as subjects, interpellating them in order that they freely accept their subjectivity and their subjection' (*Critical Practice*).

Intertextuality
A term first introduced into critical theory by the French ▷ psychoanalytical writer ▷ Julia Kristeva, relating specifically to the use she makes of the work of ▷ Mikhail Bakhtin. The concept of intertextuality implies that literary texts are composed of dialectically opposed utterances, and that it is the function of the critic to identify these different strands and to account for their oppositions within the text itself. Kristeva notes that Bakhtin's '"dialogism" does not strive towards transcendance . . . but rather towards harmony, all the while implying an idea of rupture (of opposition and analogy) as a modality of transformation' (*Desire and Language*, trans. 1980). Similarly, no text can be entirely free of other texts. No work is written or read in isolation, it is located, in Kristeva's words, 'within the totality of previous . . . texts'. This is a second important aspect of intertextuality.

▷ Feminism; Psychoanalytical criticism.
Bib: Worton, M. and Still, J. (eds.), *Intertextuality: Theories and Practices*

Irish fiction in English
Ireland – England's first and closest colony – presents a recent history of literary movements and concerns that is very differently paced from that of its colonist. From 1171, the year of Ireland's conquest by Henry II, until the latter years of the 19th century, the history of Irish literature in English is, largely speaking, part of the general history of Engish literature. Since the Irish Literary Revival began in the 1880s, however, the existence and the memory of a literature in Ireland's original tongue, ▷ Gaelic, has interacted with the country's adopted vernacular at every level: in the detail of syntax; in the choice – or rejection – of subject-matter; and in each writer's wrestle with identity.

Throughout the 18th and 19th centuries – and into the 20th – writers from Anglo-Irish Ireland made a rich and vigorous contribution to English literature: ▷ Jonathan Swift, ▷ Oliver Goldsmith, ▷ Oscar Wilde and George Bernard Shaw are amongst the better-known. Their writings were not primarily concerned with the matter of Ireland or their authors' own Irishness. Those who did write of Ireland, like Dion Boucicault (1820–90), who is held by many to be the inventor of the 'stage Irishman', and ▷ Thomas Moore (1779–1852), the purveyor to the drawing-rooms of London of an Ireland sugared by sentiment and exile, capitalized on what looks with hindsight like caricature. All these writers of the Anglo-Irish Ascendancy, coming from their background of landed privilege, seemed to be unaware of the still surviving Gaelic tradition of native Irish literature, with its long ancestry and close connections with mainland Europe – a tradition eloquently evoked in Daniel Corkery's *Hidden Ireland* of 1924, and recently made available anew in Seán Ó Tuama's and Thomas Kinsella's 1981 anthology *An Duanaire: Poems of the Dispossessed*.

Moreover, during this pre-Revival period only a handful of creative writers mirrored the growing interest that folklorists like T. Crofton Croker (1798–1849), travellers (again, many of them from Europe) and diarists were taking in Irish peasant life outside the 'Pale' around Dublin. ▷ Maria Edgeworth (1767–1849) and William Carleton (1794–1869) stand almost alone in the seriousness with which they looked at their native land and its inhabitants. Edgeworth's *Castle Rackrent* (1800) and Carleton's *Traits and Stories of the Irish Peasantry* (1830–3) are isolated landmarks; and Carleton, an adopted member of Ascendancy culture who was born a Catholic peasant, has been read in recent years with renewed interest and recognition.

In the decades that followed the devastation of native Gaelic culture by the famine and mass emigration of the 1840s, a new sense of Ireland's nationhood began, paradoxically, to emerge. The poets and dramatists of the Literary Revival of the 1880s and 1890s regarded Standish O'Grady (1846–1928) as its prime mover. His two-volume history of Ireland – *The Heroic Period* (1878) and *Cuchullin and His Contemporaries* (1880) – sent them back with a new authority to the ancient matter of Ireland. And it was on this material, and on a new attention to the distinctive English actually spoken in Ireland, that the renaissance of Irish letters was founded. Its chief authors – the most notable being W. B. Yeats (1865–1939), J. M. Synge (1871–1909) and Lady Gregory (1852–1932) – were still, to begin with, the sons and the daughters of the Ascendancy, but before long they were joined in their work of forging the soul of the soon-to-be-independent nation by writers who sprang from the native and Catholic population. A common task was perceived.

The history of Irish literature in English is closely linked, then, to the political history of the nation that (except for the six counties in its north-east corner) won its independence from British rule in 1921, and declared its Republican status when leaving the Commonwealth in 1949. Irish writers since the Revival have had to reconsider and redefine ideas of continuity and cultural identity that are quite different from those that face English writers in the post-colonial period, though there are affinities with the experience of the other Celtic nations of Britain – the Welsh and the Scots. (▷ Scottish fiction)

In the hundred-odd years since the poet and translator Douglas Hyde (1860–1949) gave a lecture to the newly formed National Literary Society in Dublin entitled 'The Necessity of De-Anglicising Ireland' (1892), Irish writers have had continually to ask themselves and each other quite how, and to what extent, de-Anglicization is to be carried out – and who they are when they have done it. Questions of national identity cross over with questions of personal identity in this distinctive version of the 20TH-century artist's problematic relation to society.

Ireland's writers began by looking to their country's heroic past and its idealized idea of the west, the non-anglicized land of saints, scholars and a noble peasantry; but they also looked, from the very start, to the literatures of Europe, and cast a cold and realist eye at their own urban and rural present. ▷ James Joyce (1882–1941) taught himself enough Norwegian as a schoolboy to write a letter to his hero, Ibsen, who was already a profound influence on the playwrights of Dublin's Abbey Theatre; George Egerton (Mary Dunne, 1859–1945) translated Knut Hamsun's *Hunger* and wrote about the 'New Woman' in her novel *Keynotes* (1893) before the old century ended. Kate O'Brien (1897–1974) and Maura Laverty (1907–66) found inspiration and objectivity by living for a time in Spain, Ireland's old ally. For many Irish writers – Joyce, ▷ Samuel Beckett and Francis Stuart (b 1902) are early examples – this looking outside Ireland necessarily became a longer physical exile: the required distance from which to practise their art – or indeed to have it published and read. For during the first half-century of independence, the Irish state's narrow, inward-looking patriotism and the tight grip of a reactionary Catholic clerisy directly impoverished cultural life within Ireland: ▷ censorship meant that most works of serious literature by Irish men and women were banned in their own country.

Those who stayed, returned, or at least kept a foothold in the place, were able to refine and multiply the means of reclaiming or repairing an Irish heritage. They worked from an intimate knowledge of place, like Patrick Kavanagh (1904–67), who immotalized his townland of Mucker in *The Great Hunger* (1942) and *Tarry Flynn* (1948); others, like Austin Clarke (1896–1974) and later Thomas Kinsella (b 1928), worked from a more scholarly knowledge of the Gaelic-language heritage than was available to the Revivalists. By the mid-20th century many writers were recognizing the impossibility of

bridging the gap to the past, and were finding that the fractured state of Irish culture itself offered a fruitful area of exploration for the isolated and disillusioned artist/commentator. Flann O'Brien (Brian O'Nolan, 1911–66) created a comic and fantastic Gaelic/modernist world in his novel *At Swim-Two-Birds* (1939) as his response to this artistic dilemma.

It tended to be the novelists and short-story writers who recorded the day-to-day reality of life in the young state. ▷ Sean O'Faolain (b 1900) and ▷ Frank O'Connor (Michael O'Donovan, 1903–66) demonstrated, in their short stories of the Troubles and after, not just a consummate art, but a seminal understanding of the why and the how of that wished-for 'de-Anglicization'. Written from the fringes, but courageously central in their concerns, the novels and short stories of the Aran Islander ▷ Liam O'Flaherty (1897–1984) are eloquent accounts of the dignity and constraints of life in the no-longer idealized rural west; and Patrick McGill's *Children of the Dead End* (1914) is a classic account of the reality of land-hunger and migratory labouring.

At home and abroad, then, Irish writers were grappling with the question of identity, and a body of remarkable writing was being assembled into a tradition of its own. But the achievements of three writers in particular placed a burden of success on subsequent generations. In poetry, the novel and drama, the work of Yeats, Joyce and Synge proved difficult to build on directly. Over the years a pattern can be discerned in which Ireland's vigorous – but even in the 1980s essentially naturalistic – tradition of fiction has more in common with the elegiac and story-telling parts of Yeats's *oeuvre* than with Joyce's modernism. Conversely, poets have found in ▷ *Ulysses*'s concern with the here and now of life as it is lived – and lived in the city – a more usable language than Yeats's lovely rhetoric or Synge's Gaelic-shadowed experimentalism.

During this first century of a consciously Irish literature in English, Gaelic has continued to be the linguistic bedrock of Irish writers.

One half-century into the new state, a rather less easily accommodated bedrock issue surfaced: the rekindling of violent conflict on a large scale in the Six Counties in 1968. To the chagrin of some writers south of the border, the work of many poets and playwrights of the North has been received with far more interest and critical acclaim in recent years than has been granted to writing from the South. For a time, all the artistic as well as the political action has seemed to be north of the Border. While the unprecedented prosperity of the 1960s and 70s inclined the South to a certain complacency, in the North it has seemed to both sides 'as though the whole of Anglo-Irish history has been boiled down and its dregs thrown out, leaving their poisonous concentrate on these six counties' (the final sentence of David Thomson's *Woodbrook*; 1974).

In the field of the novel, Irish women have managed, as women have in English generally, to make a substantial contribution; but the pressures of a conservative and patriarchal society have been less kind to women poets. As Irish women free

themselves from the extremes of traditional roles, all
the expected fields of women's writings are growing
rapidly, and making strong connections with writing
in England and the USA. Particularly notable are ▷
Edna O'Brien (b 1930), Julia O'Faolain (b 1932),
Jennifer Johnston (b 1930) and the promising Deidre
Madden (b 1961).

The great expansion in Irish publishing over the last
20 years, especially of contemporary work, augurs well
for the continuing vigour of all areas of Irish literature
in English, and in Gaelic too. Another hopeful sign is
the Republic's decision not to tax artists' earnings.
Bib: *Macmillan Dictionary of Irish Literature*; Kee,
R., *The Green Flag: A History of Irish Nationalism*;
Kinsella, T. (trans.), *The Tain*.

Irony
▷ Figures of Speech.

Isherwood, Christopher (1904–86)
Novelist and dramatist. Born in Cheshire and
educated at Repton School and Cambridge and
London universities. At preparatory school he met
the poet W. H. Auden (1907–73), with whom he
later collaborated on three plays, *The Dog Beneath
The Skin* (1935), *The Ascent of F6* (1936) and *On
The Frontier* (1938). These are primarily political
and psychological parables. Isherwood's first two
novels, *All The Conspirators* (1928) and ·*The Memorial*
(1932), employ ▷ modernist styles and techniques.
His experience of teaching English in Berlin from
1930 to 1933 is reflected in *Mr Norris Changes Trains*
(1935) and *Goodbye to Berlin* (1939), which employ a
more realistic mode. The latter is a series of linked
tales recording the atmosphere and characters of
a decadent Berlin in the last days of the Weimar
Republic; the narrator is characterized by a certain
passivity and detachment, summarized in his claim: 'I
am a camera with its shutter open . . .' The section
entitled 'Sally Bowles' was dramatized in 1951 as
I Am A Camera and turned into a stage musical in
1968 as *Cabaret*. Isherwood visited China in 1933
with Auden, and together they wrote *Journey to a
War* (1939). In 1939 they both emigrated to the
USA, where Isherwood became naturalized in 1946.
All his major work is written in the first person,
and his American novels draw extensively on his
own development as a theme. They are: *Prater
Violet* (1945), *The World in the Evening* (1954), *Down
There On A Visit* (1962), *A Single Man* (1964) and *A
Meeting By the River* (1967). He also wrote numerous
screenplays, and several autobiographical and
travel pieces, including *Lions and Shadows* (1938),
Christopher and his Kind (1976) and *The Condor and
the Cows: a South American Travel Diary* (1950).
He translated works relating to the mystical Hindu
philosophy of Vendanta, a philosophy which is
advocated in *A Meeting By the River*.
Bib: King, F., *Christopher Isherwood*; Summers, C. J.,
Christopher Isherwood; Bachards, D., and White, J.P.,
(eds.), *Where Joy Resides: An Isherwood Reader*.

Ishiguro, Kazuo (b 1954)
Novelist and short-story writer. Born in Nagasaki,
Japan, he has lived in Britain since 1960, where he

studied at the universities of Kent and East Anglia.
He has worked as a grouse-beater at Balmoral Castle
and as a community and social-worker in Scotland
and London. He now lives in Guildford, Surrey. His
work was included in *Introduction 7: Stories by New
Writers, 1981*. His first two novels, *A Pale View of
Hills* (1982) and *An Artist of the Floating World* (1986)
explore post-war Japanese cultural displacement
through the thoughts and memories of individuals:
a Japanese woman living in England, stirred to
retrospection by her daughter's suicide; a painter,
once employed by the pre-war Imperial regime,
living in a provincial Japanese town. In *The Remains
of the Day* (1989), which won the Booker Prize, an
English butler on a tour of Britain reassesses the
lost opportunities of his life. His work has been
widely praised for its delicacy of style and subtlety of
psychological insight.

Italian influence on English fiction
Apart from the influence of Italian literature, Italy
as a country was particularly important to England
in the 16th and early 17th century. The English
attitude to Italy was complicated – a mixture of
admiration, envy, intense interest and disapproval
amounting to abhorrence. The Italian cities were for
Englishmen the centres and summits of civilization,
and such centres in most periods are supposed to
represent not only what is most advanced in thought
and behaviour, but also what is most extravagant and
corrupt.

Two Italian books of the 16th century were
immensely fascinating to Englishmen, and the
English response to them explains much of the
contradiction in English feeling. The first was
Castiglione's *Courtier* (1528, trans 1561) which
offered a model for the virtues and accomplishments
of the perfect ▷ gentleman; this was greatly admired
by English courtly figures such as Sir Thomas Wyatt
and ▷ Sir Philip Sidney, and was approved even
by such an anti-Italian as Queen Elizabeth's private
tutor, Roger Ascham. The other was ▷ Machiavelli's
Prince (1513). This book was not translated into
English until 1640, but many educated Englishmen
knew Italian in the 16th century; in any case,
Gentillet's *Contre Machiavel* (*Against Machiavelli*,
1576) was widely known in England and translated in
1602. Machiavelli's object was to develop a political
science capable of uniting Italy; this did not interest
Englishmen, but they were deeply horrified by
Machiavelli's demonstration that for such politics to
be effective they had to disregard ordinary morality
and good faith. The work no doubt impressed
English statesmen such as Elizabeth's minister Cecil,
but it made 'politics' – 'politic' – 'politician' into
evil words for those not occupied by statecraft, and
a Machiavellian was synonymous with an atheist
or with one who had taken the devil as his master.
More superficially, travel in Italy was supposed to
induce folly and affectation and to corrupt morals.
As Roger Ascham put it in *The Scholemaster* (1570)
'what the Italian saith of the Englishman . . . *Englese
Italianato, è un diavolo incarnato*, that is to say, you
remain men in shape and fashion, but become devils
in life and condition.' Italians were poisoners and

seducers like Iachimo in Shakespeare's *Cymbeline*. It was not only because their fiction was popular that so many Elizabethan and Jacobean plays were based on Italian tales ('*novelle*'), but because Italy could be appealed to as the land where human nature was richest, darkest and brightest.

The fact that Rome was the centre of the Catholic Church was of course bad enough for Protestant Englishmen after 1540; before that date, the image was brighter, and throughout the century Englishmen did not forget that Italy was the nation of such great scholars and philosophers as Pico della Mirandola (1463–94) whose works ▷ Sir Thomas More partly translated. It was the independence of the best Italian minds that attracted the best English minds of the 16th and 17th centuries. The free-thinking Italian philosopher, Giordano Bruno (?1548–99), despised the stale traditions of the English universities on his visit (1583–5), but he admired Queen Elizabeth and made friends with men such as Sir Philip Sidney and Sir Walter Raleigh. The astronomer Galileo, who, like Bruno, came into conflict with the Inquisition, was studied by the poet John Donne, and received visits from the sceptical philosopher ▷ Thomas Hobbes and the Puritan John Milton. Milton's visit to Italy (1638–9) enriched him with encounters with scholars and patrons of learning, while at the same time he felt in danger from the papal police because of his religious opinions; this is another example of the complicated relationships of Englishmen with Italy.

After 1650 Italy by no means lost its fascination for the English, but it was Italy as a storehouse of the past, rather than a challenging present, that drew Englishmen. In the 18th century the English invented a sort of tourism; what was called the 'Grand Tour' formed part of the education of upper-class young men and Italy was one of its principal objectives. They were drawn to the architectural and sculptural remains of the old Roman Empire, the framework of their literary education in Latin literature. In the second half of the 19th century the art critic ▷ John Ruskin and the Pre-Raphaelite painters and poets turned their interest to the Italian Middle Ages.

The most important contributors to the Italian romantic novel are probably Alessandro Manzoni (1785–1873), who influenced ▷ Sir Walter Scott, and Ugo Foscolo (1778–1827), who was himself exiled in England. Foscolo's *The Last Letters of Jacopo Ortis* (1802–14) was a major contribution to the novel form. Later, *The Child of Pleasure* (1890), a novel by Gabriele D'annunzio (1863–1938), influenced the aesthetic, symbolist and Pre-Raphaelite schools in England.

The reputation of Italian authors in other countries has continued in the 20th century, often rivalling the golden age of medieval Italianate influence. The works of Italo Calvino (1923–85), Primo Levi (1919–87) and Umberto Eco (b 1932) are published in English almost as soon as in the original Italian. Levi's autobiographical accounts of his experiences in Auschwitz, as for example in *The Periodic Table* (1975), Eco's theoretical works and his best-seller *The Name of the Rose* (1981), and Calvino's neo-realist trilogy *Our Ancestors* (1952–9) have an international readership. Other 20th-century Italian writers of note are the novelist Alberto Moravia (the pen name of Alberto Pincherle), who, like Calvino, wrote neo-realistic works concerned with socio-political issues, as for example, *Two Women* (1957) and Giorgio Bassani (b 1916), a confessional novelist aware of the torments of evil and morality, as in his work *The Garden of the Finzi-Contini* (1962).

Ivanhoe (1819)

A historical novel by ▷ Sir Walter Scott. It is set in the reign of Richard I, who is one of the characters; the story concerns rivalry between the king and his wicked brother John (reigned 1199–1216), and between Saxons and the ruling Norman aristocracy. Locksley (the legendary outlaw, Robin Hood) aids Richard against the rebellious Normans, and helps to bring about the union of the Saxon hero, Wilfred of Ivanhoe, and the heroine Rowena. It was the first novel by Scott to deal with an English (as distinct from a Scottish) subject, and was very popular in the 19th century. This popularity is partly due to its being one of the first attempts to write a novel about the Middle Ages with a genuine regard for history.

Jack and the Beanstalk

A well-known ▷ fairy tale based on a myth found all over the world. Jack exchanges his mother's cow for a hatful of beans. When thrown into the garden, the beans rapidly sprout stalks which reach above the clouds. Jack climbs one of the beanstalks and finds himself in a new land near the castle of a man-eating giant. Jack manages by cunning to steal the giant's wealth and when the giant pursues him down the stalk, he fells it so that the giant falls and breaks his neck.

Jack Wilton

▷ Unfortunate Traveller, The.

Jacobin

Originally a name given to Dominican friars in France, because their first convent was in the Rue St Jacques in Paris. The name was transferred to a political society which rented a room in the convent in the first year of the ▷ French Revolution. The society developed into a highly organized political party, led by Robespierre, who became practically dictator of France in 1793. The club was closed after the fall of Robespierre in 1794. The Jacobins were extreme in asserting the principle of equality and in their opposition to privilege. Later, when conservative reaction had set in, 'Jacobin' was used loosely for anyone with political radical tendencies in England as well as in France; eg the paper The Anti-Jacobin was founded to combat English liberal opinion in 1797.

Jacobson, Dan (b 1929)

Novelist, short-story writer and critic. Born in South Africa, he moved permanently to England in 1954, and is now Professor of English Literature at University College, London. His novels are: The Trap (1955); A Dance in the Sun (1956); The Price of Diamonds (1957); The Evidence of Love (1960); The Beginners (1966); The Rape of Tamar (1970); The Wonder Worker (1973); The Confessions of Joseph Baiz (1977); Hidden in the Heart (1991); The God Fearer (1992). His story collections include: A Long Way From London (1958); The Zulu and the Zeide (1959); Beggar My Neighbour (1964); Through the Wilderness (1968); A Way of Life (1971); Inklings: Selected Stories (1973). Up to and including The Beginners, the story of three generations of an immigrant Jewish family, the novels are set in South Africa, and are largely naturalistic in style. The Rape of Tamar, which inspired the play Yonadab by Peter Shaffer, is a more experimental work, much concerned with the ambiguities of narration. It has an old Testament setting, and a self-conscious, and highly characterized narrator. The Confessions of Joseph Baiz is the fictional autobiography of a man who can love only those whom he has betrayed, and is set in an imaginary totalitarian country, somewhat resembling South Africa. Recurrent concerns of Jacobson's novels and stories include power, religion, guilt and betrayal, and his work is characterized by its inventiveness and wit. His non-fiction includes: Time of Arrival and Other Essays (1967); The Story of the Stories: The Chosen People and its God (1982); Time and Time Again: Autobiographies (1985); Adult Pleasures: Essays on Writers and Readers (1988).
Bib: Roberts, S., Dan Jacobson.

Jakobson, Roman (1896–1982)

Linguist. Born in Moscow, where he was educated, Jakobson worked in Czechoslovakia for almost 20 years, between 1920 and 1939, and after the German invasion he escaped to Scandinavia, before going to the U.S.A. where he taught in a number of universities, and became Professor of Russian Literature at the Massachusetts Institute of Technology. During his formative years he was heavily influenced by a number of avante-garde movements in the Arts, but in his own work he laid specific emphasis upon the formulation of a 'poetics' which took into account the findings of ▷ structuralism, and the work of the Russian ▷ Formalists. He was an active member of the Society for the Study of Poetic Language (OPOYAZ) which was founded in St Petersburg in 1916, and in 1926 he founded the Prague Linguistic Circle. His wife Krystyna Pomorska notes, in a recent collection of his writings, that poetry and visual art became for Jakobson the fundamental spheres for observing how verbal phenomena work and for studying how to approach them (Roman Jakobson, Language and Literature, 1987).
Bib: Hawkes, T., Structuralism and Semiotics; Jakobson, R., Language and Literature and Verbal Art, Verbal Sign, Verbal Time; Bennett, T., Formalism and Marxism; Erlich, V., Russian Formalism: History-Doctrine.

James, C.L.R. (1901–89)

Political activist, theorist, novelist, short-story writer and journalist. Born in Trinidad and educated there at Queens Royal College secondary school, Port of Spain, he began his career in the 1920s as a professional cricket player, a school teacher and editor of the literary magazine Trinidad. During his long, active and eventful life he was for various periods cricket correspondent for the Manchester Guardian, editor of the Marxist journal Fight in London, a trade union organizer and Marxist activist in the USA, secretary of the West Indian Federal Labour Party in Trinidad, editor of The Nation (Port of Spain), a lecturer at various colleges and universities, a BBC cricket commentator and cricket columnist for Race Today. He was twice exiled to Britain: the first time in 1953, when the McCarthyite American government deported him because of his left-wing views, and the second time in the early 1960s when the leader of the Trinidadian Government (whose party James served as secretary and who had also once been his pupil) found his outspokenness threatening and forced him to leave. His political convictions were defined by Marxism and Pan-Africanism; in London in the 1930s he was associated with future African leaders Jomo Kenyata and Kwame Nkrumah. Pan-Africanism is explored in two of his political works: A History of Negro Revolt (1938), revised as A History of Pan-African Revolt (1969), and Nkrumah and the Ghanaian Revolution (1977). His response to Stalinism was to take a

Trotskyist line: his book *Mariners, Renegades and Castaways: The Story of Herman Melville and the World We Live In* (1953) used a parallel with Melville's novel *Moby Dick* for a critique of Stalinism.

His own fiction writing began in the 1920s with short stories which, despite his own middle-class and British-influenced family background, were naturalistic ($\triangleright$ naturalism) studies of the life of poor Trinidadians in the Port of Spain slums. His only novel, *Minty Alley* (1936), has a similar setting, examining the lives, relationships and hopes of the inhabitants of a Port of Spain boarding house. He published a large number of political and historical works, of which the most influential is *The Black Jacobins: Toussaint L'Ouverture and the San Domingo Revolution* (1938), an account of the slave revolt, led by L'Ouverture in Haiti in the 1790s and unique in the history of slavery in that it led to independence. He also wrote a play on this subject: *Toussaint L'Ouverture*, produced in London in 1936, revised as *The Black Jacobins*, and produced in Nigeria in 1967 (published in *A Time and a Season: Eight Caribbean Plays*, ed. E. Hill, 1976). His short stories are included in *The Best Short Stories of 1928* (published by Cape) and in *Island Voices* (1970). He retained his enthusiasm for cricket and wrote several books on the game, notably *Beyond the Boundary* (1963), which examines the socio-political significance of cricket in both the West Indies and Britain. Other works include: *The Life of Captain Cipriani: An Account of British Government in the West Indies* (1932); *The Future in the Present: Selected Writings of C.L.R. James* (1977); *Spheres of Existence: Selected Writings* (1981); *At the Rendezvous of Victory: Selected Writings* (1985). Bib: Said, E., *Culture and Imperialism*.

James, Henry (1843–1916)

Novelist. Born in New York; his father was an original writer on philosophy and theology, and his brother, William James, became one of the most distinguished philosophers and psychologists of his day. His education was divided between America and Europe. Europe drew him strongly, and he finally settled in Europe in 1875 after a series of long visits. He was naturalized British in 1915. Towards both continents, however, he had mixed emotions. As to America, he belonged to the eastern seaboard, New England, which had its own well-established traditions originating in English Puritanism, and he was out of sympathy with the American ardour for commercial enterprise and westward expansion. As to Europe, he was fascinated by the richness of its ancient societies and culture, but he brought an American, and especially a New England, eye to the corruption which such advanced development generated. The conflict was fruitful for his development as an artist, and it was not the only one; he was also aware of the contrast between the contemplativeness of his father's mind and the practical adventurousness characteristic of his brother's outlook and of Americans in general. And in his close study of the art of the novel, he felt the difference between the intense interest in form of the French tradition and the deeper moral interest to be found in the English tradition.

In the first period of his work, his theme is preponderantly the clash between the European and the American outlooks: *Roderick Hudson* (1875); *The American* (1877); *The Europeans* (1878); $\triangleright$ *Daisy Miller* (1879); $\triangleright$ *The Portrait of a Lady* (1881). To this period also belong two novels about American life: *Washington Square* (1881); *The Bostonians* (1886); and two restricted to English life, *The Tragic Muse* (1890); *The Princess Casamassima* (1886). His second period shows a much more concentrated and difficult style of treatment, and it concerns English society only: *The Spoils of Poynton* and $\triangleright$ *What Maisie Knew* (1897); $\triangleright$ *The Awkward Age* (1899). Between his first and second periods (1889–95) he experimented in drama; this was his least successful episode, but the experiment helped him to develop a dramatic technique in the writing of his novels. He wrote 12 plays in all. In his last period, the most intensive and subtle in style, James returned to the theme of the contrast of American and European values: $\triangleright$ *The Wings of the Dove* (1902); $\triangleright$ *The Ambassadors* (1903); $\triangleright$ *The Golden Bowl* (1904). On his death he left unfinished *The Ivory Tower* and *The Sense of the Past*. Some of his best fiction is to be found among his short stories, and he was particularly fond of the $\triangleright$ novella form – between a story and a usual novel in length; *The Europeans* and *Washington Square* come into this class, and so does his masterpiece of ambiguity, $\triangleright$ *The Turn of the Screw* (1898).

In his criticism, James is important as the first distinguished writer in English to give the novel and its form concentrated critical attention. His essays have been collected under the title *The House of Fiction* (1957), edited by Leon Edel, who has also edited his letters (4 vols., 1974–84) and, with L.H. Powers, his notebooks (1987). James also wrote books of travel, the most notable of which is *The American Scene* (1907), and autobiographical pieces – *A Small Boy and Others* (1913); *Notes of a Son and a Brother* (1914) and *Terminations* (1917). (The last is also the title of a story published in 1895.) Bib: Edel, L., *Henry James*; Matthiessen, F. O., *Henry James: The Major Phase*; Anderson, Q., *The American Henry James*; Leavis, F. R., in *The Great Tradition*; Dupee, F. W., *Henry James*; Bewley, M., in *The Complex Fate* and in *The Eccentric Design*; Wilson, E., in *The Triple Thinkers*; Krook, D., *The Ordeal of Consciousness in James*; Gard, R. (ed.), *James: The Critical Heritage*; Tanner, T., *Henry James*; Berland, A., *Culture and Conduct in the Novels of Henry James*; Woolf, J., *Henry James: The Major Novels*; Poole, A., *Henry James*; Horne, P., *Henry James and Revision*.

James, P. D. (b 1920)

Writer of crime stories and $\triangleright$ detective fiction. P. D. James's skilful and subtle detective novels have made her into one of Britain's most popular writers, not simply for the dexterity with which she handles her suspense plots, but for the complex characterization and social context of her writing. Like the great women crime writers of the previous generation ($\triangleright$ Agatha Christie, Dorothy L. Sayers, $\triangleright$ Margery Allingham and $\triangleright$ Ngaio Marsh), James has a central sleuth who figures in many of her novels – Adam Dalgleish of Scotland Yard, who first appeared in *Cover her Face* (1962). Her other works include: *A Mind to Murder* (1963); *Unnatural Causes* (1967); *An Unsuitable Job for a Woman* (1972); *The Black Tower* (1975); *Innocent Blood* (1980); *A Taste for Death* (1986).

Jane Eyre (1847)

A novel by ▷ Charlotte Brontë. It is in the form of a fictional ▷ autobiography, with some authentic autobiographical experience. The experiences of the penniless, unattractive child, at first in the household of her unfeeling aunt Mrs Reed and later at Lowood Asylum – a charitable school – are the subject of the earlier and most generally admired part of the book. Later she becomes governess to the ward of a rich landowner, Mr Rochester, whose terrible secret is his mad wife; this part of the story is a mixture of romantic love, romantic horror and social naivety, together with a truthfulness to feeling which still keeps the heroine convincing and interesting. In the third section, Jane is sought in marriage by a clergyman, St John Rivers, a man of rigorous honour and ideals, whom she refuses after a telepathic communication from Rochester because, unlike the passionate but morally imperfect Rochester, he does not love her. Her marriage to Rochester at the end of the book is again oddly compounded of naivety, romanticism, self-deception and truthfulness. The novel was in more than one respect an innovation: it ran contrary to the puritanic tradition that a good woman did not need to feel physical passion or require it in her lover; it presented a romantic heroine whose nature and appearance it is impossible to sentimentalize or idealize; it is the first novel told in the first person in which the narrator's personality is not just a window through which the events are seen but also defines the quality of the events as we experience them through her mind. *Jane Eyre* was the text which acted as a catalyst in ▷ feminist criticism in the 1980s through the medium of S. Gilbert and S. Gubar's *The Madwoman in the Attic* (1979), in which the unstable female characters in texts written by women were seen as doubles of the sane heroine and products of the suppression of the feminine.

▷ Jean Rhys's 1966 novel *Wide Sargasso Sea* tells the earlier life of the first Mrs Rochester, implying a feminist critique on the basis of that which is excluded from *Jane Eyre*.

Janet's Repentance

One of ▷ George Eliot's ▷ *Scenes of Clerical Life*.

Jefferies, Richard (1848–87)

Essayist and novelist. He wrote about the English countryside and its life and presented it plainly, without affection but with force. This has caused his reputation to rise in the 20th century, with its intensified interest in preserving natural surroundings and in understanding their environmental influence on society. He is well known for his volumes of essays: *Gamekeeper at Home* (1878); *Wild Life in a Southern County* (1879); *Round about a Great Estate* (1880); *Wood Magic* (1881); *The Life of the Fields* (1884). His novels are *Greene Ferne Farm* (1880);

The Dewy Morn (1884); *Amaryllis at the Fair* (1887); *After London, or Wild England* (1885). His best-known books are probably *Bevis* (1882), a children's story, and his autobiography, *The Story of my Heart* (1883).

▷ Essay; Children's books.

Bib: Taylor, B., *Richard Jefferies*.

Jekyll and Hyde

▷ *Strange Case of Dr Jekyll and Mr Hyde, The*.

Jerome, Jerome K. (1859–1927)

Novelist. Born in Walsall and brought up in the East End of London, where his father was an ironmonger, Jerome worked as an actor and journalist. His *Three Men in a Boat* (1889) is a comic ▷ picaresque tale of a rowing holiday on the Thames, and its popular success encouraged Jerome to write a sequel, *Three Men on the Bummel* (1900), in which the characters are taken to Germany. Other works include the autobiographical *Paul Kelver* (1902) and the autobiography *My Life and Times* (1926).

Jews in England

The Jews first settled in England after the Norman Conquest and, as elsewhere, undertook the occupation of lending money on interest which in the earlier Middle Ages was forbidden to Christians. They were expelled from England by Edward I in 1290. Neither in the Middle Ages nor later was anti-Semitism as strong in England as in some other countries, but the baseless myth that the Jews made ritual sacrifices of Christian boys is exemplified by the *Prioress's Tale* in ▷ Chaucer's ▷ *Canterbury Tales*. Between 1290 and 1655, when they were readmitted by Oliver Cromwell, a few Jews were admitted by special licence, and a number of rich Jews were living in London in the reign of Elizabeth I.

Jews returned to England after 1655 in fair numbers; by the end of the 18th century there were about 20,000 living in London. Anti-Semitism was inconspicuous – this fact has been attributed to the assiduous Bible-reading of the English middle classes – but unless they renounced their religion they suffered restrictions on political rights and entry into certain professions (*eg* the Law) similar to those of other denominations outside the ▷ Church of England. These restrictions were not entirely removed until the middle of the 19th century, although by that time ▷ Benjamin Disraeli, a Jew who had been received into the Church of England, was already one of the country's leading statesmen. In 19th-century fiction Jews are commonly depicted in extremes of good or bad; as against the evil criminal Fagin of ▷ Charles Dickens's ▷ *Oliver Twist* there is his Riah of ▷ *Our Mutual Friend*, ▷ George Eliot's idealized Daniel Deronda, the godlike Sidonia in Disraeli's ▷ *Coningsby*, and Rebecca, the secondary heroine of ▷ Walter Scott's ▷ *Ivanhoe*. Some of ▷ Anthony Trollope's novels portray a confirmed anti-Semitism in established society. In the 20th century, Leopold Bloom in ▷ James Joyce's ▷ *Ulysses* is partly a representation of the myth of the Wandering Jew.

Jewsbury, Geraldine Endsor (1812–80)
Daughter of a merchant from Manchester, Geraldine Jewsbury was born, the fourth of six children, in Measham, Derbyshire. Her elder sister, also a writer, cared for the family until her marriage, when Geraldine took over, caring for her father until his death in 1840 and her brothers till her marriage in 1853. Her ill-health prevented her becoming a journalist, but she contributed to and was a reader for *Bentley's*, influencing the choice of books in Mudie's Circulating Library (▷ Mudie, Charles): novels were to have moral tone and nothing 'unpleasant'. An intimate friend of the ▷ Carlyles, Jewsbury was known for brilliant wit and conversation, and the houses in Manchester and London were visited by many celebrities. She published articles in, among other magazines, ▷ *The Athenaeum* and the ▷ *Westminster Review*, and wrote six novels, including *Zoe* (1845), *The Half Sisters* (1848), *Marian Withers* (1851), *The Sorrows of Gentility* (1856), and two stories for children. *A Selection from the letters of Geraldine Jewsbury to Jane Carlyle* was published in 1892 (ed. Mrs A. Ireland). ▷ Virginia Woolf wrote an article about this: 'Geraldine and Jane' (*TLS* 28 Feb. 1929). The women had wanted the letters destroyed.
Bib: Howe, S., *Geraldine Jewsbury*.

Jhabvala, Ruth Prawar (b 1927)
Novelist, short-story writer, and writer of screenplays. She was born in Germany of Polish parents who came to England as refugees in the year of her birth. She studied at London University and in 1951 married the Indian architect C. S. H. Jhabvala. From 1951 to 1975 she lived in India, and since then has lived in New York. Many of her novels are based on her own ambiguous position in India as a European with an Indian family. They explore the tensions of contemporary Indian society, such as the conflict of ancient and modern ideas and the interaction of Westernized and non-Westernized Indians. They are based on witty but sympathetic observation of social manners, largely in domestic settings. Some of the sharpest satire is reserved for the naive and superficial enthusiasm of certain visiting Europeans, who are frequently exploited by a manipulative swami. *Heat and Dust* (1975) employs a double narrative consisting of the experiences of a contemporary English girl in India, and the love affair of her grandfather's first wife with an Indian prince in 1923. *In Search of Love and Beauty* (1983) reflects Jhabvala's change of home; it is a story of German Jewish emigrés in 1930s New York. Her other novels are: *To Whom She Will* (1955); *The Nature of Passion* (1956); *Esmond in India* (1958); *The Householder* (1960); *Get Ready For Battle* (1962); *A Backward Place* (1965); *A New Dominion* (1972); *In Search of Love and Beauty* (1983); *Three Continents* (1988); *Poet and Dancer* (1993). Story collections are: *Like Birds, Like Fishes* (1963); *A Stronger Climate* (1968); *An Experience of India* (1971); *How I Became A Holy Mother* (1976); *Out of India: Selected Stories* (1987). She has written a number of screenplays, some of which are based on her own works, as part of a highly successful film-making team with James

Ivory as director and Ismail Merchant as producer: *The Householder* (1963); *Shakespeare Wallah* (with Ivory; 1965); *The Europeans* (1979) (based on the novel by ▷ Henry James); *Quartet* (1981) (based on the novel by ▷ Jean Rhys); *Heat and Dust* (1983); *The Bostonians* (1984) (based on the ▷ Henry James novel); *A Room with a View* (1986) and *Howards End* (1992) (based on the novels by ▷ E. M. Forster).
Bib: Sucher, L., *The Fiction of Ruth Prawar Jhabvala*; Long, R. E., *The Films of Merchant Ivory*.

John Bull
A personification of England, dating from a political allegory *The History of John Bull* (1712) by John Arbuthnot. The character is there described as honest but quarrelsome, his temper depending on the weather; he understands business and is fond of drinking and the society of his friends. He is intended to represent the national character.

Johnson, Bryan S. (1933–73)
Novelist, poet and dramatist. His novels were highly experimental, taking as their main subject his own life as a novelist and the nature of the novel. He employed a whole range of ▷ post-modernist narrative devices for questioning the boundaries of fact and fiction. He claimed to write, not fiction, but 'truth in the form of a novel'. *Travelling People* (1963) uses a different viewpoint or narrative mode for each chapter, including a film scenario, letters and typographical effects. In *Alberto Angelo* (1964) the 'author' breaks into the narrative to discuss his own techniques, aims and sources. *The Unfortunates* (1969) is a loose-leaf novel of 27 sections, 25 of which can be read in any order. Johnson committed suicide at the age of 40, soon after completing *See the Old Lady Decently* (1975), which is based around the death of his mother in 1971, and incorporates family documents and photographs. His other novels are: *Trawl* (1966); *House Mother Normal* (1971); *Christie Malry's Own Double Entry* (1973). He also wrote plays, screenplays, television scripts and several collections of poems.

Johnson, Pamela Hansford (1912–81)
Novelist. Perhaps her best-known work is the trilogy composed of *Too Dear for my Possessing* (1940), *An Avenue of Stone* (1947) and *A Summer to Decide* (1949). These extend from the late 1920s to the late 1940s, and combine observation of events and society with the study of intricate relationships arising from the attractions for each other of unlike characters. The formal quality reflects the influence of ▷ Marcel Proust, on whom Pamela Hansford Johnson composed a series of radio programmes, *Six Proust Reconstructions* (1958). Some of her later novels were more comic and satirical (*eg, Who is Here?*, 1962 *Night and Silence*, 1963; *Cork Street*, 1965 and *Next to the Hatter's*, 1965) but *An Error of Judgement* (1962) concerns the problem of apparently motiveless evil in modern society, and relates to her non-fictional investigation of the Moors Murder case, *On Iniquity* (1967). Pamela Hansford Johnson was married to the novelist ▷ C. P. Snow. Her other novels are:

The Survival of the Fittest (1968); *The Honours Board* (1970); *The Holiday Friend* (1972); *The Good Listener* (1975); *The Good Husband* (1978); *A Bonfire* (1981).
Bib: Burgess, A., *The Novel Now*; Lindblad, I., *Pamela Hansford Johnson*.

Johnson, Samuel (1709–84)
Critic, poet, lexicographer, essayist. Born at Lichfield to elderly parents, Johnson's childhood was marred by ill health; a tubercular infection from his wetnurse affected both his sight and hearing, and his face was scarred by scrofula or the 'King's Evil'. He was educated at Lichfield Grammar School, and in 1728 went up to Pembroke College, Oxford; his studies at the university were, however, cut short by poverty, and in 1729 he returned to Lichfield, affected by melancholy depression.

After a brief period as a schoolmaster at Market Bosworth, Johnson moved to Birmingham, where he contributed articles (now lost) to the *Birmingham Journal*. In 1735 he married Elizabeth Porter, a widow greatly his senior, and using her money attempted to start a school at Edial, near his home town. The school quickly failed, and in 1737 Johnson set off to London accompanied by one of his pupils, the actor David Garrick. Lack of a university degree hindered him from pursuing a profession, and he determined to make a living by writing.

Edward Cave, the founder of *The Gentleman's Magazine*, allowed him to contribute articles, and for many years Johnson lived by hack writing. His *Parliamentary Debates* were published in this magazine, and were widely believed to be authentic. In 1738 the publication of his poem, *London*, revealed his literary abilities. But the project of compiling the ▷ *Dictionary of the English Language* which was to occupy the next nine years testifies to Johnson's concern to produce saleable material. Lacking a patron, he approached Lord Chesterfield with the plan; the resulting snub is a notorious episode in the decline of the patronage system. In 1749, the poem *The Vanity of Human Wishes* was published, and his play *Irene* staged by Garrick. In 1750 he began the twice-weekly periodical ▷ *The Rambler*, to add to his income but also as a relief from the *Dictionary* work.

The death of his wife in 1752 returned Johnson to the melancholy depression he had suffered after leaving Oxford. However, he continued to contribute to periodicals, and in 1755 the *Dictionary* was published, bringing him wide acclaim which also included, by the intervention of friends, an honorary degree from Oxford. From 1758–60 he wrote the ▷ *Idler* essays for the *Universal Chronicle*, and in 1759 ▷ *Rasselas* was published. In 1762 a Crown pension relieved some of the financial pressure, and the following year he met ▷ James Boswell, who was to become his biographer.

In 1765 Johnson's spirits were much lifted as he made the acquaintance of the ▷ Thrales, and over the next few years he spent much time at their home in Streatham. In the same year, his edition of Shakespeare, for which he wrote a famous Preface, appeared.

Johnson's desire to travel was partly fulfilled by journeys made in his later years. In 1773 he and Boswell made their ▷ *Journey to the Western Islands of Scotland* (1775), and in 1774 Johnson went to Wales with the Thrale family. The following year he accompanied the Thrales to Paris, his only visit to the Continent.

In 1777 Johnson began work on ▷ *The Lives of the Poets* (1779–81), at the request of booksellers. In 1784, estranged from his friend Mrs Thrale by her remarriage, he died in his home in Bolt Court. He is buried in Westminster Abbey.
Bib: Boswell, J. (ed. Hill, G. B.; revised Powell, L. F.), *The Life of Samuel Johnson*; Bate, W. J., *Samuel Johnson*; Hardy, J. P., *Samuel Johnson: A Critical Study*.

Johnson, The Life of Samuel (1791)
▷ Boswell, James.

Johnson's Dictionary
▷ *Dictionary of the English Language, A*.

Jonathan Wild the Great, The Life of (1743)
A satirical romance by ▷ Henry Fielding. His purpose was to ridicule 'greatness' by telling the story of a 'great' criminal in apparently admiring terms. The subject makes clear that the admiration is ironical, but the reader is reminded that eminent statesmen and other 'respectable' men of power – all those, in fact, who are normally regarded as great – commonly pursue their aims with as little scruple. Wild was a historical character who had been executed in 1725, and made the subject of a narrative by ▷ Defoe.

In Fielding's fictional satire, Wild begins his career by being baptized by the conspirator Titus Oates – also a criminal character – and takes to a career of crime in childhood. He becomes the leader of a gang of thieves, among whom he keeps discipline by threatening them with denunciation, while himself avoiding incrimination. The vilest of his crimes is the systematic ruin of his former schoolfriend, the jeweller Heartfree, whom he nearly succeeds in having executed. In the end it is Wild who is executed, but he is sent to his death with the same mock-heroic impressiveness as has characterized Fielding's treatment of him throughout.
▷ Picaresque.

Jones, David Michael (1895–1974)
Poet and artist. His paintings, engravings and woodcuts are probably now better known than his writing, with the exception of *In Parenthesis* (1937), an account of his experiences in World War I that combines verse and prose. See also *The Anathemata* (1952), Jones's most important work, and *Epoch and Artist* (selected writings, 1959).

Joseph Andrews (1742)
A novel by ▷ Henry Fielding. It was begun as a parody of ▷ Samuel Richardson's novel ▷ *Pamela*. In Richardson's novel the heroine, Pamela Andrews, is a chaste servant girl who resists seduction by her master, Mr B, and eventually forces him to accept her in marriage. Fielding ridicules Richardson by

opening his novel with an account of the resistance by Pamela's brother Joseph to seduction by his employer, the aunt of Mr B, whose name Fielding maliciously extends to Booby (= clumsy fool). Joseph is dismissed for his obstinate virtue, and sets out in search of his own sweetheart. On the journey he is befriended by his old acquaintance, a clergyman, Parson Adams. At this point Fielding seems to have changed the plan of his novel; Adams, instead of Joseph, becomes the central character on whom all the interest centres. With the change, the novel becomes something like an English ▷ *Don Quixote*, since Adams is a learned but simple-hearted, single-minded Christian whose trust in the goodness of human nature leads him into constant embarrassments.

Josipovici, Gabriel (b 1940)

Novelist, short-story writer and critic. Born in France, educated in Cairo, Cheltenham and at Oxford University, Josipovici is a lecturer and (since 1984) Professor of English at the University of Sussex. His novels are ambiguous and experimental works of ▷ post-modernist fiction, conveying a sense of fragmentation and uncertainty. *The Inventory* (1968), *Words* (1971) and *The Echo Chamber* (1980) are almost entirely in dialogue; *The Present* (1975) uses a present-tense narration and interweaves a number of stories; *Migrations* (1977) and *The Air We Breathe* (1981) are structured by the repetition of scenes and images. His other novels are: *Conversations in Another Room* (1984); *Contre-Jour* (1986); *In the Fertile Land* (1987); *The Big Glass* (1991). Story collections are: *Mobius the Stripper: Stories and Short Plays* (1974); *Four Stories* (1977). Plays include: *Evidence of Intimacy* (1972); *Echo* (1975); *Marathon* (1977); *A Moment* (1979); *Vergil Dying* (broadcast 1979). Criticism includes: *The World and the Book: A Study of Modern Fiction* (1971); *The Lessons of Modernism and Other Essays* (1977); *Writing and the Body* (1982); *The Book of God: A Response to the Bible* (1988); *Text and Voice: Essays 1981–1991* (1992). In 1990 he published *Steps: Selected Fiction and Drama*.

Journal of a Tour to the Hebrides, The (1785)

▷ James Boswell's account of the tour to the Hebrides which he made with ▷ Samuel Johnson in 1773 (cf. ▷ *A Journey to the Western Islands of Scotland*). The tour gave Boswell the opportunity to encourage Johnson's consideration of many topics, and the narrative, which he showed to Johnson, records Johnson's opinions and perorations on many matters. Boswell was partly motivated in undertaking the tour by the desire to show Johnson his homeland, but he also saw it as a good occasion to collect material for his *Life of Samuel Johnson*.

Journal of the Plague Year, The (1722)

Written by ▷ Daniel Defoe, the *Journal* purports to be the record of 'H.F.', a survivor of the plague in London of 1664–5. The initials have suggested to critics that Defoe's uncle, Henry Foe, may have provided some of the first-hand information.

The narrative tells of the spread of the plague, the suffering of the Londoners, and the attempts by the authorities to control the disease. Defoe incorporates statistical data, some of which is taken from official sources, to demonstrate the extent of the plague and its effects on the life of the capital. The 'factual' nature of the statistics stands in grim juxtaposition to the vivid recreation of death and disease, the inhabitants imprisoned in their own homes by danger and terror, and the mass burial sites and death-carts which became a familiar part of everyday existence.

Journalism

The distinction between journalism and literature is not always clear, and before the rise of the modern newspaper with its mass circulation in the second half of the 19th century, the two forms of writing were even more difficult to distinguish than they are today. The most superficial but also the most observable difference has always been that journalism puts immediacy of interest before permanency of interest, and easy readability before considered qualities of style. But of course what is written for the attention of the hour may prove to be of permanent value; a good example is ▷ William Cobbett's ▷ *Rural Rides* in his weekly *Political Register* in the early 19th century.

The ▷ 'pamphlets' of writers such as ▷ Thomas Nashe and Thomas Dekker in the 1590s, and those on the controversial religious matters of the day such as the Marprelate pamphlets, are no doubt the earliest work with the stamp of journalism in English. However, the profession began to take shape with the wider reading public and the regular periodicals of the early 18th century. In that period we can see that it was the attitude to writing that made the difference – at least on the surface – between the journalist and the serious man of letters. Joseph Addison (1672–1719) considered himself a serious man of letters, whereas ▷ Defoe, writing incessantly on matters of practical interest without concerning himself with subtleties and elegance of style, is more our idea of a journalist. The 18th century was inclined to disparage such writing as ▷ Grub Street, though this term included all kinds of inferior, merely imitative 'literature', that we would not accept as journalism. The trade of journalism taught Defoe the realism that went into his fiction. A good example of the combination of facts and fiction is his ▷ *Journal of the Plague Year* (1722) which is both a fine example of journalistic reporting (from other people's accounts) and a fine achievement in imaginative realism. (Such a combination has a post-modernist equivalent in the form of ▷ faction, together with film and television dramatized documentaries.)

Defoe in the 18th century and Cobbett in the 19th century both assumed that the main function of their writing was to *enlighten* their readers. In the 1890s, however, the 'popular press' arose in which the desire to entertain was as strong as the desire to inform, and profitability was a major concern. The distinction between the serious and popular press is still current in the division between newspapers such as *The Times* and *The Guardian* and the tabloid press papers such as *The Sun* and *The Mirror*.

▷ Newspapers; Reviews and Periodicals.

Journey to the Western Islands of Scotland, A (1775)

▷ Samuel Johnson's account of the tour which he and ▷ James Boswell made in 1773 (cf. ▷ *Journey of a Tour to the Hebrides*). The tour gave rise to Johnson's meditations on the life, culture and history of the Scottish people, as well as on the Scottish landscape. Its publication aroused the wrath of the poet James Macpherson, whose work *Ossian* (or *Oisin*) Johnson rightly regarded as inauthentic.

Joyce, James (1882–1941)

Novelist. He was Irish, and born at a time when Irish nationalism was moving into its fiercest, most desperate phase. Joyce was born into a Catholic family, was educated by the Jesuits, and seemed destined for the Catholic priesthood, yet he turned away from the priesthood, renounced Catholicism, and in 1904 left Ireland with Nora Barnacle, with whom he spent the rest of his life and had two children. They lived in Trieste, in Zurich and, after World War I, in Paris. But although he took no part in the movement for Irish liberation, Joyce did not renounce Ireland; the setting for all his fiction is the capital city (and his home town) of Dublin. This and his own family relationships were always his centres, and from them he drew increasingly ambitious imaginative conceptions which eventually extended to the whole history of European culture.

His first important work was a volume of stories, ▷ *Dubliners*, published after long delay in 1914. The collection has artistic unity given to it by Joyce's intention 'to write a chapter of the moral history of my country . . . under four of its aspects: childhood, adolescence, maturity and public life'. The method combines an apparent objective realism with a subtle use of the symbolic and the mimesis of Dublin speech idiom and is based on Joyce's idea of 'epiphanies' – experiences, often apparently trivial, presenting to the observer deep and true insights. His first novel, ▷ *A Portrait of the Artist as a Young Man* (1916), is largely autobiographical and describes how, abandoning his religion and leaving his country, he discovered his artistic vocation. Its original method of narration – a form of ▷ stream of consciousness – causes the reader to share the hero's experience by having it presented to him with a verbal equipment which grows with the hero's development, from infancy to young manhood.

The next novel, ▷ *Ulysses* (1922), is still more original in the use of language. First serialized in the *Little Review* in 1918, its subject is apparently small – a single day in the life of three Dubliners – but Joyce's treatment of it makes it vast. The characters are made to correspond to the three main characters of ▷ Homer's ▷ *Odyssey*, and the 18 episodes are parallels to the episodes in that epic. The past is thus made to reflect forward on to the present, and the present back on to the past, revealing both with comic irony and endowing the apparently trivial present with tragic depth. In this book, modern man in the modern city is presented with unprecedented thoroughness and candour.

In his last book, ▷ *Finnegans Wake* (1939), Joyce attempts an image of modern 'Everyman' with all the forces of his experience released – in other words it concerns one night of a character who, because he never fully wakes up, is not restricted by the inhibitions of normal daylight consciousness. To express this night consciousness Joyce uses a special dream language by which words are fused together to give instantaneous multiple allusiveness; the same technique had been used by the mid-19th-century children's writer ▷ Lewis Carroll in the poem called 'Jabberwocky' (*Through the Looking-Glass*, 1872). However, because Joyce wishes to use the public-house keeper who is his hero as the representative of modern European man, he often fuses English words with those of other European languages, thus increasing the difficulty for the reader. Despite the support of friends such as Harriet Shaw Weaver (editor of *The Egoist*), and the poets W. B. Yeats and Ezra Pound, Joyce suffered from poverty all his life, as well as from severe eye problem. He had many difficulties with publishers and the authorities because of the alleged obscenity of his work; the unexpurgated edition of *Ulysses* was not published in Britain until 1937.

He published three volumes of poetry, which show his sense of poignant verbal beauty: *Chamber Music* (1907); *Gas from a Burner* (1912); *Pomes Penyeach* (1927). His *Collected Poems* appeared in 1936. His single play, *Exiles* (1918), is interesting chiefly for showing his admiration for the Norwegian dramatist Ibsen. An early version of his *Portrait of the Artist* was published in 1944 (enlarged 1955) as *Stephen Hero*.

▷ Catholicism in English literature; Irish fiction in English.

Bib: Ellmann, R., *James Joyce* (biography), *Ulysses on the Liffey* and *The Consciousness of Joyce*; Burgess, A., *Joysprick*; Peake, C. H., *James Joyce: the Citizen and the Artist*; Kenner, H., *Joyce's Voices and Ulysses*; Tindall, W. Y., *A Reader's Guide to Finnegans Wake*; Joyce, S., *My Brother's Keeper*; Levin, H., *Joyce: a Critical Introduction*; Budgen, F., *James Joyce and the Making of Ulysses*; Gilbert, S., *James Joyce's Ulysses: a Study*; Denning, R. H. (ed.), *Joyce: The Critical Heritage*; McCabe, C., *James Joyce and the Revolution of the Word*; Kime Scott, B., *Joyce and Feminism*.

Jude the Obscure (1895)

The last novel by ▷ Thomas Hardy. In Hardy's words the theme is the 'deadly war . . . between flesh and spirit' and 'the contrast between the ideal life a man wished to lead and the squalid real life he was fated to lead'. Jude Fawley is a village mason (like Hardy's father) who has intellectual aspirations. He is seduced into marriage by Arabella Donn; when she abandons him, he turns back to learning, but falls in love with Sue Bridehead, whose contradictory nature seeks freedom and yet frustrates her own desire. She runs away from her schoolmaster husband, Phillotson, who disgusts her, and joins with Jude in an illicit union. Their children die at the hands of Jude's only child by Arabella, who takes his own and their lives because he believes that he and they had no right to be born. Sue returns in remorse to Phillotson, while Jude is beguiled back by Arabella, who deserts him on his deathbed.

The setting and the four main characters are so

representative that the novel is almost an allegory. Jude's native place is Marygreen, a run-down village which is a kind of emblem of decayed rural England. His ambition is to enter the university of Christminster, which is Oxford, but so named as a reminder by Hardy that the way of learning had once also been a goal of the spirit. Jude uproots himself from Marygreen but is unable to enter the university because of his social origins, though he lives in the town (where he meets Sue) and works there as a mason. Hardy is concerned, not only to criticize the social elitism of the old universities of Oxford and Cambridge but also to show that the decay of spiritual goals in the England of his day matches the decay of the countryside. Jude himself is a complete man – physically virile as well as spiritually aspiring; it is his very completeness which the modern world, both Marygreen and Christchurch, is unable to accept. Sue Bridehead represents the 'new woman' of the day, emancipated in her own theory but not in body. Sue is all mind; Arabella all body, and Phillotson a kind of walking death – a man of the best intentions who is nonetheless helplessly destructive in consequence of his lack of both physical and spiritual vitality. The novel epitomizes Hardy's longing for spiritual values and his despair of them; its pessimism has strong poetic quality, and after completing it he gave himself entirely to poetry. Like many of Hardy's novels, *Jude the Obscure* is set in the recent past – about 20 years before the time of writing. Publication of the book caused an uproar; after its hostile reception Hardy wrote no further novels.

Jung, Carl (1875–1961)

Swiss psychiatrist. He was part of the group surrounding ▷ Sigmund Freud between 1907 and 1913, but because of disagreements with Freud, he left to form his own school of 'Analytical Psychology'. Jung attributed less importance to the sexual, and saw the unconscious as containing, not only repressed material, but also undeveloped aspects of the personality, which he divided into thinking, feeling, sensuous and intuitive aspects. The personal unconscious he held to be the reverse of the persona, or outer self, and to perform a compensatory function. Furthermore, beneath the personal unconscious lay the racial and collective unconscious, the repository of the beliefs and myths of civilizations, which at the deepest level were all united. Jung termed the themes and symbols which emerged from this collective unconscious, archetypes, and Jungian therapy uses dream interpretation to connect the patient with the healing power of these archetypes. Jung saw the libido as a non-sexual life force, and neuroses as imbalances in the personality. He made a comparative study of the myths, religions and philosophies of many cultures, and his thought has a religious and mystical tenor. He is also the originator of the terms 'introvert', 'extrovert' and 'complex'. Many of his ideas and experiences are referred to in the autobiographical *Memories, Dreams, Reflections* (ed. Amelia Jaffé, translated 1963).

His influence on 20th-century literature results particularly from the importance he gave to myths and symbols as universal and creative modes of understanding. The creation, or reworking, of myths is a feature of the work of writers such as ▷ James Joyce (▷ *Ulysses*, about which Jung wrote an essay; 'Ulysses: A Monologue', 1932), T. S. Elliot and ▷ David Jones.

▷ Psychoanalytical criticism.
Bib: Jacobi, J., *The Psychology of C. J. Jung*.

Kant, Immanuel (1724–1804)
German philosopher of Scottish descent. His
most important works include: *Critique of Pure
Reason* (1781 and 1787); *Prolegomena to every future
Metaphysic* (1783); *Foundation for the Metaphysic
of Ethic* (1785); *Critique of Practical Reason* (1788);
Critique of Judgement (1790). He counteracted
Leibnitzian rationalism and the scepticism of ▷
David Hume by asserting the 'transcendence' of
the human mind over time and space (hence
'transcendental philosophy'). Time and space
are forms of our consciousness: we can know
by appearances but we cannot know 'things in
themselves'. On the other hand, it is in the nature of
our consciousness to have inherent in it an awareness
of design in nature, and of moral and aesthetic value
under a Divine moral law. His philosophy, continued
and modified by other German philosophers (Fichte,
Schelling, Hegel), profoundly influenced the poet
and philosopher ▷ Coleridge; through Coleridge,
it provided a line of thought which, in 19th-century
England, rivalled the sceptical materialistically
inclined tradition stemming from ▷ Locke, Hume
and ▷ Bentham.
▷ German influence on English fiction.

Kavanagh, Julia (1824–77)
Novelist. Born in Thurles and educated at home,
Julia Kavanagh was the daughter of a writer who
later claimed to have written her novels and that
his own worst work (a novel called *The Hobbies*)
was by her. She lived with her parents in France,
until they separated in 1844, when she returned to
England with her mother, whom she then supported
by her writing. French character and way of life
are reflected in her novels, and on the death of her
mother she returned to France and lived in Nice
until her death. Her first novel, *The Montyon Prizes*
(1846) was very popular. The best known are perhaps
Madeleine (1848), *Nathalie* (1850) and *Adèle* (1858).
Her biographical sketches, *French Women of Letters*
(1862) and *English Women of Letters* (1863), have
been much praised. Her other publications include a
volume of short stories, *Forget-me-nots* (1878).

Keane, Molly (b 1904)
Novelist and playwright. Born into an upper-middle-
class world of country life, Keane's witty novels are
concerned with the narrow interests of the privileged
and leisured Anglo-Irish community. Her career
has had two phases: up to her mid-30s and then
from the early 1980s onwards, punctuated by twenty
years of non-production. Her works include: *Taking
Chances* (1929); *Conversation Piece* (1932); *Devoted
Ladies* (1934); *The Rising Tide* (1937); *Spring Meeting:
A Comedy in Three Acts* (1938); *Loving Without Tears*
(1951); *Good Behaviour* (1981, shortlisted for the
Booker Prize); and *Time After Time* (1983).

Kelman, James (b 1946)
Novelist, short-story writer and playwright. Kelman was
born and educated in Glasgow, where he attended the
University of Strathclyde. He has worked in various
labouring and semi-skilled jobs. He has been seen,

along with ▷ Alasdair Gray, ▷ Janice Galloway
and Tom Leonard, as contributing to 'the new
Glasgow writing'. His fiction, like that of Gray, has
its roots firmly in the urban landscape of Glasgow
and combines a bleak view of contemporary culture
and of human experience with linguistic exuberance
and technical inventiveness, including a the use of
variable ▷ focalization: his novels *The Busconductor
Hines* (1984) and *A Disaffection* (1989) gain some
of their ironic effects from the way in which they
shift between internal focalization on the narrator
(using a form of stream of consciousness) and a
relatively detached reporting of events, whereas the
latter technique is used throughout in *A Chancer*
(1985). Volumes of short stories: *An Old Pub Near
the Angel* (1973); *Three Glasgow Writers* (with Tom
Leonard and Alex Hamilton, 1976); *Short Tales from
the Nightshift*; *Not Not While the Giro* (1983); *Lean
Tales* (with Alasdair Gray and Agnes Owens, 1985);
Greyhound for Breakfast (1987); *The Burn* (1991).
Plays: *The Busker* (1985); *Le Rodeur* (adapted from
a play by Enzo Corman, 1988); *In the Night* (1988).
Radio play: *Hadie and Baird: The Lost Days* (1978).
He has won the Cheltenham Prize (1987) and the
James Tait Black Memorial Prize (1990).

Keneally, Thomas (b 1935)
Novelist and playwright. Keneally was born in
Sydney and educated at St Patrick's College,
Strathfield, New South Wales. He studied law,
trained for the Catholic priesthood, served in the
Australian armed forces, and has worked as a school
teacher and university lecturer in drama. His novels
employ a wide range of genres and settings: his
first novel, *The Place at Whitton* (1964) is a horror
story; *Blood Red, Sister Rose* (1974) is a historical
novel about Joan of Arc; *Confederates* (1979) is set
during the American Civil War and *Schindler's Ark*
(1982) during the Second World War. However,
a number of his novels have specifically Australian
themes, exploring relations between Europe and
Australia and between whites and aborigines in
Australia: *The Chant of Jimmie Blacksmith* (1972)
concerns a half-aborigine who, after experiencing
racial hostility, turns to ritual killing, while *Bring
Larks and Heroes* (1967) and *The Playmaker* (1987)
are both set in the penal colony period in Australia.
The second of these, about a group of convicts
staging George Farquhar's Restoration satire of
army life, *The Recruiting Officer*, has recently been
adapted for the stage by Timberlake Wertenbaker
as *Our Country's Good*. Keneally's other novels
are: *The Fear* (1965, revised as *By the Line*); *Three
Cheers for the Paraclete* (1968); *The Survivor* (1969);
A Dutiful Daughter (1971): *Gossip from the Forest*
(1975); *Moses the Lawgiver* (1975); *Season in Purgatory*
(1976); *Passenger* (1979); *The Cut-Rate Kingdom*
(1980); *A Family Madness* (1985); *Towards Asmara*
(1989); *Flying Hero Class* (1991). His plays include:
Halloran's Little Boat (1966); *Childermass* (1968); *An
Awful Rose* (1972); *Victim of the Aurora* (1977); *Bullie's
House* (1980); *Woman of the Inner Sea* (1992). He has
also written plays and documentaries for television,
film screenplays, books for children and non-fiction
writing on Australia. He has acted in films, including

the film of his own novel *The Chant of Jimmie Blacksmith*.
Bib: Quartermaine, P., *Thomas Keneally*.

Kilvert, Robert Francis (1840–79)

Diarist. He was curate in the village of Clyro, Radnorshire. His candour and responsiveness to people and environment make his diaries valuable records of rural environment in the mid-Victorian era. Selections were published in 1938–40, edited by William Plomer.
▷ Diaries.

Kim (1901)

A novel by ▷ Rudyard Kipling. Kim, whose real name is Kimball O'Hara, is the orphan son of an Irish soldier in India, and he spends his childhood as a waif in the city of Lahore. He meets a Tibetan holy man in search of a mystical river, and accompanies him on his journey. Kim falls in with his father's old regiment, and is adopted by them, eventually becoming an agent of the British secret service under the guidance of an Indian, Hurree Babu. In spite of Kipling's British chauvinism, conspicuous in the later part of the book, the earlier part is an intimate and graphic picture of the humbler reaches of Indian life.

King, Sophia (c 1782–?)

Novelist and poet. Sister to ▷ Charlotte Dacre and, like her, overawed by their powerful father, John King. Her melodramatic novels centre upon repressed heroines and dark destructive fathers and lovers: *Cordelia, or The Romance of Real Life* (1799), published by ▷ Minerva, has a daughter who devotes her life to her wicked father; *The Fatal Spectre, or Unknown Warrior* (1801) has a male protagonist who ruins his mistress and is discovered to be the devil; and *The Adventures of Victor Allen* (1805) has a hero who displays biting cruelty towards women, even though the psychological reasons for this are later uncovered. This latter work is often there to anticipate ▷ *Frankenstein*. King described her writing as a place where, 'the fantastic imagination roves unshackled'.
Bib: Tompkins, J.M.S., *The Popular Novel in England 1770–1800*.

King, William (1663–1712)

Author of satirical and burlesque works in both prose and verse, including (with Charles Boyle) *Dialogues of the Dead* (1699) and *The Art of Cookery* (1708), imitating Horace's *Art of Poetry*.

Kingsley, Charles (1819–75)

Novelist; clergyman; reformer. He belonged to a movement known as Christian Socialism, led by F. D. Maurice. He is now remembered chiefly for his ▷ children's book, ▷ *The Water Babies* (1863). His novels *Yeast* (1848) and *Alton Locke* (1850) are concerned with the theme of social injustice. *Hypatia* (1853), *Westward Ho!* (1855) and *Hereward the Wake* (1865) are historical novels. His retelling for the young of Greek myths, *The Heroes* (1856) is still well known.
Bib: Pope-Hennessy, U., *Canon Charles Kingsley*;

Martin, R. B., *The Dust of Combat: A Life of Kingsley*; Thorp, M. F., *Life*; Barry, J. D., in *Victorian Fiction* (ed. L. Stevenson); Chitty, S., *The Beast and the Monk: A Life of Charles Kingsley*; Collom, S. B., *Charles Kingsley: The Lion of Eversley*.

Kipling, Rudyard (1865–1936)

Poet, short-story writer, novelist. He was born in India, educated in England, and returned to India at 17 as a journalist. In 1889 he came to England to live.

Kipling's poetry is striking for his success in using, vividly and musically, popular forms of speech, sometimes in the Browning tradition of the ▷ dramatic monologue, *eg McAndrew's Hymn*, or in the ballad tradition, *eg Barrack-Room Ballads* (1892). He was also able to write poetry appropriate to public occasions and capable of stirring the feelings of a large public, *eg* his famous *Recessional* (1897). His poetry is generally simple in its components but, when it rises above the level of doggerel, strong in its impact. It needs to be read in selection: *A Choice of Kipling's Verse* (ed. T. S. Eliot), has a very good introductory essay.

Kipling's stories brought him fame, and, partly under French influence, he gave close attention to perfecting the art of the short story. The volumes include *Plain Tales from the Hills* (1887), *Life's Handicap* (1891); *Many Inventions* (1893); *The Day's Work* (1898); *Traffics and Discoveries* (1904); *Actions and Reactions* (1909); *A Diversity of Creatures* (1917); *Debits and Credits* (1926) and *Limits and Renewals* (1932). The early stories in particular show Kipling's capacity to feel with the humble (common soldiers, Indian peasants) and the suffering. But he admired action, power, and efficiency; this side of his character brought out much of the best and the worst in his writing. Some of his best stories show his enthusiasm for the triumphs of technology, and are about machines rather than people, *eg* in *The Day's Work*. On the other hand he was inclined to be crudely chauvinistic, and to show unpleasant arrogance towards peoples ruled by or hostile to Britain, though he also emphasized British responsibility for the welfare of the governed peoples. Yet again, he sometimes engaged in delicate if sentimental fantasy, as in *They* and *The Brushwood Boy* (1925); some of his later stories show a sensitive and sometimes morbid insight into abnormal states of mind, *eg Mary Postgate* (1917). The stories, like the poems, are best read in selection: *A Choice of Kipling's Prose* (ed. Somerset Maugham).

Kipling is not outstanding as a full-length novelist. His best novel is ▷ *Kim* (1901), based on his childhood in India; *Stalky and Co* (1899) is well-known as a tale about an English public school, and is based on Kipling's own schooldays at the United Services College. *The Light that Failed* (1890) shows his more sensitive and sombre aspect. An autobiographical fragment, *Something of Myself*, was published in 1937.

Kipling's children's stories are minor classics of their kind: *The Jungle Books* (1894–5); *Just So Stories* (1902); *Puck of Pook's Hill* (1906). *Rewards and Fairies* (1910) is less celebrated.

▷ Children's books; Imperialism.

Bib: Birkenhead, Lord, *Rudyard Kipling* (biography); Page, N., *A Kipling Companion*; Carrington, C. E., *Life*; Dobree, B., *Kipling*; Orwell, G., in *Critical Essays*; Wilson, E., in *The Wound and the Bow*; Green, R. L. (ed.), *Kipling: The Critical Heritage*; Wilson, A., *The Strange Ride of Rudyard Kipling*; Kemp, S., *Kipling's Hidden Narratives*; Seymour-Smith, M., *Rudyard Kipling*.

Kipps (1905)

A novel by ▷ H. G. Wells. It describes the social rise of a shop-assistant through an unexpected legacy, his engagement to a vulgarly snobbish young lady who has hitherto been out of his reach, and his painful acquisition of the false standards and cares which are forced upon him. He escapes the marriage by marrying suddenly a girl of his own former class, but he only escapes his worries when he loses his money. The book contains acute social observation and comedy in the Dickens tradition, though Wells's style is quite his own.

Koestler, Arthur (1905–83)

Novelist and philosopher. He was born in Hungary and educated at the University of Vienna. From 1932–8 he was a member of the Communist Party (▷ Communism). He went to Spain as a correspondent during the Spanish Civil War, and was imprisoned by the Nationalists. Subsequently imprisoned in France during 1939–40, he joined the Foreign Legion before escaping to Britain in 1941. After World War II he became a British subject. From the 1930s to the 1950s his work was primarily concerned with political issues; his novel *Darkness At Noon* (1940) exposed Stalinist methods through the story of the imprisonment and execution of a former Bolshevik leader. From the 1950s onwards his writings were more concerned with the philosophical implications of scientific discoveries. His non-fiction trilogy, *The Sleepwalkers* (1959), *The Act of Creation* (1964) and *The Ghost in the Machine* (1967) considered the effect of science on man's idea of himself, and defended the concept of mind. A persistent feature of his work was a sense of horror at the barbarities of 20th-century Europe. Koestler, who had advocated the right to euthanasia, and who was suffering from leukaemia and Parkinson's disease, committed suicide together with his third wife, Cynthia Jefferies, in 1983. His other novels are: *The Gladiators* (1939); *Arrival and Departure* (1943); *Thieves in the Night* (1946); *The Age of Longing* (1951); *The Call Girls* (1972). Autobiographical writings include: *Arrow in the Blue* (1952); *The Invisible Writing* (1954). Other prose writings include: *The Yogi and the Commissioner* (1945); *The Roots of Coincidence* (1972).
Bib: Hamilton, I., *Koestler: A Biography*; Pearson, S. A., *Arthur Koestler*.

Kristeva, Julia (b 1941)

French psychoanalyst, philosopher and linguistic theorist. Julia Kristeva was born and grew up in Bulgaria, and moved to Paris to study in 1966. She writes in French, and is now a naturalized French citizen, but she has often drawn on the language and psychology of exile in her work – in 1970 ▷ Roland Barthes was one of the first theorists to respond enthusiastically to her work, calling her 'L'étrangère'. Kristeva's earlier work is more strongly concerned with ▷ semiotics and linguistic theory (*Séméiotiké*, 1969, outlines Kristeva's own brand of 'semanalysis'; see also *Desire in Language: A Semiotic Approach to Literature and Art*, 1980), and as her interest in psychoanalysis has burgeoned she has undertaken a series of studies of literature, poetics and abnormal psychology, and the relationship between language and the body (particularly *Powers of Horror*, 1982, *Tales of Love*, 1983, and *Black Sun*, 1980). Her long-term interest in symbolist and ▷ modernist writers continues to animate her work (Mallarmé and ▷ Lautréamont are the subject of *Revolution in Poetic Language*, 1974, and Céline figures centrally in *Powers of Horror*), and she has also had a profound impact on the development of the so-called 'New French Feminist' movement (see essays and interviews with her in *New French Feminisms*, ed. E. Marks and I. de Courtivron, as well as *Desire in Language* and *About Chinese Women*, trans. 1977). Kristeva is a long-term member of the editorial board of the radical journal ▷ *Tel Quel*, and is a practising psychoanalyst.
Bib: Moi, T. (ed.), *The Kristeva Reader*, Lechte, J., *Julia Kristeva*; Moi, T., *Sexual/Textual Politics*.
▷ Feminism; post-structuralism; psychoanalytic criticism; *écriture féminine*.

Kureishi, Hanif (b 1954)

Novelist, playwright and screenplay writer. Born in Kent and educated at King's College London, he was appointed Writer in Residence at the Royal Court Theatre in 1982 after winning the George Devine Award for his play *Outskirts* (1981). He has written two screenplays: *My Beautiful Laundrette* (filmed 1985) and *Sammy and Rosie Get Laid* (filmed 1987). He also wrote the screenplay for (and directed) the film *London Kills Me* (1991). His first novel, *The Buddha of Suburbia* (1989), is a comic, satirical story about growing up in south-east London.

L

La Fayette, Marie-Madeleine Pioche de la Vergue, Comtesse de (1634–93)

French novelist, whose (anonymously published) third work, *The Princess of Clèves* (1678), represents an important early stage in the development of the European novel. As a prototype of the ▷ *Bildungsroman* and of the psychological novel, this story of an unhappy but faithful wife at the 16th-century court of Henri II of France marks the point at which the novel as such emerges in France as a form distinct from the romance. La Fayette was a member of a literary circle in Paris which included La Rochefoucauld, famous for his aphorisms.

La Guma, Alex (1925–85)

South African writer and political activist. He worked as a clerk, bookkeeper and factory hand and was a committee member of the Cape Town Communist Party until its banning in 1950. In 1956 he helped to organize the Freedom Charter and as a result was one of the 156 people accused in the Treason Trial. He began writing for *New Age* in 1960, was placed under house arrest in 1962 and, after the passing of the No Trial Act, was put in solitary confinement. He fled from South Africa in 1967, initially to Britain and then to Cuba, where he was African National Congress representative and where he died in 1985. His novels, set in the black townships and prisons of South Africa under the apartheid regime in the 1960s, are powerful works of protest, showing police violence on the streets and torture in prison, and emphasizing the development of political consciousness as necessary to any better future. The novels include: *A Walk in the Night* (1962); *And A Threefold Cord* (1964); *The Stone Country* (1967); *In The Fog of the Season's End* (1972); *Time of the Butcherbird* (1979).

Lacan, Jacques (1901–81)

French psychoanalyst whose re-readings of ▷ Freud have become influential within the area of literary criticism. Lacan's *The Four Fundamental Concepts of Psychoanalysis* (trans. 1977), and his *Ecrits: A Selection* (trans. 1977) outline the nature of his revision of Freudian psychoanalytic method. A further selection of papers has appeared under the title of *Feminine Sexuality* (trans. 1982). It is to Lacan that we owe the terms ▷ 'imaginary' and ▷ 'symbolic order'. Similarly, it is to his investigation of the operations of the unconscious according to the model of language – 'the unconscious is structured like a language' – that we owe the notion of a 'split' human subject. For Lacan the 'imaginary' is associated with the pre-Oedipal (▷ Oedipus complex) and pre-linguistic relationship between mother and child (the 'mirror' stage) where there appears to be no discrepancy between identity and its outward reflection. This is succeeded by the entry of the infant into the 'symbolic order', with its rules and prohibitions centred around the figure of the father (the phallus). The 'desire of the mother' is then repressed by the child's entry into language and the 'symbolic order'. The desire for 'imaginary' unity is also repressed to form the unconscious, which the interaction between analyst and patient aims to unlock. Some of the fundamental divisions that Lacan has located in the 'subject' have proved highly adaptable for a range of ▷ materialist literary criticisms, including (more controversially) ▷ feminism.

Bib: Bowie, M., *Lacan* and *Freud, Proust and Lacan: Theory as Fiction*; Felman, S., *Jacques Lacan and the Adventure of Insight*; Grosz, E., *Jacques Lacan: A Feminist Introduction*; Gallop, J., *Reading Lacan*.

Lady Chatterley's Lover (1928)

▷ D.H. Lawrence's last novel. Constance Reid ('Connie') is the daughter of late-Victorian, highly cultured parents with advanced views. She marries Sir Clifford Chatterley in 1917, when he is on leave from the army; soon afterwards he is wounded, and permanently crippled from the waist down. Connie finds herself half alive, as though she has not been fully awakened; her dissatisfaction, however, does not proceed merely from her husband's disability, but from the impotence of civilization which the disability symbolizes. She is rescued from it by her husband's gamekeeper, Mellors, who fulfils her as a lover and as a human being. For Lawrence, the sexual relationship was potentially the profoundest human relationship: to treat it lightly was to trivialize the whole human being, and to regard it with shame was to repress essential human energies. He saw that 'advanced' young people took the former attitude, and that the older generation took the latter; he regarded both attitudes as leading symptoms of decadence in our civilization. He did not suppose that the sexual relationship could in itself constitute a renewal of civilization, but he considered that such a renewal depended on the revitalization of relationships, and that this revitalization could never take place without the recovery of a true and healthy sexual morality. 'I want men and women to be able to think sex, fully, completely, honestly and cleanly.' (*Apropos of Lady Chatterley's Lover*, 1930.)

This aim led Lawrence to use unprecedentedly explicit language in conveying the love affair between Connie and Mellors, and the novel thus acquired unfortunate notoriety. In Britain, the full version was suppressed for immorality, but an expurgated version was published in 1928. An unabridged edition came out in Paris in 1929; the first British unabridged edition was published by Penguin Books in 1959. This led to an obscenity trial, the first test of the 1959 Obscene Publications Act, at which many distinguished authors and critics (including ▷ E.M. Forster) testified in defence of the novel. The acquittal of Penguin had important consequences for subsequent publishing. Lawrence's defence of the novel, *Apropos of Lady Chatterley's Lover*, is one of the finest of his essays.

▷ Censorship.

Lagado

In ▷ Swift's ▷ *Gulliver's Travels* (Part III) capital of the island of Balnibarbi, and its neighbouring flying island Laputa.

Lamb, Charles (1775–1834)

Essayist and critic. His best-known work is his two volumes of the *Essays of Elia* (1823 and 1833), in which he discourses about his life and times. His *Specimens of English Dramatic Poets who lived about the Time of Shakespeare* directed interest towards Shakespeare's contemporaries, who had been somewhat neglected in the 18th century, although perhaps not so much ignored as Lamb thought. His friends included many writers of his time, and this fact gives a special interest to his letters. He collaborated with his sister Mary in adapting Shakespeare's plays into stories for children – *Tales from Shakespeare* (1807). His poems are unimportant but one or two, *eg The Old Familiar Faces* (1798) and the prose-poem, *Dream Children*, recur in anthologies. Lamb seems to have been a man of unusual charm and of gifts which he never allowed himself to display fully and energetically, perhaps because he was haunted by the fear of insanity, to which both he and his sister were subject.

▷ Children's books.

Bib: Lucas, E. V., *Life*; Tillyard, E. M. W. (ed.), *Lamb's Criticism*; Blunden, E., *Charles Lamb and his Contemporaries*; Cecil, D., *A Portrait of Charles Lamb*.

Lamb, Lady Caroline (1785–1828)
Novelist and poet. The only daughter of the 3rd Earl of Bessborough, she was taken to Italy at the age of three and brought up mostly in the care of a servant. Educated at Devonshire House School, she was then looked after by her maternal grandmother, Lady Spencer, who worried about her instability and 'eccentricities'. She married the statesman William Lamb (later the 2nd Viscount Melbourne), but in 1812, just after her marriage, became desperately infatuated with Byron, of whom she wrote in her diary that he was 'mad, bad and dangerous to know'. After he broke with her, she became increasingly unstable and violent-tempered, and her husband sued for separation, becoming temporarily reconciled, however, on the day fixed for the execution of the deed. Meeting Byron's funeral cortège seems to have hastened her disintegration and she ended up living with her father-in-law and only surviving son, an invalid. Her first novel, *Glenarvon* (1816), had a significant, though brief success, due no doubt to its portrayal of Byron and herself in a wild and romantic story. It was published anonymously, though she courted notoriety, being impulsive, vain and excitable to the point of insanity, as well as highly original. She wrote two further novels, *Graham Hamilton* (1822) and *Ada Reis* (1823), and poetry, some of which has been set to music.

Bib: Jenkins, E., *Lady Caroline Lamb*.

Lamb, Mary Ann (1764–1847)
Sister to ▷ Charles Lamb and daughter of a lawyer, she was brought up in poor circumstances, helping her mother, who worked as a needlewoman. In 1796, overworked and stressed, she pursued her mother's apprentice round the room with a knife in a fit of irritation, and when her mother interposed she killed her. The verdict was one of insanity and she was given into the custody of her brother Charles who took charge of her, finding suitable accommodation for her during her periodic bouts of illness and maintaining a close and affectionate relationship.

With Charles, she wrote *Tales from Shakespeare* (1807), designed to make Shakespeare's stories accessible to the young; *The Adventures of Ulysses* (1808), which was an attempt to do the same for ▷ Homer; and *Mrs Leicester's School* (1809), a collection of short stories.

▷ Children's books.

Lamming, George (b 1927)
Barbadian novelist. After teaching in Trinidad he moved to Britain in 1950, though he was later to return to the West Indies. His novels are concerned with the West Indian identity, both individual and collective, and the aftermath of colonialism and slavery. *The Emigrants* (1954) is a bleak portrayal of identity sought and lost among black emigrants to England in the 1950s; *Season of Adventure* (1960) represents the awakening to a new and more liberal consciousness of the daughter of a West Indian police officer; *Water with Berries* (1971) uses parallels with the colonial symbolism of Shakespeare's *The Tempest* to represent the historical consequences of colonialism through the personal crises of three West Indian artists living in London. His other novels are: *In the Castle of my Skin* (1953); *Of Age and Innocence* (1958); *Natives of my Person* (1972); *The Pleasures of Exile* (1984).

Bib: Paquet, S. P., *The Novels of George Lamming*.

Langue
This term appears throughout ▷ Ferdinand de Saussure's *Course in General Linguistics* (1915) to denote the system of ▷ signs which makes up any language structure. According to Saussure, individual utterances (▷ parole) are constructed out of elements which have no existence 'prior to the linguistic system, but only conceptual and phonetic differences arising out of that system'. This observation is fundamental to ▷ structuralism, which is concerned with the positioning of particular elements within a nonvariable structure. 'Langue' is the term used to denote the linguistic structure itself, that is the rules which lie behind particular linguistic events.

Laputa
In ▷ Jonathan Swift's ▷ *Gulliver's Travels*, the flying island in the satire against the ▷ natural philosophers of Part III.

Last Chronicle of Barset, The (1867)
The last of the ▷ Barsetshire novels, about the politics of the imaginary cathedral town of Barchester, by ▷ Anthony Trollope. It centres on one of Trollope's best characters – the Reverend Josiah Crawley, the curate of Hogglestock. A poor, proud, isolated man with rigorous standards, he is accused of theft and persecuted by the arrogant Mrs Proudie, wife of the bishop. A minor theme is the engagement of Major Grantly to Mr Crawley's daughter, Grace, in defiance of the wishes of his father the Archdeacon. It is often considered to be the best of Trollope's novels.

Laurence, Margaret (1926–87)
Canadian novelist and short-story writer. She was educated at United College (now the University of

Winnipeg) and worked as a reporter before marrying and moving to England and then to Africa. She wrote a series of novels and short stories centred on Manawaka, Manitoba, a fictional small-town on the Canadian prairies: *The Stone Angel* (1964); *A Jest of God* (1966); *The Fire Dwellers* (1969); *A Bird In The House* (stories; 1970); *The Diviners* (1974). These works were written in England, where Laurence lived with her children for 12 years, after separating from her husband in 1962. They explore the social history of Canada, through the lives of several generations of women, dealing with themes such as the claustrophobia of small town life, the force of social inhibitions, the quest for identity and the importance of a sense of the past. *A Jest of God* was filmed in 1968 as *Rachel, Rachel*. Laurence's earlier work reflects the seven years which she spent in Somalia and Ghana between 1950 and 1957. *A Tree For Poverty* (1954) is a translation of Somali oral poetry and prose; *This Side Jordan* (1960) is a novel about racial tension in the Gold Coast (now Ghana); *The Tomorrow Tamer* (1963) is a collection of stories; *The Prophet's Camel Bell* (1963) is a travel narrative. She published several children's books and two collections of essays: *Long Drums and Cannons: Nigerian Dramatists and Novelists 1952–66 (1968)* and *Heart of a Stranger* (1976). The autobiographical *Dance on the Earth* was published in 1989.

▷ Post-colonial literature.

Bib: Thomas, C., *Laurence*; Gunnars, K. (ed.), *Crossing the River: Essays in Honour of Margaret Laurence*; Morley, P., *Margaret Laurence: The Long Journey Home*; Thomas, C., *The Manawaka World of Margaret Laurence*; Woodcock, G. (ed.), *A Place to Stand On: Essays By and About Margaret Laurence*; New, W.H. (ed.), *Margaret Laurence: The Writer and Her Critics*.

Lautréamont, Comte de (pseudonym of Isidore-Lucien Ducasse) (1846–70)

French writer of lyrical prose pieces which appeared under the title *Les Chants de Maldoror* in 1868, with a slightly expanded posthumous version in 1890. The hero, Maldoror, is a demonic figure and his world is one of delirium and nightmare interspersed with blasphemy and eroticism. The hallucinatory quality of this work attracted the interest of the Surrealists (▷ Surrealism), who claimed Lautréamont as one of their own and promoted his work. Their interest has been carried forward into contemporary French criticism.

Lawrence, D.H. (David Herbert) (1885–1930)

Novelist, poet, critic. The son of a coal-miner, he passed through University College, Nottingham, and for a time worked as a teacher. He eloped to Italy with Frieda Weekley, the German wife of a Nottingham professor, in 1912, and married her in 1914. His hatred of World War I, together with the German origins of his wife, caused them unhappiness in 1914–18; after the war they travelled about the world, visiting especially Australia and New Mexico. Lawrence died of tuberculosis at Vence in France in 1930. His reputation has grown

gradually, and he is likely always to remain a controversial figure.

Lawrence's life, art, criticism, poetry, and teaching were all so closely related that it is unusually difficult to distinguish one aspect of his achievement from all the others. Misunderstandings about his supposed obsession with sexuality and the needless legal action for obscenity in connection with two of his novels (▷ *The Rainbow* and ▷ *Lady Chatterley's Lover*) initially distorted judgement of his work, but he is now firmly established as a major ▷ modernist novelist. On the other hand, he has been the subject of irrelevant hero-worship which is equally distorting, and which he would have repudiated. He was a deeply religious – though not a Christian – writer who believed that modern man is perverting his nature by the wilful divorce of his consciousness from his spontaneous feelings. He has been accused of social prejudice. It is true that he was keenly critical of society; but he was the first major English novelist to have truly working-class origins, and this, together with his wide range of friendships with men and women of all classes, gave him unusual perceptiveness into the contradictions of English society. His attitude to women has been severely critized (see K. Millett, *Sexual Politics*; 1970 and Anna Wickham, 'The Spirit of the Lawrence Women', in R.D. Smith (ed.) *The Writings of Anna Wickham*), as have the general political implications of his ideas (see J. Carey 'D.H. Lawrence's Doctrine' in S. Spender (ed.), *D.H. Lawrence: Novelist, Poet, Prophet*; 1973).

Novels: *The White Peacock* (1911); *The Trespasser* (1912); ▷ *Sons and Lovers* (1913), an autobiographical novel, was his first distinguished work, and it was followed by what are generally regarded as his two masterpieces, *The Rainbow* (1915) and ▷ *Women in Love* (1921); *The Lost Girl* (1920); *Aaron's Rod* (1922); *Kangaroo* (1923) about Australia; *The Plumed Serpent* (1926) about New Mexico; *Lady Chatterley's Lover* (1928), banned except for an expurgated edition until 1959. The unfinished *Mr Noon* was published in 1984. He also wrote several volumes of short stories and novellas which include much of his best fiction. Among the best known of these are *St Mawr*, *The Daughters of the Vicar*, *The Horse Dealer's Daughter*, *The Captain's Doll*, *The Prussian Officer*, *The Virgin and the Gipsy*.

One of Lawrence's most distinguishing features as an artist in fiction is his use of natural surroundings and animals realistically and yet symbolically, to express states of experience which elude direct description. This 'poetic' element in his fiction is reflected in much of his verse; some of this is in rhymed, metrical stanzas, but a great deal of it is free of verse conventions and close to the more condensed passages of his prose. Lawrence began writing poetry at the time when Imagism was seeking more concrete expression, and he contributed to Imagist anthologies.

Lawrence's descriptive, didactic, and critical prose is also important. His psychological essays, *Psychoanalysis and the Unconscious* (1921) and *Fantasia of the Unconscious* (1922) are imaginative, not scientific works, and contribute to the understanding of his creative mind. His descriptive volumes, *Sea and Sardinia* (1921), *Mornings in Mexico* (1927) show his outstanding powers of presenting scenes with sensuous immediacy, and his characteristic concentration of all his interest – moral and social, as well as aesthetic – on to natural environment. The same concentration is to be seen in his critical and didactic writing; he brought moral, aesthetic, and social judgements into play together. Much of his best critical writing is contained in the posthumous volumes *Phoenix* I and II; the *Study of Thomas Hardy* is of particular importance for the understanding of Lawrence's own work. His letters were published in 7 volumes (vols 1–3, 1979–91).

Lawrence wrote eight plays including: *The Widowing of Mrs Holroyd* (1920); *Touch and Go* (1920); *David* (1927); *A Collier's Friday Night* (1965); *The Daughter in Law* (1967); *The Fight for Barbara* (1967). These have never received the attention accorded the rest of his work. He was an excellent letter-writer: *Letters* (ed. Aldous Huxley).
Bib: Leavis, F.R., *D.H. Lawrence, Novelist*; E.T., *D.H. Lawrence, a Personal Record*; Lawrence, F., *Not I, but the Wind*; Moore, H.T., *The Intelligent Heart*; Nehls, E., (ed.) *Lawrence: a Composite Biography*; Spilka, M., *The Love Ethic of D.H. Lawrence*; Draper, R.P., *Lawrence: The Critical Heritage*; Hough, G.G., *The Dark Sun*; Kermode, F., *Lawrence*; Burgess, A., *Flame Into Being*; Sagar, K., *The Life of D.H. Lawrence* and *D.H. Lawrence: Life Into Art*; Feinstein, E., *Lawrence's Women*; Bell, M., *D.H. Lawrence: Language and Being*.

Lawrence, G. A. (George Alfred) (1827–76)
Novelist. Lawrence's first novel was the enormously successful *Guy Livingstone* (1857), whose fighting, hunting, womanizing hero was the most extreme example of the glorification of masculinity common to a group of writers in the 1840s and 1850s sometimes known as the 'muscular' school (other novelists included ▷ Charles Kingsley and ▷ Thomas Hughes). Lawrence had attended ▷ Thomas Arnold's ▷ Rugby, and his portrayal of the school in *Guy Livingstone* is even more violent than that in Hughes's *Tom Brown's Schooldays*, published the same year. His subsequent novels were largely written in a similar vein, and include *Maurice Derring* (1864) and the nationalistic *Brakespeare* (1868), set in the Hundred Years' War.

Lawrence T. E. (Thomas Edward) (1888–1935)
Soldier and author, T. E. Lawrence is more popularly known as 'Lawrence of Arabia'. This title was inspired by his guerilla leadership activities in Arabia during World War I, of which he subsequently gave an epic and heroic account in the classic *Seven Pillars of Wisdom* (1926) – a shortened version of this book was later published as *Revolt in the Desert* (1927).

In many ways Lawrence epitomizes the image of the 'boy's own hero'; organizing in 1916 the Arab revolt against the Turks and developing imaginative and risky guerilla tactics, he was offered, but refused, both the Victoria Cross and a knighthood. After the war he went on to enlist in the ranks of the R.A.F. under two pseudonyms. His

diaries for this period were published in 1955 as *The Mint*.

Lawrence was also something of an archaeologist and translator; in 1932 he published a translation of ▷ Homer's ▷ *Odyssey*. In 1962 the film director David Lean turned Lawrence's life and work with the Arab freedom movement into the cinema classic *Lawrence of Arabia*.

Le Carré, John (David John Moore Cornwell) (b 1931)
Le Carré is one of the most intriguing of Cold War novelists, managing to write challenging and sophisticated work for a popular audience. Le Carré's work is grim, bitter and unromantic, and his characters are brilliantly bleak psychological cases of individuals (often secret service workers) in morally compromised situations. His reputation was established with this third novel, *The Spy Who Came In From The Cold* in 1963, in which Le Carré's most famous character, George Smiley appears. Although most of his works – including *Call for the Dead* (1961); *The Looking-Glass War* (1965); *A Small Town in Germany* (1968); *Tinker, Tailor, Soldier, Spy* (1974); *The Honorable Schoolboy* (1977); *Smiley's People* (1980) and *The Perfect Spy* (1986) – are concerned with espionage, in *The Naive and Sentimental Lover* (1971) and *The Little Drummer Girl* (1983), he turned to the Middle East and explored the Palestinian situation. Le Carré's work is eminently filmable, and many of his works have been translated into feature films or television dramas. In 1990 a film was made of Le Carré's 'glasnost' novel *The Russia House* (1988); scripted by Tom Stoppard, it was the first Hollywood film to be made on location in the (former) Soviet Union.
Bib: Barley, Tony: *Taking Sides: The Fiction of John Le Carré*.

Le Fanu, J. (Joseph) S. (Sheridan) (1814–73)
Novelist and journalist. Born in Dublin of an old Huguenot family related by marriage to the Dramatist Sheridan's family, he wrote poetry as a child, including a long Irish poem at the age of 14. After education by his father and tutors, he went to Trinity in 1833, writing for the *Dublin University Magazine* and in 1837 joining the staff. He later became editor and proprietor. In 1837 he published some Irish ballads and in 1839 was called to the bar, although he did not practise, soon turning to journalism. He bought *The Warden*, *Evening Packet* and part of the *Dublin Evening Mail*, later amalgamating the three into the *Evening Mail*. In 1844 he married Susan Bennett and withdrew from society after her death in 1858, when he wrote most of his novels, many in bed, on scraps of paper. His writing is ingeniously plotted, shows an attraction to the supernatural and has been increasingly well received this century. The novels include *The House by the Churchyard* (1863), *Wylder's Hand* (1864), *Uncle Silas* (1864), *Guy Deverell* (1865), *The Tenants of Malory* (1867), *A Lost Name* (1868), *The Wyvern Mystery* (1869), *Checkmate* (1871), *The Rose and the Key* (1871) and *Willing to Die* (1873), which was finished a few days before his death. The collection

of stories, *In a Glass Darkly*, appeared in 1872 and included *Carmilla*, a vampire novel with lesbian overtones which influenced ▷ Bram Stoker's *Dracula*. A collection of neglected stories, *Madam Crowl's Ghost and Other Tales of Mystery* was published in 1923.

Leavis, Frank Raymond (1895–1978)

Critic. From 1932 till 1953 he edited ▷ *Scrutiny*, a literary review with high critical standards, and pervaded by his personality. It maintained that the values of a society in all its activities derive from its culture, and that central to British culture is English literature; that a literature can be sustained only by discriminating readers, and therefore by a body of highly trained critics working together, especially in the collaborative circumstances of a university (*Education and the University*; 1943). The need for the testing of judgements by collaborative discussion is important in Leavis's view of criticism. However, collaboration may become uncritical discipleship, and this was one of the two unfortunate consequences of the exceptional force of Leavis's personality. The other unfortunate consequence was the hostility which this force of personality aroused in many critics who were not among his collaborators and followers. He maintained that true critical discernment can be achieved only by a total response of the mind – intellectual, imaginative and moral; thus a critical judgement reflects not only the work of literature being judged, but the worth of the personality that makes the judgement, so that Leavis's censure of critics with whom he strongly disagreed was sometimes extraordinarily vehement, as in his *Two Cultures?: The Significance of C. P. Snow* (1962). However this vehemence was a price he paid for his determination to sustain a living tradition of literature not only by assessing contemporary writers with the utmost rigour, but also by reassessing the writers of the past, distinguishing those he thought had a vital relevance for the modern sensibility from those that stand as mere monuments in academic museums. Such evaluative treatments caused him to be widely regarded as a destructive critic; his attack on the three-centuries-long prestige of Milton (*Revaluation*, 1936 and *The Common Pursuit*, 1952) gave particular offence.

Leavi's intense concern with the relationship between the kind of sensibility nourished by a literary culture and the quality of a society as a whole has a historical background that extends to the beginning of the 19th century. It first appears in Wordsworth's *Preface to the Lyrical Ballads* (1800), is to be felt in the writings of the 19th-century philosopher ▷ John Stuart Mill (see *Mill on Bentham and Coleridge*, ed. by Leavis, 1950), and is explicit in ▷ Matthew Arnold's writings, especially *Culture and Anarchy* (1869). Later the theme is taken up by the novelists, *eg* in ▷ Gissing's ▷ *New Grub Street* and, both in his novels and in his criticism, by ▷ D.H. Lawrence. The outstanding importance of novels in connection with the theme has caused Leavis to be foremost a critic of the novel; perhaps his most important single book is *The Great Tradition: George Eliot, Henry James, Joseph Conrad* (1948), but this

should be read in conjunction with his books on Lawrence and (with Q.D. Leavis) on *Dickens the Novelist* (1971). The critical writings of T.S. Eliot were a significant influence on Leavis's work; as critics, they share a tendency to make absolute value judgments supported by authority of tone rather than evidence. Although still influential, Leavis must now be considered together with more contemporary literary theory, such as ▷ post-structuralism, which has tended to challenge radically and contradict vehemently his criticism.

Leavis, Q.D. (1906–81)

Literary critic, Q.D. Leavis was educated at Cambridge in the 1920s (she was a student of I.A. Richards), and became a central figure in what came to be known as 'Cambridge criticism', the 'traditional' form of moral criticism (as distinct from Richards's ▷ New Criticism), which is more readily associated with her husband, ▷ F.R. Leavis. As one of the founders of the journal ▷ *Scrutiny* and writer of the influential *Fiction and the Reading Public* (1932), Q.D. Leavis helped to establish English literature as a discipline in its own right and in the form it took from the 1930s onwards, *Fiction and the Reading Public* is primarily a sociological and psychological account of popular reading patterns, which consolidates her more fundamental celebration of great literary classics as the primary source of our culture's essential humane values. Leavis's work is thus often read as the direct descendant of the cultural criticism of Victorian critic ▷ Matthew Arnold, but it is also important for a psychological dimension, and, in her essays, for a serious interest in the work of women writers, which is not generally seen as characteristic of her *Scrutiny* contemporaries. In tandem with bringing up a family, she also wrote *Dickens the Novelist* (1970) with her husband, and a wide range of essays, which are collected in three volumes as *Collected Essays* (1983).

Lee, Harriet (1757–1851)

Novelist and playwright. The sister of ▷ Sophia Lee, with whom she wrote *Canterbury Tales* (twelve tales, two by Sophia, published 1797–1805). The tales cover conventional material: for example, one is a ▷ Gothic romance and another offers a sensational account of the ▷ French Revolution. One story, however, *Kruitzer, The German's Tale* (1801), depicts the suffering of a woman unable either to escape her weak husband, or to reform her evil, but Romantic son, and was acknowledged by Byron as the source of his *Werner* (1821). Lee's dramatic output achieved much less recognition. *The New Peerage, or Our Eyes may Deceive Us* (1787) and *The Mysterious Marriage, or the Heirship of Roselva* (1795–8) are unremarkable in their plots, and the characters are somewhat ▷ flat and stereotyped. She was proposed to by ▷ Godwin, but turned him down.

Bib: Punter, D., *The Literature of Terror: A History of Gothic Fictions from 1765 to the Present Day*; Rodgers, K., *Feminism in Eighteenth-century England*.

Lee, Sophia (1750–1824)

Novelist and dramatist. Sister of ▷ Harriet Lee, whom she collaborated with in the series of *Canterbury Tales* (1797–1805), contributing the stories for 1798 and 1799, both of which were unremarkable. Sophia, however, had more success than her sister in the literary world; her play *The Chapter of Accidents* (1780) was staged regularly, and her novel, *The Recess, or A Table of Other Times* (1783–5) ran to five editions over the following nine years. The novel deals with two women who are the unacknowledged daughters of Mary Queen of Scots, and attempts to show how history ignores the roles that women have played in important political events (▷ Histories and Chronicles). Lee earned a considerable amount of money from *The Chapter* and set up a school at Bath with her sister on the proceeds.

Bib: Punter, D., *The Literature of Terror: A History of Gothic Fictions from 1765 to the Present Day*; Rodgers, K., *Feminism in Eighteenth-century England*.

Lehmann, Rosamond (1901–90)

Novelist and short-story writer. The poet and critic John Lehmann was her brother. Her novels depict the experience of educated and sensitive women, focusing in particular on infatuation, betrayal and the contrast between the relative safety of childhood and the disillusionment of adolescence and adulthood. They make considerable use of memories and impressions, rendered in a lyrical prose style. She was initially associated with ▷ Virginia Woolf and ▷ Elizabeth Bowen for her rendering of the consciousness of women, but her work is generally regarded as narrower in scope. Her novels are: *Dusty Answer* (1927); *A Note in Music* (1930); *Invitation to the Waltz* (1932); *The Weather in the Streets* (1936); *The Ballad and the Source* (1944); *The Echoing Grove* (1953); *A Sea-Grape Tree* (1976). Story collection: *The Gipsy's Baby* (1946). She also published an autobiography, *The Swan in the Evening* (1967).

Lennox, Charlotte (?1727–1804)

Charlotte Lennox was probably born in America, and grew up in New York. From an early age she is known to have been in London trying, unsuccessfully, to make a career on the stage. In 1747 she published *Poems on Several Occasions*, and in 1750, the year in which her appearance on the stage is last reported, she brought out her first novel, *The Life of Harriot Stuart*.

Lennox's literary talent was enthusiastically supported by ▷ Samuel Johnson and ▷ Henry Fielding. In 1752 *The Female Quixote* established her name as a writer; the novel tells of a naive heroine, Arabella, whose view of the world is foolishly filtered through the romances she reads. Lennox uses this framework to satirize sexual stereotypes and the social conventions of courtship.

Johnson's help in finding publishers for Lennox was probably partly motivated by his knowledge of her circumstances as well as her literary achievements. Her husband, Alexander, was a constant drain on the family's finances, and Lennox's writing provided their only support.

She worked on translations and adaptations to supplement their income, and produced three volumes of Shakespeare's sources, with Johnson's encouragement. Her final novel *Euphemia* (1790) explores the position of women in marriage, reflecting her own experience with the spendthrift husband she eventually left.

Lesage, Alain-René (1668–1747)

French novelist and playwright. He wrote two important ▷ picaresque narratives, both set in Spain and offering a cynical but humorous view of human desires and motives: *Gil Blas* (1715–35), which influenced such novelists as ▷ Fielding and ▷ Smollett, and *The Devil Upon Two Sticks* (1707), in which the devil removes the roofs from the houses of Madrid to reveal the greed of the inhabitants. Lesage was a professional writer who produced a large number of comic plays.

Lesbian and Gay Writing

Many major literary figures throughout history have depicted same-sex relations and/or expressed sexual desire for members of the same sex: for example, ▷ Plato, Shakespeare, Thomas Mann, ▷ Marcel Proust, ▷ Oscar Wilde, ▷ E.M. Forster, ▷ Virginia Woolf, ▷ Patrick White (to name only a few). The definitions accorded to such practices and feelings, and the extent to which they have been subject to oppression, have varied. In Ancient Greece male homosexuality was accepted within a particular framework: the teaching relationship between experienced men and boys. In pre-19th-century Britain same-sex relations were defined (and oppressed) largely in terms of practices rather than identity. The term 'homosexual' emerged in the 19th century, and the term 'heterosexual' followed it; the tragic case of Oscar Wilde focused a great deal of public attention (and prejudice) on male homosexuality. During most of the period during which the novel has flourished there has been widespread persecution and oppression of homosexual people and homophobia in many of the discourses of culture. Hence homosexuality has tended to be accorded a marginal place in literary representation, and when it has been shown, has usually been hedged about with implications of the exotic, the abnormal or at least the exceptional. When ▷ Radclyffe Hall published her plea for the recognition and acceptance of lesbianism, *The Well of Loneliness*, (1928) – even though it had a sympathetic preface from the sexologist ▷ Havelock Ellis, testifying to its scientific accuracy – the book was condemned as obscene and banned. This is in line with official attempts to promote heterosexual activity within marriage as the healthy norm. In the 1950s and 1960s aversion therapy was used in an effort to impose or restore this norm in homosexuals – The Kinsey Reports on *Sexual Behaviour in the Human Male* (1948) and *Female* (1953), however, showed that what had been defined as deviant behaviour was far more widespread than had been believed, thus challenging the 'naturalness' of heterosexuality. Homosexual behaviour in certain circumstances defined as private was decriminalized, but not until ten years after the Wolfenden report recommended it. E.M. Forster's *Maurice*, which ends with the protagonist choosing a life of freedom rather than repression, was not published until 1971, after Forster's death. However, novelistic discussions of homosexuality tended to promote toleration. There have been important fictional presentations from outside England, for example by Jean Genet (*Our Lady of the Flowers*), William Burroughs (*The Naked Lunch*) and James Baldwin (*Giovanni's Room*). Recent scholarship has identified gay and lesbian communities as important centres of innovation; see Shari Benstock, *Women of the Left Bank*, an account of women writers in Paris in the early years of this century, which identifies a close connection between the writers' political experience as lesbians and their readiness to experiment with representation. Since the 1960s the active assertion of gay and lesbian rights and identities in Europe and the USA have contributed to a rich and diverse field of fiction, including the work of such contemporary novelists as ▷ Sara Maitland, Michelene Wandor, ▷ Alan Hollinghurst, ▷ Maureen Duffy and ▷ Jeanette Winterson.

Bib: Dollimore, J., *Sexual Dissidence: Augustine to Wilde, Freud to Foucault*; Bristow, J., *Sexual Sameness: Textual Differences in Lesbian and Gay Writing*; Sedgwick, E., *Epistemology of the Closet*; Fuss, D., *Inside/Out: Lesbian Theories, Gay Theories*; Meyers, J., *Homosexuality and Literature 1890–1930*; Jay, K. and Glasgow. J (eds.), *Lesbian Texts and Contexts: Radical Revisions*.

Lessing, Doris (b 1919)

Novelist and short-story writer. Born in Persia (now Iran) and brought up in Southern Rhodesia (now Zimbabwe), she settled in London in 1949. Her writing spans an exceptionally wide range of genres, settings and narrative techniques, but is unified by certain persistent concerns: the analysis of contemporary culture and of social process; a sense of 20th-century history as catastrophic and an attempt to link this to personal unhappiness; a mystical and sometimes utopian emphasis on higher states of consciousness; an intense anger at social injustice; an interest in radical revisions of the self and of personal and sexual relations.

Her first novel, *The Grass is Singing* (1950) is the story of a relationship between a white woman and a black man in Rhodesia, and was followed by the *Children of Violence* series, a *Bildungsroman* about a young Rhodesian girl in revolt against the establishment, ending in England with a vision of future chaos and a tentative hope for a utopian future. The series consists of: *Martha Quest* (1952); *A Proper Marriage* (1954); *A Ripple from the Storm* (1958); *Landlocked* (1965); *The Four Gated City* (1969). ▷ *The Golden Notebook* (1962) exemplifies the element of ▷ post-modernist experiment in Lessing's work, in its use of multiple narratives and its concern with fiction and the reconstruction of the self, but it also addresses social issues of the 1960s: the crisis in radical politics, women's liberation, the value of psychoanalysis. During the 1970s Lessing started to write ▷ science fiction, and has remained

a fierce exponent of its value as a literary form. Her series *Canopus in Argus: Archives* comprises: *Shikasta* (1979); *The Marriages Between Zones Three, Four and Five* (1980); *The Sirian Experiments* (1981) *The Making of the Representative for Planet 8* (1982); *Sentimental Agents* (1983). These novels attempt to set human history and human relationships in the context of a battle between good and evil in the universe and an evolutionary quest for a higher state of being. Lessing has continued to show her inventiveness and flexibility with *The Diary of Jane Somers* (1984), a critique of society's treatment of the old, *The Good Terrorist* (1985), a study of the making of a terrorist, and *The Fifth Child* (1988), which uses elements of the horror story genre to explore problems in liberal ideals. Her other novels are: *Briefing for a Descent into Hell* (1971); *The Summer Before Dark* (1972); *Memoirs of a Survivor* (1974). Story collections include: *This Was the Old Chief's Country* (1951); *Five: Short Novels* (1953); *The Habit of Loving* (1957); *A Man and Two Women* (1963); *African Stories* (1964); *Winter in July* (1966); *The Black Madonna* (1966); *The Story of a non-Marrying Man* (1972).

Her other works include: *Going Home* (1957), a study of Southern Rhodesia; *In Pursuit of the English* (1960), a study of England in (1960), *A small Personal Voice: Essays, Reviews, Interviews* (1974); *African Laughter: Four Visits to Zimbabwe* (1992); *London Observed: Stories and Sketches* (1992). *The Making of the Representative for Planet 8* has been turned into an opera, with music by Philip Glass (1988).

Bib: Sage, L., *Doris Lessing*; Sprague, C., and Tiger, V. (eds.), *Critical Essays on Doris Lessing*; King, J., *Doris Lessing*; Sprague, C., *Rereading Doris Lessing*; Taylor, J. (ed.), *Notebooks, Memoirs, Archives*.

Lesson of the Master, The (1892)

A story by ▷ Henry James. Its theme is the barrier set up against the true artist by supposedly cultivated society, which can understand nothing about the artist's dedication and can therefore only hinder him by its unintelligent praise based on false standards.

Letter-writing

This is clearly an important branch of literature even when the interest of the letters is essentially historical (*eg* the 15th-century Paston Letters) or biographical. Letters may also be, by intention or by consequence of genius, works of intrinsic literary value. The 18th century (the age of the epistolary novel) was more than any other the period when letter-writing was cultivated as an art: see, above all, the letters of ▷ Horace Walpole and those to his son by Lord Chesterfield – the former a record of events and the latter consisting of moral reflections. Earlier than the 18th century, postal services were not sufficiently organized to encourage regular letter-writing, and the art of familiar prose was inadequately cultivated; by the mid-19th century, communications had improved enough to make frequent and full letter-writing redundant. By then letters had intrinsic, literary interest chiefly by virtue of the writers' talent for literary expression in other modes of writing, added to the accident that they found letters a congenial means of communication. The letters of the poet

Gerard Manley Hopkins and the novelist ▷ D. H. Lawrence are examples. In the first 30 years of the 19th century the Romantic habit of introspection resulted in a quantity of extremely interesting letters: those of Keats, Byron, ▷ Coleridge and ▷ Lamb are outstanding.

Despite the telephone, many 20th-century writers have had large collections of their letters published ▷ Virginia Woolf produced a copious correspondence and Sylvia Plath's *Letters Home* (to her mother) is a famous later anthology.

▷ Biography.

Lever, Charles James (1806–72)
Irish novelist. Famous in the 19th century for his vigorous comic novels about Irish country life and life in the army, *eg Harry Lorrequer* (1837), *Charles O'Malley* (1841), *Tom Burke of Ours* (1843). He was criticized for perpetuating the Englishman's comic notion of the Irish character – the 'stage Irishman' caricature, but ▷ William Makepeace Thackeray, who was a friend of Lever and parodied him in *Novels by Eminent Hands*, declared (in *A Box of Novels*) that Lever was true to Irish nature in being superficially humorous but sad at heart.
Bib: Stevenson, L., *Dr Quicksilver: The Life of Charles Lever.*

Leviathan (1651)
▷ Hobbes, Thomas.

Lewes, George Henry (1817–78)
Philosopher and critic. He wrote on a wide variety of subjects but his most remembered work is his *Life of Goethe* (1855), researched with ▷ George Eliot's help. Other works include *The Biographical History of Philosophy* (1845–6), studies in biology such as *Studies in Animal Life* (1862), two novels, *Ranthrope* (1847–6) and *Rose, Blanche and Violet* (1848), critical essays on the novel and the theatre, and, his most important philosophical book, *Problems of Life and Mind* (1873–8), the last volume of which was completed by George Eliot after his death. He collaborated with Thornton Leigh Hunt in founding the *Leader* and was first editor of the *Fortnightly Review* 1865–6. In 1854 he left his wife, who had had three sons by Hunt, and lived with Mary Ann Evans (George Eliot) until his death.
Bib: Kitchell, A. T., *George Lewes and George Eliot*; Ashton, R., *G.H. Lewes.*

Lewis, Alethea (1750–1827)
Novelist. A ▷ didactic writer whose works are thoughtful but often heavily moralistic and naïve in style. Her novels include: *Plain Sense* (1795) for ▷ Minerva, and the ▷ Gothic *The Nuns of the Desert, or The Woodland Witches* (1805). She also wrote a philosophical treatise under the pen-name 'Eugenia De Acton', *Essays on the Art of Being Happy* (1803).

Lewis, C.S. (Clive Staples) (1808–1963)
Novelist, critic, poet and writer on religion. Born in Belfast, Lewis served in France during World War I. From 1925 until 1954 he was a Fellow of

Magdalen College, Oxford and tutor in English, and from 1954 was Professor of Medieval and Renaissance Literature at Cambridge. His fiction reflects an interest in fantasy, myth and fairytale with an underlying Christian message. He wrote a ▷ science-fiction trilogy: *Out of the Silent Planet* (1938); *Perelandra* (1943) (as *Voyage to Venus*, 1953); *That Hideous Strength* (1945). *The Lion, The Witch, and The Wardrobe* (1950) was the first of seven fantasy stories for children. His popular theological works include: *The Problem of Pain* (1940); *Miracles* (1947) and *The Screwtape Letters* (1942), which takes the form of letters from an experienced devil to a novice devil. *A Grief Observed* (1961) is a powerful autobiographical work, an account of his grief at the death of his wife. He also wrote such classics of literary history as *The Allegory of Love* (1936) and *A Preface to Paradise Lost* (1942).

▷ Children's books.

Lewis, Matthew Gregory (1775–1818)
Novelist, poet and playwright, often known as 'Monk Lewis' after his most famous work, *The Monk* (1796), an extravagant ▷ Gothic novel. Set in a monastery in Madrid, it is a sensational story of murder, incest, rape and damnation, which was attacked for indecency at the time of publication and became a *succès de scandale*. Lewis, whose family were wealthy members of the political establishment, was educated at Westminster School and Christ Church, Oxford and became a diplomat and later a Member of Parliament. He died of yellow fever caught on a visit to his estates in Jamaica.

Lewis, Percy Wyndham (1882–1957)
Painter, novelist, critic and polemical journalist. Born in the USA, he came to England as a child and studied art at the Slade School in London and then in Paris. Before 1914 he was leader of the Vorticist movement in painting, which, drawing on the French Cubist movement and the Italian Futurist movement, advocated dynamic, semi-abstract representation of angular, precise and rhythmical forms. Lewis carried over this predilection for vigour and energy into literature, taking a boldly independent attitude to modern culture, rather like that of the poet Ezra Pound with whom he edited the review *Blast* (1914–15), and asserted the right and the power of the intellect to take command in the cultural crisis. He was opposed to domination by political ideology (though he wrote favourably of Hitler in 1931), by psychological cults and by the bureaucratic and welfare state; he made it his principal aim to expose the confusion of mind which he considered to be overwhelming 20th-century man, and the hollowness of humanity which he believed to be the consequence of encroaching mechanization. He had something in common with his friend T. S. Eliot (see *The Waste Land*, for example) but never became a Christian; with ▷ D. H. Lawrence whose mysticism he nevertheless despised; with ▷ James Joyce, though he was strongly opposed to his subjective ▷ stream of consciousness technique; with ▷ F. R. Leavis and the other ▷ *Scrutiny* critics, who, however, rejected him as brutally negative. He prided himself on his

very distinctive style of expression, which is energetic and concentrates on presenting the externals of human nature with icy clarity.

His outstanding writings are probably his novels and stories: *Tarr* (1918); *The Wild Body* (stories; 1927); *The Apes of God* (1930 – a satire); *Snooty Baronet* (1932); *The Revenge for Love* (1937 – considered by some critics to be his best novel); *The Vulgar Streak* (1941); *Rotting Hill* (stories; 1951); *Self Condemned* (1954); and the four-part fable *The Human Age – The Childermass* (1928), *Monstre Gai* (1955), *Malign Fiesta* (1955) to have been completed by *The Trial of Man* which he did not live to finish.

His ideas are expounded in his philosophical work *Time and Western Man* (1927) and his autobiographies *Blasting and Bombardiering* (1937) and *Rude Assignment* (1950). He wrote notable literary criticism in *The Lion and the Fox: the Role of Hero in the Plays of Shakespeare* (1927), *Men Without Art* (1934) and *The Writer and the Absolute* (1952).
Bib: Grigson, G., *A Master of Our Time*; Kenner, H., *Wyndham Lewis*; Meyers, J., *The Enemy*; Materer, T., *Wyndham Lewis: the Novelist*; Meyers, J. (ed.), *Wyndham Lewis: a Revaluation*; Jameson, F., *Fables of Aggression: Wyndham Lewis, the Modernist as Fascist*; Symons, J. (ed.), *The Essential Wyndham Lewis: An Introduction to His Work*.

Liberty, On (1859)

A political essay by ▷ John Stuart Mill, in which he discusses how far and in what ways the state is entitled to interfere with the liberty of individuals. He concludes that in general this interference should be restricted to the protection of other individuals, and of individuals collectively considered as society. Mill was mainly alarmed lest a new tyranny should arise from democratic majorities who might be indifferent to minority rights.

Life and Death of Mr Badman, The (1680)
▷ *Badman, The Life and Death of Mr.*

Life of Jonathan Wild the Great, The (1743)
▷ *Jonathan Wild the Great, The Life of.*

Life of Samuel Johnson, The (1791)
▷ Boswell, James.

Lilliput

The island in Part I of ▷ Swift's ▷ *Gulliver's Travels*; the Lilliputians are diminutive in body, and their corresponding pettiness of mind is intended as satirical comment on the pettiness of contemporary English politics and society.

Linton, Eliza Lynn (1822–98)

Novelist and critic. Born in Keswick, Cumberland, she was a baby when her mother died. She did not agree with the ideas of her family and moved to London in 1845, entering the London literary scene with two historical novels, *Azeth the Egyptian* (1846) and *Anymone* (1848). She wrote for the ▷ *Morning Chronicle* 1848–51, publishing *Realities* in 1851, when she moved to Paris until 1854. She married a widower with children, William James

Linton, in 1858, adding his name to hers; but they were incompatible and separated in 1867. Her fiction changed from being romantic and imaginative, becoming well-constructed and vigorous, though without the early enthusiasm and sentimentalism. She had friends in the literary world including Walter Landor, and sold the house she inherited at Gad's Hill to ▷ Charles Dickens. From 1866 she wrote for the *Saturday Review* and offended many women with her attacks on ▷ feminism and the ▷ New Woman in an article called 'The Girl of the Period' (1868). Her other works include *Ourselves: essays on women* (1869), *Rebel of the Family* (1880), *The True History of Joshua Davidson, Christian and Communist* (1872) and *The Autobiography of Christopher Kirkland* (1885), which contains much of her own autobiography but portrayed through a masculine persona. Her own memoir, *My Literary Life*, appeared posthumously in 1899, showing her generosity, but also her acid tendency in an attack on ▷ George Eliot.
Bib: Layard, G.S. (ed.), *Mrs Eliza Lynn Linton. Her Life, Letters and Opinions.*

Litotes
▷ Figures of Speech.

Little Dorrit (1855–7)

A novel by ▷ Charles Dickens. It centres on the theme of imprisonment, both literal and symbolic. William Dorrit (with his children and his brother Frederick) has been so long in the Marshalsea Prison for debtors that he is known as 'the Father of the Marshalsea' – a title that gives him a spurious social prestige. Arthur Clennam, who befriends him in the belief that the Dorrit family has been victimized by the commercial interests of his own family, is eventually confined in the same prison. But outside, the characters inhabit prisons without visible walls: William Dorrit inherits a fortune, and he and his family are constricted by social ambition under the gaolership of Mrs General who instructs them in fashionable ways; Mrs Clennam, Arthur's supposed mother, inhabits a gloomy house, confined to her chair and her bad conscience, under the gaolership of her servant Flintwinch who knows her guilty secrets; Merdle, the financier of reputedly enormous wealth, is the prisoner of his false position, and his gaolers are his fashionable wife and his arrogant butler; the servant girl, Tattycoram, is at first the prisoner of the well-intentioned but misguided Mr and Mrs Meagles, and then escapes to the worse prison of Miss Wade, herself a prisoner of her self-inflicted loneliness. The nation is under the imprisoning control of a government department, the Circumlocution Office, which exists to gratify the interests of the enormous Barnacle family. Three characters stand out in independence of this conspiracy to confine and frustrate: Frederick Dorrit, who lives out an existence of passive misery by refusing to share (in or out of the Marshalsea) the self-deceptions of his brother William; Amy ('Little Dorrit') who consistently follows the compassion of her affections and the duties this imposes on her; and Daniel Doyce, the engineer whose enterprise is baffled by the Circumlocution Office but who perseveres in his vocation with humble and disinterested reverence for the demands that it makes on him. The self-interested Circumlocution Office at the top of society is balanced by the inhabitants of Bleeding Heart Yard, people who are themselves prisoners of the exorbitant property owner, Casby, but who live in the freedom of their own equal and open-hearted society. The blackmailer Rigaud is a figure of menacing evil and a dramatic counterpart to Mrs Clennam's hypocrisy and pretence, which is at the heart of the imaginative scheme of the novel. *Little Dorrit* is often regarded as Dickens's finest work, both in dramatic impressiveness and in richness of psychological insight.

Lively, Penelope (b 1933)

Novelist and short-story writer. Born in Egypt, Lively came to England in 1945 and was educated at St Anne's College Oxford. She has worked as a reviewer and BBC radio presenter. She writes elegant and perceptive novels about the moral dilemmas and intellectual development of middle-class characters, with a particular focus on the importance of the past and its reassessment for the understanding of the present. This concern is often presented through characters professionally preoccupied with the past, such as archaeologists, biographers and historians. Her novels are: *The Road to Lichfield* (1977); *Treasures of Time* (1979); *Judgement Day* (1980); *Next to Nature, Art* (1982); *Perfect Happiness* (1983); *According to Mark* (1984); *Moon Tiger* (1987); *Passing On* (1989); *City of the Mind* (1991); *Cleopatra's Sister* (1993). Volumes of short stories: *Nothing Missing But the Samovar* (1978); *Corruption* (1984); *Pack of Cards: Stories 1978–1986* (1989). She has also written television plays, books for children and *The Presence of the Past: An Introduction to Landscape History* (1976).

Lives of the Poets, The (1779–81)

By ▷ Samuel Johnson; originally entitled *Prefaces biographical and critical to the Works of the English Poets*. Johnson began work on the project at the request of a number of booksellers, who required essays on the poets which could be prefaced to editions of their works. The essays developed so successfully that it was decided to issue them in their own right. The essays are interesting both for their critical insight and because they embody both the literary tastes of the time. They are idiosyncratic and prejudiced, but always lively; Johnson's bias against the Metaphysical poets in particular has been challenged by changing literary tastes.

Locke, John (1632–1704)

Philosopher. He follows ▷ Thomas Hobbes in his sceptical ▷ rationalism, but he is the direct opposite of Hobbes in his optimistic view of human nature and in the moderation and flexibility of his social and political ideas. Hobbes was born in the year of the attempted invasion by the Armada (1588) and was painfully aware of the human propensity to violence from the decade of civil wars (1642–52); Locke's sympathies were identified with the moderation of

the bloodless Revolution of 1688 and the climate of reasonableness which followed it.

In his two *Treatises of Government* (1690), Locke, like Hobbes, presupposes a state of nature preceding a social contract which was the basis of political society. But whereas Hobbes saw the state of nature as a state of war, Locke saw it as a peaceful condition in which the Law of Nature and of Reason was spontaneously observed; his idea of the social contract was not, as for Hobbes, that human existence was intolerable without it, but that it merely provided additional assurance that life and property would be respected. For Hobbes sovereignty had to be single and absolute, but for Locke it was merely a public service always responsible to society, which may at any time remove it. Similarly, in his *Letters concerning Toleration* (1689, 1690, 1692 and a fourth published posthumously) Locke, unlike Hobbes, held that the state has no right to interfere in religious matters and that oppression of religion by governments caused religion to spark civil violence.

Locke's advocacy of religious toleration was consistent with his sceptical attitude to faith and knowledge. Man must first discover what he can know before he persecutes others for publishing false beliefs, and this inquiry he conducts in his ▷ *Essay concerning Human Understanding* (1690). This shows man's capacity for knowledge to be distinctly limited, but the existence of God turns out to be a necessary hypothesis discoverable by reason. Christianity therefore is inherently reasonable (*Reasonableness of Christianity*, 1695) and faith by revelation is indispensable only because the use of reason is unavailable to the majority of mankind; 'nothing that is contrary to . . . reason has a right to be urged or assented to as a matter of faith' (*Human Understanding*, Bk. IV).

In his *Thoughts on Education* Locke extols reason at the expense of imagination and therefore (by implication) of the imaginative arts. When he applies his philosophy to politics or education, Locke is always guided by standards of practical utility, and in his abstract speculation he refrains from carrying his reasoning so far (as ▷ David Hume was to seem to do) that the logical basis for the conduct of practical life by the light of reason was undermined. His philosophy dominated the 18th century and is at the back of such 19th-century rationalist movements as ▷ Utilitarianism.
Bib: Cranston, M., *Life*; MacLean, K., *John Locke and English Literature in the Eighteenth Century*; Willey, B., *The Seventeenth Century Background*; *English Moralists*; James, D. G., *The Life of Reason: Hobbes, Locke, Bolingbroke*.

Lodge, David (b 1935)

Novelist and critic, born in London and educated at London University. Since 1976 he has been Professor of Modern English Literature at the University of Birmingham. His novels are: *The Picturegoers* (1960); *Ginger, You're Barmy* (1962); *The British Museum is Falling Down* (1965); *Out of the Shelter* (1970); *Changing Places* (1975); *How Far Can You Go?* (1980); *Small World* (1984); *Nice Work* (1988); *Paradise News* (1991). His earlier novels are

views of English society in a light, realistic mode, but *The British Museum is Falling Down* introduces extensive use of parody and a farcical element. He is best known for *Changing Places* and *Small World*, inventive, humorous tales of academic life, full of jokes, puns, allusions, parodies and reflexive comments on the nature of narrative which reflect his interest in critical theory. They have affinities with the campus novels of ▷ Malcolm Bradbury. *Out of the Shelter* is a ▷ *Bildungsroman*, and *How Far Can You Go?* explores the personal struggles of a group of Catholics from the 1950s to the 1970s, concentrating in particular on the issue of contraception. Criticism includes: *Language of Fiction* (1966); *The Novelist at the Crossroads* (1971); *The Modes of Modern Writing* (1977); *Working With Structuralism* (1981).
Bib: Morace, R. A., *The Dialogic Novels of Malcolm Bradbury and David Lodge.*

Lodge, Thomas (1558–1625)

Poet and man of letters. He was one of the group now known as the ▷ University Wits; university scholars who used their learning to make a career as professional writers for the expanding reading public of the late 16th century. In many ways his career is representative of this new kind of Elizabethan professional writer.

He was the son of Sir Thomas Lodge, a Lord Mayor of London, and was educated at Merchant Taylors School and Trinity College, Oxford. He then became a student of law at Lincoln's Inn, London, in 1578. The law students of the Inns of Court in the reign of Elizabeth were a leading element of the literary public, and others besides Lodge found these law colleges a nursery for literary rather than legal talent. During the next 20 years he practised all the kinds of writing which were popular at the time. His first work (1580) was a ▷ pamphlet entitled *A Defence of Plays*, written in answer to Stephen Gosson's attack on theatrical literature, *Schoole of Abuse* (1580). Besides other pamphlets, he wrote prose romances interspersed with lyrics (*eg Rosalynde, Euphues Golden Legacy*, 1590, and *A Margarite of America*, 1596), verse romances (*eg Scilla's Metamorphosis*, 1589, reissued as *Glaucus and Scilla*, 1610), a sonnet sequence (*Phillis*, 1593), and a collection of epistles and satires in imitation of the Roman poet Horace, *A Fig for Momus* (1595). He also wrote plays, or at least collaborated with playwrights, *eg* a chronicle play *The Wounds of Civil War* (printed 1594) and, probably with ▷ Robert Greene, *A Looking Glass for London and England* (1594). Besides this writing activity, he joined two piratical expeditions against Spain, the first to the Canary Isles in 1588, and the second to Brazil in 1591. It was on the first that he wrote his most famous work, the romance *Rosalynde*, later used by Shakespeare as the story for *As You Like It*, and on the second that he wrote *A Marguerite of America*. After 1596, when he published the penitential and satirical pamphlets (*Wit's Misery* and *World's Madness*), he became converted to Roman Catholicism and took to the study of medicine, receiving the degree of M.D. from Oxford University in 1603. His literary works during the remainder of his life were serious and chiefly translations, (*eg* of

Josephus, 1602, and Seneca, 1614), and religious and medical treatises.
Bib: Sisson, C. J., *Lodge and Other Elizabethans.*

London Magazine, The

Three periodicals of this name have existed: the first ran 1732–85; the second, 1820–29; and the third, founded in 1954, still exists. The second is the most famous. It was founded as the political opponent of the right-wing ▷ *Blackwood's Magazine*, and its first editor, John Scott, was killed in a duel in consequence of the rivalry. It had unusual literary distinction, with ▷ Lamb, Hazlitt, Hood and ▷ De Quincey on its staff; it published the first version of De Quincey's ▷ *Confessions of an English Opium-Eater.*

Lord Jim (1900)

A novel by ▷ Joseph Conrad. It is narrated by Marlow, an officer in the Merchant Navy who also appears in Conrad's other works, ▷ *Heart of Darkness, Chance* and *Youth.* The first 35 chapters we are to suppose recounted to companions after dinner; the rest is in the form of a letter and written narrative subsequently posted to one of these friends. Jim is a young sailor, the son of an English country parson, who dreams of being a hero. He becomes chief mate of the *Patna*, a decrepit ship with second rate officers, carrying pilgrims from Singapore to Jeddah. When the ship seems about to sink he loses his nerve and, at the last moment, jumps into a small boat with the other officers. When they reach land they discover that the *Patna* has stayed afloat and been towed to safety. The other officers disappear, but Jim stays to face disgrace at the official inquiry. He meets Marlow, to whom he tells his story and subsequently, persecuted by his sense of lost honour, Jim takes up humble employment as a water clerk in various Eastern ports (it is thus that Marlow introduces him to us at the start of the novel). Through the intervention of Marlow, Jim is sent by Stein, a benevolent trader, to a remote trading post in the jungle called Patusan. There, in alliance with a local chief called Doramin, who is Stein's friend, Jim defeats in battle the forces of Sherif Ali, a half-caste Arab bandit leader, and becomes a venerated figure. However, when a party of European adventurers led by the scoundrelly Gentlemen Brown appears in Patusan, the memory of his past dishonour fatally weakens Jim's resolve. He asks Doramin to let them go free, pledging his own life for their good behaviour. They massacre a party of the villagers, including Doramin's son, and Jim allows himself to be shot by Doramin, leaving behind Jewel, the local woman with whom he has been living, as a sad and lonely figure.

Lowry, Malcolm (1909–57)

Novelist. He was educated in England, but spent most of his later life in Mexico, the United States, and British Columbia. His first novel, *Ultramarine*, was published in 1933. His reputation chiefly rests on his second and only other completed novel, *Under the Volcano* (1947). The central character, Geoffrey Firmin, is British Consul in a Mexican city situated under two volcanoes, just as in ancient times the Underworld, Tartarus, was supposed to be situated beneath the Sicilian volcano, Etna. Firmin is an alcoholic who has rejected the love of his wife and his friends and taken to drink as escape from the inhumanity of the modern world (the events take place in 1938) and his own sense of guilt and failure. The novel is highly allusive and symbolic, with metaphysical and mythical overtones, and the narrative is partly ▷ stream of consciousness. It shows the influence of ▷ Joseph Conrad and ▷ James Joyce and it has been described as the most distinguished work of fiction produced by an English novelist since 1945. A number of works were published posthumously, including: two novels entitled *Dark as the Grave Wherein My Friend is Laid* (1968) and *October Ferry to Gabriola* (1970), which were put together from Lowry's drafts by his widow; *Selected Poems* (1962) and a volume of short stories, *Hear Us, O Lord, from Heaven Thy Dwelling Place* (1961). This *Selected Letters* have been edited by Harvey Breit and Margerie Bonner Lowry (1965). Bib: Woodcock, G., *Lowry: the Man and His Work*; Day, D., *Lowry, a Biography*; Cross, R. K., *Malcolm Lowry: a Preface to His Fiction*; Binns, R., *Malcolm Lowry*.

Lucian (2nd century AD)
Greek satirist. He is especially known for his satirical dialogues and for his *True History*, an account of imaginary voyages which ▷ Jonathan Swift may have used as a model for his ▷ *Gulliver's Travels*.

Luggnagg
A country in Part III of ▷ Swift's ▷ *Gulliver's Travels*. It is inhabited by the Struldbrugs who have immortality, and find it a curse.

Lyell, Sir Charles (1797–1875)
Geologist. His principal work, *The Principles of Geology* (1830–33) revolutionized ideas about the age of the earth, and was a challenge to current theological thinking as ▷ Darwin's *Origin of Species* (1859) was to be. He also contributed the idea of change as continuous and ceaseless instead of sudden, intermittent and catastrophic, which had

been the prevailing view. This added to the sense of flux and instability which haunted such contemporary imaginative writers as ▷ Matthew Arnold and Tennyson, whose *In Memoriam* (1850) shows traces of Lyell's influence.

Lytton, Edward George Earle Lytton Bulwer- (1st Baron Lytton) (1803–73)
Novelist. He was the son of General Bulwer and added his mother's surname of Lytton on inheriting her estate in 1843. He was educated at Trinity and Trinity Hall, Cambridge, and was made a Baron in 1866. His novels were very famous in his lifetime, and their range is an indication of the literary variety and changes in the Victorian period. His political outlook was radical when he was young; he was then a friend of the philosopher ▷ William Godwin, whose influence is evident in his early novels, *Paul Clifford* (1830) and *Eugene Aram* (1832). On the other hand, he was a member of fashionable society and his first success (*Pelham*, 1828) is closer to ▷ Benjamin Disraeli's political novels of high society, for example ▷ *Coningsby*. Then in mid-career, under the influence of the strict Victorian moral code, he wrote domestic novels such as *The Caxtons – A Family Picture* (1848). He showed the influence of ▷ Sir Walter Scott on the Victorians in his historical novels such as *The Last Days of Pompeii* (1834), *Rienzi* (1835) and *The Last of the Barons* (1843), and the current ▷ German influence in the didacticism of his early novels and in fantasies such as *The Pilgrims of the Rhine* (1834). Bulwer-Lytton was a friend of ▷ Charles Dickens (see the biography of Dickens by Jack Lindsay) and satirized Lord Tennyson in his poem *The New Timon* (1846). He wrote some successful plays – *The Lady of Lyons* (1838), *Richelieu* (1838) and *Money* (1840). Like Disraeli, he combined his literary with a political career, for which he was rewarded with a peerage as Baron Knebworth (his mother's estate), but in his case literature had priority. His work is now little respected (he is considered as neither sincere nor original) but he is interestingly representative of his period.
Bib: Sadleir, M., *Bulwer: A Panorama*; Christensen, A. C., *Edward Bulwer-Lytton: The Fiction of New Regions*.

M

Mabinogion

A collection of medieval Welsh tales, some from
the 14th-century *Red Book of Hergest*. A *mabinog*
was a bard's apprentice. 11 tales were translated
by Lady Charlotte Guest (1838); four of these are
versions of still older Celtic myths and are called
the 'Four Branches of the Mabinogi'. These are the
true *Mabinogion*. The others are old British tales of
Roman times, British tales of King Arthur, and later
tales of medieval romance.

Macaulay, Thomas Babington (1800–59)

Historian, ▷ essayist, politician and poet. He was
actively on the ▷ Whig side politically; that is
to say, without being a radical reformer, he had
strong faith in the virtue of British parliamentary
institutions. He was, from the publication of his
essay on Milton in 1825, a constant contributor
to the main Whig periodical, the ▷ *Edinburgh
Review*, and his *History of England* (1848 and 1855)
is strongly marked by his political convictions. He
was trained as a lawyer and became an eloquent
orator; his writing has corresponding qualities of
persuasiveness and vividness. As a historian he was
best at impressionistic reconstruction of the past, and
the same gift served him in his biographical essays
on ▷ John Bunyan, ▷ Oliver Goldsmith, ▷ Samuel
Johnson, ▷ Fanny Burney and the younger William
Pitt. He represented the most optimistic strain of
feeling in mid-19th-century England – its faith in the
march of progress.

Macaulay's *Lays of Ancient Rome* (1842) were an
attempt to reconstruct legendary Roman history in
a way that might resemble the lost ballad poetry of
ancient Rome. Though not major poetry, they are
very vigorous verse with the kind of appeal that is to
be found in effective ballad poetry.

Macaulay was raised to the peerage in 1857.
▷ Histories; *Macaulay's History of England*.

Bib: Trevelyan, G.M., *Life and Letters*; Bryant, A.,
Macaulay; Firth, C., *A Commentary on Macaulay's
History of England*; Trevelyan, G. M. in *Clio: a
Muse*; Stephen, L., in *Hours in a Library*; Clive,
J., *Thomas Babington Macaulay: The Shaping of the
Historian*.

Macaulay's History of England from the Accession of James II

The history (Vols. 1 & 2, 1848; 3 & 4, 1855; 5, 1861)
is a thorough, detailed account of two reigns: James
II and William III. It is unfinished and was originally
intended to extend to the time of George I (1714–27)
and further. The period covered is perhaps the most
crucial for English political development. James II,
a Catholic, tried to enforce his will in the Catholic
interest against Parliament, which frustrated him
and expelled him from the throne in the Revolution
of 1688. Parliament then summoned William from
Holland to reign jointly with his wife, who was also
James's daughter, Mary II (1689–94). William was
the champion of the Protestant cause in Europe, and
Mary was also Protestant.

Macaulay's politics were strongly in the ▷ Whig
parliamentary tradition and his history is an epic of
the triumph of the ideas which to him gave meaning
to English history. Considered as history, the work
is accordingly one-sided, much more a work of
historical art than of historical science; it represents
what historians have come to call 'the Whig
interpretation of history'.

Macauley, Dame Rose (1881–1958)

Novelist, poet, travel writer and critic. Born in
England, she spent part of her childhood in Italy,
but returned to England for her education at Oxford
High School and Somerville College Oxford.
She had early experience of loss: her brother was
murdered and the poet Rupert Brooke, who was
her friend, died in 1915 on his way to the front in
the Dardanelles. During World War I she worked
as a civil servant and began a long-term relationship
with a married man (until his death in 1942), which
caused her exile from the Anglican Church. In
London from 1916 she attended a literary salon
where she met such writers as W.B. Yeats, ▷ Arnold
Bennett, ▷ Aldous Huxley and ▷ Walter de la
Mare. In the 1930s she became a close friend of
▷ Virginia Woolf. She wrote war fiction, including
the autobiographical *Non-Combatants and Others*
(1916) and *Told By an Idiot* (1923) and, later, *And No
Man's Wit* (1940), set in civil war Spain; a historical
novel, *They Were Defeated* (1932); satire, in *Potterism*
(1920). During the 1940s she published no fiction,
but returned to the novel with *The World My Witness*
(1950) and *The Towers of Trebizond* (1956), the first
about the after-effects of World War II, as seen in
the mind of a young woman living in London, and
the second a more humorous work about Islam and
Anglicanism.

Bib: Babington Smith, C. (ed.), *Letters to a Friend*
(1961–62); *Rose Macauley* (1972); Kime Scott, B.
(ed.), *The Gender of Modernism*.

Machiavelli, Nicolo di Bernardo dei (1409–1527)

Italian political theorist and historian. Machiavelli
can be thought of as having two discrete existences.
One is that of the Florentine diplomat, author of
a comedy *La Mandragola* (1518) and of a series of
important treaties on politics and statecraft: *The
Prince* (1513), *Art of War* (1520) and *The Discourses*
(1531). The other existence, however, is that which
haunted the imagination of English writers in the
16th century and later, when Machiavelli's reputation
as a cynical, cunning and diabolic figure emerges. In
fact, Machiavelli's own works were very little known
in England (other than by unreliable report) until a
translation of *The Prince* appeared in 1640, though
translations of his *Art of War* and portions of his
historical works had been translated and published
in 1560 and 1593, respectively. Nevertheless, it is
the image of Machiavelli which became influential in
England as is evidenced by Christopher Marlowe's
creation of the stage-figure Machevill in his play
The Jew of Malta. We can perhaps best understand
this image of the Italian thinker in England as the
embodiment, or focus, of a network of anxieties
experienced within the emergent ▷ Protestant state,
and directed outwards on the threatening presence of
continental (and Catholic) Europe.

Bib: Gilmore, M. P. (ed.), *Studies on Machiavelli*.

Mackenzie, Compton (1883–1972)

Novelist. Son of a British actor-manager and an American actress. A very prolific writer of great popularity; his best-known novels are probably *Sinister Street* (1913–14) and *The Four Winds of Love* – a sequence composed of *The East Wind* (1937), *The South Wind* (1937), *The West Wind* (1940), *West to North* (1940), *The North Wind* (1944–5). When he began writing, ▷ Henry James regarded him as one of the most promising of younger novelists, and ▷ Ford Madox Ford thought *Sinister Street* perhaps a work of genius. However, other critics have rarely given him much extensive attention.

Bib: Dooley, D. T., *Compton Mackenzie*; Linklater, A., *Compton Mackenzie: A Life*.

Mackenzie, Henry (1745–1831)

Scottish novelist and magazine editor. His novel *The Man of Feeling* (1771) epitomized the 18th-century cult of ▷ sensibility. His second novel, *The Man of the World* (1773), has a villainous hero in contrast to the sensitive, benevolent and unworldly hero of his first book. He also published *Julia de Roubigné* (1777), which shows the influence of ▷ Richardson, and a play, *The Prince of Tunis* (1773).

Macmillan's Magazine

It was founded in 1859 and published a variety of material, including pieces by Tennyson, ▷ Matthew Arnold, ▷ Henry James and ▷ Thomas Hardy. It folded in 1907.

Magazine

Originally meaning 'storehouse', the word has also denoted, since the 18th century, a periodical containing miscellaneous material, *eg* the *Gentleman's Magazine* (founded 1731): 'a Monthly Collection to store up, as in a Magazine, the most remarkable pieces on the subjects above-mentioned' (from the introduction to the first number). In the 18th and early 19th century magazines only differed from other serious periodicals (*eg* the ▷ *Edinburgh Review* and the ▷ *Quarterly*) in having greater variety of content and being open to imaginative writing. Distinguished magazines of this kind include ▷ *Blackwood's* and the second ▷ *London Magazine* (1820–29). Later in the 19th century, magazines became predominantly popular periodicals devoted principally to fiction. Since World War II magazines have often been seen as synonymous with reading matter specifically directed at women; examples are *Vogue*, *Cosmopolitan*, and the feminist magazines *Spare Rib* and *Everywoman*. During the 1980s the number of magazine titles increased very considerably. See *Wellesley Index to Periodicals*.

▷ Reviews and Periodicals.

Magic realism

A term applied in literature primarily to Latin American novelists such as ▷ Jorge Luis Borges (1899–1987), Gabriel García Márquez (b 1928) and Alejo Carpentier (b 1904), whose work combines a realistic manner with strong elements of the bizarre, supernatural and fantastic. This technique has influenced novelists such as ▷ John Fowles, ▷ Angela Carter and ▷ Salman Rushdie.

▷ Spanish influence on English fiction.

Maitland, Sara (b 1950)

Novelist, short-story writer. She was educated at St Anne's College Oxford, and is a member of the Feminist Writers Group, a group of women writers who share socialist and feminist convictions. Another member is ▷ Michèle Roberts, who shares with Maitland an interest in the relations of Christianity with feminism and women's sexuality, an interest reflected in Maitland's novel *Virgin Territory* (1984), about tension between lesbian love and Christianity. The group also includes Michelene Wandor (with whom Maitland co-wrote a post-modernist epistolary novel, *Arky Types*, 1987), ▷ Zoë Fairbairns and Valerie Miner. They collectively produced a volume of short stories, interspersed with direct political statements and entitled *Tales I Tell My Mother* (1978); the stories were written individually but discussed and revised collectively. The blending of realism and fantasy which has emerged as an important feminist strategy (for example in the work of ▷ Angela Carter) is apparent in Maitland's novel *Three Times Table* (1990), which explores the lives of three women in London but includes dragons as well as dialogue. Maitland's other works include her novel *Daughter of Jerusalem* (1978), *Very Heaven: Looking Back at the Sixties* (1988) and *The Rushdie File* (1989), edited with Lisa Appignanesi.

Malapropism

▷ Figures of Speech.

Malgonkar, Manohar (b 1913)

Indian novelist and short-story writer. Educated at Bombay University, he has been an officer in the Maratha Light Infantry, a big game hunter, a civil servant, a mine owner and a farmer, as well as standing for parliament. He is primarily a novelist of action and adventure, with a Conradian (▷ Joseph Conrad) stress on the stuggles of the individual; he uses Indian historical settings such as the Indian Munity, the last years of the Raj and the aftermath of Independence and Partition in 1947. His novels are: *Distant Drum* (1960); *Combat of Shadows* (1962); *The Princes* (1963); *A Bend in the Ganges* (1964); *The Devil's Wind: Nana Saheb's Story* (1972); *Shalimar* (1978); *The Garland Keepers* (1980); *Bandicoot Run* (1982). Volumes of short stories: *A Toast in Warm Wine* (1974); *In Uniform* (1975); *Bombay Beware* (1975); *Rumble-Tumble* (1972). He has also written biography, popular history and a screenplay.

Bib: Naipaul, V.S., *An Area of Darkness*; Dayananda, J.Y., *Manohar Malgonkar*.

Mallock, W. H. (1849–1923)

A Catholic controversialist now best known for his satirical novel *The New Republic*, portraying leading members of the Victorian intelligentsia, including ▷ John Ruskin, ▷ Matthew Arnold, ▷ Walter Pater and ▷ Thomas Huxley. He wrote a number of books on social questions against socialism. His *Memoirs of Life and Literature* was published in 1920.

Bib: Adams, A. B., *The Novels of W. H. Mallock*; Wolf, R. L., *Gains and Losses: Novels of Faith and Doubt in Victorian England*.

Malthus, Thomas Robert (1766–1834)
Economist; particularly famous for his *Essay on Population* (1798), which he reissued in an expanded and altered form in 1803. Its orginal title was: *An Essay on the Principle of Population as it affects the Future Improvement of Society, with Remarks on the Speculations of Mr Godwin, M. Condorcet, and other Writers.*

The essence of his view was that social progress tends to be limited by the fact that population increases more rapidly than means of subsistence, and always reaches the limits of subsistence, so that a substantial part of society is doomed to live beyond the margin of poverty. The 'natural checks' which prevent population increase from exceeding the means of subsistence are war, famine, and pestilence, to which he added human misery and vice. In the second edition he added a further possible check by 'moral restraint', *ie* late marriages and sexual continence. These arguments made a strong impression on public opinion; an important practical consequence of them was the replacement of the existing haphazard methods of poor relief by the harsh but reasoned and systematic ▷ Poor Law system of 1834.

Malthus's relentless and pitiless reasoning led to political economy becoming known as the 'gloomy science'. His conclusions were contested by humanitarians, and later seemed belied by factors he did not foresee, such as cheap imports of food from newly exploited colonies like Canada. Since 1918 'Malthusian' theories of the dangers of over-population have revived.

Manchester Guardian, The
It was started in 1821 as a weekly paper, becoming daily in 1855. As the leading Liberal publication outside London, it was edited from 1872 to 1929 by C. P. Scott. Its title was changed to *The Guardian* in 1959, and since 1961 it has been published from London. It is considered to be one of the more liberal or left-wing papers.

Manley, Delarivière (?1663–1724)
Playwright and novelist. Manley's unconventional lifestyle led to many scandalous strictures. She married her cousin John Manley at an early age, only to find he was already married, and on making this discovery left him, although she was pregnant and had no means of support. For some months she lived in the household of the Duchess of Cleveland, acting as secretary and companion, but left her patronage after rumours of an affair with the Duchess's son.

For some time she seems to have lived in the country, returning to London in 1696, when two of her plays were performed: *The Lost Lover or the Jealous Husband* and *The Royal Mischief*. At this time she became the mistress of John Tilly, the Warden of Fleet Prison.

In 1705 Manley's novel *The Secret History of Queen Zarah* appeared, and proved an enormous success. In its use of a mythical society to satirize contemporary English life, it set the pattern for her later *roman à clef*, *The New Atalantis* (1709). In 1711 Manley succeeded ▷ Jonathan Swift as editor of *The Examiner*, and in the course of her writing career produced many political pamphlets. In 1714 *The Adventures of Rivella*, apparently a fictionalized autobiography, appeared. Her final achievement was a series of novels, *The Power of Love*, published in 1720.

Manning, Olivia (1915–80)
Novelist and short-story writer. Her major work is *The Balkan Trilogy*, set in Romania, Greece and Egypt during the early stages of World War II, and which consists of: *The Great Fortune* (1960); *The Spoilt City* (1962) and *Friends and Heroes* (1965). It is told primarily through the consciousness of a newly married English woman, and builds up a strong sense of place and of history through the portrayal of a wide range of characters and the accumulation of details of daily experience. The story is continued in *The Levant Trilogy*: *The Danger Tree* (1977); *The Battle Lost and Won* (1978); *The Sum of Things* (1980). Other novels: *The Wind Changes* (1937); *Artist Among the Missing* (1949); *School for Love* (1951); *A Different Face* (1953); *The Doves of Venus* (1955); *The Rain Forest* (1974). Story collections: *Growing Up* (1948); *My Husband Cartwright* (1956); *A Romantic Hero* (1967).

Mansfield, Katherine (1888–1923)
Short-story writer. Born (Katherine Mansfield Beauchamp) in Wellington, New Zealand; married the critic ▷ John Middleton Murry in 1913. Her story collections are: *In a German Pension* (1911); *Je Ne Parle Pas Français* (1918); *Bliss* (1920); *The Garden Party* (1922); *The Dove's Nest* (1923); *Something Childish* (1945); *The Aloe* (1930); *Collected Stories* (1945). Her *Journal* (1927, enlarged edition 1934) and *Letters* (1928) were edited by Murry. The stories resemble in their form those of the Russian writer ▷ Chekhov, and ▷ James Joyce's ▷ *Dubliners*; they do not have a distinct plot with a definite beginning and ending and a self-sufficient action, conveying instead an impression of continuity with ordinary life, and depending for their unity on delicate balance of detail and feeling. She contributed to the development of the ▷ stream of consciousness technique, and to the ▷ modernist use of multiple viewpoints. Her *Collected Letter* have been edited in two volumes (1984, 87) by V. O'Sullivan.
Bib: Alpers, A., *The Life of Katherine Mansfield*; Hanson, C., and Gurr, A., *Katherine Mansfield*; Tomalin, C., *Katherine Mansfield: A Secret Life*; Fullbrook, K., *Katherine Mansfield*.

Mansfield Park (1814)
A novel by ▷ Jane Austen. The theme is the conflict between three different styles of moral feeling. The first is that of Sir Thomas Bertram, owner of Mansfield Park; it stands for a system of conservative, orderly principle, a tradition inherited from the 18th century, emphasizing stability and discounting the feelings. The second style of moral feeling is embodied in Fanny Price, Sir Thomas's niece whom he takes into his household because her parents are poor and their family too large; although

she is timid, withdrawn and overawed by her new surroundings, she posseses a highly developed sensibility and capacity for affection both of which are foreign to the Bertrams, except to the younger son, Edmund, who to some degree appreciates her. The third style is represented by Henry and Mary Crawford, half-brother and half-sister to the wife of the village parson. They are rich, independent, attractive; they do not share Sir Thomas's cold theories, and they do possess Fanny's capacity for ardent feeling; on the other hand, they are without Sir Thomas's dedication to conscience and without Fanny's reverence for consistency of moral with affectionate and aesthetic sensibilities. The difference between the three styles of life becomes overt while Sir Thomas is absent in the West Indies; the Crawfords virtually take over Mansfield Park in order to rehearse, with the Bertram children and two guests, a performance of Kotzebue's *Lovers' Vows*. Henry Crawford is by this time conducting a flirtation with Maria Bertram, who is engaged to one of the guests, Mr Rushworth, and Mary Crawford is in love with Edmund; these relationships are in effect parodied in the play (popular in Jane Austen's time) so that the characters can perform on the stage what they desire to enact in real life. Fanny, knowing that Sir Thomas would disapprove of amateur acting, refuses to take part, but the situation is painful to her because she is secretly in love with Edmund herself. The rehearsals are stopped by Sir Thomas's sudden return, but a new crisis occurs in Fanny's life when Henry, awakened to the reality of her diffident charms, proposes marriage to her. She refuses him, much to Sir Thomas's uncomprehending disapproval, and is not in a position to explain to him the grounds of her refusal: that she disapproves of Henry morally and is in love with his son. She is exiled to her own family at Portsmouth, where disorder and strong emotion, often reduced to callous bad temper by poverty and overcrowding, are the rule. Henry is for a time constant, but he disgraces himself, the Bertrams and his sister by eloping with Maria after she has married. By degrees, both Sir Thomas and Edmund came to appreciate Fanny at her true value, and at the end of the novel she is to become Edmund's wife.

Of Jane Austen's completed works *Mansfield Park* is the most direct criticism of the ▷ Regency style of sensibility (represented by the Crawfords), with its tendency to reject continuity with the best elements of the past; at the same time the criticism is balanced by a recognition of the importance of the sensibility if morality is to receive true life from the feelings. It is also a bold challenge to the romantic style of fiction: Mary Crawford, antagonist to the heroine Fanny, is not only shown as friendly to her and in all but the deepest sense appreciative of her; she is also the possessor of genuine social attractions which Fanny lacks.

Markandaya, Kamala (b 1924)

Pen name of Kamala Durnauja, Indian novelist. Educated at Madras University, she has worked as a journalist, but is now a full-time writer and lives in London. Her novels are set in contemporary India; they deal with a range of subjects and settings, but tend to emphasize relationships and personal dilemmas, including the tension between Indian and European cultural influences. Her novels are: *Nectar in a Sieve* (1954); *Some Inner Fury* (1955); *A Silence of Desire* (1960); *Possession* (1963); *A Handful of Rice* (1966); *The Coffer Dams* (1969); *The Nowhere Man* (1973); *Two Virgins: A Novel* (1974); *The Golden Honeycomb* (1977); *Pleasure City* (1982).
Bib: Banerji, N., *Kamala Markandaya: A Critical Study*.

Marriage

According to Laurence Stone, in England marriage only gradually acquired its function of regulating sexual chastity in wedlock: up to the 11th century polygamy and concubinage were widespread and divorce was casual. Even after that time divorce by mutual consent followed by remarriage was still widely practised. In the 13th century, however, the Church developed its control, asserting the principles of monogamy, defining and outlawing incest, punishing fornication and adultery and ensuring the exclusion of bastards from property inheritance. In 1439 weddings in church were declared a sacrament and after 1563 in the Roman Catholic Church the presence of a priest was required to make the contract valid. In this way, what had been a private contract between two families concerning property exchange – Claude Lévi-Strauss was the first to point out in 1948 women's universal role in such transactions between men – became regulated. Ecclesiastical law always recognized the formal exchange of oral promises (spousals) between the parties as a legally binding contract; as the Church got more powerful it exerted greater control over the circumstances in which those promises were made. In 1604 the hours, place and conditions of church weddings were defined and restricted; notice and publicity (the calling of the banns) were required, as a guard against bigamy and other abuses. One effect of this was to create a demand for clergymen willing to perform weddings outside the specified conditions. In 1753 Lord Hardwicke's Marriage Act was designed to close these loopholes: weddings had to be in church, duly registered and signed, verbal spousals would not be legally binding and marriages already contracted in breach of the 1604 conditions were declared invalid. No-one under 21 could marry without parental consent and there were heavy penalties for clergymen who defied these injunctions. After this, the Civil Marriage Act of 1836 was passed to regulate all marriages solemnized other than in accordance with the rites of the Church of England. Divorce, with the option of remarriage, was not available except by private Act of Parliament, which only the rich could afford: there were only 131 cases between 1670 and 1799. The poor used a ritualized wife-sale (as in ▷ Thomas Hardy's ▷ *The Mayor of Casterbridge* – the last recorded example was in 1887) or desertion. In 1857 the Matrimonial Causes Act introduced civil divorce for adultery: again only the rich could afford it and only men could do the divorcing. Wives were not permitted to divorce their husbands for adultery until 1923. In 1937 three additional grounds for divorce were introduced, cruelty, desertion and insanity. Further liberalization of the divorce laws took place in the 1960s: recognition of the concept of marital breakdown has allowed a less punitive and accusatory procedure.

▷ Divorce; Women, Status of.

Marryat, Frederick, Captain (1792–1848)
Novelist. He was a Captain in the Royal Navy and his novels are chiefly about the sea. The best-known of them are: *Frank Mildmay* (1829); *Peter Simple* (1834); *Jacob Faithful* (1834); *Mr Midshipman Easy* (1836). *Japhet in Search of a Father* (1836) is the story of a child of unknown parents who eventually achieves prosperity. Others of his books were intended for boys; the best-known of these is *Masterman Ready* (1841). Marryat continued the 18th-century realistic tradition of narrative.

▷ Realism.
Bib: Marryat, F., *Life and Letters of Captain Marryat*; Conrad, J., 'Tales of the Sea' in *Notes on Life and Letters*; Warner, O., *Captain Marryat: a Rediscovery*.

Marsh, Ngaio (1899–1982)
Detective novelist. Her works include: *A Man Lay Dead* (1934); *Enter a Murderer* (1935); *Death in Ecstasy* (1936); *Death at the Bar* (1940); *Died in the Wool* (1945); *Opening Night* (1951); *Singing in the Shrouds* (1958); *Hand in Glove* (1962); *Black Beech and Honeydew* (1965); *A Clutch of Constables* (1968); *Tied up in Tinsel* (1972); *Last Ditch* (1977); *Photo Finish* (1980). Ngaio Marsh is frequently bracketed with her three female ▷ detective-writing contemporaries (▷ Margery Allingham, ▷ Agatha Christie, Dorothy L. Sayers) who together comprise the formidable bed-rock of classic inter-war crime writing. Although she was born, educated and lived in New Zealand (her name is Maori), Marsh's novels are nevertheless often set in the English country house, or in the theatre, which she loved and dedicated much of her working life to: she was a successful director, and the action of her last novel (*Light Thickens*, 1982) takes place in the middle of a production of *Macbeth*. Marsh's 'serial detective' is Roderick Alleyn, a character of some complexity whose role is nevertheless always set out as a function of plot and narrative mystery, for Marsh the primary factors in detective writing.

Martin Chuzzlewit, The Life and Adventures of (1843–44)
A novel by ▷ Charles Dickens. The Chuzzlewit family includes old Martin, a rich man grown misanthropic owing to the selfishness and greed of the rest of his family; young Martin, his grandson, who begins with the family selfishness but is eventually purified by hardship and the good influence of his servant, Mark Tapley; Anthony, old Martin's avaricious brother, and Jonas, Anthony's son, who, by the end of the book, has become a figure of the blackest evil; Pecksniff, at first a trusted friend of old Martin, is one of Dicken's most effective hypocrites; Mrs Gamp, the disreputable nurse, is one of his most famous comic creations. The novel is divided rather sharply by the episode

in which young Martin temporarily emigrates to America. This episode is a self-sufficient satire on American life; moreover, not only is young Martin's character radically changed by it but the story thereafter takes on a denser substance. Pecksniff, Jonas and the fraudulent financier Tigg Montague cease to be merely comic and become substantially evil. These changes mark the transition from the earlier Dickens, the comic entertainer, into the later Dickens, of sombre power. The novel is thus a transitional work but it is also, as his comic masterpiece, the climax of Dicken's first phase.

Martineau, Harriet (1802–76)
Critic and ▷ essayist; also ▷ biographer and novelist. The sixth of eight children of a manufacturer of camlet and bombazine, she was born in Norwich where she was educated, at home and later in school. She had no sense of taste or smell and was a sickly child, gloomy, jealous and morbid, suffering from her parents' discipline and domestic scrimping, necessitated by their desire to educate their children to earn their own living. She supported herself initially partly by needlework and partly by writing reviews for the *Monthly Repository*. A devout ▷ Unitarian, she first published *Devotional Exercises* (1823), and in 1830 and 1831 won all three prizes in a competition set by the Central Unitarian Association for essays intended to convert the Roman Catholics, Jews and Mahommedans. Between 1832 and 1834 she wrote *Illustrations of Political Economy*, social reformist stories influenced by ▷ Jeremy Bentham and ▷ John Stuart Mill, along with stories for 'Brougham's Society for the Diffusion of Useful Knowledge', of which some 10, 000 copies were sold. She became a celebrity, living with her mother and aunt in Westminster, dining out every day except Sunday with friends such as ▷ Malthus, Sydney Smith, Milnes and politicians whom she advised; she suggested and managed ▷ Thomas Carlyle's first course of lectures in 1837. In 1834 she visited the US partly for her health, supporting the Abolitionists despite threats and difficulties, publishing in 1837 *Society in America* and, a lighter and more popular product of her trip, *A Retrospect of Western Travel*. In 1839 she toured abroad again, but had to return quickly from Venice and was ill for some six months. In 1843 she published *Life in the Sick Room*, which she came to despise when her views on religion developed. She was cured of a serious illness by mesmerism in 1844 and went on to practice it herself, giving an account in *Letters on Mesmerism* (1845). She travelled in Egypt and Palestine in 1846–7. By now she had rejected all religion.

She wrote numerous articles in the *Daily News* and some for the ▷ *Edinburgh Review*. Her other works include: *Deerbrook* (1839), her first novel and her favourite, *The Hour and The Man* (1840) on Toussaint l'Ouverture, a popular volume of children's stories (▷ Children's books) *The Playfellow* (1841), *The History of England During the Thirty Years' Peace* (1849) and *Laws of Man's Social Nature*. She was influenced by ▷ Comte, of whose philosophy she produced a free translation and condensation, *The Philosophy of Comte* (1853). She wrote a hurried

autobiography in 1855 when diagnosed terminally ill, *An Autobiographical Memoir*, published eventually in 1876. She attributed her power to 'earnestness and intellectual clearness within a certain range', although she had 'no approach to genius' due to her lack of imagination. Her *Selected Letters* have been edited by V. Sanders (1990).
Bib: Pichanick, V. K., *Harriet Martineau, the Woman and Her Work*; Webb, R. K., *Harriet Martineau, a Radical Victorian*; Sanders, V., *Reason Over Passion: Harriet Martineau and the Victorian Novel*; David, D., *Intellectual Women and Victorian Patriarchy*.

Marx, Karl (1818–83)
Born in Trier of German-Jewish parentage, he attended university in Berlin and Bonn where he first encountered Hegelian dialectic. He met Friedrich Engels (1820–95) in Paris in 1844, and in 1848, the Year of Revolutions, they published *The Communist Manifesto* together. In that year Marx returned to Germany and took part in the unsuccessful revolution there before fleeing to Britain where he was to remain until his death in 1883. In 1867 he published *Capital*, the voluminous work for which he is best known. Marx is justly renowned for his adaptation of the Hegelian dialectic for a ▷ materialist account of social formations, which is based upon an analysis of the opposition between different social classes. He is, arguably, the most influential thinker and social commentator of the 19th century whose work has had far-reaching effects on subsequent generations of scholars, philosophers, politicians and analysts of human culture. In the political ferment of the 1960s, and especially in France, his work has been subject to a series of extraordinarily productive re-readings, especially by philosophers such as ▷ Louis Althusser which continue to affect the understanding of all aspects of cultural life. In Britain Marx's work is what lies behind a very powerful literary and historical tradition of commentary and analysis, and has informed much work in the areas of sociology, and the study of the mass media. *Capital* and a range of earlier texts, have come to form the basis of the materialist analysis of culture.
▷ New historicism.

Mary Barton **(1848)**
The first novel by ▷ Elizabeth Gaskell. Written while she was in deep distress over the death of her infant son, it is a plea for greater understanding between the employing class and the industrial proletariat of the north. It is set in Manchester in the decade in which she wrote; this was known as 'the Hungry Forties' because of the distress among the working classes. The most interesting character creation is John Barton, a sober and intelligent workman, whose perception of the social injustice which surrounds him and of which he is a victim drives him into bitter resentment. A group of workers draw lots to assassinate Henry Carson, one of the younger and most callous of the employers, as a warning to the rest of the class. The lot falls on Barton, who commits the murder. Suspicion, however, falls on his daughter's lover, Jem Wilson, who is brought to trial and saved from the death penalty only by Mary

Barton's strenuous efforts. John Barton confesses to the murder to Henry Carson's father, who forgives him on his deathbed. Despite implausibilities, the novel is one of the most sensitive studies of industrial working-class life in Victorian fiction; as such, it suffered angry criticism from some of the employing class whom it was intended to convert. It was admired by ▷ Thomas Carlyle and ▷ Charles Dickens.

Masefield, John (1878–1967)
Poet and novelist. He went to sea in 1893, and published his first volume of poems, *Salt-Water Ballads* in 1902. He was a prolific poet; the first edition of his *Collected Poems* came out in 1923, and the collection increased steadily until 1964. His work has immediate appeal, and is strongest in narrative verse: *The Everlasting Mercy* (1911); *The Widow in the Bye Street* (1912); *Dauber* (1913); *The Daffodil Fields* (1913); *Reynard the Fox* (1919). He was chosen as Poet Laureate in 1930. His novels have romantic charm, eg *Sard Harker* (1924); *Odtaa* (1926). *The Midnight Folk* (1927) is a classic of children's literature.
▷ Children's books.
Bib: Babington Smith, C., *John Masefield, a Life*; Spark, M., *John Masefield*.

Master Humphrey's Clock
The title of what ▷ Charles Dickens intended to be an inclusive serial linking distinct tales – ▷ *The Old Curiosity Shop* and ▷ *Barnaby Rudge*. Master Humphrey is the narrator of the early pages of the former, but Dickens abandoned the idea.

Materialism
The philosophical theory that only physical matter is real and that all phenomena and processes can be explained by reference to it. Related to this is the Marxist doctrine that political and social change is triggered by change in the material and economic basis of society.
▷ Marx, Karl.

Maturin, Charles Robert (1782–1824)
Irish novelist and dramatist. Like ▷ Matthew 'Monk' Lewis and ▷ Mrs Radcliffe he belonged to the school of writers who exploited the emotions of terror and love of mystery among readers in the late 18th and early 19th centuries. *The Fatal Revenge, or The Family of Montorso* (1807), *The Wild Irish Boy* (1808) and *The Milesian Chief* (1812) were ridiculed but admired for their power by ▷ Walter Scott. Scott and Byron secured the production of Maturin's tragedy *Bertram* in 1816, which was a great success. His other tragedies were less successful, and he returned to the novel. The best of his later novels is *Melmoth the Wanderer* (1820), to which the French novelist ▷ Balzac wrote a sequel *Melmoth réconcilé à l'église* (1835). His last novel was *The Albigenses* (1824).

Maugham, William Somerset (1874–1965)
Novelist, short-story writer and dramatist. Educated at King's School, Canterbury, and Heidelberg

University; he then studied medicine in London. His first novel, *Liza of Lambeth* (1897) shows the influence of ▷ Zola, an example of the growing importance of French influence on English fiction at the end of the 19th century. His semi-autobiographical novel *Of Human Bondage* (1915) made his name. Other novels include: *The Hero* (1901); *The Moon and Sixpence* (1919); *The Painted Veil* (1925); *The Casuarina Tree* (1926); *Cakes and Ale* (1930). The professional accomplishment of his novels gave him a wide foreign public, and after 1930 his reputation abroad was greater than at home, though interest in him revived here towards his 80th birthday. He celebrated his 80th year by the special republication of *Cakes and Ale*, a novel which satirizes the English propensity for admiring the 'Grand Old Men' among their writers. Some of his best fiction is in his short stories, in volumes such as *The Trembling of a Leaf* (1921), *The Mixture as Before* (1940). His plays were successful, but have lost interest now. They include: *Our Betters* (1917); *Caesar's Wife* (1919); *East of Suez* (1922); *The Constant Wife* (1926); *The Letter* (1927); *The Breadwinner* (1930); *Sheppey* (1933).

Bib: Maugham, R., *Somerset and All the Maughams*; Morgan, T., *Somerset Maugham*; Brander, L., *Somerset Maugham: A Guide*.

Mayor of Casterbridge, The (1886)

A novel by ▷ Thomas Hardy. Its hero is the country labourer, Michael Henchard. At the beginning of the book, when times are hard, he gets drunk at a fair and sells his wife and child to a sailor called Newson. He bitterly repents and renounces strong drink for 20 years. His wife returns after 18 years, supposing Newson to be drowned, and by this time Henchard has prospered so far as to have become Mayor of Casterbridge (Dorchester). At the same time as her return, Henchard takes on as his assistant in his business of corn-dealing a wandering Scotsman, Donald Farfrae. The rest of the novel is the story of the rivalry between Farfrae and Henchard. Farfrae is never deliberately his enemy, yet merely by virtue of living in the same town he deprives Henchard of everything, and the latter leaves the place at the end of the novel as poor as when he started, and far more wretched. Hardy seems to have intended a kind of Darwinian study of the survival of the fittest among human beings. Henchard is a monolithic character, who puts all his energy and passion into every relationship and activity; Farfrae has a flexible personality and is able to devote to every predicament exactly what it demands, without excess. Henchard's crowning sadness is the loss of the girl he has supposed to be his daughter but who is in fact Newson's; he loves her nonetheless but Newson returns and claims her.

McEwan, Ian (b 1948)

Novelist and short-story writer. His first collection of stories, *First Love, Last Rites* (1975) gained immediate notoriety for its exploration of the erotic, perverse and macabre themes which also figure in *In Between the Sheets* (1978). His first novel, *The Cement Garden* (1978) is a story of adolescent guilt, while *The*

Comfort of Strangers (1981) is a dream-like narrative set in Venice and ending in violence. His recent work includes: *The Child in Time* (1987); *The Innocent* (1990); and *Black Dogs* (1992). He has also written a television play, *The Imitation Game* (1981) and a screenplay, *The Ploughman's Lunch* (1983).

McGahern, John (b 1934)

Irish novelist and short-story writer. Educated at University College Dublin, he has worked as a primary school teacher and been a Research Fellow at the University of Reading, a visiting professor in the USA and Northern Arts Fellow at Newcastle University; he lives in Ireland. In one of his short stories a character makes television documentaries about 'the darker aspects of Irish life' and this might serve as a description of McGahern's own fiction, which explores family tensions, and minor, mundane tragedies of loss, alienation and unfulfilment in domestic Irish settings, using a language which is generally sparse and understated, but is illuminated by colloquial vividness and humour and sometimes modulates into lyricism. His novels are: *The Barracks* (1963); *The Dark* (1965); *The Leavetaking* (1974); *The Pornographer* (1979); *Amongst Women* (1990). Volumes of short stories: *Nightlines* (1970); *Getting Through* (1978); *High Ground* (1985); *The Collected Short Stories* (1992).

Meiosis

▷ Figures of Speech.

Melincourt, or Sir Oran Haut-ton (1817)

A novel by ▷ Thomas Love Peacock. Sir Oran Haut-ton is an orang-outang of delightful manners and a good flute-player for whom the young philosopher, Mr Sylvan Forester, has bought the title of baronet and a seat in Parliament. 'Haut ton' is a French phrase then used in English for 'high tone', *ie* fashionable, refined, and aristocratic. Peacock is developing the idea of Lord Monboddo (1714–90), an early anthropologist, who describes such a creature in his books, as an example of 'the infantine state of our species'; Peacock's ape, however, compares favourably with the aristocracy. The book is a satire on the right-wing (Tory) establishment, and especially those writers who had once been Radicals: Southey (Mr Feathernest); Wordsworth (Mr Paperstamp); ▷ Coleridge (Mr Mystic). Mr Vamp and Mr Killthedead are Tory reviewers, and Mr Fax may represent ▷ Malthus. Sylvan Forester may be the poet Shelley; and Simon Sarcastic, Peacock himself.

Memoir novel

A novel which is presented as an autobiographical account but is in fact partly or wholly fictitious, such as ▷ Defoe's ▷ *Moll Flanders* (1722) or ▷ Charlotte Brontë's ▷ *Jane Eyre* (1847).

Memoirs of a Cavalier (1724)

A work of fiction by ▷ Daniel Defoe, though it was thought that the memoirs were possibly genuine. They describe the career of a professional soldier, Colonel Andrew Newport, born in 1608. He sees military service in Europe during the Thirty Years' War, and then joins the English Royalist army in the Civil War.

Meredith, George (1828–1909)

Novelist and poet. Born at Portsmouth, the son of a tailor and naval outfitter; his grandfather, Melchizedeck, had had the same business and is the basis of the character Old Mel in the novel *Evan Harrington* (1861). George Meredith was educated in Germany and his writings were influenced by Germans, especially the novelist Jean Paul Richter (1763–1825), who stimulated his conception of comedy. Meredith was even closer to French culture, especially the radical thinking of the 18th-century Philosophes (▷ Encyclopaedists). On his return to England he began to study law but soon took to journalism and serious literature.

He began by publishing verse: *Poems* (1851). In 1855 he published his eastern romance *Shaving of Shagpat*, and in 1857 a romance in German style, *Farina, a Legend of Cologne*. ▷ *The Ordeal of Richard Feverel* (1859) was his first real novel, followed by *Evan Harrington*, which is now regarded as one of his best. In 1862 he produced his most famous volume of poems, *Modern Love*. Other publications included: *Sandra Belloni* (1864; originally called *Emilia in England*); *Rhoda Fleming* (1865); *Vittoria* (1867 – a sequel to *Sandra*); *The Adventures of Harry Richmond* (1871); *Beauchamp's Career* (1875 – his own favourite); *The Idea of Comedy* (1877 – a critical essay, important for understanding his work); ▷ *The Egoist* (1879 – one of his best known novels); *The Tragic Comedians* (1880); *Poems and Lyrics of the Joy of Earth* (1883); *Diana of the Crossways* (1885 – the first of his novels to reach a wide public); *Ballads and Poems of Tragic Life* (1887); *A Reading of Earth* (1888 – verse); *One of Our Conquerors* (1891); *The Empty Purse* (1892 – a poem); *Lord Ormont and his Aminta* (1894); *The Amazing Marriage* (1895). His concluding works were all poetry: *Odes in Contribution to the Song of French History* (1898); *A Reading of Life* (1901); *Last Poems* (published in 1910 after his death). His unfinished novel, *Celt and Saxon*, was also published posthumously.

Meredith's reputation at present rests chiefly on his novels but, like ▷ Thomas Hardy, he seems to have been a novelist who preferred poetry. His prose is poetic in its use of metaphor and symbolism, and both his poetry and his prose are often expressed in concentrated and difficult language which invites comparison with Robert Browning. The impulsiveness and ruggedness of his prose also recalls ▷ Thomas Carlyle, whom Meredith resembled in his hostility to the mechanistic qualities of his age. Of all the Victorian novelists who ever had a major reputation, his has perhaps sunk the lowest in this century: both his prose and his poetry tend to be regarded as intolerably mannered and he is accused of fixing his attention on style as an end, instead of using it as a medium. Nonetheless, his intense interest in psychological exploration (again recalling Browning), his use of metaphor and symbol from the natural world to express states of mind and the freshness of some of his characters (especially

women) were all original in his own time and keep him from being forgotten.

▷ French and German influence on English fiction

Bib: Stevenson, L., *Life*; Lindsay, L., *Life*; Trevelyan, G. M., *Poetry and Philosophy of George Meredith*; Sassoon, S., *Meredith*; Sitwell, O., *Novels of Meredith*; Lees, F. N., in *Pelican Guide 6: Dickens to Hardy*; Cline, C. L., *Letters*; Woolf, V., in *Common Reader*; Williams, D., *George Meredith: His Life and Lost Love*; Beer, G., *Meredith: A Change of Masks*.

Metafiction

This term is applied to fictional writing which questions the relationship between reality and fiction through deliberately and self-consciously drawing attention to its own status as a linguistic construct. Examples would include ▷ John Fowles's *The French Lieutenant's Woman*, ▷ Salman Rushdie's *Midnight's Children* and ▷ Dan Jacobson's *The Rape of Tamar*.

▷ Historiographic metafiction.

Metalanguage

A term coined by the linguist L. Hjelmslev to describe a language which refers to *another language* rather than to non-linguistic objects, situations or events. In the words of ▷ Roland Barthes it is 'a second language in which one speaks about the first' (*Mythologies*). In this sense, metalanguage can be used as a means of reflecting on language itself.

▷ Metafiction.

Metaphor

▷ Figures of Speech.

Metonymy

▷ Figures of Speech.

Microcosmographie

▷ Characters, Theophrastian.

Middlemarch, a Study of Provincial Life (1871–2)

A novel by ▷ George Eliot. The events it describes occur just before the ▷ Reform Bill of 1832 but its content of ideas is more relevant to the mid-Victorian period when it was written. The material was originally intended for two novels, one centred on Dorothea Brooke and the other a study of provincial life in the town of Middlemarch, based on Coventry. Unity is achieved by the fusion of the two senses of 'provincial': the geographical sense of 'situated outside the capital' and the cultural one of the 'ignorant of the central current of ideas'. Dorothea, the daughter of a country gentleman, aspires to a high spiritual conduct of life; she is however isolated geographically, socially and intellectually, like most females of her time, and she finds no scope for her ambitions. In consequence she is led into an infatuation with Mr Casaubon, an elderly parson-scholar whose life-work is the writing of his 'Key to all Mythologies', in which he expects to demonstrate the centrality of the Christian scriptures among human beliefs. Unfortunately, his work is reduced to futility by his ignorance of the leading (German) scholarship in his field, and his egotism and narrowness of human experience prevent him from appreciating the quality of Dorothea's ardour and potentiality. Dorothea finds her marriage a total disillusionment. This marital failure runs parallel to that of Tertius Lydgate and Rosamund Vincy. Lydgate, a young medical scientist, is engaged in equally radical research into the possible existence of a 'basic tissue.' Unlike Casaubon, he is alert to the intellectual centre of his thought (Paris) and he has chosen to live in a provincial town only because he supposes that by so doing he can escape the social involvements and professional rivalries of the metropolis. But Rosamund, the daughter of a Middlemarch manufacturer who has the typically provincial ambition to raise his family to the level of metropolitan fashion, has been attracted to Lydgate only because he has aristocratic relations. Rosamund has no understanding of her husband's intellectual promise and does nothing but frustrate it. Moreover, he has been beguiled into the marriage by his own emotional immaturity, which has misled him into assuming that a beautiful wife is a mere ornament to the life of an intellectual man, without a will of her own; his mistake, in fact, is a youthful equivalent of Casaubon's when the latter marries Dorothea. Lydgate is also mistaken in supposing that the provincialism of Middlemarch will leave him free to conduct his own affairs: he becomes unwittingly involved in the intrigues of the chairman of the Hospital Board, Nicholas Bulstrode, a banker and a bigoted Dissenter who supposes himself to have a divine mission to direct the lives of others and a heavenly dispensation which enables him to balance his moral accounts with God, as his clients balance their financial accounts with himself. Bulstrode is ruined by the consequences of his own criminal past and his ruin nearly drags down Lydgate, already faced with financial disgrace by the expensive tastes of his wife.

These are the novel's themes of public failure arising from individual inadequacies which are a result of a personal blindness in the characters and their failure to discern the central truths of their life and work. The themes of failure are counter-balanced by those of fulfilment. Dorothea loses her spiritual arrogance by learning from her own mistakes; after the death of her husband, she acquires a capacity for humble and open-minded human sympathy, which helps to save Lydgate and even momentarily redeems Rosamund. Her frustration is released by the gradual awakening of sexual love between herself and Casaubon's young relative, Will Ladislaw, who differs from the other characters by being essentially cosmopolitan in his background and outlook. Another centre of judgement is that of the Garth family, who acknowledge their provinciality and by avoiding illusions achieve balanced insights and clear directions for their energies in ways that are really less provincial than those of their superiors in wealth and social status. Mary Garth manages to rescue Fred Vincy, Rosamund's brother, from the unreal values which obsess his family. A minor character but one central to George Eliot's valuations is the free-thinking parson Farebrother, condemned to a life of

self-sacrifice by external causes and yet able to live it not only without either bitterness or unctuousness but also without any narrowing down of his capacity for human sympathy.

At first sight *Middlemarch* seems to be as narrow in its environmental setting as it is complex in its structure, but George Eliot touches upon so many aspects of 19th-century experience as to make it one of the richest and most spacious of all English novels.

Mill, John Stuart (1806–73)

Writer on economics, politics, psychology, logic and ethics. He did not invent the word ▷ Utilitarian, but was the first to apply it to the reform movement which had been started by his father's friend ▷ Jeremy Bentham and of which his father, James Mill, was one of the leaders. The movement derived from 18th-century ▷ rationalism and the group was known as 'the philosophical radicals' because of the intellectual thoroughness with which they reasoned out their political and social standpoints. James Mill educated his son strenuously from a very early age (he began Greek at the age of 3) but the education, wide as it was, ignored the imaginative and emotional needs of his son's character. J. S. Mill describes in his *Autobiography* (1873) how this neglect produced in him a spiritual crisis when he was 21, after he had already made a brilliant start to his career. He discovered that he was emotionally indifferent to the ends for which he was working. He recovered partly through his discovery of the poetry of Wordsworth and the crisis enabled him to develop a far more sympathetic and balanced outlook on human needs than had been possessed by his father or Bentham.

Mill's literary output was very large and his influence on his time was great, though much of his writing (for instance his psychology, which he based on 18th-century associationism) has now been superseded by subsequent thinking. However, his *Autobiography* and a number of his essays have permanent value, for instance his essay ▷ *On Liberty* (1859) and those on Bentham (1838) and ▷ Coleridge (1840), whom he described as the two great formative influences of his age. His most massive work was his *Principles of Political Economy* (1848). He was an early leader of the movement for the emancipation of women and published *The Subjection of Women* (1869). His *Utilitarianism* (1863) was a reasoned defence of his philosophy.

A peculiarity of his upbringing, considering its period, is that that he was educated against the Christian faith.

▷ Women, Education of.

Bib: Packe, M. St J., *Life*; Leavis, F. R., *Mill on Bentham and Coleridge*; Wishy, B., *Preface to Liberty*; Halévy, E., *The Growth of Philosophic Radicalism*; Abrams, M. H., *The Mirror and the Lamp*; Anschutz, R. P., *The Philosophy of J. S. Mill*; Bain, A., *J. S. Mill: a Criticism*; Stephen, L., *Utilitarianism*; Neff, E., *Carlyle and Mill*; Britton, K. W., *Mill*.

Mill on the Floss, The (1860)

A novel by ▷ George Eliot. It is set in the English midlands and its central character is Maggie Tulliver, the daughter of a miller. She is intelligent and richly imaginative beyond the understanding of her relatives and in particular of her brother, Tom, a boy of limited intelligence and sympathies to whom she is devoted. The novel is divided into seven parts; the first three lead up to Mr Tulliver's bankruptcy and make a rich and comic study of English country life in the mid-19th century with deep insights into the psychology of the rural middle class. The last three deal with the tragic love of Maggie for Philip Wakem, the deformed son of the lawyer through whom Mr Tulliver has been ruined, the compromising of her reputation by the educated and agreeable Stephen Guest and her alienation from her brother, with whom she is, however, reconciled by means of the flood which drowns them both. The earlier chapters contain some of Eliot's best writing, though not sustained in the later part.

Milne, A. A. (Alan Alexander) (1882–1956)
Novelist, dramatist, children's writer. He was for many years assistant editor of *Punch*, and he became widely popular as the author of light comedies and novels. His earliest play is *Wurzel-Flummery* (1917) and his best known *Mr Pim Passes By* (1919). However he achieved fame by four ▷ children's books, centring on his son, Christopher Robin. Two of these are verse: *When We Were Very Young* (1924) and *Now We Are Six* (1927). The other two are prose stories, with Christopher Robin's teddy bear Winnie the Pooh as hero: *Winnie the Pooh* (1926); *The House at Pooh Corner* (1928). They have been translated into many languages; *Winnie the Pooh*, rather to its advantage, into Latin.

Mimesis
In ▷ Plato's *Republic* 'mimesis' is used to designate 'imitation', but in a derogatory way. The term is given a rigorous, positive meaning in ▷ Aristotle's *Poetics* where it is used to describe a process of selection and representation appropriate to tragedy: 'the imitation of an action'. Literary criticism from ▷ Sir Philip Sidney onwards has wrestled with the problem of the imitative function of literary texts, but after ▷ structuralism with its questioning of the referential function of all language, the term has taken on a new and problematic dimension. Mimesis has frequently been associated with the term ▷ 'Realism', and with the capacity of language to reflect reality. At particular historical moments, *eg* the Renaissance, or the present time, when reality itself appears to be in question, then the capacity of language to represent reality is brought to the fore. The issue becomes even more complex when we realize that 'reality' may be something other than our experience of it. The debate has been carried on most vigorously at a theoretical level in the exchanges earlier this century between the Hungarian critic Georg Lukács, and the dramatist Bertolt Brecht. The nub of the debate between these two Marxist thinkers (▷ Marx, Karl) was how best to represent 'the deeper causal complexes of society' (Brecht). Brecht rejected the view propounded by Lukács that the novel was the literary form which pre-eminently represented social process, arguing that realism was a major political, philosophical and practical issue and

should not be dealt with by literature alone. Such a view rejected the metaphysical implications which lay behind the Aristotelian notion of mimesis, in favour of a more historical analysis which saw literature as part of the process of social change.

In ▷ narratology, the distinction between mimesis (showing) and diegesis (telling) is considered under the heading of ▷ mood. For example, if the speech of a fictional character is given in full, in quotation marks, this is considered mimetic, whereas a summary of what was said would be relatively diegetic.
Bib: Auerbach, E., *Mimesis*; Genette, G., *Narrative Discourse*.

Minerva Press
Established in London in 1790 by William Lane, it combined a press with a ▷ circulating library, and published mainly women authors for a primarily female readership. It is often identified with the worst kind of ▷ Gothic and sentimental excess, and probably equates most closely to the Mills and Boon pulp novels published in the late 20th century. Yet the authors did produce some interesting work, perhaps more by accident than design, and Minerva certainly provided the means for women to earn their living as authors.
Bib: Blakey, D., *The Minerva Press 1790–1820*.

Mise en abyme
The *mise en abyme* is a feature specially characteristic of the French ▷ *nouveau roman* and of ▷ metafiction. It means a throwing into the abyss, and occurs when some element within the text mirrors the structure of the text as a whole, creating an interpretative 'abyss' as the part seems to contain the whole. A visual analogy would be a painting of a room, in which a copy of the same painting hangs on the wall. The device and the term were developed by the French novelist ▷ André Gide, whose novel *The Counterfeiters* (1949) contains a clear example: a character who is writing a novel resembling *The Counterfeiters*.

Mistry, Rohinton (b 1952)
Indian novelist. Mistry was brought up in Bombay, and moved to Canada in 1975, where he studied at the University of Toronto and has since worked in a bank. His first work was *Tales from Firozsha Baag* (1987), a collection of short stories set in the middle-class Parsi suburbs of Bombay. His first novel, *Such a Long Journey* (1991), is the story of a Bombay family; it has an extravagant plot, vivid, often humorous characters and elements of ▷ magic realism.

Mo, Timothy (b 1953)
Novelist. Born in Hong Kong of an English mother and a Cantonese father and educated at St John's College, Oxford, Mo has worked as a journalist. His first novel was *The Monkey King* (1978), a lively story of family and business intrigue, set in Hong Kong and the New Territories on the Chinese Mainland. *Sour Sweet* (1982) is the touching story of a Chinese family, first-generation immigrants in London,

whose initial isolation is mitigated when they open a take-away, leading to comic cross-cultural confusions, until the father accidentally becomes involved in the world of the Triad gangs in Soho (the subject of a parallel narrative in the novel). *An Insular Possession* (1986) blends history and fiction in its account of conflicts between Britain and China over the opium trade in the 1830s and 1840s, as does *The Redundancy of Courage* (1991), which concerns an initially uncommitted Chinese hotel-proprietor who becomes involved in the resistance movement after the American-backed Indonesian invasion of East Timor in 1975.

Modernism

The term 'modern' first appears (as '*modernus*') in 6th-century latin, while 'modernism' is not found until the early 18th-century Quarrel between the Ancients and the Moderns. However 'modernism' is now generally agreed to mean the influential international movement in literature, drama, art, music and architecture which began in the latter years of the 19th century and flourished until at least the 1920s; it can usefully be distinguished from 'modernity', which refers to the broader social, political and economic conditions of the modern world, often seen as starting at a much earlier date than 'modernism' in the arts. Modernism can be seen as a reaction to the urbanization, bureaucratization and rapid social change associated with modernity, but it can also been seen in specifically aesthetic terms as a reaction to ▷ realism and ▷ naturalism, undermining the representationalism (▷ mimesis) associated with those movements. In fiction the ▷ stream of consciousness novel was a prime example of modernism, and it was associated with multiple, subjective or unreliable narratives, formal experiment and symbolic or mythic structures. The apocalyptic and pessimistic strains in modernist writing may be related to the impact of World War I on the idea of civilization, but the innovative strength of women's writing within modernism suggests a more positive form of ideological change. (See Kime Scott, B. (ed.), *The Gender of Modernism*). In critical terms, modernist writing challenged the approaches of students and critics alike and so contributed to the development later in the century of new approaches to literature and reading.

▷ Post-modernism; Deconstruction.
Bib: Bradbury, M. and McFarlane, J., *Modernism*; Calinescu, M., *Five Faces of Modernity*; Berman. M., *All That Is Solid Melts Into Air: The Experience of Modernity*; Bell, M., *The Context of English Literature, 1900–1930*.

Modernity
▷ Modernism.

Modest Proposal, A (1729)
A satirical ▷ pamphlet by ▷ Jonathan Swift, written when he was Dean of St Patrick's Cathedral, Dublin. The full title is *A Modest Proposal for Preventing Children of Poor People from being a Burden to their Parents or the Country*. Indignant at the extreme misery of the Irish poor under English government,

Swift, in the guise of an economic 'projector', calmly recommends that it would be more humane to breed up their children as food for the rich. The pamphlet is an example of the controlled but extreme savagery of Swift's irony, and the fierceness of his humanitarianism.

Molesworth, Mary Louisa (1839–1921)
Children's writer and novelist. Born Stewart, in Rotterdam where her father was a merchant, she was educated at home by her mother in Manchester where they moved in 1841. In 1861 she married Major Richard Molesworth, and first told stories to her own seven children, writing stories for and about them from a child's viewpoint, in which she portrayed a disciplined but loving world. In 1878 she separated from her husband, whose personality had been changed by a head wound sustained in the Crimean War, and from then on wrote to support her family. Using the pseudonym Ennis Graham, she wrote a large number of novels and stories. Her own childhood is described in *The Carved Lions* (1895) but perhaps the most famous and popular children's book is *The Cuckoo Clock* (1877). Others include *The Tapestry Room* (1879), *Tell Me a Story* (1875), *Carrots* (1876) and *Two Little Waifs* (1883).

▷ Children's books.
Bib: Avery, G., *Nineteenth-Century Children*; Lancelyn Green, R., *Tellers of Tales*.

Moll Flanders (1722)
A novel by ▷ Daniel Defoe, and his most famous, after ▷ *Robinson Crusoe* (1719). Its full title was *The Fortunes and Misfortunes of the Famous Moll Flanders*, and its substance is the adventures of an orphan girl from her early seduction through her various love affairs and her career of crime, to her transportation to Virginia and her final prosperity there. It is a realistic, episodic narrative with keen social and psychological perception in certain incidents. The book has no unifying structure, however, and none of the characters is fully established imaginatively. The conclusion is an example of Defoe's crude and superficial morality, Puritan in its tradition, but less profound and subtle than that of his predecessor ▷ John Bunyan. The Puritanism has become simplified to commercialism, especially evident in Moll's final 'repentance'.

▷ Picaresque.

'Monk' Lewis
▷ Lewis, Matthew Gregory.

Monologic
▷ Bakhtin, Mikhail.

Montaigne, Michel de (1533–92)
French essayist, and inventor of the ▷ essay form. His life was lived partly at court, or performing the office of magistrate in the city of Bordeaux, and partly in retirement. During retirement, he wrote his *Essais* ('experiments'), the first two volumes of which were published in 1580, and the third in 1588. He was a scholar, well-read in ▷ humanist literature and in the works of the ancient Greeks and Romans. His favourite author was Plutarch.

The Essays seem to have been begun as commentaries on his reading, perhaps to assist his exceptionally bad memory. From this grew a desire to arrive at a complete image of man; as a means to this, he tried to develop a portrait of himself, since 'each man bears the complete stamp of the human condition'. The sentence shows the still-prevailing view of his time, that human beings followed general principles in the structure of their personalities – a view quite unlike the view that grew up in the 18th century and came to predominate in the 19th, that each individual is unique (see ▷ Rousseau). He recognized, however, the difficulties in arriving at conclusive ideas about human nature, and the essays are characterized by the scepticism with which he weighs contradictions and opposing views.

Montaigne was translated into English by John Florio in 1603. The essays had an extensive influence upon English literature and the Montaigne tradition of essay writing was taken up by Abraham Cowley (*Essays in Verse and Prose*, 1668), ▷ Sir William Temple (*Miscellanea*, 1680, 1692, 1701) and, after the more formal period of the 18th century, ▷ Charles Lamb's *Essays of Elia* (1823).

Mood

One of the five categories in which ▷ Genette analyses narrative discourse, mood is described by him as 'the regulation of narrative information' through the control of 'distance' and 'perspective'. The analysis of mood in a novel therefore includes the question of ▷ focalization.

Moonstone, The (1868)

A novel by ▷ Wilkie Collins. It is one of the earliest stories of detection and concerns the mysterious disappearance of a valuable diamond, formerly sacred to the Moon-god in one of the Indian temples. The novel is told in the first person by various participants in the events; it is plotted with skill, psychological ingenuity and a typically Victorian delight in characterization. Sergeant Cuff, the first detective in English fiction, appears in it.

▷ Detective fiction.

Moore, Brian (b 1921)

Novelist. Born in Belfast, Moore emigrated to Canada in 1948 and now lives in California. His Northern Irish Catholic upbringing provides the background for much of his work, which deals with themes of Irish migration, failure, guilt, isolation and loss of faith. His novels are characterized by narrative clarity and a sensitivity to the female point of view (notably his first and perhaps most famous novel, *The Lonely Passion of Judith Hearne*, 1955). *Black Robe* (1985) reflects contemporary Ulster by describing the confrontation between the settlers and native Indians in 17th-century Canada. Other novels include: *I Am Mary Dunne* (1968); *The Revolution Script* (1971); *Catholics* (1972); *The Great Victorian Collection* (1975); *The Doctor's Wife* (1976); *The Colour of Blood* (a political and theological thriller, 1987); *Lies of Silence* (1990); and *No Other Life* (1993). Moore also writes detective fiction as Michael Bryan and Bernard Marrow.

▷ Irish fiction in English.
Bib: Dahlie, H., *Brian Moore*.

Moore, G. E. (1873–1958)

Philosopher. He lectured on philosophy at Cambridge from 1911 to 1925, when he became professor. His principal book is *Principia Ethica* (1903); he also wrote *Ethics* (1912) and *Philosophical Studies* (1922). His philosophy was that of the 'New Realism', in opposition to the idealism of ▷ F. H. Bradley who was in the tradition of Hegel. Where the ▷ Idealists tended to a poetic conception of truth and ethics, rhetorically expressed and appealing to the emotions as much as to the reason, Moore appealed to the reason only, basing his arguments on common sense, and holding it to be the function of philosophy to clarify statements and arrive at fully intelligible definitions. At the same time, he argued that all experience is to be enjoyed, and that the richest possessions are aesthetic experience and personal friendship. He consequently had two kinds of influence, philosophical and literary. Philosophically, he was one of the starting points of ▷ Russell and the Logical Positivists such as A. J. Ayer, but in literary circles he had considerable personal influence on the ▷ Bloomsbury Group, centred on the novelist ▷ Virginia Woolf and her husband Leonard. The Bloomsbury Group owed its cohesiveness to a cult of personal relations such as Moore advocated, and some of its members regarded the state of mind of perfect aesthetic appreciation as one of the aims of life.
Bib: Schilpp, P. A., *The Philosophy of Moore*; Johnstone, J. K., *The Bloomsbury Group*.

Moore, George (1852–1933)

Irish novelist. He combined an ▷ aestheticism in tune with the aesthetic movement at the end of the 19th century, and the Celtic revivalism that went with a part of it, with a ▷ naturalism which showed the influence of late 19th-century French literature, especially from the novelist ▷ Zola. His most famous novels are: *A Mummer's Wife* (1885); *Esther Waters* (1894); *Evelyn Innes* (1898); *Sister Theresa* (1901); *The Brook Kerith* (1916); *Héloïse and Abélard* (1921). He was equally well known for his autobiographical studies: *Confessions of a Young Man* (1888); *Avowals* (1919, 1926); *Hail and Farewell* (1911–14) and *Conversations in Ebury Street* (1924). His carefully worked style was more admired in his own day than it is now.

▷ Celtic Twilight.
Bib: Korg, J., in *Victorian Fiction* (ed. L. Stevenson); Brown, M. J., *Moore: a Reconsideration*; Sechler, R. P., *George Moore: 'a Disciple of Walter Pater'*; Yeats, W. B., in *Dramatis Personae*; Hough, G., in *Image and Experience*.

Moore, Thomas (1779–1852)

Born in Dublin, Moore studied law at the Middle Temple and became a popular drawing-room singer. Later he was for a time Admiralty Registrar in Bermuda. His early pseudonymous volume, *The Poetical Works of the late Thomas Little Esq.* (1801) was referred to by Lord Byron in *English Bards and*

Scotch Reviewers (1809), and the two poets became close friends. Moore received many letters from Byron, though he shamefully expurgated them after Byron's death, and agreed to destroy the *Memoirs* which Byron had left to him. Moore's own writings range from lyric to satire, from prose romance to history and biography. The extremely popular *Irish Melodies*, which contain his most enduring work, appeared in ten parts between 1807 and 1835, and in 1813 he published a group of satires aimed at the Prince Regent, *The Twopenny Post Bag*. His long narrative peom in the Byronic mode, *Lalla Rookh: An Oriental Romance* (1817), achieved an international reputation, but in his next work *The Fudge Family in Paris* (1818) he returned to satire, aiming his shafts against the Englishman abroad. His *Loves of the Angels* (1823) became notorious for its eroticism. He also wrote a prose romance set in 3rd-century Egypt, *The Epicurean* (1827), a *History of Ireland* (1835–46), and biographies of Thomas Sheridan (1825), and (ironically in view of his destruction of his friend's own autobiographical work) of Byron (1830).
Bib: White, T. de V., *Tom Moore: The Irish Poet*.

More, Hannah (1745–1833)
An eminent ▷ Bluestocking, More settled in London in 1774, where she became the friend of Garrick, ▷ Johnson, ▷ Burke and ▷ Richardson. She was a conservative Christian feminist who opposed ▷ Mary Wollstonecraft on women's rights. As well as tragedies, such as *Percy* (1777), poetry and writings about social reform, such as *Village Politics* (1793), she published *Coelebs in Search of a Wife* (1809), a novel which, despite hostile reviews, proved an immense success. Her correspondence is lively and entertaining.
Bib: Jones, M. G., *Hannah More*.

More, Sir Thomas (St Thomas More) (1478–1535)
Scholar, thinker and statesman. He was the leading ▷ humanist of his day, and a friend of ▷ Erasmus. For some time he was a particular favourite of Henry VIII, who raised him to the Lord Chancellorship, the highest office in the state. However, More firmly refused to recognize the king's divorce from Queen Katharine and the Act of Supremacy (1534). For this the king executed him, and the Catholic Church canonized him exactly 400 years later.

More's *History of King Richard III* (1513) has been called the first masterpiece of ▷ history and biography in English, but his principal work ▷ *Utopia* (1516) was in Latin, translated into English in 1551. Famous as a patron of letters and the arts, he invited the painter Holbein to England.
▷ Catholicism (Roman) in English literature.
Bib: Surtz, E. (ed.), *Selected Works*, Sylvester, R. S., Harding, D. P. (eds.), *The Life of Sir Thomas More*; Hexter, J. H., *More's 'Utopia': The Biography of an Idea*; Greenblatt, S., *Renaissance Self-fashioning*.

Morier, James Justin (1780–1849)
Travel writer and novelist. Morier was a diplomat stationed in Persia and his ▷ travel books, *A Journey Through Persia* (1812) and *A Second Journey Through Persia* (1818) describe his experiences there. In 1817

he resigned his post and devoted himself to writing novels which also reveal the influence of his life in Persia: *The Adventures of Hajji Baba of Ispahan* (1824) is a ▷ picaresque tale of an ordinary Persian artisan, and made an important contribution to the growing fashion of Orientalism.

Morning Chronicle
A London ▷ Whig ▷ newspaper founded in 1769; its contributors included Sheridan, ▷ Lamb, James Mill, ▷ John Stuart Mill, ▷ Dickens, and ▷ Thackeray. It came to an end in 1862.

Morning Herald, The
A London ▷ newspaper, 1780–1869. It had a large circulation, and published police cases, illustrated by the famous artist ▷ George Cruikshank, illustrator of Dickens's novel ▷ *Oliver Twist*.

Morning Post, The
A conservative but highly independent London newspaper, founded 1772, ceased 1936. Wordsworth, ▷ Coleridge and Southey contributed to it.

Morris, William (1834–96)
Poet, socialist thinker, designer and printer. He was one of the leading artists of his day, associated with, though not a member of, the Pre-Raphaelite Brotherhood, which sought to recover the cultural unity of medieval society. It is a designer of textiles and wallpapers that he is most admired today. His aim was to counteract the industrial squalor of Victorian England, and to correct the major social injustice by which the proletariat were cut off from beauty of any sort by the nature of their environment: 'I don't want art for a few, any more than education for a few, or freedom for a few.' Paradoxically his campaign against aesthetic barbarism went with rejection of the machine and insistence on handwork, which cut him off from the economic realities of his age.

This withdrawal from social and political complexities is in keeping with his poetry which expresses withdrawal into the romances of the Middle Ages (*Defence of Guinevere*, 1858; *Earthly Paradise*, 1868–70); into ancient Greek ▷ epic (*Life and Death of Jason*, 1867; translation of Virgil's ▷ *Aeneid*, 1875, and of ▷ Homer's ▷ *Odyssey*, 1887); and into Icelandic epic (*Sigurd the Volsung*, 1876). His verse (the majority of it translation) was voluminous, fluent, decorative and musical in the Spenserian tradition current in the Victorian period.

Nonetheless, his socialism was a reality. He was one of the founders of the Socialist League (1884) and edited its monthly periodical *Commonweal*, until in 1890 the anarchist wing of the movement drove him out. His *News from Nowhere* (1891 – previously contributed to *Commonweal*) is a prose 'utopia' describing England at a future date after the establishment of socialism. It is one of the most read of his works today. Another work of socialist inspiration, in mixed prose and verse, is *A Dream of John Ball* (1888).
Bib: Henderson, P., *Life*; Mackail, J. W., *Life*; Hough, G., *The Last Romantics*; Jackson, H., *Morris: Craftsman-Socialist*; Thompson, E. P.,

Morris: Romantic to Revolutionary; Lewis, C. S., in
Rehabilitations.

Morrison, Arthur (1863–1945)

Novelist and short-story writer. Born in Poplar,
Morrison worked as a journalist, contributing tales of
East End life to ▷ *Macmillan's Magazine* (published
as *Tales of Mean Streets*, 1894). His subsequent
novels *A Child of the Jago* (1896) and *The Hole in
the Wall* (1902) are also ▷ naturalistic accounts of
slum life. Morrison also wrote ▷ detective fiction
(*The Dorrington Deed Box*, 1897, in the manner of
▷ Conan Doyle), and later became a distinguished
Orientalist.

Mphahlele, Es'kai (b 1919)

South African novelist, short-story writer and critic.
He was educated at the University of South Africa
in Pretoria and the University of Denver, USA. He
worked as a clerk and as an English teacher in South
Africa and was fiction editor of *Drum* magazine
(1955–57) before leaving on an exit permit (which
forbade re-entry to the country) in 1957; he was not
to return for 20 years. In the 1960s he was director
of African cultural programmes in Paris and in
Nairobi, Kenya and then edited the journals *Black
Orpheus* and *Journal of New African Literature and the
Arts* in Ibadan, Nigeria. He held lecturing posts at
universities in Nigeria, Kenya, Zambia and the USA
before returning to South Africa in 1987, where
he lectured at the University of Witwatersrand,
Johannesburg and became director of a community
education project in Soweto. His early short stories,
collected in *Man Must Live* (1947), portrayed life
in the urban black ghettos of South Africa with a
degree of humour; later stories, in *The Living and
Dead* (1961) and *In Corner B* (1967), have a stronger
element of protest. He has written two novels, *The
Wanderers* (1971), a partly autobiographical account
of South African intellectuals in exile, and *Chirundu*
(1979), a political novel about a post-independence
African state. His critical work *The African Image*
(1962) was an early and influential account of African
fiction and he also edited *Modern African Stories*
(1964, with E. Komey) and *African Writing Today*
(1967); Mphahlele has played an important role in
developing and promoting African literature. His
most recent work of fiction is the volume of short
stories *Renewal Time* (1988). He has published two
autobiographical works: *Down Second Avenue* (1959)
and *Afrika My Music: An Autobiography 1957–1983*
(1984) as well as essays, books for children and
works on education and creative writing; see *The
Unbroken Song: Selected Writing of Es'kai Mphahlele*
(1981). His letters have been published as *Bury
Me at the Crossroads: Selected Letters of Es'kai
Mphahlele* (1984).
Bib: Barnett, U. A., *Es'kai Mphahlele*; Manganyi,
N. C., *Exiles and Homecomings: A Biography of Es'kai
Mphahlele*.

Mrs Dalloway (1925)

A novel by ▷ Virginia Woolf. Set in London, it is the
story of one day in the life of Clarissa Dalloway, the
wife of Richard Dalloway, a Member of Parliament

(the Dalloways appeared in Woolf's earlier novel,
The Voyage Out). Clarissa spends the day preparing
for a party she is to give that evening, a party which
provides the culmination of the novel. The ▷ stream
of consciousness narrative represents the thoughts
of Clarissa and a range of other characters with
whom she is acquainted, or connected by chance
occurrences of the day. Throughout the novel,
memories of the past are blended with present
sensations, and the narrative builds up a highly
poetic evocation of the atmosphere of London and
of the interaction of different lives. The principal
characters, apart from the Dalloways, are: their
daughter Elizabeth and her embittered and envious
tutor, Miss Kilman; Peter Walsh, with whom Clarissa
was in love during her youth; Sally Seton, Clarissa's
girlhood friend, and Lady Bruton, a society hostess.
In contrast to this group, whose lives are linked,
are Septimus Warren Smith and his wife Rezia;
Septimus is in a highly disturbed state after his
experiences during World War I and the news of
his suicide intrudes on Clarissa's party, brought by
Sir William Bradshaw, a manipulative psychiatrist
whom Septimus had consulted. The novel ends with
the affirmation of life joined to an awareness of loss
and death.

Mudie, Charles Edward (1818–90)

Son of a bookseller, Mudie founded Mudie's
Circulating Library, which loaned books to the public
for a fee. Beginning in Bloomsbury, he expanded to
Oxford Street where the business ran for many years.
Along with other ▷ circulating libraries, Mudie's
exercised a noticeable moral censorship in the
selection of books.

Muir, Edwin (1887–1959)

Autobiographer, critic, poet, and novelist. He spent
his childhood on a farm in the Orkney Islands,
from which his father was compelled by economic
hardship to move to Glasgow. For several years
Muir struggled to earn his living in Glasgow as a
clerk in various businesses; he became interested in
socialism, and started writing. In 1919 he married,
moved to London, and became a journalist.
Thereafter, he travelled widely in Europe, and held
a number of teaching posts. In 1940 he produced
the first version of his autobiography, *The Story
and the Fable*, expanded, revised and republished as
Autobiography in 1954. The experiences of his own
lifetime afforded him deep insight – social, cultural,
spiritual. He had moved from a pre-industrial
society in Orkney to 20th-century industrialism at its
grimmest in Glasgow. He was deeply aware of the
Scottish roots of his culture, and was liberated from
their limitations partly through ▷ German literature
and thought – ▷ Nietzsche, Heine, Hölderlin; in
the 1930s he and his wife Willa translated Kafka.
Experience of psychoanalysis liberated the deeper
levels of his imagination, and led him, through
illumination about the relationship of man to his
natural environment, to strong and unusually
lucid religious feeling. His *Autobiography* is a
modern classic.

His birthplace, Orkney, has had some measure of

detachment from the history of the rest of Scotland, and it is partly this that enabled him to show some of the most penetrating perceptions about modern Scottish culture in *Scottish Journey* (1935) and *Scott and Scotland* (1936). His critical works include: *Latitudes* (1924); *Transition* (1926); *The Structure of The Novel* (1928); *The Present Age* (1939); *Essays on Literature and Society* (1949).

His poetry includes: *Journeys and Places* (1925); *Variations on a Time Theme* (1934); *The Narrow Place* (1943); *The Labyrinth* (1949); and *One Foot in Eden* (1956).

His novels are: *The Marionette* (1927); *The Three Brothers* (1931); *Poor Tom* (1932). Biography: *John Knox* (1929).

▷ Autobiography; Scottish fiction in English.
Bib: Knight, R., *Edwin Muir; an Introduction to His Work*; Butter, E., *Edwin Muir, Man and Poet*.

Murdoch, Iris (b 1919)
Novelist and philosopher. Her novels are: *Under the Net* (1954); *Flight from the Enchanter* (1955); *The Sandcastle* (1957); *The Bell* (1958); *Bruno's Dream* (1960); *A Severed Head* (1961; dramatized 1963); *An Unofficial Rose* (1962); *The Unicorn* (1963); *The Italian Girl* (1964; dramatized 1967); *The Red and the Green* (1965); *The Time of the Angels* (1966); *The Nice and the Good* (1968); *A Fairly Honourable Defeat* (1970); *An Accidental Man* (1971); *The Black Prince* (1973); *The Sacred and Profane Love Machine* (1974); *A Word Child* (1975); *Henry and Cato* (1976); *The Sea, The Sea* (1978); *Nuns and Soldiers* (1980); *The Philosopher's Pupil* (1983); *The Good Apprentice* (1985); *The Book and the Brotherhood* (1987); *A Message to the Planet* (1989).

Iris Murdoch is one of the most prolific and the most popular of serious contemporary novelists. Born in Dublin and educated at Somerville College Oxford and Newnham College Cambridge, she has lectured in philosophy. Her husband is the critic John Bayley. Her profession as a philosopher is reflected in many aspects of her fiction. She has written a study of the work of Jean-Paul Sartre (*Sartre, Romantic Rationalist*, 1953) and her interest in, and dissent from Sartre's ▷ existentialism is evident in her first two novels, which treat existential issues of identity and freedom. These concerns have persisted in her work, but *The Bell* and *The Time of the Angels* introduce religious themes, while since *The Nice and the Good* many of her novels have directly addressed ethical questions. *The Good Apprentice*, for example, explores the idea of a character who, without explicit religious faith, sets out to be good. Although her works are novels of ideas, they combine this with exciting and sometimes macabre plots, elements of the grotesque and supernatural and touches of social comedy. They are highly structured, both by the use of symbolism, and by the patterning of shifting personal relationships.

Her plays include: *The Three Arrows* (1970); *The Servants and the Snow* (1973); *Art and Eros* (1980). Other works are: *The Sovereignty of Good* (1970); *The Fire and the Sun: Why Plato Banished the Artists* (1977); *Acastos: Two Platonic Dialogues* (1986); *Metaphysics as a Guide to Morals* (1992).

Bib: Conradi, P., *Iris Murdoch: the Saint and the Artist*; Johnson, D., *Iris Murdoch*; Todd, R., *Iris Murdoch*; Byatt, A.S., *Degrees of Freedom: The Novels of Iris Murdoch*.

Murry, John Middleton (1889–1957)
Critic. His own struggles to achieve personal integration, his close relationship with
▷ D. H. Lawrence, and his marriage to the story-writer ▷ Katherine Mansfield, led him to write about a number of writers relating their personal lives to their art: *Dostoevsky* (1916), *Keats and Shakespeare* (1925), *Studies in Keats* (1930), *William Blake* (1933), *Shakespeare* (1936), *Jonathan Swift* (1954). He is perhaps best known for his controversial study of D. H. Lawrence, *Son of Woman* (1931), and for the *The Problem of Style* (1922). He was editor of the ▷ *Athenaeum* from 1919 to 1921, and published the work of a number of major writers, including ▷ Virginia Woolf.
Bib: Lea, F. A., *The Life of John Middleton Murry*.

Musgrave, Agnes (fl. c 1800)
Novelist. Little is known of Musgrave's life, but she was a best-selling ▷ Minerva novelist from 1795 to 1801. Intriguingly, her first work is a supposed history of the Musgrave family through the female line from medieval times to her own age; it is supposedly discovered and recounted by the author. *Edmund of the Forest* (1797), *The Solemn Injunction* (1798) and *The Confession* (1801) followed Musgrave's first novel, but they are all conventionally sensational and ▷ Gothic.

Myers, Leopold Hamilton (1881–1944)
Novelist. His father, F. W. H. Myers (1843–1901) was a characteristic product of the 19th-century ▷ agnosticism so prominent among the educated classes; his reaction against it took the form of attempts to prove the existence of the soul by scientific experiment; he was one of the founders of the Society for Psychical Research. The son's concern with the spiritual life took the form of seeking answers to the question 'Why do men choose to live?'. His chief opponents in his pursuit of the answer were not scientific rationalists in the tradition of ▷ T. H. Huxley, but aesthetes of the Bloomsbury tradition, who left moral experience to look after itself while they cultivated enjoyment of 'states of mind'. He also regarded the great influence on English writing of the French novelist, ▷ Marcel Proust (1871–1922) as pernicious, because Proust likewise esteemed experience aesthetically and not morally. Myers considered that this led to the trivializing of life, and his novels dramatize the opposition between those who interpret experience through moral discrimination and those who vulgarize it by regarding it as a means to aesthetic experience only; from the latter evil arises. He regarded civilized society as corrupted by its moral indifference.

His first novel, *The Orissers* (1922) presents the issue in bare terms, but his principal work was the sequence of novels about 16th-century India, published together as *The Near and the Far* in 1943.

Myers chose the remote setting of India under the Emperor Akbar because he wanted to escape from the secondary preoccupations of daily life in modern England, and to treat moral and spiritual issues with the large scope which the India of that date, with its multiplying religions and philosophies, afforded him. Evil is represented in the novel through Akbar's son Prince Daniyal, intelligent, artistic, but morally nihilistic, and rival of his merely stupid brother Salim for succession to the throne. Good is expressed through the character of the Guru (teacher) of the last section (*The Pool of Vishnu*): 'All communion', he says, 'is through the Centre. When the relation of man and man is not through the Centre it corrupts and destroys itself.' In his later years he became a ▷ Communist. He committed suicide in 1944. Other novels include: *The Clio* (1925); *Strange Glory* (1936).
▷ Bloomsbury Group.
Bib: Bantock, G. H., *L. H. Myers: A Critical Study*.

Mysteries of Udolpho, The (1794)

A novel by ▷ Mrs Ann Radcliffe. It achieved great fame in its own day, and is often cited as the typical ▷ Gothic novel. It is mainly set in a sombre castle in the Apennine mountains in Italy. The atmosphere is of secret plots, concealed passages, abductions, and the supernatural. ▷ Jane Austen satirized the taste for such sensational literature in ▷ *Northanger Abbey*.

N

Naipaul, Shiva (1945–85)
Trinidadian novelist, travel writer and journalist.
Born in Port of Spain, Trinidad, the brother of
▷ V. S. Naipaul, he was educated at Queens Royal
College, Trinidad, St Mary's College, Trinidad
and at University College Oxford. His first two
novels are both set among the Hindu community in
Trinidad: *Fireflies* (1970 and *The Chip-Chip Gatherers*
(1973), which won the Whitbread Award. *A Hot
Country* (1983) is a study of English expatriates in
a fictional South American country. *North of South:
An African Journey* (1978) presents a critical view of
East African societies, showing racism, corruption
and inequality. *Journey to Nowhere: a New World
Tragedy*, first published as *Black and White* (1980), is
about the 1978 Jonestown Massacre in Guyana, in
which 900 sect members committed suicide on the
orders of their leader. *Beyond the Dragon's Mouth:
Stories and Pieces* (1984) includes essays, stories and
autobiographical fragments.

Naipaul, V. S. (Vidiahar Surajprasad) (b 1932)
Trinidadian novelist of Indian descent. Educated at
Queens Royal College, Port of Spain, Trinidad, and
Oxford University, he settled in England in 1950.
His brother was the novelist ▷ Shiva Naipaul. V.
S. Naipaul is the most admired of contemporary
Caribbean novelist writing in English and has won
many literary awards, including, in 1993, the first
David Cohen British Literature Prize. His work is
concerned with personal and political freedom, the
function of the writer and the nature of sexuality,
and is characterized by fastidiousness, clarity,
subtlety, and a detached irony of tone. His earlier
novels, *The Mystic Masseur* (1957), *The Suffrage of
Elvira* (1958) and *Miguel Street* (1959) convey both
the vitality and the desolation of Trinidadian life.
The Mimic Men (1967) is a satirical examination of
the economic power structure of an imaginary West
Indian island. *A House for Mr Biswas* (1961), often
regarded as his masterpiece, tells the tragicomic
story of the search for independence and identity
of a Brahmin Indian living in Trinidad. His other
novels are: *Companion* (1963); *In A Free State* (1971);
Guerillas (1975); *A Bend in the River* (1979); *The
Enigma of Arrival* (1987). Naipaul has also produced
essays, criticism, journalism, autobiography and travel
writing, including: *The Middle Passage* (1962); *An Area
of Darkness* (1964); *A Congo Diary* (1980); *The Return
of Eva Peron* (1980); *Among the Believers: An Islamic
Journal* (1981); *India: A Million Mutinees Now* (1981);
Finding the Centre (1984).
Bib: Hamner, R. D. (ed.), *Critical Perspectives
on V. S. Naipaul*; Theroux, P., *V. S. Naipaul: An
Introduction to His Work.*

Namjoshi, Suniti (b 1941)
Indian short-story writer and poet. Namjoshi was
born in Bombay and educated at the University
of Poona in India and at Missouri and McGill
Universities in the USA. Drawing on Indian legends,
fables, poems and oral story-telling traditions, she has
written feminist fables and versions of fairy stories,
a practice she shares with a number of English
feminists such as ▷ Angela Carter. Prose works:
Feminist Fables (1981); *The Conversations of Cow*
(1985); *Aditi and the One-Eyed Monkey* (1986); *The
Blue Donkey Fables* (1988); *The Mothers of Maya Diip*
(1989). Her volumes of poetry include: *The Jackass
and the Lady* (1980); *The Authentic Lie* (1982); *Flesh
and Paper* (1986); *Because of India* (1989).

**Narayan, R. K. (Rasipuran Krishnaswami)
(b 1906)**
Indian novelist and short-story writer. His novels
are: *Swami and Friends* (1935); *The Bachelor of Arts*
(1937); *The Dark Room* (1938); *The English Teacher*
(1945); *Mr Sampath* (1949); *The Financial Expert*
(1952); *Waiting for the Mahatma* (1955); *The Guide*
(1958); *The Man Eater of Malgudi* (1961); *The Vendor
of Sweets* (1967); *The Painter of Signs* (1976); *A Tiger
for Malgudi* (1983); *Talkative Man* (1986). His novels
are set in the imaginary southern Indian community
of Malgudi, based on the town of Mysore, which
he uses to epitomize Indian culture from the days
of the Raj to the present. The early novels show the
continuing influence of British culture, in particular
on the education system, and contain elements of
▷ autobiography. His work attains a new seriousness
with *The English Teacher*, which is based on his
own marriage and the early death of his wife. His
mature work deals with spirituality and with human
weakness, corruption, failure and lack of fulfilment
in an ironic and sceptical manner, supported by the
vivid realization of the life of the town. *The Guide*,
the story of a con man who becomes a saint, is one
of his outstanding works, while *A Tiger for Malgudi*
represents an excursion into a fantasy mode; drawing
on the Hindu doctrine of reincarnation, it has a
tiger as its hero and narrator. Story collections are:
Malgudi Days (1943); *Dodu* (1943); *Cyclone* (1944); *An
Astrologer's Day* (1947); *Lawley Road* (1956); *A House
and Two Goats* (1970); *Old and New* (1981); *Malgudi
Days* (1982) (not the same as the 1943 volume);
Under The Banyan Tree (1985); *Mr Sampath – The
Printer of Malgudi* (1990). Narayan has also written
travel literature, memoirs, essays and versions of the
Indian epics *The Ramayana* and *The Mahabharata;
Gods, Demons and Others* (1990) is based on Indian
myths and legends.
Bib: Walsh, W., *R. K. Narayan: a Critical Appreciation.*

Narrating or narration/narration (French)
Terms in ▷ narratology denoting the act of telling a
▷ story, which takes place in a ▷ narrative.

Narrative or text/récit (French)
Terms denoting the objects of study in ▷ narratology.
The narrative informs the reader of the ▷ story and
implies the existence of the act of ▷ narrating.

Narratology
The systematic study of the structures, forms and
modalities of narrative, including questions of
temporal arrangement or tense (▷ order, ▷ duration,
▷ frequency), ▷ mood (the manner of narration
and point of view, including ▷ focalization), and
▷ voice (the identity and relationship to the action
of the ▷ narrator and narratee). Early considerations

of narratological questions are found in ▷ Henry James's Prefaces (1907–9) and ▷ E.M. Forster's book ▷ *Aspects of the Novel* (1927). Wayne Booth's *The Rhetoric of Fiction* (1961) inaugurated a more wide-ranging and systematic approach, while the influence of ▷ structuralism produced the rigorous analysis of categories of narrative typified by ▷ Gérard Genette's *Narrative Discourse* (1980). There is a more accessible summary of this approach in Shlomith Rimmon-Kenan's *Narrative Fiction: Contemporary Poetics* (1983).

Narrator

A fictional person or consciousness who narrates all or part of a text. A narrator may be a character within a story, who then tells a story, such as Marlow in ▷ Conrad's ▷ *Heart of Darkness*; this is known as an intradiegetic narrator. Alternatively, a narrator may be extradiegetic, that is, outside the story that he or she narrates, like the narrator of ▷ Fielding's ▷ *Tom Jones* (who has a strong personality, but does not participate in the story as such), or like the largely impersonal and uncharacterized narrator of ▷ Henry James's ▷ *The Ambassadors*. Such extradiegetic narrators are different from the ▷ implied author since they may be unreliable narrators (▷ Narrator, unreliable).

Narrator, unreliable

A ▷ narrator who cannot be relied upon to provide accurate information, so that the reader is obliged to try to deduce, from the possibly misleading account given by such a narrator, the true facts of the case. A narrator may be unreliable because of limited knowledge or understanding (*eg* the idiot Benjy in the first section of William Faulkner's *The Sound and the Fury*), because of being in a disturbed state of mind (*eg* the governess, in one possible reading of ▷ *The Turn of the Screw* by ▷ Henry James), because of personal bias or dubious moral values (*eg* Dowell in ▷ Ford Madox Ford's *The Good Soldier*), or out of sheer wilfulness (*eg* the narrator of ▷ Peter Carey's *Illywhacker*). Unreliable narration tends to emphasize the subjective nature of truth and the technique often tends towards the implication that there is no such thing as an objective viewpoint.

Nashe, Thomas (1567–1601)

Pamphleteer, poet and playwright. He spent six years at St John's College, Cambridge, and is numbered among the University Wits who made the decade 1590–1600 an unusually lively period in literature. Two features of this liveliness were ▷ satire and prose romance (sometimes called 'the Elizabethan novel'). Nashe contributed to both: his best known work, ▷ *The Unfortunate Traveller, or the Life of Jack Wilton* (1594), is one of the outstanding romances of the decade, and it includes some of his best satire, often in the form of ▷ parody of some of the contemporary styles of fine writing. Most of the rest of his satire was also in prose. *Pierce Penniless, His Supplication to the Devil* (1592) is a satire in the tradition of the allegorical Morality plays; an attack on the qualities that made for success in the London of his day, and a denunciation of them as new

versions of the Seven Deadly Sins; the method looks forward to Ben Johnson's Comedy of Humours. His last work, *Lenten Stuff* (1599), is a comic extravaganza on Yarmouth, a fishing town, and the red herring. Other prose work includes his early ▷ pamphlets attacking the Puritan side in the Marprelate controversy and vigorous disagreement with Gabriel Harvey on literary and moral questions between 1593 and 1596. His *Christ's Tears over Jerusalem* (1593) records his repentance for religious doubts.

Nashe was sent to prison in 1597 for an attack on abuses in his play *The Isle of Dogs*, which has been lost. The only play of his sole authorship which survives is *Summer's Last Will and Testament* (1592). This defends the traditional festivities of the countryside against Puritan condemnation of them, and at the same time attacks the useless extravagance of courtiers. It includes some very fine lyrics, especially *In Plague Time* and *Autumn*.

Nashe is chiefly known as a prose writer; his prose is notable for the abundance of its energy which compensates for the confusion of its organization. His gift for parody and the rapidity and vividness of his expression show that the greater coherence and lucidity which English prose was to achieve in the 17th century was not all gain. The freedom and zest of his comic writing owe something to earlier Renaissance writers – the Italian poet and comedian Pietro Aretino and the great French satirist ▷ François Rabelais.

Bib: McKerron, R. B. (rev.), *The Works of Thomas Nashe* (5 vols); Hibbard, G. R., *Nashe: A Critical Introduction*; Ryan, K., 'The Extemporal Vein; Thomas Nashe and the Invention of Modern Narrative' in J. Hawthorn (ed.), *Narrative from Malory to Motion Pictures*.

Nationalism

The emotion or the doctrine according to which human egotism and its passions are expanded so as to become identical with the nation state. As a widespread phenomenon it is usually dated from the American War of Independence (1775–83) and from the ▷ French Revolution and the wars that followed it. This makes it an especially 19th and 20th-century phenomenon, which it undoubtedly is, but on the other hand intense national self-consciousness existed among the older European nations before, though without the fanaticism which has been characteristic of it since 1790. Thus strong national feeling arose in England and France, in consequence of the Hundred Years' War in the 15th century; it arose again in the 16th and 17th centuries under the English queen Elizabeth I and the French king Louis XIV respectively. Possibly these earlier emotions should be distinguished as patriotism, but the distinction is vague. During the 1990s nationalism in Europe seems to be becoming a renewed force, and a renewed danger, following the break-up of the old Soviet power-bloc.

Natural Law

According to theologians (*eg* Richard Hooker, 1533–1600), that part of the Divine Will that manifests itself in the order of the material world:

distinguishable from but of a piece with human and divine law. Modern scientists define it as the principles of uniformity discernible in the behaviour of phenomena, making such behaviour predictable. For the 18th century, the existence of Natural Law was important as the basis for ▷ Natural Religion.

Natural Philosophy

In the 17th and 18th centuries, the study of physics and kindred sciences. Interest in Natural Philosophy became organized and heightened with the establishment in 1662 of the Royal Society, which took the whole of knowledge as its province. The natural philosophers included such eminent persons as Isaac Newton (1642–1727), the chemist Robert Boyle (1627–91), and the naturalist John Ray (1627–91), and the naturalist John Ray (1627–1705). They were religious men and made their religion accord with their science. However, in spite of the respect accorded to some of them, especially Newton, intellectuals in the period 1660–1730 tended to react against natural philosophy with angry contempt. They were provoked not so much by the fear of the injury such thought might do to religious faith – this was much more a 19th-century reaction – as by disgust at the triviality of much scientific inquiry, the technical fruits of which were slow to appear. The most notable satire was Swift's 'Laputa' in Part III of ▷ *Gulliver's Travels*. Other examples were Samuel Butler's *Elephant in the Moon*, some of the ▷ *Spectator* essays of Addison and Steele, and the *Memoirs of Martinus Scriblerus*, published with the works of Alexander Pope in 1741, though the principal author seems to have been John Arbuthnot (1667–1735).

Natural Religion

A belief first taught by Lord Herbert of Cherbury (1583–1648); according to him, belief in God and right conduct are planted in human instincts. This Christian doctrine was the basis for deistic thought in the later 17th and 18th centuries, and contributed to the growth of religious toleration, though also to passivity of religious feeling and hence to indifference. Herbert's aim was to resolve the doubts arising out of the religious conflicts of his time. For the reaction against Deism, see William Blake's propositions in *There is No Natural Religion* (1788).

Naturalism

In literature, a school of thought especially associated with the novelist ▷ Emile Zola. It was a development of ▷ Realism. The Naturalists believed that imaginative literature (especially the novel) should be based on scientific knowledge, and that imaginative writers should be scientifically objective and exploratory in their approach to their work. This means that environment should be exactly treated, and that character should be related to physiological heredity. Influential in France and Germany, the movement counts for little in Britain; the novelists ▷ George Gissing and ▷ Arnold Bennett show traces of its influence in the treatment of environment in relation to character.

▷ French influence on English fiction.

Nature

The word is used throughout English literature with meanings that vary constantly according to period or to mode of expression, *eg* philosophic, religious or personal. This note is intended to guide the student by showing some of the basic approaches to the idea.

1 *Creation and the Fall.* Fundamental to all conceptions of Nature is traditional Christian doctrine. This influences English writers even when they are using a more or less agnostic or atheistic approach. The doctrine is that Nature is God's creation, but by the fall of man, symbolized by the story of Adam's disobedience in the book of *Genesis*, earthly nature is self-willed and destructive, though not to the extent that the Divine Will and Order is obliterated in it.

2 *All-embracing Nature.* Nature is sometimes seen as the whole of reality so far as earthly experience goes. For instance, the opening 18 lines of ▷ Chaucer's *Prologue to the Canterbury Tales* show Nature as the great reviver of life. This use of the word has a different kind of significance in the 18th century when scientific Reason has replaced the religious imagination as the familiar vehicle for the interpretation of reality. See **4** *Nature and Truth*.

3 *Nature and God.* In line with traditional Christian doctrine, Natural Law is linked to Human Law and Divine Law as a manifestation of the Divine Will, in such works as Hooker's *Laws of Ecclesiastical Polity* (1597). However, from the beginning of the 17th century, there was a new interest in the function of human reason as an instrument for the acquisition of knowledge independently of religious feeling. Men like Ralegh (*History of the World*, 1614) and Bacon (*The Advancement of Learning*, 1605) began to ask what, given that God was the Primary Cause of Nature, were the Secondary, or Immediate, Causes of natural phenomena. Newton's work on gravitation (*Principia Mathematica*, 1687) and ▷ Locke's ▷ *Essay concerning Human Understanding* seemed to solve the problem, causing people to see God as the Divine Artificer whose Reason could be discerned in the government of even the smallest phenomena, as well as in the great original act of Creation.

4 *Nature and Truth.* Nature is, in the 18th century, Truth scientifically considered. 'To follow Nature' (*eg* in works of imaginative literature) may mean: (i) to present things and people (*eg* an imagined character) as they really are; (ii) to reveal truths that lie beneath appearances; (iii) to follow rational principles. It was the attempt to 'follow Nature' in these ways that constituted the main discipline of the novelists ▷ Defoe, ▷ Richardson, ▷ Fielding, ▷ Smollett.

5 *Nature as Moral Paradox.* The Christian conception of Nature as both God-created and spoilt by the fall of man led at various times to the problem that Nature is both good and evil. According to the medieval conception, maintained until the middle of the 17th century, human society was itself the outcome of the Divine Natural Order, so that it was by Natural Law that children should honour their parents, subjects their sovereigns, etc. On the other hand, the natural passions of men and beasts, unrestrained by reason, were the source of rapacity and ruin. Thus Shakespeare's King Lear begins by relying on the former conception of Nature, but he is exposed to the reality of the latter.

19th-century natural science revived the feeling that Nature was essentially destructive, and hostile or at best indifferent to men; this is the 'Nature red in tooth and claw' image of Tennyson's *In Memoriam* (1850), set against the idea of the love of God. The atheistic ▷ Thomas Hardy saw men as subjected to the irony of indifferent fates, and the natural environment as governed in the same way.

6 *Nature for Man's Use.* Implicit in Christian doctrine was the belief that Nature was created *for* man; that it was his birthright to exploit and use it. This begins with the conception of Nature as the Great Mother, originating in pre-Christian times but pervasive in medieval verse and later, *eg* in much Elizabethan pastoral poetry. It took a more active significance when the 17th- and 18th-century 'natural philosophers' from Bacon onwards sought methods by which man could increase his power over Nature; 18th-century poetry commonly shows Nature as beautiful when she is productive under the ingenuity of human exploitation.

7 *Nature and Art.* 'Art' in earlier contexts often includes technology, *eg* in Polixenes' remarks on cultivation to Perdita in *The Winter's Tale* IV. iii; here art is seen as itself a product of nature. But art was often set against nature in Shakespeare's time and afterwards, *eg* in ▷ Sidney's *Apology for Poetry*: 'Her [*ie* Nature's] world is brazen; the Poets only deliver a golden'; here the function of imaginative art seems to be the opposite of the 18th-century poets' and novelists' conception of 'truth to nature', but Sidney meant that poetry should improve on Nature, not falsify it; the creation must be ideal but consistent with Nature.

8 *Nature opposed to Court and City.* 'Art', however, was not necessarily an improvement. The city and the court, in Shakespeare's time, were the centres of new financial forces generating intrigue and 'unnatural' (*ie* inhuman) behaviour. There was also a kind of pastoral made by idealizing the life of the great country houses, *eg* Ben Jonson's *Penshurst*. In the 18th century poets like James Thomson wrote about natural surroundings for their own sake, and sometimes included wild nature as their subject, but it was Wordsworth who gave to wild nature its importance as the principal subject of what later came to be known as 'nature' poetry.

9 *Nature in Communion with the Individual.* Wordsworth was to some extent anticipated in the 18th century by such a poet as William Cowper, and his teacher was especially ▷ Jean-Jacques Rousseau. It was Wordsworth above all, however, who gave to Nature its modern most familiar sense – as the non-urban, preferably wild environment of man, to which the depths of his own nature always respond. Here he finds a communion which refreshes the loneliness of his spirit in a relationship which underlies and gives meaning to his human relationships.

Nennius

Welsh monk and reputed compiler of a 9th-century *Historia Brittonum* (*History of the Britons*), which provides an outline of British history, from the founding of the island by Brutus, used by ▷ Geoffrey of Monmouth as a framework for his historical narrative. Arthur is mentioned as a British battle leader (not a king), who fights 12 battles, culminating in the battle of Badon, in which he fells 960 men at one charge.

New Atlantis, The (1626)

A philosophical tale by Francis Bacon 1561–1626, in the tradition of ▷ Sir Thomas More's ▷ *Utopia* (1615). It was left unfinished at Bacon's death, and published in 1626. The title is an allusion to the mythical island described by ▷ Plato in his dialogue *Timaeus*. Bacon's island is called Bensalem (*ie* an analogous place to Salem or Jerusalem, the holy city) and its chief glory is its university, 'Solomon's House'. Unlike the English universities of Bacon's day, this is devoted to scientific research – 'the knowledge of causes, and secret motions of things; and the enlarging of the bounds of human empire, to the effecting of all things possible'. The boundless optimism of this Baconian ideal was to be reflected in the work of 17th-century science in general.

New Criticism

This term is given to a movement which developed in the late 1940s in the USA, and which dedicated itself to opposing the kind of criticism that is associated with Romanticism, and 19th-century realism. The 'practical criticism' of I. A. Richards (1893–1979) was an influential stimulus to this movement in which emphasis was placed upon the self-contained nature of the literary text, as were the critical writings of T. S. Eliot. In the work of 'new' critics such as Cleanth Brooks, W. K. Wismatt, John Crowe Ransom, Allen Tate, and R. P. Blackmur, concern with the 'intention' of the writer was replaced by close reading of particular texts, and depended upon the assumption that any literary work was self-contained. New Criticism placed a particular emphasis upon poetry, and asserted that the individual poem 'should not mean but be'.

New Grub Street (1891)

A novel by ▷ George Gissing. The title refers to ▷ Grub Street, which was inhabited in the 18th century by journalists of a low order, who wrote to gain a living without seriousness of intention or artistic standards. The living they earned was generally a mean one, but since 1875 the new periodicals and newspapers had found a way to achieve massive circulations by printing material which had an immediate appeal although its intrinsic quality was trivial or merely sensational. This commercialization of journalism had spread to the production of books. Gissing's novel is about the difficulties of the serious literary artist faced by successful competition from the now very well rewarded commercial writer without scruples, either moral or artistic. The serious writer in the book is Edwin Reardon (a self-portrait) and his successful competitor is Jasper Milvain. Commercial success is also illustrated by Whelpdale, editor of the magazine *Chit-Chat* (based on the actual magazine *Titbits* founded in 1881) which never publishes articles longer than two inches in length. At the other extreme is the novelist Biffen, who has the artistic fastidiousness of the French novelist ▷ Flaubert and writes the same kind of book. Biffen and Reardon both end in failure but Gissing's novel was fairly popular, which perhaps argues against the extreme pessimism of his thesis.

▷ Journalism; Newspapers.

New historicism
A theoretical movement which developed in America in the 1980s, partly as a reaction against the ahistorical approaches of ▷ New Criticism and the unselfconscious historicism of earlier critics. New historicism draws upon Marxist criticism in its emphasis upon political and social context and rejection of individual aspiration and universalism, but at the same time it insists that historical context can never be recovered objectively. New historicists do not assume that literature reflects reality and that these 'reflections' enable the reader to recover without distortion the past presented in the texts. Rather, they look for an interplay between text and society, which can never be presented neutrally. Moreover, readers must be aware of their *own* historical context: we read texts from the perspective of our own age and can never perfectly re-create history.

▷ Cultural materialism; Marx, Karl; Poetics.
Bib: Greenblatt, S., *Renaissance Self-fashioning*; Howard, J. E. and O'Connor, M. F., *Shakespeare Reproduced*; Tennenhouse, L., *Power on Display*; Veeser, H. A., *The New Historicism*.

New Monthly Magazine
It started in 1814 and had editors of considerable literary note such as the poets Thomas Campbell and Thomas Hood, the novelists ▷ Harrison Ainsworth and ▷ Bulwer-Lytton, and the essayist Theodore Hook. It gave considerable space to criticism. It closed in 1884.

New Statesman and Society, The
The leading left-wing weekly periodical of the intelligentsia. It was founded in 1913; its Conservative counterpart is ▷ *The Spectator*. In politics it has always followed a general line of ▷ Fabian socialism.

New Woman, The
A term popularized in the 1890s by journalists and literary reviewers, it was used in a general and often ill-defined way to describe the modern ▷ feminist figure who was emerging in the press and in novels (though to a lesser extent in real life) and who caused considerable shock to conventional opinion by the radicalism of her ideas. Although there was never any identifiable single movement with which she was associated, the New Woman was thought to embody all that was most advanced in feminist ideology. Broadly, her beliefs included rejection of marriage, a more honest and direct approach to female sexuality, and a demand for the reorganization of society so as to give women economic and personal independence. Early literary representations of the New Woman are found in Henrick Ibsen's play *The*

Doll's House (produced in England in 1889) and in ▷ Olive Schreiner's *The Story of An African Farm* (1883). During the 1890s a type of novel known as 'The New Woman Fiction' enjoyed considerable notoriety, several of its kind becoming best-sellers. Amongst these were ▷ Sarah Grand's *The Heavenly Twins* (1893), ▷ George Egerton's *Keynotes* (1893) and ▷ Grant Allen's *The Woman Who Did* (1895). Several established novelists were also accused of embodying New Woman figures in their novels of the 1890s, including ▷ Thomas Hardy in ▷ *Jude the Obscure* and ▷ George Gissing in *The Old Women*. The New Woman as a popular stereotype did not outlast the Victorian age and early 20th-century feminism concentrated its energies more on the suffrage movement than on the New Woman's ideals of personal integrity and sexual freedom.
Bib: Cunningham, G., *The New Woman and the Victorian Novel*; Stubbs, S., *Women and Fiction: Feminism and the Novel 1880–1920*; Showalter, E., *Sexual Anarchy*.

Newcomes, The (1853–5)
A novel by ▷ William Makepeace Thackeray; it was published in instalments. The characters are drawn from the middle and upper classes, and the book is a study of the vices and virtues of such mid-19th-century society. The vices are shown in the worldly cynicism of Lady Kew who seeks a fashionable marriage for her grand-daughter Ethel Newcome; in the mean snobbery of Ethel's brother Barnes, who frustrates her marriage with her cousin Clive Newcome; in the hypocrisy, intrigue and viciousness of Clive's eventual mother-in-law Mrs Mackenzie, and in the philistinism and arrogance of the social world as a whole. The virtues are less successfully presented. Clive Newcome's father, Colonel Newcome, is the honourable, single-minded soldier who loses his fortune and is subjected to the tyranny of Mrs Mackenzie. Thackeray was inclined to see decency as overwhelmed by materialism.

Newgate novel
Strictly speaking, a novel of which the characters and/or elements of plot are taken from *The Newgate Calendars*, which were records of notorious crimes, named after Newgate Prison in London and published at various dates between 1773 and 1826. Examples are *Rookwood* (1834) by ▷ William Harrison Ainsworth and *Paul Clifford* (1830) by ▷ Bulwer-Lytton, and, more loosely, a novel about criminals, such as ▷ *Oliver Twist* (1837) by ▷ Charles Dickens. Newgate novels provoked a furious debate in the 1830s and 40s, because they often showed some sympathy for criminals and suggested that social conditions contributed to crime; they were attacked as morally corrupting by some critics, including the novelist ▷ Thackeray.

Newman, John Henry (1801–90)
Writer on religion and education. From 1833 to 1842 he was one of the most influential and controversial leaders of the Church of England, but in 1845 he was received into the Roman Catholic Church. As a Catholic convert he was

even more influential, and he was made a Cardinal in 1879.

His first period of activity (1833–42) was as leader of the Tractarian Movement – more or less identical with the ▷ Oxford Movement – whose aim was to defend the Church of England against encroachments by the state on the one hand, and against adulteration of its doctrines by the Broad Church tendencies on the other. The Church of England was founded in the 16th century on a central position between the Catholicism of Rome and the whole-hearted ▷ Protestantism of Luther and Calvin. This had always been both its strength and its weakness; it was able to accommodate a variety of believers, but it was inclined to lose itself in vagueness and become subservient to the state. Newman's *Tracts for the Times* tried to secure a firm basis for Anglican doctrine and discipline, as against supporters of the Broad Church party (such as ▷ Thomas Arnold) who cared less for doctrine than for social ethics. Newman's tracts led him steadily towards Roman Catholicism, however, until his *Tract XC* went so far as to say that the Anglican 39 Articles – which all clergy had to accept – were not incompatible with essential Roman Catholic beliefs, but only with distortions and exaggerations of them.

As a Roman Catholic, Newman's first valuable literary work was *The Scope & Nature of University Education* (1852), a collection of lectures to the new Catholic University of Dublin, of which he became Rector in 1854. These were combined with further lectures delivered in 1859 to make *The Idea of a University Defined* (1873). His spiritual autobiography, defending the sincerity of his Catholic beliefs against the accusations by the Broad Churchman, ▷ Charles Kingsley, came out with the title *Apologia pro Vita sua (Defence of his Life)* in 1864. It was not only very persuasive in convincing the public of the genuineness of his faith; it was also an eloquent and lucid presentation of the nature of religious belief at a time when much religious thinking in English was muddled, superficial and entangled in irrelevant controversies with scientific agnostics such as ▷ T. H. Huxley. His *Grammar of Assent* (1870) was a more strictly philosophical account of religious belief.

Newman also wrote some minor poetry, including the famous hymn *Lead Kindly Light*, and the ▷ dramatic monologue *The Dream of Gerontius*, better known for the music set to it by Elgar. He also wrote two religious novels – *Loss and Gain* (1848) and *Callista* (1856).

As a writer he is famous for the lucidity and grace of his style. His wide influence, still very powerful, arose from his ability to understand the tragic extremity of the emotional and intellectual bewilderment of his contemporaries, while refusing to compromise his beliefs.

▷ Agnosticism.
Bib: Harold, C. F., *Newman: an Expository and Critical Study of his Mind, Thought and Art.*

Newspapers
Periodicals resembling newspapers began in a small way in the reign of James I; in the decades of the Civil War and the Interregnum they increased in number owing to the need of either side to engage in propaganda. From 1695 press ▷ censorship was abandoned; newspapers and weekly periodicals began to flourish.

The first English daily, the *Daily Courant*, a mere news-sheet, began in 1702, but in the earlier part of the 18th century papers more nearly resembling what we now know as the weekly reviews were of greater importance, and leading writers conducted them, *eg* ▷ Defoe's *The Review* (thrice weekly – 1704–13); ▷ Steele's *Tatler* (thrice weekly – started 1709); Steele and Joseph Addison's ▷ *Spectator* (daily – started 1711); and the ▷ *Examiner* (started 1710), to which the chief contributor was ▷ Jonathan Swift. ▷ Samuel Johnson's ▷ *Rambler* (1750) was of the same kind. Of these men, only Defoe resembled fairly closely what we nowadays regard as a journalist as distinct from a man of letters.

The first attempt to reach a mass circulation was made through this kind of periodical by ▷ William Cobbett with his *Weekly Political Register* (started 1802), and in 1808 Leigh Hunt's weekly *Examiner*, directed to a more educated public through with less remarkable literary merit, began to rival Cobbett's paper as a medium of radical comment and criticism.

Of daily papers founded in the 18th century, the ▷ *Morning Post* (started 1772) survived until 1936, and ▷ *The Times* (started 1785) is today the daily with the greatest prestige, though it has a comparatively small circulation. Other important dailies with a shorter life were the ▷ *Morning Chronicle* (1769–1862), and the ▷ *Morning Herald* (1780–1869). Both reached peak circulations of about 6,000. To reach the very large circulations of today, newspapers had to await the abolition of the stamp duty – a tax on newspapers – in 1855. The Stamp Tax was started in 1712. It was a method of restricting circulations by raising the prices of newspapers. The government of the day resented criticism of its policies but did not dare revive the Licensing Act, the lapsing of which in 1695 was really the start of the British freedom of the press. The abolition of the tax, together with the advent of cheap paper and a nationwide potential public thanks to universal literacy, led to a new kind of newspaper at the end of the 19th century. Alfred and Harold Harmsworth; later Lord Northcliffe and Lord Rothermere, founded the *Daily Mail* in 1896; by 1901 it was selling a million copies. Other popular newspapers followed it with steadily increasing circulations.

Several unfortunate consequences have followed this development:

1 Much ▷ journalism has degenerated into mere commerce, so that news is regarded as what is most saleable, *ie* what appeals most readily to the baser and more easily roused human appetites.

2 Newspapers, in order to keep their prices down, have come to rely on advertising revenue, which is attracted chiefly to those with very large circulations so that some with smaller circulations have been eliminated.

3 The British newspapers have divided rather sharply into the serious ones with a large influence but a small circulation, and the popular ones or

tabloids, which often achieve their large circulations by irresponsible appeals to the baser public tastes. Finally, modern newspapers, as great capitalistic enterprises, tend to be right-wing politically, so that left-wing opinion is under-represented in the daily press. However, British newspapers are jealous of their independence: they are quick to resist any tendency by the government to check their freedom of expression. Since the war, the Press Council has been established for the purpose of limiting the abuse of this freedom by, for instance, the infringement of personal privacy; however, its powers are limited to public rebuke, and it has no power to penalize or censor newspapers. In 1990 the Press Complaints Commission was established.

The 20th-century weekly reviews have seldom been able to compete with the daily papers in the size of their circulations. However, the strong tradition of weekly journalism inherited from the 18th and 19th centuries ensures that the 'weeklies' have large influence among the intelligentsia. The oldest of the influential weeklies is the *Spectator* which has no connection with Addison's periodical, but was founded in 1828. It is conservative and is counter-balanced by ▷ *The New Statesman and Society* on the left. The most influential literary periodicals in Britain are *The Times Literary Supplement*, a weekly which is published by *The Times* newspaper and the *London Review of Books*, published every two weeks.

Ngcobo, Lauretta (b 1932)

South African novelist and critic. Ngcobo now lives in Britain having escaped from South Africa during the 1960s, when she was threatened with arrest as a member of the Pan-African Congress. Her two novels are about black resistance to the apartheid regime and to white oppression in South Africa: *Cross of Gold* (1981) is about a revolutionary fighter, while *And They Didn't Die* (1990) is about a woman's struggle for life and autonomy. Ngcobo edited *Let It Be Told* (1987), a collection of essays by black women writers in Britain.

Ngugi wa Thiong'o (b 1938)

Kenyan novelist, short-story writer and playwright. Educated at the universities of Makere in Kenya and Leeds in Britain, Ngugi was a fierce critic of the Kenyan regime and campaigner for the rights of the rural poor in Kenya, and was held in solitary confinement after the performance of his play *Ngaahika Ndeenda* (written with Ngugi wa Mirii, translated as *I Will Marry When I Want*, 1982) and the publication of his novel *Petals of Blood* (1977), which attacks economic exploition from a Marxist perspective. Ngugi has lived in exile since 1982. He published four novels in English, a fifth in both English and Gikuyu (the language of the people of the Kenyan highlands) and since 1982 has not written in English. Some of his work was published under the name James T. Ngugi. *Weep Not, Child* (1964) and *The River Between* (1965) were both written while the author was still a student; the first is the story of a boy growing up during the period of the Mau Mau rebellions, while the second is based around the symbolic separation of two

villages and set during the rebellion of the 1920s; *A Grain of Wheat* (1967) portrays the time leading up to Independence. These novels combine realism with elements of the symbolic and of parable and, explore collective values through the thoughts and experiences of individuals. *Devil on the Cross* (1982) represents a shift towards a more allegorical and fantastic mode, used for a direct polemical attack on bourgeois exploitation. The novel *Matigari* (1986) was translated into English in 1987. Plays: *The Black Hermit* (1962); *This Time Tomorrow* (1966); (with Micere Githae Mugo) *The Trial of Dedan Kimathi* (1976). Short stories: *Secret Lives* (1975). Other writings include: *Homecomings: Essays on African and Caribbean Literature, Culture and Politics* (1972); *Writers in Politics: Essays* (1981); *Detained: A Writer's Prison Diary* (1981); *Barrel of a Pen: Resistance to Repression in Neo-Colonial Kenya* (1983); *Decolonising the Mind: The Politics of Language in African Literature* (1986).

Nicholas Nickleby (1838–9)

A novel by ▷ Charles Dickens; like his other novels, it was first published in serial parts. Nicholas, his sister Kate and their mother are left penniless and struggle for a living under the oppressive guardianship of Ralph Nickleby, an avaricious financier, the dead Mr Nickleby's brother. Morally, the tale is in black and white; Nicholas stands for ardent and youthful virtue, Ralph for meanness and cruelty. Nicholas is sent to teach at Dotheboys Hall, an iniquitous school run by Wackford Squeers to whom Nicholas gives a vigorous thrashing. Kate is apprenticed to Madame Mantalini, a dressmaker, where she is exposed to the vicious advances of Ralph's associate, Sir Mulberry Hawk. Nicholas beats him too. Ralph's evil intentions are eventually exposed by his eccentric but right-minded clerk, Newman Noggs, and the Nickleby family are befriended by the Cheeryble brothers. The novel is in Dickens's early, episodic and melodramatic style but many of the episodes are presented with great vividness and comedy. It was dramatized, with huge success, by the Royal Shakespeare Company in 1980.

Nichols, Grace (b 1950)

Poet and novelist. Born in Guyana where she worked as a teacher, journalist and information assistant, and educated at the University of Guyana, Nichols came to live in Britain in 1977. Her publications include a biting attack on colonialism in *i is a long memoried woman* (1983) (which won the Commonwealth Poetry Prize), and the playfully ironic *The Fat Black Woman's Poems* (1984). Her first novel was *Whole of a Morning Sky* (1986), set in Guyana in the 1960s. She also writes ▷ children's books.

▷ Post-colonial fiction.

Nietzsche, Friedrich Wilhelm (1844–1900)

German philosopher. He challenged the concepts of 'the good, the true, and the beautiful' as, in their existing form of abstract values, a decadent system at the mercy of the common man's will to level distinctions of all kinds. He set his hope on the will to power of a new race of men who would assert their own spiritual identities. Among his more famous works are a book on the philosopher Schopenhauer and the composer Wagner, whom he regarded as his own teachers: *Unzeitgemässe Betrachtungen* ('Thoughts out of Season'; 1876); *Die Fröhliche Wissenschaft* ('The Joyful Wisdom'; 1882); *Also sprach Zarathustra* ('Thus spake Zarathustra'; 1891).

Nietzsche was one of the important progenitors of ▷ existentialism, and he had a considerable influence on some of the major English writers in the first quarter of this century. His ideas inspired George Bernard Shaw (1856–1950) in the latter's belief in the Superman-hero as the spearhead of progress, *eg* his conception of Joan of Arc in his play *Saint Joan*, and ▷ D. H. Lawrence wrote in Nietzsche's spirit in his affirmation of spontaneous living from deep sources of energy in the individual – human 'disquality' (see ▷ *Women in Love*, ch. 8) as opposed to democratic egalitarianism. The Irish poet W. B. Yeats (1865–1939) also affirmed a natural aristocracy of the human spirit, and saw in Nietzsche a continuation of the message of the poet William Blake, who preached the transcendence of the human 'identity' over the 'self', which is defined and limited by the material environment. After 1930, Nietzsche's influence declined because he was seen as a prophet of the more vicious forms of ▷ fascism. However, in recent criticism Nietzsche's work has been re-evaluated by ▷ post-structuralist theory, especially with regard to his discussion of metaphor and metonymy (▷ Figures of Speech) and the privileging of a rhetorical reading of philosophical texts.

▷ German influence on English fiction.

Nightmare Abbey (1818)
A novel by ▷ Thomas Love Peacock. It is a satire on the current taste for ▷ Gothic mystery and Romantic despair. Mr Glowry and his son Scythrop own the Abbey; Scythrop is in love with two girls, like Peacock's friend, the poet Shelley. Mr Flosky is a satirical portrait of ▷ Coleridge in his aspect as a transcendental mystic, and Mr Cypress represents Byron's self-centredness. There are other characters of cheerful temperament to counteract the Romantic sombreness of these. The plot is slight, but the comic fantasy is sustained by it and by the conversations which are always the greater part of a Peacock novel.

Nineteenth Century, The
A monthly review founded in 1877 by J. T. Knowles, its first editor. It was renamed *The Nineteenth Century and After* in 1900, and *The Twentieth Century* in 1950. It was distinguished for bringing together leading antagonists of opposing views. Contributors included ▷ Ruskin, Gladstone, ▷ T. H. Huxley, ▷ Beatrice Webb, ▷ William Morris, ▷ Ouida and ▷ Oscar Wilde.

Nominalism
One of the two main schools of late medieval philosophy, the other being ▷ realism. The nominalists argued that terms naming things according to their kinds ('animal', 'vegetable', etc) and abstract terms ('beauty', 'goodness', etc) are merely names describing the qualities of things and do not refer to things that have reality in themselves. The realists argued that on the contrary such 'universals' alone have an ultimate reality and that the reality of individual objects depends upon them. The nominalist viewpoint is represented in modern philosophy by such thinkers as ▷ John Stuart Mill and other 'empiricist' philosophers who reason that reality can only be known by particular experience of it, and argue against any theory of implanted ideas such as the Deists believed in. In 20th-century political philosophy, nominalism has been opposed to essentialism (which resembles realism by believing in transcendent universals); see Karl Popper, *The Poverty of Historicism*.
Bib: Knowles, D., *The Evolution of Medieval Thought*.

Nonsense literature
This covers several kinds of literature, which have in common that they all in some way deliberately defy logic or common sense, or both. In English folk literature, many nursery rhymes come into the category. The most important kind, however, is undoubtedly in ▷ children's literature, especially the poems of Edward Lear and the *Alice* stories by ▷ Lewis Carroll, both of which are to be taken seriously as literature. Both writers are Victorian and this perhaps accounts for their imaginative depth; they wrote in a period of intense mental restlessness before the time of ▷ Freud and thus they gave themselves wholly to their fantasies, undisturbed by the idea that they might be betraying secrets of their own nature. Modern writers, *eg* ▷ James Joyce in his ▷ *Finnegans Wake*, will as fearlessly reveal their depths, but it will not be to children. Another reason why nonsense literature reached its peak in the Victorian period is perhaps that this was almost the earliest period when intelligent minds considered that children were worth writing for merely in order to amuse them, and not to elevate their minds. 20th-century writers in plenty have thought children worth amusing but the child-public is now a recognized one, whereas Lear and Carroll wrote for a few young friends; they were thus as much concerned with their own interest and amusement as with that of their audience.

North and South (1854–5)
A novel by ▷ Elizabeth Gaskell published serially (1854–5) by ▷ Charles Dickens in his periodical ▷ *Household Words*. The heroine, Margaret Hale, moves from the rural south of England to the industrial north, Lancashire. The sharp contrast between the two halves of England is equalled by the misunderstandings and savage opposition between employers and employees in the northern town. Margaret becomes involved in the affairs of one of the employers, John Thornton, with whom she too has deep misunderstanding. Suffering eventually brings them together and teaches Thorton the necessity of treating his workers as human beings and not merely as factors in industrial calculation. Like her earlier ▷ *Mary Barton*, this novel is a

courageous penetration of the industrial jungle which she knew at first hand; both are attempts, like Dickens's ▷ *Hard Times*, to modify the harshness of the industrial world with humane values, though Gaskell's unwillingness to question the so-called laws of *laissez-faire* economics weakens her analysis politically, while the romantic conclusion to the novel diverts attention into the personal realm.

North Briton, The

It was a radical political weekly, started in 1762 by ▷ John Wilkes and Charles Churchill. It opposed the government of George III and his Prime Minister, the Scotsman Lord Bute, and was aimed particularly against Bute's journal *The Briton*, edited by the Scottish novelist, ▷ Tobias Smollett. After 45 issues it was suppressed.

North, Sir Thomas (?1535–?1601)

Translator. He is especially known as the translator of Plutarch's *Lives* of the ancient Greek and Roman heroes. The translation was from the French of Amyot, and was published in 1579. It was not close, but very clear and vigorous, and constituted one of the masterpieces of English prose. It was widely read in Shakespeare's day, and was used by Shakespeare himself as the basis for his plays *Julius Caesar, Antony and Cleopatra*, and *Coriolanus*. Other translations by him were: the *Dial of Princes* (from *Reloj de Príncipes* by Guevara) published in 1557, which set the fashion for ornate writing culminating in Lyly's ▷ *Euphues*; and *The Moral Philosophy of Doni* (1570), an Italian collection of Eastern fables.

Northanger Abbey (1818)

A novel by ▷ Jane Austen. It was stated in 1798 and incompletely revised when it was published (in 1818 after her death) with her last completed novel ▷ *Persuasion*.

The book is in part a satire on the sensational and sentimental literature of the time, particularly of the enormously popular ▷ *Mysteries of Udolpho* by ▷ Mrs Radcliffe. The heroine is an ingenuous young girl, Catherine Morland, who visits the fashionable resort of Bath and afterwards, with some friends she has made there, the country house of Northanger Abbey. She is healthy-minded and trusting but very suggestible; on the one hand she is entirely deceived by the worldly flattery of her scheming friend, Isabella Thorpe, who tries to marry Catherine's brother under the mistaken impression that he is very rich, and on the other hand she suspects (under the influence of Mrs Radcliffe's novel) that Northanger Abbey conceals terrible secrets. Its owner, General Tilney, is the father of the man she loves and is in fact almost as cold-hearted and inhumane as she suspects him of being, but in quite a different way; he has not, as she at first suspected, murdered his wife, but he turns Catherine out of the house at very short notice from purely mercenary motives. The theme of the book is partly the danger of confusing literature and life, a theme to which Jane Austen returns in ▷ *Sense and Sensibility* and ▷ *Emma*; it is also that life is as surprising and remorseless as the most Romantic literature but in quite a different way.

Northcliffe, Alfred Harmsworth Viscount (1865–1922)

One of the principal founders of the 'popular press' with its very large circulation, and in particular of the *Daily Mail* (1896).
▷ Newspapers.

Nostromo (1904)

A novel by ▷ Joseph Conrad. The setting is an imaginary South American state called Costaguana, intended to be typical of that continent; all the events occur in or near Sulaco, capital city of the Occidental Province in Costaguana. At the beginning of the novel, Costaguana is ruled by a brutal and corrupt dictator after a short period of enlightened and liberal rule. The Occidental Province, however, remains a refuge of enlightenment and comparative prosperity, thanks partly to its geographical isolation from the rest of the country, and mainly to the existence of a large silver mine, run by an Englishman, Charles Gould, who secures the financial support of an American millionaire. In outline, the story is the history of how the Occidental Republic establishes its independence of the rest of the country, but at the same time loses the ideals which inspired it in the struggle.

Each of five main characters serves as a focus for a strand of narrative:

1 Charles Gould (nicknamed 'King of Sulaco'), in his struggles to save the mine from ruin by the corrupt government, becomes the centre of the party of freedom and justice; but he becomes increasingly dehumanized by his preoccupations, and estranged from his wife, whose values of humaneness and compassion are betrayed, despite the eventual triumph of her husband's party.

2 Captain Mitchell, the Harbourmaster, is another Englishman; stupid, but honest and courageous, he is unable to see beneath the surface of events, and is used by Conrad to record these deceptive appearances.

3 Gian'Battista Fidanza, the Italian chief of the dockworkers, is universally known as 'Nostromo' ('Our Man'). He has a romantic pride in the devotion of his men, and in the knowledge that Mitchell, Gould, and their associates have complete confidence in his integrity. His spiritual downfall, unknown to any but himself, is due to his desire to preserve the appearance of integrity while yielding to secret dishonesty.

4 Martin Decoud is the journalist of the Sulacan revolution; he is totally French by education and culture, though not by descent. He is cynically entertained by the spectacle of Costaguaneran politics, but romantically attached to Antonia Avellanos, daughter of José, a Sulacan scholar and liberal politician. He dies of the physical isolation brought upon him by circumstances, since his highly cultivated consciousness is incapable of sustaining a sense of his own reality when the spectacle of events and the woman he loves are removed from him.

5 Dr Monygham is an Irishman, embittered by his self-contempt arising from his betrayal, under torture, of his political associates. His humanity is preserved by his devotion to Mrs Gould, who is for

him the uncontaminated embodiment of what is good in human nature.

These are only the chief characters, and they do not exhaust the novel's large cast. They are united by the theme of individual isolation even in co-operation with one another, and by a discrete pattern of symbols, of which the chief is the silver of the mine. This operates at first as an instrument of liberation, and later as a force of corruption; all the time it is a symbol of the illusiveness of human idealism. The novel depicts the pervasive and debasing effects of 'material interests' (primarily the economic power of US business). The narrative structure is highly complex, and uses shifts of chronology and retrospective narration to combine a detailed account of 17 days of crisis with a sense of the broad sweep of historical events.

Nouveau roman (new novel)
A French literary movement originating in the late 1950s and associated principally with Nathalie Sarraute (b 1902), Claude Simon (b 1913), Michel Butor (b 1926), Robert Pinget (b 1919) and Alain Robbe-Grillet (b 1922). Their common concern was a challenge to narrative assumptions based on strictures of the orderly unfolding of plot and life-like characters moving in a recognizable universe. These assumptions, however widely held, suppose that literature is mimetic, that it imitates life. The *nouveau roman* set out to challenge the illusion of reference (that the novel 'refers' to life) insofar as reference is tied to representation. It held that the so-called naturalness of narrative was a set of artifices to which we had become accustomed and that narrative order and significance were an illusion fostered by the omniscient author. For the 'new' novelists, representation is not an a priori given; it is produced. Drawing on the work of ▷ André Gide and ▷ Marcel Proust, notably Gide's ▷ *mise en abyme* technique, the *nouveau roman* will therefore expose its own means of production and raise the problem of its own narrative existence. Correspondingly, the role of the reader is also revised. He or she is called upon to co-author the text, to act not as a passive recipient of information, but as an active producer of meanings. Indeed, given the fragmentary or elliptical nature of *nouveau roman* narrative presentation, the reader's search for meaning is often thematized as an (impossible) attempt to solve an enigma (the *nouveau roman* frequently adopts the detective story format).

The impact of the *nouveau roman* was greatly magnified by the fact that the practice of novel writing was accompanied by thorough-going critical reflection on that practice. The novelists themselves were also heavily engaged in theory and frequently worked alongside professional academic theoreticians or were allied to magazines such as ▷ *Tel Quel*. Of the original group of new novelists, Robbe-Grillet and Simon are still strong practitioners. While the mainstream of the English novel has been little affected, the techniques of the *nouveau roman* have influenced writers such as ▷ Christine Brooke-Rose and ▷ Brigid Brophy. In the 1970s there emerged

the new new novel (*nouveau nouveau roman*), centring on the novelist and theorist Philippe Sollers (b 1936) and displaying many of the traits of ▷ deconstructive and ▷ post-structuralist principles.
Bib: Robbe-Grillet, A., *Pour un Nouveau Roman*.

Novel in verse
The novel in verse is not a recognized or clearly defined genre; most candidates for inclusion in this category belong to other, well-established genres: ▷ *The Odyssey* is an epic; ▷ *Sir Gawain and the Green Knight* (late 14th century) is an alliterative romance; Wordsworth's autobiographical *magnum opus*, *The Prelude* (1805), is a philosophical poem; Byron's ▷ *Don Juan* (1819–24) is a mock-epic satire. The category is worth proposing only because it indicates a fruitful area of overlap between the novel and other genres, including some curiosities such as *Amours de Voyage* (1858) by Arthur Hugh Clough, which is a short epistolary novel in verse. ▷ David Jones's *In Parenthesis*, a sustained narrative about the First World War, is partly in verse and partly in prose that is so poetic it might be termed a prose poem; the poet Ezra Pound described his modernist sequence of poems, *Hugh Selwyn Mauberley* (1920), as 'an attempt to condense the [Henry] James novel'. There have been some remarkable recent achievements in this area: *Omeros* (1990), by the poet Derek Walcott, is a lyrical and poetic reworking of Homeric epic in a Caribbean context, but contains some richly novelistic description, characterization and episode. *Love, Death and the Changing of the Seasons* (1987), by the American poet Marilyn Hacker, is the story of a lesbian relationship, recounted with a witty intensity that places it in the tradition of the Renaissance sonnet sequence, whereas ▷ Vikram Seth's *The Golden Gate* (1986), although written entirely in a variation of sonnet form, is essentially a novel: plot and character predominate, rather than linguistic artifice and meditation.

Novella
In modern usage the novella is a long short story or short novel, such as ▷ Joseph Conrad's ▷ *Heart of Darkness* (1902), or ▷ Henry James's *The Aspern Papers* (1888). The French term '*nouvelle*' is sometimes used with the same meaning. The *novella* (Italian), or *nouvelle* (French), was also a Renaissance genre, a short prose narrative of the sort found in ▷ Boccaccio's ▷ *Decameron*, and was one of the forms out of which the novel developed.

Nwapa, Flora (b 1931)
Nigerian novelist and short-story writer. Much of Nwapa's fiction is concerned with questions of isolation, support and autonomy, as it bears on women. Her novels are: *Efuru* (1966); *Idu* (1970); *One is Enough* (1981 – the title refers to husbands); *Women Are Different* (1986). Volumes of short stories: *This Is Lagos* (1986); *Wives at War* (1980).
Bib: James, A., *In Their Own Voices: Interviews with African Women Writers*.

O

O'Brien, Edna (b 1932)
Novelist and short-story writer, born in County
Clare, Ireland. Novels include: *The Country Girls*
(1960); *The Lonely Girl* (1962) (as *Girl With Green
Eyes*, 1964); *Girls in Their Married Bliss* (1964); *August
is a Wicked Month* (1965); *Casualties of Peace* (1967);
A Pagan Place (1970); *Night* (1972); *Johnny I Hardly
Knew You* (1977); *The High Road* (1988); *Time and
Tide* (1992). Her novels are concerned primarily with
women's experience of loss, guilt and self-division;
they are characterized by a certain lyricism and
nostalgia, combined with a detached humour which
has become more bitter as her work has developed.
Her first three novels form a trilogy about the lives
of two contrasted women, and use a realistic mode
which is replaced by internal monologues in some
of her later work. Her style is very effective in the
short-story form: *The Love Object* (1968); *A Scandalous
Woman* (1974); *Mrs Reinhardt* (1978); *Returning*
(1982); *A Fanatic Heart: Selected Stories* (1984);
Lantern Slides (1990). She has also written plays,
screenplays and television plays.

O'Brien, Flann (1911–66)
Pseudonym of Brian Nolan, author of hilarious,
learned, parodic, linguistically exuberant novels,
which anticipate many features of ▷ post-modernist
metafiction: *At Swim-Two-Birds* (1939), which
incorporates pastiche and parody of Irish folklore;
An Béal Bocht (1941 in Gaelic, translated 1973
as *The Poor Mouth*); *The Third Policeman* (written
1940, published 1967). O'Brien was born in County
Tyrone and educated at University College Dublin;
he was a civil servant and also wrote a weekly
satirical column in the *Irish Times*.

Observer, The
A ▷ newspaper published only on Sundays, started
in 1792. It is central in its politics, and aims to appeal
to a liberal and left-wing readership. In 1993 it was
bought by the daily newspaper The *Guardian*.

**O'Connor, Frank (pen name of Michael
O'Donovan) (1903–66)**
Irish writer, especially famous for his short stories.
He was born in Cork, received little education, and
for some time worked as a librarian in Cork and
Dublin. He was encouraged to write by the Irish
poet A.E. (George Russell), and his publisher,
Harold Macmillan (later the English Conservative
Party leader) influenced him in deciding on a literary
career. He participated in the Irish Rebellion after
World War I. His first volume of short stories, *Guests
of the Nation*, was published in 1931. Other volumes
are: *Bone of Contention* (1936), *Three Tales* (1941),
Crab Apple Jelly (1944), *The Common Chord* (1948),
Traveller's Samples (1951), *My Oedipus Complex*
(1963). His translations of poetry and legends from
the Irish are also famous: *A Golden Treasury of Irish
Poetry* (1967). He wrote two novels which have less
repute than his short stories: *The Saint and Mary
Kate* (1932) and *Dutch Interior* (1966). His critical
works include one of the best studies of the art of the
short story, *The Lonely Voice*, and a study of the novel,

The Mirror in the Roadway. He also published two
volumes of an uncompleted autobiography, *An Only
Child* and *My Father's Son*. From 1952 he taught in
an American university.

O'Connor's stories are remarkable for their
insight, comedy, pathos and compassion. His field
was the lower ranges of Irish society, which he
understood profoundly, and which he universalized
by his generous intelligence and sympathies in a way
that recalls Chekhov's treatment of Russian life.
Bib: Sheehy, Maurice (ed.), *Michael/Frank*.

Odyssey
An ▷ epic by the ancient Greek poet ▷ Homer. The
hero, Odysseus King of Ithaca, is on his way home
after the Trojan war, but he is blown off course and
the return journey takes him ten years. The principal
episodes of his voyage are as follows:

1 The land of the Lotus-Eaters. Those who eat of
the lotus plant forget their homeland.

2 The land of the Cyclops. These are a race of
one-eyed giants. Odysseus puts out the eye of the
Cyclops Polyphemus, who is son of Poseidon, god
of the sea; it is to punish him for this that Poseidon
sends him wandering for ten years.

3 The Isle of Aeolus, king of the winds. Odysseus
steals from him the bag in which the winds are
contained, but his companions open it too soon, and
the winds escape.

4 Telepylus, the city of the cannibal
Laestrygonians. They destroy his fleet except one
ship, in which he escapes.

5 The Isle of Circe. She transforms his men into
swine, but with the aid of the god Hermes, he resists
her enchantments, compels her to restore his men,
and remains in the island as her lover for a year.

6 He visits the Underworld, Hades, to learn
from the prophet Tiresias the way home. Tiresias
warns him against harming the cattle of the sun-
god, Helios.

7 He evades the enchanting songs of the Sirens,
who try to lure him on to the rocks.

8 He passes through the strait of Scylla and
Charybdis – a treacherous rock and a whirlpool.

9 He comes to the Island of Thrinacia (Sicily)
where the cattle of Helios live, which the ghost of
Tiresias has warned him not to harm, but overcome
by hunger, his companions devour them.

10 In punishment, his ship is wrecked and all
his men perish, but Odysseus reaches the island
of the goddess Calypso, who keeps him prisoner
for seven years as her lover. He eventually
escapes, with the aid of the goddess Athene,
and reaches the lands of the Phaeacians where
Nausicaa and her father, the king of the country,
befriend him. The narrative of all the above
events comes to the reader through Odysseus,
who tells them to the king. The king helps
him back to Ithaca. There, with the help of
his son Telemachus, he kills the suitors who
have been pestering the chaste Penelope, his
queen.

The *Odyssey* has had a considerable influence
on the novel, most notably ▷ *Ulysses*, by ▷ James
Joyce.

Oedipus

In Greek myth, a character first mentioned by ▷ Homer as having (unknown to himself) killed his own father and married his own mother. In later versions the story was filled out: his father, King Laius of Thebes, was warned by an oracle that his son would kill him, and ordered that the child Oedipus should be destroyed; he was accordingly exposed in a waste place, but a shepherd rescued him; ignorant of his parentage, he later returned to Thebes, and on the way there, killed his father in consequence of a wayside quarrel; on his arrival at Thebes, he saved the city from the Sphinx and married his mother, Jocasta. Sophocles's *Oedipus the King*, tells of his subsequent discovery of his parentage and the consequences of this discovery; Sophocles also dramatized Oedipus' death in *Oedipus at Colonus*.

The ▷ 'Oedipus Complex' is the name for a discovery by the psychoanalyst ▷ Sigmund Freud that children tend to feel sexual attraction to the parent of the opposite sex, and corresponding jealousy towards the parent of the same sex.

▷ Psychoanalytical criticism.

Oedipus complex

In ▷ Freudian psychoanalysis Sophocles's story of ▷ Oedipus who killed his father and married his mother, is used as a model of the way in which human desires and feelings are structured during the passage from infancy to adulthood. The triangular relationship modelled on Sophocles's text can be used to explain relationships within the family which is the model of socialization available to the child. In order for successful socialization to occur, the child must emerge from the position of desiring an incestuous relationship with individual parents – for which in the case of the male, the penalty would be castration – and to transfer the affections for the mother onto another. The difficulties which this sometimes causes are illustrated in novels such as ▷ D. H. Lawrence's ▷ *Sons and Lovers* where Paul Morell is faced with having to transfer his affections for his mother onto other women. The Oedipus complex, and the model of triangulated desire upon which it is built, must be overcome in order for individual gendered human subjects to take their place in a world of which they are not the centre. This process of 'decentring' is explained by ▷ Jacques Lacan as an acceptance of the repression of desire imposed upon the subject by the father, an acceptance of a 'symbolic castration'. This raises a number of difficulties in the case of the gendered *female* subject who can never break free of the castration complex imposed upon her by a phallocentric ▷ symbolic order. Basically the Oedipus complex is used to account for a particular hierarchy of relationships within the family unit. It is a process through which the male is expected to pass in order to reach mature adulthood, and it seeks to offer an explanation of the ways in which authority operates as a system of constraints and laws.

O'Faolain, Sean (1900–91)

Irish novelist and writer of short stories. He was born in Dublin and attended the National University of Ireland and Harvard University in the USA. He participated in the Irish Rebellion following World War I, and later lived in England as a teacher. His novels include *A Nest of Simple Folk* (1933) and *Bird Alone* (1936). His first volume of stories, *Midsummer Night Madness* (1932), vividly reflects the atmosphere of the Irish disturbances. A collected edition of the stories was published in 1958, and in 1966 he published a further volume, *The Heat of the Sun*. Among his other writings are two biographies which are studies of Irish leaders, one on Daniel O'Connell entitled *King of the Beggars* (1938), and *The Great O'Neill* (1942). His critical work includes *The Short Story* (1948). His autobiography *Vive Moi!* appeared in 1965. He was made Director of the Arts Council of Ireland in 1957.

O'Flaherty, Liam (1897–1984)

Irish novelist and writer of short stories. Born in the Aran Islands he was educated for the Roman Catholic priesthood, but did not enter it. He fought in World War I, and settled in England in 1922. His first volume of stories, *Spring Sowing*, was published in 1926; it contains stories of Irish peasant life and wild nature. At his best, his stories have the intensity of fine lyric poetry, and he is peculiarly gifted at representing the exhilaration and poignancy of life directly exposed to natural forces. Other volumes of stories include: *The Mountain Tavern* (1929), *The Wild Swan* (1932), *Two Lovely Beasts* (1948). His novels include *The Informer* (1925) – made into a film in 1935 and the historical *Famine* (1937). His autobiography is entitled *Shame the Devil* (1934).

Okri, Ben (b 1959)

Novelist and short-story writer, educated in Nigeria and at the University of Essex. During the 1980s he was poetry editor of *West Africa* magazine and worked for the BBC World Service 1984–5. *The Famished Road* (1991), which brought him widespread recognition, is narrated by a 'spirit child' and combines social realism with elements of the supernatural and of ▷ magic realism, producing a dream-like quality also found in many of his short stories, collected in *Incidents at the Shrine* (1986) and *Stars of the New Curfew* (1989). His other novels are: *Flowers and Shadows* (1980); *The Landscape Within* (1981); *Songs of Enchantment* (1993, sequel to *The Famished Road*).

Old Curiosity Shop, The (1840–1)

A novel by ▷ Charles Dickens; it was serialized as part of ▷ *Master Humphrey's Clock* in 1840–1 and published in book form in 1841.

The Curiosity Shop (a shop which sells second-hand goods of ornamental or rarity value) is kept by the grandfather of little Nell Trent. The old man has been impoverished by the extravagances of his son-in-law and those of Fred Trent, Nell's brother. He is forced to borrow money from Quilp, a grotesque and malevolent dwarf, who believes the old man to be a miser with a hidden store of wealth. Quilp gets possession of the shop, and Nell and her grandfather take to wandering about the countryside. Eventually Nell dies, too late to be saved by her grandfather's brother, who has returned from abroad and finds them after a long search. Quilp is drowned while attempting to escape arrest. Other characters include Sampson Brass, Quilp's unscrupulous lawyer, his sister Sally and 'the Marchioness', a child whom the Brasses keep as a servant in vile conditions.

The novel shows Dickens's extraordinary vitality of imagination and also exemplifies the vulgarity which was part of his vitality. This vulgarity tended to display itself in melodrama and in sentimentality, here exhibited in the characters of Quilp and Little Nell respectively. The death of Little Nell is often regarded as Dickens's most notorious sentimental indulgence.

Oliphant, Margaret (M.O.W.) (1828–97)
Novelist and biographer. The daughter of a Scots Customs clerk named Wilson, Margaret Oliphant was born in Wallyford, near Musselburgh. The father was somewhat indifferent to his family, the mother energetic, eager and sarcastic, with a similarity to Jane ▷ Carlyle recognized by her daughter. She went to London in 1851 to take care of an 'unsatisfactory' brother and in 1852 married her cousin, an artist. From 1852 she wrote novels in ▷ Blackwood's Magazine and reviewed for them. Her husband died of consumption in 1859, three months before the birth of their third child, leaving her dependent on her writing. After the death of her daughter in 1864 she took on her widowed brother and his three children and provided for their education and maintenance as well as that of her own sons. She produced a constant stream of writing: ▷ biography, fiction and reviews, and published nearly 100 different works. She wrote vividly and inventively, with pathos and humour, but the struggle to meet her financial obligations, her disappointments and griefs constantly oppressed her and she expressed regret at having to write such quantities. Her works include: Passages in the Life of Mrs Margaret Maitland (1849), Caleb Field (1851), a historical novel, Merkland (1851) which was a great success, The Athelings (1857), one of several domestic romances. Her Chronicles of Carlingford' series perhaps owes something to ▷ George Eliot, and ▷ Anthony Trollope, comprising Salem Chapel (1863), The Rector and the Doctor's Family (1863), The Perpetual Curate (1864), Miss Marjoribanks (1866) and Phoebe Junior (1876). Stories of the Seen and Unseen deal with experiences of death and matters of the soul, including elements of mysticism, and include A Beleaguered City (1880) and A Little Pilgrim (1882). Her Literary History of England (1882) was much praised. Annals of a Publishing House, about Blackwood's was published in 1897 and a posthumous ▷ autobiography in 1899.
Bib: Coghill, A. L. (ed.), The Autobiography and Letters of Mrs M.O.W. Oliphant, Colby, V. & R., The Equivocal Virtue: Mrs Oliphant and the Victorian Literary Market Place; Cunningham, V., Everywhere Spoken Against: Dissent in the Victorian Novel (chapter).

Oliver Twist (1837–9)
A novel by ▷ Charles Dickens, published in instalments in 1837–9. Oliver is a child of unknown parents, born in a ▷ workhouse where he leads a miserable existence under the tyranny of Bumble, a beadle, ie a parish council official. He runs away to London and becomes mixed up in a gang of thieves led by Fagin and including the brutal burglar, Bill Sikes, Nancy his whore and a young pickpocket called the 'Artful Dodger'. He is temporarily rescued by the benevolent Mr Brownlow but a mysterious character called Monks, who has an interest in keeping Oliver's parentage a secret, induces the gang to kidnap him. He is finally rescued through the action of Nancy, who in consequence is brutally murdered by Sikes.

The novel shows the mixture of sentimentality and melodrama characteristic of early Dickens but in Bumble especially he exhibits keen social satire, and the London underworld is presented vividly. It was written at a time when a number of novelists (eg the 'Newgate School', especially ▷ Harrison Ainsworth) had written romances about crime but Dickens dissociated it from these in the preface to the 3rd edition, and it was realistic enough to startle the educated public into a new consciousness of the unprivileged and the criminal level of society, and to show how lack of compassion in the more privileged helped to make poverty a nursery of crime.

Ondaatje, Michael (b 1943)
Novelist and poet, born in Sri Lanka (then Ceylon). At the age of eighteen he arrived in Canada, where he attended Bishop's University in Quebec, the University of Toronto and Queens University, Kingston, Ontario. He taught at the University of Western Ontario (1967–71) and subsequently at York University in Toronto. His fiction has a strong element of technical experiment, combined with strong feeling and political concerns: Coming Through Slaughter (1976) uses a form of ▷ faction, portraying the life of the jazz cornet player Buddy Bolden through a combination of narrative techniques, including transcripts of interviews, song lyrics, biographical summaries and subjective narration. Ondaatje has written a stage version of this novel. In the Skin of a Lion (1987) explores the lives of marginalized people in Canadian society using both mythic and ▷ metafictional devices. His most recent novel is: The English Patient (1992), which was joint winner of 1992's Booker Prize. His volumes of poetry include: The Dainty Monsters (1967); The Man With Seven Toes (1969); The Collected Works of Billy the Kid: Left Handed Poems (1970); Rat Jelly (1973); Elimination Dance (1978); Secular Love (1984); The Cinnamon Peeler: Selected Poems (1989). He has also directed films and edited books of verse and stories. Running in the Family (1982) is autobiographical.
Bib: Solecki, S., (ed.), Spider Blues: Essays on Michael Ondaatje.

Onomatopoeia
The use of verbal sound to evoke the sound of what the word represents. Thus a cuckoo is a bird whose

song resembles the two syllables of its name, which is therefore onomatopoeic.

Opie, Amelia (1769–1853)

Novelist and poet. Opie began to participate in London society in 1794, and soon became acquainted with and admired by the more radical members of the literary groups, in particular ▷ Elizabeth Inchbald, ▷ William Godwin and ▷ Mary Wollstonecraft (whom Opie depicts in her novel *Adeline Mowbray, or The Mother and Daughter*, 1804). Other novels include *The Father and Daughter* (1801), *Valentine's Eve* (1816) and *Madeline* (1822); they are all sentimental domestic novels and bear out Opie's own stated purpose in writing: 'I like to make people cry, indeed, if I do not do it, all my readers are disappointed.' Her ceaseless literary outpouring is of questionable quality, and this led to her being satirized as Miss Poppyseed by ▷ Peacock in his novel *Headlong Hall*. She married the painter John Opie in 1798 (her maiden name was Alderson), but at his death in 1807 moved to Norwich where, in 1825, she became a Quaker, devoting herself to spiritual writing, notably *Lays for the Dead* (1833). Bib: James, A.H., *Best Sellers of Jane Austen's Age*; Menzies, J., and Lloyd, H., *Amelia: The Tale of a Plain Friend*.

Ordeal of Richard Feverel, The (1859)

A novel by ▷ George Meredith. Sir Austin Feverel prides himself on the 'system' which he has devised for the upbringing and education of his motherless son, Richard; he is, however, a self-satisfied egotist who lacks disinterested understanding of his son's character. The 'system' breaks down in Richard's adolescence, when the boy falls in love with Lucy Desborough, a girl of lower social background than Sir Austin's ideal for his son's bride. They are secretly married but Sir Austin manages to separate them by egotistically exploiting Richard's love for him. Richard becomes involved with a beautiful woman of loose morals; he begins this new relationship with characteristically romantic and idealistic motives of redeeming her but he partly falls under her spell. Lord Mountfalcon, who is interested in permanently separating Lucy and Richard, is chiefly responsible for Richard's betrayal of her, and in remorse for his infidelity Richard fights a duel with him and is wounded. Lucy has meanwhile become reconciled with Sir Austin but the shock of the duel kills her. The novel – Meredith's first important one – exemplifies his combination of romantic intensity with psychological analysis.

Order

One of the five categories in which ▷ Genette analyses narrative discourse, order is concerned with the relationship between the chronological order of fictional events and their order in the narrative (eg 'flashbacks'). Order, ▷ duration and ▷ frequency are matters of temporal arrangement or 'tense'; the other two categories are ▷ mood and ▷ voice.

Origin of Species, The

▷ Darwin, Charles.

Orlando (1928)

A fantasy by ▷ Virginia Woolf in which the evolution of poetic genius is traced through the Sackville family and their country mansion of Knole from Thomas Sackville (1536–1608) to the poet Victoria Sackville-West (1892–1962). This is done through an immortal character Orlando, who changes sex from a man into a woman in the 17th century, after growing to male adulthood in Elizabethan times. She then discovers that life as a woman in the 18th and 19th centuries offers different and limited freedoms. The book is a parodic combination of historical novel and biographical fantasy which explores the themes of androgyny and women's creativity. It is thus perhaps the closest Woolf gets in her fiction to an exploration of the ideas she outlines in *A Room of One's Own* (1931) and *Three Guineas* (1938). A film version of *Orlando*, directed by Sally Potter, was released in 1993.

Orwell, George (pseudonym of Eric Blair) (1903–50)

Novelist, journalist and critic. Born into a poor but proud middle-class family, he was sent to a private school, from where he won a scholarship to Eton. His snobbish upbringing, and the uneasiness he felt in living with boys richer than himself, gave him a distaste for middle-class values and, in relation to the working-classes, a sense of guilt which was intensified by the large unemployment of the 1930s. He served in the Burma Police (1922–7), and then resigned from dislike of what he interpreted as ▷ imperialist oppression – *Burmese Days* (1934). He then tried to appease his sense of social guilt by living for 18 months in the utmost destitution – *Down and Out in London and Paris* (1933). At the height of the economic Depression in the 1930s, he was commissioned by a left-wing publisher, Gollancz, to make a personal investigation of conditions in the north of England – *The Road to Wigan Pier* (1937). By the time of its publication, Orwell was fighting for the Republicans in Spain, where he was wounded in the throat – *Homage to Catalonia* (1938). He came to regard himself as an independent and democratic socialist. During World War II, he was rejected for the army on medical grounds, and worked for the Indian service of the BBC. In 1945 he published his masterpiece, the fable *Animal Farm*, a satire on Stalinism. After the war he wrote his most famous work, *1984* (1949), a vision of a world ruled by dictatorships of the Stalinist style, taken to an extreme in which private life and private thought are all but eradicated by surveillance, propaganda, and the systematic perversion of language.

His other novels are: *A Clergyman's Daughter* (1935); *Keep the Aspidistra Flying* (1936); *Coming Up For Air* (1939). Among his best works are his social and literary critical essays: *Inside the Whale* (1940); *The Lion and the Unicorn* (1941 – subtitled *Socialism and the English Genius*); *Critical Essays* (1946); *Shooting an Elephant* (1950). Recurrent themes in his work are the effect of poverty on the spirit, the difficulty of reconciling public demands with private desires and conscience, and the danger of corrupted language. He was literary editor of *Tribune* 1943–5.

His Collected Essays, Journalism and Letters were published in 1968 (ed. S. Orwell and I. Angus).
Bib: Woodcock, G., *The Crystal Spirit*; Williams, R., *Orwell*; Crick, B., *George Orwell, a Life*; Meyers, J., *George Orwell: the Critical Heritage*; Shelden, M., *Orwell: The Authorised Biography*.

Ouida (1839–1908)

The pseudonym of Marie Louise de la Ramée, 'Ouida' originates in a childish failure to say 'Louise'. She was born in Bury St Edmunds of an English mother and French father, was educated in local schools and then in Paris, where her father disappeared during the Paris Commune of 1871. From 1860 she lived mostly in Italy, an expensive and affected life with dogs and frequent hopeless infatuations. She had a high opinion of her own genius, writing 45 novels of an unreal fashionable world, rebelling against the moral tone of contemporary literature. Her powerful novels were very popular for a time, despite their extravagance and inaccuracies, and her ridiculous portrayals of men. However, she became less popular from 1890 and ultimately died in destitution in Viareggio. Her stories appeared in *Bentley's Miscellany* 1859–60. Her first success was *Held in Bondage* (1863) but *Strathmore* (1865) really established her reputation. Her other novels include *Under Two Flags* (1867), *Folle-Farine* (1871), *Two Little Wooden Shoes* (1874), *A Village Commune* (1881) dealing with peasant life, *In Maremma* (1882) and the animal stories, *A Dog of Flanders* (1872) and *Bimbi, Stories for Children* (1882).
Bib: Ffrench, Y., *Ouida: A Study in Ostentation*; Bigland, E., *Ouida: The Passionate Victorian*; Stirling, M., *The Fine and the Wicked: The Life and Times of Ouida*.

Our Mutual Friend (1864–5)

The last complete novel by ▷ Charles Dickens, published serially 1864–5.

The principal plot starts from the will of a deceased refuse-collector, Old Harmon, who bequeaths his fortune to his son, John Harmon, on condition that he marries a certain girl, Bella Wilfer. Young Harmon wishes to discover what she is like before he discloses himself. He intends to adopt a disguise but his identity is obscured beyond his intention when circumstances point to his death by murder. Since he is believed dead, the father's property goes instead to Mr Boffin, old Harmon's foreman. Boffin adopts Bella, and young Harmon, disguising himself as John Rokesmith, becomes engaged as Boffin's secretary. Bella becomes spoilt by wealth and contemptuously rejects Rokesmith-Harmon as a lover; she is, however, reformed by Boffin, who pretends himself to undergo complete debasement of character through his accession of wealth and thus gives Bella, who has been devoted to him, a violent distaste for the evils of money. Rokesmith's true identity as young Harmon is at length brought to light. With this main plot goes a minor story of Silas Wegg's attempt to blackmail Boffin. In addition there is a parallel main plot concerning the rival lovers of Lizzie Hexam, daughter of a Thames boatman; one of her lovers is the aristocratic young barrister, Eugene Wrayburn, and the other the embittered schoolmaster of low social origins, Bradley Headstone. Headstone tries to murder Wrayburn, and nearly succeeds, but he is drowned in a struggle with Rogue Riderhood, another waterman who is also a blackmailer. Wrayburn, physically wrecked, marries Lizzie for whom he at last comes to have a real need. The two main plots are linked through the waterside characters who are connected with young Harmon's supposed murder at the beginning of the book. The novel extends through the Wrayburn-Lizzie story into upper-middle-class circles which include the arrogant Podsnaps, the Veneerings who attempt to climb into wealthy society and fall out of it again, the fraudulent social adventurers Mr and Mrs Lammle, the mean and ruthless financier Fledgeby. Through Fledgeby on the one side and Lizzie on the other, the lower social circles include Riah, the benevolent Jew, and Jenny Wren, the bitter-sweet doll's dressmaker. The book is thus given an unusually wide variety of character and social environment, even for Dickens, and it is pervaded by a rich symbolism arising from the use made of the River Thames and the dust-heaps out of which the Harmon fortunes have been made. The motive of special social reform, more characteristic of early Dickens (eg ▷ *Oliver Twist*, 1838) is evident in the episode of Betty Higden, the poor woman who dies by the roadside sooner than enter a workhouse.

Overbury, Sir Thomas (1581–1613)

Essayist and poet; as a writer he is chiefly remembered as the author of one of the most widely read collections of 'Theophrastian' character-sketches, published in 1614; John Webster, Thomas Dekker, John Donne and others made additions to subsequent issues of the collection between 1614 and 1622.

Overbury was also the victim of one of the most sensational murders in English history. He tried to oppose a love intrigue between James I's royal favourite, Thomas Carr, Earl of Somerset, and the young Countess of Essex. The lovers conspired to have Overbury poisoned; the crime came to light, and the prosecution was conducted by Francis Bacon. Carr and the Countess were convicted and disgraced, but their agents who actually administered the poison were hanged.

▷ Characters, Theophrastian.

Owen, Robert (1771–1858)

Social reformer, and a leading socialist thinker in the early 19th century. He became part-owner of the New Lanark Cotton Mills in 1800, and found that its workers were living in the degraded and nearly desperate conditions common in the earlier phase of the ▷ Industrial Revolution. He set about improving their housing and working conditions, and established infant schools. His reforms were a success, but his expenditure on them caused resentment among his partners, and in 1813 he established a new firm, with ▷ Jeremy Bentham as one of his partners. In the same year he published a volume of essays, *A New View of Society*, in which he sought to prove that the human character is entirely created by its environment. In 1817, in a report to the House of Commons, Owen pointed out that the existing social misery was caused by men competing unsuccessfully with machines, and he recommended the establishment of socialist working communities in the country; they were to vary from 500 to 3,000 in size, and were to be partly industrial. His views were received favourably by, among other people, the Duke of Kent, the father of Queen Victoria, but Owen spoilt his case with public opinion in general by mixing his proposals with anti-religious propaganda. Nonetheless two experiments were attempted in 1825, one in England and one in America; both failed in under two years. Owen now became the leader of a socialist-secular movement, through which he sought to replace the emphasis on political reform by emphasis on economic action. His influence led to the Grand National Consolidated Trades Union in 1833 ($\triangleright$ Trade Union), but this also failed owing to bad organization. The word 'socialism' originated through discussions centred on the Association of all Classes of all Nations, which Owen founded in 1835. The only permanent success among Owen's experiments was his establishment of the Co-operative Movement, which nowadays is affiliated to the Labour Party.

Oxford Movement (Tractarian Movement)
A religious movement within the $\triangleright$ Church of England; it had its origin and main centre in Oxford and ran from 1833, when it began with a sermon by Keble until 1845 when its most

eloquent leader, $\triangleright$ John Newman, entered the Roman Catholic Church. Some of the leaders of the Church of England realized (especially after the Act of Catholic Emancipation, 1829) that the Church was by its constitution largely at the mercy of the state, and was in danger of becoming in essentials a department of the state. The Oxford Movement preached that the Church had its independent, spiritual status, was in direct descent from the medieval Catholic Church, and represented a 'middle way' between post-Reformation Catholicism and $\triangleright$ Protestantism. The movement's propaganda was conducted through $\triangleright$ tracts, many of them by John Newman, and culminated in *Tract XC* which asserted that the Thirty-Nine Articles, on which Anglican doctrine is based, are compatible with Roman Catholic doctrine. The tracts divided Anglican opinion severely, and Newman's secession to the Church of Rome, followed by the secession of other High Anglican clergy, brought the movement into discredit with the majority of Anglican opinion. Edward Pusey, Professor of Hebrew at Oxford, was the leader of the Oxford Movement, which was in consequence often called Puseyite. An indirect result of the movement was to focus attention on the medieval background of the Church, and to encourage that reification of the Middle Ages which emerged in much victorian literature, in the artistic movement known as Pre-Raphaelitism and in Victorian neo-Gothic architecture.

Oxymoron
$\triangleright$ Figures of Speech.

P

Paine, Thomas (1737–1809)
Political author. The son of a small farmer, his early career in England as an official ended in failure, and he sailed for America in 1774. In 1776 he published the republican pamphlet *Common Sense*, which set the colonists openly on the road to independence. After the start of the American War of Independence, he maintained the morale of the rebels with a series of pamphlets called *The Crisis* (1776–83). The opening sentence was 'These are the times that try men's souls' – words which became a battle-cry.

In 1787 he returned to Europe to carry on his fight for republican democracy. When ▷ Burke published his ▷ *Reflections on the Revolution in France* in 1790, Paine replied with Part I of his *Rights of Man* (1791). The Government was making the preparations for his trial for treason in 1792 when the poet William Blake got him out of the country to France, where the French revolutionary government had elected him a member of the republican Convention. In France he published his *Age of Reason* (1793) which defended a rational, abstract form of deism against orthodox Christianity. This caused him to lose his popularity in England and in America. He also lost favour with the French for his injudicious criticisms, and for a time he was imprisoned, though he was later restored to his seat in the Convention. In 1802 he returned to America to find that he had lost his influence there and he died at his farm in New Rochelle in 1809. Ten years later the English radical ▷ William Cobbett returned to England with Tom Paine's bones. For some time his works remained a text-book for English radicalism.

Palindrome
▷ Figures of Speech.

Palinode
The withdrawal in a piece of writing of ideas or attitudes expressed in another by the same writer: or the expression in one work of ideas which are in direct opposition to those which the author has expressed in a previous one.

Pamela (1740–1)
Subtitled 'Virtue Rewarded', *Pamela* is an epistolary novel by ▷ Samuel Richardson. The story of a young servant girl who evades her master's attempts at seduction, Richardson's novel was a great contemporary success, yet sophisticated readers were quick to see its ambiguous message. By her insistence on her country simplicity, Pamela persuades the squire to marry her; yet her self-conscious parade of 'artless' virtue suggests a level of sexual innuendo of which Richardson may or may not have been aware. ▷ Henry Fielding's ▷ *Shamela* and ▷ *Joseph Andrews* parody this element of *Pamela*.

Pamphlet
Any short treatise published separately, usually without hard covers. It is usually polemical, *ie* written to defend or attack some body of ideas, especially religious or political ones. In the 16th century and especially towards the end of the reign of Elizabeth I pamphleteering became a widespread literary industry, the beginning of journalism. ▷ Thomas Nashe and Thomas Dekker were amongst the most famous pamphleteers, and the Presbyterian Marprelate controversy was the most famous of the 'pamphlet wars'. In the 17th century Milton was the most famous writer of pamphlets, and his *Areopagitica* (1644) is his masterpiece. In the 18th century some of ▷ Swift's finest prose was in pamphlet form, *eg* ▷ *A Modest Proposal* (1729), and ▷ Defoe was a prolific pamphleteer. The 18th century, however, saw the rise of the weekly periodicals, which reduced the need for the pamphlet form of literature.
▷ Journalism.

Pandosto (1588)
A prose romance by ▷ Robert Greene, used by Shakespeare as the basis for his late play, *The Winter's Tale*.

Pantagruel
A comic romance by ▷ François Rabelais, published in its first version in 1532. Pantagruel is the son of ▷ Gargantua; *Gargantua* (1534) and *Pantagruel* are the first two volumes of a five-volume series of such romances. With their allusiveness, parodic energy and physicality they represent a significant influence on such novelists as ▷ Swift, ▷ Sterne and ▷ Joyce.

Pantheism
A term used to cover a variety of religious and philosophical beliefs, which have in common that God is present in Nature, and not separable from it in the sense in which a cause is separable from its effect, or a creator from his creation. Pantheism is implicit in doctrines derived from ▷ Plato, *eg* in some of the neo-Platonists of the 16th century, and in some poetry inspired by the natural environment. Amongst English poets, the most famous example is Wordsworth in his earlier phase (1797–1807), notably in the first two books of his 1805 version of *The Prelude*. In his revised version of this autobiographical poem, Wordsworth tried to eliminate the pantheistic tendencies, since they are not in accordance with most forms of Christian doctrine.

Paradiso
The third and final section of ▷ Dante's great poem, the ▷ *Divina Commedia*. Dante has been led through the Inferno and the Purgatorio by the spirit of the Roman poet ▷ Virgil. Now his guide is Beatrice, the woman who had inspired Dante's love. As the Inferno had been divided into circles, so Paradise is divided into spheres: the sphere of the Moon, of Mercury, Venus, the Sun, Mars, Jupiter, Saturn, the Fixed Stars, and the Primum Mobile, or First Mover. Each sphere contains the kind of spirit which the ancient Greek and Roman myths had caused to be associated with it: Mars, the Christian warriors and martyrs; Jupiter, the just rulers; Saturn, the holy contemplatives, etc. The spheres are in ascending order of merit, and culminate in Dante's remote, ecstatic vision of God Himself. In each, Dante has conversations on philosophical and spiritual matters with the men and women from history whom he conceives to have been assigned there.

▷ *Inferno*; *Purgatorio*.

Paradox
▷ Figures of Speech.

Parody
A literary form which constitutes a comic imitation
of a serious work, or of a serious literary form. Thus
▷ Fielding's ▷ *Joseph Andrews* is partly a parody of
▷ Richardson's ▷ *Pamela*, and ▷ Cervantes's ▷ *Don
Quixote* parodies chivalric romance. It is difficult
to draw a line between parody and burlesque;
the latter is more obviously comic in its style of
imitation. Together with pastiche, parody has played
a significant role in ▷ post-modernist fiction.

Parole
In the work of ▷ Ferdinand de Saussure, the
founder of ▷ structuralism, this is usually translated
as 'speech' or 'speech act'. It refers to a particular
instance of speech. '*Parole*' is to be distinguished
from ▷ '*langue*' (language) which is the linguistic
system which underpins every utterance (*parole*).
Speakers of a language (*langue*) avail themselves of
parts of that system and reactivate it each time they
engage in speech (*parole*).
▷ Sign.

Pascal, Blaise (1623–62)
French religious philosopher and
mathematician. In 1646 he became a devout
adherent of the Jansenist movement which had its
headquarters at the nunnery of Port-Royal near Paris.
Jansenism (started by Cornelius Jansen, 1585–1638)
maintained, like the Protestant predestinarians,
that salvation through the love of God was possible
only for those whom God pleased to love, *ie* an
individual was predestined to salvation or to
damnation; however it also emphasized the necessity
of belonging to the Roman Catholic Church. The
movement was strongly attacked by the Jesuit
Order, and when its leading exponent, Antoine
Arnauld, was being threatened with dismissal
from his academic post, Pascal wrote *Provincial
Letters* (1656) in his defence. This was his first
important work, a masterpiece of lucid, ironical
controversy; in particular, Pascal advocated moral
austerity and criticized Jesuit libertinism. His *Pensées*
('Thoughts' – pub. 1670) is his more famous work;
it consists of notes for a book on religion intended
to demonstrate the necessity of the religious life.
Though fragmentary, the notes have great aphoristic
power; with an intellect as powerful and a style as
lucid as that of ▷ Descartes, Pascal criticizes the
earlier philosopher's notion of the supreme power of
human reason, and shows the limitations of reason in
dealing with ultimate mysteries.

Passage to India, A (1924)
A novel by ▷ E. M. Forster. It had originally been
planned ten years earlier, and its picture of India
belongs partly to that period. The scene is the city of
Chandrapore on the banks of the Ganges, and India
is under British rule. The background characters
consist mainly of the British officials and their

wives, and the local Indian intelligentsia. The main
characters are as follows: Aziz, a Muslim Indian
doctor; Godbole, a Hindu professor; Fielding, the
headmaster of the Government College; Ronald
Heaslop, another of the British officials; and two
visitors from Britain, Mrs Moore, the mother of
Heaslop by her first marriage, and Adela Quested,
who is engaged to him. Both women have strong
liberal principles, and make friends easily with
Fielding, the only liberal in the resident British
colony. Fielding is also a friend of Aziz, and a
colleague of Godbole. Aziz issues an impulsive
invitation to the British visitors to visit the local
Marabar Caves; these have a strong significance
for the Hindus, although Godbole, when he is
asked about them, is unable to explain it. The
climax of the book occurs when this visit takes
place. Heat, discomfort, and the caves themselves
cause Mrs Moore and Adela to suffer traumatic
experiences. Mrs Moore loses all her faith and
idealism; Adela has an attack of hysteria which
temporarily convinces her that Aziz has attempted
to rape her. This supposed rape brings the already
strained relations between the British and the Indians
to a crisis, but the crisis is resolved (not without
disgracing the more reactionary British officials)
by Adela's return to sanity in the witness-box.
Mrs Moore, although she is now selfish, hard and
disillusioned, whereas before she had been generous,
kind and idealistic, is in touch with a new kind
of truthfulness which helps Adela's restoration.
Only Mrs Moore and Godbole understand the true
nature of Adela's experience in the caves, and they
understand it from opposite, though complementary,
points of view.
   The novel has psychological, political, and
religious dimensions. The Christianity, or the
sceptical liberalism, of the more enlightened of
the British is shown to be adequate for normal
relationships and practical affairs, but they have
become too shallow for the interpretation of deeper
human experience; Aziz's Muslim faith is stronger,
but it is more an aesthetic and cultural tradition
than a binding spiritual faith. Godbole's Hinduism,
on the other hand, is profound and intelligent,
though it is no guide to the daily conduct of affairs.
This religious dimension is presented by constant
symbolism, ranging in character from unobtrusive
(though often important) details, to the conspicuous
and suggestive image of the caves themselves. *A
Passage to India* is Forster's most ▷ modernist work
and is usually regarded as his masterpiece.
▷ Imperialism.

Pater, Walter Horatio (1839–94)
Scholar, essayist and critic. He was elected to a
fellowship in Brasenose College, Oxford, in 1864.
He was connected with the Pre-Raphaelite group,
shared their idealistic worship of beauty and became
an important influence in the cult of art which led to
the ▷ Aesthetic Movement at the end of the century;
▷ Oscar Wilde was among those profoundly affected
by the Paterian sensibility. His most important work
was *Studies in the History of the Renaissance* (1873),
a collection of essays on Italian painters and writers

from the 14th to 16th centuries; the Conclusion
to these essays, in which he advocates a fusion of
psychic, moral and sensuous ecstasy, became a kind
of manifesto of the aesthetic movement. His next
most famous work is the philosophic romance *Marius
the Epicurean* (1885). Other works: *Imaginary Portraits*
(1887); *Appreciations with an Essay on Style* (1889);
Plato and Platonism (1893); *The Child in the House*
(1894); *Greek Studies and Miscellaneous Studies* (1895);
an unfinished romance, *Gaston de Latour* (1896).
Pater wrote with immense care for beauty of style,
which became for him and end in itself.
Bid: Levey, M., *The Case of Walter Pater*; Monsman,
G., *Walter Pater*; Iser, W., *Walter Pater: The Aesthetic
Moment*; Seiter, R. M. (ed.) *Walter Pater: The Critical
Heritage*; Loesberg, J., *Aestheticism and Deconstruction:
Pater, Derrida and De Man*.

Pathetic fallacy
▷ Figures of Speech.

Payn, James (1830–98)
Novelist. Educated at Eton and Cambridge, Payn
launched his literary career by contributing to
▷ Dicken's ▷ *Household Words*. His highly popular
novels tapped into the vogue for the ▷ sensation
novel of the 1860s and 1870s, melodramatically
dealing with scheming relatives, disputes over wills
and strange disappearances of these, the best known
are *Lost Sir Massingberd* (1864) and *By Proxy* (1878).
Between 1883 and 1896 Payn edited the ▷ *Cornhill
Magazine*.

Peacock, Thomas Love (1785–1866)
Novelist and poet. After unsuccessful attempts in
poetry and the theatre, he found his special form
in the 'discussion novel': *Headlong Hall* (1816);
▷ *Melincourt* (1817); ▷ *Nightmare Abbey* (1818); *Maid
Marian* (1822); *The Misfortunes of Elphin* (1829);
▷ *Crotchet Castle* (1831); *Gryll Grange* (1861). These
consist almost entirely of conversation and have very
little plot; the characters represent outlooks, ideas,
and attitudes such as arouse Peacock's derision,
and the prevailing tone is comic and satirical. The
conversations are interspersed with songs, often of
great charm, and hilarious and extravagant episodes.
His sceptical essay *The Four Ages of Poetry* (1820)
provoked Shelley's famous *Defence of Poetry* (1821).
Bib: Van Doren, C., *Life*; Priestley, J.B., *Life*; Able,
A. H., *Meredith and Peacock – A Study in Literary
Influence*; House, H., in *All in Due Time*; Brett-Smith,
H. F. B. (ed.), *Life in Works*, Vol I; Jack, I., Chap
VII in *Oxford History of English Literature*; Butler, M.,
Peacock Displayed: A Satirist in His Context.

Peake, Mervyn (1911–68)
Novelist, dramatist, poet and painter. Peake was born
in China, but his family returned to England in 1923,
where he subsequently trained as an artist. He is
best known for his trilogy *Gormenghast*, a fantasy epic
set in a grotesque world, consisting of *Titus Groan*
(1946), *Gormenghast* (1950) and *Titus Alone* (1959). In
form it is a ▷ *Bildungsroman* with multiple subplots,
and it is distinguished by a rich vocabulary and
by the effects of Peake's strong visual imagination.
Peake's work met a mixed critical reception, but

gained a considerable cult following, aided by the
increasing popularity of fantasy fiction associated with
the work of ▷ J. R. R. Tolkien.
Bib: Batchelor, J., *Mervyn Peake: A Biographical and
Critical Exploration*.

Pendennis, The History of
A novel by ▷ William Makepeace Thackeray,
published serially 1848–50. It is about worldly
upper-class society in London and the fortunes of a
young man, Arthur Pendennis, whose 'bad angels'
are his cynical, materialistic uncle, Major Pendennis,
and the pretty but selfish Blanche Amory whom he
nearly marries. Blanche's father, an escaped convict
who is thought to be dead but is in fact – as Major
Pendennis knows – still alive, haunts the book in the
guise of Colonel Altamont. Arthur's 'good angels'
are his widowed mother, Helen; Laura Bell, whom
he eventually marries and whom his mother has
adopted; and George Warrington, a friend with
whom he shares rooms. The good influences are,
however, less imaginatively presented than the bad
ones, and the distinctiveness of the novel depends on
its amusing portrayal of the vulgarity, intrigue, and
materialism of London society and the journalistic
and literary world of Fleet Street.

Pepys, Samuel (1633–1703)
Diarist. He was an industrious and highly efficient
official in the Admiralty Office, and a man who
had musical culture and persistent, if amateurish,
scientific and literary interests. As secretary to his
cousin, Edward Montagu, Earl of Sandwich, he
was aboard the fleet which brought Charles II back
to England at the Restoration in 1660. His official
position in the Admiralty gave him the confidence
of the king's brother, James Duke of York, who
was Lord High Admiral, and an opportunity for
direct observation of court life. He was elected to
Parliament and knew the world of politics, was a
friend of a number of leading writers and musicians,
and held distinguished appointments in the City of
London. He was thus centrally placed to observe his
age, and with all his seriousness he was pleasure-
loving and witty.
His diary (kept 1660–9) is a unique document
not only because he brought to it these qualities and
advantages (many of which were shared by his friend
the diarist ▷ John Evelyn) but because he kept it for
his eye alone, and consequently wrote with unusual
candour and objectivity. To prevent his servants
and family from prying into it, he used a kind of
shorthand cypher, which was not interpreted until
1825, when part of the diary was first published. The
first more or less complete edition was in 1896. Of
all diaries in English, it has the greatest appeal to the
general reader, as well as having outstanding value
for the historian.
▷ Diaries.
Bib: Lives by J. R. Tanner, A. Bryant, and J. H.
Wilson. Letters edited by J. R. Tanner, A. Bryant,
and J. H. Wilson. Letters edited by J. R. Tanner,
A. Bryant, and J. H. Wilson. Marburg, C., *Mr Pepys
and Mr Evelyn*; Latham, R. and Mathews, W.,
(eds.), *Diary*.

Peregrine Pickle, The Adventures of (1751)

A novel by ▷ Tobias Smollett. The hero is an adventurer seeking his fortune in England and on the Continent. Its form is a succession of episodes without a uniting structure, depending for its interest on the vigour of depiction of the characters and incidents. It contains various eccentric characters, especially the retired sailor and his associates, Commodore Trunnion, Lieutenant Hatchway, and Tom Pipes. The episodes give opportunity for much social and political satire, from English village life upwards, and show an awareness of social structure like that found in the novels of ▷ Henry Fielding. Trunnion and his circle were an inspiration to ▷ Laurence Sterne's Uncle Toby in ▷ Tristram Shandy.

▷ Picaresque.

Perfectibilism

The optimistic doctrine that individuals and society are capable of achieving perfection in living. The ▷ French Revolution, with its reliance on reason for the solution of all human problems, encouraged perfectibilism, and the philosopher ▷ William Godwin was an English example. ▷ Peacock, in ▷ Headlong Hall (1816), presents a humorous version of a perfectibilist in Mr Foster.

Periodicals

▷ Reviews and Periodicals.

Perrault, Charles (1628–1703)

French author, known in England chiefly for his collection of ▷ fairy tales published in 1697, Histoires et Contes du Temps Passé ('Stories and Tales from the Past') subtitled Contes de ma Mère l'Oie ('Tales of Mother Goose'). They were translated into English by Robert Samber (1729), and have remained the best known fairy tales among English children. They were retold by Perrault from popular sources, and are as follows: ▷ Sleeping Beauty; ▷ Red Riding Hood; Blue Beard; ▷ Puss in Boots; The Fairy; ▷ Cinderella; Riquet with the Tuft; Hop o' my Thumb. Several of them provide the themes for modern Christmas pantomimes.

Personification

▷ Figures of Speech.

Persuasion (1818)

The last completed novel by ▷ Jane Austen; it was published, incompletely revised, in 1818, the year following her death. The theme is the coming together of the heroine, Anne Elliott, and the hero, Captain Wentworth, in spite of social obstacles, the selfishness and foolishness of her father (Sir Walter) and sisters, and the rival attraction of the more obviously seductive Musgrove sisters. Anne, before the novel begins, had already refused Wentworth on the counsel of Lady Russell, who stands in place of mother to her; Lady Russell had misunderstood Wentworth's character and feared his poverty. Anne's personality is diffident and humble but at the opening of the story she has begun to realize that the refusal was a mistake, likely to ruin her happiness. The renewal of Wentworth's love and his eventual marriage to Anne is a victory: their strong and distinctive but quiet and reticent qualities overcome the cruder and shallower social characteristics of their circumstances.

Philistines

In the original sense, a race inhabiting the coast of Palestine in biblical times.

In a secondary meaning, the term is applied to those who are indifferent or actively hostile to artistic and cultural values. This common use was introduced by ▷ Matthew Arnold (Culture and Anarchy 1869; ▷ Essays in Criticism I – essay on Heine). Arnold divided the English society of his day into three classes of cultural indifference: the upper class were barbarians; the middle class, philistines; the working class, the populace. By this he meant that the upper class underestimated cultural values, the middle class ignored them, and the populace was ignorant of them. Arnold had derived this use of 'philistines' from the Germans, who applied it to townspeople as opposed to students in university towns.

Phillips, Caryl (b 1958)

Novelist, playwright, travel writer. Born in St Kitts, West Indies, brought up in Leeds, England, and educated at Oxford, he has been writer-in-residence at the Factory Community Centre, London, at the Literary Criterion Centre, Mysore, India and at the University of Stockholm, Sweden. His most recent novel, Crossing the River (1993), is the story of the disparate lives of three characters, sold into slavery in different countries and different centuries. His other novels are: The Final Passage (1985); A State of Independence (1986); Higher Ground (1989); Cambridge (1991). Plays: Strange Fruit (1981); Where There is Darkness (1982); The Shelter (1984); The Wasted Years (1985); Playing Away (1987). Travel writing: The European Tribe (1987).

Philosophes

▷ Encyclopaedists.

Phiz (Browne, Hablot Knight) (1815–82)

Illustrator. He was the principal illustrator for the novels of ▷ Charles Dickens (especially ▷ David Copperfield, ▷ The Pickwick Papers, ▷ Dombey and Son, ▷ Martin Chuzzlewit, ▷ Bleak House). He also illustrated the works of other Victorian novelists, notably ▷ Harrison Ainsworth and ▷ Charles Lever.

Picaresque

From the Spanish picaro, 'rogue' or 'cunning trickster'. The term is especially applied to a form of prose fiction originating in Spain in the 16th century, with such works as the anonymous Lazarillo de Tormes (1553), and dealing with the adventures of such characters in loose episodic form, often involving a journey.

The first distinctive example in English is ▷ Thomas Nashe's The Unfortunate Traveller (1594). In the 18th century, examples include ▷ Daniel

Defoe's ▷ *Moll Flanders*, ▷ Henry Fielding's ▷ *Jonathan Wild* and ▷ Tobias Smollett's *The Adventures of Ferdinand Count Fathom*. Other traditions combine with the picaresque: the mock romance in the tradition of ▷ *Don Quixote*, and the tradition of religious pilgrimage (cf. ▷ *The Pilgrim's Progress*).

Bib: Sieber, H., *The Picaresque*.

Pickwick Papers, The (1836–7)

The first novel by ▷ Charles Dickens, published serially 1836–7. The story is the adventures of Mr Pickwick and his friends Tupman, Snodgrass and Winkle, who go on a journey of observation of men and manners on behalf of the Pickwick Club, of which Mr Pickwick is the founder and the chairman. The episodes are predominantly comic and Mr Pickwick seems at first to be intended as a mere figure of fun, destined always to be made a fool of owing to his extreme innocence of the ways of the world. Fairly early on, however, he acquires a servant, Sam Weller. Sam is the ideal servant; he is practical, good-humoured, resourceful and devoted. Pickwick now begins to be endowed with a new dignity; still very innocent, he is no longer a mere figure of fun, for he is also shown to have positive moral qualities, such as a determination to stand by the values of truth and justice. He becomes, in fact, a kind of 19th century English middle-class Don Quixote with Sam Weller as a Sancho Panza, without any of the ridiculousness of Sancho, but with a great deal of comedy derived from his highly developed and typically Cockney sense of humour. At first there is a story but no plot; about half-way through, however, a semblance of a plot develops with Mrs Bardell's conspiracy to obtain £750 from Mr Pickwick for breach of promise of marriage. Assisted by a firm of unscrupulous lawyers, she is at first successful and Mr Pickwick goes to prison. This is the beginning of Dickens's constant preoccupation with prison and with the parasitic qualities of the legal profession. Various episodes illustrate the kinds of social viciousness which Dickens was to enjoy ridiculing or dramatizing – the cheerful roguery of Mr Jingle; the hypocrisy of the 'shepherd', Mr Stiggins; the demagogic Mr Potts in the parliamentary election at Eatanswill, etc. By contrast, Mr Wardle represents the opulent philanthropy and cordial 'religion of Christmas' which were also to figure in Dickens's novels to the end but especially in the earlier ones. In the outcome, Mr Pickwick and Sam Weller emerge as a kind of ideal alliance between the middle and working classes – complete sincerity and integrity in moral guidance on Pickwick's part, total devotion and most useful practical capacity on Weller's side. The values of the book are representative of the older rural England; Dickens has not yet entered the darkness, mystery and dramatic evil of 19th-century urban civilization.

Picturesque, The Cult of the

A term used in the late 18th and early 19th centuries to describe a certain kind of scenery, where cultivation was employed to produce artificially 'wild' nature. Landscape gardeners incorporated 'wildernesses' into their prospects, often with fake ruins suggesting the decay of classical civilization. The writer most identified with the 'picturesque' was William Gilpin (1724–1804), who wrote a series of illustrated picturesque tours. ▷ Jane Austen in ▷ *Mansfield Park* parodies the cult, and ▷ Thomas Love Peacock's *Headlong Hall* satirizes a contemporary dispute about its qualities.

Pilgrim's Progress, The

A prose ▷ allegory by ▷ John Bunyan. *The Pilgrim's Progress from this World to that which is to come* is in two parts: Part I (1678) tells of the religious conversion of Christian, and of his religious life – conceived as a pilgrimage – in this world, until he comes to the River of Death, and the Heavenly City which lies beyond it; Part II (1684) describes the subsequent conversion of his wife Christiana and their children, and their similar journey with a group of friends.

Both parts contain episodes which symbolize real life experiences: thus, Christian, soon after the way has been pointed out to him, falls into the ▷ Slough of Despond – a bog which represents the depression which overcomes the new convert when he has passed the stage of first enthusiasm; later he has to pass through phases of spiritual despair and terror, symbolized by the ▷ Valleys of Humiliation and the Shadow of Death; he has to face the derision and anger of public opinion in the town of Vanity Fair, and so on. Christiana and the children have an easier time; perhaps Bunyan wished to show that God in his mercy shields the weaker pilgrims, or perhaps that public opinion is harsher to pioneers than to those that follow them.

The 'pioneer pilgrims' – Christian and his associates – belong to the ▷ Puritan sects, of one of which Bunyan was himself a member, who were undergoing persecution in the reign of Charles II, especially during the earlier years, when English society was in strong reaction against the previous Puritan regime of Oliver Cromwell. Yet *The Pilgrim's Progress* is much more than merely a dramatization of the Puritan spirit. By its allegorical content, it is related to the tradition of the allegorical sermon which, in village churches, survived the Reformation of the 16th century, and some of the adventures (Christian's fight with Apollyon, the Castle of Giant Despair, the character of Greatheart) are related in spirit to popular versions of medieval and 16th century romances, surviving in the ▷ chapbooks. These aspects give it a close relation with popular traditions of culture to an extent unequalled by any other major literary work. Another element of popular culture shows in Bunyan's assimilation of the English translation of the ▷ Bible, and this reminds us that for many households the Bible was the only book constantly read, and that during the next century Bunyan's allegory took its place beside it. Still more important than these links with the past is Bunyan's anticipation of the kind of vision of human nature which in the 18th and 19th centuries was to find its scope in the novel: his allegorized characters do not, as in past allegories, merely simplify human virtues and vices, but reveal how an individual destiny can be shaped by the predominance in a personality of an outstanding quality, good or bad; the adventures of the pilgrims are conditioned by the differences of these qualities. Thus, Christian and Faithful, fellow pilgrims, have radically different temperaments and correspondingly different experiences.

▷ Celestial City; City of Destruction; Doubting Castle; Vanity Fair.

Pix, Mary (1666–1709)
Dramatist and novelist, one of the so-called 'Female Wits' satirized in a play of that name in 1696. Pix's first play, a heroic tragedy called *Ibrahim, the Thirteenth Emperor of the Turks*, was produced at Drury Lane in 1696, the same year as her novel, *The Inhuman Cardinal, Or: Innocence Betrayed*, and a comedy following ▷ Aphra Behn, *The Spanish Wives*. Another comedy, *The Innocent Mistress*, was staged at Lincoln's Inn Fields in the following year. Later plays include *The Deceiver Deceived* (1697), *The False Friend* (1699), *The Beau Defeated* (1700), *The Double Distress* (1701); and *The Conquest of Spain* (1705); Pix wrote a dozen plays in all, of which the comedies are generally considered far superior to the tragedies.
Bib: Steeves, E. L. (ed.), *The Plays of Mary Pix and Catharine Trotter*; Clark, C., *Three Augustan Women Playwrights*; Morgan, F. (ed.), *The Female Wits*.

Plath, Sylvia (1932–63)
Poet and novelist. She was brought up in the United States; her father, who died when she was nine, was of Prussian origin and her mother Austrian. Her university education was at Smith College, Massachussetts, and Newnham College, Cambridge. She married the English poet, Ted Hughes, in 1956. For a time she taught at Smith College, but in 1959 she settled in England. In 1960 she published her first volume of poetry, *The Colossus*, and in 1963 her only novel, *The Bell Jar*, under the pen-name of Victoria Lucas. Her reputation was established on the posthumous publication of her book of poetry, *Ariel* (1965). This volume aroused more interest in Britain than any other since Dylan Thomas's *Deaths and Entrances* (1946). The poems combine bold imagery and original rhythms with strenuous artistic control; their themes concern states of mind in extremity. In a commentary recorded for the ▷ British Council, she declared: 'One should be able to control and manipulate experiences, even the most terrifying . . . with an informed and intelligent mind.' Plath committed suicide in 1963. Other important posthumous publications are *Crossing the Water* (1971) and *Winter Trees* (1972); Plath also wrote a radio play, *Three Women*, broadcast in 1962. *Collected Poems* (ed. Ted Hughes; 1981); *Letters Home* (1978).
Bib: Alvarez, A., in *Beyond All This Fiddle* and *The Savage God*; Uroff, M. D., *Sylvia Plath and Ted Hughes*; Stevenson, A., *Bitter Fame: A Life of Sylvia Plath*; *The Art of Sylvia Plath: A Symposium* (ed. Charles Newman) contains a bibliography.

Plato (?428–?348 BC)
Greek philosopher. He was a follower of the Athenian philosopher Socrates, and his dialogues

represent conversations in which Socrates takes the lead. The most famous of these 'Socratic' dialogues are *Protagoras, Gorgias, Phaedo, Symposium,* ▷ *Republic, Phaedrus, Timaeus.* His longest work, the *Laws*, does not include Socrates as a character. His central conception is that beyond the world of transient material phenomena lies another eternal world of ideal forms which the material world represents in the form of imitations. His figure for this in the *Republic* is that men in the material world are like people watching shadows moving on the wall of a cave; they see only these shadows and not the realities which cast the shadows. Plato is one of the two most influential philosophers in European thought, the other one being ▷ Aristotle, who was at first his pupil.

Platonic Love
A term which has come to possess three distinct, if related, senses: **1** A love between individuals which transcends sexual desire and attains spiritual heights. This is the most popularly understood sense of the term. **2** The complex doctrine of love which embraces sexuality, but which is directed towards an ideal end, to be found discussed in ▷ Plato's *Symposium*. **3** A reference to homosexual love. This third sense is derived from the praise of homosexual love to be found in the *Symposium*.

Play on words
▷ Figures of Speech.

Pleonasm
The use of unnecessary words in the expression of a meaning, *eg* in the phrase 'a deceitful fraud', 'deceitful' is pleonastic, since a fraud is by definition a kind of deceit.

Plumptre, Anne (1760–1818) and Annabella (1761–1838)
Translators and novelists. The two Plumptre sisters were well-educated and were prolific authors, usually in tandem, for most of their lives, beginning with two ▷ Minerva novels. Anne wrote *Antoinette* (1796), the story of a beautiful and intelligent woman philosopher, while Annabella (commonly known as Bell) published *Montgomery, or Scenes in Wales* (1796). Shortly afterwards they began translating from German, Anne undertaking seven plays by Kotzebue, and Bell, Iffland's play *The Foresters* (1799) and Kotzebue's *The Guardian Angel* (1802). Other novels include Bell's *The Western Mail* (1801) and Anne's *Something New* (1801). In 1802, Anne travelled to France to see the effects of the ▷ French Revolution with ▷ Amelia Opie, and the two sisters parted ways; Anne wrote ▷ travel and ▷ autobiographical works (*Narrative*, 1810, and *History of Myself and My Friends*, 1813), and Bell produced children's stories and domestic material (*Stories for Children*, 1804; *Domestic Management, or the Healthful Cookery Book*, 1804). They returned to collaborative work just before Anne's death in 1818, writing the strange and fascinating collection *Tales of Wonder, of Humour, and of Sentiment*.

Poetics

In ▷ Aristotle's *Poetics* the rules of 'tragedy' are abstracted from a collection of specific instances to form a theoretical model. The function of 'poetics', therefore, has always been to organize formally details of poetic structures, and to this extent it is both prescriptive and descriptive. This Aristotelian usage persists, though in considerably extended form, in the titles of works of critical theory, such as Jonathan Culler's *Structuralist Poetics* (1975). The theoretical works also address the issue of an organized system of analytical methods, as well as aesthetics of artistic construction. More recently, for example in the work of ▷ new historicist critics such as Stephen Greenblatt, the phrase 'cultural poetics' is used to designate an investigation into 'how the boundaries were marked between cultural practices understood to be art forms and other, contiguous, forms of expression' (*Shakespearean Negotiations*; 1988). Such investigations seek to explain how particular aspects of general cultural life are given artistic expression. Whereas Aristotle's Poetics can be said to have a ▷ formalist bent, one of the ways in which the term has come to be used today locates the formal aspects of literary texts within a social context.

Point of view

Term often used in the analysis of ▷ narrative to refer to the perspectives from which the events are seen and narrated. Since these two may be different (the ▷ focal character may differ from the ▷ narrator), the term 'point of view' has been abandoned in more recent ▷ narratology, and its elements separated out into aspects of ▷ mood and ▷ voice.

Political Register, The

A weekly journal started by ▷ William Cobbett in 1802, and continued until the year of his death, 1835. It was singularly bold and independent in opinion, and had a wide circulation especially among the poor of rural England. In 1803, Cobbett was fined £500 for his criticism of the government's Irish policy, and in 1809 he was sent to prison for two years for his criticism of military punishments. He continued to edit the paper from prison. From 1821 it included serial publication of ▷ *Rural Rides*.
▷ Journalism.

Polyphonic

▷ Bakhtin, Mikhail.

Poor Laws

Laws which gave public relief to those among the poor who could not earn their own living and were not supported by others. The first great Poor Law was that of 1601, under Elizabeth I. The dissolution of monasteries and other Church institutions which had undertaken the care of the destitute, together with a number of causes of unemployment (*eg* enclosures) caused a series of poor laws to be passed in the 16th century, of which the law of 1601 was the climax. Every parish was required to appoint overseers, whose task it was to provide work for the able-bodied unemployed, and relief (through a local tax called a 'poor rate') for those who were unable to work. The law survived until the 19th century, when problems of poor relief had become too great for it to be an efficient solution. Local magistrates employed a method known as the 'Speenhamland System', from the place of its origin, by which the unemployed were given enough money to enable them to survive; the disadvantage of this system was that it demoralized those who were employed in very hard labour but unable to earn more than the unemployed who were given relief. In 1834, the New Poor Law was passed. Parishes were grouped into Unions under Boards of Guardians. The main principle of this was that the able-bodied poor were only given relief in ▷ workhouses and that these were not to be so agreeable as to make them inviting to such unemployed as were merely lazy and unwilling to work. The workhouses were in consequence often very disagreeable places, and bitterly unpopular. The law was replaced in 1925 by a more complicated and humane system. In the 1930s, when there was extensive unemployment in Britain, the most unpopular feature of relief to the unemployed was the 'Means Test', involving detailed investigation into whatever means a family might possess to support itself without state aid. The system of National Insurance, set up by the Labour Government of 1945-50, avoided this cause of resentment by making relief available to everyone whatever their income, in return for a universal weekly payment. What is an appropriate level of relief continues to be a matter of debate.

Pornography

This is generally understood to mean representations or literature which is intended to produce sexual excitement. There is, however, a considerable degree of dispute about pornography and it has become the subject of legal cases and public campaigns. The most notorious of these must be the trial concerning ▷ D. H. Lawrence's ▷ *Lady Chatterly's Lover* in 1960. On the right wing are those moralists who wish to police public standards and ban all sexual material, arguing that it depraves and corrupts. Some ▷ feminists also attack pornography at all levels, saying that it is male violence against women; they have particularly broad categories, including advertising; other feminists have sought to offer alternative erotic representations in literature, photography and art, which will be appealing to women. The liberal viewpoint, summed up by the Williams Committee of 1979, draws a distinction between public and private pornography, and if it is not hurting anyone will not interfere legally, though definitions of what is 'private' and what constitutes hurt remain contentious.
▷ Censorship.
Bib: Dworkin A., *Pornography: Men Possessing Women*; Kappeller, S., *Pornography of Representation*; special *Screen* edition on Pornography (1982) (Lawrence, D. H., 'Pornography and Obscenity' in *Phoenix*; Betterton, R. (ed.), *Looking On: Images of Feminity in the Visual Arts and Media*.

Portrait of a Lady, The (1881)

A novel by ▷ Henry James. The heroine, Isabel Archer, is brought from America to England by her aunt, Mrs Touchett, the wife of a retired American banker. Isabel has the candour and freedom conspicuous among American girls of the period; she also has beauty, intelligence, and a spirit of adventure and responsiveness to life. She refuses offers of marriage from both Lord Warburton, a 'prince' of the English aristocracy, and Caspar Goodwood, a 'prince' of American industry. In the meantime her cousin, Ralph Touchett, has fallen in love with her, but he is slowly dying of consumption and dare not become her-suitor. Instead, he tries to play the 'fairy godmother' by persuading his father to leave her the money which would have been due to himself. His action has two unfortunate results: it awakens Isabel's New England Puritan conscience through the sense of responsibility which the possession of wealth entails, and it attracts the rapacious Madame Merle, whose guilty secret is that she is looking for a rich stepmother for her daughter by her former lover, Gilbert Osmond. Osmond (like Madame Merle herself) is an artistic but cold-blooded and totally self-centred expatriate American. Isabel in her humility is easily made to feel her own cultural inferiority to the exquisite exterior qualities of Osmond, whom she sees as the prince she has been looking for – a man deprived of noble potentialities by the unjust circumstance of his poverty. She marries him, only to discover his hollowness, and that her marriage is imprisonment in the ogre's castle.

The novel, sometimes regarded as James's masterpiece, shows his conception of the relationship of the American consciousness to European influences. The Americans who are new to Europe have integrity, the will to live, and good will towards humanity, but they lack richness of tradition and are restricted by the limitations of the New England puritan inhibitions; the American expatriates have rich cultural awareness but this commonly corrupts their integrity, and instead of good will they have immense rapacity, while a European such as Lord Warburton lacks the energy of the Americans. On the other hand the best kind of American expatriate (Ralph Touchett) combines the best of both worlds.

Portrait of the Artist as a Young Man, A (1916)

An autobiographical novel by ▷ James Joyce. The theme is the life of a middle-class Irish boy, Stephen Dedalus, from his infancy in the strongly Catholic, intensely nationalistic environment of Dublin in the 1880s to his departure from Ireland some 20 years later. In his boyhood he sees his elders bitterly divided in consequence of the Church's rejection of Parnell, the nationalist leader, owing to the scandal of his private life. As he grows up he is repelled by the pettiness, treacheries and vindictiveness of Irish nationalism, and for a time is drawn towards the rich spirituality of the Catholic tradition. The Irish Catholic Church, however, also suffered from provincialism and narrowness, and a moment of revelation on the seashore shows him that the largeness of an artistic vocation will alone suffice for him to harmonize the spiritual and fleshly sides of

his nature, and enable him to rise above the vulgarity of his environment; but the choice brings with it the decision to leave Ireland.

The originality of the novel consists in its presentation of the hero's experience from within his own consciousness. The language gradually expands from the fragmentary diction of an infant on the first page through the connected but limited range of expression characteristic of a schoolboy to the sophistication of a fully articulate university student.

▷ Irish fiction in English; stream of consciousness.

Positivism

▷ Comte, Auguste.

Post-colonial fiction

One of the most abiding consequences of British imperialism has been the legacy of the English language bequeathed to the former colonies of the Empire. It is a legacy that has at best proved a mixed blessing, but one which makes it possible to speak of a unity running through the literary production of countries as different from one another as Jamaica and New Zealand, as India and Canada. The writing of each of these countries has been strongly influenced by English cultural norms; at the same time the fact that English was the language of the colonizer has always made it a problematic medium for the Commonwealth or post-colonial writer. The St Lucian poet Derek Walcott (b 1930) encapsulates the essence of the problem in a poem entitled 'A Far Cry From Africa' which, while on one level dramatizing his own personal *Angst* as a Caribbean person of mixed racial descent, responding to the Mau Mau uprising in Kenya in the 1950s, also addresses the sense of cultural schizophrenia he feels. He asks how, 'divided to the vein', he can 'choose/ Between this Africa and the English tongue I love?'

This dilemma is present, to a greater or lesser degree, in virtually all post-colonial fiction in English, and texts are frequently written in hybrid modes that demonstrate some kind of cross-cultural fusion between English and the value-systems of the local culture.

The nature of the local cultures varies considerably, but it is possible to identify two main types; those of the disrupted Third World society and the transplanted New World society. In the former category belong the primarily oral ancestral cultures of Africa and the part-scribal, part-oral cultures of the Indian sub-continent, as well as a variety of myth-centred cultures in South-East Asia and Oceania and other parts of the globe. In all of these societies there has been a disruption of age-old traditions during the period of colonialism, and in the post-independence era an urge to reconstruct which has had to come to terms with the fact that it is impossible simply to turn back the clock but which nevertheless insists that the age-old traditions become a cornerstone in the process of rebuilding. Thus, in West Africa, writers like the Nigerians ▷ Wole Soyinka (b 1934) and ▷ Chinua Achebe (b 1930) have insisted that the artist has a crucial part to play in the process of reconstruction and have seen the author's role as a modern-day equivalent of that of the *griot*, or oral repository of the tribe's history; they have taken the view that he or she must be a spokesperson for the community, not an individualist in the Western Romantic tradition of the artist, and Achebe has particularly stressed the importance of the artist's role as a teacher. In works like *Arrow of God*, (1964) Achebe, like many of his West African contemporaries, has re-examined the historical past of his society and, without sentimentalizing it, implied that a dialogue between past and present is a *sine qua non* for progress in the future.

In the latter category, that of the transplanted New World society, belong the cultures of Canada, Australia and New Zealand, where in each case the majority population is of European origin and has had to adapt, transform or subvert Old World cultural forms and genres in order to make them relevant to very different landscapes and social situations. The Canadian writer ▷ Margaret Atwood (b 1939) dramatizes the problem of constructing an identity in a new land in a poem entitled 'Progressive Insanities of a Pioneer' (in *The Animals in That Country*; 1968) in which the eponymous settler finds himself 'a point/ on a sheet of green paper/ proclaiming himself the centre', but finding he has staked his plot 'in the middle of nowhere' is unable even to name the 'unstructured space' of his New World environment. Later, in her novel *Surfacing* (1972), Atwood offers a more positive approach to the same theme in a work which charts the spiritual odyssey of a contemporary Canadian woman who has constructed a false identity for herself as a result of having internalized a set of rationalist values that are particularly identified with the neo-imperialism of American patriarchal and technological society, but seen to be endemic in the modern world. Women and Canadians are represented as suffering from a common victim syndrome and needing to transform themselves by becoming 'creative non-victims'. The protagonist of *Surfacing* manages to achieve regeneration through reverting to an animal-like identity, regressing to a pre-linguistic mode of existence in which she sees herself as establishing contact with the gods of the original Amerindian inhabitants of Canada and the natural world of the country. Similarly, in ▷ Patrick White's *Voss* (1957) the hero's 19th-century exploration of the interior of Australia, an endeavour which is sharply contrasted with the complacent lives of the country's middle-class coastal dwellers, is only complete once he has died and his blood has seeped into the parched soil of the outback. In both novels the metamorphoses of identity and attitudes to the country that lie at the heart of the texts are complemented on a formal level by a complex metaphorical style that suggests linguistic quest. ▷ Peter Carey's writing offers a more nightmarish, post-modern vision of the contemporary Australian landscape, particularly in his collection of fragmentary short stories, *Exotic Pleasures* (1981).

Simply to label Canadian and Australasian cultures as 'transplanted' is, of course, finally simplistic, since it involves a perspective which confines itself to the majority population. In each case an indigenous population (Amerindians in Canada; Aborigines in Australia; and Maoris in New Zealand), which has been the victim of various kinds of brutalization and discrimination, continues to make a very important contribution to the national culture and in recent years has been doing so through the medium of English. For these groups the struggle for social justice and cultural survival has been – and is – the crucial cultural issue, as it is for the blacks of South Africa. It permeates the writing of Aborigines like Colin Johnson (b 1938), Kath Walker (b 1920), Kevin Gilbert (b 1933) and Jack Davis (b 1917), as well as the prize-winning novels of the Maori writers Witi Ihimaera (b 1944) and ▷ Keri Hulme (b 1947). Generally the criterion for Aboriginality has been self-definition and interestingly many writers who are only a small part Maori or Aborigine, like Keri Hulme and, in Australia, Archie Weller (b 1958), have chosen to identify with this aspect of their ancestry and have generally been accepted by the indigenous group in which they have chosen to locate themselves.

The notion of transplantation also comes to be of less value in the contemporary period, when the original phase of settlement is so far in the past that the sense of displacement has long ceased to operate for most of the country's inhabitants. Nevertheless, new waves of migrants (particularly southern European and south-east Asian immigrants into Australia, and middle European, Italian and East and West Indian immigrants into Canada) continue to experience numerous problems occasioned by transplantation. Yet, for the writers of these countries, the twin pulls of the overseas metropolis (the United States as much as Britain in the case of Canada) and the home country – internationalism and nationalism – have continued to be exercised in a variety of ways, not least through the dominance, until recently, of British and American publishing houses and the problem that local publication, when available, frequently meant a far more restricted readership. Place of publication has, of course, in many cases determined the range and nature of writers' references to local culture and their use of varied English linguistic forms.

The writing of one region, the West Indies, is the product of *both* disruption and transplantation; the region can be classified as *both* Third World *and* New World. The population of the contemporary Commonwealth Caribbean is almost entirely made up of descendants of peoples transplanted from the Old World (the original Carib and Arawak Indian inhabitants have been almost completely exterminated). The most important population group, the descendants of the slaves who were brought from West Africa to work on the West Indian sugar plantations, underwent a very different experience of transplantation from Europeans who went to the Americas or Australasia, since they were forcibly transported and had their culture systematically destroyed in the New World. Family and tribal groups were generally split up on arrival and this led to the emergence of Creolized forms of English as the *lingua franca* through which the slaves communicated with one another and with their masters. So, while the influence of English culture, imposed through the colonial educational curriculum and a range of other institutions has been dominant until recently, the struggle to throw off this culture and replace it by local folk forms has been of a different kind to similar endeavours in other Anglophone New World societies.

Caribbean writing is characterized by a variety of rhetorical devices that take issue with the norms of English literature. Most prominent among these is a range of oral forms that illustrate the complex Creole language situation of the various Caribbean territories – in each case the spoken language is a continuum, with a variety of registers.

Different Caribbean writers have taken a range of stands on the question of Caribbean aesthetics and while some have stressed the importance of the African legacy in the West Indies, others like the Guyanese novelist ▷ Wilson Harris (b 1921) have put the emphasis on the mixed multi-cultural heritage of the region. In a series of complex and hermetic novels, beginning with *Palace of the Peacock* (1960), which break all the rules of European classic ▷ realism, Harris has argued for a cross-cultural vision of consciousness, which he sees as bringing about both psychic and social integration. Walcott takes a similar view in arguing for a 'creative schizophrenia' and thus turning the fragmented cultural legacy occasioned by colonialism into a source of strength rather than divisiveness. It is a position which has analogues in each of the post-colonial literatures.

The essence of contemporary Aboriginal writing has been seen to inhere in *bricolage* (a phrase coined by Claude Lévi-Strauss), using the bits and pieces of the various 'means at hand' in a flexible way to produce something new, and this model can be applied to the literary production of most of the post-colonial countries. While all forms of discourse work in this way – traditional ideas of inspiration functioning in a vacuum have been seriously challenged in recent years – this view of how texts are originated has particular relevance for post-colonial writing and oral forms, where cross-cultural connections abound and where English almost always functions in an ambiguous way. It is especially marked in the work of a complex, post-modernist writer like ▷ Salman Rushdie (b 1947) whose *Midnight's Children* (1981) draws on a vast range of Hindu, Islamic and Western, classical and modern, 'serious' and 'popular' traditions to produce a highly original collage. This takes on the qualities of a 'Bombay Talkie', the eclectic, decorum-confounding dominant film genre of India, a form that is frequently referred to in *Midnight's Children* and which provides a metaphor for the novel's structure. Yet *bricolage* is also a quality of Indian writing in English, such as the novels of ▷ R. K. Narayan (b 1907) and ▷ Nayantara Sahgal (b 1927) that exhibits less technical virtuosity on the surface. In the work of both of these writers there is a fusion of traditional and Western elements (the novel itself is not an indigenous genre in India) which produces a hybrid mode of expression that

exists at the interface of two or more cultures. Contemporary Indian writing in English is a paradox in that it is written in a tongue that is not the dominant spoken language anywhere in India (as a result Indian drama in English hardly exists) and yet it is perhaps the only modern Indian literature able to cross cultural boundaries and give a sense of pan-Indian identity. This situation is, however, only a particular manifestation of the complex cultural predicament of the various post-colonial literatures. Despite their diversity, they have all had to respond to the alien cultural forms imposed during the period of colonialism and to mediate between these forms and modes of expression that have their origins in local or ancestral traditions.

Bib: Atwood, M., *Survival: A Thematic Guide to Canadian Literature*; Baugh, E. (ed.), *Critics on Caribbean Literature*; Goodwin, K., *A History of Australian Literature*; Gérard, A. (ed.), *European-Language Writing in Sub Saharan Africa* (2 vols.); Mukherjee, M., *The Twice-Born Fiction: Themes and Techniques of the Indian Novel in English*. Ashcroft, B. et al., *The Empire Writes Back: Theory and Practice in Post-Colonial Literature*; Nasta, S. (ed.), *Motherlands: Black Women's Writing from Africa, the Caribbean and South Asia*; Said, E. W., *Culture and Imperialism*.

Post-modernism

A term widely used in philosophy and many areas of cultural theory since the 1970s, sometimes with reference to a period in cultural history, sometimes to a philosophical approach and sometimes to a mode within literature, architecture, film, music, dance, television, video, art and a whole range of other cultural practices and forms.

The earliest occurrences of the term are a subject of some debate: there are examples of its use in late 19th-century art criticism and, in the 1930s (as '*postmodernismo*') in relation to Spanish poetry of the period around 1910. However, its earliest applications in English to history and to literature seemed to have occurred roughly simultaneously in 1946, when the historian Arnold Toynbee applied it to the period of Western civilization since 1875 and the American poet and critic Randall Jarrell applied it to the poetry of his compatriot Robert Lowell. In the 1960s the term began to be more widely used in association with 1960s counter-culture and in the late 1970s was taken up within philosophy by French ▷ post-structuralist thinkers. Works influential in the spread of the concept included those listed below by Ihab Hassan (1971), Jean-Francois Lyotard (1979) and Charles Jencks (1977).

There is much debate about the existence, nature and meaning of post-modernism. As the name implies, it involves a relationship to ▷ modernism. Sometimes post-modernism is seen as a reaction *against* modernism, sometimes as a continuation of modernism by other (or more extreme) means and sometimes simply as a chronological successor. When post-modernism is used as a period term, its beginning is generally dated much later than in Toynbee's use: sometime between 1940 and 1975. Whether it is still continuing is also debatable: a stong candidate for successor has not emerged, except perhaps the *fin de siècle* (a term borrowed from the end of the 19th century). Ideas commonly associated with post-modernism include the following: a scepticism about the 'grand narratives' of history, science and philosophy (Lyotard); an emphasis on indeterminacy, multiplicity and playfulness; a breaking-down of the barriers between 'high' and 'popular' culture; a new relationship to the past, involving neither respect nor rejection but an allusive, free borrowing of various elements so as to create a 'double coding' of past and present (Jencks); a new phase of 'late' capitalism marked by the worldwide dominance of American-centred consumerism and the commodification of culture (Jameson); the loss of 'historicity' or an authentic sense of the past in favour of a predominantly 'spatial' mode of understanding (Jameson); other forms of transformation in our understanding of space and time (Harvey); pastiche; a new depthlessness in which the rhetoric of 'deep' (or 'transcendent') meaning and truth is abandoned; the dominance of the 'simulacrum', the copy or imitation which undermines the very idea of originality or authenticity, producing the hyperreal (Baudrillard).

In literature, post-modernism is associated with self-reference, paradox, playfulness, pastiche, allusion and sometimes minimalism. In fiction, the term is usually applied to novels which foreground their own fictionality (▷ metafiction; see Hutcheon); to novels which construct self-consciously fictional versions of history (▷ historiographic metafiction); and to novels which invent separate, parallel or imaginary worlds (see McHale). Novelists such as Kafka, ▷ Beckett and Genet have been identified as precursors of post-modernism, as well as much earlier writers such as ▷ Cervantes and ▷ Sterne.

Critics of post-modernism often claim that it is either a spurious idea or a pernicious doctrine; such critics include ▷ humanists who may regard the whole notion as a fashionable bandwagon with little substance, and ▷ Marxists, who tend to see post-modernism as selling out to consumerism and abandoning the ▷ enlightenment project of the rational liberation of humanity: see Callinicos, Habermas, Norris. Recently the relationship of post-modernism to ▷ feminism (see Waugh) and to post-colonial theory (see Connor) has received much attention.

Bib: Connor, S., *Postmodernist Culture: An Introduction to Theories of the Contemporary;* Hassan, I., *The Dismemberment of Orpheus: Toward a Postmodern Literature;* Lyotard, J.-F., *The Postmodern Condition: A Report on Knowledge;* Hutcheon, L., *A Poetics of Postmodernism: History, Theory, Fiction* and *The Politics of Postmodernism;* Harvey, D., *The Condition of Postmodernity;* Calinescu, M., *Five Faces of Modernity;* Callinicos, A., *Against Postmodernism: A Marxist Critique;* Bernstein, R.J. (ed.), *Habermas and Modernity;* Norris, C., *What's Wrong with Postmodernism: Critical Theory and the Ends of Philosophy;* Waugh, P., *Feminine Fictions: Revisiting the Postmodern.*

Post-structuralism

At first glance, the term post-structuralism seems to imply that the post-structuralists came after the structuralists and that post-structuralism was the heir of ▷ structuralism. In practice, however, there is not a clear-cut division between structuralism and post-structuralism. Although the two have different focuses of interest and preoccupations, many of their concerns bind them together. Structuralism encompasses approaches to criticism which use linguistic models to enable critics to focus not on the inherent meaning of a work but on the structures which *produce* or generate meaning. Post-structuralism focuses on the ways in which the texts themselves subvert this enterprise; the structuralist emphasis on ▷ difference as constructing relatively stable systems of meaning is displaced in post-structuralism by ▷ Derrida's concept of *différance*: a French term which puns on the words for 'difference' and 'deferral', thus suggesting the endless displacement of unstable meaning along a chain of signifiers. Leading post-structuralists include Derrida, ▷ Lacan, Gilles Deleuze, J. Hillis Miller and ▷ Paul de Man.

▷ Deconstruction; Feminism.

Bib: Culler, J. *On Deconstruction;* Norris, C, *Deconstruction: Theory and Practice;* Sturrock, J. (ed.), *Structuralism and Since.*

Potter, Beatrix (1866–1943)

Writer for children. One of the most famous and widely-translated writers of children's stories, Potter's anthropomorphic tales of animal adventures have been famously praised by ▷ Graham Greene for their lack of sentimentality. Beginning with *The Tale of Peter Rabbit* (1901) (published and printed – as well as, of course, illustrated – by Potter herself), her simple stories have become classics of ▷ children's writing. Potter was also an accomplished naturalist, artist (illustrating all her own work), and (later) sheep farmer. Her numerous works hardly need listing; they include: *The Tale of Squirrel Nutkin* (1903); *The Tailor of Gloucester* (1903); *The Tale of Jemima Puddle-Duck* (1908); *The Tale of Mr Tod* (1912). See also *The Journals of Beatrix Potter* (1966) and *Dear Ivy, Dear June: Letters from Beatrix Potter* (1977).
Bib: Godden, R., *The Tale of the Tales;* Greene, G., 'Beatrix Potter' in *Collected Essays;* Linder, L., *The History of the Writings of Beatrix Potter,* Taylor, J., *Beatrix Potter: Artist, Storyteller, Countrywoman.*

Powell, Anthony (b 1905)

Novelist. He writes sophisticated comedy of upper-class life in England since 1920; his approach may be compared with the different treatment of the same society by ▷ Aldous Huxley, ▷ Evelyn Waugh, and by ▷ D. H. Lawrence in *St Mawr.* Early novels are: *Afternoon Men* (1931); *Venusberg* (1932); *From a View to a Death* (1933); *Agents and Patients* (1936); *What's Become of Waring* (1939).

In 1948 he produced a study of ▷ John Aubrey, the 17th-century anecdotal biographer, author of *Brief Lives.* He then began his major work which, it has been suggested, owes something to Aubrey as it clearly does to the sequence *A la Recherche*

du Temps Perdu by the French novelist ▷ Marcel Proust. Powell's sequence of novels is called *A Dance to the Music of Time*. The narrator, whose personality is kept in detachment but not eliminated, is an upper-class young man with whose life various circles of friends intertwine in a kind of dance, and in a way that is only conceivable in the upper levels of any society. The characters make a pattern of contrasts, the most serious and interesting being that of the man of distinction – Stringham – who evokes the high style of an Elizabethan courtier such as Ralegh, but who is in the worldly sense a failure, and Widmerpool, the man of grotesque and crude manners and feeling, who is yet a worldly success owing to his insensibility and the force of his ambition. *A Dance to the Music of Time* consists of: *A Question of Upbringing* (1951); *A Buyer's Market* (1952); *The Acceptance World* (1955); *At Lady Molly's* (1957); *Casanova's Chinese Restaurant* (1960); *The Kindly Ones* (1962); *The Valley of Bones* (1964); *The Soldier's Art* (1966); *The Military Philosophers* (1968); *Books Do Furnish a Room* (1971); *Temporary Kings* (1973); *Hearing Secret Harmonies* (1975). The sequence begins in 1921 at the narrator's public school; it ends after the war with the death of Widmerpool in circumstances of sinister pathos. Powell has followed up his novel sequence with a sequence of memoirs entitled *To Keep The Ball Rolling*: *Infants of the Spring* (1978); *Messengers of Day* (1978); *Faces in My Time* (1980); *The Strangers All Are Gone* (1982). Other novels: *O, How the Wheel Becomes It!* (1983); *The Fisher King* (1986).
Bib: Bergonzi, B., *Anthony Powell*; Spurling, H., *Invitation to the Dance*; Tucker, J., *The Novels of Anthony Powell*; Mc Ewan, N., *Anthony Powell*.

Powys, John Cowper (1872–1963)
Novelist, poet and essayist. Principal novels are: *Wolf Solent* (1929); *A Glastonbury Romance* (1932); *Weymouth Sands* (1934); *Maiden Castle* (1936); *Owen Glendower* (1940); *Porius* (1951). Works of criticism and thought: *Visions and Revisions* (1915; revised 1935); *Psychoanalysis and Morality* (1923); *The Religion of a Sceptic* (1925); *The Meaning of Culture* (1929); *In Defence of Sensuality* (1930); *The Art of Happiness* (1935); *The Pleasures of Literature* (1938). One of his most famous books is his *Autobiography* (1934), developed from his contribution to the *Confessions of Two Brothers* (1916) written with Llewelyn Powys.

Like his brother, ▷ T. F. Powys, his fiction is influenced by his background in the English west country, but his prose is contrasted with his brother's by its expansiveness and diffuseness. His writing combines a strongly physical sensationalism with a fascination for the intangible and mysterious reaches of human experience. He is concerned with the transformation of ordinary life by a contemplative intensity which generates a mythical sense of the individual's relation to his natural environment. His work shows the influence of ▷ Thomas Hardy, with whom he was acquainted. Critics are divided as to whether Powys is an overrated or an underrated novelist.
Bib: Graves, R. P., *The Brothers Powys*; Cavaliero, G., *John Cowper Powys, Novelist*; Churchill, R. C., *The Powys Brothers*.

Powys, Theodore Francis (1875–1953)
Novelist and short-story writer; brother of ▷ John Cowper Powys. His novels and fables were set in the rural south-west of England; the characters are presented with a simplicity and poetry resembling the style of the Old Testament of the Bible, but the individuality of the expression is too distinct for the resemblance to be obvious, and the tone is naïve on the surface but sophisticated in its pagan, often cynical implications. At its best, *eg* in *Mr Weston's Good Wine* (1927) and *Fables* (1929), Powys's art rose to exquisite tragic poetry; at its worst it descended to brutality and cruelty. His fiction is a very late and unusual example in English of a writer using purely rural traditions and environment; the tragic pessimism, less humane and more sophisticated than ▷ Thomas Hardy's, is perhaps a reflection of the disappearing vitality of that way of life. Some other works: *Mark Only* (1924); *Mr Tasker's Gods* (1925); *Kindness in a Corner* (1930). *Fables* was republished as *No Painted Plumage* in 1934.
Bib: Coombes, H., *T. F. Powys*; Hunter, W., *The Novels and Stories of T. F. Powys*.

Predestination
A theological doctrine which holds that, since God in his eternal wisdom has foreknown the events of time since before the creation of the world, he has foreseen and chosen those individuals who are damned and those who are saved for eternal life after death. Those who are saved are called 'the elect', and those who are damned 'the reprobate'.

Pride and Prejudice (1813)
A novel by ▷ Jane Austen. Mr and Mrs Bennet belong to the minor gentry and live at Longbourne near London. Mr Bennet is witty and intelligent, and bored with his foolish wife. They have five daughters, whose marriage prospects are Mrs Bennet's chief interest in life, since the estate is 'entailed' – *ie* by the law of the period it will go on Mr Bennet's death to his nearest male relation, a sycophantic clergyman called Mr Collins. The main part of the story is concerned with the relationship between the witty and attractive Elizabeth Bennet and the haughty and fastidious Fitzwilliam Darcy, who at first considers her beneath his notice and later, on coming to the point of asking her to marry him, finds that she is resolutely prejudiced against him. His friend Charles Bingley is in love with the eldest daughter, Jane, but they are kept apart by the jealous snobbishness of his sisters and (at first) the fastidious disapproval of Darcy. Meanwhile, Elizabeth is subjected to an insolent offer of marriage by Mr Collins and the arrogant condescension of his patroness, Lady Catherine de Bourgh, Darcy's aunt. Those who regard the Bennet family as foolish and vulgar have their opinion justified when Lydia Bennet elopes with an irresponsible young officer, George Wickham. By this time, however, Darcy and Elizabeth have been chastened by finding in one

another a fastidiousness and pride that equal their own and, despite the family scandal, they are united.

The novel has always been one of the most liked of Jane Austen's, and it contains excellent social comedy, but in some respects it stands apart. She herself said of it 'The work is rather too light, and bright, and sparkling; it wants to be stretched out here and there with a long chapter of sense.' Elizabeth Bennet was, however, her own favourite heroine.

Priestley, J. B. (John Boynton) (1894–1984)
British novelist and playwright, whose first success as a novelist was *The Good Companions* (1929) an entertaining story of theatrical touring, and as a playwright with *Dangerous Corner* in 1932, a thriller dealing with the theme of time. This was followed by two other 'time' plays, *Time and the Conways* and *I Have Been Here Before*, in 1937. His many other novels include *Angel Pavement* (1930), *Bright Day* (1946) and *The Image Man* (1968). In his drama he is notable for experimenting with a variety of dramatic subjects and styles, from the popular thrillers such as those mentioned above and *An Inspector Calls* (1945), to conventional comedies like *Laburnum Grove* (1933) and *When We are Married* (1938), the ▷ Chekhovian *Eden End* (1934) and the expressionistic *Johnson over Jordan* (1939). One of his later works was a dramatization with ▷ Iris Murdoch of her novel, *A Severed Head* (1963).

Prince, Mary (c 1788–c 1833)
Autobiographer. Mary Prince was a slave who, on being abandoned in London in 1831, was befriended by Susannah Moodie (shortly to become one of the first Canadian women writers) who acted as her amanuensis, and by Thomas Pringe who campaigned for her emancipation. Her story was published in that year as part of the campaign, (reprinted in 1987, edited by Moira Ferguson). Prince was born in Bermuda in the household of a kindly family, but she was sold separately from her family when she was eleven and her new owners were savagely cruel to her. Over the next eighteen years Prince was flogged, put to work at salt production (particularly harsh), and probably sexually abused. But by 1826 she was in Antigua, had converted to Methodism, had learned to read and had married Daniel Jones, a free man. Her owners appeared to have attempted to break this new sense of independence by taking her to London, but when that failed, they simply threw her out on to the streets. Prince's narrative is part of a tradition of slave narratives which began at the beginning of the 18th century and were an important contribution to the political movement against slavery.
    ▷ Autobiography.

Pritchett, V. S. (Victor Sawdon) (b 1900)
Novelist, short-story writer, critic and travel writer. He left school at 15 to work in the leather trade, and also worked in the photographic trade in Paris before becoming a journalist. Since 1926 he has been a regular critic for the ▷ *New Statesman*, and since 1946 a director. He is best known for his short stories, which are economical and understated,

employing colloquial dialogue. His work is primarily in a ▷ realist mode, and consists of ironic observation of society and human eccentricity. Story collections are: *Collected Stories* (1982); *More Collected Stories* (1983). His novels are: *Clare Drummer* (1929); *Shirley Sanz* (1932); *Nothing Like Leather* (1935); *Dead Man Leading* (1937); *Mr Beluncle* (1951). Criticism includes: *The Living Novel* (1946); *Balzac: A Biography* (1973); *The Myth Makers: Essays on European, Russian and South American Novelists* (1979).
Bib: Baldwin, D. R., *V. S. Pritchett*.

Professor, The (1857)
The first novel by ▷ Charlotte Brontë. She offered it for publication in 1846 but it was refused and not published until 1857 after her death. In the meantime she recast the material, which was based on her experience as a teacher in Brussels in 1843, and made it into ▷ *Villette*, which came out in 1853. *The Professor* has a man, William Crimsworth, for its central character, whereas *Villette* has a young woman, Lucy Snowe. William Crimsworth has a love affair with an Anglo-Swiss woman teacher analogous to Lucy's with Monsieur Paul Emmanuel but the relationship is less intricate and profound.

Protestantism
A term used for all varieties of Christian belief which broke away from Roman Catholicism during the Reformation in the 16th century, or for religious communities not in agreement with Roman Catholicism but originating since the Reformation. It was first used in regard to those who protested against the Emperor Charles V's condemnation of the reformers in Germany at the Diet of Spires, 1529. Protestants in Britain include Anglicans, Presbyterians, Methodists and Baptists.

Proust, Marcel (1871–1922)
French writer. Early in his career, he was the author of critical works, *Les Plaisirs et les jours* (1896; translations from Ruskin), *Pastiches et mélanges* (1919) and two posthumously published works *Contre Sainte-Beuve* (1981), and the incomplete novel *Jean Santeuil* (1952). Proust is nonetheless known for one book, his major work, *A la recherche du temps perdu*. It runs to 3,000 printed pages and was originally published in eight parts between 1913 and 1927. The novel was first translated by C. K. Scott-Moncrieff under the title *Remembrance of Things Past*, but a recent and much improved version has been completed by Terence Kilmartin.

A la recherche is the story of an artistic vocation, the attempt to write a novel which is similar to (though not the same as) that which the reader has before him. The novel itself is full of artist-figures, and the narrator's own endeavours to perceive pattern in disorder and fragmentation centre crucially on a discovery, a discovery about time and memory. The attempt to resurrect and recapture time past through voluntary memory cannot but fail, for voluntary memory is sifted for its relevancies. The past can consequently only be reached by involuntary memory, itself triggered by the most apparently innocuous and circumstantial of objects: a madeleine dipped in tea, a starched napkin, an uneven paving-stone. These objects are associated with forgotten events in the past, and those instants when the bond between past and present is recovered and the past reborn are 'privileged moments' (*moments privilégiés*). The novel jettisons a unilinear plot, while the central focus for narration is restricted to that of Marcel (not to be confused with Proust himself); impressions and sensations are fed through his consciousness which evolves over time and constitutes a devolved, perceptually-limited human subject. Proust's portrayal of social and above all sexual relations, moreover, intensify the sense of a self unable to know others, until the narrator realizes that only art gives access to others, since only in art is there the 'real residue' of the personality.

Proust's novel aroused two kinds of reactions. His minuteness in rendering human consciousness, for example, recalls both ▷ Henry James and ▷ James Joyce. His perception that the insignificance of an incident at the time of experiencing it contrasts with the importance it may come to have in the memory anticipates ▷ Virginia Woolf. The design by which relationships amplify through a lifetime into a pattern evocative of musical composition was emulated by ▷ Anthony Powell in *A Dance to the Music of Time*. On the other hand other 20th-century novelists, such as ▷ D. H. Lawrence and ▷ L. H. Myers, have rejected Proust on the grounds that his principles are merely aesthetic.

Psychoanalytical criticism

Psychoanalysis and literary criticism both seek to interpret their respective objects of enquiry, and both involve the analysis of language. In its early manifestations psychoanalytical criticism (*eg* Ernest Jones's *Hamlet and Oedipus*; 1949) sought to apply the methods of psychoanalysis to particular texts, in order to uncover their 'unconscious'. Jones's claim was to reveal the causes of Hamlet's behaviour, beginning from the assumption that 'current response is always compounded partly of a response to the actual situation and partly of past responses to older situations that are unconsciously felt to be similar'. The French psychoanalyst ▷ Jacques Lacan's re-reading of ▷ Freud has sought to render problematical this relationship between patient and analyst, and, by implication, between text and reader. Lacan's description of the unconscious as being structured 'like a language' raises fundamental questions for the authoritative role usually ascribed to the literary critic. To this extent the 'unconscious' of the literary text is brought into confrontation with the unconscious of the critic.

Many of the terms taken from psychology which are associated with Lacan's reading of Freud have been incorporated into the language of literary criticism; for example, the decentred subject of psychoanalysis, ▷ condensation, ▷ displacement, the realm of the ▷ 'imaginary', the ▷ symbolic order, all refer in some way to textual mechanisms.
Bib: Laplanche, J. and Pontalis, J-B., *The Language of Psychoanalysis*; Lacan, J., *The Four Fundamental Concepts of Psychoanalysis*; Wright, E., *Psychoanalytical Criticism*; McCabe, C., *The Talking Cure: Essays*

in Psychoanalysis and Language; Layton, L. and Schapiro, B.A. (eds.), *Narcissism and the Text: Studies in Literature and the Psychology of Self*; Freud, S., *The Pelican Freud Library*, vol 14: *Art and Literature*.

Public schools

In Britain these are not and have never been either schools under the state, or entirely non-feepaying schools. They are distinguished from 'private' schools in not being run for private profit by individual owners; like the colleges of Oxford and Cambridge, they were founded and endowed for the public good, often for poor scholars. Until the Education Act of 1944, they were often hard to distinguish from endowed Grammar Schools; the latter were, however, more likely to draw on the immediate locality for their pupils, whereas the public schools drew on the whole nation, with varying provision for 'poor scholars'. Since, until the 19th century, education was largely restricted to study of the classics – ancient Greek and Latin language and literature – they tended to attract, in the Middle Ages, those who were to enter the Church and the learned professions; from the 16th century it became increasingly regarded as indispensable to 'a gentleman' that he should possess a firm classical culture, and from the 18th century, public schools began to be aristocratic educational institutions. The middle classes often had little use for the education they provided, or they were excluded as Dissenters and went to a Dissenting Academy instead, where in any case the education was wider and more practical. A change came in the 19th century when the middle classes had enormously increased in wealth and numbers and many of them aspired to be or regarded themselves as 'gentlemen' and required a 'gentleman's education' for their sons. Several other causes extended public school education to much of the middle class: Dissenting Academies declined and public school education broadened; ▷ Thomas Arnold as headmaster of ▷ Rugby (1828–42) imbued it with strong religious and moral feeling, suited to the traditions of the middle classes, in which Puritanism was a large element; the country needed a large governing class for its rapidly growing empire. Now that this empire has gone, various motives, creditable and less creditable, cause the English upper and middle classes to maintain the public schools; sometimes the motive may be snobbery, but it is often the educational prestige that some public schools have acquired. The nature of this prestige varies greatly, since 20th-century public schools do not conform to a model. In the 19th century the inspiration of Arnold tended to make the public schools somewhat narrow; leadership and fair-mindedness were cultivated at the expense of wide culture and intellectual flexibility. When Arnold's son, the poet and critic ▷ Matthew Arnold, described the English upper classes as 'barbarians', he was thinking of the products of the public schools.

Some public schools date from the 19th century, but those with most prestige are usually much older: Winchester (founded 1382); Westminster (1560); Eton (1440); Harrow (1571); Rugby (1567). The public school system is 'English' rather than 'British', since it has flourished mainly in England, and has never become characteristic of Scotland, Wales or Ireland, though distinguished public schools exist in those countries. It was at one time a predominantly masculine system, although there are now a large number of girls' public schools and a number of boys' schools have begun to admit girls, especially into their sixth forms.

Punch

A weekly comic periodical, founded in 1841. Thomas Hood and ▷ Thackeray were early members of its staff, and it employed a number of distinguished illustrators in the 19th century including Leech, Tenniel, Keene, and ▷ George Du Maurier. From 1849 for a century it kept the same cover picture – of Punch of the puppet-shows. It was at first a radical paper, but as it became more and more an upper-class 'institution', so in politics, tone and taste it began to represent an influential but increasingly narrow section of the upper middle class. It has published the work of many famous cartoonists, including, in latter years, Ronald Searle, Michael Heath, Bill Tidy and Gerald Scarfe. It closed down in 1992.

Purbeck, Elizabeth and Jane (c 1789–1802)

Novelists. The Purbeck sisters wrote collaborative novels which balanced romantic narratives with gentle social and political comment. *History of Sir George Warrington, or The Political Quixote* (1797) and *Neville Castle* (1802) show a certain sympathy for the ideals of equality and use characters from real life, such as ▷ Tom Paine, and historical backdrops, like the ▷ French Revolution, in order to test their protagonists' devotion to their political and philosophical commitments. The latter novel also provides interesting critical material on ▷ Fanny Burney, ▷ Fielding, ▷ Sophia Lee, and ▷ Richardson.

Purgatorio

The second book of the ▷ *Divina Commedia* by ▷ Dante. Having emerged from the Inferno, the poet, still accompanied by ▷ Virgil, follows a spiral up to the Mount of Purgatory, where the souls of the dead are purged of the stains of their sins as they await release into Heaven. They encounter various groups of repentant sinners on the seven circular ledges of the mountain, who suffer punishments and pain, but do so more willingly, knowing the suffering will pass in the end. On its summit is the Earthly Paradise where the poet meets Beatrice, who is to guide him through the spheres of Heaven.

▷ *Inferno; Paradiso.*

Puritanism

The term is used in a narrow sense of religious practice and attitudes, and in a broad sense of an ethical outlook which is much less easy to define.

1 In its strict sense, 'Puritan' was applied to those Protestant reformers who rejected Queen Elizabeth's religious settlement of 1560. This settlement sought a middle way between Roman Catholicism and the extreme spirit of reform of Calvin's Geneva. The

Puritans, influenced by Geneva, Zurich, and other Continental centres, objected to the retention of bishops and to any appearance of what they regarded as superstition in church worship – the wearing of vestments by the priests, and any kind of religious image. Apart from their united opposition to Roman Catholicism and their insistence on simplicity in religious forms, Puritans disagreed among themselves on questions of doctrine and church organization. The principal sects were: Presbyterians, Independents (at first called Brownists, and later Congregationalists), Baptists, and (later) ▷ Quakers. They were strong in the towns, especially in London, and in the University of Cambridge, and socially they were widespread, and included members of the aristocracy and of the working classes, as well as the middle, commercial classes where they had their chief strength. Puritanism was very strong in the first half of the 17th century and reached its peak of power after the Civil War of 1642–6 – a war which was ostensibly religious, although it was also political. Matters of church government were much involved with matters of state government, since Presbyterians and Independents, who believed in popular control of the church, were not likely to tolerate royal control of Parliament's political affairs. Puritanism was both religiously and politically supreme in the decade 1650–60, but on the Restoration of the monarchy Puritans were denied participation in the Church of England, and refused rights of free religious worship. The last was granted them by the Toleration Act of 1689, and during the 18th century both Puritanism and the official attitude to it were modified under the influence of Rationalism. Nonetheless, the Methodist movement of that century had many of the characteristics of the older Puritan sects. It was, moreover, only in 1829 that Nonconformists (as they were now called) were allowed to offer themselves as candidates for seats in Parliament, and only in 1871 did the Universities of Oxford and Cambridge cease to be the monopoly of the Church of England.

2 In the broader sense of a whole way of life, puritanism has always represented strict obedience to the dictates of conscience and strong emphasis on the virtue of self-denial. In this sense individuals can be described as 'puritan' whether or not they belong to one of the recognized Puritan sects, or even if they are atheists.

The word 'Puritan' is often thought to imply hostility to the arts, but this is not necessarily true. In the reign of Elizabeth I poets such as Edmund Spenser and ▷ Sidney combined a strong puritan moral tone (without any Puritan doctrine in the sectarian sense) with an intense delight in artistic form; in the 17th century John Milton was an ardent Puritan, but his poetry is one of the climaxes of English Renaissance art. However, it is true that the strict Puritans of the age of Shakespeare were commonly opponents of the art of the theatre; this was partly because the theatres were sometimes scenes of moral licentiousness and disorder, and partly because the strict Puritan, in his intense love of truth, was very inclined to confuse fiction with lying. Thus in the later 17th century ▷ Bunyan was criticized by some of his Puritan comrades for writing fiction in his allegory, ▷ *Pilgrim's Progress*, and in the early 18th century ▷ Defoe had to defend his ▷ *Robinson Crusoe* against similar charges. Nonetheless, in the 18th and 19th centuries, Puritanism, or attitudes derived from it, did tend to encourage 'philistinism', or contempt for culture. This was because Puritanism had always encouraged an essentially practical attitude to worldly affairs, and when religion slackened as a driving force, the practical virtues came to be regarded as the principal, if not the only ones. Art, on the other hand, encourages the contemplative virtues, which the practical man of Puritan tradition was inclined to regard as unnecessary, therefore frivolous, and so, in a puritan sense, 'sinful'. There is continuity of development from Priestley, the 18th-century scientist and preacher, through the practical philosophy of ▷ Bentham, to James Mill, the ▷ Utilitarian leader, who was an atheist.

What is called the 'Puritan conscience', on the other hand, had an important influence on one kind of art form – the novel. Puritans believed that the good life could only be lived by 'the inner light' – the voice of God in the heart – and to discern this light it was necessary to conduct the most scrupulous self-enquiry. This produced the kind of spiritual autobiography that was common in the mid-17th century, and of which the best example is Bunyan's ▷ *Grace Abounding*. Such self-knowledge had two important consequences: it increased interest in, and understanding of, the human heart in others as well as the self, and the first results of this are apparent in Bunyan's *Pilgrim's Progress*; but it also encouraged a sense of the loneliness of the individual – a sense that was supported by the growing economic individualism of the later 17th century. These are important constituents of the novelist's vision, and when one adds to them the preoccupation with moral values with which Puritanism is so bound up, and which are such a permanent feature of the English

novel, it is possible to think that without Puritanism the novel form would never have developed indigenously in England.

Puss in Boots
A folk tale, translated into English in 1720 from the French collection by ▷ Charles Perrault. The cat is the property of a poor man, the third son of a miller. By the animal's ingenuity, the miller's son marries the king's daughter. The story is a popular theme of Christmas pantomimes.

Pym, Barbara (1913–80)
Novelist. Educated at Oxford University, she served with the W.R.N.S. during World War II, and subsequently worked at the International African Institute in London. Between 1950 and 1961 she published six novels: there then followed 16 years during which she could not find a publisher. After praise from Lord David Cecil and the poet Philip Larkin in 1977 her work received renewed attention, and she published a further three novels. Since then her work has enjoyed considerable popularity. Her novels are sensitive, shrewd, ironical portraits of English middle-class life, with a particular focus on the lives of women; the social contexts are frequently academic and clerical. She is often said to write in the tradition of ▷ Jane Austen. A further three novels were published posthumously. Her novels are: *Some Tame Gazelle* (1950); *Excellent Women* (1952); *Jane and Prudence* (1953); *Less Than Angels* (1955); *A Glass of Blessings* (1958); *No Fond Return of Love* (1961); *Quartet in Autumn* (1977); *The Sweet Dove Died* (1978); *A Few Green Leaves* (1980); *An Unsuitable Attachment* (1982); *Crampton Hodnet* (1985); *An Academic Question* (1986).
Bib: Benet, D., *The Life and Work of Barbara Pym*; Weld, A., *Barbara Pym and the Novel of Manners*; Liddell, R., *A Mind at Ease: Barbara Pym and Her Novels*.

Q

Quakers

Originally a derisive name for the members of a religious society properly called the Society of Friends; the Friends are still known as Quakers, but the term has lost its contemptuous significance. The Society was founded by ▷ George Fox, who began his preaching career in 1647. He preached the truth came from an inner spiritual light, and declared that no special class of men (*ie* priests) or buildings (*ie* churches) should be set apart for religious purposes. This individualism at first attracted a number of mentally disturbed followers whose ecstasies are perhaps responsible for the nickname 'Quaker', though Fox himself declared that it was first used in 1650 because he taught his followers to 'Tremble at the World of the Lord'. They held a view, unusual among ▷ Puritans, that it was possible to gain complete victory over sin in this life. Such a doctrine, in addition to their refusal to accept those religious institutions that the other Puritans accepted, made them intensely unpopular for the first ten years of their existence. Later they became influential far beyond their numbers, which have remained comparatively few. Owing to the freedom of mind which is the essence of the movement, it is difficult to define their doctrine, which seems to vary greatly among individuals. On the other hand they are well known for a range of characteristic virtues: humanitarianism (they were amongst the first to protest against slavery – 1688); non-resistance to violence; respect for individuals regardless of race, sex, or religion; sobriety of conduct and tranquillity of mind. One of the most important of their early members was William Penn (1644–1718), the founder of the American colony of Pennsylvania. Like other Puritans, they were prominent in commerce, but took care to engage in activities that were not harmful; in consequence Quaker names are particularly well known in connection with the manufacture of chocolate. However, in the 18th century their outstanding importance was in banking: their sober-mindedness and strictness of morality counteracted the speculative manias of the time, and did much to establish secure financial foundations for the rapid expansion of British trade.

Quarterly Review, The

Founded by John Murray in 1809 as a moderate Tory rival to the ▷ *Edinburgh Review*. The first editor was the irrascible traditionalist William Gifford, and later editors included ▷ Samuel Taylor Coleridge's nephew, Sir J. T. Coleridge, and John Lockhart. ▷ Sir Walter Scott, Robert Southey and Samuel Rogers were early contributors. Scott's approving review of ▷ Jane Austen's ▷ *Emma* appeared in the *Quarterly* in March 1816, and a hostile article by John Wilson Croker on John Keats's *Endymion* (Sept. 1818) provoked Lord Byron's squib (written in 1821):

> *Who kill'd John Keats?*
> *'I,' says the* Quarterly,
> *So savage and Tartarly:*
> *'Twas one of my feats.'*

Rabelais, François (?1495–1553)

French comic writer. He was successively a Franciscan friar, then Benedictine monk, before abandoning the religious life and turning to the study of medicine (he became a Bachelor of Medicine at Montpellier in 1535). He was protected by the powerful Du Bellay family in his censorship disputes with the Sorbonne. His famous works are all in prose, but difficult to classify because of their kaleidoscopic forms of narrative and plot. ▷ *Pantagruel* (1533) and ▷ *Gargantua* (1535) were later reversed in sequence, Gargantua being the father of Pantagruel. Ten years and more later come *Tiers Livre* (*Third Book*, 1545) and *Quart Livre* (*Fourth Book*, first version 1548, expanded version 1552). The authenticity of the *Cinquiesme Livre* (1564) remains disputed, though the opening section, *L'Isle Sonnante* ('Ringing Island'), was published separately in Rabelais's lifetime and is accepted by some as his work.

There is in Rabelais an exuberant command of linguistic mechanisms which underpin the entire range of comedy he deploys, from simple pun to obscenity, and slapstick and absurdity to invective and satire. Among English writers consciously indebted to Rabelais, Sir John Harington's (?1560–1612) *Metamorphosis of Ajax* and *Anatomy* follow his style, using coprological humour and mock encomia; the Elizabethan journalist ▷ Thomas Nashe has much of Rabelais's vitality; Robert Burton's *Anatomy of Melancholy* (1621–51) has a comparable amplitude of language; and Samuel Butler's bitter attack on the Puritans (▷ Puritanism), the mock-epic *Hudibras* (1663), is more than Rabelaisian in its bitter humour. ▷ Swift shares Rabelais's indignation, but his disgust is un-Rabelaisian, while ▷ Sterne has a similar expansiveness, yet the prurience of his humour has no counterpart in Rabelais. Rabelais was notably translated by the Scotsman, Sir Thomas Urquhart (c 1611–60) (Books I–II, 1653; Book III, 1693), with continuations by Peter Motteux (1663–1718) (Books IV–V, 1693–94).

Radcliffe, Mrs Ann (1764–1823)

Novelist. She was one of the most famous of the writers of ▷ Gothic novels, which sought to gain their effect through mystery and the supernatural in a setting of grand scenic description. She was immensely popular in her own day for her four novels: *The Sicilian Romance* (1790); *The Romance of the Forest* (1791); ▷ *The Mysteries of Udolpho* (1794), and *The Italian* (1797). *Udolpho* is the most remembered, owing to satirization through an account of its effect on a young girl in ▷ Jane Austen's ▷ *Northanger Abbey*.
Bib: Cotton, D., *The Civilized Imagination: A Study of Ann Radcliffe, Jane Austen and Sir Walter Scott.*

Radicalism

The political views of Radicals, who believe in the need for thorough reform going right to the roots (the meaning of 'radical') and origins of undemocratic abuses. The term probably originated in 1797 with the declaration of Charles James Fox that 'radical reform' was necessary. In the early 19th century it had the pejorative connotation that 'extremist' has today.

Rainbow, The (1915)

A novel by ▷ D. H. Lawrence. It is set in Lawrence's own background, the English Midlands; the subject is three generations of the Brangwen family extending from the middle of the last century to the early years of the present one.

The Brangwens are a family of farmers and have for generations lived on their own land which, by the time at which the novel begins, is near an encroaching industrial area. The men of the family are depicted as concentrating their minds earthwards, on their work and surroundings; the women have tended to look outwards to society, and to emulate their social superiors. Tom Brangwen, the first of the main characters, is sent to a grammar school by his ambitious mother; the experience both frustrates him and arouses him. His awakened need for what is strange and mysterious attracts him to Lydia Lensky, an aristocratic but impoverished Polish exile, a widow, and the mother of a small daughter. They marry and although their marriage meets difficulties it becomes a happy one. Lydia and Tom remain ignorant of much in each other's nature, but Lydia finds confidence in Tom's established way of life, while he finds enlargement precisely in what, for him, is mysterious in his wife. Tom's stepdaughter, Anna, is attracted to his nephew, Will Brangwen, who has had an urban upbringing and has a strong artistic imagination and profound religious instincts inherited from his forefathers. This marriage is much less happy. Anna is suspicious and jealous of her husband's religious spirit, and since he himself cannot relate it to a way of life, she succeeds in destroying it. In doing so, she unintentionally transforms him from an original artist into a craftsman in the ▷ William Morris style. They are united in a passionate night-time sensuality, but have no daylight union. Their daughter, Ursula, belongs to the first generation of the modern woman: she sets out to be a teacher, and after an intense struggle in one of the characteristically inhuman English board schools, she succeeds in affirming her independence. A lesbian relationship with a teacher does not last and her love affair with Skrebensky, a thoroughly Anglicized descendant of another Polish exile, ends in frustration. She inherits from her mother a capacity for passion which expresses her full nature, whereas his nature is divided between a dead conformity to society and a sensuality which is incapable of real passion. Ursula tries to compromise by suppressing her instincts, but a concluding scene, in which she is exposed to the menace of restless horses, on to which she projects her disturbed emotions, shows that she is wrong in attempting this solution. The story of Ursula and her sister Gudrun is continued in ▷ *Women in Love*, originally conceived as part of the same novel. The title of the novel refers to its central symbol of a rainbow, or arch. This symbol signifies an ideal which modifies with time, from the stability of an achieved relationship in the first generation to the

transcendant hope of a collective rebirth at the end
of the novel.

The novel was for a time suppressed on grounds
of immorality, but is now regarded as one of
Lawrence's greatest achievements.

Rambler, The

A twice-weekly periodical produced by ▷ Dr Samuel
Johnson from March 1750 to March 1752. All except
five were written by Johnson himself. The papers
were in the tradition of *The Tatler*, and *The Spectator*
essays by Joseph Addison and ▷ Sir Richard Steele
40 years before. The essays cover a wide variety
of subjects, including Eastern tales, criticisms and
allegories. Johnson's moral seriousness in the
work is indicated by the prayer that he wrote on its
commencement. *The Rambler* was pirated and copied,
evidence of its great popularity, and in Johnson's
lifetime ran to ten reprintings.

Rasselas, Prince of Abyssinia, The History of (1759)

A prose work by ▷ Samuel Johnson. Tradition has
it that Johnson composed the work rapidly to pay for
the cost of his mother's funeral. Its theme has often
been compared by critics to that of Johnson's poem
The Vanity of Human Wishes.

The theme of *Rasselas* is 'the choice of life', a
phrase which occurs repeatedly. The prince, son of
the emperor of Abyssinia, is tired of the pleasant life
in the 'happy valley', and in the company of his sister
Nekayah, her attendant Pekuah, and the philosopher
Imlac, escapes to Egypt.

Imlac's advice demonstrates to the youth the
transient nature of human happiness, a state which
is in any case unobtainable. Imlac also voices
Johnson's views on 'the business of a poet', which
is to 'examine not the individual, but the species'.
The poet should aim to be 'the interpreter of nature,
and the legislator of mankind', not to 'number the
streaks of the tulip'. *Rasselas* often parallels Voltaire's
Candide, published in the same year, and when
Johnson later read this work he commented on the
similarities.

Rationalism

1 In philosophy, the belief that reason, rather than
sensation, is the only certain guide to knowledge.

2 In religion, the practice of seeking explanations
which satisfy reason for what had been accepted as
supernatural.

Reade, Charles (1814–84)

Novelist and playwright. The seventh of 11 children,
Reade was born in Oxfordshire and educated
largely at home. In 1831 he went to Oxford and
in 1843 was called to the bar, but preferred music
and the theatre. In 1845 he was made Dean of Arts
at Magdalen and in 1851 was made vice-president
of his college, and began a long and prolific
career as writer and dramatist. He met the actress
Mrs Seymour in 1854 and they lived together
until her death in 1879, after which he wrote little,
turning to religion. He was a philanthropic man,
both impulsive and impatient. He remained a theatre
manager to 1882.

His writing career began with a stage version of
▷ Tobias Smollett's *Peregrine Pickle* in 1851. He
co-wrote and produced *Masks and Faces* in 1852,
turning it into the novel *Peg Woffington* the following
year, when the 'reforming' novel about prisons,
Christie Johnstone, also appeared. *It is Never Too Late
to Mend*, in similar vein, followed in 1856, as well
as the play *Gold!*; the novel was later dramatized
and the play rewritten as the novel *Foul Play* (1869).
He wrote short stories, pieces of journalism and
plays at the same time. In 1858 he published *The
Autobiography of a Thief* and *Jack of all Trades*, and in
1859 *Love Me Little, Love Me Long*. *The Cloister and
the Hearth* was published in 1861. *Hard Cash* (1863)
tackled the disgrace of lunatic asylums and in 1866
Griffith Gaunt triggered scandal and litigation by its
frank attitude to sexual problems. From this time on,
Reade was a controversial and litigious figure. *Put
Yourself in His Place* (1870) attacked enforced ▷ trade
union membership; *The Simpleton* (1873) gave rise to
a libel action and a quarrel with ▷ Anthony Trollope.
Other novels and plays include *The Wandering
Heir* (1873) and *A Woman Hater* (1877). Reade
was both famous and successful, being regarded as
the natural successor to ▷ Charles Dickens, and
by ▷ Henry James and Swinburne as superior to
▷ George Eliot. He commented on himself, 'I am
a painstaking man, and I owe my success to it.' His
writing is now considered overburdened with detail,
melodramatic and superficial in characterization. His
most successful work is *The Cloister and the Hearth*,
for which he is largely remembered.
Bib: Elwin, M., *Charles Reade: A Biography*; Burns,
W., *Charles Reade: A Study in Victorian Authorship*;
Hughes, W., *The Maniac in the Cellar: Sensation
Novels of the 1860s*.

Reader-response criticism

▷ Reception theory.

Realism

A term used in various senses, both in philosophy
and in literary criticism. Three principal meanings,
two of them philosophical and one literary, are
particularly worth distinction.

1 In medieval philosophy, the realists were
opposed to the ▷ nominalists. Realism here means
that classes of things ('universals') have reality
whereas individuals have not, or at least have
less: *eg* individual birds take their reality from the
classification 'bird'. The nominalists considered
that only the individual bird has reality, and that the
classification 'bird' is only a formulation in the mind.

2 Since the Middle Ages, realism has become
opposed to ▷ idealism. Here realism means that
reality exists apart from ideas about it in the mind,
and idealism represents the view that we can know
nothing that is not in our minds.

3 Literary realism is a 19th-century conception,
related to 2 and coterminous with industrial
capitalism. In general, it means the use of the
imagination to represent things as common sense
supposes they are. Realism was often associated
with the representation of immoral or transgressive
behaviour, notably in the fiction of French

19th-century realist novelists such as ▷ Balzac and ▷ Flaubert, who defended themselves from charges of immorality by claiming fidelity to reality. Realism does not apply only to 19th-century literature; ▷ Defoe is commonly called a realist because of his factual description and narration. 19th-century realism in literature arose, however, from a reaction against 19th-century Romanticism, and it is related to ▷ naturalism; for a discussion of late 20th-century critiques of realism as a vehicle of ▷ ideology, see Catherine Belsey, *Critical Practice*. Realism is also used in modern literature in opposition to what is regarded as sentimentalism – the disposition to represent feelings (*eg* the various forms of love) as nicer than we know them to be; an illogical extension of this use of the term is sometimes to apply it to literature that represents experience as nastier than we know it to be. Finally, realism in literature is sometimes related to nominalism, *ie* the realist writer is he who represents individuals rather than types; in this sense, modern literary realism is the opposite of the realism of medieval philosophy.

Reception theory

This movement is associated pre-eminently with the German contemporary literary theorists Wolfgang Iser and Hans-Robert Jauss, and is often linked with reader-response criticism. Reception theory emphasizes the reader's consumption of the literary text over and above the question of the sum total of rhetorical devices which contribute to its structure as a piece of literature. The work of reception (*Rezeptionästhetik*) causes the reader constantly to rethink the canonical value of texts, since it involves noting the history of a text's reception as well as the current value which it may possess for the critic. Insofar as reception theory concerns itself with larger historical questions, it emphasizes histories of response which help to account for the reception of particular texts in the present. The approach to 'history' outlined here is pragmatic, and the emphasis is laid firmly on the matter of the interaction between text and reader and on the way cultural context is required to make sense of literature.
Bib: Iser, W., *The Act of Reading*; Fish, S., *Is There a Text in This Class? The Authority of Interpretive Communities*; Freund, E., *The Return of the Reader: Reader-Response Criticism*.

Red Riding Hood, Little

A popular fairy tale, originally derived from the French version by ▷ Perrault, translated into English in 1729. The little girl is so called because of the red hood that she wears. A wolf meets her in the forest while she is on her way to her grandmother. Having discovered the purpose of her journey, he goes on ahead and eats the grandmother and takes her place in bed; when Red Riding Hood arrives he eats her as well. In modern versions, she and her grandmother are subsequently cut out of the wolf's stomach, alive and well, by her father, a woodcutter.

Redgrove, Peter (b 1932)

Poet and novelist. Redgrove is a prolific writer whose work straddles many forms – he has worked as a scientific journalist, and has written many novels, poems, plays (he won the Italia prize in 1981) and non-fiction (including *The Wise Wound* with poet Penelope Shuttle, with whom he lives in Cornwall). His poetic work was originally associated with that of the Group, the 'school' of post-Movement poets which included his contemporaries at Cambridge in the late 1950s, Ted Hughes and ▷ Sylvia Plath. Redgrove is now also a lay psychoanalyst. His poetry publications include: *The Collector* (1960); *The Force* (1966); *Sons of my Skin* (1975); *The Weddings at Nether Powers* (1979); *The Applebroadcast* (1981) and *The Man Named East* (1985). His fiction includes: *In the Country of the Skin* (1973); *The Beekeepers* (1980) and, with Shuttle, *The Terrors of Dr Treviley* (1974). Both fiction and poetry are notable for powerful, dense images and a preoccupation with both physicality and spirituality.

Reeve, Clara (1729–1807)

Novelist. Important for her contribution to the ▷ Gothic novel, Reeve wrote *The Champion of Virtue* in 1777, which was revised and republished as *The Old English Baron* in 1778. This book was hugely successful, catching the tone of ▷ Walpole's popular ▷ *The Castle of Otranto* (1764), to which she was directly and self-confessedly indebted. Reeve wrote that in *The Old English Baron* she had tried to unite 'the most attractive and interesting circumstances of ancient Romance and modern Novel'. However, she criticized Walpole for the excessive violence of his text, he retaliated by referring to her work as insipid. The female characters in the novel appear incidental, and indeed Reeve's writing became increasingly conservative as she grew older; for example, she commented that ▷ women's education should consist of, 'virtue, modesty and discretion'. Nevertheless, in her critical volume, *The Progress of Romance* (1785), she claims that ▷ romance is ideally suited to women writers, and deals in some detail with those female authors she considers interesting. Reeve's other novels follow similar Gothic or sentimental patterns and include: *The Two Mentors* (1783); *The Exiles* (1788); *The School for Widows* (1791). Her early work includes the unjustly neglected *Original Poems on Several Occasions* (1769).
Bib: Punter, D., *The Literature of Terror: A History of Gothic Fiction from 1765 to the Present Day*.

Reflections on the Revolution in France (1790)

A political treatise by ▷ Edmund Burke. Burke attacks the principles on which the ▷ French Revolution was being conducted, denies that the English Revolution of 1688 was based on the same principles, and insists that a society is an organic growth like a tree, requiring the same kind of careful surgery in accordance with its principles of growth. The book was provoked by a sermon in praise of the French Revolution, preached by a Nonconformist minister, Dr Price; Burke is in effect not merely attacking the French revolutionaries, but the reverence for abstract, rational, scientific enlightenment which, during the 18th century, had increasingly transformed the 17th-century Puritans into the 18th-century rationalistic Dissenters or

Nonconformists, and had found disciples among many others of the educated classes. The *Reflections* is a great work of conservative political philosophy, as well as a masterpiece of polemical prose. It represents the French Revolution as a turning-point in history: 'The age of chivalry is gone. That of sophisters, economists and calculators has succeeded; and the glory of Europe is extinguished for ever.'

Reform Bills, Parliamentary

In English history, a succession of laws passed in the 19th and 20th centuries for the reform of the system of election of Members of Parliament. The system has always been based on towns and rural districts, grouped into constituencies, each electing one or (until recently) sometimes more than one candidate as Member. The most important Reform Bill was the first, passed through Parliament in 1832, because it reduced the electoral confusion into a rational system. Most constituencies had remained unchanged since the Middle Ages; in consequence, some towns had grown to great size with inadequate representation in Parliament, or none at all, while others were represented by more than one Member although they had sunk into insignificance or even, in a few cases, had ceased to exist. This meant great power for the landed aristocracy, and great deprivation of power for the large and growing middle class. Some boroughs ('towns' – but often mere villages) were called 'pocket boroughs' because they were virtually owned by one landlord, who had them 'in his pocket', *ie* caused them to elect the Members of his choice; others were called 'rotten boroughs' because few inhabitants possessed the right to vote, and they were easily and habitually bribed. The law of 1832 redistributed Members of Parliament so as to correspond to the great centres of population, but limited the franchise (right to vote) to those who possessed a level of income such as ensured that electors belonged at least to the middle class.

The Reform Bill of 1867 extended the franchise to all male members of the working class in the towns, and that of 1884 to the rural working class. The delay in extending the franchise to the working class was bound up with the absence of any official state system of education; this was introduced in 1870. The town working classes received the vote before the rural ones owing to their greater experience in organization gained through ▷ trade unions and the running of Nonconformist chapels.

The vote was now possessed by all men over 21 (with few exceptions, such as lunatics, criminals, and peers who had seats in the House of Lords) but not by women. Women over 30 were enfranchised in 1918 thanks to the campaigning by ▷ Suffragette movements and the services performed by women in World War I. Women over 21 received the vote in 1928. The same laws enabled women to stand for Parliament. A 1969 Act lowered the voting age for both men and women to 18.

Much of the intimidation and corruption of voters was a consequence of votes being made openly; secret voting or 'voting by ballot', was introduced in 1872.

Regency

In English history, the period 1811–20 when George. Prince of Wales, later George IV (1820–30), took the title of Prince Regent during the final illness of his father, George III (1760–1820). In British cultural history, the term is often applied to cover the first 20 years of the 19th century during which a certain style of taste in art and architecture prevailed. It was inspired by the taste of the first French Empire which itself arose from French revolutionary cultivation of ancient Greece, especially the republic of Athens. Architecture was austerely classical (the 'Greek style'), and dress was similarly modelled on long, graceful lines suitable for men and women with slender figures.

In literature, the term covers the working life of the second generation of Romantic poets (Byron, Shelley and Keats), the work of the essayists ▷ Lamb and Hazlitt, and that of the novelists ▷ Jane Austen and ▷ Walter Scott. The word is applied, however, more to architecture, dress and furniture than to literature, the principal architects being John Nash (1752–1835) and John Soane (1753–1837), architect of the Bank of England.

Regional novel

A novel (often one of a series) which portrays the life of a specific region. For a novel to be termed regional, the specific characteristics of that region generally need to be a significant focus of attention in the text. Examples are the Potteries novels of ▷ Arnold Bennett (for example, *Anna of the Five Towns*, 1902) and the ▷ Wessex novels of ▷ Thomas Hardy (for example, *The Return of the Native*, 1878).

Relativism

A philosophical theory, according to which beliefs and truths are neither universal nor timeless, but dependent upon the assumptions and situation of the individual or group that maintains them. A moderate form of relativism holds that an objective world exists, but that it must always be seen and interpreted differently by different persons. A more extreme form, adopted by ▷ Nietzsche and sometimes termed perspectivism, holds that it is only perspectives which exist and that there is no objective reality, knowable or otherwise.

Renault, Mary (1905–1983)

Writer of popular historical novels. Renault was born and educated in England, working as a nurse during World War II, after which she emigrated with her life-long partner Julie Mullard to South Africa where she was an active anti-apartheid campaigner until her death in Cape Town. Most of Renault's highly successful novels deal with the classical world, and, in their exploration of the transition from matriarchal social systems and religion to more modern partriarchy, they show the influence of ▷ Robert Graves's *The White Goddess*. All of Renault's novels are distinguished by the meticulous research and accuracy of historical details which underpins them. Her best-known books are the homoerotic Alexander trilogy (which covers the life of Alexander the Great:

Fire from Heaven, 1970; *The Persian Boy* 1972; and *Funeral Games*; 1981), and two novels narrated by Theseus (*The King Must Die*, 1958, and *The Bull from the Sea*, 1962). Her other works include: *Purposes of Love* (1939); *The Charioteer* (1953); *The Last of the Wine* (1956); *The Mask of Apollò* (1966); *The Praise Singer* (1978).
Bib: Dick, B. F., *The Hellenism of Mary Renault*; Wolf, P., *Mary Renault*.

Republic, Plato's
A Philosophical dialogue by the Greek philosopher ▷ Plato. Socrates discusses with his friends the nature of justice, and the conversation leads to an outline of the ideal state. Public life must exhibit the highest virtues of private life, and justice is achieved if the classes work together to contribute to society the virtues in which each excels. Democracy (the rule of the people), oligarchy (the rule of a small powerful group), and timocracy (the rule of men of property) are in turn rejected, in favour of aristocracy – the rule of the best, trained by an exacting system of education. The aristocrat will seek wisdom, whereas the man of action seeks honour, and the merchant gratifies his appetites. Wisdom is a direct apprehension of the good conceived as a system of ideal forms; Book VII contains the famous parable of men sitting with their backs to these forms (the only substantial reality) watching the shadows on the wall of the cavern – *ie* phenomena apprehended by the senses – and supposing these shadows to be the only reality. Book X contains Plato's notorious rejection of poetry: poets must be expelled, though with honour, because they frustrate the pursuit of true wisdom by extolling the illusory phenomena of this world, and weaken the mind by stimulating wasteful sympathy with the misfortunes of men.

Resurrection man; Resurrectionist
A term in use in the late 18th and early 19th centuries for one who made a living by digging up dead bodies and selling them to anatomists to use for dissection; such a person is Jerry Cruncher in Dickens's novel about the French Revolution, ▷ *A Tale of Two Cities*.

Return of the Native, The (1878)
A novel by ▷ Thomas Hardy. Its setting is Egdon Heath, a wild tract of country in Dorset, in the south-west of England. The atmosphere of the Heath prevails over the whole book; as an environment, it repels some characters and absorbs others; those who are absorbed achieve a sombre integration with it but those who are repelled and rebel suffer disaster. The central character – 'the Native' – is Clym Yeobright, a Paris diamond merchant who has returned to the Heath in revulsion from the futility of his urban life and occupation. He intends to become a schoolmaster and marries the restless, self-seeking Eustacia Vye who is unfaithful to him; her affair with the unscrupulous Damon Wildeve leads to the death of both. Other characters include Thomasin Yeobright whom Wildeve marries, to her misfortune and the grief of Diggory Venn, the travelling sheep-dyer (or 'reddleman') who represents a primitive

sincerity and truthfulness, and Mrs Yeobright, Clym's mother, whom Eustacia estranges from her son. Clym becomes a furze-cutter on the Heath and eventually a travelling preacher. The novel is an example of Hardy's preoccupation with the relationship of characters with natural environment but it suffers from a weak conception of the central character, Clym.

Review, The
It was written by ▷ Daniel Defoe and published three times weekly from 1704 to 1713. It expressed Defoe's opinion on current political events, and also on literature and manners. Defoe has been called the inventor of the leading article, a feature of modern newspapers.

Reviews and Periodicals
The English periodical press arose gradually from the controversial religious and political pamphleteering of the late 16th and 17th centuries. It became established as a recognized institution early in the 18th century, and it was also in the 18th century that the review, which expresses opinion, became distinguished from the newspaper, which gives priority to information on current events. The great age for the periodical press was, however, 1800–1914; this was the period when the quarterlies and the monthlies had their widest influence, and the weeklies their largest circulation proportionately to the size of the reading public. Since 1914, the influence of the quarterlies and monthlies has declined; the weeklies have remained important, but they have had to compete on the one side with the tendency of newspapers to include a large amount of material originally restricted to reviews, and on the other with the medium of broadcasting.

Reynolds, G. W. M. (George William MacArthur) (1814–79)
Novelist and journalist. A political radical, Chartist sympathizer and republican, Reynolds built up a substantial niche for himself in publishing and the newspaper business by writing specifically for the growing urban working-class readership: in 1846, he founded the penny weekly magazine *Reynolds's Miscellany* and in 1850 launched *Reynold's Weekly Newspaper* (which ran until 1967). One of the most successful purveyors of the so-called 'penny-dreadful' fiction (sensational stories issued in 1d serial form), he initiated the series *The Mysteries of London* (1846–50; based on Eugene Sue's *Les Mystères de Paris*, 1842–3), the Regency romance *The Mysteries of the Court of London* (1849–56), and various of the many ▷ Dickens plagiarisms and continuations that poured out in the 1840s, including *Pickwick Abroad* (1839), *Pickwick Married* (1841) and *Master Timothy's Book-Case* (1842).
Bib: James, L., *Fiction for the Working Man*; Sutherland, J., *The Longman Companion to Victorian Fiction*.

Rhetoric
Rhetoric in the medieval period was a formal skill of considerable importance. It was taken to mean the effective presentation of ideas with a set of rules or

style, and was founded in the classical tradition of ▷ Aristotle and Cicero. It was taught in monastic schools as part of the *trivium*, Rhetoric, Logic and Grammar, which used as its basic text Geoffrey de Vinsauf's *Poetria Nova* (1200). Rhetoric not only formed patterns in which texts should be written, but it also governed how the works should be received and allocated them to particular categories, *eg* epic, debate or sermon. The system of rhetoric was paramount to the operation of literature in the medieval period.

Similarly, almost all of the practice or theory of writing in the Renaissance period was touched by what became known as the 'Art of Rhetoric'. Rhetorical theory formed an important part of the educational syllabus at the universities, and almost every major writer of the 16th and 17th centuries would have undergone some training in rhetoric. Rhetoric was learned first through reading the classical text-books on rhetoric, in particular the works of Quintillian (especially the *Institutio Oratore*) and Cicero. Secondly, practical rhetorical exercises were performed by the student in which a particular topic was debated. In these debates, the student was expected to be able to organize an argument according to set formulae, producing examples with which to sustain the analysis which themselves would be derived from a suitable store of words, images, fables and metaphors discovered in reading classical texts.

But the production of arguments was only one part of the rhetoricians' skills. Rhetoric also involved the classification of language – in particular the classification and analysis of ▷ figures of speech. Further, it was understood as an enabling tool by which ▷ discourse could be reproduced. In essence, therefore, it offered a system for producing both speech and writing. This system can be considered under five distinct parts: 1 'invention', which signifies the discovery of arguments applicable to a given case; 2 'arrangement' or 'disposition', which governed the ordering of the arguments to be used; 3 'style' or the actual choice of words and units of expression; 4 the important area of 'memory', which helped the rhetorician develop skills in recalling the order and substance of the argument being deployed; 5 'delivery', which was applicable mainly to spoken discourse but which governed such details as the appropriate facial expressions or gestures which might be used.

Whilst rhetoric was understood as a way of facilitating the classification of the various parts of an argument it was also a powerful tool in the analysis of discourse and it can thus be understood as a form of literary criticism. It was, however, in its abiding influence on stylistic forms that it was of most importance to the Renaissance writer. Numerous text-books on rhetoric were published throughout the 16th century in England. Perhaps the most important were: Leonard Cox, *The Art or Craft of Rhetoric* (1624); Richard Sherry, *A Treatise of Schemes and Tropes* (1550); Thomas Wilson, *Art of Rhetoric* (1553); Henry Peacham, *The Garden of Eloquence* (1577); and Abraham Fraunce, *Arcadian Rhetoric* (1584). But many other texts were written with the art of

rhetoric either governing the structure or informing the language. ▷ Sir Philip Sidney's *An Apologie for Poetrie* (1595), for example, is structured according to rhetorical principles of organization.

Recent developments in critical theory have sought to re-emphasize rhetoric as a form of critical practice, particularly in relation to the *effects* that any verbal construction may have on those to whom it is addressed. In this respect rhetoric is closely associated with some of the larger issues which surface in relation to the theory of 'discourse'. The recent emphasis upon the *structure* of discourse draws attention away from language as a means of *classifying* to one of examining the way discourses are constructed in order to achieve certain effects. Here the emphasis would be on the different *ways* in which particular figures are presented in language, and what that presentation may involve. This form of rhetorical analysis has been undertaken by ▷ Jacques Derrida in volumes such as *Of Grammatology* (1974), by ▷ Paul De Man in his *Blindness and Insight* (1971), by ▷ Terry Eagleton in *Criticism and Ideology* (1976), and in a whole range of texts by ▷ Michel Foucault.

Rhys, Jean (1894–1979)

Adopted name of novelist, born Jean Williams on the West Indian island of Dominica. Brought up speaking both English and the Dominican French dialect, she lived in Europe from the age of 16, moving between London, Vienna and Paris before finally settling in Devon. *The Left Bank* (1927), a series of sketches of Bohemian life in Paris, was followed by four novels which tell the stories of isolated, poor, victimized women, adrift in London or Paris, in a laconic, lucid style which combines the tragic and the absurd. These are: *Postures* (1928) (in the U.S.A. as *Quartet*; 1929); *After Leaving Mr Mackenzie* (1931); *Voyage in the Dark* (1934) and *Good Morning Midnight* (1939). After a considerable period of critical neglect, *Wide Sargasso Sea* (1966) reawakened widespread interest in her work, especially among ▷ feminists. It recounts the early life of the first Mrs Rochester from ▷ Charlotte Brontë's ▷ *Jane Eyre*, rendering the alienation and suffering of an isolated consciousness with great power. Set mostly in the West Indies, it is richer in imagery and symbolism than her earlier work, combining lyricism and psychological insight with an exploration of political, racial and sexual oppression. She has written two books of short stories: *Tigers Are Better Looking* (1968) and *Sleep It Off Lady* (1976). *Quartet* was made into a film (with a screenplay by ▷ Ruth Prawar Jhabvala) by the director James Ivory in 1981. A selection of her letters was edited by Francis Wyndham and Diana Melly in 1984, and *Smile Please: An Unfinished Autobiography* was published in 1979.

Bib: Stanley, T.F., *Jean Rhys: A Critical Study*. Frickey, P.M (ed.), *Critical Perspectives on Jean Rhys*; Emery, M.L., *Jean Rhys at "World's End": Novels of Colonial and Sexual Exile*; Harrison, N.R., *Jean Rhys and the Novel as Women's Text*.

Richard Feverel
▷ *Ordeal of Richard Feverel, The*.

Richardson, Dorothy (1873–1957)
Novelist. Born in Abingdon, Berkshire, she worked as a governess from the age of 17, before moving to London where she became an intimate of ▷ H.G. Wells and part of a circle of socialists and intellectuals. She took up journalism, and for the rest of her life earned a meagre living by this means, while dedicating herself to her long novel, *Pilgrimage*, which consists of the following volumes: *Pointed Roofs* (1915); *Backwater* (1916); *Honeycomb* (1917); *The Tunnel* (1919); *Interim* (1919); *Deadlock* (1921); *Revolving Lights* (1923); *The Trap* (1925); *Oberland* (1927); *Dawn's Left Hand* (1931); *Clear Horizon* (1935); *Dimple Hill* (1938); *March Moonlight* (1967). It is a semi-autobiographical work, recounting the life of the heroine, Miriam Henderson, through concentration on her continuous subjective experience of the present moment. Richardson, together with ▷ Virginia Woolf and ▷ James Joyce was responsible for the development of the ▷ stream of consciousness technique (though she disliked this term) which was an important aspect of the ▷ modernist revolution in narrative.
Bib: Rosenberg, J., *Dorothy Richardson: the Genius They Forgot*; Radford, J., *Dorothy Richardson*; Fromm, G.G., *Dorothy Richardson: A Biography*; Hanscombe, G. E., *The Art of Life: Dorothy Richardson and the Development of Feminist Consciousness*.

Richardson, Henry Handel (1870–1946)
Pseudonym of Australian novelist and short-story writer Ethel Florence Lindesay Richardson Robertson. She studied music in Leipzig from 1887–90, lived in Strasbourg 1895–1903, and in England from 1903. Her trilogy *The Fortunes of Richard Mahony* uses elements of her father's life, and is the sombre tale of an emigrant doctor's rise to riches and unexpected loss of fortune. It consists of *Australia Felix* (1917); *The Way Home* (1925); *Ultima Thule* (1929). Her work shows the influence of ▷ Goethe and the German Romantic tradition. Her other novels are: *Maurice Guest* (1908); *The Getting of Wisdom* (1910); *The Young Cosima* (1939). Story collections include: *The End of Childhood and Other Stories* (1934). The autobiographical *Myself When Young* was published posthumously in 1948.
Bib: Mcleod, K., *Henry Handel Richardson: A Critical Study*.

Richardson, Samuel (1689–1761)
Novelist. Richardson was the son of a furniture-maker, born near Derby, though most of his childhood was spent in London as the family returned to live there. Little is known of his education, though by the age of 13 he is known to have written love letters on behalf of his friends, an activity relevant for his later choice of the epistolary genre.

In 1706 Richardson was apprenticed to a printer, and in 1715 became a freeman of the Stationers' Company. In 1721 he began his own business, which proved successful for the rest of his life. In the same year he married the daughter of his former master, though his wife died ten years later, and in the early 1730s he suffered the deaths of all the six children born to the marriage.

In 1733 he remarried, again to the daughter of a colleague, and four of their daughters survived. In the same year he published *The Apprentice's Vade Mecum*, a conduct guide to moral behaviour. In 1730 his own, deliberately moral, version of *Aesop's Fables* appeared.

The moral intention of his early works is evident in his fiction, though the creations of his imagination frequently escape any strict schemata. ▷ *Pamela*, begun in the same year as *Aesop's Fables* appeared, began as a series of conduct guides or 'Familiar Letters', which his friends encouraged him to write. Richardson's professional life, meanwhile, was proving rewarding. In 1723 he had begun to print *The True Briton*, an influential ▷ Tory journal, and in 1733 the House of Commons was using his presses. In 1742 he gained a lucrative contract as printer of the Parliamentary Journals.

His social life was proving equally enjoyable. He particularly relished the company of young women, whom he referred to as his 'honorary daughters', and while writing ▷ *Clarissa* (probably begun in 1744) he frequently asked them for their comments and teased them with speculations about the fate of his heroine. The first two volumes appeared in 1747 and were widely acclaimed; five more followed in 1748. The novel was praised, but readers were uneasy about its sexual elements, and its popularity proved less than that of *Pamela*.

About 1750 Richardson embarked on a new project, which was to be centred on the 'good man'. In 1752 ▷ Samuel Johnson read the draft manuscript of the work, ▷ *The History of Sir Charles Grandison*, and the novel appeared in seven volumes in 1753–4. Again, there was some doubt about the morality of the book, an ironic fate for a writer with Richardson's intentions.

In 1755 Richardson published a volume of selections from his three novels, in a form which he considered contained the essence of his writing; he was constantly concerned about the length of his fictions, and continually worked on revisions. His novels develop the epistolary style to a great degree of psychological subtlety, and he has long been regarded as one of the chief founders of the English novel.
Bib: Eaves, T. C. D. and Kimpel, B. D., *Samuel Richardson*; Kinkead-Weekes, M., *Samuel Richardson, Dramatic Novelist*; Flynn, C. H., *Samuel Richardson, A Man of Letters*.

Rights of Man
▷ Paine, Thomas.

Riley, Joan (b 1958)
Novelist. Born in Jamaica, and educated at the universities of Sussex and London, she teaches black history and culture and works for a drugs advisory agency. Her novels are: *The Unbelonging* (1985); *Waiting in the Twilight* (1987); *Romance* (1988). Her work is concerned with the hardships, and the search for a sense of meaning and identity, of people born in Jamaica and living in Britain.

Rob Roy (1817)
A novel by ▷ Sir Walter Scott, giving a picture of
Scotland just before the first Jacobite rebellion of
1715. The plot concerns the rivalry in love of the
cousins Francis and Rashleigh Osbaldistone for
Diana Vernon. Rashleigh, the villain, is involved in
Jacobite intrigue. Their adventures are interwoven
with the fortunes of Rob Roy Macgregor, a historical
character whom Scott romanticizes. He is the chief
of the Clan Macgregor in the Scottish Highlands,
and a convicted outlaw who lives by plunder. In the
novel he acts on the side of the hero, Francis, at
Diana's earnest appeal. As usual in Scott's novels,
the notable parts are those which concern Scottish
common life, and such characters as Bailie Nicol
Jarvie and Francis's servant Andrew Fairservice.

Roberts, Michèle (b 1949)
Poet, short-story writer and novelist. Roberts is a
prolific writer, has appeared widely on television,
radio and in anthologies, and regularly gives
readings of her work as well as teaching creative
writing. She has been very influential on the
development and recognition of contemporary
poetry in her capacity as poetry editor of *Spare Rib*
(1975–77) and of the London listings magazine,
City Limits (1981–83). She was one of the founders
of the Feminist Writers Group, with ▷ Sara
Maitland, ▷ Zoë Fairbains and Michelene
Wandor; the group collectively wrote the short-
story collection *Tales I Tell My Mother* (1978).
Roberts shares with Maitland an interest in the
relationship of female sexuality to religion, a
concern apparent in her novels, which include:
The Visitation (1983); *The Wild Girl* (1984); *The
Book of Mrs Noah* (1987). Her volumes of poetry
include: *Licking the Bed Clean* (1978); *Smile,
Smile, Smile, Smile* (1980); *The Mirror of Mother*
(1986). Her most recent novel, *Daughters of the
House* (1992), was shortlisted for the Booker
Prize.

Robinson, Mary (1758–1800)
Novelist, poet and actress. Although Mary
Robinson is now known for her ▷ Gothic novels,
during her lifetime she was infamous for her
affair with the Prince of Wales. He saw her act
the role of Perdita in 1779 and fell in love with
her. The relationship lasted just over a year,
leaving Robinson the butt of crude satire and
with the lasting nickname 'Perdita'. In 1783
she became paralysed from the waist down
after a miscarriage and from then on she was
forced to earn her living by writing. Her poetry
was never very original, picking up populist
sentiment in relation to current events, such
as the storming of the Bastille, and when her
collection *Lyrical Tales* (1800) was published,
Wordsworth considered changing the title of his
own work. In comparison her novels are sharp and
witty, tinged with liberal sentiment; they include
Vancenza (1792), *Angelina* (1795) and *Hubert de
Sevrac* (1796).
Bib: Bass, P., *The Green Dragon*; Rodgers, K.,
Feminism in Eighteenth-century England.

*Robinson Crusoe, The Life and strange
surprising Adventures of* (1719)
A novel by ▷ Daniel Defoe. The first part was based
on the experiences of a sailor, Alexander Selkirk,
who went ashore on the uninhabited island of Juan
Fernandez in 1704, and remained there until he
was rescued in 1709. Crusoe runs away to sea (as
Selkirk had done) and after a number of adventures
is wrecked on an uninhabited island, where he
remains for 20 years. Defoe describes the industrious
and methodical way in which he builds up a life for
himself, how he is endangered by the periodic visits
of a race of cannibals, how he tames one of them
into an ideal servant, Man Friday. The island is
eventually visited by a ship in the hands of mutinous
sailors; he subdues the mutineers and rescues the
officers, who take him back to England, leaving the
repentant mutineers behind as a colony, together
with some Spaniards whom he had previously
rescued from the cannibals.

In *The Farther Adventures of Robinson Crusoe*,
published in the same year, Crusoe revisits the
colony and relates its fortunes; he also travels
elsewhere, visits China, and returns to England
across Siberia and Russia. The third part, *The Serious
Reflections of Robinson Crusoe* (1720), consists of moral
essays in which Defoe represents the book as an
▷ allegory of his own life. This was partly a defence
against the disapproval of his fellow ▷ Puritans
who regarded fiction as hardly distinguishable from
lies; on the other hand, Defoe's tale is certainly an
image of the loneliness and arduousness of the life of
individual economic enterprise which was becoming
increasingly typical of society; Crusoe is made to
say that he has been more lonely since his return to
London than he ever was on his island.

Modern critics have noticed how Crusoe sees
human beings merely in terms of their economic
virtues, and seen the narrative as a paradigm of
▷ colonialism. The book has always been praised
for its detailed verisimilitude, which caused it to
be received at first as an authentic account; the
descriptions are almost entirely in terms of what the
philosopher ▷ John Locke had distinguished as the
objectively discernible 'primary qualities' (▷ *Essay
concerning Human Understanding*) as opposed to the
subjectively experienced 'secondary qualities' (colour,
beauty, etc.) which it is difficult to verify. The style
of the writing is extremely plain, in keeping with
the principles that Thomas Sprat had laid down
for the Royal Society in 1667 (*History of the Royal
Society*): 'the language of Artisans, Countrymen, and
Merchants'. That Crusoe appears much less religious
than Defoe means him to is also often remarked; on
the other hand, if there is a principle of unity in the
long, episodic narrative, it is the function of God as
the basic Providence, subjecting chaos so that man
may use his constructive virtues for the building of
an orderly world.

Roche, Regina Maria (1764–1845)
Novelist. A prolific Irish novelist, Roche wrote
sentimental tales about the injustices done to her
various protagonists and their families. The tone,
however, was predictably ▷ Gothic, and she became

one of the stalwarts of the ▷ Minerva Press. Her novels include *The Vicar of Lansdowne, or Country Quarters* (1789), *The Children of the Abbey* (1796) and *Clermont* (1798). The last work was satirized by ▷ Jane Austen in ▷ *Northanger Abbey*.

Roderick Random, The Adventures of (1748)
A novel by ▷ Tobias Smollett. It is based on Smollett's own experience as a naval doctor at the siege of Cartagena in 1741; it is episodic in form, and vivid but somewhat brutal in manner. In the Preface, the author pays tribute to the comic genius of ▷ Cervantes, author of ▷ *Don Quixote*.

Roman-à-clef
A novel which describes real people and events, but using invented names, so that it can be decoded using a key (French, '*clef*'). Examples are ▷ Peacock's *Nightmare Abbey* (1818), which contains caricatures of Shelley, Byron and Coleridge, and ▷ Aldous Huxley's *Point Counter Point*, which includes characters based on ▷ Middleton Murry and ▷ D.H. Lawrence. Since novelists very frequently base their characters to some extent on real people, the boundaries of the form are not clearly defined, although some authors have actually published a key.

Roman à these/Tendenzroman
A novel which is dominated by its treatment of a particular issue (French '*these*' = proposition, argument; German '*Tendenz*' = tendency, trend). Frequently this involves an attack on a particular social injustice. The ▷ social problem novels of the 1840s in England are examples of the *roman à these*.

Roman feuilleton
A novel published in serial form in a newspaper.

Roman-fleuve
A sequence of novels in which some of the same characters reappear, and in which the plot of each novel continues or complements that of others in the sequence. Well-known examples are ▷ Balzac's *The Human Comedy* and ▷ Galsworthy's *The Forsyte Saga* (1922); the latter, since it is about a family, could also be termed a saga novel.

Romance
The term romance is derived from the Latin word *romanice*, meaning 'in the Romance language' and is used, somewhat confusingly, in a range of literary senses, of which at least five can usefully be distinguished, although they are historically related in various ways:
1 Medieval romances, such as ▷ *Sir Gawain and the Green Knight*, were verse narratives on courtly and chivalric subjects, in most cases based on legends and stories about the courts of King Arthur and the Emperor Charlemagne or classical tales of heroism. Many were translations or versions of French originals. Generically and historically distinct from the novel, they nevertheless, as extended fictional narratives, can be seen as one of its antecedents.

Chivalric romance made a major contribution to the novel via ▷ *Don Quixote*, partly a satire on the form.
2 Prose romances became common in English from the 15th century and flourished in the Elizabethan era; for example ▷ Thomas Lodge's *Rosalynde, Euphues Golden Legacy* (1590) and ▷ Mary Wroth's *Urania*. These tend to be notable for elegance of style, elaborate description and intellectual discussions rather than plot interest, but ▷ picaresque romances, such as ▷ Thomas Nashe's ▷ *The Unfortunate Traveller* have stronger links to the novel.
3 17th-century French romances, or *romans de longue haleine* (literally, 'romances of long breath'; *ie* sustained romances), such as ▷ Madeleine de Scudéry's ten-volume *Artamène, or the Great Cyrus*, were interminable episodic narratives of love and honour; they were part of the literary context out of which the French novel emerged (▷ Marie-Madeleine de La Fayette), and a form with which English novelists of the 18th century, such as ▷ Samuel Richardson and ▷ Clara Reeve, were given to contrasting with their own works.
4 The term romance has continued to be applied, regularly though not systematically, to novels involving fantastic or supernatural events, such as the ▷ Gothic novel, and to adventure novels, such as the historical romances of ▷ Sir Walter Scott, ▷ Robert Louis Stevenson's *Kidnapped* or the novel simply entitled *Romance*, by ▷ Joseph Conrad and ▷ Ford Madox Ford. ▷ H.G. Wells called his ▷ science fiction novels 'scientific romances', and science fiction is one of the contemporary inheritors of this tradition of writing.
5 In post-war fiction, romances, more often termed romantic fiction, are novels about love, sex and adventure, written for a mass market and in many cases aimed particularly at women readers. This form of writing has traditionally been given a low valuation by literary critics, but some feminist critics have sought to revise this (see Modleski, T., *Loving with a Vengeance: Mass-Produced Fantasies for Women*; Elam, D., *Romancing the Postmodern*).
    ▷ Romanticism.

Romantic Fiction
    ▷ Romance.

Romanticism
Romanticism in Britain is more associated with poetry than with the novel, although Continental novels were among the key sources of the Romantic movement, notably ▷ Jean-Jacques Rousseau's *Julie, or the New Héloïse* (1761) and ▷ Johann Wolfgang von Goethe's *The Sorrows of Young Werther* (1774). The most significant manifestation of Romanticism in the British novel is the ▷ Gothic novel, with its emphasis on extreme states of feeling, its use of the supernatural and its evocation of the medieval. The 18th-century Gothic novels of ▷ Horace Walpole and ▷ Matthew Gregory Lewis anticipated aspects of Romantic taste and sensibility, while ▷ Mary Shelley's ▷ *Frankenstein* is one of the most lastingly influential Romantic works. The historical novels of ▷ Sir Walter Scott reflect the Romantic fascination

with the past. ▷ Autobiography took a new impetus and new forms from the Romantic emphasis on subjectivity, notably in the work of ▷ Charles Lamb, and ▷ Thomas De Quincey. Among later novelists, it is probably Charlotte and Emily ▷ Brontë who are most indebted to Romanticism. ▷ Jane Austen wrote during the Romantic period but the term ▷ Regency might seem more appropriate for her fiction, which contains many anti-Romantic elements, such as the satire on the Gothic novel in ▷ *Northanger Abbey*; however, ▷ *Sense and Sensibility* explores elements of Romantic sensibility, although not necessarily sympathetically. Romantic fiction (the capital letter is used to denote the literary/historical period, as opposed to the more general and colloquial use of the term romantic) should not be confused with romantic fiction (▷ romance).

Romola (1863)

A historical novel by ▷ George Eliot, serialized in ▷ *Cornhill Magazine* (1862–3). It is set in late 15th-century Florence at the time of the predominance of the reforming monk Savonarola. Romola is a high-minded girl who marries a self-indulgent and unscrupulous Greek, Tito Melma. Repelled by her husband and disillusioned by the course of Savonarola's career, she eventually finds her salvation in self-denial. In writing the novel, George Eliot was putting forward the principle that it is as important to actualize the society in which the characters move as to give reality to the characters themselves. The novel has been praised for the thoroughness of research which established the Florentine scene; on the other hand, by comparison with the later novels (▷ *Middlemarch* and ▷ *Daniel Deronda*) set in England, modern readers feel that medieval Florence did not touch the author in the sense that she participated imaginatively in its life, with the result that of all her novels, *Romola* is probably the least read.

Ross, Mrs (c 1811–25)

Novelist and writer of short stories. Published by ▷ Minerva among others, Mrs Ross is one of few prose writers to balance ▷ rationalism and Romanticism, 'sense and sensibility' as it were, and combine them with relatively frank descriptions of sexuality. Her plots and characters are ingenious, and her novels often possess tough moral conclusions. Her work includes: *The Cousins, or A Woman's Promise and A Lover's Vow* (1811); *The Balance of Comfort, or The Old Maid and Married Woman* (1817); *The Woman of Genius* (1821).

Rousseau, Jean-Jacques (1712–78)

French-Swiss thinker. His chief works were: *Discourse on the Influence of Learning and Art* (1750), in which he argues that progress in these has not improved human morals; *Discourse on Inequality* (1754), in which society is considered to have spoilt the liberty and virtue natural to primitive peoples; a novel, *The New Héloïse* (1761), in which the return to primitive nature is considered in relation to the relationships of the sexes and the family; ▷ *The Social Contract* (1761), a political treatise with the theme that the basis of society is artificial, not binding on individuals when society ceases to serve their interests; *Emile* (1762), advocating education through the evocation of the natural impulses and interests of the child, and the *Confessions*, an autobiography which was self-revealing without precedent, published after his death.

Rousseau was immensely influential, not only in France but throughout Europe. His praise of nature and protests against society were significant contributions to the creation of a revolutionary state of mind, culminating in the ▷ French Revolution of 1789. Education from nature, his conception of nature as a life-giving force, was of great importance in the background of Wordsworth, and through Wordsworth, of much of English 19th-century imaginative thinking, and linked with his devotion to nature was his equally influential reverence for childhood. As an autobiographer, Rousseau was one of the first to base the importance of individual experience on its uniqueness, not on its moral excellence or intellectual attainment. This was quite contrary to the characteristic 18th-century view, expressed in works like Samuel Johnson's ▷ *Rasselas*, in which the valuable experience was conceived to be only that which was true of and for humanity at large.

Roxana, or the Fortunate Mistress (1724)

A novel by ▷ Daniel Defoe presented as a fictional autobiography. 'Roxana', the daughter of French Protestant refugees, is deserted and left destitute by her first husband, and, with a taste for the finer things in life, sees prostitution as her only lucrative profession. A second marriage to a Dutch merchant leaves her widowed, but she climbs to a state of social importance by a series of increasingly grand affairs, one of which is hinted to be with the king. Like ▷ Moll Flanders, she repents; but the penitence of Roxana is also ambiguous, and her thoughts are haunted by the illegitimate daughter whose death is on her conscience.

Rugby School

One of the most famous of the English ▷ Public Schools. It was founded in 1567, but its importance begins with the headmastership of ▷ Thomas Arnold (father of the poet and critic ▷ Matthew Arnold) from 1828 to 1842. Hitherto, the ancient Public Schools had imparted education (chiefly in the Greek and Latin languages and literatures) but without any consistent moral instruction. Rugby became a pioneer of 'character-building', which came to be regarded as the most typical quality of the English 'public school tradition'. The virtues were supposed to be those of physical and moral discipline, leadership and fair-mindedness. A large number of public schools were founded in the second half of the 19th century, and they were modelled on Arnold's ideals. Since the large Empire of which Britain was the centre required an extensive class of administrators, these ideals were eminently useful in producing them. A once-popular novel, *Tom Brown's Schooldays* (1857) by Thomas Hughes, describes life at Rugby under Arnold.

Rural Rides (1820–30)
Reports of rural conditions by ▷ William Cobbett.
He disapproved of certain remedies proposed by
an official body to the Government for agricultural
distress resulting from the Napoleonic War. He
decided to make a number of tours on horseback in
order to find out the facts for himself, and published
his impressions in his journal, the ▷ *Political Register*,
between 1820 and 1830, when they were collected
into book form. The essays are in vivid, direct prose,
full of acute comments, lively incident, and strong
if prejudiced argument. They are early examples
of direct journalistic reporting and are raised to
permanent value as literature by the energy of
Cobbett's conviction and the simplicity and vigour of
his prose, which he had modelled on the writings of
▷ Jonathan Swift.
▷ Journalism.

Rushdie, Salman (b 1947)
Indian novelist. Born in Bombay and educated
at Cambridge University, he now lives in Britain.
His second novel, *Midnight's Children* (1981) won
the Booker Prize and became a best-seller. It is
a voluminous work, ranging in time from World
War I to 1977, and combining a realistic portrayal
of poverty and suffering with magic, fantasy, farce,
symbolism and ▷ allegory in a manner which
associates it with ▷ magic realism. Its many narrative
strategies compete with, and undermine, each other,
and serve to question the relation of history to
fiction; in this respect Rushdie is a ▷ post-modernist
writer. In particular, narrative multiplicity functions
in his work as a form of resistance to the unitary
nature of ▷ imperialist ideology and political control.
He is an inventive, self-conscious and versatile writer,
with a flamboyant style which at times verges on the
self-indulgent. His other novels are: *Grimus* (1975);
Shame (1983), and ▷ *The Satanic Verses* (1988) which
aroused worldwide controversy and criticism from
Muslims for its alleged blasphemy. His has also
provoked death threats, as a result of which Rushdie
has been obliged to live in hiding. His recent
publications have included a book for children,
Haroun and the Sea of Dreams (1990), and *Imaginary
Homelands: Essays and Criticism 1981–1991* (1991).
Travel writing: *The Jaguar Smile: A Nicaraguan
Journey* (1987).
Bib: Ruthven, M., *A Satanic Affair: Salman Rushdie
and the Rage of Islam*; Weatherby, W.J., *Salman
Rushdie: Sentenced to Death*; Ahsan, M.M. and Kidwa
A.R., *Sacrilege Versus Civility: Muslim Perspectives on
the Satanic Verses Affair*.

Ruskin, John (1819–1900)
Writer on art and on its relationship with society.
His central inspiration was that great art is moral,
and the corollary that the working men of industrial
England were spiritually impoverished. Like the
Pre-Raphaelites (he was a patron of D. G. Rossetti,
their leader), he found the contrast to the England
of his day in the freedom of individual response
to environment among the medieval artists, and he
expressed this view in the famous chapter called
'The Nature of Gothic' in *The Stones of Venice*. In

the field of design, Ruskin, like ▷ William Morris,
advocated a return to handicrafts and to medieval
conditions of production.
The latter part of his life was much concerned
with attacks on the social philosophies of political
economists, such as ▷ John Stuart Mill, to whom he
did less than justice, and in endeavours to awaken
the working classes to the nature of their combined
artistic and moral impoverishment. He wrote his
artistic books in a style of elaborate but precise and
delicate eloquence but his social gospel had more
concentrated and direct fervour. His puritanical
mother (he was an only child) had given him a
concentrated education in the Bible and though
his religious views as an adult were not explicit, his
conception of art as fundamentally spiritual arose out
of the intensity of his early religious training. Though
a supporter of the Pre-Raphaelites, Ruskin did not
lean like them towards 'art for art's sake' but towards
'art for the spiritual health of man'. In his campaign
against the mediocre aspects of industrial culture,
he was a disciple and admirer of ▷ Thomas Carlyle
but he extended Carlyle's vision of greatness and has
proved to be a writer of more permanent interest.
Nonetheless, he wrote so voluminously that, like
Carlyle, he is best read in selections.
His principal works are: *Modern Painters* (1843–60)
in which he champions Turner, one of the greatest
of English painters and at the time one of the most
controversial; *The Seven Lamps of Architecture* (1849)
leading to *The Stones of Venice* (1851–3) in which
he makes his discovery of 'the Nature of Gothic';
this took him towards problems about the nature of
civilized society in *The Political Economy of Art* (1857),
The Two Paths (1859) and, one of his most famous
books, ▷ *Unto This Last* (1862). *Sesame and Lilies*
(1865), *Ethics of the Dust* (1866), *The Crown of Wild
Olive* (1866) are essays in criticism on the age, and
Fors Clavigera (1871–84) is composed of 96 letters
to an educated artisan in which he shows himself
distrustful of liberal democracy. *Praeterita* (1885–9) is
one of the celebrated ▷ autobiographies in English,
although it is fragmentary and incomplete. Its most
famous section is the first, in which Ruskin describes
his unusual, in some ways unnatural, yet fertilizing
childhood.
Bib: Selections by Quennell, P.; Clark, K.;
Rosenberg, J. D.; Leon, D., *Life*; Evans, J., *Life*;
Ladd, H., *The Victorian Morality of Art*; Rosenberg,
J. D., *The Darkening Glass*; Wilenski, R. H., *John
Ruskin*; Lippincott, B., *Victorian Critics of Democracy*.

**Russell, Bertrand Arthur William, Lord
(1872–1970)**
Philosopher. Russell's important work on mathematical
philosophy and logic is one of the foundations of
20th-century Anglo-Saxon philosophy. His most
influential texts are *The Principles of Mathematics*
(1903); *Principia Mathematica* (1910–13, written
in collaboration with his Cambridge tutor, A. N.
Whitehead); *The Problems of Philosophy* (1912); his
epistemological works *Mysticism and Logic* (1918),
Analysis of Mind (1921) and *Human Knowledge* (1948);
and the accessible *History of Western Philosophy*
(1945). As this indicates, Russell's working life was

long and illustrious; he was a fringe member of the ▷ Bloomsbury Group (writing on aesthetics, and a famous sparring-partner for ▷ D. H. Lawrence). Later in life Russell was a founder member of CND. He was married to writer Dora Russell.

Russian Formalism
▷ Formalism.

Russian influence on English fiction
The international importance of Russian literature belongs chiefly to its achievements in the 19th century. Until the middle of the 19th century, the influence was chiefly from Britain upon Russia: ▷ Laurence Sterne, ▷ Walter Scott, Lord Byron and, later, ▷ Charles Dickens all made an important impression on Russian writers. Since about 1850, however, the balance of influence has been in the opposite direction, although Russian literature has chiefly been known in translation, which has limited extensive public knowledge to prose works, especially the novels. These have been widely read, especially in the famous translations by Constance Garnett, who translated ▷ Tolstoy, ▷ Dostoevsky, ▷ Turgenev, ▷ Chekhov and ▷ Gogol in the decades before and after 1900.

Tolstoy and Turgenev were the first Russian novelists to receive wide acclaim in Britain and Tolstoy is still considered the supreme novelist. His reputation in Britain owed much to ▷ Matthew Arnold, whose essay in praise of Tolstoy appeared in 1887, and is included in ▷ *Essays in Criticism, Second Series* (1888). His tribute is the more noticeable because he otherwise ignored novelists in his criticism, and it made its mark because he was the most influential critic of his day. However, other critics contributed their admiration for the Russians in the last quarter of the 19th century. This interest was awakened by the feeling that the Russians, besides the French, were the only nation to produce a range of major novelists comparable to those writing in English and that, unlike the French, they shared with the British and Americans a moral concern with human nature in society. There was also the feeling that the Russian novelists went beyond the British and Americans, excelling in their rendering of religious experience, though the full force of this was not felt until Constance Garnett produced her translation of Dostoevsky's *Brothers Karamazov* in 1912.

In America, interest in Russian writing seems to have gone deeper, because of a feeling that these two great continental nations shared comparable experiences in the disorderly variety of their rapid growth. It was not merely this, however, that made the great Anglo-American novelist ▷ Henry James a lifelong admirer of Turgenev. Turgenev was already well known in England from the middle of the century when he became the friend of ▷ George Eliot. These two novelists were the predominant influences on James's own work. He admired both for the depth of their moral insights but he admired Turgenev for what he saw as his superior artistic strictness in handling the elusive novel form. Turgenev thus combined for James the virtues of the French novelists with those of the English novelist he most admired. Gilbert Phelps, in *The Russian Novel in English Fiction* (1956), traces Turgenev's influence in some of the detail of James's novels and suggests his further influence on ▷ George Gissing, ▷ George Moore, ▷ Arnold Bennett, ▷ John Galsworthy and ▷ Joseph Conrad. Conrad is the most doubtful instance of these writers showing the Russian influence; as a Pole, he felt antagonistic to Russia and he did not know Russian, and yet it is impossible not to think of both Turgenev and Dostoevsky when reading ▷ *Under Western Eyes*.

Chekhov's influence on the short story and on the drama seems evident, although it may be that the distinctive development of the ▷ short story in English (for instance in ▷ James Joyce's ▷ *Dubliners* and in ▷ Katherine Mansfield) is as much an example of parallel development in the form as owing to Chekhov's initiation. In the drama, Chekhov's original handling of human speech as a medium has been developed in the works of ▷ Samuel Beckett and Harold Pinter.

The prestige of Russian literature in the mid-20th century remains very high in Britain, especially Boris Pasternak's *Doctor Zhivago* (1957) and the works of Alexander Solzhenitsyn. What is admired is the rendering of human experience and suffering on an heroic scale, and the courage and vitality of literary productivity in the face of adverse and repressive conditions. In the 1980s, however, with the more liberal regime in Russia, more, possibly dissident, literature has become available to the West. The break-up of the Soviet Union in the 1990s has clearly transformed the situation of Russian literature, especially its relations with the rest of the world.

Rutherford, Mark
▷ White, William Hale.

Sackville-West, Hon. Victoria Mary ('Vita')
(1892–1962)
Poet, novelist, travel-writer. Born at Knole, Kent,
to one of the oldest families in England, she was
married to Harold Nicolson, and travelled with
him during his diplomatic career before settling
at Sissinghurst Castle, Kent in 1930. From 1918
until 1921 her relationship with Violet Keppel (later
Violet Trefusis) was of great importance in her life.
In 1922 she met ▷ Virginia Woolf and began a
correspondence and friendship that inspired Woolf's
novel, ▷ *Orlando* (1928). Her earlier novels were:
Heritage (1919); *The Dragon in Shallow Waters* (1921);
Challenge (1923); *Grey Wethers* (1923); *Seducers
in Ecuador* (1924). Her next three novels were
best-sellers: *The Edwardians* (1930); *All Passion Spent*
(1931); *Family History* (1932). *Thirty Clocks Strike the
Hour* (1932) was a collection of short stories, while
her remaining four novels were: *The Dark Island*
(1934); *Grand Canyon* (1942); *The Easter Party* (1953);
No Signposts in the Sea (1962). Her fiction evokes
a social world in realistic detail and, while largely
traditional in mode, explores themes such as the
duality within the gender identity of the individual
and the assertion of women's rights. Her volumes
of poetry were: *Constantinople* (1915); *Poems of West
and East* (1917); *Selected Poems* (1941); *Collected
Poems* (1933). *The Land* (1926), which belongs to
the pastoral genre, *Solitude* (1938) and *The Garden*
(1946) were all long poems. Her other works include
a family history, entitled *Knole and the Sackvilles*
(1922), travel books on Persia, gardening books and
biography.
Bib: Watson, S.R., *V. Sackville-West*; Nicolson, N.,
Portrait of a Marriage; Nicolson, N. and Trautman,
J., (eds.), *The Letters of Virginia Woolf, Vol. III
1923–1928*; De Salvo, L. and Leaska, M.A., *The
Letters of Vita Sackville-West to Virginia Woolf*;
MacKnight, N. (ed.), *Dearest Andrew: Letters from Vita
Sackville-West to Andrew Reiber, 1951–1962*; Leaska,
M.A. and Phillips, J., *The Letters of Violet Trefusis to
Vita Sackville-West*; Glendinning, V., *Vita: The Life of
Vita Sackville-West*; Raitt, S., *Vita and Virginia*.

Sade, Donatien Alphonse, Marquis de (1740–1814)
French novelist and poet. His belief that his
destructive impulses were part of his nature, and
yet uncontrollable, counterbalanced the doctrine of
▷ Rousseau, according to whom man undistorted
by social forces was naturally good. Sade's ideas
profoundly influenced the dark side of Romanticism
but, with the exception of Swinburne, were less
pervasive in England. Sade has recently received
renewed attention in France (*eg* ▷ Roland Barthes,
Sade, Fourier, Loyola; 1971), where he has fed into
a ▷ Nietzschean strain of literary and theoretical
thinking.

Sahgal, Nayantara (b 1927)
Indian novelist and journalist, born in Allahabad,
Uttar Pradesh, India and educated at schools in
India and at Wellesley College, Massachusetts, USA.
She is a member of one of India's most powerful
political families, the Nehrus, the niece of India's
first prime minister, Jawaharlal Nehru, and daughter
of a prominent politician and diplomat, Nehru's
sister Vijaya Lakshmi Pandit. Her earliest writings
were autobiographical, drawing on her experience
of Indian politics before and after Independence:
Prison and Chocolate Cake (1954); *From Fear Set Free*
(1962). Most of Sahgal's earlier novels concern the
lives of upper-middle-class women, with political
events providing the context: *A Time to be Happy*
(1958); *This Time of Morning* (1965); *Storm in
Chandigarh* (1969); *The Day in Shadow* (1971); *A Voice
for Freedom* (1977); *A Situation in New Delhi* (1977).
Her later fiction is more explicitly focused on the
political and historical: *Rich Like Us* (1985), which
won the Sinclair Prize for fiction, shows concern
for human rights issues in its portrayal of political
violence during the state of emergency of the late
1970s. *Plans for Departure* (1985), which won the
Commonwealth Prize for fiction (Eurasia category) is
set in India during the period of World War I, with
a Danish suffragette as protagonist, while *Mistaken
Identity* (1988), about a woman who rejects a life in
purdah, is set in the 1930s. Sahgal has also written
historical and political non-fiction, including two
books on Indira Ghandi and *The Freedom Movement
in India* (1970).
Bib: Krishna Rao, A.V., *Nayantara Sahgal: A Study of
Her Fiction and Non-Fiction.*

Saintsbury, George Edward Bateman (1845–1933)
Literary historian and critic. His works include:
A Short History of French Literature (1882); *A Short
History of English Literature* (1898); *A History of
Criticism* (1900–4); *A History of English Prosody*
(1906–21); *The History of English Criticism* (1911); *A
History of the French Novel* (1917–19). He also wrote
studies of Dryden, ▷ Walter Scott, and ▷ Matthew
Arnold. His treatment of literary study was historical;
that is to say, principles of evaluation or critical
theory were for him secondary to coherent narration.

Sand, George (1804–76)
Pseudonym of Amandine-Aurore Lucille Dupin,
baronne Dudevant, she was born in Paris and
brought up at her paternal grandmother's country
property at Nohant (later hers), following the death
of her father, in an atmosphere of quarrels between
her mother and grandmother. After a convent
education in Paris, she ran wild again at Nohant,
reading avidly ▷ Rousseau, Byron, Shakespeare
and Chateaubriand among others. She married the
baron Dudevant, a retired army officer, and had
two children, but by 1831 was living an independent
life in Paris, writing to earn her living. Her work
reflected the men and ideas in her personal life,
and her catholic enthusiasm for humanitarianism,
Christian socialism, Republicanism, etc. She also
wrote idealized romances of rustic life, set around
Nohant. *Indiana* (1832) was the first of many
successes and was followed by *Valentine* (1832),
Lélia (1833), *Jacques* (1834) and *Mauprat* (1837).
These championed the rights of women to follow
their desires and ignore convention. *Spiridion* (1839)
and others reflect her ideas, and the country tales
include *La Mare au Diable* (1846) and *La Petite
Fadette* (1848). Her relationship with the poet Alfred

de Musset is fictionalized in *Elle et lui* (1859) and incidents in her nine-year liaision with the composer Chopin are portrayed in *Un hiver à Majorque* (1841). She also wrote some political articles, biographical and critical essays, unsuccessful drama and an autobiography in four volumes, *Histoire de ma vie* (1854–5).

Sansom, William (1912–76)

Short-story writer, novelist and travel writer. He served in the London Fire Brigade in World War II, an experience which gave rise to *Fireman Flower* (1944), a volume of short stories, which was the form in which he was most successful. His work covers a wide range of subject matter and styles, from documentary realism to macabre fantasy. In *The Body* (1949) the mental stability of the first-person narrator gradually disintegrates as a result of obsessive jealousy.
Bib: Michel-Michot, P., *Sansom: A Critical Assessment*.

Sargeson, Frank (1903–82)

New Zealand novelist, short-story writer and dramatist. His stories tend to deal with a small group of characters and to be narrated from within the consciousness of one of them, often a character with limited powers of self-expression, like the narrator of the ▷ novella *That Summer* (1946). His novels are more various in tone, but render the sense of a claustrophobic and somewhat Puritan New Zealand society by means of irony, comedy and a skilful rendering of idiom. His novels are: *I Saw In My Dream* (1949); *I For One . . .* (1954); *The Hangover* (1967); *Joy of the Worm* (1969); *Sunset Village* (1976). Story collection: *Collected Short Stories* (1965). Autobiography: *Memoirs of a Peon* (1965).
Bib: Copland, R. A., *Frank Sargeson*.

Sartor Resartus: The Life and Opinions of Herr Teufelsdröckh (1833–4)

A disguised spiritual ▷ autobiography by ▷ Thomas Carlyle. It was serialized (1833–4) in *Fraser's Magazine* and published in book form in Boston, USA, in 1836 and in Britain in 1838, Carlyle was under the influence of the ▷ German Romantics, *eg* Jean Paul Richter. The title is Latin for 'the tailor re-patched': Carlyle offers the fable that human beliefs and institutions are like clothes and need renewing. Against Byron's attitude of doubt, isolation and suffering, Carlyle calls for the affirmativeness of the German poet ▷ Goethe; heroic qualities such as sacrifice and devotion to duty must redeem the inner man and, through men, the directionless age in which Carlyle felt himself to be living – the age of flux and the decay of unquestioning religious faith. Besides the drive of German influence, Carlyle felt the force of the old-fashioned Scottish Calvinism such as had animated his father. The three crucial chapters are 'The Everlasting No', 'Centre of Indifference' and 'The Everlasting Yea'. Despite the difficulty he had in getting the book published in Britain, it marks the beginning of his exposition of the creed of heroism, which made Carlyle an inspiring figure in commerce-dominated mid-19th-century Britain.

Sartre, Jean-Paul (1905–80)

French writer. His areas of activity and influence covered philosophy, the novel, drama, literary criticism and political commitment. He was the major exponent of atheistic ▷ existentialism in France and made an early impact with his novels *La Nausée* (1938) and *Les Chemins de la liberté*, a projected tetralogy of which only three volumes were published: *L'Age de raison* (1945), *Le Sursis* (1945) and *La Mort dans l'âme* (1949). In *La Nausée*, the central character, Roquentin, discovers that far from being central to the nature of things, man is metaphysically superfluous (*de trop*) in the universe. *Les Chemins de la liberté* are set at the outbreak of World War II and portray the urgent necessity of commitment, especially in the form of political action, to secure personal and collective freedom. The same themes run through Sartre's drama, which is more accessible than the fiction and has proved more enduringly popular (*Les Mouches*, 1943, a version of the Orestes story; *Huis Clos*, 1945; *Les Mains sales*, 1948). The philosophical background to existentialism was expounded in *L'Etre et le néant* (1943) and *Critique de la raison dialectique* (1960).

Satre also wrote a number of existentialist-orientated biographies, of Baudelaire, of Jean Genet (1910–86) and of ▷ Flaubert. His volumes of *Situations* contain mainly essays on politics, literature and society and in 1945 he founded the important literary and political review, *Les Temps modernes*. In 1964 he published his autobiography, *Les Mots*, which seeks to expose the ideology of the autobiographical genre and views with irony his years of childhood under his grandfather Charles Schweitzer (Sartre was the cousin of Albert Schweitzer (1875–1965). In the same year, Sartre was awarded and refused the Nobel Prize for Literature.

Sassoon, Siegfried (1886–1967)

Poet and autobiographer. His *Memoirs of a Foxhunting Man* (1928) and *Memoirs of an Infantry Officer* (1930) are accounts of his life as a country gentleman before World War I, and of his experiences during it. He also became famous for his savagely satirical poems written during his military service, his first and most famous volume of anti-war poems being *Counter-attack* (1918). He was a friend of Wilfred Owen, and influenced Owen's writing. The two volumes of memoirs were put together as *The Complete Memoirs of George Sherston* (1937), which includes an additional section, *Sherston's Progress*. His poems, including volumes published since World War I, are in a collected edition (1961).

Satanic Verses, The (1988)

Novel by ▷ Salman Rushdie which received mixed reviews on its publication in 1988. Controversy erupted when Muslims protested that the book was blasphemous. Copies were burned in Bradford and demonstrations took place there and elsewhere in Britain, Pakistan and the USA. In Iran mass demonstrations against the author, book and publisher caused international tension to rise. The Ayatollah Khomeini passed a death sentence on Rushdie, who went into hiding. The novel returned to the ▷ best-seller lists in the wake of the controversy, which raised many issues of freedom of speech and expression, and the freedom to publish.

Satire

A form of attack through mockery; it may exist in any literary medium, but is often regarded as a medium in itself. The origins of the word help to explain the manifestations of satire. It derives from the Latin 'satura' = a vessel filled with the earliest agricultural produce of the year, used in seasonal festivals to celebrate harvest; a secondary meaning is 'miscellany of entertainment', implying merry-making at such festivals, probably including verbal warfare. This primitive humour gave rise to a highly cultivated form of literary attack in the poetry of Horace, Persius (1st century AD) and Juvenal. Thus from ancient Roman culture two ideas of satire have come down to us: the first expresses a basic instinct for comedy through mockery in human beings, and was not invented by the Romans; the second is a self-conscious medium, implying standards of civilized and moral rightness in the mind of the poet and hence a desire on his or her part to instruct readers so as to reform their moral failings and absurdities. The two kinds of satire are inter-related, so that it is not possible to distinguish them sharply. Moreover, it is not easy to distinguish strict satire in either of its original forms from other kinds of comedy.

1 Strict satire, *ie* satire emulating the Roman poets. This was one of the outcomes of Renaissance cultivation of ancient Latin literature. Between 1590 and 1625 several poets wrote deliberate satires with Juvenal, Persius and Horace in mind; the most important of these were Donne and Ben Jonson. The great age of the strict satire was the 18th century, notably in the work of Alexander Pope who emulated the relatively genial satire of Horace, and ▷ Samuel Johnson, who emulated the sombre style of Juvenal. Satire of this sort makes its object of attack the social forms and corruptions of the time.

2 Comedy of Humours and Comedy of Manners. These are the most easily distinguishable forms of dramatic satire. The former is associated chiefly with Ben Jonson. The 'humours' in Jonson's conception are the obsessions and manias to which the nature of human beings invites them to abandon themselves; they have a close relation to the medieval Seven Deadly Sins, such as lust, avarice and gluttony. The Comedy of Manners belongs to the period 1660–1800, and, especially, to the first 40 years of it. Its most notable exponents are Congreve at the end of the 17th century and Sheridan at the end of the 18th. This comedy is less concerned with basic human dispositions and more with transient social ones; rational social behaviour is the standard in the mind of the dramatist. Both these forms of satire were taken over by novelists; the 18th-century novelist ▷ Fielding began as a writer of dramatic comedies of manners, but Dickens in the 19th century writes more distinctly in the tradition of the comedy of humours, with a strong addition of

social stagnation. Satire in the theatre has, since the 1960s, been replaced by television satire, with radical programmes such as *Beyond the Fringe* and more recently, *Spitting Image*.

3 Satire of ▷ parody and irony (▷ Figures of speech). The most notable practitioner in prose of ironic and parodic satire was ▷ Swift. Works such as ▷ *A Modest Proposal* and ▷ *Gulliver's Travels* aim to ambush the reader's expectations and to undermine complacency through shock, laughter and incongruity.

4 Flytings, and other traditional forms. The Middle Ages took from its popular festivals a strong tradition of verbal combat (flytings) and sardonic criticism of the established social order. One aspect of this emerges in popular ballads (especially in the printed form of broadsides which developed after the medieval period) and in the work of educated writers such as Langland and ▷ Chaucer – grimly in the former's *Piers Plowman*, and genially in the latter's ▷ *Canterbury Tales*. Dunbar was another eminent practitioner of flytings, *eg* his *Flyting of Dunbar and Kennedy*.

5 Novelistic satire. Much satire in novels from the 18th to the 20th century cannot be summed up under comedy of manners. The novels of ▷ Peacock, for example, establish a tradition of comic discussions mocking at contemporary trends of thought; Peacock's example was partly followed by ▷ Meredith and ▷ Aldous Huxley. Another variant is the 'anti-utopia', using an imaginary country to satirize actual tendencies in contemporary Britain. The most notable examples of this are ▷ *Erewhon* by ▷ Samuel Butler and *Brave New World* by ▷ Aldous Huxley. Apart from these examples, it is difficult to find a novelist who does not use satire at least intermittently, usually as social comment. Eminent examples are: Fielding, ▷ Jane Austen ▷ Thackeray, ▷ Dickens, ▷ Wells, ▷ Forster, and more recently ▷ Angus Wilson, ▷ Evelyn Waugh, ▷ George Orwell, and the 'campus novels' of ▷ Malcolm Bradbury and ▷ David Lodge.

Saturday Review

It was founded in 1855 and noted for the brilliance of its contributors and the severity of its criticism. Later it took a greater interest in literature and included contributions from ▷ Thomas Hardy, Max Beerbohm, Arthur Symons and ▷ H. G. Wells. George Bernard Shaw was dramatic critic from 1895 to 1898 and Agate from 1921 to 1923.

Saussure, Ferdinand de (1857–1913)

Swiss linguist, generally regarded as the founder of ▷ structuralism. Saussure's *Course in General Linguistics*, was published two years after his death, in 1915, and represents a reconstruction of three series of lectures which he gave at the University of Geneva during the years 1906–7, 1908–9, and 1910–11. It was Saussure who pioneered the distinction between ▷ 'langue' and ▷ 'parole', and who sought to define the operations of language according to the principles of combination and ▷ difference. Although ▷ deconstruction has done much to undermine the Structuralist base of Saussure's

thinking, the concept of 'difference' as a determining principle in establishing meaning ('signification') remains one of the key concepts in modern critical theory. Moreover, Saussure's work provided the foundation for the methodological analysis of ▷ sign systems (▷ semiotics), and the types of linguistic investigation which he undertook have been successfully appropriated by literary critics, as well as by social anthropologists such as Claude Lévi-Strauss (b 1908).
Bib: Culler, J. D., *Ferdinand de Saussure*.

Sayers, Dorothy L. (Leigh) (1893–1957)
▷ Detective fiction.

Scenes of Clerical Life (1857)
Three tales by ▷ George Eliot, and her earliest work in fiction: *The Sad Fortunes of the Rev. Amos Barton*; *Mr Gilfil's Love-Story*; and *Janet's Repentance*. The hero of each is a clergyman. They were published first in ▷ *Blackwood's Magazine* in 1857 and collected as *Scenes of Clerical Life* in 1858.

Schreiner Olive (Emilie Albertina) (1855–1920)
Daughter of a Methodist missionary of German descent and an English mother, Olive Schreiner was born in Basutoland, the sixth of 12 children. Self-educated, she became governess to a Boer family at the age of 15 and began to write. She came to England in 1881 to seek a publisher and in 1884 met ▷ Havelock Ellis with whom she developed a close friendship. Ten years later she returned to South Africa and married the politician Samuel Cron Crowright who became her literary assistant and later literary executor. They took trips to England and travelled around Africa together. Her first and most acclaimed work is *The Story of an African Farm* (1883), which was published under the pseudonym Ralph Iron. Its unorthodox religious views and ▷ feminist standpoint caused a considerable stir. She wrote most after her return to South Africa: *Trooper Peter Halket of Mashonaland* (1897), *From Man to Man* (1926) and *Undine* (1929), all with feminist themes, and short stories, *Dreams* (1891), *Real Life* (1893) and *Stories, Dreams and Allegories* (1920). She also wrote *Woman and Labour* (1911). See also: *Letters* (1924).
Bib: Schreiner, S. C. C., *The Life of Olive Schreiner*; First, R. & Scott, A., *Olive Schreiner*.

Science Fiction
The term 'science fiction' was coined in the mid-19th century, though it was 'reinvented' and given wider currency in the late 1920s by the American magazine editor Hugo Gernsback, who popularized the stories deriving from, pre-eminently, ▷ H. G. Wells and Jules Verne. To Gernsback a science fiction story was 'a charming romance intermingled with scientific fact and prophetic vision' (editorial, *Amazing Stories*, 1926). Wells had called what would now be dubbed his science fiction 'scientific romances', and the relation between romance, particularly Gothic romance (▷ Gothic novels), and science fiction has often been remarked on by definers of the form. ▷ Kingsley Amis in *New Maps of Hell* (1960), a work which did much to encourage

serious critical attention to this branch of popular literature, allows for a broadening of the speculative base of science fiction through reference to sciences, or 'pseudo-sciences', like sociology, psychology, anthropology, theology and linguistics.

Darko Suvin (*Metamorphoses of Science Fiction*, 1979) remarks that 'cognition' would be a more appropriate word than science in defining this literary genre, and his emphasis on estrangement, or alienation, provides a useful direction for the discussion of science fiction in terms of recent critical theory, which has given new life to the ▷ Russian Formalist assertion that literature 'defamiliarizes' conventional assumptions. Science fiction, which is a product of and response to an era of rapid scientific and technological development, has often been concerned to promote new ways of seeing appropriate to, for example, the human consequences of industrialization, the implications of Darwinian (▷ Charles Darwin) evolutionary theory, Einstein's theory of relativity, and the second law of thermodynamics concerning the ultimate entropy of a closed system like the universe. Though the popularity of science fiction may result from the withdrawal of much modern mainstream fiction from traditional forms of storytelling, its concerns as speculative, defamiliarizing literature set it apart from the conventions of classic realism with its emphasis on, for example, characterization. Critics hostile to the science fiction genre have complained that its presentation of human character compared unfavourably with that of realist fiction, whereas others have argued that this represents a response to a world dehumanized by technology, or a radically different viewpoint for asking the question 'What constitutes the human?'

▷ Mary Shelley's ▷ *Frankenstein, Or The Modern Prometheus* (1817) is centrally concerned with this question of defining the human through its treatment of artificially created life and offers the polar opposites of the human as idealist romantic hero and as mere mechanism. This duality is figured in a wide range of subsequent science fiction, most obviously in the genre's obsession with robots and other forms of artificial life and intelligence. In constructing a nameless 'other', Frankenstein's creation or 'monster', *Frankenstein* deals with another obsessively pursued theme of science fiction – confrontation with the alien. Mary Shelley's text, in its repeated patterns of dualism, of attempted completion of incomplete individuals, suggests the possibility, dear to much recent science fiction, that Earth is the alien planet and 'otherness' is the repressed in the human psyche or in human society.

Frankenstein may be regarded as a significant root work of science fiction, but it is the scientific romances of H. G. Wells which established the genre in the 1890s. Many of these share with *Frankenstein* an unsettling pessimism deriving from a perception of the destructive and alienating uses to which technological development might be put, while much American science fiction, at least in the period before World War II, suggested an optimistic faith in the possibilities of scientific and technological development, springing, perhaps, from a culture defining itself through reference to an expanding frontier. Wells established an influential British tradition of bleaker Darwinism, emanating from an imperial culture already in decline.

Wells's *The Time Machine* (1895) provides a model for a range of subsequent science fiction. It introduces, in almost comic pseudo-scientific discourse, a technological means of travel through time; it facilitates sociological criticism and prediction through the use of utopian and dystopian discourses; it treats the theme of confrontation with the alien, of the last man on earth, of the entropic death of the world; it provides new contexts for old myths; and it defamiliarizes the cosy certitudes of the late Victorian male world in which it starts. *The War of the Worlds* (1898), repeatedly adapted and imitated in the 20th century, may be regarded as the genesis of the bulk of science fiction treatments of interplanetary war or invasion by the alien. *Mr Blettsworthy on Rampole Island* (1928), which employs the traditional device of the dream as a means of transport in place of a time-machine, involves an inversion of dream and reality of a kind familiar in a wide range of science fiction. *The Shape of Things to Come* (1933), widely known through the Alexander Korda film version, represents a more optimistic element in Wells's science fiction in that it suggests the possibility of redemption through an enlightened, technologically oriented élite; yet images of global disorder and collapse are, perhaps, most vividly projected in this text.

Mark Rose, in *Alien Encounters: Anatomy of Science Fiction* (1981), approaches the definition of science fiction through its phases of development. Thus the scientific romances of such as Wells transform earlier kinds of romance, like the Gothic, and fill a gap left by the predominance of realistic fiction. Later phases manifest a generic self-consciousness, in that science fiction texts come to be based on an explicit form. Rose provides the example of ▷ C. S. Lewis, whose science fiction output is in part a response to the fiction of Wells. The settings of Lewis's space trilogy, *Out of the Silent Planet* (1943), *Perelandra* (1943) and *That Hideous Strength* (1945), are respectively Mars, Venus and Earth, but Lewis's preference for angels rather than space-ships as a means of interplanetary travel has led to some questioning of their status as science fiction. The trilogy evinces an attachment to supernatural Christianity rather than to science, in opposition to the element of pessimistic materialism in Wells; but some variant of such mysticism is not uncommon in the genre. For example, Lewis's near-contemporary, Olaf Stapledon, in works like *Last and First Men* (1930), *Last Men in London* (1932) and *Star-Maker* (1937), projected what he called 'myths' of future history on a scale that goes beyond beyond Wells's scientific romances.

▷ Aldous Huxley acknowledged that his *Brave New World* (1932) started out as a parody of H. G. Wells's *Men Like Gods*, and it has become, in the words of Brian Aldiss (b 1925) (*Billion Year Spree*, 1973) 'arguably the Western World's most famous science fiction novel'. The status accorded this satirical dystopian text, like that enjoyed by the still controversial *1984* (1949) by ▷ George Orwell,

may result from the fact that, in the context of the author's novel output outside the field of science fiction, it can be regarded as somehow 'mainstream' fiction. Both of these works have been regarded as more 'serious' than most science fiction, though this may be based on questionable assumptions about intrinsic literary merit.

A number of British writers were regular contributors to the pre-World War II American science fiction magazine which did much to create a persistent downmarket image for the genre in the popular imagination. The first magazine devoted entirely to science fiction was Hugo Gernsback's *Amazing Stories* (published from 1926), which made an effort to appear respectably scientific and educational in a market which often relied upon lurid presentation. It was followed by such titles as *Science Wonder Stories*, *Wonder Stories* and *Astounding Stories* in the late 1920s and early 1930s. Besides Wells, British contributors included John Russell Fearn, Eric Frank Russell and John Beynon Harris. Fearn, whose work appeared in *Amazing Stories* first in 1933, produced a staggering quantity of novels and short stories under no less than 25 pseudonyms as well as editing two British science fiction magazines. Russell, whose output was modest compared to Fearn's, began publishing in *Astounding Stories* in 1937 and went on to contribute to British magazines like *Tales of Wonder* and *Fantasy*. Harris is better known as John Wyndham, though he also wrote as John Beynon, J. B. Harris and Johnson Harris. He published short stories and novels from 1930 on, though his reputation rests on the novels he produced as John Wyndham from 1951, the year in which *The Day of the Triffids* was published.

'Exiles on Asperus' (in *Wonder Stories Quarterly*, 1933) by John Beynon Harris demonstrates how Wyndham was not temperamentally drawn to the 'space-opera' conventions of the American magazines or to their attachment to science fiction 'gadget' stories. He was happier, and more successful, developing the Wellsian tradition of science fiction in novels centring on an imagined disaster arising from the upsetting of the natural and social orders, generally through the agency of technology. His catastrophe stories, including *The Day of the Triffids*, *The Kraken Wakes* (1953) and *The Midwich Cuckoos* (1957), belong to a class of British science fiction stretching from Wells to the present, including New Wave science fiction which in some ways represented a reaction against Wyndham's formulae. *The Day of the Triffids* makes uses of the traditional science fiction theme of the Last Man/Last Woman, a new Adam and Eve faced with the arduous complexities of an unfamiliar world. The treatment evokes a characteristically English romantic nostalgia, reminiscent of ▷ Richard Jefferies's vision of the ruined capital in *After London* (1885). The remaking of a new world out of the scraps of the old in *The Day of the Triffids* also suggests a debt to ▷ Daniel Defoe's ▷ *Robinson Crusoe* (1719), but Wyndham's novel is predominantly Wellsian, though it retains a safe, genteel quality not so typical of Wells.

▷ Arthur C. Clarke, one of the most celebrated science fiction writers of the 20th century, combines meticulous attention to the scientific and technological aspects of the genre, in the tradition of Jules Verne, with a lyrically didactic commitment to the benign evolutionary potential of technology that owes much to the impact of Clarke's early reading of Stapledon. Both were powerfully expressed in Stanley Kubrick's film *2001* (1968), for which Clarke wrote the screenplay. The kind of wondering transcendence conveyed at the end of that film is characteristic of Clarke's work, encountered in, for example, one of his most popular novels, *Childhood's End* (1953); while *The Deep Range* (1957) develops into a lesson in respect for the non-human creatures of the earth as the prospect of contact with beings from other worlds approaches.

The first novel of Brian Aldiss, *Non-Stop* (1958), gave an indication of the exhilarating variety which has proved a feature of his subsequent fictional output. *Hothouse* (1962) and *Greybeard* (1964) treat the well-established theme of imagined catastrophe, but combine a playful abundance of exotic science fiction invention with romantic nostalgia. A Swiftian satirical mode characterizes *The Dark Light Years* (1964), while the alienating detachment of *Report on Probability A* (1968) draws the techniques of the French ▷ *nouveau roman* into the orbit of science fiction. *Frankenstein Unbound* (1973) and *Moreau's Other Island* (1980) reinvent seminal science fiction texts for a new context, while the abundance of Aldiss's Helliconia trilogy (1982–5) defies brief categorization. The epilogue to the third volume, *Helliconia Winter* (1985), a translated extract from Lucretius, *De Rerum Natura*, might be applied to Aldiss's *oeuvre*: 'Everything must pass through successive phases. Nothing remains forever what it was.'

Aldiss's commitment to science fiction, his urge to experiment and enjoy, and to extend the possibilities of the genre, gave him a respected place in the so-called New Wave science fiction writing associated with the magazine *New Worlds* under the editorship of Michael Moorcock (b 1939) from 1964. Until then *New Worlds* had been edited by E. J. Carnell, who was also responsible for *Science Fantasy*. Carnell's magazine published a wide range of British science fiction, including the work of such prolific authors as Kenneth Bulmer, who employed 15 pen-names in addition to his own name, and John Brunner, who began publishing science fiction at the age of 17. The scale of Brunner's output may have resulted in his work being critically underrated, though his dystopian novels *Stand on Zanzibar* (1968), *The Jagged Orbit* (1969) and *The Sheep Look Up* (1972) achieved critical acclaim. Like Brunner, Moorcock is a prolific author who started young; he was editing *Tarzan Adventures* at the age of 17. His 'sword and sorcery' fantasies embody the apocalyptic theme which runs through much of his later science fiction, in which he reconstructs the past as well as imagining the future; this kind of reconstruction may be seen as a way of deconstructing the present. Works like *War Lord of the Air* (1971) and *The Land Leviathan* (1974) present a past manufactured from a range of literary reference, to, for example, Verne, Wells and ▷ Joseph Conrad, and demonstrate Moorcock's

attachment to the concept of the 'multiverse', which proposes a variety of separate realities which can sometimes interact. His fondness for series of novels and a modernist tendency to fragment his narratives are particularly evident in his Jerry Cornelius novels, including *The Final Programme* (1969), *A Cure for Cancer* (1971), *The English Assassin* (1972) and *The Condition of Muzak* (1977).

New Worlds under Moorcock represented a spirited reaction against the continuing influence of American pulp science fiction, and a number of American authors were attracted to its programme. But it was a British author, J. G. Ballard (b 1930), who was championed most consistently by the magazine. The Conradian tone of much of Ballard's science fiction contrasts with the racier products of some *New Worlds* writers, influenced by the current 'rock' culture; he has never been much interested in the traditional science fiction fare of space travel and the distant future, preferring to focus on something challengingly closer to the present, defamiliarizing the familiar earth into the alien planet, and insisting that the outward thrust of science fiction be matched by an inward journey. The estranging, detritus-strewn landscapes of much of his fiction indicate Ballard's fascination with surrealist art, though his *Empire of the Sun* (1983), a novel drawing on his boyhood experience of World War II in the Far East, reveals a source closer to home for his images of collapse and desolation. Ballard's catastrophe novels, like *The Drowned World* (1962), *The Drought* (1965) and *The Crystal World* (1966), bear some relation to the disaster stories of John Wyndham and John Christopher, though there is little in the way of romantic nostalgia in his treatment of 'biospheric' disasters. What might be seen as his post-imperial pessimism has not generally endeared Ballard to an American audience. His experimental 'condensed' novels, which first began appearing in *New Worlds*, were published together in *The Atrocity Exhibition* (1970) and, again, did not find favour in the U.S. The disturbing presentation of perverse urban nightmares in *Crash!* (1973), *Concrete Island* (1974) and *High Rise* (1975) bring the concept of the science fiction catastrophe even closer to our own time, as if the irreversible disaster had already occurred in our culture.

▷ Doris Lessing, who turned to science fiction in the early 1970s when her reputation as a mainstream novelist was already established, is also drawn towards visions of the decline and breakdown of society. The last volume of the 'Children of Violence' novels, *The Four-Gated City* (1969), ultimately projects into the future, but from the publication of *Briefing for a Descent into Hell* (1971) Lessing has shown a firm commitment to the exploratory, speculative potential of science fiction, with particular reference to questions of gender and the theme of spiritual awakening. The evocations of collapse and depletion in Lessing's science fiction, which, in the 1980s, turns to space fiction on the grand galactic scale, are set against the possibility of a utopian alternative, and its emphasis is more mystical than scientific. In *Briefing and Memoirs* the alternative might amount to no more than dreams; but in

Shikasta (1979) utopian society is destroyed by a malign galactic empire, while in *The Marriages between Zones Three, Four, and Five* (1980) it is confirmed that the project of utopian evolutionary development, through, for example, the use of psychic powers, lies within the province of women.

A number of ▷ Angela Carter's novels may be classed as science fiction, though, like Lessing, she tends not to focus primarily on science. *Heroes and Villains* (1970) is set in the familiar terrain of a post-catastrophe world and, using the structure of romantic fantasy, explores a variety of dualities, including fantasy/reality, beauty/barbarism, love/hate, male/female. Carter's particular skill, evident in *The Infernal Desire Machines of Dr Hoffman* (1972), *The Passion of New Eve* (1977) and *Nights at the Circus* (1983), lies in her exuberantly self-conscious, inventive storytelling in which romance, satire, horror and comedy interact exotically.

Ian Watson is also adept in exotic narrative, for example, *Whores of Babylon* (1988), but his reputation has been for intellectual, speculative brilliance. His texts, like Lessings's, have a tendency to the mystical and transcendent, and approach the possibility of such transcendence through the discourses of science, linguistics, mysticism and myth, as is impressively demonstrated by his first four novels: *The Embedding* (1973), *The Jonah Kit* (1976), *The Martian Inca* (1977) and *Alien Embassy* (1977).

Christopher Priest also built up during the 1970s a reputation as a thoughtful and inventive science fiction author through such works as *Inverted World* (1974) and *A Dream of Wessex* (1977).

The next new wave of science fiction is already upon us. Science fiction might be said to have begun with the work of a woman and, looked at one way, Mary Shelley's *Frankenstein* is a coded analysis of female experience. The women's movement of recent years, with a strong lead from the United States, has led to a powerful reaction against science fiction's traditional marginalization of women, and Lessing is not unique in turning to science fiction from a different novel tradition. Michèle Roberts, for example, adopts the dystopian mode in *The Book of Mrs Noah* (1973), while ▷ Zoë Fairbairns uses science fiction's speculative resources to consider the issue of wages for housework in *Benefits* (1979). The Women's Press boasts a growing list of feminist science fiction, and one of the editors responsible for this, Sarah Lefanu, has written a study of feminism and science fiction, *In the Chinks of the World Machine* (1988). Commenting on the value of science fiction, Lefanu has said: 'It deals with the possibility of change, and allows the investigation of radical ideas.' **Bib:** Aldiss, B., *Billion-Year Spree*; Kuhn, A., *Alien Zones*; Nicholls, P., *Encyclopedia of Science Fiction*; the journal, *Science Fiction Studies*.

Scott, Hugh Stowell (1862–1903)

Writer of adventure romances, which he published under the name 'Henry Seton Merriman'. Most of them have rapid, exciting plots and exotic settings, which Scott researched on his extensive travels. The son of a shipowner in Newcastle-upon-Tyne, Scott abandoned a business career early on to pursue writing and travelling; it has been suggested that he worked for the British intelligence services, and some of his work is strongly pro-imperialist. His novels include: *The Slave of the Lamp* (1892); *With Edged Tools* (1894); *The Grey Lady* (1895); *In Kedar's Tents* (1897); *The Isle of Unrest* (1900); *Barlasch of the Guard* (1902); *The Last Hope* (1904).

Scott, Paul (1920–78)

Novelist. He served in India, Burma and Malaya during World War II and subsequently worked in publishing. His major achievement was *The Raj Quartet*, a tetralogy consisting of: *The Jewel in the Crown* (1966); *The Day of the Scorpion* (1968); *The Towers of Silence* (1971); *A Division of the Spoils* (1975). A portrait of Indian society at the time of Independence in 1974, it uses a range of narrative forms, including letters, journals, reports and memories. The story is built around the consequences of the rape of an English girl; consequences which serve to reveal corruption and racism in the Raj adminstration and the roots of the political unrest and intercommunal violence at the Partition of India. Scott was accorded little critical recognition until *Staying On* (1977), a gentle satire set after Independence, won the Booker Prize. His work is notable for its combination of complex narrative technique with historical accuracy. *The Raj Quartet* was televised as *The Jewel in the Crown* in 1984 and *Staying On* was adapted for television in 1981. Scott's earlier novels include *The Birds of Paradise* (1962).

Scott, Sir Walter (1771–1832)

Scottish poet and novelist. The son of an Edinburgh lawyer, he was descended from famous families on the Scottish side of the border with England. This ancestry early attracted him to the drama and tragedy of Anglo-Scottish border history; he became an antiquarian, and a very romantic one. His Romanticism was stimulated further by reading the poetry of the contemporary Germans, Bürger and ▷ Goethe; he hoped to do for the Scottish border what they had done for the German Middle Ages, and make its past live again in modern romance. A widespread taste was already developed for the Middle Ages and was manifesting itself in the ▷ Gothic novel. He collaborated with the most famous of the Gothic novelists – ▷ Matthew 'Monk' Lewis – in producing *Tales of Wonder* in 1801. A little later Coleridge's poem *Christabel*, inspired him to write poems in the same metre, and between 1805 and 1815 he produced the succession of narrative poems which made him famous. He began to feel himself outdone as a narrative poet by Byron, however, and from 1815 he devoted himself to the novels for which he is now better known. Publishing enterprises in which he had begun to involve himself in 1809 left him with a debt of £130,000 to pay off, when the London publisher Constable went bankrupt. Scott was immensely proud, and determined to pay off the debt by his own literary efforts. By writing very prolifically for the rest of his life, he nearly succeeded; he was by then a very sick man, and his efforts are a legend of literary heroism.

Scott's most famous poems are *The Lay of the Last*

Minstrel (1805); *Marmion* (1808), and *The Lady of the Lake* (1810). The first two are from Anglo-Scottish border history and legend; the third is about the equally bitter enmity of Scottish Highlander for Scottish Lowlander. The readability of these poems makes it easy to account for their popularity, but the kind of interest they offer – the dramatization of the life of a whole society – was not such as Scott was able to work out in the verse-narrative medium.

His novels show a double interest: he was the first novelist in English to present characters as part of a society, and not merely against the background of a particular society, the nature of which is taken for granted; he was also the inventor of the true historical novel. His best work is contained in the Waverley novels and in the first three series of *Tales of My Landlord*: ▷ *Waverley* (1814), ▷ *Guy Mannering* (1815), *The Antiquary* (1816), *Old Mortality* (1816), ▷ *Rob Roy* (1817), ▷ *The Heart of Midlothian* (1818), *The Bride of Lammermoor* and *The Legend of Montrose* (1819). All these concern 17th- and 18th-century Scotland, and the religious and dynastic struggles that shaped the nation as Scott knew it. From then onwards he was writing with excessive haste in order to pay off his debts, and he commonly chose English and medieval subjects, *eg* ▷ *Ivanhoe* (1819), *Kenilworth* (about English Elizabethan times – 1821), *Quentin Durward* (1823) and some 16 others, only one of which, *St Ronan's Well* (1823), was set in Scott's own time.

Not only was Scott's influence, both in Britain and Europe, very large in shaping literary taste, but he had an extensive influence in encouraging non-literary taste, such as that for wild landscape (especially of the Highlands) and more intelligent interest in the past. As a critic he was among the first to recognize the genius of ▷ Jane Austen. In politics he was strongly right wing (Tory), and he helped to found the great Tory review, the ▷ *Quarterly*, in 1809.

Bib: Buchan, J., *Life*; Davie, D., *The Heyday of Sir Walter Scott*; Hayden, J. O., *Scott: The Critical Heritage*; Hillhouse, J. T., *The Waverley Novels and their Critics*; Lewis, C. S., in *They Asked for a Paper*; Lockhart, J. G., *Memoirs*; Muir, E., *Scott and Scotland*; Ferris, I., *The Achievement of Literary Authority: Gender, History and the Waverley Novels*.

Scottish fiction in English

This belongs above all to the Lowlands; it is a distinctive branch of literature in the English language, the Lowland Scottish form of which had originally a close resemblance to that spoken in the north of England. Racially, linguistically and culturally, Lowland Scottish ties with England were close, despite the constant was between the two countries between the late 13th and mid-16th centuries. In contrast, until the 18th-century destruction of Highland culture, the Lowlanders had little more than the political bond of a common sovereign with their Gaelic-speaking fellow-countrymen of the north. While it is not true to say that Scottish literature is a branch of English literature, the two literatures have been closely related.

Scottish prose literary tradition may be seen in Medieval philosophers such as Duns Scotus and Renaissance ▷ humanists such as George Buchanan (16th century) who wrote principally in Latin. Thereafter the great Scottish writers (especially from the 18th century) were mainly anglicized in their prose expression; ▷ David Hume and ▷ Adam Smith in the 18th century, ▷ Walter Scott and ▷ Thomas Carlyle in the 19th. Apart from Scott, other writers participated in the adventurous prose narrative, such as ▷ Robert Louis Stevenson and R. M. Ballantyne (1825–94) who are both well known for their escapist fantasies often read as ▷ children's fiction. In a similar supernatural vein ▷ Margaret Oliphant produced several novels with Scottish backgrounds.

The 20th century has seen what is often described as the Scottish Renaissance, which suggests a revival in cultural production and political identity. There have been three waves in this redevelopment, the first, in the early part of this century with a growth in nationalistic sentiment. In this period the work of Hugh MacDiarmid is most seminal, from his early Scottish propaganda in the *Scottish Chapbook* (started 1922) to his most famous poem *A Drunk Man Looks at the Thistle* (1926) and later poetical works. MacDiarmid rejected the earlier nostalgic approach and placed Scottish literature firmly in the European ▷ modernist movement. Other important writers of the first wave include the poet Edwin Muir, and the novelists ▷ Lewis Grassic Gibbon and Neil M. Gunn (1891–1973). Muir adopts a mythopoeic discourse which Gibbon and Gunn take up as a sense of Celtic inheritance, although while Gibbon uses myth fatalistically, Gunn sees in it a possibility for Scottish self-regeneration. Like MacDiarmid, all actively reject nostalgia and evoke social and political themes.

The second wave which occurred during the 1940s and 1950s saw a continuation, but rejuvenation of the earlier themes, primarily in the work of poets such as George Mackay Brown (b 1921), Edwin Morgan (b 1920) and ▷ Ian Hamilton Finlay.

The third period in the Scottish Renaissance is still happening and takes the broadest sense of national literary identity to its utmost limits. Novelists such as William McIlvanney (b 1936) focus upon the political unrest and tension of modern urban life in Scotland. Like McIlvanney, the novelists ▷ Muriel Spark and Robin Jenkins (b 1912) have taken advantage of the expansion of publishing in the 1980s to reach a wider and more international market. The 1980s and 90s have seen the emergence of 'the new Glasgow writing', including the culturally-specific, technically inventive ▷ post-modernist fiction of ▷ Alasdair Gray, ▷ James Kelman and ▷ Janice Galloway.
Bib: Watson, R., *The Literature of Scotland*.

Scriblerus Club

Formed in 1713 by Alexander Pope, ▷ Jonathan Swift, John Gay, Thomas Parnell, John Arbuthnot, and the Tory politician, Lord Oxford. The aim was to satirize 'false tastes' through the fictional memoirs of a conceited and arrogant 'modern' writer, Martinus Scriblerus. The club's members were scattered when the Tories fell from power after Queen Anne's death in 1714. Only the first volume of the memoirs was completed, and this was published in Pope's works in 1741. However, the ideas initiated at this time saw fruit in various later works, in particular Pope's *Dunciad*, many of the notes of which are signed 'Scriblerus', and in the satire on science and learning in the third book of Swift's ▷ *Gulliver's Travels*.

Scrutiny

A literary critical review published in Cambridge from 1932 to 1953; its principal editor was ▷ F. R. Leavis. *Scrutiny* was famous for its intellectual energy, the coherence of outlook among its contributors, and the urgency and purposefulness of its tone. This purposefulness was a response to a Leavisite analysis of the contemporary cultural scene which may be summarized as follows. The quality of Western (more particularly, British) civilization was deteriorating because of the influence upon it of commercial vulgarization. Such vulgarization could only end in the complete loss of those standards by which life in any organized society can be seen and felt to be valuable. The importance of a great literary tradition is that it constitutes a form of spiritual life that sustains high values and withstands vulgarization. However, such a tradition must itself be sustained by constant, sensitive and scrupulous critical activity carried on by alert and active intellects within the society. But the British literary tradition no longer possessed this kind of cultural leadership; the leading men of letters, on the contrary, with a few exceptions, regarded literature as an elegant pastime for a fashionable elite (such as the ▷ Bloomsbury Group) and they employed slack and inadequate standards in their judgements. *Scrutiny*, therefore, was intended to demonstrate the exacting standards which are required of criticism if a lively and effective literary tradition is to be sustained. The example to be followed was that of the recently defunct review, *The Calendar of Modern Letters* (1925–27) edited by Edgell Rickword.

The strongest part of *Scrutiny's* critical attack was directed towards literary education. It sought to counteract the kind of academic inertia which tends to the passive acceptance of some literary reputations and the equally passive neglect of other writers. This policy led to an extensive revaluation of the writers of the past. In regard to poetry, this revaluation took the direction already pursued by T. S. Eliot (*Selected Essays*, 1932); in regard to the novel, the dominant influences were those of F. R. Leavis himself, and his wife ▷ Q. D. Leavis. *Scrutiny* had a pervasive influence in Britain and the USA, especially among teachers at all levels of education.
Bib: Mulhern, F., *The Moment of Scrutiny*; Baldick, C., *The Social Mission of English Criticism*.

Scudéry, Madeleine de (1607–91)

French writer. De Scudéry was a prominent member of a salon and author of romances such as *Artamène, or the Great Cyrus* (10 volumes, 1649–53), a heroic story of immense length about war and love in the 5th century BC, and *Clélia, a Roman Story* (10 volumes, 1654–60), which included a famous 'map of tenderness', charting the course of gallantry in love. Such romances were very fashionable in the late 17th century, in England as well as France, but were criticized by many 18th-century novelists such as ▷ Clara Reeve, who described them as 'the books that pleased our grandmothers'.

Secret Agent, The (1907)

A novel by ▷ Joseph Conrad. The subject is revolution and counter-revolution in western Europe; the scene is London; the 'secret agent' is Mr Verloc, of mixed nationality. He is employed by the embassy of an unnamed foreign power (Czarist Russia) to mix with anarchist conspirators who have taken refuge on British soil, and to report their activities. Between the embassy and the conspirators are the London police, represented by Chief Inspector Heat, whose work is to watch the anarchists but not to interfere with them until they commit crimes. The embassy wishes to force the British government and its police to suppress the anarchist colony, and uses Verloc to organize a bomb outrage (against Greenwich Observatory) so as to arouse public concern. Verloc's seedy shop in Soho is a meeting place for the motley group of political fanatics, including Karl Yundt, a malevolent old terrorist, Ossipan, a scientific materialist who lives off women, Michaelis, a utopian Marxist and the Professor, the most ruthless of the anarchists, who always carries with him a bomb to prevent arrest. The Professor is disquieted by the inability of the British masses to see politics in terms of violence; if violence were used by the government, the masses would believe that counter-violence was their only hope, and a revolutionary situation would exist in Britain. In addition to this political level, the novel has a psychological one: if either revolution or counter-revolution is to be accomplished successfully, the human instruments must be disinterested, but in fact both the revolutionaries and their opponents are dominated by self-regard. The only characters capable of full disinterest are those who are so wretched as to be incapable of reflecting on their own condition. Mrs Verloc's half-witted brother Stevie rises to one idea only: 'bad life for poor people'. He thus becomes the willing tool of Mr Verloc, who charges him with the task of placing the bomb. In the event, Stevie causes no damage to the Observatory but he is himself blown up. Mrs Verloc, who has married Mr Verloc solely to provide support for Stevie, though her husband supposes her entirely devoted to himself, murders him from rage and grief. She tries to flee the country with Ossipan and, when he deserts her, she throws herself overboard from a Channel ferry. In contrast to Winnie Verloc and Stevie, characters simplified by misery and elementary development, is the Assistant Commissioner of Police, who neither acts disinterestedly nor has any belief that he can, but lives by the awareness that self-knowledge is the only antidote to the poison of self-regard. He solves the mystery of the outrage, and thus frustrates the destructive folly of Mr Vladimir, the ambassador. The novel is distinguished by the use of a pervasive irony to expose the futility of political extremism, the strength of human illusions, and the suffering and chaos prevailing in a supposedly civilized society.

Selborne, Natural History and Antiquities of
▷ White, Gilbert.

Selkirk, Alexander (1676–1721)
A sailor, whose experiences on the uninhabited island of Juan Fernandez, where he was landed at his own request and remained from 1704 to 1709, are the basis of the desert island part of ▷ Daniel Defoe's ▷ *Robinson Crusoe.*

Selvon, Sam (b 1923)
Novelist, playwright (radio and theatre), screenwriter and short-story writer. Born in Trinidad, he served in the Royal Naval Reserve in the Caribbean during World War II, worked as a journalist for the *Trinidad Guardian* from 1946 until 1950, and then moved to London, working for three years as a civil servant in the Indian High Commission and then as a freelance writer, particularly for BBC drama. Since 1978 he has lived in Canada. His novels are: *A Brighter Sun* (1952); *An Island is a World* (1955); *The Lonely Londoners* (1956); *Turn Again Tiger* (1958); *I Hear Thunder* (1963); *Housing Lark* (1965); *The Plains of Caroni* (1969); *Those Who Eat the Cascadura* (1972); *Moses Ascending* (1975); *Moses Migrating* (1983). *Ways of Sunlight* (1958) is a collection of short stories. His work is set in Trinidad and London, and many of his novels are concerned with the experience of cultural displacement, racism and economic hardship of those moving to Britain from the West Indies, an experience treated with wit, humour and affirmation of growing confidence and assertion, as well as with indignation. Similar themes, and some of the same characters, appear in *Eldorado, West One,* a sequence of seven one-act plays (written 1969; published 1988). He has also written many radio plays, and *Switch* (1977), a play for the theatre. He was co-author of the film *Pressure* (1978) and has published a prose collection, *Foreday Morning: Selected Prose 1946–1986* (1989).

Semiology, Semiotics
The term 'semiology' was used in ▷ Ferdinand de Saussure's *Course in General Linguistics* (published 1915) to describe 'a science of ▷ signs', whose objective is 'to investigate the nature of signs and the laws governing them'. The more current term, semiotics, was associated originally with the American philosopher C. S. Peirce. Peirce's tripartite division of signs into 'icon' (a sign possessing a similarity to its object), 'symbol' (a sign arbitrarily linked to the object), and 'index' (a sign physically associated with its object), has more recently been revised in Umberto Eco's *A Theory of Semiotics* (1976) where the emphasis throughout is upon the complex mechanisms and conventions which govern the production of signs.

Senior, Olive (b 1943)
Jamaican short-story writer, novelist, poet and dramatist. She was born one of ten children of a poor family living in a rural part of Jamaica and brought up by a relative. She has worked as as Publications Officer at the University of West Indies Institute of Social and Economic Studies and as editor of *Jamaica Journal*. Senior has stressed her interest in orality, oral narrative and the sound of the speaking voice, and her short stories, collected in *Summer Lightning* (Commonwealth Writers Prize, 1987) and *Arrival of the Snake Woman* (1989), make rich and complex use of the variety of forms of spoken English in Jamaica to explore social and personal relations. Poetry: *Talking of Trees* (1985). Plays: *Down the Road Again* (1968). Other works: *The Message is Change: A Perspective on the 1972 General Election*; (1972); *A–Z of Jamaican Heritage* (1983); *Working Miracles: Women's Lives in the English-Speaking Caribbean* (1989).
Bib: Pollard, V., 'Mothertongue Voices in the Writing of Olive Senior and Lorna Goodison', in Nasta, S. (ed.), *Motherlands.*

Sensation, Novel of
Popular from about 1860, sensation novels included extravagant, often horrible events, and may be considered the precursors of the modern thriller. Examples are ▷ Wilkie Collins's *The Woman in White* ▷ Mrs Henry Wood's *East Lynne,* ▷ Mary Elizabeth Braddon's *Lady Audley's Secret* and even some of ▷ Charles Dickens's novels.
▷ Reade, Charles.
Bib: Hughes, W., *The Maniac in the Cellar: Sensation Novels of the 1860s*; Pykett, L., *The 'Improper' Feminine: The Women's Sensation Novel and the New Woman Writing.*

Sense and Sensibility (1811)
A novel by ▷ Jane Austen. A youthful version, *Elinor and Marianne,* has been lost. The revised novel was published in 1811.

The two heroines, Elinor and Marianne Dashwood, are fatherless sisters who live with their mother in comparative poverty, having been defrauded of more substantial income by their stepbrother, John Dashwood, and his arrogant and selfish wife. The title of the novel indicates the difference between the sisters: Elinor is practical and watches after the family affairs with sober good sense, and Marianne prides herself on the strength of her feelings and her contempt for material interests. Elinor is in love with a depressed and apparently dull young man, Edward Ferrars (brother of Mrs John Dashwood), while Marianne loves the handsome and glamorous John Willoughby. The superficial contrast between the sisters and their lovers is shown to be deceptive: Elinor's feelings are as deep as Marianne's but her sense of responsibility is greater and she keeps her sorrows to herself, whereas Marianne makes almost a virtue of the public exhibition of her grief, thus becoming a burden on her sister and her mother. In the end, the romantic-seeming Willoughby turns out to have given up Marianne from fear of losing a legacy, while the prosaic Edward gladly sacrifices the favour of a rich relative for the sake of marriage to Elinor.

Sensibility

The term 'sensibility', indicating the tendency to be easily and strongly affected by emotion, came into general use in the early 18th century. At this time writers and thinkers, such as the third ▷ Earl of Shaftesbury, in reaction against the practical, materialist philosophy of ▷ Hobbes, began to promote an idealistic, spiritual alternative, based on personal feeling. Joseph Addison in 1711 defined modesty as 'an exquisite Sensibility', 'a kind of quick and delicate Feeling in the Soul'. By the middle of the 18th century the word 'sensibility' had grown in stature, indicating the capacity for compassion or altruism, and also the possession of good taste in the arts. Joseph Warton in 1756 declines to explain a subtle point since 'any reader of sensibility' will already have taken it ▷ Laurence Sterne in his ▷ *Sentimental Journey* (1768) eulogizes 'Dear Sensibility! source unexhausted of all that's precious in our joys or costly in our sorrows!' The word remained fashionable in this sense in the early 19th century when ▷ Jane Austen used it in the title of her novel *Sense and Sensibility* (1811).

The cultivation of sensibility also led to exoticism and medievalism, such as in the 'Gothic story', ▷ *The Castle of Otranto* (1765) by ▷ Horace Walpole. The new intensity of feeling took a less exotic form in the profuse sentiment of ▷ Samuel Richardson's novels, and also in the cult of sentimentalism promoted by Sterne's *A Sentimental Journey* and Henry Mackenzie's *The Man of Feeling* (1771).
Bib: Todd, J., *Sensibility*; Hilles, F. W., and Bloom, H. (eds.), *From Sensibility to Romanticism*; Frye, N., *Towards Defining an Age of Sensibility*.

Sentiment or Sensibility, novel of
▷ Sensibility.

Sentimental Journey through France and Italy, A (1768)

A narrative, part novel and part travel book, by ▷ Laurence Sterne (under the pseudonym of 'Mr Yorick' – the name of a character in Sterne's ▷ *Tristram Shandy*), based on his stay in France, 1762–64. It was intended to be longer, but Sterne died after the publication of the first two volumes in 1768.

Seth, Vikram (b 1952)

Poet, novelist, travel-writer. Born in Calcutta, India, and educated at Corpus Christi College Oxford, Stanford University and Nanjing University, China, he trained as an economist. His volumes of poetry are *Mappings* (1980); *The Humble Administrator's Garden* (1985); *All You Who Sleep Tonight* (1990). *The Golden Gate* (1986) is a witty and accomplished novel, written in a form of sonnet borrowed from Pushkin's *Eugene Onegin*, and portrays the Californian life-style through the story of the relationships of a group of young professionals. His most recent work is a novel largely in prose, although with poems scattered through it, *A Suitable Boy* (1993). It is a vast, optimistic, comic tale of Indian life, centred on four extended upper-class families. As in *The Golden Gate*, the writing varies in intensity but the novel has an irresistible exuberance and liveliness. Seth has also published *From Heaven Lake: Travels through Sinkiang and Tibet* (1983).

Sewell, Anna (1820–70)

The author of *Black Beauty* (1878), a novel written with the aim of improving the treatment of horses and presented in the form of 'The Autobiography of a Horse, Translated from the Original Equine.' Sewell came of an impoverished ▷ Quaker family and suffered from a damaged ankle and poor health; she wrote the book during the last years of her life, when she was an invalid. The success of the book was largely posthumous; Sewell was paid only £20 for it.
Bib: Chitty, *Life*.

Shaftesbury, Lord (Anthony Ashley Cooper, 3rd Earl of Shaftesbury) (1671–1713)

A moral philosopher, with great influence in the first half of the 18th century. His main beliefs are contained in his *Characteristics of Men, Manners, Opinions, Times* (1711; revised edition, 1713). He was a Deist a Churchman, and a Platonic idealist. His optimistic philosophy was in direct oppositon to that of ▷ Thomas Hobbes, author of *Leviathan*. He believed that men have 'natural affections' which are capable of going beyond self-interest. The cultivation of disinterested affection for others will produce virtue and the true social morality. His concept of these 'natural affections' seemed to make the supernatural elements of Christian doctrine unnecessary to the acquirement of true religion. On this ground he was opposed by Bishop Butler in his *Analogy of True Religion* (1736). On a purely theoretical level, Shaftesbury anticipated the beliefs about Nature of the poet William Wordsworth, and he encouraged the growing emphasis on sentiment and sensibility in criticism and poetry in the 18th century.
Bib: Willey, B., in *Eighteenth-century Background* and *The English Moralists*; Brett, R. L., *The Third Earl of Shaftesbury: a Study in Eighteenth-century Literary Theory*.

Shamela (1741)

An Apology for the life of Mrs Shamela Andrews, published pseudonymously by ▷ Henry Fielding, parodies ▷ Samuel Richardson's, ▷ *Pamela* of the preceding year. The plot and characters are taken from Richardson's novel, yet the tone reveals what Fielding saw as Richardson's hypocritical morality, where virtue is rewarded by worldly wealth and status.

Sharp, William (1855–1905)

Scottish novelist and poet, who published much of his better work in the 1890s under the name 'Fiona Macleod', supposedly his cousin, an alter ego whose real existence he always maintained (she appeared in *Who's Who*) and may even have believed in. The novels of Fiona Macleod are mystical, nostalgic tales of Celtic peasant life, such as *Pharais: A Romance of the Isles* (1894), *The Mountain Lover* (1895), *The Sin Eater* (1895) and *Green Fire* (1896). Sharp also

wrote novels under his own name, including the
▷ epistolary novel *A Fellowe and his Wife* (1892),
jointly authored with the American writer Blanche
Willis Howard. After early, uncongenial work as
a clerk, Sharp had begun his literary career in the
1880s as a journalist, and by writing commissioned
biographies and poetry, but in the 1890s spent much
of his time travelling. The dual personality provoked
a nervous crisis in 1897.

Shelley, Mary Wollstonecraft (1797–1851)

The only daughter of feminist ▷ Mary Wollstonecraft
and radical philosopher ▷ William Godwin, her
mother having died a few days after her birth.
Her father remarried in 1801 but Mary found her
stepmother unsympathetic and remained rather close
to her father despite his cold manner. She idolized
her own mother, and educated herself through
contact with her father's intellectual circle and her
own hard study. She met Percy Bysshe Shelley in
1812 and on return from an extended visit to friends
in 1814 became very close to him. He was in the
midst of separating from his wife Harriet, and
within a couple of months he and Mary left England
together, marrying in 1816 after Harriet's suicide.
They had a devoted but difficult relationship, only
one of their children surviving childhood, Godwin
pressing them for loans and Shelley's father Timothy
making only a small allowance for the child, Percy.
After Shelley's death in 1822 Mary stayed a short
while in Italy, then returned to London where she
continued to write novels, produced an account of
her travels with Percy in Europe and edited Shelley's
poetry and prose, but proved too exhausted to write
his biography, which she abandoned. ▷ *Frankenstein,
or the Modern Prometheus* (1817) was her first and
most famous novel, apparently inspired by a dream.
The Last Man (1826) has characters based on Shelley
and Byron, and *Lodore* (1835) contains much that is
autobiographical. *Mathilda* (1819) and *Valperga* (1823)
are among her other novels; *Rambles in Germany and
Italy* (1844) was well received; she also published
many short stories in annuals like *The Keepsake*.
Bib: Jones, F. L. (ed.), *Mary Shelley's Journal* and
The Letters of Mary Shelley; Lyles, W. H., *Mary
Shelley: An Annotated Biography*; Nitchie, E., *Mary
Shelley*; Poovey, M., *The Proper Lady and the Woman
Writer*; Gilbert, S. and Gubar, S., *The Madwoman
in the Attic*; Fleenor, J., *The Female Gothic*; Baldick,
C., *In Frankenstein's Shadow: Myth Monstrosity and
Nineteenth-Century Writing*; Bennett, B. T. (ed.),
Letters; St Clair, W, *The Godwins and the Shelleys*;
Spark, M., *Mary Shelley*.

Sherwood, Mary Martha (1775–1851)

Novelist, diarist, autobiographer, and children's
author. Mary Sherwood began writing at seventeen
in order to help fund the school in which she was
a pupil (*The Traditions* was published by ▷ Minerva
in 1795), and she continued working on novels in
order to support her parents and siblings, and later
her husband and children. She married her cousin,
Henry Sherwood, in 1805 and they went to India
where she pursued her writing in addition to their
evangelical work. Her two most famous books are

Little Henry and His Bearer (1815) and *The Fairchild
Family* (1818; second and third parts were published
in 1842 and 1847). This last book was immensely
popular, partly because its overtly moralizing tone is
neatly undercut with a delight in gruesome details
and genuinely scary passages. In the later, Victorian,
editions these parts were considered too unpleasant
for the young and were expurgated. From then on
the book declined in popularity.
Bib: Cutt, M. N., *Mrs Sherwood and Her Books for
Children*.

Shields, Carol (b 1935)

Novelist and short-story writer, born in America
and educated at Hanover College. In 1957 she
married a Canadian and settled in Canada, where
she attended the University of Ottowa and wrote an
MA dissertation on the nineteenth-century Canadian
writer Susanna Mudie, published as *Susanna Moodie:
Voice and Vision* (1976). Many of her novels are
concerned with marriage, love and the details of
domestic experience, including *Small Ceremonies*
(1976), *The Box Garden* (1977), *Happenstance* (1980),
A Fairly Conventional Woman (1982) and *The Republic
of Love* (1992), the last of these with a suggestion
of the magical. *Mary Swann* (1987) is a literary
mystery story which uses a range of narrative forms:
letters, diaries, poems, a film script; generically it is
comparable to ▷ A. S. Byatt's *Possession*. Shields's
work shows a fondness for enigmas with hinted
solutions: the sender of a bizarre wedding present
in *The Republic of Love*; the identity and motives
of a literary thief in *Mary Swann*. Shields has also
written a novel jointly with Blanche Howard, *A
Celibate Season* (1991), and drama. She has lived
in Vancouver, Toronto and Ottowa, and now lives
in Winnipeg, Manitoba. Volumes of short stories:
Various Miracles (1985); *The Orange Fish* (1989).
Poetry: *Others* (1972); *Intersect* (1974).

Shinebourne, Janice (b 1947)

Novelist. Shinebourne was born in Guyana of
Chinese and Indian ancestry, and educated at the
University of Georgetown and in Britain, where
she moved in the early 1970s. She has worked as a
lecturer, editor and community worker. Her first
novel, *Timepiece* (1986) is about the move from rural
to urban Guyana and its effect on the consciousness
of the young woman protagonist. Her second novel
is *The Last English Plantation* (1989). She has also
written short stories.

Shirley (1849)

A novel by ▷ Charlotte Brontë. It is set in the north
of England and deals with the bad labour relations
of the time of the Napoleonic Wars (1803–15). A
mill-owner, Robert Gérard Moore (half Belgian and
half English), introduces labour-saving machinery
against the opposition of his workers, who threaten
to destroy the mill. He attempts to gain money
by marrying the rich and proud Shirley Keeldar,
who refuses him and eventually marries his brother
Louis, opposed to Robert. The end of the war
releases Robert from his financial difficulties and
he marries Caroline Helstone, whom he really loves

and who loves him. The novel was characteristic of a number written during the 1840s and early 1850s (by ▷ Charles Dickens, ▷ Benjamin Disraeli, ▷ Mrs Gaskell) on the social problems of class hostility. It is also much concerned with the need for useful employment for women. In the character of Shirley Keeldar, Charlotte portrayed her sister ▷ Emily Brontë as she might have been.

Short Story

This very early kind of fiction was first taken seriously in the 19th century as an independent literary form, making different demands on the writer and the reader from the demands of longer works of fiction such as the novel. Three writers originated this serious practice of the art of the short story: the American, Edgar Allan Poe (1809–49); the Frenchman, Poe's disciple, Guy de Maupassant (1850–93); and the Russian, ▷ Anton Chekhov. These writers evolved the qualities especially associated with the short story: close texture, unity of mood, suggestive idiom, economy of means. Such qualities associate the short story with the short poem, and we find that in English the verse story anticipated the prose story in works such as the tales of George Crabbe and Arthur Hugh Clough's *Mari Magno* (1862). However, no relationship can be established between the verse of such writers and the prose of ▷ Rudyard Kipling, with Maupassant behind him, or that of ▷ Katherine Mansfield, who was strongly influenced by Anton Chekhov. These two wrote little else in prose except stories (Kipling wrote two novels), but the greatest masters of the short story form – ▷ Henry James, ▷ Joseph Conrad, ▷ James Joyce, and ▷ D. H. Lawrence – were predominantly novelists. Their stories were perhaps formed less by the example of the foreign writers mentioned than by the structure of their own novels. These had a less distinctly marked plot line than those of earlier novelists, and yet a closer coherence; chapters from them can be extracted showing many of the essential qualities of short stories (*eg* 'Rabbit' in Lawrence's ▷ *Women in Love*, or the Christmas dinner in Joyce's ▷ *Portrait of the Artist*) in spite of their relationship to their respective novels as wholes. It seems therefore that the best stories of these writers were by-products of their novels, which by their structure suggested the evolution of stories as separate entities.

It is difficult to make a clear distinction between the short story and the *nouvelle* (novella or long story); it is difficult also to say at what point a *nouvelle* stops short of being a novel; on the whole the *nouvelle* or 'long short story' seems to share with the short story as generally understood a unity of mood, which is not so likely to be found in a true novel, however short. All the masters of the short story who have been mentioned were also masters of the *nouvelle*, but not necessarily (*eg* Chekhov) of the novel form.

The period 1880–1930 was the flowering time of the short story in English; besides the English writers already mentioned, it included the early and best work of ▷ A. E. Coppard, who was one ∙of the few English fiction-writers of any note

(Katherine Mansfield being another) who have restricted themselves to the short-story form. Later short-story writers have been numerous, but they have mostly practised the art as an alternative and often subsidiary form to that of the novel. In Ireland, where the art of the novel has scarcely taken root, the art of the short story has flourished more distinctively. It begins with the stories of ▷ George Moore (*The Untilled Field*, 1903), but the Irish tradition becomes really outstanding in the first books of ▷ Liam O'Flaherty (*Spring Sowing*, 1926), ▷ Sean O'Faolain (*Midsummer Night Madness*, 1932), and ▷ Frank O'Connor (*Guests of the Nation*, 1931). In his book on the art of the short story, *The Lonely Voice* (1964), O'Connor offers an explanation as to why the short story should be the more natural form of fiction for Irish literary culture.

Since O'Connor, William Trevor has continued the Irish connection with the short story. Other contemporary writers who excel at the form include ▷ Peter Carey, whose early stories are collected in *Exotic Pleasures* (1980) and ▷ Ian McEwan, whose collections *First Love, Last Rites* (1975) and *In Between the Sheets* (1977) attracted great critical attention, ▷ Angus Wilson, ▷ Muriel Spark, ▷ Nadine Gordimer, ▷ Margaret Atwood, ▷ Desmond Hogan and Shena Mackay have also used the genre to interesting effect.

Bib: Bates, H. E., *The Modern Short Story*; O'Connor, F., *The Lonely Voice*; O'Faolain, S., *The Short Story*; Bayley, J., *The Short Story: Henry Ian to Elizabeth Bowen*; Lohafer, S. and Clarey, J. E., *Short Story Theory at a Crossroads*.

Shorthouse, Joseph Henry (1834–1903)

Novelist, whose *John Inglesant* (1880), a historical and philosophical romance set in England and Italy during the 17th century, was initially rejected by publishers but later became a ▷ best seller and acquired something of a cult following. Shorthouse was brought up as a ▷ Quaker but converted to the Church of England, and religious loyalties and conversion play a large part in the novel. Shorthouse worked in business despite poor health; his other literary works were relatively minor historical romances, such as *The Countess Eve* (1888) and two novels set in the present: *Sir Percival* (1886) and *Blance Lady Falaise* (1891).

Sidney, Sir Philip (1554–86)

Poet, courtier, soldier and statesman. A member of a distinguished noble family, he was a fine example of the Renaissance ideal of aristocracy in his ability to excel in all that was regarded as fitting for a nobleman. He thus became a pattern for his age, as is shown by the numerous elegies to him, including one by Edmund Spenser (*Astrophel*) and one by James I of England. he was wounded at the battle of Zutphen in Flanders in characteristic circumstances, having discarded leg armour on finding that a comrade in arms had neglected to wear any; as he lay mortally wounded in the leg, he is reputed to have passed a cup of water to a dying soldier with the words, 'Thy need is greater than mine.'

Sidney's writings date mostly from the period

1580–83, when he was temporarily out of favour with Elizabeth I for political reasons, and was living with his sister, Mary Herbert, Countess of Pembroke at Wilton House near Salisbury; they were published after his death. His most famous poetry, the sonnet sequence *Astrophil and Stella*, was published in 1591, and inspired the numerous other sonnet sequences of the 1590s, including Shakespeare's.

Apart from his sonnets, Sidney's poetic reputation rests on the verse interludes in ▷ *The Arcadia*, Sidney's prose romance, started in 1580 and published in 1590. His prose work also includes the most famous piece of Elizabethan criticism, *An Apologie for Poetrie* published in 1595. A collaboration with his sister, the verse paraphrase of the *Psalms*, was not published till 1823. He also wrote two pastoral poems published in Davison's *Poetical Rhapsody* (1602) and partly translated from the French Du Plessis Mornay's *A Work Concerning the Trueness of the Christian Religion* (1587).
Bib: McCoy, R. C., *Sir Philip Sidney: Rebellion in Arcadia*; Hamilton, A. C., *Sir Philip Sidney*; Waller, G. F. and Moore, M. D. (eds), *Sir Philip Sidney and the Interpretation of Renaissance Culture*.

Sign

This is the term used by ▷ Ferdinand de Saussure in his *Course in General Linguistics* (1915) to refer to any linguistic unit through which meaning is produced. In Saussure's theory, the *sign* is the combination of two discrete elements, the *signifier* (form which signifies) and the *signified* (idea signified). In the phrase 'A rose by any other name would smell as sweet', the word 'rose' is the signifier and the 'concept of a rose' is the signified.

Signifier and signified are distinct aspects of the sign, but exist only within it. One important aspect of Saussure's definition of the sign is that any particular combination of signifier and signified is *arbitrary*. So a 'rose' could be called a 'chrysanthemum' or a 'telephone', but would still be as aromatic. Saussure's perceptions have been extremely influential in the development of ways of discussing the processes through which meaning is achieved.

▷ Langue; Parole; Structuralism; Post-structuralism; Discourse; Barthes, Roland; Derrida, Jacques.

Signified
▷ Sign.

Signifier
▷ Sign.

Silas Marner (1861)

A novel by ▷ George Eliot. Silas is a weaver who has been driven out of a small community of dissenters in a northern industrial town, in consequence of false information that he has stolen some of the community's funds. He emigrates to a midland village where he is in all essential respects 'a foreigner'. He sets up again as a weaver but he has no relationship with his neighbours beyond the commercial one; having also lost his religious faith, he lives only for money and acquires a store of it. This is stolen from him by Dunstan Cass, son of the

local squire, but Silas's despair is later obliterated by the mysterious arrival in his cottage of a little girl, whom he adopts, calls Eppie and devotes himself to. His love for her gradually brings to him the affection and respect of his neighbours. It turns out that Dunstan, who had vanished after the theft, had drowned immediately afterwards and that Eppie is really the daughter of Dunstan's elder brother, Godfrey, by a low-class, drunken woman, now dead, to whom Godfrey was secretly married. Godfrey, now happily married but childless, claims Eppie when she is nearly grown up but she refuses to part from Silas. The plot of the novel thus resembles a fable about living and deathly attachments.

Sillitoe, Alan (b 1928)

Novelist and poet. The son of a labourer in a cycle factory, he left school at 14 to work in a similar factory. His birthplace was the Midlands town of Nottingham, near which ▷ D. H. Lawrence also grew up. Sillitoe, like Lawrence, writes from the standpoint of one whose origins are outside London and the middle classes, and he is the best known of a group of post-war novelists from similar backgrounds, including ▷ Stan Barstow, ▷ John Braine and ▷ David Storey. The influence of Lawrence on these writers is inevitably strong, and especially so in the case of Sillitoe, but he presents a narrow spirit of social rebellion from which Lawrence is free. At present, his fame rests chiefly on his first novel, *Saturday Night and Sunday Morning* (1958), which has been filmed. The novel's hero, Arthur Seaton, has become a type-figure of the post-1945 industrial, welfare state working man, born into an economic fabric against which his strong impulses rebel. More original and equally well known is the tale *The Loneliness of the Long-Distance Runner* (1959), a kind of fable of anarchic social rebellion. He has also written stories: *The Ragman's Daughter* (1963); *Guzman Go Home* (1968); *Men Women and Children* (1973); *Down to the Bone* (1976); *The Second Chance* (1980); and poems: *The Rats* (1960); *A Falling Out of Love* (1964); *Snow on the North Side of Lucifer* (1979); *Sun before Departure: poems 1974 to 1982* (1984); *Tides and Stone Walls* (1986); and more novels: *The General* (1960), about the war in Malaya, in which Sillitoe served; *Key to the Door* (1961); *The Death of William Posters* (1965); *A Tree on Fire* (1967); *A Start in Life* (1970); *Travels in Nihilon* (1971); *Raw Material* (1972); *The Flame of Life* (1974); *The Widower's Son* (1976); *The Storyteller* (1979); *Her Victory* (1982); *The Last Flying Boat* (1983); *Down From the Hill* (1984); *Life Goes On* (1985); *Out of the Whirlpool* (a novella; 1987). In 1978 he published three plays: *This Foreign Field* (1970), *Pit Strike* (1977), *The Interview* (1978).
▷ Realism.
Bib: Atherton, S., *Alan Sillitoe: a Critical Assessment*.

Silver-fork Novels

Novels of fashion which took as their setting the society of the wealthy upper classes and which were popular at the beginning of the 19th century. Even at the time there was debate as to whether these novels unquestioningly praised the seemingly empty lives of their heroes and heroines (the term comes from

'silver-fork polisher', which means to compliment those wealthy enough to possess such cutlery), or whether they were in fact subtle satires. The two sides of this debate may be seen to be represented by William Hazlitt who referred to silver-fork novelists as 'dandy writers' (*The Examiner*, 1827), and by the novelist ▷ Edward Bulwer-Lytton, who defended his own work as an exposé of the fashionable classes, rather than an accolade to them. Other silver-fork novelists include: ▷ Marguerite Blessington, ▷ Susan Ferrier, ▷ Catherine Gore, ▷ Lady Caroline Lamb, ▷ Frances Trollope.
Bib: Adburgham, A., *Silver Fork Society: Fashionable Life and Literature 1814–1840*; Rosa, M.W., *The Silver-fork School*.

Simile
▷ Figures of Speech.

Sinbad the Sailor
The hero of one of the Eastern tales called ▷ *Arabian Nights*. Also spelt Sindbad. His best-known adventure is that with the huge sea-bird called the Roc.

Sinclair, Andrew (b1935)
Novelist. Like ▷ David Caute, Sinclair is interested in ▷ post-modernist experimental narrative. *Gog* (1967), the epic journey through England of an alienated, semi-mythical character, blends realism and fantasy, and employs a variety of narrative forms, including critical essay, comic strip and film script. Sinclair's work has affinities with that of American writers such as Kurt Vonnegut. Other novels include: *Magog* (1972); *A Patriot for Hire* (1978).

Sinclair, May (1863–1946)
Novelist, poet and critic. She was brought up by her mother and educated largely at home, though she spent one year at Cheltenham Ladies College. Her novels include: *The Divine Fire* (1904); *The Judgment of Eve* (1907); *The Helpmate* (1907); *Kitty Tailleur* (1908); *The Creators: A Comedy* (1910); *The Combined Maze* (1913); *The Three Sisters* (1914); *The Tree of Heaven* (1917); *Mary Olivier: a Life* (1919); *The Romantic* (1920); *Anne Severn and the Fieldings* (1922); *The Life and Death of Harriet Frean* (1922); *The Dark Night* (1924); *The Rector of Wyck* (1925); *Far End* (1926); *The Allinghams* (1927); *The History of Anthony Waring* (1927). They reveal her interest in psychoanalysis, philosophy and feminist issues and her concern with problems of social and psychological repression faced by women; some, such as the ▷ *Bildungsroman*, *Mary Olivier* and *The Life and Death of Harriet Frean* use ▷ stream of consciousness narrative (a term which Sinclair herself applied to the work of ▷ Dorothy Richardson). Sinclair supported herself financially by writing reviews and translations; she published *The Three Brontës* (1912), a biography; *Feminism* (1912); two works on idealist philosophy, *Defense of Idealism* (1917) and *The New Idealism* (1922); and articles and reviews about the work of contemporary poets such as T.S. Eliot and ▷ H.D.
Bib: Boll, T.E., *Miss May Sinclair, Novelist*; Zegger,

H., *May Sinclair*; Gillespie, D.F., in Kime Scott, B. (ed.), *The Gender of Modernism*.

Sir Charles Grandison, The History of (1753–4)
The last of the three novels presented through letters by ▷ Samuel Richardson. It is an attempt to present the type of the perfect gentleman, just as its predecessor, ▷ *Clarissa* had represented the perfect woman. It prescribes the kind of behaviour which Addison had preached in his periodical ▷ *The Spectator*. However, it suffers much more than does *Clarissa* from the excessive idealization of its central character. The theme is right conduct in acute sentimental and ethical dilemma; Grandison is in love with Harriet Byron (whom he rescues from the vicious Sir Hargrave Pollexfen), but has obligations to Clementina Porretta, member of a noble Italian family. Among other lessons, Sir Charles shows how a gentleman can avoid fighting a duel without losing his honour. The book has some good minor characters, and is an interesting study in manners, though Richardson did not understand the Italian aristocracy of his period. As a psychological study, it is much inferior to *Clarissa* but it influenced the work of ▷ Jane Austen.

Sketches by Boz (1836)
Early journalism by ▷ Charles Dickens. The sketches, 'Illustrative of Everyday Life and Everyday People', were begun in 1833, published in various magazines, and collected into book form in 1836.

Sleath, Eleanor (fl. c 1800)
Novelist. Sleath wrote six ▷ Gothic novels for ▷ Minerva. Mocked by ▷ Jane Austen for their unsophisticated style, Sleath's novels are packed full of all the conventional Gothic devices – ghosts, castles, disguises and villainy – and have fast-paced narratives. *Orphan of the Rhine* (1798) and *The Nocturnal Minstrel, or The Spirit of the Wood* (1810) have historical settings and beautiful heroines who, although crossed by fate and deceived by scoundrels, triumph in the end. *The Bristol Heiress, or The Errors of Education* begins as a satire of polite society, though the plot transfers as a strange, haunted castle in Cumberland.

Sleeping Beauty, The
A famous fairy story in the collection made by ▷ Charles Perrault, translated into English in 1729. A baby princess is doomed by a wicked fairy to prick herself on the finger and die, but a good fairy changes death into a hundred years' sleep, from which the princess is awakened by the kiss of a prince.

Slough of Despond
A boggy place in ▷ John Bunyan's allegory ▷ *Pilgrim's Progress*. Christian sinks into it immediately after taking flight from the ▷ City of Destruction. It signifies the period of depression into which a convert is liable to fall after the first enthusiasm of his conversion.

Smart, Elizabeth (1913–1986)
Canadian novelist and poet. Smart is best known for *By Grand Central Station I Sat Down and Wept*

(1945), a novel in an extravagant, highly poetic style influenced by the surrealist poetry of George Barker, with whom she had four children, though she never became one of his several wives. This relationship, begun when Smart wrote to Barker and continued over many years, is portrayed in the latter part of the novel. Smart moved to England in 1943, working as a journalist, an advertising copy-writer and literary editor of *Queen*. Her later works include two volumes of poetry, *A Bonus* (1977) and *Eleven Poems* (1982); an autobiographical prose piece, *The Assumption of the Rogues and Rascals* (1977); *In the Meantime* (1984), poems and prose pieces. Her journals have been published as *Necessary Secrets* (1991) as well as her *Early Writings* (1987)

Bib: Sullivan, R., *By Heart. Elizabeth Smart: A Life*.

Smiles, Samuel (1812–1904)

Journalist: philosopher of 'self-help'. Born at Haddington in Scotland, one of eleven children, his early life was a struggle, dominated by the vigour of his widowed mother. He graduated in medicine at Edinburgh University in 1832, and began practising as a doctor in his home village. Competition was severe however, and he exchanged medicine for ▷ journalism, becoming editor of the *Leeds Times*. He also became secretary to railway companies, and in this capacity he made acquaintance with George Stephenson (1781–1848), inventor of the steam railway engine. His *Life of Stephenson* was published in 1857, and was followed by the lives of other famous 19th-century engineers: *James Brindley* (1864); *Boulton and Watt* (1865); *Telford* (1867). But the book that made him famous was *Self-Help* (1859); it sold 20, 000 copies in the first year, and was translated into at least 17 languages. He followed it by similar books, all demonstrating the worldly advantages of certain moral virtues: *Character* (1871); *Thrift* (1875); *Duty* (1880). The success of these books was due to their optimism, and to the simple, practical expression of his ideas. His international prestige is illustrated by his reception of the Order of St Sava from the King of Servia in 1897. Smiles represents the vigorous and hopeful aspect of the ▷ Industrial Revolution, as it affected ordinary people, in contrast to the sceptical view of it taken by many other writers.

Smith, Adam (1723–90)

Political economist. His important work was *An Enquiry into the Nature and Causes of the Wealth of Nations* – always referred to as *The Wealth of Nations* – published in 1776, at the outbreak of the rebellion of the American colonists, who, he predicted, 'will be one of the foremost nations of the world'. The especial influence of this book comes from his discussion of the function of the state in the degree and kind of control it should exercise over the activities of society, and in particular, of trade. He concluded that the traditional mercantile system (nowadays called 'protection') was based on a misunderstanding of the nature of wealth, and that nations prospered to the extent that governments allowed trade to remain freely competitive, unrestrained by taxes intended to protect the economy of a nation from competition from other nations. His opinions became increasingly influential and eventually dominant in British economics during the first half of the 19th century; his opposition to *unnecessary* interference by the government in trade and society became harmful in that it was interpreted by later governments as an excuse not to remedy social abuses arising from industrialism.

▷ Free Trade.

Smith, Charlotte (1749–1806)

Novelist and poet. Charlotte Smith's poetry, including *Elegiac Sonnets, and Other Essays* (1784) and *The Emigrants* (1793), was admired by ▷ Leigh Hunt, while her novels – which she wrote to support her large family after her husband had been imprisoned for debt – were praised by ▷ Sir Walter Scott and influenced ▷ Ann Radcliffe. Her ironic and spare writing was often autobiographical: for example, *Emmeline, The Orphan of the Castle* (1788) presents the male characters as weak in comparison to the strong and mutually supportive female protagonists, and *The Banished Man* (1794) satirizes a woman writer who is surmounted by difficulties.

Of all her novels, *The Old Manor House* (1793) is considered her best work, and is the most readily accessible to a 20th-century readership. She also translated Prevost's *Manon Lescaut* (1786), though this was withdrawn because it was considered too immoral.

Bib: Bowstead, D., *Fettered or Free? British Women Novelists, 1670–1815*; Hillbish, F.M.A., *Charlotte Smith, Poet and Novelist*; Kelly, G., *The English Jacobin Novel*; Todd, J., *Sensibility: An Introduction*.

Smith, Stevie (Florence Margaret) (1902–71)

Poet and novelist. Her 'unpoetic' life as an office worker who cared for her elderly aunt in a London suburb is well-known as the context for the production of her concise but anarchic poetry. Much of her work is animated by themes of sexual anxiety and an ambivalence towards Christianity which belies its popular image of comic whimsy. Of her novels, *Novel on Yellow Paper* (1936) is the most widely known, her several collections of witty, understated poems being accompanied by her own drawings. Works include: *Collected Poems* (1975); *Me Again: Uncollected Writings* (ed. Barbera, J. and McBrien, W.; 1983).

Smith, W.H. and Sons

A firm of newsagents, stationers, booksellers and (from 1860 until 1961) owners of a ▷ circulating library, the rival of Mudie's (▷ Mudie, Charles Edward). Founded in 1792 in a small newsvendor's shop in London, the firm flourished through its station bookstall concessions (the first at Euston in 1848) and its involvement in publishing. Like Mudie's, Smith's exercised some moral censorship over the material they sold (and still do). The two firms were rivals but combined to kill off the ▷ triple-decker novel in 1894. Unlike Mudie's, however, Smith's are still flourishing and in 1959 established the W.H. Smith Literary Award.

Smollett, Tobias George (1721–71)

Born near Dumbarton, the son of a Scots laird, Smollett studied at Glasgow University and was then apprenticed to a surgeon. In 1739 he moved to London, trying to stage his play *The Regicide*, but the attempt was unsuccessful, and he joined the navy as a surgeon's mate, sailing for the West Indies.

In 1744 Smollett returned to London and set up a medical practice in Downing Street, though never making a living out of medicine. His first publication, a poem entitled *The Tears of Scotland* appeared in 1746, and later that year he published a satire on London life, *Advice*. In 1747 a further satire, *Reproof*, appeared, and he wrote the novel ▷ *The Adventures of Roderick Random*, published to great acclaim in 1748. Further novels, which draw on his experiences in the navy and his Continental travel, include ▷ *The Adventures of Peregrine Pickle* (1751) and *The Adventures of Ferdinand Count Fathom* (1753).

Smollett, now married and a father, struggled to support his family by editorial work, working on *The Critical Review* from 1756–63, and publishing his translation of ▷ *Don Quixote* in 1755. Finally, his *Complete History of England* proved a commercial success, and was followed by *Continuation* volumes. In 1760 Smollett began *The British Magazine*, where *The Life and Adventures of Sir Lancelot Greaves* was run as a serial; in the same year he was fined and imprisoned for a libellous article in the *Critical Review*.

Smollett had been suffering from ill health for several years, and in 1753 he began to show symptoms of consumption. In 1763 his daughter died, and he abandoned literary work to travel with his wife in Italy and France. On their return in 1765 he wrote the epistolary work *Travels through France and Italy*, which drew from ▷ Sterne the nickname 'Smelfungus'. His final major work was ▷ *The Expedition of Humphry Clinker*, published shortly before his death in 1771.

Bib: Knapp, L. M., *Tobias Smollett: Doctor of Men and Manners*; Boucé, P. G., *The Novels of Tobias Smollett*.

Snobs, The Book of (1848)

A collection of satirical sketches by the novelist ▷ William Makepeace Thackeray, first published in the periodical ▷ *Punch* in 1846–7 as *The Snobs of England by one of themselves*. The title is based on a Cambridge student paper, *The Snob*, to which he contributed as an undergraduate in 1829.

Snow, C. P. (Charles Percy 1905–80)

Novelist; author of the sequence *Strangers and Brothers* comprising *Strangers and Brothers* (1940), *The Light and the Dark* (1947), *Time of Hope* (1949), *The Masters* (1951), *The New Men* (1954), *Homecomings* (1956); *The Conscience of the Rich* (1958), *The Affair* (1960), *Corridors of Power* (1964); *The Sleep of Reason* (1968); *Last Things* (1970).

He also played a large part in public affairs; he was created Baron (Life Peerage) in 1964, and served as a junior minister (Ministry of Technology) from 1964 till 1966. Trained as a scientist, he held strong views about the intellectual cleavage between men trained in the sciences and those trained in liberal studies in the modern world. His Rede Lecture at Cambridge, *The Two Cultures and the Scientific Revolution* (1959) became famous, partly because it provoked an exceptionally ferocious retort from the critic ▷ F. R. Leavis. Other novels include: *The Malcontents* (1972); *In Their Wisdom* (1974).

Bib: Cooper, W., *C. P. Snow*; Leavis, F. R., *Two Cultures? The Significance of C. P. Snow*; Halptrin, J., *C. P. Snow: an Oral Biography*

Social contract

A doctrine about the origins of society especially associated with the English thinkers ▷ Thomas Hobbes and ▷ John Locke, and the French thinker ▷ Jean-Jacques Rousseau. Hobbes (in *Leviathan*) argued that people were naturally violent and rapacious, and that they contracted to put themselves under strong government in order to make the continuance of life and property possible. Locke (*Treatise on Government*) thought the social contract was a convenience rather than a necessity, arguing that private property could have existed in pre-social humanity, but that people contracted to accept government to make themselves secure. Humanity for Locke was not necessarily violent, and government should be tolerant and humane. Rousseau (*Social Contract*) argued that primitive peoples were above all timid, and that they contracted to form governments which rested on the consent of the people, who should overthrow them if they were inefficient or tyrannical. Rousseau's view supported the action of the French revolutionaries and encouraged the growth of democratic ideas in the 19th century. All three opposed the beliefs maintained until the mid-17th century everywhere, that rulers owed their authority to the will of God.

Social Problem novel (Condition of England novel)

A type of novel which came to prominence in the 1840s (known as the 'Hungry Forties' because of starvation among the urban working classes). These novels addressed the social and economic problems arising from the Industrial Revolution, including urban poverty, unemployment and industrial conflict, and attempted to promote reform. Notable examples are ▷ *Mary Barton* (1848) and ▷ *North and South* (1854–5) by ▷ Mrs Gaskell, ▷ *Coningsby* (1844) by ▷ Disraeli and *Alton Locke* (1950) by ▷ Charles Kingsley. The phrase 'condition of England' was coined by ▷ Carlyle in his work *Chartism* (1839).

Socrates (?470–399 BC)

Greek philosopher. He taught entirely by word of mouth, the so-called 'Socratic method' being the discovery of the truth by putting appropriate questions. Because he wrote nothing, all information about him depends on the writings of two contemporaries – the historian Xenophon (*Memorabilia*) and the philosopher ▷ Plato, who stands in relation to Socrates somewhat as St Paul does to Jesus Christ, except that Plato was personally taught by Socrates. Plato puts his own ideas into the mouth of Socrates in his philosophical dialogues, and it is of course difficult to know just how much and in what ways he expanded the Socratic philosophy. This philosophy declared that the true end of philosophy was not to discover the nature of the world but the nature of goodness and how to lead the good life; related to this is the doctrine of Forms, according to which reality is seen as fundamentally spiritual, and the real in a person is their soul.

Socrates is said to have had a beautiful soul in an ugly body; he was married to a woman called Xanthippe. He fell out of favour with the ruling party of Athens, his native city, because he befriended enemies of the party; he was accordingly made to put himself to death by drinking hemlock.

Somerville and Ross

Edith Oenone Somerville (1858–1949) and Violet Martin ('Martin Ross', 1862–1915) were second cousins from Irish families who collaborated on many works of fiction, most notably *Some Experiences of An Irish RM* (1899), a series of comic, satirical and sentimental stories linked by the narrator, a Resident Magistrate in south-west Ireland. The work sold out in a month, and its popularity prompted two sequels: *Some Further Experiences of an Irish RM* (1908) and *Mr Knox's Country* (1915). Somerville and Ross wrote many other novels (mostly set in Ireland), together and separately, and corresponded extensively with each other. *The Real Charlotte* (1894), about the ruining of an innocent Irish girl by a jealous older rival, is generally thought to be their best work. Both women were involved with the women's suffrage movement and with Irish nationalism; Somerville continued to publish work in their joint names after Ross's death, claiming contact with her spirit, and was still writing and publishing in her eighties.

Sons and Lovers (1913)

The first of ▷ D. H. Lawrence's major novels. It is based on his own early life in the Midlands coal-mining village of Eastwood (Nottinghamshire), on his relationships with his mother and with his father who was a mineworker, and on those with his early women friends.

Eastwood is called Bestwood in the novel: the character who corresponds to Lawrence himself is Paul Morel. The strongest relationship is the close tie between Mrs Morel and Paul, who has two brothers and a sister. Mrs Morel comes of a proud, Dissenting middle-class family with memories of ancestors who fought against Charles I. She inherits the uncompromising traditions of English Dissent, and, though her family has been impoverished, she has an inherent aristocracy of temperament derived from her family tradition of high standards. The father, Walter Morel, a miner, is a contrast to his wife, both in his background (he is the grandson of a French refugee and an English barmaid) and in his easy-going, pleasure-loving, spontaneous temperament. The marriage is an unhappy one: Mrs Morel's strictness and truthfulness are outraged by her husband's slackness and deceitfulness. In the war between them, the children take the side of the mother.

The closeness between Mrs Morel and Paul

develops after the death of her eldest son, William, and Paul's own serious illness. He goes to work in a Nottingham factory, but he has his mother's intellectual seriousness and artistic sensitivity, and has ambitions to become an artist. Mrs Morel invests in him all her pride of life and the hopes and passions that her marriage has disappointed. She finds a rival in Miriam Leivers, the shy and intensely serious daughter of a local farmer, and bitterly opposes her friendship with Paul. He is affected by his mother's opposition, and at the same time he resents what he considers to be Miriam's emotional demands upon him, since he believes them to be a barrier to the sensual release for which he craves. He reacts against Miriam by engaging in a sensual love affair with Clara Dawes, a married woman who has quarrelled with her husband. This relationship is not opposed by Mrs Morel, since it is a physical one and does not compete with her own emotional possessiveness. Paul, on the other hand, finds that Clara affords him no more release than Miriam had done; he is unconsciously subjected, all the time, to his mother. The mother's protracted illness and death, and Paul's fight with Baxter Dawes, Clara's husband, are complementary climaxes of the novel. Both together constitute his release, although the death leaves him with a sense of complete dereliction: he has to face the choice of willing himself to live or surrendering to his own desire for death.

The book was early regarded as a vivid presentation of the working of the ▷ Oedipus Complex. Lawrence was not acquainted with ▷ Freud's theories when he started work on the novel in 1910, but had come into contact with them before completing the final version in 1912. It is in its own right a major novel, but it certainly constitutes Lawrence's attempt to release himself from the problems of his own early development. He later declared that his study of his father had been unfair and one-sided. Jessie Chambers, the woman on whom Miriam was based, wrote a study of Lawrence as a young man: *D. H. Lawrence, A Personal Record* by E. T. (1935).

Sophists

In ancient Greece of the 5th century BC, professional educators, who claimed to train men for civic life, but not for any particular trade or profession. They differed from philosophers in that they professed to teach, whereas philosophers professed to know; it is the difference between victory by argument and discovery through argument. By degrees the Sophists fell into disrepute, and today the term 'sophistry' means an ingenious argument deliberately intended to mislead the audience.

Soyinka, Wole (b 1934)

Nigerian playwright, novelist and poet, educated at the Government College, Ibadan and the University of Leeds. After his degree at Leeds, he worked as a reader for the Royal Court Theatre in London before returning to Nigeria in 1959, where he subsequently held various research and teaching posts in drama at the universities of Ibadan, Ife and Lagos as well as working for Nigerian radio and television. He was imprisoned 1967–69 for alleged pro-Biafra activities, an experience recorded in his *The Man Died: Prison Notes* (1972). In 1975 he became Professor of Comparative Literature at the University of Ife. Soyinka is primarily a dramatist, his work ranging from the early comedy of village life, *The Swamp Dwellers* (1958), to *The Road* (1965), a Beckettian drama set in a Lagos 'motor park', and *The Bacchae: A Communion Rite* (1973), based on the classical tragedy by Euripides. Much of his drama uses mime, dance, myth and supernatural elements; for example, *The Road* involves characters, masks and ceremonies from the Yoruba Festival of the Dead. Soyinka has, however, also published two novels: *The Interpreters* (1965), which explores hopes for the future of Africa through the activities of a group of young Nigerian artists, and *Season of Anomy* (1973), a bleak portrayal of war, tyranny and poverty in post-colonial Africa, using ▷ modernist techniques such as highly symbolic and figurative language and an open ending. Soyinka has also published several volumes of verse and critical works such as *Myth, Literature, and the African World* (1976). In 1976 he became the first African to win the Nobel Prize for Literature.

Spanish influence on English fiction

The earliest translation of a Spanish masterpiece into any language was that of ▷ Cervantes's ▷ *Don Quixote* (1605–15) by Thomas Shelton in 1612 (Part I) and 1620 (Part II). Of all Spanish texts, *Don Quixote* was to have the most profound influence on English literature: in the 17th century Francis Beaumont's *The Knight of the Burning Pestle* (1607) and Samuel Butler's *Hudibras* (1663) utilize the comic elements of the novel, while Philip Massinger's *The Renegado* (1624) combines material from *Don Quixote* together with Cervantes's play, *Los Baños de Argel* (1615). In the 18th century ▷ Henry Fielding's *Don Quixote in England* (1734) and ▷ Laurence Sterne's ▷ *Tristram Shandy* (1760–7), and in the 19th century the novels of ▷ Walter Scott and ▷ Charles Dickens perpetuate English indebtedness to Cervantes.

The 16th and 17th centuries in Spain are known as the Golden Age, which paralleled in quality, but greatly exceeded in abundance of texts, the creativity of the Elizabethan and Jacobean ages in England. In this period Spanish influence was felt primarily in the drama.

The 17th-century translations of James Mabbe further facilitated Spanish literary influence in England; works translated by Mabbe include Cervantes's *Novelas ejemplares* (1613; *Exemplary Novels*, trans. 1640), and Mateo Alemán's (1547–?1614) ▷ picaresque novel, *Guzmán de Alfarache* (trans. 1622). The latter text, with *Don Quixote*, formed part of the broader, generic development of the picaresque novel in Spain, England and elsewhere in Europe. The tradition of translating Iberian masterpieces into English continues through to the 20th century: Joan Martorell's novel, *Tirant lo Blanc* (1490), was translated in 1984 by D. H. Rosenthal.

In the 20th century Spanish texts in English have become more readily available, for example,

the works of Federico García Lorca (1898–1936), especially his dramas *Blood Wedding* (perf. 1933) and *The House of Bernada Alba* (perf. 1945), enjoy regular revivals in Britain. Lorca's work has had far greater impact on post-war American fiction than on English literature. Perhaps fittingly, in recent years it is Latin-American literature which has had the most pronounced effect on English writing and on the reading public in England. The ▷ 'magic realism' novels of Gabriel García Márquez (b 1928), such as *Cien Años de Soledad* (*One Hundred Years of Solitude*, 1967), and the novels, essays and criticism of Carlos Fuentes (b 1928), such as *Terra Nostra* (1975), are now internationally famous in English as well as Spanish.

Spark, Muriel (b 1918)

Before becoming a novelist, she was a poet (*Collected Poems*, 1967). Her first novel was *The Comforters* (1957), which she has described as 'a novel about writing a novel' *ie* an experiment in, and exploration of what it means to write fiction. At about the same time she became a convert to Roman Catholicism, and her novels since have tended to take a parabolic form (characteristic of other contemporary novelists, *eg* ▷ Iris Murdoch, ▷ William Golding) combining overt, often wittily satirical ▷ realism with implications of an extra-realist, spiritual dimension. One of her best-known works is *The Prime of Miss Jean Brodie* (1961), the story of the influence over a group of schoolgirls of a progressive spinster schoolteacher in Edinburgh. It is characteristic of Spark's work in its combination of the comic and the sinister, and the skilful use of anticipations of later events. Her three ▷ novellas, *The Public Image* (1968); *The Driver's Seat* (1970) and *Not to Disturb* (1971) exemplify the economy, precision and hardness of her work; they invite little sympathy for their characters, but rather convey a strong sense of pattern and fate underlying an apparent contingency of event. Her other novels are: *Robinson* (1958); *Memento Mori* (1959); *The Ballad of Peckham Rye* (1960); *The Bachelors* (1960); *The Girls of Slender Means* (1963); *The Mandelbaum Gate* (1965); *The Hothouse by the East River* (1972); *The Abbess of Crewe* (1972); *The Takeover* (1976); *Territorial Rights* (1979); *Loitering with Intent* (1981); *The Only Problem* (1984); *A Far Cry From Kensington* (1988); *Symposium* (1990).

Other writings include a stage play *Doctors of Philosophy* (1962), radio plays collected in *Voices at Play* (1961), a further volume of poetry, *Going Up to Sotherby's* (1982) and short stories in *Collected Stories I* (1967); *The Stories of Muriel Spark* (1985). In 1992 she published *Curriculum Vitae* (memoirs).

Bib: Stanford, D., *Muriel Spark: A Biographical and Critical Study*; Stubbs, P., *Muriel Spark* (Writers and their Work series); Kemp, P., *Muriel Spark*; Bold, A., *Muriel Spark*.

Spectator, The

The name of two periodicals, the first appearing daily (1711–12 and 1714), and the second a weekly founded in 1828 and still continuing. The earlier is the more famous of the two, owing to the contributions of its famous editors, Addison and

▷ Steele; it had an important influence on the manners and culture of the time. The later *Spectator* has also had a distinguished history, however; it began as a radical journal, but is now the leading intellectual weekly periodical of the right.

▷ Reviews and Periodicals.

Spence, Elizabeth Isabella (1768–1832)

Novelist and travel writer. Spence began writing for amusement, but when she was orphaned in 1786 she gradually began to use her writing as a means of support. Her early work consists of accounts of her travels within Britain and of the people she met, including *Summer Excursions* (1809; England and Wales) and *Letters From the Highlands* (1816; Scotland). The novels which followed attempted to retain the tone of ▷ travel writing by mixing regional history and descriptions of local scenes with fictional characters and narrative. She published *A Traveller's Tale of the Last Century* (1819), *Old Stories* (1822) and *How to be Rid of a Wife* (1823).

Spencer Herbert (1820–1903)

Philosopher. He was representative of one aspect of the Victorian period in his faith in ▷ Darwin's theory of evolution and his trust in scientific progress. Politically he was individualist, and ethically ▷ Utilitarian. Some of his more influential works were: *First Principles* (1862); *Principles of Biology* (1854); *Principles of Psychology* (1870–2); *Principles of Sociology* (1877–9); *Principles of Ethics* (1893).

Stead, Christina (1902–83)

Australian novelist. Educated at Sydney University Teacher's College, she moved to Europe in 1928, and to the U.S.A. in 1935, travelling with the American political economist William James Blake, whom she married in 1952. She worked as a Hollywood screen-writer before moving to England and, in 1968, returning to Australia. Many of her novels are concerned with the experience of women, and in particular the quest for love. They are notable for their stylistic power, richness of observation, and vivid characterization, and contain an element of the fantastic. Her first works were collections of stories: *The Salzburg Tales* and *Seven Poor Men of Sydney*, both published in 1934. Of her novels, *House of All Nations* (1938) reflects her left-wing views in its account of a glittering, amoral world of financial speculation, while *The Man Who Loved Children* (1940), a novel of American family life, shows an interest in the causes of genius. In *For Love Alone* (1944) a girl escapes to Australia in search of love and freedom.

▷ Post-colonial fiction.

Bib: Williams, C., *Christina Stead: A Life in Letters*; Lidoff, J., *Christina Stead*; Sheridan, S., *Christina Stead*; Brydon, D., *Christina Stead*.

Steel, Mrs Flora Annie (1847–1929)

Novelist. Brought up in London and Scotland, she married at twenty and lived for some twenty-one years in the Punjab, India, where her husband was a civil servant. For a member of the colonial administration she was exceptionally sympathetic to the Indians and did extensive work for the health and education of Indian women, founding a school for Indian girls and working as a school inspector. She started writing after returning to England on her husband's retirement in 1889, and most of her fiction is set in India: *On the Face of the Waters* (1896), about the Indian mutiny; *Wide Awake Stories* (1884), tales set in the Punjab; *Hosts of the Lord* (1900), about Indian religions; and *The Curse of Eve* (1929), which advocates birth control. She was involved with the suffragette movement and wrote an autobiography, *The Garden of Fidelity* (1929).

Bib: Powell, V., *Flora Annie Steel: Novelist of India*

Steele, Sir Richard (1672–1729)

Essayist and journalist. He was educated (with Joseph Addison) at Charterhouse School and at Oxford University. On graduation he entered the army. His prose treatise *The Christian Hero* (1701) attracted the favour of King William III, but caused Steele the inconvenience of finding that he was expected to live up to his own precepts. This his pleasure-loving nature did not find convenient, and he redressed the balance by his comedy *The Funeral* (1701). He wrote other comedies: *The Lying Lover* (1703); *The Tender Husband* (1705), an imitation of Molière's *Sicilienne*; *The Conscious Lovers* (1722). It is not, however, for his comedies that he is now read, but for a new kind of periodical ▷ essay of which he was practically the inventor, and which he published in *The Tatler*, started in 1709, and appearing three times weekly. Although since the lapsing of the Licensing Act in 1695 there was no active ▷ censorship of political opinion, Steele found it safer to avoid politics, at least after the Tory party came to power in 1710, since he was a consistent ▷ Whig. His essays treated daily life, manners and behaviour, in a way calculated to educate middle-class readers and win the approval of people of virtue, and yet always to entertain them. These motives, and the kind of interest that his essays inspired, anticipate the character of later 18th-century novels, especially those of ▷ Samuel Richardson. *The Tatler* was already a success when Joseph Addison started to collaborate with Steele, but they closed it down in 1711, and started the still more famous ▷ *Spectator* (1711–12). The crisis of succession to the throne grew intense in 1713–14: the Whigs favoured the Protestant House of Hanover and a powerful Tory faction was ready to support Anne's half-brother James if he would turn Protestant, though other Tories remained loyal to the Act of 1701 in favour of Hanover. Steele was consequently attacked by the Tory journalist, ▷ Jonathan Swift, both for his conduct of his next paper, *The Guardian* (1713), and for his ▷ pamphlet in favour of the Protestant succession, *The Crisis* (1714). In 1714 the Whigs returned to power and Steele's political fortunes revived; he was knighted in 1715, and received various official posts. In 1714 he produced his autobiographical *Apology for Himself and his Writings*; he also edited a number of other periodicals, all of them short-lived, and none with the fame of *The Tatler* and *The Spectator*: *The Englishman, The Reader, Town Talk, Tea-Table, Chit Chat, Plebeian.*

The last, a political paper, led to a quarrel with Addison in 1718.

▷ Coverley, Sir Roger de.

Bib: Aitken, G. A., *Life*; Hazlitt, W., *The English Comic Writers*; Dobree, B., *Variety of Ways*.

Stendhal (pseudonym of Henri Beyle) (1788–1842)
French writer, known for his novels *Armance* (1822), *La Chartreuse de Parme* (1830) and *Lucien Leuwen* (unfinished and published posthumously in 1894). Considered the first of the French realists (▷ realism), Stendhal is renowned for his exact depiction of milieu and for his close attention to psychological verisimilitude and motivation. However, his realism is neither a simple fidelity to detail nor does it underwrite the values and representations which aristocratic and bourgeois society makes of itself. Stendhal depicts the conflict of social verisimilitudes with narrative inventions which contravene such verisimilitudes; so the mainspring of *Le Rouge et le Noir* is the socially unacceptable love of the aristocratic Mathilde and the commoner Julien, while *Armance* raises the 'shocking' issue of homosexuality before its Byronic conclusion. On the author's side, irony is his means of refusing to endorse such values. Irony here is not as a purely corrosive negativity. It discreetly raises the issue of the ethics of representation itself, moving outwards from the hero and society to ask whether the novel can hold together that encounter of social and individual forces it narrates.

Stendhal's interests were wide and he was likewise the author of travel books, journalism and controversial literary pamphlets (*Racine et Shakespeare*, 1823 and 1825, in which he declared his support for the Romantics. Three volumes of autobiographical writing were published after his death: his *Journal* (1888), *La Vie de Henry Brulard* (1890) and *Souvenirs d'égotisme* (1892).

Stephen, Sir Leslie (1832–1904)
Critic and biographer. He began his career as a tutor at Trinity Hall, Cambridge, and university rules demanded that he should be in orders as an Anglican clergyman. His philosophical studies led him to the religious scepticism so frequent among intellectuals of the middle and later 19th century, and he renounced his orders in 1875. From 1866 he contributed critical essays to the ▷ *Cornhill Magazine* and political ones for the *Nation*; he also wrote for the *Saturday Review* and helped to found the *Pall Mall Gazette* (1865). In 1871 he became editor of the *Cornhill*; the 11 years of his editorship made it one of the most distinguished literary reviews of the later 19th century. His critical essays were published in book form in *Hours in a Library* (1874–9). He wrote philosophical essays, defining his agnostic position: *Essays on Free Thinking and Plain Speaking* (1873). He contributed a number of ▷ biographies to the *English Men of Letters* series: *Johnson* (1878); *Pope* (1880); *Swift* (1882); *George Eliot* (1902), and *Hobbes* (1904). His most distinguished work is firstly his editorship of the *Dictionary of National Biography*, started in 1882, to which he contributed many of the articles, and his book on *The English Utilitarians*

(1900). His last book, *English Literature and Society in the Eighteenth Century*, was published on the day of his death.

Today, Stephen is one of the most respected among critics of the later 19th century; the rigour and sincerity of his thinking make him a link between the Victorians and 18th-century rationalist traditions of thought which continued into the 19th century in the ▷ Utilitarian school of thinkers. He has twice been used as the basis of a character in the masterpieces of distinguished novelists: Vernon Whitford in ▷ *The Egoist* by ▷ Meredith, and Mr Ramsay in ▷ *To the Lighthouse* by ▷ Virginia Woolf, his daughter by his second wife. His first wife had been a daughter of the novelist ▷ William Makepeace Thackeray.

▷ Agnosticism; Reviews and Periodicals.
Bib: Lives by F. W. Maitland; Noel Annan.

Sterne, Laurence (1713–68)
Sterne was born at Clonmel in Ireland, the son of an improvident army officer. After leaving Cambridge University he became an Anglican priest near York, where his great-grandfather had been Archbishop. His celebrated novel ▷ *The Life and Opinions of Tristram Shandy* appeared in successive volumes from 1760 until 1767. Opinions have always been divided about the qualities of this book, although Sterne's reputation rests principally upon it. ▷ Samuel Johnson found it eccentric and shallow, declaring, 'Nothing odd will do long. *Tristram Shandy* did not last'; but in the 20th century the critic Viktor Schlovsky has argued that '*Tristram Shandy* is the most typical novel of world literature.' ▷ *A Sentimental Journey through France and Italy*, which demonstrates many of the same stylistic idiosyncracies, appeared in 1768, the last year of Sterne's life. His *Journal to Eliza*, published posthumously, is a curious, quasi-autobiographical work that hovers uneasily between fact and fiction, tragedy and farce. The same blend of seriousness and whimsicality is evident in Sterne's sermons, he published under the name of one of the characters from *Tristram Shandy* as *The Sermons of Mr Yorick*. A contemporary review took offence at this jesting allusion. 'We have read of a Yorick likewise in an obscene romance,' it thundered. 'But are the solemn dictates of religion fit to be conveyed from the mouths of buffoons and ludicrous romancers?'

Sterne's characteristic blending of sentimentality and farce, although distinctive in style, is not without precedent. His main literary influences can be found in ▷ Rabelais, ▷ Cervantes, and ▷ Montaigne, although there are also debts to ▷ Burton's *Anatomy of Melancholy*, ▷ Locke's *Essay on Human Understanding*, and ▷ Swift's *Tale of a Tub*. From Rabelais Sterne derived not only his bawdy humour, but also his fascination with exuberant word-play, his love of lists and puns, his delight in the sonorous malleability of words and his absurd parodies of learned debates. From Locke he borrowed and parodied the theory of the association of ideas, a theory which allows him to present each of his characters trapped in a private world of allusions. ▷ Thackeray objected to the self-indulgence of

Sterne's wit; 'He is always looking on my face, watching his effect, uncertain whether I think him an impostor or not; posture-making, coaxing and imploring me.' Yet it is precisely this fictional virtuosity that has recommended Sterne as a model to later writers keen to assert not only that all art is artifice, but that history and biography too are merely varieties of elaborate fiction.

Bib: Cash, A. H., *Lawrence Sterne*; New, M., *Laurence Sterne as Satirist*; Howes, A. B., *Sterne: the Critical Heritage*; Lamb, J., *Sterne's Fiction and the Double Principle*.

Stevenson, Robert Louis Balfour (1850–94)

Novelist, essayist, poet. The son of an engineer, he intended to take up the same profession, for which he showed early talent, but bad health prevented this. Partly because of his health and partly for love of travel, he spent much of his life abroad and some of his best writing is in essays of travel, *eg An Inland Voyage* (1878) and *Travels with a Donkey in the Cevennes* (1879). His most famous works, however, are the fantasy, so often used as an emblem of divided personality, ▷ *The Strange Case of Dr Jekyll and Mr Hyde* (1886) and his adventure story ▷ *Treasure Island* (1883). Still well known are his Scottish historical romances, in the tradition of ▷ Walter Scott: *Kidnapped* (1886), *The Master of Ballantrae* (1889), and *Catriona* (1893); it has been said that *Weir of Hermiston*, also in this style but left unfinished, would have been his masterpiece. Other works of fiction: *New Arabian Nights* (1882); *Prince Otto* (1885); *The Black Arrow* (1888); *The Wrong Box* (1889); *The Wrecker* (1892); *Island Nights Entertainments* (1893); *The Ebb Tide* (1894); *St Ives*, also left unfinished at his death. Essays: *Virginibus Puerisque* (1881); *Familiar Studies of Men and Books* (1882); *Vailima Letters* (1895). His *A Child's Garden of Verses* (1885) was for long considered a minor children's classic (▷ children's books), and he published other poetry in *Underwoods* (1887). Stevenson was strongly influenced by French ideas of literary style and his preoccupation with style apart from the substance that is being expressed was characteristic of the ▷ aestheticism of the later 19th century although he had too much love of the world of action and simplicity of mind to make it possible to class him with the aesthetes. He has had a wide popular readership which has perhaps denied him critical attention; critics have detected a darker side to his writing beneath the swashbuckling, and dualism is a theme in evidence.

Bib: Balfour, G., *Life*; Daiches, D., *Robert Louis Stevenson*; Elwin, M., *The Strange Case of Stevenson*; Furnas, J. C., *Voyage to Windward* (life); Eigner, E. M., *Robert Louis Stevenson and Romantic Tradition*; Calder, J. (ed.), *Stevenson and Victorian Scotland*; Miller, K., *Doubles*.

Stoics

A school of philosophy founded by the Greek Zeno of Citium, in the 4th century BC. It later extended to Rome, where its leaders became Epictetus and Seneca (both 1st century AD) and the Roman Emperor Marcus Aurelius (2nd century AD). They reasoned that all being is material, and therefore the soul is, and so are the virtues. The soul, however, is an active principle which sustains the body, and proceeds from God; only the active principle has significance, and the wise person is therefore indifferent to material suffering and cares only for virtue governed by judgement which is in accordance with the principles of wisdom. Some of the ethical principles of Stoicism were in accordance with Chrisianity (which Marcus Aurelius nevertheless persecuted) and, abstracted from religious doctrine, they appealed to the Renaissance ideal of the noble soul; hence the recurrence of Stoic attitudes in the drama of Shakespeare and his contemporaries.

Stoker, Bram (1847–1912)

Irish novelist and short-story writer, now remembered principally for the universally known, much parodied and frequently filmed *Dracula* (1897), which was influenced by ▷ J. Le Fanu's vampire novel *Carmilla* (1872). Stoker spent most of his career as secretary and business manager to the actor Henry Irving; he wrote many horror stories, other novels of the supernatural, such as *The Lady of the Shroud* (1909), and adventure novels such as *The Snake's Pass* (1890).

Storey, David (b 1933)

Novelist and dramatist. His novels include: *This Sporting Life* (1960); *Flight into Camden* (1961); *Radcliffe* (1963); *Pasmore* (1972); *A Temporary Life* (1973); *Saville* (1976); *A Prodigal Child* (1982); *Present Times* (1984).

Before he became a novelist and playwright Storey was an art student, and to pay for his studies in London he played at weekends in professional Rugby League football for a northern team. The son of a miner, Storey is the most interesting of a number of novelists in modern Britain who have in common that their social viewpoint is outside the middle class and centred geographically outside London; they include ▷ Alan Sillitoe, ▷ John Braine and ▷ Stan Barstow. Their obvious antecedent is ▷ D. H. Lawrence. Storey is distinguished from his contemporaries with a similar background by the absence of social belligerence and an ability to reach across from a provincial-industrial world denuded of art to a world of highly cultivated sensibility without playing false to the social experience that shaped him. His first novel, which has been filmed, is about his background world, in which sport is the principal cultural force; the next two are in different ways more ambitious and less successful, but their faults are interesting as the price paid for their serious experimental boldness. *Radcliffe* modifies 1950s ▷ realism with elements of the ▷ Gothic, allegorical and fantastic, while retaining a concern with class and social mobility; *Pasmore* continues this development by linking social instability to a personal crisis of identity. His plays often explore class antagonism and social dislocation: *Restoration of Arnold Middleton* (1966); *In Celebration* (1969); *The Contractor* (1969); *Home* (1970); *The Changing Room* (1971); *The Farm* and *Cromwell* (both 1973): *Life Class* (1974); *Mother's Day* (1976); *Sisters* (1978); *Early Days* (1980).

Bib: Taylor, J. R., *David Storey*.

Story/*histoire* (French)
Term used in ▷ narratology for the events described
in a fiction (in chronological order), as the reader
deduces them from the ▷ narrative.
▷ Narrating.

Story of an African Farm, The
▷ Schreiner, Olive.

Stow, Randolph (b 1935)
Australian novelist, born in Western Australia and
educated at the University of Western Australia
and the University of Sydney. He has worked
as a storeman in an Anglican Mission, as an
anthropologist in Papua New Guinea and as a
lecturer in English at the universities of Leeds and
Western Australia. In 1966 he moved to Britain,
living in Suffolk and later in Essex. He won the
Patrick White Award in 1979, and Stow's portrayal of
a spiritual journey in *To The Islands* (1958), which is
about the quest of an ageing Christian missionary for
the aboriginal 'island of the dead', invites comparison
with ▷ Patrick White's *Voss*. His other novels
are: *A Haunted Land* (1956); *The Bystander* (1957);
Tourmaline (1963); *The Merry-Go-Round in the Sea*
(1965); *Visitants* (1979); *The Girl Green as Elderflower*
(1980); *The Suburbs of Hell* (1984). His volumes of
poetry include: *Act One* (1957); *Outrider: Poems
1956–1962* (1962): *A Counterfeit Silence: Selected
Poems* (1969). He has also written opera libretti for
the composer Peter Maxwell Davies (*Eight Songs for
a Mad King*, 1969, and *Miss Donnithorne's Maggot*,
1974), edited *Australian Poetry 1964* and written for
children.
Bib: Hassall, A. J. (ed.), *Visitants, Episodes from Other
Novels, Poems, Stories, Interviews and Essays*; Hassall,
A. J., *Strange Country: A Study of Randolph Stow*.

Strachey, (Giles) Lytton (1880–1932)
Biographer. His best-known works are *Eminent
Victorians* (1918) – short biographical studies of
Cardinal Manning, Florence Nightingale and
General Gordon – and *Queen Victoria* (1921). He
also wrote *Elizabeth and Essex* (1928), and criticism:
Landmarks in French Literature (1912) and *Books
and Characters* (1992). Strachey regarded most
biographies of the 19th century as dull monuments
to the subject, whereas he considered biography to
be an art form, presenting the subject as a human
being and showing him or her from unexpected
aspects. Strachey was a prominent member of the
▷ Bloomsbury Group.
▷ Biography.
Bib: Sanders, C. P., *Strachey: His Mind and Art*;
Johnstone, J. K., *The Bloomsbury Group*; Holroyd, M.,
Lytton Strachey.

Strawberry Hill
▷ Walpole, Horace.

Stream of consciousness
A term which was used by William James in his
Principles of Psychology but was first applied to
literature in a 1918 review by May Sinclair of
volumes of ▷ Dorothy Richardson's *Pilgrimage*. Since

then it has been used for the narrative technique
which attempts to render the consciousness of a
character by representing as directly as possible
the flow of feelings, thoughts and impressions.
The term 'interior monologue' is also sometimes
used. The classic exponents of the technique, apart
from Richardson, are ▷ Virginia Woolf, ▷ James
Joyce and the American novelist William Faulkner
(1897–1962). Joyce attributed his initial discovery of
the technique to his reading of the novel *Les Lauriers
sont coupés* by the French novelist Edouard Dujardin.

Structuralism
A form of critical theory chiefly derived from
the work of ▷ Ferdinand de Saussure and from
Russian ▷ Formalism. Structuralism rejects the
notion that the text expresses an author's meaning
or that it reflects society and, instead, treats it as an
independent unit which activates various objective
relationships with other texts. Structuralism, then,
concentrates upon the relationship between cultural
elements, especially those in binary oppositions,
without which, it is claimed, meaning cannot exist.
▷ Post-structuralism.
Bib: Culler, J., *Structuralist Poetics*.

Subjectivity
In its use in the language of literary criticism this
concept is not to be confused with the notion of
'individual response' with which it has customarily
been associated. ▷ Louis Althusser and ▷ Jacques
Lacan develop the notion of human beings as
'subjects', that is points at which all of those social,
cultural, and psychic forces which contribute to
the construction of the individual, come together.
Implicit in the concept of the 'subject' is the idea of
the grammatical positioning of the personal pronoun
in a sentence: the 'I' being referred to as 'the
subject of discourse'. Also, implicit in the concept
of 'subjectivity' is the notion of 'subjection', which
raises fundamental questions about the ways in which
the behaviour of individual 'subjects' is conditioned
by external forces. Within the boundaries of critical
theory the 'subject' is never unified (except through
the functioning of an ▷ ideology which is designed
to efface contradiction), but is, in reality split, or
'decentred'. This is part of a movement away from
the kind of philosophical ▷ humanism which would
place the individual at the centre of attention. It
would attribute to him or her an autonomy of action
as well as an authority arising out of the suggestion
that he or she is the origin and source of all
meaning. 'Subjectivity' is an indispensable category
of analysis for ▷ feminism, ▷ psychoanalytical
criticism and for the various kinds of ▷ materialist
analysis of texts.

Sublimation
This term is used in ▷ Freudian psycho-analysis to
describe the process whereby activities which have
their origins in the unconscious, and which can be
traced to primal issues of sexuality, are diverted
and surface in other areas of human endeavour,
as something else. This concept is of particular
use to literary criticism, not only because it can

provide an explanation of the mechanisms of artistic creation itself, but because it assists in the analysis of literary representations of human motives and actions. Implicit in sublimation is the notion of an unconscious whose operations, distorted as desires, rise to the level of the conscious.

Subversion

This is a term usually associated with the sphere of political action, but applied to literary texts it points towards the relationship between a particular text, or even a part of a text, and what is generally regarded as the prevailing order. Individual texts are capable of challenging dominant orthodoxies (eg ▷ James Joyce's ▷ *Ulysses* or ▷ D. H. Lawrence's ▷ *Lady Chatterley's Lover*), either at the level of literary form, or at the level of discernible content. Thus, they may be said to subvert expectations or dominant values. A more complex kind of subversion may take place within the boundaries of a particular text which otherwise would be accepted as conforming to prevailing values and attitudes. Where this happens, negotiation takes place (which can be analysed as part of the text's structure) whereby that which is dominant in the text seeks to contain and control those forces which could subvert it. Such a process is particularly evident in relation to sexual difference, where a potentially subversive 'feminity' is often seen to threaten the dominant masculine discourses which seek to contain it. Very often potentially subversive energies are only ever permitted to enter a text in marginalized forms, eg female promiscuity, as various forms of 'evil' all of which are shown to be a danger to the status quo. An acceptance of the judgements implied in these moral categories is usually a precondition of a reading which is complicit with its dominant discourses and structures. A more critical reading will seek to reinstate the text's 'subversive' elements in order to show precisely how certain values, and the literary structures which sustain them, are produced.

Suffragette Movement

Colloquial term for the Women's Suffrage Movement which pursued violent action to secure political rights for women before and during the First World War. Specifically they wanted equal rights with men to have the vote (suffrage) in parliamentary elections and to be candidates for election. Among the famous leaders of the movement were Mrs Pankhurst and her two daughters, Sylvia and Christabel. The movement ended in 1918 when votes were given to women at the age of 30; in 1928 they received equal rights with men.

▷ Women, Status of.

Bib: Tickner, L., *The Spectacle of Women*.

Surrealism

Inaugurated in Paris in 1924 by André Breton's first *Surrealist Manifesto* (two further manifestos were to follow in 1930 and 1934), its founding members included Louis Aragon (1897–1982), Robert Desnos (1900–45), Paul Eluard (1895–1952), Benjamin Péret (1899–1959) and Philippe Soupault (b 1897). The movement's ambition was a radical programme, extending beyond art and literature to embrace social

and political reform. To advertise and propagate their aims, the Surrealists created a 'Bureau de recherches surréalistes' and a number of reviews: *Littérature* (1919), *La Révolution surréaliste* (1924), *Le Surréalisme au service de la Révolution* (1930) and *Minotaure* (1932). Purely within France, Surrealism's roots lay in Guillaume Apollinaire's (1880–1918) experiments with poem-objects and in the cubist poetry of Pierre Reverdy (1889–1960). More broadly, as the first *Manifesto* made clear, it was especially indebted to Freudian (▷ Freud) theories of dream and sought to overthrow rationalism, in favour of unconscious mental states, so giving rise to an expanded sense of the psychic life. Such unconscious processes could best be liberated by activities such as 'automatic writing'. By this technique, a writer's faculty of conscious censorship is laid aside, allowing the chance encounter between two otherwise unrelated elements which might produce the surreal image and intimate the incursion of dream into reality.

Just as Surrealism travelled easily between forms of artistic production and ostensibly external forms such as psychology and philosophy, so its own artistic manifestations span poetry, prose and painting, though it is best known for and possibly most representatively manifested in the first and last of these. Max Ernst (1891–1976), René Magritte (1898–1967) and Joan Miró (1893–1983) helped establish the movement in art and Salvador Dali (1904–89) provided greater impetus still when he associated himself with Surrealism in 1929; his dream-like work was plainly inspired by Freud, while his surreal objects such as the lobster-telephone amuse and shock our sense of the everyday propriety of such objects. Louis Aragon (1897–1982), the foremost of Surrealism's several communists (Eluard was another), made an early contribution with his *Feu de joie* (1920) and *Le Mouvement perpétuel* (1925) as well as major novels. However, Aragon's commitment to communism from 1927 onwards finally led to his break with Surrealism in 1932, even though Breton's *Second Manifesto* of 1930 had called for the harmonization of Freud and ▷ Marx. World War II caused an hiatus in Surrealism's activities and despite the success of the various Surrealist Exhibitions (eg London, 1936; Paris 1938, 1947, 1959), by the 1950s the movement's force was to all intents and purposes spent.

The widespread influence of French Surrealism between the Wars gave rise to two corresponding movements, Belgian Surrealism and English Surrealism.

Surtees, Robert Smith (1805–64)

Novelist. In 1832 he helped to found the *New Sporting Magazine*, which he edited for five years and to which he contributed sketches collected in 1838 under the title of *Jorrocks's Jaunts and Jollities*. It was this book which suggested to the publishers, Chapman and Hall, the idea that ▷ Charles Dickens might write a similar series of sketches about a Nimrod Club of amateur sportsmen. Dickens adapted this idea to the Pickwick Club and thus started ▷ *The Pickwick Papers*, issued in 20 parts

in 1836–7 and published in book form in 1837. Surtees's most famous foxhunting novel is probably *Handley Cross* (1843), still regarded as a minor classic. He published eight novels in all.
Bib: Cooper, L., *R. S. Surtees*; Welcome, J., *The Sporting World of R. S. Surtees*.

Swift, Graham Colin (b 1949)
Novelist and short-story writer. Born in London and educated at the universities of Cambridge and York, he worked as a part-time teacher of English in London colleges from 1974–83. *Waterland* (1983) reflects on the significance of historical knowledge and the influence of the environment on human identity, through the tragi-comic story of several generations of a Fenland family, interspersed with material about the history and geography of the area. His other fiction is: *The Sweet-Shop Owner* (1980); *Shuttlecock* (1981); *Learning to Swim and Other Stories* (1982); *Out of This World* (1988); *Ever After* (1992).

Swift, Jonathan (1667–1745)
Satirist. He was of an old English family, but his grandfather seems to have lost his fortune on the Cavalier side in the Civil Wars of the mid-17th century. The poet John Dryden (1631–1700) was his cousin. Swift was educated in Ireland, where he had the future playwright ▷ Congreve as a schoolfellow, and took his degree at Trinity College, Dublin. He began his working life as secretary to the statesman and writer ▷ Sir William Temple in 1689, left him to take orders as a priest in the Church of England in 1694 (receiving a small ecclesiastical office in Ireland), and returned to remain in Temple's service until Temple's death in 1699. Throughout the reign of Queen Anne (1702–14) he played a large part in the literary and the political life of London, though he was dividing his time between England and Ireland. He contributed some numbers to Addison and ▷ Steele's journals, *The Tatler* and ▷ *The Spectator*, and together with Alexander Pope and Arbuthnot founded the ▷ Scriblerus Club. Politically he at first served the ▷ Whig party, but in 1710 he changed over to the Tories, led by Edward Harley, Earl of Oxford, and the brilliant but unreliable Bolingbroke. He served the Tories by his ▷ pamphlet *The Conduct of the Allies* (1711) advocating peace in the War of the Spanish Succession, and by his conduct of the journal *The Examiner* (1710–11). His assistance was invaluable to the Tory party, who held power from 1711 until the death of the Queen; in 1713 Swift was rewarded by being made Dean of St Patrick's Cathedral, Dublin, an office which he at first held as an absentee. By this time, however, the Queen was dying, and Harley and Bolingbroke, divided over the succession to the throne, were opponents: Bolingbroke offered Swift great rewards for his support, but Swift preferred to remain with Harley, who had lost power and for a time was even in danger of losing his life. In 1714 the Queen died, the Whigs returned to power, Bolingbroke fled, and George I came over from Germany as King. Swift left England for his Deanery in Ireland. At first he had few friends there, but between 1720 and 1730 he wrote a number of eloquent pamphlets in the interests of the oppressed Irish, and ended by achieving great popularity. The same decade saw the crisis of his relationships with the two women who loved him: Esther Johnson, the 'Stella' of his *Journal to Stella*, compiled 1710–13, and Esther Vanhomrigh, whom he called 'Vanessa'. The relationship with the latter was tragically concluded with her death in 1723; Stella died in 1728. Swift lived as a conscientious and efficient Dean almost to the end of his life, unselfishly disposing of most of his wealth for the poor, but he went out of his mind in 1742.

Swift wrote a great deal of prose, chiefly in the form of pamphlets, and not all of it is satire: *The Conduct of the Allies* is not, for instance, nor are his sermons. However, his great reputation rests principally on his prose satire, and he is especially admired for the very subtle and powerful form of his irony. The surface of his prose is limpidly clear and beguilingly placid, but his use of it is to enforce by close logic an impossible and often very shocking proposition, which is driven home with distinct and startling imagery. His position is that of a sincere Christian who advocates reason; he despises alike the emptiness of the ▷ Deists and the emotionalism of ▷ Puritans. He is at the same time a strong humanitarian, who is revolted by injustices leading to so much suffering, but despairs of the capacity of the human race to rid itself of its tendency to bestiality and heartlessness. Though a believer in reason, he despised the pedantry of so many scholars, and the irrelevances of the 'natural philosophers' in their pursuit of science. He has been censured on two grounds: first, the minor but undoubted one that his disgust at some aspects of human existence derived from his own morbidity, and secondly, the much more controversial one that his vision is in the end negative and destructive. His most famous works are as follows: ▷ *The Battle of the Books* (written 1697, published 1704), a contribution to the dispute between the relative merits of the ancients and the moderns in literature; ▷ *A Tale of a Tub* (1704), a satire on 'corruption in religion and learning' and one of his masterpieces; *Argument against Abolishing Christianity* (1708), a satire on the irreligion of the time; ▷ *Drapier's Letters* (1724), against the monopoly granted by the English government to William Wood to provide the Irish with a copper coinage; ▷ *Gulliver's Travels* (1726); and ▷ *A Modest Proposal* (1729), a most forceful exposure of the conditions of the Irish poor. Swift's poetry has only recently received the critical attention that it deserves. His most admired poem is *Verses on the Death of Dr Swift* (1731), a partly satirical poem in which he imagines public reaction to the news of his death, and then gives his own deliberately deceptive assessment of his life and achievements. *Cadenus and Vanessa* is an equally deceptive poem which purports to give an account of his love affair with Esther Vanhomrigh. It was published, at her request, after her death in 1723. ('Cadenus' is an anagram of 'Decanus' = Dean.)
Bib: Ehrenpreis, I., *Swift, The Man, His Works and The Age*; Nokes, D., *Jonathan Swift, A Hypocrite Reversed*; Eilon, D., *Faction's Fictions: Ideological closure*

in Swift's Satire; Rawson, C. J., *Gulliver and the Gentle Reader: Studies in Swift and our Time*; Reilly, P., *Jonathan Swift: The Brave Desponder*; Steele, P., *Jonathan Swift: Preacher and Jester*.

Sybil, or The Two Nations (1845)

A novel by ▷ Benjamin Disraeli. The 'two nations' are the rich and the poor. The country is shown to be governed by the rich in the interests of the rich – *ie* the landlords and the employers. Sybil is the daughter of Gerard, a ▷ Chartist leader; she is loved by an enlightened young aristocrat, Charles Egremont, younger brother of an oppressive landlord, Lord Marney. Disraeli gives romantic historical background to his theme by causing Sybil to belong to the same family as the last abbot of Marney, whose lands Lord Marney's ancestors had seized at the time of the dissolution of the monasteries under Henry VIII. The poor nation is likewise identified with the ▷ Anglo-Saxons, despoiled of their land by the Norman conquerors of the 11th century. This novel, like ▷ *Coningsby* (1844) is part of Disraeli's campaign to renew the Tory party through the Young England movement by inspiring it with a true and disinterested ideology. The novel combines a rather comic element of operatic romanticism with shrewd observation and social satire.

Syllepsis
▷ Figures of Speech.

Symbolic order
A psychoanalytical term now frequently used in literary criticism. 'Symbolic' in this context refers initially to the notion that language itself is comprised of symbols which stand for things. But, the French psychoanalyst ▷ Jacques Lacan observes that: 'It is the world of words that creates the world of things', and in so doing introduces an 'order' into what would otherwise be disparate units. That process of ordering is motivated by a series of impulses and desires which are not usually available to the conscious mind. Thus, the symbolic order is that order of representations through whose organization the child enters into language and the social order as a gendered human 'subject'. In the case of ▷ Freudian psychoanalysis each symbol refers back to an Oedipal stage (▷ Oedipus complex) which the infant passes through on the way to maturity.

In Lacan, the 'unconscious' is said to be structured like a language, already a system of representations through which the individual gendered subject realizes his or her identity. In some respect all literary texts traverse the realm of the symbolic order in that they represent and articulate those images through which reality is grasped discursively.

Symbolism
As a movement, Symbolism is primarily associated with poetry, and notably a group of French poets of the late 19th century, including Stephane Mallarmé (1842–98), Paul Verlaine (1844–96) and Arthur Rimbaud (1854–91). Symbolist poets sought to use poetic language and symbols in a manner analogous to music to express personal feelings through suggestion and mood rather than direct statement. The American writer Edgar Allen Poe and the composer Ricard Wagner also played an important role in the Symbolist movement, which was a key influence on Anglo-American ▷ modernism, most obviously in poetry, but also in the fiction of ▷ James Joyce, who combines symbolism with naturalism. The general emphasis on subjectivity, on the flux of consciousness and on the ineffable in much modernist fiction owes something to Symbolism, as does the interest in the imitation of musical form (for example in the novels of ▷ Virginia Woolf). In relation to the novel, the term 'symbolism' is often used more loosely, to refer to the way in which objects, phenomena, people or animals are given special meaning within a text: for example the symbol of the rainbow in ▷ D.H. Lawrence's novel of that title.

Synchronic
Adjective used by ▷ Ferdinand de Saussure to describe the analysis of the meaning of a ▷ sign in relation to the other current elements of the language system ▷ *langue*. Saussure juxtaposes the synchronic study of language with the *diachronic* study of language which looks at the historical development of language. This is one of the important polarities in Saussure's theories.
▷ Parole.

Synecdoche
▷ Figures of Speech.

Tacitus, Cornelius (AD ?55–120)

Roman historian. He was eminent in Roman political and social life, and the son-in-law of Gnaeus Julius Agricola, the governor of Britain who effectively transformed the decay of island into an orderly Roman province. His surviving works are the *Dialogue on Orators*, consisting of conversations about the decay of Roman education; the *Life of Agricola*, including an account of Britain under the rule of his father-in-law; *Germany*, an account of the characteristics of the land and its people, contrasting their freedom and simplicity with the degeneracy of Rome; the *Histories*, a fragment of an account of the Roman Empire during the last 30 years of the 1st century; the *Annals*, a fragment of a history of the Empire in the first half of the century.

Tacitus was a contemporary of the satirical poet Juvenal; together they represent the last significant phase of classical Latin literature; both have a strong ethical concern with the condition of Roman civilization, and Tacitus reveres the austere virtues of the pre-imperial republic, though he accepts the Empire as a political necessity. His style is distinguished for its brevity, and his works were an outstanding constituent of English education from the 16th to 19th centuries.

Tale of a Tub, A (1704)

A prose satire by ▷ Jonathan Swift. The title is the same as that of one of the last and least interesting comedies by Ben Jonson, but Swift ironically explains it in his Preface as derived from the practice of sailors of tossing a tub to a whale in order to divert it from attacking the ship. The ship, Swift explains, is an image of the state, and the whale is *Leviathan*, ▷ Hobbes's political treatise, from which the wits of the age drew their dangerous armament of scepticism and satire; he pretends that he has been employed to divert these attacks by his engaging nonsense. For the next edition (1710) Swift added *An Apology*, in which he discloses his true aim – to satirize 'the numerous and gross corruptions in Religion and Learning'. The real meaning of the title is that Swift is beguiling readers so as to expose them the more effectively to the ferocity of irony. The central fable of the *Tale* is the story of three brothers, Martin, Peter and Jack, who inherit three simple coats from their father, whose will enjoins that the coats must in no way be altered. Under the leadership of Peter, however, the brothers find it convenient to alter the coats beyond recognition to comply with fashion. Peter's authority eventually becomes so insanely domineering that Martin and Jack revolt against him; Martin tears off the ornaments on his coat, but stops before he altogether disfigures it; Jack, however, reduces his to a squalid rag. The fable is an allegory of the Reformation: Peter represents the Church of Rome, Martin the Church of England, in which Swift was a priest, and Jack the extremer Protestants, or Dissenters; the coat is the Word of God as expressed in the New Testament. Swift's main object of attack is Jack, since he regarded the Dissenters, with their claim to receipt of divine inspiration and their resistance to authority, as the principal threat to the rule of right reason, true religion, and fine

civilization in his time. The fable is interspersed with digressions, satirizing the arrogance of those who set up their private intellects or privileged inspiration as guides to their fellow-men; by Section XI the digressions come together with the fable, and Jack is declared to be the leader of the Aeolists, who expound their doctrines through 'wind', from Aeolus, Greek god of the winds. The satire is essentially an attack on the 'windiness' that Swift discerned in the more pretentious philosophical and religious teaching of his time.

Tale of Two Cities, A (1859)

A novel by ▷ Charles Dickens. The cities are London and Paris, and the tale is a romance of the ▷ French Revolution. The hero is a young French nobleman, Charles Darnay, who has renounced his status as nephew of the Marquis de St Evrémonde from hatred of the pre-revolutionary aristocratic oppression, exemplified by his uncle. He marries the daughter of Dr Manette, who at the beginning of the novel has just been released from the Paris prison of the Bastille, where he was confined 18 years before by the secret influence of the Marquis. Darnay, owing to his aristocratic descent, nearly falls victim to the ▷ Terror but he is saved by the dissolute Englishman, Sydney Carton, who redeems himself by sacrificing his life for Darnay; this is made possible because Carton and Darnay exactly resemble each other, so that the former is able to substitute himself for the latter. The novel is notable for its scenes of revolutionary violence, for which Dickens was indebted to ▷ Thomas Carlyle's *History of the French Revolution* (1837). The revolutionaries Monsieur and Madame Defarge, and the English body-snatcher Jerry Cruncher, who makes a living by stealing corpses and selling them for medical dissection, are memorable characters.

Tel Quel

A magazine, for many years the leading French *avant-garde* journal. Its name was taken from a work by Paul Valéry (1871–1945) and it was edited by Philippe Sollers (b 1936), novelist, theorist and husband of the feminist writer, ▷ Julia Kristeva. In political terms, the magazine's sympathies were Marxist-Leninist-Maoist. It welcomed the student demonstrations of May 1968 with an issue entitled 'The Revolution, here and now' and its programme for a French 'Cultural Revolution' was backed by figures such as the composer Pierre Boulez (b 1925) and the novelist and theoretician Jean Ricardou (b 1932). *Tel Quel* provided a forum for left-wing intellectuals and gave rise to the *Tel Quel* group. Their joint publication, *Théorie d'ensemble* (1968), contained *inter alia* ▷ Jacques Derrida's essay 'La Différance', ▷ Michel Foucault's piece 'Distance, aspect, origine' (discussing Alain Robbe-Grillet and Sollers) and ▷ Roland Barthes's 'Drame, poème, roman' (on Sollers). Alongside its support for radical political and theoretical positions, the magazine did much to promote the cause of a literary counter-orthodoxy, represented by ▷ Sade, ▷ Lautréamont, Georges Bataille and Robbe-Grillet.

In the late 1970s, *Tel Quel* began to lose its

radical impetus. Sollers renounced his theoretical persuasions, sympathized with the right-wing group, Les Nouveaux Philosophes, and embraced Catholicism. From 1982, the magazine changed its name to *L'Infini* and found itself a new publisher.

Temple, Sir William (1628–99)

Statesman, diplomatist, essayist. In English literature he is especially known as the patron of ▷ Jonathan Swift, who lived at his house (Moor Park) as Temple's secretary from 1689 to 1694, and again from 1696 till Temple's death. Temple's most famous ▷ essay was his contribution to the controversy about the relative merits of ancient (*ie* Greek and Latin) and modern literature. Entitled *Of Ancient and Modern Learning*, it praised the *Letters of Phalaris* as a notable example of ancient work. Unfortunately the great scholar Bentley exposed the Letters as a forgery. Temple's embarrassment provoked Swift to come to his aid with his first notable essay, ▷ *The Battle of the Books*. Temple was a model of the cultivated aristocracy of his time, and his essays (chiefly on political matters) were regarded as setting standards for correctness and elegance of expression. His wife was Dorothy Osborne and her letters to him before their marriage (in 1655) were first published in 1888; Temple's memoirs were published by Swift in 1709.
Bib: Lives by C. Marburg and H. E. Woodbridge.

Tennant, Emma (b 1937)

Novelist. Her work combines a ▷ feminist perspective with a ▷ post-modernist use of allusion, parody, and fantasy, and in these respects has some affinity with that of ▷ Angela Carter. *The Time of the Crack* (1973) and *The Last of the Country House Murders* (1974) are both set in the future; the former is an apocalyptic satire, while the latter is a black comedy which parodies country house detective fiction. *The Bad Sister* (1978) satirizes the divisive effect upon women of social roles and expectations: the heroine finds herself inhabited by a demented other self, and the book itself is split between a prosaic account of contemporary society and a realm of dreams and fantasy. The expression of feminist revolt through a disturbed mental state has antecedents in *The Golden Notebook* by ▷ Doris Lessing, and in the work of ▷ Virginia Woolf. Many of Tennant's novels rework elements of literary classics: *The Adventures of Robina, by Herself* (1986) updating ▷ Defoe's *Roxana* and ▷ Cleland's *Fanny Hill*; *The Two Women of London* (1989) using the ▷ Jeckyll and Hyde theme of doubles; and *Faustine* (1992), creating a feminist version of the Faust story. Her other novels are: *The Colour of Rain* (1964); *Hotel de Dream* (1976); *Wild Nights* (1979); *Alice Fell* (1980); *Queen of Stones* (1982); *Woman Beware Woman* (1983); *Black Marina* (1985); *The House of Hospitalities* (1987).

Terror, The (Reign of)

The period in the ▷ French Revolution from June 1793 to July 1794 under the dictatorship of Robespierre, when many people were executed without trial merely because they were suspected of opposition to the Revolution. The term has since been applied to similar regimes in other periods and countries.

Tess of the D'Urbervilles, A Pure Woman (1891)

A novel by ▷ Thomas Hardy. The heroine is Tess Durbeyfield, daughter of a poor west-country peasant who learns that he may be a descendant of the aristocratic D'Urbervilles. The novel is about her tragic predicament between two men: Alec D'Urberville, by whom she becomes pregnant after what is effectively a rape, and Angel Clare, whom she later meets and marries. Both Alec and Angel are intruders into Tess's environment. Alec (who has no proper title to his aristocratic surname) is the son of a north-country businessman who has bought his way into the class of gentry; Angel is the son of a conventional clergyman and has dissociated himself from his background by acquiring vague liberal ideas. When Tess confesses to him that she is not a virgin, his old-fashioned prejudices overcome him and he casts her off, repenting when it is too late. Forsaken by her husband, Tess is faced by renewed assaults from Alec, whom she eventually murders. After a period of hiding with Angel, Tess is tried, condemned and executed for murder. The finest passages of the book are the episodes set in the peaceful environment of Talbothays Dairy Farm, where Tess meets Alec, and the grim surroundings of Flintcomb Ash, where she works when Angel has forsaken her. Tess is represented as the victim of cruel chance – an example of Hardy's belief that the world is governed by ironical fate – but as usual in his work it is the intruders who are the instruments of the destructive force.

Thackeray, William Makepeace (1811–63)

Novelist. He had a conventional upper-class education at a public school – Charterhouse – and Cambridge University, which he left in 1830 without taking a degree. For the next 16 years he worked as a comic illustrator and journalist, writing satirically humorous studies of London manners in *The Yellowplush Correspondence (Fraser's Magazine* 1837–8), and *Snob Papers* (▷ *Punch* 1846–7) – later published as ▷ *The Book of Snobs*; parodies of the contemporary fashion for the criminal-hero (*Catherine*, 1839, and *Barry Lyndon*, 1844); humorous travel books (*The Paris Sketch-Book* and *The Irish Sketch-Book*, 1840 and 1843), tales of humour and pathos (*The Great Hoggarty Diamond*, 1841).

His first major novel, ▷ *Vanity Fair*, came out in the year 1848 (it was published serially, as were most of his novels, and the date given is that of completion); it was a social panorama of the English upper-middle classes, satirizing their heartlessness and pretentiousness at the height of their prosperity; it was followed by novels in a similar field: ▷ *Pendennis* (1850), and ▷ *The Newcomes* (1853–5). ▷ *Henry Esmond* (1852) is a historical novel set in the reign of Queen Anne (1702–14) and represents Thackeray's strong taste for the 18th century; *The Virginians* (1859) is its sequel in 18th-century England and America. The same taste for 18th-century England is expressed in his historical lectures, *The Four Georges*, published in 1860. In 1855 he published his comic-romantic ▷ children's story, *The Rose and the Ring*. In 1860 he became editor of the famous ▷ *Cornhill Magazine*, and contributed to it *The Adventures of Philip* (1861–2), his essays *Roundabout Papers* and the novel, unfinished at his death, *Denis Duval*.

Thackeray was once considered the great counterpart to ▷ Charles Dickens in the mid-Victorian novel (the years 1850–70). Dickens conveyed a panorama of the lower half of society and Thackeray of the upper half; both were great humorists, with a strong bent for ▷ satire and a capacity for social indignation. Thackeray is now chiefly remembered for *Vanity Fair*. His imaginative intensity is seen to be less than that of Dickens and the sentimentality with which he counterbalanced his satire is the more conspicuous. Like Dickens, he opposed the ▷ utilitarianism of his age by an appeal to spontaneous affection and he tried to counterbalance it by an appeal to 18th-century proportion and elegance, but he also felt impulses of ▷ Romanticism, which in Dickens are far more uninhibited.
Bib: Ray, G. N., *Life*; Tillotson, G., *Thackeray the Novelist*; Stevenson, L., *The Showman of Vanity Fair*; Stevenson, L., (ed.) in *Great Victorians*; Studies by J. Dodd, L. Ennis, J. Y. T. Greig and G. N. Ray; Tillotson, G., and Hawes, D. (eds.), *The Critical Heritage*; Carey, J., *Thackeray: Prodigal Genius*.

Thiong'o, Ngugi wa
   ▷ Ngugi wa Thiong'o.

Thirty-nine Articles
The code of religious doctrine which all clergy of the ▷ Church of England have to accept. In 1553 42 articles were laid down; these were reduced to 39 in 1571.

Thomas, D. M. (Donald Michael) (b 1935)
Novelist and poet. His best-known work is *The White Hotel* (1981), a fictional account of the life of one of ▷ Freud's patients, making extensive use of fantasy and controversial use of the Holocaust, a subject to which he returns in *Pictures at an Exhibition* (1993). His other works include *Ararat* (1983); *Swallow* (1984); *Selected Poems* (1983); *Flying into Love* (1992).

Thrale, Hester Lynch (1741–1821) (later Hester Thrale Piozzi)
Born Hester Salusbury, she married Henry Thrale in 1763. Thrale was a wealthy brewer with political ambitions, and when in the following year they made the acquaintance of ▷ Samuel Johnson, Johnson assisted Thrale by writing election addresses. The friendship between Johnson and Hester Thrale became very close, and at various times Johnson lived with the family in their home at Streatham. When Thrale died in 1781, Hester Thrale remarried. Gabriel Piozzi, her second husband, was an Italian musician, and her friends and family vociferously disapproved. The marriage ended the friendship with Johnson, who sent her an anguished letter on the subject.

Hester Thrale's biography of Johnson, *Anecdotes of the late Samuel Johnson*, was strongly contested by ▷ Boswell when it appeared in 1786; his motives in challenging her account probably stem from literary rivalry. Hester Thrale was also an energetic letter writer, and *Thraliana*, a selection of anecdotes, poems, jests and journal entries, covers the period 1776–1809.
Bib: Clifford, J. L., *Hester Lynch Piozzi*.

Times, The
British newspaper. It was founded in 1785 as *The Daily Universal Register*, and took its present name in 1788. In the 19th century it took the lead in contriving new methods of collecting news (notably through the employment of foreign correspondents), and its succession of distinguished editors and contributors gave it an outstanding status among British newspapers. Though always in private ownership, it has always claimed to be an independent newspaper rather than a party one. The literary style of one of its staff writers caused it to be nicknamed 'The Thunderer' in the 19th century; the novelist ▷ Anthony Trollope consequently refers to it as *The Jupiter* in his novels, since this king of the gods was known as the Thunderer by the ancient Romans. *The Times* publishes *The Times Literary Supplement* and *The Sunday Times* weekly. Its outlook is traditional and often conservative in political terms. In 1981 it was bought by Rupert Murdoch's News International Group, which also publishes the tabloid newspaper *The Sun*.
   ▷ Newspapers.

Titles of nobility
The main titles of nobility, or peerages, in Britain are as follows, from lowest to highest in order of seniority:
Baron. A title originating with the Norman aristocracy after the Conquest.
Viscount. Originating in 1440.
Earl. As old as the title of Baron, and equivalent to the title of Count in other countries of Europe. An Earl's wife is known as a Countess.
Marquess. Originating in 1385.
Duke. Originating in 1337, when the title Duke of Cornwall became a title regularly awarded to the heir to the throne. The title of Duke was restricted to the royal family until the end of the 14th century.
   All the above-mentioned titles are hereditary, with the exception of life peerages (always Baron or Baroness) originally awarded for political purposes. Whether inherited or awarded for the life of the holder, such a title carried with it the right to sit in the House of Lords.
   The title of knight or baronet (hereditary knighthood) is not a title of nobility; the holder is, politically speaking, a commoner, *ie* represented in accordance with his vote in the House of Commons, and entitled to seek election as a member of it.

To the Lighthouse (1927)
A novel by ▷ Virginia Woolf. The setting is a house used for holidays by Mr and Mrs Ramsay. The household consists of themselves, their eight

children, and a number of their friends, of whom
the most important is the painter Lily Briscoe.
The novel dispenses with plot and is organized
into three parts, dominated by two symbols – the
lighthouse out at sea, and Lily's painting of the
house, with Mrs Ramsay sitting in the window with
her son James. The parts are entitled 'The Window',
'Time Passes', and 'The Lighthouse'. The first
part is dominated by Mrs Ramsay, who is intuitive,
imaginative, and possesses a reassuring and vitalizing
influence upon people and their emotions. The
mysterious lighthouse flashing through the darkness
is associated with her. In the interval represented
by the second part of the novel, corresponding to
the war years 1914–18, she dies, and the third part
is dominated by Mr Ramsay who is intellectual,
philosophical, and lonely. The lighthouse seen as a
practical instrument, close at hand and by daylight,
is associated with him. The middle section concerns
the empty house, subject to the flux of time and its
changes. Lily Briscoe, the artist, stands aloof from
Mrs Ramsay's embracing influence and seeks to
fix the constantly changing relationships of people
and objects in a single composition; she completes
the picture in the last sentence of the book, when
the Ramsay son, James, achieves reconciliation
with his father and with the lighthouse seen as
fact. Mrs Ramsay, in her role as wife and mother,
and Lily, single and an artist, represent alternative
possibilities for a woman's way of life.

The story is told through the ▷ stream of
consciousness technique – in the minds of the
characters, especially James, Lily, and Mrs
Ramsay. The novel, one of the most original of the
many fictional experiments in the 1920s, is partly
autobiographical, and based on Virginia Woolf's
own family. Mr and Mrs Ramsay are her father and
mother, ▷ Leslie Stephen and his second wife.

Toft, Eric John (b 1933)

Novelist and short-story writer. Born and brought
up in Hanley, Stoke-on-Trent, in the Potteries
district of the English Midlands, he was educated at
Hanley High School and Magdalen College Oxford,
and taught at Brighton College of Education. In a
sequence of powerful ▷ realist novels, set primarily
in the Potteries, he has created a story of change
and development in English working-class life from
1917 to the present: *The Bargees* (1969); *The Wedge*
(1972); *The Underground Tree* (1978); *The Dew* (1981).
The House of the Arousing (1973), a volume of short
stories, draws on the author's experience of travelling
in Malaysia.

Tolkien, J. R. R. (John Ronald Reuel) (1892–1973)

Novelist, philologist and critic. From 1925 to 1945 he
was Professor of Anglo-Saxon at Oxford University,
and during the 1930s belonged to 'The Inklings',
a literary society whose other members included
▷ C. S. Lewis. From 1945 to 1959 he was Merton
Professor of English Language and Literature at
Oxford. His large-scale fantasy of another world
The Lord of the Rings (1954–6) has gained enormous
popularity. His other novels are: *The Hobbit* (1937)
and *The Silmarillion* (1977).

Tolstoy, Count Leo Nikolaevitch (1828–1910)

Russian novelist, dramatist and moral philosopher.
What are usually considered his two greatest novels,
War and Peace (1865–9) and *Anna Karenina* (1875–7),
have a spaciousness, profundity and balance of sanity
which have caused them to be used as a standard
by which the achievements of other novelists can be
measured. The scale of greatness is to be accounted
for not only by the depth of Tolstoy's mind but by
the breadth of his experience, which in turn owes
something to Tolstoy's position in Russian society
and the critical phase of history through which
Russia was passing during his lifetime. He belonged
to the class of Russian landed gentry and was partly
educated by French tutors, a fact which, taken with
the sensitivity of the Russian intelligentsia to West
European culture, gave him a broader understanding
of the issues of civilization in his time than was
characteristic of most Western novelists. Tolstoy
frequented the intellectual and fashionable classes of
Russian society, travelled abroad and spent the years
1851–7 in the Russian army, seeing service in the
Crimean War against Britain, France and Turkey.
Two other absorbing aspects of his experience were
the problems of Russia's vast peasantry, emancipated
from serfdom in 1861, and the prominence of
religion in Russian life.

Tolstoy was early influenced by the thought of
▷ Jean-Jacques Rousseau and this, combined with
his own direct experience of peasant life, developed
in him a strong faith in spontaneous, simple
living in contrast to the sophisticated, fashionable,
educated society which he also knew well. From
1876, disillusioned by worldliness and inspired by
the example of the peasants, he thought increasingly
about the religious interpretation of experience,
but his thinking turned him away from the Russian
Orthodox Church to a religion of his own, based on
the words of Christ (in *Matthew* 5:39) 'that ye resist
not evil'. Tolstoy's religion was thus pacifistic and
on the side of self-abnegation; it did not admit the
existence of life after death nor a personal God, his
belief being that the kingdom of God is within man.
He described his religion in *What I believe in* and *A
Short Exposition of the Gospels*; a complete account of
his conversion is given in *A Confession* (1879–82), and
he also published stories inspired by his inner life at
the time, *The Memoirs of a Madman* and *The Death of
Ivan Ilyich*. In *What is Art* (1896), he expounded his
doctrine that good art works by re-creating in the
reader the fine emotions of the writer, bad art by
similarly conveying the bad ones. Tolstoy's influence
may be seen in the works of G.B. Shaw, ▷ E.M.
Forster and ▷ D.H. Lawrence.

▷ Russian influence on English fiction.

Tom Brown's Schooldays

▷ Rugby School.

Tom Jones, a Foundling (1749)

A novel by ▷ Henry Fielding. The central character
begins life as a baby of unknown parentage (*ie* 'a
foundling') who is discovered in the mansion of the
enlightened landowner, Squire Allworthy. Allworthy
adopts him, and he grows up a handsome and

generous-hearted youth, whose weakness is his excess of animal spirits and inclination to fleshly lusts. He falls in love with Sophia Western, daughter of a neighbouring landowner, Squire Western, who is as gross, ignorant and self-willed as Allworthy is refined and enlightened. Western intends Sophia for Blifil, Allworthy's nephew, a mean and treacherously hypocritical character, who is supported against Tom by two members of Allworthy's household, the pedantic chaplain Thwackum and the pretentious philosopher, Square, who counterbalance each other. They succeed in disgracing Tom, whom Allworthy is persuaded to disown. The central part of the novel describes his travels and amorous adventures in the company of a comic follower, Partridge. Sophia also leaves home, to escape from Blifil, and nearly falls victim to a plot by Lady Bellaston, with whom Tom has become amorously entangled, to place her in the power of Lord Fellamar. Tom is eventually identified as the son of Allworthy's sister; the plots against him are brought to light; he is received again by Allworthy, and marries Sophia.

The novel, like its predecessor by Fielding, ▷ *Joseph Andrews*, is a 'comic epic', offering a wide range of social types of the age, all of whom are presented as permanent human types rather than as unique individuals, as 19th-century novelists would show them. Fielding's method is expository; he does not attempt to create illusions of characters with interior lives of their own, but expounds behaviour, with the aid of prefatory essays to his chapters, always light-heartedly, but always with a view to exhibiting basic human motives as they have always existed, rather in the manner of the 17th-century comedies of humours and of manners. He owes much to ▷ Cervantes's comic romance ▷ *Don Quixote* and to the studies of contemporary morals and manners by the painter ▷ William Hogarth. To some extent the book was written in rivalry to ▷ Samuel Richardson's ▷ *Clarissa*, a novel written in a tragic spirit and in a strenuous and idealistic moral tone. It was Fielding's tendency to 'correct' Richardson's idealism and partly self-deceiving moral rigour by reducing events to more usual human experience and intrepreting this in the light of tolerant comedy instead of grand tragedy; for instance, Lovelace, in *Clarissa* is a human fiend (though also an interesting psychological study) where Tom is merely a healthy young man whose licentiousness is bound up with his virtue of outgoing sympathy and generosity. Thus, *Tom Jones* is both one of the first important English novels, a new kind of imaginative work, and one that embodies highly traditional values.

Tory
▷ Whig and Tory.

Tract
An ▷ essay or treatise, usually short but published singly and usually on a religious subject. The most famous in English are the *Tracts for the Times* (1833–41) by a group of devout Anglicans, Hurrell Froude, Pusey, Keble, and ▷ Newman. Their purpose was to increase the spiritual dignity and independence of the ▷ Church of England by the revival of doctrines stressed in the 17th century but since then largely neglected, with the consequence, as the authors believed, that the Church was losing its spiritual identity and was exposing itself more and more to secular ▷ utilitarianism and domination by the state. Newman's was the predominating spirit in the group; he started the series, and he wrote *Tract XC*, which caused scandal by emphasizing the closeness of the Anglican to the older Catholic tradition, and thus ended the series.
▷ Oxford Movement.

Tractarian Movement
▷ Oxford Movement; Tract.

Trade Union
The history of British trade unionism may be divided into four main phases.

1 Impulses to start trade union associations arose from the early development in England of capitalist industrialism and the congregation of workers in factories in the later 18th century. At first workers associated chiefly in small ways for such purposes as mutual insurance against unemployment in what were known as 'Friendly Societies'. Nonetheless the movements were regarded with suspicion by the government as possible centres of revolution, especially after the ▷ French Revolution of 1789–93. Consequently Parliament passed the Combination Acts of 1799–1800 to forbid the formation of unions. These laws were repealed in 1824, and thereafter the activity of forming associations amongst employees was a lawful one, but this did not include striking.

2 The next phase was a brief one, and ended in failure. An attempt was made, at first successfully, to form a national union of workers called the Grand National Consolidated Trades Union; this came to nothing after the trial and transportation of six Dorsetshire agricultural labourers in 1834 on the charge of administering false oaths; they are the so-called 'Tolpuddle Martyrs' whose memory is still revered.

3 For 30 years industrial relationships remained stormy, but until 1890 working-class energies were taken up with other movements such as the ▷ Chartist Movement and the Anti-Corn Law League. A respectable kind of Trade Unionism developed among skilled workers, such as the Amalgamated Society of Engineers. In the 1860s a number of outrages in the industrial north of England again alerted public suspicion of trade unions, and the government appointed an inquiry into their activities. This was so reassuring that unionism began to prosper. In 1868 the Trades Union Congress (T.U.C.) was started; thus began a new phase in which trade unionism again had a national organization capable of coordinating the interests of industrial workers.

4 The last phase, since 1870, has been the development of Unionism to its present state: for a time it was one of the most powerful factors of national life. Two laws gave the movement new legal security; that of 1871 legalized action through strikes, and that of 1876 gave unions the right to exist as

corporations, able to own property and to defend their rights corporatively (*ie* not as mere collections of individuals) in courts of law. Two important developments followed in the last 20 years of the century: the growth of unions where they were most needed, among unskilled workers; and the formation of a political party, the Labour Party, which had union interests at heart and strong financial support from the T.U.C. Modern unions federated in the T.U.C. have a membership of around 9 million, and unions have tended to amalgamate, so that, while they are much larger than in the 19th century, they are fewer in number. The Industrial Relations Act, which came into force in 1972, was a move towards bringing the question of industrial action within a legal framework. By the late 1980s Union power was severely diminished, owing to opposition by the Tory government.

▷ Industrial Revolution.

Transference

This is the term used in ▷ Freudian psychoanalysis, along with others such as ▷ 'condensation' and ▷ 'displacement', to describe one of the mechanisms whereby unconscious desires enter into ▷ consciousness. It is given a more specific meaning in the relationship between analyst and patient (analysand) in psychoanalysis, as part of the process of removing those impediments to the recollection of repressed impulses on the part of the latter. Situations and emotions are relived during the treatment and these ultimately express the indestructibility of unconscious fantasies. In the structure of a literary work, repetitions of particular situations and events, and even the duplication of 'character', can be explained as kinds of transference of the 'unconscious fantasies' of the writer. In this way desires and feelings which in psychoanalysis occur in the life of the patient, are *transferred* onto the analyst/reader, producing a repetition or re-enactment of them. For example, in Shakespeare's *Hamlet* 'madness' is transferred from the hero onto Ophelia, and an analysis of that process situates the reader/spectator within a complex process of the construction of male/female subjectivity as a result. The issue can be complicated further if the writer 'Shakespeare' is taken to be the 'analysand' projecting unconscious desires and feelings through his 'characters' onto the 'analyst' (reader/spectator).

Transferred epithet

▷ Figures of Speech.

Transgression

As a term used in contemporary literary criticism, it is generally associated with the concept of ▷ 'subversion' insofar as it denotes the act of crossing accepted boundaries. Applied to literary texts it is usually taken to refer to any form of behaviour or representation which challenges the dominant values encoded within that text.

Translation

The life of English literature has always issued from a combination of strong insular traditions and participation in wider European traditions. Translation has always been the principal means of assimilating European literatures into the English idiom, and it was particularly important before the 18th century, when the main streams of European cultural life were flowing through other languages. The aim of translators was then less to make an accurate rendering than to make the substance of foreign work thoroughly intelligible to the English spirit; the character of the translation thus proceeded as much from the mind of the translator as from the mind of the original writer. If the translator had a strong personality, the translation often became a distinguished work of English literature in its own right. Translators with less individuality often produced work of historical importance because of its contemporary influence on English writing.

From the 14th to the 18th centuries, English writers were constantly absorbing the ancient and contemporary Mediterranean cultures of Europe, and worked on the literatures of France, ancient Rome, Italy, ancient Greece, and Spain. There is no distinct boundary between translation and adaptation; ▷ Chaucer brought English poetry into accord with French and Italian poetry partly by freely adapting work in those languages. His outstanding work of translation is his version of Guillaume de Lorris's *Roman de la Rose*. French ceased to be the first language of the English upper classes in Chaucer's lifetime, but the English nobility continued to have strong ties with French aristocratic culture, and thus translations from French prose were in demand in the 15th and 16th centuries. Caxton, the first English printer, published many English versions of French romances. The outstanding 15th-century work of English prose was Malory's *Morte d'Arthur*, which Caxton published, and which is partly a translation and partly an adaptation. The work of translation was an important influence on the development of a fluent English prose medium, and this is evident in the difference between Wycliff's 14th-century translation of the Latin Bible and ▷ Tyndale's version of the New Testament from the Greek (1525). Lord Berner's translation of Froissart's *Chronicles* is another distinguished example of English prose development in the 15th and early 16th centuries.

Printing, the Renaissance, and the rise of new educated classes, all helped to expand translation in the 16th century, which was the first major period for translation of classical writers. These had been of central importance in the Middle Ages too (King Alfred and later Chaucer had translated ▷ Boethius's *De Consolatione Philosophiae*) but knowledge of them had now widened and standards of scholarship had advanced. The first important rendering in English of a great classical poem is that of ▷ Virgil's ▷ *Aeneid* by the Scots poet, Gavin Douglas (1553).

Chapman's ▷ *Iliad* (1611) and ▷ *Odyssey* (1615) are impressive, but have less intrinsic merit as English literature. Ovid had long been a favourite poet, and translations were made of his poems by Arthur Golding (1565–67) and Christopher Marlowe (published 1597). But in the 17th and 18th centuries the best-known English version of

Ovid was George Sandys's version of *Metamorphoses*, completed in 1626. Ovid had an extensive influence on poets, including Shakespeare; the Roman dramatist Seneca's influence on the poetic drama, both as a philosopher and as a dramatist, was equally conspicuous, and it was no doubt helped by the historically important but otherwise undistinguished *Ten Tragedies*, translated by various hands and published between 1559 and 1581. Among the most distinguished prose translators of ancient literature in this period was Philemon Holland, remembered especially for his version of Pliny's *Natural History*, which he published in 1601. The best known of all, especially for his value to Shakespeare but also for the quality of his writing, is ▷ Thomas North, whose version (1579) of Plutarch's *Lives* was made not from the original Greek but from the French of Jacques Amyot.

Translations from the contemporary European languages were also numerous in the 16th and early 17th centuries, and indicate the constant interest of English writers in foreign literatures. Sir John Harington translated Ariosto's *Orlando Furioso* in 1591. Tasso's *Jerusalem Delivered* was translated as *Godfrey of Bulloigne* or *The Recovery of Jerusalem* (1600); Castiglione's very influential *Il Cortegiano* was translated by Sir Thomas Hoby (1561). The best known of all these contemporary works is John Florio's rendering of the *Essays* of ▷ Montaigne, published in 1603. Part I of Cervantes's ▷ *Don Quixote* was translated in 1612 before Part II was written; the whole work was three times translated in the 18th century, by Motteux (1712), Jarvis (1742) and ▷ Smollett (1755). The first three books of ▷ Rabelais's *Gargantua and Pantagruel* were translated notably by Thomas Urquhart; two were published in 1653, and the third in 1694. The fourth and fifth books were added by Motteux in 1708.

Many of the translations made before 1660, especially those in prose, were marked by a super-abundance of words, characteristic of much English writing in the 16th and 17th centuries: the originals tended to be amplified rather than closely rendered. After the Restoration in 1660, writers attached importance to discipline and control, and to emulating these virtues as they were exemplified in the old Latin poets and in contemporary French writers of verse and prose.

Some of the more distinguished translations of the first 30 years of the 19th century, such as Cary's translation in blank verse of ▷ Dante's ▷ *Divine Comedy* (1805–12), and ▷ Coleridge's version of Schiller's *Wallenstein* (1800), show the new kinds of influence on the Romantic writers. After 1830, translation became a kind of net for hauling in exotic writings, and its field became very wide, *eg* ▷ Richard Burton's ▷ *Arabian Nights* (1885–88) and ▷ William Morris's translation of the Icelandic Sagas (beginning in 1869), as well as many new versions of the ancient Greek and Latin authors. Two vices of the period were a tendency to make a foreign work express essentially English 19th-century sentiment and to use peculiarities of style under the mistaken impression that because they gave strangeness to the work, therefore they gave the translation

an air of authenticity – a fault which ▷ Matthew Arnold criticizes in his fine essay *On Translating Homer* (1861). The really influential translations were more often of contemporary writers, such as those by Constance Garnett of the Russian novelists ▷ Tolstoy and ▷ Turgenev (▷ Russian influence on English fiction); William Archer's translations of Ibsen; and Scott Moncrieff's fine rendering of ▷ Proust's great novel under the title of *Remembrance of Things Past*. These works bring us into the 20th century, in which translation has been cultivated with a new sense of its importance and difficulties. Among the most eminent of modern translations are Ezra Pound's *Cathay* (from the Chinese) and his version of the Old English *The Seafarer* (1912), and Willa and ▷ Edwin Muir's translations of Kafka (1930–49). In the 20th century translation has become more widespread, making texts in many languages readily available, and this has included critical as well as fictional works. However, while providing us with an international ▷ best-seller list, regularly including writers such as Umberto Eco (▷ Italian influence on English fiction) and Gabriel García Marquez (▷ Spanish influence on English fiction), there is a danger that a new saleable canon will be created and more marginal texts will remain trapped by linguistic barriers.

Travel literature

This large branch of English literature may be conveniently discussed under these headings: **1** fantasy purporting to be fact; **2** factual accounts; **3** travel experiences regarded as material for art.

1 *Literature of fantasy purporting to be fact.* So long as extensive travel was rarely undertaken, it was possible for writers to present accounts of fantasy journeys and to pass them off as fact without much fear of being accused of lying. Thus a 14th-century French writer wrote the *Travels of Sir John de Mandeville*, which is a work of fiction or compilation from narratives by other travellers, but purporting to be an account of genuine journeys written by Mandeville himself. The work was translated into English in 1377, became extremely popular, and was long regarded as genuine. Long after the extravagances of the story were seen to be falsehoods, Mandeville, a purely fictional English knight, was thought to be the genuine author.

2 *Literature of fact.* By the second half of the 16th century, the great Portuguese, Spanish and Italian explorers had discovered the Americas and greatly extended knowledge of eastern Asia. Liars could still find large, credulous audiences, but the facts were marvellous enough to require no distortion. Writers also began to feel strong motives for publishing truthful accounts. Thus ▷ Richard Hakluyt published his *Principal Navigations, Voyages and Discoveries of the English Nation* in 1589, partly for patriotic reasons. The English had been slow to start on exploratory enterprises, although by this time they were extremely active. Hakluyt, finding that the reputation of his nation stood low among foreigners in this field, wanted to demonstrate the reality of the English achievement, and at the same time to stimulate his fellow-countrymen to further endeavours. His book is really a compilation of accounts by English explorers; an enlarged edition came out in 1598, and a still further enlarged edition was published under the title of *Hakluytus Posthumus, or Purchas his Pilgrims* by Samuel Purchas in 1625. The accounts vary from those by accomplished writers like Sir Walter Raleigh to others by writers with little or no experience of writing; they constitute an anthology of early English descriptive writing in which the writers are concerned with the truthfulness of their accounts rather than with entertaining or deceiving the reader. Other examples of this new kind of honest and truthful handling of descriptive language are Captain John Smith's history of the founding of the colony of Virginia, *General History of Virginia, New England, and the Summer Isles* (1624). The contrast between this newer, plainer style more characteristic of the ▷ pamphleteers can be seen in accounts of travels in Europe by Thomas Coryate (?1577–1617), author of *Coryate's Crudities*, and Fynes Morison (1556–1630), author of *Itinerary*: Coryate is deliberately strange and fanciful, though an acute observer, but Morison is much more straightforward.

The steady growth of English overseas trade kept alive a taste for accounts of great voyages throughout the 17th and 18th centuries. At the end of the 17th century Captain William Dampier published three books which included the imaginations of ▷ Defoe and ▷ Swift: *New Voyage Round the World* (1697), *Voyages and Descriptions* (1699), and *Voyage to New Holland* (1703). Dampier was an excellently direct and clear writer of his own books, but Lord George Anson's voyage round the world (1740–44) was written up from his journals by his chaplain, R. Waters, and depends on the singularly dramatic events for its force of interest. The last of these outstanding accounts of great voyages were the three undertaken by Captain James Cook, *A Voyage Round Cape Horn and the Cape of Good Hope* (1773), *A Voyage Towards the South Pole and Round the World* (1777), and *A Voyage to the Pacific Ocean* (1784). With the discovery of the coastlines of Australia and New Zealand, the main outlines of world geography became known, and the interest of both explorers and their readers passed to the mysteries of the great undiscovered interiors of the continents. With this change in subject matter, a change also came over the style of travel literature.

3 *Travel literature as material for art*. Mungo Park's *Travels in Central Africa* preserves the plain, unaffected style of 18th-century travel literature, but subsequent work, for instance ▷ Richard Burton's book about India, *Scinde or the Unhappy Valley* (1851), and his later books about his exploration of East and Central Africa (*First Footsteps in East Africa*, 1856; *The Lake Region of Central Africa*, 1860) bear more of the stamp of the author's personal feelings and reactions. Partly, no doubt, this arose from the new importance attached to authorial personality due to ▷ Romanticism; also the contact with strange physical environments and peoples (in contrast to the emptiness and impersonality of the ocean) inevitably drew out authorial response. At all events, travel literature began to draw nearer to autobiography. Not only 'darkest Africa', but the Arabian peninsula

fascinated writers. Burton was one of the first Englishmen to visit the holy city of Mecca, and wrote an account of it in *Pilgrimage to Al-Medinah and Mecca* (1855). Later Charles Doughty tried to restore the vividness of 16th-century to 19th-century prose in his *Arabia Deserta* (1888), and ▷ T. E. Lawrence's *Seven Pillars of Wisdom* (1926), an account of the Arab struggle against the Turks in World War I belongs to the same tradition of art made from travel in Arabia. George Borrow (1803–81) did not go so far for his material, but he went a stage further than these writers in combining travel literature and imaginative art, so that it is difficult to know whether or not to classify his books with the novel. They are full of personal encounters with individuals, chiefly among the common people; he was particularly interested in the ▷ gipsies (*The Gypsies in Spain*, 1841; *Lavengro*, 1851; *Romany Rye*, 1857) and he was talented at conveying the intimate texture of the life of a country (*The Bible in Spain*, 1843; *Wild Wales*, 1862). James Kingslake's account of his travels in the lands of the Eastern Mediterranean, *Eothen* (1844), and Lafcadio Hearn's *Glimpses of Unfamiliar Japan* (1894) are two other examples of travel literature which owe their classic status as much to the author's art and personality as to their subject matter. Thus travel literature became a natural subsidiary form for the novelists; it is among the best writing of ▷ R. L. Stevenson and ▷ D. H. Lawrence. ▷ Joseph Conrad, who, as a sailor, was a professional traveller during the first part of his adult life, may be said to have completely assimilated the literature of travel into the art of the novel.

Increasing ease of travel since World War II has greatly increased the amount of travel writing. Eric Newby's *A Short Walk in the Hindu Kush* (1959) has became a classic. Other important contemporary travel writers include Bruce Chatwin (1940–89).

Treasure Island (1883)
A romance by the novelist ▷ Robert Louis Stevenson, perhaps his best known work. It is set in the 18th century and the plot concerns the search for hidden treasure buried in a desert island by an actual 18th-century pirate, Captain Kidd. The story contains the basic elements of a traditional English romance – treasure, pirates, adventure, a desert island – and belongs to a line of desert island literature descending from ▷ *Robinson Crusoe*.

Treatise of Human Nature
▷ Hume, David.

Tremain, Rose (b 1943)
Novelist, playwright and short-story writer. Educated at the Sorbonne and the University of East Anglia, she has worked as a teacher, assistant editor and researcher and since 1980 has been a full-time writer and part-time lecturer in creative writing. Her novels are in most cases unsentimental accounts of the loneliness and emotional relationships of ageing or unfulfilled characters: *Sadler's Birthday* (1976); *Letter to Sister Benedicta* (1978); *The Cupboard* (1981); *The Swimming Pool Season* (1985); *Sacred Country* (1992). *Restoration* (1989) is a historical novel, set in

the Restoration period and narrated by the King's fool. Volumes of short stories: *The Colonel's Daughter* (1984); *The Garden of the Villa Mollini* (1987). Drama: *Mother's Day* (1980); *Yoga Class* (1981); *Temporary Shelter* (1984). She has also written books for children, a biography of Stalin and *The Fight for Freedom for Women* (1973).

Tressell, Robert (pseudonym of Robert Noonan) (? 1870–1911)

Novelist. Tressell worked as a painter and decorator, and is remembered for his posthumously published novel *Ragged Trousered Philanthropists* (1918; first full edition 1955). A ▷ naturalistic account of a year in the life of a town's working men (in the decorating and undertaking businesses), the novel is a powerful attack on the greed of employers (the philanthropy in the title is an ironic reference to the exploited workers), and has become a classic of working-class and left-wing fiction.

Bib: Alfred, D. (ed.), *The Robert Tressell Lectures, 1981–88.*

Tricoteuses

The 'knitters', from the French *tricoter* = to knit. A name given to the women who brought their knitting to the debates in political assemblies during the ▷ French Revolution. In English fiction, Madame Defarge in Dicken's novel ▷ *A Tale of Two Cities* knits the names of those who are to meet death by the guillotine into an endless scarf.

Trilby (1894)

Novel, written and illustrated by ▷ George du Maurier. It tells the story of Trilby O'Ferrall, an artists' model in Paris with whom all the art students fall in love. She comes under the mesmeric influence of Svengali, a German-Polish musician who makes her famous. His spell is so strong that when he dies she loses her voice, fails and dies herself. The novel enjoyed enormous popularity and was dramatized in 1895. Trilby's soft felt hat with an indented crown is the original 'trilby'.

Triple-decker/three decker

A novel published in three volumes. This was the dominant form of fiction during the period from the 1820s until 1894, and the novels were distributed primarily via the ▷ circulating libraries, such as ▷ Mudie's.

Tristram Shandy, The Life and Opinions of (1760–7)

A novel by ▷ Laurence Sterne, published in successive volumes, I to IX from 1760 to 1767. Any attempt to paraphrase the 'plot' of this eccentric masterpiece would be doomed, like trying to net the wind. Sterne deliberately flaunts his freedom to tease and surprise the reader with his interruptions and digressions. 'If I thought you was able to form the least judgement or probable conjecture to yourself, of what was to come in the next page,' he writes, 'I would tear it out of my book.' Tristram, the nominal hero, plays little part in the action of the book, though as the authorial voice of the narrative his random associations determine its form. As a

character he is not born until volume IV, and never gets beyond infancy. The bulk of the novel is taken up with the theories and hobby-horses of Tristram's father, Walter Shandy, and his uncle Toby; these two brothers appear like comic caricatures of ▷ Locke's theory of the association of ideas. Each of them is trapped in his own private world of associations; for Walter these centre on his obsessions with noses and names; for Toby they are based on military science and his quest to determine the circumstances of the wound in the groin which he suffered at the siege of Namur. The other characters, Dr Slop, Corporal Trim, parson Yorick, Mrs Shandy and the Widow Wadman are swept up in the general associations – many of them sexual – of noses and wounds, breeches and ballistics.

'Shandy' is an old Yorkshire dialect word meaning crackbrained, odd or unconventional, and it suits this book perfectly. With its black and marbled pages, its flash-backs and interpolations, its asterisks, blanks and dashes, this novel defies any attempts to unscramble a straightforward narrative theme. The effect on the reader is to suggest that the conventional notion of a biographical narrative, with a distinct beginning, sequence of events and ending, is untrue to human experience which finds that beginnings do not really exist, and orderly sequences are frustrated by every kind of distraction. Tristram Shandy has been called 'the greatest shaggy-dog story in the language' and a satiric essay on human misunderstanding. It is a joyous, exuberant cock-and-bull story, in which the juggler Sterne shamelessly leads the reader by the nose on an endless quest for the elusive copula that links cause and effect, intention and achievement.

Troilus and Criseyde

▷ Chaucer composed *Troilus and Criseyde* some time in the 1380s (before 1388). His contribution to the medieval Troy story was not to produce an English version of the history of Troy, from beginning to end (in the tradition of Benoît de Sainte-Maure and Guido de Columnis), but to refract the Troy story through that of the relationship between Troilus ('little Troy') and Criseyde, organized as an epic love-tragedy, with a five-book division and elaborate apostrophes and a palinode. The siege of Troy and past Trojan and Greek history form a significant backdrop to, and determining influence on, the conduct and outcome of their affair.

The outline of Chaucer's narrative is taken from ▷ Boccaccio's *Il Filostrato* but in addition to developing the background to their story, Chaucer changes some aspects of the presentation of its key characters, not least in the role of the narrator himself, who no longer presents Troilus's experience as a cipher for his own but adopts the familiar 'ineffectual' Chaucerian role. Pandaro, the go-between figure in Boccaccio's version, is a cousin of Criseyda and a peer of Troilus; in Chaucer's version, Pandarus is Criseyde's uncle and, though still a lover himself, plays the role of an avuncular confessor to Troilus. His engineering power is increased on a local domestic scale and his role as stage-manager of their affair is enhanced, but his controlling powers are markedly circumscribed at the same time: he may be on hand literally to help Troilus into bed with Criseyde but his resources diminish as the larger context of the siege intervenes in the lovers' lives. Criseyde is more vulnerable, naive and sensitive to the pressures around her than her counterpart in Boccaccio; there is no precedent for her presentation as a woman under siege within a siege. Troilus is a more bookish lover in Chaucer's version, who has a lyrical tradition of love sentiments at his command, and his songs and monologues in Book III celebrate his relationship with Criseyde in metaphysical terms. However, Chaucer is not presenting a Divine Comedy in this narrative but a pagan history, and one in which human love is subject to the forces of time and change.

The organization of the poem into five books reflects the progress of the love affair: the broad opening panorama of Book I gives Troilus and Criseyde a place in the wider history of Troy; the focus narrows in Books II and III, which chart the increasing self-involvement of the lovers as they create their own private world within Troy. Book IV marks the interruption of the historical world into their affairs, with the plan to exchange Criseyde; and the final Book sketches the 'changing' of Criseyde, her transferral to the Greek camp and engagement with Diomedes, Troilus's reluctant perception of her change, and his final change, as he ascends the spheres after his death and laughs at the behaviour of mortals, their loves and longings, on little earth. The book ends with its 'maker' committing it to the care of his peers 'Moral Gower', and 'philosophical Strode'.

Bib: Windeatt, B. (ed.), *Troilus and Criseyde*; Salu, M. (ed.), *Essays on Troilus and Criseyde*.

Trollope, Anthony (1815–82)

Novelist. The unbusinesslike qualities of his father, a barrister who forsook the law and ruined himself in farming, caused his childhood to be poverty-stricken, although his mother, ▷ Frances Trollope kept her family from the worst hardships by writing. Trollope himself was a prolific novelist, and though he worked seriously his *Autobiography* (1883) deeply offended the taste of the time by his frank statement that the writing of novels was a craft and a business, like making shoes, with nothing exalted or inspired about it. He was a strong admirer of the novels of ▷ Thackeray and shared Thackeray's contempt for the commercial arrogance of the British upper-middle classes. On the other hand, unlike Thackeray, Trollope had also strong faith in the traditional virtues and values of the English gentry, and several of his novels are about how the gentry class opened its ranks (through marriage, and after a struggle) to the best elements of less-privileged classes. His first novel was published in 1847, but it was in 1855 that he published the first of his most famous series, the Barsetshire novels – ▷ *The Warden*. The series continued with *Barchester Towers* (1857); *Dr Thorne* (1858); *Framley Parsonage* (1864); *The Small House at Allington* (1864); ▷ *The Last Chronicle of Barset* (1867). It is in these books that he displays his very conservative values most winningly and convincingly;

they present a world of very solidly portrayed church dignitaries and landed gentry and show a loving care for fully-rounded characterization. The world he shows with such conviction was perhaps already passing, and in presenting it Trollope does not forget the weaker side of its values nor the assaults and encroachments upon it of political adventurers and the more vulgar of the middle class. His later work became more political, for instance *Phineas Finn* (1869); *The Eustace Diamonds* (1873); *Phineas Redux* (1874); *The Way We Live Now* (1875); *The Prime Minister* (1876); *The Duke's Children* (1880). Some critics consider that this group of his novels is unduly neglected; the setting is commonly London, which Trollope thought a source of evil, and the tone is more critical of society. *The Way We Live Now* reflects his disillusionments most strongly; it includes a powerful portrait of a fraudulent tycoon in Melmotte, and is not so much political as a devastating social study.

Trollope lost favour after his death, but regained strong popularity in the mid-20th century. This was because this period of insecurity and war made Trollope's world of traditional values seem very reassuring. Yet critics seldom allow him rank equal to his contemporary ▷ George Eliot; he does not even pretend to insight as deep, or tragic vision, though he is often subtle and fond of pathos.

Bid: Sadleir, M., *Life*; Bowen, E., *Trollope: a new Judgement*; Cockshut, A.O.J., *Anthony Trollope: a Critical Study*; Gerould, W.G. and J.T., *Guide to Trollope*; Smalley, D. (ed.). *The Critical Heritage*; Wall, S., *Trollope and Character*; Glendinning, V., *Trollope*.

Trollope, Frances (1780–1863)

Born Frances Milton in Somerset, the daughter of a vicar, she married in 1809 and had six children, including the future novelist ▷ Anthony Trollope. She began writing when she was over 50 to support the family in the face of her husband's financial disasters and published in all some 114 books on travel, and novels. Despite the financial success of her first book she worked extremely hard, from before dawn each day, writing and caring for her family. She visited America for an extended period and lived in France, Austria and Italy (meeting the Brownings, ▷ Dickens and Walter Landor) for a few years. Her writing owed its popularity perhaps to her scathing views of Americans, also to its exuberant quality and her rather coarse, humorous women. *Domestic Manners of the Americans* (1832) brought her fame and popularity; *Paris and the Parisians* (1835), *Vienna and the Austrians* (1838) and *A Visit to Italy* (1842) were also successful. Her novels include *The Vicar of Wrexhill* (1837), portraying a mixture of vice and religion, *The Widow of Barnaby* (1838) and *The Life and Adventures of a Clever Woman* (1854).

Bib: Trollope, F.E., *Frances Trollope: Her Life and Literary Work from George III to Victoria*; Johnston, J., *The Life, Manners and Travels of Fanny Trollope: A Biography*.

Turgenev, Ivan Sergeevich (1818–83)

Novelist and playwright. Born in Orel, central Russia, educated at Moscow and St Petersburg

Universities and Berlin, Turgenev, after a brief spell in the civil service, devoted himself to literature. In 1852 he was imprisoned for a month for his article on the death of ▷ Gogol and was subsequently banished to his estate. He left Russia in 1861 and, apart from a few visits, remained in self-imposed exile, largely in Baden Baden and Paris, where he died, although he continued to write of Russia and his own class, which he perhaps sensed was doomed. The novels have something of an autumnal character. He fell in love with the singer Pauline Garcia Viardot who did not give him an easy life, and this is also reflected in the novels in the theme of a strong woman and rather weak man. He knew ▷ Flaubert, ▷ George Sand and other French writers, and from 1847 visited England. He was widely read in English, admiring Shakespeare greatly; he knew and valued ▷ Charles Dickens and ▷ George Eliot, and was acquainted with ▷ William Thackeray, ▷ Anthony Trollope, ▷ Thomas Carlyle, Robert Browning, Alfred Tennyson, the Rossettis and others. He admired, met and influenced ▷ Henry James, and influenced many writers including ▷ George Moore, ▷ Joseph Conrad and ▷ Virginia Woolf. He published a little poetry in 1838 but his first published prose was *A Hunter's Notes* (1847–51). He wrote a series of novels illuminating social and political issues: *Rudin* (1856), *A Nest of Gentlefolk* (1859), *On the Eve* (1860), *Fathers and Sons* (1862), *Smoke* (1867) and *Virgin Soil* (1877). His short stories include 'Asya' (1858), 'First Love' (1860) and 'Torrents of Spring' (1870); his most famous and critically acclaimed play is *A Month in the Country* (1850).

▷ Russian influence on English fiction.

Turn of the Screw, The (1898)
A ▷ novella by ▷ Henry James, published in *The Two Magics*. It is a ghost story, about a governess given sole charge of two children, Miles and Flora, in a country house named Bly. She comes to believe that she has to contend with the evil, ghostly influence of two dead servants, Peter Quint and Miss Jessell, over the children, who are ostensibly angelic but invisibly corrupted. Flora is taken away to London by the housekeeper, but Miles, when confronted by the governess with her belief, dies in her arms. The possibility that the governess is an hysteric who hallucinates the ghosts and herself manipulates the children provides a second layer of meaning. This layer is, however, in Benjamin

Britten's opera of the same title, weakened by the fact that the 'ghosts' are given singing parts and appear on stage. James's story, which he described as 'a trap for the unwary', is a masterpiece of ambiguity throughout.

Turpin, Richard (Dick) (1706–39)
A famous English highwayman and thief, hanged at York for horse-stealing. He was greatly romanticized by the novelist ▷ Harrison Ainsworth in his novel *Rookwood* (1834), in which Turpin's famous ride from London to York on his mare, Black Bess, is described. The ride, like other romantic episodes told about him, is fictional.

Tutuola, Amos (b 1920)
Nigerian novelist. Tutuola was born in Abeokuta, Western Nigeria, where he was educated at an Anglican school. He served in the RAF in Lagos (1943–46) and later worked for the Nigerian Broadcasting Corporation. His first novel, *The Palm-Wine Drinkard and His Dead Palm-Wine Tapster in the Dead's Town* (1952), was one of the first Nigerian novels in English and received praise for its vivid and playful use of language. The patronizing tone of some early critical treatments of his work provoked hostility to it in Africa, but it was defended by ▷ Chinua Achebe in *Morning Yet on Creation Day* (1975). His other novels are: *My life in the Bush of Ghosts* (1954); *Simbi and the Satyr of the Dark Jungle* (1955); *The Brave African Huntress* (1958); *The Feather Woman of the Jungle* (1962); *Abaiyi and His Inherited Poverty* (1967); *The Witch-Herbalist of the Remote Town* (1981); *Pauper, Brawler and Slanderer* (1987). Stories: *The Village Witch Doctor* (1990). Other publications: *Yoruba Folktales* (1986).
Bib: Lindfors, B., *Critical Perspectives on Amos Tutuola*.

Tyndale, William (? 1492–1536)
A translator of the Bible; his version was a principal basis for the Authorized Version of 1611. He was a convinced ▷ Protestant. His other works include: *Parable of the Wicked Mammon* (1528), *Obedience of a Christian Man* (1528), and *Practice of Prelates* (1530). These works influenced the forms that extreme Protestantism, ▷ Puritanism, took in England. While on a visit to the Netherlands, he was arrested in 1535 and burned as a heretic.

▷ Bible in England.

U

Ulysses

A novel by ▷ James Joyce. It was first published in
Paris in 1922, but was banned in England for its
alleged obscenity until 1936. In a number of ways
the book is an innovation in methods of presenting
human experience through the novel form, and
it is also the most ambitiously comprehensive
attempt to do so, except perhaps for Joyce's next
book, ▷ Finnegans Wake (1939). 1 It is an attempt
to present a character more completely than ever
before. The story shows in immense detail the life
of a man during a single day of 24 hours. The
man is Leopold Bloom, a Jew of Hungarian origin
living in Dublin; the day is 16 June 1904. 2 To do
this requires a method of conveying the process of
thinking; Joyce's method has become known as the
▷ stream of consciousness technique, suggested to
him by the work of a French novelist, Dujardin. 3
At the same time as seeking to create imaginatively
'a whole individual', Joyce seeks to make this
individual representative, by setting him against
the background of the oldest extended portrait of a
man in European literature. He does this by making
Bloom analogous with ▷ Homer's Odysseus, and
by dividing the book into episodes, each of which
corresponds to one in the ▷ Odyssey, though not in
the same order.

4 Joyce varies the technique of written expressions
so as to make his language as close an analogy as
possible to the modes of modern human experience.
Thus in the fierce drunken episode 15 (Circe),
the method is dramatic dialogue; in the fatigued
anti-climax of 17 (Ithaca), the questionnaire is
used; in the final episode 18 (Penelope), the
stream of consciousness is used to the full, without
punctuation.

No human experience is complete without
relationship; Bloom is a lonely man, with numerous
casual acquaintanceships. However, two deeper
relationships dominate his story: there is the
physical relationship with his wife, Molly,
whose fidelity he more than mistrusts, and a
spiritual affinity with Stephen Dedalus, whom
he does not meet till near the end, but who
is a lonely young man unconsciously seeking
a father, as Bloom is a lonely middle-aged
man wanting a son. Molly is analogous to
Penelope in the Odyssey and Stephen relates to
Telemachus, the wife and son respectively of
Odysseus.

In some respects Joyce is carrying the artistic
devotion of the French novelists to an extreme:
Ulysses is an elaborate formal construction of
immense seriousness, showing a dedication
to art for its own sake comparable to that of
the novelist ▷ Flaubert; it is also a realistic
exercise, carrying to extreme the naturalism of
▷ Zola.

Uncommercial Traveller, The

A collection of tales, sketches and essays,
descriptive of places, society and manners, by
▷ Charles Dickens. They were published in ▷ All
the Year Round and reissued in book form in 1861
and 1868.

Under the Greenwood Tree (1872)

The first of the ▷ Wessex novels by ▷ Thomas
Hardy. The story is a village love affair between a
schoolmistress, Fancy Day, and Dick Dewy, son of
a 'tranter' or carrier of goods. It includes the theme
of the rivalry of the village orchestra, who have
hitherto played the music in church services, with
Fancy, who takes over from them by substituting
the harmonium. The story is thus slight and idyllic
compared to Hardy's later Wessex stories but it is
written with delicacy and insight. The title is the
first line of a song in Shakespeare's As You Like It.

Under the Volcano

▷ Lowry, Malcolm.

Under Western Eyes (1911)

A novel by ▷ Joseph Conrad. It is set in pre-
revolutionary Russia and in Switzerland, and is
told through the character of the English-language
teacher, who witnesses many of the events in
Switzerland, and reconstructs those in Russia
from the notebooks of the central character, Kyrilo
Sidorovitch Razumov. Razumov is the illegitimate
son of a Russian nobleman, and has been brought
up in the household of a Russian priest. He is
given to understand that if he behaves well, his
real father will assist him in his career; accordingly
he is studious at the university, and keeps himself
rigorously isolated from student politics. His
enigmatic silence on political subjects, however, is
misinterpreted by the radical students as signifying
that he is a strongly committed supporter of
revolutionary activity; thus, when one of them,
Victor Haldin, commits a political assassination
and takes refuge with him, Razumov tries to
disembarrass himself by betraying Haldin to the
police. The police, however, will not allow him
to return to his solitary studies; instead they send
him to Switzerland, ostensibly as a revolutionary
emissary, but actually to spy on the Russian
revolutionaries in exile there. He finds them to be
a circle composed partly of flamboyant or brutal
self-seekers, such as Peter Ivanovitch, Madame de
S., and Nikitin (nicknamed Necator, the killer).
But there are also idealists of complete integrity,
including Victor Haldin's sister, Nathalie Haldin.
Nathalie is a pupil and friend of the English
language teacher, who thus becomes involved in the
story. She welcomes Razumov as a revolutionary
hero, and the friend of her brother, for whose
death he has in fact been responsible. Razumov
is tormented by his guilt, his love and admiration
for Nathalie, his horror and contempt of the
debased elements among the revolutionaries, and
the seeming impossibility of recovering his integrity
and living otherwise than by false appearance.
Eventually he confesses the truth to Nathalie and to
the revolutionaries, and is reduced to total deafness
by two blows from Nikitin. Nathalie is appalled, but
understands him. She has told her English friend:
'You belong to a people which has made a bargain
with fate, and wouldn't like to be rude to it.' The
Western (British and Swiss) attitude to politics and
the individual is such that fateful choices such as

the one forced on Razumov are not demanded. His drama 'under the Western eyes' of the English language teacher is the drama of a nation where the individual is not permitted to withdraw from political decision into private life. Razumov spends the rest of his days as a sick man in Russia, respected by the best of the revolutionary circle whom he has known in Switzerland, and cared for devotedly by one of them.

Unfortunate Traveller, or the Life of Jack Wilton, The (1594)

A ▷ romance by ▷ Thomas Nashe, published in 1594. Wilton begins as a page in the court of Henry VIII, and then travels through Europe as adventurer, soldier of fortune, and hanger-on of the poet Henry Howard Surrey. It is one of the first notable ▷ picaresque tales in English. Among other historical figures, apart from Surrey, Wilton meets ▷ Sir Thomas More, ▷ Erasmus and Pietro Aretino; he witnesses historical events, such as the struggle between the Anabaptists of Munster and the Emperor Charles V, and describes a plague in Rome. The book is extremely episodic, and Jack himself has no consistent character. The narrative begins as a sequence of mischievous pranks in the manner of the popular 'jest-books' of Nashe's time, and at the other extreme goes into brutally realistic descriptions of rape and of the plague in Rome. Nashe's story is remarkable for its creation of a self-conscious narrative voice, and in its awareness of its status as a text which is created by the activity of a reader. At the same time, its delight in the grotesque, and in a constantly reiterated discourse of bodily distortion and pain, serves to make the work one of the most vivid attempts at linguistic refashioning in the 16th century.
Bib: Rhodes, N., *Elizabethan Grotesque*.

Unitarianism

A doctrine of religion that rejects the usual Christian doctrine of the Trinity, or three Persons in one God (the Father, the Son, and the Holy Ghost), in favour of a belief in the single person of God the Father. It originated in Britain in the 18th century and was in accord with the rationalistic approach to religion of that century. The first Unitarian church opened in London in 1774; many English Presbyterians (in the 16th and 17th centuries one of the largest sects outside the Church of England) became Unitarians.

Universities

Until 1828, England possessed only two universities, those of Oxford, founded from Paris in the 12th century, and of Cambridge, founded largely by an emigration from Oxford in the early 13th century. Scotland's first university was St Andrew's (1411), followed by Glasgow (1451), Aberdeen (two – 1494 and 1593) and Edinburgh (1582). That of Dublin (Trinity College) was opened in 1591. Medieval universities were in the hands of the clergy, which mattered little when the Church was undivided and Christian belief was almost universal.

After the Reformation in the mid 16th century, Catholics were excluded, and from 1660 (the Restoration) all Protestants who were not members of the ▷ Church of England were excluded from the English universities, though not from the Scottish ones, since the Anglican Church was not established there.

Dissenters established their own academies in the 18th century, and in the early 19th century a movement was started among prominent Dissenters to establish the University of London, which opened in 1828.

Since then, numerous universities have been founded, many of them since 1945; there is one in Wales, and there are forty-one in England, eight in Scotland, and two in Northern Ireland. The university population in 1985–6 was 310,000.

This rapid rise of new universities has reduced the pre-eminence of Oxford and Cambridge (sometimes referred to jointly as 'Oxbridge') which preserved their superior prestige at least until 1945. The universities of the 19th and earlier 20th centuries were disdainfully designated 'provincial', and were popularly known as 'red-brick' in allusion to their architecture.

Oxford and Cambridge, which became open to the members of all religious sects in 1871, represented an aristocracy of intellect, but their students were also drawn disproportionately from the richer classes, since, until 1945, state grants of money to poorer students were relatively few, and life at these ancient universities was comparatively expensive. Attendance at prestigious colleges, especially when preceded by attendance at one of the more important ▷ public schools (eg Eton, Harrow, Winchester, ▷ Rugby) was regarded by many people as of even greater social than intellectual importance. It was not uncommon for commercial families (like the Vincys in George Eliot's ▷ Middlemarch) to send their sons to Oxford and Cambridge to acquire no more than the manners of their social superiors. In the 1960s, however, the prevailing radicalism among students led them to react violently against this kind of 'Oxbridge' appeal, and some elements in Oxford and Cambridge are themselves seeking to free their reputations from the suggestion of social privilege and conservatism.

Before 1945, British universities were singularly independent of state control; this independence is now threatened by their extensive and growing dependence on government finance. In the 1980s severe cutbacks and even departmental closures have been enforced, though it is still felt politically unacceptable to force the closure of a whole institution.

University Wits

A group of young men in the reign of Elizabeth I who were educated at either Oxford or Cambridge Universities, and then embarked on careers as men of letters. Their names were John Lyly, dramatist and writer of the kind of romance known as the ▷ Elizabethan novel; George Peele, dramatist; ▷ Robert Greene, dramatist; ▷ Thomas Lodge, who tried most of the branches of contemporary literature; ▷ Thomas Nashe, novelist and ▷ pamphleteer; Christopher Marlowe, dramatist. To these, the name of Thomas Kyd is sometimes added, although he is not known to have attended a university. Lyly was a writer for court circles, but the others were representative of a new kind of writer (of which Shakespeare was also an example) who sought his fortune with the general public. Most of them had some kind of influence on, or relationship with, Shakespeare: Lyly used the kind of sophisticated diction which Shakespeare partly emulated and partly parodied in *Love's Labour's Lost* and elsewhere; Greene wrote a mellifluous blank verse which anticipates some qualities in the earlier verse of Shakespeare, and was the author of the 'novel' *Pandosto*, source of *The Winter's Tale*; Lodge wrote *Rosalynde*, the source of *As You Like It*; Marlowe was the greatest architect of the dramatic blank verse medium; Kyd possibly wrote the first version of *Hamlet*.

Unreliable narrator
▷ Narrator, unreliable.

Unsworth, Barry (b 1930)
Novelist. Unsworth was born in Durham and educated at Manchester University. He worked for several years for the British Council in Athens and Istanbul, and Greece and Turkey have often provided the settings for his fiction, which deals with the passions and moral ambiguities arising from the meetings of cultures and ideologies. His novels include: *The Partnership* (1966); *The Hide* (1970); *Mooncranker's Gift* (1974); *The Big Day* (1976); *Pascali's Island* (1980); *The Rage of the Vulture* (1982); *Stone Virgin* (1985); *Sugar and Rum* (1988). The Booker Prize winning *Sacred Hunger* (1992) is a sea-tale in the tradition of ▷ Conrad and > Golding, recounting the voyage of an 18th-century slaver; its wealth of historical detail and strongly sustained narrative make for a powerful indictment of the slave trade, and, by implication, the exploitation engendered by an unfettered and amoral free market.

Unto This Last (1860–2)
Four essays on political economy by ▷ John Ruskin. They were intended to be part of a larger treatise, but their publication in the ▷ *Cornhill Magazine* aroused so much hostility that the editor (▷ William Thackeray) discontinued them. The reason for the anger was that Ruskin (an art critic) was, as it seemed to the public, stepping out of his professional function in order to attack the predominant economic theory of trading relationships, which he was considered by the middle-class public unqualified to do. The middle classes were inclined to believe that the subject had been reduced to the clear elements of a science by the political economists and ▷ utilitarian thinkers of the first half of the 19th century – men such as ▷ Jeremy Bentham, Ricardo, ▷ Malthus, James and ▷ John Stuart Mill. Ruskin pointed out that

what was called 'political economy' was really 'commercial economy' and that it was untrue since it omitted facts of human nature, unjust since it unduly favoured the employing middle class and uncivilized since it omitted the cultural values that ought to underlie wealth. He found space to praise ▷ Charles Dickens's novel ▷ *Hard Times*, itself an attack on Utilitarianism. In spite of the hostility and scorn of Ruskin's contemporaries, much of his thinking in these essays has been accepted by later sociologists and economists. The Indian leader Mahatma Gandhi admitted a debt to *Unto This Last*, as did a number of the early leaders of the British Labour Party.

Utilitarianism
A 19th-century political, economic and social doctrine which based all values on utility, *ie* the usefulness of anything, measured by the extent to which it promotes the material happiness of the greatest number of people. It is especially associated with ▷ Jeremy Bentham, at first a jurist concerned with legal reform and later a social philosopher. Followers of the movement are thus often called 'Benthamites' but Bentham's disciple ▷ John Stuart Mill used the term 'Utilitarians'. Owing to their habit of criticizing social concepts and institutions on strictly rational tests, the leaders of the movement were also known as Philosophical Radicals.

Utilitarianism dominated 19th-century social thinking, but it had all its roots in various forms of 18th-century ▷ rationalism. In moral philosophy, ▷ David Hume had a strong influence on Bentham by his assumption that the supreme human virtue is benevolence, *ie* the disposition to increase the happiness of others. Psychologically, Bentham's principle that humans are governed by the impulses to seek pleasure and avoid pain derives from the associationism of David Hartley. But Bentham and his associates believed that the virtue of benevolence, and human impulses towards pleasure, operate within social and economic laws which are scientifically demonstrable. Bentham accepted ▷ Adam Smith's reasoning in *The Wealth of Nations* (1776) that material prosperity is governed by economic laws of supply and demand, the beneficial operation of which is only hindered by governmental interference. ▷ Malthus, in his *Essay on the Principle of Population* (1798), maintained that it is mathematically demonstrable that population always tends to increase beyond the means of subsistence, and Ricardo, a friend of Bentham's, applied Malthus's principle to wages, arguing that as the population increases wages will necessarily get lower, since the increase is more rapid than that of the wealth available to support the workers. Smith, Malthus and Ricardo were masters of what was called the science of Political Economy, and the inhuman fatalism with which they endowed it caused it to be known as the ▷ dismal science. However, it was not dismal for the industrial middle class of employers, whose interests it suited; they were already 'utilitarians' by self-interest and thus willing converts to the theory.

Thus the operation of Utilitarianism in the 19th century was paradoxical. It liberated society from laws which were inefficient survivals from the past (the Elizabethan ▷ Poor Laws) but it replaced them by laws that often operated with cold inhumanity (*eg* the Poor Law of 1834). It reduced senseless government interference with society but its concern with efficiency encouraged a bureaucratic civil service. It liberated the employers but it was often unsympathetic to the interests of the employees. Its principle was benevolent but its faith in reason often made it indifferent to individual suffering. The inhumanity of the creed, and its indifference to cultural values unless they could be shown to be materially useful, caused it to be vigorously attacked by leading writers between 1830 and 1870, including ▷ Thomas Carlyle, ▷ Charles Dickens, ▷ John Ruskin and ▷ Matthew Arnold. But perhaps its sanest and most lucid critic was John Stuart Mill; though himself a Utilitarian to the end of his life, he saw the philosophical limitations of the movement and exposed them in his essays in 1838 on Bentham, and on ▷ Samuel Taylor Coleridge whom he admired as the father of the opposing tendency of thought. Mill's essay *Utilitarianism* (1863) emphasized that some kinds of pleasure are better than others – a distinction Bentham failed to make – and that the highest virtue in humanity is 'the desire to be in unity with our fellow creatures'. Mill was aware, as Bentham had not been, of the importance of the artistic imagination, in particular of poetry, in a civilization.

Our society is still in many ways utilitarian but as a systematic philosophy Utilitarianism did not outlast the 19th century. The last important figures connected with the movement are the philosophers ▷ Herbert Spencer and ▷ Leslie Stephen.

▷ *Unto This Last.*

Utopia (1516)

A political and philosophical treatise by ▷ Sir Thomas More, in the form of an account of an imaginary, newly discovered country. It was written in Latin, and translated into English (after More's death) in 1551; it had already been translated into French (1530), and such was the European fame of the book that Italian, Spanish and German versions also appeared.

The idea of a fictional country was no doubt stimulated by recent Italian, Portuguese, and Spanish exploration, and in particular by ▷ travel literature such as Amerigo Vespucci's account of his travels (1507). Philosophically, the book is a pure product of Renaissance ▷ humanism, and like other products of that movement, it was inspired by the ancient Greek philosopher ▷ Plato. The land of Utopia is the Platonic ideal of a country, only to be realized on the assumption that man is basically good. Private property is replaced by communal ownership; there is complete freedom of thought; war is regarded as abominable, and to be used only in the last resort, when it should be waged as effectively as possible, even, if necessary, by unscrupulous means. Earthly happiness is glorified;

the good life is the life of mental and physical fulfilment, rather than the medieval Christian life of self-denial and asceticism, but the Utopians are humane and benevolent, not self-indulgent. There is perfect mutual respect, and women receive the same education as men.

Utopian fiction

More's ▷ *Utopia* introduced into the English language the word 'utopian' = 'imaginary and ideal', and started a succession of 'utopias' in English literature. The idea of inventing an imaginary country to be used as a 'model' by which to judge earthly societies did not, however, originate with More, but with his master the Greek philosopher ▷ Plato, who did the same in his dialogues *Timaeus* and the *Republic*. *Utopia*'s most notable successors in the 17th century were Bacon's unfinished *New Atlantis* (1626), in which science is offered as the solution for humanity, and James Harington's *Oceana* (1656), which put forward political ideas that were to have a powerful influence in America. In the 20th century, ▷ H. G. Wells was, in his earlier days, a vigorous utopian: *Anticipations* (1901), *A Modern Utopia* (1905), and *New Worlds for Old* (1908). Just before Wells, ▷ William Morris's *News from Nowhere* (1890) is a noteworthy socialistic utopia.

However, from the 18th century, much utopian literature is satirical, intended to give warning of vicious tendencies of society rather than to exemplify ideals. An example of this is Bernard de Mandeville's (1670–1733) *Fable of the Bees* (1714), about the downfall of an ideal society through the viciousness of its inhabitants; and Swift's ▷ *Gulliver's Travels* (1726) can be put in the same class. In the 19th century the best known examples are Samuel Butler's ▷ *Erewhon* (1872) and *Erewhon Revisited* (1901). In the 20th century, fears for the future of mankind have predominated over the optimism about inevitable progress which was more typical of the 19th century, and this has led to a new kind of utopian writing, portraying our own society set in the future, showing our fears realized. For this kind of work, the term 'dystopia' has been invented. The first striking example was ▷ Aldous Huxley's *Brave New World* (1932), about the deadness of a civilization which has come to be dominated by scientific technology; ▷ E. M. Forster's tale *The Machine Stops* has a similar theme, and both are written in reaction against H. G. Wells's optimism about technology. ▷ George Orwell's *1984* is a nightmare about 20th-century political totalitarianism, the grimmer, because Orwell brought the date of his anticipated society so close to the time of writing. A number of 20th-century women writers have explored utopian and dystopian worlds as a means of satirizing or criticizing sexual relations in the modern world, or as a way of exploring new possibilities for gender relations and identities. ▷ Doris Lessing's science fiction explores utopianism, while Marge Piercy's *Woman On The Edge of Time* juxtaposes an ideal future with the grim present. American feminist writer Charlotte Perkins Gilman's *Herland* (1916) is perhaps the most famous feminist utopia, whilst ▷ Margaret Atwood's *The Handmaid's Tale* is a feminist dystopia.

▷ Science Fiction.

Valley of Humiliation; Valley of the Shadow of Death

Two places of trial through which pilgrims had to pass in ▷ John Bunyan's ▷ *Pilgrim's Progress*. The Valley of the Shadow of Death is a reference to Psalm 23 in the Bible (Authorized Version).

Vanity Fair

A town through which the pilgrims pass in ▷ John Bunyan's ▷ *Pilgrim's Progress*. It is a vivid representation of the pleasure-loving worldliness of society in the reign of Charles II, seen from a ▷ Puritan point of view. 'Vanity' in the biblical sense is equivalent to triviality and worthlessness, and it includes all the good things of this world, when compared to the values of the heavenly world of the spirit: 'Vanity of vanities, saith the Preacher, vanity of vanities; all is vanity.' (*Ecclesiastes* 1:2). The town is a great market (fair) for these vanities; the townsmen are not only trivial but heartless, and also bitterly resentful when the pilgrims despise their vanities. Faithful is martyred there, but in Part II he has left disciples behind him and they are to some extent tolerated. Perhaps this is Bunyan's way of acknowledging that the spirit of his age was becoming more tolerant of the Puritans.

Vanity Fair (1847-8)

A satirical historical novel by ▷ William Thackeray published in monthly issues. The title, borrowed from ▷ John Bunyan's ▷ *Pilgrim's Progress*, shows that Thackeray's subject matter is the worldly, materialistic society of his time. He shows his men of religion to be either hypocrites or deluded. Dissenters, the descendants of Bunyan, include old Osborne, the arrogant, sombre and unfeeling businessman; ▷ evangelicalism is represented by the hypocritical Bute Crawley.

The novel is subtitled 'A Novel without a Hero' and there is in fact nothing heroic about the society that Thackeray presents. However, its heartlessness and snobbery are skilfully manipulated by the central character, Becky Sharp, an ingenious and vigorous adventuress of poor parentage. She begins her socially ambitious career with a friendship with Amelia Sedley, the soft-hearted, weakly sentimental heroine of the book. Becky tries to marry Jos Sedley, Amelia's brother, a foolish but rich 'nabob'. Frustrated in this, and reduced to being a governess, she then makes love to the mean and avaricious Sir Pitt Crawley, but makes the mistake of marrying his second son, Rawdon, a gallant but ignorant and dissolute man who, despite his incapacity, is later made Governor of the unhealthy Coventry Islands. Her marriage does not prevent her from pursuing her social ambitions still further by becoming the mistress of the aristocratic and degenerate Lord Steyne. Her ambitions are eventually defeated but she manages to end up as a respected member of society.

Amelia Sedley first marries the worthless young officer, George Osborne, who is killed at the battle of Waterloo. The only fine human values are characterized by his friend, Dobbin, an English ▷ gentleman in the moral rather than the social sense, who eventually becomes Amelia's second husband. The novel is an impressive, if negative, landscape of upper-class society in the first half of the 19th century; its best parts are those that concentrate on Becky Sharp and are written with a keen, sardonic humour. The novel is commonly regarded as Thackeray's most successful work.

Verne, Jules (1828-1905)

French author of adventure stories and ▷ science fiction, notably *Voyage to the Centre of the Earth* (1864), *Twenty Thousand Leagues Under the Sea* (1869) and *Round the World in Eighty Days* (1873).

Vicar of Wakefield, The (1761-2)

A novel by ▷ Oliver Goldsmith written 1761-2 but not published until 1766. Dr Primrose, a good-natured and innocent vicar, lives in comfortable circumstances with his wife and six children. Then their life is overturned by a series of disasters, reducing them to poverty and disgrace; the vicar endures his troubles with sweetness and stoicism. Eventually, they are restored to prosperity by the friendship of a benefactor, Mr Burchill, who turns out to be Sir William Thornhill, whose nephew had originally caused their misfortunes. The novel has conventionally been interpreted as a simplistic moral fable, the chief virtue of which is its sentimentality. Recent critics however suggest an element of satiric irony, drawing parallels with Goldsmith's complex creations in other genres.

Victoria

Queen of Britain, 1837-1901. She came to the throne at 17, and had the longest reign in British history. It was also a highly successful reign, for it re-established the prestige of the monarchy, which at her accession was neither popular nor respected. The political conflicts between the monarchy and Parliament between 1603 and 1714 has concluded with the victory of Parliament, and England was a constitutional monarchy, with the king reduced to symbolic status. However, Victoria's grandfather, George III (1760-1820) was insane for the last ten years of his life; her uncle George IV (1820-30) had disgusted the nation by his immoral conduct, thus leaving a bad impression which the reign of his successor and brother, William IV (1830-37), had been too short to redeem. The other members of the royal family, including Victoria's father, the Duke of Kent, were also in low esteem. Yet when Victoria died in 1901, the monarchy was more popular and respected than ever before, and she succeeded in establishing a model of behaviour for the sovereign which has preserved the popularity of royalty to the present day.

Victoria had dignity and a fine sense of behaviour on public occasions; moreover, she could be pointed to as setting a standard for the domestic virtues of rectitude of personal conduct and devotion to her husband and family, virtues greatly esteemed by the middle classes at the period when these classes dominated national life. She married Prince Albert of Saxe-Coburg-Gotha in 1840; he died in 1861, by which time they had had nine children. Their court was dull, but it was dignified and decorous.

Victoria was able to perform the role of a monumental symbol for the nation during the 60 years of the greatest prosperity, power and influence that it had ever known. During her reign the British Empire was built up to its greatest extent, and for an empire a monarchy is a much more effective symbolic head than a president. This her Prime Minister, ▷ Benjamin Disraeli, well understood when he induced Victoria to adopt the title Empress of India in 1877. Her relationships with her ministers were not always as happy as they were with Disraeli, but the disagreements were mainly behind the scenes. Her jubilees of 1887 and 1897 were great national occasions, on which the sovereign was identified with the nation as never before since the reign of Elizabeth I.
    ▷ Victorian period.

Victorian period
The period coinciding with the reign of Queen Victoria (1837–1901) is commonly divided into three.
    1 *1837–1851: the Early Victorian period.* This was a time of struggle and growth; the age of the ▷ Chartist Movement and the Anti-Corn Law League (▷ Corn Laws), but also of the building of railways. The ▷ 'Hungry Forties' ended with the Great Exhibition in 1851, the culmination of the ▷ Industrial Revolution, which Britain achieved earlier than any other nation.
    2 *1851–1870: the Mid-Victorian period.* Britain had passed the time of the worst popular discontents, and was at her height in wealth, power, and influence.
    3 *1870–1901: the Late Victorian Period.* A less fortunate period, when other nations (especially Germany and the United States) were competing with Britain industrially. Britain had acquired much territory in consequence of her pursuit of trade; she now became imperialist in her jealousy and mistrust of other imperialist nations, and the period ended with the imperialist South African War (Boer War) of 1899–1901. Economically, Britain was becoming less the 'workshop of the world' than the world's banker. Domestically, partly in consequence of the second Parliamentary ▷ Reform Bill (enfranchising the town workers – 1867) and the Education Act (establishing a state system of education – 1870) it was a time of popular political and social movements which included the building up of ▷ trade unions and the formation of the Labour Party.
    Culturally, the Victorian period was the age when change rather than stability came first to be accepted as normal in the nature of human outlook. Ancient foundations of religious belief were eroded, among intellectuals, by scientific advances, especially the biological discoveries of ▷ Darwin (▷ Agnosticism). The educated classes and their leaders sought to establish guiding values for living; it was the period of the 'Victorian Sage' – ▷ Carlyle, ▷ Mill, ▷ Arnold, ▷ Ruskin, and Tennyson – educating the social conscience.

The relationship of the individual to himself, to other individuals, and to society at large is the study to which the novel is admirably adapted; the English novel developed in the works of ▷ Gaskell, ▷ Thackeray, ▷ Trollope, the ▷ Brontës, ▷ Dickens, ▷ George Eliot and ▷ Henry James into the art form of the age. Culturally and in many ways socially, the Victorian period saw the outset and display of the problems which the 20th century has had to solve.

Villette (1853)
A novel by ▷ Charlotte Brontë. The title is the name by which the author disguises Brussels, capital of Belgium, where she had been employed as a teacher in a school kept by Monsieur and Madame Héger. The novel is based on her experiences and is told in the first person by the central character, Lucy Snowe. Lucy is a young girl who begins life in secure circumstances and then, as the result of disasters, finds herself deprived of family and means of financial support. After a period of living as companion to an old lady, who dies, she sets forth to seek her fortune in the foreign city of Villette, where she is first nursery governess to the children of Madame Beck, who keeps a school, and then one of the teachers. The main part of the novel is the story of her stormy relationship with Paul Emmanuel, Madame Beck's cousin and her colleague in running the school. She ends up with her own school, established by Monsieur Paul, and as his fiancée, but the conclusion is left uncertain. The novel is remarkable in three respects. First, like Charlotte Brontë's ▷ *Jane Eyre*, it is ▷ autobiographical in a new and interesting sense: the reader experiences the events entirely through the mind and feelings of Lucy, who thus provides the psychological atmosphere, while at the same time allowing the reader to make judgements of events independently of Lucy's prejudices. Secondly, the love affairs are so presented that they are shown to be a process of self-discovery by which the lovers learn to know themselves and thus enlarge their personalities. This is especially true of Lucy and Paul but it is also true of secondary affairs in the book; only the trivial personalities fail to undergo this development and are proved trivial by their failure. Thirdly, the novel shows the clash of two cultures – the Protestant ▷ Anglo-Saxon culture of Lucy Snowe and the Latin, Catholic culture of Paul Emmanuel – and the ways in which the personalities of each transcend their differences so as to achieve mutual admiration and love, although their cultural opposition remains as strong at the end as at first.
Bib: Newton, J., 'Villette' in *Feminist Criticism and Social Change* (ed. Newton and Rosenfelt).

Vindication of the Rights of Woman
    ▷ Wollstonecraft, Mary.

Virgil (Publius Vergilius Maro) (70–19 BC)
Roman poet. He was born on a farm not far from Mantua in northern Italy, and is often referred to as 'the Mantuan'. He greatly esteemed the

farming section of society to which he belonged, and valued the farming way of life. He was not, from the place of his origin, of Roman descent, but belonged to the first generation of Italians who felt a consciousness of nationhood, with Rome as their capital. By 40 BC he was in Rome, under the patronage of the wealthy Roman patrician (nobleman), Maecenas. He wrote the first work for which he is famous, the *Eclogues* or *Bucolics*, between 42 and 37 BC; their title merely means short, selected pieces, but his intention was to praise the Italian countryside as the Greek poet, Theocritus had praised the countryside of Sicily. The *Georgics* (37–30 BC), written at the instigation of Maecenas to encourage a sense of the value of a stable and productive society, is devoted to the praise of the farming way of life. The ▷ *Aeneid* written during the remainder of his life, is an ▷ epic about the travels of Aeneas the Trojan, and emulates ▷ Homer's ▷ *Odyssey*. Its purpose is not merely this, but to relate the Romans to the great civilization of the Greeks, on which their own civilization was so much based, by making Aeneas the ancestor of the Roman nation. The *Aeneid*, with the epics of Homer, is one of the basic poems in the culture of Europe and is taken as a standard for what was, perhaps until the 19th century, regarded as the noblest form of literature.

Not even Homer exceeds Virgil in the extent of his influence and prestige in the 20 centuries of European culture. He did not, like all the Greek poets and many of the Roman ones, have to wait for the Renaissance to 'discover' him, for he was esteemed in the Middle Ages, when, indeed, he became a legend. This was partly owing to his *Fourth Eclogue* which celebrated the birth of a child who was to restore the Golden Age, a poem which in the Christian centuries was supposed to be a prophetic vision of the birth of Christ. He was thus regarded as more than merely a pagan poet, and ▷ Dante chose him as his guide through Hell and Purgatory in his 13th-century Christian epic, the *Divine Comedy* (▷ *Divina Commedia*). In direct literary influence, he was, even more than Theocritus, the pattern for pastoral poetry, and even more than Homer, for the epic, although he was himself a student of both.

Voice

One of the five categories in which ▷ Genette analyses narrative discourse, voice is concerned with the way in which the act of narrating is 'implicated in the narrative'; the study of voice in a novel therefore attends to the identity and nature of the ▷ narrator and the real or implied audience or narratees.

W

Wain, John (b 1925)
Novelist, poet and critic. Prose fiction: *Hurry on Down* (1953); *Living in the Present* (1955); *The Contenders* (1958); *A Travelling Woman* (1959); *Nuncle and Other Stories* (1962); *The Young Visitors* (1965); *Death of the Hind Legs and Other Stories* (1966); *The Smaller Sky* (1967); *A Winter in the Hills* (1970); *The Life Guard* (1971); *The Pardoner's Tale* (1978); *Young Shoulders* (1982); *Where the Rivers Meet* (1988); *Comedies* (1990). Criticism: *Preliminary Essays* (1957); *Essays on Literature and Ideas* (1963); *The Living World of Shakespeare* (1964). His first novel showed him to be a leading member of the school of novelists who concern themselves with the changed surface and social texture of the post-war world. His novels are distinguished by unusual narrative force and economy, and his criticism by the clarity and forthrightness of his judgements. As a poet, Wain's work was associated with that of the Movement and with later 'movements' of the 1960s. He published: *A Word Carved on a Sill* (1956); *Weep Before God* (1961); *Wildtrack* (1965); and *Feng* (1975).

Walpole, Horace (1717–97)
Letter-writer, antiquarian, connoisseur. He was son of the powerful statesman, Robert Walpole, and for a short time followed a political career, but he abandoned it, though he continued his interest in politics. His father's influence procured for him three sinecures (*ie* posts under the government which carried salaries though they required very little work) and these enabled him to pass his life as an assiduous spectator and man of pleasure. He developed a strong taste for the Gothic style in all its forms, converting his house (Strawberry Hill, Twickenham, where he settled in 1747) into what he called 'a little Gothic castle', and writing the first of the ▷ Gothic novels, ▷ *The Castle of Otranto* (1764). He is chiefly famous for his letters, however, and is regarded as one of the best correspondents in the best period of ▷ letter-writing. Their main quality is their liveliness, humour, and vividness of observation.
Bib: Lives by Ketton-Cremer and Lewis, W. S.; Stephen, L., in *Hours in a Library*.

Walton, Izaac (1593–1683)
Biographer. Izaac Walton's popular reputation has rested on his *The Compleat Angler* (1653, with revised editions in 1658 and 1661) – ostensibly a fishing manual. The comprehensive nature of the work is, however, hinted at in its subtitle: *The Contemplative Man's Recreation* – an evocation of an idyllic, reflective, pastoral nostalgia. As a biographer Walton was the author of a series of important 'lives' of 17th-century poets and divines. His *Life of John Donne* was published in 1658, and was followed by lives of Richard Hooker (1665), George Herbert (1670) and Robert Sanderson (1678). The *Life of Sir Henry Wotton* first appeared appended to a posthumous edition of Wotton's poetry in 1640 and was published separately in 1651. The two biographies of Donne and Herbert are the most renowned. Walton is concerned with recording his subjects' piously Anglican Christian virtue, but they are, nevertheless, important statements concerning the contemporary perception of these major writers, and instances of a 17th-century art of hagiographic ▷ biography.
Bib: Keynes, G. L. (ed.), *The Compleat Walton*; Novarr, D., *The Making of Walton's Lives*.

Ward, Edward ('Ned') (1667–1731)
Tavern-keeper and ▷ Grub Street writer, specializing in doggerel verses and humorous sketches of London life. His prose work *The London Spy* (1698–1709) takes us on a tour of the sights of London, and is full of humorous anecdotes and eccentric characters. His *Hudibras Redivivus* was published 1705–7.

Ward, Mrs Humphry (Mary Augusta) (1851–1920)
Novelist. Her most famous novel, *Robert Elsmere* (1888), was a study of religious conflict. Elsmere is a clergyman who loses his faith through a study of the 'higher criticism' of Bible texts. (The novelist ▷ George Eliot lost her faith in Christianity by the same influence.) The purport of the book is that the revitalization of Christianity required more attention to the social obligations of the Church and the abandonment of its supernatural – or at least its miraculous – constituents of belief. The book was very widely read in Britain and America, partly in consequence of a review of it in the *Nineteenth Century* by the statesman, W. E. Gladstone. In accordance with the ideas expressed in the novel, Mrs Ward was a very active philanthropist. She was also an active opponent of the Women's Suffrage Movement (the ▷ Suffragettes). She wrote a number of other novels, and translated Amiel's *Journal Intime* into English.
Bib: Trevelyan, J. P., *The Life of Mrs Humphry Ward*; Jones, E. H., *Mrs Humphry Ward*; Peterson, W. S., *Victorian Heretic: Mrs Humphry Ward's Robert Elsmere*; Sutherland, J. A., *Mrs Humphry Ward: Eminent Victorian, Pre-Eminent Edwardian*.

Warden, The (1855)
A novel by ▷ Anthony Trollope, the first to be a success with the public, and the first of his ▷ Barsetshire series.
 The theme of the novel is the two aspects of the problem of the reform of public abuses. It shows how an office which brings to its holder an income much in excess of his duties may nonetheless be conducted usefully and with integrity, so that to abolish the office may be an act of personal injustice although the abolition may be justifiable on public grounds.
 The novel is set in the cathedral city of Barchester in Barsetshire. A clergyman, the Reverend Septimus Harding, is Warden of Hiram's Hospital, a long-established charitable institution for maintaining 12 poor old men in comfort. For this he draws an income which in the course of time has increased to £800 a year, although his actual duties are almost non-existent. However, he maintains with the old men affectionate

relationships which are inestimable financially. The wardenship is attacked as a public abuse by John Bold, a Barchester surgeon, although Bold is in love with Harding's daughter Eleanor. Bold is opposed (on the wrong grounds) by the worldly churchman Archdeacon Grantly, who is Harding's son-in-law. Harding resigns his office as a matter of conscience, but the Bishop refuses to appoint a new Warden, and the old men of the Hospital lose the chief solace of their old age.

Warner, Marina (b 1946)

Novelist, critic and cultural historian, educated at Lady Margaret Hall, Oxford. Her novels are much concerned with history and its bearing on the present: *In A Dark Wood* (1977) is about a Jesuit who is writing a biography of a 17th-century missionary; in *The Lost Father* (1988) the narrator is writing a novel, set in Italy and based on her own family history. Other novels: *The Skating Party* (1982); *Indigo, or Mapping the Waters* (1992). Television play: *Tell Me More* (1991). Libretto: *The Legs of the Queen of Sheba* (1991). She has also written cultural criticism, studies of history and myth, biography and children's writing.

Warner, Rex (1905–86)

Novelist, poet and translator. He was educated at Oxford University, where he met W. H. Auden and Cecil Day Lewis. His allegorical first novel, *The Wild Goose Chase* (1937) examines the political issues of the 1930s through a fantastic imaginary world and concludes with a ▷ communist ▷ Utopia. *The Professor* (1938) and *The Aerodrome* (1941) are similarly concerned with political power, and the conflict of love and personal integrity with totalitarianism. Warner's work is frequently compared with that of Kafka, but also shows the influence of classical literature, of which he made many translations. He also wrote several historical novels, including *The Young Caesar* (1958) and *Imperial Caesar* (1958), which are written in the form of supposed autobiography.
Bib: Reeve, N. H., *The Novels of Rex Warner: An Introduction.*

Warner, Sylvia Townsend (1893–1978)

Novelist, poet, short-story writer, musicologist and biographer. Born in Harrow, Middlesex, she worked in a munitious factory during World War I and in 1922 became one of the editors of the Oxford University Press's *Tudor Church Music*. She lived in Dorset with the poet Valentine Ackland from 1932 until the latter's death in 1969; together they served as Red Cross Volunteers in Spain in 1930. Her novels are: *Lolly Willowes: or, The Loving Huntsman* (1926); *Mr Fortune's Maggot* (1927); *The True Heart* (1929); *Summer Will Show* (1936); *After the Death of Don Juan* (1938); *The Corner That Held Them* (1948); *The Flint Anchor* (1954). Her novels are notable for their imaginative scope, including as they do elements of the supernatural, mystical and historical and embracing fantasy, comedy and satire; their settings include a South Sea Island, a

medieval nunnery, the Paris of the 1848 revolution and the Essex marshes. She also published ten volumes of short stories, books on Somerset (1949) and on ▷ Jane Austen (1951), a biography of T.H. White (1967) and volumes of poetry, including: *The Espalier* (1925); *Time Importuned* (1928); *Opus 7* (1931, a long narrative poem); *Rainbow* (1932); *Whether a Dove or a Seagull* (1933, with Valentine Ackland); *Boxwood* (1957); *Two Poems* (1945); *King Duffus* (1968); *Azrael* (1978); *Twelve Poems* (1980). Her *Collected Poems* were published in 1982, edited by Claire Harman, and her *Letters* in 1982, edited by William Maxwell.
Bib: Harman, C., *Sylvia Townsend Warner: a biography;* Mulford, C., *This Narrow Place: Sylvia Townsend Warner and Valentine Ackland: Life, Letters and Politics 1930–1951.*

Water Babies, The (1863)

A moral fantasy for children, by ▷ Charles Kingsley, subtitled *A Fairy Tale for a Landbaby*. The little boy Tom is employed as a chimney-sweep by the brutal Mr Grimes; he falls into the river, gets turned into a water baby and is carried down to the sea. He meets a number of fabulous creatures and undergoes ordeals which effect moral instruction. He emerges purified, on equal terms with Ellie, the little girl in whose house he once swept the chimneys. Grimes is sent away to a penance of sweeping out Etna. The book is partly an attack on the exploitation of child labour and on the brutalization of the poor, and partly a fable about their moral education. Some of the moralizing is offensive, socially and psychologically, to modern readers but the book remains a children's classic for the sake of the ingenuity of its fantasy.
▷ Child labour; Children's books.

Waugh, Evelyn (1903–66)

Novelist. Born in London and educated at Hertford College Oxford, he worked for a while as an assistant schoolmaster, an experience which provided the basis for his first novel, *Decline and Fall* (1928). His satires of the late 1920s and 1930s up to and including *Put Out More Flags* (1942), present the modern world as anarchic and chaotic, and are a blend of farce and tragedy. His technique included the extensive use of dialogue, and rapid changes of scene. Many of the early novels recount the ▷ picaresque and outrageous experiences of a naive central character, such as Paul Penny feather in *Decline and Fall*, and William Boot in *Scoop* (1938), a hilarious story of Western journalists in Africa. Waugh became a Catholic in 1930; this was initially reflected in his work only in a sense of the transience and emptiness of worldly concerns. But World War II, during which Waugh served with the Royal Marines in Crete and Yugoslavia changed the character of his work; it became more explicitly Catholic, serious to the point of sombreness, and more three-dimensional in his portrayal of his characters. The first novel to show these qualities was *Brideshead Revisited* (1945). In 1961 he completed his most considerable work, a trilogy about the war entitled *Sword of Honour*.

Among others of his novels that have achieved fame are *The Loved One* (1948), a satire on American commercialism, extending to the commercialization of death, and *The Ordeal of Gilbert Pinfold* (1957), a pseudo-autobiographical caricature of a 50-year-old Catholic novelist. His post-war work expresses a distaste for, and rejection of, modern civilization, and a pervasive sense of the vanity of human desires. All Waugh's work is marked by an exquisite sense of the ludicrous and a fine aptitude for exposing false attitudes. His comedy is closely dependent on the carefully calculated urbanity of his style. Other novels are: *Vile Bodies* (1930); *Black Mischief* (1932); *A Handful of Dust* (1934); *Scott-King's Modern Europe* (1947); *Tactical Exercise* (1954); *Basil Seal Rides Again* (1963). Story collections are: *Mr Loveday's Little Outing* (1936); *Work Suspended* (1949).

Waugh also wrote travel books, selections from which have been collected under the title *When the Going Was Good* (1946), and biographies of the 19th-century poet and painter D. G. Rossetti (1928), and of the 16th-century Catholic martyr, Edmund Campion (1935).

▷ Catholicism in English literature.
Bib: Bradbury, M., *Evelyn Waugh* (Writers and Critics Series 1964); Stannard, M., *Evelyn Waugh: the Critical Heritage*; Sykes, C., *Evelyn Waugh: a Biography*.

Waverley (1814)

The first of ▷ Sir Walter Scott's novels, subtitled *'Tis Sixty Years Since*. The hero, Edward Waverley, is a young English officer who visits the Highlands of Scotland just before the Jacobite Rebellion of 1745. Here he falls in love with Flora, the Jacobite daughter of a Highland chieftain. He joins the Jacobite forces. When these are eventually defeated, Waverly is saved from execution by a senior English officer on the other side, whom he has saved in a battle. *Waverley* is the first historical novel of distinction in English literature, and Scott's vivid description of Scottish society and scenery caused it to be received with great enthusiasm.

Waves, The (1931)

A novel by ▷ Virginia Woolf. It is the story of six characters, each of whom tell his or her own story in monologue, and reflects images of the others in his or her own mind. The monologues occur in groups, at different stages of their lives, and each group is preceded by a passage describing a time of day, from dawn to nightfall. It is a poetic, lyrical and highly patterned work, and presents human existence as an organic process, uniting individuals like waves on the sea. *The Waves* is the climax of Virginia Woolf's experiments in fictional form.

Way of All Flesh, The (1903)

A novel by ▷ Samuel Butler, written 1873–5 and published after his death, in 1903. It is one of the few purely satirical works of distinction of the ▷ Victorian period; the satire is directed against the Victorian cult of the family as the sacred and blessed nucleus of society, and (as so often in ▷ Charles Dickens) the refuge from the harshness of the world. The arrogant, self-righteous, intolerant and stupid kind of Victorian parent is exemplified in the clergyman Theobald Pontifex, father of Ernest Pontifex. Victorian authoritarianism and repressiveness is also attacked in Theobald, seen as a religious humbug, and in Dr Skinner, headmaster of the ▷ public school that Ernest attends. The first 50 chapters of the books are autobiographical; Butler even includes actual letters in the text. The narrative is not told through Ernest (Butler as a boy) but in the first person through his friend the middle-aged Overton, who represents a more tolerant aspect of Butler; by this means, Butler conveys criticism of his intolerant younger self, in the person of Ernest. The book was much praised, especially by G. B. Shaw.

▷ Autobiography.

Wealth of Nations
▷ Smith, Adam.

Webb, Beatrice (1858–1943)

Sociologist. She was the daughter of Richard Potter, a railway director and friend of the philosopher, ▷ Herbert Spencer, who exercised a guiding influence over her education. Her mother was a product of the 19th-century ▷ Utilitarian school of thought. She early developed a strong social conscience, which led her to choose as her career the almost unprecedented one of 'social investigator'. Victorian sensitiveness to social abuses was strong amongst the intelligentsia, but she realized that constructive action was hampered by lack of exact information: 'The primary task is to observe and dissect facts.' In order to do so, she took bold steps for a Victorian girl of the prosperous middle class, such as disguising herself as a working girl and taking employment under a tailor in the East End of London. She and her husband were among the early members of the ▷ Fabian Society, and among the founders of the Labour Party. Her autobiographies *My Apprenticeship* (1926) and *Our Partnership* (1948) are in the tradition of ▷ John Stuart Mill's *Autobiography* (1873) in being essentially histories of the growth of opinions and ideas; *My Apprenticeship*, however, is very enlightening about social backgrounds in the 1880s, and a valuable addition to the Victorian novels, which, she said, were the only documents for the study of society available in her youth. She and her husband were among the founders of the weekly journal ▷ *New Statesman*, still a leading left-wing journal.

Weldon, Fay (b 1931)

Novelist, dramatist and television screenwriter. Her novels include: *The Fat Woman's Joke* (1967); *Down Among the Women* (1971); *Female Friends* (1975); *Remember Me* (1976); *Words of Advice* (1977); *Praxis* (1978); *Little Sisters* (1978); *Puffball* (1980); *The President's Child* (1982); *The Life and Loves of a She-Devil* (1983); *The Shrapnel Academy* (1986);

The Rules of Life (1987); *The Heart of the Country* (1987); *Leader of the Band* (1988); *The Cloning of Joanna May* (1990); *Darcy's Utopia* (1990); *Moon over Minneapolis* (1991); *Growing Rich* (1992); *Life Force* (1992). Story collections are: *Watching Me, Watching You* (1981); *Polaris* (1985). The ▷ feminism of her work is concentrated in the portrayal of the exploitation of women by men in domestic situations, and in relationships. Her tragi-comic novels are powerful stories of pain, loss and betrayal, and their desperation is accentuated by the sense of a controlling social and biological pattern which negates the characters' attempts to make choices about their lives. The endings of her books, however, often hint at the emergence of a new and more liberated woman.

Welfare State
A term currently in use to describe the national system of social security brought into being by the Labour government of 1945–50 and based on W. A. Beveridge's *Report on Social Insurance and Allied Services* (1942). The system depends on National Insurance payments which are obligatory for all adult members of the community apart from Old Age Pensioners and family dependants. It is also funded from general taxation. In return for these payments, made weekly, the state grants financial assistance in the form of family allowances, payments made during sickness and unemployment and to maintain those who have been permanently incapacitated by injury, and pensions for the old. Medical attention is partly free and partly assisted. State education, from the nursery school level for children under five to university level, is also frequently assumed in the concept of the Welfare State.

The Welfare State is thus the opposite of the *laissez faire* concept of the state which prevailed in the 19th century. According to the latter, the state was expected to allow society to develop freely according to 'natural' economic forces. Its function was merely to prevent interference with these in the shape of crime or insurrection. The *laissez faire* concept was never quite supreme; the state always assumed some responsibility for the very poor, for instance in the provision of ▷ workhouses. Nevertheless, *laissez faire* ideas prevailed to the extent that the state was assumed to have no basic responsibility for the individual material welfare of its citizens. The opposite 'Welfare' concept of the state's duties arose partly from the 19th-century religious thinking about society, and partly from the growth of socialist philosophies. The modern Welfare State is generally considered to have had its beginnings under the Liberal government of Campbell Bannerman and Asquith (1905–14); this introduced old-age pensions, some Unemployment and Health Insurance, and other measures. Since the 1980s *laissez faire* concepts of the state have been reasserted and responsibility for individual welfare repudiated as the market economy is encouraged.

Well of Loneliness
▷ Hall, Radclyffe.

Wells, H. G. (Herbert George) (1886–1946)
Novelist and journalist. He was brought up in the lower middle class, the son of a professional cricketer; in 1888 he took an excellent degree in science at London University. His social origins and his education explain much of his approach to life as a writer. The great novelist of the 19th-century lower middle classes is ▷ Dickens, and some of H. G. Wells's best fiction is about the same field of society; novels such as ▷ *Kipps* (1905) and *The History of Mr Polly* (1910) are of this sort, and they have the kind of vigorous humour and sharp visualization that is characteristic of early Dickens. On the other hand, rising into the educated class at a time of rapid scientific and technical progress, he ignored the values of traditional culture and art, and became fascinated with the prospects that science offered, for good as well as for ill. This side of him produced a different kind of writing: Wells was one of the inventors of ▷ science fiction. *The Time Machine* (1895), *The Invisible Man* (1897), *The War of the Worlds* (1898) and *The First Men in the Moon* (1901) are examples of his fantasies. But his social experience and his interest in technology also drew him to writing fictional-sociological studies in which he surveyed and analysed, often with the same Dickensian humour, the society of his time; *Tono-Bungay* (1908) is perhaps the best of these. Other examples are *Ann Veronica* (1909) about the problems connected with newly emancipated women, *The New Machiavelli* (1911) about socialist thinking – Wells had joined the ▷ Fabians in 1903 – and *Mr Britling Sees It Through* (1916) about World War I seen from the point of view of the 'Home Front'. But the interest in science also made him a ▷ utopian optimist, and this point of view caused him to write such didactic works as *A Modern Utopia* (1905) and *New Worlds For Old* (1908). There was always a great deal of naivety in Wells's optimism, and later in his life he paid the penalty by reacting into excessive gloom, in *Mind at the End of its Tether* (1945). He declared that *The Open Conspiracy* (1928) contained the essence of his philosophy. He was never a deep thinker, however; his work lives by the vitality of his humour and by the urgency with which he pressed his ideas. This urgency necessarily made him a popularizer, and his most notable work of popularization was *The Outline of History* (1920).

In some ways Wells resembles his contemporary, the dramatist George Bernard Shaw; both were socialists, both felt the urgency to enlighten mankind as quickly as possible, and both cared more that their works should have immediate effect than that they should be works of art – Wells told the novelist ▷ Henry James that he would rather be called a journalist than an artist. Possibly the most penetrating remark on Wells was that addressed to him by the novelist ▷ Joseph Conrad: 'You don't really care for people, but you think they can be improved; I do, but I know they can't.'
Bib: Mackenzie, N. and J., *The Time Traveller:*

Life of H. G. Wells; Bergonzi, B., *The Early H. G. Well* and *H. G. Wells: Twentieth-Century Views*; Parrinder, P. (ed.), *H. G. Wells: the Critical Heritage*; Hammond J. R., *H. G. Wells and Rebecca West*.

Welsh fiction in English (Anglo-Welsh literature)

To define Anglo-Welsh fiction as that produced in English by Welsh writers is too simplistic. Writers' claims on Welsh ancestry vary enormously. Some even adopt Welshness as, for example, Raymond Garlick (b 1926), an Englishman who identified with Welsh political causes and became founder-editor of the literary magazine *Dock Leaves* (later *The Anglo-Welsh Review*, 1957–88) and a critic and poet firmly within the Welsh context. Thus poet and novelist Glyn Jones's criterion of Anglo-Welshness – expressed in his critical work *The Dragon Has Two Tongues* as involvement in the Welsh situation – seems justifiable. ▷ Richard Hughes and ▷ John Cowper Powys have received the accolade of critical studies in the *Writers of Wales* series through their eventually permanent residence in, and lifelong empathy with Wales. From Powys's Wessex came Jeremy Hooker (b 1941), whose 19 years in Wales made him a leading critic in the Anglo-Welsh field and temporarily changed his poetic direction. Thus a widely debatable area of Anglo-Welsh acceptability exists.

Historically, poetry is the dominant genre of Anglo-Welsh literature, prose a mainly 20th-century growth. Moreover, the growth of Anglo-Welsh literature is a concomitant of the historical process that weakened the influence of the Welsh language.

Anglo-Norman settlements of the Marches and South Wales were followed by Henry I's 12th-century Flemish settlement of South Pembroke, subsequently augmented by English settlements in Gower and around Laugharne. Edwardian castles protected English merchants who were granted privileges within town walls, as at Caernafon and Conwy. Itinerant drovers and weavers soon forged linguistic links with England. The establishment of the Tudor dynasty brought Welsh influence into England, though Henry VIII's Acts of Union insisted on Welsh office-holders' proficiency in English, eventually producing an anglicized squirearchy. Three centuries later, Victorian government policy further weakened the hold of the Welsh language by encouraging 'The Welsh Not', prohibiting Welsh language conversation in schools. A piece of wood or slate with the letters 'WN' cut into it was hung round the neck of the last pupil caught speaking Welsh in class – whoever was left wearing it at the end of the school day would be punished. From the early 19th century, the increasing influx into the South Wales valleys not only drained the rural areas of the west and north but brought in labouring or technological expertise for pit-sinking, blast furnace, canal, tramroad, railway and docks construction. The ultimate figure of English-speaking immigrants in the South Wales valleys accounted for at least 40 per cent of the population, swamping the native Welsh speakers. The subsequent foundation of county schools from

1895 onwards provided secondary education in the medium of English. This explains why Glyn Jones, an early pupil at Merthyr's Cyfarthfa Castle Grammar School, though from a Welsh-speaking family, developed into an Anglo-Welsh writer. It was these socio-economic pressures that helped to create the 'first flowering' of Anglo-Welsh literature.

Many young provincial writers departed for London between the wars to find publishers who encouraged them to adapt their work for the metropolitan market. Caradoc Evans (1878–1945), according to the novelist and critic Professor Gwyn Jones the 'first distinctive ancestral voice' of Anglo-Welsh writing, produced the first London-published best-seller. In *My People* (1915) and subsequent short-story collections, Caradoc Evans invented grotesqueries of character and speech for his Cardi peasantry whose lust, greed and hypocrisy established a false Welsh stereotype that amused Londoners but gave unmitigated and lasting offence to the Welsh-speaking literary establishment. Notwithstanding, Caradoc Evans's commercial success encouraged a vein of fantasy among the 'first flowering' of Anglo-Welsh writers, Rhys Davies, Glyn Jones, and Dylan Thomas, which was continued in the post-war period by Gwyn Thomas. Moreover, the eccentric and grotesque provided a diversion from painfully harsh living conditions in decaying rural and unemployment- ravaged industrial communities. Beneath this surface, however, industrial realism encapsulates a political message – socialist in the 'first flowering', nationalist in the 'second flowering' in the 1960s. This idealism motivates an inevitably doomed nationalist military uprising in Glyn Jones's ▷ novella, *I Was Born in the Ystrad Valley*, as early as 1937. ▷ Communist political activism inspires Lewis Jones's *Cwmardy* (1937) and *We Live!* (1939), Jack Jones paints panoramic historical canvases behind his family epics in *Black Parade* (1935) and *Rhondda Roundabout* (1934), whereas Gwyn Jones employs a briefer time-scale in *Times Like These* (1936) where he examines the social and familial crises precipitated by the General Strike. However, it was Richard Llewellyn's *How Green Was My Valley* (1939) which became the popular stereotype of the Valleys' industrial novel despite its inaccuracies and sentimentality, a far cry from Gwyn Thomas's rejected pre-war novel *Sorrow For Thy Sons* (eventually published in 1986, five years after his death). Gwyn Thomas's post-war hyperbolic wit, farcical situations and eccentric characters create a Valleys' world where laughter is the only antidote to poverty and unemployment. Meanwhile, short stories between the wars mediate between a poetic vision of Welsh-speaking Wales, Lawrentian-influenced in Rhys Davies and Geraint Goodwin, and the realistic depiction of industrial communities, infused with wit and humour.

Meic Stephens (b 1938) was the prime mover behind the 'second flowering' which gathered momentum in the 1960s when nationalist ideas were superseding socialist politics. He founded *Poetry Wales* in 1965 with support from Harri Webb, and in 1967 became Literature Director of the newly constituted *Welsh Arts Council* whose financial support for writers and publishers gave tremendous impetus to Welsh and Anglo-Welsh writing. An unfortunate effect, however, was that London publishers and reviewers disregarded Anglo-Welsh writing when it developed independently from metropolitan influences, leading to a critical undervaluing that still persists in England. In 1968 Meic Stephens led a move to create the English section of *Yr Academi Gymreig*, originally a literary society founded for Welsh-language writers only, but from then on providing invaluable encouragement to Anglo-Welsh writers. Concluding an exciting decade, Ned Thomas launched *Planet* in 1970, a magazine whose political thrust was left-wing and nationalist, and which also published literary material.

Recently, an updated view of Valleys society has informed the short stories and novels of Alun Richards (b 1929) and Ron Berry (b 1920). Alun Richards illuminates social tensions among the migratory professional classes, nuances between the Valleys and Cardiff, and Cardiff and London. His sensitive ear for dialogue contributed to the effectiveness of his work for the theatre (published in *Plays for Players*; 1975) and television. Ron Berry has explored Valleys sexual mores with lively humour. Closely associated with the border country of his upbringing, ▷ Raymond Williams's novels present the tensions of nationalism, social mobility, working-class solidarity and conflicting loyalties, though the political and socio-economic dimensions of his critical *oeuvre* are more familiar. The novelists with Anglo-Welsh connections who have achieved most recent critical acclaim are Bernice Rubens, Alice Thomas Ellis, Stuart Evans and Peter Thomas, a newcomer as a novelist extending Gwyn Thomas's hyperbolic vision.

With a higher concentration of writers in Wales than anywhere else in Britain, the vigorous growth of Anglo-Welsh literature is assured, particularly since, though it has retained its traditionally distinguishing characteristics, it has developed a more outward-looking stance. Happily, there are indications that the Anglo-Welsh literary movement may eventually receive its long overdue recognition from the English critical establishment.
Bib: Stephens, M. (ed.), *The Oxford Companion to the Literature of Wales*; Adams, S. and Hughes, G. R., *Essays in Welsh and Anglo-Welsh Literature*; Conran, A., *The Cost of Strangeness*; Garlick, R., *An Introduction to Anglo-Welsh Literature*; Hooker, J., *The Poetry of Place*; Jones, G., *The Dragon Has Two Tongues*; Jones, G. and Rowlands, R., *Profiles*; Mathias, R., *A Ride Through the Wood*; Mathias, R., *Anglo-Welsh Literature*; Curtis, T. (ed.), *Wales: the Imagined Nation*.

Wessex
The kingdom of the West Saxons from the 6th century till the reign of Alfred at the end of the 9th, after which it developed into the kingdom of England. The capital was the town of Winchester in Hampshire, and the area also included Dorset, Somerset, Wiltshire, and Berkshire. The name

of Wessex was revived by the novelist and poet ▷ Thomas Hardy for his regional novels.

West, Jane (1758–1852)
Poet, novelist and dramatist. A prolific author, whose restrained prose style and dry sense of humour brought admiration from ▷ Jane Austen and ▷ Mary Wollstonecraft. Her poetry and plays were published in 1791, but thereafter she concentrated on novels, which include material that is anti-sentimental (*The Advantages of Education, or The History of Maria Williams*, 1793), anti-radical (*A Tale of the Times*, 1799) and anti-feminist (*Letters to a Young Lady*, 1806). Her historical novels, *The Loyalists* (1812) and *Alicia de Lacey* (1814), are perhaps the most readable today.
Bib: Butler, M., *Jane Austen and the War of Ideas*; Rendall, J., *The Origins of Modern Feminism 1780–1860*.

West, Dame Rebecca (1892–1983)
Novelist, journalist, feminist writer and critic. Born Cecily Isabel Fairfield, she named herself Rebecca West at the age of 19, after the strong-willed and independent protagonist of *Rosmersholm*, a play by the Norwegian dramatist Ibsen. She was educated in Edinburgh and began her writing career with work for feminist and socialist journals such as *The Freewoman* and *Clarion*. She had a long affair with the novelist ▷ H.G. Wells (after writing a highly critical review of his work) and had a son by him; in 1930 she married a banker. In 1916 she published a study of ▷ Henry James and in 1918 her first novel, *The Return of the Soldier*, appeared. This uses ▷ modernist narrative techniques to explore the psychological and social nuances of the relationship between three women and a man who returns from World War I with memory loss. Much of her fiction is centred on the contemporary experience of women and emphasizes the special qualities of women as she sees them: *Harriet Hume* (1929); *The Harsh Voice* (1935); *The Thinking Reed* (1936); *The Fountain Overflows* (1956). She also deals with political issues, such as the suffrage movement in *The Judge* (1922) and the Russian Revolution in *The Birds Fall Down* (1966). A journey to Yugoslavia resulted in a travel diary, *Black Flag and Grey Falcon: A Journey through Yugoslavia* (1941), and she published *The New Meaning of Treason* (1949), based on her observation of the Nuremberg trials, *McLuhan and the Future of Literature* (1969) and a biography of St Augustine (1933). See also: *Rebecca West: A Celebration* (1977); *The Strange Necessity: Essays by Rebecca West* (1928); *The Young Rebecca: Writings of Rebecca West 1911–1917* (1982, ed. Jane Marcus).
Bib: Glendinning, V., *Rebecca West: A Life*; Weldon, F., *Rebecca West*; Deakin, M., *Rebecca West*; Wolfe, P., *Rebecca West: Artist and Thinker*; Orel, H., *The Literary Achievement of Rebecca West*; Ray, G.N., *H.G. Wells and Rebecca West*.

Westminster Review
It was founded in 1823 as a vehicle for the Benthamite (otherwise known as the ▷ Utilitarian)

school of thought, and at first kept severely to
its principles. Its politics of ruthless, scientific
institutional reform made it not only a strong
opponent of the Tory ▷ *Quarterly Review* but
put it well to the left of the ▷ *Edinburgh Review*.
It appealed to a narrower public, and tended,
in the Utilitarian manner, to regard the arts
with disdain. In 1836 it combined with the now
livelier Utilitarian *London Review*, and continued
as the *London and Westminster Review*, under the
editorship of the distinguished Utilitarian ▷ John
Stuart Mill. Mill wanted to broaden Utilitarian
thinking, and writers who were not followers of
the movement were brought in, such as ▷ Carlyle
and the novelist ▷ George Eliot, who was assistant
editor 1851–54. Later contributors varied as greatly
as > Walter Pater, father of the ▷ Aesthetic
movement, and the positivist Frederic Harrison.
It continued to advocate scientific progress,
and by the end of the century it ceased to be
literary.

What Maisie Knew (1897)

A novel by ▷ Henry James. Its theme is the
survival of innocence in a world of adult corruption,
the influence of adults on a child, and her influence
on them.

Maisie Farange is a small girl whose parents
have divorced each other with equal guilt on both
sides. The parents are heartless and indifferent to
their daughter, except as a weapon against each
other and in their farcical, though not wholly vain,
struggles to maintain acceptable social appearances.
Maisie is passed from one to the other, and each
employs a governess to take responsibility for her
welfare. Both parents marry again, and eventually
relinquish Maisie herself. By the end of the book
Maisie finds herself torn between two prospective
'step-parents', each formerly married to her real
parents, divorced from them, and about to marry
each other, Maisie herself having been the occasion
of their coming together. Her 'stepfather', Sir
Claude, is charming and sweet-natured, but weak
and self-indulgent; her 'stepmother', Mrs Beale, is
genuinely fond of Maisie (as Sir Claude is) but is
basically selfish and rapacious. In addition, the child
has a simple-minded plain and elderly governess,
Mrs Wix, who is herself in love with Sir Claude,
and devoted to Maisie. The affection of none of
them, however, is single-minded, as hers is for
each one of them. The pathos of the novel arises
from the warm responsiveness, deep need, and pure
integrity of Maisie, from whose point of view all
the events are seen. Its irony arises from the way
in which the child's need for and dependence on
adult care and love is transformed into responsibility
for the adults themselves, who become dependent
on her decisions. In the end these decisions
lead her to choose life alone with Mrs Wix, who
naively hopes to imbue her with a 'moral sense',
unaware that beside Maisie's innocence her
own idea of a moral sense represents modified
corruption.

The novel is written in James's late, compressed
and dramatic style, and is one of his masterpieces.

Whig and Tory

Political terms distinguishing the two parties
which were the forebears of the present Liberal
and Conservative parties respectively. They were
originally terms of abuse, provoked by the attempt
of ▷ Lord Shaftesbury in 1679 to exclude James
Duke of York (later James II) from succession to
the throne because he was a Catholic. Shaftesbury
and his party were called Whigs because their
preference for the ▷ Protestant religion over the
law of hereditary succession caused their opponents
to liken them to the Scottish Presbyterian rebels
of the time – called derisively 'whigs' from the
nickname given to Scottish drovers. They retaliated
by calling the supporters of James, 'tories', from the
Irish term for robbers, implying that they no more
cared about safeguarding the Protestant religion
than did the Irish Catholic rebels. The Exclusion
question was settled in favour of James, but not for
long, since the Tories did in fact care greatly about
the maintenance of the ▷ Church of England,
and when James II was clearly seen to be acting
in Catholic interests, the Tories united with the
Whigs in deposing him in 1688. The political terms
remained because, though not very consistently,
the parties remained; and the parties survived
because they represented distinct social interests
in the country, though also not very consistently.
The Whigs were especially the party of the landed
aristocracy, who cared less for the institutions of the
Crown and the Church of England than for their
own power; since this was allied to the commercial
interests of the country, they tended to gain support
from the merchants of the towns, many of whom
were Dissenters opposed to the Church of England.
The principal Tory support came from the smaller
landed gentry, or squirearchy, whose interests
were conservative, and whose fortunes seemed best
protected by introducing as little change in the
established institutions, whether of Church or of
State, as possible. In the major crises the Tories
were generally defeated, but they had extraordinary
survival capacity by virtue of their willingness to
accept changes once they had become inevitable.
Their first major defeat was in 1714 when
the Tory party was split between Bolingbroke's
anti-Hanoverian faction and those loyal to the 1701
Act of Settlement by which the throne went to
the House of Hanover and not to Anne's Catholic
half-brother.

Whigs were then supreme for 40 years (though
they disintegrated into rival groups), until after
the accession of George III in 1760. George tried
then to revive the power of the throne by securing
supporters for his politics in Parliament; these
supporters were known as 'the King's Friends'
or 'New Tories'. This policy was also defeated,
however, by their loss of prestige as a result of
the victory of the American rebels in the War of
American Independence (1775–83). The country
was not then in a mood to see the return of the
restless and corrupt Whigs, and Tory governments
continued in power until 1832.

About 1830 the names Liberal and Conservative
began to replace Whig and Tory in popular use,

and these terms were officially adopted some 30 years later. 'Tory' survives, to some extent, as interchangeable with Conservative (it is shorter for newspaper headlines), but 'Whig' has been altogether superseded.

White, Antonia (1899–1980)

Novelist and translator. She was intially named Eirene Botting, White being her mother's surname. Her parents were converts to Catholicism and she was sent to the Convent of the Sacred Heart, Roehampton; after she began writing her novel *Frost in May* (1933) at the age of 15 her father withdrew her from the school (telling her she had been expelled) and sent her to St Paul's School for Girls (where he was classics master). After doing some teaching and clerical work she attended drama school in 1919 and worked as an actress. She was married three times, two of the marriages being annulled; she experienced periods of mental disturbance (and spent nine months in an asylum) but also supported herself and her children for periods through work as a journalist and advertising copy-writer. She is best known for her four autobiographical novels: *Frost in May*; *The Lost Traveller* (1950); *The Sugar House* (1952); *Beyond the Glass* (1954). These depict her experiences at school and her subsequent mental disturbances as well as her continuing complex and ambivalent relationship with Catholicism. *The Hound and the Falcon* (1965) describes, in letter form, her reconversion to Catholicism. Her other writings include: *Strangers* (1954), a volume of short stories; *Three in a Room* (1957); *Minka and Curdy* and *Living with Minka and Curdy* (1970) about her much-loved cats. *As Once in May* (1983) includes stories, essays, poems, autobiographical fragments and parts of a sequel to her tetralogy of novels and was edited by her daughter Susan Chitty, who also published *Now to My Mother: A Very Personal Memoir of Antonia White*. Bib: Marcus, J., in Kime Scott, B. (ed.), *The Gender of Modernism*; Showalter, E., *A Literature of their Own*.

White, Gilbert (1720–93)

Writer on natural history. He was born at Selborne, a village in Hampshire. After spending some years as a Fellow of Oriel College, Oxford, he became a country curate, and spent the last nine years of his life in the village of his birth. His *Natural History of Selborne* (1789) is a record of the plant, animal, and bird life there, inspired by genuine scientific curiosity and showing great delicacy and charm of expression. The book has been described as the first to raise natural history to the level of literature, and is the fruit of the development of 17th- and 18th-century natural science, partly initiated by the greatest of English naturalists, John Ray (1627–1705), author *The Wisdom of God Manifested in the Works of his Creation* (1691), a scientist who shared Newton's intellectual curiosity and his religious awe at the spectacle of divine organization in the universe. Another tradition leading to White was the newly awakened sensibility for natural surroundings in the poetry of William Collins,

▷ Oliver Goldsmith and William Cowper. The poetic movement culminated in the 19th century in the work of Wordsworth and Clare. Bib: Holt-White, R., *Life and Letters*.

White, Patrick (1912–1990)

Australian novelist, dramatist and poet. Born in London, educated in Australia, and at Cheltenham College and Cambridge University. He travelled widely in Europe and the USA, served in the Royal Air Force during World War II, and then returned to live in Australia. His work combines an intense spirituality with social comedy and a distaste for human pretension and egotism. His first novel, *The Happy Valley* (1939), set in remote New South Wales, shows the influence of ▷ Joyce, while *The Living and the Dead* (1941) is primarily a condemnation of English society of the 1920s and 1930s. White established his reputation with *The Tree of Man* (1955) and *Voss* (1957). Both concern man's confrontation with the inhuman forces of nature in Australia, the former through the struggles of a young farmer, the latter through the journey among the Aborigines of a mid-19th-century German explorer. White's last works of fiction were two collections, each containing three short pieces: *Memoirs of Many in One* (1986) and *Three Uneasy Pieces* (1988). His other novels are: *The Aunt's Story* (1948); *Riders in the Chariot* (1961); *The Solid Mandala* (1966); *The Vivisector* (1970); *The Eye of the Storm* (1973); *A Fringe of Leaves* (1976); *The Twyborn Affair* (1979). Drama includes: *Return to Abyssinia* (1947); *Four Plays* (1965) (*The Ham Funeral*, 1961; *The Season at Sarsaparilla*, 1962; *A Cheery Soul*, 1963; *Night on Bald Mountain*, 1964); *Big Toys* (1977); *Signal Driver* (1983). Story collections are: *The Burnt Ones* (1964); *The Cockatoos* (1974). Verse: *The Ploughman and Other Poems* (1935).
▷ Post-colonial fiction
Bib: Walsh, W., *Patrick White's Fiction*; Marr, D., *Patrick White: A Life*; Bliss, C., *Patrick White's Fiction: The Paradox of Fortunate Failure*; Tacey, D. J., *Patrick White: Fiction and the Unconscious*.

White, William Hale (1831–1913) (pseudonym: Mark Rutherford)

Novelist. His father was a ▷ Dissenter and intended his son to be a Dissenting clergyman. However, he could not reconcile his ideas and the religious doctrines that he was required to believe, and instead he had a civil service career in the Admiralty. His three famous novels were *The Autobiography of Mark Rutherford* (1881), *Mark Rutherford's Deliverance* (1885) and *The Revolution in Tanner's Lane* (1887). The first two are ▷ autobiographical and concerned with loss of faith. White makes Rutherford more outwardly unfortunate than he was himself, since he had a successful career both as a writer and as a civil servant; the reason seems to be that he makes his character represent not only his own loss of Christian faith but the sense of impoverishment that accompanied it. In his study of ▷ John Bunyan (1905), he makes the statement: 'Religion is dead when imagination deserts it.' White's own

questioning of his belief started from reading Wordsworth in *Lyrical Ballads* (1798–1800) and the subsequent feeling that nature stirred him as 'the God of the Church' could not. As studies of spiritual loss and contention with it, the Mark Rutherford novels have wide human relevance. The third novel is concerned with radical movements in the early 19th century and shows White's political intelligence, which comes out directly in his pamphlet on the political franchise. His other novels are *Miriam's Schooling* (1890), *Catherine Furze* (1893) and *Clara Hopgood* (1896). Other works: *Pages from a Journal* and *More Pages from a Journal* (1900 and 1910); *Last Pages* (1915).
▷ Agnosticism.
Bib: Maclean, C. M., *Life*; Stone, W., *Life*; Stock, I., *William Hale White*; Lucas, J., *The Literature of Change: Studies in the Nineteenth-Century Provincial Novel*.

Who's Who
An annual biographical dictionary of eminent contemporary men and women. First published in 1849.
▷ Biography.

Wide Sargasso Sea, The
▷ Rhys, Jean.

Wilde, Oscar Fingal O'Flahertie Wills (1856–1900)
Dramatist, poet, novelist and essayist. He was the son of an eminent Irish surgeon and a literary mother. At Oxford University his style of life became notorious; he was a disciple of ▷ Pater, the Oxford father of ▷ aestheticism, and he carried the doctrine as far as to conduct his life as an aesthetic disciple – a direct challenge to the prevailing outlook of the society of his time, which was inclined to regard overt aestheticism with suspicion or disdain. In 1888 Wilde produced a volume of children's fairy tales very much in the melancholy and poetic style of the Danish writer Hans Christian Andersen – *The Happy Prince*. He followed this with two other volumes of stories, and then the novel, *The Picture of Dorian Grey* (1891), whose hero is an embodiment of the aesthetic way of life. More commonly known were his comedies, *Lady Windermere's Fan* (1892), *A Woman of No Importance* (1893), *An Ideal Husband* (1895), and above all the witty *Importance of Being Earnest* (1895). The plays are apparently light-hearted, but they contain strong elements of serious feeling in their attack on a society whose code is intolerant, but whose intolerance is hypocritical. In 1895, by a libel action against the Marquis of Queensberry, he exposed himself to a countercharge of immoral homosexual conduct, and spent two years in prison. In 1898 he published his *Ballad of Reading Gaol* about his prison experience, proving that he could write in the direct language of the ballad tradition, as well as in the artificial style of his *Collected Poems* (1892). His *De Profundis* (1905) is an eloquent statement of his grief after his downfall, but modern critics are equally as impressed by the intelligence of his social essays, such as *The Critic*

as *Artist* (1891) and *The Soul of Man under Socialism* (1891). The paradox of Wilde is that, while for his contemporaries he represented degeneracy and weakness, there is plenty of evidence that he was a brave man of remarkable strength of character who made an emphatic protest against the vulgarity of his age and yet, artistically, was himself subject to vulgarity of an opposite kind.
▷ Lesbian and Gay Writing.
Bib: Critical studies by Roditi, E., Ransome, A.; Lives by Lemmonier, L.; Ervine, St J.; Pearson, H.; Bentley, E. R., in *The Playwright as Thinker*; Beckson, K. (ed.), *The Critical Heritage*; Bird, A., *The Plays of Oscar Wilde*; Worth, K., *Oscar Wilde*; Dollimore, J., *Sexual Dissidence: Augustine to Wilde, Freud to Foucault*; Hart-Davis, R. (ed.), *Letters*; Ellman, R., *Oscar Wilde* and *Four Dubliners*.

Wilkes, John (1727–97)
Journalist and politician. He was dissolute, and notorious for his membership of the scandalous Hell-Fire Club at Medmenham Abbey, with its motto 'Fay ce que voudras' = 'Do as you will'. Politically he was radical and courageous, and a popular hero. In 1762 he attacked George III's administration under Lord Bute in *The North Briton*, a periodical which countered *The Briton* edited by the novelist, ▷ Tobias Smollett. As an M.P., he was twice expelled from the House of Commons for libel, and in 1769 he was three times elected to Parliament by the county of Middlesex, the election each time being annulled. He was allowed to sit in 1774, in which year he was Lord Mayor of London. His character was such as to win the respect of ▷ Dr Johnson, a man of opposite moral and political principles: 'Jack has great variety of talk, Jack is a scholar, Jack has the manners of a gentleman.' (Quoted in ▷ Boswell's *Life of Johnson*.)

Wilkinson, Sarah (d c 1830)
Novelist. By Wilkinson's own account she published a novel, *The Thatched Cottage*, opened a school on the proceeds, and taught intermittently after that time. Much influenced by ▷ Ann Radcliffe, her novels include all the required ▷ Gothic ingredients. *The Spectre of Lanmere Abbey* (1820) is one of her best. However, Wilkinson was unable to take the ghosts, hauntings and other paraphernalia seriously, and a mocking irony always undercuts, quite pleasurably, the required overladen and exaggerated prose. Wilkinson is otherwise known for her ▷ chapbooks, which consist of condensed forms of popular works as well as simplified translations of foreign literature. she scrupulously acknowledged the authors of the works she treated in his manner (▷ Henry Fielding, ▷ Matthew Lewis, Ann Radcliffe and ▷ Sir Walter Scott), but her own ironic tone is evident in the main body of the text and the resulting combination provides a sense of witty self-consciousness.

Williams, Raymond (1921–87)
One of the most influential of radical thinkers in Britain in the 20th century. Williams's work spans

literary criticism, cultural studies, media studies, communications and politics, and he also wrote plays and novels. In *Culture and Society 1780–1950* (1958) and *The Long Revolution* (1961) he laid the foundation for a wide-ranging analysis of modern cultural forms, and can justly be accredited with the foundation of cultural studies as an interdisciplinary field of enquiry. In books such as *Modern Tragedy* (1966) and *Drama from Ibsen to Brecht* (1968), which was a revision of his earlier *Drama from Ibsen to Eliot* (1952), he challenged accepted ways of evaluating drama and dramatic forms, and in 1968 he was a guiding spirit behind the New Left's *Mayday Manifesto* (1968). For Williams writing was primarily a social activity, deeply implicated in politics. Through books such as *The Country and The City* (1973), *Marxism and Literature* (1977), *Politics and Letters* (1979), *Problems in Materialism and Culture* (1980), *Writing in Society*, *Towards 2000* (1983) and his *John Clare's Selected Poetry and Prose* (1986), he pursued these themes with an intellectual rigour which refused easy formulations. His was the intellectual force behind the current movement of ▷ cultural materialism, the British equivalent of American ▷ new historicism. Williams's novels are about the people, geography and history of the Welsh borders where he grew up: *Border Country* (1960); *Second Generation* (1964); *The Fight for Manod* (1979); *People of the Black Mountains: 1 The Beginning* (1989); 2. *The Eggs of the Eagle* (1990).
Bib: Eagleton, T., *Raymond Williams: Critical Perspectives*.

Wilson, Angus (1913–91)

Novelist and short-story writer. Born in Durban, South Africa, Wilson was educated at Westminster School in London and at Merton College, Oxford. He worked for many years in the British Museum Reading Room, served in the Foreign Office during World War II, and, from 1963, taught English literature at the University of East Anglia. He was primarily a satirist, with a particularly sharp ear for the way in which hypocrisy, cruelty and smugness are betrayed in conversation. His first published works were short stories, *The Wrong Set* (1949) and *Such Darling Dodos* (1950), depicting English middle-class life around the time of World War II. His early work was traditional in form, inspired by his respect for the 19th-century English novel and a reaction against the dominance of post-Jamesian narrative techniques in the ▷ modernist novel. *Hemlock and After* (1952), *Anglo-Saxon Attitudes* (1956) and *The Middle Age of Mrs Eliot* (1958) deal with such issues as responsibility, guilt and the problem of loneliness. The surface is satirical, and at times highly comic, but, as the protagonist of *Anglo-Saxon Attitudes* comments, 'the ludicrous was too often only a thin covering for the serious and the tragic'. *The Old Men at the Zoo* (1961) represents a considerable change of mode: it is a bizarre fable concerning personal and political commitment, set in the London Zoo at a time of international crisis. From this point on Wilson's work became more experimental: *Late Call* (1964) makes use of pastiche, while *No Laughing Matter*

(1967) reflects the influence of ▷ Virginia Woolf, employing multiple interior monologues, as well as parodic dramatic dialogue and stories by one of the characters. It has a broad historical and social sweep, setting the story of a family between 1912 and 1967 in the context of British society as a whole. Like *Anglo-Saxon Attitudes* and *Late Call* it traces personal and public concerns back to the period immediately before World War I. *Setting the World on Fire* (1980) is another new departure in form; it is a complex and highly patterned work in which the myth of Phaeton is re-enacted in modern London. His other novels are: *As If By Magic* (1973). Story collections: *Death Dance* (1969); *Collected Stories* (1987). Travel writing: *Reflection in a Writer's Eye* (1986). Critical works include: *Emile Zola* (1952); *The World of Charles Dickens* (1970); *The Strange Ride of Rudyard Kipling* (1977).
Bib: Cox, C. B., *The Free Spirit*; Halio, J. L. (ed.), *Critical Essays on Angus Wilson*; Gardener, A., *Angus Wilson*; Faulkner, P., *Angus Wilson, Mimic and Moralist*.

Wilson, Colin (b 1931)

Novelist and critic. He is known primarily as the author of the ▷ existentialist work *The Outsider* (1956), which was much acclaimed at the time of its publication. He is the author of 15 novels, and over 50 works of non-fiction. His novels feature violence, sexuality and the idea of the outsider in society, and seek to acknowledge fictionality by using genres such as the detective story with a deliberate incongruity.

Wilson, Harriette (1786–1845)

Autobiographer. Infamous for her racy ▷ autobiography, *Memoirs* (1825), in which she describes her life as a courtesan and her affairs with many of the leading figures of her day. She planned the book with her husband William Henry Rochfort (whom she married in 1823), as a form of blackmail and, indeed, when it was published it caused an immediate sensation amongst those mentioned (including Beau Brummell and the Duke of Wellington), as well as amongst the outraged upholders of morality. She followed this with two ▷ romans-à-clef which are immensely readable, fast-paced accounts of London life: *Paris Lions and London Tigers* (1825) and *Clara Gazul* (1830).

Wings of the Dove, The (1902)

A novel by ▷ Henry James. The scene is principally London and Venice. Kate Croy and Merton Densher, a young journalist, are in love, but without the money to marry. Kate's rich aunt, Maud Lowder, takes into her circle Milly Theale, a lonely American girl of great single-mindedness, eagerness for life, and capacity for affection, and also a millionairess. Milly is travelling in Europe with Susan Stringham, an old friend of Mrs Lowder's. Mrs Stringham learns from Milly's doctor that the girl is suffering from a fatal illness, that her death cannot be long delayed, and that it can only be delayed at all if she achieves happiness.

Mrs Stringham communicate this to Kate, who conceives a plot with a double purpose: Merton is to engage Milly's love, the bringing her the happiness that she needs, and at the same time securing her money when she dies, so that Kate's own marriage to Merton can at last take place. Milly's love for Merton is very real; because of it, however, she refuses another suitor, Lord Mark, who knows Kate's plot and in revenge betrays it to Milly. She dies, broken-hearted, but she leaves Merton her money. Merton and Kate, however, find that they are for ever separated by the shadow of the dead Milly between them.

The story is an example of James's 'international theme': in this case, the openness and integrity which he saw as strengths of the American personality are opposed to the selfishness and deviousness which he saw as part of the decadent aspect of European culture. It is written in the condensed, allusive style which is characteristic also of ▷ *The Ambassadors* and ▷ *The Golden Bowl*.

Winterson, Jeanette (b 1959)

Novelist. Winterson's works have been praised for their originality of subject matter and form. Her first novel, the autobiographical *Oranges are not the only fruit* (1985), is a witty account of her upbringing as the child of fundamentalist Christians and her development as a lesbian in a town in the north of England; it won the Whitbread Award for First Novel and was translated into an enormously popular television series. Her subsequent novels have been more experimental and formally complex; these are *Boating for Beginners* (1986); *The Passion* (which won the John Llewelyn Rhys Prize in 1987); *Sexing the Cherry* (1989); *Written on the Body* (1992). ▷ Lesbian and gay writing.

Wives and Daughters (1864–6)

A novel by ▷ Mrs Gaskell, published serially in the ▷ *Cornhill Magazine* and not completed at her death. It is a study of two families, the Gibsons and the Hamleys, in a small country town and the relationships of the parents and the children in each. The central character is Molly Gibson, whose liberal, frank, sincere and deeply responsible nature is painfully tested by the marriage of her widowed father (a country doctor) to a silly, vain widow. The widow brings with her, however, her own daughter, Cynthia, a girl with her mother's outward charm but without her illness and with feelings guided more by her discerning intelligence than by spontaneous loyalties. Cynthia at 16 has become engaged to a coarse but astute man, Mr Preston, who is a local land-agent. The two girls become involved with the two sons of Mr Hamley, the local squire. The elder boy, Osborne, is superficially brilliant and charming and much overestimated by his father. The younger son, Roger, has much less showy qualities but a deeper nature and eventually wins the academic success expected of but not achieved by the elder, who makes an unfortunate marriage, is cast off by the father and dies young. The novel thus brings out the differences between superficial and deep natures, and the perils that result from consequent false estimates of character, made even by the intelligent.

Wodehouse, Sir Pelham Grenville (1881–1975)

Writer of humorous short-stories and novels. Born in Guildford, Surrey and educated at Dulwich College, London, he was brought up partly by aunts in England, since his father was a judge in Hong Kong. Known always as P. G. Wodehouse, his most famous creations were the good-natured but disaster-prone young man about town, Bertie Wooster, and his ever-resourceful 'gentleman's gentleman' (manservant), Jeeves, first introduced in *The Man With Two Left Feet* (1917). The Jeeves and Wooster books included: *My Man Jeeves* (1919); *The Inimitable Jeeves* (1923); *Carry On Jeeves* (1925); *Right Ho Jeeves* (1934); *The Code of the Woosters* (1938); *Jeeves in the Offing* (1960); *Stiff Upper Lip Jeeves* (1963). Wodehouse depicted a range of other comic characters, evoking a charming escapist myth of upper-class England of the 1920s. He also wrote school-stories such as *Mike* (1909), sentimental romances such as *Love Among the Chickens* (1906), song lyrics and works for the theatre and cinema. Despite a scandal when he broadcast from Germany during World War II, after having been captured, he remained immensely popular and widely read. He lived in Britain, France and the USA, becoming an American citizen in 1945.
Bib: Donaldson, F., *P.G. Wodehouse*.

Wollstonecraft, Mary (1759–97)

Pamphleteer and novelist. Wollstonecraft is notable for her outspoken views on the role of women in society, and on the part played by education in woman's oppression. After running a school in London with her sister, she set out her ideas in the early pamphlet *Thoughts on the Education of Daughters* (1787). The following year her novel, *Mary*, developed this theme, together with a satirical perspective on the manners of the aristocracy, possibly based on her own experiences as governess with the family of Lord Kingsborough in Ireland.

Wollstonecraft's most famous work, *A Vindication of the Rights of Woman* (1792) now stands as one of the major documents in the history of women's writing. Attacking the 'mistaken notions of female excellence' which she recognized in contemporary attitudes to 'femininity' and the cult of the sentimental, Wollstonecraft argued that women were not naturally submissive, but taught to be so, confined to 'smiling under the lash at which [they] dare not snarl'. Although widely caricatured by critics for her own 'immoral' life – an affair with Gilbert Imlay, and subsequent marriage with ▷ William Godwin – Wollstonecraft's ideas are closely related to the moralist tradition of writing addressed to young women. Arguing that the true basis of marriage must be not love but friendship, she continues the rational proposals outlined by the 17th-century pamphleteer ▷ Mary Astell in such works as *A Serious Proposal to the Ladies*. The most radical of her thoughts concern the treatment by society of unmarried mothers, whom she believed were worthy of the respect and support of their

families and lovers. Her novel *Maria: or, The Wrongs of Woman* (1798) remained unfinished and was published posthumously, but develops the ideas of *A Vindication* in a more complex and experimental context. The philosophical tradition behind her writings is evident in *A Vindication of the Rights of Man* (1790), a reply to ▷ Burke, and in the dedication of *Rights of Woman* to Talleyrand.
Bib: Tomalin, C., *The Life and Death of Mary Wollstonecraft*.

Women, Education of

In medieval convents, nuns often learned and received the same education as monks. Thereafter, women's intellectual education was not widely provided for until the later 19th century, though much would depend on their social rank, their parents, or their husbands. Thomas More in ▷ *Utopia* advocated equal education for both sexes; ▷ Swift in the 'Land of the Houyhnhnms' (▷ *Gulliver's Travels*) causes his enlightened horse to scorn the human habit of educating only half mankind, and yet allowing the other half (*ie* women) to bring up the children. On the other hand, in the 16th century the enthusiasm for education caused some highly born women to be very highly educated; this is true of the two queens, Mary I and Elizabeth I, of the 'ten-days queen' Lady Jane Grey (whose education is described in Ascham's *Schoolmaster*, 1570), and of the Countess of Pembroke, Sidney's sister. In the 17th century we see from ▷ Pepys's Diary how he tried to educate his French wife, and ▷ Evelyn, the other well-known diarist, describes his highly educated daughter. Rich women were expected to have some social and some artistic accomplishments, but Pepys's for example did not expect his wife to share his scientific interests.

It is often difficult to interpret the evidence from the past as it is sometimes based on assumptions or fears about women's education that enlightened people do not now share.

Boarding schools for girls came into existence in the 17th century and became more numerous in the 18th, but either they were empty of real educational value or they were absurdly pretentious, like Miss Pinkerton's Academy described in Thackeray's ▷ *Vanity Fair* (1847–8); Upper-class girls had governesses for general education, music masters, dancing masters, and teachers of 'deportment', *ie* in the bearing of the body; lower class women were illiterate, unless they learned to read and write at 'charity schools'. On the other hand they had a much wider range of domestic skills than is usual with modern women, and among the poor, a rich store of folklore. However, in the 18th century there was already a shift in values. Swift, in his letter to a young lady about to enter marriage, points out that the way to keep a husband's affections was to grow in maturity of mind, and the ▷ bluestocking women of the middle of the century were entertainers of the intellectual elite of their society.

The big change dates from the mid-19th century. Tennyson's *The Princess* (1850), for example,

advocates educational opportunities for women and the eponymous heroine actually founds a university for this purpose. Actual colleges were founded for the higher education of women (beginning with Queen's College, London, 1848), and schools (*eg* Cheltenham Ladies' College) comparable to the ▷ public schools for boys were founded. The women's colleges Girton (1869) and Newham (1875) were founded in Cambridge, and others followed at Oxford. Societies were also founded for the advancing of women's education. All this in spite of warnings from medical men that cerebral development in the female must be at the cost of physiological, *ie* child-bearing, aptitude. Since the commencement of state education in 1870, the status of women teachers has been brought equal to that of men teachers, and since 1902 equal secondary education has been provided for both sexes.

Women, Status of

Unmarried women had few prospects in Britain until the second half of the 19th century. In the Middle Ages they could enter convents and become nuns, but when in 1536–9 Henry VIII closed the convents and the monasteries, no alternative opened to them. Widows like Chaucer's Wife of Bath in ▷ *The Canterbury Tales* might inherit a business (in her case that of a clothier) and run it efficiently, or like Mistress Quickly in Shakespeare's *Henry IV, Part II* they might run inns. The profession of acting was opened to women from the Restoration of the Monarchy in 1660, and writing began to be a possible means of making money from the time of ▷ Aphra Behn. Later the increase of interest in education for girls led to extensive employment of governesses to teach the children in private families; such a position might be peaceful and pleasant, like Mrs Weston's experience in the Woodhouse family in Jane Austen's ▷ *Emma*, but it was at least as likely to be unpleasant, underpaid, and despised, as the novelist ▷ Charlotte Brontë found. Nursing was also open to women, but nurses had no training and were commonly a low class of women like Betsey Prig and Mrs Gamp in Dickens's ▷ *Martin Chuzzlewit* until Florence Nightingale reformed the profession.

Wives and their property were entirely in the power of their husbands according to the law, though in practice they might take the management of both into their own hands, like the Wife of Bath. A Dutch observer (1575) stated that England was called the 'Paradise of married women' because they took their lives more easily than Continental wives. Nonetheless, a middle-class wife worked hard, as her husband's assistant (probably his accountant) in his business, and as a mistress of baking, brewing, household management and amateur medicine.

The 19th century was the heroic age for women in Britain. No other nation before the 20th century has produced such a distinguished line of women writers as the novelists ▷ Jane Austen, ▷ Elizabeth Gaskell, Charlotte and ▷ Emily Brontë and ▷ George Eliot (Mary Ann Evans). In addition there was the prison reformer, Elizabeth Fry; the reformer of the nursing profession, Florence Nightingale; the explorer, Mary Kingsley; the sociologist, ▷ Beatrice Webb, pioneers in education, and the first women doctors. The Married Women's Property Act of 1882 for the first time gave wives rights to their own property which had hitherto been merged with their husbands'. Political rights came more slowly, and were preceded by an active and sometimes violent movement, led by the Suffragettes (▷ Suffragette Movement), who fought for them. Women over 30 were given the vote in 1918 as a consequence of their success in taking over men's work during World War I, but women over 21 (the age at which men were entitled to vote or stand for Parliament) had to wait until 1928. Now most professions are nominally open to women, including the law and even the pending ordination of women to the priesthood of the ▷ Church of England.

The position of women at work is still not equal to men: the success of a few women does not alter the fact that the average wage of women is about three-quarters that of men. Women are disproportionately under-represented in positions of security and power, for example in high level management jobs.

Women in Love (1921)

A novel by ▷ D. H. Lawrence. It continues the lives of two of the characters in ▷ *The Rainbow*. Ursula Brangwen is a schoolteacher, and her sister Gudrun is an artist. The other two main characters are Gerald Crich, a mine-owner and manager, and Rupert Birkin, a school-inspector. The main narrative is about the relationships of these four: the union of Rupert and Ursula after conflict, the union of Gerald and Gudrun ending in conflict and Gerald's death, the affinities and antagonisms between the sisters and between the men. The settings include Shortlands, the mansion of the mine-owning Crich family; Breadalby, the mansion of Lady Hermione Roddice, a meeting-place of the leading intellectuals of the day; the Café Pompadour in London, a centre for artists, and a winter resort in the Austrian Tyrol. The theme is human relationships in the modern world, where intelligence has become the prisoner of self-consciousness, and spontaneous life-forces are perverted into violence, notably in Gerald, Hermione, and the German sculptor Loerke. Symbolic episodes centred on animals and other natural imagery are used to present those forces of the consciousness that lie outside rational articulation, and personal relationships are so investigated as to illuminate crucial aspects of modern culture: the life of industry, the life of art, the use and misuse of reason, and what is intimate considered as the nucleus of what is public. Rupert Birkin is a projection of Lawrence himself, but he is objectified sufficiently to be exposed to criticism.

Women's movement, The

The women's movement – under many names – is dedicated to the campaign for political and legal rights for women. It wishes to prevent discrimination on the grounds of gender and is, generally, a movement for social change.

There is no single source, although the history of women's quest for equality is a long one. The *Querelle des Femmes* in the medieval period, ▷ Aphra Behn and Mary Astell in the 17th century, and ▷ Mary Wollstonecraft in the Romantic Age all furthered women's rights. In the Victorian period ▷ feminism became linked with other social movements such as anti-slavery campaigners, evangelical groups and ▷ Quakers. The ▷ suffragette movement (1860–1930) united women and their solidarity was to re-emerge in the radicalization of the 1960s. The important works of this later stage in the women's movement are ▷ Simone de Beauvoir's *Le Deuxième Sexe* (1949), Kate Millett's *Sexual Politics* (1969) and ▷ Germaine Greer's *The Female Eunuch* (1970). The 1970s and beyond have witnessed the second stage of the women's movement and seen its diversification into separate pressure groups – *eg* lesbianism, Third World – and its partial metamorphosis into post-feminism. This latter term has become popularized and takes for granted that women now have equality with men, but the mainstream of the women's movement denies this emphatically and perseveres with its campaign.

▷ Women, Status of.

Bib: Mitchell, J. and Oakley, A. (eds.), *What is Feminism?*; Eisenstein, H., *Contemporary Feminist Thought*; Faludi, S., *Backlash*.

Wood, Ellen (Mrs Henry), 1814–87

Novelist. Daughter of a glove manufacturer of scholarly tastes, Ellen Price was born in Worcester and lived as a child with her maternal grandmother. Curvature of the spine affected her health all her life and she wrote her novels in a reclining chair. In 1836 she married Henry Wood, head of a banking and shipping firm, and they lived in France until 1856 when they returned and remained in London. She was a very orthodox churchwoman and strongly conservative. Her first novel, *East Lynne* (1861), was enormously successful and has been much dramatized, translated and filmed. She wrote numerous other novels, though none other so famous, including *Mrs Halliburton's Troubles* (1862), *The Channings* (1862), *The Shadow of Ashlydyat* (1863), *Lord Oakburn's Daughters* (1864), *Within the Maze* (1872) and many more. The *Johnny Ludlow* series of stories (1868–89) drew on local and family history from her early life, and lacked some of the melodramatic and sensational elements of many of her other novels. Despite the heavy moralizing as well as careless and inaccurate writing, her novels were immensely popular, especially at first. She also took on contemporary issues: *A Life's Secret* (1867) portrayed a negative side of ▷ trade unionism and caused her publisher's office to be mobbed by a hostile crowd.

▷ Sensation novel.

Bib: Wood, C. W., *Memorials of Mrs Henry Wood*; Hughes, W., *The Maniac in the Cellar: Sensation Novels of the 1860s*.

Woodlanders, The (1887)

A novel by ▷ Thomas Hardy. The setting is
Dorset in the south-west of England and the human
relationships are a kind of movement upwards,
downwards and upwards again from the primitive
rural base. The primitive peasant girl, Marty
South, is in love with the young cider-maker,
Giles Winterbourne, who is as simple in his
background as she is herself but has great natural
delicacy of feeling. Giles is himself in love with
Grace Melbury, the daughter of a local timber
merchant, who has had a 'lady's' education. She
has not been spoiled by this but her sensibilities
have spoiled her for the primitive environment to
which Giles belongs. Her parents marry her to
the young doctor, Edred Fitzpiers, who, however,
is enticed away by the great lady of the district,
Felice Charmond. Grace takes refuge in the woods
with Giles, who, though a sick man, abandons his
cottage to her and lives in a hut nearby, where he
dies. Grace and Marty South mourn together over
his grave but Grace becomes reconciled to Fitzpiers
and Marty is left to mourn alone. Neither Fitzpiers
nor Mrs Charmond belongs to the rural background
and their intrusion into it is disruptive of its values,
embodied above all in Giles Winterbourne.

Woolf, Virginia (1882–1941)

Novelist and critic. She was the daughter of
▷ Leslie Stephen, the literary critic; after his death
in 1904, the house in the Bloomsbury district of
London which she shared with her sister Vanessa
(later Vanessa Bell) became the centre of the
▷ Bloomsbury Group of intellectuals, one of whom,
the socialist thinker Leonard Woolf, she married in
1912. Together they established the Hogarth Press
which published much of the most memorable
imaginative writing of the 1920s. She experienced
recurrent bouts of depression, and during one of
these took her own life by drowning herself in the
River Ouse, near her home at Rodmell, Sussex.

Her first two novels, *The Voyage Out* (1915)
and *Night and Day* (1919), are basically ▷ realist
in their technique, but in the next four – *Jacob's
Room* (1922), ▷ *Mrs Dalloway* (1925), ▷ *To the
Lighthouse* (1927) and ▷ *The Waves* (1931) – she
became increasingly experimental and innovatory.
Her attitude was formed by three influences: the
negative one of dissatisfaction with the methods
and outlook of the three novelists who, in the
first 20 years of this century, dominated the
contemporary public, ▷ H.G. Wells, ▷ Arnold
Bennett, and ▷ John Galsworthy (see Woolf's
essay 'Mr Bennett and Mrs Brown', 1923), the
outlook of the Bloomsbury circle, with their strong
emphasis on the value of personal relations and the
cultivation of the sensibility; the sense of tragedy
in the 19th-century Russian novelists, ▷ Tolstoy
and ▷ Dostoevsky, and the short-story writer
▷ Chekhov. She sought to develop a technique
of expression which would capture the essence
of the sensibility – the experiencing self – and to
do this, she reduced the plot-and-story element of
novel-writing as far as she could and developed a
▷ stream of consciousness narrative to render inner

experience. The last two of the four experimental
novels mentioned are usually considered to be her
most successful achievements, especially *To the
Lighthouse*. In her later novels, *The Years* (1937)
and *Between the Acts* (1941), she again used a
more customary technique, though with stress on
symbolism and bringing out the slight incident as
possibly that which is most revelatory. She is now
generally regarded as one of the greatest of the
modernist innovators, and is also an important focus
for feminist debate.

▷ *Orlando* (1928) is a composite work, ostensibly
a biography of a woman poet (▷ Victoria Sackville-
West), but in part a brilliantly vivid historical novel
(though her subject was her contemporary) and
in part literary criticism. Her more formal literary
criticism was published in two volumes *The Common
Reader* (1925) and *The Common Reader, 2nd Series*
(1932). In these she expressed her philosophy of
creative writing (for instance in the essay *Modern
Fiction*, 1925) and her response to the writers
and writings of the past that most interested her.
She had a partly fictional way of re-creating the
personalities of past writers which is sensitive and
vivid. In her social and political attitude she was
feminist, *ie* she was much concerned with the rights
of women and especially of women writers. This is
one of the basic themes of *Orlando* but it comes out
most clearly in *A Room of One's Own* (1931). *Flush*
(1933) is another experiment in fictional biography
(of Elizabeth Barrett Browning's spaniel) and she
wrote a straight biography of her friend the art
critic Roger Fry (1940). Apart from *The Common
Reader*, her volumes of essays and criticism include:
Three Guineas (1938); *The Death of the Moth* (1942);
The Captain's Death Bed (1950); *Granite and Rainbow*
(1958). Her *Collected Essays* were published in
1966, her *Letters* between 1975 and 1980 and her
diaries (*The Diary of Virginia Woolf*) between 1977
and 1984. *Moments of Being* (1976) is a selection of
autobiographical writings. Her stories are collected
in *A Haunted House* (1943).

Bib: Woolf, L., *Autobiography*; Bell, Q., *Virginia
Woolf, A Biography*; Gordon, L., *Virginia Woolf: A
Writer's Life*; Clements, P., and Grundy, I. (eds.),
Virginia Woolf: New Critical Essays; Daiches, D.,
Virginia Woolf; Johnstone, J. K., *The Bloomsbury
Group*; Marcus, J. (ed.), *New Feminist Essays on
Virginia Woolf*; Naremore, J., *The World Without
a Self*; Rosenthal, M., *Virginia Woolf*; Barrett, M.
(ed.), *Virginia Woolf: Women and Writing*; Marcus,
J., *Art and Anger: Reading like a Woman*; De Salvo,
L.A., *Virginia Woolf: The Impact of Childhood Sexual
Abuse on Her Life and Work*; Bowlby, R., *Virginia
Woolf: Feminist Destinations*; Roe S., *Writing and
Gender: Virginia Woolf's Writing Practice*.

Workhouses

Institutions to accommodate the destitute at public
expense, and to provide them with work to ensure
that they were socially useful. They were first
established under the ▷ Poor Law of 1576; they
increased in number, but by the 18th century
the administration of them, the responsibility
of the parish, had become seriously inefficient,

Select Critical Bibliography

Note

The critical books listed here have been chosen from the huge number of works about the novel for one of the following reasons: (a) because they provide useful overviews, introductions or source material; (b) because they have been influential in the history of novel criticism and theory; (c) because they deal with areas or aspects of fiction which are of particular importance or which are relatively neglected.

Allott, Miriam	*Novelists on the Novel* (London: Routledge & Kegan Paul, 1959)
Bakhtin, M.M.	*The Dialogic Imagination: Four Essays*, edited by Michael Holquist, translated by Caryl Emerson and Michael Holquist (Austin: University of Texas Press, 1981)
Barthes, Roland	*S/Z*, translated by Richard Miller (1974; Oxford: Blackwell, 1990)
Bergonzi, Bernard	*The Situation of the Novel* (London: Macmillan, 1970)
Booth, Wayne C.	*The Rhetoric of Fiction* (Chicago and London: University of Chicago Press, 1961)
Bradbury, Malcolm	*Possibilities: Essays on the State of the Novel* (London: Oxford University Press, 1973)
Bradbury, Malcolm	*The Novel Today: Contemporary Writers on Modern Fiction*, revised edition (Glasgow: Fontana, 1990)
Brooks, Peter	*Reading for the Plot: Design and Intention in Narrative* (Cambridge, MA and London: Harvard University Press, 1984)
Day, Geoffrey	*From Fiction to the Novel* (London: Routledge, 1987)
Forster, E.M.	*Aspects of the Novel* (London: Edward Arnold, 1927)
Genette, Gérard	*Narrative Discourse*, translated by Jane E. Lewin (Oxford: Blackwell, 1980)
Gibson, Andrew	*Reading Narrative Discourse: Studies in the Novel from Cervantes to Beckett* (Basingstoke and London: Macmillan, 1980)
Gilbert, Sandra M. and Gubar, Susan	*The Madwoman in the Attic: The Woman Writer and the Nineteenth-Century Literary Imagination* (New Haven and London: Yale University Press, 1979)
Gilbert, Sandra M. and Gubar, Susan	*No Man's Land: the Place of the Woman Writer in the Twentieth Century*, 3 volumes (New Haven and London: Yale University Press, 1988, 1989 and forthcoming)
Hardy, Barbara	*The Appropriate Form: An Essay on the Novel*, revised edition (London: Athlone Press, 1971)
Hawthorn, Jeremy	*Studying the Novel: an Introduction*, 2nd edition (London: Edward Arnold, 1992)
Hillis Miller, J.	*Fiction and Repetition: Seven English Novels* (Oxford: Basil Blackwell, 1982)
Hillis Miller, J.	*Ariadne's Thread: Story Lines* (New Haven and London: Yale University Press, 1992)
Hunter, J. Paul	*Before Novels: the Cultural Contexts of Eighteenth-Century English Fiction* (London: W.W. Norton, 1990)
Hutcheon, Linda	*Narcissistic Narrative: the Metafictional Paradox* (1980; New York and London: Methuen, 1984)

James, Henry — *The Critical Muse: Selected Literary Criticism*, edited by Roger Gard (London: Penguin, 1987)

Jameson, Fredric — *The Political Unconscious: Narrative as a Socially Symbolic Act* (London: Methuen, 1981)

Kermode, Frank — *The Sense of an Ending: Studies in the Theory of Fiction* (London: Oxford University Press, 1966)

Kermode, Frank — *Modern Essays* (London: Fontana, 1971)

Kettle, Arnold — *An Introduction to the English Novel*, 2 volumes (London: Hutchinson, 1951, 1953)

Kettle, Arnold (ed.) — *The Nineteenth Century Novel: Critical Essays and Documents*, revised edition (London: Heinemann, 1981)

Kime Scott, Bonnie (ed.) — *The Gender of Modernism: A Critical Anthology* (Bloomington and Indianapolis: Indiana University Press, 1990)

King, Bruce (ed.) — *The Commonwealth Novel Since 1960* (Basingstoke and London: Macmillan, 1991)

Kundera, Milan — *The Art of the Novel* (London: Faber, 1990)

Leavis, F.R. — *The Great Tradition: George Eliot, Henry James, Joseph Conrad* (1948; Harmondsworth: Penguin, 1972)

Lodge, David — *Language of Fiction: Essays in Criticism and Verbal Analysis of the English Novel*, 2nd edition (London: Routledge & Kegan Paul, 1984)

Nasta, Susheila (ed.) — *Motherlands: Black Women's Writing from Africa, the Caribbean and South Asia* (London: Women's Press, 1991)

Rimmon-Kenan, Shlomith — *Narrative Fiction: Contemporary Poetics* (London and New York: Routledge, 1983)

Seymour-Smith, Martin — *Novels and Novelists: A Guide to the World of Fiction* (New York: St Martin's Press, 1980)

Showalter, Elaine — *A Literature of Their Own: British Women Novelists from Brontë to Lessing* (1977; London: Virago, 1978)

Sutherland, John — *The Longman Companion to Victorian Fiction* (Harlow, Essex: Longman, 1988)

Watt, Ian — *The Rise of the Novel: Studies in Defoe, Richardson and Fielding* (1957; Harmondsworth: Penguin, 1972)

Chronology

This chronology gives a breakdown of important dates, both literary and historical. The literary dates are listed in the left-hand column and the historical events in the right-hand column. The listing is necessarily selective.

c. 2000 BC
Story of Sinahue (Egyptian novel)

c. 1400 BC
Epic of Gilgamesh

c. 600 BC
Odyssey; Iliad (written down)

c. AD 50
Petronus: *Satyricon*

c. 160
Apuleius: *The Golden Ass*

c. 200
Longus: *Daphis and Chloe*

c. 900
The Arabian Nights

	1066 Battle of Hastings, Victory of William, Duke of Normandy **1086** Domesday Book compiled
c. 1136 Geoffrey of Monmouth: *History of the Kings of Britain*	
	c. 1209 After riots at Oxford some students move to Cambridge **1215** The Magna Carta signed
c. 1220 Laʒamon: *Brut* **c. 1230** *The Romance of the Rose*	
	1231 Establishment of the Chancellorship as most important office of state **1295** Edward I forms the Model Parliament
Dante: began *Divine Comedy* (? 1307)	**1337** Beginning of the Hundred Years War
1348–53 Boccaccio: *The Decameron*	**1349** The Black Death
c. 1360 *Gawain and the Green Knight, Patience* and *Pearl Morte Arthure* **1375–99** Chaucer: *Canterbury Tales* (? 1373–93) *Troilus and Criseyde* Wycliffe: Trans of the bible (1380)	**1377** Richard II **1381** The Peasants' Revolt: Wat Tyler's rebellion **1399** Henry IV
1400–24 Paston Letters (1422–1507) Caxton: *Recuyell of the Histories of Troy* (? printed 1474) Malory: *Morte d'Arthur* (printed 1485) Caxton: trans. of Aesop's *Fables* Henryson: *Moral Fables of Aesop*	**1413** Henry V **1415** Battle of Agincourt **1422** Henry VI

1429
Joan of Arc raises the Seige of Orleans
1461
Edward IV
1475
Richard III
1476/7
Establishment of Caxton's printing press in England
1485
Henry VII
1492
Columbus lands in America
1498
Erasmus in England

1509
Henry VIII succeeds as King of England on death of
Henry VII

1513
Gavin Douglas: trans. of Virgil's *Aeneid* (written; printed
1553)
1516
Sir Thomas More: *Utopia*

1517
Luther's '95 Theses': start of the Reformation
1520
Meeting at the Field of the Cloth of Gold between Henry
VIII and Francis I
1521
Henry VIII Defender of the Faith
Luther appears before the Diet of Worms

1525
Tyndale: trans. of the New Testament

1526
Burning of Tyndale's trans. of the New Testament
1531
Henry VIII declared Head of the Church in England
1532
Submission of the clergy (to Henry VIII; begins English
Reformation)
1533
Jan. Henry VIII secretly married to Anne Boleyn
Apr. Divorce of Henry VIII from Catherine of Aragon
June Coronation of Anne Boleyn
July Henry VII excommunicated by the Pope
Sept. Birth of Princess Elizabeth to Anne Boleyn
1534
England's final break with Rome
More's refusal to take oath to the succession
Parliament passes Act of Supremacy: Pope's powers in
England taken over by Henry VIII

1533-35
Rabelais: *Pantagruel and Gargantua*

1535
Coverdale: trans. of the Bible

1535
Henry VIII named 'Supreme Head of the Church'
Trial and execution of Sir Thomas More
1536
Execution of Anne Boleyn
1539
Act of the Six Articles passed, 'abolishing diversity of
opinions'
Marriage treaty between Anne of Cleves and Henry VIII
1540
Annulment of Henry VIII's marriage to Anne of Cleves
Marriage between Henry VIII and Catherine Howard
1542
Execution of Catherine Howard
Mary Queen of Scots accedes on death of James V of
Scotland

1543
Marriage of Catherine Parr and Henry VIII
1545
The Council of Trent: beginning of the Counter-
Reformation
1547
Death of Henry VIII: succeeded by Edward VI (aged 9)
Repeal of Act of Six Articles (1539)

1548
Book of Common Prayer

1549
New Book of Common Prayer to be used from this date
1553
Gavin Douglas: trans. of Virgil's *Aeneid* (written 1513)

1553
Death of Edward VI
Lady Jane Grey proclaimed queen
Mary proclaimed queen in place of Lady Jane Grey

1554
Lazovillo de Tormes

1554
Roman Catholicism re-established in England by
Parliament
1556
Stationers' Company gains monopoly of English printing

1557
Earl of Surrey: trans. of Virgil's *Aeneid* (Books II and
IV)
1558
Knox: *First Blast of the Trumpet*
1559
Mirror for Magistrates (first edition)

1558
Death of Mary; accession of Elizabeth I
1559
Coronation of Elizabeth I
Act of Supremacy and Act of Uniformity

1563
Foxe: *Acts and Monuments* (Foxe's Book of Martyrs)
1565
Golding: trans. of Ovid's *Metamorphoses* (Books I–IV)

1563
The Plague in London kills many thousands

1566
Birth of James VI of Scotland
1567
Abdication of Mary Queen of Scots

1570
Ascham: *The Schoolmaster*

1572
St Bartholomew's Day massacre in Paris
1577
Holinshed: *Chronicles*
1578
Lyly: *Euphues, the Anatomy of Wit* Part One
1579
North: trans. of Plutarch's *Lives* (from French)
1580
Lyly: *Euphues and his England*
1581
Joseph Hall: *Ten Books of Homer's Iliads*

1577
Francis Drake starts his circumnavigation of the globe
1578
James VI takes over government of Scotland

1580
Francis Drake returns to England
1581
Laws against Roman Catholics passed
1583
Discovery of the Somerville plot to assassinate Elizabeth
I
Discovery of the Throgmorton plot for Spanish invasion
of England

1584
Knox: *History of the Reformation in Scotland*
Peele: *Arraignment of Paris*

1585
Raleigh establishes his first colony at Roanoke, Virginia
1586
Camden: *Britannia*

1586
The Star Chamber condemns Mary Queen of Scots to
death
1587
Mary Queen of Scots executed

1588
Greene: *Pandosto*

1590
Lodge: *Rosalynde*
Sidney: *Arcadia*
Spenser: *Faerie Queene* (Books I–III)
1591
Sir John Harington: trans. of Ariosto's *Orlando Furioso*
Sidney: *Astrophel and Stella* (posthumous)
Spenser: *Complaints*
1592
Greene's *Groatsworth of Wit*
Lyly: *Galatea*
1593
Henryson: *The Testament of Cresseid* (published)
1594
Hooker: *Ecclesiastical Polity* (Books I–IV)
Nashe: *The Unfortunate Traveller*

1596
Spenser: *Faerie Queene* (Books IV–VI)
         Four Hymns
1597
Bacon: *Essays*
Joseph Hall: *Virgidemiarum* (Books I–III)
Deloney: *Jack of Newbury*
1598
Chapman: trans. of Homer's *Iliad* (Books I–II; VII–XI)

1600
Fairfax: trans. of Tasso's *Jerusalem Delivered*

1605
Cervantes: *Don Quixote* (Part I)

1610
Chapman: trans. of the *Iliad* Books I–XII
1611
Authorised Version of the Bible
Chapman: trans. of the *Iliad* Books XIII–XXIV

1614
Chapman: trans. of *The Odyssey* Books I–XII
1615
Chapman: trans. of the *Odyssey* Books XIII–XXIV

1588
19 July Spanish Armada sighted off the Cornish coast
29 July The Battle of Gravelines: the Armada defeated

1592
Establishment of the Presbyterian Church in Scotland

1595
Death of Sir Francis Drake

1599
Birth of Oliver Cromwell

1601
The execution of Earl of Essex
1602
Bodleian Library founded
Re-conquest of Ireland begun
1603
Queen Elizabeth I dies and is succeeded by James VI of
    Scotland as King James I of England and Ireland
1604
The Hampton Court conference: James supports new
    traslation of Bible
James VI and I proclaimed king of 'Great Britain, France
    and Ireland'
1605
The Gunpowder plot
1606
Suppression of Roman Catholics by English Parliament
1607
English colony founded in Virginia

1611
The colonisation of Ulster

1613
Poisoning of Sir Thomas Overbury
1614
'The Addled Parliament'

1618
Start of Thirty Years War
Execution of Sir Walter Raleigh

1621
Wroth: *Urania* (Part I)

1626
Sandys: trans. of Ovid's *Metamorphoses*

1634
Thomas Carew: *Coelum Britannicum*
1642
Sir Thomas Browne: *Religio Medici*

1644
Milton: *Areopagitica*

1651
Hobbes: *Leviathan*

1653
Izaak Walton: *Compleat Angler*
Scudéry: *Artamène* (1649–53)

1660
Pepys: *Diary* (begun 1 Jan.)

1668
Aphra Behn: *Oroonoko*

1678
Bunyan: *Pilgrim's Progress* (Part One)
La Fayette: *The Princess of Clèves*
1681
Aphra Benn: *The Rover* Part Two

Pilgrim's Progress

1620
Freedom of worship granted to Roman Catholics in
England in terms of marriage treaty between England
and Spain
Pilgrim Fathers depart from Plymouth, England, in
Mayflower

1625
Accession of Charles I
Marriage of Charles I and Henrietta Maria

1633
William Laud appointed Archbishop of Canterbury

1642
Civil War starts
Battle of Edgehill

1645
Prohibition of the Prayer Book by Parliament
Execution of Archbishop Laud
1649
Execution of Charles I
Abolition of the monarchy
Declaration of the Commonwealth
1651
Battle of Worcester

1653
Long Parliament expelled by Cromwell
Establishment of the Protectorate: Oliver Cromwell Lord
High Protector
1654
Union of England, Scotland and Ireland
1658
3 Sept. Death of Oliver Cromwell: succeeded by Richard
Cromwell, his son, as Lord Protector
1660
16 Mar. Dissolution of the Long Parliament
Charles II invited to return to England by Convention
Parliament
1661
Corporation Act: magistrates' oath of allegiance
1662
Act of Uniformity: revises Prayer Book; Licensing Act
forbids import of anti-Christian literature
1665
The Great Plague
1666
2 Sept. Great Fire of London

1674
Rebuilding of the Theatre Royal, Drury Lane
1678
The Popish Plot: the Pope, France and Spain are accused
of conspiracy to defeat Charles

1683
Rye House plot to kill Charles II and his brother, James,
Duke of York

1685
Death of Charles II; succeeded by James II
The Monmouth Rebellion
1688
The Glorious Revolution
William of Orange invited to England by Whig lords
1689
Abdication of James II declared by Parliament
Coronation of William and Mary
Act of Toleration (for Dissenters)
1690
Battle of the Boyne

1691
Congreve: *Incognita*

1693
The National Debt established
1694
Establishment of the Bank of England
1695
End of Press Censorship

1701
Protestant succession to British throne established by the
     Act of Settlement
1702
Death of William III. Accession of Queen Anne
1704
Marlborough achieves victory over the French at the
     Battle of Blenheim
1707
The Union of England and Scotland as Great Britain

1704
Swift: *Battle of the Books*
     Tale of a Tub

1709
Steele: *The Tatler* (Apr. 1709–Jan. 1711)
1711
Addison (and Steele): *The Spectator* (1 Mar. 1711–6 Dec.
     1712)

1714
1 Aug. Death of Queen Anne: succeeded by George I
     (Elector of Hanover)
1715
Jacobite uprising

1719
Defoe: *Robinson Crusoe*

1720
South Sea Bubble
1721
Robert Walpole becomes Prime Minister

1722
Defoe: *Journal of the Plague Year*
     Moll Flanders
1724
Defoe: *Roxana*
1726
Swift: *Gulliver's Travels*

1727
Death of George I: succeeded by his son George II

1730
The Grub Street Journal (–1737)
1735
Le Sage: *Gil Blas* (1715–35)
1740
Richardson: *Pamela* (Volumes I–II)
1741
Fielding: *Shamela*
Hume: *Essays Moral and Political* (Volume I)
Richardson: *Pamela* (Volumes III–IV)
1742
Fielding: *Joseph Andrews*

1747
Richardson: *Clarissa* (Volumes I–II)
1749
Cleland: *Fanny Hill*
Fielding: *Tom Jones*

1752
Adoption of the Gregorian calendar: 2 September
followed by 14 September
1753
Apr. Charter granted for the foundation of the British
Museum

1755
Johnson: *Dictionary of the English Language*
1760
Sterne: *Tristram Shandy* (Volumes I–II)

1760
25 Oct. Death of George II. Accession of George III

1761
Sterne: *Tristram Shandy* (Volumes III–IV and V–VI)

1763
16 May Boswell meets Johnson

1764
Horace Walpole: *The Castle of Otranto*
1765
Sterne: *Tristram Shandy* (Volumes VII–VIII)
1766
Goldsmith: *The Vicar of Wakefield*
1767
Sterne: *Tristram Shandy* (Volume IX)
1768
Chatterton: *Rowleyan Writings* (composed)

1769
Opening of the Royal Academy
1770
Lord North becomes Prime Minister
Import duties on all goods except tea removed
1772
Start of Captain Cook's second voyage of discovery

1773
Diderot: *Jacques the Fatalist*
1775
Reeve: *The Progress of Romance*

1773
The Boston Tea Party
1775
Defeat of the British at the Battle of Lexington: start of
the American War of Independence
George Washington becomes Commander-in-Chief of
American forces

1776
Gibbon: *Decline and Fall of the Roman Empire* (Volume I)
1778
Fanny Burney: *Evelina*
1779
Johnson: *Lives of the Poets* (Volume I)
1780
Bentham: *Principles of Morals and Legislation* (privately
printed)
1781
Johnson: *Lives of the Poets* (Volume II)
1782
Fanny Burney: *Cecilia*

1782
Resignation of Lord North
Preliminaries for peace between Britain and America
1783
Pitt's first ministry (–1801)
1784
John Wesley founds Methodism
William Pitt becomes Prime Minister
1788
First colony founded in Australia
The Times first published

1789
The Storming of the Bastille: Start of the French Revolution

1790
Burke: *Reflections on the Revolution in France*
1791
Boswell: *The Life of Johnson*
Tom Paine: *The Rights of Man* (Part I)
1792
Tom Paine: *The Rights of Man* (Part II)

1792
Paris Commune established
Trial of Tom Paine
1793
Godwin: *Political Justice*
1794
Ann Radcliffe: *The Mysteries of Udolpho*
1796
Fanny Burney: *Camilla*
M. G. Lewis: *The Monk*

1793
Louis XVI executed

1798
The Irish rebellion
Nelson beats the French fleet at the Battle of the Nile
1799
Hannah More: *Modern Female Education*

1799
Newspaper Act

1800
Bill of Union of Great Britain and Ireland
1804
Napoleon crowned emperor
1805
Wordsworth: *The Prelude* (completed)
1807
C. and M. Lamb: *Tales from Shakespeare*

1805
Battle of Trafalgar: Nelson defeats French fleet

1809
Battle of Corunna: death of Sir John Moore
1811
Jane Austen: *Sense and Sensibility*

1811
The Regency Act makes the Prince of Wales Prince Regent (George III insane)
Luddite riots

1812
Byron: *Childe Harold* (Cantos I and II)
1813
Jane Austen: *Pride and Prejudice*
1814
Jane Austen: *Mansfield Park*
Fanny Burney: *The Wanderer*
Maria Edgeworth: *Patronage*
Scott: *Waverley*

1815
Passage of Corn Law prohibiting imports when price low
Battle of Waterloo: Wellington defeats Napoleon

1816
Jane Austen: *Emma*
Byron: *Childe Harold* (Canto III)
Scott: *Old Mortality*
1817
Blackwood's Magazine (established)
Coleridge: *Biographia Literaria*
Mary Shelley: *Frankenstein*
1818
Jane Austen: *Northanger Abbey*
                Persuasion
Byron: *Childe Harold* (Canto IV)
Peacock: *Nightmare Abbey*
Scott: *Heart of Midlothian*

1818
5 May Birth of Karl Marx

1819
Byron: *Don Juan* (Cantos I and II)
Scott: *Bride of Lammermoor*

1820
Lamb: *Essays of Elia* (begun)
Scott: *Ivanhoe*
1821
Byron: *Don Juan* (Cantos III and V)
De Quincey: *Confessions of an English Opium Eater*
Scott: *Kenilworth*

1823
Byron: *Don Juan* (Cantos XV–XVI)
Hazlitt: *Liber Amoris*
Scott: *Quentin Durward*
Lamb: *Essays of Elia* (second series)
Westminster Review (established)
1824
Byron: *Don Juan* (Cantos XV–XVI)
1828
The *Spectator* (established)
1830
Cobbett: *Rural Rides*
Stendhal: *The Red and the Black*
1831
Peacock: *Crotchet Castle*

1833
Carlyle: *Sartor Resartus* (in *Frazer's Magazine*; completed 1834)

1834
Dickens: *Sketches by Boz*

1836
Dickens: *Pickwick Papers* (completed 1837)
1837
Dickens: *Oliver Twist* (completed 1838)

1838
Dickens: *Nicholas Nickleby* (completed 1839)
1840
Browning: 'Sordello'
Dickens: *Old Curiosity Shop*
1841
Dickens: *Barnaby Rudge*

1843
Carlyle: *Past and Present*
Dickens: *Martin Chuzzlewit* (completed 1844)
Macaulay: *Essays* (reprinted from *Edinburgh Review*)
Ruskin: *Modern Painters* (Volume I)

min Disraeli: *Sybil, or The Two Nations*

1819
The Peterloo Massacre: Manchester reform meeting broken up
Parliament passes the Six Acts to suppress possible disorder
1820
Death of George III: succeeded by George IV (the Prince Regent)
1821
Greek War of Independence
Legislation regarding free trade

1822
George Canning becomes Leader of the House of Commons and Foreign Secretary
1823
Catholic association established in Ireland by Daniel O'Connell
Robert Peel permits transportation of convicts
The Monroe doctrine: United States refuses to tolerate European political intervention in American states

1828
Tory administration formed by Wellington
1830
26 June Death of George IV: William IV comes to the throne

1832
The Reform Bill becomes law (start of electoral reform process)
1833
29 Aug. Controls placed upon child labour by passage of Factory Act

1834
Formation of the Grand National Consolidated Trades Union
The Tolpuddle Martyrs sentenced to transportation
Abolition of slavery in territories governed by Britain
1836
Chartist movement founded
1837
Death of William IV; Queen Victoria succeeds to the throne

1841
Conservative ministry formed by Robert Peel
1842
Parliament rejects Chartist petition
Mines Act: regulates employment of women and children underground
Chartist uprisings

1846
Balzac: *Cousin Bette*
Dickens: *Dombey and Son* (completed 1848)
1847
A. Brontë: *Agnes Grey*
C. Brontë: *Jane Eyre*
E. Brontë: *Wuthering Heights*
1848
Elizabeth Gaskell: *Mary Barton*
Thackeray: *Vanity Fair* (completed)
1849
C. Brontë: *Shirley*
Dickens: *David Copperfield*
Thackeray: *Pendennis* (completed 1850)
1850
Ruskin: *Pre-Raphaelitism*
Wordsworth: 'The Prelude' (written 1805)

1852
Dickens: *Bleak House*
1853
C. Brontë: *Villette*
Elizabeth Gaskell: *Cranford*
1854
Dickens: *Hard Times*

1855
Browning: 'Men and Women'
Dickens: *Little Dorrit* (completed 1857)
Trollope: *The Warden*
1857
C. Brontë: *The Professor*
Elizabeth Barrett Browning: 'Aurora Leigh'
Trollope: *Barchester Towers*
Flaubert: *Madame Bovary*
1859
Darwin: *Origin of Species*
Dickens: *Tale of Two Cities*
George Eliot: *Adam Bede*
1860
Wilkie Collins: *Woman in White*
Dickens: *Great Expectations* (completed 1861)
George Eliot: *Mill on the Floss*
1861
George Eliot: *Silas Marner*
1862
J. S. Mill: *Utilitarianism* (in *Frazer's Magazine*)
1863
George Eliot: *Romola*
Thomas Huxley: *Man's Place in Nature*
Kinglsey: *Water Babies*
1865
Matthew Arnold: *Essays in Criticism*
Lews Carroll: *Alice's Adventures in Wonderland*
Dickens: *Our Mutual Friend* (completed)

1866
Elizabeth Gaskell: *Wives and Daughters*
Dostoevsky: *Crime and Punishment*

1867
Matthew Arnold: *The Study of Celtic Literature*

1846
May Repeal of the Corn Laws

1849
Benjamin Disraeli becomes Conservative leader

1851
Palmerston resigns
1852
Lord John Russell resigns
1853
Free Trade budget introduced by Gladstone

1854
Britain and France declare war on Russia (Crimean War)
The Battle of Balaclava: the charge of the Light Brigade

1859
Benjamin Disraeli's Reform Bill
Liberal administration formed by Palmerston

1861
American Civil War starts

1865
The Confederate army surrenders at Shreveport: end of
the United States Civil War
Palmerston dies; Lord John Russell becomes Prime
Minister

1867
Fenian disturbances
The Dominion of Canada established by the British
North America Act
Suffrage extended by Parliamentary Reform Act

1868
Wilkie Collins: *The Moonstone*
George Eliot: *The Spanish Gypsy*

1869
Blackmore: *Lorna Doone*
Tolstoy: *War and Peace* (1863–9)
1870
Dickens: *Mystery of Edwin Drood*
1871
George Eliot: *Middlemarch* (completed 1872)

1872
Hardy: *Under the Greenwood Tree*
1873
Pater: *Studies in the History of the Renaissance*
1874
Hardy: *Far from the Madding Crowd*

1876
George Eliot: *Daniel Deronda*
1877
Henry James: *The American*
1878
Hardy: *The Return of the Native*
1879
Henry James: *Daisy Miller*
Meredith: *The Egoist*
1880
Benjamin Disraeli: *Endymion*
1881
Hardy: *A Laodicean*
Henry James: *Portrait of a Lady*
1882
Matthew Arnold: *Irish Essays*
1883
Burton: trans. of *Arabian Nights Entertainments*
Stevenson: *Treasure Island*
Schreiner: *Story of an African Farm*

1886
Henry James: *The Bostonians*
Stevenson: *Dr Jekyll and Mr Hyde*
     Kidnapped

1888
Matthew Arnold: *Essays in Criticism* (second series)

1891
Gissing: *New Grub Street*
Hardy: *Tess of the D'Urbervilles*
William Morris: *News from Nowhere*
Wilde: *The Picture of Dorian Gray*
1893
Gissing: *The Odd Woman*

1894
Kipling: *The Jungle Book*
William Morris: *The Wood beyond the World*
Ella Hepworth Dixon: *The Story of a Modern Woman*
Annie Holdsworth: *Joanna Traill, Spinster*

1868
Benjamin Disraeli becomes Prime Minister
Liberal victory in General Election: Gladstone forms
     ministry
1869
Opening of the Suez Canal
Birth of Gandhi

1871
Religious tests for entry to universities of Oxford and
     Cambridge abolished by the Universities Tests Act
Trade Unions legalized by Act of Parliament
1872
Voting by secret ballot introduced by the Ballot Act
1873
Judicature Act, reforming courts of law
1874
Conservative victory in General Election
Benjamin Disraeli forms ministry
1875
Public Health Act

1877
Queen Victoria becomes Empress of India

1880
Liberal administration formed by Gladstone

1883
Karl Marx dies

1885
General Gordon dies at Khartoum
1886
Gladstone brings in Home Rule Bill for Ireland
Second reading of Home Rule Bill brings Liberal defeat

1887
The Golden Jubilee of Queen Victoria
1888
Local Government Act (establishes local councils)
1890
Parnell resigns as Irish Nationalist leader

1893
Jan. Independent Labour Party formed by Keir Hardie at
     Bradford conference

1895
Hardy: *Jude the Obscure*
H. G. Wells: *The Time Machine*
Wilde: *The Importance of Being Earnest*
Grant Allen: *The Woman Who Did*
1897
Henry James: *What Maisie Knew*
H. G. Wells: *The Invisible Man*
Bram Stoker: *Dracula*
1898
Conrad: *The Nigger of the Narcissus*
Henry James: 'The Turn of the Screw'
H. G. Wells: *The War of the Worlds*
1899
Henry James: *The Awkward Age*

1898
19 May Gladstone dies

1899
Boer War begins

1900
Conrad: *Lord Jim*
Saintsbury: *History of Criticism*
1901
Kipling: *Kim*
Shaw: *The Devil's Disciple*
1902
Conrad: *Heart of Darkness*
Henry James: *Wings of a Dove*

1903
Henry James: *The Ambassadors*

1904
Henry James: *The Golden Bowl*
1905
Wilde: *De Profundis*
1907
Conrad: *The Secret Agent*
            Nostromo
1908
Forster: *A Room with a View*

1910
Forster: *Howards End*

1911
Conrad: *Under Western Eyes*
Lawrence: *The White Peacock*

1913
Lawrence: *Sons and Lovers*

1914
Joyce: *Dubliners*

1900
British Labour Party founded
Commonwealth of Australia proclaimed
1901
Queen Victoria dies and Edward VII accedes to the
    throne
1902
Boer War ends
Secondary schools established by Education Act for
    England and Wales
1903
Emmeline Pankhurst founds the Women's Social and
    Political Union
Orville and Wilbur Wright's first flight
1904
Entente Cordiale between Britain and France
1905
Unrest in Russia

1909
Institution of a system of old age pensions for all persons
    over 70 years of age
1910
Death of Edward VII; accession of George V
Commons resolution to reduce the life of Parliament from
    seven to five years with restrictions on the power of the
    Lords' veto
1911
Passage of the Copyright Act: copies of all British
    publications go to the British Museum and five other
    copyright libraries
National Insurance Bill introduced by Lloyd George
Suffragette riots in London
1912
Commons reject Women's Franchise Bill
1913
Commons pass Irish Home Rule Bill, rejected by the
    Lords
Suffragette demonstrations in London
'Cat and Mouse' Act
1914
Germany declares war on Russia: start of the First World
    War
Britain declares war on Germany

1915
Buchan: *The Thirty-Nine Steps*
F. Maddox Ford: *The Good Soldier*
Lawrence: *The Rainbow*
Somerset Maugham: *Of Human Bondage*
Dorothy Richardson: *Pointed Roofs*
Woolf: *The Voyage Out*
1916
Joyce: *A Portrait of the Artist as a Young Man*

1917
Henry James: *The Ivory Tower*

1918
Rebecca West: *The Return of the Soldier*
Mansfield: 'Prelude'

1919
May Sinclair: *Mary Olivier*

1920
Pound: *Hugh Selwyn Mauberley*

1921
Lawrence: *Women in Love*
1922
Galsworthy: *The Forsyte Saga*
Aldous Huxley: *Mortal Coils*
Joyce: *Ulysses*

1924
Forster: *A Passage to India*
1925
I. A. Richards: *Principles of Literary Criticism*
Woolf: *Mrs Dalloway*
1926
Lawrence: *The Plumed Serpent*

1927
Woolf: *To the Lighthouse*

1928
Lawrence: *Lady Chatterley's Lover*
Radclyffe Hall: *The Well of Loneliness* (banned)
Evelyn Waugh: *Decline and Fall*
Virginia Woolf: *Orlando*
1929
R. Graves: *Good-bye to All That*
I. A. Richards: *Practical Criticism*

1930
Lawrence: *The Virgin and the Gypsy*
Sol Plaatje: *Mhudi*
1931
Virginia Woolf: *The Waves*

1932
Aldous Huxley: *Brave New World*
Evelyn Waugh: *Black Mischief*

1915
Second Battle of Ypres
English and French forces land at Gallipoli

1916
The Battle of Verdun
Lloyd George becomes Prime Minister
1917
Abdication of Czar Nicholas II
United States declares war on Germany
The October revolution: Lenin leads Bolsheviks against Kerensky in Russia
1918
Second Battle of the Somme
Second Battle of the Marne
Execution of Nicholas II
Women over 30 given the vote
1919
Peace conference at Versailles adopts Covenant of the League of Nations
The Treaty of Versailles signed
1920
The League of Nations formed
The Government of Ireland Act passed: providing for North and South to have their own Parliaments

1922
Proclamation of the Irish Free State
Mussolini joins Fascist government in Italy

1923
Establishment of the USSR
Equality in divorce proceedings given to women by the British Matrimonial Causes Act
1924
Ramsay MacDonald forms first Labour government
1925
British Unemployment Insurance Act

1926
May General Strike
Germany joins the League of Nations
1927
German financial and economic crisis
Rise of Stalin: expulsion of Trotsky
1928
Minimum voting age for women reduced to 21 from 30 years

1929
General Election victory for the Labour Party
The Wall Street Crash: collapse of the US Stock Exchange
1930
Gandhi begins his campaign of civil disobedience
Nazis win seats from moderates in German elections
1931
The New Party formed by Oswald Mosley
National government formed by Ramsay MacDonald
Invergordon naval mutiny
1932
Hunger marches in Britain
Nazis gain majority in German parliament

1933
Orwell: *Down and Out in Paris and London*
H. G. Wells: *The Shape of Things to Come*
1934
Evelyn Waugh: *A Handful of Dust*

1936
Aldous Huxley: *Eyeless in Gaza*

1937
Karen Blixen: *Out of Africa*
Orwell: *The Road to Wigan Pier*
1938
Beckett: *Murphy*
G. Greene: *Brighton Rock*
Evelyn Waugh: *Scoop*
1939
Isherwood: *Goodbye to Berlin*
Joyce: *Finnegans Wake*

1940
G. Greene: *The Power and the Glory*

1941
Virginia Woolf: *Between the Acts*

1943
G. Greene: *The Ministry of Fear*

1945
Isherwood: *Prater Violet*
Orwell: *Animal Farm: A Fairy Story*
Evelyn Waugh: *Brideshead Revisited*

1946
Orwell: *Collected Essays*

1947
Lowry: *Under the Volcano*

1948
G. Greene: *The Heart of the Matter*
F. R. Leavis: *The Great Tradition*

1933
Adolf Hitler becomes Chancellor of Germany
Persecution of the Jews in Germany begins
1934
The British Union of Fascists addressed by Oswald
    Mosley
Adolf Hitler becomes Führer
Purge in the Russian Communist Party
1936
Penguin Books founded
Accession of Edward VIII on death of George V
Spanish Civil War starts
The abdication of Edward VIII
1937
Irish Free State becomes Eire

1938
Munich Conference

1939
Franco secures the surrender of Madrid: end of the
    Spanish Civil War
Britain and France declare war on Germany: start of the
    Second World War
1940
National government formed, Churchill becomes Prime
    Minister
Evacuation of Dunkirk
Battle of Britain
Start of the Blitz: German night-time raids on London
1941
Japanese bomb Pearl Harbour
United States declares war on Germany and Italy
1943
Germany surrenders at Stalingrad
Surrender of Italy
1944
Butler's Education Act
'D-Day' landings on the Normandy beaches
1945
The Yalta conference: meeting between Churchill,
    Roosevelt and Stalin
Mussolini dies
Death of Hitler
'VE' day
The Potsdam conference: meeting between Churchill and
    Attlee, Stalin, Truman
The United States drops atomic bombs on Hiroshima
    and Nagasaki
The surrender of Japan; end of Second World War
Labour wins General Election
1946
United Nations General Assembly holds its first meeting
Arts Council founded
National Insurance comes into effect
1947
Nationalisation of the Coal Industry
Independence of India and Pakistan founded
1948
National Health Service founded
Nationalization of British Railways
Berlin blockade and airlift
British Citizenship Act: Commonwealth citizens granted
    subject status
UN convention on human rights and genocide

1949
Radclyffe Hall: *The Well of Loneliness* (republished)
Stevie Smith: *The Holiday*

1950
G. Greene: *The Third Man*
Doris Lessing: *The Grass is Singing*

1952
Amos Tutuola: *The Palm-Wine Drinkard*
Doris Lessing: *Martha Quest*

1953
Orwell: *England, Your England*
George Lamming: *In the Castle of My Skin*
1954
Kingsley Amis: *Lucky Jim*
Golding: *Lord of the Flies*
1955
G. Greene: *The Quiet American*

1956
Samuel Selvon: *The Lonely Londoners*

1957
Iris Murdoch: *The Sandcastle*
Patrick White: *Voss*

1958
G. Greene: *Our Man in Havana*
C. Achebe: *Things Fall Apart*
1959
Alan Sillitoe: *The Loneliness of the Long-Distance Runner*
Muriel Spark: *Memento Mori*
1960
Wilson Harris: *Palace of the Peacock*

1961
G. Greene: *A Burnt-out Case*
Cyprian Ekwensi: *Jaguar Nana*
Iris Murdoch: *A Severed Head*
Muriel Spark: *The Prime of Miss Jean Brodie*
V. S. Naipaul: *A House for Mr Biswas*

1962
Anthony Burgess: *A Clockwork Orange*
Margaret Drabble: *A Summer Bird-Cage*
Doris Lessing: *The Golden Notebook*
David Storey: *This Sporting Life*
1963
Iris Murdoch: *The Unicorn*
C. P. Snow: *Corridors of Power*

1964
Ngugi wa Thiong'o: *Weep Not, Child*

1949
Beginning of South African apartheid
North Atlantic Treaty signed by Britain, France,
   Belgium, Netherlands, Italy, Portugal, Denmark,
   Iceland, Norway, United States and Canada
Proclamation of the Republic of Eire
Proclamation of the Communist People's Republic of
   China
1950
Korean War begins

1951
The Festival of Britain
Conservatives win British General Election
1952
Death of George VI; accession of Elizabeth II
British atomic bomb announced
Mau Mau troubles in Kenya
1953
Death of Stalin
Coronation of Elizabeth II
1954
Nasser becomes Egyptian Premier

1955
West Germany admitted to NATO
Universal Copyright Convention
1956
Suez crisis
Russian invasion of Hungary
1957
The Common Market founded when Treaty of Rome
   signed
The Wolfenden report on homosexuality and prostitution
Launch of Sputnik I
Independence of Ghana (formerly Gold Coast)
1958
The appearance of Beatniks

1959
Obscene Publications Act

1960
'Wind of Change' speech made by Macmillan
Kennedy wins US Presidential election from Nixon
1961
Yuri Gagarin becomes first man in space
Britain applies for membership of the EEC
East Germany closes the border between East and West
   Berlin
The Berlin Wall
Mass CND rally in Trafalgar Square
1962
The United States blockades Cuba: the 'Cuban missile
   crisis'

1963
The Beatles become popular
Britain refused Common Market entry
The Profumo scandal: Profumo resigns
The assassination of President Kennedy
1964
Harlem race riots in US
Martin Luther King awarded Nobel peace prize
Wilson forms Labour administration on resignation of
   Alec Douglas-Home
Fighting in Vietnam

1965
John Fowles: *The Magus*

1966
G. Greene: *The Comedians*
Tom Stoppard: *Rosencrantz and Guildenstern are Dead*
1967
Angela Carter: *The Magic Toyshop*
V. S. Naipaul: *The Mimic Men*

1969
John Fowles: *The French Lieutenant's Woman*
G. Greene: *Travels with My Aunt*
Margaret Atwood: *The Edible Woman*
Booker Prize first awarded
1970
Nuruddin Farah: *From a Crooked Rib*

1971
Forster: *Maurice*
Kofi Awoonor: *This Earth, My Brother*
Iris Murdoch: *An Accidental Man*
1972
Margaret Drabble: *The Needle's Eye*
Margaret Atwood: *Surfacing*
1973
Iris Murdoch: *The Black Prince*

1974
Bessie Head: *A Question of Power*
Doris Lessing: *The Memoirs of a Survivor*

1975
Bradbury: *The History Man*
Lodge: *Changing Places*
1976
R. K. Narayan: *The Painter of Signs*
1977
Ngugi wa Thiong'o: *Petals of Blood*
1978
Ama Ata Aidoo: *Our Sister Killjoy*
Iris Murdoch: *The Sea, The Sea*
Emma Tennant: *The Bad Sister*
Fay Weldon: *Praxis*
1979
Andre Brink: *A Dry White Season*

1980
Anthony Burgess: *Earthly Powers*
William Golding: *Rites of Passage*
1981
Alasdair Gray: *Lanark*
Salman Rushdie: *Midnight's Children*

1983
Keri Hulme: *The Bone People*
William Golding wins the Nobel Prize for Literature
J. M. Coetzee: *Life and Times of Michael K*
Fay Weldon: *The Life and Loves of a She-Devil*

1965
Edward Heath becomes Leader of the Conservative Party
Death penalty abolished
1966
Labour win British General Election
Cultural Revolution in China
1967
Legalization of homosexuality and abortion

1968
Assassinations of Bobby Kennedy and Martin Luther
   King
Civil Rights Bill passed in the United States
United Nations adopts Nuclear Non-proliferation Treaty
Richard M. Nixon elected President of the United States
1969
First American moon landings

1970
Lowering of the voting age in Britain to 18
Conservative win in British General Election
1971
Anti-Vietnam War demonstration in Washington

1972
Direct rule by British government in Northern Ireland

1973
Signing of Vietnam peace agreement
Britain joins the EEC
1974
Solzhenitsyn's expulsion from the USSR
General Election in Britain with no overall majority
Labour wins General Election
The 'Watergate' scandal: Nixon resigns

1975
End of the Vietnam War

1979
Winter of Discontent
Conservatives win General Election
1980
Soviet invasion of Afghanistan
American hostages in Iran
1981
Riots in London, Liverpool and Manchester

1982
The Falklands War
1983
Conservative victory in General Election
Anti-nuclear protests at Greenham Common
The Ballykelly Bombing

1984
Kingsley Amis: *Stanley and the Women*
Anita Brookner: *Hôtel Du Lac*
Angela Carter: *Nights at the Circus*
Janet Frame: *An Angel at My Table*
David Lodge: *Small World*

1985
Peter Ackroyd: *Hawksmoor*
Peter Carey: *Illywhacker*
Janette Turner Hospital: *Borderline*
Jeanette Winterson: *Oranges Are Not The Only Fruit*
Fay Weldon: *Polaris*

1986
Kingsley Amis: *The Old Devils*
Margaret Atwood: *The Handmaid's Tale*
Flora Nwapa: *Women are Different*
Wole Soyinka wins Nobel Prize for Literature

1987
Peter Ackroyd: *Chatterton*
Wandor and Maitland: *Arky Types*
Chinua Achebe: *Anthills of the Sahara*
Michael Ondaatje: *In the Skin of a Lion*

1988
Alan Hollinghurst: *The Swimming-Pool Library*
Peter Carey: *Oscar and Lucinda*
Shashi Despande: *That Long Silence*
David Lodge: *Nice Work*
Marina Warner: *The Lost Father*
Salman Rushdie: *Satanic Verses*

1989
Margaret Atwood: *Cat's Eye*
Peter Ackroyd: *First Light*
Anthony Burgess: *Any Old Iron*
Buchi Emecheta: *Gwendolen*
Kazuo Ishiguro: *The Remains of the Day*
Martin Amis: *London Fields*

1990
Peter Ackroyd: *Dickens*
A. S. Byatt: *Possession*
Nadine Gordimer: *My Son's Story*
Brian Moore: *Lies of Silence*
J. M. Coetzee: *Age of Iron*

1991
Martin Amis: *Time's Arrow*
Margaret Atwood: *Wilderness Tips*
Angela Carter: *Wise Children*
J. G. Ballard: *The Kindness of Women*
Dan Jacobson: *Hidden in the Heart*
Nadine Gordimer wins Nobel Prize for literature and
    publishes *Jump*

1992
Malcolm Bradbury: *Doctor Criminale*
Barry Unsworth: *Sacred Hunger*
Angela Carter: *Expletives Deleted*
Doris Lessing: *African Laughter*
A. S. Byatt: *Angels and Insects*

1993
Ben Okri: *Songs of Enchantment*
Nuruddin Farah: *Gifts*
Angela Carter: *American Ghosts and Old World Wanderers*

1984
Miners' strike

1985
Famine in Ethiopia – Live Aid concerts raise money for
    famine relief

1986
Chernobyl nuclear power station explosion – radioactive
    cloud over much of Europe

1987
Conservative party wins third term of office
British government attempts to ban publication of Peter
    Wright's *Spycatcher*
'Black Monday' – British stock market crash

1988
Bicentenary of Australia

1989
Russian troops complete withdrawal from Afghanistan
Controversy over *Satanic Verses* results in death threat to
    Salman Rushdie, who goes into hiding
Revolutions in Eastern Europe and beginning of the
    break-up of the Warsaw Pact

1990
Nelson Mandela freed in South Africa and ANC
    unbanned
Iraq invades Kuwait
John Major replaces Margaret Thatcher as Conservative
    Prime Minister of Britain
Reolutions in Eastern Europe continue
Reunification of Germany

1991
Gulf War
Attempted coup in USSR; Mikhail Gorbachev resigns
    and Boris Yeltsin oversees break-up of Soviet Union.
    Soviet regions recognised as independent countries
British hostages Jackie Mann, John McCarthy and Terry
    Waite released in the Lebanon

1992
Trades barriers within European Community lifted to
    form single market
General Election in Britain results in fourth term of office
    for Conservative Party
Presidential election in USA won by Democratic
    candidate Bill Clinton
War in the former Yugoslavia

1993
Landslide victory in French elections for right-wing
    parties